Film and Theory

Film and Theory

An Anthology

Edited by

Robert Stam and Toby Miller

Department of Cinema Studies, New York University

Blackwell
Publishing

© 2000 by Blackwell Publishing Ltd
Editorial selection, arrangement and apparatus © 2000 by Robert Stam and
Toby Miller

BLACKWELL PUBLISHING
350 Main Street, Malden, MA 02148-5020, USA
9600 Garsington Road, Oxford OX4 2DQ, UK
550 Swanston Street, Carlton, Victoria 3053, Australia

First published 2000

4   2007

Library of Congress Cataloging-in-Publication Data

Film and theory: an anthology / edited by Toby Miller and Robert Stam.
p.cm.
Includes bibliographical references and index.
ISBN 0-631-20625-6 — ISBN 0-631-20626-4 (pbk. : alk. paper)
1. Motion pictures. I. Miller, Toby. II. Stam, Robert, 1941–()
PN1994. F4382 1999   791.4301 — dc21   99–19390 CIP

ISBN-13: 978-0-631-20625-5 — ISBN-13: 978-0-631-20626-2 (pbk. : alk. paper)

A catalogue record for this title is available from the British Library.

Set in 10 on 12 pt
by Kolam Information Services Pvt. Ltd, Pondicherry, India
Printed and bound in Singapore
by Markono Print Media Pte Ltd

The publisher's policy is to use permanent paper from mills that operate a sustainable
forestry policy, and which has been manufactured from pulp processed using acid-
free and elementary chlorine-free practices. Furthermore, the publisher ensures that
the text paper and cover board used have met acceptable environmental accreditation
standards.

For further information on
Blackwell Publishing, visit our website:
www.blackwellpublishing.com

Contents

Part III   The Image and Technology

Part IV   Text and Intertext

Part V   The Question of Realism

Part VI   Alternative Aesthetics

Acknowledgments

The editors and publishers gratefully acknowledge the following for permission to reproduce copyright material:

Altman, Rick, "A Semantic/Syntactic Approach to Film Genre," *Cinema Journal* 23: 3, pp. 6–18. Copyright © 1984 by the University of Texas Press. All rights reserved.

Andrew, Dudley, "The Unauthorized Auteur Today," from (ed. Jim Collins, Hilary Radner, and Ava Preacher Collins) *Film Theory Goes to the Movies*, copyright © 1993. Reproduced by permission of Routledge Inc. New York.

Caldwell, John T., "Modes of Production: The Televisual Apparatus," from *Televisuality*, copyright © John T. Caldwell. Reprinted by permission of Rutgers University Press.

Carroll, Noël, "The Specificity of the Media in the Arts," from *Theorizing the Moving Image* (Cambridge University Press, Cambridge, 1996).

Chion, Michel, "Projections of Sound On Image," from *Audio Vision: Sound on Screen* by Michel Chion © 1994 Columbia University Press. Reprinted with the permission of the publisher.

Churchill, Ward, "Fantasies of the Master Race: Categories of Stereotyping of American Indians in Film," from (ed. M. Annette Jaimes) *Fantasies of the Master Race: Literature, Cinema and the Colonization of American Indians* (Common Courage Press, Monroe, 1992).

Collins, Jim, "Television and Postmodernism," from (ed. Robert C. Allen) *Channels of Discourse Reassembled: Television and Contemporary Criticism*. Copyright © 1992 by the University of North Carolina Press. Used by permission of the publisher.

Copjec, Joan, "The Orthopsychic Subject: Film Theory and the Reception of Lacan," *October*, 49 (Summer, 1989), pp. 53–71. © 1989 by October Magazine Ltd and the Massachusetts Institute of Technology.

Coward, Rosalind, "Dennis Potter and the Question of the Television Author," *Critical Quarterly*, vol. 29, no. 4, 1987, courtesy of Blackwell Publishers, Oxford.

Cunningham, Stuart, "The 'Force-Field' of Melodrama," *Quarterly Review of Film Studies*, vol. 6, no. 6, Fall 1981.

de Lauretis, Teresa, "Rethinking Women's Cinema: Aesthetics and Feminist Theory," *New German Critique*, no. 34 (Winter 1985).

Diawara, Manthia, "Black American Cinema: The New Realism," copyright © 1993, from *Black American Cinema* by Manthia Diawara. Reproduced by permission of Routledge Inc.

Doane, Mary Ann, "Film and the Masquerade: Theorizing the Female Spectator," *Screen*, 23, nos. 3–4 (September–October 1982).

Dyer, Richard, "Introduction," from *Heavenly Bodies: Film Stars and Society* (St Martin's Press Inc., New York, 1986).

Dyer, Richard, "White," *Screen*, 29, no. 4 (1988).

Enzensberger, Hans Magnus, "Constituents of a Theory of the Media," *New Left Review*, no. 64, November/December 1970, pp. 13–36.

Espinosa, Julio García, "For An Imperfect Cinema," from (ed. Coco Fusco) *Reviewing Histories: Selections from New Latin American Cinema* (Hallwalls, Buffalo, 1987).

Flitterman-Lewis, Sandy, "To Desire Differently: Feminism and the French Cinema" (University of Illinois Press, 1990).

Gabriel, Teshome H., "Towards a Critical Theory of Third World Films," *Third World Quarterly*, 1983, copyright © Carfax Publishing Limited, Abingdon, Oxford.

Gaines, Jane, "White Privilege and Looking Relations," *Cultural Critique*, no. 4, Fall 1985.

Gunning, Tom, "The Cinema of Attraction: Early Film, Its Spectator and the Avant-Garde," *Wide Angle*, vol. 8, nos. 3–4, Fall 1986: pp. 1–14 © 1986 Ohio University: Athens Center for Film and Video. Reprinted by permission of the Johns Hopkins University Press.

Hall, Stuart, "Cultural Identity and Cinematic Representation," *Framework*, no. 36, 1989.

Hill, John, "Ideology, Economy and the British Cinema," from (ed. Michele Barrett, Philip Corrigan, Annette Kuhn, and Janet Wolff) *Ideology and Cultural Production* (Croom Helm, London, 1979).

hooks, bell, "The Oppositional Gaze," from *Black Looks: Race and Representation* (South End Press, Boston, 1992).

Jenkins, Henry, "Conclusion," from *Textual Poachers: Television Fans and Participatory Culture*, copyright © 1992. Reproduced by permission of Routledge, Inc.

Joyrich, Lynne, "Critical and Textual Hypermasculinity," from (ed. Patricia Mellencamp) *Logics of Television* (Indiana University Press, Bloomington and Indianapolis, 1990).

Metz, Christian, "The Imaginary Signifier" (trans. Ben Brewster), *Screen*, vol. 16, no. 2 (Summer 1975), courtesy the John Logie Baird Centre.

Mulvey, Laura, "Visual Pleasure and Narrative Cinema," *Screen*, vol. 16, no. 3 (Autumn 1975), courtesy the John Logie Baird Centre.

Naremore, James, "Marlon Brando in *On the Waterfront*," from *Acting in the Cinema* (University of California Press, 1988, copyright © The Regents of the University of California).

Neale, Steve, "Questions of Genre," *Screen*, 31, no. 1, 1990.

Odin, Roger, "For a Semio-Pragmatics of Film," from (ed. Warren Buckland) *The Film Spectator: From Sign to Mind* (Amsterdam University Press, Amsterdam 1995).

Penley, Constance, "Feminism, Film Theory, and the Bachelor Machines," from *m/f*, no. 10, 1985.

Petro, Patrice, "Mass Culture and the Feminine: The 'Place' of Television in Film Studies," *Cinema Journal*, 25: 3, pp. 5–21. Copyright © 1986 by the University of Texas Press. All rights reserved.

Rowe, Kathleen K., "Roseanne: Unruly Woman as Domestic Goddess," *Screen*, vol. 31, no. 4 (Winter 1990), reprinted by permission of Oxford University Press.

Shively, JoEllen, "Cowboys and Indians: Perceptions of Western Films Among American Indians and Anglos," *American Sociological Review*, 57, no. 6, December 1992, reproduced by permission of the American Sociological Association.

Shohat, Ella, "Gender and Culture of Empire: Toward a Feminist Ethnography of the Cinema," *Quarterly Review of Film and Video*, vol. 13, nos. 1–3, pp. 45–84, 1991, with permission of Gordon and Breach Publishers.

Sobchack, Vivian, "The Scene of the Screen: Envisioning Cinematic and Electronic 'Presence'," from (ed. Hans Ulrich Gumbrecht and K. Ludwig Pfeiffer: trans. William Whobrey) *Materialities of Communication* (Stanford University Press, Stanford, 1994, with the permission of the publishers, Stanford University Press, © 1994 by the Board of Trustees of the Leland Stanford Junior University).

Solanas, Fernando and Gettino, Octavio, "Towards a Third Cinema: Notes and Experiences for the Development of a Cinema of Liberation in the Third World" (trans. from *Cineaste*) (first published Michael Chanan ed.) *25 Years of Latin American Cinema* (British Film Institute, London, 1983).

Stam, Robert, "Television News and Its Spectator," from (ed. E. Ann Kaplan) *Regarding Television* (American Film Institute, Fredericksburg, 1983).

Straayer, Chris, "The She-Man: Postmodern Bi-Sexed Performance in Film and Video," from (ed. Jane Gaines) *Classical Hollywood Narrative: The Paradigm Wars* (Duke University Press, Durham, 1992).

Vasudevan, Ravi S., "Addressing the Spectator of a 'Third World' National Cinema: The Bombay 'Social' Film of the 1940s and 1950s," *Screen*, vol. 36, no. 4, Winter 1995, reprinted by permission of Oxford University Press.

Williams, Linda, "Film Bodies: Gender, Genre, and Excess" *Film Quarterly*, vol. 44, no. 4, Summer 1991, pp. 2–13 © 1991 by The Regents of the University of California.
Winston, Brian, "Introduction: Necessities and Constraints: A Pattern of Technological Change," from *Technologies of Seeing: Photography, Cinematography and Television* (British Film Institute, London, 1996).
Žižek, Slavoj, "Looking Awry," *October*, 50 (Fall, 1989), pp. 31–55, © 1989 by October Magazine Ltd and the Massachusetts Institute of Technology.

The publishers apologize for any errors or omissions in the above list and would be grateful to be notified of any corrections that should be incorporated in the next edition or reprint of this book.

Introduction

Robert Stam

Film and Theory forms part of a trilogy of books which try to chart the shifting terrain of film theory. *Film and Theory* anthologizes some of the most interesting and influential work from the late 1970s to the present. *A Companion to Film Theory* maps present and future trends as seen by some of the leading figures in the field. And *Film Theory: An Introduction* provides a historical overview of theory during the "century of the cinema."

Obviously, no single anthology could possibly do justice to such a prolific and variegated field as "film theory." No field featuring such a wide spectrum of approaches – auteurism, semiotics, psychoanalysis, reception theory, feminism, cognitive theory, neo-formalism, semio-pragmatics, postcolonial theory – could ever be "covered" in the narrow frame of a single book. Nevertheless, *Film and Theory* does attempt, perhaps quixotically, to trace out some of the major strands of the film and media theory of the last few decades. To make the task more manageable, we pass over the period known as "classical film theory," i.e. the film theory prior to the advent of structuralism in the 1960s. Our introductions to specific sections do review, however, some of the basic issues. To avoid redundancy with other anthologies, we also bypass many of the widely antho-logized texts of the semiotic and psychoanalytic–semiotic phases of film theory. While hardly exhaustive, the volume does present diverse styles and genres of film-related theorizing, with emphasis on the period from the late 1970s to the present.

Rather than look at film theory in terms of "schools" and "allegiances," *Film and Theory* charts the diverse currents and tendencies in terms of orienting "questions" and "problematics:" What is the cinema? What distinguishes it from neighboring arts? Can the filmmaker be compared to an author? What is the cinematic apparatus? Does the cinema inherently favor certain kinds of content or modes of expression? What is realism? What are the alternatives to realism? How does genre operate in film? What are the parameters of filmic style? What does the spectator want? How do spectators understand narrative or identify with characters? How are spectators differentiated in their desires?

What are the modes of narration in the cinema? How is the cinema raced? gendered? sexualized?

This methodological *parti pris* for questions rather than answers allows for what we trust is a more ecumenical approach. Different schools can be seen as responding to the same question, even when the schools were not in any obvious sense responding to one another. Thus psychoanalysis, reception theory, cognitive theory, semio-pragmatics, race theory, and feminism all shed light on the question: what does the spectator want? Our goal is to facilitate a multilateral polylogue among theorists and schools which have too often ignored or maligned one another. Without papering over differences in a facile Muzak-like harmony, or exciting them into needlessly hostile confrontation, our approach attempts to open up theory to dialogical interaction and even "miscegenation" among apparently opposite theoretical "tribes."

Theoretical "truth," in our view, does not lie exclusively with one camp; rather, truth is contingent, mediated, collectively forged in the "in-between" of a polyvocal conversation. This is especially true in a field like film theory, where theorists see film through cultural, ideological, and personal grids, and where only very technical questions can be answered conclusively. Our project therefore counterpoints voices and discourses, avoiding both dogmatism (which brooks no disagreement and thus makes dialogue impossible) and relativism (which embraces all opinions and thus makes dialogue pointless).

Film and Theory offers a kind of cubist collage of theoretical grids; each grid brings its quantum of illumination. As the products of specific cultural and discursive moments, all theories are situated; they embody a "standpoint" in time and space which entails both blindnesses and insight. The objects in the center of their field of vision may stand out clearly, while those on the edges tend to blur, whence the need for the "excess seeing" of other theoretical grids. The diverse grids are therefore necessarily complementary and in need of mutual completion. While some argue that we can do film theory *without* recourse to linguistics or psychoanalysis or critical race theory, we are more interested in "doing *with*" than in "doing *without*." The Hobson's choice of cognitivism *or* psychoanalysis, rationality *or* irrationality, for example, leaves no room for the ways in which the rational and the irrational, the denotative and the connotative, interpenetrate both film spectatorship and film theory. Both cognitive theory and psychoanalysis, then, can illuminate specific dimensions of the cinematic experience.

At the same time this volume implicitly tries to rethink the whole issue of what qualifies as theory. Our hope here has been to gather theoretical essays which offer precise, subtle, general and open-ended understanding of the film medium specifically and of the audio-visual media generally. We do not generally include textual analyses unless they give voice to some larger theoretical or methodological ambition, i.e. unless they are meant to construct, verify, perfect, or contest – as opposed to merely illustrate – a theory. Since earlier periods of film theory, at least up through the 1970s, have already been widely disseminated, we have not reproduced many of the already anthologized classic semiotic and psychoanalytic essays, except when they have been absolutely seminal for discussions that are still going on, as in the case of Laura Mulvey's "Visual Pleasure and Narrative Cinema" and Metz's "The Imaginary Signifier." Unlike many existing anthologies, *Film and Theory* does reflect the general shift from film theory per se into emerging fields such as "cultural studies," "visual culture," and "postcolonial theory."

A historical structuring, sometimes overt, sometimes subliminal, undergirds *Film and Theory*. The brief introductory essays preceding each cluster of essays overview the history of discussion of specific questions. They do not introduce the essays themselves or adjudicate between them, but rather stand alongside the other essays, sketching out what we see as useful background. The clusters of reproduced essays, meanwhile, are in most cases arranged internally in more-or-less chronological order so as to give a sense of the trajectory of the debates, of how the conversation has evolved over time, without, of course, endorsing any notion of linear progress postulating "later" answers as necessarily "better."

In the 1970s much film theory came to consist in ritualistic invocations (and crude summaries) of Lacan and other poststructuralist gurus, often presuming a quasi-religious initiation into the sacred texts of the then-reigning *maîtres à penser*. Current theory, thankfully, is more epistemologically modest and less authoritarian. Semioticians themselves have abandoned their totalizing ambitions, while theorists like Noël Carroll and David Bordwell have called for "middle-level theorizing" which would "countenance as film theory any line of inquiry dedicated to producing generalizations pertaining to, or general explanations of, filmic phenomena, or devoted to isolating, tracking, and/or accounting for any mechanisms, devices, patterns, and regularities in the field of cinema" (Bordwell and Carroll, 1996: 41). Film theory, then, refers to any generalized reflexion on the patterns and regularities (or significant irregularities) to be found in relation to film as a medium, to film language, to the cinematic apparatus or to the nature of the cinematic text, or to cinematic reception. Instead of Grand Theory, then, only theories and the "activity of theorizing," and the workmanlike production of general concepts, taxonomies, and explanations.

While we agree with Bordwell and Carroll that we should rethink the issue of what qualifies as theory, and while we endorse the "modesty" of their perspective, this modesty should not become an alibi for censuring larger philosophical or political questions about the cinema. There is a danger that "middle-range" theory, like "consensus history" or "end-of-ideology" discourse, will assume that the big questions have all been settled, leaving us only with small-scale inquiries susceptible to direct empirical verification. That some questions, such as the role of the cinematic apparatus in engendering ideological alienation, were answered ineptly, does not mean that such questions were not worth asking. Even unanswerable questions might be worth asking, if only to see where they take us and what we discover along the way. Film theory, to put it paradoxically, might generate productive fallacies and regrettable successes. Modesty, furthermore, can lead in many directions not necessarily acknowledged by Bordwell and Carroll. The patterns and regularities noted in the field of cinema, for example, might have to do not only with predictable stylistic or narratological procedures but also with patterns of gendered, racialized, sexualized, and culturally inflected representation. Why are materials on "race," for example, or on "third cinema" not seen as "theoretical?" Could this elision be traced to the colonialist hierarchy which associates Europe with reflecting "mind" and non-Europe with unreflecting body? Our hope is to expand the realm of film theory to include such diverse schools as multicultural media theory, postcolonial theory, queer theory, in short the entire gamut of all the complex, subtle, and theoretically sophisticated film-related work performed under a wide variety of banners.

Although we try to survey the field of film theory somewhat impartially, our own views inevitably come into play not only in our introductions to the various sections but also in the very selection of texts, the rubrics chosen, the sequencing, the omissions, and so forth. Our goal is not merely to passively register the trajectories of recent film theory but also to have a creative impact on the field, not through the brilliance or audacity of our own interventions but rather through our coordinating role as orchestrators of pre-existing texts, our way of juxtaposing the familiar and the unfamiliar in ways which we hope will provoke fresh discussion.

Our criteria for inclusion of essays were quite varied. At times we included essays because of their enormous influence (the case of Laura Mulvey's "Visual Pleasure and Narrative Cinema" and Christian Metz's "Imaginary Signifier," Enzensberger on the "consciousness industry"). Other essays were included because they both sum up and critique a foundational argument (e.g. Noël Carroll on "media specificity," Constance Penley on apparatus theory). Other essays survey the current state of a debate (Dudley Andrew on auteurism), or exemplify a method (James Naremore on acting, Kathleen Rowe on "unruly" feminism), or represent a current of research (Ward Churchill on stereotypes of Native Americans, Roger Odin on semio-pragmatics, John Caldwell on "televisuality").

We have also wanted to "deprovincialize" theory in disciplinary terms. Film theory can learn not only from linguistics, psychoanalysis, and literary theory but also from the social sciences generally and from cultural studies in the broadest sense. Film theory, we would add, now "exports" ideas as well as importing them, within an increasingly favorable "balance of trade." Film theoretical treatments of issues of narrative and narration, the gendered gaze, subject positioning, spectatorship, and racialized and sexualized representations have by now had wide impact on other fields, even if these other fields do not always acknowledge their debt. Although it is important to be media-specific, to discern what traits are unique to film, it is also important not to seal off the theorizing of the cinema from the history or theorizing of the other arts or, for that matter, from history *tout court*.

In this anthology, we are highly aware of our own intertext, i.e. the diverse anthologies and collections (included in the bibliography) which have preceded our own, and which we regard with respect and gratitude, but which were conceived at a different time and in pursuit of distinct goals. The specific "difference" of this book, however, lies in (1) its ecumenical incorporation of a wide spectrum of film-theoretical grids; (2) its attempt to reconcile diachrony and synchrony, history and system; and (3) its attempt to register the shift toward cultural studies, a field where film theory is at once an "insider" and an "outsider." In this process, we have tried to avoid a number of counterproductive "ghettoizations" of (1) media – here we treat cinema, television, and video as "closely neighboring languages"; (2) grids – here materialist, psychoanalytic, feminist, and cognitive grids all have something to offer; and (3) social subjects of representation. For us, issues of race, gender, and sexuality, as well as issues of methodology, cannot be confined to tokenistic "special sections;" since they are "everywhere," they crop up in diverse sections.

Theories do not supersede one another in a linear progression. Indeed, there are Darwinian overtones in the view that theories can be "retired," that they can "fall by the wayside," or be "eliminated" in competition. Theories do not fall into disuse like old automobiles, relegated to a conceptual junkyard. They do not die; they transform themselves, leaving traces and reminiscences. There are shifts in emphasis, of course, but many of the major themes – mimesis, authorship, spectatorship – have been there from the beginning. Theory, like all writing, is palimpsestic; it forms a mosaic of traces of earlier theories and the impact of neighboring discourses. We have tried in this book to set up a polyphonic play of theoretical voices. Rather than an innocuous pluralism, we have sought for a strong counterpoint of voices, in which diverse answers are marshaled in relation to the same question. This volume demonstrates, we think, that there is something to be learned from virtually every critical school. While some voices are perhaps more persuasive than others, none of the voices annihilates the others. Each has something to say.

Part I
The Author

Introduction

Robert Stam

A product of the conjunction of the cinephilia of the cinemateque and the "cultural field" of the Parisian bohemians and intellectuals, auteurism as a movement first emerged in postwar France. Philosophically, auteurism was aligned with a romantic strain of existentialism; paraphrasing Sartre, Bazin claimed that the cinema's "existence precedes its essence." Auteurism was summed up by André Bazin in a 1957 article – "La Politique des auteurs" – as the analytical process of "choosing in the artistic creation the personal factor as a criterion of reference, and then postulating its permanence and even its progress from one work to the next" (Bazin, 1957 in Hillier, 1985).

Although auteurism came into vogue only in the 1950s, the root idea itself was in some ways a traditional one, part of cinema's search for artistic legitimation. The characterization of the cinema as the "seventh art" had already implicitly given film artists the same status as writers and painters. Directors like Griffith and Eisenstein had compared their own cinematic techniques to the literary devices of writers like Flaubert and Dickens. Already in 1921, the filmmaker Jean Epstein, in "Le Cinéma et les lettres modernes," used the term "author" to apply to filmmakers, while Louis Delluc analysed the films of Griffith, Chaplin, and Ince in what might be called a "proto-auteurist" manner (Crofts in Hill and Gibson, 1998: 312).

In postwar France the auteurist metaphor became a key structuring concept in film criticism and theory. Alexandre Astruc in "The Birth of a New Avant-Garde: The Camera Pen" (1948) asserted that the cinema was a means of personal expression, suggesting that the filmmaker should be able to say "I" like the novelist or poet. A kind of graphological trope, from Astruc's "camera-stylo" (camera-pen) to Metz's discussion of "cinema and écriture" in *Language and Cinema*, dominated the period. The French New Wave directors, many of whom began as film critics who saw writing articles and making films as simply two forms of expressive writing, were especially fond of the scriptural metaphor. "We are always alone," Godard (1958) wrote somewhat melodramatically, "whether in the studio or before the blank page." Agnès Varda, about to make *La Pointe courte*, announces that she "will make a film exactly as one writes a book" (cited in Philippe, 1983: 17). At the same time the New Wave directors were profoundly ambivalent about literature, which was both a model to be emulated, and, in the form of overly literary scripts, the enemy to be shunned. In aesthetic–ideological terms, auteurism formed a kind of palimpsest bearing the traces of diverse periods: romantic in its adulation of the creative genius of authors, it was also modernist in its aesthetic taste, while simultaneously displaying some of the symptoms of a "postmodern sensibility in its dissolving of the boundaries between 'high' and 'low' art" (see Naremore, in Miller and Stam, 1999).

With its first issue in 1951, *Cahiers du cinéma* became a key auteurist organ. *Cahiers* used a number of weapons to spread auteurist ideas: the mock-canonical "ten best" lists; the "allegorical" praise of some directors and the denigration of others; and interviews with its favorite directors. *Cahiers* wrote about and interviewed both French (Renoir, Cocteau, Bresson) and American auteurs (Hawks, Hitchcock, Welles). *Cahiers* defended the American films of Lang against the prejudice that his work declined in Hollywood. In the case of Hitchcock, *Cahiers* not only supported his American films, but two of its members, Eric Rohmer and Claude Chabrol, also wrote a book arguing that Hitchcock was both a technical genius and a profound metaphysician whose work revolved around the theme of the "transfer of guilt."

One of the pleasures of auteurist criticism was discerning style and individuality where it had not been detected before. The "scandal" of the auteur theory lay not so much in glorifying the director as the equivalent in prestige of the literary author but rather in exactly *who* was granted this prestige. Filmmakers like Eisenstein, Renoir, and Welles had always been regarded as auteurs because they were known to have had artistic control over their own productions. The novelty of auteur theory was to suggest that studio directors like Hawks and Minnelli were also auteurs, even though they worked within a system traditionally regarded as a powerful machine destructive of individual talents. But intrinsically strong directors, auteur theory suggested, will exhibit, over the years, a recognizable stylistic and thematic personality, *even* when working in the Hollywood "dream factory."

In his landmark 1957 article, Bazin warned against any aesthetic "cult of personality" which would erect favored directors into infalible masters. Auteurism, Bazin argued, must be complemented by other approaches – technological, historical, sociological. Great films, he argued, arise from the fortuitous intersection of talent and historical moment. Occasionally a mediocre director – Bazin cites Curtiz and *Casablanca* – might vividly capture a historical moment, without qualifying as an authentic auteur. The quality control guaranteed by the well-oiled Hollywood industrial machine, furthermore, virtually assured a certain competence and even elegance.

"La Politique des auteurs" translates literally as the "auteur policy" rather than "theory." In France, auteurism formed part of a strategy for opening the way to a new kind of filmmaking. Critic–directors like Truffaut and Godard were dynamiting a place for themselves by attacking the established system, derisively labeled the "cinéma de papa," with its rigid production hierarchies, its preference for studio shooting, and its conventional narrative procedures. Disseminated internationally by journals such as *Film Culture* in the United States, *Movie* in Britain, and *Filme Cultura* in Brazil, auteurism took on new coloring in different locations, affiliating with Leavisite criticism in Britain, and with "new criticism" in the United States. In "Notes on the Auteur Theory in 1962," Andrew Sarris turned the auteur theory into a nationalist instrument for asserting the superiority of American cinema. Sarris declared himself ready to "stake his critical reputation" on the notion that American cinema has been "consistently superior" to what Sarris dismissively and ethnocentrically called the "rest of the world." Sarris proposed three criteria for recognizing an auteur: (1) technical competence; (2) distinguishable personality; and (3) interior meaning arising from tension between personality and material (Sarris, 1971).

Pauline Kael debunked the three criteria in her response article "Circles and Squares" (1963). Technical competence, she argued, was hardly a valid criterion, since some directors, such as Antonioni, were *beyond* competence; they questioned the very idea of technical competence. "Distinguishable personality" was meaningless since it favors repetitious directors whose styles are recognizable because they rarely try anything new. The distinctive smell of skunks, she analogized, does not make that smell pleasant or superior to that of roses. Kael dismissed "interior meaning," finally, as impossibly vague and favoring "hacks who shove style into the crevices of plots" (Kael, 1963/1966). But the heat of the Sarris–Kael debate masked their shared premise – to wit, the idea that film theory/criticism should be evaluative, concerned with the comparative ranking of films and directors. At its most crass, this approach led to sterile quarrels about comparative merit and a reckless gambling on critical reputations. Arbitrary tastes were elevated into supposedly rigid hierarchies.

Auteurism was both displaced and driven underground by the linguistically oriented semiotics which emerged in the late 1960s and early 1970s, a body of theory which was much less interested in film as the expression of the creative will of individual auteurs. Auteurism introduced a kind of system which consisted in seeking out and constructing an authorial personality out of surface clues and symptoms. This systematic side of auteurism made it reconcilable with a certain structuralism, resulting in an awkward marriage-of-convenience called "auteur–structuralism," exemplified by Geoffrey Nowell-Smith's study *Visconti* (1967), Peter Wollen's *Signs and Meaning in the Cinema* (1998), and Jim Kitses's *Horizons West* (1969). The auteur–structuralists placed the director's name in quotation marks to highlight the idea of an auteur as a critical construct rather than a flesh-and-blood person. They looked for hidden structuring oppositions which subtended the thematic leitmotifs and recurrent stylistic figures typical of certain directors – for example the culture/nature binarism of garden and desert in John Ford's films – as the key to their deeper meaning. (One detects here the power of structuralism's arbitrary privileging of the number two).

But the hyphen in "auteur–structuralism" was ultimately a stressful one, as theory was torn between the individualism of authorship and the collectivity of myth. The structuralist claim that "language speaks the author" and "ideology speaks the subject" left little room for authorial agency. Structuralists and poststructuralists scorned auteurism for formulating the theory in such a way as to make the cinema the last outpost of a quasi-religious romanticism long discarded by other arts (Sarris's term "pantheon" evokes this veneration for the god-like artist). Both structuralism and poststructuralism relativized the notion of the author as the sole originating and creative source of the text, preferring to see the author as "site" rather than point of origin. For Roland Barthes the "author" became a kind of byproduct of writing. The author was never more than the instance writing, just as linguistically the subject/shifter "I" is nothing more than the instance saying "I." A text's unity, for Barthes, derived not from its origin but from its destination. Barthes spoke, somewhat demogogically, of the "death of the author" and the consequent "birth of the reader."

Foucault, meanwhile, located the emergence of the author in the cultural context of the eighteenth century, an example of the "individualization" of the history of ideas. Foucault preferred to speak of the "author function," seeing authorship as an ephemeral time-bound institution which would soon give way to a future "pervasive anonymity of discourse." The film author, as a consequence, tended to shift from being the generating source of the text to becoming a shifting discursive configuration produced by the intersection of a group of films with historically constituted ways of reading and viewing. The author, in this anti-humanist reading, was diasporized, dissolved into more abstract, theoretical instances such as "enunciation," "subjectification," and "écriture." (Skeptics pointed out that the poststructuralist authors who had decreed the author's death were themselves consecrated authors, even stars, and that they did not neglect to collect their royalty checks).

Auteurism was also criticized on more practical grounds. Auteurism, it was pointed out, underestimates the impact of production conditions. The filmmaker is not an untrammeled artist; he/she is immersed in material contingencies, surrounded by a Babel of voices and the buzz of technicians, cameras, and lights. While the poet can write poems on a napkin in prison, the filmmaker requires money, camera, film. The film author also requires collaborators. Even a low-budget feature can involve more than a score of people working over an extended period. A genre like the musical requires the strong creative participation of composers, musicians, choreographers, and set designers. Writers, cinematographers, composers, stars, corporate executives all collaborate in film authorship. Industry-oriented critics like Thomas Schatz, meanwhile, spoke not of the genius of authors but rather of what Bazin had called the "genius of the system," i.e. the capacity of a well-financed and talent-filled industrial machine to turn out high-quality films. While auteurists emphasized *personal* style and mise-en-scène, Bordwell, Staiger, and Thompson in their work on "classical Hollywood cinema" emphasized the *impersonal* and standardized "group style" of a homogeneous corpus whose main features were narrative unity, realism, and invisible narration. Any coherent theory of authorship, in sum, had to take into account these diverse intrications in terms of material circumstances and personnel within filmic authorship.

Auterism also required modification to apply to neighboring media such as television. In television, some argued, the real auteurs were the producers like Norman Lear and Stephen Bochco (see Rosalind Coward's essay here). What happens to their status as authors when TV commercial directors (e.g. Ridley Scott, Alan Parker) move into feature films, or when prestigious directors (e.g. David Lynch, Spike Lee, Jean-Luc Godard) move into commercials, or when Michelangelo Antonioni choreographs a psychedelic spot for Renault? Are they always and in every circumstance still auteurs, or does their auteur status depend on the medium, the context, the format?

Auteur theory tended to be oriented toward both Hollywood commerical and European art cinema, and was somewhat discomfited by alternative practices. Partisans of the avant-garde, such as Pam Cook, censured auteurism for failing to leave room for experimental cinema. Auteurism thus falters when confronted with the work of a Michael Snow or a Hollis Frampton. It also breaks down completely with political film collectives like Grupo Cine de la Base. Indeed, leftist film activists who preferred more collective and egalitarian models were naturally suspicious of the hierarchical and authoritarian assumptions undergirding auteurism. Marxists also criticized auteurism's ahistorical assumption that talent will eventually "out" no matter what political or economic conditions prevail. Third World critics, meanwhile, gave auteurism a mixed reception. Brazilian filmmaker/critic Glauber Rocha wrote in 1963 that "if commercial cinema is the tradition, auteur cinema is the revolution" (Rocha, 1963). But in 1969 the Argentinian leftist filmmakers Fernando Solanas and Octavio Getino mocked auteur cinema (their "second cinema") as politically innocuous and easily cooptable by the establishment, favoring instead a "third cinema" which is collective, militant, and activist (Solanas and Getino, in Chanan, 1983).

Feminist analysts too expressed ambivalence about auteurism. On the one hand, they pointed out the phallocentric overtones of such tropes as the "camera pen" and the patriarchal and Oedipal substratum implicit in the reviling of the "cinéma de papa" and the "death of the author." On the other hand, theorists like Sandy Flitterman-Lewis and Judith Mayne called for the recognition of such female auteurs as Germaine Dulac, Ida Lupino, and Dorothy Arzner (see Sandy Flitterman-Lewis's essay here). As early as 1973, Claire Johnston argued that auteur theory marked an important intervention: "stripped of its normative aspects the classification of films by director has proved an extremely productive way of ordering our experience of the cinema" (Johnston, 1973).

In the present day, auteurism no longer triggers violent polemics; indeed, some, like Dudley Andrew in this volume, even speak of a "renaissance" of auteurism. But auteurism no longer provokes polemics partially because it has *won*. Auteurism is now widely practiced even by those who have reservations about the "theory," not least by those film academics who imagine their affective relation to film as an ongoing dialogue with the personae imagined to lie "behind" the films of an Ingmar Bergman, a Woody Allen, or a Pedro Almodóvar. Whatever the objections to auteur theory, museums still offer retrospectives in the work of specific directors, film courses revolve around directors, and film publishing tends to privilege auteur studies. For David Bordwell, "the institutional context of academic film studies has been the result of explicatory, chiefly auteur-centered criticism" (Bordwell, 1989: 52). And a steadily increasing portion of the general public tends to choose films on the basis of auteurs rather than of stars or genres. Auteurism, for Timothy Corrigan, has become "a commercial strategy for organizing audience reception, as a critical concept bound to distributing and marketing aims that identify and address the potential cult status of an auteur" (Corrigan, 1991: 103).

Auteurism, in any case, clearly represented an improvement over the critical methodologies which preceded it, notably impressionism (a kind of neuroglandular response to films based solely on the critic's sensibilities and tastes), and sociologism (an evaluative approach based on a reductive view of the perceived progressive or reactionary political qualities of the characters or story line). Auteurism also performed an invaluable rescue operation for neglected films and genres. It discerned authorial personalities in surprising places – especially in the American makers of B-films like Samuel Fuller and Nicholas Ray. It rescued entire genres – the thriller, the Western, the horror film – from literary high-art prejudice against them. Auteurism has clearly made a substantial contribution to film theory and methodology. Auteurism forced attention to the films themselves and to mise-en-scène as the stylistic signature of the director. Auteur studies now tend to see a director's work not as the expression of individual genius but rather as the site of encounter of a biography, an intertext, an institutional context, and a historical moment. Within a Bakhtinian "translinguistic perspective," for example, artists are creative but they do not create *ex nihilo*; rather, they "orchestrate" pre-existing voices, ideologies, and discourses, without losing an overall shaping role. Most contemporary auteur studies have jettisoned the romantic individualist baggage of auteurism to emphasize the ways a director's work can be both personal *and* mediated by extrapersonal elements such as genre, technology, studios, and the linguistic procedures of the medium.

1
Dennis Potter and the Question
of the Television Author

Rosalind Coward

Introduction

The question of the author poses particularly difficult problems for any attempt to understand the mass media by reference to critical models drawn from literary studies. While 'authorship' may not be the only or indeed the most crucial factor in the academic study of literature, it would be hard to deny its significance as a way of organizing the disparate elements that constitute the study of literature. As Stephen Heath said in the *Nouveau Roman*:

> the institutionalization of 'literary criticism' (in faculties, journals, newspaper reviews, etc.)...depends on and sustains the author (enshrined in syllabi and examinations, interviews and television portraits). The task of criticism has been precisely the construction of the author. It must read the author in texts grouped under his name. Style in this perspective is the result of the extraction of marks of individuality, and creation of the author and the area of his value.

Conceived thus, the study of the author seems a peculiarly limiting way of approaching the mass media, encompassing as it does the popular, commercial and above all *collective* productions of film, radio and television. Such forms of production, requiring division of labour, disparate skills and shared responsibilities have more immediately in common with industrial production than with the literary image of the individual author or artist. However, although these forms of production seem to suggest that almost any criteria other than the study of the individual author might be more appropriate, it would be misleading to suggest that the question of the author has been irrelevant to the study of mass media. It is an interesting reflection on the interdependency of the idea of art and the idea of the individual artist, that the higher the valuation of the medium *as an art*, the more likely you are to find the quest to establish an author for a work. Indeed with the recent 'season' of Dennis Potter plays and films on television we can witness the simultaneous 'literary' commitment to the idea of an individual author, and the desire to elevate the status of television through the existence of 'great' television writers.

The Author in Film Studies

This quest for the idea of the individual author has particularly marked the critical study of film. Apart from one or two isolated attempts to treat film as an art, such as Gilbert Seldes's 1937 book *Movies for the Millions*, film (and particularly Hollywood film) was regarded as not worthy of serious study before the 1950s. Much of this attitude derived, as in the case of television today, from an unwillingness to treat an industrial, collective and popular medium as likely to be worthy of serious critical attention, and again it is worth noting here the way in which criticism inscribes the creative individual as the crucial factor, differentiating art from mass entertainment. In the late 1950s and early 1960s the film journal, *Cahiers du cinéma*, produced a manifesto arguing for what it called a *politique des auteurs*, which was regrettably mistranslated into English as "auteur theory". The motive behind the position of *Cahiers du cinéma* was twofold. On the one hand there was a desire to challenge some of the snobbish hostility to American cinema, and on the other there was a move against studying film only for its sociological contents and themes without any regard to *how* a film might produce its effects.

The journal argued on behalf of the existence of distinctive *auteurs* in cinema who could be seen to stamp their work with marks of their own personality. The cinematic author was taken to be the director (or *cinéaste*) who, through the translation of the script and the overall arrangement of the disparate elements which make up film, could be seen to be determining the overall shape and meaning of the film. Clear examples could be found in the popular genre works of John Ford, Howard Hawks and Nicholas Ray. What this approach offered was a serious study of film technique, with attention to the codes of shooting, lighting, editing and how these were combined by individual directors to produce their distinctive styles. In paying attention to these factors, the writers for *Cahiers* drew attention to the particularities of cinematic language, and especially to the concept of *mise-en-scène*. *Mise-en-scène* was seen as the most usual method the director used to imprint his distinctive style on the film. *Mise-en-scène* was understood as the various elements that went into the staging of a shot, including the scene arrangement, the camera movement, details of dialogue and the style of its delivery and the transitions from shot to shot.

The limitations of the *auteur*ist approach were considerable. Most serious was the fact that it introduced a whole new hierarchy in the critical study of film. Only those films, or groups of films, which could be demonstrated to bear the distinctive marks of an 'individual' author became worthy of serious study (even if the canon did now include some Hollywood directors). And as a concomitant it followed that the quest to establish the author also became a method of evaluation. Individual personality, or distinctive traits of personal style, became methods of establishing value.

The criticism which Roland Barthes levelled at the obsession with the idea of the individual author of the written text is just as relevant to cinema. Barthes challenged the obsession with the idea of the individual creative genius as the explanation for the meanings revealed in a text. For him, the idea of individual creativity blinded critics to the process of production and the characteristics of the material in which that production was accomplished, be it film or writing. In *auteur*ist approaches to film, this elevation of the individual at the expense of understanding the processes by which meaning is arrived at took a particularly romantic turn. Given the collective and industrial nature of film production, it was regarded as all the more remarkable that individuality could be achieved against such odds. Just as in the study of literature, the pre-eminence given to the individual as the explanation for meaning acted as a closure on what could be said about a film in terms of the social forces in which it was produced.

The same tides which brought Barthes's criticisms to bear on the literary text and the enshrinement of the individual also turned against the *auteur*ist approach to cinema. But it is generally recognized that the *politique des auteurs* did something for film studies which is rarely accomplished in literary studies when it focuses on the individual author as a means of understanding that text. What *auteur*ism accomplished in film was in fact the beginnings of an elaboration of film language. In attending to *how* the individual *auteur* transformed the elements of the raw material into a meaning and a style which was distinctive, this approach to film did in fact bring critics into a close *textual* analysis of the visual image. Perhaps for the first time, the idea of the transparency of the photographic image was effectively challenged. (By this I refer to the prevailing 'common-sense' belief that the camera simply records what is there and is therefore the medium most likely to accurately record reality.) In studying the elements which are arranged in a shot to produce its particular meaning, in studying the codes of lighting, of how shot follows shot, of the positioning of figures and objects within a shot, and the general composition of the image, what began to emerge were the tools of material analysis of film which deals with codes, ideologies, orders of discourse (the social factors in determining meaning rather than the life or personality of an individual). To some extent *auteur*ist approaches to film laid the groundwork for the approaches which superceded it, approaches influenced by semiology which insisted on studying *how* meaning comes about in a filmic text, in the combination of all its signifying elements or codes – including as a minor, but rather privileged code, the '*auteur*ist' interpretation, relating one film to others 'by' a particular director.

Television Authorship

The situation with television is peculiarly pointed. The history of broadcast television certainly shows an institutional sympathy to the idea of the author, perhaps even greater than that of film. Probably deriving its direct descent from radio, television carries with it a firm belief in the value of the written word, and with that come the inevitable ideologies about the significance of the individual author. The history of BBC radio is marked not only by an extreme reverence to the great authors of the literary establishment, but also by 'episodes' where significant literary figures were courted by the new mass medium. What is more, much of radio's history is marked by a denial of the essential characteristics of the medium of radio and an insistence that radio was simply a spoken 'version' of the written text, involving very little technical interference between the written word and its delivery to the audience. Even if it may not have appeared so to the average listener, the author, both in the form of literary figures and in the form of the individual scriptwriter, was enormously important in radio's self-perception.

Television at its inception acquired wholesale a series of values from radio in which the 'writer' is privileged above any of the 'technical' tasks such as direction and production. Yet in spite of this willingness to found its more 'serious' productions on the idea of authorship, this has proved a relatively intractable task. For the average consumers such as ourselves, television is virtually an anonymous medium. The bulk of its output – news, documentaries, soap-operas, serials, adverts, come to us without any obvious 'organizing consciousness'. Indeed, very often quite other criteria apply in what we consider to be the most important factor in an individual programme. Even in programmes such as sit-coms where the *cognoscenti* might recognize authorship in the form of scriptwriters, the significance of character actors is often thought to at least equal, if not outweigh, the significance of the scriptwriter in determining the meaning of a production. Here television shares some of the same problems as film in terms of ascribing authorship. For film critics often felt that the 'star' of a film was perhaps finally the crucial factor in the film's meaning. For example, we are far more likely to think of a Garbo film than know the name of Clarence Brown, who in fact directed seven of Garbo's films.

In fact, many of the constraints on an easy recognition of television authorship are similar to those of film. Radio can inspire the illusion of very little technical intervention between the written words of the author and the audience's reception of these words. But film and television both present us with a complexity of production, and division of labour within that, which makes the image of the transparent communication between one author and his or her audience, hard to credit. But in spite of this, television itself and television critics do struggle hard to retain a regime of individuality. Indeed it is a fundamental value of television. At moments this regime of individuality is quite different from that of literature, as in the inscription of the idea of the television personality attaching to frivolous and serious alike, encompassing presenters like Wogan at one end, and a 'personality' reporter like John Pilger at the other. At other moments, however, the idea of the individual author derived directly from literary models reigns supreme. First, much of television's quality output is based on 'dramatizations' of authors – Dickens and Shakespeare are favourites but there are many others, like the Bröntes, Jane Austen or more modern writers like Malcolm Bradbury. These productions reinforce the idea of the text (and create the idea of the programme) as the emanation of one individual mind. *The History Man* is far more likely to be remembered as a dramatization of Malcolm Bradbury's novel than by any specifically televisual attribute it might have acquired in the process of dramatization. These productions are much more common than a second relation which television has to the literary author, which is the commissioning of original works by 'quality' writers. There is surprisingly little traffic between, say, the Booker Prize shortlist writers and television. Fay Weldon's successful incursion on to TV with *The Heart of the Country* and Alan Bennett's TV plays are the exception rather than the rule.

It is rare for something originating from within television itself to be regarded as 'quality' entertainment in the same way. In fact that notion of quality seems curiously parasitic on the literary establishment. The only hope which television offers itself for claiming an intrinsic cultural quality is through the notion of the playwright. And this notion of the playwright owes nothing to specific skills within the medium of television, and everything to the institution of literature. The playwright is the lure held up to television. If the playwright is good enough, television too might become an art.

Dennis Potter and *The Singing Detective*

The example of Dennis Potter is both timely and relevant. Critics are claiming that with the success of his last production, *The Singing Detective*, he has established himself as the first 'great' television writer. Television itself was last to respond to the critical success which *The Singing Detective* accomplished in the press. Firstly, Dennis Potter became the subject of an Arena programme, which has previously expressed a clear commitment to a highly traditional notion of the Arts. Secondly, and more recently, there has been a Dennis Potter retrospective, showing work, of rather variable quality, dating from the 1960s. Both of these are indeed high accolades for a writer who has worked almost exclusively within the medium of television. In so far as television does reflect on itself, it has been (especially recently) the presentation of television as social history, and with little claim for 'cultural achievement'.

The elevation of Dennis Potter to television *auteur* is not without a hidden agenda. The retrospective of his plays has allowed inclusion of *Brimstone and Treacle*, a play banned under the previous BBC regime of Alisdair Milne (in 1972). By constructing Potter as the first great television playwright, the new regime at the BBC can mark its distance from the previous one, but without having to defend the play itself. It simply becomes an important example of the *oeuvre* of Dennis Potter. But long before the retrospective, the Arena programme made it quite clear that Potter had already been claimed by the ideologies surrounding the individual author in literary criticism. Potter was interviewed by Alan Yentob, Head of Arts Programmes for the BBC, whose questions emphasized the importance of Dennis Potter's life as the way of understanding his work. The questions sought to establish recurrent themes in Potter's output and, in particular, they revealed the desire to relate those themes to the individual's autobiography. Much of the programme was geared to understanding Dennis Potter's previous output, in the light of *The Singing Detective*, as if *The Singing Detective* was the laying bare of the themes and obsessions which previous works began to explore.

In criticizing this approach to *The Singing Detective*, I am in no way trying to lessen its significance. Far from it. Watched by eight million people (and source of offence to a sizeable minority) it was certainly an important cultural event, putting forward extremely complex, perhaps even radical, ideas about male sexuality, fantasy and history in a highly entertaining way. Indeed, it could be argued that the series was far more important and searching than anything which has appeared on these subjects in the literary text over the last decade. However, far from 'authorship' being necessary to guarantee this significance, the concept, if anything, seems to get in the way, and block recognition of some of the truly radical aspects of the series.

The Singing Detective

The reception of *The Singing Detective* shows up the inadequacies which the search for authorship imposes on a medium like television. The Arena programme attempted to construct the television *auteur*, with snippets of previous productions, with questions designed to tell the story of his own life, and then an attempt to find the points of contact between these two. The retrospective series has offered a number of disparate programmes, linked by the author, in which we are invited to find recurrent themes, and distinctive stylistic traits. Both these approaches limit what can be said about texts. They attempt to impose one meaning on Dennis Potter's work, either a meaning which can be explained by his life (themes) or by his character and distinctiveness (style). By this operation, his most important series, *The Singing Detective*, can be understood as the apotheosis of these themes. But just like the attempts to establish the author in early *auteur* writing about the cinema, even these questions open up onto another, more important approach to television. For in attempting even to talk about the author's style in relation to *The Singing Detective*, we are forced into questions about the nature of the medium of television itself. The questions which present themselves here are about how the meaning is produced in a text which is using visual, verbal and musical language, which moves complexly between fantasy and 'reality', and which self-consciously refers to the conventions and styles of television and film.

What is striking about *The Singing Detective* is the mixing of televisual or film genres. Scenes of intense, almost documentary realism set in the hospital are quickly replaced by perfect parodies of *film noir*, or give way to musical numbers. A perfect example of this occurs in the first episode. During the consultant's ward round, the stark, alienating reality of the hospital is suddenly transformed into a *smoky* where the entire hospital staff perform the musical number 'Dem bones, dem bones, dem dry bones'. The sequence returns with surprising ease to the painful 'reality' of Marlow embarrassing the doctors by weeping bitterly about his condition. Although Marlow's head is the point which we gradually learn unifies the disparate fragments of memory, fantasy and experience, there is no hierarchy of discourses, where for example the scenes of hospital realism are given greater significance than other scenes. The first episode starts firmly located in the fantasy thriller genre, and it is only some time into the episode that we are given a 'realistic' location, the hospital ward where Philip Marlowe, writer of second-rate detective fiction, is incapacitated with a horrific skin complaint. The juxtaposition marks a series of significant oppositions (between fantasy and reality, between 'art' and life) which dominate the series in the very process of their breaking down.

In attempting to analyse the style and effect of these passages, the links to be made with 'previous Dennis Potter productions' and with 'the life of Dennis Potter' are rather limiting. Much more important is an attention to the text which reveals very precisely the culminative impression of meaning formed by the juxtaposition of known film and television genres with each other. There is no clear unilinear narrative development; scenes are juxtaposed rather than being connected in any linear 'cause' and 'effect' sequence. Throughout the series, the genres shift as the scenes shift; often 'scenes' are played out in a mixture of genres. In conventional TV production, a programme either stays within one genre for its duration or makes clear how we can evaluate a hierarchy of genres, that is, it observes the conventions of television realism, unless it clearly marks its departure into dream or day-dream (even then, the fantasy insert often remains in the same style as the so-called reality sequences). In *The Singing Detective* the switch between genres is crucial to exploring the themes of reality and fantasy; often the distinction between the two is only marked by quite subtle changes in television style.

Episode five provided a particularly good example of the intercutting between genres, both marking and blurring the distinction between fantasy and reality, and used for cumulative effect. The sequence starts as a ward scene with a strong connotation of hospital realism, signalled by the loud soundtrack of hospital noises. The scene continues with a move into close-up and focus on the dialogue of Philip Marlowe and his girlfriend Nicola. The predominating style is that of TV drama, with an emphasis on acting and witty repartee between the protagonists. Very quickly the scene moves to fantasy; at first this is clearly marked, but gradually the distinctions become harder and harder to maintain. The distinction between Philip and Nicola's 'real' exchange in the hospital, and Philip's fantasy of her involvement with Mark Binney, is at first easy to maintain. However, the distinction becomes increasingly untenable. Nicola does indeed seem to be trying to 'cheat' on Marlowe just as his fantasy suggests, and the Mark Binney figure starts appearing in the hospital setting. At one point, two figures who had previously clearly inhabited Marlowe's fantasy world as writer, signified by their heavy (heavy-handed) connotations of *film noir*, merge into the hospital realism, culminating in a strange and inexplicable chase from the hospital (again whose unreality is only signified by knowledge of the American TV thriller drama). At moments the rapid shift from genre to genre, from fantasy to reality, is foregrounded, as in one moment where Nicola and Mark Binney are interrupted by the sound of Nicola's voice in the hospital and turn towards the interruption as disgruntled actors.

There is no guiding or explanatory voice through sequences like this. Meaning arrives only through the culmination of juxtaposed scenes. Over the six episodes there are repetitions. Certain scenes begin to appear in shorthand, such as the scene of the woman's body being brought out of the river, or the scene of his mother making love to an unknown soldier in the woods. These scenes, or parts of these scenes, are repeated, set first against one scene then against another, beginning to transfer meaning from the first scene to the third. At first the woman's body appears closely in relation to Marlowe's fantasies, in particular his thriller and detective fantasies. Gradually the scene begins to reappear more and more in relation to other more personal memories, of his childhood and of his mother's 'betrayal'. Only at certain moments in the entire six episodes is there any definitive linking and locating of the various memories and fantasies. This occurs in a scene where Marlowe is dragged into an unwilling word game with a psychotherapist which leads at increasing pace to 'shit', 'women', 'sex', 'death'. And as those words arrive, so too do the various recurrent visual themes. This scene foregrounds one of the important aspects of *The Singing Detective* – precisely this use of repetition and rhythm. The only overall comprehension which is possible for the series derives from recognizing the pattern of repetition and recognizing the build-up of rhythm to the significant moments where memories and fantasies are linked together.

What is important about this approach to the series is that it emphatically reveals the importance of the viewer as the place where the meaning of the text ultimately (if anywhere) resides. What we need to recognize is that viewers of this series are being called on to recognize (and use) television genres and codes in order to recognize the differences between fantasies, and between fantasy and reality. No text could more vividly illustrate Barthes's description of what makes up all texts, 'the text is a tissue of quotations drawn from inummerable centres of culture' (*S/Z*). Each element is a trace of what has previously gone before, a reworking of previous cultural usages; the programme is 'an intertextual space'

(Kristeva). But unlike most television and popular entertainment, which simply repeats previous cultural usages in worn stereotypes, *The Singing Detective* takes up these 'quotations', and by juxtaposition and repetition, uses them to explore themes of memory, repression, the past and the present. And what is revealed by Dennis Potter's particular exploration of these themes through the medium of television is how complex and sophisticated is the ability of the average television audience to 'read' the codes of television. Nothing could more dramatically reveal the continued disregard of the television audience's intelligence than the fact that such a 'complex' programme (in the aesthetic terms of television management) could be so popular. None of these things can be said from a form of criticism which is determined to explain *The Singing Detective* by reference only to the author Dennis Potter.

In a sense *The Singing Detective* is 'about authorship', about a writer, Philip Marlowe, his need to fantasize to assuage his personal pain, and his desire to impose (or at least present) his fantasies on others. But if we see the series as simply governed by the central character's consciousness (a central character, as the press kept telling us, who is very like Potter), then we miss the point – the final episode where the petty gangsters come in search of their author, and Nicola has apparently murdered Binney. These cannot be seen as simply emanations of the author, Philip Marlowe. The characters have gained a life of their own – and only the inadequacies of that life are the author's responsibility. Perhaps then, Potter himself, doyen of TV 'authors', is telling us that authorship is a relatively unimportant, if ego-inflating, critical question. Or, as he put it in the Arena programme: 'Nowhere but nowhere in the script did I mention the Forest of Dean' (Potter's own birthplace). So who set the series there? It must have been the producer Kenith Trodd – a great promoter of Potter as author. Such are the tangles that the hunt for the television will snare us in.... The 'author' is an external and uncomfortable import in television criticism. Nevertheless the existence of the author is being made a condition of television being taken seriously as a cultural product. I hope to have shown that neither film nor television can usefully be forced into that particular obsession, which only serves to hide knowledge of the media from us and therefore make us complicit in the belief that film and television are not in fact constructs but are instruments of personal expression.

2

To Desire Differently: Feminism and the French Cinema

Sandy Flitterman-Lewis

Femininity and Authorship

All of this becomes extremely complicated when we apply the enunciative model of authorship to women's work – when we attempt, in fact, to consider this theoretical apparatus in terms of the feminine – for the consideration of films made by women adds another, absolute, crucial, dimension to these discussions. An important paradox arises when we think of feminist filmmakers, because although the effort to define the terms of a feminist counter-tradition must, of necessity, focus on the work of women, the power of the theories heretofore elaborated shifts the discussion of authorship away from actual individuals and toward relations of unconscious desire generated by the text. Yet this does not mean that cinematic production is somehow gender-neutral; indeed to ignore sexuality in considerations of authorship is to, in essence, support the masculine status quo. As Stephen Heath observes, "Any discourse which fails to take account of the problem of sexual difference in its enunciation and address will be within a patriarchal order, precisely indifferent, a reflection of male domination."[1] This raises a number of complex questions, each suggesting a different level of analysis: How can we define a "desiring look" when the position of looking is feminine? What are the parameters and articulations of a "female discourse" as it traverses a particular text? And how can we conceptualize a "woman's desire" from the triple standpoint of the author, text, and viewer?

To consider female authorship within these theoretical parameters is to pose the problem of sexual difference across the field of cinematic enunciation. Enunciative positioning must be conceived in a *different* way when the female is taken into account, but specific definitions of female enunciation are currently only in the process of being elaborated, and much work still remains to be done. While a feminist cinema must necessarily posit its enunciative position as feminine, this does not simply mean that there is a feminine "content" or "expression" that emanates directly from the woman's place. Rather, the notion of authorship/enunciation in the feminine raises the question of female *desire*, indicating a terrain of representation from which various new positions can be engaged, scopic modalities which imply alternative conceptions of female subjectivity and desire. These supersede either individual filmmakers or particular fictional characters. Within this context, a film made by a woman (even one with strong female models) might still organize its vision according to masculine structures. This is because, regardless of a film's content, it is always taken up in the unconscious processes of desire which negotiate the cinematic text. Feminist analyses of the cinema must work at this level of complexity because it is here that the cultural (unconscious) and the representational (cinematic) intersect, and it is only in these terms that the impasses of biology and of content analysis can be avoided. However, defining the "I" who speaks cinematically – as a woman – is a deceptive and difficult task.

Another complication that sexual difference suggests concerns the theoretical assumption that the enunciative apparatus itself is masculine. Yet while Bellour's work on Hitchcock and enunciation does focus on the way that *male* desire is articulated, the debated "masculinity" of enunciation refers more to the kind of analysis in which Freud defined the libido itself as "masculine" than to the presumed sex of the enunciator. In fact, there is often a confusion between actual men (male filmmakers) and the global system of enunciation, in which the circulation of desire is interpreted and examined in terms of the psychoanalytic category of masculinity. More important for feminists, however, is the fact that Bellour defines *the place* of the enunciator as that which monitors the different types of scopic relation to the object, classifying the relative positions of the camera-look in relation to what is represented. It is a splitting of vision which inscribes the enunciation of a film's textual system, and the delegation of "the look" is what makes this splitting of vision possible. Therefore, although a masculine standard might be implied by the theoretical construct (its elaboration, in fact, having come about precisely in terms of the generation of masculine desire), the question of enunciation *in the feminine* recasts the very terms and relations of sexuality, vision, authorship, and text. This suggests a number of possibilities for female enunciation: a problematization of the enunciating subject itself and the indication of alternative positions, a denaturalization of the gaze structured according to phallic logic, a shift of emphasis in the quality and intensity of the controlling look – as well as in its object, a new recognition of what Chantal Akerman calls "*la jouissance du voir*" (the erotics of vision unhampered by the strictures of voyeuristic definition), and, at the level of the diegesis, differing structures of point-of-view and identification as well as the creation of new possibilities for destabilizing the inevitability and homogeneity of the patriarchal narrative.

A closer look at the paradox of authorship reveals some productive contradictions. On the one hand, theory's dissolution of the concept of authorship into questions of enunciation and subjectivity means an end to the idea of the author as source and guarantee of meaning – a refusal to see the film as the manifestation of the personal vision of a unique artist – in favor of a notion of the text which implies both signifying and psychic operations in its construction. On the other hand, the study of any specific individual filmmaker will take into account *history* (the historical moment when the filmmaker lived and worked) and *biography* (the specific personal history, including the gender of the filmmaker, particularly – and emphatically – if a woman). A film's preoccupations, interests, and stylistics will be shaped by the individual *and* her time, and will indicate what we might consider a feminine voice. A theoretical position must incorporate this – it is a political necessity for feminists – and cannot obviate it altogether in a general theory of the apparatus. The problem, specifically for this book, becomes one of critically discussing the work of particular female authors while remaining within the context of enunciative theory. If the author is no longer understood as an expressive, fully self-present individual whose conscious intentions are manifested in film, still feminism necessitates that films and filmmakers be looked at in terms of how they treat the feminist problematic, how they (and we) define a "female perspective," "feminine desire," "feminist discourse," the "woman's film" – in short, how they pose the *difference* of women's filmmaking. However, the border between those definitions and authorial intentionality becomes quite thin, while it is that very intentionality which the theory seeks to displace.

At least three solutions to the contradiction between the textual instance of enunciation and the "author as individual" present themselves. Although both history (culture) and biography (gender) crystallize in the latter notion, these important elements must be inserted into a theoretical context which denies such individuality. The resolution of the paradoxical emphases of authorship is achieved by combining both tendencies to produce "authorship" as a tripartite structure, comprising (1) authorship as a historical phenomenon, suggesting the cultural context; (2) authorship as a desiring position, involving determinants of sexuality and gender; and (3) authorship as a textual moment, incorporating the specific stylistics and preoccupations of the filmmaker. At the same time, each of these components of authorship implies the other two, for they exist in a perpetually dynamic relation.

Following from this, if one recognizes that the textual author – understood as an enunciative source – is a feminist filmmaker, then her function as controller of the discourse (the one who organizes the narrative logic, negotiates the disparate visions) can be seen as one which attempts to originate the representation of her own (female) desire. Janet Bergstrom offers a series of questions posed from this perspective, questions that suggest a feminist reformulation of authorship in enunciative terms: "Who 'speaks' beneath the deceptively neutral and objective voice of the 'third person' narration? According to what logic(s) does the film make sense? In whose interest are the images and sounds recorded and ordered in a specific way, as one particular system? Who controls the look, and with it, the diegesis, and what kind of spectator does this presuppose?"[2]

The third avenue out of the paradox involves making a link between the historical discourse (which contextualizes a particular filmmaker's work in terms of production and aesthetics) and the discourse of textual analysis (which focuses on processes of desire) in such a way as to maintain the integrity of each while emphasizing the necessity of their interrelation. Thus the construction of a history – a usable tradition of alternative feminist film practice – would be possible in terms of forms of textual resistance to the dominant cinematic model. Feminist cinema would be defined, then, not according to the biological gender of the filmmaker, but according to specific textual and enunciative processes that posit the work as alternative cinema. In this way, an articulation of both forms of authorship – individual and textual – could be forged.

Given the conditions imposed by formulating cinematic production in terms of enunciation, then, what are the possibilities for an alternative feminist cinematic practice? What happens when a female enunciating subject is posed, when the desiring look articulates a different economy of vision? If we accept the theory's founding premise – that meaning is located not in the film-text itself, but in the relationship between author, spectator, and text, or more specifically in the enunciating instance of the text – how can we then specify precisely what is "feminine" (or feminist, in fact) about a particular film? How can we articulate the terms of feminine desire and female specificity both within a text and at its enunciative source? For one thing, a feminist cinema will attempt to restore the marks of cinematic enunciation so carefully elided by the concealing operations of patriarchal cinema, or at least it will work to undermine them. In any case, it will foreground sexual difference in the enunciative relay, focusing on the status and nature of the representation of the woman – her desire, her images, her fantasms. In so doing, a counter-cinema will attempt to reinsert the subject – a sexed subject – into the process of meaning-production, thereby allowing its structures to subvert, rework, or offer alternatives to the pervasive logic of masculine desire articulated by dominant cinema. As a consequence, new spectator-text relation-ships – ones which render problematic the pleasures of cinematic voyeurism – might be generated, new subjective structures obtained. For it is never a question of films having been made by individual men or women or of a specific content speaking to the needs of a particular sex. Rather, as Stephen Heath maintains, "What one has is always a structure of representation in and from the terms of which position enunciations can be engaged, specified as 'masculine,' 'feminine,' with the possibility of reappropriating the latter as site of resistance to the domination, the definitions, the assignments of the former."[3]

Notes

1   Stephen Heath, "Difference," *Screen* 19:3 (Autumn 1978): 50–127.
2   Janet Bergstrom, "The Avant-Garde: Histories and Theories," *Screen* 19:3 (Autumn 1978): 119–27.
3   Heath, "Difference," p. 103.

3
The Unauthorized Auteur Today

Dudley Andrew

Breathe easily. *Epuration* has ended. After a dozen years of clandestine whispering we are permitted to mention, even to discuss, the auteur again.[1] Since 1990 *Hors cadre* has devoted an entire issue to "L'Etat de l'auteur"; *Film Quarterly* has published James Naremore's "Authorship and the Cultural Politics of Film Criticism"; and Rutgers has brought out Timothy Corrigan's *A Cinema Without Walls*, a book that reads like a compendium of contemporary directorial talent and that includes a specific chapter on the status of the auteur today.[2]

No matter what each of us thought, or thinks, of ideological criticism, it was ruthless when it came to proper names, most ruthless of all toward those names that authorized naming in the first place: Truffaut, Rohmer, and behind them, André Bazin. Without trying to settle scores, I am happy to call attention once more to what may be Bazin's most significant insight into the medium he so loved: the cinema, he felt, was congenitally impure. No effort to purify it could long succeed: not the Dadaists of the twenties nor the Lettrists of his own day, not the Cinema-Verité movement of the sixties nor the political avant-garde that after 1968 marched in step with the changing of the guard at *Cahiers du cinéma*.

In fact, *Cahiers* in its first years had religiously pursued purity, latching onto Sartre's notion of "authenticity," where an individual authors his or her life in choice and where writers and filmmakers authenticate their work in style. Even though auteurism had been fostered as a way of recovering a large number of otherwise disposable studio-made movies, it carried with it the aura of elitism emanating from the French ciné-clubs of the postwar years and from festivals where auteurs were annually inducted and honored as individuals with strong (invariably masculine) personalities producing art capable of transcending its conditions of production and reception. The *Cahiers* critics promised to rectify the distracted attention of earlier audiences with a reverential viewing of films that in some cases they treated as sacramental objects, harboring the genuinely spiritual values conferred on them by their makers. As we will see, this sentiment toward cinema continues to be entertained today in France, though in a sophisticated and self-conscious manner.

Bazin, it is usually forgotten, was a drag on this policy, suspicious of its vocabulary.[3] He was most likely to mention an auteur in conjunction with a genre or a national trend or a social movement. When he allowed himself to indulge in the excesses of existential auteurism, as in his essay "*Le Journal d'un curé de campagne* and the Stylistics of Robert Bresson," he multiplied the names of authors. Recall this remarkable sentence from that more remarkable analysis: "The sound of a windshield-wiper against a page of Diderot is all it took to turn it into Racinian dialogue."[4] Bazin faced up to the question of adaptation and translation with all the economic, and ideological ramifications these terms imply. In this cultural ecology the auteur certainly played the most noticeable function but nevertheless was treated as a function within a system of forces. To stop one's analysis at the auteur, as Bazin accused his friends at *Cahiers*, was to stop inquiring of the cinema.[5] It was to fetishize an imagined purity of spirit or core of being beneath the images of a film. Bazin's taste for impure cinema, for hybrids and eccentricities, would have salivated at this volume's Table of Contents, and at postmodern cinema generally. For despite his commitment to the integral humanism of Rossellini and Renoir, no one was more adept than he at teasing out the multiple strands woven into any film experience. The author may have been primary for him, but only as a tortion in the knot of technology, film language, genre, cultural precedent, and so forth, a knot that has in the past decades grown increasingly tangled.

Structuralism came to study systematically the textual knot and to suppress the search for its human source. Language alone could be credited with authoring those linguistic configurations we call texts. Peter Wollen discussed Hawks and Ford not as complex men with worldviews but as names for certain regularities in textual organization, although in the first (1969) edition of *Signs and Meaning in the Cinema* he still felt required to append his pantheon of rich auteurs, holding it up against that of Andrew Sarris. By the time of the second edition (1972), flush with Foucault, he retracted the retrograde appendix. Still, Wollen's structuralism (which he compares to meteorology and implicitly to chemistry) made room for the individual as "catalyst," that is, as an element, innocuous in itself, having the potential to initiate a complex reaction when dropped into the proper mix of other elements.[6] This scientistic analogy did not keep Wollen from proclaiming the primacy of interpretation, of "reading the codes," and from confessing that some films yield nothing when read deeply while others (the great films?) reward such reading by supporting a supplement of meaning read into them. The auteurist in him was sustained by this belief in the importance of locating in the confused and contradictory activity of texts those structures that, under analysis, invariably precipitate out when the same catalyst is known to have been employed. We name these structures "von Sternberg," "Fuller," "Cukor," and so on. Isolating the auteur's signal within the noise of the text carried for Wollen a strategic function, by initiating further analyses to disentangle other signals – other codes – that contribute to the textual (dis)organization. Critics may begin by appreciating the intentions and achievements of a bold individual, but persistent structural analysis should lead them to distinguish numerous other factors (codes of genre, studio, technicians, culture) that support or more often vie with that of the director. The vibrancy of the text, its fertility as a site for productive reading, outlives the illusory vibrancy of some genius standing behind or before the text.

The two editions of Wollen's important book, the first reluctantly auteurist, the second Foucauldian, stand as mileage markers in the short trail of academic film studies, a trail that we know leads quickly to psychoanalysis, ideological critique, and the study of audiences in popular culture. One might call this a tiresome tale of academic fads, were it not for the fact that the identical issues (the status of the auteur, the discipline of the system, competition within the text, and competition within audiences) can be seen at play in real-world cultural arenas. With the demise of the confident studio system, American films joined those of other national cinemas in more readily displaying the tensions that went into their making and the anxieties that attended their reception. In the late sixties one can monitor cinema systems and their disruption worldwide. Let's look to Japan in 1968 where the notorious Seijun Suzuki affair staged a drama of business and expression as colorful as in a Kabuki play.[7]

When a Tokyo ciné-club announced its intention to hold a retrospective of most of Suzuki's forty B-movies, his studio, Nikkatsu, pulled the prints from circulation and fired the director ostensibly for making incomprehensible films. At issue, as the subsequent court proceedings brought to light, was the right of a studio to shape the appeal of its products. The elite reception to which Suzuki would have been treated in this retrospective undermined the regulated flow of images in the culture industry.

In the years following the trial the studio has been vindicated in that ciné-clubs have lost the substantial cultural weight they attained in the late sixties. Today they are invoked as a warm memory of a more innocent, more human age. On the other hand, the ciné-club proved to be a vanguard of a general uprising, for it breached the ramparts of the studio walls by declaring its right to use films in any way it might choose. The fragmentation of the mass audience into uncoordinated subgroups has been the story of global culture since 1980 and it is the story of postmodernism as well, with well-known consequences for the intentions of authors, agents, and even governments.

Suzuki constitutes a preeminent case because of the ostensibly apolitical nature of his films. Nikkatsu was concerned not so much about the power of auteurs and their renegade texts but about that of audiences to break up the meaning of texts and to break up the system Nikkatsu believed it controlled. This same shift became evident in the West in the 1970s with the canon-bashing that occurred in the wake of feminism and multiculturalism: while a great many films and some new auteurs may have climbed into the pantheon, they have done so at deflated value. For the most advanced cultural critics have sold their stock in auteurs and even in texts, buying heavily into audiences and the cultures they comprise.[8]

But the Suzuki story continues: today he is indeed a genuine force in Japanese cinema. Special issues of journals have been consecrated to him. While he no longer turns out three films a year, but more like one every three years, each now causes a stir. Nikkatsu on the other hand is inert. The auteur has outlasted the industry, or rather he has adapted to a fragmented audience, one small but passionate portion of which will pay to see, and see repeatedly, whatever it is that Suzuki signs.

Auteurism, in short, is far from dead.[9] As Timothy Corrigan says, it may

> in fact be more alive now than at any other point in film history.... within the commerce of contemporary culture it [auteurism] has become, as both a production and interpretive position, more critically central yet massively different from what it once may have been. Since the early 1970s, the commercial conditioning of this figure has successfully evacuated it of most of its expressive power and textual coherence; simultaneously, this commercial conditioning has called renewed attention to the layered pressures of auteurism as an agency that establishes different modes of identification with its audiences.[10]

What has happened since the early seventies, since the Wollen book and the Suzuki affair, to produce these different modes of identification? Among other factors, the incessant flow of televisual images has eroded the stability of texts and seeped like an acid to break up the last signs of their authors as authorities who hover over the experience of their work and exert a moral pressure on its interpretation. Auteurs may exist but they do so by the grace of spectators. Today critics feel the need to be concerned with the cultural environment within which a diverse citizenry moves, takes pleasure, and jockeys for position. They must be concerned with Tokyo, London, São Paulo, and Rome, where, out of control, a superabundance of images is taken up willy-nilly by the myriad groups wandering the streets at cross-purposes or to no purpose at all.

Critics like Corrigan, who are fascinated or bewildered by the rapidly shifting movements in culture since Vietnam, recognize the importance of the auteur in the proliferation of texts and meanings, but treat that auteur not as an individual with a vision or even a program but as a dispersed, multi-masked, or empty name bearing a possibly bogus collateral in the international market of images, a market that increasingly trades in "futures." This reduction of the auteur to a single relay in the economic flow of images has the effect of superimposing representations onto reality, reversing the traditional model. "To begin to write," Edward Said claimed, "is to redirect human energy away from the 'world' to the page."[11] If the cinema had ever been worthy to be taken as a page on which something once begun was written, Corrigan would have us believe this is no longer the case today, that we are in the midst of "A Cinema Without Walls" spilling out into the world. If they once did so, auteurs today turn not away from the world but toward it, and the world, if we dare to speak of it at all anymore, is a salad of possibilities in which images and representations are included as first-order elements. Not long ago one aptly referred to Fellini's "world," or Ingmar Bergman's or John Ford's, indicating thereby an abstracted set of elements systematically interrelated in a structure to be projected on a screen somewhere to the side of the daily life from which those elements were culled. But today, should we speak of Spike Lee's "world," when his is designed to fold itself inside our world? Appearing on talk shows and Nike shoe ads, Lee is familiar in our living rooms, just as pizza and Public Enemy fit comfortably within his films. Indeed those films are likely to be invited into our living rooms on tape. This is more than a matter of new technologies of distribution; it stems from a recognition that nature and culture and the representation of both are increasingly experienced homogeneously. Do tourists today distinguish their trip to the Epcot Center from their visit to Florida?

The global commercialization of culture validates Corrigan's viewpoint, money serving as the great equalizer. Not only does it equalize Spike Lee, Ridley Scott, and Robert Bresson at the Video Rental store, but it places even the most intentional auteur (Coppola is Corrigan's well-chosen example) inside a system that is larger than he, a system that quickly and crudely exchanges his value on the market in its own way. American film critics like Corrigan who once looked to Europe for models of films and criticism, must now be increasingly attentive, like their country itself, to Japan and what it represents in economy and culture. For Japan stands for neon and simulacra, not for texts and authors, despite the proliferation of print in that country. In the postwar era the auteur was the strongest tie linking cinema to the literary function; the auteur proved that Film could be an art, an expression of personal thought and feeling, opposed to the externality of spectacle, opposed also perhaps to the universal appeal of most movies. The mention of literature calls to mind a cinema that is viewed in private, meditatively, one that is reflected upon and discussed and from which ideas may be taken, in short a cinema to be read rather than consumed.[12]

Are even books still read in such a way? To think about the author in Japan is to think nostalgically, to think of Soseki and Tanizaki and the refined world of sensibility that they represented and to which they contributed. Whereas today, in Tokyo's Jonmocho district – the world's greatest concentration of bookstores – magazines and manga increasingly dominate the shelves. Thousands of browsers move from rack to rack, flipping pages. They edge distractedly to the cashier where they riffle through their wallets and exchange thousand-yen notes featuring portraits of Soseki for picture books of humanized robots or more often of robotic nubile girls (drawn or photographed, it hardly matters). A leading critic of Japanese literature concludes his last book with a meditation on post-literacy in the midst of a booming publishing culture.[13] Japanese books are designed to be disposable. In that country the author is recruited into a commerce of swift exchange where even in scholarly writing the topos of ideas are scanned with the rapidity of a simplified line drawing.[14]

Cinema is part of the media economy that has reduced the auteur to a sign, indeed precisely to a signature. But cinema is also a victim of this economy, its carefully painted images losing out on (and to) the electronic pictures flowing like tap water or sewage down twelve or thirty-four or a hundred channels around the globe. Looked at from the perspective of Tokyo, literature and cinema have in common the futile and pathetic struggle to preserve the value of thought, of feeling, of art, in a world that decreasingly cares about such things.

But let me return to Europe where such things are discussed and apparently still cared about. For the auteur has returned to academic respectability today, as Corrigan's book demonstrates, and it has done so thanks to heretical Foucauldians like Edward Said and Gilles Deleuze. Said's sensitivity to the micro-structures of power and knowledge didn't keep him from writing a book called *Beginnings* and from retaining a belief that critical humanism (that is, strategic interventions by individuals) could alter such massive and dispersed ideological formations as the one he identified as "Orientalism." To "begin" a project is not to originate a work, but rather to deflect a flow, to branch off in a direction. This limited sense of novelty retains the power of individual effort and critique while recognizing the greater power of the social system within which anything that makes a difference must begin. We credit this view to the likes of Alexander Kluge and Fernando Solanas. Why not apply it in some degree, too, to a Ridley Scott, whose attempt to branch out from the road picture in *Thelma and Louise* (1991) seems more heroic for its collapse in the film's final chase sequences.[15]

Less moderate than Said, Gilles Deleuze returns to Nietzsche and especially to Bergson in insisting on "the new," on "creative evolution." Deleuze's influential books on cinema depend on auteurs, on their muscular expansion of the repertoire of cinematic representation, and effectively on what we once called their "visions of the world." In a symptomatic moment he locates in the films of Akira Kurosawa a configuration of camera movements that double as a fictive graphic sign – a kanji – for Kurosawa's own name.[16] Always a problematic and very special sign, the signature of the author is a mark on the surface of the text signaling its source. The signature embeds within it – as in hypertext – a genuine fourth dimension, the temporal process that brought the text into being in the first place.[17] The signature moors the film image to a submerged reef of values by means of the slender line drawn by camera or pen. It is visible in the credits of films, in the literal appearance in the midst of their films of auteurs like Hitchcock, and after him of Truffaut, Godard, and Rohmer.

An auteur may be surrounded by the images for which it is claimed he is responsible, while not directing their reading. This would be Deleuze's point regarding Kurosawa and Hitchcock, whose use of the figure of the spiral in *Vertigo* he identifies as a graphic signature as well. The spectator is free to employ these figures as he or she wishes because, for Deleuze, one doesn't "read" a movie anyway, rather one subsists within its duration and its flow, carried by it, but not carried to any pre-given destination. The auteur marks the presence of temporality and creativity in the text, including the creativity of emergent thought contributed by the spectator.

Deleuze's resolute stance against the semiology of cinema may be responsible for the French reassessment of the auteur in terms no longer of literature but of painting. Several of France's most significant films of late take as their subject the creative instant of the artist. Jacques Rivette's *La Belle Noiseuse* and Maurice Pialat's *Van Gogh* confirm the relation between cinema and painting that theorists like Jacques Aumont and Raymond Bellour have been insisting upon, particularly in relation to Godard's recent work.[18] Godard has always understood that the image of the auteur as a writer before a blank page must be followed by the more disappointing image of those pages filled out in a language whose net inevitably surrounds and constricts the expressive impulse that pushes the stylus into the paper. But the image of the painter before an empty canvas retains the lure of pre-linguistic purity, the moment when representation and perception interact in ways that are potentially fresh. *Passion* (1982) takes originality for its subject; *Je Vous Salue Marie* (1984) meditates on the virgin birth by simulating the untrammeled perception of nature. One might consider Godard, Rivette, and even Pialat as special cases, but when a popular success like *Touts les matins du monde* (1991), starring Gérard Depardieu, burrows into the stillness of a Baroque composer before the act of composing, one must credit a significant backlash against the massive successes of American action cinema (*Terminator 2* [1991]) and of the simulations of international postmodernism (*La Femme Nikita* [1991]) that form the backdrop of contemporary culture.[19]

In their theory and films, then, the French remind us even today that properly speaking the author is not one who employs a completed language system but stands as the function that reaches back to the silence before language and draws out in birth pangs an expression shaped to feeling and thought. To read a poem or a novel is to participate again in this struggle for expression, what today we call *écriture*, the quest for the state of wordlessness through words.[20] *Écriture* (and paradoxically these "painting films")[21] involves temporality and interiority, whereas the postmodern media world is one of pure spatiality and externality, the display – the spectacle – of the social.

The term *écriture* inevitably turns my conclusion toward Marguerite Duras. *Le Camion* (1977) opens with a shot of an intersection. When a truck (*the* truck of the title) centers itself in focus, the credits begin to identify those responsible for this text, including Marguerite Duras as author and director. But where, or which, is the text of those listed as responsible for it? We ask this when the credits are interrupted by a shot of Duras herself reading a written text to Gérard Depardieu. When the truck returns along with the remainder of the credits we are led to realize that this film is an exemplification of a reading that we are intermittently allowed to be present at. No prior literary work is translated by the cinema. The cinema in fact imagines a piece of writing that is simultaneously under construction. The author is present in the text as a cinematic effect.

Atop this fertile image of the auteur in the text, however, we must impose a second image, more recent and far more normal: on the cover of a popular monthly journal a black-and-white photo of a fetching teenager, hat cocked

1930s style, with the caption inviting the reader to open and enter "La vraie vie de Marguerite Duras."[22] In the midst of a biographical assemblage, a crucial page is devoted to the recent adaptation of her most popular novel *L'Amant* (1992). Duras, we learn, wrote a screen version of *L'Amant* at the request of its producer Claude Berri by composing a parasitic novel, *L'amant de la Chine du Nord* that contains references to its possible realization in motion pictures. The second chapter begins: "C'est un livre, c'est un film, c'est la nuit."[23] Producing more "literature," this adaptation only brought her into dispute with Berri and with the film's director, Jean-Jacques Annaud, a dispute whose notoriety has even now become part of the promotion of a film that Duras repudiates. Yet Duras's name and her adolescent photograph are integral to the advertising of this film and presumably to the pleasure of the public standing in line to watch what is in every sense a hybrid artifact.

L'Amant (as writing, text, film, supplemental text, and cultural phenomenon) strains the issues of purity and hybridity with which I began. *L'Amant* requires Duras and requires her absence; this is the paradox of auteurism.[24] We want to believe in Duras, though few authors disappear more mysteriously behind a screen of words. This is a struggle of faith in an atheist world, for the author is surely an analogue of God, the creator and source of the world. With the disappearance of God we are left with the body of the world: so, with the disappearance of the author, we are left with the material body of the text. Since Nietzsche, we have been tempted to play with that body as we choose, for readers exist and the text exists, but the author is an effect of both, an effect, moreover, brought about by distance and invisibility. Nevertheless, despite Nietzsche and the freeplay he ushered in, the word "auteur," and the occasional signs left by whatever this word signals, can thicken a text with duration, with the past of its coming into being and with the future of our being with it.

Notes

1   *Epuration* refers to the period in France just following World War II when certain personalities in the film world were for a time forbidden to practice their trade because of hints of collaboration with the Nazis. Henri-Georges Clouzot and Arletty were the most famous names taken out of circulation for a time.

2   *Hors cadre* 8 (Spring, 1990); James Naremore, "Authorship and the Cultural Politics of Film Criticism," *Film Quarterly* 44, no. 1 (Fall 1990); Timothy Corrigan, *A Cinema Without Walls* (New Brunswick: Rutgers University Press, 1991). Naturally none of the authors of these texts wants to return to the critical paradigm of the 1950s and 1960s; all of them complicate the issue, but all of them discuss it too. Naremore does so sheepishly, a bit ashamed to bring it up in these sophisticated days. Corrigan more courageously accords the auteur a role in the new system of textual production that goes by the name postmodernism. Many of the contributors to *Hors cadre* gladly return to the concept if not the flesh and blood of the author (seen now as split, or absent, or constructed, or as a mere signature) in their efforts to probe

ever more deeply into the peculiar, and I would say hybrid, medium known as the cinema.

3 Someone who does not forget this is Jim Hillier whose collection *Cahiers du Cinéma: The 1950s* (Cambridge, Mass.: Harvard University Press, 1988) is indispensable to the history of auteurism.

4 André Bazin, *What is Cinema?*, trans. Hugh Gray, Vol. 1 (Berkeley: University of California, 1968), p. 130.

5 André Bazin, "La Politique des auteurs," in Hillier, *Cahiers du Cinéma.*

6 Peter Wollen, *Signs and Meaning in the Cinema* (London: Secker and Warburg, 1972), p. 168.

7 I am indebted here to Aaron Gerow's unpublished 1991 paper "Spectating in the Postmodern: The Suzuki Seijun Mondai."

8 Competing values complicate the situations, as when filmmakers such as Helke Sander and Tomás Gutiérrez Alea loudly disdain cinema as "art" in the traditional sense, yet are canonized as auteurs who have opened up new options in the social production and reception of cinema.

9 Naremore declared auteurism dead on page 20 of his *Film Quarterly* essay, adding that debates about it (his and mine included, I suppose) were likewise finished.

10 Corrigan, *A Cinema Without Walls*, p. 135.

11 Edward Said, *Beginnings* (Baltimore: Johns Hopkins University Press, 1975), p. 24.

12 Eric Rohmer relates viewing films to reading books in a library in his *The Taste for Beauty* (Cambridge University Press, 1989), p. 157.

13 Maseo Miyoshi, *Off Center: Power and Cultural Relations between Japan and the United States* (Cambridge, Mass.: Harvard University Press, 1991), p. 217.

14 Masao Miyoshi notes that the scholarly essay is increasingly being replaced by the transcript of the round-table discussion, the latter satisfying a need for quick summaries of positions, for the illusion of immediacy and of the "event" rather than of reflection, and of course for the illusion of contact with the auteurs of the intellectual sphere.

15 To all appearances, a disproportionate share of the film's $16,000,000 budget went into the final quarter of the movie, complete with daring, but familiar helicopter shots. Our interest in the female characters and their perceptions is swept into the chase, re-masculinized. Still, in its very title *Thelma and Louise* gives a conscience to the rather standard road picture it becomes. The genre perhaps has always contained its own critique, though it may seldom have been so visible.

16 Gilles Deleuze, *Cinema I: The Movement-Image* trans. Hugh Tomlinson (Minneapolis: University of Minnesota Press, 1989), p. 21.

17 See Cl. Gandelman and N. Greene, "Fétichisme, signature, cinéma," *Hors cadre* 8 (Spring, 1990), pp. 147–62.

18 Jacques Aumont, *L'Oeil interminable* (Paris, Séguir 1989), and *L'Image* (Paris: Fernand Nathan, 1990); Raymond Bellour, ed., *Cinéma et peinture: approaches* (Paris: Presses Universitaires de France, 1990), and *L'Entre-image* (Paris: 1990).

19 Pierre Corneu, the director of *Tous les matins du monde*, does not hesitate to discuss the Straub/Huillet *Chronicle of Anne Magdelena Bach* in assessing his own achievement in *Cahiers du cinéma* 451 (January, 1992). *Tous les matins du monde* grossed more money than any other film in Paris in the first weeks of 1992. While the French may have pushed the notion of the artist-creator the furthest, an international interest in

this topos can be seen by scanning recent films such as *Angels at my Table* (Campion, 1991), *Vincent and Theo* (Altman, 1990), *Prospero's Books* (Greenaway, 1991), and so on.

20 Marc Le Bot, "L'Auteur anonyme ou l'état d'imposteur," *Hors cadre* 8 (Spring, 1990), p. 19.

21 Paradoxical because the term "*écriture*" which has haunted cinema since 1950 at first did so under the spirit of literature. Today those films – specifically Rivette's and Godard's – that take up the struggle of language and expression, increasingly do so under the spirit of painting and art history. This would be Raymond Bellour's point, and I agree with it.

22 *Lire* 193 (October, 1991).

23 Marguerite Duras, *L'Amant de la Chine du Nord* (Paris: Gallimard, 1991), p. 17.

24 The phenomenon is notable enough to have received mention (with a photo!) in *Newsweek*, February 17, p. 8.

Part II

Film Language/Specificity

Introduction

Robert Stam

Throughout the century of the cinema's existence, theorists have reflected on two interrelated questions: (1) whether or not film constituted a language, and (2) what was the "essence" or specificity of that language. To begin with the first concept, the notion of "film language" appears already in the 1910s and 1920s in the writings of Riccioto Canudo and Louis Delluc, both of whom saw the language-like nature of the cinema as linked, paradoxically, to its non-verbal nature, its status as a "visual esperanto" transcending the barriers of national language.[1] Also in the 1920s, the Russian Formalists, in their anthology *Poetica Kino* (1927), developed the analogy between language and film in a somewhat more systematic way. Tynanov, for example, spoke of the cinema as offering the visible world in the form of semantic signs generated by cinematic procedures.[2]

Since the beginnings of film as a medium, analysts have also sought the unique and distinguishing features, the "essence," as it were, of the "seventh art." For some this essence was rooted in photography, or in montage, or in some quality of cinematic representation such as movement. The etymological meanings of the original names given the cinema, interestingly, "envision" this specificity differently and even foreshadow later theories of the cinema: "biograph" and "animatographe" emphasize the recording of life itself (a strong current in the writings of Bazin and Kracauer); "vitascope" emphasizes the *looking* at life (and thus shifts emphasis to the spectator and scopophilia); the "cinematographe," and later "cinema," call attention to the transcription of movement. Virtually all the names include some variant on "graph" (Greek: "writing" or "transcription") and thus implicitly anticipate later tropes of filmic "authors" and processes of écriture. Questions of media specificity also lurk in the background when critics (or ordinary spectators) call films "too theatrical" or "too talky" or "too literary."

When spectators confidently announce, as if they were themselves inventing the idea rather than receiving it spoon-fed from the industry, that they believe that "film is entertainment," they too are proffering a medium-specificity argument, albeit a peculiarly unreflective one.

There are many ways to address the question of cinematic specificity. It can be approached (a) *linguistically*, i.e. in terms of film's "materials of expression," (b) *historically*, i.e. in terms of its origins (daguerrotypes, dioramas, kinetoscopes), (c) in terms of its *processes of production* (collaborative rather than individual), or (d) in terms of its *processes of reception* (isolated individual readers versus gregarious reception in movie theatres). Some early theorists argued for a cinema "untainted" by contaminations from the other arts. Jean Epstein spoke of "pure cinema," while Dziga Vertov defended a newspaper-like *kino pravda* ("cinema-truth"), a reference both to "truth" and to the communist newspaper *Pravda*, which would eschew staging and drama. Other theorists and filmmakers, in contrast, stressed the *links* between cinema and the other arts. Griffith claimed to have borrowed some of his techniques from painters like Rembrandt (chiaroscuro), or novelists like Dickens (narrative cross-cutting). Eisenstein found prestigious literary antecedents for cinematic devices, for example the narrative "cross-cutting" in the agricultural fair chapter in *Madame Bovary*. The insistence on both the similarities and the differences between cinema and the other arts provided a Janus-faced way of legitimizing a fledgling medium, a way of saying simultaneously both that the cinema was just as good as the other arts, but also that it should be judged in its own terms, in relation to its own potentials.

Thinkers as diverse as André Bazin, Siegfried Kracauer, and Christian Metz have all been concerned, in their distinct fashions, with the issue of cinematic specificity. Bazin asked the question in his title *What is Cinema?* and answered his own question by rooting cinema in photography's charismatic indexicality, its existential link to the pro-filmic referent. It was only with the advent of structuralism and semiotics in the 1960s, however, that the two questions – film language and film specificity – merged to be explored in depth and in relation to one another. Partially in response to Metz's seminal essay "Le Cinéma: langue ou langage" (Cinema: Language System or Language), a number of important book-length studies were published on the language of film, notably Metz's *Essais sur la signification au cinéma* (1968, translated as *Film Language* in 1974); Metz's *Langage et cinéma* (published in French in 1971); Pasolini's *L'Experience heretique: langue et cinéma* (1968 but translated into French only in 1989); Eco's *La Struttura Assente*; Emilio Garroni's *Semiotica ed Estetica* (*Semiotics and Aesthetics*, 1968); Gianfranco Bettetini's *Cinema: Lingua e Scrittura* (*The Language and Technique of Film*, 1968); and Peter Wollen's *Signs and Meaning in the Cinema* (1969). Pasolini, for example, argued that cinema formed a "language of reality" with its own double articulation, to wit of "cinemes" (by analogy to phonemes) and its "im-signs" (by analogy to morphemes). The minimal unit of cinematic language, for Pasolini, is formed by the diverse real-world signifying objects in the shot. Umberto Eco and Emilio Garroni criticized Pasolini's "semiotic naivete" for confusing what was cultural production with natural reality. Eco, whose work on the cinema was part of his work on "articulations" in language generally, argued against the idea of "double articulation" in the cinema, arguing instead for thee articulations: first, iconic figures; second, iconic figures combined into semes; and third, semes combined in "kinemorphes."

Metz's self-declared purpose was to "get to the bottom of the linguistic metaphor," by testing it against the most advanced concepts of contemporary linguistics. Metz took the metaphor seriously, but also skeptically, in order to discern its quantum of truthfulness. (It is often forgotten that Metz stressed *dis*analogies as well as analogies between film and language). For Metz, the object of cine-semiology was to disengage the cinema's signifying procedures, its combinatory rules, in order to see to what extent these rules resembled the doubly-articulated diacritical systems of "natural languages."

Metz's well-known conclusion to his own question about whether cinema was *langue* or *langage* was that the cinema was not a *langue* (language system) but that it was a *langage* (language). Although the cinema lacks the arbitrary sign, minimal units and double articulation typical of language systems, it nevertheless manifests a language-like systematicity. For Metz, the question "Is film a language?" is inseparable from the question "What is specific to the cinema?" For Metz, cinema is a language, first of all, as a "technico-sensorial unity" grounded in a given "matter of expression." While verbal language deploys two expressive materials (phonic sound for oral language, graphic traces for written language), cinematic language is the set of messages whose matter of expression consists of five tracks or channels: moving photographic image, recorded phonetic sound, recorded noises, recorded musical sound, and writing (credits, intertitles, written materials in the shot). Cinema is a language, in sum, not only in a broadly metaphorical sense but also as a set of messages grounded in a given matter of expression.

Film became a discourse, Metz argued, by organizing itself as narrative and thus producing a body of signifying procedures. Both language and film produce discourse through paradigmatic and syntagmatic operations. Language selects and combines phonemes and morphemes to form sentences; film selects and combines images and sounds to form "syntagmas," i.e. units of narrative autonomy in which elements interact semantically. The "Grand Syntagmatique" was Metz's attempt to isolate the principal syntagmatic figures or the spatiotemporal orderings of the narrative cinema; it comes in response to the question: "How does film constitute itself as narrative discourse?"

In Metz's most thoroughgoing exercise in filmo-linguistics, *Langage et cinéma*, first published in French in 1971 and translated (badly) into English in 1974,[3] he sheds the vestigial Bazinianism of his early period (film's base in photography, its manipulation of blocks of "reality"), developing instead the concept of cinema as a necessarily "pluri-codic" medium. By emphasizing "code" rather than language, Metz moved from a specifically linguistic approach to a broad semiotic approach. Unlike language, film has no "master code" shared by all films. Filmic texts, for Metz, form a structured network of codes; they are produced by the interweaving of (1) "specifically cinematic codes" i.e. codes that appear only in the cinema, and (2) "non-specific codes, i.e. codes shared with languages other than the cinema. Cinematic language, for Metz, is the totality of cinematic codes and subcodes in so far as the differences separating these various codes are provisionally set aside in order to treat the whole as a unitary system.

Much of semiotic work has as its goal distinguishing film from the other media in terms of its means of expression. Metz, for example, distinguishes between film and theater by the physical presence of the actor in the theater versus the deferred absence of the performer in the cinema, a "missed rendezvous" that paradoxically makes film spectators *more* likely to "believe" in the image. It is precisely the "imaginary" nature of the filmic signifier that makes it so powerful a catalyst of projections and emotions. (Marshall McLuhan implied something similar in his contrast of "hot" and "cool" media). Metz also compares film to television, concluding that despite differences in technology (photographic versus electronic), differences in social status (cinema by now a consecrated medium, television still deplored as a "wasteland"), differences in reception (domestic small screen versus theatrical large screen), the two media constitute virtually the same language. They share important linguistic procedures (scale, sound effects, camera movements, etc.). Thus they are two closely neighboring systems; the specific codes which also belong to the other are much more numerous and important than those which do not belong to it; and inversely, those which separate them are much less numerous and important than those which separate them, in common, from other languages. One might of course argue that evolving technologies and reception conditions are more important than Metz suggests. The cinema in its long-heralded specificity now seems to be dissolving into the larger stream of the audio-visual media, be they photographic, electronic, or cybernetic. Losing its hard-won privileged status as "king" of the popular arts, the cinema must now compete with television, video, video games, computers, virtual reality. Film is now seen as on a continuum with television, rather than being its antithesis, with a good deal of cross-fertilization in terms of personnel, financing, and even aesthetics. But what is methodologically important, in the end, is the differential, diacritical approach: constructing or discerning film's specificity by exploring *both* the analogies and disanalogies, within an evolving history, between it and other media.

Thinking on the issue of medium specificity since the 1960s has moved from essentialism to anti-essentialism. In this sense, there is surprising agreement between what would seem to be two contradictory currents: Metzian semiotics and the analytic/cognitive theory of Noël Carroll, both of whom share an anti-essentialist approach to medium specificity. Both Metz and Carroll agree that one cannot read out a single legitimate aesthetic from the material traits of the medium, as if artforms, as Carroll puts it, were "natural kinds outfitted with gene-like programs that mandate stylistic developments" (Carroll, 1996: 53). Carroll speaks not of essences but rather of "necessary conditions" for film, or as he prefers to put it – in a formulation which elides sound – the "moving image." These conditions are, first, *detached display*, a visual array "whose source is such that on the basis of the image alone we are unable to orient ourselves toward it in the space that is continuous with our own bodies." (This point recalls Metz's in "The Fiction Film and its Spectator" that the spectator has a strong impression, but never the *illusion*, of reality). The second necessary condition is that film belongs to the "class of things from which the impression of movement is technically possible." The third necessary condition is that film, or "moving image," involves performance generated by a template that is a token, while the fourth is that the performance in moving-image art is not an artwork in its own right but rather in subordination to a larger whole (we do not go to *Moby Dick* to see Gregory Peck perform but to see a performance of *Moby Dick*). The fifth and final necessary condition is that a moving image must be two-dimensional. Moving images can be instantiated, for Carroll, in a variety of media. Though born with film, the moving image can undergo transformation as new media are invented. The five conditions, unlike previous medium-essentialism arguments, dictate no particular style as norm.

Given all these interrogations, the "essence" of cinema is now seen as a question of not having any essence at all. As a multi-track and changing medium, the cinema is heir to all the antecedent arts and discourses. While the matter of expression of literature is words, and only words, cinema is a composite language by virtue of its diverse matters of expression and thus "inherits" all the art forms associated with these matters of expression. Given the synesthetic multiplicity of material signifiers and intertextual traditions available to it, the cinema can absorb virtually any kind of pre-existing discourse or expression.

The Metzian approach to film specificity and film language was largely pre-missed on just one version of linguistics, namely, that of the "Saussurean diaspora," i.e. the linguistics of Saussure and his latter-day descendants such as Martinet and Hjelmslev. A number of other important traditions have also focused on these questions. First, a strong semiotic movement has been operating in the former Soviet Union, one drawing strength from Russian Formalism, the Bakhtin School, and from Prague Structuralism – a movement centered especially in Moscow and Tartu (Estonia). These scholars, some direct heirs of the Form-alist movement, have worked in the area of what they call "secondary modeling systems." In this perspective, natural language is a "primary modeling system," i.e. a grid which shapes our apprehension of the world, while artistic languages constitute "secondary modeling systems," i.e. apparatuses, existing at a higher level of abstraction, through which the artist perceives the world and that model the world for the artist. In *Semiotics of Cinema*, Yuri Lotman, the most active and representative of this school, discusses cinema both as language and as secondary modeling system, while trying to integrate the analysis of cinema into a broader cultural theory.

There have also been attempts to apply Noam Chomsky's transformational linguistic models to the cinema. Chomsky's "generative grammar" emphasizes the syntactic more than the semantic dimension of language; more specifically, it is concerned with the speaker's capacity to both generate and understand "new" sentences. Rather than restrict itself to "surface structures," i.e. the syntactic organization of the sentence as it occurs in speech, it seeks the "deep structures," i.e. the fundamental mechanisms of language, the grammar or underlying logic, which makes possible the engendering of an infinity of grammatical sentences. The major American proponent of a transformationalist approach to the cinema has been John M. Carroll. In "A Program for Cinema Theory," (Carroll, 1988) Carroll argues that cinema does indeed have a grammar, that its "deep structure" consists of events while its "surface structure" consists of actualized film sequences, felt by ordinary viewers to be "grammatical" or "ungrammatical." His goal is to create a grammar of film capable of enumerating all sequential constructions which are "acceptable" to the spectator. Carroll's normative view has the effect, unfortunately, of naturalizing and universalizing one historically bound set of film practices – those of dominant cinema – while devaluing all transgressive experiments as "incorrect."

Beginning in the 1980s, the goal of the Franco-Italian tradition of semio-pragmatics, especially associated with the names of Franco Casetti in Italy and Roger Odin in France, was to study the production and reading of films in so far as they constitute programmed social practices. The goal of semio-pragmatics, according to Odin, is to show the mechanisms of producing meaning, to understand how a film is understood. Within this perspective, both the production and the reception of film are institutional acts involving roles shaped by a network of determinations generated by the larger social space. Semio-pragmatics pursues the Metzian project of studying how filmic meaning is produced but places this production within a more social and historical "space." For Odin, the "space of communication" (Odin, 1983) constituted by producer and spectator of film together is highly diverse, ranging from the pedagogic space of the classroom, the familial space of the home movie, to the fictional-entertainment space of mass-mediated culture (see chapter 5, this volume).

In many of these currents, the American semiotician C. S. Peirce has also been an influential figure. The application of Peircean "pragmatist" semiotics to the cinema has not been limited to the explication and extrapolation of Peirce's trichotomy of icon, index, and symbol. Peirce's ideas were first taken up by Peter Wollen in the late 1960s, and have subsequently been taken up with interest by such theorists as Kaja Silverman, Teresa de Lauretis, Gilles Deleuze, Julia Kristeva, and David Rodowick. Gilles Deleuze in *Image/Movement*, especially, deploys Peirce, in conjunction with Bergson, in a defiantly non-linguistic but still semiotic manner. For Deleuze, structural linguistics is incapable of accounting for the fluidity of the cinema.

Despite a certain backlash against the film-language metaphor – Gregory Currie delineates some of the objections in his essay "Languages of Art and

Languages of Mind" (1995) – that metaphor is still productive in some ways. As Roger Odin points out in *Cinéma et production de sens* (1990), linguistics offers three advantages for film theory: (1) it provides a contrastive, differential point-of-comparison between film and language; (2) it provides a battery of methods and tools which help us comprehend the functioning of the filmic medium; and (3) it offers a sophisticated way of interrogating artistic languages, a kind of "epistemological guarantee." At the same time, Odin calls for new directions in the approach to these questions, involving (1) increased understanding of the cognitive work of the spectator; and (2) renewed attention to the constraints of filmic comprehension, restraints which are in appearance exterior to film but which still have impact on the spectatorial "reading" of film.

In conclusion, it is wrong to say that a linguistic approach necessarily *reduces* film to language; rather, it reveals the languaged *dimension* of film, without suggesting that is the only dimension. Nevertheless, we can now see that the question of the relations between film and language was seen in a very partial manner by the pioneer film semiologists. The discussion tended to focus on questions grounded in Saussurean categories: Is film a language system? a language? like a language? But in fact questions having to do with film and language, and the potential contribution of linguistically inflected methods, are infinitely more diverse. To what extent do we know the visual world through language, and how does this "knowing" inflect the cinematic experience? What is the role of "inner speech?" What is the link between the broad intertext of verbal recounting and the conventional modalities of filmic recounting? How does the fact of cinema's involvement with a number of natural languages impinge on film as a discursive practice? How can we characterize the broad intersection of language, film, and culture? (Those hostile to all language-based discussion of the cinema tend to lump all these questions together.) When we think of this range of questions, we realize that first-phase cine-semiology was both too linguistic – i.e. too constrained by the Saussurean model – and not linguistic enough. If we scrutinize cinema as a multileveled discursive and communicative practice, and not just as a signifying system, we can see cinema and language as being even more thoroughly imbricated than cine-semiology managed to suggest.

Notes

1 Language-related citations from Canudo and Delluc can be found in a number of classical anthologies: Marcel Lapierre, *Anthologie du cinéma* (Paris: La Nouvelle edition, 1946); Marcel L'Herbier, *Intelligence du cinématographe* (Paris: Ed. Correa, 1946) and Pierre L'Herminier, *L'Art du cinéma* (Paris: Seghers, 1960). See also Richard Abel (1988).

2 For an English version, see Herbert Eagle (ed.), *Russian Formalist Film Theory* (Ann Arbor: Michigan Slavic Publications, 1981).

4
The Specificity of Media in the Arts

Noël Carroll

I

The idea – which I shall call the medium-specificity thesis – that each art form, in virtue of its medium, has its own exclusive domain of development was born in the eighteenth century, almost at the same time that the distinctions between the aesthetic and the nonaesthetic and between the fine arts and the practical arts crystallized. Yet despite its age, the medium-specificity thesis continues to exercise a tenacious grip on the imaginations of artists and theorists alike. On the contemporary art scene, this is perhaps most evident in the arena of video aesthetics, where one group, the image processors, advocate their stylistic explorations on the grounds that they are concerned with the basic attributes of video. Summarizing their position, Shelley Miller writes: "Electronic image processing uses as art-making material those properties inherent in the medium of video. Artists work at a fundamental level with various parameters of the electronic signal, for example, frequency amplitude or phase, which actually define the resulting image and sound."[1]

Undoubtedly many video avant-gardists are predisposed toward the medium-specificity thesis because, given backgrounds in the fine arts, their thinking has been and is swayed by the still influential tenets of Modernism à la Clement Greenberg. This approach to painting and sculpture is strongly essentialist. Greenberg proclaims:

> A modernist work of art must try, in principle, to avoid dependence upon any order of experience not given in the most essentially construed nature of its medium. This means, among other things, renouncing illusion and explicitness. The arts are to achieve concreteness, "purity," by acting solely in terms of their separate and irreducible selves.
>
> Modernist painting meets our desire for the literal and positive by renouncing the illusion of the third dimension.[2]

For Greenberg, optical, two-dimensional effects are the medium-specific domain of painting, while tactile, three-dimensional effects are the domain of sculpture. And video artists, influenced by this version of Modernism, believe that the proper direction of their art form will be involved in the isolation and definition of the quiddity of the video medium. Moreover, with Greenberg, these medium-specificity proponents are advocating that the differences between media should supply us with a standard of what art should and should not be made. And, if medium-specificity is transgressed, the medium-specificity critic is thought to have a reason to evaluate a given work of art negatively.

Contemporary photographic criticism also shows some recurrent tendencies toward upholding the medium-specificity thesis. For example, in his extremely popular book, *Camera Lucida*, Roland Barthes argues that photographic representation is essentially different from representation based on analogy or copying, i.e. the kind of representation found in painting. Barthes writes: "The realists, of whom I am one and of whom I was already one when I asserted that the Photograph was an image without code – even if obviously, certain codes do infect our reading of it – the realists do not take the photograph for a copy of reality, but for an emanation of *past reality*: a *magic*, not an art."[3] Furthermore, realist aesthetic preferences appear connected to Barthes's realist account of photographic representation – specifically, his taste for photos that afford the opportunity for the spectator actively to discover uncoded details.[4]

The persistence of the medium-specificity thesis has significance for educational policy as well. For when video makers and photographers strive to form their own academic departments or divisions, a prospect already before us, they are likely to do so by asserting their autonomy from other arts on the basis of medium-specificity arguments.

II

The medium-specificity thesis holds that each art form has its own domain of expression and exploration. This domain is determined by the nature of the medium through which the objects of a given art form are composed. Often the idea of "the nature of the medium" is thought of in terms of the physical structure of the medium. The medium-specificity thesis can be construed as saying that each art form should pursue those effects that, in virtue of its medium it alone – i.e. of all the arts – can achieve. Or the thesis might be interpreted as claiming that each art form should pursue ends that, in virtue of its medium, it achieves most effectively or best of all those effects at its disposal. Most often the medium-specificity theorist unconsciously relies upon (and conflates) both these ideas. Each art form should pursue *only* those effects which, in virtue of its medium, it excels in achieving. The thesis holds that each art form should pursue ends distinct from other art forms. Art forms should not overlap in their effects, nor should they imitate each other. Also, each art form is assumed to have some range of effects that it discharges best or uniquely as a result of the structure of its physical medium. Each art form should be limited to exploiting this range of effects, which the nature of the medium dictates.

The idea that each art form has its own domain and that it should not overlap with the effects of other art forms hails from the eighteenth century, when theorists such as Jean Baptiste Dubos, James Harris, Moses Mendelsohn, and most famously, Gotthold Ephraim Lessing revolted against the kind of art theory proposed in Charles Batteux's tract entitled *The Fine Arts Reduced to the Same Principle*.[5] As Batteux's title should suggest, pre-Enlightenment art theorizing tended to treat all arts as the same – e.g. as striving for the same effect, such as the imitation of the beautiful in nature. Enlightenment proponents such as Lessing, possessed by the epoch's zeal for distinctions, sought to differentiate the arts in terms of their medium-specific ingredients. Using the concept of a *sign* in advance of semiology, Lessing felt that the proper subject matter of each medium could be extrapolated from the physical properties of its constituent signs: poetry, whose words are encountered *sequentially*, is a temporal art, specializing in the representation of events and processes, while painting, whose signs, daubs of paint, are encountered as only spatially contiguous, should represent moments.[6]

The impression that proponents of the medium-specificity thesis impart is that one need only examine the physical structure of the medium, and the sort of effects the art form based in that medium should traffic in, more or less jumps out at one. Paint is the major ingredient in painting. Therefore, painting should primarily exemplify flatness (or, at least, be constrained to exemplify only effects that are consistent with flatness). However, it is far from clear that one can move so neatly from the physical medium to the *telos* of the art form. For example, if anything can lay claim to being the physical trait that essentially defines film, it is its flexible celluloid base. But what does this suggest to us about the kinds of things that could or should be represented or expressed in the medium? Indeed, why suppose that the essential characteristics of a medium necessarily have any directive consequences for the art made in that medium? Of course, this point also pertains when we are speaking of other than essential aspects of the physical medium. If some sort of writing instrument, e.g. a typewriter (or, to be more up-to-date, a word processor), and some material surface, say paper, are the customary, basic materials of the novelist, what can we extrapolate from this about the proper range of effects of the novel?[7]

Perhaps we will be told that language rather than print is the novelist's basic material. But then what different effects should poetry and the novel pursue, insofar as they have the same basic material? Maybe a move will be made to suggest that sound is the basic material of poetry, whereas events and actions are the basic material of the novel. Of course, it is very difficult to understand why we are to construe actions and events as *physical* constituents of a medium on a par with candidates like the paint of paintings. And, undoubtedly, the medium-specificity theorist, at this point, will tell us that we need not be committed to a simple notion of the medium restricted solely to its physical characteristics. But once we abandon a supposedly physicalist account of the medium, how are we to determine what the basic elements or constituents of the medium are? Whether or not it is true that actions and events are the basic elements of the novel, of course, is not my concern. My interests in the preceding dialectic lie in what it reveals about medium-specificity arguments, viz. that it is not an easy task to identify the basic materials of a medium, let alone to move from a simple enumeration of a medium's physical elements to the effects the art form embodied in the medium should be committed to explore. Indeed, it is often difficult to know at what level of analysis we should focus our attention *vis-à-vis* medium-specificity accounts. For though they generally suggest that their starting point is some physical element or constituent, medium-specificity discourse also easily drifts into consideration of nonphysicalistic elements or constituents: space and time, for example, are often said to be the basic ingredients of film. But why are these more pertinent to the medium-specificity theorist than the flexible-celluloid base of cinema?

Of course, if we already have a specific use for a medium, say poetry, then we may be able to say that features of the medium, even what physical features, are relevant for serving that purpose. However, here it pays to note that a feature, like sound in language, might be better characterized as a feature relevant for the purposes of poetry rather than as the basic, determinant feature of the medium. Basic-feature talk seems to imply or connote that prior to any uses of the medium, a medium could have a feature that would be more important and more indicative than any other of its features concerning what ranges of expression the art form embodied in the medium should explore. But, in fact, we have no idea of what features of the medium are important unless we have a use for the medium.

Furthermore, once we realize that it is our purposes that mold the medium's development and not the medium that determines our artistic purposes, we realize that the problem of overlaps between media is vitiated. We may have a purpose, such as the dramatic portrayal of human action, that will cross media, selecting the features of each medium that best facilitate our purpose. These features in each medium, in turn, either may resemble or may sharply contrast with those of other media. The provisional purposes we designate for a medium may in fact be *best* pursued by imitating another medium. Thus, Jean-Marie Straub, in his film *The Bridegroom, the Actress, and the Pimp*, mimes theater outright in order to make – quite effectively, I might add – his reflexive point that all film is "staged." Moreover, it is likely that when we introduce a new medium like video or photography, we will have to begin by attempting to adapt it to already existing purposes and strategies, e.g. portraiture, whose implementation perforce will recall the effects of other media. With such incipient arts, that is, practitioners will have to begin somewhere. The evolution of the medium will depend on the purposes we find for it. The medium has no secret purpose of its own.

Another way to approach this point is to remember that all media have more than one constituent component. To simplify, let us say that paint, paint brushes, and canvases are the basic materials of painting. How does the medium-specificity theorist know to identify paint as the pertinent element in this group? And, having identified paint as the lead element, how does the Modernist know to identify the potential for flatness, as opposed to impastos of ever-widening density, as the relevant possibility of paint that is to be exploited? Clearly paint itself cannot dictate how it is to be used – paint can be adapted for covering houses, covering canvases, portraying funerals, or proffering color fields. Paint does not determine how it will be used, but the purposes for which paint is used – art and/or Modernism – determine the relevant features of the medium for the task at hand. Flatness, for example, could be made to express Modernist ideals of purity and rigor. In short, the purposes of a given art – indeed, of a given style, movement, or genre – will determine what aspects of the physical medium are important. The physical medium does not select a unique purpose, or even a delimited range of purposes, for an art form.

The fact that a medium is generally composite in terms of its basic constituents leads to other complications for the medium-specificity thesis. For different features of the medium may suggest radically different directions of artistic development. Film has photography as a basic element, which has led many to designate it as a realist art. But the appearance of movement generated by the sequential structure of the film strip is equally basic to cinema, and it has led some to champion cinema as a magical art. In such cases, which aspect of the medium should be emphasized? Can the medium-specificity theorist offer a nonarbitrary basis for selecting the program suggested by one basic feature of the medium over another? Perhaps the medium-specificity theorist will opt for the program suggested by that element of the medium that is a *sine qua non* of the medium. But in our film example, both photography and the sequential structure of the film strip are *sine qua nons*.

Of course, the medium-specificity theorist may argue that no problem arises for him because basic elements of the medium suggest different lines of development. For, it may be said, the artist can pluralistically pursue more than one line of development. However, there are often cases where the candidates for the basic features of the medium suggest programs of development that conflict with each other. Both cinematography and editing are counted as among the basic elements of cinema, ones purportedly enjoining radically opposed styles: realism versus montage. Here it is impossible that the artist can fully explore the range of effects his medium excels in, because it is impossible simultaneously to exploit the cinematic potentials of rapid editing and deep-focus, realist cinematography. Similarly, video's capacity for immediate transmission makes it a useful device for creating certain news documents, while its potential for instant feedback enables it to be employed for abstract image processing. But one cannot make an abstract, image-processed news document.

A medium may excel in more than one effect, and these effects may be incompatible, thus making it impossible for the artist to abide by the medium-specificity thesis by doing what the medium does best. For it is not possible to do all that the medium does best. Nor does the medium-specificity thesis have a nonarbitrary way to decide which of conflicting "medium-based" styles is to be preferred. Obviously, one will gravitate toward the technique that serves one's purposes best. What aspects of the medium are to be emphasized or exploited will be determined by the aims of the artists and the purposes of the art form. If poetry is to be read silently on the page, then it makes sense to emphasize certain aspects of the medium, such as where each line ends; if poetry is primarily to be declaimed aloud by bards, however, line endings will not be a very determinant feature of the medium, even if our poets compose their songs ahead of time on paper. A medium is used to serve the purposes of an art form, a style, or a genre. Those purposes make different aspects of the medium relevant, rather than vice versa.

In response to my claims about the priority of use, it may be asserted that there are certain uses to which a medium cannot be put. And this, it might be said, is the basic truth of the medium-specificity claim. However, if the force of *cannot* here is that of either logical or physical impossibility, then the medium-specificity thesis is nothing but a truism, one irrelevant to art criticism or art making. For if it is literally impossible for a given medium to be put to a given use, then it never will be. Thus, since there is never any likelihood that media will over-step themselves in terms of what is logically or physically possible for them to do, there is no reason to warn them to be wary in this regard.

Clearly the existing output of any medium will only consist of objects designed to serve uses that it is logically and physically possible for the medium to perform. Use determines what aspects of the medium are relevant for aesthetics, rather than some essential trait of the medium determining the proper use of the medium. But if the use of the medium is key, then effects will be evaluated in terms of how well they serve presiding purposes. Some uses of painting, land-scape, for example, enjoin the exploitation of *pictorial* depth – obviously a logical and physical possibility of the medium. Such instances of pictorial depth, then, will be evaluated in light of the degree to which they serve the purposes to which they are connected. Our landscape paintings with their depth cannot be rejected on the grounds that paintings *cannot* disregard the essential flatness of the medium. Quite clearly some paintings do and, therefore, can ignore the Modernist's constraints concerning pictorial flatness. In such cases, excellence in the service of a definable purpose – e.g. accurately portraying recognizable land-scapes – will be our leading criterion for accepting each modification of the medium, at least where there is agreement about how to use the medium. Moreover, where there is not agreement, reference to traits of the medium will have little sway concerning alternative styles, since traits of the medium are only significant *vis-à-vis* uses. Rather, we will have to find other reasons for advocating one use over others.

It may be felt that whatever persuasiveness the foregoing account has, it can be resisted on the grounds that there are straightforward examples where artistic failure can be incontestably ascribed to ignoring the medium-specificity thesis. Imagine a silent film drama in which we see a gun pointed at X, followed by an intertitle reading "Bang!," followed by an image of a prostrate, dead X. One explanation of what has gone wrong here is that the filmmaker has failed to execute the scene in terms of what the medium does best – viz. showing things. However, we must ask whether the putative error here would be an error in any kind of film or only in certain types or genres of film with very special purposes. Put this way, I think we see that the sequence just described might be a brilliant invention in a comedy or in a film striving after Brecht's vaunted alienation effect. On the other hand, the sequence is an error within the Hollywood style of the action genre for which, among other things, considerations of pacing as well as of spectacular effects would favor showing the gunshot. Style, genre, and art form, and the purposes rooted therein, determine what elements of the medium will and will not be relevant. That is, contra the medium-specificity thesis, there are no techniques that are unavailable to an artist because of a failure to exploit certain characteristics of a given medium (or because of overlaps with other media). Rather there are styles, genres, art forms, and their presiding purposes, which determine the viability of a technique within a context of use. Where certain artistic failures occur – such as in cases of canned theater – we are not confronting transgressions of the medium but errors within prevailing styles that cannot be recuperated by references to other existing styles or other defensible purposes.

Earlier I assumed that the "cannot" in the medium-specificity thesis – i.e. "Make no medium do what it cannot do" – signaled either logical or physical impossibility. However, there is another sense of "cannot" that the medium-specificity theorist is banking on. According to the medium-specificity approach, we are told that if one wants to identify the aspects of the medium that a given art is to exploit, then one must look to those aspects that differentiate the medium in question from all other media. Thus, it is the purported flatness of paint that distinguishes it from sculpture. So painting-as-surface is the painter's proper arena. Here we see that the medium-specificity thesis is to be read normatively – "Do not make an art form do what it cannot do" means "Do not make it do what it ought not do because some other art does it." Thus, the medium-specificity formula is an injunction.

As an injunction, the medium-specificity thesis has two components. One component is the idea that there is something that each medium does best – alternatively, best of everything else a given medium does or best in comparison with other media. On both counts, Lessing thought that painting represented moments best and poetry actions. Rudolf Arnheim thinks that films represent animated action best.[8] Also, the medium-specificity thesis holds that each of the arts should do that which differentiates it from the other arts. We can call these two components of the medium-specificity thesis the excellence requirement and the differentiation requirement, respectively. There are many problems with the medium-specificity thesis. Some of these are a direct result of the combination of the differentiation and excellence requirements.

An underlying assumption of the medium-specificity thesis appears to be that what a medium does best will coincide with what differentiates media (and art forms). But why should this be so? For example, many media narrate. Film, drama, prose, and epic poetry all tell stories. For argument's sake, let us say it is what each of these arts does best – i.e. what each does better than anything else it does. Yet, narrative will not differentiate these art forms. What does the medium-specificity thesis tell us to do in such a situation?

If film and the novel both excel in narration, (1) should neither art form narrate since narration fails to differentiate them? or (2) should film not narrate since narration will fail to differentiate it from the novel and the novel claimed the domain of narration first? or (3) should the novel give up narration and let the newcomer have its chance?[9]

The first alternative is simply absurd. It would sacrifice a magnificent cultural invention – narration – for whatever bizarre satisfaction we can derive from adherence to the differentiation requirement. That is, to what end would we be forgoing artistic excellence in cases like this? Clearly attainable excellence will always be more important to us than differentiation for its own sake.

The second alternative is also unattractive. In this case, the medium-specificity theorist would appear to confuse history with ontology. Film is to forswear narrating just because literature already has that turf staked out. But surely this is only an accident of history. What if movies had arisen before writing? Then would novels have to find some occupation other than narrative? And what might that have been?

Clearly, accidents of history should not preclude an artistic medium from exploring an area in which it excels. Nor should accidents of history be palmed off as ontological imperatives, another proclivity of the medium-specificity thesis. That is, according to one very natural construal of the medium-specificity thesis, the special subject matter of each art form follows from the nature of the medium it is embodied in. However, in fact, we have seen that the medium-specificity thesis is even more complicated than this because a medium is supposed to specialize in what it excels in as a result of its nature, but only where that area of special achievement differentiates the medium in question from other media. So, the question of differentiation is not simply a question about the nature of what a medium in isolation excels in, but a question about the comparison of arts. And it is quite possible that a new art may be invented which excels in an area where an older art already excels.[10] To award the older art the domain just because it is already established seems arbitrary, as does the third alternative above – awarding the domain to the younger art just because it is younger. If two arts both excel in an area it seems natural to permit them both to explore it. What reason do we have to be against this option? Following this policy, we will enrich ourselves by multiplying the number of excellent things we have. This is surely the case with narrative. The world is richer for having novels *and* fiction films *and* epic poems *and* dramas *and* operas *and* comic books *and* narrative paintings, etc., though the differentiation component of the medium-specificity thesis would seem to urge us to forsake some if not all of these treasures should we choose to regard the medium-specificity thesis as a guideline for deciding what art can and cannot be made.

The specificity thesis has both an excellence component and a differentiation component. Perhaps one interpretation of the theory is that each art form should pursue those projects which fall in the area of intersection between what the art form excels in and what differentiates the art form from other art forms. But this does not seem to be an acceptable principle because, among other things, it entails that an art form might not be employed to do what it does best just because some other art form also does it well or, for that matter, can merely do it passingly. Again, the specificity thesis seems to urge us willingly to sacrifice excellence in art on principle. But I think that excellence is always the overriding consideration for deciding whether or not a particular practice or development is acceptable.

Indeed, I believe that what could be called the priority of excellence is the central telling point against the specificity thesis. To dramatize this, let us imagine that for some reason the only way that G. B. Shaw could get backing for *Pygmalion* was to make it as a talking picture – perhaps in the possible world we are imagining, Shaw was only reputed as a successful screenwriter. Let us also suppose that in some sense it is true that theater is a better showcase for aesthetically crafted language than talking pictures. Would we decide that *Pygmalion* should not be made, even though film will afford an adequate mode of presentation for it? I think our answer is "no," because our intuitions are that the medium-specificity thesis should not be allowed to stand between us and excellence.

Nor need the excellence be a matter of the highest excellence achievable in a given medium. One interpretation of the medium-specificity thesis urges that a medium pursue only that which it does best of all the things it does. But if a medium does something well and the occasion arises, why should an art form be inhibited especially just because there is something that the art form does better? Certain magical transformations – weaklings into werewolves – can be most vividly executed in cinema. But it can also be done quite nicely on stage. Should this minor excellence be forgone in a stage adaptation of *Dr Jekyll and Mr Hyde* either because language, not transformation, is what theater handles best or because film can make the metamorphosis more graphic?

The medium-specificity thesis guides us to sacrifice excellence in art. We should eschew Groucho Marx's movie monologues because they more appropriately belong to theater, just as the *Laocoön* should have been poetry. But is there reason to give up all this real and potential excellence? There is the medium-specificity argument conceived of as a rule that tells us what art should or should not be made. But on what grounds? It is not a moral imperative. So what is its point? What do we gain from abiding by the medium-specificity dictum that compensates or accounts for the sacrifices of excellence the medium-specificity theorist calls for? Here it is important to recall that the medium-specificity thesis has often been mobilized to discount acknowledged artistic accomplishments.[11]

The medium-specificity theorist may maintain that his position is basically committed to the proposition that each medium should only pursue those effects that it acquits better than any other medium. This not only raises the question of why a medium should only pursue that which it is thought to do better than any other (in opposition to what it is merely thought to do as well as other media, or what it does well but not as well as other media are thought to do); it also raises the question of whether it makes sense to compare arts in terms of whether they are more or less successful in performing the same generic functions. Can we say whether film, drama, or the novel narrates best, or is it more appropriate to say they narrate differently? Moreover, the relevant issue when commending a given artwork is not whether it is an instance of the medium that is best for the effect the artwork exemplifies, but whether the artwork in question achieves its own ends.

Surprisingly, there is little by way of defense for the medium-specificity thesis, especially when it is thought of as a way of determining what art should and should not be made. The thesis usually succeeds by appearing to be intuitively self-evident. Undoubtedly, the medium-specificity theorist leads listeners to accept the thesis through an implicit analogy with tools. Tools, for example, a Phillips-head screwdriver, are designed with functions in mind, and efficiency dictates that we use the tool for what it is designed for. If you wish to turn a screw with an x-shaped groove on top, use a Phillips-head screwdriver. If you wish to explore the potentials of aesthetically crafted, dramatic language, employ theater. If your topic is animated action, use film. Likewise, just as you should not, all things being equal, use a Phillips-head screwdriver as a church key (though it can open a beer can), you should not, all things being equal, use cinema to perform theater's task and vice versa.

But I think that to carry over the tool analogy to an art form is strained. Art forms are not tools, designed and invented to serve a single, specific purpose, nor are they even tools with a delimited range of functions. Most art forms were not self-consciously invented and, therefore, they are not designed.[12] Painting was not invented to celebrate flatness. Moreover, even with self-consciously invented arts like photography, film, and video, it was soon realized that these media could perform many more tasks than they were expressly and intentionally designed for. Indeed, our interest in an art form is in large measure an interest in how artists learn or discover new ways of using their medium. But the idea of the artist discovering new ways of using the medium would make no sense if the medium were designed for a single, fixed purpose, as the strongest variants of the medium-specificity thesis seem to suggest.

An art form is embodied in a medium which, even in the cases of the self-consciously invented arts, is one whose many potentials remain to be discovered.

But discovery would not be a relevant expectation to have of artists, nor would an interest in it be relevant to an art form if the task of the art form were as fixed as that of a Phillips-head screwdriver. A correlative fact against the idea of the fixedness of function of art forms is the fact that art forms continue to exist over time, obviously because they are periodically reinvented and new uses are found for them. But if art forms were as determinately set in their function as are things like Phillips-head screwdrivers, one would expect them, like most tools, to pass away as their function becomes archaic. That art forms are constantly readapted, reinvented, and redirected bodes ill for the central metaphor suggested by the medium-specificity thesis: that of the art form as specialized tool.

Furthermore, the notion of "efficiency" as it figures in the allure of the medium-specificity thesis is suspect. For it is not clear that if film undertakes the task of painting – showing a still setting – it will be inefficient in the sense of incurring more labor. Nor is it obvious that expenditures of time, material, or labor are really relevant in the appraisal of artworks. Excellence of effect is what we care about. Moreover, if "efficiency" is thought of as "operating competently," then it is difficult to see how the medium-specificity theorist can employ it in a non-question-begging fashion since things such as the *Laocoön* do support some measure of aesthetic experience even if they supposedly transgress their medium.

One way to attempt to defend the medium-specificity thesis is by asking, "Why else would there be different art media if they were not supposed to pursue different ends?" The medium-specificity thesis is, in this light, an inference to the best explanation. Given the fact that we have a number of arts, we ask "why?" The answer that seems most reasonable is: "Because each art has, or should have, a different function." Again, there is some underlying idea of efficiency.

An important presupposition of this argument is that it is legitimate to ask why we have different arts. It also supposes that it is legitimate to expect as an answer to this question something like a rational principle.

To paraphrase Wittgenstein, where there is no question, there is no answer. We can, I think, use this principle to rid ourselves of the preceding argument. For its question, when stated nonelliptically, is not "Why are there diverse arts?" but "What is the rationale that explains or justifies our possession of exactly the diverse arts we have?" Now there may be an answer, or, better, a *series* of answers to the former question – answers of an historical and/or an anthropological variety. For example, we have film because Edison wanted an invention to supplement the phonograph. Perhaps we have painting because one day a Cro-Magnon splashed some adhesive victuals on a cave wall and the result looked strikingly like a bison. And so on. But we have no answer to the second question – "What is the rationale for having exactly the several arts we have?" Rather, each art arose due to a chain of events that led to its discovery or invention and to its subsequent popularization. The result is the *collection* of arts we have, which we only honorifically refer to as a system. The arts are not systematic, designed with sharply variegated functions, as the medium-specificity thesis holds. Rather, they are an amalgamation of historically evolved media whose effects often overlap. There is no rationale for the system, for in truth, it is only a collection. Thus, we have no need for the explanation afforded by the medium-specificity thesis.

As I mentioned earlier, one area where it will be tempting to resort to medium-specificity arguments is in the justification of the formation of new arts-educational departments, such as film, video, photography, holography, and so on. Proponents of such departments will argue that their medium is distinct from the other arts in such a way that it will not receive its due if condemned to existence in departments dominated by specialists in literature, theater, and fine art. Furthermore, it may be added that the medium-specificity thesis is of great heuristic value insofar as it entreats students to think deeply about the specific elements of their trade.

I do not wish to demean the fact that the medium-specificity myth has and can have useful results. But I wonder whether the students who benefit from this myth are really doing something as simple as considering the materials of their arts rather than the "state-of-the-art" techniques, conventions, and styles that dominate their practices. And, furthermore, the medium-specificity thesis can result in undesirable consequences. Students can become mired in the prevailing traditions of their medium, closed to the possibility of innovating inspiration from the other arts. Indeed, my own prejudice is to suspect that once students have mastered the basic techniques of their medium, their best strategy is to explore not only the history of their art, but other arts and culture at large for new and stimulating ideas.

Concerning the usefulness of medium-specificity arguments for the justification of new academic departments, it can be said that this is a rhetorical matter, not a logical one. That administrators may be persuaded by such arguments, or that the proponents of new arts-educational disciplines feel they need such arguments, does not show that the medium-specificity thesis is valid. On the other hand, such departmental realignments can be defended without reference to medium-specificity. We may argue that the practice in question has become or is becoming so important to the life of our culture that it warrants intensive and specialized study, even if the enterprise does overlap with the practices of preexisting forms such as theater, literature, or fine art.

III

In concluding, I would like to emphasize that the strongest and most pervasive instances of the medium-specificity argument maintain that the various media (that art forms are embodied in) have unique features – ostensibly identifiable in advance of, or independently of, the uses to which the medium is put – and, furthermore, these unique features determine the proper domain of effects of the art form in question. However, it seems to me that what are considered by artists, critics, and theorists as aesthetic flaws, traceable to violations of the medium, are in fact violations of certain styles, the purposes of those styles, and their characteristic modes of handling the medium. That medium-specificity arguments are often connected with advancing the cause of one artistic movement or use of the medium should indicate that what is urged under the banner of medium specificity is linked to implicit conceptions of preferred artistic styles.

Even when analysts are not concerned with saying how a medium should be used but are only attempting to describe the unique, artistically pertinent features of a medium, I suspect that they are really speaking of styles within the medium. If we are told, for example, that temporal manipulation is the artistically relevant, unique feature of film, our informant clearly is thinking of film in relation to certain styles of filmmaking. For real-time exposition is also a feature of the medium, one pertinent to alternate styles of filmmaking, which, of course, have different purposes.[13]

Similarly, if we are told that the potential for wordless action and spectacle, rather than ornate language, is the key element of an authentic, nonliterary theater, then it is evident, I think, that we are being asked to advocate one style of theater while being confused about the reasons for doing so. We are led to believe that our decision is based upon some facts about the nature of the theatrical medium rather than assessing the purposes of the style of the nonliterary theater we are asked to endorse.

The task of the theorist of an art is not to determine the unique features of the medium but to explain how and why the medium has been adapted to prevailing and emerging styles and, at times, to either defend or condemn the prevailing or emerging purposes artists pursue. Such debate should not proceed by arguments about what the medium dictates, but rather by finding reasons – artistic, moral, and intellectual – that count for or against those styles, genres, artworks, and their subtending purposes which confront us in the thick of the life of the culture.

Notes

1   Shelley Miller, "Electronic Video Image Processing: Notes toward a Definition," *Exposure* 21, no. 1 (1983): 22.
2   Clement Greenberg, "The New Sculpture," from his *Art and Culture* (Boston: Beacon, 1961), p. 139.
3   Roland Barthes, *Camera Lucida*, trans. Richard Howard (New York: Hill and Wang, 1981), p. 88. I criticize this position on photography in my "Concerning Uniqueness Claims for Photographic and Cinematic Representation," in the journal *Dialectics and Humanism*, no. 2 (1987).
4   See Barthes's discussion of the photographic *punctum* in *Camera Lucida*, esp. pp. 51–60.
5   The historical remarks here follow the account offered by Monroe C. Beardsley in his *Aesthetics: From Classical Greece to the Present* (New York: Macmillan, 1966), pp. 160–3.

6   Gotthold Ephraim Lessing, *Laocoön*, trans. E. Frothingham (New York: Noonday Press, 1969), pp. 91–2.

7   In the paragraph above, I am accepting the frequent presupposition of specificity theorists that media can be individuated on the basis of their physical structures. But this does seem problematic. Why claim that daguerreotypes should be grouped in the same medium as celluloid-based photography? The physical structure and certain of the physical potentials of these processes are so different. Why not claim there are at least two media here? Obviously, the question of individuating media is not simply a matter of physicalistic considerations. Media are cultural and historical constructions. The topic of the way in which media are individuated is too large to include in this paper. For the purposes of my argument, I am hypothetically assuming the adequacy of our present distinctions between media. But for further discussion, see my "Defining the Moving Image."

8   Rudolf Arnheim, *Film*, trans. L. M. Sieveking and F. D. Morrow (London: Faber and Faber, 1933).

9   It is interesting to note that most often when medium-specificity claims are advanced in support of the program of a particular art, generally, the theorist does not contrast the art he champions with every other art – which one would expect given the theory – but only with selected arts. Thus, painting is contrasted with sculpture, or video with film, or photography with painting, or film with theater, etc. Film, for example, is not usually contrasted with the narrative novel in order to find film's proper domain of effects, nor is video contrasted with music. The theory is only applied to certain neighbors of the art in question, normally ones with which the art in question is competing for attention and for audiences. The differentiation requirement, in such contexts, does not seem to be a matter of ontology but a rhetorical lever in aesthetic power struggles. This is discussed at greater length in my "Medium Specificity Arguments and Self-Consciously Invented Arts: Film, Video and Photography," in *Millennium Film Journal* nos. 14/15 (Fall/Winter, 1984–5).

Parenthetically, it is worth pointing out that most frequently medium-specificity arguments are used in the context of comparing only two arts. This may be the cause of the fact that it is difficult to find elaborately articulated statements of the general thesis. Rather, the general thesis is most commonly assumed as a premise for the purposes of a more local argument.

10 Here we are not speaking of the arts excelling relative to each other but excelling in terms of one thing that they do compared to other things that they do.

11 For example, see Erwin Panofsky's attack of *The Cabinet of Dr. Caligari* in his "Style and Medium in the Motion Pictures," in *Film Theory and Criticism*, ed. Gerald Mast and Marshall Cohen (New York: Oxford University Press, 1970), p. 263.

12 Here an analogy with human beings may be helpful. Human beings are not designed with a fixed function and, as a result, we do not attempt narrowly to constrain the ways in which they can fruitfully develop. We accept a range of alternative, even competing, life-styles. Likewise with the artforms embodied in artistic media.

13 Another reason that I advocate the priority of stylistic considerations over mediumistic ones is that our stylistic aims, needs, and purposes lead to changes in the very physical structure of media. It is because we are committed to certain stylistic aims that we mold dancers' bodies in a certain way; it is because we already are committed to certain styles of realism that various technical innovations, like cinemascope, are

introduced into the film medium. The physical structure of a medium does not remain static. It is modified as a result of the needs and imperatives of our existing and emerging styles, genres, and art movements. Those often literally shape the medium, rather than the medium dictating style.

5

For a Semio-Pragmatics of Film

Roger Odin

A necessary starting point is the definition of our aim. Semiology means two things to us:

(a) An attempt to 'understand how a film is understood' (to use Christian Metz's expression).[1]

(b) An attempt to understand the mechanisms of the film–spectator relationship.

We are convinced that this programme can only be carried out if we see *pragmatics* as playing the *leading part* in the production of *meaning* and *affects*.

It is probably possible, albeit slightly over-simplistic, to distinguish three main current trends in the attitudes of linguists towards pragmatics.

Some prefer a complete separation between the fields of linguistics and pragmatics, and see any aspect of the latter as being part of a theory of action (pragmatics being then considered as the study of the application of linguistic formulas to a given context);[2] others try and implement some sort of 'integrated pragmatics'.

The latter current seems to embrace two distinct trends: for some linguists, linguistic analysis consists in identifying the informational content characterizing the utterance, then in determining its value and its illocutionary force[3] – this is what Alain Berrendonner calls the 'theory "in Y"';[4] others prefer to renounce the notion of 'literal meaning',[5] and largely reduce the utterance to 'instructions' given to its potential interpreters, 'expecting them to search the discourse for relevant information, and use it in such a way as to reconstruct the meaning intended by the speaker'.[6]

Although the latter position seems the most acceptable within the field of linguistics, it does not seem possible to apply it unaltered to film as a subject for analysis.

The language of images is, indeed, characteristically devoid of any such instructions on the level of the utterance: an image never indicates what procedures are to be followed for its reading. In order to understand an image, therefore, it is necessary to follow procedures with no indication, within the image itself, 'of their nature, or of the order in which they are to be carried out'. In other words, any reading of an image consists of 'applying' to it processes that are essentially external to it. This reading does not result from an internal constraint, but from a cultural constraint.[7]

The sequential nature of film, which enables it to record 'the chronicle of a series of events', does not contradict the above remarks: a filmic chronicle follows a 'series of states, but without extracting or stressing the transformation processes: it is indeed a dynamic product, and therefore completely different from the static views offered by photography or by drawing, but it is nothing more than a series of states'.[8]

Consequently, the only internal constraints involved in filmic communication are the obligation of *compatibility* between the procedures through which meaning is produced, and the form, disposition and consecution of the permanent marks imprinted[9] on the film, which are accurately reproduced every time the film is projected.[10]

We must, therefore, confront the shocking fact that not only does a film produce no meaning by itself,[11] but all it can do is to *block* a number of possible investments of meaning.[12] The only effect of internal constraints is to prevent the application of certain reading rules.

Seen from this angle, the elementary mechanism of the production of meaning could be described as follows:

(a)   The spectator proposes a meaning, and puts it to the test in the structure of the image.
(b)   If this proposition seems compatible with the constraints of the structure of the image, meaning is then produced.

It must, however, be stressed that where film is concerned, these constraints are extremely flexible, and always easy to evade. Filmic images, which disappear as soon as they appear, are fundamentally changeable, transitory, evanescent; they have to be seized as they rush past, on the spur of the moment, and with no hope of ever retrieving them; they follow one another relentlessly, allowing us no rest, no chance to take control, making it impossible for us to check and verify them (at least under normal projection conditions).[13] Predictably, the spectator is prone to deviant constructions, which do not even respect the disposition and the order of the marks imprinted on the film.[14] He has every reason to infringe the rules.

Although internal constraints are never imperative, some films, because of their structure, impose greater constraints than others (blocking the application of certain rules on the production of meaning more or less stringently).

In some experimental films, for instance, the configuration of the marks changes randomly between two frames. Under such conditions, the application of rules in the production of meaning is practically impossible, except on a very punctual level (such films are not in fact intended to function as forms of communication, even though they still carry some meaning: no film can totally block the production of meaning).

In classic narrative film, on the contrary, any alterations occurring between two frames, between two shots, between two sequences, obey certain rules of coherence. The marks are imprinted on the film in keeping with the operation of these rules. This does not mean, of course, that the spectator is forced to apply the rules – since they are not incorporated into the film itself – but that nothing in the film itself will oppose an application of the rules by the spectator.

What is meant by *spectator* needs some explanation, since all propositions on the production of meaning seem to emanate from him.

The definition given by Christian Metz in his interview with Marc Vernet and Daniel Percheron is, to a certain degree, relevant to us: 'For me, the spectator is not the individual who goes to the cinema as a whole, concrete person, but only a part of him which goes there. It is the psychological mechanism necessary to the functioning of the institution, but only for the duration of the show'.[15]

For us, the *spectator* is a constructed entity, an actant; more precisely, he can be defined as the *point of passage of a bundle of determinations*.

Seen from this angle, the production of meaning is entirely based on *external* determinations. It is, indeed, exclusively through these determinations that the process of filmic communication can become operational: the closer the link between the determinations affecting the spectator and those affecting the direction, the more likely it is that the spectator-actant's constructions will match those of the director-actant.

All things considered, it is precisely because the Subjects producing the meaning (director and spectator) are not free to produce any odd discourse (because they can only express themselves by obeying the constraints of the 'discursive practice'[16] characterizing their time and background) that communication can take place.

All determinations do not, however, have the same field of temporal and spatial application.

Some of them operate in a fairly stable way, and cover a vast geographical area (this is the case of determinations affecting the analogical reading of images, and narrative reading). Others, on the contrary, are particularly short-lived and/or limited in space (for instance, determinations affecting the interpretation of historical clues: recognition of certain characters or events). These determinations (and the processes of production of meaning that they trigger off) seem to be what M. Tardy describes as 'semiogeneses': the 'emergence of original modes of signification, furtive codes which only last for a moment'.[17]

Yet others are directly linked to language learning: the recognition of objects involves semes and semantemes[18] and there is, as Michel Colin points out, a 'discourse' in film.[19]

Others, finally, arise from the institutions constituting the filmic field: fiction film, documentary film, pedagogic film, home movies, industrial film, experimental film, etc.

By *institution*, we mean a structure activating a whole bundle of determinations. What we call a 'spectator' is simply the *point of passage*[20] of the determinations characterizing a given institution.

It is, of course, these institutional determinations that primarily interest the specialist in film semio-pragmatics, for they are the ones most specific to the filmic field (other determinations relate to the general cultural space).

Let us give some examples of what these institutions can directly affect.

1   The institution affects the hierarchical ordering of relevant features in the material of expression, but also of codes. This order provides the basis for the evaluation of the *degree of cinematic specificity* of the productions presented to the spectator.

The dominant filmic institution is thus characterized, from the point of view of the definition of film according to relevant features in the material of expression, by the predominance of the following features:

- iconicity (figurative images);
- mechanical duplication of reality;
- reproduction of motion.[21]

Any occurrence of a feature of sub-categorization other than one of these three features, in the context of dominant film, is perceived by the spectator as a lowering of the degree of cinematic specificity of the passage in question.

The experimental filmic institution, on the other hand, applies a reversal of this hierarchical system. In this context, film productions of the highest degree of cinematic specificity are those that would be deemed to have the lowest specificity according to the dominant filmic institution. Here, priority is given to:

- non-figurative images;
- fixed images, or images manipulating the deconstruction or construction of motion;
- and images produced by other means than the mechanical duplication of reality (for instance, images drawn by hand onto the film itself, as in some films by MacLaren).

The same observations apply to codes: whereas the dominant film institution considers productions that obey the rules of narrative coding as being of the highest degree of cinematic specificity,[22] the experimental film institution reserves this recognition to films that block the process of production of a narrative.[23]

Each institution is thus characterized by a certain definition of the filmic object in terms of material and codes.

2 The institution determines certain aspects of the *production of meaning*. For instance, the same phenomenon, such as an absence of sound, will be interpreted as devoid of significance in the institution of silent film, and as a mistake (a mechanical failure) or a special effect, in the context of the institution of sound film. However, it must be said at this point that linguistic determinations, which are not exclusive to a film institution, are predominant. Institutions nevertheless have the power to block or facilitate the application of these linguistic determinations (thus, the experimental institution tries to block certain discursive determinations).

3 The institution determines the way in which the spectator produces *the image of the director*. In the institution of experimental film, for instance, which is a subdivision of the 'artistic' institution, the spectator acts in the Author's name (as Benjamin said, 'art is a question of surnames'). The institution of fiction film, on the contrary, demands the obliteration of any such marks of enunciation (the film is meant to function by itself, as if it had never been produced by a director). In the institution of pedagogic film,[24] the director is constructed by the spectator as the one possessing Knowledge, whereas in the institution of newsreel film, he is constructed as the one possessing Sight, the one who has seen. In this sense, the instruction given by the institution of newsreel film can be described as follows:

(a) The director and the camera were there when the events happened; they saw them.
(b) These events would have happened in the same way if the director and the camera had not been there.[25]

This last point is one of the differences between fiction film and newsreel film: the spectator watching a fiction film knows that the events that he sees happening on screen have been specially produced by the director, in front of the camera, even if he agrees, as long as the projection lasts, to pretend that the events existed by themselves (this reminds us of the familiar question on the suspension of disbelief: 'I know very well . . . but all the same').

4 The institution also determines the spectator's *affective positioning*. As Metz has shown, the dominant film institution produces a spectator-actant at once isolated, motionless and dumb, whose psychological positioning lies somewhere between the waking state, day-dreaming and dreaming, and who is willing to produce this comprehensive imaginary construction: the diegesis.[26] As for us, we have tried to show how the institution of home movies produces a spectator who is more a 'participant' than a real spectator: he takes part in the direction of the

film (having held the camera), in the action taking place on screen (having been filmed), in the installation of the projection equipment (having set up the screen and projector), and, finally, in this type of event that consists of the collective creation of a memorial diegesis by the members of the family.[27]

Thus, each institution has its own specific way of positioning its spectator. Hence the necessity, when analysing a film, of specifying which institutional framework one takes as a viewpoint; also the necessity, for the theoretician of film, of analysing the different ways in which institutions produce their spectator: which largely remains to be done.

Remarks on Terminology

We propose calling '*reader-actant*' the arch-lexeme subsuming the different ways in which institutions produce their spectator, and reserving the term '*spectator*' for the '*reader-actant*' produced by the institution of dominant film. We will, of course, have to find appropriate denominations for the '*reader-actants*' of other film institutions.

The choice of the arch-lexeme 'reader-actant' is explained by our wish to avoid, as much as possible, denominations implying that the production of meaning rests exclusively with the director-actant (such as the transmitter-recipient and sender-addressee pairs). In this respect, the notion of 'reader' seems less loaded, implying more of a really active process of production.

Alongside these denominations (reader-actant vs director-actant), we shall refer to the *directing space* and to the *reading space*. We shall also call '*direction-film*' the film endowed with meaning produced within the directing space by the director-actant, and '*reading-film*', the film endowed with meaning produced within the reading space by the reader-actant. This terminology seems more adequate to us than the traditional notion of 'filmic text' (which gives the misleading impression that the film is in itself endowed with meaning), in that it clearly states that meaning is produced in both spaces, that these two productions are quite independent from each other, and are directly linked to the work of the actants concerned: the 'direction-film' and the 'reading-film' are thus opposed (as pro-ductions endowed with meaning) to the '*reel-film*' (the film as a series of marks imprinted on the film base) and to the '*projection-film*' (the film as a series of light or sound resonances, as it appears on screen awaiting an investment of meaning on the part of the 'reader-actant').

5 Finally, the institution determines *the production of affects by the film itself*. Indeed, at every stage of the projection, the 'reading-film', as it is constructed by the reader-actant under the influence of determinations, retroacts on this reader-actant, triggering positive or negative emotional reactions, which are themselves conditioned by the influence of institutional determinations. The film analyst, having determined the institutional context which constitutes his

viewpoint (having, therefore, specified the rules influencing the construction of the reader-actant by the relevant institution), will be expected to examine the way in which the 'reading-film' plays with the reader-actant's affects. It could be argued ·that this implies a return to Charles Bally's 'stylistics of effects', but, of course, with a different set of presuppositions, for the analysis does not aim to reveal the feelings of the 'speaker' (in our terminology, the director-actant), but only to show how the 'reading-film' shapes the affective reactions of the reader-actant in a certain institutional context.

For the purpose of our work on fiction film, we choose to designate, by the notion of 'mise en phase', the specific affective relationship produced by this type of film, in the framework of the dominant filmic institution.[28]

By '*mise en phase*', we mean the following: at every major stage in the story being told, the film produces a relationship between itself and the spectator (an affective positioning of the latter) which is *homologous* with the relationships occurring in the diegesis.

In Lacanian terms, the 'mise en phase' could be said to activate the inscription of the spectator on the imaginary axis.[29] Indeed, the power of the 'mise en phase' is such that it enables the imaginary axis to benefit from figures which would otherwise be perceived as more or less strong marks of enunciation counteracting the spectator's fictional positioning. In other words, no figure is in itself inappropriate on the level of the imaginary axis: even a direct look into the camera (probably the most loaded figure from the point of view of the utterance, and the biggest taboo in fiction film)[30] can be put to use on the imaginary axis, as long as it corresponds to a homologous relationship within the diegesis (this applies to the glance directed at the camera during Henri's defloration of Henriette in Jean Renoir's *Partie de campagne*).[31] In *La Jetée* by Chris Marker, everything points in this direction: this film, at first sight, shows all the hallmarks of an experimental film, relying almost entirely on the freeze frame[32] – a highly loaded figure from the point of view of the utterance, in the context of the dominant filmic institution – and yet it succeeds, thanks to the 'mise en phase', in producing a highly intense fictional effect.[33]

Conversely, certain films that should, *a priori*, operate on the fictional level (since they tell a story) block the process of 'mise en phase', and so fail to produce a satisfactory film–spectator relationship in the context of the dominant filmic institution; such films are then perceived by the spectator as 'bad' films. This is the case of *Le Tempestaire* by Jean Epstein, which both triggers off and blocks the process of 'mise en phase'.[34] We propose to call 'phase displacement' [*déphasage*] the series of processes counteracting the 'mise en phase'.

Finally, it must be said that a film that has been rejected by the dominant filmic institution due to such 'phase displacement' can operate in the context of some other institution, for which no 'mise en phase' is compulsory. For this reason, *Le Tempestaire* comes into its own with institutions that allow a second reading (such as film clubs or courses on film study); it then operates on a 'performative' level. Let us remember that the term 'performative' applies to 'texts that are characterized by a relative change of focus, from the content being told to the process of telling'.[35] Viewed from this angle, *Le Tempestaire* can be seen as a remarkable parable on how fictional film operates (but not as a fiction film).

These observations on the functioning or malfunctioning of a film in a given institutional context lead to the introduction of the notion of *sanction* into the notion of institution.

The notion of sanction is, indeed, central to the notion of institution: 'The institution is a symbolic network, liable to social sanctions', as Castoriadis wrote in *L'institution imaginaire de la société*.[36] Similarly, Berrendonner defines the institution as a 'normative power, subjecting the individuals to certain mutual practices on pain of sanctions'.[37]

The displeasure felt by the spectator viewing *Le Tempestaire* from within the institution of the fiction film is the sanction pronounced by this institution against a film that blocks the process of 'mise en phase'. In the same way, boredom will be the sanction pronounced by someone going to see a documentary in the frame of mind of someone going to see a fiction film. Inversely, someone going to see a fiction film in the frame of mind of the reader-actant of a documentary would probably be considered 'insane', for he would be accused of confusing different levels of reality.

It can be seen that the sanction may apply to the film itself, if its treatment of the material is unacceptable to the institution within which it is meant to operate, or the reader-actant, if he infringes the institutional determinations that are imposed on him (this reminds us of the necessity of the distinction between the spectator in the flesh, and the reader-actant as constructed by the institution: for conflicts may arise between these two entities).

We have just demonstrated the existence of different filmic institutions, and (too briefly, no doubt) outlined a framework for possible further reflection. The next question is: should we distinguish between *several* 'film' objects necessitating very distinct semiological approaches (corresponding to the diversity of filmic institutions), or should we, on the contrary, construct *one* film semiology, integrating variations of instructions and treatment within a single approach?

The answer is far from obvious. For instance, Eric de Kuyper's comment on experimental film (which he renames the 'bad form') is that 'this deconstruction of film may be done with film, but should probably be excluded from the filmic field proper. The deconstruction . . . is so successful that, let's face it, it no longer belongs to the cinema'.[38] Dominique Noguez (though not hostile to experimental film) supports a similar solution, wondering whether it might not be sensible to question the very idea of a 'single corpus', 'the very idea that there is one cinema'.[39]

This position seems to encounter a number of problems, of which we only recently became aware. One of them is that everything does not change as one moves from one institution to another.

One finds, for instance, the same filmic treatment (basically strong and discontinuous) in home movies, experimental films and documentary films. It is the reading instructions that change: production of a family fiction,[40] with the institution of home movies; production of the experimental effect, with the institution of experimental film,[41] and production of an authentic effect, with the institution of the documentary film.[42]

Inversely, the same instruction (at least on a certain level) can be compatible with different, not to say opposite treatments. This is what happens, in our opinion, between the institution of home movies and the dominant filmic institution: both institutions instruct their reader-actant to produce a fiction (a family fiction, a really 'fictional' fiction) and this fiction is actually constructed in both institutions, although the figures through which this fiction is constructed in the institution of home movies are precisely those that would prevent it in the dominant filmic institution (broken up narrative, jumps, blurred images, address to the camera . . .); and, inversely, movies constructed in the style of the fiction film (continuity, coherence, no address to the camera . . .) provokes a reaction of rejection in the reader-actant as a member of the family.[43]

Finally, even when two institutions are differentiated by instructions and by the filmic treatment which is being applied, this does not mean that they operate independently of each other. There exists, paradoxically, a strong link between the dominant filmic institution and the institution of experimental film. Eric de Kuyper stresses this particular point, and proposes, consequently, the term 'marginal' film as a substitute for 'experimental' film: 'This cinema will be called *marginal*. Simply in order to remind us that what is written in the margin of a text bears a relation (any relation, but some relation) to this text, to the large corpus to which it is linked, on which it depends, on which it is commenting or which it is refuting by means of notes and arguments. But it is in the margin, whether it likes it or not'.[44]

Experimental film could be considered, to a certain extent, as the negative of classic fictional film,[45] justifying the formulation of appropriate transformation rules.

It is in fact probable that the institution of classic fiction film enjoys a privileged position in the filmic field, for everyone has assimilated the norms of fiction film. There is therefore a risk, whenever we watch a documentary or an experimental film, of a conflict between the fictional determinations that we all carry within ourselves, and the determinations characterizing these institutions. No theoretician can afford to ignore this phenomenon.

We shall therefore state the existence of a law of *co-determination* between institutions, and consider that the institutional *heterogeneity* of the filmic field is a *structured* one.

This idea of heterogeneity is not self-evident. We know that Ferdinand de Saussure, for instance, saw heterogeneity and systematicity as being in contradiction. Since then, a number of linguists (Labov, Weinreich, Herzog . . .) have attempted to reconcile the two;[46] it does seem that if one wants to avoid being out of touch with what is really happening in linguistic communication, if one refuses, in other words, to abandon the level of performance, the notion of free variable should be replaced by that of *variable structures* contained in the language and *determined by different social functions*. In this respect, a language is a *diasystem* composed of several *dialects*, and every speaker has a number of different codes at his disposal; competence then appears to be the command of a *regularly* differentiated system.[47]

In the same way, the heterogeneity of the filmic field can be described as a structure within which each institution uses a specific filmic 'dialect' and fulfils a specific *social function*. This notion of function actually needs some clarification, for we may well have to distinguish, along with Michel Pêcheux,[48] between the *apparent* function and the *implicit* function. The institution of home movies, for instance, fulfils the apparent function of storing memories, and the implicit function of strengthening family bonds (and therefore a certain social order).

Our semio-pragmatic bias therefore leads us to contemplate the construction of a sort of *polylectal* grammar of film. By way of conclusion, we shall point to one major problem which has so far been ignored: the problem of the origin of institutions, and of their very existence.

Notes

1 Christian Metz, *Language and Cinema*, trans. Donna Jean-Umiker Sebeok, The Hague: Mouton, 1974, p. 74.

2 This is the neopositivist attitude (Morris, Carnap) recently revived by Alain Berrendonner: *Eléments de pragmatique linguistique*, Editions de Minuit, 1981.

3 The main representatives of this trend are Austin, Searle, Ducrot, Recanati, Orecchioni.

4 Berrendonner, ibid., p. 11.

5 For an examination of this concept, see John R. Searle: *Expression and Meaning*, Cambridge: Cambridge University Press, 1979.

6 Oswald Ducrot, *Les Mots du discours*, Editions de Minuit, 1980, p. 12.

7 F. Bresson, 'Compétence iconique et compétence linguistique', in *Communications* No. 33, 1981, pp. 187–9.

8 Ibid., p. 188.

9 Approaching this question during Metz's seminar, one of the participants (the experimental film director Giovanni Martedi) remarked that this statement was questionable: the quality of the film is affected by time, and the marks may change quite considerably after a long period.

10 This also needs qualifying: the marks vary depending on the power generated by the projector, the dimensions of the projector gate, etc.

11 Sol Worth was already expressing the same idea: 'There is no meaning in a film itself', in 'The Development of a Semiotic of Film', *Semiotica*, 1969, 1–3, p. 289.

12 Paul Willemen also remarks: 'Texts can restrict readings (offer resistance), they can't determine them', in 'Notes on Subjectivity. On Reading Edward Branigan's "Subjectivity Under Siege"', *Screen*, 19, 1, 1978.

13 Obviously, things happen quite differently if the reading takes place at the editing table.

14 Raymond Bellour quotes some significant examples of deviant reading in the introduction to his study *L'Analyse du film*, Paris: Albatros, 1979, 'D'une histoire', in particular p. 13.

15 'Entretien avec Ch. Metz', in *Ça Cinéma*, special Christian Metz issue, 7/8, 1975, p. 37.

16 Discursive practice: 'a set of anonymous, historical rules, always determined in time and space, which have defined, at a certain time and for a given social, economic, geographical or linguistic field, the working procedures of the utterance process'. Michel Foucault, *The Archaeology of Knowledge*, trans. A. M. Sheridan-Smith, New York: Pantheon Books, 1972.

17 M. Tardy, 'Sémiogénèse d'encodage, sémiogénèse de décodage', in *The Canadian Journal of Research Semiotics*, Spring 1979, Vol. VI, No. 3; VII, No. 1, p. 111.

18 On this point, see Metz, 'Le Perçu et le nommé', in *Vers une esthétique sans entrave*, Mélanges Mikel Dufrenne, 10/18, 1975, pp. 345–78; and my own article: 'Quelques réflexions sur le fonctionnement des isotopies minimales et des isotopies élémentaires dans l'image', in *Versus*, 14/3, pp. 69–91.

19 Michel Colin, *Prolégomènes à une 'sémiologie générative' du film*, Thèse de Doctorat ès Lettres, 1979. [Published as *Langue, film, discours: Prolégomènes à une sémiologie générative du film*, Paris: Klincksieck, 1985.]

20 E. Veron: 'The subject is therefore, in our opinion, the *point of passage* of the rules on production and recognition processes', in 'Semiosis de l'idéologie et du pouvoir', *Communications* 28, 1978, p. 19.

21 On this definition of film in terms of relevant features of the material of expression, see Metz, *Language and Cinema*, pp. 227–35; and the chapter 'Préliminaire' in my thesis: 'L'Objet cinéma', in *L'Analyse sémiologique des films*.

22 'The basic formula, which has never changed, is the one that consists in making a large continuous unit that tells a story, a "movie"'. Metz, *Film Language: A Semiotics of the Cinema*, trans. Michael Taylor, New York: Oxford University Press, 1974, p. 45.

23 On this point, see Dominique Noguez, *Eloge du cinéma expérimental*, Publication du Centre Georges Pompidou, 1979.

24 On the functioning of the pedagogic film, see Geneviève Jacquinot, *Images et Pédagogie*, Paris: PUF, 1977.

25 On the functioning of the news report, or documentary film, see Bill Nichols, *Ideology and the Image*, Bloomington: Indiana University Press, 1981, chapters 6, 7 and 8.

26 Metz, 'The Fiction Film and its Spectator', trans. Alfred Guzzetti, in Metz, *Psychoanalysis and Cinema: The Imaginary Signifier*, London: Macmillan, 1982, pp. 99–147.

27 See my own article, 'Rhétorique du film de famille' in *Rhétoriques sémiotiques, Revue d'Esthétique*, 1979, 1/2, 10/18, pp. 340–73.

28 On this point, see my own study, *Partie de campagne: un exemple de 'mise en phase'*.

29 This notion of 'mise en phase' seems to correspond quite accurately to what Michel Colin calls 'secondary identification'; indeed, the 'mise en phase' attempts to get the

spectator to enter into the relational system, in other words the discourse, of the film (see *Langue, film, discours*, Paris: Klincksieck, 1985).

We also discovered at a later date that the expression 'mise en phase' was also used by Ph. Hamon to explain what happens in a realistic text, and especially descriptions; Hamon mentions an 'aesthetics of the process of mise en phase (set/character/spectator)', and points out that 'the description is a kind of tonal operator (producing a positive or negative effect, euphoria or dysphoria) orientating the consumption of the text by the reader in the light of a global aesthetics of homogeneity' (Ph. Hamon, *Introduction à l'analyse du descriptif*, Hachette Université, 1981, p. 20). This coincidence is all the more interesting as the realistic text is the equivalent, within the literary space, of the classic fiction film within the filmic space.

30 On this taboo, see, for example, Alain Bergala, *Initiation à la sémiologie du récit en images*. Les Cahiers de l'audio-visuel, pp. 31–2, and Francesco Casetti 'Les Yeux dans les yeux', *Communications*, 38, 1983, pp. 78–97.

31 The look directed at the camera, which is a kind of rape of our spectatorial self, is actually simultaneous with the 'rape' of Henriette by Henri.

32 The only exception to the systematic use of the freeze-frame is shot No. 282, which actually shows the woman opening her eyes (reproducing the movement).

33 On this point, see my own article: 'Le Film de fiction menacé par la photographie et sauvé par la bande-son. A propos de *la Jetée* de Chris Marker', in Dominique Chateau, André Gardies, and François Jost (eds), *Cinémas de la modernité, films, théories*, Colloque de Cerisy, Paris: Klinsieck, 1981, pp. 147–72.

34 On this point, see my own article 'Mise en phase, déphasage et performativité dans *Le Tempestaire* de Jean Epstein', *Communications* 38, 1983, pp. 213–38.

35 C. Kerbrat Orecchioni, 'Note sur les concepts d'Illocutoire et de Performatif' in *Linguistique et sémiologie*, 4, 1977, p. 82.

36 C. Castoriadis, *L'Institution imaginaire de la société*, Paris: le Seuil, 1975, p. 184.

37 Berrendonner, ibid., p. 95.

38 Eric de Kuyper, 'Le Mauvais genre. II', in *Ça Cinéma*, 19, p. 33.

39 Dominique Noguez, 'Théorie(s) du (ou des) cinéma(s)?', in *Cinémas de la modernité*, p. 43.

40 According to this instruction, the breaks play the part of a 'stimulant' of memorial activity; at the same time, they enable each participant to reconstruct *his* own diegesis fairly free of constraints. On the concept of 'family fiction', see my own article 'Rhétorique du film de famille', pp. 364–7.

41 It seems as if the instructions given by experimental film could be summarized as follows: read the breaks as a deliberate attempt, on the part of this type of film, to distinguish itself from classic fiction film, as manifestations of the desire to produce 'another' type of film; and enjoy these breaks. The 'experimental' effect certainly deserves a more detailed analysis; some relevant comments can be found in Noguez, *Eloge du cinéma expérimental*, especially in chapter 1: 'Qu'est-ce que le cinéma expérimental?'

42 Here, unlike what happens in experimental and home movies, the instruction orders the reader to consider the breaks as signs of the cameraman's presence on site, and of the difficulty of shooting live events. Once again, a detailed analysis of the 'filmic document' effect is needed; a few comments can be found in Nichols, *Ideology and the Image*.

43 Many an amateur film director, 'corrupted' by the fetishism characterizing fiction films and prevailing in amateur film clubs, has learnt this the hard way, after a few family quarrels.

44 Eric de Kuyper; 'Le Mauvais genre. I. (Une affaire de famille)', in Ça Cinéma, 18, p. 45.

45 This emerges very clearly from the first chapter of Noguez's study: *Eloge du cinéma expérimental*.

46 See 'Empirical Foundation for a Theory of Language Change', by U. Weinreich, W. Labov, M. I. Herzog, in W. P. Lehmann and Y. Malkiel (eds), *Directions for Historical Linguistics, A Symposium*, Austin and London: University of Texas Press, 1968.

47 Similar comments can be found in: A. Delveau, H. Huot, F. Kerleroux, 'Questions sur le changement linguistique', *Langue française* No. 15, 1972, and S. Lecointre and J. Le Galliot, 'Le Changement linguistique: problématiques nouvelles', *Langages*, 32, 1973.

48 Michel Pêcheux, *Analyse automatique du discours*, Paris, Dunod, 1969, pp. 13–14.

6
The Scene of the Screen: Envisioning Cinematic and Electronic "Presence"

Vivian Sobchack

It is obvious that cinematic and electronic technologies of representation have had enormous impact upon our means of signification during the past century. Less obvious, however, is the similar impact these technologies have had upon the historically particular significance or "sense" we have and make of those temporal and spatial coordinates that radically inform and orient our social, individual, and bodily existences. At this point in time in the United States, whether or not we go to the movies, watch television or music videos, own a video tape recorder/player, allow our children to play video and computer games, or write our academic papers on personal computers, we are all part of a moving-image culture and we live cinematic and electronic lives. Indeed, it is not an exaggeration to claim that none of us can escape daily encounters – both direct and indirect – with the *objective* phenomena of motion picture, televisual, and computer technologies and the networks of communication and texts they produce. Nor is it an extravagance to suggest that, in the most profound, socially pervasive, and yet personal way, these objective encounters transform us as *subjects*. That is, although relatively novel as "materialities" of human communication, cinematic and electronic media have not only historically *symbolized* but also historically *constituted* a radical alteration of the forms of our culture's previous temporal and spatial consciousness and of our bodily sense of existential "presence" to the world, to ourselves, and to others.

This different sense of *subjective* and *material* "presence" both signified and supported by cinematic and electronic media emerges within and co-constitutes *objective* and *material* practices of representation and social existence. Thus, while cooperative in creating the moving-image culture or "life-world" we now inhabit, cinematic and electronic technologies are quite different from each other in their concrete "materiality" and particular existential significance. Each offers our lived-bodies radically different ways of "being-in-the world." Each implicates us in different structures of material investment, and – because each has a particular affinity with different cultural functions, forms, and contents – each stimulates us through differing modes of representation to different aesthetic responses and ethical responsibilities. In sum, just as the photograph did in the last century, so in this one, cinematic and electronic screens differently demand and shape our "presence" to the world and our representation in it. Each differently and objectively alters our subjectivity while each invites our complicity in formulating space, time, and bodily investment as significant personal and social experience.

These preliminary remarks are grounded in the belief that, during the last century, historical changes in our contemporary "sense" of temporality, spatiality, and existential and embodied presence cannot be considered less than a consequence of correspondent changes in our technologies of representation. However, they also must be considered something more, for as Martin Heidegger reminds us, "The essence of technology is nothing technological." That is, technology never comes to its particular material specificity and function in a neutral context for neutral effect. Rather, it is always historically informed not only by its materiality but also by its political, economic, and social context, and thus always both co-constitutes and expresses cultural values. Correlatively, technology is never merely "used," never merely instrumental. It is always also "incorporated" and "lived" by the human beings who engage it within a structure of meanings and metaphors in which subject–object relations are cooperative, co-constitutive, dynamic, and reversible. It is no accident, for example, that in our now dominantly electronic (and only secondarily cinematic) culture, many human beings describe and understand their minds and bodies in terms of computer systems and programs (even as they still describe and understand their lives as movies). Nor is it trivial that computers are often described and understood in terms of human minds and/or bodies (for example, as intelligent, or as susceptible to viral infection) – and that these new "life forms" have become the cybernetic heroes of our most popular moving image fictions (for example, *Robocop* or *Terminator II*).[1] In this sense, a qualitatively new techno-logic can begin to alter our perceptual orientation in and toward the world, ourselves, and others. And as it becomes culturally pervasive, it can come to profoundly inform and affect the socio-logic, psycho-logic, and even the bio-logic by which we daily live our lives.

This power to alter our perceptions is doubly true of technologies of representation. A technological artifact like the automobile (whose technological function is not representation but transportation) has profoundly changed the temporal and spatial shape and meaning of our life-world and our own bodily and symbolic sense of ourselves.[2] However, representational technologies of photography, the motion picture, video, and computer inform us twice over: first, like the automobile, through the specific material conditions by which they latently engage our senses at the bodily level of what might be called our *microperception*, and then again through their explicit representational function by which they engage our senses textually at the hermeneutic level of what might be called our *macroperception*.[3] Most theorists and critics of the cinematic and electronic have been drawn to macroperceptual analysis, to descriptions and interpretations of the hermeneutic–cultural contexts that inform and shape both the materiality of the technologies and their textual representations.[4] Nonetheless, "all such contexts find their fulfillment *only* within the range of microperceptual possibility" (Ihde, 1990: 29; my emphasis). We cannot reflect upon and analyze either technologies or texts without having, at some point, engaged them *immediately* – that is, through our perceptive sensorium, through the materiality (or *immanent mediation*) of our own bodies. Thus, as philosopher of technology Don Ihde puts it, while "there is no microperception (sensory–bodily) without its location within a field of macroperception," there can be "no macroperception without its microperceptual foci" (ibid.). It is important to note, however, that since perception is constituted and organized as a bodily and sensory *gestalt* that is always already meaningful, a microperceptual focus is not the same as a physiological or anatomical focus. The perceiving and sensing body is always also a *lived-body* – immersed in and making social meaning as well as physical sense.

The aim of this essay, then, is to figure certain microperceptual aspects of our engagement with the technologies of cinematic and electronic representation and to suggest some ways in which our microperceptual experience of their respective material conditions informs and transforms our temporal and spatial sense of ourselves and our cultural contexts of meaning. Insofar as the cinematic and the electronic have each been *objectively constituted* as a new and discrete techno-logic, each also has been *subjectively incorporated*, enabling a new perceptual mode of existential and embodied "presence." In sum, as they have mediated our engagement with the world, with others, and with ourselves, cinematic and electronic technologies have transformed us so that we currently see, sense, and make sense of ourselves as quite other than we were before them.

It should be evident at this point that the co-constitutive, reversible, and dynamic relations between objective material technologies and embodied human subjects invite a phenomenological investigation. Existential phenomenology, to use Ihde's characterization, is a "philosophical style that emphasizes a certain interpretation of human *experience* and that, in particular, concerns *perception* and *bodily* activity" (1990: 21). Often misunderstood as ungrounded "subjective" analysis, existential phenomenology is instead concerned with describing, thematizing, and interpreting the structures of lived spatiality, temporality, and meaning that are co-constituted dynamically as embodied human subjects perceptually engage an objective material world. It is focused, therefore, on the *relations between* the subjective and objective aspects of material, social, and personal existence and sees these relations as constitutive of the meaning and value of the phenomena under investigation.[5]

Existential phenomenology, then, attempts to describe, thematize, and interpret the *experiential* and *perceptual field* in which human beings play out a particular and meaningful structure of spatial, temporal, and bodily existence. Unlike the foundational, Husserlian transcendental phenomenology from which it emerged, existential phenomenology rejects the goal of arriving at universal and "essential" description, and "settles" for a historicized and "qualified" description as the only kind of description that is existentially possible or, indeed, desirable. It is precisely *because* rather than *in spite of* its qualifications that such a description is existentially meaningful – meaningful, that is, to human beings who are themselves particular, finite, and partial, and thus always in culture and history, always open to the world and further elaboration. Specifically, Maurice Merleau-Ponty's existential phenomenology departs from the transcendental phenomenology most associated with Edmund Husserl in that it stresses the *embodied* nature of human consciousness and views bodily existence as the original and originating *material premise* of sense and signification. We sit in a movie theater, before a television set, or in front of a computer terminal not only as *conscious* beings but also as *carnal* beings. Our vision is not abstracted from our bodies or from our other modes of perceptual access to the world. Nor does what we see merely touch the surface of our eyes. Seeing images mediated and made visible by technological vision enables us not only to see technological images but also to see technologically. As Ihde emphasizes, "the concreteness of [technological] 'hardware' in the broadest sense connects with the equal concreteness of our bodily existence," and, in this regard, "the term 'existential' in context refers to perceptual and bodily experience, to a kind of 'phenomenological materiality'" (1990: 26).

This correspondent and objective materiality of both human subjects and worldly objects not only suggests some commensurability and possibilities of exchange between them, but also suggests that any phenomenological analysis of the existential relation between human subjects and technologies of representation must be semiological and historical even at the microperceptual level. Description must attend both to the particular materiality and modalities through which meanings are signified and to the cultural and historical situations in which materiality and meaning come to cohere in the praxis of everyday life. Like human vision, the materiality and modalities of cinematic and electronic technologies of representation are not abstractions. They are concrete and situated and institutionalized. They inform and share in the spatiotemporal structures of a wide range of interrelated cultural phenomena. Thus, in its attention to the broadly defined "material conditions" and "relations" of production (specifically, the conditions for and production of existential meaning), existential phenomenology is not incompatible with certain aspects of Marxist analysis.

In this context, we might turn to Fredric Jameson's useful discussion of three crucial and expansive historical "moments" marked by "a technological revolution within capital itself" and the particular and dominant "cultural logic" that correspondently emerges in each of them (1984: 77). Historically situating these three "moments" in the 1840s, 1890s, and 1940s, Jameson correlates the three major technological changes that revolutionized the structure of capital – by changing market capitalism to monopoly capitalism and this to multinational capitalism – with the emergence and domination of three new "cultural logics":

those axiological norms and forms of representation identified respectively as realism, modernism, and postmodernism. Extrapolating from Jameson, we can also locate within this conceptual and historical framework three correspondent technologies, forms, and institutions of visual (and aural) representation: respectively, the photographic, the cinematic, and the electronic. Each, we might argue, has been critically complicit not only in a specific "*technological* revolution within capital," but also in a specific and radical *perceptual* revolution within the culture and the subject. That is, each has been co-constitutive of the very temporal and spatial structure of the "cultural logics" Jameson identifies as realism, modernism, and postmodernism. Writing about the nature of cultural transformation, phenomenological historian Stephen Kern suggests that some major cultural changes can be seen as "*directly* inspired by new technology," while others occur relatively independently of technology, and still others emerge from the new technological "metaphors and analogies" that *indirectly* alter the structures of perceptual life and thought (Kern, 1983: 6–7). Implicated in and informing each historically specific "technological revolution in capital" and transformation of "cultural logic," the technologically discrete nature and phenomenological impact of new "materialities" of representation co-constitute a complex cultural *gestalt*. In this regard, the technological "nature" of the photographic, the cinematic, and the electronic is graspable always and only in a qualified manner – that is, less as an "essence" than as a "theme."

Although I wish to emphasize the technologies of cinematic and electronic representation, those two "materialities" that constitute our current *moving-* image culture, something must first be said of that culture's grounding in the context and phenomenology of the *photographic*. The photographic is privileged in the "moment" of market capitalism – located by Jameson in the 1840s, and cooperatively informed and driven by the technological innovations of steam-powered mechanization that allowed for industrial expansion and the cultural logic of "realism." Not only did industrial expansion give rise to other forms of expansion, but expansion itself was historically unique in its unprecedented *visibility*. As Jean-Louis Comolli points out:

> The second half of the nineteenth century lives in a sort of frenzy of the visible.... [This is] the effect of the social multiplication of images.... [It is] the effect also, however, of something of a geographical extension of the field of the visible and the representable: by journeys, explorations, colonizations, the whole world becomes visible at the same time that it becomes appropriatable. (Comolli, 1980: 122–3)

Thus, while the cultural logic of "realism" has been seen as primarily represented by literature (most specifically, the bourgeois novel), it is, perhaps, even more intimately bound to the mechanically achieved, empirical, and representational "evidence" of the world constituted by photography.

Until very recently, the photographic has been popularly and phenomenologically perceived as existing in a state of testimonial verisimilitude – its film emulsions analogically marked with (and objectively "capturing") material traces of the world's concrete and "real" existence.[6] Photography produced images of the world with a perfection previously rivaled only by the human eye. Thus, as Comolli suggests, with the advent of photography, the human eye loses its "immemorial privilege" and is devalued in relation to "the mechanical eye of the photographic machine," which "now sees *in its place*" (1980: 123). This replacement of human with mechanical vision had its compensations however – among them, the material control, containment, and actual possession of time and experience.[7] Abstracting visual experience from a temporal flow, the photographic chemically and metaphorically "fixes" its ostensible subject as an *object* for vision, and concretely reproduces it in a *material* form that can be possessed, circulated, and saved, in a form that can over time accrue an increasing rate of interest, become more *valuable* in a variety of ways. Thus, identifying the photograph as a fetish object, Comolli links it with gold, and aptly calls it "the money of the 'real' " – of "life" – the photograph's materiality assuring the possibility of its "convenient circulation and appropriation" (1980: 142).

In his phenomenological description of human vision Merleau-Ponty tells us, "To see is *to have at a distance*" (1964: 166). This subjective activity of *visual* possession is objectified and literalized by the materiality of photography, which makes possible its *visible* possession. What you see is what you get. Indeed, this structure of objectification and empirical possession is doubled, even tripled. Not only does the photograph materially "capture" traces of the "real world," not only can the photograph itself be possessed concretely, but the photograph's culturally defined semiotic status as a mechanical reproduction (rather than a linguistic representation) also allows an unprecedentedly literal and material, and perhaps uniquely complacent, form – and ethics – of self-possession. Family albums serve as "memory banks" that authenticate self, other, and experience as empirically "real" by virtue of the photograph's material existence as an object and possession with special power.[8]

In regard to the materiality of the photograph's authenticating power, it is instructive to recall one of a number of particularly relevant ironies in *Blade Runner* (Ridley Scott, 1982), a science fiction film focusing on the ambiguous ontological status of a group of genetically manufactured "replicants." At a certain moment, Rachel, the film's putative heroine and the latest replicant prototype, disavows the revelation of her own manufactured status by pointing to a series of keepsake photographs that give "proof" to her mother's existence, to her own existence as a little girl, to her subjective memory. Upon being told that both her memory and their material extroversion "belong to someone else," she is both distraught and ontologically re-signed as someone with no "real" life, no "real" history – although she still remembers what she remembers and the photographs still sit on her piano. Indeed, the photographs are suddenly fore-grounded (for the human spectator as well as the narrative's replicant) as utterly suspect. That is, when interrogated, the photographs simultaneously both reveal and lose that great material and circulatory value they commonly hold for *all* of us as the "money of the 'real.'"

The structures of objectification and material possession that constitute the photographic as both a "real" trace of personal experience and a concrete extroversion of experience that can "belong to someone else" give specific form to its temporal existence. In capturing aspects of "life itself" in a "real" object that can be possessed, copied, circulated, and saved as the "currency" of experience, the appropriable materiality and static form of photography accomplish a palpable intervention in what was popularly perceived in the mid-nineteenth century to be time's linear, orderly, and teleological flow from past to present to future. The photograph freezes and preserves the homogeneous and irreversible *momentum* of this temporal stream into the abstracted, atomized, and secured space of a *moment*. But at a cost. A moment cannot be inhabited. It cannot entertain in the abstraction of its visible space, its single and static *point* of view, the presence of a lived-body – and so it does not really invite the spectator *into* the scene (although it may invite contemplation *of* the scene). In its conquest of time, the photographic constructs a space to hold and to look at, a "thin" insubstantial space that keeps the lived-body out even as it may imaginatively catalyze – in the parallel but temporalized space of memory or desire – an animated drama.

The radical difference between the transcendental, posited moment of the photograph and the existential momentum of the cinema, between the scene to be contemplated and the scene to be lived, is foregrounded in the remarkable short film *La jetée* (Chris Marker, 1962).[9] A study of desire, memory, and time, *La jetée* is presented completely through the use of still photographs – except for one extraordinarily brief but utterly compelling sequence in which the woman who is the object of the hero's desire, lying in bed and looking toward the camera, blinks her eyes. The space between the camera's (and the spectator's) gaze and the woman becomes suddenly habitable, informed with the real possibility of bodily movement and engagement, informed with a lived temporality rather than an eternal timelessness. What, in the film, has previously been a mounting accumulation of nostalgic moments achieves substantial and present presence in its sudden accession to momentum and the consequent possibility of effective action.

As did André Bazin (1967), we might think of photography, then, as primarily a form of mummification (although, unlike Bazin, I shall argue that cinema is not). While it testifies to and preserves a sense of the world and experience's real presence, it does not preserve their present. The photographic – unlike the cinematic and the electronic – functions neither as a coming-into-being (a presence always presently constituting itself) nor as being-in-itself (an absolute presence). Rather, it functions to fix a being-that-has-been (a presence in the present that is always past). Paradoxically, as it objectifies and preserves in its acts of possession, the photographic has something to do with loss, with pastness, and with death, its meaning and value intimately bound within the structure and investments of nostalgia.

Although dependent upon the photographic, the cinematic has something more to do with life, with the accumulation – not the loss – of experience. Cinematic technology *animates* the photographic and reconstitutes its visibility and verisimilitude in a difference not of degree but of kind. The *moving picture* is a visible representation not of activity finished or past, but of activity coming-into-being – and its materiality came to be in the 1890s, the second of Jameson's transformative moments of "technological revolution within capital itself." During this moment, the internal combustion engine and electric power literally reenergized market capitalism into the highly controlled yet expansive structure of monopoly capitalism. Correlatively, the new cultural logic of "modernism" emerged, restructuring and eventually dominating the logic of realism to represent more adequately the new perceptual experience of an age marked by the strange autonomy and energetic fluidity of, among other mechanical phenomena, the motion picture. The motion picture, while photographically verisimilar, fragments, reorders, and synthesizes time and space as animation in a completely new "cinematic" mode that finds no necessity in the objective teleo-logic of realism. Thus, although modernism has found its most remarked expression in the painting and photography of the futurists (who attempted to represent motion and speed in a static form) and the cubists (who privileged multiple perspectives and simultaneity), and in the novels of James Joyce, we can see in the cinema modernism's fullest representation.[10]

Philosopher Arthur Danto tells us, "With the movies, we do not just see *that* they move, we see them *moving*: and this is because the pictures themselves move" (1979: 17). While still objectifying the subjectivity of the visual into the visible, the cinematic qualitatively transforms the photographic through a materiality that not only claims the world and others as objects for vision but also signifies its own bodily agency, intentionality, and subjectivity. Neither abstract nor static, the cinematic brings the *existential activity* of vision into visibility in what is phenomenologically experienced as an *intentional stream* of moving images – its continuous and autonomous visual production and meaningful organization of these images testifying to the objective world and, further, to an anonymous, mobile, embodied, and ethically invested *subject* of worldly space. This subject (however physically anonymous) is able to inscribe visual and bodily changes of situation, to dream, hallucinate, imagine, and re-member its habitation and experience of the world. And, as is the case with human beings, this subject's potential mobility and experience are both open-ended and bound by the existential finitude and bodily limits of its particular vision and historical coherence (that is, its narrative).

Here, again, *La jetée* is exemplary. Despite the fact that the film is made up of what strike us as a series of discrete and still photographs rather than the "live" and animated action of human actors, even as it foregrounds the transcendental and atemporal non-becoming of the photograph, *La jetée* nonetheless phenomenologically *projects* as a temporal flow and an existential becoming. That is, *as a whole*, the film organizes, synthesizes, and enunciates the discrete photographic images into animated and intentional coherence and, indeed, makes this temporal synthesis and animation its explicit narrative theme. What *La jetée* allegorizes in its explicit narrative, however, is the transformation of the moment to momentum that constitutes the ontology of the cinematic, and the latent background of every film.

While the technology of the cinematic is grounded, in part, in the technology of the photographic, we need to remember that "the essence of technology is nothing technological." The fact that the technology of the cinematic *necessarily* depends upon the discrete and still photograph moving intermittently (rather than continuously) through the shutters of both camera and projector does not *sufficiently* account for the materiality of the cinematic as we experience it. Unlike the photograph, a film is semiotically engaged in experience not merely as a mechanical objectification – or material *reproduction* – that is, not merely as an object for vision. Rather, the moving picture, however mechanical and photo-graphic its origin, is semiotically experienced as also subjective and intentional, as *presenting representation* of the objective world. Thus perceived as the subject of its own vision as well as an object for our vision, a moving picture is not precisely a *thing* that (like a photograph) can be easily controlled, contained, or materially possessed. Up until very recently in what has now become a dominantly electron-ic culture, the spectator could share in and thereby, to a degree, interpretively alter a film's presentation and representation of embodied and enworlded experi-ence, but could not control or contain its autonomous and ephemeral flow and rhythm, or materially possess its animated experience. Now, of course, with the advent of videotape and VCRs, the spectator can alter the film's temporality and easily possess, at least, its inanimate "body." However, the ability to control the autonomy and flow of the cinematic experience through "fast forwarding," "replaying," and "freezing"[11] and the ability to possess the film's body and animate it at will at home are functions of the materiality and technological ontology of the electronic – a materiality that increasingly dominates, appropri-ates, and transforms the cinematic.

In its pre-electronic state and original materiality, however, the cinematic mechanically projected and made visible for the very first time not just the objective world but the very structure and process of subjective, embodied vision – hitherto only directly available to human beings as that invisible and private structure we each experience as "my own." That is, the materiality of the cinematic gives us concrete and empirical insight and makes objectively visible the reversible, dialectical, and social nature of our own subjective vision. Speaking of human vision, Merleau-Ponty tells us: "As soon as we see other seers... henceforth, through other eyes we are for ourselves fully visible.... For the first time, the seeing that I am is for me really visible; for the first time I appear to myself completely turned inside out under my own eyes" (1968: 143–4). The cinematic uniquely allows this philosophical turning, this objective insight into the subjective structure of vision, into oneself as both viewing subject and visible object, and, remarkably, into others as the same.

Again, the paradoxical status of the "more human than human" replicants in *Blade Runner* is instructive. Speaking to the biotechnologist who genetically produced and quite literally manufactured his eyes, replicant Roy Baty says with an ironic concreteness that resonates through the viewing audience even if its implications are not fully understood, "If you could only see what I've seen with your eyes." The perceptive and expressive materiality of the cinematic through which we engage this ironic articulation of the "impossible" desire for intersubjectivity is the very materiality through which this desire is visibly and objectively fulfilled.[12] Thus, rather than merely replacing human vision with mechanical vision, the cinematic mechanically functions to bring to visibility the reversible structure of human vision (the system visual/visible) – a lived-system that necessarily entails not only an enworlded object but always also an embodied and perceiving subject.

Indeed, through its motor and organizational agency (achieved by the spatial immediacy of the mobile camera and the reflective and temporalizing editorial re-membering of that primary spatial experience), the cinematic inscribes and provokes a sense of existential "presence" that is as synthetically centered as it is also mobile, split, and decentering. The cinematic subject (both film and spectator) is perceived as at once introverted and extroverted, as existing in the world as both subject and object. Thus, the cinematic does not evoke the same sense of self-possession as that generated by the photographic. The cinematic subject is sensed as never completely self-possessed, for it is always partially and visibly given over to the vision of others at the same time that it visually appropriates only part of what it sees and, indeed, also cannot entirely see itself. Further, the very mobility of its vision structures the cinematic subject as always in the act of displacing itself in time, space, and the world – and thus, despite its existence as embodied and centered, as always eluding its own (as well as our) containment.

The cinematic's visible inscription of the dual, reversible, and animated structure of embodied and mobile vision radically transforms the temporal and spatial structure of the photographic. Consonant with what Jameson calls the "high-modernist thematics of time and temporality," the cinematic thickens the photographic with "the elegiac mysteries of *durée* and of memory" (Jameson, 1984: 64). While its visible structure of "unfolding" does not challenge the dominant realist perception of objective time as an irreversibly directed stream (even flashbacks are contained by the film's vision in a forwardly directed momentum of experience), the cinematic makes time visibly *heterogeneous*. That is, we visibly perceive time as differently structured in its subjective and objective modes, and we understand that these two structures *simultaneously* exist in a demonstrable state of *discontinuity* as they are, nonetheless, actively and con-stantly *synthesized* in a specific lived-body experience (i.e. a personal, concrete, and spatialized history and a particularly temporalized narrative).

Cinema's animated presentation of representation constitutes its "presence" as always presently engaged in the experiential process of signifying and coming-into-being. Thus the significant value of the "streaming forward" that informs the cinematic with its specific form of temporality (and differentiates it from the atemporality of the photographic) is intimately bound to a structure not of possession, loss, pastness, and nostalgia, but of accumulation, ephemerality, and anticipation – to a "presence" in the present informed by its connection to a collective past and to a future. Visually (and aurally) presenting the subjective temporality of memory, desire, and mood through flashbacks, flash forwards, freeze framing, pixilation, reverse motion, slow motion, and fast motion, and the editorial expansion and contraction of experience, the cinema's visible (and audible) activity of *retension* and *protension* constructs a subjective temporality different from the irreversible direction and momentum of objective time, yet simultaneous with it. In so thickening the present, this temporal simultaneity also extends cinematic presence spatially – not only by embracing a multiplicity of situations in such visual/visible cinematic articulations as double exposure, superimposition, montage, parallel editing, but also primally, by expanding the space in every image between that Here where the enabling and embodied cinematic eye is situated and that There where its gaze locates itself in its object.

The cinema's existence as simultaneously presentational and representational, viewing subject and visible object, present presence informed by both past and future, continuous becoming that synthesizes temporal heterogeneity as the conscious coherence of embodied experience, transforms the thin abstracted space of the photographic into a thickened and concrete *world*. We might remember here the animated blinking of a woman's eyes in *La jetée* and how this visible motion transforms the photographic into the cinematic, the flat surface of a picture into the lived space of a lover's bedroom. In its capacity for movement, the cinema's embodied agency (the camera) thus constitutes visual/visible space as always also motor and tactile space – a space that is deep and textural, that can be materially inhabited, that provides not merely a ground for the visual/visible but also its particular *situation*. Indeed, although it is a favored term among film theorists, there is no such abstraction as *point of view* in the cinema. Rather, there are concrete *situations of viewing* – specific and mobile engagements of embodied, enworlded, and situated subjects/objects whose visual/visible activity prospects and articulates a shifting field of vision from a world whose horizons always exceed it. The space of the cinematic, in-formed by cinematic time, is also experienced as heterogeneous – both discontiguous and contiguous, lived from within and without. Cinematic presence is multiply located – simultaneously displacing itself in the There of past and future situations yet orienting these displacements from the Here where the body at present is. That is, as the multiplicity and discontinuity of time are synthesized and centered and cohere as the *experience* of a specific lived-body, so are multiple and discontiguous spaces synopsized and located in the spatial *synthesis* of a particular *material* body. Articulated as separate shots and scenes, discontiguous spaces and discontinuous times are synthetically gathered together in a coherence that is the cinematic lived-body: the camera its perceptive organ, the projector its expressive organ, the screen its discrete and material center. In sum, the cinematic exists as a visible performance of the perceptive and expressive structure of lived-body experience.

Not so the electronic, whose materiality and various forms and contents engage its spectators and "users" in a phenomenological structure of sensual and psychological experience that seems to belong to *no-body*. Born in the USA with the nuclear age, the electronic emerged in the 1940s as the third "technological revolution within capital itself," and, according to Jameson, involved the unprecedented and "prodigious expansion of capital into hitherto uncommodified areas," including "a new and historically original penetration and colonization of Nature and the Unconscious" (1984: 78). Since that time, electronic technology has "saturated all forms of experience and become an inescapable environment, a 'technosphere'" (Landon, 1987: 27). This expansive and totalizing incorporation of Nature by industrialized culture, and the specular production and commodification of the Unconscious (globally transmitted as visible and marketable "desire"), restructures capitalism as multinational. Correlatively, a new cultural logic identified as "postmodernism" begins to dominate modernism, and to alter our sense of existential presence.

A function of technological pervasion and dispersion, this new electronic sense of presence is intimately bound up in a centerless, network-like structure of instant stimulation and desire, rather than in a nostalgia for the past or anticipation of a future. Television, video cassettes, video tape recorder/players, video games, and personal computers all form an encompassing electronic representational system whose various forms "interface" to constitute an alternative and absolute world that uniquely incorporates the spectator/user in a spatially decentered, weakly temporalized, and quasi-disembodied state. Digital electronic technology atomizes and abstractly schematizes the analogic quality of the photographic and cinematic into discrete pixels and bits of information that are then transmitted serially, each bit discontinuous, discontiguous, and absolute – each bit being-in-itself even as it is part of a system.[13]

Once again we can turn to *Blade Runner* to provide illustration of how the electronic is neither photographic nor cinematic. Tracking Leon, one of the rebellious replicants, the human protagonist Deckard finds his empty rooms and discovers a photograph that seems, itself, to reveal nothing but an empty room. Using a science fictional device, Deckard directs its electronic eye to zoom in, close up, isolate, and enlarge to impossible detail various portions of the photograph. On the one hand, it might seem that Deckard is functioning like a photographer working in his darkroom to make, through optical discovery, past experience significantly visible. (Indeed, this sequence of the film recalls the photographic blow-ups of an ambiguously "revealed" murder in Michelangelo Antonioni's 1966 classic, *Blow-up*.) On the other hand, Deckard can be and has been likened to a film director, using the electronic eye to probe photographic space intentionally and to animate a discovered narrative. Deckard's electronic eye, however, is neither photographic nor cinematic. While it constitutes a series of moving images from the static singularity of Leon's photograph and reveals to Deckard the stuff of which narrative can be made, it does so serially and in static, discrete "bits." The moving images do not move themselves, and they reveal no animated and intentional vision to us or to Deckard. Transmitted to what looks like a television screen, the moving images no longer quite retain the concrete and material "thingness" of the photograph, but they also do not achieve the subjective animation of the intentional and prospective vision objectively projected by the cinema. They exist less as Leon's experience than as Deckard's information.

Indeed, the electronic is phenomenologically experienced not as a discrete, intentional, and bodily centered projection in space but rather as simultaneous, dispersed, and insubstantial transmission across a network.[14] Thus, the "presence" of electronic representation is at one remove from previous representational connections between signification and referentiality. Electronic presence asserts neither an objective possession of the world and self (as does the photographic) nor a centered and subjective spatiotemporal engagement with the world and others accumulated and projected as conscious and embodied experience (as does the cinematic). Digital and schematic, abstracted both from *reproducing* the empirical objectivity of Nature that informs the photographic and from *presenting* a representation of individual subjectivity and the Unconscious that informs the cinematic, the electronic constructs a metaworld where ethical investment and value are located in *representation-in-itself*. That is, the electronic semiotically constitutes a system of *simulation* – a system that constitutes "copies" lacking an "original" origin. And, when there is no longer a phenomenologically perceived connection between signification and an "original" or "real," when, as Guy Debord tells us, "everything that was lived directly has moved away into a representation" (1983: n.p.), referentiality becomes *intertextuality*.

Living in a schematized and intertextual metaworld far removed from reference to a real world liberates the spectator/user from what might be termed the latter's moral and physical gravity. The materiality of the electronic digitizes *durée* and situation so that narrative, history, and a centered (and central) investment in the human lived-body become atomized and dispersed across a system that constitutes temporality not as the flow of conscious experience but as a transmission of random information. The primary value of electronic temporality is the bit or *instant* – which (thanks to television and videotape) can be selected, combined, and instantly replayed and return to such a degree that the previously irreversible direction and stream of objective time seems overcome in the creation of a recursive temporal network. On the one hand, the temporal cohesion of history and narrative gives way to the temporal discretion of chronicle and episode, to music videos, to the kinds of narratives that find both causality and intentional agency incomprehensible and comic. On the other hand, temporality is dispersed and finds resolution as part of a recursive, if chaotic, structure of coincidence. Indeed, objective time in postmodern electronic culture is perceived as phenomenologically discontinuous as was subjective time in modernist cinematic culture. Temporality is constituted paradoxically as a *homogeneous* experience of *discontinuity* in which the temporal distinctions between objective and subjective experience (marked by the cinematic) disappear and time seems to turn back in on itself recursively in a structure of equivalence and reversibility. The temporal move is from *Remembrance of Things Past*, a modernist remembering of experience, to the recursive postmodernism of a *Back to the Future*.

Again "science fiction" film is illuminating.[15] While the *Back to the Future* films are certainly apposite, Alex Cox's postmodern, parodic, and deadpan *Repo Man* (1984) more clearly manifests the phenomenologically experienced homogeneity of postmodern discontinuity. The film is constructed as both a picaresque, episodic, loose, and irresolute tale about an affectless young man involved with car repossessors, aliens from outer space, Los Angeles punks, government agents, and others, and a tightly bound system of coincidences. Individual scenes are connected not through narrative causality but through the connection of literally material signifiers. A dangling dashboard ornament, for example, provides the acausal and material motivation between two of the film's otherwise disparate episodes. However, the film also re-solves its acausal structure through a narrative recursivity that links all the characters and events together in what one character calls both the "cosmic unconsciousness" and a "lattice of coincidence." Emplotment in *Repo Man* becomes diffused across a vast relational network. It is no accident that the car culture of Los Angeles figures in *Repo Man* to separate and segment experience into discrete and chaotic bits (as if it were metaphysically lived only through the window of an automobile) – while the "lattice of coincidence," the "network" of the Los Angeles freeway system, reconnects experience at another and less human order of magnitude.

The postmodern and electronic "instant," in its break from the temporal structures of retension and protension, constitutes a form of absolute presence (one abstracted from the continuity that gives meaning to the system past/present/future) and changes the nature of the space it occupies. Without the temporal emphases of historical consciousness and personal history, space becomes abstract, ungrounded, and flat – a site for play and display rather than an invested situation in which action "counts" rather than computes. Such a superficial space can no longer hold the spectator/user's interest, but has to stimulate it constantly in the same way a video game does. Its flatness – a function of its lack of temporal thickness and bodily investment – has to attract spectator interest at the surface. Thus, electronic space constructs objective and superficial equivalents to depth, texture, and invested bodily movement. Saturation of color and hyperbolic attention to detail replace depth and texture at the surface of the image, while constant action and "busyness" replace the gravity that grounds and orients the movement of the lived-body with a purely spectacular, kinetically exciting, often dizzying sense of bodily freedom (and freedom from the body). In an important sense, electronic space disembodies.

What I am suggesting is that, ungrounded and uninvested as it is, electronic presence has neither a point of view nor a visual situation, such as we experience, respectively, with the photograph and the cinema. Rather, electronic presence randomly disperses its being *across* a network, its kinetic gestures describing and lighting on the surface of the screen rather than inscribing it with bodily dimension (a function of centered and intentional projection). Images on television screens and computer terminals seem neither projected nor deep. Phenomenologically they seem, rather, somehow just there as they confront us.

The two-dimensional, binary superficiality of electronic space at once disorients and liberates the activity of consciousness from the gravitational pull and orientation of its hitherto embodied and grounded existence. All surface, electronic space cannot be inhabited. It denies or prosthetically transforms the spectator's physical body so that subjectivity and affect free-float or free-fall or free-flow across a horizontal/vertical grid. Subjectivity is at once decentered and completely extroverted – again erasing the modernist (and cinematic) dialectic between inside and outside and its synthesis of discontinuous time and discontiguous space as conscious and embodied experience. As Jameson explains:

> The liberation . . . from the older *anomie* of the centered subject may also mean, not merely a liberation from anxiety, but a liberation from every other kind of feeling as well, since there is no longer a self present to do the feeling. This is not to say that the cultural products of the postmodern era are utterly devoid of feeling, but rather that such feelings – which it might be better and more accurate to call "intensities" – are now free-floating and impersonal, and tend to be dominated by a peculiar kind of euphoria. (Jameson, 1984: 64)

Brought to visibility by the electronic, this kind of euphoric "presence" is not only peculiar. At the risk of sounding reactionary, I would like to suggest that it is also dangerous. Its lack of specific interest and grounded investment in the human body and enworlded action, its saturation with the present instant, could well cost us all a future.

Phenomenological analysis does not end with the "thick" description and thematization (or qualified reduction) of the phenomenon under investigation. It aims also for an interpretation of the phenomenon that discloses, however partially, the lived meaning, significance, and non-neutral value it has for those who engage it. In terms of contemporary moving-image culture, the material differences between cinematic and electronic representation emerge as significant differences in their meaning and value. Cinema is an objective phenomenon that comes – and becomes – before us in a structure that implicates both a sensible body and a sensual and sense-making subject. In its visual address and movement, it allows us to see what seems a visual impossibility: that we are at once intentional subjects and material objects in the world, the seer and the seen. It affirms both embodied being and the world. It also shows us that, sharing materiality and the world, we are intersubjective beings.

Now, however, it is the electronic and not the cinematic that dominates the form of our cultural representations. And, unlike cinematic representation, electronic representation by its very structure phenomenologically denies the human body its fleshly presence and the world its dimension. However significant and positive its value in some regards, the electronic trivializes the human body. Indeed, at this historical moment in our particular society and culture, the lived-body is in crisis. Its struggle to assert its gravity, its differential existence and situation, its vulnerability and mortality, its vital and social investment in a concrete life-world inhabited by others is now marked in hysterical and hyperbolic responses to the disembodying effects of electronic representation. On the one hand, contemporary moving images show us the human body relentlessly and fatally interrogated, "riddled with holes" and "blown away," unable to maintain its material integrity or gravity. If the Terminator doesn't finish it off, then electronic smart bombs will. On the other hand, the current popular obsession with physical fitness manifests the wish to transform the human body into something else – a lean, mean, and immortal "machine," a cyborg that can physically interface with the electronic network and maintain material presence in the current digitized life-world of the subject. (It is no accident that body builder Arnold Schwarzenegger played the cyborg Terminator.)

Within the context of this material and technological crisis of the flesh, one can only hope that the hysteria and hyperbole surrounding it is strategic – and that through it the lived-body has, in fact, managed to reclaim our attention to forcefully argue for its existence and against its simulation. For there are other subjects of electronic culture out there who prefer the simulated body and a virtual world. Indeed, they actually believe the body (contemptuously called "meat" or "wetware") is best lived only as an image or as information, and that the only hope for negotiating one's presence in our electronic life-world is to exist on a screen or to digitize and "download" one's consciousness into the neural nets of a solely electronic existence. Such an insubstantial electronic presence can ignore AIDS, homelessness, hunger, torture, and all the other ills the flesh is heir to outside the image and the datascape. Devaluing the physically lived body and the concrete materiality of the world, electronic presence suggests that we are all in imminent danger of becoming merely ghosts in the machine.

Notes

A much shorter version of this paper was published in *Post Script: Essays in Film and the Humanities* 10, no. 1 (Fall 1990): 50–9, under the title "Toward a Phenomenology of Cinematic and Electronic Presence: The Scene of the Screen."

1   *Robocop* (1987) was directed by Paul Verhoeven; *Terminator II: Judgment Day* (1991) by James Cameron.

2   Reference here is not only to the way in which automotive transportation has changed our lived sense of distance and space, the rhythms of our temporality, and the hard currency that creates and expresses our cultural values relative to such things as class and style, but also to the way in which it has changed the very sense we have of our

bodies. The vernacular expression of regret at "being without wheels" is profound, and ontologically speaks to our very real incorporation of the automobile as well as its incorporation of us.

3   These terms are derived from Ihde. Ihde distinguishes two senses of perception: "What is usually taken as sensory perception (what is immediate and focused bodily in actual seeing, hearing, etc.), I shall call microperception. But there is also what might be called a cultural, or hermeneutic, perception, which I shall call macroperception. Both belong equally to the lifeworld. And both dimensions of perception are closely linked and intertwined."

4   Two types of theory that are, to some degree, attempts at microperceptual analysis are, first, psychoanalytic accounts of the processes of cinematic identification in which cinematic technology is deconstructed to reveal its inherent "illusionism" and its retrogressive duplication of infantile and/or dream states and, second, neo-Marxist accounts of both photography's and cinema's optical dependence upon a system of "perspective" based on an ideology of the individual subject and its appropriation of the "natural" world. One could argue, however, as I do here, that these types of theory are not microperceptual *enough*. Although both focus on the "technological" construction of subjectivity, they do so abstractly. That is, neither deals with the technologically constructed temporality and spatiality that *ground* subjectivity in a sensible and sense-making *body*.

5   For the history, philosophy, and method of phenomenology, see Spiegelberg, 1965; Carr, 1967; and Ihde, 1979.

6   The very recent erosion of "faith" in the photographic as "evidence" of the real in popular consciousness has been a result of the development of the *seamless electronic manipulation* of even the tiniest "bits" of the photographic image. While airbrushing and other forms of image manipulation have been around for a long while, they have left a discernible "trace" on the image; such is not the case with digital computer alterations of the photographic image. For an overview, see "Ask It No Questions: The Camera Can Lie," *New York Times*, Aug. 12, 1990, sec. 2, pp. 1, 29.

7   Most media theorists point out that photographic (and later cinematic) optics are structured according to a norm of perception based upon Renaissance perspective, which represented the visible as originating in and organized by an individual, centered subject. This form of representation is *naturalized* by photography and the cinema. Comolli says: "The mechanical eye, the photographic lens ... functions ... as a guarantor of the identity of the visible with the normality of vision ... with the norm of visual perception" (1990: 123–4).

8   It must be noted that the term "memory bank" is analogically derived in this context from electronic (not photographic) culture. It nonetheless serves us as a way of reading backward that recognizes a literal as well as metaphorical *economy* of representation and suggests that attempts to understand the photographic in its "originality" are pervasively informed by our contemporary electronic consciousness.

9   For readers unfamiliar with the film, *La jetée* is a narrative about time, memory, and desire articulated in a recursive structure. A survivor of World War III has a recurrent memory of a woman's face and a scene at Orly airport where, as a child, he has seen a man killed. Because of his vivid memory, his post-apocalyptic culture – underground, with minimal power and without hope – attempts experiments to send him back into his vivid past so that he can, perhaps, eventually time-travel to the future. This

achieved, aware he has no future in his own present, the protagonist, with the assistance of those in the future, ultimately returns to his past and the woman he loves. But his return to the scene of his original childhood memory at Orly reveals, first, that he (as an adult) has been pursued by people from his own present and, second, that his original memory was, in fact, the vision of his own adult death.

10   James Joyce, in 1909, was "instrumental in introducing the first motion picture theater in Dublin" (see Kern, 1983: 76–7).

11   In the traditional cinema, an image can be "frozen" only by replicating it many times so that it can continue moving through the projector to appear frozen on the screen.

12   For a complete and lengthy argument supporting this assertion, see Sobchack, 1992.

13   It is important to point out that although all moving images follow each other serially, each cinematic image (or frame) is projected analogically rather than digitally. That is, the image is projected *as a whole*. Electronic images, however, are transmitted digitally, each bit of what appears as a single image sent and received as a discrete piece of information.

14   "Network" was a term that came into common parlance as it described the electronic transmission of television images. Now, we speak of our social relations as "networking." In spatial terms, however, a "network" suggests the most flimsy, the least substantial, of grounds. A "network" is constituted more as a lattice between nodal points than as grounded and physical presence.

15   It is no accident that all the films used illustratively here can be identified with the generic conventions and thematics of science fiction. Of all genres, science fiction has been most concerned with poetically mapping the new spatiality, temporality, and subjectivities informed and/or constituted by new technologies. As well, science-fiction cinema, in its particular materiality, has made these new poetic maps concretely visible. For elaboration of this mapping, see ch. 4, "Postfuturism," of Sobchack (1987).

Part III
The Image and Technology

Introduction

Toby Miller and Robert Stam

In this introduction, we move between linguistic and formalist approaches to the image, followed by an investigation of debates about technology and film theory. After a discussion of attempts to uncover the language of cinema, we look at what formalism and technique have made of the shot and how the means of constituting cinema technically have changed over time. The essays that follow cover the history of film technology (Winston), the advent of sound (Chion), and the changes brought about by the TV and video screen (Caldwell).

Our trajectory takes us from questions of meaning, where "there are nothing but signs" to be read (Derrida, 1976: 50), to practice, where signs are made. Throughout, we suggest you bear in mind the simplest explanation of the image, from the language philosopher Ludwig Wittgenstein. He understands it as "a situation in logical space, the existence and non-existence of states of affairs." Those "states" position the picture "against reality like a measure." The picture touches reality through "correlations...with things" (Wittgenstein, 1981: 8–10). Truth and falsehood, understanding and misunderstanding, depend on this process of comparison and measurement and their communication between filmmakers and spectators. Photographs have the power of indexicality, a sense of objective record, especially when they appear to be unedited or unposed. At the same time, they embody two highly subjective moments: the moment of composition, with the photographer imposing a producing vision; and the moment of interpretation, when the viewer imposes a receiving vision. Images are about depicting and seeing: occasions of sight that are doubled, as filmmakers and spectators try to imagine each other's point-of-view, one after the other. Wittgenstein argues for a tripartite analysis of images: as objects in themselves versus the objects they depict; as referring to real objects versus the mental picture of those objects; and as material versus mental images (Mitchell, 1986: 15–16).

Applying such an analysis to film theory necessitates both an understanding of the formal properties of the image and the technology that generates and exhibits it.

Wittgenstein's trichotomy involves a constant circling and return to the key questions for semiotic analysis: signifier, signified, and interpreter. Michel Foucault analyses Velázquez's painting *Las Meninas* in this way: the painter within the image looks out at the spectator, a fact discernible because the spectator is looking into it, at him. But the position the spectator must adopt in order to notice this is identical to that of the spectator within the image who is his subject. The model and painter – and the spectator – exchange glances ceaselessly. While the spectator has the power to move away from or into this image-plane, she is unable to note what the people in the picture are actually looking at – another painting, which she sees only from behind. This is a self-reflexive spectacle, one that implicates painter, image, and spectator, both inside the text and as part of it. But more than that, it carries an extra-textual history, a residue that is about the actual historical occasion of its creation, which involves royalty and a system of cultural and social patronage; but even this determining feature of the image's conditions of existence can at times become subordinate for the spectator to its sheer reflexivity, as the implication of sign, referent, and interpreter appears to all of us (Foucault, 1973: 4–5, 8, 16). André Bazin notes that the image is always about capturing and commemorating a moment that has been lost: in representing it, we preserve it, with corresponding points of tension between style, resemblance, and reception. At the same time, Bazin saw the mechanical reproduction of images as a crucial watershed. For the first time, "an image of the world is formed automatically, without the creative intervention of man." The play of presence and absence noted by Foucault went into full swing, with the outcome a seemingly natural event that carried the objective resonances of nature (Bazin, 1967: 10, 13).

Roland Barthes (1996) points out that the image tends to be characterized by polysemy (literally, many "semes" or meanings). Captions that accompany photographs, or written materials in a film, serve as verbal devices that discipline polysemy by encouraging preferred "readings" by spectators. The anchoring words "fix the floating chain of signifieds." Christian Metz (1974) suggests that the analogy is less between filmic signifier and signified than in the parallel perception common to everyday experience and the cinema. It is important to remember that Metz, in suggesting that cinema lacks the arbitrary sign of linguistics, is not suggesting that the concept of sign, or of the signifier/signified as composing the sign, is irrelevant. It is only the relation between signifier and signified that differs, being arbitrary in one case and motivated in the other. A play of light and shadow on a screen (the signifier) has a motivated relation to the signified triggered by that play of light. In his psychoanalytically inflected work, Metz came to insist on the doubly "imaginary" nature of the cinematic signifier, imaginary in what it happens to represent and imaginary in its very constitution as presence/absence.

Metz explores the notion that the shot is like a word while the sequence is like a sentence. He points out the differences which render such an analogy problematic: (1) shots are infinite in number, unlike words (since the lexicon is in principle finite) but like statements, an infinity of which can be constructed on the basis of a limited number of words; (2) shots are the creations of the filmmaker, unlike words (which pre-exist in lexicons) and again are like statements; (3) even relatively straightforward shots provide an inordinate wealth of semantic information; (4) unlike the word, which is a purely virtual lexical unit to be used as the speaker wishes, shots are actualized units. The word "dog" can be associated with any breed, while a filmic shot of a dog tells us, at the very minimum, that here is a certain kind of dog of a certain size and appearance, shot from a specific angle with a specific lens. While it is true that filmmakers might "virtualize" the image of a dog through backlighting, soft focus, or decontextualization, Metz's general point is that the cinematic shot more closely resembles an utterance or an assertion "here is the backlit silhouetted image of what appears to be a large dog" than a word; (5) unlike words, shots do not gain meaning by paradigmatic contrast with other shots that might have occurred at the same point of a syntagmatic chain. In a typical sentence, one imagines a limited number of substitutions at each point on the syntagmatic chain, whereas images in film are opposed to an open list of alternatives.

Metz adds a further disanalogy between the cinema and natural language: film is not widely available as a code. To speak a language is simply to use it, while to "speak" cinematic language is always to a certain extent to invent it. One might argue, of course, that this asymmetry is itself culturally and socially determined; one can hypothesize a society in which all citizens would be provided the opportunity to master the code of filmmaking. But in society as we know it, Metz's point must stand. There is, furthermore, a fundamental difference in the diachrony of natural as opposed to cinematic language. Cinematic language can be suddenly prodded in a new direction by innovatory aesthetic procedures such as those introduced by a film like *Citizen Kane* (Orson Welles, 1941), for example, or made possible by a new technology such as the zoom or steadicam. Natural language shows a more powerful inertia and is less open to individual initiative and creativity.

Peter Wollen takes up the Peircean trichotomy of semiotics in *Signs and Meaning in the Cinema* (1972), arguing that cinema deploys three categories of sign: the icon (which resembles images and sounds); the index (a photo-chemical registering of the "real"); and the symbol (speech and writing). Umberto Eco (1983) also draws on Peirce and the notion of "codes" in his analysis of the filmic analogon. Eco lists these codes as operative within the iconic sign: (1) perceptive codes (the domain of the psychology of perception); (2) codes of recognition (culturally disseminated taxonomies); (3) codes of transmission (the dots of a news photo or scan lines of a televisual image); (4) tonal codes (connoted elements having to do with stylistic convention); (5) iconic codes proper, subdividable into (a) figures, (b) signs, and (c) semes; (6) iconographic codes; (7) codes of taste and sensibility; (8) rhetorical codes, subdividable into (a) figures, (b) visual premises, and (c) visual arguments; (9) stylistic codes; and (10) codes of the unconscious.

In *A Theory of Semiotics* (1976) Eco rejects the idea that the iconic sign "has the same properties" as its referent. If this were true, Eco argues, a portrait of the Queen of England would be composed of skin and bones. The physical materiality of sign and referent are quite different, but perceived as similar. The queen and the portrait share a perceptual structure, a system of relations between parts, so that the queen herself and the portrait provoke similar perceptual reactions. Eco maintains that spectators recognize objects and their representation as similar because we select pertinent features, a decision which requires a certain cultural training. (The documentary filmmaker Robert Flaherty claimed that the protagonist of *Nanook of the North* (1922) had to learn to recognize himself in a photographic portrait.) The impression of similarity is historically informed and culturally coded. Artistic representation, in this sense, responds to other representations rather than to "real-life" referents. For Alec McHoul, this means "there is a relation between a photograph and 'what it is a picture of,' but that relation has to do with effective historical elements rather than with the necessary properties of any photographic sign" (McHoul, 1996: 19). These "effective historical elements" are the framing devices of the process that created the image plus the framing devices that it experiences while moving through space and time – here, realism meets political economy meets the audience.

Having established the arbitrary but ultimately anchored nature of film-as-sign, we need a means of describing the individual units of cinema as they are deployed by filmmakers. The Soviet filmmaker and theorist Sergei Eisenstein defined the shot in film as "the minimum 'distortable' fragment of nature" (1977: 5). In the early days of cinema, "films consisted of only one shot." The 80 feet of negative in each roll was used to record a single set-up (Salt, 1996: 171). David Bordwell et al.'s (1988) study of classical Hollywood to 1960 suggests that post-Renaissance painting was the principal guide for determining the content of the shot. Composition in the frame is centered, with the erect human form a model and the face its apex. Characters are generally shot along a horizontal line, allowing for gender differences and other distinctions of power that draw upon and form cultural convention. Extreme long-shots often draw attention to the bottom half of the screen, as per landscape art, but other shots privilege the upper third and the central vertical third of the frame as the site of action. The closer the shot is, the more critical it becomes. This is a model of expressive totality, with the body positioned in the center of the image as a compositional axis. The Renaissance painter's deployment of the concept of frontality from Graeco-Roman theatrical history was also a determining influence on classical film's understanding of how to illustrate action. The face and body of the subject are to be available at all times. Groups of people do not form ranks, as in everyday life. Instead, they move into semi-circles or horizontal or diagonal lines. A sense of depth is conveyed through visual overlap, focus, pattern, color, and lighting via the three-point system of key, back, and fill-lights (ibid.: 50–2).

In early Hollywood, a 75-minute feature would comprise anywhere between 240 and 1,000 shots, but mostly under 500. But by the post-World War I period, the majority of films had over 500 shots. In addition, the average shot length had gone from 5 to 10 seconds (ibid.: 60–1). Today, determinations on shot-length vary with the type of shot and its contents, and the selection will give a distinct rhythm to the text: brief shots with lots of cuts emphasize pace and action rather than panoramic vision. In addition to timing and rhythm, there are numerous methods of transition from one form of shot to another. Dissolves merge the conclusion of one scene with the beginning of another to indicate the passage of time and place or shift the viewer into another diegesis, such as a flashback. Fading in and out involves a gradual movement between a black screen and an image of action; it may signal a moment for reflection or the transition between events or spaces that are only loosely connected. The wipe sees one shot literally pushing the previous one out of the frame (Ayres et al., 1990: 182–3). The developing importance of the TV screen has changed the look of the shot. The medium shots and close-ups that work best on television are more frequent, and there is less use of the wide ratio of luminescence that film can deliver, but video cannot reproduce (Wasko, 1994: 166).

Eisenstein utilized a Marxist dialectic to understand both the single shot, which he called a "cell," and its combination with other shots. This dialectic, a relationship of struggle, was expressed in the concept of montage as a "collision." The complex, conflictual assignation of two elements produced a "concept." To justify his valorization of this process as a force for making meaning, Eisenstein told the tale of a re-edited film in which a woman is condemned to death. A man runs up to another man in great distress, who turns away and wipes a tear from his face. The intertitle reads: "In the name of freedom I had to sacrifice a friend." But in the original, the alarmed man had spat in his face, which had motivated the wiping motion; this had disappeared in a version that remade the entire meaning of the scene by removing one shot and inserting a particular intertitle (Eisenstein, 1977: 36–7, 11). In his "Types Instead of Actors" talk from 1929, V. I. Pudovkin relates an "experiment" conducted by Lev Kuleshov that stresses the insignificance of pro-filmic events by comparison with their combination after the fact. Editing can produce new meanings barely prefigured on location or the set by altering the sequence of shots. For instance, intermingling smiling and frightened looks with a revolver radically transforms facial subjectivity: depending on the choice of image bracketing the weapon, the actor is ascribed a range of interiorities from cowardice to bravery. Although there is controversy about this experiment qua historical event, it has canonical status in screen studies and much film production. Alfred Hitchcock calls the Kuleshov effect "pure cinema." He admires the capacity of editing to alter a person's interiority simply by reordering a sequence (Pudovkin, 1978: 167–8; Holland, 1992: 79–82; Prince and Hensley, 1992; Hitchcock, 1995: 215).

The shot makes the micro-politics of the screen more available to inspection and evaluation than is the case with other art. Eisenstein divided the shot in two.

The old method, which we might associate with the metteur-en-scène director, involved the "artificial spatial organization of an event in front of the lens." This could mean directing a sequence of actions, or simply placing a tableau before the lens. The newer method, which we might associate with the auteur who shifts from a generic code to a signed message, called for what Eisenstein named "a 'picking-out' by the camera" that sees the use of the lens as an "ax . . . hewing out a piece of actuality" (Eisenstein, 1977: 41). "Hewing" intervenes in the pro-filmic event. This can be achieved within a single shot by a variety of camera moves. The camera may pan across a horizontal plane in order to illustrate the spatial relationship between figures. It can "follow the action" or move between an establishment or master shot – which sets the scene by indicating the condition of the actants and their physical relationship – and a two-shot. Another option is to tilt the camera vertically, which can provide height and depth to both spatial relationships and action coverage.

Gilles Deleuze (1986: ix) distinguishes between "the perception-image [P-I], the affection-image [Af-I] and the action-image [Ac-I]" of film. P-I concerns the objective fact of what is in a frame and the spectator's act that grasps and makes sense of it. Af-I describes images that encourage a reading of characters' internal states of mind. Ac-I covers events within a shot. Deleuze's model is useful for understanding point-of-view editing. This uses two shots, concentrating in turn on a character's glance off-screen and then on the object apparently being looked at. It relies on a perceptual cue in the spectator so as to remove the need for a third camera. Point-of-view editing also produces an awareness that the physiognomy of the person can be interpreted through her possible relationship to the object that is being contemplated. In Eisenstein's *Battleship Potemkin* (1925), a sailor's look of anger at the plate in front of him not only explains his decision to break it; it also illustrates, and is added to by, the film's context of socialist politics. The initial shot of his glance lets us know about an emotion; the cut to what is being thought about focuses attention on what produced this feeling (Carroll, 1978: 126, 128, 133, 135).

Martin Scorsese's *Goodfellas* (1990) features the shot on the move. The ease with which Henry (Ray Liotta) escorts his future wife Karen (Lorraine Bracco) into the Copacabana contributes to her seduction. In a four-minute steadicam hand-held take, Scorsese is also seducing spectators with Henry's vision of this life and its headiness (Keyser, 1992: 210). As Scorsese has said of the film as a whole, "it was one long trailer, where you just propel the action and you get an exhilaration" (quoted in DeCurtis, 1992: 432). (The same fluency and power are evident in Welles's *Touch of Evil* (1958), which opens with a bravura camera movement that takes us all the way from Mexico to the United States at the same time as it introduces the hero, heroine, and the animating crime for the narrative.) Freeze-frames are explanations in *Goodfellas*, moments of interiorization for Henry Hill as he closes in on himself prior to a return to the unfurling of the story at normal speed (Smith, 1993).

The more conventional method of conveying movement is through the zoom, dolly, or tracking shot. The zoom increases the focal length of the lens and the size of the image. The dolly is a machine on wheels which physically transports the camera and its tripod towards and away from the action. The dolly conveys an overt sense of the camera traveling past objects. This gives an appearance of depth rather than the actual flatness of two-dimensional images. A tracking shot is produced by the movement of the camera to either side of the action, next to or in front of moving figures (Ayres et al., 1990: 82–4; Bordwell et al., 1988: 52, 63–4). Scorsese has spoken of how the storehouse of audience knowledge and experience makes the panning shot a thing of the past, of a langorous time before visual cross-cutting (Smith, 1993).

How important is the shot to the way we understand film? Noël Burch (1981a: 17–21) argues that screen texts have two kinds of cinematic space: what is inside the frame and what is beyond it. Screen space is, straightforwardly, what we can see in any given image. But many different forms of off-screen space are implied by the camera. Each of the frame's four sides represents only a partial boundary. It presumes that objects and activities lie just beyond, either in a room where we can see half a person to the left, or in a house where we can hear helicopters roaring overhead. Then there is the space occupied by the camera itself. Characters may gaze into – or most often beyond – the camera, or brush past it. In doing so, they are also gazing into a space beyond (and meta-textually above) the screen, which they can occupy as vocal narrators through a voice-over that traces their own movement in the image from the vantage-point of recollection. Whenever actants appear or depart by a transition out of the frame, they are explicitly moving away from the camera, but not from the space of the text itself, as such movements tend to be motivated entrances and exits. Similarly, the intensity generated by an on-screen gaze at an off-screen presence, or vice versa, can make what is outside the frame be, paradoxically, very much inside the space. This leads to a further division between two types of off-screen space: the concrete and the imaginary. When objects come into frame and have an impact, but we cannot quite make them out or understand why they are there, they have come from imaginary space. If we then receive additional information about this event, the off-screen space becomes concrete.

Similarly, FBI agents and their foes in *The X-Files* television series are made mysterious not only through narrative devices, but also through visual ones: seen through mirrors, from their own points of view (thus not revealing them) or from a victim's distorted point of view, they are regularly hard to discern. Filmed frames that include them are sometimes skipped (as they were to great effect in *Alien* (Ridley Scott, 1979)) – or the "thing" can be seen from the rear – or through speed-ups or blurs – through incomplete scenes or half views. On the other hand, we might see the effects of their activities, but not the method of perpetration. So in the "Humbug" *X-Files* episode, the first shot of the mysterious creature terrorizing Gibsontown is shown through a heavily greased lens.

The look of the lens itself reminds us that film is a meta-technological device: it has encouraged a fascination with technology as both a means of communication and a space of performance. As we see in Part VIII, Teresa de Lauretis (1989) and others use the notion of cinema as a sexual technology, a site where practices are instantiated that construct sex and desire through such techniques as confession, concealment, and the drive for truthful knowledge about motivation, character, and occasion. The reproducibility of virtuosic performance provided by electronic technology has produced an era of performativity. Both simultaneity of instant reception and longevity of recorded life come with electronic media. The technology of visual reproduction enables a multiplicity of personalized perspectives inside a world of commodity reproduction. The first occurred alongside a transition from concentrating on technology – the wonder of the apparatus – and on to the issue of visible labor and hence personality.

De Lauretis's point about performance technology segues into issues of technical innovation. The meeting-ground is played out in Burch's film *Correction Please, or How We Got into Pictures* (1981), which derives from the director's participation at a conference on early cinema and archiving in the late 1970s, where he was part of a group that watched all available footage up to the year 1906. That experience produced the drive towards an allegorical account of the move from the first moments of cinema through to the incorporation of, or domination by, continuity editing and matched sound. *Correction Please* enacts a story five times, supplemented on each occasion by a stylistic and technical innovation. The characters are named after early filmmakers, and ten archival inserts from 1900 to 1906 are also included (Christie, 1981). The five sequences allude to the period up to 1905, D. W. Griffith's Biograph work from 1910, Reginald Barker's films (1915), Fritz Lang's 1922 *Mabuse*, and the emergence of dialogue-inflected narration. As additional overlays of semiosis are appended to enrich the text, the mystery of meaning is removed, adding a certain mundanity via all this information: the multiple sign systems of vision, continuity, story, and sound produce a nostalgia for non-redundancy and indeterminacy.

Performance technology and mechanical technology are mutually constitutive during early cinema, when there is no assumption that films should tell a self-evident tale that can be comprehended at one sitting. Instead, a lecturer is required as a key component at screenings, to explain the text to audiences – useful work for professors! As the camera moves closer to actants from about 1913, adopting a variety of angles rather than a theatrical frontality in order to move in and pan across scenes, lighting privileges certain elements in the frame while blurring others. Cutting comes to be centered around action, the standardization of narrative methods is well in play, and the lecturer is dismissed until the advent of cinema studies, just at the moment that stage actresses are walking into the previously prurient low-life of the photoplay, claiming the representation of femininity that had been the province of cross-dressing men or women prepared to be part of the peep-hole disrobing genre that had been so prominent (Burch, 1981b: 24, 26–32).

The technology of the railways offered early film both motion and excitement – the Lumière brothers' *L'Arrivée d'un train en gare de la ciotat* (1895) had French audiences bobbing and weaving as the train approached the station. By 1913, newsreels and long-form narrative cinema had synchronized with forces from science and religion that were turning the very human body into technology: neurology and moralism. *The Times* of London feared that the moving image's "new form of excitement . . . massacres, horrible catastrophes, motor-car smashes, [and] public hangings" would appeal to the "greedy eyes" of children, rendering them immune to the affect right-minded youth ought to experience on exposure to such horrors. But there was a counter-discourse. D. W. Griffith defended *The Birth of a Nation* (1915) against accusations of racism through a revealing mixture of truth and/as distraction: previously restricted access to "the truths of history" policed by the university system would be broken down by cinema, even as it brought "diversion to the masses" (*The Times*, quoted in Barker, 1993: 11; Griffith, quoted in Gross et al., 1988: 31).

What is the intellectual foundation to these alternately dystopic and utopic positions? Bazin locates the emergence of film as the outcome of an inspirational imagination that attains its physical realization with the necessary technological developments. In other words, the idea of cinema exists before the means to make it have a material form. As this idea could only have an imaginary existence, Bazin calls his provocative essay "The Myth of Total Cinema" (1967). He argues that film was principally the product of "the imagination of those carrying on the search," rather than social relations of economics and technology. In other words, the "ideological superstructure" brought forth the conditions of possibility for an "economic infrastructure." The inventors and fantasists had desires first and foremost. So, for Bazin, "the cinema is an idealistic phenomenon." From the first, he says, inventors sought to produce "a picture of life and a faithful copy of nature." This necessitated all the new technology that took a century to become standard: sound, relief, movement, and colour (Bazin, 1967: 17–18). The cinema arrived because these heroic male figures wanted "a recreation of the world in its own image." Each complicating development of technology, each additional component of machinery or labor piled on top of one another, appeared as part of the search for a reduction in the space between the pro-filmic event and the filmic record. The image was to be freed progressively of a dependence on artistic "interpretation" and "the irreversibility of time," in keeping with these inventors' deep commitment to realism (ibid.: 21). This position requires Bazin to explain the transition from silent to sound features as a logical movement to bring the fantasy into truth. So here we have a version of history that seeks to account for the contemporary screen in terms of a totalizing history, predicated on the formative power of desire that works away at the economic and technical borders of possibility in order to produce truth.

Most accounts of the emergence of color film follow the Bazinian mimetic fallacy, with a glorious match of audience and business, united in the drive towards an ever greater realism. Certain historical researches have complicated this cosy account. For example, the development of film stock privileged certain skin tones over others via the selection of specific chemical dye-couplers – a particular kind of whiteness can be reproduced much more easily with most industrial and domestic filmmaking technology than darker-toned human skin. This is a matter of aesthetic, chemical, commercial, and racist choice, not a teleological march on accuracy (Winston, 1996: 40–3).

This touches on the criticism of Bazin that his insistence on consumer desires producing technical dreams neglects the intensive capitalist politics that surrounded the beginning of cinema. Movies could have come about much earlier than they did. The fact that they did not is due to investment patterns and plans, not to the absence of innovation. Equally, the story of 3-D cinema is about Polaroid challenging Eastman's hegemony over film stock but being defeated by the unwillingness of exhibitors to risk refitting their theaters (Wollen, 1985: 19). It is assuredly not to do with brilliant men devising new ways to meet the wishes of audiences and then finding they had miscalculated. At the same time, we need models that allow for commercial, governmental, and aesthetic forces at play, since doctrines of realism inherited from the stage, ideas about public performance, urbanization, US immigration, and the rising role of the state are as crucial as issues of inventiveness or business (Winston, 1996: 26–34).

The technical knowledge to bring sound to pictures existed years before it happened. As usual with communications technology, war and its associated bureaucracy stimulated research via encouragement, funds, and testing/playgrounds, as Paul Virilio (1989) points out. World War I problematized the model of scientific progress through the lone individual in the white coat, struggling to master nature. Instead, this boffin-like figure was supplanted by the defence-funded and/or profit-centered corporate entity that pioneered through capital. The US was paramount here. When the state ceased to offer vast sums in telecommunications support after the war, private industry maintained the momentum that had been established. But the interdependence of telephone research with sound research cut the film industry's potential link to sound. It gave research and development a referent outside the cinema. The film studios had commercial reasons for a lack of interest: the 1920s were times of vertical expansion by Hollywood producers. They broadened their involvement in cinema by investing in stars, theaters, and directors, predicated on the relative stability of the industry's methods and mechanisms of narration. The American exportation of people and film texts as a result of World War I (a movement that decimated the French and German cinemas, which had lived successfully without America until the war) would have been jeopardized by the addition of the spoken word to the image track. It took a studio that lacked the capital to have bought many exhibitionary outlets – Warner Brothers – to invest in the new technology. The others were soon forced by domestic box-office pressures to follow this lead, despite the impact on their recent, suddenly obsolete, theatrical refits. But once sound was universal, and adjustments were made to personnel and material, it actually cut costs, reducing the number of shots and the call on actors' time. Films were made more quickly and resources deployed more continuously (Neale, 1985: 77–82).

Idealist arguments continue to be profoundly influential, as per predictions for new audio-visual technologies. While electronic mail is hailed as a renewal of epistolary culture and a democratization of salon conversation, fiber optics and accelerated communication also threaten written signs, as economies of scale make digital video and audio equipment standard for personal computers. This new anonymity is likened to the chaotic publishing conditions of the French Revolution, when the expression of ideas left no signature. Such moments await legislation to identify thoughts with their authors. The arrival of the state on the scene marks a medium's power, when it has induced sufficient moral panic or potential for profit to generate regulation. Radical aspiration and conservative anxiety meet in utopic and dystopic projections that take commercial, governmental, and theoretical flight. In the nineteenth century the telegraph was regarded as dangerously libertarian in its implications for individual communication, a threat to the domination of newspapers. They responded by forming Associated Press (AP). In a repeat move a century later, AP began to use the World Wide Web to distribute material (Markoff, 1994 and 1995). Inventions that might loosen corporate control of information as a commodity are soon redisposed by oligopolistic organization and the law of property.

The domain of the digital is heralded as the ultimate refinement of film and television; a second chance, the one that defines the screen as an "activity center" and makes it "a good cultural object" (Boddy, 1994: 116, 107). Al Gore claims that the National Information Infrastructure (the NII) will "educate, promote democracy, and save lives" (quoted in Gomery, 1994: 9). In the policy documentation about the NII, readers are asked to envisage a world in which "no matter where you went or what time it was, your child could see and talk to you . . . the best schools were available to all" and "art, literature, and science were available everywhere." There are parallels with the space programs of the 1960s, another bold liberal frontier. John F. Kennedy's foundational remarks to Congress in 1961 are eerily akin to those of Gore and the other credulous NIIists. Kennedy referred to the capacity of "the wonders of science . . . to explore the stars, conquer the deserts, eradicate disease, tap the ocean depths and encourage the arts and commerce." Thirty years on, Gore has turned this into a less distanced rhetoric. In one sense, alienation is complete, because no one will suffer the privations of the desert other than via simulation; in another sense, alienation will be ended forever as, in his words, "each person will move from being just a consumer to being a consumer and a provider," via "another kind of empowerment . . . one of the most powerful revolutions in the entire history of humankind" (Gore, quoted in Lauria and White, Jr, 1995: 64–5, 72). Echoes of Marx, Godard, and video access here!

Informatics is inflected with the phenomenological awe of a precocious child who can be returned to Eden. The redeemed version of the screen will heal the wounds of the modern, reconciling private and public, labor and leisure, commerce and culture, individuality and collectivity. The digital will permit the subject to re-experience all the precision of feeling that analogic forms provided only via encoding aberrations and noise. But while the new "digital individual" has his or her persona defined through computerized forms that offer some freedom of representation inside screen space, they also subject the person to surveillance and definition via governmental and corporate identification, and they operate in a privatized way that is restricted financially to the upper social echelon (Gomery, 1994: 17). Of the 80 million users of personal computers in the world, half live and work in the US (Lauria and White, Jr, 1995: 73). The sales trends internationally for hardware are downwards, however, and central control over networks is increasing quickly. Broadcast television and mass-market video and film will continue to be what they are today for many people around the world: "a consolation prize" (Gitlin, 1993: 48). And they will have a very different phenomenology, because the body will be at rest in front of the screen, unemployed, or laboring for low wage rates.

If we look back to Kennedy's first budget for space exploration, under the binary heading he drew "between freedom and tyranny," we find that something much more interesting than a contest with Soviet dogs was being put into play. Following the money shows that almost all the funds were committed to producing business- and surveillance-related satellites: men on the moon were truly epiphenomenal. As with satellites, tax money created the Internet via defense funding from 1969 to 1984. Science research kept up the development of the system for a decade, until the risk capital provided by the state had produced an audience that corporations could take over (Lauria and White, Jr, 1995: 65, 80). This is a further encouragement to depart from a utopic, non-institutional account of new technology.

Unpacking the Clinton Administration's policy on the NII reveals a familiar trend in its three founding *données*. The first principle, universal service, is the same as we saw with color television: a combination of inter-operability to ensure that everyone can be a customer, but a careful demarcation of terrain that cuts out new competitors. The second principle, free-market capitalism, is aimed at transcending the NII and remaking it into a GII (sounds like "guy"): the Global Information Infrastructure. This model follows on from how the US established its hegemony in screen trade, but with a bonus: unlike the cinema, where domestic anti-trust legislation broke up vertically integrated film production, distribution, and exhibition while permitting cartel behavior internationally, the new rules allow both. Carriers can become producers. The final principle, flexible regulation, enshrines this cross-ownership in a confused screen of public-interest rhetoric (Lauria and White, Jr, 1995: 76–7). These are the real changes that Gore is referring to: institutional, corporate persons, not human subjects, can "move from being just a consumer to being a consumer and provider." We are witness to the realization by a heavily indebted, deindustrialized sovereign-state which happens to own the world's communications infrastructure that it must make national economic policy function as it has always made international economic policy do: via the precepts of monopoly capital. The governmental reaction against allowing First Amendment rights to the NII or the GII, combined with CIA oversight of all electronic mail as part of its new focus on industrial espionage, perfectly models a combination of export that will not offend anti-liberal societies, and offers the prospect of domestic political control and technical innovation.

In film, the move from analog to digital technology means several things. Along with the NII and developments in fiber optics, we are promised dial-up cinema, an infinite selection of films from across time and space at instant call. The shift to the digital makes reproducibility infinite, with no risk of a degraded image. Since the picture is stored as pixels, it does not suffer from being copied – the same encoded information is simply being downloaded – and for special effects, the possibilities are imposing. In *Clear and Present Danger* (Phillip Noyce, 1994), Harrison Ford drives up to the White House gates. His identification established by a soldier, the camera pans up to the White House in a single, unedited move. Or does it? In fact, the government prohibited shooting inside the grounds, so a motion-control shot was constructed digitally. The White House gates were photographed with a computerized camera that recorded the information which would have been in a shot from the character's (absent) car up to the entrance and digitally matched that with footage of the real car pulled up at a full-size model of the gates in a car park. An identical process was used elsewhere in the film to pan down from the White House to Ford going out through the checkpoint (Weiner, 1994: 10).

This is simply one more moment in the history of film and illusion. Digitization makes the appearance of a person in a place look actual when it is not. Is the intent or effect different from matting-in or rear projection? No, the degree of spectacle is what differs, and doctrines of verisimilitude and customer expectations shift along with them. When we turn to documentary genres, the concern about falsification is intense, just as it has been for a century. Most anxieties associated with this return to the notion of mimesis assume pictures were once unalloyed truth, neutral archives of record. But viewers of high-technology action-adventure cinema know about stunts – they always have – and the work of digital imaging is increasingly part of the sales pitch that promotes such movies. Capitalism is not unfairly pretending to show what really happened – it is fetishizing innovation and difference, pointing out the fallacy in mimesis to the audience as part of its product differentiation. Similarly, one of the most controversial technological innovations of recent times has been colorization, a process whereby black-and-white texts are re-released in color. Critiques have come in terms of both standards and ethics: are the images of good quality, and how do they relate to the intentions of the original filmmakers? The idea behind the process is to generate new lives for texts, making them more saleable on video and to television, but audience reaction is very mixed (Auter, 1997: 22–3, 25).

What are we to make of an epoch that promises computer-generated actors, desktop computers that can produce feature films, films distributed digitally rather than on celluloid, simultaneous work on the same text across time zones via fiber optics, and dial-up home video access on demand? *Star Trek II: The Wrath of Khan* (Nicholas Meyer, 1982) was the first feature film to have an entirely computer-generated sequence, *Willow* (Ron Howard, 1988) the first morph, and *Terminator 2: Judgment Day* (James Cameron, 1991) the first computer-generated principal character, while Disney employed six times the number of animators in 1998 than a decade earlier – all of which goes to show the cost and complexity of new technology to this point, and the strange impact it can have on employment patterns. Clearly, this is a time of flux, slow in terms of computer generation on film until the mid-1990s, fast in terms of the development and spread of electronic norms since then.

Even those writers familiar with the dangers of technological determinism, however, suggest that we may be entering a new narrational era, similar to the one ushered in by the studio system's standardization of fiction film and its technologies on show in *Correction Please*. It is true that the past century has seen filmmaking dominated by processes of assemblage, whereby norms of continuity demand that one shot relate to another in sequence, in such a way that a narrative builds towards resolution. Today, the digital era and associated audience sensibilities and commercial dictates may be steering us towards what Robert Rosen terms "flow and transformation," such that special effects drive storytelling, perhaps transcending rather than being components of it. Analog filmmaking's tendency to privilege overt signage identifying time and space transitions may be under critique from new notions of discontinuity, via a generation reared on hypertextuality and the hugely popular non-narrative norms of video clips. Rosen stresses the failure of most video games adapted from successful feature releases. The lucrative games market is constructed around interactivity, which is unsuited to linear narratives as per most Hollywood movies. This may be an indication that there are limits to audience interest in being assigned responsibility, or that new pressures will emerge on the basic organization of film texts (Rosen, 1997: 57, 59). The technophilic magazine *Wired* (1997) dubbed this potentially new epoch "Hollywood 2.0," troping a computer-generation term for software upgrading to argue for a sea-change from the settled world of "Hollywood 1.0" and its supposedly unitary, homogeneous narrative and industrial organization. At the same time, evidence from cognitive theory and analysis suggests stringent limitations to audience engagement with hypertext (Boiarsky, 1997). Meanwhile, the more optimistic among documentarists foresee a world where electronic subscription finances new projects and high-capacity connections and multimedia computers find consumers directly downloading, copying, and viewing documentaries through electronic fund transfers, even as web cameras add to and subtract from versions of actuality texts (Krieg, 1997).

Whatever happens in the next few years, we must bear in mind certain constant facts. Film is a service industry, predicated on communication as a good. The audio-visual media deny the primacy of personal, physical experience through their promiscuous journalism and eyeline tourism. From the morphed special effect to the hand-painted video clip, they are about simulation, the sense that setting up replicas is not merely a displacement of personal/material art and experience, but actually preferable to them. But none of this is about visionary inventors finding means to satisfy the existing curiosity of audiences, or the operation of a consumer-driven market. It is about the uncertain dance of finance, law, the state, monopoly capital, and performance norms, in a complex and shifting mix of power relations.

Works Cited

Auter, Philip 1997. "'A Fine Mess': A Preliminary Look at the Effect of Colorization on Audience Interaction with a Comedy Program," *Feedback* 38, no. 4: 22–6.

Ayres, Rowan, Martha Mollison, Ian Stocks, and Jim Tumeth 1990. *Guide to Video Production.* Sydney: Allen & Unwin/Australian Film, Television & Radio School.

Barker, Martin 1993. "Sex, Violence, and Videotape," *Sight and Sound* 3, no. 5: 10–12.

Barthes, Roland 1996. *Camera Lucida: Reflections on Photography.* Trans. Richard Howard. New York: Hill and Wang.

Bazin, André 1967. *What is Cinema?* Trans. Hugh Gray. Berkeley: University of California Press.

Boddy, William 1994. "Archaeologies of Electronic Vision and the Gendered Spectator," *Screen* 35, no. 2: 105–22.

Boiarsky, Greg 1997. "The Psychology of New Media Technologies: Lessons from the Past," *Convergence* 3, no. 3: 107–26.

Bordwell, David, Janet Staiger, and Kristin Thompson 1988. *The Classical Hollywood Cinema: Film Style and Mode of Production to 1960.* London: Routledge.

Burch, Noël 1981a. *Theory of Film Practice.* Trans. Helen R. Lane. Princeton: Princeton University Press.

—— 1981b. "How We Got into Pictures: Notes Accompanying *Correction Please*," *Afterimage* nos. 8–9 (Spring): 24–38.

Carroll, Noël 1978. "Toward a Theory of Film Editing," *Millennium Film Journal* no. 3: 79–99.

Christie, Ian 1981. "How We Got Into Pictures," *Afterimage* nos. 8–9 (Spring): 22.

de Lauretis, Teresa 1989. *Technologies of Gender: Essays on Theory, Film and Fiction.* Bloomington: Indiana University Press.

DeCurtis, Anthony 1992. "Interview with Martin Scorsese," *South Atlantic Quarterly* 91, no. 2: 427–58.

Deleuze, Gilles 1986. *Cinema 1: The Movement-Image.* Trans. Hugh Tomlinson and Barbara Habberjam. Minneapolis: University of Minnesota Press.

Derrida, Jacques 1976. *Of Grammatology.* Trans. Gayatri Chakravorty Spivak. Baltimore: Johns Hopkins University Press.

Eco, Umberto 1976. *A Theory of Semiotics.* Bloomington: Indiana University Press.

—— 1983. "Critique of the Image," in *Thinking Photography*, ed. Victor Burgin. London: Macmillan, 32–8.

Eisenstein, Sergei 1977. *Film Form: Essays in Film Theory.* Trans. and ed. Jay Leyda. San Diego: Harcourt Brace Jovanovich.

Foucault, Michel 1973. *The Order of Things: An Archaeology of the Human Sciences*. New York: Vintage.

Gitlin, Todd 1993. "Flat and Happy," *Wilson Quarterly* 17, no. 4: 47–55.

Gomery, Douglas 1994. "In Search of the Cybermarket," *Wilson Quarterly* 18, no. 3: 9–17.

Gross, Larry, John Stuart Katz, and Jay Ruby (eds) 1988. "Introduction: A Moral Pause," in *Image Ethics: The Moral Rights of Subjects in Photographs, Film, and Television*. New York: Oxford University Press, 3–33.

Hitchcock, Alfred 1995. "Film Production," in *Hitchcock on Hitchcock: Selected Writings and Interviews*, ed. Sidney Gottlieb. Berkeley: University of California Press, 210–26.

Holland, Norman N. 1992. "Film Response from Eye to I: The Kuleshov Experiment," in *Classical Hollywood Narrative: The Paradigm Wars*, ed. Jane Gaines. Durham, NC: Duke University Press, 79–106.

"Hollywood 2.0." 1997. *Wired* 5, no. 11: 200–15.

Keyser, Les 1992. *Martin Scorsese*. New York: Twayne.

Krieg, Peter 1997. "Docs Go Digital," *Dox* no. 11 (Summer): 12–13.

Kuleshov, Lev 1974. *Kuleshov on Film: Writings of Lev Kuleshov*. Trans. and ed. Ronald Levaco. Berkeley: University of California Press.

Lauria, Rita and Harold M. White, Jr 1995. "Mythic Analogues of the Space and the Cyberspace: A Critical Analysis of U.S. Policy for the Space and the Information Age," *Journal of Communication Inquiry* 19, no. 2: 64–87.

McHoul, Alec 1996. *Semiotic Investigations: Towards an Effective Semiotics*. Lincoln, NB: University of Nebraska Press.

Markoff, John 1994. "The Rise and Swift Fall of Cyber Literacy," *New York Times* 13 March: E1, E5.

——1995. "If Medium is the Message, the Message is the Web," *New York Times* 20 November: A1, D5.

Metz, Christian 1974. *Film Language: A Semiotics of the Cinema*. Trans. Michael Taylor. New York: Oxford University Press.

Mitchell, W. J. T. 1986. *Iconology: Image, Text, Ideology*. Chicago: University of Chicago Press.

Neale, Steve 1985. *Cinema and Technology: Image, Sound, Colour*. London: BFI/Macmillan.

Prince, Stephen and Wayne E. Hensley 1992. "The Kuleshov Effect: Recreating the Classic Experiment," *Cinema Journal* 31, no. 2: 59–75.

Pudovkin, V. I. 1978. *Film Technique and Film Acting*. Trans. and ed. Ivor Montagu. New York: Grove Press.

Rosen, Robert 1997. "Teaching Film in a Company Town: An Agenda for Discussion in the Digital Age," *Metro* no. 112: 55–9.

Salt, Barry 1996. "Cut and Shuffle," in *Cinema: The Beginnings and the Future: Essays Marking the Centenary of the First Film Show Projected to a Paying Audience in Britain*, ed. Christopher Williams. London: University of Westminster Press, 171–96.

Smith, Gavin 1993. "Interview with Martin Scorsese," *Film Comment* 29, no. 6.

Virilio, Paul 1989. *War and Cinema: The Logistics of Perception*. Trans. P. Cammiler. London: Verso.

Wasko, Janet 1994. *Hollywood in the Information Age: Beyond the Silver Screen*. Cambridge: Polity Press.

Weiner, Rex 1994. "Special F/X: Hollywood Splices Mother Nature," *Variety* 29 August–4 September: 7, 10.

Winston, Brian 1996. *Technologies of Seeing: Photography, Cinematography, and Television*. London: BFI.

Wittgenstein, Ludwig 1981. *Tractatus Logico-Philosophicus*. Trans. D. F. Pears and B. F. McGuinness. London: Routledge and Kegan Paul.

Wollen, Peter 1972. *Signs and Meaning in the Cinema*. London: Secker & Warburg.

——1985. "Cinema and Technology: A Historical Overview," in *The Cinematic Apparatus*, ed. Teresa de Lauretis and Stephen Heath. Basingstoke: Macmillan, 14–22.

7

Necessities and Constraints: A Pattern of Technological Change

Brian Winston

On Technological Determinism

Fernand Braudel puts it thus:

> First the accelerator, then the brake: the history of technology seems to consist of both processes, sometimes in quick succession: it propels human life onward, gradually reaches new forms of equilibrium on higher levels than in the past, only to remain there for a long time, since technology often stagnates, or advances only imperceptibly between one 'revolution' or innovation and another.[1]

The crucial question, however, is: who is the driver here? Within the dominant framework of the idea of progress, the commonly held assumption is that it is the technologist who has control of the pedals. This view does not imply approval. There are those (the ecologically minded, for example) who might say the technologist drives badly. The more extreme might say that the technologist has fallen asleep at the wheel. But whatever our opinion of the driver, there is a clear understanding that, happy or alarmed, the rest of us are all passengers and, therefore, more or less powerless.

This position can be termed 'technological determinism'. Technological determinism, as Raymond Williams explained,

> is an immensely powerful and now largely orthodox view of the nature of social change. New technologies are discovered by an essentially internal process of research and development, which then sets the conditions of social change and progress. Progress, in particular, is the history of these inventions, which 'created the modern world'. The effects of the technologies whether direct or indirect, foreseen or unforeseen, are as it were the rest of history.[2]

The technological determinist vision is important not simply as a powerful and somewhat unexamined explanation of the world in which we live. It also intervenes directly in that world at the level of political policy-making and thereby impacts on all our lives. Politicians of all persuasions profess a belief in it. It allows them, elegantly, to disguise their own agendas; to pretend that they are in the grip of forces both elemental and unnatural. Man-made the forces might be, but they are not of the politicians' making. Thus, when a politician, in this random example the late President of France François Mitterrand, says 'Science and technology are going to develop forcing humans to conceive of a different society',[3] he appears to be as much in the grip of these forces as the next president.

And so are captains of industry such as Rupert Murdoch. His search for world multimedia domination has nothing to do with the logics of capitalism, much less personal ambition. On the contrary, as one British socialist politician put it: "Technological changes are *driving* different sectors of the industry – newspapers, television, telephony, video, computers, cable and satellite – closer together" (emphasis added).[4] So what is poor Murdoch to do? He is as much the victim of technology as is President Mitterrand or you and I. These examples are chosen absolutely at random and could be endlessly duplicated because technological determinism is a truth universally acknowledged. It suffuses the computer/technology and editorial pages of the quality press as much as it permeates the corridors of political and business power.

But, despite its pervasiveness, it seems to me clearly absurd to suggest that technological determinism renders Mitterrand and Murdoch powerless (for all that it indisputably works to convince the rest of us that our self-evident powerlessness is inevitable, unavoidable and without human agency). 'The basic assumption of technological determinism', wrote Williams, 'is that a new technology – a printing press or a communications satellite – "emerges" from technical study and experiment. It then changes the society or the sector into which it has "emerged". "We" adapt to it, because it is the new modern way.'[5] To dispute that this is indeed what happens is heretical, self-evidently absurd. The devices tumble out of the laboratory, the products of untrammelled human creativity, and they change our world. Denying the technological determinist vision runs not only against the grain of the times but also the risk of being dismissed as Luddite.[6] Nevertheless I wish to do this. I wish to suggest that such an obvious understanding is wrong. Holding a technological determinist view is, I would claim, like believing that it is the movement of the leaves on the trees which creates the wind.[7]

Let us take an opposing position, one which proposes that the technologist is – if not merely a passenger – then no more than the mechanic servicing a vehicle designed and built to society's specification. We, collectively, are in the driver's seat. This is certainly Braudel's view: although science and technology, as they are commonly understood, are 'uniting today to dominate the world – such unity *depends necessarily* upon the role played by present-day societies, which may encourage or restrain progress, today as in the past' (emphasis added).[8] In other words, in the dance of history society always leads technology.

The science and technology that produced the set of phenomena known as the industrial revolution were all to hand centuries before they were actually applied to achieve that effect. It was the socio-economic configurations of Britain in the eighteenth century that accelerated the application of the technologies involved, just as the socio-economic conditions in, say, southern Germany or northern Italy two centuries earlier put a brake on the same applications of those identical technologies. In a narrow sense, technological development is always as Braudel says it was of the industrial revolution: 'Innovations were quite clearly dependent on the state of the market: they were introduced only when they met persistent demand from consumers.'[9]

I want to argue that this sort of historical pattern holds true for current (and, almost certainly, short-term future) innovations – at least in the field of communications. To do this we need first to go beyond 'the market' which is but a subset of the social. As Braudel himself warns, economics are no better, by themselves, at explaining these phenomena than is technology. He is not suggesting substituting economics as an alternative monocausal explanation for change (*pace* a vulgar Marxism) because all monocausal explanations are inadequate. Rather, he demonstrates the need for complex, 'thick' explanations. Second, this insight into the primacy of society as the main agent in setting technology's agenda applies more widely than just to what we might see as the more overtly social deployments of technological developments, such as the industrial revolution. What is less clearly perceived is that the sort of prefiguration Braudel points to in the industrial revolution occurs (indeed, necessarily occurs) with all innovations great and small. The state of the market, or better, of society is the crucial factor in enabling the development and diffusion of any communications technology or in hindering it. That is as true of the computer chip and the Internet as it was of the telegraph and the telephone. Thus, innovations are the creatures of society in a general sense.

Again let me stress that I am only concerned with *communications* technologies. That is to say, this claim is without prejudice to what might or might not be the case in other fields. With these communications technologies, though, I observe a sequence of events with a more or less regular pattern which allows me to propose a model to describe the underlying nature of their introduction and diffusion over the past two centuries and more. The pattern displayed by the model is perforce quite complicated since it needs to take account of the uneven nature of the phenomenon – the accelerators as well as the brakes. It also needs to absorb Williams's fundamental insight as to the primacy of the social sphere.

Modelling Technological Change

The pattern is, first and foremost, historic; that is, in Saussurean terms, diachronic. But, just as Saussurean linguistics has both a diachronic and synchronic dimension, so too, it seems to me, does the pattern of technological change in communications. At any given discrete moment the situation of a technology can be represented by the synchronic intersection of three fields: science, in its original sense of fundamental knowledge (which might or might not encompass theoretical concepts); technology – the application of such knowledge 'in the metal' (as the engineers say, when actually meaning in any material, of course); and, encompassing and framing all, society.

A good way to think about how these three intersect is offered by carrying the analogy of the Saussurean model further. Just as utterance, in Saussurean linguistics, is a surface expression of deep-seated mental competence, so too can technology be thought of as a species of 'utterances' in a 'language' called science. Utterance is the surface expression of the deeper structure and, therefore, stands in a structural relationship to language. Chomsky's terms, 'performance' for 'utterance' and 'competence' for 'language', make this clearer. Technology is a performance of a competence arising from science (or knowledge). Technology stands in a structural relationship to science.

In the original linguistic model, the transformation from mental competence to physical performance is rule-governed. In this analogous application, the structural relationship between scientific competence and technological performance can still be thought of as a transformation, but it would be foolish, given the messiness of the social sphere in which a myriad of factors are in play, to describe it as rule-governed. I would want to split the difference between a strict rule-governed relationship (in linguistics, a grammar) and a totally random relationship. The pattern is too regular to be random but not so regular as to be completely predictive.

A technology moves from inchoate scientific knowledge (which itself is conditioned by society) to wide diffusion in society via a number of transformations. The first and most obvious is the business of translating scientific understanding into a device that exists in the world. This requires a transformation in the mind of the technologists who are, remember, themselves the products, and indeed the prisoners, of their cultures.

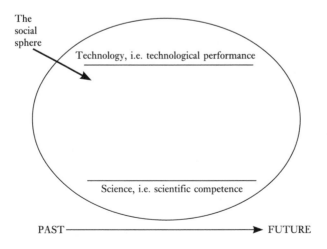

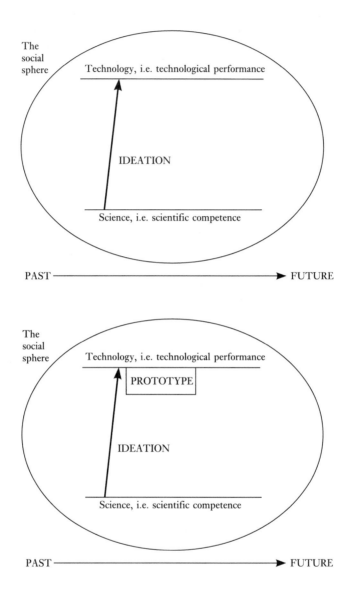

Crudely, this is the idea of the device – and in the model we can describe this as a transformation termed "ideation". This work of "ideation" produces the technological performances we call prototypes.

What then transforms the prototype into the invention? We are here dealing with Braudel's observation that technologies can remain unexploited for long periods of time. They languish, as it were, in the prototype phase, conceived and produced because the technologist, as a social being, sees a possibility of a use but the rest of society does not. Braudel's accelerator is not activated. In this model, acceleration can be thought of as an external social force, or combination of such forces, acting on the production of prototypes. When these forces come into play, they transform the prototype.

In effect, these accelerating social forces can be described as supervening social necessity, transforming prototype into an invention and enabling its diffusion.

This introduction of supervening social necessity explains the phenomenon of simultaneous 'invention'. Obviously, if technologists are working to an agenda determined by society and subject to further social forces such as their own conditioning, they are not as likely (as popular accounts suggest) to make 'eureka' discoveries. They are, as the historical record demonstrates, more likely to find similar or identical solutions for the same social need and to do so more or less at the same time. (This is literally true, for example, of the telephone. Alexander Graham Bell and his rival Elisha Gray both arrived at the Washington patent office on the same February day in 1876 with designs for such a thing.)

It is also the case that the difference between prototype and invention is more complex than is usually assumed to be the case. It is not, for example, always true that the invention works better and that the prototype or prototypes work less well. For instance, patents existed for the use of magnetic tape as a memory or storage medium for calculators from 1943. But, almost certainly because these were German (indeed, 'Nazi'), the earliest diffused computer memory systems were based on glass tubes filled with mercury, cathode ray tubes or nickel or iron-oxide plated metal drums.[10] The stated reasons for avoiding tape

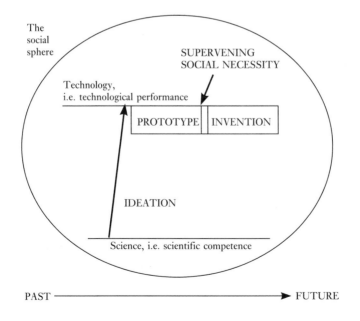

PAST ⟶ FUTURE

included, for example, the dirt problem; but this would be solved within another five years by nothing more complex than a dust-free cabinet housing for the tape deck.[11]

Further, it could be that on occasion neither prototype nor invention works very well. Again, the telephone is a case in point. Bell was legally awarded the patent but Gray's device was closer to solving the problem of 'the electric speaking telephone'. In effect, neither was to be diffused. The telephone technology that was actually to work in the world was created in an intense research and development phase involving these two, Watson, Edison, Berliner and others over the next three years to 1879.[12] Further examples to prove these points are laid out, as are descriptions of different classes of prototypes, inventions and supervening social necessities in *Misunderstanding Media*.[13]

New technologies contain considerable disruptive power. Many believe that this power is exercised in an untrammelled way and that our world is utterly transformed by these technologies. But what is transformed? Our economic system is, fundamentally, unchanged by these devices. Indeed they are the creatures and products of that system. Our political structures remain largely recognizable as does our cultural life and, despite hyperbolic discourse that claims otherwise, our sense of ourselves. It all depends on where you stand. For a technological determinist, whether of conservative or radical bent, the impact of the technology looms large and the changes wrought are great. The potential changes (which are always apparently to occur within the next five years to ten years) are greater yet, quite often wholly transformative.

But I would take a different view. I still see, after two centuries (at least) of these supposedly transformative technologies impacting on our world, patriarchy, capitalism, nations (and tribes), the Queen, the Stars and Stripes, wars of religion, exploitation of labour, leisure versus work and so on. So, for example, what interests the technological determinist is that the American radical right endlessly exploits the Internet; what interests me is that these folks use the technology to push a social vision two centuries out-of-date. In short, stand close to the technologies and they loom very large; stand away and they blend into the fabric of society. Being digital becomes no big deal.

This is not to argue that new communications technologies (or indeed other areas of technology) have nil effect, occasion no changes. Of course they do. Nor is it to argue that those changes are insignificant. Of course they can be very significant (although even a cursory knowledge of history will very often reduce the scale of change involved.) Rather, it is simply to suggest that these effects and changes are slow to work their way into society. To account for this in the model, the transformation that covers the move of the invention out into the world is conditioned by a social brake not an accelerator. New technologies are constrained and diffused only in so far as their potential for radical disruption is contained or suppressed. That is the brake. The technologies are made to 'fit' into society by this last transformation. This can therefore be termed 'the suppression of radical potential'.

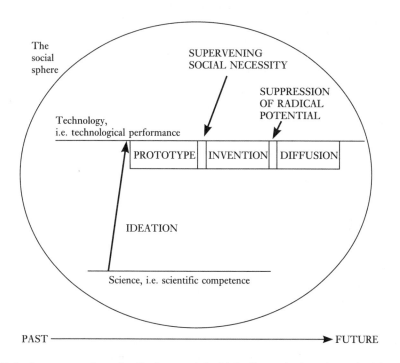

It is the suppression of radical potential which allows the broad continuities of our civilization to survive the stream of innovations. This suppression is the factor which primarily accounts for Braudel's delays.

The suppression of the radical potential of any technology is so well established as to begin to give the appearance of inevitability. So much does diffusion depend on such suppression that, despite the model not being regular enough to produce rule-governed transformations, we can nevertheless think of this transformation as being almost a law – the 'law' of the suppression of radical potential. Television, for instance, was available for full-scale diffusion two decades or so before that actually took place, and not all these lost years can be accounted for by the Second World War. More significant are the complex strategies deployed by the radio and film industries both to control the new medium's effect on their enterprises and to adjudicate their rival ownership claims on it. Again, the complex operation of this transformation and the resultant complexities within the diffusion phase are described more fully in *Misunderstanding Media*.

The purpose of all this is simply to enable us to elucidate the nature of technological progress in communications in a way that meshes with the complexities of these histories. Of necessity, doing this requires rethinking the received accounts of these technological developments in a critical way. The case studies in this book are concerned with image technologies – technologies of seeing, and primarily the technologies of the moving image. I shall take, as the first case, the history of the development of the cinema itself and ask some basic questions: Why did this happen in 1895? Why was film 35mm wide?

Issues of this sort are fundamental to the ways in which we have applied technology to the human act of seeing. These technologies of seeing, and how they are introduced and develop, are the concerns of this book. Why can't colour films photograph black people very easily? Why did 16mm take thirty years to become a professional film stock? Why is high-definition television not available today? How long before we have holographic films and television?

Notes

1 Fernand Braudel, *Civilisation and Capitalism, 15th–18th Century. Volume 1. The Structures of Everyday Life: The Limits of the Possible* (New York: Harper Row, 1979), p. 430.

2 Raymond Williams, *Television: Technology and Cultural Form* (London: Fontana, 1974), p. 13.

3 Quoted in the *Guardian*, 1 May 1995.

4 Mo Mowlam, 'Paper Tigers', *New Statesman & Society* vol. 7 no. 319/vol. 90 no. 1642, 9 September 1995, p. 24.

5 Raymond Williams, *The Politics of Modernism* (New York: Verso, 1989), p. 120.

6 This easy insult is itself an expression of technological determinism and concomitant historical ignorance in that it betrays a serious misunderstanding of the Luddites' actual campaign which was less to do with machines than with terms of trade. See E. P. Thompson, *The Making of the English Working Class* (Harmondsworth: Penguin, 1968), p. 600.

7 I am conscious of hearing Guy Cumberbatch use this image in connection with those who believe it is violent media material which causes violence in society. It seems to me to fit just as well here.

8 Braudel, *Civilisation and Capitalism. Volume 1*, p. 431.

9 Fernand Braudel, *Civilisation and Capitalism, 15th–18th Century. Volume 3. The Perspective of the World* (New York: Harper Row, 1979), p. 567.

10 Simon Lavington, *Early British Computers* (Manchester: Manchester University Press, 1980), pp. 16–22.

11 Brian Winston, *Misunderstanding Media* (London: Routledge & Kegan Paul; Cambridge, Mass.: Harvard University Press, 1986), pp. 159–60.

12 Ibid., pp. 315–37.

13 Ibid.

8
Projections of Sound on Image

Michel Chion

The house lights go down and the movie begins. Brutal and enigmatic images appear on the screen: a film projector running, a close-up of the film going through it, terrifying glimpses of animal sacrifices, a nail being driven through a hand. Then, in more "normal" time, a mortuary. Here we see a young boy we take at first to be a corpse like the others, but who turns out to be alive – he moves, he reads a book, he reaches toward the screen surface, and under his hand there seems to form the face of a beautiful woman.

What we have seen so far is the prologue sequence of Bergman's *Persona*, a film that has been analyzed in books and university courses by the likes of Raymond Bellour, David Bordwell, Marilyn Johns Blackwell. And the film might go on this way.

Stop! Let us rewind Bergman's film to the beginning and simply *cut out the sound*, try to forget what we've seen before, and watch the film afresh. Now we see something quite different.

First, the shot of the nail impaling the hand: played silent, it turns out to have consisted of three separate shots where we had seen one, because they had been linked by sound. What's more, the nailed hand in silence is abstract, whereas with sound, it is terrifying, real. As for the shots in the mortuary, without the sound of dripping water that connected them together we discover in them a series of stills, parts of isolated human bodies, out of space and time. And the boy's right hand, without the vibrating tone that accompanies and structures its exploring gestures, no longer "forms" the face, but just wanders aimlessly. The entire sequence has lost its rhythm and unity. Could Bergman be an overrated director? Did the sound merely conceal the images' emptiness?

Next let us consider a well-known sequence in Tati's *Monsieur Hulot's Holiday*, where subtle gags on a small bathing beach make us laugh. The vacationers are so amusing in their uptightness, their lack of fun, their anxiety! This time, let's cut out the visuals. Surprise: like the flipside of the image, another film appears that we now "see" with only our ears; there are shouts of children having fun, voices that resonate in an outdoor space, a whole world of play and vitality. It was all there in the sound, and at the same time it wasn't.

Now if we give Bergman back his sounds and Tati his images, everything returns to normal. The nailed hand makes you sick to look at, the boy shapes his faces, the summer vacationers seem quaint and droll, and sounds we didn't especially hear when there was only sound emerge from the image like dialogue balloons in comics.

Only now we have read and heard in a different way.

Is the notion of cinema as the art of the image just an illusion? Of course: how, ultimately, can it be anything else? This book is about precisely this phenomenon of *audio-visual illusion*, an illusion located first and foremost in the heart of the most important of relations between sound and image, as illustrated above with Bergman: what we shall call *added value*.

By *added value* I mean the expressive and informative value with which a sound enriches a given image so as to create the definite impression, in the immediate or remembered experience one has of it, that this information or expression "naturally" comes from what is seen, and is already contained in the image itself. Added value is what gives the (eminently incorrect) impression that sound is unnecessary, that sound merely duplicates a meaning which in reality it brings about, either all on its own or by discrepancies between it and the image.

The phenomenon of added value is especially at work in the case of sound/image synchronism, via the principle of *synchresis*, the forging of an immediate and necessary relationship between something one sees and something one hears. Most falls, blows, and explosions on the screen, simulated to some extent or created from the impact of nonresistant materials, only take on consistency and materiality through sound. But first, at the most basic level, added value is that of text, or language, on image.

Why speak of language so early on? Because the cinema is a vococentric or, more precisely, a verbocentric phenomenon.

Value Added by Text[1]

In stating that sound in the cinema is primarily vococentric, I mean that it almost always privileges the voice, highlighting and setting the latter off from other sounds. During filming it is the voice that is collected in sound recording – which therefore is almost always voice recording – and it is the voice that is isolated in the sound mix like a solo instrument – for which the other sounds (music and noise) are merely the accompaniment. By the same token, the historical development of synch sound recording technology, for example, the invention of new kinds of microphones and sound systems, has concentrated essentially on speech since of course we are not talking about the voice of shouts and moans, but the voice as medium of verbal expression. And in voice recording what is sought is not so much acoustical fidelity to original timbre, as the guarantee of effortless intelligibility of the words spoken. Thus what we mean by vococentrism is almost always verbocentrism.

Sound in film is voco- and verbocentric, above all, because human beings in their habitual behavior are as well. When in any given sound environment you hear voices, those voices capture and focus your attention before any other sound (wind blowing, music, traffic). Only afterward, if you know very well who is speaking and what they're talking about, might you turn your attention from the voices to the rest of the sounds you hear. So if these voices speak in an accessible language, you will first seek the meaning of the words, moving on to interpret the other sounds only when your interest in meaning has been satisfied.

Text structures vision

An eloquent example that I often draw on in my classes to demonstrate value added by text is a TV broadcast from 1984, a transmission of an air show in England, anchored from a French studio for French audiences by our own Léon Zitrone.[2] Visibly thrown by these images coming to him on the wire with no explanation and in no special order, the valiant anchor nevertheless does his job as well as he can. At a certain point, he affirms, "Here are three small airplanes," as we see an image with, yes, three little airplanes against a blue sky, and the outrageous redundancy never fails to provoke laughter.

Zitrone could just as well have said, "The weather is magnificent today," and that's what we would have seen in the image, where there are in fact no clouds. Or: "The first two planes are ahead of the third," and then everyone would have seen *that*. Or else: "Where did the fourth plane go?" – and the fourth airplane's absence, this plane hopping out of Zitrone's hat by the sheer power of the Word, would have jumped to our eyes. In short, the anchor could have made 50 other "redundant" comments; but their redundancy is illusory, since in each case these statements would have guided and structured our vision so that we would have seen them "naturally" in the image.

The weakness of Chris Marker's famous demonstration in his documentary *Letter from Siberia* – already critiqued by Pascal Bonitzer in another context[3] – where Marker dubs voice-overs of different political persuasions (Stalinist, anti-Stalinist, etc.) over the same sequence of innocuous images, is that through his exaggerated examples he leads us to believe that the issue is solely one of political ideology, and that otherwise there exists some neutral way of speaking. The added value that words bring to the image goes far beyond the simple situation of a political opinion slapped onto images; added value engages the very structuring of vision – by rigorously framing it. In any case, the evanescent film image does not give us much time to look, unlike a painting on a wall or a photograph in a book that we can explore at our own pace and more easily detach from their captions or their commentary.

Thus if the film or TV image seems to "speak" for itself, it is actually a ventriloquist's speech. When the shot of the three small airplanes in a blue sky declares "three small airplanes," it is a puppet animated by the anchorman's voice.

Value Added by Music

Empathetic and anempathetic effects

In my book *Le Son au cinéma* I developed the idea that there are two ways for music in film to create a specific emotion in relation to the situation depicted on the screen.[4] On one hand, music can directly express its participation in the feeling of the scene, by taking on the scene's rhythm, tone, and phrasing; obviously such music participates in cultural codes for things like sadness, happiness, and movement. In this case we can speak of *empathetic music*, from the word empathy, the ability to feel the feelings of others.

On the other hand, music can also exhibit conspicuous indifference to the situation, by progressing in a steady, undaunted, and ineluctable manner: the scene takes place against this very backdrop of "indifference." This juxtaposition of scene with indifferent music has the effect not of freezing emotion but rather of intensifying it, by inscribing it on a cosmic background. I call this second kind of music *anempathetic* (with the privative *a-*). The anempathetic impulse in the cinema produces those countless musical bits from player pianos, celestas, music boxes, and dance bands, whose studied frivolity and naiveté reinforce the individual emotion of the character and of the spectator, even as the music pretends not to notice them.

To be sure, this effect of cosmic indifference was already present in many operas, when emotional pitch was so high that it froze characters into inaction, provoking a sort of psychotic regression. Hence the famous operatic convention of madness, with the dumb little music that a character repeats while rocking back and forth.... But on the screen the anempathetic effect has taken on such prominence that we have reason to consider it to be intimately related to cinema's essence – its mechanical nature.

For, indeed, all films proceed in the form of an indifferent and automatic unwinding, that of the projection, which on the screen and through the loudspeakers produces simulacra of movement and life – and this unwinding must hide itself and be forgotten. What does anempathetic music do, if not to unevil this reality of cinema, its robotic face? Anempathetic music conjures up the mechanical texture of this tapestry of the emotions and senses.

Finally, there also exist cases of music that is neither empathetic nor anempathetic, which has either an abstract meaning, or a simple function of presence, a value as a signpost: at any rate, no precise emotional resonance.

The anempathetic effect is most often produced by music, but it can also occur with noise – when, for example, in a very violent scene after the death of a character some sonic process continues, like the noise of a machine, the hum of a fan, a shower running, as if nothing had happened. Examples of these can be found in Hitchcock's *Psycho* (the shower) and Antonioni's *The Passenger* (an electric fan).

Influences of Sound on the Perception of Movement and Perception of Speed

Visual and auditory perception are of much more disparate natures than one might think. The reason we are only dimly aware of this is that these two perceptions mutually influence each other in the audio-visual contract, lending each other their respective properties by contamination and projection.[5]

For one thing, each kind of perception bears a fundamentally different relationship to motion and stasis, since sound, contrary to sight, presupposes movement from the outset. In a film image that contains movement many other things in the frame may remain fixed. But sound by its very nature necessarily implies a displacement or agitation, however minimal. Sound does have means to suggest stasis, but only in limited cases. One could say that "fixed sound" is that which entails no variations whatever as it is heard. This characteristic is only found in certain sounds of artificial origin: a telephone dial tone, or the hum of a speaker. Torrents and waterfalls can produce a rumbling close to white noise too, but it is rare not to hear at least some trace of irregularity and motion. The effect of a fixed sound can also be created by taking a variation or evolution and infinitely repeating it in a loop. As the trace of a movement or a trajectory, sound thus has its own temporal dynamic.

Difference in speed of perception

Sound perception and visual perception have their own average pace by their very nature; basically, the ear analyzes, processes, and synthesizes faster than the eye. Take a rapid visual movement – a hand gesture – and compare it to an abrupt sound trajectory of the same duration. The fast visual movement will not form a distinct figure, its trajectory will not enter the memory in a precise picture. In the same length of time the sound trajectory will succeed in outlining a clear and definite form, individuated, recognizable, distinguishable from others.

This is not a matter of attention. We might watch the shot of visual movement ten times attentively (say, a character making a complicated arm gesture), and still not be able to discern its line clearly. Listen ten times to the rapid sound sequence, and your perception of it will be confirmed with more and more precision.

There are several reasons for this. First, for hearing individuals, sound is the vehicle of language, and a spoken sentence makes the ear work very quickly; by comparison, reading with the eyes is notably slower, except in specific cases of special training, as for deaf people. The eye perceives more slowly because it has more to do all at once; it must explore in space as well as follow along in time. The ear isolates a detail of its auditory field and it follows this point or line in time. (If the sound at hand is a familiar piece of music, however, the listener's auditory attention strays more easily from the temporal thread to explore spatially.) So, overall, in a first contact with an audio-visual message, the eye is more spatially adept, and the ear more temporally adept.

Sound for "spotting" visual movements and for sleight-of-hand

In the course of audio-viewing a sound film, the spectator does not note these different speeds of cognition as such, because added value intervenes. Why, for example, don't the myriad rapid visual movements in kung fu or special effects movies create a confusing impression? The answer is that they are "spotted" by rapid auditory punctuation, in the form of whistles, shouts, bangs, and tinkling that mark certain moments and leave a strong audio-visual memory.

Silent films already had a certain predilection for rapid montages of events. But in its montage sequences the silent cinema was careful to simplify the image to the maximum; that is, it limited exploratory perception in space so as to facilitate perception in time. This meant a highly stylized visual mode analogous to rough sketches. Eisenstein's *The General Line* provides an excellent example with its close-ups in the cream separator sequence.

If the sound cinema often has complex and fleeting movements issuing from the heart of a frame teeming with characters and other visual details, this is because the sound superimposed onto the image is capable of directing our attention to a particular visual trajectory. Sound even raises the possibility of sleight-of-hand effects: sometimes it succeeds in making us see in the image a rapid movement that isn't even there.

We find an eloquent example in the work of sound designer Ben Burtt on the *Star Wars* saga. Burtt had devised, as a sound effect for an automatic door opening (think of the hexagonal or diamond-shaped automatic doors of sci-fi films), a dynamic and convincing pneumatic "shhh" sound. So convincing, in fact, that, in making *The Empire Strikes Back*, when director Irving Kershner needed a door-closing effect he sometimes simply took a static shot of the closed door and followed it with a shot of the door open. As a result of sound editing, with Ben Burtt's "pssht," spectators who have nothing before their eyes besides a straight cut nevertheless think they see the door slide open. Added value is working full steam here, in accordance with a phenomenon specific to sound film that we might call faster-than-the-eye.

Deaf people raised on sign language apparently develop a special ability to read and structure rapid visual phenomena. This raises the question whether the deaf mobilize the same regions at the center of the brain as hearing people do for sound – one of the many phenomena that lead us to question received wisdom about distinctions between the categories of sound and image.

The ear's temporal threshold

Further, we need to correct the formulation that hearing occurs in continuity. The ear in fact listens in brief slices, and what it perceives and remembers *already* consists in short syntheses of two or three seconds of the sound as it evolves. However, within these two or three seconds, which are perceived as a *gestalt*, the ear, or rather the ear–brain system, has minutely and seriously done its investigation such that its overall report of the event, delivered periodically, is crammed with the precise and specific data that have been gathered.

This results in a paradox: we don't hear sounds, in the sense of recognizing them, until shortly after we have perceived them. Clap your hands sharply and listen to the resulting sound. Hearing – namely the synthesized apprehension of a small fragment of the auditory event, consigned to memory – will *follow* the event very closely, it will not be totally simultaneous with it.

Influence of Sound on the Perception of Time in the Image

Three aspects of temporalization

One of the most important effects of added value relates to the *perception of time in the image*, upon which sound can exert considerable influence. An extreme example, as we have seen, is found in the prologue sequence of *Persona*, where atemporal static shots are inscribed into a time continuum via the sounds of dripping water and footsteps. Sound temporalizes images in three ways.

The first is temporal animation of the image. To varying degrees, sound renders the perception of time in the image as exact, detailed, immediate, concrete – or vague, fluctuating, broad.

Second, sound endows shots with temporal linearization. In the silent cinema, shots do not always indicate temporal succession, wherein what happens in shot B would necessarily follow what is shown in shot A. But synchronous sound does impose a sense of succession.

Third, sound *vectorizes* or dramatizes shots, orienting them toward a future, a goal, and creation of a feeling of imminence and expectation. The shot is going somewhere and it is oriented in time. We can see this effect at work clearly in the prologue of *Persona* – in its first shot, for example.

Conditions necessary for sound to temporalize images

In order to function, these three effects depend on the nature of the sounds and images being put together.

First case: *the image has no temporal animation or vectorization in itself*. This is the case for a static shot, or one whose movement consists only of a general fluctuating, with no indication of possible resolution – for example, rippling water. In this instance, sound can bring the image into a temporality that it introduces entirely on its own.

Second case: *the image itself has temporal animation* (movement of characters or objects, movement of smoke or light, mobile framing). Here, sound's temporality *combines* with the temporality already present in the image. The two may move in concert or slightly at odds with each other, in the same manner as two instruments playing simultaneously.

Temporalization also depends on the type of sounds present. Depending on density, internal texture, tone quality, and progression, a sound can temporally animate an image to a greater or lesser degree, and with a more or less driving or restrained rhythm.[6] Different factors come into play here:

1 *How sound is sustained.* A smooth and continuous sound is less "animating" than an uneven or fluttering one. Try accompanying an image first with a prolonged steady note on the violin, and then with the same note played with a tremolo made by rapidly moving the bow. The second sound will cause a more tense and immediate focusing of attention on the image.

2 *How predictable the sound is as it progresses.* A sound with a regular pulse (such as a basso continuo in music or a mechanical ticking) is more predictable and tends to create less temporal animation than a sound that is irregular and thus unpredictable; the latter puts the ear and the attention on constant alert. The dripping of water in *Persona* as well as in Tarkovsky's films provide good examples: each unsettles our attention through its unequal rhythm.

   However, a rhythm that is too regularly cyclical can also create an effect of tension, because the listener lies in wait for the possibility of a fluctuation in such mechanical regularity.

3 *Tempo.* How the soundtrack temporally animates the image is not simply a mechanical question of tempo. A rapid piece of music will not necessarily accelerate the perception of the image. Temporalization actually depends more on the regularity or irregularity of the aural flow than on tempo in the musical sense of the word. For example, if the flow of musical notes is unstable but moderate in speed, the temporal animation will be greater than if the speed is rapid but regular.

4 *Sound definition.* A sound rich in high frequencies will command perception more acutely; this explains why the spectator is on the alert in many recent films.

Temporalization also depends on the *model of sound-image linkage* and on the *distribution of synch points* (see below). Here, also, the extent to which sound activates an image depends on how it introduces points of synchronization –

predictably or not, variously or monotonously. Control over expectations tends to play a powerful part in temporalization.

In summary, for sound to influence the image's temporality, a minimum number of conditions are necessary. First, the image must lend itself to it, either by being static and passively receptive (cf. the static shots of *Persona*) or by having a particular movement of its own (microrhythms "temporalizable" by sound). In the second case, the image should contain a minimum of structural elements – either elements of agreement, engagement, and sympathy (as we say of vibrations), or of active antipathy – with the flow of sound.

By visual *microrhythms* I mean rapid movements on the image's surface caused by things such as curls of smoke, rain, snowflakes, undulations of the rippled surface of a lake, dunes, and so forth – even the swarming movement of photographic grain itself, when visible. These phenomena create rapid and fluid rhythmic values, instilling a vibrating, trembling temporality in the image itself. Kurosawa utilizes them systematically in his film *Dreams* (petals raining down from flowering trees, fog, snowflakes in a blizzard). Hans-Jürgen Syberberg, in his static and posed long takes, also loves to inject visual microrhythms (smoke machines in *Hitler*, the flickering candle during Edith Clever's reading of Molly Bloom's monologue, etc.), as does Manoel de Oliveira (*Le Soulier de satin*). It is as if this technique affirms a kind of time proper to sound cinema as a recording of the microstructure of the present.

Sound cinema is chronography

One important historical point has tended to remain hidden: we are indebted to synchronous sound for having made cinema an art of time. The stabilization of projection speed, made necessary by the coming of sound, did have consequences that far surpassed what anyone could have foreseen. Filmic time was no longer a flexible value, more or less transposable depending on the rhythm of projection. Time henceforth had a fixed value; sound cinema guaranteed that whatever lasted x seconds in the editing would still have this same exact duration in the screening. In the silent cinema a shot had no exact internal duration; leaves quivering in the wind and ripples on the surface of the water had no absolute or fixed temporality. Each exhibitor had a certain margin of freedom in setting the rhythm of projection speed. Nor is it any accident that the motorized editing table, with its standardized film speed, did not appear until the sound era.

Note that I am speaking here of the rhythm of the finished film. Within a film there certainly may be material shot at non-standard speeds – accelerated or slow-motion – as seen in works of Michael Powell, Scorsese, Peckinpah, or Fellini at different points in sound film history. But if the speed of these shots does not necessarily reproduce the real speed at which the actors moved during filming, it *is* fixed in any case at a precisely determined and controlled rate.

So sound temporalized the image: not only by the effect of added value but also quite simply by normalizing and stabilizing film projection speed. A silent film by

Tarkovsky, who called cinema "the art of sculpting in time," would not be conceivable. His long takes are animated with rhythmic quiverings, convulsions, and fleeting apparitions that, in combination with vast controlled visual rhythms and movements, form a kind of hypersensitive temporal structure. The sound cinema can therefore be called "chronographic": written in time as well as in movement.

Temporal linearization

When a sequence of images does not necessarily show temporal succession in the actions it depicts – that is, when we can read them equally as simultaneous or successive – the addition of realistic, diegetic sound imposes on the sequence a sense of real time, like normal everyday experience, and above all, a sense of time that is linear and sequential.

Let us take a scene that occurs frequently enough in silent film: a crowd reacting, constructed as a montage of close-ups of scowling or grinning faces. Without sound the shots that follow one another on the screen need not designate actions that are temporally related. One can quite easily understand the reactions as being simultaneous, existing in a time analogous to the perfect tense in grammar. But if we dub onto these images the sounds of collective booing or laughter, they seem magically to fall into a linear time continuum. Shot B shows someone who laughs or jeers *after* the character in shot A.

The awkwardness of some crowd scenes in the very earliest talkies derives from this. For example, in the opening company dinner of Renoir's *La Chienne*, the sound (laughter, various verbal exchanges among the partygoers) seems to be stuck onto images that are conceived as inscribed in a kind of time that was not yet linear.

The sound of the spoken voice, at least when it is diegetic and synched with the image, has the power to inscribe the image in a real and linearized time that no longer has elasticity. This factor explains the dismay of many silent film-makers upon experiencing the effect of "everyday time" at the coming of sound.

Synchresis, which we shall discuss at greater length in chapter 3, is a powerful factor in linearizing and inscribing images into real time.

Vectorization of real time

Imagine a peaceful shot in a film set in the tropics, where a woman is ensconced in a rocking chair on a veranda, dozing, her chest rising and falling regularly. The breeze stirs the curtains and the bamboo windchimes that hang by the doorway. The leaves of the banana trees flutter in the wind. We could take this poetic shot and easily project it from the last frame to the first, and this would change essentially nothing, it would all look just as natural. We can say that the time this shot depicts is real, since it is full of microevents that reconstitute the texture of the present, but that it is not vectorized. Between the sense of moving from past to future and future to past we cannot confirm a single noticeable difference.

Now let us take some sounds to go with the shot – direct sound recorded during filming, or a soundtrack mixed after the fact: the woman's breathing, the wind, the chinking of the bamboo chimes. If we now play the film in reverse, it no longer works at all, especially the windchimes. Why? Because each one of these clinking sounds, consisting of an attack and then a slight fading resonance, is a finite story, oriented in time in a precise and irreversible manner. Played in reverse, it can immediately be recognized as "backwards." Sounds are vectorized.

The same is true for the dripping water in the prologue of *Persona*. The sound of the smallest droplet imposes a real and irreversible time on what we see, in that it presents a trajectory in time (small impact, then delicate resonance) in accordance with logics of gravity and return to inertia.

This is the difference, in the cinema, between the orders of sound and image: given a comparable time scale (say two to three seconds), aural phenomena are much more characteristically vectorized in time, with an irreversible beginning, middle, and end, than are visual phenomena.

If this fact normally eludes us, it is because the cinema has derived amusement from exceptions and paradoxes by playing on what's visually irreversible: a broken object whose parts all fly back together, a demolished wall that reconstructs, or the inevitable gag of the swimmer coming out of the pool feet first and settling upon the diving board. Of course, images showing actions that result from non-reversible forces (gravity causes an object to fall, an explosion disperses fragments), is clearly vectorized. But much more frequently in movies, images of a character who speaks, smiles, plays the piano, or whatever are reversible; they are not marked with a sense of past and future. Sound, on the other hand, quite often consists of a marking off of small phenomena oriented in time. Isn't piano music, for example, composed of thousands of little indices of vectorized real time, since each note begins to die as soon as it is born?

Stridulation and tremolo: naturally or culturally based influence

The temporal animation of the image by sound is not a purely physical and mechanical phenomenon: cinematic and cultural codes also play a part in it. A music cue or a voice-over that is culturally perceived as not "in" the setting will not set the image to vibrating. And yet, the phenomenon still has a non-cultural basis.

Take the example of the string tremolo, a device traditionally employed in opera and symphonic music to create a feeling of dramatic tension, suspense, or alarm. In film we can get virtually the same result with sound effects: for example, the stridulation of nocturnal insects in the final scene of Randa Haines's *Children of a Lesser God*. This ambient sound, however, is not explicitly coded as a "tremolo"; it is not in the official repertoire of standard devices of filmic writing. Nevertheless it can have on the dramatic perception of time exactly the same effect of concentrating attention and making us sensitive to the smallest quivering on the screen, as does the tremolo in the orchestra. Sound editors and mixers frequently do utilize such nocturnal ambient sounds, and parcel out the effect like orchestra conductors, by their choices of certain sound-effects recordings and the ways they blend these to create an overall sound. Obviously the effect will vary according to the density of the stridulation, its regular or fluctuating quality, and its duration – just as for an orchestral effect.

But what exactly is there in common, for a film spectator, between a string tremolo in a pit orchestra, which the viewer identifies as a cultural musical procedure, and the rustling of an animal, which the viewer perceives as a natural emanation from the setting (without dreaming, of course, that the latter could have been recorded separately from the image and expertly recomposed)? Only an acoustic identity: that of a sharp, high, slightly uneven vibrating that both alarms and fascinates. It appears, then, that we have a universal and spontaneous effect operating here. It is also, however, a very fragile effect, which the slightest thing – bad sound balance, a spectator's loss of confidence in the audio-visual contract due to a fault in production – suffices to compromise.

This also holds true for all effects of added value that have nothing of the mechanical: founded on a psychophysiological basis, they operate only under certain cultural, aesthetic, and emotional conditions by means of a general interaction of all elements.

Reciprocity of Added Value: The Example of Sounds of Horror

Added value works reciprocally. Sound shows us the image differently than what the image shows alone, and the image likewise makes us hear sound differently than if the sound were ringing out in the dark. However, for all this reciprocity the screen remains the principal support of filmic perception. Transformed by the image it influences, sound ultimately reprojects onto the image the product of their mutual influences. We find eloquent testimony to this reciprocity in the case of horrible or upsetting sounds. The image projects onto them a meaning they do not have at all by themselves.

Everyone knows that the classical sound film, which avoided showing certain things, called on sound to come to the rescue. Sound *suggested* the forbidden sight in a much more frightening way than if viewers were to see the spectacle with their own eyes. An archetypal example is found at the beginning of Aldrich's masterpiece *Kiss Me Deadly*, when the runaway hitch-hiker whom Ralph Meeker picked up has been recaptured by her pursuers and is being tortured. We see nothing of this torture but two bare legs kicking and struggling, while we hear the unfortunate woman's screams. There's a typical use of sound, we might say. Of course – as long as it's clear that what makes the screams so terrifying is not their own acoustic properties but what the narrated situation, and what we're allowed to see, project onto them.

Another traumatic aural effect occurs in a scene in *The Skin*, by Liliana Cavani (1981, based on Malaparte's novel). An American tank accidentally runs over a little Italian boy, with – if memory does not fail me – a ghastly noise that sounds like a watermelon being crushed. Although spectators are not likely to have heard the real sound of a human body in this circumstance, they may imagine that it has some of this humid, viscous quality. The sound here has obviously been Foleyed in, perhaps precisely by crushing a melon.

As we shall see, the figurative value of a sound in itself is usually quite non-specific. Depending on the dramatic and visual context, a single sound can convey very diverse things. For the spectator, it is not acoustical realism so much as synchrony above all, and secondarily the factor of verisimilitude (verisimilitude arising not from truth but from convention), that will lead him or her to connect a sound with an event or detail. The same sound can convincingly serve as the sound effect for a crushed watermelon in a comedy or for a head blown to smithereens in a war film. The same noise will be joyful in one context, intolerable in another.

In Franju's *Eyes Without a Face* we find one of the rare disturbing sounds that the public and critics have actually remarked upon after viewing: the noise made by the body of a young woman – the hideous remains of an aborted skin-transplant experiment – when surgeon Pierre Brasseur and his accomplice Alida Valli drop it into a family vault. What this flat thud (which never fails to send a shudder through the theater) has in common with the noise in Cavani's film is that it transforms the human being into a thing, into vile, inert, disposable matter, with its entrails and osseous cavities.

But it is an upsetting noise also in that within the film's rhythm it constitutes an *interruption of speech*, a moment where the two perpetrators' speech is absent. At the cinema or in real life certain sounds have this resonance because they occur at a certain place: in a flow of language, where they make a hole. A ghastly example of this idea can be seen in Tarkovsky's *Andrei Rublev*. A Russian prince emerges from being tortured by the Tartars; he is covered with bandages, which hide his mutilated body and leave nothing visible but his lips. Abandoned on a bed, he curses his torturers; but just after, the torturer's hand brings a ladle full of boiling oil which is poured down his throat. This action is masked from view by the back of the torturer, who has mercifully (or rather cleverly) interposed himself at that moment between the spectator and the victim's head. What we hear is the atrocious sound of gargling, which makes the skin crawl. All the same, as with the crushing sound mentioned above, this could be the same sound Peter Sellers might make as he gargles in a Blake Edwards comedy.

Here, the effect of the sound is so strong because it represents human speech felled at its physical core: what has been destroyed are a larynx and a tongue, which have just spoken.

Notes

1 Chion's terminology, referring as it does to the register of political economy, is based on a pun: *value added by text* plays on the *value added tax* imposed on purchases of goods and services in France and the rest of the EC (*trans*).

2 Léon Zitrone: French TV anchor, a household word in France since the early years of television. Zitrone did commentary for horse races, figure skating, official ceremonies such as royal weddings, and air shows.

3 Pascal Bonitzer, *Le Regard et la voix*, pp. 37–40.

4 Michel Chion, *Le Son au cinéma*, chapter 7, "La Belle Indifférente," pp. 119–42, especially pp. 122–6.

5 Throughout this book I use the phrase *audio-visual contract* as a reminder that the audio-visual relationship is not natural, but a kind of symbolic contract that the audio-viewer enters into, agreeing to think of sound and image as forming a single entity.

6 Here by *density* I mean the density of sound events. A sound with marked and rapid modifications in a given time will temporally animate the image in a different way than a sound that varies less in the same time.

9
Modes of Production: The
Televisual Apparatus

John T. Caldwell

These radio news pictures projected from magic lantern slides onto the screens of the best picture theaters in the cities ... [mean that] no newspaper can possibly put news events before the public as quickly as the theater can with radio news pictures.
Technical proposal for theatrical television, SMPE Journal, *May 1923[1]*

Although some parts of the program technic may parallel the technics of the stage, motion pictures and sound broadcasting, it will be distinct from any of these. In effect, a new art form must be created.
Modernist aesthetic espoused by RCA engineer R. R. Beal, 1937[2]

Television engineers have often acted as closet artists. From the very beginning, developers of production technology have seldom shied away from offering aesthetic theorizations about their new and constantly developing technologies. Even a cursory survey of the technical literature from the 1920s and 1930s shows that television might have ended up radically different from the form that we now know. Engineers hawked various visions of the artform: as a cinematic type of theatrical television, as a facsimile system, as radio photographs that produced paper prints, as a visual newswire, and as a video phone.[3] From the perspective of the 1990s, these early and alternative technical proposals, along with alternative economic proposals – like pay per view and a system of programming subsidized by TV set license fees – all seem incredibly forward-thinking. Each prototype, after all, now plays an important part in the contemporary multinational, multimedia environment. Yet, by 1950, each prototype had been written off as a failure.

This shepherding and attrition of technological and artistic prototypes suggests two things. First, media technologies are not easily dichotomized as either deterministic (forces that effect change) or symptomatic (phenomena that reflect cultural needs and ideologies), as Raymond Williams suggests.[4] As the above epigraphs indicate, prewar RCA and Society for Motion Picture Engineers (SMPE) aestheticians actively broached and bartered different aesthetic models in a give-and-take process of negotiation with stockholders, with government regulators, and with the supposed needs and tastes of the American people. William Boddy has shown incisively how government-sanctioned monopolistic practice in the postwar era was a clear incursion into technological development – an exclusionary process of control that benefited specific business interests.[5] To the deterministic–symptomatic model, then, one must also then add a third axis: the interventionist. History shows that mass-cultural processes are not always as subtle as some cultural studies suggest, nor are they always as ambiguous and contradictory as ideological criticism implies. Explicit aesthetic and theoretical discourses – as well as overt interventions of power – have always accompanied new media technologies and will continue to do so. Political and economic interests have never been queasy about publicly flexing corporate muscle to control paradigm shifts. These manifest tendencies in television's mode of production had an effect on televisual style as well.

Having surveyed the historical and ideological functions of aesthetic television, that is, the conditions and precedents for stylistic exhibitionism, I want to examine here some of the industrial conditions behind the emergence of televisuality. A consideration of the televisual mode of production – its production technology, methods, personnel, and organizational form – shows that the excessive looks of primetime television in the 1980s were not just illustrations of a stylistic or postmodernist sensibility, but were rather indications of substantive changes within the televisual industry and its production apparatus. To understand these changes, it is important to look at several key televisual technologies, their affect on production practice, and two major influences on televisual programming: the film-style look and the style-obsessed world of primetime commercial advertising. . . .

Televisual Labor

Although students of cultural studies now flock to the audience and to the domestic living room in order to better explain television, few consider the practitioners or makers of what is transmitted over the TV a source for productive analysis. This academic oversight may be logical, given the problematic nature of much in the industry. The primetime production world, for example, is still in many ways an exclusionary old-boys network, fueled by patriarchy and by discourses that institutionalize anecdotes about "the ways things are done." There are those, for example, who celebrate the masculinist virtues of production technology. The latest full-page ads from Panavision in Hollywood show musclebound and loosely clothed male production studs erecting a tripod-mounted 35mm camera – all in a pictorial tableau clearly modeled on the bloody WWII Marine Corp flag-raising on Iwo Jima.[6] *Semper fi, Panavision.*

Film and television production accomplishment is, apparently, still very much fueled by testosterone. In recent and official how-to production publications by the Directors Guild, veterans teach television aspirants and newcomers the essential tricks of the directing trade: "Travel for [the director] becomes an adventure that no money can buy. Wherever he goes, he becomes involved with the natives at the location. ... The relationship the director has with prominent people offers a different satisfaction than the one he has with the 'common' man. ... I do not give brown envelopes with cash or cash in any form; I do not supply anyone with members of the opposite sex for any purpose."[7] In the old Hollywood, then, television commercial directing can be couched as a middle-aged forerunner of the "sex, drugs, and rock-and-roll" ethos. Straight-shooting, insider production books like this one cannot resist acknowledging the industry's important lifestyle functions and lures – travel, elitism, bribery, and illicit sex – as part of the director's professional package. This production patriarch has spoken, by substantiating each lifestyle concern with pregnant anecdotes from inside the production industry.

Compare this old-school *Weltanschauung* with an emblematic quote from a newer director, one more typical of the wave that entered television on terms very different from those laid down by the venerable Directors Guild of America: "I see my background in semiotic theory as the main reason why I've been able to cross over from such a radical avant-garde position to such a commercial medium. ... Godard meets *Monterey Pop* is my ideal."[8] The references to semiotics and Godard are curious to say the least. These are not the references high theory expects to find in the *day-to-day workings* of the television industry. The remarks do show, however, that some parts of the industry are capable of viewing their work as a process of reflexive stylization and as a sign system. Semiotic and film historical consciousness counteract the way that the earlier industry overprivileged the maker's intentions as the key to a program's meaning. From a semiotic perspective, meanings are constructed by the program text through plays of image and sound, rather than predetermined by the program makers. The program, in short, is no longer construed as a neutral vehicle that transmits messages for its senders. Rather, the formal elements of the program themselves are the content. This particular homage to master-deconstructionist Godard, to the avant-garde, and to semiotic theory implies that some directors no longer dutifully accept the industry's received production wisdom and orthodox style. This degree of intellectual self-consciousness was not always a part of production.

Before the 1970s the production industry seemed to have little need for intellectual speculations on its form. After all, the industry's formal methods were self-evident, naturalized and codified through widespread use. Academic training, in fact, could be a definite mark against aspiring applicants to the primetime program production industry in Hollywood. The reason for this prejudice, of course, was that the only persons qualified to talk about or explain the industry were thought to be the practitioners and industry professionals themselves. The problem with this view, though, is the same one argued in philosophical aesthetics against the so-called intentionalist fallacy.[9] That is, critics of the fallacy argue that the meaning of an artistic work cannot logically be limited to the original *intent and expression* of the work's maker. If it is, the viewer is locked into a tautology, a closed loop. A work of art or film is not a work of art or film simply because their makers say so. Against the traditional view that privileged the originators of the artwork over its perception, Godardian consciousness presupposes the text as an (inter)active stylistic operation; that films and videos work as an array of signals and codes that are manipulated and orchestrated by producers and viewers. For a TV director to invoke Godard, and then to apply him to popular culture, is not just an exercise in the faddish, but empty, lingo of postmodernism. The behavior suggests instead a fairly widespread knowledge of film history, deconstruction, and stylistics.

I am suggesting that a new generation of production personnel in television is more stylistically *and* more theoretically inclined. Many production approaches in primetime are now premeditated rather than rote. One might counter this perception, however, by arguing that only those filmmakers tainted by the excesses of MTV or features actually evidence greater theoretical focus. After all, many in the industry tended to view with distaste the excessive style, hypervisuality, and self-consciousness of newcomer MTV. For example, *American Cinematographer* defined high-quality programs by setting them apart from MTV: "Pete Townshend's Deep End, *overcomes MTV special effects and overproduction* and exists on its own terms" (italics mine).[10] Notice here that excessive visuality – overproduction – seems to be a trait that producers should overcome. What the trade review argues for is stylish production, but only if it can be linked to a show's essential objectives, that is, to its own terms. The reference suggests that the industry is interested, not in excessive or empty style, but in stylistic originality and *motivated* style. Overproduction for *American Cinematographer*, then, might more accurately be described as special effects for special effects' sake, as canned looks that work apart from particular references or program objectives.

This example shows that even competing ideologies within the industry are reprivileging production style. On the one hand, the new generation of MTV-bred television and commercial directors play with the limits of style and radical theory. On the other hand, even the more conservative and older imagemakers associated with the feature film industry revalue style, but do so in a different way. *American Cinematographer* does not have an aversion to the stylish image – far from it. What it wants is *smart style*, rather than empty or unmotivated stylistic effect. Even this apparently reactionary critique against MTV stylishness is actually a call for stylistic heterogeneity. That is, it assumes that each work should be uniquely stylized according to its own objectives – neither wallpapered with special effects, nor forced to bear a standard and unmotivated industry look.

The industry's semiotic self-consciousness goes deeper than its various cutting edges and avant-gardes. Take for example the following trade account of production style in the popular primetime soap *Dallas*. Director of photography (DP) "Caramico sees his work as following the [series] look that's been established – of continuing the *tropes* laid down by previous cinematographers and by producer

Leonard Katzman."[11] The reference to program tropes is not the kind of language one finds in earlier generations of books based on *prescriptive* rules and biblical production principles. Once one has viewed the look of a show through the lens of narrative theory – as figures of speech, as stylistic quotes, as smart references – form is no longer seen as a neutral vehicle. It is easy to foreground stylishness in unorthodox program genres. But here, even in the conservative and classical Hollywood style used in primetime dramas like *Dallas*, the look of the show presents itself as if derived from a well-stocked menu of possible stylistic figures.[12] Even if such programming does not invoke Metz's semiotic terminology, its utilization of tropes from a stylistic menu suggests that television is being theorized-in-practice as a visually coded formal system, as a semiotic smorgasbord. In this way, even conservative shows not originally pitched as stylistic can still be self-conscious about their visual poses.

The determining stylistic role that production personnel play is most evident at high-volume primetime production studios like Universal. With numerous episodic and serial shows simultaneously in production at any one time, visual style becomes both formulaic and very much tied to the tools assigned to each show. By 1993, Universal was still cutting conservative workhorse series like *Murder She Wrote* and *Columbo* on film. Flatbed film editing, after all, fits well the 1970s zero-degree telefilm style that is still used in both of these series. On more flashy and contemporary series though – *Law and Order, Crime and Punishment*, and the very hip and premediated *Miami Vice* – like 1993 spin-off *South Beach* – the producers at Universal chose a much newer and flashier editing tool.[13] Universal Studio executives praised the stylistic possibilities offered by the newer, nonlinear CMX-6000 editing system, but described the ultimate choice of editing technology as the series producer's call. Style, however, was not the only thing on the vice president's mind. Electronic editing also promised to be more cost effective – something the old-guard studios have always understood better than anybody else. Significantly, the new tools were tied directly to specific crafts people and to off-the-lot, third-party postproduction houses – all tied together in what the studio described as a new interpersonal relationship.[14] In Universal's eyes, then, televisual production technology cannot be distinguished from a new kind of producer and a new kind of extra-studio corporate relationship.

One of the most provocative illustrations of changes in televisual style comes from changes in the kind of background expected of directors. Television directing is no longer necessarily dominated by actors' directors. Veterans with decades of production experience, in fact, now argue that the best training for second-unit directing, a prerequisite for first-unit work, comes not from writing or producing, but from working as a cinematographer. "You have to be a director of photography before you can [direct] second unit, because you have to be able to shoot in any style. [As a director] you have to match what the main cinematographer does."[15] From the perspective of this director on the 1992 network series *Covington Cross*, then, one of the chief directorial tasks in primetime is to construct coherent stylistic worlds, on command, and from a wide variety of visual styles. Facility with rote, classical montage and blocking is no longer the issue. Requiring a cinematography pedigree for television directing could not be more alien to the script- and acting-sensitivity celebrated by many earlier television directors. John Frankenheimer and Delbert Mann in the 1950s could not have cared less about the grade of fog filter used on the set or the characteristic curves of their primetime kinescope stocks.

Televisual Technologies

Simply looking at television's flow of ads, shows, and promos on any given night reveals the importance and consciousness of the televisual mode of production and its technologies. If many primetime shows now use all of their available "bells and whistles," then ads and music videos actually make production equipment a crucial part of their dramatic action as well. When director David Fincher, for example, used the new Raybeam, a lighting grid with thirty 1Ks on a recent Nike commercial, he liked the polished high-tech look so much that he included it as a prop in the background. From then on he had to re-rent the light as a prop to insure continuity among the other spots in the entire Nike television campaign.[16] The production tool became a fetishized toy in the hip urban world that Nike fantasized for its audience.

But new production tools not only influenced what was seen by viewers within television images, they also had a profound influence on how those images were constructed, altered, and displayed. It is important to see the emergence of stylistic exhibitionism in the 1980s alongside the growing popularity of six new technical devices in the televisual production world: the video-assist, motion control, electronic nonlinear editing, digital effects, T-grain film stocks, and the Rank-Cintel. The development and availability of digital video effects, for example, has always promised (or threatened) to replace conventional production methods – a potential celebrated both by techno-futurists and production executives looking to save money in primetime by getting rid of real (and expensive) locations and sets.[17] Chapter 5 analyses this virtual world of excessive videographics in more detail. In addition, a case study at the conclusion of chapter 9 examines portable videotape, another influential industrial component in the rise of televisuality, and a technology directly implicated by new forms of electronic editing and digital videographics. Before considering the broader implications of these televisual technologies, however, a closer look at their importance in primetime production discourse is needed.

Video-assist

If one observes a film-based shoot for television today, one frequently confronts a production spectacle notably different from the way things used to be done. It is not uncommon today to see production personnel clustered around a glowing video monitor, entranced by the electronic image rather than by the actors or the action in front of the film camera. The video-assist makes possible this radical shift of the production group's gaze. In the old days, the nature of the image was really the business of only one or two people on a telefilm shoot: the director of photography and the camera operator. Although ultimately responsible for the show, the director was more concerned with acting and could only engage with the image as it was being shot, through the vague visual approximation offered by a neck-strung director's finder. Reinforcing the invisible nature of the television image during the shoot was the fact that the director and crew had to wait for projection of the film dailies – work-prints made from the camera original negative – which came back from the lab well after the day's shoot was over. As with feature filmmaking, sometimes the results were acceptable, sometimes they were not. For many years, television's 35mm Mitchell cameras did not even have reflex viewing. Camera people were forced to develop complicated "rack-over" systems to shift the camera away from the lens to enable the operator to frame a shot. This shift allowed the camera people to predict what the camera was seeing. Later, "reflex-viewing" on Panavision cameras allowed the operators to see the action exactly as it was being shot, but no one else at the time, including the director of photography, had any *certainty* about whether the shot worked, that is, whether it was exposed or framed correctly. The image was always in some ways a mystery, one that revealed its secrets only after a return journey from the lab's dark, chemical soup. This invisibility lent itself well to the mystique of the cinematographer's difficult craft and to the cult of professionalism.

With the introduction and availability of fiber optics, however, there was but a short and logical leap to the video-assist. Tiny fiber optics were tapped into the reflex viewfinder, fed out into a video pick-up device (a tiny video camera), and electronically fed to a monitor on the set. This device, then, allowed one and all on the set simultaneous and critical access to the once-mysterious camera image. What occasionally results from its use is a kind of team visualization, where every one of the key creative personnel has access to the composed image. This device, of course, saves money: a lot of takes never need to be printed, because flaws in acting or blocking become immediately apparent as the shot is being made or when videotape recorded from the video-assist is played back between takes. Yet the *displacement of the production gaze from the proprietary mysterium of the cinematographer* to the public consumption of the entire crew makes everyone an expert on the image. The video-assist allows extreme precision during a setup, and saves money, but it can also be the bane of image makers when gaffers, actors, grips, and other "experts" offer suggestions about better ways to compose the image. Construction of the televised image before video-assist was based primarily on verbal commands between key personnel and mathematical calculations made by the cinematographer and his assistant(s). The video-assist, by contrast, allows everyone on the set to be highly conscious and concerned about visual quality. For better or worse, now everyone seems to be a master of the image.

Motion control

Another type of equipment that complements the video-assist, in both the *dispersal and intensification of the image*, is motion control. I include in this category not just the computer-controlled units that automatically program cameras to perform and reduplicate complicated camera moves, but also the Steadicam, Camrail, robotic-controlled studio cameras, and much less cybernetic devices like jib arms and motorized cranes. All of these devices are alike in one important way: they physically *take the camera away from the camera operator's eyes and move it through space in very fluid ways*. The resulting effect can be eerily nonhuman, as with the Steadicam – a body-mounted camera harness governed by a gyroscopic control that minimizes jerkiness and vibration. By taking out even the sensation of human steps when the operator moves, the camera eye seems to float through space with a mind of its own. Popularized in excessively styled feature films by the Coen brothers (*Blood Simple, Raising Arizona*) and by Stanley Kubrick (*Full-Metal Jacket*), the Steadicam has been a workhorse in television commercial production, and an almost obligatory rental unit in music video shoots, for over ten years. Because of the Steadicam's extreme spatial fluidity in and around the body, the operator typically gauges his or her shot with the aid of the video-assist and a camera-mounted video monitor. Recognizing widespread demand, manufacturer Cinema Products has developed smaller versions of the Steadicam; lighter units specifically designed for television's video electronic field production (EFP) workhorse Betacam, and even the newer guerrilla format, high-8mm.

Everybody seems to want disembodied camera fluidity, not just feature film-makers. The jib arm, a less sophisticated leverlike extension that mounts and pivots on the head of a tripod or dolly, also takes the camera eye far away from the operator's head. With video-assisted monitoring, television shots can now start far above a cameraperson's eye level and sweep laterally, vertically, or diagonally through a shot even as the camera rolls. Periscopic lenses on jib- or dolly-mounted cameras allow television cinematographers to shift from sweeping renditions of exterior action to snaking arterial moves through microscopic spaces as well. Programmed, computerized control of these moves allows directors to repeat identically the same complicated shots for one or one hundred takes, all without the inevitable flaws and subtle differences that a human operator brings. Even outside of film-origination television, for example, at NBC network news and CNN, robotic control has had a profound effect on the way that live three-camera studio production is orchestrated. During John Williams's elegiac orches-tral score at the start of NBC's nightly news, high-end robotic studio cameras glide subtly and smoothly around Tom Brokaw at center stage. One station technical director mused uneasily about his experience with the new automated studios: "Robocams – made 'em look so good, it's costing me my job."[18] As well as being stylish, then, television's robotic and autonomous eyes also have dire labor implications. Even the extensive and highly stratified camera crews in primetime production stand back and watch as a single composite operator (cameraman/DP/assistant cinematographer/grip) coaxes the Steadicam eye through its dramatic flight-like apparitions.

This family of motion-control devices all do one thing for the television image: they automate an inherently omniscient point of view and subjectivize it around a technological rather than human center. If anything reflects the ontological death of photographic realism in television, it is surely this gang of new and automated motion-control devices. The ideological effect of this basic televisual apparatus is one of airless and high-tech artifice. The televisual image no longer seems to be anchored by the comforting, human eye-level view of the pedestal-mounted camera, but floats like the eye of a cyborg.

Electronic and nonlinear editing: "Thirty-two levels of undo"

If video-assist and motion control effected stylistic consciousness and disembodied fluidity *within the frame*, then a third group of technologies – electronic editing – helped shatter the *sequential and temporal* straitjacket necessitated by conventional forms of editing. Electronic editing of videotape has been pervasive since the early 1970s, first as control-track editing, and then as frame-accurate SMPTE (Society for Motion Picture and Television Engineers) "time-code" editing.[19] From the start, many telefilm producers despised these options. While video editing was acceptable for short network news stories, it proved impractical for longer forms, since video editing allowed no flexibility for change, modification, or revision once a succession of shots was laid down. If 25 minutes of the final program had been edited and an early scene needed to be shortened or replaced, then the entire show back to that point had to be rebuilt and re-edited. This system of online editing meant that creative impulse had little place in the on-line suite. Directors and associate producers in charge of editing had to know the exact duration and sequence of each shot in the show. Mid-session changes of even a few shots could mean doubling the on-line editing costs. This was not, obviously, a creative or user-friendly system. Editing film, on the other hand, might be slower, but it allowed for numerous editorial reworkings. Telefilm editors could start cutting scenes in the middle of a program and work out from there with no negative effect. The total running time would simply expand as the editor added, deleted, or reversed scenes. The program's form grew and breathed with editorial changes. Telefilm editors were not locked into the rigid temporal sequences necessitated by videotape editing.

In the face of this uneven industrial reception by the primetime producers, major video equipment manufacturers – masters in the 1970s and 1980s of a high-tech industrial world obsessed with research and development – announced ever more highly sophisticated videotape editing systems. By 1993 even Sony's industrial and low-end broadcast editing systems had become proficient at loading up the television image with multiple simultaneous images and slow motion. Sony boasted that their "BVE-2000 editor connects to as many as 12 VTRs, controlling up to 6 in any one edit."[20] This was the very kind of extreme visual facility that telefilm editors failed to find in the earlier variants of videotape editing. In some ways, the six-plus layered images simultaneously available even on this basic industrial video system allowed for a denser and more complicated image than those of film. Telefilm producers, after all, were limited to the two layers available during any one edit (due to the A and B rolls in 16mm film negative; or the A roll and effects roll in 35mm). Videotape editing, then, has become hyperactive and visually dense with or without the endorsement of primetime telefilm producers. The production company for *Arsenio Hall* boasted that their hip and kinetic opening collaged visual fragments from a number of diverse sources: 35mm, 16mm, 8mm, black and white, and color. Anything and everything could be slammed together in the highly developed world of electronic videotape editing. Even before the wide acceptance of nonlinear cutting, then, videotape editing had provided practitioners with an apt tool for the new collage style favored in the 1980s.

The resistance to cutting on tape by the major telefilm producers began to loosen in the mid and late 1980s, with the development of newer random-access memory electronic editing systems, like Lucasfilm's Editdroid, the EMC2, the Montage Picture Processor, and the CMX-6000. All promised primetime program producers the ability to do film-style editing for television. The technological breakthrough that made this possible, was the increasing cost effectiveness and memory-storage power of newer recording media: electronic video discs and greatly expanded computer hard drives. As alternatives to videotape-based recording or editing, films or tapes were loaded into a computer's RAM, video discs, or hard drives and any part of the original source material could be called up at any time within a microsecond. Shows cut on these systems could provide half-hour or hour-long screenings for producers even though no show actually or physically existed, either on tape or on work-print. The production footage was merely volatile, stored electronic information. The edited versions of shows were really software-driven computer files that pulled up scenes instantaneously and in a sequence on command. The ability to move scenes around endlessly was the promise of these devices.

At first, the claim to fame of this editing equipment was its ability to show your producer or client ten different completed versions of the same scene or program during the same screening session. The broader implications, however, also became clear: *nothing visual was set in stone*. Again, the majors at Universal and Warners were willing to consider the technology, not just because they wanted to ape the flashy style of MTV, but because it promised serious production economies. Grady Jones, vice president of postproduction at Walt Disney Television, rationalized about the nonlinear technology: "We're always trying to bring costs down. We don't have much padding anywhere. The only thing that we can do is try to control the length of time it takes to complete the editorial and sound effects cutting."[21] By 1993, one of the newest and least expensive nonlinear systems – the Mac-base Avid – received the kind of acclaim that indicated its new and extensive popularity. Avid was awarded an Emmy for technical accomplishment by the Academy of Television Arts and Sciences. Nonlinear Avids were, after all, being utilized everywhere: in New York-based commercial postproduction houses, in music videos, in primetime program production. The reason? The trades boasted about its ability to provide limitless reworkings. "The bottom line is that this system gives me enormous creative freedom. I can edit unlimited versions and save them all. The Avid has *thirty-two levels of undo* and that completely frees up the editor to *experiment*."[22] Even mainstream television people in Los Angeles, then, saw and valued the dramatic experimental potential of the new systems. Forget orthodox editing wisdom, the whole point for editors now frequently is to demonstrate how far one can push the editing syntax on a project or scene, and how many stylistic variations one can showcase. After all, with nonlinear, there is no risk. Nothing is stylistically set in stone. Nonlinear encouraged, or fed, the televisual appetite for stylistic volatility and infinite formal permutations.

The two other crucial televisual technologies – the Rank-Cintel telecine and new high-speed film stocks – are best understood within the broader context of two emergent obsessions in 1980s television: the film-style look and primetime commercial advertising.

Playing with Limits: Self-Conscious Primetime Practice

Lighting for features, lighting for television, the light is identical.
George Spiro Dibie, president, American Society of Lighting Directors[23]

On television, you can't be Vittorio Storaro. But what you can do is like music.
Oliver Wood, director of photography, *Miami Vice*[24]

One of the central working concerns in television production in the 1980s concerned the formal potential of the television image, and especially the question of what can be done within the constraints and confines of the limited television frame. Consider the diametrically opposed views outlined above. Some DPs saw in primetime Bertolucciesque cinematic potential; others, melodic sensitivity. TV was inherently like film; TV and film were antithetical. Such contradictory answers – about what television can and cannot do, and what it can do best – abounded, but the question became more and more pervasive in the working and marketing discourse of the industry. Academic high theory, on the other hand, was working from two very different and problematic assumptions: first, that producers–practitioners could not be aware of the deep structure or ideological implications of their work, and second, that producers–practitioners used aesthetic criteria that were incomplete or naive. Evidence for this bias is found in the widespread penchant that high theory has for inventing its own frameworks, aesthetic categories, and critical terminology.

Even a limited examination of recent literature from the industry, however, shows that these assumptions and write-offs of the industry are misguided. Not only is television currently stylish, but it can be stylish in an extremely self-conscious and analytical way. While high theory was speculating on television as a distracting verbal–aural phenomenon, something very different was happening within the producing industry. There, in producer story sessions, in conversations between DPs and gaffers on sets, and among editors in postproduction suites, an awareness was growing of television as a style-driven phenomenon heavily dependent upon the visual.

Since the systematic approach to visual style is very much on the minds of some practitioners, and evident in the practice of many others, it is worth examining how media producers conceptualize this visuality.[25] Two areas of industrial debate – film-style programming and videographic programming – correspond roughly to a major generic programming division in television. That is, the division mirrors an institutional split between primetime dramatic and comedy series on the one hand – producer-dominant genres that use *film* pervasively – and the other extensive array of director–editor-dominant program forms and genres that are heavily dependent upon extensive *electronic* postproduction. Before turning to an indepth study of videographic embellishment in chapter 5 – an electronic practice that dominates both off-primetime and interstitial material in primetime – a further clarification of cinematic televisuality is needed.

The film look

The issue of image superiority in the film versus video debate and questions about the merits of film-style production methods for television have received much attention in the 1980s and 1990s. Landmark work in this area was produced by Harry Matthias and Richard Patterson, and other works have followed.[26] I am not interested so much in the technical aspects of this debate as in the ways that practitioners interpret and explain the film look in television. To understand this kind of discourse, however, it is important to survey some of the technical issues that have become central for those television production people that make heavy use of film technology. A discussion of more fully electronic variants of televisuality will follow.

New film stocks

Predictions to the contrary, film origination in television has not been replaced by video imaging. Far from it, film origination has thrived and prospered in two major areas of television: (1) primetime programming (episodic shows, movies for television, and miniseries), and (2) commercial advertising for television. By the late 1980s, Eastman Kodak boasted about an increase, rather than a decrease, in film consumption in television. With "80 percent of prime evening time schedules for the three major networks made of programs originated on film . . . this

[was] one of our best years ever in terms of original negative used for TV production."[27] Even as the aesthetic and formal possibilities offered by film increased, the popularity of shooting television on film stock also increased. Film-tape manufacturers argued that certain TV scripts in fact call for quality "production values that are more appropriate for film," especially any genre requiring "fantasy" rather than "immediacy."[28]

Not only did shows shot on film dominate television in the late 1980s, the quality of the film stocks allowed for a kind of visual sophistication impossible during the zero-degree telefilm years of the 1960s and 1970s.[29] In the early 1980s first Fuji, then Eastman, and then Agfa all introduced new lines of film negative stock with dramatic improvements in both sensitivity to light and graininess. Chemically engineered around new and less visible T-grain silver halide particles in the emulsion, the new stocks could be used in extremely low-light situations, could be easily "push processed" one or two stops, had more saturated color rendition, and provided a greater range of contrast and tonality within a single image than any of the earlier stocks. When primetime DPs boasted that "of course, not every television show is shot at ten footcandles," they were both showing off that they could shoot primetime at that unheard of level of darkness and also making stark contrasts to earlier, prestige production stocks.[30] Other primetime DPs tied the new speed and sensitivity to production mobility and freedom. "Technicolor was great but very slow – [it required] 900 footcandles at F/2 to get an exposure, and a camera and blimp so big and so heavy it was totally impractical to use it in real locations. Nowadays we can turn up with a little camera and some film and shoot anywhere."[31] High-speed film stocks, then, also meant improved logistical mobility and more flexible production scheduling.

By 1990, Eastman provided a vast menu of professional negative stocks for telefilm producers, from grainless, color-saturated daylight stocks to nighttime stocks that could be pushed to 1000 ASA or higher. These were overwhelming options for television cinematographers trained in the 1960s and early 1970s, a period when one or two stocks were typically available and when high-speed negative was defined as a mere 64 ASA. Film stocks, therefore, had a direct impact on the ability of producers and cinematographers to marshal variant visual looks. The reasons were not just photochemical, however. With the increased use of computer technology – for design, engineering, and quality control of new emulsions during the 1980s and 1990s – film stock companies like Agfa, Eastman, and Fuji were now able to make potentially limitless numbers of stocks. Technical representatives from Rochester, New York, now continuously circulate among DPs and operators in their quest to formulate new stocks and discover new needs. If a stock with a particular look is not currently available for a commercial need, Eastman will now consider customizing one. This is not the development-lazy and cash-rich Fortune 500 company of the 1970s. Extreme international competition by Fuji and Agfa have changed the way that both business and engineering is done in the industry. But the facility with engineering endless photographic looks is not just an economic consequence, it is also an outgrowth of interaction between computerized emulsion engineering and the publicized stylistic needs of a new generation of primetime and feature cinematographers.

By 1991, filter manufacturer Tiffen had created a host of designer-color filters: "grape, chocolate and tropic blue – all available in three densities, and all available in half-color and graduated to half-clear."[32] Not only did the new film stocks have a direct impact on camera mobility, low-light sensitivity, and photographic tonality, they also allowed *a new level of visual detail in front of the camera*. Televisual sets and locations got visually denser and more complicated after Ridley Scott's *Blade Runner* and Chiat Day's Macintosh television spots in 1984, even as the ability to render such images by new film stocks – and higher resolution color television monitors at home – improved. In addition, the whole optical film industry was revolutionized by the improved resolution and chrominance abilities of television. Far from the days when primetime DPs were locked into the polar world of filters limited mostly to color and density corrections between tungsten light and daylight, the new filters and stocks were designed to render both wild variations and subtle nuances of color within a single image. When industrial players like Tiffen baptize their new "grape" glass as a "designer filter," the association is complete. The designer televisuality of Michael Mann's *Miami Vice* is matched by the designer optics of Tiffen's lense-mounted glass. When television cameramen now ask for more coral rather than simply more orange, the televisual revolution symbolically betrays its technical as well as producerly roots.

Rank-Cintel

The desire to infuse video with a visual style more typical of film was enabled by one technical development as much as by any other. In 1977, the first Rank-Cintel "flying spot scanner" was installed in the United States. Several generations of design improvements followed, and other companies marketed their own versions of the chip-based film-to-video transfer machines. Higher quality images could be rendered on videotape, since the Rank-Cintel was able to reproduce and take advantage of film's unique look and "incredible dynamic range."[33] Practitioners boasted that the Rank meant that "film provides an ability to record as much as a 400 : 1 range of brightness which is the difference between the brightest and darkest elements in any scene. This allows a talented cinematographer to use light to paint very subtle details which establish mood and setting."[34] Consider the not so subtle conceptual transformation that takes place here, from a purely technical description of contrast to an aesthetic theorization. Mere television transfer technique is redefined in terms of painting and cinematography. This simple verbal deduction undercuts the way that television image technology has traditionally been defined: as amorphous, low-resolution, flat, and crudely contrasty.

Television's marked shift toward using film negative was based in part on the promise that Rank-type transfer units could reduce electronic noise in the picture, while at the same time maintaining details in the darkest shadow areas of the television image. Rank-Cintel now offers producers a menu of various and distinctive looks depending on the type of film format being transferred: original camera negative, interpositive, dupe negative, or low-contrast projection prints all demand different setups and parameters on the Rank-Cintel. Each variety of stock affords the producer a different visual look. The producers of *Love Boat*, for instance, continued to transfer their shows from Eastman color *projection* print stock 5384, even though projection prints give much less subtlety and tonality than do transfers from negative.[35] For the producers of that show, the contrasty, saturated look of the print film gave the show a look that its fantasy needed and that its audience was thought to expect.

Transfer technology in the 1980s, then, did not just make the image *better* visually, it actually multiplied the various visual looks of television into discrete codes that could be tied to specific program ends. For *Love Boat*, projection-print Rank transfers *signified* fantasy. For other shows, transfers from negatives gave the subtlety associated with painterly chiaroscuro. Transfer technology, then, helped codify the look of television even before the artisans of postproduction were fully involved in a given program.

Once these two technical conditions existed in television (origination in film and transfer via flying spot scanner), pressures to change production aesthetics itself would intensify. Achieving the so-called film-look in shooting style became a production cliché in the 1980s. Originally, film-style video simply referred to the shift from three-camera live in-studio TV to remote single-camera shooting that became popular in the late 1970s. Electronic news gathering (ENG) changed to electronic field production (EFP) for more discriminating producer–practitioners. But this early shift in the way that video shoots in the field were organized – to ENG and EFP – was mostly logistical, since it had as much to do with camera and recorder placement as anything else. It was not until the 1980s that a more intensive change began to occur within the visual frame itself.

Improvements in lighting developed alongside EFP, and a subsequent shift to charged-couple devices (CCD) in cameras (rather than conventional tubes) afforded producers greater subtlety in visualizing their images.[36] It is, obviously, unlikely that technical changes alone intensified the image in television. Formal changes in genre and narrative greatly impacted the rise of televisuality. Industry-wide though, there was an increased interest in transforming television images into complex, subtle, and malleable graphic fields. It is likely, given this shift, that formal and narrational changes provided the ideational resource required by an industrial transformation of this scale.[37] MTV and *Miami Vice* certainly were landmark programming developments that changed the way that television looked.[38] These changes have been discussed in detail elsewhere, so I will merely reiterate that distinctive programming forms and shows like these provided the conceptual framework – that is, the audience expectation and the cultural capital – needed to effect a shift in the televisual discourse. If film origination and Rank-Cintel transfers provided, in Brian Winston's terms, the "technical competence" needed for a change in the television industry, then the new highly stylized shows like *Miami Vice* and *Crime Stories* and MTV provided the ideational requirement for industry changes in the 1980s.[39] By the time feature-film director Barry Levinson was showcased on network television in 1993, the importance of televisual transfer technology was clear. Each episode of Levinson's *Homicide* opened with stitched-together footage shot on a primitive, spring-wound cast-off 16mm Bolex camera and feature-style images shot on 35mm. This mixing and matching of emulsion and format types, and the manipulation of colored filtered effects and black-and-white stock, were all possible because Rank-style transfers provided extreme options for stylistic control and reworking, even after the primetime footage was in the can.[40]

Notes

1   C. F. Jenkins, "Radio Photographs, Radio Movies, and Radio Vision," *Journal of Society of Motion Picture Engineers* (May 1923), 81.

2   R. R. Beal, "RCA Developments in Television," *Journal of Society of Motion Picture Engineers* (August 1937), 143.

3   A good and accessible source for this early technical literature is Jeffrey Friedman, ed., *Milestones in Motion Picture and Television Technology: The SMPTE 75th Anniversary Collection* (White Plains, NY: Society of Motion Pictures and Technical Engineers, 1991), especially 97–233. The word "television" was later added to the professional organization's prewar name, SMPE.

4   Raymond Williams, *Television, Technology and Cultural Form* (New York: Schocken Books, 1974).

5   William Boddy, *Fifties Television* (Urbana: University of Illinois Press, 1990), especially chapter 1.

6   *American Cinematographer* (June/July 1993).

7   Ben Gradus, *Directing the Television Commercial* (Los Angeles: Directors Guild of America, 1981), 4, 5, 34.

8   "Close-ups: Michael Oblowitz," *Millimeter* (February 1989), 196.

9   The most notable critique of intentionalist theory is the work of Monroe Beardsley and William K. Wimsatt, "The Intentionalist Fallacy," in *Problems in Aesthetics*, ed. Morris Weitz (New York: Macmillan, 1987), 347–60. The irony of raising this issue is that while the industry assumes it is the guarantor of the meanings of its productions, academic theory ignores even provisional discourses by the industry in favor of the spectator's supposed meanings and reception. My study focuses on the terrain between these two polarities. I aim to reconsider the theorization of the industry, but also to take that theorization as a mythology and framing practice that legitimates, naturalizes, and explains its operations.

10   From a review in *American Cinematographer* (January 1987), 94.

11   From *Millimeter* (April 1988), 148.

12   The most extensive explication of the classical Hollywood style is found in David Bordwell, Janet Staiger, and Kristin Thompson, *The Classical Hollywood Style: Film Style and the Mode of Production to 1960* (New York: Columbia University Press,

1985). This relatively neutral-looking style still pervades much of the serious dramatic programs in primetime television.

13 Katherine Stalter, "Working in the New Post Environment," *Film and Video* (April 1993), 100. A couple of universal shows – *Murder She Wrote*, and *Columbo* MOW's – are still cutting film. "They do that on *Murder She Wrote* because the producer who was associated with that show from the beginning was a film person ... we're still cutting film because that's how its been done. Other studio shows, like *Law and Order* is cut on the CMX-6000. Dick Wolf and the other producers like that system; it works well for them. But they are also conscious of trying to reduce expenses," claims Bruce Sandzimier, vice president of editorial, Universal Television.

14 Bruce Sandzimier, VP of editorial, Universal Television continues: "A case in point would be *South Beach*, a new one-camera dramatic series we just put into production. The executive producer ... also produces *Law and Order* and *Crime and Punishment* for Universal. His shows have been editing on the CMX-6000, which you get through the Post Group. So he – and we, the studio – developed a relationship with the Post Group." Stalter, *Film and Video* (April 1993), 100.

15 Arthur Wooster, second unit director, *Covington Cross*, as quoted in Josephine Ober, "Cover Story: Team Work on *Covington Cross*," *In Camera*, Eastman Kodak (Spring 1992–1993), 4.

16 From comments by Ray Peschke, quoted in *Film and Video* (November 1991), 74.

17 "Episodic Television has always had to narrow its scope because of lack of money, but digital technology can open up all kinds of possibilities," states Hal Harrison, vice president of postproduction, Viacom. Stalter, "Working in the New Post Environment," 100.

18 WRAL-TV5, Raleigh, North Carolina, advertisement, "Situations Wanted Technical," *Broadcasting* (November 30, 1992).

19 SMPTE time-code editing refers to an electronic timing and identification scheme standardized by the Society for Motion Picture and Television Engineers. This time-code system laid down a stream of digital audio blips onto an existing audio or address track on the recorded videotape stock. Once done, each video frame had now been assigned an identifying address that any standardized editing controller could find and cut on automatically. Frame accuracy in editing was but one of the advantages of this system.

20 Sony, direct-mail advertising insert, included as a promotional insert in *Video Systems* (June 1993), 16–17.

21 Stalter, "Working in the New Post Environment," 100.

22 Iain Blair, "*Needful Things*: Producer Jack Cummins, Director Fraser Heston and Cinematographer Tony Westman Bring Their production of the Stephen King Novel to the Pacific Northwest," *Film and Video* (April 1993), 99.

23 Quote from "Small Screen Shooters: Four Distinguished Cinematographers Discuss the Craft of Shooting Film for Episodic Television," *Millimeter* (April 1988), 143.

24 Ibid., 142.

25 I have organized my analysis of the status of the image in the industry around two poles that correspond to the current film versus video look debate. Whereas in chapter 5 I will address one major area implicating visual style as central in the practice of television (that is, the industrial discourse centered around electronic post and videographic effects), I will in this chapter limit my analysis to the discourse surrounding a

more conventional production arena (that is, the ways that producers and directors talk about shooting television programs for primetime and advertising).

26 See especially Harry Matthias and Richard Patterson, *Electronic Cinematography: Achieving Photographic Control Over the Video Image* (Belmont, Calif.: Wadsworth, 1985), and Anton Wilson, *Anton Wilson's Cinema Workshop* (Los Angeles: American Society of Cinematographers, 1983), 243–97. Other books that examine both technical and aesthetic issues in the film versus video image discourse include David Viera, *Lighting for Film and Electronic Cinematography* (Belmont, Calif.: Wadsworth, 1993), and the introductory text, Larry Ward, *Electronic Moviemaking* (Belmont, Calif.: Wadsworth, 1990).

27 Quote of Eastman Kodak executive from "Electronic Imagery," *American Cinematographer* (June 1987), 89. "Through most of the current season, some 80 percent of prime evening time schedules for the three major networks have been made up of programs originated on film. In addition, we are now seeing more fourth network and pay channel movies and other specialized programming originated on film. This might be one of our best years ever in terms of original negative used for TV production."

28 Ibid., 89.

29 I am, of course, comparing only the quality of *color* film stocks between the two periods. Some of the 35mm black-and-white negative stocks used in the 1950s, while much slower in light sensitivity than many modern color stocks, could achieve the kind of rich tonality impossible for any color stock to render, if lit properly. But this comparison is a bit like comparing apples and oranges.

30 Stuart Allen, "Lighting for Television: Faster Filmstocks Are Changing the Ways that Cinematographers Approach Their Work," *Film and Video* (June 1990), 47.

31 Alan Hume, DP, quoted by Ober, "Cover Story: Team Work on *Covington Cross*," 4.

32 Ad for Tiffen filters, *Film and Video* (November 1991), 71.

33 From Richard Schafer, "Choice of Transfers: Film to Tape," *American Cinematographer* (September 1986), 97.

34 Ibid., 97.

35 Shafer, "Choice of Transfers: Film to Tape," 99.

36 In practical terms CCDs replaced vacuum tubes in cameras with rectangular chips that were comprised of grids of light-sensitive microscopic materials. This field of points corresponded roughly to the pixels that make up the grid on a computer screen. The more points or pixels in a grid, the higher the visual resolution.

37 It is also likely that this transformation – this intensive reinvestment in primetime production – may be related to the slowly atrophying number of feature films that were being produced each year during the early 1980s. The availability of both ideational and labor surpluses in Hollywood during this period might partly explain the renewed focus on primetime production practice in the 1980s. The complexities of this relationship between feature film and primetime are, of course, beyond the scope of this book.

38 For an in-depth analysis of the ideology of MTV's visual style, see E. Ann Kaplan, *Rocking Around the Clock*; Todd Gitlin gives an excellent feel for the visual look and demeanor of *Miami Vice* in *Watching Television*.

39 Brian Winston, *Misunderstanding Media* (London: Routlege, Kegan Paul, 1986), discussed and applied to video in Roy Armes, *On Video* (New York: Routlege, Chapman & Hall), 206–8.

40 *Film and Video* (May 1993), 112–14.

Part IV
Text and Intertext

Introduction

Robert Stam

"Textual analysis" traces its long-term antecedents to biblical exegesis, to nine-teenth-century hermeneutics and philology, to the French pedagogical method of close reading (*explication de texte*), and to American New Criticism's "immanent" analysis. Its short-term antecedents include Lévi-Strauss's work on myth, Umberto Eco's study of the "open work," Roland Barthes's distinction between "work" and "text," and Althusser's "symptomatic readings." The "film text" transferred from literature to film the traditional respect accorded "the sacred word" (first religious and then secular, literary), in a delegation of "aura" aimed at winning prestige for what was still seen as a fledgling medium. Film texts, the trope implies, are worthy of the same serious attention normally given to litera-ture. The notion of the film "text" is also a logical corrolary of the move from filmmaker to "auteur;" what would "authors" write, if not texts?

The concept of "text," etymologically "tissue" or "weave," emphasizes film not as an imitation of reality but rather as an artifact, a construct. In "From Work to Text," Barthes distinguished between the "work" defined as the phenomenal object (for example, the book one holds in one's hand), i.e. a completed product conveying a pre-existent meaning, as opposed to the "text," defined as a meth-odological field of energy, a production absorbing writer and reader together. "We now know," Barthes writes, "that the text is not a line of words releasing a single 'theological' meaning (the 'message' of an Author-God) but a multidimen-sional space in which a variety of writings, none of them original, blend and clash" (Barthes, 1977: 146).

In *Language and Cinema* Metz (1974), who had been Barthes's student, devel-oped the notion of the "textual system," i.e. the undergirding organization of a film text considered as a singular totality. For Metz, every film has a particular structure or network of meaning around which it coheres – even if the system chosen, as in the case of *Un Chien andalou*, is one of deliberate incoherence. The structure is a configuration arising from the choices made from the diverse codes available to the filmmaker. The textual system does not inhere in the text; it is constructed by the analyst. The concept of the textual system helps Metz define the task of the film analyst as opposed to that of the theorist. While "cinematic language" is the object of cine-semiological *theory*, the text is the object of filmo-linguistic *analysis*. (In practice, the distinction is not always so clear.)

Metz was not concerned, in *Language and Cinema*, with providing a "how-to" book for textual analysis, but rather with determining its theoretical status, its "place." The role of textual analysis, for Metz, is to explore the work of cinematic codes (camera movement, off-screen sound) and extra-cinematic codes (ideological binarisms of nature/culture, male/female) either across a number of texts or within a single text. All films, for Metz, are mixed sites; they all deploy cinematic and non-cinematic codes. No film is constructed uniquely out of cinematic codes; films always speak of something, even if, as in the case of many avant-garde films, they speak only about the apparatus itself, or about the film experience, or about our conventional expectations concerning that experience.

In *Language and Cinema* Metz tended to oscillate between a more neutral notion of text as any finite, organized discourse intended to realize communication, on the one hand, and the more programmatic avant-garde deconstructionist sense of text on the other. Stated differently, there exists a clear tension between a static, taxonomic, structuralist–formalist view of textual systems, and a more dynamic poststructuralist Barthesian–Kristevan view of text as "productivity," "displacement," and "écriture." It is this latter view of the text as a "non-finalized" perpetual displacement that constitutes the more dynamic pole in *Language and Cinema*. A film's text is not the "list" of its operative codes, then, but rather the labor of constant restructuration by which the film "writes" its text, modifies and combines its codes, playing some codes off against others, and thus constitutes its system. The textual system, then, is the instance which displaces the codes so that they come to inflect and substitute one another. What matters is the passage from code to code, the way in which signification is relayed from lighting, for example, to camera movement, from dialogue to music, or the way that music plays against dialogue, or lighting against music, or music against camera movement. Filmic écriture works with and against the various codes in order to constitute itself as text. This formulation has the advantage of "socializing," as it were, the artistic process of creation. By foregrounding écriture as the re-elaboration of codes, Metz envisions film as a signifying practice not dependent on romantically connoted entities such as "inspiration" and "genius" but rather as a reworking of socially available discourses.

The publication of *Language and Cinema* was followed by an international deluge of textual analyses of films in journals such as *Screen* and *Framework* in England, *Iris* and *Vertigo* and *Ça* in France, *Camera Obscura*, *Wide Angle* and *Cinema Journal* in the United States, *Contracampo* in Spain, and *Cadernos de*

Critica in Brazil. Such analyses investigated the formal configurations making up textual systems, usually isolating a small number of codes and then tracing their interweavings across the film. Among the more ambitious textual analyses were Kari Hanet's analysis of *Shock Corridor*, Stephen Heath's of *Touch of Evil*, Pierre Baudry's of *Intolerance*, Thierry Kuntzel's of *The Most Dangerous Game*, and *Cahier*'s of *Young Mr Lincoln*.

What then, was new in the semiotic approach to textual analysis? First, the new method demonstrated a heightened sensitivity to the filmic signifier and to specifically cinematic formal elements as opposed to an emphasis on character and plot. In this sense, it rendered film analysis less naive, less caught up in the make-believe world of the story of the film. Second, the analyses tended to be methodologically self-aware; they were at once about their subject – the film in question – and about their own methodology. Each analysis thus became an exemplum of a possible approach. These analyses also presupposed a radically different emotional stance toward films, one characterized by a kind of Brechtian distantiation whereby the analyst was supposed to both love and not love the film. Third, rather than take in the film at a single screening, the analyst scrutinized the film shot-by-shot. (The existence of VCRs has to a certain extent democratized the practice of close analysis of film.) Analysts such as Marie-Claire Ropars and Michel Marie developed elaborate schemas for notation, registering such codes as angle, camera movement, movement in the shot, off-screen sound and so forth.

Many analyses focused on synecdochic fragments of films. Thus Marie-Claire Ropars devoted 40 pages to the first two minutes of Eisenstein's *October*, while Thierry Kuntzel dedicated long analyses to the ouverture sequences of films such as *M*, *King Kong* and *The Most Dangerous Game*, seen as condensed matrices of meaning. The dedication of many pages of critical writing to a brief segment also made a point *vis-à-vis* high art elitists, as if the analysts were trying to demonstrate that the same medium despised by others was actually the scene of veritable cornucopias of meaning. The analysis also varied widely in scale. The limits of the text might be defined by a single image (for example, the Ronald Levaco and Fred Glass analysis of the MGM logo), by the segment (Bellour on *The Birds*), by an entire film (Heath on *Touch of Evil*, Bellour on *North by Northwest*), by the entire oeuvre of a filmmaker as examples of a "plurifilmic textual system" (Rene Gardies on Glauber Rocha), or even by a vast corpus of films (Andre Gaudreault and Tom Gunning on silent cinema 1900–8).

Textual analyses rejected the traditional evaluative terms of film criticism in favor of a new vocabulary drawn from structural linguistics, narratology, psychoanalysis, Prague School aesthetics, and literary deconstruction. Although most of the analyses generated by this wave belonged, broadly speaking, to the general semiotic current, not all of them were rigorously based on Metzian categories. Marie-Claire Ropars-Wuilleumier's extremely intricate analyses of such films as *India Song* and *October* synthesized semiotic insights with a more personal project, partially inspired by Derridean grammatology, concerning montage as the key to filmic "writing." Many textual analyses were influenced by literary textual analyses, for example Julia Lesage's extrapolation of Barthes's "five codes" to Renoir's *Rules of the Game*. Some textual analyses were inspired by Proppian narratological methods (Peter Wollen on *North by Northwest*), or by psychoanalysis (Bellour on *North by Northwest*), or by other theoretical currents such as Bakhtinian "translinguistics." Kristin Thompson's *Ivan the Terrible: A Neo-formalist Analysis* (1981), for its part, offers a programmatic *tour de force*, performed both with and against the grain of semiotics, and meant to demonstrate an alternative neo-formalist method of textual analysis.

In the 1980s textual analysis came under attack from a number of directions. Poststructuralist currents, first of all, destabilized textual meaning, shaking early semiology's scientist faith that analysis might definitively "capture" a film's meaning by exhaustively delineating all its codes. The shift in interest from text to spectator, meanwhile, also devalorized textual analysis per se in favor of the study of spectatorial positioning and the impact of texts on audiences. Some proponents of "cultural studies," meanwhile, expressed hostility to textual analysis. In their Introduction to *Cultural Studies* Cary Nelson, Paula Treichler, and Lawrence Grossberg suggest that "textual analysis in literary studies carries a history of convictions that texts are properly understood as wholly self-determined and independent objects" (Grossberg et. al., 1992)

But while cultural studies advocates like these see textual analysis in literary studies as *under*politicized, David Bordwell in *Making Meaning* seems to see textual analysis in film as *over*politicized. In "post-1968 symptomatic criticism," Bordwell argues,

> the theme of fate is replaced by the duality power/subjection. Love is replaced by desire, or law/desire. Instead of the individual there is subject/object or phallus/ lack. Instead of art there is signifying practice. Instead of society there is nature/ culture or class struggle. (Bordwell, 1989: 109)

Bordwell laments, in quasi-elegiac terms, the shift from what he himself calls "the individualist perspective," to "an analytical, almost anthropological detachment that sees sexuality, politics, and signification" as the key areas of meaning. Film interpreters, for Bordwell, root out symbolic meanings by bringing into play "semantic fields" assumed in advance rather than emerging inductively from the analysis itself. While claiming to do theory, interpreters merely "apply" it in a "piecemeal, ad hoc, and expansionist manner" (ibid.: 250). Bordwell critiques the predominance in film criticism of two tendencies linked to textual analysis: thematic explanation and symptomatic reading (usually politically symptomatic reading). Both tendencies, for Bordwell, share an interpretative logic and rhetoric, when in fact "the great days of interpretation-centered criticism are over." The epidemic of interpretation, for Bordwell, "attests to the powerful role of literature departments in transmitting interpretative values and skills" (ibid.: 17). Bordwell here deploys two formalist schemata: (1) the demand for media specificity, or better academic/disciplinary specificity (film studies should not borrow from literature departments); and (2) the critique of the "routinization" of symptomatic reading. (The role of art for the formalists, we recall, was to challenge automatized perceptions.) It was better, Bordwell concluded, *not* to "read" films at all, if reading means the ascription of symptomatic meanings. (Ironically, Bordwell's conclusion was the result of his own symptomatic reading of a vast corpus of textual analyses.)

In their *L'Analyse des films* (1989), Jacques Aumont and Michel Marie outline four possible critiques of textual analysis: (1) that its relevance is limited to narrative cinema; (2) that it "murders to dissect," favoring dissection for the sake of dissection; (3) that it reductively "mummifies" film by reducing it to its systemic skeleton; and (4) that it elides film's context, its conditions or production and reception. Of these four critiques, the first misfires (since textual analysis is applicable to any object), while the second seems rooted in hostility to analysis per se, especially when performed in relation to an "unworthy" medium. But the last two charges have some force, and in fact are interrelated. When textual analyses are reductive, it is precisely *because* they are ahistorical and fail to take production and reception into account. And the charge of "ahistoricism" is not answered, as Aumont and Marie answer it, with a suggestion that analysts "also" do history. The roots of the "decontextualization" of some textual analysis lie in the ahistoricism of two of the source movements of semiotics: Saussurean linguistics – particularly its tendency to cut off language from history – and Russian formalism, with its preference for a purely immanent "intrinsic" analysis. For a truly "sociological poetics," in contrast, all artistic languages, given their inherently dialogical quality and the fact that they are addressed to socially situated interlocutors, are "always already" social and historical.

Film analysis is an open medium. It is a method rather than an ideology; it is a genre of film writing open to diverse influences (from Barthes to Jameson to Deleuze), to diverse grids (psychoanalysis, Marxism, feminism), to diverse "schemata" (reflexivity, excess, carnival), and to diverse principles of pertinence, both cinematic (camera movement, editing), and extra-cinematic (representation of women, blacks, gays and lesbians). The announced "death" of textual analysis, and of interpretation, therefore, is decidedly premature. Any perusal of the pages of *Screen, Camera Obscura*, or *Cinema Journal* reveals scores of close analyses of films, and major publication series like the BFI Classics or Rutgers Film Analysis Series will guarantee the role of film analysis well into the future. We now even have CD-ROMs not only on film analysis in general (the work of Henry Jenkins and Ben Singer) but also analyses of specific film such as Hitchcock's *Rebecca* and Mario Peixoto's *Limite*. While we might lament the abuses of some textual analyses, we cannot impose "law-and-order" on the unruly anarchy of interpetation. We all bring our interpretative standpoints to film, even when we try to hide them. Films are open to our desires and projections, even when these desires are sublimated into an apparatus of positivist objectivity. It is also hard to imagine that we will ever get completely "beyond" interpretation. While it is right to critique the totalizing ambitions or the epigonic predictability of textual analysis, and to suggest that there is much to do *besides* analysis, that does not mean that analysis (and its inevitable fellow traveler interpretation) is not worth doing. That textual analysis can be flat, stale, and derivative does not discredit the enterprise *in toto*.

Like "text," "genre" too constitutes a very ancient approach to artistic texts. Etymologically drawn from the Latin *genus* ("kind"), "genre" criticism began as the classification of the diverse kinds of literary texts. Aristotle's *Poetics*, for example, proposed to treat "poetry in its various kinds, noting the essential quality of each." Aristotle's definition of tragedy touched on diverse aspects of genre: the kinds of events portrayed (an action of a certain magnitude); the social rank of the characters (nobles, better than ourselves); the ethical qualities of the characters (their "tragic flaws"); narrative structure (dramatic reversals); and audience effects (the purging of pity and fear through "catharsis").

Questions of generic classification have also interested later philosophers. The eighteenth-century neo-classicists, for example, turned genre into a rigid set of rules, such as the "three unities" of tragedy: time, place, and action. For the romantics, in contrast, such ossified rules were tyrannical straitjackets imposed on the creative flow of individual feelings. Within film, this romantic rebellion against the constrictions of genre is recapitulated in the existentialism-tinged work of the French New Wave, where the phenomenal "existence" of the film precedes the "essence" implied by generic categories.

In film discourse, genre is the theory that never really went away. From the beginning, long before the pioneering essays on the Western by Robert Warshow and André Bazin, there was always a consciousness, however rudimentary, of the various "types" of films. Some were inherited from literature: comedy, tragedy, melodrama. Others were more specifically cinematic: "views," "travelogues," "animated cartoon." The word "genre" has been traditionally used in at least two senses: (1) in an inclusive sense which sees all films as participating in genre; and (2) in a more restricted sense of the Hollywood "genre film," i.e. the less prestigious and lower-budget productions or "B" films. Genre in this sense is a corollary of the industrialized mode of production of Hollywood (and its imitators), an instrument of simultaneous standardization and differentiation. Genre in this sense has institutional force and density; it implies a generic divison of labor, whereby studios specialized in specific genres (MGM and the musical, for example), while within each studio, each genre had not only its sound-stages but also its daylaborers: scriptwriters, directors, costume designers.

While some genres represent established categories of studio production (Westerns, musicals) recognized by both producers and consumers, others were *ex post facto* designations constructed by critics. No producer in the 1940s set out to make a "film noir." The term itself was coined retrospectively by French film critics on the analogy of the *serie noire*. By the time of *Body Heat* (1981), however, after the genre had been popularly consecrated, Lawrence Kasdan could consciously strive for a "noir effect" in his remake of *Double Indemnity*.

A number of perennial doubts plague genre theory. Are genres really "out there" in the world, or are they merely the constructions of analysts? Is there a finite taxonomy of genres or are they in principle infinite? Are genres timeless Platonic essences or ephemeral, time-bound entities? Should genre analysis be descriptive or proscriptive? Genre taxonomies in film have been notoriously imprecise and heterotopic, having some of the qualities of Foucault's Chinese encyclopedia. While some genres are based on story content (the "war film"), others are borrowed from literature (comedy, melodrama) or from other media (the musical). Some are performer-based (the Astaire–Rogers films), or budget-based ("blockbusters"), or based on artistic status (the "art film"), or based on a somewhat nebulous "mood" or style (film noir), or based on sexual ("Queer cinema") or racial affiliation ("Black cinema"). Some, like "documentary" and "satire," might better be seen as "transgenres." Subject matter is perhaps the weakest criterion for generic grouping because it fails to take into account *how* the subject is treated. The subject of nuclear war, for example, has been generically rendered as satire (*Dr Strangelove*), docu-fiction (*War Game*), porn (*Café Flesh*), melodrama (*Testament*, *The Day After*), and satiric compilation documentary (*Café Flesh*). The Hollywood-on-Hollywood film can be a melodrama (*A Star is Born*), a comedy (*Show People*), a musical (*Singin' in the Rain*), a verité documentary (*Lion's Love*), a parody (*Silent Movie*), and so on.

Genre analysis provides a commutational backdrop of comparison which allows us to discern aesthetic lineage and affiliation. We need only compare *New York, New York* to *On the Town* to appreciate both the continuities and the breaks between it and the traditional musical. Genre analysis at its best orchestrates a wide variety of concerns, not only with story and types of characters but also with modes of representation, rhetorical and stylistic protocols, and the contractual relationship with the audience.

At the same time, genre analysis tends to have certain pitfalls. First, there is the question of extension. Some generic labels, such as comedy, are too broad to be useful, whereas others, say "biopics about Sigmund Freud" or "disaster films concerning earthquakes," are too narrow. Second, there is the danger of *normativism*, of having a preconceived *a priori* idea of what a genre film *should* do, rather than seeing genre merely as a trampoline for creativity and innovation. Thus *Flashdance* is dismissed as not a "real" musical. Third, genre is sometimes imagined to be *monolithic*, as if films belonged only to *one* genre. The "law of genre" presumably forbids miscegenation *between* genres, yet as Bordwell, Staiger and Thompson demonstrate, even classical Hollywood films hybridized diverse generic strands, if only for commercial reasons (Bordwell et. al., 1985: 16–17). Godard, to take a more flagrant example, was notoriously fond of oxymoronic genre collages: *Breathless* as an "existentialist gangster film," *A Woman is a Woman* as a "cinema verité musical," and *Numero Deux* as "feminist pornography." Fourth, genre criticism is often plagued by *biologism*, the assumption that genres have a life cycle, moving from birth to maturity and parodic decline. But in fact we find parody at the very beginning of art forms (for example, the relation between Richardson's *Pamela* and Fielding's *Shamela* in the novel, or between Griffith and Keaton in film). Genres, furthermore, are permanently available for resuscitation and reconfiguration, as in the perennial flowerings of carnivalesque conventions going at least as far back as the Middle Ages. Much genre criticism suffers from *Eurocentrism*: the tendency to restrict discussion of genre to Hollywood and its European relatives. But why should studies of the musical not include the Brazilian chanchada, the Bombay musical, the Mexican *cabaretera* film, the Argentinian *tango* film, and the Egyptian musicals of Leila Mourad?

Genres can also be *submerged*, as when a film appears on the surface to belong to one genre yet on a deeper level belongs to another, as when analysts argue that *Taxi Driver* is "really" a Western. Here genre criticism becomes an exploratory cognitive instrument: what do we learn if we regard *Taxi Driver* as a Western? What happens if we regard *Spartacus* as an allegory about the Civil Rights struggle? What features of these texts become visible through such a strategy? Politically repressive circumstances can lead to the submerging of genre, as when political allegories like dos Santos's *A Very Crazy Asylum* hide their serious intentions behind a facade of farce. Genres can also be kidnapped by the director (the dubbing of *What's Up Tiger Lily?*) or audience (*The Rocky Horror Picture Show*). At times, analysts commit "genre mistakes," mistakenly transferring standards appropriate to one genre to another, as when critics found *Dr Strangelove* "cynical" because it had no admirable characters, when in fact "lack of admirable characters" is a constitutive feature of satire. Woody Allen's films, especially those in which he appears as an actor/character, are often mistaken for self-indicting autobiography, the critical equivalent of equating Shakespeare with Iago. Genre mistakes also occur when "carnivalesque" films are criticized for not offering "positive images," when in fact carnival's "grotesque realism" entails alternative, more debauched protocols of representation. There is also the danger of *acinematic* analysis, of not taking into account the filmic signifier. Indeed, genre study needs more work on the matching between genre and the specifically cinematic codes: the role of lighting in film noir, of color in musicals, camera movement in the Western.

Particularly unfortunate is the tendency to see films as belonging to a single genre; everything in the film that does not fit the generic label is cut off, when in fact most films interweave multiple genres. Preston Sturges's *Sullivan's Travels* provides a hyperbolic instance of this process. The genre references begin with the title, with its Swiftian evocations of (1) picaresque and (2) satire, where a voyage becomes the trampoline for a critique of diverse milieux, professions, and institutions. But there are other strains in this meta-cinematic generic weave: (3) the Hollywood film about Hollywood; (4) Sennett-style slapstick; (5) the screwball comedy; (6) the depression documentary à la Pare Lorentz; (7) chain-gang films like *I am a Fugitive from a Chain Gang*; (8) the all-black musical like *Hallelujah*; (9) the social consciousness film like The *Grapes of Wrath* (here *O Brother Where Art Thou?*); and (10) the animated cartoon. In many national traditions generic "impurity" is the norm. Bombay (Bollywood) films follow a general "formula" – songs and dances, strong emotions – but easily mix melodrama with comedy in what is called a "masala" (the mixing of spices) approach.

In the late 1960s and 1970s film analysts like Jim Kitses, Ed Buscombe, and Will Wright brought genre theory to a new level of sophistication. Buscombe (1970) called for more attention to the iconographic elements of films, while Kitses in *Horizons West* (1969) set out a table of binary oppositions (Individual/Community; Nature/Culture) which structured the Western. Will Wright (1975) took a Proppian approach in *Sixguns and Society*, arguing that the oppositions set up in earlier Westerns actually evolve into very different configurations in later Westerns. Steve Neale argues in chapter 10 of this volume that genres are "systems of orientations, expectations and conventions that circulate between industry, text, and subject" (Neale, 1980: 19). And in chapter 11 Rick Altman calls for a complementary approach which would be both "semantic," having to do with narrative content, and "syntactic," having to do with the structures into which narrative elements are inserted, with the caveat that many films can innovate by mixing the syntactics of one genre and the semantics of another (see Altman, 1984).

Genre is also rich in social implication. The entire course of Western literature, according to Erich Auerbach, has worked to erode the elitist "separation of styles" implicit in the Greek tragic model, through a democratizing impulse (rooted in the Judaic notion of "all souls equal before God") by which the dignity of a noble style was gradually accorded to ever "lower" classes of people. And indeed genres come equipped with clear class connotations. Within literary history the romance, rooted in aristocratic notions of courtliness and chivalry, is challenged by the novel, rooted in the common-sense world of bourgeois facticity. Art constantly revitalizes itself by drawing on previously marginalized forms and genres through what Shklovski calls the "law of the canonization of the junior branch." Some films explicitly connect class and genre. King Vidor's *Show People*, for example, pits homegrown vaudevillian slapstick against Frenchified costume drama, portraying comedy as the genre of the unpretentious people, and costume drama as the genre of the "let-them-eat-cake" elite.

Because it deals with "types," genre theory always runs the triple risk of static taxonomism and essentialism. Genre might therefore be more usefully regarded as a specific aspect of the broader and more open question of "intertextuality." Like genre, intertextuality too has a venerable pedigree, implicit already in Montaigne's observation that "more books are written about other books than about any other subject," and in T. S. Eliot's notion of "tradition and the individual talent." But the term itself was first introduced in the 1960s as Kristeva's translation of the Bakhtinian notion of "dialogism," defined as "the necessary relation of any utterance to other utterances." (An "utterance," for Bakhtin, can refer to any "complex of signs," from a spoken phrase to a poem, or song, or play, or film.) For Bakhtin, every utterance is immersed in the memory of prior utterances and emitted in anticipation of the response of an interlocutor. The concept of dialogism suggests that every text forms an intersection of textual surfaces. All texts are tissues of anonymous formulae embedded in the language, variations on those formulae, conscious and unconscious quotations, conflations and inversions of other texts. In the broadest sense, intertextual *dialogism* refers to the infinite and open-ended possibilities generated by all the discursive practices of a culture, the entire matrix of communicative utterances within which the artistic text is situated, and which reach the text not only through recognizable influences but also through a subtle process of dissemination. The intertext of the work of art, then, may be taken to include not just other art works in the same or comparable form, but also all the "series" within which the singular text is situated. Or, to put it more crudely, any text that has slept with another text has also slept with all the texts that the other text has slept with.

"Intertextuality" has a number of advantages over "genre." First, intertextuality relates the singular text principally to other systems of representation rather than to an amorphous "context." Second, intertextuality avoids the circular, tautological tendency of generic taxonomies: a film is a Western because it has the characteristics of a Western. Intertextuality is less interested in essentialist definitions than in the active inter-animation of texts. Third, intertextuality implies a more dynamic relation to the tradition; whereas a film simply "belongs" to a genre rather like an individual "belongs" to a family, or a plant "belongs" to a genus, intertextuality is more proactive: the artist actively orchestrates pre-existing texts and discourses rather than simply following a formula. Fourth, intertextuality allows for dialogic relations with other arts and media, both popular and erudite. Fifth, intertextuality is less "Hollywoodcentric" in that it avoids the association with "Hollywood genre film."

Bakhtin's notion of the "chronotope" (literally "time–space") is also useful for our discussion of filmic genre. The "chronotope" refers to the constellation of distinctive temporal and spatial features within a genre defined as a "relatively stable type of utterance." In "Forms of Time and Chronotope in the Novel" Bakhtin (1986) suggests that time and space in the novel are intrinsically connected since the chronotope "materializes time in space." Although Bakhtin does not refer to the cinema, his category seems ideally suited to it as a medium where "spatial and temporal indicators are fused into one carefully thought-out concrete whole." Bakhtin's description of the novel as the place where time "thickens, takes on flesh, becomes artistically visible" and where "space becomes charged and responsive to the movements of time, plot and history" seems in some ways even more appropriate to film than to literature, for whereas literature plays itself out within a virtual, lexical space, the cinematic chronotope is quite literal, played out concretely across a screen with specific dimensions and unfolding in literal time (usually 24 frames per second), quite apart from the fictive time–space specific films might construct. A number of analysts, notably Vivian Sobchack, Arlindo Castro, Kobena Mercer, Michael Montgomery, Robert Stam, Paul

Willemen, and Paula Massood have seen the notion of the chronotope as having the potential to historicize the discussion of filmic genre. (See, for example, Sobchack's "Lounge Time: Post-War Crises and the Chronotope of Film Noir," in Browne, 1997)

Building on Bakhtin and Kristeva, Gérard Genette in *Palimpsestes* (1982) proposed the more inclusive term "transtextuality" to refer to "all that which puts one text in relation, whether manifest or secret, with other texts" and posited five types of transtextual relations: intertextuality, paratextuality, meta-textuality, architextuality, and hypertextuality. Although Genette restricts him-self to literary examples, one might easily imagine filmic instances of the same procedures (see Stam, 1989, for an extrapolation of Genette's categories for the cinema). Strategies of transtextual allusion are central to postmodern popular culture. As Gilbert Adair put it in a title, "the postmodernist always rings twice." Thus commercials for Diet Coke feature long-deceased Hollywood actors, updating and commercializing the Kuleshov experiments in montage. The music video for Madonna's "Material Girl" encodes *Gentlemen Prefer Blondes*, even though some of Madonna's contemporary fans might not be aware of the fact.

Finally, contemporary genre theory needs to take new audio-visual and computer technologies into account, not only because the new media will inevit-ably generate new forms of textuality and therefore new forms of intertextuality, but also because a number of theorists have posited a kind of "match" between intertextuality theory itself and new media and computer technologies. First, electronic or virtual textuality is necessarily different from print or celluloid textuality. "Hypermedia" combines sound, graphics, print, and video, allowing for extraordinary new combinations. For one thing, some films now come accompanied by parallel digital texts. The CD-ROM associated with Isaac Julien's documentary on Fanon, *Black Skin White Mask*, for example, provides a digital version of the intertext of the film, with source materials on Fanon, Algeria, psychoanalysis and so forth. The film's paratext, for example the parts of the interviews not included in the film proper, can now be "seen" in their entirety on the CD-ROM. Second, a language of links, networks, and interweav-ing is shared by Barthesian semiotics, Bakhtinian dialogics, Derridean decon-struction, and hypertext and multimedia discourse. Designers of computer software, Landow argues, recognize themselves in the split-writing of Derrida, and when Derrida spoke of a new kind of writing, he did not realize he was speaking of cybernetic écriture. The interactive nature of computers turns their users into producer–bricoleurs. Conceivably, cybernetically aware hypertexters could take a well-known novel like *Madame Bovary*, turn it from print to a hypertext version, then add music and graphics to create a kind of hybrid adaptation, a quasi-film. As Gregory Ulmer points out, electronic culture allows diverse cultural formats – oral, written, and visual – to coexist interactively, facilitating the technological realization of Walter Benjamin's dream of a book composed entirely of quotations (Ulmer, in Truman, *Literary Online* 139–64).

Replacing single-entry linear texts with fluid texts with multiple points of entry, as well as hypertext's openness to multiple temporalities and perspectives, also has positive implications for a polycentric, polychronic view of film, one that substitutes an image of infinite passageways and pathways for the exclusivist logic of the "final word."

10
Questions of Genre

Steve Neale

This article will discuss some of the issues, concepts, and concerns arising from work on film genres published over the last decade or so. It seeks to highlight a number of questions and problems that may pinpoint some possible directions for future research. I will be particularly concerned with the constitution of generic corpuses – the extent to which they are constituted by public expectations as well as by films, and the role of theoretical terms, on the one hand, and industrial and institutional terms, on the other, in the study of genres. The concept of verisimilitude is central to an understanding of genre, as is the question of the social and cultural functions that genres perform. These, too, will be discussed. Throughout I shall stress the changing, and hence historical, nature, not just of individual genres, but of generic regimes as well.

I shall be referring to several books and articles (thus, to some extent, this piece will serve as an extended review). But at a number of key points I shall be taking my cue, explicitly or otherwise, from an article by Alan Williams entitled "Is a Radical Genre Criticism Possible?" (an article that is itself a review of Thomas Schatz's *Hollywood Genres* and, to some extent, of my own book, *Genre*).[1]

Despite, or perhaps because of, the fact that it raises so many fundamental questions, Williams's article has not been discussed as much as it deserves. In saying this, however, I should note that, insofar as I shall be concentrating here on American cinema and American genres, I shall be ignoring (or at least setting to one side) one of Williams's most important points – that "'genre' is not exclusively or even primarily a Hollywood phenomenon" and that "we need to get out of the United States."[2] I concentrate on American cinema partly because, as Williams himself notes elsewhere in his article, there is still an enormous amount of research to be done on what is still the most powerful national cinema in the world, and partly because most of the work published on genre to date has tended overwhelmingly to concern itself with Hollywood. In order to engage with this work, it is necessary to engage with its object. However, I should like to note too that a number of the more general, conceptual points I wish to make are equally applicable to film genres in India or Japan or Italy or Britain.

Expectation and Verisimilitude

There are several general, conceptual points to make at the outset. The first is that genres are not simply bodies of work or groups of films, however classified, labeled, and defined. Genres do not consist only of films: they consist also, and equally, of specific systems of expectation and hypothesis that spectators bring with them to the cinema and that interact with films themselves during the course of the viewing process. These systems provide spectators with a means of recognition and understanding. They help render films, and the elements within them, intelligible and therefore explicable. They offer a way of working out the significance of what is happening on the screen: why particular events and actions are taking place, why the characters are dressed the way they are, why they look, speak, and behave the way they do, and so on. If, for instance, a character in a film bursts into song for no reason (or no otherwise explicable reason), the spectator is likely to hypothesize that the film is a musical, a particular kind of film in which otherwise unmotivated singing is likely to occur. These systems also offer grounds for further anticipation. If a film is a musical, more singing is likely to occur, and the plot is likely to follow certain directions rather than others.

Inasmuch as this is the case, these systems of expectation and hypothesis involve a knowledge of – indeed they partly embody – various regimes of verisimilitude – various systems of plausibility, motivation, justification, and belief. *Verisimilitude* means "probable" or "likely."[3] It entails notions of propriety, of what is appropriate and therefore probable (or probable and therefore appropriate).

Regimes of verisimilitude vary from genre to genre. (Bursting into song is appropriate, therefore probable – therefore intelligible, therefore believable – in a musical. Less so in a thriller or a war film.) As such, these regimes entail rules, norms, and laws. (Singing in a musical is not just a probability; it is a necessity. It is not just likely to occur; it is bound to.) As Tzvetan Todorov has insisted, there are two broad types of verisimilitude applicable to representations: generic verisimilitude and a broader social or cultural verisimilitude. Neither equates in any direct sense to "reality" or "truth":

> If we study the discussions bequeathed us by the past, we realize that a work is said to have verisimilitude in relation to two chief kinds of norms. The first is what we call *rules of the genre*: for a work to be said to have verisimilitude, it must conform to these rules. In certain periods, a comedy is judged "probable" only if, in the last act, the characters are discovered to be near relations. A sentimental novel will be probable if its outcome consists in the marriage of hero and heroine, if virtue is rewarded and vice punished. Verisimilitude, taken in this sense, designates the work's relation to literary discourse: more exactly, to certain of the latter's subdivisions, which form a genre.

But there exists another verisimilitude, which has been taken even more frequently for a relation with reality. Aristotle, however, has already perceived that the verisimilar is not a relation between discourse and its referent (the relation of truth), but between discourse and what readers believe is true. The relation is here established between the work and a scattered discourse that in part belongs to each of the individuals of a society but of which none may claim ownership; in other words, to *public opinion*. The latter is of course not "reality" but merely a further discourse, independent of the work.[4]

There are several points worth stressing here. The first is the extent to which, as the example of singing in the musical serves to illustrate, generic regimes of verisimilitude can ignore, sidestep, or transgress these broad social and cultural regimes.

The second is the extent to which this "transgression" of cultural verisimilitude is characteristic of Hollywood genres. This has implications for conventional notions of realism. There is, of course, always a balance in any individual genre between purely generic and broadly cultural regimes of verisimilitude. Certain genres appeal more directly and consistently to cultural verisimilitude. Gangster films, war films, and police procedural thrillers, certainly, often mark that appeal by drawing on and quoting "authentic" (and authenticating) discourses, artifacts, and texts: maps, newspaper headlines, memoirs, archival documents, and so on. But other genres, such as science fiction, Gothic horror, or slapstick comedy, make much less appeal to this kind of authenticity, and this is certainly one of the reasons why they tend to be despised, or at least misunderstood, by critics in the "quality" press. For these critics, operating under an ideology of realism, adherence to cultural verisimilitude is a necessary condition of "serious" film, television, or literature. As Todorov goes on to argue, realism as an ideology can partly be defined by its refusal to recognize the reality of its own generic status or its own adherence to a type of generic verisimilitude.

A third point to be made is that recent uses of the concept of verisimilitude in writing on genre tend to blur the distinction between generic and cultural verisimilitude, vitiating the usefulness of the term. Both Christine Gledhill and Kathryn Kane, for instance, in writing about melodrama and the war film respectively, tend to use "verisimilitude" simply as a synonym for "realism" or "authenticity."[5] This is a pity because, as both Gledhill and Kane implicitly demonstrate, melodrama and the war film are genres that often seek to blur the distinction between the cultural and the generic, and they are often particularly marked by the tensions between the different regimes.

The fourth point is that, at least in the case of Hollywood, generic regimes of verisimilitude are almost as "public," as widely known, as "public opinion" itself. It is not simply in films or in genres that the boundaries between the cultural and the generic are blurred: the two regimes merge also in public discourse, generic knowledge becoming a form of cultural knowledge, a component of "public opinion."

Fifth, and finally, it is often the generically verisimilitudinous ingredients of a film, those elements that are often least compatible with regimes of cultural verisimilitude – singing and dancing in the musical, the appearance of the monster in the horror film – that constitute its pleasure and thus attract audiences to the film in the first place. They too, therefore, tend to be "public," known, at least to some extent, in advance.

These last two remarks lead on to the next set of points, which concern the role and importance of specific institutional discourses, especially those of the press and the film industry itself, in the formation of generic expectations, in the production and circulation of generic descriptions and terms, and, therefore, in the constitution of any generic corpus.

Genre and Institutional Discourse

As John Ellis has pointed out, central to the practices of the film industry is the construction of a "narrative image" for each individual film: "An idea of the film is widely circulated and promoted, an idea which can be called the 'narrative image' of the film, the cinema's anticipatory reply to the question, 'What is the film like?' "[6] The discourses of film-industry publicity and marketing play a key role in the construction of such narrative images; but important too are other institutionalized public discourses, especially those of the press and television, and the "unofficial," "word of mouth" discourses of everyday life.

Genre is, of course, an important ingredient in any film's narrative image. The indication of relevant generic characteristics is therefore one of the most important functions that advertisements, stills, reviews, and posters perform. Reviews nearly always contain terms indicative of a film's generic status, while posters usually offer verbal generic (and hyperbolic) description – "The Greatest War Picture Ever Made" – as anchorage for the generic iconography in pictorial form.

These various verbal and pictorial descriptions form what Gregory Lukow and Steven Ricci have called the cinema's "intertextual relay."[7] This relay performs an additional, generic function: not only does it define and circulate narrative images for individual films, beginning the immediate narrative process of expectation and anticipation; it also helps to define and circulate, in combination with the films themselves, what one might call "generic images," providing sets of labels, terms, and expectations that will come to characterize the genre as a whole.

This is a key point. It is one of the reasons why I agree with Lukow and Ricci on the need to take account of all the component texts in the industry's intertextual relay when it comes to studying not only films but genre and genres. And it is one of the reasons why I would disagree with Rick Altman, in *The American Film Musical*, on the limited significance he assigns to the role of industrial and journalistic discourses in establishing a generic corpus.[8] (One of the many merits of Altman's book, however, is that he devotes the best part of a chapter to this issue. Most books and articles on genre fail to discuss it at all.)

For Altman, the role of industrial and journalistic terms is crucial in establishing the presence of generic consistencies but of limited use in defining them:

> The fact that a genre has previously been posited, defined, and delimited by Hollywood is taken only as *prima facie* evidence that generic levels of meaning are operative within or across a group of texts roughly designated by the Hollywood term and its usage. The industrial/journalistic term thus founds a hypothesis about the presence of meaningful activity, but does not necessarily contribute a definition or delimitation of the genre in question.[9]

The identification of an industrial/journalistic term, then, is for Altman merely the first step in a multistage process. Having established a preliminary corpus in this way, the role of the critic is next to subject the corpus to analysis, to locate a method for defining and describing the structures, functions, and systems specific to a large number of the films within it. Then the critic, using this method as a basis, reconstitutes and redefines the corpus:

> Texts which correspond to a particular understanding of the genre, that is, which provide ample material for a given method of analysis, will be retained within the generic corpus. Those which are not illuminated by the method developed in step three will simply be excluded from the final corpus. In terms of the musical, this would mean admitting that there are some films which include a significant amount of diegetic music, and yet which we will refuse to identify as musicals in the strong sense which the final corpus implies.[10]

Having thus established a final corpus, the critic is finally in a position to produce a history of the genre and to analyze "the way in which the genre is molded by, functions within, and in turn informs the society of which it is a part."[11]

Before explaining my disagreement with this reasoning, it is important to recognize, along with Altman, that it is not possible to write about genres without being selective, and that many of the deficiencies of a good deal of writing on genre stem from defining and selecting on the basis of pre-established and unquestioned canons of films. As Alan Williams points out, this is one of the central deficiencies of Schatz's book, in which coverage of any given genre

> depends not on historical or theoretical even-handedness but on tacitly agreed-upon landmarks. Thus the chapter on the musical covers mainly Warner Brothers/Busby Berkeley, Fred Astaire at RKO, and the Freed Unit at MGM. So where is Lubitsch and the operetta? (Maybe the latter is not a "Musical," but *Hollywood Genres* does not explain.) Al Jolson and the crucially important melodramatic musicals of the early sound years? Who decided that these points alone would suffice?[12]

In contrast, Altman's book is impressively wide in its range of references and refreshingly free from established canons of taste and categorization, including not only Jolson, operetta, and Lubitsch, but also the Elvis Presley films of the fifties and sixties and films like *Grease* (Randal Kleiser, 1978) and *Flashdance* (Adrian Lyne, 1983). It is important to say, too, that I agree with Altman that journalistic and industrial labels rarely, on their own, provide a conceptual basis for the analysis of genres or for the location of generic patterns, structures, and systems, just as I agree that such analysis is vitally important.

Where I disagree, however, is on Altman's assertion that the importance of industrial/journalistic terms is restricted to the first step of generic analysis. I disagree with this because I do not believe the aim of generic analysis is the redefinition of a corpus of films. Such an aim is in the end no different, in effect if not in intention, from the highly selective categorizations of Schatz or from the worst pigeonholing inheritances of neo-classical literary theory. We can easily end up identifying the purpose of generic analysis with the rather fruitless attempt to decide which films fit, and therefore properly belong to, which genres. We can also end up constructing or perpetuating canons of films, privileging some and demoting or excluding others. (Thus even Altman, despite his broad range and the power of his method, finds himself excluding films like *Dumbo* [Ben Sharpsteen, 1941] and *Bambi* [David Hand, 1942] and nearly excluding *The Wizard of Oz* [Victor Fleming, 1939].)

Such an aim is, therefore, inherently reductive. More than that, it is in danger of curtailing the very cultural and historical analysis upon which Altman rightly insists as an additional theoretical aim. The danger lies not only in the devaluation of industrial/journalistic discourses, but in the separation of genre analysis from a number of the features that define its public circulation. These features include the fact that genres exist always *in excess* of a corpus of works; the fact that genres comprise expectations and audience knowledge as well as films; and the fact that these expectations and the knowledge they entail are public in status. As Todorov has argued (while himself tending to equate genres solely with works):

> One can always find a property common to two texts, and therefore put them together in one class. But is there any point in calling the result of such a union a "genre"? I think that it would be in accord with the current usage of the word and at the same time provide a convenient and operant notion if we agreed to call "genres" only those classes of texts that have been perceived as such in the course of history. The accounts of this perception are found most often in the discourse on genres (the meta-discursive discourse) and, in a sporadic fashion, in the texts themselves.[13]

As far as the cinema is concerned (Todorov here is writing about literature – and High Literature at that), this meta-discursive discourse is to be found in its intertextual relay. Clearly, generic expectations and knowledge do not emanate solely from the film industry and its ancillary institutions; and, clearly, individual spectators may have their own expectations, classifications, labels, and terms. But these individualized, idiosyncratic classifications play little part, if any, in the public formation and circulation of generes and generic images. In the public sphere, the institutional discourses are of central importance. Testimony to the existence of genres, and evidence of their properties, is to be found primarily there.

A distinction needs to be made, then, between those studies of genres conceived as institutionalized classes of texts and systems of expectation and those studies that use critically or theoretically constructed terms as the basis for discussing classes of films. (Studies of film noir are obvious examples of the latter.) A distinction also needs to be made between institutionally recognized subgenres, cycles, and categories (operetta and the singing Western) and theoretical or scholarly classifications (the fairy tale musical, the show musical, and the folk musical). This is not to argue that theoretical studies and classifications are somehow illegitimate. (Far from it. These examples all illustrate how productive they can be.) It is, however, to insist on the pertinence of Todorov's distinction for an understanding of what it is that is being studied.

Institutional Discourses and Genre History

Not only do industrial and journalistic labels and terms constitute crucial evidence for an understanding of both the industry's and the audience's generic conceptions in the present; they also offer virtually the only available evidence for a historical study of the array of genres in circulation, or of the ways in which individual films have been generically perceived at any point in time. This is important for an understanding of the ways in which both the array and the perceptions have changed.

Let me give some examples. Both "the Western" and *The Great Train Robbery* (Edwin S. Porter, 1903) are firmly established in genre studies, the latter as an early, highly influential example of the former. However, in his *Dictionary of Slang and Unconventional English*, Eric Partridge dates the first colloquial use of the term *Western* in anything other than an adjectival sense to around 1910. The first use of the term cited in the *Oxford English Dictionary* with reference to a film dates from 1912, occurring in a review of *The Fight at the Mill* (1912) in a July 1912 issue of the trade magazine *The Moving Picture World*. This was nine years after *The Great Train Robbery* was released.

Now it may be argued, of course, that this is merely quibbling. While the specific term *Western* may not have been available to audiences in 1903, Westerns themselves, in the form of dime novels, Wild West shows, paintings, illustrations, short stories, and the like (as well as one or two films), had been around for some time.[14] Thus audiences of *The Great Train Robbery*, well accustomed to these forms, would have drawn on the paradigms they provided in understanding and locating the film. Charles Musser, however, has convincingly argued that this was not the case, that the paradigms used both by the industry and its audiences were different and that it was the confluence of paradigms provided by melodrama, the chase film, the railway genre, and the crime film, rather than the Western, that ensured the film's contemporary success:

> Kenneth MacGowan attributed this success...to the fact that the film was "the first important Western," William Everson and George Fenin find it important because it is "the blueprint for all Westerns." These, however, are retrospective readings. One reason for *The Great Train Robbery*'s popularity was its ability to incorporate so many trends, genres and strategies fundamental to the institution of cinema at that time. The film includes elements of both re-enactment of contemporary news events (the train hold-up was modeled after recently reported crimes) and refers to a well-known stage melodrama by its title. Perhaps most importantly, *The Great Train Robbery* was part of a violent crime genre which had been imported from England a few months earlier. Porter was consciously working (and cinema patrons viewing) within a framework established by Sheffield Photo's *Daring Daylight Burglary*, British Gaumont/Walter Haggar's *Desperate Poaching Affair [Affray]* and R. W. Paul's *Trailed by Bloodhounds....* [Thus,] when initially released, *The Great Train Robbery* was not primarily perceived in the context of the Western. Its success did not encourage other Westerns but other films of crime – Lubin's *Bold Bank Robbery* [Jack Frawley, 1904], Paley and Steiner's [*Avenging a Crime; Or,*] *Burned at the Stake* [1904], and Porter's own *Capture of the Yegg Bank Robbers* [1904]....It was only when the Western genre emerged as a vital force in the nickelodeon era that *The Great Train Robbery* was interpreted from this new perspective.[15]

Musser's argument here serves to indicate, in addition to the change in generic status of *The Great Train Robbery*, the extent to which different periods in the history of the American cinema have been marked by different generic systems, different "generic regimes." It is an important theoretical point that genres "do not exist by themselves; they are named and placed within hierarchies or systems of genres, and each is defined by reference to the system and its members."[16] Furthermore, "Each era has its own system of genres."[17] Company catalogues are a particularly useful resource in establishing the generic regimes of the earliest years of the cinema. Their terminology and their groupings indicate the considerable differences between these regimes and the regimes of the studio era. Thus, instead of the Westerns, horror films, and war films of later years, the Kleine Optical Company's catalogue for 1905 lists films in the following groupings:

1   Story
    (a) historical
    (b) dramatic
    (c) narrative
2   Comic
3   Mysterious
4   Scenic
5   Personalities[18]

Meanwhile, Biograph's "Advance Partial List" of films for sale in 1902 lists its "subject" under the following titles and headings: Comedy Views, Sports and Pastime Views, Military Views, Railroad Views, Scenic Views, Views of Notable Personages, Miscellaneous Views, Trick Pictures, Marine Views, Children's Pictures, Fire and Patrol Views, Pan-American Exposition Views, Vaudeville Views, and Parade Pictures.[19] (The number of "documentary" or "actuality" categories here is, of course, indicative of the extent to which these genres far outweighed fiction in the period prior to 1903–4.)

In demonstrating the degree to which genre categories and generic regimes have changed, these examples illustrate the historical character of all genres. Genres are inherently temporal: hence, their inherent mutability on the one hand and their inherent historicity on the other. In disagreeing with Altman on the significance of institutional discourses, I now wish to focus attention on a further aspect of that temporality.

Genre as Process

It may at first sight seem as though repetition and sameness are the primary hallmarks of genres, as though, therefore, genres are above all inherently static. But as Hans Robert Jauss and Ralph Cohen (and I myself) have argued, genres are, nevertheless, best understood as *processes*.[20] These processes may, for sure, be dominated by repetition, but they are also marked fundamentally by difference, variation, and change.

The process-like nature of genres manifests itself as an interaction between three levels: the level of expectation, the level of the generic corpus, and the level of the "rules" or "norms" that govern both. Each new genre film constitutes an addition to an existing generic corpus and involves a selection from the repertoire of generic elements available at any one point in time. Some elements are included; others are excluded. Indeed, some are mutually exclusive: at most points in its history, the horror film has had to characterize its monster *either* supernaturally – as in *Dracula* (Tod Browning, 1930) – *or* psychologically – as in *Psycho* (Alfred Hitchcock, 1960). In addition, each new genre film tends to extend this repertoire, either by adding a new element or by transgressing one of the old ones. Thus, for instance, *Halloween* (John Carpenter, 1979) transgressed the division between psychological and supernatural monsters, giving its monster the attributes of both. In this way the elements and conventions of a genre are always *in* play rather than being simply *re*played;[21] and any generic corpus is always being expanded.

Memories of the films within a corpus constitute one of the bases of generic expectation. So, too, does the stock of generic images produced by advertisements, posters, and the like. As both corpus and image expand and change with the appearance of new films, new advertising campaigns, and new reviews, so also what Jauss has termed the "horizon of expectation" appropriate to each genre expands and changes as well:

> The relationship between the individual text and the series of texts formative of a genre presents itself as a process of the continual founding and altering of horizons. The new text evokes for the reader (or listener) the horizon of expectations and "rules of the game" familiar to him from earlier texts, which as such can then be varied, extended, corrected, but also transformed, crossed out, or simply reproduced.[22]

This is one reason why it is so difficult to list exhaustively the characteristic components of individual genres, or to define them in anything other than the most banal or tautological terms: a Western is a film set on the American western frontier; a war film is a film that represents the waging of war; a detective film is a film about the investigation of criminals and crime; and so on. More elaborate definitions always seem to throw up exceptions. Altman provides an example. He cites Jean Mitry's definition of the Western as a "film whose action, situated in the American West, is consistent with the atmosphere, the values and the conditions of existence in the Far West between 1840 and 1900."[23] He then goes on to cite an exception, the "Pennsylvania western":

> To most observers it seems quite clear that films like *High, Wide and Handsome* (Rouben Mamoulian, 1937), *Drums along the Mohawk* (John Ford, 1939), and *Unconquered* (Cecil B. DeMille, 1947) have definite affinities with the western. Employing familiar characters set in relationships similar to their counterparts west of the Mississippi, these films construct plots and develop a frontier structure clearly derived from decades of western novels and films. But they do it in Pennsylvania and in the wrong century.[24]

Exclusive definitions, lists of *exclusive* characteristics, are particularly hard to produce. At what point do Westerns become musicals like *Oklahoma!* (Fred Zinnemann, 1955) or *Paint Your Wagon* (Joshua Logan, 1969) or *Seven Brides for Seven Brothers* (Stanley Donen, 1954)? At what point do singing Westerns become musicals? At what point do comedies with songs (like *A Night at the Opera* [Sam Wood, 1935]) become musical comedies? And so on.

These examples all, of course, do more than indicate the process-like nature of individual genres. They also indicate the extent to which individual genres not only form part of a generic regime, but also themselves change, develop, and vary by borrowing from, and overlapping with, one another. Hybrids are by no means the rarity in Hollywood many books and articles on genre in the cinema would have us believe. This is one reason why, as Marc Vernet has pointed out, "a guide to film screenings will often offer to the spectator rubrics like: western, detective film, horror film, and comedy; but also: dramatic comedy, psychological drama, or even erotic detective film."[25] Indeed, in Hollywood's classical era, as Bordwell, Staiger, and Thompson have shown, nearly all its films were hybrids insofar as they always tended to combine one type of generic plot, a romance plot, with others.[26] Moreover, it is at least arguable that many of the most apparently "pure" and stable genres, both inside and outside the cinema, initially evolved by combining elements from previously discrete and separate genres either within or across specific generic regimes. Ernest Mandel, for example, has argued that the detective genre emerged in this way by combining three such generically disparate elements: the "reverse story," developed by Godwin (*Caleb Williams*, 1794); the divination deduction technique, which originated in Persia and was introduced into modern literature by Voltaire (*Zadig*); and the *coup de théâtre*, borrowed from melodrama.[27] Similarly, Richard Traubner has shown, in painstaking detail, how operetta emerged by combining the features of *opera buffa*, German *Singspiel*, and British ballad opera and how it subsequently evolved by replacing some of these features with elements of burlesque and revue; then, in America at least, these were displaced in turn, until the genre finally emerged as the "musical play" with shows (and films) like *Show Boat* (filmed in 1936 by James Whale and in 1951 by George Sidney), *Oklahoma!*, *Brigadoon* (filmed in 1954 by Vincente Minnelli), *Carousel* (filmed in 1956 by Henry King), *West Side Story* (filmed in 1961 by Robert Wise), and *My Fair Lady* (filmed in 1964 by George Cukor).[28]

Hence the importance of *historicizing* generic definitions and the parameters both of any single generic corpus and of any specific generic regime. For it is not that more elaborate definitions are impossible to provide, just that they are always historically relative and therefore historically specific. It is not that the process-like nature of genres renders generalizations invalid. Genre films, genres, and generic regimes are always marked by boundaries and by frameworks, which always have limits. Thus even hybrids are recognized as hybrids – combinations of specific and distinct generic components – not as genres in their own right. (This is why I would prefer not to say, as Jim Collins has recently done, that a genre text always "remakes" norms, but rather that a genre text always either reworks them, extends them, or transforms them altogether.)[29] The point, though, is that if these limits are historically specific, they can be determined only empirically, not theoretically.

Genre History: Three Approaches

There currently seem to exist three major ways in which genre history has been conceived. The first is what Jauss has called "the evolutionary schema of growth, flowering, and decay."[30] This schema is open to several objections: it is teleological; it is (for all its organic metaphors) highly mechanistic; and it treats genres in isolation from any generic regime.

Similar objections apply to a second model of evolutionary development, used by Thomas Schatz, in which genres progress toward self-conscious formalism. Here is Williams's description of Schatz's approach:

As genres change over time, and their audiences become more and more self-conscious, genres progress from transparency to opacity, "from straightforward storytelling to self-conscious formalism" (p. 38). Not all genres complete this cycle unimpeded. Gangster Films, for example, were disrupted by the threat of censorship as were, at various points, War Films.

To this Williams poses a theoretical objection:

> Note that Schatz locates this shift to opacity *within individual genres*, such that a "new" genre in the 1980s would have to go through a "classical" stage before evolving into self-conscious formalism. It is not the filmmaking system or the social context that has changed, but the genres that have evolved. (In my opinion, this is clearly wrong.)

And here is an empirical objection: "One can find self-conscious Westerns, such as Fairbanks' *Wild and Woolly* [John Emerson, 1917], as early as the late teens. In fact, the entire mid-to-late silent cinema seems remarkably 'formalistic,' which is possibly one reason it is wholly absent from Schatz's book."[31] (A similar point has been made at greater length, and to equally devastating effect, in an article by Tag Gallagher.)[32]

The third historical model is the one provided by the Russian formalists.[33] It has the virtue of embedding the history of individual genres within the history not just of generic formations but of wider cultural formations as well. It is perhaps best known for Tynyanov's concept of "the dominant" (with its correlative concept of genre history as the displacement of one dominant genre by another),[34] and by Shklovsky's idea that such displacements occur according to a principle known as "the canonization of the junior branch": "When the 'canonized' art forms reach an impasse, the way is paved for the infiltration of the elements of non-canonized art, which by this time have managed to evolve new artistic devices."[35] Quoting from Juri Streidter's introduction to a German anthology of Russian formalist texts, Jauss describes the formalists' conception as a whole:

> The Formalist conception of genre as a historical system of relations participates in the attempt to replace the classical notion of literary tradition – as a steady, unilinear, cumulative course – with the dynamic principle of literary *evolution*, by which they do not mean an analogy to organic growth or to Darwinian selection. For here "evolution" is supposed to characterize the phenomenon of literary "succession" "not in the sense of a continuous 'development,' but rather in the sense of a 'struggle' and 'break' with immediate predecessors through a contemporary recourse to something older." In the historical evolution of literature thus understood, literary genres can be grasped in the periodic alternation of the dominating role as well as in a sequence of rivalries.

In addition,

From a diachronic perspective the historical alternation of the dominating genre manifests itself in the three steps of canonization, automation, and reshuffling. Successful genres... gradually lose their effective power through continual reproduction; they are forced to the periphery by new genres often arising from a "vulgar" stratum if they cannot be reanimated through a restructuring (be it through the playing up of previously suppressed themes or methods, or through the taking up of materials or the taking-over of functions from other genres).[36]

There is clearly a great deal here that is both attractive and useful. As a theory or model, it takes account of the historicity not only of genres but of specific generic regimes; it takes account of their process-like nature; and, in its insistence on the importance of an interplay between canonized and non-canonized forms of representation and between canonized and non-canonized genres, it takes account both of the transience of generic hierarchies as well as the role of hybridization in the formation and dissolution of individual genres.

In sketching the application of this model to the American cinema, one could argue, for instance, that the cinema itself arose in and as the conjunction of a variety of art forms – canonized and otherwise: from photography, through pictorial entertainments and spectacles like the diorama, the zoëtrope, and the magic lantern show, to magic itself and to the vaudeville routine. Its earliest generic regime, in America as elsewhere, was dominated by the genres associated with these forms: the moving snapshot or "view," re-enacted and reconstructed news, trick films, and slapstick and gag-based comedy. Subsequent to this, there is a shift to a predominance of fiction, in particular melodrama (whether in its thrilling, mysterious, domestic, or spectacular guise) on the one hand and comedy on the other. With accompanying subdivisions and with the addition of genres like the musical, this "dominant" came to be stabilized in the era of oligopoly and studio control. Later, in a period of crisis and readjustment, "adult" drama and "epic" values – marked by, and derived principally from, the epic itself and spreading from there to the Western, the war film, the musical, and even, with films like *The Great Race* (Blake Edwards, 1965) and *It's a Mad, Mad, Mad, Mad World* (Stanley Kramer, 1963), to slapstick comedy – gained a position of dominance, though by now they were beginning to jockey for position with "exploitation" genres and the "juvenilization" of Hollywood's output. Finally, more recently, the process of juvenilization has continued, with the emergence of the "teenpic" and the predominance of science fiction and horror. Meanwhile, in exemplary illustration of Shklovsky's thesis, some of these genres, in combination with serial-derived individual films like *Raiders of the Lost Ark* (Steven Spielberg, 1981) and *Romancing the Stone* (Robert Zemickis, 1984), have been promoted from the "junior branches" of Hollywood's output to achieve hegemony within the realms of the family blockbuster.

What is particularly valuable about the formalists' model is that it neither prescribes the conditions for generic outmodedness nor specifies any single mechanism by which non-canonized forms, devices, or genres might find a place within generic regimes or assume a position of dominance within them. It allows for a variety of factors and reasons. This is especially important in the case of the cinema, where, for example, the initial predominance of actuality genres is as much a consequence of technological factors as it is of their popularity or "canonization" elsewhere in the contemporary culture and where, on the other hand, the promotion and predominance of "juvenile" genres is as much a consequence of market research, the targeting of audiences, and, in some cases, of new special-effects techniques as it is of any new-found aesthetic vitality.[37]

What is particularly striking about this historical sketch, meanwhile, is the extent to which many genres either originated in forms and institutions of entertainment other than the cinema or were (and are) circulated additionally by them. Melodrama, for example, originated on the stage. It fed from there, in a process of increasing and mutual interaction, first into written fiction and then into the cinema. All the while, in all three fields, it generated subdivisions like the crime story, the mystery, the adventure story, the romance, and domestic drama. Comedy came from vaudeville, the circus, burlesque, and the newspaper cartoon strip as well as from the "legitimate" stage and, later, from radio and television. The musical came from Broadway (and its songs from Tin Pan Alley). Cheap hardback and paperback books, meanwhile, together with both "slick" and "pulp" magazines, comic books, comic strips, and mass-produced fiction of all kinds, helped in some cases to originate, and in all cases to circulate, genres like the Western, the detective story and the thriller, horror, science fiction, war, and romance. This generic fiction often appeared in series or serial format with precise generic titles and names: *Adventure Library* (1897), *The Detective Library* (1917), *Western Story Magazine* (1919), *Thrill Book* (1919), *Love Story Magazine* (1921), *Love Story Library* (1926), *War Stories* (1922), *Gangster Stories*, *The Magazine of Fantasy and Science-Fiction* (1942), *Bestseller Mysteries* (1942), *The Vault of Horror* (1950), and so on.[38]

At this point it is worth signaling the need for a great deal more research both on cross-media generic formation and circulation and, as a corollary, on the particular contributions of individual institutions and forms.[39] More research is needed, too, on the aesthetically specific transformations and adaptations that each genre undergoes in each institution and form.[40]

Aesthetics and Ideology

Finally, I should like to move on to discuss a set of questions about the aesthetic characteristics of mass-produced genres, their institutional functions within the cinema, and their putative social, cultural, and ideological significance.

The first point to make here is, again, a historical one. It concerns the provenance, and status, of the term "genre" itself, its applicability to the cinema, and its role in characterizing not only the cinema but mass-produced art and entertainment in general. It is a point that, once more, has usefully been focused by Williams:

> Perhaps the biggest problem with genre theory or genre criticism in the field of cinema is the word *genre*. Borrowed, as a critical tool, from literary studies... the applicability of "genre" as a concept in film studies raises some fairly tough questions. Sample genres are held to be Westerns, Science Fiction Films, more recently Disaster Films, and so on. What do these loose groupings of works – that seem to come and go, for the most part, in ten- and twenty-year cycles – have to do with familiar literary genres such as tragedy, comedy, romance, or (to mix up the pot a bit) the epistolary novel or the prose poem?

He continues,

> For the phrase "genre films," referring to a general category, we can frequently, though not always, substitute "film narrative." Perhaps *that* is the real genre. Certainly there is much more difference between *Prelude: Dog Star Man* [Stan Brakhage, 1961] and *Star Wars* than there is between the latter and *Body Heat* [Lawrence Kasdan, 1981]. It's mainly a question of terminology, of course, but I wonder if we ought to consider the principal genres as being narrative film, experimental/avant-garde film, and documentary. Surely these are the categories in film studies that have among themselves the sorts of significant differences that one can find between, say, epic and lyric poetry. If we reserve this level for the term *genre*, then film genres will by definition have the kind of staying power seen in literary genres. What we presently call film genres would then be *sub-genres*.[41]

In many ways, it seems to me, Williams is right about this. However, apart from the fact that, as he says, it is "probably too late" to change things, there is an important qualification to be made.

As Ralph Cohen has pointed out, the term *genre* is a nineteenth-century term.[42] Thus, although the concept is clearly much older, the term itself emerges precisely at the time that popular, mass-produced generic fiction is making its first appearance (its genres, incidentally, just as susceptible to Williams's strictures). At the same time also there began to emerge a distinct shift in the value placed on generic literature by High Culture artists and critics. As Terry Threadgold has explained, prior to the advent of romanticism "it was *literature* that was generic":

> The rest, the "popular culture" of political pamphlets, ballads, romances, chapbooks, was not only *not* literature, but also *not* generic; it escaped the law of genre, suffering a kind of rhetorical exclusion by inclusion in the classical distinction between high, middle, and low styles. It was seen as a kind of anarchic, free area, unconstrained by the rules of polite society and decorum, by *genre* in fact.[43]

With the emergence of new technologies, new capital, mass production, and new means of distribution (notably the railway), with the formation of a relatively large literate (or semi-literate) population (with the formation, therefore, of a market), and with the commodification of all forms of leisure and entertainment, the equation is reversed. Now it is "popular culture," mass culture, that is generic, ruled as it is by market pressures to differentiate to a limited degree in order to cater to various sectors of consumers and to repeat commercially successful patterns, ingredients, and formulas. By contrast, "true literature" is marked by self-expression, creative autonomy, and originality, and hence by a freedom from all constrictions and constraints, including those of genre.

It is at this point absolutely crucial to disentangle a number of assumptions and conflations, for this is where a great deal of "genre theory" (indeed "popular cultural theory" in general) tends to go astray. First, of course, it has to be recognized that no artist, in whatever sphere of aesthetic production, at whatever period in history, in whatever form of society, has ever been free either of aesthetic conventions and rules or of specific institutional constraints (whether he or she has reacted against them or not). Second, as Geoffrey Nowell-Smith has recently re-emphasized, *all* cultural and artistic production in Western societies is now, and has been for some time, subject to capitalist conditions of production, distribution, and exchange, hence to commodification.[44] (This means, among other things, that High Cultural art, whether it still draws upon "traditional," precapitalist genres like lyric poetry or eschews both "traditional" and modern, popular genres is still itself "generic" insofar as it is thereby still engaged in catering for a sector of the market and still involved in a form of product differentiation.)[45] The third point, therefore, is that mass-produced, popular genres have to be indeed understood within an economic context, as conditioned by specific economic imperatives and by specific economic contradictions – in particular, of course, those that operate within specific institutions and industries. That is why it is important to stress the financial advantages to the film industry of an aesthetic regime based on regulated difference, contained variety, pre-sold expectations, and the reuse of resources in labor and materials. It is also why it is important to stress the peculiar nature of films as *aesthetic* commodities demanding at least a degree of novelty and difference from one to another, and why it is necessary to explore the analogies and the distinctions between cycles and genres in the cinema, on the one hand, and models and lines in the field of non-artistic commodity production, on the other.

Failure to recognize these points results in approaches to genre that are inadequate and simplistic. It is worth specifying two such approaches here. The first is what Altman has called the "ritual" approach, exemplified again by Thomas Schatz (along with Will Wright and John Cawelti, a pioneer of this particular approach).[46] Here is Williams's summary of this approach: "The repetitive nature of genre production and consumption produces active but indirect audience participation; successful genres are 'stories the audience has isolated through its collective response.' Hence genre filmmaking can be examined as 'a form of collective cultural expression'" (pp. 12–13).[47] Quite apart from the doubtful assumption that consumer decision-making can be considered a form of "cultural expression" and quite apart from the tendency of such an approach to conflate the multiplicity of reasons for consumer "choices" and a multiplicity of readings of these "choices," the ritual theory of genres is open to question on other grounds. Principal among these is that it ignores the role of institutional determinations and decisions, bypassing the industry and the sphere of production in an equation between market availability, consumer choice, consumer preference, and broader social and cultural values and beliefs. This is an equation open to challenge on its own grounds. During the studio era, for instance, Westerns were regularly produced in large numbers, despite the fact that, as Garth Jowett has shown, such market research as was conducted at this time indicated that the genre was popular only with young adolescent boys and sectors of America's rural population and that it was *actively disliked* more than it was liked by the viewing population as a whole.[48]

Second, objections can also be made to what Altman calls the "ideological" approach to genre, which recognizes the capitalist nature of the film industry and the status of its films as commodities but which treats genres simply as vehicles for "capitalist" (or the "dominant") ideology.[49] This approach is open to the charges of reductivism, economism, and cultural pessimism.[50] It tends to presume, in the final analysis, that representations reflect their social and economic conditions of existence, that institutions and social formations necessarily secure their own reproduction, and, in Colin MacCabe's words, that "the meanings of texts . . . are always finally anchored in a class struggle which is not to be understood in cultural terms."[51] As both MacCabe and Geoffrey Nowell-Smith have insisted, each in his different way, "Stressing the capitalist character of modern cultural production is in itself neither optimistic nor pessimistic."[52] The ideological significance of any text – or any genre – is always to be sought in a context-specific analysis. It cannot simply be deduced from the nature of the institution responsible for its production and circulation, nor can it ever be known in advance.

Both these theories, for all their differences, suffer from the fact that they pay little attention to aesthetics – for them, form is always, and only, a wrapping for the cultural or ideological content in which they are almost exclusively interested. Insofar as they do discuss form, they tend to stress the repetitive, stereotypical aspects of genres, setting aside the differences within and between them in order to provide themselves with a stable corpus and in order to substantiate their underlying premise: that the reasons for the popularity and longevity of genres are relatively uniform, as are, aside from a few Lévi-Straussian antinomies, the genres themselves, the meanings they convey, and the culture (or ideology) that underpins them. While it may be that repetition is important, it is also true that, as we have seen, variation and difference are crucial. Equally, while it may be that Hollywood genres are in most instances best considered as subgenres of narrative film, and while these subgenres may not be marked by the kinds of apparent discursive peculiarities that tend to differentiate the narrative film from documentary or the structuralist avant-garde, there is still a great deal of scope for the investigation of specific discursive characteristics. Aside from my own attempt, in *Genre*, to explore the ways in which different genres exploit in different ways the features and characteristics of the narrative film (an attempt somewhat marred by an over-schematic approach, by a lack of attention to hybridization, and, above all, by a lack of attention to history), the basis for an approach can perhaps be found in the Russian formalist idea that genres can each involve a "dominant" (or dominating) aesthetic device (or ideological element).[53]

On this basis, particular genres can be characterized not as the only genres in which given elements, devices, and features occur, but as the ones in which they are dominant, in which they play an overall organizing role.

Approaches to individual genres – and to individual genre films – that draw centrally on the notion of a generic dominant are few and far between. However, it could be argued, for example, that the epic is marked by the dominance of spectacle; that the thriller and the detective genre, especially as discussed by Dennis Porter and Kristin Thompson, are dominated by the devices of suspense, narrative digression, and hermeneutic delay;[54] and that, as the Russian formalists themselves have argued, melodrama involves the subordination of all other elements "to one overriding aesthetic goal: the calling forth of 'pure,' 'vivid' emotions."[55] In doing so, however, emphasis must again be placed on the fact that dominant elements are not necessarily exclusive elements, occurring only in the genre concerned. Clearly, spectacle, digression, suspense, and the generation of passion and emotion are properties common to all Hollywood films.

By way of conclusion, I would like to stress the need for further research, for further concrete and specific analyses, and for much more attention to genres hitherto neglected in genre studies, such as the adventure film, the war film, and the epic. In stressing this, I can do no better than to quote Williams for the last time. In his own summation, he calls for a "return to film history," for "genre studies with real historical integrity." This would mean, he says, three things: "(1) starting with a genre's 'pre-history,' its roots in other media; (2) studying all films, regardless of perceived quality; and (3) going beyond film content to study advertising, the star system, studio policy, and so on in relation to the production of films."[56] I would merely add that the scope of this investigation needs to be extended beyond individual genres to encompass specific generic regimes both inside and outside the cinema.

Notes

1 Alan Williams, "Is a Radical Genre Criticism Possible?" *Quarterly Review of Film Studies* 9, no. 2 (Spring 1984): 121–5; Thomas Schatz, *Hollywood Genres: Formulas, Filmmaking, and the Studio System* (New York: Random House, 1981); Steve Neale, *Genre* (London: BFI, 1980).

2 Williams, "Is a Radical Genre Criticism Possible?" p. 124.

3 For discussions of verisimilitude and genre, see Ben Brewster, "Film," in *Exploring Reality*, edited by Dan Cohn-Sherbok and Michael Irwin (London: Allen & Unwin, 1987), esp. pp. 147–9; Gérard Genette, "Vraisemblance et motivation," in *Figures*, vol. 3 (Paris: Seuil, 1969); and Tzvetan Todorov, "The Typology of Detective Fiction" and "An Introduction to Verisimilitude," in *The Poetics of Prose* (Ithaca, NY: Cornell University Press, 1977), and *Introduction to Poetics* (Brighton: Harvester Press, 1981), esp. pp. 118–19.

4 Todorov, *Introduction to Poetics*, pp. 118–19.

5 Christine Gledhill, "The Melodramatic Field: An Introduction," in *Home Is Where the Heart Is: Studies in Melodrama and the Woman's Film*, edited by Christine Gledhill (London: BFI, 1987), esp. p. 9: "As a bourgeois form, melodrama is constrained by the same conditions of verisimilitude as realism. If the family melodrama speciality is generational and gender conflict, verisimilitude demands that the central issues of sexual difference and identity be 'realistically' presented." Kathryn Kane, *Visions of War: Hollywood Combat Films of World War II* (Ann Arbor, Mich.: UMI Research Press, 1976), esp. p. 121: "The achievement of [*The Story of*] G. I. *Joe* [William Wellman, 1945] however is not really one of historical data providing the truth of what is portrayed.... Rather, its power is the result of an insistence on *verisimilitude*, the stylistic groundwork on which the authenticity props rest."

6 John Ellis, *Visible Fictions: Cinema, Television, Video* (London: Routledge, 1981), p. 30.

7 Gregory Lukow and Steve Ricci, "The 'Audience' Goes 'Public': Intertextuality, Genre, and the Responsibilities of Film Literacy," *On Film*, no. 12 (Spring 1984): 29.

8 Rick Altman, *The American Film Musical* (Bloomington and Indianapolis: Indiana University Press, 1989).

9 Ibid., p. 13.

10 Ibid., p. 14.

11 Ibid., pp. 14–15.

12 Williams, "Is a Radical Genre Criticism Possible?" p. 123.

13 Tzvetan Todorov, "The Origin of Genres," *New Literary History* 8, no. 1 (Autumn 1976): 102.

14 On the Western prior to the emergence of the cinema and on all these forms, see *The BFI Companion to the Western*, edited by Edward Buscombe (New York: Atheneum, 1988), pp. 18–22.

15 Charles Musser, "The Travel Genre in 1903–04: Moving Toward Fictional Narratives," *Iris* 2, no. 1 (1984): 56–7. The references here are to Kenneth MacGowan, *Behind the Screen* (New York: Delacorte, 1965), p. 114; and George Fenin and William K. Everson, *The Western: From Silents to Cinerama* (New York: Orion Press, 1962), p. 49.

16 Ralph Cohen, "History and Genre," *New Literary History* 17, no. 2 (Winter 1986): 207.

17 Todorov, "The Origin of Genres," p. 103.

18 *Complete Illustrated Catalog of Moving Picture Machines, Stereoptikons, Slides, Films* (Chicago: Kleine Optical Company, November 1905), p. 36.

19 *Biograph Bulletins, 1896–1908*, compiled by Kemp R. Niver (Los Angeles: Locaire Research Group, 1971), pp. 59–73.

20   Cohen, "History and Genre," pp. 205–6; Hans Robert Jauss, *Towards an Aesthetic of Reception* (Brighton: Harvester Press, 1982), p. 80; Neale, *Genre*, p. 19.

21   I owe this phrase to an unpublished lecture on genre by Elizabeth Cowie.

22   Jauss, *Towards an Aesthetic*, p. 79.

23   Jean Mitry, *Dictionnaire du cinéma* (Paris: Larousse, 1963), p. 276; quoted in Altman, *American Film Musical*, p. 95.

24   Altman, *American Film Musical*, p. 96. See also Altman's discussion of the definition of the Western in "A Semantic/Syntactic Approach to Film Genre," reprinted in this volume.

25   Marc Vernet, "Genre," *Film Reader* 3 (February 1978): 13.

26   David Bordwell, Janet Staiger, and Kristin Thompson, *The Classical Hollywood Cinema: Film Style and Mode of Production to 1960* (New York: Columbia University Press, 1985), pp. 16–17.

27   Ernest Mandel, *Delightful Murder: A Social History of the Crime Story* (London and Sydney: Pluto Press, 1984), p. 18.

28   Richard Traubner, *Operetta: A Theatrical History* (New York: Oxford University Press, 1989).

29   Jim Collins, *Uncommon Cultures: Popular Culture and Post-Modernism* (New York and London: Routledge, 1989), p. 46.

30   Jauss, *Towards an Aesthetic*, p. 88.

31   Williams, "Is a Radical Genre Criticism Possible?" pp. 123–4.

32   Tag Gallagher, "Shoot-Out at the Genre Corral: Problems in the 'Evolution' of the Western," *Film Genre Reader*, edited by Barry K. Grant (Austin: University of Texas Press, 1986), pp. 202–16.

33   See, in particular, Boris Eikenbaum, "The Theory of the Formal Method," and Jury Tynyanov, "On Literary Evolution," both in *Readings in Russian Poetics: Formalist and Structuralist Views*, edited by Ladislav Matejka and Krystyna Pomorska (Ann Arbor: Michigan Slavic Publications, 1978); and Viktor Shklovsky's views as summarized both in these works and in Victor Erlich, *Russian Formalism: History-Doctrine* (New Haven and London: Yale University Press, 1981), pp. 259–60.

34   Tynyanov, "On Literary Evolution," pp. 72–3.

35   Quoted in Erlich, *Russian Formalism*, p. 260.

36   Jauss, *Towards an Aesthetic*, pp. 105–6.

37   On exploitation, juvenilization, and the emergence of the teenpic, see Thomas Doherty, *Teenagers and Teenpics: The Juvenilization of American Movies in the 1950s* (Boston: Unwin Hyman, 1988). On the role of special effects, see Steve Neale, "Hollywood Strikes Back – Special Effects in Recent American Cinema," *Screen* 21, no. 3 (1981): 101–5.

38   Dates for series titles indicate initial year of publication. On mass-produced fiction, series, and genres, see, among others, Christine Bold, *Selling the Wild West: Popular Western Fiction, 1860–1960* (Bloomington and Indianapolis: Indiana University Press, 1987); *The Pulps: Fifty Years of American Pop Culture*, edited by Tony Goodstone (New York: Chelsea House, 1970); Ron Goulart, *Great History of Comic Books* (Chicago and New York: Contemporary Books, 1986); Theodore Peterson, *Magazines in the Twentieth Century* (Urbana: University of Illinois Press, 1956); Janice A. Radway, *Reading the Romance: Women, Patriarchy and Popular Literature* (Chapel Hill: University of North Carolina Press, 1984); Quentin Reynolds, *The Fiction Factory, or*

From Pulp Row to Quality Street (New York: Random House, 1955); Frank L. Schick, *The Paperbound Book in America* (New York: R. R. Bowker, 1958); and Piet Schreuders, *The Book of Paperbacks: A Visual History of the Paperback* (London: Virgin Books, 1981).

39 The only books dealing with a number of genres across a variety of institutions and forms are, so far as I am aware, John G. Cawelti, *Adventure, Mystery, and Romance* (Chicago and London: University of Chicago Press, 1976); and Robert C. Toll, *The Entertainment Machine: American Show Business in the Twentieth Century* (Oxford: Oxford University Press, 1982). Research is also needed on the institutional connections between the cinema, the theater, radio, television, and popular music, which in part enable cross-media generic circulation. For a summary and bibliography of some of the work to date, see Calvin Pryluck, "Industrialization of Entertainment in the United States," in *Current Research in Film: Audiences, Economics and Law*, vol. 2 edited by Bruce A. Austin (Norwood, NJ: Ablex, 1986).

40 The kind of studies I have in mind are best represented, to date, by Altman's *American Film Musical*, especially his emphasis on edited alternation in constructing a "dual focus" narrative and his concepts of the "audio" and "video" dissolve, esp. pp. 16–27 and 59–89; John Mueller's *Astaire Dancing: The Musical Films* (New York: Knopf, 1985), esp. "Astaire's Use of the Camera," pp. 26–34; and Christine Saxton's *Illusions of Grandeur: The Representation of Space in the American Western* (Ann Arbor, Mich.: University Microfilms, Inc., 1988).

41 Williams, "Is a Radical Genre Criticism Possible?" pp. 121–2.

42 Cohen, "History and Genre," p. 203.

43 Terry Threadgold, "Talking about Genre: Ideologies and Incompatible Discourses," *Cultural Studies* 3, no. 1 (January 1989): 121–2.

44 Geoffrey Nowell-Smith, "Popular Culture," *New Formations*, no. 2 (Summer 1987): 79–90.

45 For a discussion of this idea in relation to the cinema, see Steve Neale, "Art Cinema as Institution," *Screen* 22, no. 1 (1981): 11–40.

46 Cawelti, *Adventure, Mystery, and Romance*; Schatz, *Hollywood Genres*; Will Wright, *Sixguns and Society: A Structural Study of the Western* (Berkeley: University of California Press, 1975).

47 Williams, "Is a Radical Genre Criticism Possible?" p. 123.

48 Garth S. Jowett, "Giving Them What They Want: Movie Audience Research before 1950," in *Current Research in Film*, vol. 1, edited by Austin.

49 Altman, *American Film Musical*, p. 94.

50 Possibly the worst example I have come across is Judith Hess Wright, "Genre Films and the Status Quo," *Jump Cut*, no. 1 (May–June 1974): 1, 16, 18.

51 Colin MacCabe, introduction to *High Theory/Low Culture: Analysing Popular Television and Film*, edited by MacCabe (Manchester: Manchester University Press, 1986), p. 4.

52 Nowell-Smith, "Popular Culture," p. 88.

53 See Tynyanov, "On Literary Evolution."

54 Dennis Porter, *The Pursuit of Crime: Art and Ideology in Detective Fiction* (New Haven, Conn.: Yale University Press, 1981); Kristin Thompson, *Breaking the Glass Armor: Neoformalist Film Analysis* (Princeton: Princeton University Press, 1988), esp. pp. 49–86.

11
A Semantic/Syntactic Approach
To Film Genre

Rick Altman

What is a genre? Which films are genre films? How do we know to which genre they belong? As fundamental as these questions may seem, they are almost never asked – let alone answered – in the field of cinema studies. Most comfortable in the seemingly uncomplicated world of Hollywood classics, genre critics have felt little need to reflect openly on the assumptions underlying their work. Everything seems so clear. Why bother to theorize, American pragmatism asks, when there are no problems to solve? We all know a genre when we see one. Scratch only where it itches. According to this view, genre theory would be called for only in the unlikely event that knowledgeable genre critics disagreed on basic issues. The task of the theorist is then to adjudicate among conflicting approaches, not so much by dismissing unsatisfactory positions, but by constructing a model which reveals the relationship between differing critical claims and their function within a broader cultural context. Whereas the French clearly view theory as a first principle, we Americans tend to see it as a last resort, something to turn to when all else fails.

Even in this limited, pragmatic view, whereby theory is to be avoided at all costs, the time for theory is nevertheless upon us. The clock has struck thirteen; we had best call in the theoreticians. The more genre criticism I read, the more uncertainty I note in the choice or extent of essential critical terms. Often, what appears as hesitation in the terminology of a single critic will turn into a clear contradiction when studies by two or more critics are compared. Now, it would be one thing if these contradictions were simply a matter of fact. On the contrary, however, I suggest that these are not temporary problems, bound to disappear as soon as we have more information or better analysts. Instead, these uncertainties reflect constitutive weaknesses of current notions of genre. Three contradictions in particular seem worthy of a good scratch.

When we establish the corpus of a genre we generally tend to do two things at once, and thus establish two alternate groups of texts, each corresponding to a different notion of corpus. On the one hand we have an unwieldy list of texts corresponding to a simple, tautological definition of the genre (e.g. Western =

film that takes place in the American West, or musical = film with diegetic music). This *inclusive* list is the kind that gets consecrated by generic encyclopedias or checklists. On the other hand, we find critics, theoreticians, and other arbiters of taste sticking to a familiar canon which has little to do with the broad, tautological definition. Here, the same films are mentioned again and again, not only because they are well known or particularly well made, but because they somehow seem to represent the genre more fully and faithfully than other apparently more tangential films. This *exclusive* list of films generally occurs not in a dictionary context, but instead in connection with attempts to arrive at the overall meaning or structure of a genre. The relative status of these alternate approaches to the constitution of a generic corpus may easily be sensed from the following typical conversation:

> I mean, what do you do with Elvis Presley films? You can hardly call them musicals.
> Why not? They're loaded with songs and they've got a narrative that ties the numbers together, don't they?
> Yeah, I suppose. I guess you'd have to call *Fun in Acapulco* a musical, but it's sure no *Singin' in the Rain*. Now there's a real musical.

When is a musical not a musical? When it has Elvis Presley in it. What may at first have seemed no more than an uncertainty on the part of the critical community now clearly appears as a contradiction. Because there are two competing notions of generic corpus on our critical scene, it is perfectly possible for a film to be simultaneously included in a particular generic corpus and excluded from that same corpus.

A second uncertainty is associated with the relative status of theory and history in genre studies. Before semiotics came along, generic titles and definitions were largely borrowed from the industry itself; what little generic theory there was tended therefore to be confused with historical analysis. With the heavy influence of semiotics on generic theory over the last two decades, self-conscious *critical* vocabulary came to be systematically preferred to the now suspect *user* vocabulary. The contribution of Propp, Lévi-Strauss, Frye, and Todorov to genre studies has not been uniformly productive, however, because of the special place reserved for genre study within the semiotic project. If structuralist critics systematically chose as object of their analysis large groups of popular texts, it was in order to cover over a basic flaw in the semiotic understanding of textual analysis. Now, one of the most striking aspects of Saussure's theory of language is his emphasis on the inability of any single individual to effect change within that language. The fixity of the linguistic community thus serves as justification for Saussure's fundamentally synchronic approach to language. When literary semioticians applied this linguistic model to problems of textual analysis, they never fully addressed the notion of interpretive community implied by Saussure's linguistic community. Preferring narrative to narration, system to process, and *histoire* to *discours*, the first semiotics ran headlong into a set of restrictions and contradictions that eventually spawned the more process-oriented second semiotics. It is in this context that we must see the resolutely synchronic attempts of Propp, Lévi-Strauss, Todorov, and many another influential genre analysts.[1] Unwilling to compromise their systems by the historical notion of linguistic community, *these theoreticians instead substituted the generic context for the linguistic community*, as if the weight of numerous "similar" texts were sufficient to locate the meaning of a text independently of a specific audience. Far from being sensitive to concerns of history, semiotic genre analysis was by definition and from the start devoted to bypassing history. Treating genres as neutral constructs, semioticians of the sixties and early seventies blinded us to the discursive power of generic formations. Because they treated genres *as the interpretive community*, they were unable to perceive the important role of genres in exercising influence *on the interpretive community*. Instead of reflecting openly on the way in which Hollywood uses its genres to short-circuit the normal interpretive process, structuralist critics plunged headlong into the trap, taking Hollywood's ideological effect for a natural ahistorical cause.

Genres were always – and continue to be – treated as if they spring full-blown from the head of Zeus. It is thus not surprising to find that even the most advanced of current genre theories, those that see generic texts as negotiating a relationship between a specific production system and a given audience, still hold to a notion of genre that is fundamentally ahistorical in nature.[2] More and more, however, as scholars come to know the full range of individual Hollywood genres, we are finding that genres are far from exhibiting the homogeneity which this synchronic approach posits. Whereas one Hollywood genre may be borrowed with little change from another medium, a second genre may develop slowly, change constantly, and surge recognizably before settling into a familiar pattern, while a third may go through an extended series of paradigms, none of which may be claimed as dominant. As long as Hollywood genres are conceived as Platonic categories, existing outside the flow of time, it will be impossible to reconcile *genre theory*, which has always accepted as given the timelessness of a characteristic structure, and *genre history*, which has concentrated on chronicling the development, deployment, and disappearance of this same structure.

A third contradiction looms larger still, for it involves the two general directions taken by genre criticism as a whole over the last decade or two. Following Lévi-Strauss, a growing number of critics throughout the seventies dwelled on the mythical qualities of Hollywood genres, and thus on the audience's ritual relationship to genre film. The film industry's desire to please and its need to attract consumers was viewed as the mechanism whereby spectators were actually able to designate the kind of films they wanted to see. By choosing the films it would patronize, the audience revealed its preferences and its beliefs, thus inducing Hollywood studios to produce films reflecting its desires. Participation in the genre film experience thus reinforces spectator expectations and desires. Far from being limited to mere entertainment, film-going offers a satisfaction more akin to that associated with established religion. Most openly championed by John Cawelti, this ritual approach appears as well in books by Leo Braudy, Frank McConnell, Michael Wood, Will Wright, and Thomas Schatz.[3] It has the merit not only of accounting for the intensity of identification typical of American genre film audiences, but it also encourages the placing of genre film narratives into an appropriately wider context of narrative analysis.

Curiously, however, while the ritual approach was attributing ultimate authorship to the audience, with the studios simply serving, for a price, the national will, a parallel ideological approach was demonstrating how audiences are manipulated by the business and political interests of Hollywood. Starting with *Cahiers du cinéma* and moving rapidly to *Screen*, *Jump Cut*, and a growing number of journals, this view has recently joined hands with a more general critique of the mass media offered by the Frankfurt School. Looked at in this way, genres are simply the generalized, identifiable structures through which Hollywood's rhetoric flows. Far more attentive to discursive concerns than the ritual approach, which remains faithful to Lévi-Strauss in emphasizing narrative systems, the ideological approach stresses questions of representation and identification previously left aside. Simplifying a bit, we might say that it characterizes each individual genre as a specific type of lie, an untruth whose most characteristic feature is its ability to masquerade as truth. Whereas the ritual approach sees Hollywood as responding to societal pressure and thus expressing audience desires, the ideological approach claims that Hollywood takes advantage of spectator energy and psychic investment in order to lure the audience into Hollywood's own positions. The two are irreducibly opposed, yet these irreconcilable arguments continue to represent the most interesting and well defended of recent approaches to Hollywood genre film.

Here we have three problems which I take not to be limited to a single school of criticism or to a single genre, but to be implicit in every major field of current genre analysis. In nearly every argument about the limits of a generic corpus, the opposition of an inclusive list to an exclusive canon surfaces. Whenever genres are discussed, the divergent concerns of theorists and historians are increasingly obvious. And even when the topic is limited to genre theory alone, no agreement can be found between those who propose a ritual function for film genres and those who champion an ideological purpose. We find ourselves desperately in need of a theory which, without dismissing any of these widely held positions, would explain the circumstances underlying their existence, thus paving the way for a critical methodology which encompasses and indeed thrives on their inherent contradictions. If we have learned anything from poststructuralist criticism, we have learned not to fear logical contradictions but instead to respect the extraordinary energy generated by the play of contradictory forces within a field. What we need now is a new critical strategy enabling us simultaneously to understand and to capitalize on the tensions existing in current generic criticism.

In assessing theories of genre, critics have often labeled them according to a particular theory's most salient features or the type of activity to which it devotes its most concentrated attention. Paul Hernadi thus recognizes four general classes of genre theory: expressive, pragmatic, structural, and mimetic. In his extremely influential introduction to *The Fantastic*, Tzvetan Todorov opposes historical to theoretical genres, as well as elementary genres to their complex counterparts. Others, like Frederic Jameson, have followed Todorov and other French semioticians in distinguishing between semantic and syntactic approaches to genre.[4] While there is anything but general agreement on the exact frontier separating semantic from syntactic views, we can as a whole distinguish between generic definitions which depend on a list of common traits, attitudes, characters, shots, locations, sets, and the like – thus stressing the semantic elements which make up the genre – and definitions which play up instead certain constitutive relationships between undesignated and variable placeholders – relationships which might be called the genre's fundamental syntax. The semantic approach thus stresses the genre's building blocks, while the syntactic view privileges the structures into which they are arranged.

The difference between semantic and syntactic definitions is perhaps at its most apparent in familiar approaches to the Western. Jean Mitry provides us with a clear example of the most common definition. The Western, Mitry proposes, is a "film whose action, situated in the American West, is consistent with the atmosphere, the values, and the conditions of existence in the Far West between 1840 and 1900." Based on the presence or absence of easily identifiable elements, Mitry's nearly tautological definition implies a broad, undifferentiated generic corpus. Marc Vernet's more detailed list is more sensitive to cinematic concerns, yet overall it follows the same semantic model. Vernet outlines general atmosphere ("emphasis on basic elements, such as earth, dust, water, and leather"), stock characters ("the tough/soft cowboy, the lonely sheriff, the faithful or treacherous Indian, and the strong but tender woman"), as well as technical elements ("use of fast tracking and crane shots"). An entirely different solution is suggested by Jim Kitses, who emphasizes not the vocabulary of the Western but the relationships linking lexical elements. For Kitses the Western grows out of a dialectic between the West as Garden and as Desert (between culture and nature, community and individual, future and past). The Western's vocabulary is thus generated by this syntactic relationship, and not vice versa. John Cawelti attempts to systematize the Western in a similar fashion: the Western is always set on or near a frontier, where man encounters his uncivilized double. The Western thus takes place on the border between two lands, between two eras, and with a hero who remains divided between two value systems (for he combines the town's morals with the outlaws' skills).[5]

Now, in passing we might well note the divergent qualities associated with these two approaches. While the semantic approach has little explanatory power, it is applicable to a larger number of films. Conversely, the syntactic approach surrenders broad applicability in return for the ability to isolate a genre's specific meaning-bearing structures. This alternative seemingly leaves the genre analyst in a quandary: choose the semantic view and you give up *explanatory power*, choose the syntactic approach and you do without *broad applicability*. In terms of the Western, the problem of the so-called "Pennsylyania Western" is instructive here. To most observers it seems quite clear that films like *High, Wide and Handsome* (Mamoulian, 1937), *Drums Along the Mohawk* (Ford, 1939), and *Unconquered* (DeMille, 1947) have definite affinities with the Western. Employing familiar characters set in relationships similar to their counterparts west of the Mississippi, these films construct plots and develop a frontier structure clearly derived from decades of Western novels and films. But they do it in Pennsylvania, and in the wrong century. Are these films Westerns because they share the syntax of hundreds of films we call Westerns? Or are they not Westerns, because they don't fit Mitry's definition?

In fact, the "Pennsylvania Western" (like the urban, spaghetti, and sci-fi varieties) represents a quandary only because critics have insisted on dismissing one type of definition and approach in favor of another. As a rule, semantic and syntactic approaches to genre have been proposed, analyzed, evaluated, and disseminated separately, in spite of the complementarity implied by their names. Indeed, many arguments centering on generic problems have arisen only when semantic and syntactic theoreticians have simply talked past each other, each unaware of the other's divergent orientation. I maintain that these two categories of generic analysis are complementary, that they can be combined, and in fact that some of the most important questions of genre study can be asked only when they *are* combined. In short, I propose a semantic/syntactic approach to genre study.

Now let us return to the three contradictions delineated earlier, in order to discover whether the proposed semantic/syntactic approach provides any new understanding. First, the split corpus that characterizes current genre study – on the one side an inclusive list, on the other an exclusive pantheon. It should now be quite clear that each corpus corresponds to a different approach to generic analysis and definition. Tautological semantic definitions, with their goal of broad applicability, outline a large genre of semantically similar texts, while syntactic definitions, intent as they are on explaining the genre, stress a narrow range of texts that privilege specific syntactic relationships. To insist on one of these approaches to the exclusion of the other is to turn a blind eye on *the necessarily dual nature of any generic corpus*. For every film that participates actively in the elaboration of a genre's syntax there are numerous others content to deploy in no particular relationship the elements traditionally associated with the genre. We need to recognize that not all genre films relate to their genre in the same way or to the same extent. By simultaneously accepting semantic and syntactic notions of genre we avail ourselves of a possible way to deal critically with differing levels of genericity. In addition, a dual approach permits a far more accurate description of the numerous inter-generic connections typically suppressed by single-minded approaches. It is simply not possible to describe Hollywood cinema accurately without the ability to account for the numerous films that innovate by combining the syntax of one genre with the semantics of another. In fact, it is only when we begin to take up problems of genre history that the full value of the semantic/syntactic approach becomes obvious.

As I pointed out earlier, most genre theoreticians have followed the semiotic model and steered clear of historical considerations. Even in the relatively few cases where problems of generic history have been addressed, as in the attempts of Metz and Wright to periodize the Western, history has been conceptualized as nothing more than a discontinuous succession of discrete moments, each characterized by a different basic version of the genre, that is by a different syntactic pattern which the genre adopts.[6] In short, genre theory has up to now aimed almost exclusively at the elaboration of a synchronic model approximating the syntactic operation of a specific genre. Now, quite obviously, no major genre remains unchanged over the many decades of its existence. In order to mask the scandal of applying synchronic analysis to an evolving form, critics have been extremely clever in their creation of categories designed to negate the notion of change and to imply the perpetual self-identity of each genre. Westerns and horror films are often referred to as "classic," the musical is defined in terms of the so-called "Platonic ideal" of integration, the critical corpus of the melodrama has largely been restricted to the postwar efforts of Sirk and Minnelli, and so on. Lacking a workable hypothesis regarding the historical dimension of generic syntax, we have insulated that syntax, along with the genre theory that studies it, from the flow of time.

As a working hypothesis, I suggest that genres arise in one of two fundamental ways: either a relatively stable set of semantic givens is developed through syntactic experimentation into a coherent and durable syntax, or an already existing syntax adopts a new set of semantic elements. In the first case, the genre's characteristic semantic configuration is identifiable long before a syntactic pattern has become stabilized, thus justifying the previously mentioned duality of the generic corpus. In cases of this first type, description of the way in which a set of semantic givens develops into a henceforth relatively stable syntax constitutes the history of the genre while at the same time identifying the structures on which genre theory depends. In dealing with the early development of the musical, for example, we might well follow the attempts during the 1927–30 period to build a backstage or night club semantics into a melodramatic syntax, with music regularly reflecting the sorrow of death or parting. After the slack years of 1931–2, however, the musical began to grow in a new direction; while maintaining substantially the same semantic materials, the genre increasingly related the energy of music-making to the joy of coupling, the strength of the community, and the pleasures of entertainment. Far from being exiled from history, the musical's characteristic syntax can be shown by the generic historian to grow out of the linking of specific semantic elements at identifiable points. A measure of continuity is thus developed between the task of the historian and that of the theoretician, for the tasks of both are now redefined as the study of the interrelationships between semantic elements and syntactic bonds.

This continuity between history and theory is operative as well in the second type of generic development posited earlier. When we analyze the large variety of war-time films that portray the Japanese or Germans as villains, we tend to have recourse to extra-filmic events in order to explain particular characterizations. We thus miss the extent to which films like *All Through the Night*, *Sherlock Holmes and the Voice of Terror*, or the serial *Don Winslow of the Navy* simply transfer to a new set of semantic elements the syntax of the righteous cops-punish-criminals genre which the gangster genre of the early thirties had turned into starting with *G-Men* in 1935. Again it is the interplay of syntax and semantics that provides grist for both the historical and the theoretical mill. Or take the development of the science-fiction film. At first defined only by a relatively stable science-fiction semantics, the genre first began borrowing the syntactic relationships previously established by the horror film, only to move in recent years increasingly toward the syntax of the Western. By maintaining simultaneous descriptions according to both parameters, we are not likely to fall into the trap of equating *Star Wars* with the Western (as numerous recent critics have done), even though it shares certain syntactic patterns with that genre. In short, by taking seriously the multiple connections between semantics and syntax, we establish a new continuity, relating film analysis, genre theory, and genre history.

But what is it that energizes the transformation of a borrowed semantics into a uniquely Hollywood syntax? Or what is it that justifies the intrusion of a new semantics into a well defined syntactic situation? Far from postulating a uniquely internal, formal progression, I would propose that the relationship between the semantic and the syntactic constitutes the very site of negotiation between Hollywood and its audience, and thus between ritual and ideological uses of genre. Often, when critics of opposing persuasions disagree over a major issue, it is because they have established, within the same general corpus, two separate and opposed canons, each supporting one point of view. Thus, when Catholics and Protestants or liberals and conservatives quote the Bible, they are rarely quoting the same passages. The striking fact about ritual and ideological genre theoreticians, however, is that they regularly stress the same canon, that small group of texts most clearly reflecting a genre's stable syntax. The films of John Ford, for example, have played a major role in the development of ritual and ideological approaches alike. From Sarris and Bogdanovich to Schatz and Wright, champions of Ford's understanding and transparent expression of American values have stressed the communitarian side of his films, while others, starting with the influential *Cahiers du cinéma* study of *Young Mr. Lincoln*, have shown how a call to community can be used to lure spectators into a carefully chosen, ideologically determined subject position. A similar situation obtains in the musical, where a growing body of ritual analyses of the Astaire/Rogers and postwar MGM Freed unit films is matched by an increasing number of studies demonstrating the ideological investment of those very same films.[7] The corpus of nearly every major genre has developed in the same way, with critics of both camps gravitating toward and eventually basing their arguments on the same narrow range of films. Just as Minnelli and Sirk dominate the criticism of melodrama, Hitchcock has become nearly synonymous with the thriller. Of all major genres, only the *film noir* has failed to attract critics of both sides to a shared corpus of major texts – no doubt because of the general inability of ritual critics to accommodate the genre's anti-communitarian stance.

This general agreement on a canon stems, I would claim, from the fundamentally bivalent nature of any relatively stable generic syntax. If it takes a long time to establish a generic syntax, and if many seemingly promising formulas or successful films never spawn a genre, it is because only certain types of structure, within a particular semantic environment, are suited to the special bilingualism required of a durable genre. The structures of Hollywood cinema, like those of American popular mythology as a whole, serve to mask the very distinction between ritual and ideological functions. Hollywood does not simply lend its voice to the public's desires, nor does it simply manipulate the audience. On the contrary, most genres go through a period of accommodation during which the public's desires are fitted to Hollywood's priorities (and vice versa). Because the public doesn't want to know that it's being manipulated, the successful ritual/ideological "fit" is almost always one that disguises Hollywood's potential for manipulation while playing up its capacity for entertainment.

Whenever a lasting fit is obtained – which it is whenever a semantic genre becomes a syntactic one – it is because a common ground has been found, a region where the audience's ritual values coincide with Hollywood's ideological ones. The development of a specific syntax within a given semantic context thus serves a double function: it binds element to element in a logical order, at the same time accommodating audience desires to studio concerns. The successful genre owes its success not alone to its reflection of an audience ideal, nor solely to its status as apology for the Hollywood enterprise, but to its ability to carry out both functions simultaneously. It is this sleight of hand, this strategic over-determination, that most clearly characterizes American film production during the studio years.

The approach to genre sketched out in this article of course raises some questions of its own. Just where, for example, do we locate the exact border between the semantic and the syntactic? And how are these two categories related? Each of these questions constitutes an essential area of inquiry, one that is far too complex to permit full treatment here. Nevertheless, a few remarks may be in order. A reasonable observer might well ask why my approach attributes such importance to the seemingly banal distinction between a text's materials and the structures into which they are arranged. Why this distinction rather than, for example, the more cinematic division between diegetic elements and the technical means deployed in representing them? The answer to these questions lies in a general theory of textual signification which I have expounded elsewhere.[8] Briefly, that theory distinguishes between the primary, linguistic meaning of a text's component parts and the secondary, or textual meaning which those parts acquire through a structuring process internal to the text or to the genre. Within a single text, therefore, the same phenomenon may have more than one meaning depending on whether we consider it at the linguistic or textual level. In the Western, for example, the horse is an animal that serves as a method of locomotion. This primary level of meaning, corresponding to the normal extent of the concept "horse" within the language, is matched by a series of other meanings derived from the structures into which the Western sets the horse. Opposition of the horse to the automobile or locomotive ("iron horse") reinforces the organic, non-mechanical sense of the term "horse" already implicit in the language, thus transferring that concept from the paradigm "method of locomotion" to the paradigm "soon-to-be-outmoded pre-industrial carry-over."

In the same way, horror films borrow from a nineteenth-century literary tradition their dependence on the presence of a monster. In doing so, they clearly perpetuate the linguistic meaning of the monster ("threatening inhuman being"), but at the same time, by developing new syntactic ties, they generate an import-ant new set of textual meanings. For the nineteenth century, the appearance of the monster is invariably tied to a Romantic over-reaching, the attempt of some human scientist to tamper with the divine order. In texts like Mary Shelley's *Frankenstein*, Balzac's *La Recherche de l'absolu*, or Stevenson's *Dr Jekyll and Mr Hyde*, a studied syntax equates man and monster, attributing to both the mon-strosity of being outside nature, as defined by established religion and science. With the horror film, a different syntax rapidly equates monstrosity not with the overactive nineteenth-century mind, but with an equally overactive twentieth-century body. Again and again, the monster is identified with his human counterpart's unsatisfied sexual appetite, thus establishing with the same primary "linguistic" materials (the monster, fear, the chase, death) entirely new textual meanings, phallic rather than scientific in nature.

The distinction between the semantic and the syntactic, in the way I have defined it here, thus corresponds to a distinction between the primary, linguistic elements of which all texts are made, and the secondary, textual meanings which are sometimes constructed by virtue of the syntactic bonds established between primary elements. This distinction is stressed in the approach to genre presented here not because it is convenient nor because it corresponds to a modish theory of the relation between language and narrative, but because the semantic/syntactic distinction is fundamental to a theory of how meaning of one kind contributes to and eventually establishes meaning of another. Just as individual texts establish new meanings for familiar terms only by subjecting well-known semantic units to a syntactic redetermination, so generic meaning comes into being only through the repeated deployment of substantially the same syntactic strategies. It is in this way, for example, that making music – at the linguistic level primarily a way of making a living – becomes in the musical a figure for making love – a textual meaning essential to the constitution of that syntactic genre.

We must of course remember that, while each individual text clearly has a syntax of its own, the syntax implied here is that of the genre, which does not appear as *generic* syntax unless it is reinforced numerous times by the syntactic patterns of individual texts. The Hollywood genres that have proven the most durable are precisely those that have established the most coherent syntax (the Western, the musical); those that disappear the quickest depend entirely on recurring semantic elements, never developing a stable syntax (reporter, catastrophe, and big caper films, to name but a few). If I locate the border between the semantic and the syntactic at the dividing line between the linguistic and the textual, it is thus in response not just to the theoretical, but also to the historical dimension of generic functioning.

In proposing such a model, however, I may leave too much room for one particular type of misunderstanding. It has been a cliché of the last two decades to insist that structure carries meaning, while the choice of structured elements is largely negligible in the process of signification. This position, most openly championed by Lévi-Strauss in his cross-cultural methodology for studying myth, may seem to be implied by my model, but is in fact not borne out by my research. Spectator response, I believe, is heavily conditioned by the choice of semantic elements and atmosphere, because a given semantics used in a specific cultural situation will recall to an actual interpretive community the particular syntax with which that semantics has traditionally been associated in other texts. This *syntactic expectation*, set up by a *semantic signal*, is matched by a parallel tendency to expect specific syntactic signals to lead to predetermined semantic fields (e.g. in Western texts, regular alternation between male and female characters creates expectation of the semantic elements implied by romance, while – at least until recently – alternation between two males throughout a text has implied confrontation and the semantics of the duel). This interpenetration of the semantic and the syntactic through the agency of the spectator clearly deserves further study. Suffice it to say for the present that linguistic meanings (and thus the import of semantic elements) are in large part derived from the textual meanings of previous texts. There is thus a constant circulation in both directions between the semantic and the syntactic, between the linguistic and the textual.

Still other questions, such as the general problem of the "evolution" of genres through semantic or syntactic shifts, deserve far more attention than I have given them here. In time, I believe, this new model for the understanding of genre will provide answers for many of the questions traditional to genre study. Perhaps more important still, as I hope I have shown, the semantic/syntactic approach to genre raises numerous questions for which other theories have created no space.

Notes

1   Especially in Vladimir Propp, *Morphology of the Folktale* (Bloomington: Indiana Research Centre in Anthropology, 1958); Claude Lévi-Strauss, "The Structure of Myths" in *Structural Anthropology* (New York: Basic Books, 1963); Tzvetan Todorov,

Grammaire du Décaméron (The Hague: Mouton, 1969), and *The Fantastic* (Ithaca, NY: Cornell University Press, 1975).

2   Even Stephen Neale's recent discursively oriented study falls prey to this problem: *Genre* (London: British Film Institute, 1980).

3   John Cawelti, *The Six-Gun Mystique* (Bowling Green: Bowling Green University Popular Press, 1971) and *Adventure, Mystery and Romance* (Chicago: University of Chicago Press, 1976); Leo Braudy, *The World in a Frame: What We See in Films* (Garden City: Anchor Books, 1977); Frank McConnell, *The Spoken Seen: Film and the Romantic Imagination* (Baltimore: Johns Hopkins University Press, 1975); Michael Wood, *America in the Movies, or Santa Maria, It Had Slipped My Mind* (New York: Delta, 1975); Will Wright, *Sixguns and Society: A Structural Study of the Western* (Berkeley: University of California Press, 1975); Thomas Schatz, *Hollywood Genres: Formulas, Filmmaking, and the Studio System* (New York: Random House, 1981).

4   Paul Hernadi, *Beyond Genre: New Directions in Literary Classification* (Ithaca, NY: Cornell University Press, 1972); Tzvetan Todorov, *The Fantastic*; Frederic Jameson, "Magical Narratives: Romance as Genre," *New Literary History* 7 (1975): 135–63. It should be noted here that my use of the term "semantic" differs from Jameson's. Whereas he stresses the overall semantic impact of a text, I am dealing with the individual semantic units of the text. His term thus approximates the sense of "global meaning," while mine is closer to "lexical choices."

5   Jean Mitry, *Dictionnaire du cinéma* (Paris: Larousse, 1963), 276; Marc Vernet, *Lectures du film* (Paris: Albatros, 1976), 111–12; Jim Kitses, *Horizons West* (Bloomington: Indiana University Press, 1969), 10–14; John Cawelti, *The Six-Gun Mystique*.

6   Christian Metz, *Language and Cinema* (The Hague: Mouton, 1974), 148–61; Will Wright, *Sixguns and Society*.

7   This relationship is especially interesting in the work of Richard Dyer and Jane Feuer, both of whom attempt to confront the interdependence of ritual and ideological components. See in particular Richard Dyer, "Entertainment and Utopia," in *Genre: The Musical*, ed. Rick Altman (London & Boston: Routledge & Kegan Paul, 1981), 175–89, and Jane Feuer, *The Hollywood Musical* (Bloomington: Indiana University Press, 1982).

8   Charles F. Altman, "Intratextual Rewriting: Textuality as Language Formation," in *The Sign in Music and Literature*, ed. Wendy Steiner (Austin: University of Texas Press, 1981): 39–51.

12
The "Force-Field" of Melodrama

Stuart Cunningham

Introduction

My admittedly cryptic title derives from Peter Brooks's seminal rehabilitation of melodrama, *The Melodramatic Imagination: Balzac, Henry James, Melodrama, and the Mode of Excess*:

> our concern... is not melodrama as a theme or a set of themes, nor the life of the drama per se, but rather melodrama as a mode of conception and expression, as a certain fictional system for making sense of experience, as a semantic field of force.[1]

Brooks's simile suggests melodrama as a dynamic "space" into which a variety of materials – aesthetic, religious, political – are drawn together in patterns that shift and change. I would tamper with the figure to the extent that a final determination of the ground of the "force-field" must not merely be semantic, but a complex interaction of religious, political, and aesthetic factors which, I shall argue, are inseparably implicated in any appraisal of melodrama.

Recent investigation – Brooks's book, but also the work of Eric Bentley, James Rosenberg, Robert Heilman, David Grimsted, Frank Rahill, James Smith, John Cawelti, Thomas Elsaesser, Lesley Stern and Tania Modleski among others[2] – has attempted to rehabilitate melodrama, to rescue it from its "bad reputation": "the indulgence of strong emotionalism; moral polarization and schematization; extreme states of being, situations, actions; overt villainy, persecution of the good, and final reward of virtue; inflated and extravagant expression; dark plottings, suspense, breathtaking peripety."[3] This rehabilitation of the category, however, has not necessarily led to an unproblematic set of genre classifications: melodrama has been advanced as the theatrical impulse itself (Bentley, Rosenberg) and thus coeval with the history of drama; as a sub-genre of tragedy (Steiner,[4] Rosenberg); as a sub-genre and descendant of romance and the sentimental novel (Elsaesser, Cawelti); as a specific narrative form which is peculiarly modern (Brooks, Heilman). This plethora of competing accounts could lead to the contention that "melodrama as a coherent dramatic category never existed, that it never amounted to either a total or coherent aesthetic."[5] However, the difficulties of assigning an *aesthetic* coherence to melodrama can be displayed by considering it as a category of religious, moral, political, as well as aesthetic experience.

Putting the case more strongly: definitional impasses arise only if melodrama is approached as an exclusively aesthetic category; these difficulties actually present the opportunity to amplify and broaden melodrama as a category, as many critics of melodrama have begun to do. Other "definitional" characteristics of melodrama, such as its preeminent place as a "popular cultural" form, its status as "essentially democratic,"[6] its flourishing and pervasiveness specifically in the modern age, and its inscription in numerous forms of representation and discourse – theater, the novel, opera, film, television, religious and political rhetoric – emphasize its fundamental role in social ritual and everyday life as much as Brooks's earlier list suggests its problematic aesthetic status. By mapping out a religious–political framework for the understanding of melodrama and then relating it to some contemporary examples of new Hollywood cinema, I hope to amplify the discussion of melodrama without neglecting its thorny aesthetic problems, as well as to emphasize the centrality of this framework in any account of contemporary melodramatic consciousness.

A Religious–Political Framework for Melodrama

Brooks presents an all-too-brief argument on the imbrication of the religious, political, and aesthetic dimensions of melodrama:

> The origins of melodrama can be accurately located within the context of the French Revolution and its aftermath. This is the epistemological moment which it illustrates and to which it contributes: the moment that symbolically, and really, marks the final liquidation of the traditional Sacred and its representative institutions (Church and Monarch), the shattering of the myth of Christendom, the dissolution of an organic and hierarchically cohesive society, and the invalidation of the literary forms – tragedy, comedy of manners – that depend on such a society...melodrama becomes the principal mode for uncovering, demonstrating, and making operative the essential moral universe in a post-sacred era.[7]

Coeval with the convulsive birth of modern democratic society itself, melodrama contributes to the Promethean struggle to found new orders of political and social morality and to filling the gap in the religious public sphere, as an old "Sacred" (religious *and* political order) gives way to a new.

Brooks's thesis may overly privilege the French "boulevard" melodrama of Pixérécourt, Caigniez and Ducange, and the French Revolution as exemplary melodrama and exemplary upheaval respectively; clearly there are a variety of origins of, and political–historical contexts for, melodrama – the eighteenth-century sentimental novel of Richardson and Rousseau, the French *romans noirs* and *romans frénétiques* of the same century, and the German romanticism of Lessing, Goethe, and Schiller. What is crucial, though, as Elsaesser points out, is that the origins of or models for melodrama occur in periods of intense social and ideological crisis[8] and that melodrama remains extraordinarily transparent to, or mimetic of, those crises. Moreover, it is not as if the French Revolution inaugurated, *tout simplement*, a monolithic "post-sacred" society; desacralization is dialectically responded to by operations of resacralization. This torsion constitutes a crucial part of the force-field of melodrama, as it is both a transparent recognition of, and a response to, desacralization.

Part of this torsion is the gap opened between public and private spheres. A new public order had to be constructed, but the ontological primacy of the individual fundamental to the new "sacred" expressed in romanticism and bourgeois liberalism rendered the new public order as a problematic ensemble of personalist ethics and entrepreneurial economics. Melodrama operates, as it were, "on both sides" of this torsion: it is both a projection of deeply personal, individualized beliefs, fears, longings, and hope into available forms of public discourse and a public winnowing, consolidation, and conventionalization of types of morality, belief, and praxis as they are represented in theatrical and political drama.

Thus, while melodrama's role in resacralization may have been the flawed one of propagating the new "sacred" in purely ethical and personal terms, nevertheless the manner in which this role was performed suggested and enacted a possibility of an encompassing moral universe. Melodrama's function at the privileged moment Brooks discusses was a kind of moral–aesthetic "performative": a discourse which, by virtue of its being spoken (and in this case performed popularly and ritually), accomplishes some action:[9]

> a new form of enactment and demonstration, the new creative rhetoric of moral law arises to demonstrate that it is still possible to find and to show the operation of basic ethical imperatives.... That they can be staged "proves" that they exist; the melodramatic mode not only uses these imperatives but consciously assumes the role of bringing them into dramatized and textual – provisional – existence.[10]

The melodramatists' Boulevard of Crime becomes, in this sense, a crucial part of a new religious public sphere, a populist–democratic "church."

The rationale and coherence of melodrama's aesthetic operations are clarified in this light. The pressure to enact or "prove" rather than reflect and doubt (more traditional aesthetic postures) grounds melodrama's heightened expressivity. The need to reconstruct a fundamental social morality, rather than deal in nuance and idiosyncrasy, leads to schematicism and simplicity. Rather than, as in tragedy, the *mysterium tremendum* remaining ineffable, "wholly other," melodrama strives to give it full force and expression – through dramatic nomination, overwhelming mise-en-scène, plenitude of meaning. The nineteenth-century theatrical tradition which culminated in Wagner's operas and his Bayreuth *Festspielhaus* originated in these, social as much as aesthetic, developments. There was a new, "democratic" audience for this public theater, the lower classes, who responded to a spectacular, gestic, musically extravagant public theater as they had earlier responded to the revolutionary *fêtes* such as the *Fête de l'etre suprême*, over which Robespierre had presided, with their equal commitment to visual spectacle and ritualized reenactment and vindication of the revolution.

Brooks, concluding and generalizing his study, intriguingly places melodrama as a challenging alternative to both nineteenth-century realism and twentieth-century modernism; implicitly, his account of melodrama as a "central poetry"[11] is offered as an alternative to theoretical justifications of realism and modernism:

> This is the mode of excess: the postulation of a signified in excess of the possibilities of the signifier, which in turn produced an excessive signifier, making large but unsubstantiable claims on meaning.[12]

This remains, in Brooks, a somewhat cryptic but crucial remark, but for my purposes it must suggest that melodrama, in striving to give aesthetic resonance to a range of religious and political factors, foregoes in principle any uniformly aesthetic structuration (or signification). Instead, it avowedly enters into an overdetermined (or "excessive") relation to its signifieds. Against the well-known Althusserian account of the text as overdetermined in an unconscious fashion and thus fractured by "structuring absences,"[13] melodrama may open itself up "consciously" to the torsion of these non-aesthetic "absences," making them "present." Quite as obviously, this makes for a considerable uneasiness with melodrama: it makes "large but unsubstantiable claims on meaning."

Of course, such a project – to make "absences" "present" – is compromised by the Derridean play of *différance*,[14] but this latter exhaustive relativism would deny the possibility and therefore the urgency of a textual practice like melo-drama's contribution to public discourse, which perforce must make "large but unsubstantiable claims on meaning." Only an *a priori* dismissal, like Althusser's, of an artistic text's ability to make potentially correct validity claims would reject this in principle. To be more precise, it is not because a textual practice like melodrama makes claims on meaning that it is to be suspected, but that it makes, and can make nothing but, "unsubstantiable" claims, that is, claims unable to yield the type of "scientific" knowledge which Althusser so rigorously distin-guishes from "ideology," that it is *en procès*.[15]

René Girard's work[16] allows us to amplify questions of de- or re-sacralization and focus on a specific problem which I want to take up in relation to the melodramatic structures of contemporary Hollywood cinema, that of violence. For Girard, human interaction, represented in literature (*Deceit, Desire, and the Novel*), anthropology (*Violence and the Sacred*), and central religious texts (*Des choses cachées depuis la fondation du monde*) is characterized by "mimetic desire," that is, a principle of pure reciprocity, or "eye for eye and tooth for tooth." Society cannot long survive operating on this principle of unchecked escalation of violence; human cultures arise as the focus of reciprocal violence is shifted onto a single arbitrary victim in a process of scapegoating or "victimage." The motivated and institutionalized repetition of this process leads to the centrality of sacrifice in early cultures, and to myths which support such a social structure.

The "sacred" in traditional societies is thus constituted principally as a means of controlling violence and justifying that control without demystifying it. The sacred order is therefore in itself violent both in terms of the bloody fate of the scapegoat and insofar as violence is not *understood*, merely *regulated*. Modern Western society differs from traditional societies not in that it lacks a sacred order, for resacralization is an unavoidable corollary of desacralization, but in that both the modern sacred order and the means of its violent regulation of violence constitute a qualitatively new development in the long history of human culture. First, the "new" sacred (and, with this, Girard's insights coincide directly with those of Habermas, whom I discuss below) is deracinated:

> The accelerated process of deritualization brought about by the rise of bourgeois society and its universalized system of exchange represents a qualitatively new development. As the purely commemorative models of ritual lose their significance, they are replaced no longer with new but similar manifestations of the violence of divine election, but with "rational" or more precisely rationalized discursive and aesthetic incarnations of the desires generated within the secular exchange system.[17]

So deracinated, in fact, that sacrificial disintegration appears to Girard for the first time in history irreversible.[18]

Second, and highly symptomatic of the first, is the definitive violence posed by the capacity of thermonuclear weaponry to easily annihilate humanity. This constitutes for Girard a uniquely full revelation of "things hidden since the foundation of the world," that is, the fundamental role that violence plays in the structure of human culture.[19] What corresponds in modern society to the justifying role of myth is the technicist mentality which can imagine ways to justify the definitively new scale of nuclear violence.

Further aspects of Girard's analysis will be taken up in the consideration of contemporary Hollywood films' representation of violence. If melodrama is social ritual, bound up with a culture's sacred order and potentially subversive of it, then melodrama of the postwar West must in some way register this quantum leap, these new stakes.

I said I wanted to outline a religious and political framework for melodrama, a delineation of the interaction of religious and political public spheres. The political dimension is usefully clarified in Habermas's analysis of the historical change in the public sphere produced by capitalism. The relation between the institutional framework (Girard's and Brooks's sacred) and subsystems of purposive–rational action (basically the means and relations of production) in precapitalist or traditional societies is one in which the latter is "grounded in the unquestionable underpinning of legitimation provided by mythical, religious or metaphysical interpretations of reality."[20] What distinguishes capitalism is that this relation has been radically changed: systems of purposive–rational action, the economic system, are quite independent of a traditional institutional framework. This analysis becomes pertinent for melodrama when it is considered that Habermas defines the traditional institutional framework in clear melodramatic terms:

> The older . . . world-views . . . answer the central questions of men's collective existence and of individual life history. Their themes are justice and freedom, violence and oppression, happiness and gratification, poverty, illness and death. Their categories are victory and defeat, love and hate, salvation and damnation.[21]

This framework necessitated that public discourse such as political persuasion be defined in relation to melodramatic categories: normative ethical standards, the "good life." As long as public discourse was based on such categories, it was open in principle to debate and refutation generated under the same principles. The type of public debate presupposed and generated by a classic melodramatic text like Stowe's *Uncle Tom's Cabin* exemplifies this point: undiminished melodramatic appeal here can function as potent social reformism precisely because the political–economic system which produced slavery was still subject in principle to a normative religious–ethical framework.[22] That sentimental or melodramatic moralism like Stowe's could function as effective social critique sharpens the contrast with the accomplished division in mature capitalism between the normative and the "purposive–rational" domain. Here, "technocratic consciousness reflects not the sundering of an ethical situation but the repression of 'ethics' such as a category of life."[23] The suppression of normative ethics, which were hitherto appropriately expressed in public discourse in melodramatic terms, leads to the depoliticization of public life and the reification of personal life as the only appropriate domain of the ethical: "traditional world-views and objectifications lose their power and validity *as* myth, *as* public religion, *as* customary ritual, *as* justifying metaphysics, *as* unquestionable tradition. Instead, they are reshaped into subjective belief systems and ethics which ensure the private cogency of modern value orientations."[24]

This is not to claim unqualified clarity and rectitude for melodramatic categories. As Habermas says, "their logic accords with the grammar of systematically distorted communication and with the fateful causality of dissociated symbols and suppressed motives." They are fraught with "wish-fulfillment and substitute gratification."[25] Melodramatic categories are fraught, overdetermined, and express in totalistic terms utopian longings, absolutist ideals, impossible moral purism. They appear at once outrageously naive and embarrassingly authentic: they present the trace of truth with unaccustomed lack of mediation and indirection. Thus they must be "unpacked" psychoanalytically and politically, but this must not involve their deconstruction or reductionist demythologizations as they crystallize and already embody in a sort of epistemological *gestalt* the contradictions and possibilities that such unpacking desires to clarify. They generate both "false consciousness and the power of reflection to which the critique of ideology is indebted."[26]

It is time to recapitulate by way of a working definition, and then turn to the question of film melodrama. My remarks are obviously not intended as an exercise in traditional genre criticism. On the contrary, I have tried to show the inadequacy of a purely aesthetic delimitation of the melodramatic, while at the same time historicizing its coherence within variable interactions of religious, political, and aesthetic forces. Nevertheless, distinctions are necessary – I shall propose a taxonomy of the melodrama "effect" in contemporary Hollywood cinema momentarily.

Melodrama in this account can be best understood not as genre but as a *mode*, *function*, or *effect*. These terms are far more appropriate to the sense of my master metaphor, "force-field," in that they fully allow for the examination of generic categories consensually regarded as melodramatic but also allow that they may appear in a wide variety of media, narrative structures, and aesthetic forms. They are also appropriate in terms of Northrop Frye's classic account of modes.[27] Frye's modal criticism is the closest he gets to a genuine historization of aesthetic forms – it is his "historical criticism." He emphasizes, in his delineation of myth, romance, the high and low mimetic modes, and the ironic mode, that there is constant slippage, combination, and recombination, amongst them.[28] He also proposes a distinction between a "naive" and "sophisticated" deployment of any mode.[29] Finally, however, my account of melodrama would be compromised if Frye's highly dismissive notion of melodrama were accepted – a sort of bastardized subgenre, melodrama exists merely in the interstices of the low mimetic and ironic modes, to be plundered by them toward typically unedifying ends.[30] The melodramatic function, however, may be seen as acutely responsive to socio-historical change, entering into varying combinations, the "modal counterpoint" Frye lauds,[31] and fully displaying the ambivalence created by the juxtaposition of "naive" and "sophisticated" tonality.

The Melodramatic in New Hollywood Cinema

One problem with Brooks's argument is that it is principally a piece of revisionist literary criticism, concerned with the placing of major writers like Balzac and James within a tradition (the melodramatic) to which they have seldom been related. Thus both the extra-aesthetic contexts of melodrama and its twentieth-century "avatars" receive scant attention; a fact of which the writer is of course aware.[32] This is a good part of the reason for discussing the possible amplifications Girard and Habermas contribute. Brooks's thesis may require qualification and adaptation to bear on contemporary melodramatic forms, a task which I will be able only to begin.

Discussions of the melodramatic in film also share in this set of definitional problems. Is film "essentially" melodramatic, as Lotman or Morse imply?[33] Is melodrama basically a matter of plot structures or, as Elsaesser persuasively argues, a matter of the dominance of highly articulated cinematic mise-en-scène over content?[34] The theoretical imponderables posed by melodrama are sharply focused in the forum *Wide Angle* provided recently in its special issue on melodrama.[35] Peter Lehman's editorial introduced a series of political and theoretical contexts for the contemporary study of film melodrama, but the subsequent articles did little to address the melodramatic as such and the extra-textual factors such inquiry must presuppose. If film melodrama can be approached as a type of public discourse on and within a religious–political framework, its textual problematics may be posed in a fresh way.

I want to constitute a set of films whose representations of violence may be elucidated by my account of melodrama. Naturally the melodramatic mode operates in a variety of ways in contemporary Hollywood cinema, but I foreground these films – Friedkin's *The Exorcist*, Coppola's *The Godfather* and *The Godfather II*, Schrader's *Blue Collar*, *Hardcore*, and *American Gigolo*, and Scorsese's *Mean Streets*, *Taxi Driver*, and *Raging Bull* – because their articulations of violence and the relations they pose between religious and political spheres are best elucidated within the framework I have presented. The list is of course not exhaustive, but it is possible to position this group in relation to other types of current Hollywood film in a tentative taxonomy based on representations of violence. "Impersonal/personal" is a relation in which the former will tend to stress cinematically spectacular possibilities of violence while the latter will emphasize the effects of violence on individuals. "Integrative/disintegrative/disintegrative–integrative" are more strictly Girardian categories: "integrative" films stress the cathartic or therapeutic role of violence and imply or assert that its dynamics may be overcome or resolved into a wider harmony – this type has most in common with the more traditional "naive" melodrama of which Griffith's films are the exemplar. "Disintegrative" films emphasize the spectacular and escalatory potential of violence and doubt that it can be contained

	Integrative	Disintegrative	Disintegrative–Integrative
Impersonal	*Close Encounters of the Third Kind*	"disaster" films	
Personal	*Ordinary People*	*The Warriors* *Phantom of the Paradise, Sisters, Carrie, The Fury, Dressed to Kill*	*The Exorcist, Godfather, Godfather II, Taxi Driver, Raging Bull*

(Many others films could be added to this taxonomy; this is a beginning.)

satisfactorily except in gestures toward narrative resolution. Films in the "disin-tegrative–integrative" category articulate most extensively the *dialectic* of violence which Girard's notion of mimetic desire explains. Such a category excludes the possibility that there is an "impersonal" outworking of violence, thus "imperso-nal/disintegrative–integrative" remains unfilled.

The films in this group operate within certain melodramatic conventions, although they would in many respects appear strange generic bedfellows for "naive" melodramas modeled on the representation of an Edenic state and the triumph of virtue. Conversely, melodramatic operations such as the effort at full signification, the triumph over repression, moral purism and melodrama's func-tioning as public discourse, however much transformed from earlier instances of melodrama, must be accounted for.

Directors such as Scorsese, Schrader, Hill, de Palma, and Coppola have been called "brutalists"; a widespread debate has grown over their use of violence.[36] Their critics argue that films which focus obsessively on violence as a style of life and develop a cinematic style which seems itself violent neglect the effect such representations may have on audiences and indeed encourage "the immense potential for savagery that already exists in America."[37] Their supporters argue in favor of the filmmaker's right to exercise artistic freedom and to address fraught issues in a mature and, if desired, stylized and playful way.

Girard introduces into his argument on violence, mimetic desire, and their textual representations a methodological hierarchy similar in structure to the familiar approach in film theory that distinguishes between texts which variously reproduce (for Girard, imitate), dominate ideology, achieve "moments of subver-sion" against dominance, or, best, inaugurate "strategies of subversion."[38] This group of films typifies the ambivalence of the melodramatic mode in that they give evidence of all three operations, but tend strongly toward subversion, or, in Girard's terms, "revelation," of the dynamics of mimetic desire and violence.

Girard presents in his argument the notion of "texts of mystified persecu-tion."[39] Girard has in mind texts of medieval and modern anti-Semitism, records of the Spanish Inquisition and the trials of witches, and oral texts of modern racism. The point he makes is that the more stylized, stereotypical, or outrageous the violence of these texts, the more insistently they register the contexts of real violence in which they are situated. That these texts offer seemingly unsubstanti-able claims, about the nature of Jews for instance, that they often offer contra-dictory explanations or undecidable choices about the reasons for violence, leads Girard to call them mystified, but nevertheless also means that they register the undecidability, contradictory nature, and terrifying "undifferentiation" (the col-lapse of social structure and human identity) that real violence generates.

The films under consideration are in some ways like texts of mystified perse-cution. Their stylization and excess (one aspect of the common wisdom that the "new" Hollywood directors have a highly self-conscious stance with regard to cinematic conventions and history) in no way implies that they have neglected cinema's "serious" function as public discourse, as Moss's criticism of "brutalism" asserts. Their deployment of melodramatic conventions is central to this, in that melodrama consistently strives for Brooks's "full signification," the ascendancy of the signified over the signifier which in turn produces an excessive signifier. The escalation of, or obsession with, violence in new Hollywood cinema is a mark of the need of the contemporary public sphere to deal with a situation of definitively new levels of mimeticism and violence and the lack of a framework of normative judgment to deal with such a situation.

One would expect, following Brooks, Girard, and Habermas, that this situation would generate (melodramatic) representations of religion and morality. This is certainly the case. Violence is overdetermined, or excessive, because the stakes of moral struggle are overdetermined. The central characters of the films under consideration, by Promethean *tours de force*, carve new moral equilibria out of starkly resistant worlds. Within their Promethean projects, not the slightest moral lapse can remain untransfigured. The slightest moral indulgence ("slight" from the position of bourgeois tolerance) precipitates excessive violence. The at times repulsive, fundamental physicality involved in the outworking of these projects breaks strong cinematic and social conventions in the effort to achieve full signification. Bourgeois tolerance, restraint, politeness, and rationality (and the comedies of manners so beloved by Hollywood based on them) may retain a residual trace of an ability to regulate violence, but have become increasingly inadequate to respond to the institutionalized violence the technicist economic–cultural system they purport to "manage" perpetrates on those who are not the beneficiaries of the system. Moreover, the radical absence in these films of a melodramatic staple, the family as a site of unproblematic and virtuous social order, heightens the Promethean individualism and starkness of moral oppositions. Central characters also are not stereotypically good or evil, a dominant structure of earlier "naive" melodrama, but embody within themselves Manichean oppositions. It is not that the classically Manichean structures of melodrama have broken down, but that they have on the contrary been strengthened: the absolute moral struggle of good and evil now fractures character unity as it once in earlier melodrama split families or social sub-groups. It is not the interiorized psychology of individuals that is at issue but the psychopathology of social life. Thus in several ways melodramatic structures persist but are translated in terms of contemporary realities.

These films do more than symptomatically register the contemporary dialectic of violence, however; they also work to "reveal" its mechanisms. Their narrative and thematic structures are characterized by the collapse of the "sacred," that is, the mechanisms of mediation which regulate and mitigate the escalation of violence as a result of mimetic desire. For Girard, desire is always mediated – we only desire something and know what we desire when a model "other" desires the same object and so establishes the value and direction of our desire. The more we strive to imitate the model, that is, the stronger our desire, the more the imitation is transfigured into conflictual rivalry and the more the initial object of desire diminishes in importance. Crucially, this is already a *narrative* account, which itself corresponds, as Girard recognizes, to an aesthetic text's typical structure.

A systematic collapse of mediations occurs in *The Exorcist*. Chris MacNeil is a famous actress who, as the film's main action commences after the prologue in Iraq, is playing the role of what is probably a university administrator who appeals to a crowd of chanting demonstrators that they should "work through the system" to effect change. There is some doubt in her mind, however, about her role; she asks the director the "meaning" of her part. From the first sequence of the body of the film, there is an under-cutting of the adequacy of "working within the system." The "system" is also represented explicitly as political mediation: the main action takes place at the seat of political power, suburban Washington; Chris MacNeil is an invitee of the White House, for a "small" supper. (The main "spin-off" of *The Exorcist*, *The Omen*, sharpens this exclusion of political mediation: Gregory Peck is a major American diplomat; the demonic child is born to his family so that he might be in a good position to take over the presidency.) The positivist rationality of the political sphere is included in and transcended by transcendental power, as the devil possessing Regan in his "playful" dialogues with Father Karras amply demonstrates.

The most explicit exclusion, of course, is that of medical, psychiatric, and psychological "explanations" of Regan's possession. It is perfectly appropriate, moreover, given the widespread deference to and even quasi-religious belief in, psychological and psychiatric models of explanation in the modern Western sacred order, that this is the mediation which proves most resistant to the film's climactic "revelation" of unmediated rivalry between Karras-as-Christ and the devil, who is, as Father Merrin reminds Karras, not three personalities, only one. Many critics attempted to dismiss the film as "devilishly" black humor, in the poorest taste, about a young girl's puberty. Notwithstanding this attempt to circumscribe the film within a "pop" psychological explanation (Regan is a girl with an Electra complex, her father is absent and uncaring – he doesn't even phone on her birthday, the ambivalence toward paternal authority is "internalized" as possession which permits an outworking of otherwise forbidden sexual display magnified as extreme rebellion), the film incorporates and transcends the psychological as finally another inadequate mediation.

The film goes even further in its exclusion of mediation. The rite of exorcism, that is, institutionalized religious mediation of presumably the most efficacious kind, is finally terminated, in the death of Merrin. The ultimate rivalry is between the devil and Karras, not as psychiatrist, not as priest, but as Christ, sacrificing his own life that disintegrative violence may finally cease. The true exorcist of the title is not Merrin, the "official" exorcist, but the film's hero, Karras.

The *locus classicus* of the articulation of "disintegrative–integrative" violence are the two *Godfather* films. They are "textbook" Girard. *The Godfather*'s narrative is based on the exemplary mimetic rivalry of a blood feud or "clan" warfare over an explicit "object," the control of the narcotics racket in New York.

Violence is initially represented as integrative; the Corleone "extended" family is integrated and maintained by violence directed outside itself. As any order based on violence, however, this integration is inherently unstable; violence directed against the Corleone family by other families seeking to maintain their "integrity" precipitates an escalation of unmediated violence. This is only checked by the "inauguration" of sacrifice – of the "first sons" of the Corleone and Tattaglia families.

As Girard does in his methodological move back (to the origins of the sacrificial order) and forward (to the irreversible breakdown of that order) from this "minimal unit" of mimetic desire, so *The Godfather II* is structured before and after the events of the earlier film. In the Vito Corleone sequences, we observe the violent origins of the established order presented in the first film. In the Michael Corleone sequences, the irreversible disintegration of that order unfolds. Mimetic conflict in the latter uses up and discards desired objects, potential models, and rivals and becomes increasingly internecine. Finally, Michael is left with only unbounded desire and the destruction of his family as a result of that desire.[40]

Travis Bickle in *Taxi Driver* is a contemporary avatar of Dostoevski's underground man.[41] The film's narrative progression demonstrates the arbitrariness and increasing slippage from desired object to object, model to rival. Travis's initial "relationship" with Betsy manages for a limited time to mediate the public–private torsion: the relationship offers some promise to fulfill both Travis's personal needs and give his disgust a focused object by his joining Palantine's political campaign. When the relationship breaks down, the public and private split. Model turns to rival. Palantine becomes the object of Travis's assassination attempt, and he attempts to absolutely subsume the personalized object of desire, Iris, in his increasingly transcendental project of desire. The much-disputed end of the film is an ironic display of the inadequate catharsis of Travis's paradoxical, publicly acclaimed success in "saving" Iris. Schrader, the film's scriptwriter, "reveals" these mechanisms clearly:

> What [Travis] seeks is escape, to shake off the mortal chains and die a glorious death. It's a purely suicidal mission he's on, so to give some greater meaning he fixes on the surrogate father – Betsy's boss, the candidate – then on the other surrogate father – Iris' pimp; he has to destroy that image to break free. It's a shallow, self-destructive kind of freedom. At the end of the film he is cheated because the gun is empty and he can't kill himself. But, in time, the cycle will again come around and he'll succeed the next time.[42]

The melodramtic mode is an insistent principle in these films. Frentz and Farrell point out the typically melodramatic effort at "full signification" in *The Exorcist*:

> First, by compressing and personifying the recurrent struggle between Positivistic Evil and Transcendent Good in two characters – the child, Regan, and Father

Karras, respectively – the work at once made the human consequences of the confrontation recognizable, explicit, and simple. Second, by elevating the struggle itself to an optimal transcendental level – as a battle between two almost extra-terrestrial forces – the work gave the struggle monumental popular significance.[43]

The genre of the "demon" film generally registers the desperate need for revitalized social rituals and the necessity for founding and public discourse in holistic and transcendent principles.[44] This is even more pertinent a decade after *The Exorcist* as the emergence in the last few years of the "New Right" testifies.

The apparent weakness of *Godfather II*'s "sentimentality, repetition, and melodrama"[45] in fact allows a greater concentration on the implicit social critique both *Godfather* films present, a component which cannot be contained within conventions of "good" entertainment: pace, drama, textual resolution. Melodrama and social critique here reinforce each other: *Godfather II* presents a constant interplay between melodrama's Edenic state, "the luminous bourgeois ideals of peace, freedom, opportunity, love, and community, and the harsh, brutal realities of the irrational economic system which encourages these ideals and feeds off their unobtainability."[46]

Schrader's films have been repeatedly criticized for the starkness of moral oppositions, the clumsy, implausible, almost off-handed plots, and the films' pervasive moral extremism. However, these are an enactment of the extremity of choice that faces us socially and spiritually and a refusal to craft well-rounded, harmonized resolutions of such choices, which would merely be aesthetic resolutions. Instead, the resolutions of his films *Blue Collar, Hardcore,* and *American Gigolo* abandon conventions of realist plausibility (*Blue Collar*: the freeze-frame and gestic slogan; *Hardcore*: Jake Vandorn finds his daughter, who first rejects him and then immediately changes completely and accepts him; *American Gigolo*: Michelle, who has come to love Julian Kay with a miraculous insistence, is able to hear his declaration of transcendent love for her through a soundproof window) for the deeper plausibility of the hope and desire, the wish-fulfillment, for change, resolution, and harmony.[47]

Notes

I want to thank Richard Herskowitz for his considerable personal encouragement and assistance. His work-in-progress, "Film in the Public Sphere" (Ph. D. dissertation, Communication Arts, University of Wisconsin-Madison) is a detailed application of the work of Gregory Bateson, Girard, and Habermas to film studies.

1   (New Haven, Conn.: Yale University Press, 1976), p. xiii.
2   Eric Bentley, "Melodrama," in *The Life of the Drama* (New York: Atheneum, 1964); James L. Rosenberg, "Melodrama," in *The Context and Craft of Drama*, eds. R. W. Corrigan and J. L. Rosenberg (San Francisco: Chandler, 1964); Robert B. Heilman,

Tragedy and Melodrama: Versions of Experience (Seattle: University of Washington Press, 1968); David Grimsted, *Melodrama Unveiled: American Theater and Culture 1880–1850* (Chicago: University of Chicago Press, 1968); Frank Rahill, *The World of Melodrama* (Philadelphia: University of Pennsylvania Press, 1967); James L. Smith, *Melodrama* (London: Methuen, 1973); John Cawelti, *Adventure, Mystery, Romance* (Chicago: University of Chicago: University of Chicago Press, 1960); Thomas Elsaesser, "Tales of Sound and Fury," *Monogram* No. 4 (1972); Lesley Stern, "Oedipal Opera: *The Restless Years*," *Australian Journal of Screen Theory* No. 4 (1978); Tania Modleski, "The Search for Tomorrow in Today's Soap Operas," *Film Quaterly* XXXIII, No. 1 (Fall, 1979).

3 Brooks, pp. 11–12.

4 George Steiner, *The Death of Tragedy* (New York: Oxford University Press, 1961), p. 133.

5 Russell Merritt, "Film and the Melodramatic Imagination," paper presented at MMLA Conference, Minneapolis, November 1980.

6 Brooks, p. 44.

7 Brooks, pp. 14–15.

8 Elsaesser, p. 3.

9 The notion of the "performative utterance" is developed by J. L. Austin and J. R. Searle. See Austin, *How to Do Things with Words* (Cambridge: Harvard University Press, 1975) and Searle, *Speech Acts: An Essay in the Philosophy of Language* (Cambridge: Cambridge University Press, 1969).

10 Brooks, p. 201.

11 Brooks, p. 198.

12 Brooks, p. 199. Although Brooks is coy about his theoretical *reprise*, one would expect that the postulation is made against, on the one hand, defenses of realism as capable of comprehending the social totality (i.e. the signified symmetrical with the signifier) such as Luckacs's, and on the other, structuralist and poststructuralist justifications of modernism (the signifier in excess of the signified).

13 Ben Brewster, "Overdetermination," Glossary to Louis Althusser and Etienne Balibar, *Reading Capital* (London: NLB, 1970), p. 315, and the classic by *Cahiers du cinéma* editors, "John Ford's Young Mr. Lincoln," *Screen* 13, No. 3 (Autumn 1972), reprinted in *Screen Reader* 1 (London: Sept. 1977).

14 For example, Jacques Derrida, *L'Ecriture et la différence* (Paris: Seuil, 1967).

15 Brewster, "Ideology," "Knowledge," "Practice, Economic, Political, Ideological and Theoretical," "Science," in Glossary to *Reading Capital*, pp. 314, 316, 318, and Althusser, "A Letter on Art in Reply to André Daspre" and "Creminoni, Painter of the Abstract," *Lenin and Philosophy and other essays* (London: NLB, 1977). Both Girard and Habermas, whose work is used below, build into their cultural theories an explicit recognition that *any* theory makes "large but unsubstantiable claims on meaning" – Girard's "hypothesis" of originary unanimous victimage, Habermas's validity claims based on an "ideal speech act." Their work is thus considerably more amenable to the task of advancing Brooks's arguments. I have proposed a similar argument as this with regard to propagandist texts in "Tense, Address, *Tendenz*: Questions of the Work of Peter Watkins," *Quarterly Review of Film Studies* 5, No. 4 (Fall 1980), p. 505.

16 René Girard, *Deceit, Desire, and the Novel: Self and Other in Literary Structure* (Baltimore: Johns Hopkins, 1965); *Violence and the Sacred* (Baltimore: Johns Hopkins, 1977); *Des choses cachées depuis la fondation du monde* (Paris: Grasset, 1978); "*To*

Double Business Bound:" Essays on Literature, Mimesis, and Anthropology (Baltimore: Johns Hopkins, 1978).

17 Eric Gans, "Scandal to the Jews, Folly to the Pagans" (review of *Des choses cachées*), *Diacritics* (September 1979), p. 47.

18 "An Interview with René Girard," *"To Double Business Bound,"* p. 219.

19 "An Interview with René Girard," p. 204.

20 Jürgen Habermas, "Technology and Science as 'Ideology,'" *Toward A Rational Society* (London: Heinemann, 1971), p. 95.

21 Habermas, p. 96.

22 Jane P. Tompkins, "Sentimental Power: *Uncle Tom's Cabin* and the Politics of Literary History," *Glyph* 8 (Baltimore: Johns Hopkins, 1981) demonstrates this connection between melodrama and social–political impact in detail.

23 Habermas, p. 112.

24 Habermas, pp. 98–9.

25 Habermas, pp. 96, 111.

26 Habermas, p. 111.

27 Northrop Frye, *Anatomy of Criticism: Four Essays* (Princeton: Princeton University Press, 1971), "First Essay. Historical Criticism: Theory of Modes."

28 Frye, pp. 42, 50.

29 Frye, p. 35

30 Frye, pp. 40, 47.

31 Frye, pp. 50–1.

32 Brooks, p. xiv.

33 Jurij Lotman, *Semiotics of Cinema* (Ann Arbor: University of Michigan Press, 1976, p. 90: "cliche is an organic part of cinema aesthetics;" David Morse, "every article about the cinema ought to talk about Griffith," *Monogram* No. 4 (1972), p. 16: "The cinema proved to be admirably adapted to the demands of melodrama."

34 Elsaesser, "Tales of Sound and Fury."

35 *Wide Angle* 4, No. 2 (1980).

36 Robert F. Moss, "The Brutalists: Making Movies Mean and Ugly," *Saturday Review* (October 1980). See also Philip Nobile, "Adler vs Kael," *Saturday Review* (August 1980).

37 Jean-Louis Comolli and Jean Narboni, "Cinema / Ideology / Criticism (1)," *Screen* 12, No. 1 (Spring 1971), reprinted in *Screen Reader* and Colin MacCabe, "Realism and the Cinema: Notes on Some Brechtian Theses," *Screen* 15, No. 2 (Summer 1974).

38 Girard's structure has Nietzsche and the early Dostoevski reproducing mimetic desire; Ingmar Bergman, among others, achieving "moments of subversion;" and Shakespeare, later Dostoevski, Dante, Proust, and the Bible inaugurating strategies of subversion against mimetic desire.

39 Girard, "Violence and Representation in the Mythical Text," in *"To Double Business Bound,"* p. 190. See also *Des choses cachées*, pp. 136–62.

40 See, especially, Girard, "Strategies of Madness – Nietzsche, Wagner, and Dostoevski," *"To Double Business Bound,"* ch. 4.

41 Cf. Girard, "The Underground Critic," *"To Double Business Bound,"* ch. 3.

42 "Screenwriter: *Taxi Driver*'s Paul Schrader interviewed by Richard Thompson," *Film Comment* (March–April 1976), p. 14.

43 Thomas S. Frentz and Thomas B. Farrell, "Conversion of America's Consciousness: The Rhetoric of *The Exorcist*," *Quarterly Journal of Speech* 61 (February 1975), p. 43.
44 Frentz and Farrell, p. 47.
45 John Hess, "*Godfather II*: A Deal Coppola Couldn't Refuse," in Bill Nichols (ed.), *Movies and Methods* (Berkeley: University of California Press, 1976), p. 83.
46 Hess, p. 85.
47 I develop these comments on Schrader in "Faith and Film," *Vanguard* 10, No. 6 (Nov–Dec. 1980).

13
Film Bodies: Gender, Genre, and Excess

Linda Williams

When my seven-year-old son and I go to the movies we often select from among categories of films that promise to be sensational, to give our bodies an actual physical jolt. He calls these movies "gross." My son and I agree that the fun of "gross" movies is in their display of sensations that are on the edge of respectable. Where we disagree – and where we as a culture often disagree, along lines of gender, age, or sexual orientation – is in which movies are over the edge, too "gross." To my son the good "gross" movies are those with scary monsters like Freddy Krueger (of the *Nightmare on Elm Street* series) who rip apart teenagers, especially teenage girls. These movies both fascinate and scare him; he is actually more interested in talking about than seeing them.

A second category, one that I like and my son doesn't, are sad movies that make you cry. These are gross in their focus on unseemly emotions that may remind him too acutely of his own powerlessness as a child. A third category, of both intense interest and disgust to my son (he makes the puke sign when speaking of it), he can only describe euphemistically as "the 'K' word." K is for kissing. To a seven-year-old boy it is kissing precisely which is obscene.

There is no accounting for taste, especially in the realm of the "gross." As a culture we most often invoke the term to designate excesses we wish to exclude; to say, for example, which of the Robert Mapplethorpe photos we draw the line at, but not to say what form and structure and function operate within the representations deemed excessive. Because so much attention goes to determining where to draw the line, discussions of the gross are often a highly confused hodgepodge of different categories of excess. For example, pornography is today more often deemed excessive for its violence than for its sex, while horror films are excessive in their displacement of sex onto violence. In contrast, melodramas are deemed excessive for their gender- and sex-linked pathos, for their naked displays of emotion; Ann Douglas once referred to the genre of romance fiction as "soft-core emotional porn for women" (Douglas, 1980).

Alone or in combination, heavy doses of sex, violence, and emotion are dismissed by one faction or another as having no logic or reason for existence beyond their power to excite. Gratuitous sex, gratuitous violence and terror, gratuitous emotion are frequent epithets hurled at the phenomenon of the "sensational" in pornography, horror, and melodrama. This essay explores the notion that there may be some value in thinking about the form, function, and system of seemingly gratuitous excesses in these three genres. For if, as it seems, sex, violence, and emotion are fundamental elements of the sensational effects of these three types of films, the designation "gratuitous" is itself gratuitous. My hope, therefore, is that by thinking comparatively about all three "gross" and sensational film body genres we might be able to get beyond the mere fact of sensation to explore its system and structure as well as its effect on the bodies of spectators.

Body Genres

The repetitive formulas and spectacles of film genres are often defined by their differences from the classical realist style of narrative cinema. These classical films have been characterized as efficient action-centered, goal-oriented linear narratives driven by the desire of a single protagonist, involving one or two lines of action, and leading to definitive closure. In their influential study of the Classical Hollywood Cinema, Bordwell, Staiger, and Thompson (1985) call this the Classical Hollywood style.

As Rick Altman has noted in a recent article (1989), both genre study and the study of the somewhat more nebulous category of melodrama has long been hampered by assumptions about the classical nature of the dominant narrative to which melodrama and some individual genres have been opposed. Altman argues that Bordwell, Staiger, and Thompson who locate the Classical Hollywood Style in the linear, progressive form of the Hollywood narrative, cannot accommodate "melodramatic" attributes like spectacle, episodic presentation, or dependence on coincidence except as limited exceptions or "play" within the dominant linear causality of the classical (Altman, 1989: 346).

Altman writes: "Unmotivated events, rhythmic montage, highlighted parallelism, overlong spectacles – these are the excesses in the classical narrative system that alert us to the existence of a competing logic, a second voice" (ibid.: 345–6). Altman, whose own work on the movie musical has necessarily relied upon analyses of seemingly "excessive" spectacles and parallel constructions, thus makes a strong case for the need to recognize the possibility that excess may itself be organized as a system (ibid.: 347). Yet analyses of systems of excess have been much slower to emerge in the genres whose non-linear spectacles have centered more directly upon the gross display of the human body. Pornography and horror films are two such systems of excess. Pornography is the lowest in cultural esteem, gross-out horror is next to lowest.

Melodrama, however, refers to a much broader category of films and a much larger system of excess. It would not be unreasonable, in fact, to consider all three of these genres under the extended rubric of melodrama, considered as a filmic mode of stylistic and/or emotional excess that stands in contrast to more "dominant" modes of realistic, goal-oriented narrative. In this extended sense melodrama can encompass a broad range of films marked by "lapses" in realism, by "excesses" of spectacle and displays of primal, even infantile emotions, and by narratives that seem circular and repetitive. Much of the interest of melodrama to film scholars over the last fifteen years originates in the sense that the form exceeds the normative system of much narrative cinema. I shall limit my focus here, however, to a more narrow sense of melodrama, leaving the broader category of the sensational to encompass the three genres I wish to consider. Thus, partly for purposes of contrast with pornography, the melodrama I will consider here will consist of the form that has most interested feminist critics – that of "the woman's film" or "weepie." These are films addressed to women in their traditional status under patriarchy – as wives, mothers, abandoned lovers, or in their traditional status as bodily hysteria or excess, as in the frequent case of the woman "afflicted" with a deadly or debilitating disease.[1]

What are the pertinent features of bodily excess shared by these three "gross" genres? First, there is the spectacle of a body caught in the grip of intense sensation or emotion. Carol Clover, speaking primarily of horror films and pornography, has called films which privilege the sensational "body" genres (Clover, 1987: 189). I am expanding Clover's notion of low body genres to include the sensation of overwhelming pathos in the "weepie." The body spectacle is featured most sensationally in pornography's portrayal of orgasm, in horror's portrayal of violence and terror, and in melodrama's portrayal of weeping. I propose that an investigation of the visual and narrative pleasures found in the portrayal of these three types of excess could be important to a new direction in genre criticism that would take as its point of departure – rather than as an unexamined assumption – questions of gender construction, and gender address in relation to basic sexual fantasies.

Another pertinent feature shared by these body genres is the focus on what could probably best be called a form of ecstasy. While the classical meaning of the original Greek word is insanity and bewilderment, more contemporary meanings suggest components of direct or indirect sexual excitement and rapture, a rapture which informs even the pathos of melodrama.

Visually, each of these ecstatic excesses could be said to share a quality of uncontrollable convulsion or spasm – of the body "beside itself" with sexual pleasure, fear and terror, or overpowering sadness. Aurally, excess is marked by recourse not to the coded articulations of language but to inarticulate cries of pleasure in porn, screams of fear in horror, sobs of anguish in melodrama.

Looking at, and listening to, these bodily ecstasies, we can also notice something else that these genres seem to share: though quite differently gendered with respect to their targeted audiences, with pornography aimed, presumably, at active men and melodramatic weepies aimed, presumably, at passive women, and with contemporary gross-out horror aimed at adolescents careening wildly between the two masculine and feminine poles, in each of these genres the bodies of women figured on the screen have functioned traditionally as the primary *embodiments* of pleasure, fear, and pain.

In other words, even when the pleasure of viewing has traditionally been constructed for masculine spectators, as is the case in most traditional heterosexual pornography, it is the female body in the grips of an out-of-control ecstasy that has offered the most sensational sight. So the bodies of women have tended to function, ever since the eighteenth-century origins of these genres in the Marquis de Sade, Gothic fiction, and the novels of Richardson, as both the *moved* and the *moving*. It is thus through what Foucault has called the sexual saturation of the female body that audiences of all sorts have received some of their most powerful sensations (Foucault, 1978: 104).

There are, of course, other film genres which both portray and affect the sensational body, e.g. thrillers, musicals, comedies. I suggest, however, that the film genres that have had especially low cultural status – which have seemed to exist as excesses to the system of even the popular genres – are not simply those which sensationally display bodies on the screen and register effects in the bodies of spectators. Rather, what may especially mark these body genres as low is the perception that the body of the spectator is caught up in an almost involuntary mimicry of the emotion or sensation of the body on the screen along with the fact that the body displayed is female. Physical clown comedy is another "body" genre concerned with all manner of gross activities and body functions – eating shoes, slipping on banana peels. Nonetheless, it has not been deemed gratuitously excessive, probably because the reaction of the audience does not mimic the sensations experienced by the central clown. Indeed, it is almost a rule that the audience's physical reaction of laughter does not coincide with the often dead-pan reactions of the clown.

In the body genres I am isolating here, however, it seems to be the case that the success of these genres is often measured by the degree to which the audience sensation mimics what is seen on the screen. Whether this mimicry is exact, e.g. whether the spectator at the porn film actually orgasms, whether the spectator at the horror film actually shudders in fear, whether the spectator of the melodrama actually dissolves in tears, the success of these genres seems a self-evident matter of measuring bodily response. Examples of such measurement can be readily observed: in the "peter meter" capsule reviews in *Hustler* magazine, which measure the power of a porn film in degrees of erection of little cartoon penises; in horror films which measure success in terms of screams, fainting, and heart attacks in the audience (horror producer William Castle specialized in this kind of thing with such films as *The Tingler*, 1959); and in the long-standing tradition of women's films measuring their success in terms of one-, two-, or three-hand-kerchief movies.

What seems to bracket these particular genres from others is an apparent lack of proper aesthetic distance, a sense of over-involvement in sensation and emotion. We feel manipulated by these texts – an impression that the very colloquialisms of "tear jerker" and "fear jerker" express – and to which we could add pornography's even cruder sense as texts to which some people might be inclined to "jerk off." The rhetoric of violence of the jerk suggests the extent to which viewers feel too directly, too viscerally manipulated by the text in specifically gendered ways. Mary Ann Doane, for example, writing about the most genteel of these jerkers – the maternal melodrama – equates the violence of this emotion to a kind of "textual rape" of the targeted female viewer, who is "feminized through pathos" (Doane, 1987: 95).

Feminist critics of pornography often evoke similar figures of sexual/textual violence when describing the operation of this genre. Robin Morgan's slogan "pornography is the theory, and rape is the practice" is well known (Morgan, 1980: 139). Implicit in this slogan is the notion that women are the objectified victims of pornographic representations, that the image of the sexually ecstatic woman so important to the genre is a celebration of female victimization and a prelude to female victimization in real life.

Less well known, but related, is the observation of the critic of horror films, James Twitchell, who notices that the Latin *horrere* means to bristle. He describes the way the nape hair stands on end during moments of shivering excitement. The aptly named Twitchell thus describes a kind of erection of the hair founded in the conflict between reactions of "fight and flight" (Twitchell, 1985: 10). While male victims in horror films may shudder and scream as well, it has long been a dictum of the genre that women make the best victims. "Torture the women!" was the famous advice given by Alfred Hitchcock.[2]

In the classic horror film the terror of the female victim shares the spectacle along with the monster. Fay Wray and the mechanized monster that made her scream in *King Kong* is a familiar example of the classic form. Janet Leigh in the shower in *Psycho* is a familiar example of a transition to a more sexually explicit form of the tortured and terrorized woman. And her daughter, Jamie Lee Curtis in *Halloween*, can serve as the more contemporary version of the terrorized woman victim. In both of these later films the spectacle of the monster seems to take second billing to the increasingly numerous victims slashed by the sexually disturbed but entirely human monsters.

In the woman's film a well-known classic is the long-suffering mother of the two early versions of *Stella Dallas* who sacrifices herself for her daughter's upward mobility. Contemporary filmgoers could recently see Bette Midler going through the same sacrifice and loss in the film *Stella*. Debra Winger in *Terms of Endearment* is another familiar example of this maternal pathos.

With the above genre stereotypes in mind we should now ask about the status of bodily excess in each of these genres. Is it simply the unseemly, "gratuitous" presence of the sexually ecstatic woman, the tortured woman, the weeping woman – and the accompanying presence of the sexual fluids, the blood and the tears that flow from her body and which are presumably mimicked by spectators – that mark the excess of each type of film? How shall we think of these bodily displays in relation to one another, as a system of excess in the popular film? And finally, how excessive are they really?

The psychoanalytic system of analysis that has been so influential in film study in general and in feminist film theory and criticism has been remarkably ambivalent about the status of excess in its major tools of analysis. The categories of fetishism, voyeurism, sadism, and masochism frequently invoked to describe the pleasures of film spectatorship are by definition perversions. Perversions are usually defined as sexual excesses, specifically as excesses which are deflected away from "proper" end goals onto substitute goals or objects – fetishes instead of genitals, looking instead of touching, etc. – which seem excessive or gratuitous. Yet the perverse pleasures of film viewing are hardly gratuitous. They have been considered so basic that they have often been presented as norms. What is a film, after all, without voyeurism? Yet, at the same time, feminist critics have asked, what is the position of women within this pleasure geared to a presumably sadistic "male gaze" (Mulvey, 1975)? To what extent is she its victim? Are the orgasmic woman of pornography and the tortured woman of horror merely in the service of the sadistic male gaze? And is the weeping woman of melodrama appealing to the abnormal perversions of masochism in female viewers?

These questions point to the ambiguity of the terms of perversion used to describe the normal pleasures of film viewing. Without attempting to go into any of the complexities of this discussion here – a discussion which must ultimately relate to the status of the term perversion in theories of sexuality themselves – let me simply suggest the value of not invoking the perversions as terms of condemnation. As even the most cursory reading of Freud shows, sexuality is by definition perverse. The "aims" and "objects" of sexual desire are often obscure and inherently substitutive. Unless we are willing to see reproduction as the common goal of the sexual drive, we have to admit, as Jonathan Dollimore has put it, that we are all perverts. Dollimore's goal of retrieving the "concept of perversion as a category of cultural analysis" – as a structure intrinsic to all sexuality rather than extrinsic to it – is crucial to any attempt to understand cultural forms – such as our three body genres – in which fantasy predominates.[3]

Structures of Perversion in the "Female Body Genres"

Each of the three body genres I have isolated hinges on the spectacle of a "sexually saturated" female body, and each offers what many feminist critics would agree to be spectacles of feminine victimization. But this victimization is very different in each type of film and cannot be accounted for simply by pointing to the sadistic power and pleasure of masculine subject positions punishing or dominating feminine objects.

Many feminists have pointed to the victimization of the woman performers of pornography who must actually do the acts depicted in the film, as well as to the victimization of characters within the films (Dworkin, 1979; MacKinnon, 1987).

Pornography, in this view, is fundamentally sadistic. In women's weepies, on the other hand, feminists have pointed to the spectacles of intense suffering and loss as masochistic.

In horror films, while feminists have often pointed to the women victims who suffer simulated torture and mutilation as victims of sadism (Williams, 1983), more recent feminist work has suggested that the horror film may present an interesting, and perhaps instructive, case of oscillation between masochistic and sadistic poles. This more recent argument, advanced by Carol J. Clover, has suggested that pleasure, for a masculine-identified viewer, oscillates between identifying with the initial passive powerlessness of the abject and terrorized girl-victim of horror and her later, active empowerment (Clover, 1987).

This argument holds that when the girl-victim of a film like *Halloween* finally grabs the phallic knife, or ax, or chain saw to turn the tables on the monster-killer, that viewer identification shifts from an "abject terror gendered feminine" to an active power with bisexual components. A gender-confused monster is foiled, often symbolically castrated by an "androgynous" "final girl" (ibid.: 206–9). In slasher films, identification with victimization is a roller-coaster ride of sadomasochistic thrills.

We could thus initially schematize the perverse pleasures of these genres in the following way: pornography's appeal to its presumed male viewers would be characterized as sadistic, horror films' appeal to the emerging sexual identities of its (frequently adolescent) spectators would be sadomasochistic, and women's films' appeal to presumed female viewers would be masochistic.

The masochistic component of viewing pleasure for women has been the most problematic term of perversion for feminist critics. It is interesting, for example, that most of our important studies of masochism – whether by Deleuze (1971), Silverman (1980; 1988), or Studlar (1985) – have all focused on the exoticism of masculine masochism rather than the familiarity of female masochism. Masochistic pleasure for women has paradoxically seemed either too normal – too much the normal yet intolerable condition of women – or too perverse to be taken seriously as pleasure.

There is thus a real need to be clearer than we have been about what is in masochism for women – how power and pleasure operate in fantasies of domination which appeal to women. There is an equal need to be clearer than we have about what is in sadism for men. Here the initial opposition between these two most gendered genres – women's weepies and male heterosexual pornography – needs to be complicated. I have argued elsewhere, for example, that pornography has too simplistically been allied with a purely sadistic fantasy structure. Indeed, those troubling films and videos which deploy instruments of torture on the bodies of women have been allied so completely with masculine viewing pleasures that we have not paid enough attention to their appeal to women except to condemn such appeal as false consciousness (Williams, 1989: 184–228).

One important complication of the initial schema I have outlined would thus be to take a lesson from Clover's more bisexual model of viewer identification in horror film and stress the sadomasochistic component of each of these body genres through their various appropriations of melodramatic fantasies that are, in fact, basic to each. All of these genres could, for example, be said to offer highly melodramatic enactments of sexually charged, if not sexually explicit, relations. The subgenre of sadomasochistic pornography, with its suspension of pleasure over the course of prolonged sessions of dramatic suffering, offers a particularly intense, almost parodic, enactment of the classic melodramatic scenario of the passive and innocent female victim suffering at the hands of a leering villain. We can also see in horror films of tortured women a similar melodramatization of the innocent victim. An important difference, of course, lies in the component of the victim's overt sexual pleasure in the scenario of domination.

But even in the most extreme displays of feminine masochistic suffering, there is always a component of either power or pleasure for the woman victim. In slasher horror films we have seen how identification seems to oscillate between powerlessness and power. In sadomasochistic pornography and in melodramatic woman's weepies, feminine subject positions appear to be constructed which achieve a modicum of power and pleasure within the given limits of patriarchal constraints on women. It is worth noting as well that *non*-sadomasochistic pornography has historically been one of the few types of popular film that has not punished women for actively pursuing their sexual pleasure.

In the subgenre of sadomasochistic pornography, however, the female masochist in the scenario must be devious in her pursuit of pleasure. She plays the part of passive sufferer in order to obtain pleasure. Under a patriarchal double standard that has rigorously separated the sexually passive "good" girl from the sexually active "bad" girl, masochistic role-playing offers a way out of this dichotomy by combining the good girl with the bad: the passive "good girl" can prove to her witnesses (the super-ego who is her torturer) that she does not will the pleasure that she receives. Yet the sexually active "bad" girl enjoys this pleasure and has knowingly arranged to endure the pain that earns it. The cultural law which decides that some girls are good and others are bad is not defeated but within its terms pleasure has been negotiated and "paid for" with a pain that conditions it. The "bad" girl is punished, but in return she receives pleasure.[4]

In contrast, the sadomasochistic teen horror films kill off the sexually active "bad" girls, allowing only the non-sexual "good" girls to survive. But these good girls become, as if in compensation, remarkably active, to the point of appropriating phallic power to themselves. It is as if this phallic power is granted so long as it is rigorously separated from phallic or any other sort of pleasure. For these pleasures spell sure death in this genre.

In the melodramatic woman's film we might think to encounter a purer form of masochism on the part of female viewers. Yet even here the female viewer does not seem to be invited to identify wholly with the sacrificing good woman, but rather with a variety of different subject positions, including those which empathically look on at her own suffering. While I would not argue that there is a very strong sadistic component to these films, I do argue that there is a strong mixture of passivity and activity, and a bisexual oscillation between the poles of each, in even this genre.

For example, the woman viewer of a maternal melodrama such as *Terms of Endearment* or *Steel Magnolias* does not simply identify with the suffering and dying heroines of each. She may equally identify with the powerful matriarchs, the surviving mothers who preside over the deaths of their daughters, experiencing the exhilaration and triumph of survival. The point is simply that identification is neither fixed nor entirely passive.

While there are certainly masculine and feminine, active and passive, poles to the left and right of the chart on which we might position these three genres (see below), the subject positions that appear to be constructed by each of the genres are not as gender-linked and as gender-fixed as has often been supposed. This is especially true today as hard-core pornography is gaining appeal with women viewers. Perhaps the most recent proof in this genre of the breakdown of rigid dichotomies of masculine and feminine, active and passive is the creation of an alternative, oscillating category of address to viewers. Although heterosexual hard core once addressed itself exclusively to heterosexual men, it has now begun to address itself to heterosexual couples and women as well; and in addition to homosexual hard core, which has addressed itself to gay and (to a lesser extent) lesbian viewers, there is now a new category of video called bisexual. In these videos men do it with women, women do it with women, men do it with men and then all do it with one another, in the process breaking down a fundamental taboo against male-to-male sex.[5]

A related interpenetration of once more separate categories of masculine and feminine is what has come to be known in some quarters as the "male weepie." These are mainstream melodramas engaged in the activation of the previously repressed emotions of men and in breaking the taboos against male-to-male hugs and embraces. The father–son embrace that concludes *Ordinary People* (1980) is exemplary. More recently, paternal weepies have begun to compete with the maternal – as in the conventional *Dad* (1989) or the less conventional, wild paternal displays of *Twin Peaks*.

The point is certainly not to admire the "sexual freedom" of this new fluidity and oscillation – the new femininity of men who hug and the new masculinity of women who leer – as if it represented any ultimate defeat of phallic power. Rather, the more useful lesson might be to see what this new fluidity and oscillation permits in the construction of feminine viewing pleasures once thought not to exist at all. (It is instructive, for example, that in the new bisexual pornography women characters are shown verbally articulating their visual pleasure as they watch men perform sex with men.)

The deployment of sex, violence, and emotion would thus seem to have very precise functions in these body genres. Like all popular genres, they address persistent problems in our culture, in our sexualities, in our very identities. The deployment of sex, violence, and emotion is thus in no way gratuitous and in no way strictly limited to each of these genres; it is instead a cultural form of problem solving. As I have argued in *Hard Core*, pornographic films now tend to present sex as a problem, to which the performance of more, different, or better sex is posed as the solution (Williams, 1989). In horror a violence related to sexual difference is the problem, more violence related to sexual difference is also the solution. In women's films the pathos of loss is the problem, repetitions and variations of this loss are the generic solution.

Structures of Fantasy

All of these problems are linked to gender identity and might be usefully explored as genres of gender fantasy. It is appropriate to ask, then, not only about the structures of perversion, but also about the structures of fantasy in each of these genres. In doing so, we need to be clear about the nature of fantasy itself. For fantasies are not, as is sometimes thought, wish-fulfilling linear narratives of mastery and control leading to closure and the attainment of desire. They are marked, rather, by the prolongation of desire, and by the lack of fixed position with respect to the objects and events fantasized.

In their classic essay "Fantasy and the Origins of Sexuality," Jean Laplanche and J. B. Pontalis (1968) argue that fantasy is not so much a narrative that enacts the quest for an object of desire as it is a setting for desire, a place where conscious and unconscious, self and other, part and whole meet. Fantasy is the place where "desubjectified" subjectivities oscillate between self and other occupying no fixed place in the scenario (ibid.: 16).

In the three body genres discussed here, this fantasy component has probably been better understood in horror film, a genre often understood as belonging to the "fantastic." However, it has been less well understood in pornography and women's film melodrama. Because these genres display fewer fantastic special effects and because they rely on certain conventions of realism – the activation of social problems in melodrama, the representation of real sexual acts in pornography – they seem less obviously fantastic. Yet the usual criticisms that these forms are improbable, that they lack psychological complexity and narrative closure, and that they are repetitious, become moot as evaluation if such features are intrinsic to their engagement with fantasy.

There is a link, in other words, between the appeal of these forms and their ability to address, if never *really* to "solve," basic problems related to sexual identity. Here, I would like to forge a connection between Laplanche and Pontalis's structural understanding of fantasies as myths of origins which try to cover the discrepancy between two moments in time and the distinctive temporal structure of these particular genres. Laplanche and Pontalis argue that fantasies which are myths of origins address the insoluble problem of the discrepancy between an irrecoverable original experience presumed to have actually taken place – as in the case, for example, of the historical primal scene – and the uncertainty of its hallucinatory revival. The discrepancy exists, in other words, between the actual existence of the lost object and the sign which evokes both this existence and its absence.

Laplanche and Pontalis maintain that the most basic fantasies are located at the juncture of an irrecoverable real event that took place somewhere in the past and a totally imaginary event that never took place. The "event" whose temporal and spatial existence can never be fixed is thus ultimately, according to Laplanche and Pontalis, that of "the origin of the subject" – an origin which psychoanalysts tell us cannot be separated from the discovery of sexual difference (ibid.: 11).

It is this contradictory temporal structure of being situated somewhere between the "too early" and the "too late" of the knowledge of difference that generates desire that is most characteristic of fantasy. Freud introduced the concept of "original fantasy" to explain the mythic function of fantasies which seem to offer repetitions of and "solutions" to major enigmas confronting the child (Freud, 1915). These enigmas are located in three areas: the enigma of the origin of sexual desire, an enigma that is "solved," so to speak, by the fantasy of seduction; the enigma of sexual difference, "solved" by the fantasy of castration; and finally the enigma of the origin of self, "solved" by the fantasy of family romance or return to origins (Laplanche and Pontalis, 1968: 11).

Each of the three body genres I have been describing could be seen to correspond in important ways to one of these original fantasies: pornography, for example, is the genre that has seemed to endlessly repeat the fantasies of primal seduction, of meeting the other, seducing or being seduced by the other in an ideal "pornotopia" where, as Steven Marcus has noted, it is always bedtime (Marcus, 1964: 269). Horror is the genre that seems to endlessly repeat the trauma of castration as if to "explain," by repetitious mastery, the originary problem of sexual difference. And melodramatic weepie is the genre that seems to endlessly repeat our melancholic sense of the loss of origins – impossibly hoping to return to an earlier state which is perhaps most fundamentally re-presented by the body of the mother.

Of course each of these genres has a history and does not simply "endlessly repeat." The fantasies activated by these genres are repetitious, but not fixed and eternal. If traced back to origins each could probably be shown to have emerged with the formation of the bourgeois subject and the intensifying importance to this subject of specified sexualities. But the importance of repetition in each genre should not blind us to the very different temporal structure of repetition in each fantasy. It could be, in fact, that these different temporal structures constitute the different utopian component of problem-solving in each form. Thus the typical (non-sadomasochistic) pornographic fantasies of seduction operate to "solve" the problem of the origin of desire. Attempting to answer the insoluble question of whether desire is imposed from without through the seduction of the parent or whether it originates within the self, pornography answers this question by typically positing a fantasy of desire coming from within the subject *and* from without. Non-sadomasochistic pornography attempts to posit the utopian fantasy of perfect temporal coincidence: a subject and object (or seducer and seduced) who meet one another "on time!" and "now!" in shared moments of mutual pleasure that it is the special challenge of the genre to portray.

In contrast to pornography, the fantasy of recent teen horror corresponds to a temporal structure which raises the anxiety of not being ready, the problem, in effect, of "too early!" Some of the most violent and terrifying moments of the horror film genre occur in moments when the female victim meets the psycho-killer-monster unexpectedly, before she is ready. The female victims who are not ready for the attack die. This surprise encounter, too early, often takes place at a moment of sexual anticipation when the female victim thinks she is about to meet her boyfriend or lover. The monster's violent attack on the female victims vividly enacts a symbolic castration which often functions as a kind of punishment for an ill-timed exhibition of sexual desire. These victims are taken by surprise in the violent attacks which are then deeply felt by spectators (especially the adolescent male spectators drawn to the slasher subgenre) as linked to the knowledge of sexual difference. Again the key to the fantasy is timing – the way the knowledge of sexual difference too suddenly overtakes both characters and viewers, offering a knowledge for which we are never prepared.

Finally, in contrast to pornography's meeting "on time!" and horror's un-expected meeting "too early!," we can identify melodrama's pathos of the "too late!" In these fantasies the quest to return to and discover the origin of the self is manifest in the form of the child's fantasy of possessing ideal parents in the Freudian family romance, in the parental fantasy of possessing the child in maternal or paternal melodrama, and even in the lovers' fantasy of possessing one another in romantic weepies. In these fantasies the quest for connection is always tinged with the melancholy of loss. Origins are already lost, the encounters always take place too late, on death beds or over coffins (Neale, 1986).

Italian critic Franco Moretti has argued, for example, that literature that makes us cry operates via a special manipulation of temporality: what triggers our crying is not just the sadness or suffering of the character in the story but a very precise moment when characters in the story catch up with and realize what the audience already knows. We cry, Moretti argues, not just because the characters do, but at the precise moment when desire is finally recognized as futile. The release of tension produces tears – which become a kind of homage to a happiness that is kissed goodbye. Pathos is thus a surrender to reality but it is a surrender that pays homage to the ideal that tried to wage war on it (Moretti, 1983: 179). Moretti thus stresses a subversive, utopian component in what has often been considered a form of passive powerlessness. The fantasy of the meeting with the other that is always too late can thus be seen as based upon the utopian desire that it not be too late to re-merge with the other who was once part of the self.

Obviously there is a great deal of work to be done to understand the form and function of these three body genres in relation to one another and in relation to the fundamental appeal as "original fantasies." Obviously also the most difficult

Table 13.1   An anatomy of film bodies

	Pornography	Horror	Melodrama
Bodily excess	Sex	Violence	Emotion
Ecstasy: shown by	Ecstatic sex	Ecstatic violence	Ecstatic woe
	Orgasm	Shudder	Sob
	Ejaculation	Blood	Tears
Presumed audience:	Men (active)	Adolescent boys (active/passive)	Girls, women (passive)
Perversion:	Sadism	Sadomasochism	Masochism
Originary fantasy:	Seduction	Castration	Origin
Temporality of fantasy:	On time!	Too early!	Too late!
Genre cycles: "Classic"	Stag films (20s–40s): *The Casting Couch*	"Classic" horror: *Dracula* *Frankenstein* *Dr Jekyll/Mr Hyde* *King Kong*	"Classic" women's films: Maternal melodrama: *Stella Dallas* *Mildred Pierce* Romance: *Back Street* *Letter from an Unknown Woman*
Contemporary	Feature-length hard core porn: *Deep Throat*, etc. *The Punishment of Anne* Femme Productions Bisexual Trisexual	Post-*Psycho*: *Texas Chainsaw Massacre* *Halloween* *Dressed to Kill* *Videodrome*	Male and female "weepies": *Steel Magnolias* *Stella* *Dad*

work of understanding this relation between gender, genre, fantasy, and structures of perversion will come in the attempt to relate original fantasies to
historical context and specific generic history. However, there is one thing that
already seems clear: these "gross" body genres which may seem so violent and
inimical to women cannot be dismissed as evidence of a monolithic and unchanging misogyny, as either pure sadism for male viewers or masochism for females.
Their very existence and popularity hinges upon rapid changes taking place in
relations between the "sexes" and by rapidly changing notions of gender – of
what it means to be a man or a woman. To dismiss them as bad excess whether of
explicit sex, violence, or emotion, or as bad perversions, whether of masochism or
sadism, is not to address their function as cultural problem-solving. Genres
thrive, after all, on the persistence of the problems they address; but genres
thrive also in their ability to recast the nature of these problems.

Finally, as I hope this most recent example of the melodrama of tears suggests,
we may be wrong in our assumption that the bodies of spectators simply

reproduce the sensations exhibited by bodies on the screen. Even those masochistic pleasures associated with the powerlessness of the "too late!" are not absolutely abject. Even tear jerkers do not operate to force a simple mimicry of the sensation exhibited on the screen. Powerful as the sensations of the jerk might be, we may only be beginning to understand how they are deployed in generic and gendered cultural forms.

Notes

I owe thanks to Rhona Berenstein, Leo Braudy, Ernest Callenbach, Paul Fitzgerald, Jane Gaines, Mandy Harris, Brian Henderson, Marsha Kinder, Eric Rentschler, and Pauline Yu for generous advice on drafts of this essay.

1   For an excellent summary of many of the issues involved with both film melodrama and the "women's film," see Christine Gledhill's introduction to the anthology *Home is Where the Heart Is: Studies in Melodrama and the Woman's Film*. For a more general inquiry into the theatrical origins of melodrama, see Peter Brooks's (1976) *The Melodramatic Imagination*. And for an extended theoretical inquiry and analysis of a body of melodramatic women's films, see Mary Ann Doane (1987), *The Desire to Desire*.

2   Carol J. Clover (1987) discusses the meanings of this famous quote in her essay, "Her Body/Himself: Gender in the Slasher Film."

3   Dollimore (1990: 13). Dollimore's project, along with Teresa de Lauretis's more detailed examination of the term "perversion" in Freudian psychoanalysis (in progress) will be central to any more detailed attempts to understand the perverse pleasures of these gross body genres. .

4   I discuss these issues at length in a chapter on sadomasochistic pornography in my book *Hard Core* (1989).

5   Titles of these relatively new (post 1986) hard-core videos include: *Bisexual Fantasies*; *Bi-Mistake*; *Karen's Bi-Line*; *Bi-Dacious*; *Bi-Night*; *Bi and Beyond*; *The Ultimate Fantasy*; *Bi and Beyond II*; *Bi and Beyond III: Hermaphrodites*.

Works Cited

Altman, Rick. 1989. "Dickens, Griffith, and Film Theory Today." *South Atlantic Quarterly* 88: 321–59.

Bordwell, David, Janet Staiger, and Kristin Thompson. 1985. *The Classical Hollywood Cinema: Film Style and Mode of Production to 1960*. New York: Columbia University Press.

Clover, Carol J. 1987. "Her Body, Himself: Gender in the Slasher Film." *Representations* 20 (Fall): 187–228.

Deleuze, Gilles. 1971. *Masochism: An Interpretation of Coldness and Cruelty*. Translated by Jean McNeil. New York: Braziller.

Doane, Mary Ann. 1987. *The Desire to Desire: The Woman's Film of the 1940's*. Bloomington: Indiana University Press.

Doane, Mary Ann, Patricia Mellencamp, and Linda Williams, eds. 1983. *Re-vision: Essays in Feminist Film Criticism*. American Film Institute Monograph Series, vol. 3. Frederick, MD: University Publications of America.

Dollimore, Jonathan. 1990. "The Cultural Politics of Perversion: Augustine, Shakespeare, Freud, Foucault." *Genders* 8.

Douglas, Ann. 1980. "Soft-Porn Culture." *The New Republic*, 30 August 1980.

Dworkin, Andrea. 1979. *Pornography: Men Possessing Women*. New York: Perigee Books.

Foucault, Michel. 1978. *The History of Sexuality* Vol. 1: *An Introduction*. Translated by Robert Hurley. New York: Pantheon Books.

Freud, Sigmund. 1915. "Instincts and their Vicissitudes." Vol. 14 of the *Standard Edition of The Complete Psychological Works of Sigmund Freud*. London: Hogarth. 14.

Laplanche, Jean and J. B. Pontalis. 1968. "Fantasy and the Origins of Sexuality." *The International Journal of Psycho-Analysis*. 49: 1–18.

MacKinnon. 1987. *Feminism Unmodified: Discourses on Life and Law*. Cambridge, MA: Harvard University Press.

Marcus, Steven, 1964/74. *The Other Victorians: A Study of Sexuality and Pornography in Mid-Nineteenth Century England*. New York: New American Library.

Moretti, Franco. 1983. "Kindergarten." In *Signs Taken for Wonders*. London: Verso.

Morgan, Robin, 1980. "Theory and Practice: Pornography and Rape." In *Take Back the Night: Women on Pornography*, edited by Laura Lederer. New York: Morrow.

Mulvey, Laura. 1975. "Visual Pleasure and Narrative Cinema." *Screen* 16, no. 3: 6–18.

Neale, Steve. 1986. "Melodrama and Tears." *Screen* 27 (Nov.–Dec.): 6–22.

Silverman, Kaja. 1980. "Masochism and Subjectivity." *Framework* 12: 2–9.

—— 1988. "Masochism and Male Subjectivity." *Camera Obscura* 17: 31–66.

Studlar, Gaylyn. 1985. *In the Realm of Pleasure: Von Sternberg, Dietrich and the Masochistic Aesthetic*. Urbana: University of Illinois Press.

Twitchell, James. 1985. *Dreadful Pleasures: An Anatomy of Modern Horror*. New York: Oxford.

Williams, Linda. 1983. "When the Woman Looks." In *Revision: Essays in Feminist Film Criticism*. See Doane, Mellencamp, and Williams (1983).

——1989. *Hard Core: Power, Pleasure and the "Frenzy of the Visible."* Berkeley: University of California Press.

Part V

The Question of Realism

Introduction

Robert Stam

The concept of realism, while ultimately rooted in the classical Greek conception of *mimesis* (imitation), gains programmatic significance only in the nineteenth century, when it comes to denote a movement in the figurative and narrative arts dedicated to the observation and accurate representation of the contemporary world. A neologism coined by French critics, realism was originally linked to an oppositional attitude toward romantic and neo-classical models in fiction and painting. The Realist novels of writers like Balzac, Stendhal, Flaubert, George Eliot, and Eça de Queiróz brought intensely individualized, seriously conceived characters into typical contemporary social situations. Underlying the realist impulse was an implicit teleology of social democratization favoring the artistic emergence of "more extensive and socially inferior human groups to the position of subject matter for problematic–existential representation" (Auerbach, 1953: 491). Literary critics distinguished between this deep, democratizing realism, and a shallow, reductionistic and obsessively veristic "naturalism" – realized most famously in the novels of Émile Zola – which modeled its human representations on the biological sciences. Georg Lukács, for example, saw naturalism as "lured" by observable surfaces, blind to underlying historical contradictions.

In the 1930s, realism became a key term in the debate which opposed Bertolt Brecht to Lukács. For Lukács, realist literature portrays the social totality through the use of "typical" characters. While Lukács took the novels of Balzac and Stendhal as his model for a dialectical realism, Brecht favored a theater realist in intention – i.e. aimed at exposing society's "causal network" – but modernist-reflexive in its forms. To cling to the ossified forms of the nineteenth-century realist novel, for Brecht, reflected a formalistic nostalgia which failed to acknowledge altered historical circumstances. Changing times called for changing modes of representation. Haunted by the Nazis' obsession with overwhelming spectacles which induced blind emotion, Brecht called for a fragmented, distantiated "theater of interruptions" which fostered critical distance.

In relation to cinema, the issue of "realism" has been always present, whether posited as an ideal or an object of opprobrium. The very names of many aesthetic movements ring the changes on the theme of realism: the "*sur*realism" of Buñuel and Dali, the "poetic realism" of Carné/Prévert, the "neo-realism" of Rossellini and de Sica, the "subjective realism" of Antonioni, the "bourgeois realism" denounced by Marxist critics. Several broad tendencies coexist within the spectrum of definitions of cinematic realism. The most conventional definitions of realism make claims about verisimilitude, the putative adequation of a fiction to the brute facticity of the world. These definitions assume that realism is not only possible (and empirically verifiable) but also desirable. Other definitions stress the differential aspirations of an author or school to mold what is seen as a *relatively* more truthful representation, seen as a corrective to the falseness of antecedent cinematic styles or protocols of representation. This corrective can be stylistic – as in the French New Wave attack on the artificiality of the "tradition of quality" – or social – Italian neo-realism aiming to show postwar Italy its true face – or both at once – Brazilian Cinema Novo revolutionizing both the social thematics and the cinematic procedures of antecedent Brazilian cinema. Still other definitions acknowledge a certain conventionality within realism, seeing realism as having to do with a text's degree of conformity to widely disseminated cultural models of "believable stories" and "coherent characters." Plausibility also correlates with *generic* codes. The crusty conservative father who resists his show-crazed daughter's entrance into show-business, can "realistically" be expected, in a backstage musical, to applaud her on-stage apotheosis at the end of the film.

Another psychoanalytically inclined definition of realism involves spectatorial belief, a realism of subjective response, rooted less in mimetic accuracy than in spectatorial credence. A purely formalist definition of realism, finally, emphasizes the conventional nature of all fictional codes, seeing realism simply as a constellation of stylistic devices, a set of conventions that at a given moment in the history of an art, manages, through the fine-tuning of illusionistic technique, to crystallize a strong *feeling* of authenticity. Realism, it is important to add, is both culturally relative – Salmam Rushdie claims that Bollywood (Bombay) musicals make Hollywood musicals look like neo-realist documents (Rushdie, 1992) – and historically conditioned. Generations of filmgoers found black-and-white more "realistic," for example, even though "reality" itself comes in color.

The discussion of realism in the cinema has often revolved around the opposition between "formative" theorists (such as Arnheim and Balazs), who stressed film's capacity to depart from literal mimesis, and who therefore favored montage techniques and other markers of mediation, and the "realists" like Bazin and Kracauer who stressed cinema's "vocation for realism," and who favored the long-take, deep-focus style which respected (or pretended to respect) the spatio-temporal integrity of the shot as a means of conveying the fortuitous events of life as a continuum. The anti-realism of the early formative theorists was partially motivated by the programmatic desire to establish cinema's pedigree as an *art*. Arnheim, for example, set out to "refute the assertion that film was nothing but the feeble mechanical reproduction of real life" (Arnheim, 1958: 37). Artistic progress meant moving away from realism. The work of Siegfried Kracauer and André Bazin, meanwhile, argued for precisely the opposite teleology: a movement *toward* realism in the form of clear and believable stories told in transparent language. Bazin postulated a kind of triumphal progress of realism (not unlike that posited for the novel by Auerbach), which began with Lumière, continued with Flaherty and Murnau, was revivified by Welles, and reached quasi-fulfillment with the Italian neo-realists. For both Bazin and Kracauer, realism was linked to a "democratic" respect for the viewers' right to scan the multi-planar depth of the screen in order to determine meaning.

The apparent conflict between the formative theorists and the realist theorists masks precisely how much they have in common. Both views are essentialist and exclusionary. They are essentialist in that they see their favored aesthetics as revealing the inherent potentialities of the medium, and they are exclusivist in that they feel theorists (and filmmakers) must choose *between* different aesthetics. They leave little place for aesthetic pluralism, or for the mutually relativizing counterpoint of realistic and anti-realistic styles within the same film.

Realism also evokes the corollary debate about "classical cinema" and the "classical realist text." The notion of "classical cinema," first introduced by Bazin but subsequently extended and critiqued by others, evokes certain practices of editing, camerawork, and sound that serve the reconstitution of a fictional world characterized by internal coherence, plausible causality, psychological realism, and the appearance of seamless spatial and temporal continuity. The classical realist film was "transparent" in the sense that it attempted to efface all traces of the "work of the film," making it pass for "natural." Noël Burch dubbed this kind of illusionist cinema the "Institutional Mode of Representation" (IMR), a product of the bourgeois dream of a perfect simulacrum of the perceptual world. By effacing the signs of their production, "dominant" cinema persuaded spectators to take constructed effects as transparent renderings of the real (Burch, 1990).

The overall trajectory from the realist theories of Bazin and Kracauer toward semiotics was toward a relativization and even an attack on realism in the name of a politicized reflexivity in the 1960s and 1970s, and on a less politicized "intertextuality" in the 1980s and 1990s. This trajectory takes us from an "ontological" interest in cinema as the phenomenal depiction of real-life "existents," to an analysis of filmic realism as a matter of aesthetic convention. In the 1970s the discussion of realism came to be inflected by psychoanalytic notions of scopophilia and voyeurism and by Lacan's conception of the mirror stage, the imaginary, and the symbolic. The focus shifted from the realities portrayed on the screen to the phantasies and projections of the desiring spectator. For psychoanalytically inflected theorists the combination of verisimilar cinematic representationalism and a fantasy-inducing spectatorial situation conspires to project the spectator into a dream-like state where interior hallucination is confused with real perception. In *The Imaginary Signifier* Metz argued that the doubly imaginary nature of the cinematic signifier – imaginary in what it represents and imaginary by the nature of its signifier – heightens rather than diminishes the impression of realism. The impression of reality is stronger in film than in theater because the phantom-like figures on the screen are too weak to resist our penchant to invest them with our desires. If the spectator is the site of a psychic process of largely unconscious origin, the issue of verisimilitude pales in importance next to spectatorial desire and the "will to believe." Even the frequent comparison between film and dream, in this phase of film semiology, implied that narrative films were not ultimately realistic but that they never-theless induced a strong *impression* (but never illusion) of realism.

For artistic modernism, those movements in the arts (both within Europe and outside of it) which emerged in the late nineteenth century, flourished in the first decades of the twentieth century, and became institutionalized as "high modern-ism" after World War II, the term "reflexivity" evokes a non-representational and trans-realist art characterized by abstraction, fragmentation, and the fore-grounding of the materials and processes of art. As the negation of ideas of veristic transparency, reflexivity is crucial to both poststructuralism and post-modernism, both of which share a heightened sense of problematized referenti-ality. Within the context of postmodernism, reflexivity evokes the quotation-like aspects of pastiche art, the hyperreal world of media politics, and the incessant self-consciousness of contemporary television programming, in short the refer-entless world of the simulacrum, where all of life is always already caught up in mass-mediated representation.

Much has been made of what might be called the political valences of realism and reflexivity. In the 1970s, the left wing of film theory, especially that influenced by Althusser as well as Brecht, came to regard reflexivity as a political obligation. Film theory in this period thus "relived," and specifically cited and reworked, the Brecht–Lukács debate over realism in the 1930s. The major thrust of the Althusserian movement sided with the Brechtian critique of realism. Traditional realism, based as it is on a unified and coherent narrative, obscures contradictions and projects an illusory "mythic" unity rooted in the Western desire for what Derrida calls "unmediated presence." The modernist text, in contrast, foregrounds contradiction and mediation. The tendency, in the early phase, was simply to equate on the one hand "realist" with "bourgeois," and on the other "reflexive" with "revolutionary." "Hollywood" (aka "dominant cinema") became synonymous with all that was retrograde and passivity-inducing. But all these equations call for close examination. Reflexivity and realism, first of all, are not necessarily antithetical terms. Many films (for example Godard's *Numéro deux*) can be seen as at once reflexive and realist, in the sense that they illuminate the everyday lived realities of the social conjunctures from which they emerge, while also reminding the readers/spectators of the constructed nature of their own mimesis. Realism and reflexivity are not strictly opposed polarities but rather interpenetrating tendencies quite capable of coexisting within the same text. It would be more accurate to speak of a "coefficient" of reflexivity, while recognizing that it is not a question of a fixed proportion.

Illusionism, meanwhile, has never been monolithically dominant even in the mainstream fiction film. The coefficient of reflexivity varies from genre to genre (musicals like *Singin' in the Rain* are classically more reflexive than social realist dramas like *Marty*), from era to era (in the contemporary postmodernist era reflexivity is the norm rather than the exception), from film to film by the same director (Woody Allen's *Deconstructing Harry* is more reflexive than *Another Woman*), and even from sequence to sequence within the same film. Few classical films perfectly fit the abstract category of transparency often taken to be the norm in mainstream cinema.

For many cultural critics, reflexivity is a sign of the postmodern, a point at which an "art of exhaustion" has little left to do except contemplate its own instruments or recycle past works of art. "Postmodern reflexivity," in this sense, has revealed the infinite cooptability of reflexivity when it is used as nothing more than an ironic device. Commercial television, for example, is often reflexive and self-referential, but its reflexivity is, at most, ambiguous. Films like *Pulp Fiction*, or TV shows like *The David Letterman Show* and *Beavis and Butthead*, are relentlessly reflexive, but almost always within a kind of cynical, pervasive ironic stance which looks with a jaundiced eye at all activism or political position-taking. Many of the distancing procedures characterized as reflexive in Godard's films can be found in TV commercials. Yet the self-referentiality of commercials that deconstruct themselves or parody other commercials serves only to trigger a state of relaxed expectation which renders the viewer more permeable to the commercial message. Indeed, advertisers have such faith in this kind of lucrative self-mockery that ABC took to tongue-in-cheek denunciations of the negative effects of its own programming: "8 Hours a Day, that's All we Ask," reads one panel, and the next: "Don't Worry, You've got Billions of Brain Cells." Reflexivity, in sum, does not come equipped with an *a priori* political valence; it can be grounded in art-for-art's sake aestheticism, in media-specific formalism, in commercial propagandizing, or in dialectical materialism. It can be narcissistic or intersubjective, a sign of political *engagement* or of nihilistic flippancy.

Any contemporary discussion of filmic realism must take evolving technologies and aesthetics into account. The new media can produce convincing photorealistic simulacra of events that never occurred. They can combine synthesized images with captured ones. They can promote "threshold encounters" between Forrest Gump and John F. Kennedy, or between Natalie Cole and her long-departed father. The new digital imaging technologies, as manifested in a film like *Jurassic Park*, simultaneously heighten the possibilities of mimeticism while also undermining faith in the mimesis, since spectators, in the Age of the Internet, tend to be aware of the technologies "behind" the effects. Who can say that technical innovations such as Dolby Sound provide more "faithful" renditions of sound? Rather, it seems that Dolby increases the visceral impact of sound without the spectator taking it literally as "something that happened." In aesthetic terms, similarly, the old critiques of dominant cinema in terms of linear narrative, coherent diegesis, eyeline matches, and invisible editing no longer quite "work," since recent blockbuster cinema, for example, is less interested in verisimilitude and spatiotemporal integrity than in pure sensation. Music video, similarly, does not strive for believability; rather, its purpose is to immerse the spectator in a Heraclitan flux of images and sounds registered on the pulse rather than through purely cognitive processes.

Both structuralism and poststructuralism had in common the habit of "bracketing the referent," i.e. insisting more on the interrelations of signs than on any correspondence between sign and referent. Poststructuralist theory reminds us that we live and dwell within language and representation, and have no direct access to the "real." But in their critique of realism, both movements occasionally went to the extreme of detaching art from all relation to social and historical context. The text was cut off from the author, the world, and the reader/spectator in a pan-semiotic vision of what Edward Said called "wall-to-wall text." But the constructed, coded nature of artistic discourse hardly precludes all reference to reality. Filmic fictions inevitably bring into play everyday assumptions about the nature of space and time as well as about social and cultural relationships. If language structures the world, the world also structures language; the movement is not unidirectional.

While on one level film is mimesis, representation, then it is also utterance, an act of contextualized interlocution between socially situated producers and receivers. To say that art is "constructed" should not be the end of discussion but the beginning. We have to ask "constructed for whom?" and in conjunction with "which ideologies and discourses?" In this sense, art is a representation not so much in a mimetic as in a political sense, as a delegation of voice.[1] A socio-discursive approach to the issue of realism shifts the emphasis from "is the representation mimetically correct?" to the question "which social voices and discourses are represented here?" The challenge now, perhaps, is to avoid a naively "realistic" view of artistic representation, without acceding to a "hermeneutic nihilism" whereby all texts are seen as nothing more than an infinite play of signification without reference to the social world. (For more on alternatives to realism, see Part VI).

Note

1   Kobena Mercer and Isaac Julien (1988), in a similar spirit, distinguish between "representation as a practice of depicting" and "representation as a practice of delegation."

14

The Cinema of Attraction: Early Film, Its Spectator, and the Avant-Garde

Tom Gunning

Writing in 1922, flushed with the excitement of seeing Abel Gance's *La Roue*, Fernand Léger tried to define something of the radical possibilities of the cinema. The potential of the new art did not lay in "imitating the movements of nature" or in "the mistaken path" of its resemblance to theater. Its unique power was a "matter of *making images seen*."[1] It is precisely this harnessing of visibility, this act of showing and exhibition which I feel cinema before 1906 displays most intensely. Its inspiration for the avant-garde of the early decades of this century needs to be re-explored.

Writings by the early modernists (Futurists, Dadaists, and Surrealists) on the cinema follow a pattern similar to Léger: enthusiasm for this new medium and its possibilities; and disappointment at the way it has already developed, its enslavement to traditional art forms, particularly theater and literature. This fascination with the *potential* of a medium (and the accompanying fantasy of rescuing the cinema from its enslavement to alien and passé forms) can be understood from a number of viewpoints. I want to use it to illuminate a topic I have approached before from another angle, the strangely heterogeneous relation that film before 1906 (or so) bears to the films that follow, and the way a taking account of this heterogeneity signals a new conception of film history and film form. My work in this area has been pursued in collaboration with André Gaudreault.[2]

The history of early cinema, like the history of cinema generally, has been written and theorized under the hegemony of narrative films. Early filmmakers like Smith, Méliès, and Porter have been studied primarily from the viewpoint of their contribution to film as a storytelling medium, particularly the evolution of narrative editing. Although such approaches are not totally misguided, they are one-sided, and potentially distort both the work of these filmmakers and the actual forces shaping cinema before 1906. A few observations will indicate the way that early cinema was not dominated by the narrative impulse that later asserted its sway over the medium. First there is the extremely important role that actuality film plays in early film production. Investigation of the films copyrighted in the US shows that actuality films outnumbered fictional films until 1906.[3] The Lumière tradition of "placing the world within one's reach" through travel films and topicals did not disappear with the exit of the Cinématographe from film production.

But even within non-actuality filming – what has sometimes been referred to as the "Méliès tradition" – the role narrative plays is quite different than in traditional narrative film. Méliès himself declared in discussing his working method:

As for the scenario, the "fable," or "tale," I only consider it at the end. I can state that the scenario constructed in this manner has no importance, since I use it merely as a pretext for the "stage effects," the "tricks," or for a nicely arranged tableau.[4]

Whatever differences one might find between Lumière and Méliès, they should not represent the opposition between narrative and non-narrative film-making, at least as it is understood today. Rather, one can unite them in a conception that sees cinema less as a way of telling stories than as a way of presenting a series of views to an audience, fascinating because of their illusory power (whether the realistic illusion of motion offered to the first audiences by Lumière, or the magical illusion concocted by Méliès), and exoticism. In other words, I believe that the relation to the spectator set up by the films of both Lumière and Méliès (and many other filmmakers before 1906) had a common basis, and one that differs from the primary spectator relations set up by narrative film after 1906. I will call this earlier conception of cinema, "the cinema of attractions." I believe that this conception dominates cinema until about 1906–7. Although different from the fascination in storytelling exploited by the cinema from the time of Griffith, it is not necessarily opposed to it. In fact the cinema of attraction does not disappear with the dominance of narrative, but rather goes underground, both into certain avant-garde practices and as a component of narrative films, more evident in some genres (e.g. the musical) than in others.

What precisely is the cinema of attraction? First it is a cinema that bases itself on the quality that Léger celebrated: its ability to *show* something. Contrasted to the voyeuristic aspect of narrative cinema analyzed by Christian Metz,[5] this is an exhibitionist cinema. An aspect of early cinema which I have written about in other articles is emblematic of this different relationship the cinema of attractions constructs with its spectator: the recurring look at the camera by actors. This action which is later perceived as spoiling the realistic illusion of the cinema, is here undertaken with brio, establishing contact with the audience. From comedians smirking at the camera, to the constant bowing and gesturing of the conjurors in magic films, this is a cinema that displays its visibility, willing to rupture a self-enclosed fictional world for a chance to solicit the attention of the spectator.

Exhibitionism becomes literal in the series of erotic films which play an important role in early film production (the same Pathé catalogue would advertise the Passion Play along with "scenes griviose d'un charactére piquant," erotic films often including full nudity), also driven underground in later years. As Noël Burch has shown in his film *Correction Please: How We Got into Pictures* (1979), a film like *The Bride Retires* (France, 1902) reveals a fundamental conflict between this exhibitionistic tendency of early film and the creation of a fictional diegesis. A woman undresses for bed while her new husband peers at her from behind a screen. However, it is to the camera and the audience that the bride addresses her erotic striptease, winking at us as she faces us, smiling in erotic display.

As the quote from Méliès points out, the trick film, perhaps the dominant non-actuality film genre before 1906, is itself a series of displays, of magical attractions, rather than a primitive sketch of narrative continuity. Many trick films are, in effect, plotless, a series of transformations strung together with little connection and certainly no characterization. But to approach even the plotted trick films, such as *Voyage dans la lune* (1902), simply as precursors of later narrative structures is to miss the point. The story simply provides a frame upon which to string a demonstration of the magical possibilities of the cinema.

Modes of exhibition in early cinema also reflect this lack of concern with creating a self-sufficient narrative world upon the screen. As Charles Musser has shown,[6] the early showmen exhibitors exerted a great deal of control over the shows they presented, actually re-editing the films they had purchased and supplying a series of offscreen supplements, such as sound effects and spoken commentary. Perhaps most extreme is the Hale's Tours, the largest chain of theaters exclusively showing films before 1906. Not only did the films consist of non-narrative sequences taken from moving vehicles (usually trains), but the theater itself was arranged as a train car, with a conductor who took tickets, and sound effects simulating the click-clack of wheels and hiss of air brakes.[7] Such viewing experiences relate more to the attractions of the fairground than to the traditions of the legitimate theatre. The relation between films and the emergence of the great amusement parks, such as Coney Island, at the turn of the century provides rich ground for rethinking the roots of early cinema.

Nor should we ever forget that in the earliest years of exhibition the cinema itself was an attraction. Early audiences went to exhibitions to see machines demonstrated (the newest technological wonder, following in the wake of such widely exhibited machines and marvels as X-rays or, earlier, the phonograph) rather than to view films. It was the Cinématographe, the Biograph, or the Vitascope that were advertised on the variety bills in which they premiered, not *The Baby's Breakfast* or *The Black Diamond Express*. After the initial novelty period, this display of the possibilities of cinema continues, and not only in magic films. Many of the close-ups in early film differ from later uses of the technique precisely because they do not use enlargement for narrative punctuation, but as an attraction in its own right. The close-up cut into Porter's *The Gay Shoe Clerk*

(1903) may anticipate later continuity techniques, but its principal motive is again pure exhibitionism, as the lady lifts her skirt hem, exposing her ankle for all to see. Biograph films such as *Photographing a Female Crook* (1904) and *Hooligan in Jail* (1903) consist of a single shot in which the camera is brought close to the main character, until they are in midshot. The enlargement is not a device expressive of narrative tension; it is in itself an attraction and the point of the film.[8]

The term "attractions" comes, of course, from the young Sergei Mikhailovich Eisenstein and his attempt to find a new model and mode of analysis for the theater. In his search for the "unit of impression" of theatrical art, the foundation of an analysis which would undermine realistic representational theater, Eisenstein hit upon the term "attraction."[9] An attraction aggressively subjected the spectator to "sensual or psychological impact." According to Eisenstein, theater should consist of a montage of such attractions, creating a relation to the spectator entirely different from his absorption in "illusory imitativeness."[10] I pick up this term partly to underscore the relation to the spectator that this later avant-garde practice shares with early cinema: that of exhibitionist confrontation rather than diegetic absorption. Of course the "experimentally regulated and mathematically calculated" montage of attractions demanded by Eisenstein differs enormously from these early films (as any conscious and oppositional mode of practice will from a popular one).[11] However, it is important to realize the context from which Eisenstein selected the term. Then as now, the "attraction" was a term of the fairground, and for Eisenstein and his friend Yuketvich it primarily represented their favorite fairground attraction, the roller coaster, or as it was known then in Russia, the American Mountains.[12]

The source is significant. The enthusiasm of the early avant-garde for film was at least partly an enthusiasm for a mass culture that was emerging at the beginning of the century, offering a new sort of stimulus for an audience not acculturated to the traditional arts. It is important to take this enthusiasm for popular art as something more than a simple gesture of *épater les bourgeoise*. The enormous development of the entertainment industry since the Teens and its growing acceptance by middle-class culture (and the accommodation that made this acceptance possible), has made it difficult to understand the liberation popular entertainment offered at the beginning of the century. I believe that it was precisely the exhibitionist quality of turn-of-the-century popular art that made it attractive to the avant-garde – its freedom from the creation of a diegesis, its accent on direct stimulation.

Writing of the variety theatre, Marinetti not only praised its aesthetics of astonishment and stimulation, but particularly its creation of a new spectator who contrasts with the "static," "stupid voyeur" of traditional theater. The spectator at the variety theater feels directly addressed by the spectacle and joins in, singing along, heckling the comedians.[13] Dealing with early cinema within the context of archive and academy, we risk missing its vital relation to vaudeville, its primary place of exhibition until around 1905. Film appeared as one attraction on the vaudeville program, surrounded by a mass of unrelated acts in a non-narrative and even nearly illogical succession of performances. Even when presented in the nickelodeons that were emerging at the end of this period, these short films always appeared in a variety format, trick films sandwiched in with farces, actualities, "illustrated songs," and, quite frequently, cheap vaudeville acts. It was precisely this non-narrative variety that placed this form of entertainment under attack by reform groups in the early Teens. The Russell Sage Survey of popular entertainments found vaudeville "depends upon an artificial rather than a natural human and developing interest, these acts having no necessary, and as a rule, no actual connection."[14] In other words, no narrative. A night at the variety theater was like a ride on a streetcar or an active day in a crowded city, according to this middle-class reform group, stimulating an unhealthy nervousness. It was precisely such artificial stimulus that Marinetti and Eisenstein wished to borrow from the popular arts and inject into the theater, organizing popular energy for radical purpose.

What happened to the cinema of attraction? The period from 1907 to about 1913 represents the true *narrativization* of the cinema, culminating in the appearance of feature films which radically revised the variety format. Film clearly took the legitimate theater as its model, producing famous players in famous plays. The transformation of filmic discourse that D. W. Griffith typifies bound cinematic signifiers to the narration of stories and the creation of a self-enclosed diegetic universe. The look at the camera becomes taboo and the devices of cinema are transformed from playful "tricks" – cinematic attractions (Méliès gesturing at us to watch the lady vanish) – to elements of dramatic expression, entries into the psychology of character and the world of fiction.

However, it would be too easy to see this as a Cain and Abel story, with narrative strangling the nascent possibilities of a young iconoclastic form of entertainment. Just as the variety format in some sense survived in the Movie Palaces of the Twenties (with newsreel, cartoon, sing-along, orchestra performance and sometimes vaudeville acts subordinated to, but still coexisting with, the narrative *feature* of the evening), the system of attraction remains an essential part of popular filmmaking.

The chase film shows how towards the end of this period (basically from 1903–6) a synthesis of attractions and narrative was already underway. The chase had been the original truly narrative genre of the cinema, providing a model for causality and linearity as well as a basic editing continuity. A film like Biograph's *Personal* (1904, the model for the chase film in many ways) shows the creation of a narrative linearity, as the French nobleman runs for his life from the fiancées his personal column ad has unleashed. However, at the same time, as the group of young women pursue their prey towards the camera in each shot, they encounter some slight obstacle (a fence, a steep slope, a stream) that slows them down for the spectator, providing a mini-spectacle pause in the unfolding of narrative. The Edison Company seemed particularly aware of this, since they offered their plagiarized version of this Biograph film (*How a French Nobleman Got a Wife Through the New York Herald Personal Columns*) in two forms, as a complete film, or as separate shots, so that any one image of the ladies chasing the man could be bought without the inciting incident or narrative closure.[15]

As Laura Mulvey has shown in a very different context, the dialectic between spectacle and narrative has fueled much of the classical cinema.[16] Donald Crafton in his study of slapstick comedy "The Pie and the Chase" has shown the way slapstick did a balancing act between the pure spectacle of gag and the development of narrative.[17] Likewise, the spectacle film traditionally proved true to its name by highlighting moments of pure visual stimulation along with narrative. The 1924 version of *Ben Hur* was in fact shown at a Boston theater with a timetable announcing the moment of its prime attractions:

8:35   The Star of Bethlehem
8:40   Jerusalem Restored
8:59   Fall of the House of Hur
10:29   The Last Supper
10:50   Reunion[18]

The Hollywood advertising policy of enumerating the features of a film, each emblazoned with the command "See!", shows this primal power of the attraction running beneath the armature of narrative regulation.

We seem far from the avant-garde premises with which this discussion of early cinema began. But it is important that the radical heterogeneity which I find in early cinema not be conceived as a truly oppositional program, one irreconcilable with the growth of narrative cinema. This view is too sentimental and too ahistorical. A film like *The Great Train Robbery* (1903) does point in both directions, toward a direct assault on the spectator (the spectacularly enlarged outlaw unloading his pistol in our faces) and towards a linear narrative continuity. This is early film's ambiguous heritage. Clearly in some sense recent spectacle cinema has reaffirmed its roots in stimulus and carnival rides, in what might be called the Spielberg–Lucas–Coppola cinema of effects.

But effects are tamed attractions. Marinetti and Eisenstein understood that they were tapping into a source of energy that would need focusing and intensification to fulfill its revolutionary possibilities. Both Eisenstein and Marinetti planned to exaggerate the impact on the spectator, Marinetti proposing to literally glue them to their seats (ruined garments paid for after the performance) and Eisenstein setting firecrackers off beneath them. Every change in film history implies a change in its address to the spectator, and each period constructs its spectator in a new way. Now in a period of American avant-garde cinema in which the tradition of contemplative subjectivity has perhaps run its (often glorious) course, it is possible that this earlier carnival of the cinema, and the methods of popular entertainment, still provide an unexhausted resource – a Coney Island of the avant-garde, whose never dominant but always sensed current can be traced from Méliès through Keaton, through *Un Chien andalou* (1928), and Jack Smith.

Notes

1 Fernand Léger, "A Critical Essay on the Plastic Qualities of Abel Gance's Film *The Wheel*" in *Functions of Painting*, ed. and intro. Edward Fry, trans. Alexandra Anderson (New York: Viking Press, 1973), 21.

2 See my articles "The Non-Continuous Style of Early Film" in *Cinema 1900–1906*, ed. Roger Holman (Brussels: FIAF, 1982) and "An Unseen Energy Swallows Space: The Space in Early Film and its Relation to American Avant Garde Film" in *Film Before Griffith*, ed. John L. Fell (Berkeley: University of California Press, 1983), 355–66, and our collaborative paper delivered by M. Gaudreault at the conference at Cerisy on Film History (August 1985) "Le cinéma des premiers temps: un défi a l'histoire du cinéma?" I would also like to note the importance of my discussions with Adam Simon and our hope to further investigate the history and archaeology of the film spectator.

3 Robert C. Allen, *Vaudeville and Film: 1895–1915, A Study in Media Interaction* (New York: Arno Press, 1980), 159, 212–13.

4 Méliès, "Importance du scénario" in *Georges Méliès*, Georges Sadoul (Paris: Seghers, 1961), 118 (my translation).

5 Metz, *The Imaginary Signifier: Psychoanalysis and the Cinema*, trans. Celia Britton, Annwyl Williams, Ben Brewster and Alfred Guzzetti (Bloomington: Indiana University Press, 1982), particularly 58–80, 91–7.

6 Musser, "American Vitagraph 1897–1901" in *Cinema Journal*, 22, 3 (Spring 1983), 10.

7 Raymond Fielding, "Hale's Tours: Ultrarealism in the Pre-1910 Motion Picture," in Fell, 116–30.

8 I wish to thank Ben Brewster for his comments after the original delivery of this paper which pointed out the importance of including this aspect of the cinema of attractions here.

9 Eisenstein, "How I Became a Film Director" in *Notes of a Film Director* (Moscow: Foreign Language Publishing House, n.d.), 16.

10 Eisenstein, "Montage of Attractions," trans. Daniel Gerould, in *The Drama Review*, 18, 1 (March 1974), 78–9.

11 Ibid.

12 Yon Barna, *Eisenstein* (Bloomington: Indiana University Press, 1973), 59.

13 "The Variety Theater 1913" in *Futurist Manifestos*, ed. Umbro Apollonio (New York: Viking Press, 1973), 127.

14 Michael Davis, *The Exploitation of Pleasure* (New York: Russell Sage Foundation, Dept. of Child Hygiene, Pamphlet, 1911).

15 David Levy, "Edison Sales Policy and the Continuous Action Film 1904–1906," in Fell, 207–22.

16 "Visual Pleasure and Narrative Cinema," *Screen*, 16, 3 (Autumn 1975), 6–18.

17 Paper delivered at the FIAF Conference on Slapstick, May 1985, New York City.

18 Nicholas Vardac, *From Stage to Screen: Theatrical Method from Garrick to Griffith* (New York: Benjamin Blom, 1968), 232.

15

Black American Cinema:
The New Realism

Manthia Diawara

The release of D. W. Griffith's *The Birth of a Nation* in 1915 defined for the first time the side that Hollywood was to take in the war to represent Black people in America. In *The Birth of a Nation*, D. W. Griffith, later a founding member of United Artists, created and fixed an image of Blackness that was necessary for racist America's fight against Black people. *The Birth of a Nation* constitutes the grammar book for Hollywood's representation of Black manhood and woman-hood, its obsession with miscegenation, and its fixing of Black people within certain spaces, such as kitchens, and into certain supporting roles, such as criminals, on the screen. White people must occupy the center, leaving Black people with only one choice – to exist in relation to Whiteness. *The Birth of a Nation* is the master text that suppressed the real contours of Black history and culture on movie screens, screens monopolized by the major motion picture companies of America.

Griffith's film also put Black people and White liberals on the defensive, inaugurating a plethora of historical and critical writings against *The Birth of a Nation*, and overdetermining a new genre, produced exclusively for Black audi-ences, called race films. More insidiously, however, the racial conflict depicted in *The Birth of a Nation* became Hollywood's only way of talking about Black people. In other words, whenever Black people appeared on Hollywood screens, from *The Birth of a Nation* to *Guess Who's Coming to Dinner?* to *The Color Purple*, they are represented as a problem, a thorn in America's heel. Hollywood's Blacks exist primarily for White spectators whose comfort and understanding the films must seek, whether they thematize exotic images dancing and singing on the screen, or images constructed to narrate a racial drama, or images of pimps and muggers. With *The Birth of a Nation* came the ban on Blacks participating in bourgeois humanism on Hollywood screens. In other words, there are no simple stories about Black people loving each other, hating each other, or enjoying their private possessions without reference to the White world, because the spaces of those stories are occupied by newer forms of race relation stories which have been overdetermined by Griffith's master text.

The relations between Black independent cinema and the Hollywood cinema just described above parallel those between Blackness and Americanness; the dichotomy between the so-called marked cultures and unmarked cultures; but also the relations between "high art" and "low art." The complexity of these relations is such that every independent filmmaker's dream is to make films for Hollywood where she/he will have access to the resources of the studios and the movie theaters. On the other hand, the independents often use an aesthetic and moral high ground to repudiate mainstream cinema, which is dismissed as populist, racist, sexist, and reactionary. Furthermore, a look at the relations between Oscar Micheaux and the Hollywood "race films," Melvin Van Peebles and the Blaxploitation films, Charles Burnett (*Killer of Sheep*), Haile Gerima (*Bush Mama*), and Spike Lee and the rethematization of urban life in such films as *City of Hope*, *Grand Canyon*, *Boyz N the Hood*, and *Straight Out of Brooklyn* reveals that mainstream cinema constantly feeds on independent cinema and appropriates its themes and narrative forms.

Some of the most prominent Black film historians and critics, such as Albert Johnson, Donald Bogle, and Thomas Cripps, emphasize mainly mainstream cinema when discussing Black films. With the exception of a few breatkthrough films, such as those by Micheaux, Van Peebles, and Lee, these historians are primarily concerned with the issues of integration and race relations in mainstream films, Black actors and actresses on the big screen, and the construction of stereotypes in Hollywood films. They rarely pay attention to independent cinema, which includes far more Black directors than Hollywood, and in which aesthetics, political concerns such as authorship and spectatorship, and the politics of representation with respect to Black cinema are more prevalent. Critics and historians such as Clyde Taylor, Toni Cade Bambara, Phyllis Klotman, and Gladstone Yearwood are the first to focus on Black independent cinema as a subject of study. More recently, the *Black Film Review* has assumed the pre-eminent role in Black film history and criticism.

Hollywood's block-booking system prevents independently produced films from reaching movie theaters and large audiences. This may be one reason why film historians and critics neglect independent cinema: some film magazines, such as *Cineaste*, adopt a policy of accepting only reviews of films that have been distributed and seen by their readers. It is also possible to argue that Black independent cinema has remained marginal until now because its language, not unlike the language of most independent films, is meta-filmic, often nationalistic, and not "pleasurable" to consumers accustomed to mainstream Hollywood products. Black independent cinema, like most independent film practices, approaches film as a research tool. The filmmakers investigate the possibilities of representing alternative Black images on the screen; bringing to the foreground issues central to Black communities in America; criticizing sexism and homophobia in the Black community; and deploying Afrafemcentric discourses that empower Black women. The narratives of such films are not always linear; the characters represent a tapestry of voices from W. E. B. DuBois, Frantz Fanon,

Toni Morrison, Malcolm X, Martin Luther King, Jr., Karl Marx, Angela Davis, Alice Walker, and Zora Neale Hurston. Even what passes as documentary in Black independent films, like *The Bombing of Osage Avenue* (Louis Massiah), is an artistic reconstruction of archival footage and "real" events.

What is, therefore, the Black independent cinema, and what constitutes its influence on mainstream cinema? The French appropriately refer to independent cinema as *cinema d'art et essai*. In France, the government sponsors such a cinema by imposing a distribution tax on commercial films. The *cinema d'art et essai* is less concerned about recouping its cost of production and making a profit; its main emphasis is toward artistic development, documenting an area of research, and delineating a certain philosophy of the world. In the late 1950s, a group of French youth, who were dissatisfied with commercial films and wanted to make their own films, mobilized private and personal funds along with government funds to produce low-budget films. The result is well known today as the French New Wave, considered by some as one of the pivotal moments in film history.

As an alternative to commercial cinema, which emphasized the well-made story, acting, and the personality of the actor, the New Wave put in the fore-ground the director, whom it raised to the same artistic level as the author of a painting, a novel, or a poem; the New Wave also demystified the notion of the well-made story by experimenting with different ways of telling the same story, and by deconstructing the notion of actor and acting. Jean-Luc Godard's *Breathless* (1959), for example, is famous for its reinsertion of the "jump-cut" as a valid narrative device. The jump-cut, which was avoided in Hollywood films in order not to disrupt the spectator with "unnecessary" repetitions, has today become a powerful narrative device used by directors such as Spike Lee, who redefines it and uses it to describe the repetition and the sameness in racial and sexual stereotyping. In *Do the Right Thing* (1988) Lee uses the same angle to repeat several shots of Blacks, Italians, Jews, and Koreans repeating racial stereotypes, unlike Godard, who uses the same image twice from the same angle. Lee practices the same device in *She's Gotta Have It* (1985) to construct sexual stereotypes among young Black males.

This example of the New Wave reveals that independent filmmakers come to their vocation for at least two reasons: one political, and the other artistic. Politically, they are dissatisfied with commercial cinema's lack of courage to address certain issues. They feel that they have to make their own films if they want to see those issues on the screen. Artistically, they want to explore new ways of telling stories; they want to experiment with the camera, the most powerful invention of modern times, and engage the infinite possibilities of storytelling. There are other examples of alternative or independent cinemas that occupy important places in the history of film. The Italian Neorealism, the Brazilian Cinema Novo, and the Argentinian Third Cinema have all created alternative narrative techniques that were at first unknown to commercial cinemas, but are claimed today as part of traditional narrative practices.

Similarly, the cloning of Hollywood's mind to Black history and culture, which do not revolve around White people, is the reason why most Black filmmakers since Oscar Micheaux have turned first to the independent sector. Since Oscar Micheaux, Black independents have pioneered creating alternative images of Blacks on the screen, constructing new narrative forms derived from Black literature and folklore, and denouncing racism, sexism, and homophobia in American culture.

This is not, however, to romanticize the independent practice. Micheaux made his films by selling personal property and borrowing money from friends. Still today, independent filmmaking causes many people to become poor. It takes more than six years for some filmmakers to gather the money for one film. Charles Burnett's *To Sleep With Anger*, and Julie Dash's *Daughters of the Dust* came only after arduous years of fundraising. Haile Gerima has been trying to raise funds for *Nunu* for several years now. We have not seen second features by talented directors such as Billy Woodberry (*Bless Their Little Hearts*), Larry Clark (*Passing Through*), Alile Sharon Larkin (*A Different Image*), and Warrington Hudlin (*Street Corner Stories*). Spike Lee sums up the harsh reality of independent production as follows:

> When I went to film school, I knew I did not want to have my films shown only during Black History Month in February or at libraries. I wanted them to have a wide distribution. And I did not want to spend four or five years trying to piecemeal together the money for my films. I did my first film, *She's Gotta Have It*, independently for $175,000. We had a grant from the New York State Council on the Arts and were raising money the whole time we were shooting. We shot the film in twelve days. The next stage was to get it out of the lab. Then, the most critical part was when I had to hole up in my little apartment to get it cut. I took about two months to do that. I had no money coming in, so I had to hold off the debtors because I knew if I had enough time to at least get it in good enough shape to show, we could have some investor screenings, and that's what happened. We got it blown up to 35mm for a film festival. What you have to do is to try to get a distributor. You enter as many film festivals as you can.[1]

Black independent cinema is any Black-produced film outside the constraints of the major studios. The filmmakers' independence from Hollywood enables them to put on the screen Black lives and concerns that derive from the complexity of Black communities. Independent films provide alternative ways of knowing Black people that differ from the fixed stereotypes of Blacks in Hollywood. The ideal spectators of the films are those interested in Black people's perspectives on American culture. White people and Whiteness are marginalized in the films, while central positions are relegated to Black people, Black communities, and diasporic experiences. For example, the aesthetics of uplifting the race in a film like *The Scar of Shame* (1928, The Colored Players) concern particularly Black spectators, whom the filmmakers' stated mission is to entertain and educate. The film posits Black upper-class culture as that which should be emulated by lower-class Blacks in order to humanize themselves. Unlike Hollywood films of that time, which identified with the ideal White male, the camera in *The Scar of Shame* identifies with the position of the Black bourgeoisie. The film is precious today as a document of Black bourgeois ways of being in the 1920s and 1930s. Crucially, it constitutes, with Oscar Micheaux's films, a genre of Black independent cinema which puts Black people and their culture at the center as subjects of narrative development; in these films, Black people are neither marginalized as a problem, nor singled out as villainous stereotypes such as Hollywood constructs in its films.

Contemporary independent films continue the same effort of inquiring into Black subjectivities, the heterogeneity of Black lives, the Black family, class and gender relations, and diasporic aesthetics. Recently, independent Black women filmmakers such as Kathleen Collins (*Losing Ground*), Alile Sharon Larkin (*A Different Image*), Ayoka Chenzira (*Zajota: the Boogie Spirit*), Julie Dash (*Daughters of the Dust*), and Zeinabu Davis (*A Powerful Thang*) have explored such themes as Black womanhood and spirituality, diaspora art and music, and Afrocentric aesthetics. Black manhood, the urban landscape, unemployment and the Black family are thematized in films like *Sweet Sweetback's Baadasssss Song* (Van Peebles), *Killer of Sheep* (Burnett), *Bless Their Little Hearts* (Woodberry), *Serving Two Masters* (Tim Lewis), *Street Corner Stories* (Warrington Hudlin), *Chameleon Street* (Wendell Harris), and *Ashes and Embers* (Haile Gerima). The themes of sexuality and homophobia are depicted in *Tongues United* (Marlon Riggs), *Storme: Lady of the Jewel Box* (Michelle Parkerson), *She's Gotta Have It* (Spike Lee), *Ganja and Hess* (Bill Gunn), *Splash* (Thomas Harris), and *She Don't Fade* (Cheryl Dunye). The major Black documentary artists, such as William Greaves, Louis Massiah, Camille Billops, and St. Clair Bourne, have also enriched the documentary genre by focusing their cameras on Black people in order to reconstruct history, celebrating Black writers and activists, and giving voice to people who are overlooked by television news and mainstream documentaries.

Two Paradigms of Black Cinema Aesthetics

Jane Gaines defines Oscar Micheaux's editing style as follows: "Perhaps to elude any attempt to essentialize it, we could treat this style as more of an ingenious solution to the impossible demands of the conventions of classical Hollywood style, shortcuts produced by the exigencies of economics, certainly, but also modifications produced by an independent who had nothing at stake in strict adherence to Hollywood grammar." Gaines goes on to posit that Micheaux's "freewheeling cinematic grammar" constitutes both a misreading and an improvement upon Hollywood logic. Clearly, Micheaux's "imperfect" cinema (to borrow a term from Julio Garcia Espinoza), which misreads and improves upon Hollywood logic, is a powerful metaphor for the way in which African Americans survived and continue to survive within a hostile economic and racist system, and used the elements of that survival as raw material to humanize and improve upon American modernism. Micheaux's "loose editing," like the improvisation of jazz, surprises and delights the spectator with forbidden images of America that Hollywood's America conceals from its space. In so far as the classical Hollywood narrative proceeds by concealment of space, Micheaux's "imperfect" narrative constitutes an excess which reveals the cheat cuts, the other America artificially disguised by the Hollywood logic. It is in this sense that Gaines writes of improvement of film language by Micheaux. In *Black American Cinema* Ron Green compares Micheaux's film style to Black English, and to jazz. His cinema is one of the first to endow African Americans with cinematic voice and subjectivity through his uncovering of new spaces at the threshold of dominant cinema.

The first step in interpreting a Black film aesthetic must therefore be directed towards an analysis of the composition of the new shots discovered by Micheaux, and their potential effects on spectators. In *Black American Cinema* Micheaux's films are discussed in an in-depth manner for the first time by Jane Gaines and Ron Green. Micheaux's legacy as an independent filmmaker not only includes his entrepreneurial style in raising money and making films outside the studios. He also turned his cameras towards Black people and the Black experience in a manner that did not interest Hollywood directors of race films. Crucially, Micheaux's camera positioned Black spectators on the same side as the Black middle-class ideology, acquiring for his films an aesthetic that was primarily specific to the ways of life of that class.

Similarly, in the 1970s, Melvin Van Peebles and Bill Gunn positioned spectators with respect to different imaginaries derived from the Black experience in America. In *Sweet Sweetback's Baadasssss Song*, Van Peebles thematizes Black nationalism by casting the Black community as an internal colony, and Sweetback, a pimp, as the hero of decolonization. In *Black American Cinema*, Toni Cade Bambara refers to *Sweet Sweetback* as "a case of Stagolee meets Fanon or Watermelon Man plays Bigger Thomas?" *Sweet Sweetback* is about policing and surveillance of Black communities, and the existentialist struggle of the film's main character, a Black man. As Bambara notices, Bigger Thomas is not the only literary reference in the film; it also draws on the theme of the running Black man in *Invisible Man*, which is collapsed into a transformed Hollywood stereotype of the Black stud. As such, *Sweet Sweetback* is famous as the paradigmatic text for the 1970s Blaxploitation films. The theme of the Black man running from the law or from Black-on-Black crime, which links Van Peebles to such Black American writers as Richard Wright, Ralph Ellison, and Chester Himes, is also echoed in 1990s films like *Juice*, *Straight Out of Brooklyn*, and *Boyz N The Hood*, not to mention *New Jack City*, a film directed by Van Peebles's son Mario Van Peebles.

Sweet Sweetback's aesthetic draws on the logic of Black nationalism as the basis of value judgment, and defines itself by positioning the spectator to identify with the Black male hero of the film. Bambara rightly criticizes the centrality of Black manhood at the expense of women in *Sweet Sweetback*, but recognizes nationalist narratives as enabling strategies for survival, empowerment, and self-determination. As Sweetback is helped to escape from the policy by one Black person after another, the nationalist discourse of the film transforms the ghetto, where Black people are objects, into the community, where they affirm their subjecthood. To put it in Bambara's words, "Occupying the same geographical terrain are the *ghetto*, where we are penned up in concentration-camp horror, and the *community*, where we enact daily rituals of group validation in a liberated zone."

In *Ganja and Hess*, Bill Gunn aestheticizes the Black imaginary by placing the spectator on the same side as the Black church. The spectator draws pleasure from the film through the confrontation between the ideology of the Black church and vampirism, addiction to drugs and sex, and materialism. *Ganja and Hess* is perhaps the most beautifully shot Black film, and the most daring with respect to pushing different passions to their limits. The Black artist, Meda (played by Bill Gunn himself), is a nihilist who advocates total silence because, as a Black person, his art is always already overdetermined by race in America. The love scenes in the film are commingled with vampiristic gestures that are attractive and repulsive at the same time. At the Cannes Film Festival in 1973, Gunn's daring camera angles during one of the love scenes brought spectators to joy, applauding and screaming "Bravo! Bravo!" in the middle of the film. *Ganja and Hess* also pushes the classical narrative to the threshold by framing a frontal nude image of a Black man coming out of a swimming pool and running toward a window where a woman, Ganja (Marlene Clarke), smilingly awaits him.

What is radical about both *Ganja and Hess* and *Sweet Sweetback* is their formal positioning of Black characters and Black cultures at the center of the screen, creating a sense of defamiliarization of the classical film language. The two films also inaugurate for Black cinema two narrative tracks with regard to time and space. While *Ganja and Hess* is cyclical, going back and forth between pre-Christian time and the time after Christ, *Sweet Sweetback* is a linear recording of the progress of Black liberation struggle.

With regard to Black aesthetics, it is possible to put in the same category as *Ganja and Hess* such films as *A Powerful Thang* (Davis), *Daughters of the Dust* (Dash), *Losing Ground* (Collins), *Killer of Sheep* and *To Sleep with Anger* (Burnett), *Tongues United* (Riggs), and *She's Gotta Have It* (Lee). These films are concerned with the specificity of identity, the empowerment of Black people through mise-en-scène, and the rewriting of American history. Their narratives contain rhythmic and repetitive shots, going back and forth between the past and the present. Their themes involve Black folklore, religion, and the oral traditions which link Black Americans to the African diaspora. The narrative style is symbolic.

Sweet Sweetback, on the other hand, defines its aesthetics through recourse to the realistic style in film. The story line develops within the logic of continuity editing, and the characters look ordinary. The film presents itself as a mirror on a Black community under siege. The real effect is reinforced throughout the film by events which are motivated by racial and gendered causes. The sound track and the costumes link the film to a specific epoch in the Civil Rights Movement. Unlike the first category of films, which uses the symbolic style and concerns itself with the past. *Sweet Sweetback* makes the movement toward the future-present by confronting its characters with the obstacles ahead of them. Other films in this category include *Cooley High* (Michael Schultz), *House Party* (Reginald Hudlin), *Chameleon Street* (Harris), *Passing Through* (Clark), *Do the Right Thing* (Lee), *Straight Out of Brooklyn* (Rich), *Juice* (Ernest Dickerson), and *Boyz N The Hood* (Singleton). These lists are neither exhaustive nor fixed. The realist category has more in common with the classical Hollywood narrative, with its quest for the formation of the family and individual freedom, and its teleological trajectory (beginning, middle, and end). The symbolic narratives have more in common with Black expressive forms like jazz, and with novels by such writers as Toni Cade Bambara, Alice Walker, and Toni Morrison, which stop time to render audible and visible Black voices and characters that have been suppressed by centuries of Eurocentrism.

The comparison of the narrative styles deployed by *Sweet Sweetback* and *Ganja and Hess*[2] is useful in order to link the action-oriented *Sweet Sweetback* to modernism, and the reflexive style of *Ganja and Hess* to postmodernism. *Sweet Sweetback* defines its Afro-modernism through a performative critique of the exclusion of Blacks from reaping the fruits of American modernity and liberal democracy. *Ganja and Hess* is a postmodern text which weaves together a time of pre-Christian Africa, a time of Christ's Second Coming in the Black church, and a time of liberated Black women. Crucially, therefore, the repetition of history as played out on the grid of the Black diaspora is important to the definition of Gunn's film language. Through the repetition of these Black times in the film, Bill Gunn defines a Black aesthetic that puts in the same space African spirituality, European vampire stories, the Black church, addiction to drugs, and liberated feminist desires.

The New Black Films

It is easy to see the symbolic, reflexive, and expressive styles in films such as *Killer of Sheep* and *Daughters of the Dust*, and the active, materially grounded, and linear styles in *Boyz N the Hood*. But before looking more closely at these films, it is important to put into some perspective the ways in which Black films posit their specificity by challenging the construction of time and space in Hollywood films. It is only in this sense that arguments can begin about whether they displace, debunk, or reinforce the formulaic verisimilitude of Hollywood.

The way in which a filmmaker selects a location and organizes that location in front of the camera is generally referred to in film studies as mise-en-scène. Spatial narration in classical cinema makes sense through a hierarchical disposition of objects on the screen. Thus space is related to power and powerlessness, in so far as those who occupy the center of the screen are usually more powerful than those situated in the background or completely absent from the screen. I have described here Black people's relation to spatially situated images in Hollywood cinema. When Black people are absent from the screen, they read it as a symbol of their absence from the America constructed by Hollywood. When they are present on the screen, they are less powerful and less virtuous than the White man who usually occupies the center. Hollywood films have regularly tried to resolve this American dilemma, either through token or symbolic representation of Blacks where they are absent – for instance, the mad Black scientist in *Terminator 2*: or through a substitution of less virtuous Blacks by positive images of Blacks – for instance, *Grand Canyon* or *The Cosby Show*. But it seems to me that neither symbolic representation nor positive images sufficiently address the specificity of Black ways of life, and how they might enter in relation to other Americans on the Hollywood screen. Symbolic representation and positive images serve the function of plotting Black people in White space and White power, keeping the real contours of the Black community outside Hollywood.

The construction of time is similarly problematic in the classical narrative. White men drive time from the East to the West, conquering wilderness and removing obstacles out of time's way. Thus the "once upon a time" which begins every story in Hollywood also posits an initial obstacle in front of a White person who has to remove it in order for the story to continue, and for the conquest ideology of Whiteness to prevail. The concept of beginning, middle, and end, in itself, is universal to storytelling. The difference here is that Hollywood is only interested in White people's stories (White times), and Black people enter these times mostly as obstacles to their progress, or as supporting casts for the main White characters. "Once upon a time" is a traditional storytelling device which the storyteller uses to evoke the origin of a people, their ways of life, and the role of the individual in the society. The notion of *rite de passage* is a useful concept for describing the individual's separation from or incorporation into a social time. The classical narrative in cinema adheres to this basic ideological formula in order to tell White people's stories in Hollywood. It seems that White times in Hollywood have no effect on Black people and their communities: whether they play the role of a negative or positive stereotype, Black people neither grow nor change in the Hollywood stories. Because there is a dearth of Black people's stories in Hollywood that do not revolve around White times, television series such as *Roots*, and films such as *Do the Right Thing*, which situate spectators from the perspective of a Black "once upon a time," are taken out of proportion, celebrated by Blacks as authentic histories, and debunked by Whites as controversial.

To return again to the comparison between *Sweet Sweetback* and *Ganja and Hess*, it is easy to see how important time and space are to defining the cinematic styles they each extol. The preponderance of space in films such as *Ganja and Hess* reveals the hierarchies of power among the characters, but it also reveals the preoccupation of this style of Black cinema with the creation of space on the screen for Black voices, Black history, and Black culture. As I will show later with a discussion of space in *Daughters of the Dust*, Black films use spatial narration as a way of revealing and linking Black spaces that have been separated and suppressed by White times, and as a means of validating Black culture. In other words, spatial narration is a filmmaking of cultural restoration, a way for Black filmmakers to reconstruct Black history, and to posit specific ways to being Black Americans in the United States.

The emphasis on time, on the other hand, reveals the Black American as he/she engenders him/herself amid the material conditions of everyday life in the American society. In films like *Sweet Sweetback* and *Boyz N the Hood*, where a linear narrative dominates, the characters are depicted in continuous activities, unlike the space-based narratives, where the past constantly interrupts the present, and repetitions and cyclicality define narration. Crucially, whereas the space-oriented narratives can be said to center Black characters on the screen, and therefore empower them, the Black-times narratives link the progress of time to Black characters and make times exist for the purpose of defining their needs and their desires. Whereas the space-based narratives are expressive and celebratory of Black culture, the time-based narratives are existentialist performances of Black people against policing, racism, and genocide. I would like now to turn to *Daughters of the Dust* and *Boyz N the Hood* to illustrate the point.

Space and Identity: Black Expressive Style in *Daughters of the Dust*

> I am the first and the last
> I am the honored one and the scorned one
> I am the whore and the holy one
> I am the wife and the virgin
> I am the barren one and many are my daughters....
> I am the silence that you cannot understand....
> I am the utterance of my name.
>
> *Daughters of the Dust*

I have argued that the Hollywood classical narrative often articulates time and space through recourse to a discriminating gaze toward American Blacks. When the story is driven by time and action, it is usually White times. I'll say more about this in my discussion below of *Boyz N the Hood*. Similarly, when spatial considerations dominate the production of the story, the purpose is usually to empower White men. Common sense reveals that characters that are more often on the screen, or occupy the center of the frame, command more narrative authority than those that are in the background, on the sides, or completely absent from the frame. By presence, here, I have in mind first of all the literal presence of White characters in most of the shots that constitute the typical Hollywood film, which helps to define these characters as heroes of the story.

There is also the symbolic presence through which narrative authority for the organization of space is attributed to certain characters in the story. These devices of spatial narration are effective in linking characters with spaces, and in revealing space occupancy as a form of empowerment. For example, through the character played by Robert Duval in *Apocalypse Now*, Francis Ford Coppola parodies the power associated with White male actors such as John Wayne as they are framed at the center of the screen.

There is a preponderance of spatial narration in Julie Dash's *Daughters of the Dust*. Black women and men occupy every frame of the film, linking Black identity to a place called Ibo Landing in the Sea Islands of South Carolina, and, more importantly, empowering Black women and their ways of life. On a surface and literal level, the wide appeal of the film for Black women depends on the positioning of the women characters as bigger than life in the middle of the screen, which mirrors the beautiful landscape of Ibo Landing. Black women see themselves on the screen, richly adorned, with different hues of Blackness and Black hair styles, and flaunting their culture. In *Daughters of the Dust* the screen belongs to Black women. At a deeper level, where space and time are combined into a narrative, Julie Dash emphasizes spatial narration as a conduit to Black self-expressivity, a storytelling device which interrogates identity, memory, and Black ways of life. *Daughters of the Dust* stops time at 1902, when the story was set, and uses the canvas of Ibo Landing in the Sea Islands to glance backward to slavery, the Middle Passage, African religions, Christianity, Islam, the print media, photography, moving pictures, and African-American folkways, as elements with which Black people must come to terms in order to glance forward as citizens of the United States. In other words, the film asks us to know ourselves first, know where we came from, before knowing where we are going. To put it in yet another way, Ibo Landing is a symbolic space in which African Americans can articulate their relation to Africa, the Middle Passage, and the survival of Black people and their ways of life in America. Crucially, the themes of survival, the memories of African religions and ways of life which enter into conflict with Christianity and European ways of life, and the film's proposal of syncretism as a way out, are narrativized from Black women's points of view. I want to take more time here to show how Julie Dash uses women's voices to make these themes compatible with the space of Ibo Landing.

The conflict in the film concerns the migration of the Peazant family from Ibo Landing of the Sea Islands to the North. At first the conflict is set in binary terms. For those who support the migration North, the space of Ibo Landing is primitive, full of people who worship the sun, the moon, and the river. The North therefore promises literacy, Christianity, and progress. For Grandma Nana and the Unborn Child who link their identity to the space of Ibo Landing, the North represents the destruction of the family, disconnection from the ancestors, and the loss of identity for the children. For Grandma Nana, Ibo Landing is where the ancestors watch over the living, protect them, and guide them. It is in this sense that Nana does not want the family reunion to be a farewell party between those who are leaving and those staying. She prepares herself to give them something that they "can take North with [them] along with [their] big dreams."

As filmic space, Ibo Landing is the link between Africa and America. Or, to put it another way, Ibo Landing is Africa in America. According to the film, it is where the last slaves landed. *Daughters of the Dust* also argues that it is where African Americans remained isolated from the mainland of Georgia and South Carolina, and "created and maintained a distinct imaginative and original African-American culture." The Peazant family must therefore learn the terms of their belonging to Ibo Landing, which will be an example of African-American belonging to America, and must use the space of Ibo Landing to validate their identities as Americans of a distinctive culture. It is interesting to notice here that, unlike the Hollywood narratives which claim space only as a process of self-empowerment, *Daughters of the Dust* acknowledges through the letter that Iona receives from her Indian lover that the space belonged to the Indians first.

Weaving the voices of Grandma Nana, the Unborn Child, and Eula (the mother of the Unborn Child) through the spaces of Ibo Landing, Julie Dash creates a narrative that connects Africa to America, the past to the present. Using African ancestor figures as her narrative grid, she places Grandma Nana at the center of her story, and constructs oppositional characters around her. On the one hand we have Haagar, Viola, the Bible lady, and Eli, who is Eula's husband; on the other hand we have Yellow Mary, Eula, and Iona, who is Haagar's daughter. We have characters who are alike and who constitute reincarnations of ancestor figures with similar dispositions; and characters who are contraries of one another, and therefore require the intervention of the ancestors to bring peace and harmony.

Grandma Nana is the oldest person on the island. She spends most of her time visiting the graveyard where the ancestors are buried, and by the water which is a dwelling place of the spirits of the ancestors. I do not have enough space here to discuss the significance of water in *Daughters of the Dust*. But it is crucial to point out the recurring Middle Passage theme of Africans walking on water to go back to Africa. As an intertextual religious space, the use of water by Grandma Nana to communicate with the gods echoes *Yeelen* by Souleymane Cissé, where the mother bathes with milk in the middle of the river and asks the Goddess to protect her son. *Daughters* also reminds us of *Testament* by Black Audio Film/Video Collective, in which the characters walk into the middle of the river or visit graveyards in order to unlock the secret of the past. It would also be interesting to investigate the use of water in vases and on altars as a representation of Voodoo in *Daughters* and in *Dreaming Rivers* by Sankofa Film/Video Collective.

Daughters depicts the survival of African religious practices in Ibo Landing through Grandma Nana in other ways as well. She can hear the calls of the spirits, and, therefore, works with the Unborn Child to keep the family together. She teaches Eli about the core of African ancestor worship: "It's up to the living to keep in touch with the dead, Eli. Man's power don't end with death. We just move on to another place; a place where we go and watch over our living family. Respect your elders, respect your family, respect your ancestors."

A recourse to religion is central to the understanding of *Daughters of the Dust*. For Grandma Nana, ancestor worship provides the strongest stability for the Black family in America and Africa. Unlike Christianity and Islam, which are teleological and reserve the final reward for the end in Heaven, the ancestors in Grandma Nana's belief system just move to another world and watch over their living descendants. The children are the reincarnation of the ancestors, and this makes them precious to the adults whose fathers and grandfathers have joined the land of the ancestors. The Unborn Child in the film is one such reincarnation. She is doubled not only in the figure of Grandma Nana herself, but also in the young girl with tribal scars who appears with her mother in one of the flashbacks. She travels through time, and she is present at different settings in the film: we see her among the first generation of Africans working with indigo dye, and we see her in 1902 setting among children playing in the sand. Like the ancestors, her role is one of a mediator in the family. It is in this sense that Grandma Nana states that for Africans, the ancestors and the children are the most sacred elements of society.

Julie Dash also uses the religious theme of reincarnation, and links the Unborn Child to African-American survival during slavery, genocide, and the rape of Black women. In the film, the theme of the Peazant family's disintegration entailed by the migration to the North is replayed in the subtheme of Eli's self-exile from his wife, Eula, because she's carrying a child that Eli does not consider his. Eli's first reaction to Eula's pregnancy is to become an iconoclast toward the ancestor belief system that Grandma Nana wants to maintain. He puts into question the religion and culture he has received from childhood to adulthood. In other words: How can this happen to him, who has played by the rules? How come the gods are not avenging his misfortune? Subsequently, he picks up his ax and proceeds to smash all the fetishes that he had previously revered.

Grandma Nana finds an answer to Eli's blasphemous questions in her belief system. She links Eula's pregnancy to the condition of Black women in slavery who were raped, denied motherhood rights, and treated like animals. At the same time, the power and complexity of Black people come from their ability to maintain the sacredness of the womb by restoring to the group the children of interracial rape. Grandma Nana uses ancestor worship, and the place of children in it, to appropriate the baby Eula is carrying. By doing so, she bends the filiative and patriarchal rules Eli maintains in order to disavow the Unborn Child. For Grandma Nana, Eli, too, must learn the process of cleansing rape from the child's name, and making it his own child. Grandma Nana argues that the womb is as sacred as the ancestors, and that the Unborn Child is sent by the ancestors, precisely at this critical juncture in Ibo Landing's history, to ensure survival: "You need this one, Eli, to make the family stronger like it used to be." It is interesting to note the spatial organization as Grandma Nana talks to Eli. As the oldest person in the Peazant family, her role is that of a teacher. As she speaks to Eli, the space revealed on the screen is that of children playing games on the beach. The narrative implication here is that the children are the audience of her teaching. At one point during the children's game, the film changes to a slow motion. As the children fall on top of one another, we hear screaming and groaning, which reminds us of the Middle Passage during which hundreds of Africans were piled on top of each other in the cabins of slave ships. The implication of Grandma Nana's teaching is that, just as captured Africans were thrown together during that painful time of the Middle Passage, Blacks today must see themselves in the same boat, and fight together to "make the family stronger."

Eli's questions about the paternity and, therefore, the race of the Unborn Child also touch on the issues of light skin and dark skin, pure blood and mixed blood, superior and inferior; in short, we are dealing with racism among Blacks. It is in this sense that Yellow Mary is ostracized by Haagar and Viola, who use her light complexion as a sign of betrayal and try to banish her from Ibo Landing. For Grandma Nana, Yellow Mary and the Unborn Child contribute to the survival and maintenance of Black people in America, because their presence makes Blackness diverse and complex. Black survival in America confounds and embarrasses both Whiteness and essentialist notions of pure Africans. Julie Dash puts onto stage one of the most beautiful and powerful scenes in the film to illustrate this point. Haagar and others have been chastising Yellow Mary for not being Black enough, when Eula stands up and delivers a speech worthy of an ancestor figure. The mise-en-scène of this sequence reveals Black women in all their powers, as Eula reminds Haagar that no one is Blacker or purer than anyone else, and warns her and Viola about the wrath of the gods, if they were to continue their gesture of expelling Yellow Mary out of the race. Spatial representation again becomes paramount, because Eula's speech is directed to the on-screen audience of the Peazant family, as well as the off-screen spectators.

I have discussed so far the ways in which *Daughters of the Dust* uses African belief systems as the center which enables Black women and men to articulate their identities on the space of Ibo Landing. Grandma Nana, particularly, posits the ancestor worship system as a text which holds together the world of the Ibo Landing and provides answers to practical daily problems. A crucial question remains: whether the belief in ancestors can coexist with other belief systems, such as Christianity and Islam, on and off the island? At first, religious systems seem to be opposed in *Daughters of the Dust*. Bilal, who is Muslim, is opposed to the Baptists, who think that their God is better. Viola and Haagar use Christianity to elevate themselves above Grandma Nana. They see ancestor worship as an idolatry which is confined to Ibo Landing. They look to the North as a sign of enlightenment and Christian salvation.

Clearly, Julie Dash represents all these belief systems on the space of Ibo Landing not to show the fixity of different religions, and their essentialist nature, but to propose all of them as part of what makes Black people in America complex. Toward the end of the film Grandma Nana brings together the different belief systems, when she ties together the Bible and a sacred object from her own religion, and asks every one to kiss the hybridized Bible before departing from the island. This syncretic move is her way of mixing up the religions in Ibo Landing, and activating their combined power to protect those who are moving North. Earlier in the film she commands Eli to "celebrate our ways" when he goes North. The syncretic move is therefore also a survival tactic for the African ways of life up North.

Arguably, another reason for deploying ancestor worship (and casting Grandma Nana at the center in the film) is to reveal its usable power in holding the Black family together. Placing women at the center of the frame is also Julie Dash's way of creating space for Black people in modernity, and is her redefinition of Black images in their relation to such modern tools as still photography, newspapers, and moving pictures. Julie Dash's spatial narrative style inextricably combines the identities of her characters with the landscape of Ibo Landing. Her mise-en-scène of Grandma Nana, Haagar, Yellow Mary, and Eula in the center of the frame makes the space theirs, and their possession of the space makes them bigger than life. They become so associated with the space of the Ibo Landing, through close-ups of various sorts, that it becomes difficult to imagine Ibo Landing now without the faces of these Black women. Analogically speaking, it is like imagining America in Western films without the faces of John Wayne, Kirk Douglas, and Gary Cooper.

The spatial narrative style of *Daughters of the Dust* enables Julie Dash to claim America as the land of Black people, to plot Africanism in American ways of life, and to make intelligible African voices that were rendered inarticulate. To return to the thematization of religion in the film, Julie Dash has made manifest an Africanism that was repressed for centuries, but that refused to die. As Grandma Nana states, "those African ancestors sneak up on you when you least suspect them." With her revival of ancestor worship as a narrative grid, as a point of reference for different themes in the film, Julie Dash has ignited the fire of love and caring among Black people. The path between the ancestors and the womb constitutes a Black structure of feeling, a caring handed down from generation to generation, which commands us to care for our children. In an article entitled "Nihilism and Black America," Cornel West proposes "a politics of conversion" as a way out of the carelessness of Black-on-Black crime, and as a protection against "market-driven corporate enterprises, and white supremacism." For West,

> The genius of our black foremothers and forefathers was to create powerful buffers to ward off the nihilistic threat, to equip black folk with cultural armor to beat back the demons of hopelessness, meaninglessness, and lovelessness. . . . These traditions consist primarily of black religious and civic institutions that sustained familial and communal networks of support.[3]

Perhaps Julie Dash's theory of ancestor worship should be among those institutions that constitute Black structures of feeling: as Grandma Nana puts it, let the ancestors guide us and protect us.

Black Times, Black Stories: *Boyz N the Hood*

Either they don't know, or don't show, or don't care about what's going on in the Hood.
Boyz N the Hood

To return now to *Boyz N the Hood*, I would like to illustrate its emphasis on time and movement as a way of defining an alternative Black film language different from the spatial and expressive language of *Daughters of the Dust*. Like *Daughters of the Dust*, *Boyz N the Hood* begins with a well-defined date. But unlike *Daughters of the Dust*, which is set in 1902 and looks into the past as a way of unfolding its story, *Boyz N the Hood* starts in 1984, and continues for more than seven years into the future. *Daughters of the Dust* is about Black people's reconstitution of the memories of the past: it is a film about identity, and the celebration of Black ways of life. *Boyz N the Hood*, on the other hand, is a rite of passage film, a film about the Black man's journey in America. The story line is linear in *Boyz N the Hood*, whereas *Daughters of the Dust* unfolds in a circular manner.

In films like *Boyz N the Hood*, *Juice*, *Straight Out of Brooklyn*, and *Deep Cover*, the narrative time coincides with the development of the lives of the characters of the films. Many of these films begin with the childhood of the main characters, who then enter into adulthood, and face many obstacles in their lives. These films produce an effect of realism by creating an overlap between the rite of passage into manhood and the narrative time of the story. The notion of rite of passage, which defines the individual's relation to time in terms of separation from or incorporation into society, helps us to understand the use of narrative time in a film like *Boyz N the Hood*. The beginning, middle, and end of *Boyz N the Hood* constitute episodes that mark the young protagonist's incorporation into the many levels of society. In fact, the structure of the film is common to African-American folktales, as well as to the classical cinema. It is as follows: A boy has to go on a journey in order to avert an imminent danger. He travels to the home of a relative or friend (uncle, aunt, father, mother, wise man, and so on) who teaches him, or helps him to overcome the obstacle. At the end, he removes the danger, and his nation (or community, or family) gets stronger with him. This skeletal structure is common to texts as diverse as *The Epic of Sunjata* (D. T. Niane), the *Aeneid* (Virgil), and *The Narrative of the Life of Frederick Douglass* (Douglass), as well as to the Hollywood Western genre, the martial art films, and the Rocky films with Sylvester Stallone. The literal journey in time and space overlaps with the symbolic journey of the rite of passage. Typically, this type of storytelling addresses moments of crisis, and the need to build a better society.

The moment of crisis is symbolized in *Boyz N the Hood* by the opening statistical information, which states that "One out of every twenty-one Black American males will be murdered in their lifetime. Most will die at the hands of another Black male." Thus, *Boyz N the Hood* is a cautionary tale about the passage into manhood, and about the development of a politics of caring for the lives of Black males. More specifically, it is about Tre Styles (Cuba Gouldings), the main character, and his relation to the obstacles that he encounters on his way to manhood. Crucially, the major distractive forces in the film are the police, gang life, and the lack of supervision for the youth. To shield Tre from these obstacles, his mother sends him to live with his father, whose teaching will guide him through the many rites of passage toward manhood.[4]

The film is divided into three episodes, and each episode ends with rituals of separation and transition. In the first episode the ritual ends with Tre leaving his mother (first symbol of weaning) and friends behind. The story of this episode implies that most of the friends he leaves behind will not make it. On the way to his father's house. Tre's mother says, "I don't want you to end up dead, or in jail, or drunk standing in front of one of these liquor stores." The second episode ends with Doughboy's (Ice Cube) arrest by the police, who take him to the juvenile detention camp. The third episode ends with the death of Ricky Baker, Doughboy, and many other Black males. At the end of each episode, Tre moves to a higher understanding of life.

Let us now focus on one of the episodes in order to show its internal conflicts, and the specific elements that enter into play to prevent the passage of young Black males into manhood and caring for the community. I will choose the first episode because it introduces the spectator to most of the obstacles which are complicated and repeated in the other episodes. The film opens with a shot in which the camera zooms in on a stop sign until it fills the screen. We see a plane flying over the roofs, and the next shot reveals Tre and three other young kids walking to school. The subtitles say: "South Central LA, 1984." The children walk by a one-way street sign. This sign, too, is depicted in close-up as the camera travels above to establish the crossroad. Then the four kids take a direction facing a wrong-way sign. They travel on that road and see a crime scene that is circled by a plastic ribbon with the words: "Police Line Do Not Cross." Inside the police line there are three posters of President Ronald Reagan with a sign saying: "Reagan/Bush, Four More Years." The kids cross the police line, as one of them moves closer to the Reagan posters. At that moment a rhythmic and violent editing reveals each of the posters in a close-up with the sound of a gunshot. There are bullet holes in the poster. In the next scene, the kids are in a classroom where the students, artworks on the wall reflect the imagery of policing: drawings of a Los Angeles Police Department helicopter looking down on people, a police car, a coffin, and a poster of wanted men. Tre disrupts a lesson on the Pilgrims, and when the teacher asks him to teach the class, he points to the map of Africa and states that: "Africa is the place where the body of the first man was found." This is a reference to the multiculturalism debate not only across the curriculum, but also in rap music, and in the press. Tre's lesson ends with a fight between himself and another boy. The following shot begins with Tre walking home. He passes a group of young Black males shooting dice. They break into a fight. As Tre crosses the street to go home, he is almost run over by a blue car which presumably is driven by gang members. His mother is on the telephone talking to the teacher about the fight and Tre's suspension. The editing of the soundtrack is interesting in this scene. As Tre walks past the men shooting dice, their noise is placed in the background, and we hear in the foreground the conversation between Tre's mother and the teacher. This editing device unites different spaces through their sharing of the same sound. For example, later in the film, the community is shown as one when people in different places listen to the same rap song. (Similarly, in *Do the Right Thing*, Spike Lee uses the DJ and his music to unite the community.) The last scene in this episode involves Tre and his mother driving to his father's house. They pass by liquor stores and junkies standing by the doors. The mother reassures Tre that she loves him, and will do anything to keep him from ending up in jail, or standing in the streets in front of liquor stores.

Signs (Stop, One Way, Wrong Way, LAPD, Liquor Store, Police Line Do Not Cross, and so on) play an important role in limiting the movement of people in South Central Los Angeles. Showing the airplane flying over the roofs not only indicates where we are in LA, but also suggests the freedom associated with flying away from such an enclosed space. Black American literature often draws on the theme of flying to construct desire for liberated spaces: Bigger Thomas of *Native Son* (Richard Wright) sees flying as a way out of the ghetto of South Side Chicago; Milkman of *Song of Solomon* (Morrison) reenacts the myth of flying Americans in order to free himself from an unwanted situation.

The signs become control tools for the police, in the way that they limit individual freedom of movement in the "hood." They also define the hood as a ghetto by using surveillance from above and outside to take agency away from people in the community. In fact, *Boyz N the Hood* is about the dispute over agency and control of the community that pits the protagonist and his allies against gang members and the police. The drawings of helicopters, police cars, and wanted men show how the police surveillance has penetrated the imaginary even of schoolchildren in the hood. Later on in the film, helicopter noise, police sirens, and police brutality are revealed to be as menacing and distracting to people in the hood as drugs and gang violence.

The dispute over the control of the hood is also a dispute over images. The police need to convince themselves and the media that every Black person is a potential gang member, armed and dangerous, in order to continue the policing of the hood in a terroristic and militaristic manner. For the Black policemen in the film, the life of a Black person is not worth much: "one less nigger out in the street and we won't have to worry about him." It is by making the gang members and other people in the hood accept this stereotype of themselves that the community is transformed into a ghetto, a place where Black life is not worth much. It seems to me that *Boyz N the Hood* blames the rise of crime and the people's feeling of being trapped in the hood on a conspiracy among the gang members, the police, the liquor stores, and Reagan. Indeed, the film raises questions of human rights violation when gang warfare and police brutality collude to prevent people from moving around freely, sleeping, or studying.

On the other hand, Tre's struggle to gain agency also coincides with his passage to manhood, and the development of a politics of caring for the community. *Boyz N the Hood*, in this respect, is one of the most didactic Black films. The other contenders are *Deep Cover*, and perhaps some rap videos which espouse a politics of identification with lawbreakers against the police.[5] The didacticism of *Boyz N the Hood* emanates from the film's attempt to teach Tre not to accept the police's and the media's stereotype of him and other young Black males as worthless; and to teach him to care for his community and reclaim it from both the gangs and the police. Didactic film language abounds in the film. We see it when the camera lingers on the liquor stores and homeless people, as Tre and his mother drive to his father's house. The mother, in one of the first instances of teaching Tre in the film, states that she loves him and that is why she is taking him out of this environment. Earlier in the same episode, we also saw the Reagan posters interpreted in a didactic manner, so as to blame him for the decay of the urban community. The posters are situated in the same environment as the murder scene.

However, Tre's father, more than the didactic camera and editing styles, is the central figure of judgment in the film. He calls the Black policeman "brother" in order to teach him, in the presence of Tre, how to care about other Black people; he delivers lessons on sex education, Black-on-Black crimes, the dumping of drugs in the Black community, gentrification, and the importance of Black-owned businesses in the Black community. He earns the nickname of preacher, and Tre's friends describe him as a sort of "Malcolm/Farrakhan" figure. Crucially, his teachings help Tre to develop a politics of caring, to stay in school, and more importantly, to stay alive. It is revealing in this sense that a didactic and slow-paced film like *Boyz N the Hood* can be entertaining and pleasurable at the same time.

The New Black Realism

Realism as a cinematic style is often claimed to describe films like *Boys N the Hood*, *Juice*, and *Straight Out of Brooklyn*. When I taught *Boyz N the Hood*, my students talked about it in terms of realism: "What happened in the film happens everyday in America." "It is like it really is in South Central LA." "It describes policing in a realistic manner." "The characters on the screen look like the young people in the movie theater." "It captures gang life like it is." "It shows Black males as an endangered species." "I liked its depiction of liquor stores in the

Black community." "I identified with Ice Cube's character because I know guys like that back home."

Clearly, there is something in the narrative of films like *Boyz N the Hood* and *Straight Out of Brooklyn* that links them, to put it in Aristotelian terms, to existent reality in Black communities. In my class, some students argued that these films use hip hop culture, which is the new Black youth culture and the most important youth culture in America today. Thus, the characters look *real* because they dress in the style of hip hop, talk the lingo of hip hop, practice its world view toward the police and women, and are played by rap stars such as Ice Cube. Furthermore, the films thematize an advocacy for Black males, whom they describe as endangered species, in the same way that rap groups such as Public Enemy sing in defense of Black males.

It seems to me, therefore, that the films are about Black males' initiation into manhood, the obstacles encountered that often result in death and separation, and the successful transition of some into manhood and responsibility toward the community. In *Juice*, for example, of the four young boys who perform the ritual of growing up, two die, one is seriously injured by a gun shot, and only one seems to have been successfully incorporated into society. Removing obstacles out of Black males' way is also the central theme of *Chameleon Street, Straight Out of Brooklyn, Deep Cover*, and *Boyz N the Hood*.

In *Deep Cover* the ritual of manhood involves the main character's exposure of a genocide plotted by drug dealers in Latin America and the highest officials in the US government against the Black community. The real "deep cover" in *Deep Cover* is the recipe for caring for the community against genocidal forces like White supremacists, drugs, and Black-on-Black crime. The removal of obstacles out of the main character's way leads to the discovery of the politics of caring to the Black community. In this film, as in many new Black realism films, to be a man is to be responsible for the Black community, and to protect it against the aforementioned dangers. John (Larry Fishburne), a cop working undercover as a drug dealer, enters in an intriguing relationship with a Black detective (Clarence Williams), who plays the born-again policeman. The religious policeman keeps reminding John of his responsibility to the community, and John laughs at him. Toward the end of the film, when the character played by Clarence Williams gets shot, John is united with him by the force of caring, and realizes that he must fight both the drug dealers and the police to protect his own.

A key difference between the new Black realism films and the Blaxploitation series of the 1970s lies in character development through rites of passage in the new films. Unlike the static characters of the Blaxploitation series, the characters of the new realism films change with the enfolding of the story line. As characters move obstacles out of their way, they grow into men, and develop a politics of caring for the community. The new realism films imitate the existent reality of urban life in America. Just as in real life the youth are pulled between hip hop life style, gang life, and education, we see in the films neighborhoods that are pulled between gang members, rappers, and education-prone kids. For the black youth, the passage into manhood is also a dangerous enterprise which leads to death both in reality and in film.

Notes

For all references to *Black American Cinema*, see Manthia Diawara, *Black American Cinema* (NY: Routledge, 1993).

1   Janice Mosier Richolson, "He's Gotta Have It: An Interview with Spike Lee," in *Cineaste*, Vol. 28, No. 4, (1992), p. 14.

2   For more on the aesthetics of *Sweet Sweetback* and *Ganja and Hess*, see the important book, *Black Cinema Aesthetics: Issues in Independent Black Filmmaking*, edited by Gladstone L. Yearwood, Athens: Ohio University Center for Afro-American Studies, 1982; Tommy L. Lott "A No-Theory Theory of Contemporary Black Cinema," in *Black American Literature Forum* 25/2 (1991); and Manthia Diawara and Phyllis Klotman, "*Ganja and Hess*: Vampires, Sex, and Addictions," in *Black American Literature Forum* 25/2 (1991).

3   Cornel West, "Nihilism in Black America," in *Dissent* (Spring 1991), 223.

4   Clearly, there is a put-down of Black women in the rhetoric used to send Tre to his father's house. For an excellent critique of female-bashing in the film see Jacquie Jones. "The Ghetto Aesthetic," in *Wide Angle*, Volume 13. Nos. 3 & 4 (1991), 32–43.

5   See Regina Austin, "'The Black Community,' Its Lawbreakers and a Politics of Identification," in *Southern California Law Review* (May 1992), for a thorough discussion of Black people's identification with the community and its lawbreakers.

Part VI

Alternative Aesthetics

Introduction

Robert Stam

From Greek *aisthesis* (perception, sensation), the discipline of aesthetics deals with the study of artistic beauty and related issues of the sublime, the grotesque, the humorous, and the pleasurable. In philosophy, aesthetics formed part, together with ethics and logic, of the triad of "normative" sciences devoted to devising rules concerning the Beautiful, the Good, and the True respectively. Aesthetics deals with such questions as: what is beauty in a work of art? Is beauty "real" and objectively verifiable, or subjective, a matter of taste? To what extent are notions of the beautiful time-bound and shaped by ambient social values?

In relation to film, aesthetics brings up such questions as: are aesthetics medium-specific? Should a film exploit the distinctive traits of the medium? Is "art" an honorific to be attributed only to a few films, or are all films works of art simply because of their institutionally defined social status? Do films have a natural "vocation" for realism, or for artifice and stylization? Should technique call attention to itself or be self-effacing? Is there an ideal style? A correct way of telling a story? A correct approach to image and mise-en-scène? What is filmic pleasure? To what extent is aesthetics linked to larger ethical and social issues? Has all art been irrevocably changed by Auschwitz, as Adorno suggested? Is aesthetics itself hopelessly compromised, as Clayde Taylor argues, by its origins in eighteenth-century racist discourses? Should we dispense with it altogether since the prism of the aesthetic inevitably abstracts art from life, community, and spirituality (see Taylor, 1998)? What is the relation between technique and social responsibility? Is a tracking shot, as Godard put it, always a question of morality? Are there aesthetic correlatives to specific ideologies such as fascism, discernible in the films of Leni Riefenstahl and Busby Berkeley, as Susan Sontag has suggested? Can fascist or racist films like *Triumph of the Will* or *Birth of a Nation* be "masterpieces" in artistic terms and still be repugnant in ethical/political terms?

Film aesthetics reflects on cinema as an art, focusing either on the aesthetic impact of film as a medium in general or on the aesthetic qualities of particular films. Already in the first decades of its history, the cinema was both denigrated as aesthetically vulgar and hailed as revolutionary by avant-garde artists such as Piscator, Cocteau, Mayakovsky, and Schoenberg. Despite the literary prejudice against film, the cinema in fact has available to it even greater expressive resources than literature, even if those resources are not always used. While the matter of expression of literature is words, and only words, cinema is a composite language by virtue of its diverse matters of expression (sequential photography, phonetic sound, music, noise) and thus "inherits" all the art forms and discourses associated with these matters of expression.

Aesthetics in film is therefore a highly complex matter, having to do with the multitude of choices made by film artists, often within messy and contingent circumstances. Think, for example, of the varied parameters of filmic style. In the cinema, style begins already with methods of pre-production (Fellini's quests for striking locations and physiognomies), production (rigid supervision à la Hitchcock or room for improvisation as with Altman), ways of working with actors (method technique with Kazan, elaborate collective exercises with Mike Leigh), and postproduction (elaborate reworking à la Coppola or minimal post-production as with Buñuel). Filmic style results from the orchestration of an infinity of choices involving camera movement (the geometrically calculated tracking shots of a Resnais, the vertiginously swirling camera movements of a Scorsese; angle (Welles's obliqueness, Akerman's frontality); laboratory effects (slow motion à la Peckinpah, subliminal freeze-frames à la Truffaut); decor (stylized with Minnelli, "realist" with John Ford); depth of field (multiple planes à la Renoir, flat à la Godard); characteristic editing preferences (single-shot sequences for Alain Tanner, rapid montage for Richard Lester); use of sound (Bressonian minimalism, Altman's crowded aural field).

To address the question of *alternative* aesthetics, we must first address the question of the *normative* aesthetic, and here the norm in question is dramatic realism and the dominant style of Hollywood continuity. Yet it is important to deprovincialize our notions of the normative in terms both of time and space. Realism as artistic norm, whether within the cinema or outside of it, is in some ways a provincial and relatively recent idea. Vast regions of the world, and long periods of artistic history, have shown little allegiance to or even interest in realism. Popular Indian cinema, for example, inherits a 2,000-year tradition that circles back to the classical Sanskrit drama, whose aesthetic is based less on plausible plot than on subtle modulations of mood and feeling (*rasa*). Even in the West, realist traditions have always been "shadowed" by other, more reflexive, traditions; the parodic plays of Aristophanes, the carnivalesque excesses of Rabelais, and the reflexive theatricality of Shakespeare. Realism, then, is just one of many possible aesthetics available to the narrative arts.

In dominant cinema the implicit norm is what has been called the "classical Hollywood cinema," or what Colin MacCabe, working from George Eliot's *Middlemarch*, called the "classical realist text." As we saw in Part V, the term "realism" evokes the reconstitution of a fictional world characterized by internal coherence, plausible causality, psychological realism, and the appearance of a seamless spatial and temporal continuity. This continuity was achieved, in the classical period of the Hollywood film, by an etiquette for introducing new scenes (a choreographed progression from establishing shot to medium shot to close shot); conventional devices for evoking the passage of time (dissolves, iris effects); conventional techniques to render imperceptible the transition from shot to shot (the 30° rule, position matches, direction matches, and inserts to cover-up unavoidable discontinuities); and devices for implying subjectivity (interior monologue, eyeline matches, empathetic music).

The challenge to this classical Hollywood aesthetic has come from many directions, including from "within" the mainstream tradition. In fact, the dominant model was challenged, to put it anachronistically, even before it established itself as the dominant. The conventional view that the cinema evolved inexorably and logically toward the *telos* of an ever-greater realism and verisimilitude has been questioned by scholars of silent cinema such as Noël Burch and Tom Gunning, who have argued that the so-called "primitive cinema" was not a bumbling attempt to achieve what were to become the dominant norms, but rather an alternative to those norms. Burch (1990) speaks of an international "Primitive Mode of Representation" (PMR) as the dominant practice from 1894 to 1914, the style of which was non-linear, anti-psychological, and discontinuous. Tom Gunning (chapter 14, this volume) delineates the non-linear aesthetics of what he calls a "cinema of attractions," a strong presence prior to 1908, whose aesthetics were exhibitionistic rather than voyeuristic, closer to circus and to vaudeville than to what later became the dominant story film.

Strict dramatic realism was never the only model available even within mainstream cinema. Such films as the Keaton parodies of Griffith (*The Three Ages*) and of the Western (*Go West*), the more irreverent of the Chaplin films, and certain films of the Marx Brothers, represented a homegrown anti-realist tradition rooted in the popular intertext of fairground, vaudeville, and burlesque. The "boiling anarchy" animating *Animal Crackers* and *Monkey Business*, for Antonin Artaud, led to "an essential disintegration of the real by poetry."[1] The Marx Brothers films combine an anti-authoritarian stance toward official institutions with a cinematic and linguistic "gramatica jocosa," which involves, in Patricia Mellenkamp's words, the "breaking and entering the narrative as well as houses, constantly shattering any imposed cause–effect logic."[2]

There was also the challenge offered by the "historical avant-gardes" of the 1920s and 1930s. Artisanal rather than industrial, these movements systematically challenged the dominant conventions. The term "historical avant-garde" covers a wide spectrum of practices. On the one hand, "impressionist" filmmakers like Louis Delluc, Jean Epstein, and Germaine Dulac (and Mario Peixoto in Brazil) emphasized the cinematic translation of subjective experience in fiction films. The German expressionists, for example Robert Wiene and *The Cabinet of Dr. Caligari* (1919) emphasized outlandishly subjectivized studio decors, chiarascuro lighting, and tormented performance. The Dada movement, meanwhile, expressed most notably in René Clair's *Entr'acte* (1924), sought for irrational, associative effects as part of a provocation against respectable art and conventional storytelling. The surrealists, in Dada's wake, both adopted popular cinema (as spectators) and attacked the film institution through provocative, anti-clerical, anti-bourgeois, and stylistically anarchic films (such as *L'Age d'Or*) full of oneiric space–time dislocations and the ludic undermining of social and aesthetic norms.

In the postwar period, the avant-garde continues in new locations (Deren, Brakhage, Mekas, Anger, Potter, Burch, Friedrich, Rainer) and dissolves into both the high-modernist art film (Resnais, Godard, Jarman, Greenaway, Egoyan, Angelopolos) and later even into the "post-classical" Movie Brat auteurist films of Scorsese and Coppola. Picking up on a cue from Renato Poggioli, who distinguished between the political and the cultural avant-gardes (sometimes in synch but often not), Peter Wollen distinguished between an apolitical avant-garde, concerned with "pure cinema" and "laying bare the device," and a political avant-garde, concerned with revolutionizing both film form and social practice. Similarly, in *Theory of the Avant-Garde* (1984) Peter Burger distinguishes between modernism as a broad umbrella for formal innovation in the arts, and the avant-garde as a designation for movements which go beyond merely formal subversion to attack the institutions of art itself. The more apolitical strain within the avant-garde sought to reflexively foreground the textual processes specific to film. There was an infinity of ways of doing this. Filmmakers could "flatten" the image, deprive it of the illusion of depth (arranging pro-filmic subjects in a single spatial plane, without foreground or background or vanishing point to reinforce the impression of relief). Or filmmakers could limit their pro-filmic material to a single matter of expression – written words, for example, as in Michael Snow's *So is This*. Or filmmakers could call hyperbolic attention to specifically cinematic movement, as when Michael Snow in *Wavelength* (1966–7) structures a 45-minute film around a single "zoom" movement. Or a film can deprive itself of movement in the shot, as Chris Marker does in *La Jetée* (1962). Or image and sound can be dislocated as in Hollis Frampton's *nostalgia*, where the filmmaker's commentaries are placed so as to apply not to the image we see but rather the image we are about to see.

In the 1960s theorists of innovation in the cinema picked up on some of the cues provided by Bertolt Brecht. Brecht had developed a strong Marxist-inflected critique of the dramatic realist model operative both in traditional theater and in the Hollywood film, a critique which influenced not only film theorists (Jean-Louis Commolli, Peter Wollen, Colin MacCabe) but also many filmmakers themselves (Glauber Rocha, Jean-Luc Godard, Tomas Gutiérrez Alea, Alain Tanner, Herbert Ross). Apart from the general goals of Brechtian theater – laying bare the causal network of events, the cultivation of an active, thinking spectator, the defamiliarization of alienating social realities, the emphasis on social contradiction, the immanence of meaning – Brecht also proposed specific techniques to achieve those goals. In terms of mythos (plot), Brecht proposed his own epic theater, i.e. a theater whose narrative structure was interrupted, fractured, digressive. In terms of acting, Brecht argued for a double distantiation, between the actor and the part, and between the actor and the spectator. Brecht argued as well for a thoroughgoing reflexivity, i.e. that art should reveal the principles of its own construction, to avoid the "swindle" of suggesting that fictive events were not "worked at" but simply "happened." Brechtian "alienation effects," meanwhile, served to decondition the spectator and "make strange" the lived social world, freeing socially conditioned phenomena from the "stamp of familiarity," and revealing them as striking, as calling for explanation, as other than "natural."

Brecht influenced filmmakers/theorists such as Peter Wollen in his formulations for a proposed "counter cinema." Wollen's schema pitted mainstream cinema against a counter cinema in the form of seven binary features: (1) narrative intransitivity versus narrative transitivity (i.e. the systematic disruption of the flow of the narrative); (2) estrangement versus identification (through Brechtian techniques of acting, sound/image disjunction, direct address, etc.); (3) foregrounding versus transparency (systematic drawing of attention to the process of construction of meaning); (4) multiple versus single diegesis; (5) aperture versus closure (rather than a unifying authorial vision, an opening out into an intertextual field); (6) unpleasure versus pleasure (the filmic experience conceived as a kind of collaborative production/consumption); and (7) reality versus fiction (the exposure of the mystifications involved in filmic fictions). The point was to deconstruct and "denaturalize" the operative codes and ideologies of dominant cinema in order to reveal their socially constructed nature.

These schemas, while suggestive and influential, could also be seen as simply reversing the old dyads rather than moving beyond them. In a purely reactive gesture, the avant-garde obsessively rejects the mainstream, rather like the lapsed Catholic who cannot stop denouncing the Church. While Brecht endorsed popular forms of culture such as sport and the circus, the new theories offered only a festival of negations of the dominant cinema. While usefully exposing the potential for exploitation in identification with streamlined plots, glamorous stars, and idealized characters, the theories failed to acknowledge the force of the desire that brings spectators to the cinema. A theory based simply on negations of the conventional pleasures of cinema – the negation of narrative, mimesis, identification – leads to a dead-end anhedonia, leaving little for the spectator to connect with. Any film, to be effective, must offer its quantum of pleasure, something to discover or see or feel.

Some of the avant-gardist theories offer a left version of the formalist fetishization of the artistic device. Mere reflexivity, quite apart from authorial intention, spectatorial expectation, or the contingencies of the historical moment, is assumed to be *necessarily* critical and efficacious. The imagined alternative aesthetics, furthermore, inclines toward austerity and minimalism; rarely did theorists in the 1970s think about the critical potential of exuberance and excess. In this sense, another key reference for rethinking the question of cinematic pleasure is Mikhail Bakhtin, a literary theorist who never directly addressed the cinema but whose theories have clear relevance for the seventh art. Bakhtin's notion of "carnival," for example, can easily sustain a cinema of raucous subversion. As theorized by Bakhtin, carnival embraces an anti-classical aesthetic that rejects formal harmony and unity in favor of the asymmetrical, the heterogenous, the oxymoronic, the miscegenated. Carnival's "grotesque realism" turns conventional aesthetics on its head in order to locate a new kind of popular, convulsive, rebellious beauty, one that dares to reveal the grotesquerie of the powerful and the latent beauty of the "vulgar." (In the cinema, the religious travesties so frequent in the films of Luis Buñuel, for example, forge a direct link between the avant-garde and the *parodia sacra* of which Bakhtin speaks).

Carnival favors an aesthetic of mistakes, what Rabelais called a *gramatica jocosa* ("laughing grammar"), in which artistic language is liberated from the stifling norms of correctness and decorum. Against the static, classic, finished beauty of antique sculpture, carnival counterposes mutable, transgressive "grotesque body," rejecting what might be called the "fascism of beauty," i.e. the construction of an ideal type or language of beauty in relation to which other types are seen as inferior "dialectal" variations. "Anti-canonical" carnivalesque art deconstructs not only the canon, but also the generating matrix that makes canons and grammaticality. And if carnival is anti-grammaticality, the dominant model of cinema, with its neat sequencing of beginning, middle, and end, would seem to constitute grammaticality. The problem-solving mode of the classical narrative, in which highly motivated characters work toward clear and realizable goals, instantiates an anti-carnivalesque, individualist, and competitive *weltanschauung*. Dominant cinema aesthetics relay time as a linear succession of events related through cause and effect, rather than conveying an associative time linked to rituals and festivals. In an ethos where "time is money," dominant cinema commercializes time in carefully measured sequences. And the blockbuster "entertainment" aesthetic, in this same perspective, can be seen as "productivist" in that every moment has to count, produce its specific quantum of affect and spectacle.

Another set of challenges to the dominant aesthetic tradition has come from the Third World. In the late 1960s and early 1970s, in the wake of the Vietnamese victory over the French in 1954, the Cuban revolution in 1959, and Algerian Independence in 1962, third-worldist film ideology was crystallized in a wave of militant film manifesto-essays – Glauber Rocha's "Aesthetic of Hunger" (1965), Fernando Solanas and Otavio Gettino's "Towards a Third Cinema" (1969) (chapter 17, this volume), and Julio García Espinosa's "For an Imperfect Cinema" (1969) – and in declarations and manifestos from third world film festivals calling for a tricontinental revolution in politics and an aesthetic and narrative revolution in film form. Rocha called for "sad, ugly films" expressive of an "aesthetics of hunger." Solanas–Gettino, meanwhile, forged a tripartite schema which distinguished between "first cinema" (Hollywood and its imitators), "second cinema" (the art film), and "third cinema," a revolutionary cinema composed primarily of militant guerrilla documentaries. The Cuban Espinosa, meanwhile, called for an "imperfect" cinema energized by the "low" forms of popular culture. Aesthetically, the notion of "Third Cinema" drew on currents as diverse as Soviet montage, Brechtian epic theater, Italian neo-realism and even the Griersonian "social documentary." The manifestos of the 1960s and 1970s valorized an alternative, independent, anti-imperialist cinema more concerned with provocation and militancy than with auteurist expression or consumer satisfaction. The manifestos contrasted the new cinema not only with Hollywood but also with their own countries' commercial traditions, now viewed as "bourgeois," "alienated," and "colonized."

Alternative cinemas have explored a wide spectrum of alternative aesthetics, crystallized in suggestive epithets and neologisms: Rocha's "aesthetic of hunger," Rogerio Sganzerla's "aesthetics of garbage," Claire Johnston's feminist "Counter Cinema," Paul Leduc's "salamander" (as opposed to dinosaur) aesthetic, Guilhermo del Toro's "termite terrorism," Teshome Gabriel's "nomadic aesthetics," Clyde Taylor's "Aesopian aesthetics," Kobena Mercer's "diaspora aesthetics," and Espinosa's *cine imperfecto*. These aesthetics bypass the formal conventions of dramatic realism in favor of such modes and strategies as the carnivalesque, the anthropophagic, the magical realist, the reflexive modernist and the resistant postmodernist. They are often rooted in non-realist, often non-Western or para-Western cultural traditions featuring other historical rhythms, other narrative structures, other views of the body, sexuality, spirituality, and the collective life. Many incorporate para-modern traditions into clearly modernizing or postmodernizing aesthetics, and thus problematize facile dichotomies such as traditional and modern, realist and modernist, modernist and postmodernist (see Shohat and Stam, 1994)

Contemporary video and computer technologies facilitate media jujitsu and the recycling of media detritus. Rather than the 1960s "aesthetic of hunger," videomakers can deploy a kind of cybernetic minimalism, achieving maximum beauty and effect for minimum expense. Video switchers allow the screen to be split, divided horizontally or vertically, with wipes and inserts. Keys, chroma-keys, matters and fader bars, along with computer graphics, multiply audio-visual possibilities for fracture, rupture, polyphony. An electronic "quilting" can weave together sounds and images in ways that break with linear character-centered narrative. All the conventional decorum of dominant cinema – eyeline matches, position matches, the 30° rule, cutaway shots – is superseded by proliferating polysemy. Spectator/participants have to decide what the images have in common, or how they conflict; they have to effect the syntheses latent in the audio-visual material.

The obvious fact that mainstream cinema has largely opted for a linear and homogenizing aesthetic where track reinforces track within a Wagnerian totality

16
Towards a Third Cinema

Fernando Solanas and Octavio Gettino

Just a short time ago it would have seemed like a Quixotic adventure in the colonialized, neocolonialized, or even the imperialist nations themselves to make any attempt to create *films of decolonization* that turned their back on or actively opposed the System. Until recently, film had been synonymous with show or amusement: in a word, it was one more *consumer good*. At best, films succeeded in bearing witness to the decay of bourgeois values and testifying to social injustice. As a rule, films only dealt with effect, never with cause; it was cinema of mystification or anti-historicism. It was *surplus value* cinema. Caught up in these conditions, films, the most valuable tool of communication of our times, were destined to satisfy only the ideological and economic interests of the *owners of the film industry*, the lords of the world film market, the great majority of whom were from the United States.

Was it possible to overcome this situation? How could the problem of turning out liberation films be approached when costs came to several thousand dollars and the distribution and exhibition channels were in the hands of the enemy? How could the continuity of work be guaranteed? How could the public be reached? How could System-imposed repression and censorship be vanquished? These questions, which could be multiplied in all directions, led and still lead many people to skepticism or rationalization: "revolutionary films cannot be made before the revolution"; "revolutionary films have been possible only in the liberated countries"; "without the support of revolutionary political power, revolutionary films or art is impossible." The mistake was due to taking the same approach to reality and films as did the bourgeoisie. The models of production, distribution, and exhibition continued to be *those of Hollywood* precisely because, in ideology and politics, films had not yet become the vehicle for a clearly drawn differentiation between bourgeois ideology and politics. A reformist policy, as manifested in dialogue with the adversary, in coexistence, and in the relegation of national contradictions to those between two supposedly unique blocs – the USSR and the USA – was and is unable to produce anything but a cinema within the System itself. At best, it can be the *"progressive" wing of Establishment cinema*. When all is said and done, such cinema was doomed to wait until the world conflict was resolved peacefully in favor of socialism in order to change qualitatively. The most daring attempts of those filmmakers who strove to conquer the fortress of official cinema ended, as Jean-Luc Godard eloquently put it, with the filmmakers themselves "trapped inside the fortress."

But the questions that were recently raised appeared promising; they arose from a new historical situation to which the filmmaker, as is often the case with the educated strata of our countries, was rather a late-comer: ten years of the Cuban Revolution, the Vietnamese struggle, and the development of a worldwide liberation movement whose moving force is to be found in the Third World countries. *The existence of masses on the worldwide revolutionary plane was the substantial fact without which those questions could not have been posed.* A new historical situation and a new man born in the process of the anti-imperialist struggle demanded a new, revolutionary attitude from the filmmakers of the world. The question of whether or not militant cinema *was possible* before the revolution began to be replaced, at least within small groups, by the question of *whether or not such a cinema was necessary to contribute to the possibility of revolution.* An affirmative answer was the starting point for the first attempts to channel the process of seeking possibilities in numerous countries. Examples are Newsreel, a US New Left film group, the *cinegiornali* of the Italian student movement, the films made by the *Etats Generaux du Cinéma Francais*, and those of the British and Japanese student movements, all a continuation and deepening of the work of a Joris Ivens or a Chris Marker. Let it suffice to observe the films of a Santiago Alvarez in Cuba, or the cinema being developed by different filmmakers in "the homeland of all," as Bolivar would say, as they seek a revolutionary Latin American cinema.

A profound debate on the role of intellectuals and artists before liberation today is enriching the perspectives of intellectual work all over the world. However, this debate oscillates between two poles: one which proposes to *relegate* all intellectual work capacity to a *specifically* political or political–military function, denying perspectives to all artistic activity with the idea that such activity must ineluctably be absorbed by the System, and the other which maintains an inner duality of the intellectual: on the one hand, the "work of art," "the privilege of beauty," an art and a beauty which are not necessarily bound to the needs of the revolutionary political process, and, on the other, a political commitment which generally consists in signing certain anti-imperialist manifestos. In practice, this point of view means the *separation of politics and art.*

This polarity rests, as we see it, on two omissions: first, the conception of culture, science, art, and cinema as univocal and universal terms, and, second, an insufficiently clear idea of the fact that the revolution does not begin with the taking of political power from imperialism and the bourgeoisie, but rather begins at the moment when the masses sense the need for change and their intellectual vanguards begin to study and carry out this change *through activities on different fronts.*

Culture, art, science and cinema always respond to conflicting class interests. In the neocolonial situation two concepts of culture, art, science, and cinema compete: *that of the rulers and that of the nation*. And this situation will continue, as long as the national concept is not identified with that of the rulers, as long as the status of colony or semi-colony continues in force. Moreover, the duality will be overcome and will reach a single and universal category only when the best values of man emerge from proscription to achieve hegemony, when the liberation of man is universal. In the meantime, there exist *our* culture and *their* culture, *our* cinema and *their* cinema. Because our culture is an impulse towards emancipation, it will remain in existence until emancipation is a reality: *a culture of subversion* which will carry with it an art, a science, and *a cinema of subversion*.

The lack of awareness in regard to these dualities generally leads the intellectual to deal with artistic and scientific expressions as they were universally conceived by the classes that rule the world, at best introducing some correction into these expressions. We have not gone deeply enough into developing a revolutionary theater, architecture, medicine, psychology, and cinema; into developing a culture *by and for us*. The intellectual takes each of these forms of expression as a unit to be corrected *from within the expression itself, and not from without, with its own new methods and models*.

An astronaut or a Ranger mobilizes all the scientific resources of imperialism. Psychologists, doctors, politicians, sociologists, mathematicians, and even artists are thrown into the study of everything that serves, *from the vantage point of different specialties*, the preparation of an orbital flight or the massacre of Vietnamese; in the long run, all of these specialties are equally employed to satisfy the needs of imperialism. In Buenos Aires the army eradicates *villas miseria* (urban shanty towns) and in their place puts up "strategic hamlets" with urbanized setups aimed at facilitating military intervention when the time comes. The revolutionary organizations lack specialized fronts in *the Establishment*'s medicine, engineering, psychology, and art – not to mention the development of *our own revolutionary* engineering, psychology, art, and cinema. In order to be effective, all these fields must recognize the *priorities* of each stage; those required by the struggle for power of those demanded by the already victorious revolution. Examples: creating a political sensitivity as awareness of the need to undertake a political–military struggle in order to take power, intensifying all the modern resources of medical science to prepare people with optimum levels of health and physical efficiency, ready for combat in rural or urban zones; or elaborating an architecture, a city planning, that will be able to withstand the massive air raids that imperialism can launch at any time. The specific strengthening of each specialty and field subordinate to collective priorities can fill the empty spaces caused by the struggle for liberation and can delineate with greatest efficacy the role of the intellectual in our time. It is evident that revolutionary mass-level culture and awareness can only be achieved after the taking of political power, but it is no less true that the use of scientific and artistic means, together with political–military means, prepares the terrain for the revolution to become reality and facilitates the solution of the problems that will arise with the taking of power.

The intellectual must find through his action the field in which he can rationally perform the most efficient work. Once the front has been determined, his next task is to find out *within that front* exactly what is the enemy's stronghold and where and how he must deploy his forces. It is in this harsh and dramatic daily search that a culture of the revolution will be able to emerge, the basis which will nurture, *beginning right now, the new man* exemplified by Che – not man in the abstract, not the "liberation of man", *but another man*, capable of arising from the ashes of the old, alienated man that we are and which the new man will destroy – by starting to stoke the fire *today*.

The anti-imperialist struggle of the peoples of the Third World and of their equivalents inside the imperialist countries constitutes today the axis of the world revolution. *Third cinema* is, in our opinion, the cinema that *recognizes in that struggle the most gigantic cultural, scientific, and artistic manifestation of our time*, the great possibility of constructing a liberated personality with each people as the starting point – in a word, the *decolonization of culture*.

The culture, including the cinema, of a neocolonialized country is just the expression of an overall dependence that generates models and values born from the needs of imperialist expansion.

> In order to impose itself, neocolonialism needs to convince the people of a dependent country of their own inferiority. Sooner or later, the inferior man recognizes Man with a capital M; this recognition means the destruction of his defenses. If you want to be a man, says the oppressor, you have to be like me, speak my language, deny your own being, transform yourself into me. As early as the 17th Century the Jesuit missionaries proclaimed the aptitude of the [South American] native for copying European works of art. Copyist, translator, interpreter, at best a spectator, the neocolonialized intellectual will always be encouraged to refuse to assume his creative possibilities. Inhibitions, uprootedness, escapism, cultural cosmopolitanism, artistic imitation, metaphysical exhaustion, betrayal of country – all find fertile soil in which to grow.[1]

> Culture becomes bilingual not due to the use of two languages but because of the conjuncture of two cultural patterns of thinking. One is national, that of the people, and the other is estranging, that of the classes subordinated to outside forces. The admiration that the upper classes expresses for the US or Europe is the highest expression of their subjection. With the colonialization of the upper classes the culture of imperialism indirectly introduces among the masses knowledge which cannot be supervised.[2]

Just as they are not masters of the land upon which they walk, the neocolonialized people are not masters of the ideas that envelop them. A knowledge of national reality presupposes going into the web of lies and confusion that arise from dependence. The intellectual is obliged to *refrain from spontaneous thought*; if he does think, he generally runs the risk of doing so in French or English – never in the language of a culture of his own which, like the process of national and social liberation, is still hazy and incipient. Every piece of data, every concept that floats around us, is part of a framework of mirages that it is difficult to take apart.

The native bourgeoisie of the port cities such as Buenos Aires, and their respective intellectual elites, constituted, from the very origins of our history, the transmission belt of neocolonial penetration. Behind such watchwords as "Civilization or barbarism!" manufactured in Argentina by Europeanizing liberalism, was the attempt to impose a civilization fully in keeping with the needs of imperialist expansion and the desire to destroy the resistance of the national masses, which were successively called the "rabble," a "bunch of blacks," and "zoological detritus" in our country and "the unwashed hordes" in Bolivia. In this way the ideologists of the semicountries, past masters in "the play of big words, with an implacable, detailed, and rustic universalism,"[3] served as spokesmen of those followers of Disraeli who intelligently proclaimed: "I prefer the rights of the English to the rights of man."

The middle sectors were and are the best recipients of cultural neocolonialism. Their ambivalent class condition, their buffer position between social polarities, and their broader possibilities of access to *civilization* offer imperialism a base of social support which has attained considerable importance in some Latin American countries.

> It serves to institutionalize and give a normal appearance to dependence. The main objective of this cultural deformation is to keep the people from realizing their neocolonialized position and aspiring to change it. In this way pedagogical colonialization is an effective substitute for the colonial police.[4]

Mass communications tend to complete the destruction of a national awareness and of a collective subjectivity on the way to enlightenment, a destruction which begins as soon as the child has access to these media, the education and culture of the ruling classes. In Argentina 26 television channels; one million television sets; more than 50 radio stations; hundreds of newspapers, periodicals, and magazines; and thousands of records, film, etc., join their acculturating role of the colonialization of taste and consciousness to the process of neocolonial education which begins in the university. "Mass communications are more effective for neocolonialism than napalm. What is real, true, and rational is to be found on the margin of the Law, just as are the people. Violence, crime, and destruction come to be Peace, Order, and Normality."[5] *Truth, then, amounts to subversion.* Any form of expression or communication that tries to show national reality is *subversion.*

Cultural penetration, pedagogical colonialization, and mass communications all join forces today in a desperate attempt to absorb, neutralize, or eliminate any expression that responds to an attempt at decolonization. Neocolonialism makes a serious attempt to castrate, to digest, the cultural forms that arise beyond the bounds of its own aims. Attempts are made to remove from them precisely what makes them effective and dangerous, their *politicization*. Or, to put it another way, to separate the cultural manifestation from the fight for national independence.

Ideas such as "Beauty in itself is revolutionary" and "All new cinema is revolutionary" are idealistic aspirations that do not touch the neocolonial condition, since they continue to conceive of cinema, art, and beauty as universal abstractions and not as an integral part of the national processes of decolonization.

Any dispute, no matter how virulent, which does not serve to mobilize, agitate, and politicize sectors of the people to arm them rationally and perceptibly, in one way or another, for the struggle – is received with indifference or even with pleasure. Virulence, nonconformism, plain rebelliousness, and discontent are just so many more products on the capitalist market; they are *consumer goods*. This is especially true in a situation where the bourgeoisie is in need of a daily dose of shock and exciting elements of controlled violence[6] – that is, violence which absorption by the System turns into pure stridency. Examples are the works of a socialist-tinged painting and sculpture which are greedily sought after by the new bourgeoisie to decorate their apartments and mansions; plays full of anger and avant-gardism which are noisily applauded by the ruling classes; the literature of progressive writers concerned with semantics and man on the margin of time and space, which gives an air of democratic broadmindedness to the System's publishing houses and magazines; and the cinema of "challenge," of "argument," promoted by the distribution monopolies and launched by the big commercial outlets.

> In reality the area of "permitted protest" of the System is much greater than the System is willing to admit. This gives the artists the illusion that they are acting "against the system" by going beyond certain narrow limits; they do not realize that even anti-System art can be absorbed and utilized by the System, as both a brake and a necessary self-correction.[7]

Lacking an awareness of how to *utilize what is ours for our true liberation* – in a word, lacking *politicization* – all of these "progressive" alternatives come to form the Leftish wing of the System, the improvement of its cultural products. They will be doomed to carry out the best work on the Left that the Right is able to accept today and will thus only serve the survival of the latter. "Restore words, dramatic actions, and images to the places where they can carry out a revolutionary role, where they will be useful, where they will become *weapons in the struggle*."[8] Insert the work as an original fact in the process of liberation, place it first at the service of life itself, ahead of art; *dissolve aesthetics in the life of society*: only in this way, as Fanon said, can decolonization become possible and culture, cinema, and beauty – at least, what is of greatest importance to us – become *our culture, our films, and our sense of beauty*.

The historical perspectives of Latin America and of the majority of the countries under imperialist domination are headed not towards a lessening of repression but towards an increase. We are heading not for bourgeois–democratic regimes but for dictatorial forms of government. The struggles for democratic freedoms, instead of seizing concessions from the System, move it to cut down on them, given its narrow margin for maneuvering.

The bourgeois–democratic facade caved in some time ago. The cycle opened during the last century in Latin America with the first attempts at self-affirmation of a national bourgeoisie differentiated from the metropolis (examples are Rosas' federalism in Argentina, the Lopez and Francia regimes in Paraguay, and those of Bengido and Balmaceda in Chile) with a tradition that has continued well into our century: national–bourgeois, national–popular, and democratic–bourgeois attempts were made by Cardenas, Yrigoyen, Haya de la Torre, Vargas, Aguirre Cerda, Peron, and Arbenz. But as far as revolutionary prospects are concerned, the cycle has definitely been completed. The lines allowing for the deepening of the historical attempt of each of those experiences today pass through the sectors that understand the continent's situation as one of war and that are preparing, under the force of circumstances, to make that region the Vietnam of the coming decade. A war in which national liberation can only succeed when it is sumultaneously postulated as social liberation – socialism as the only valid perspective of any national liberation process.

> At this time in Latin America there is room for neither passivity nor innocence. The intellectual's commitment is measured in terms of risks as well as words and ideas; what he does to further the cause of liberation is what counts. The worker who goes on strike and thus risks losing his job or even his life, the student who jeopardizes his career, the militant who keeps silent under torture: each by his or her action commits us to something much more important than a vague gesture of solidarity.[9]

In a situation in which the "state of law" is replaced by the "state of facts," the intellectual, who is *one more worker*, functioning on a cultural front, must become increasingly radicalized to avoid denial of self and to carry out what is expected of him in our times. The impotence of all reformist concepts has already been exposed sufficiently, not only in politics but also in culture and films – and especially in the latter, *whose history is that of imperialist domination – mainly Yankee.*

While, during the early history (or the prehistory) of the cinema, it was possible to speak of a German, an Italian, or a Swedish cinema clearly differentiated and corresponding to specific national characteristics, today such differences have disappeared. The borders were wiped out along with the expansion of US imperialism and the film model that it imposed: *Hollywood movies.* In our times it is hard to find a film within the field of commercial cinema, including what is known as "author's cinema," in both the capitalist and socialist countries, that manages to avoid the models of Hollywood pictures. The latter have such a fast hold that monumental works such as the USSR's Bondarchuk's *War and Peace* are also monumental examples of the submission to all the propositions imposed by the US movie industry (structure, language, etc.) and, consequently, to its concepts.

The placing of the cinema within US models, even in the formal aspect, in language, leads to the adoption of the ideological forms that *gave rise to precisely that language and no other*. Even the appropriation of models which appear to be only technical, industrial, scientific, etc., leads to a conceptual dependency situation, due to the fact that the cinema is an industry, but differs from other industries in that it has been created and organized in order *to generate certain ideologies*. The 35mm camera, 24 frames per second, arc lights, and a commercial place of exhibition for audiences were conceived not to gratuitously transmit any ideology, but to satisfy, in the first place, the cultural and surplus value needs *of a specific ideology, of a specific world-view: that of US financial capital*.

The mechanistic takeover of a cinema conceived as a show to be exhibited in large theaters with a standard duration, hermetic structures that are born and die on the screen, satisfies, to be sure, the *commercial interests* of the production groups, but it also leads to the *absorption of forms of the bourgeois world-view* which are the continuation of nineteenth-century art, of bourgeois art: man is accepted only as a passive and consuming object; *rather than having his ability to make history recognized, he is only permitted to read history, contemplate it, listen to it, and undergo it*. The cinema as a spectacle aimed at a digesting object is the highest point that can be reached by bourgeois filmmaking. The world, experience, and the historic process are enclosed within the frame of a painting, the same stage of a theater, and the movie screen; man is viewed as a *consumer of ideology*, and not as the creator of ideology. This notion is the starting point for the wonderful interplay of bourgeois philosophy and the obtaining of surplus value. The result is a cinema studied by motivational analysts, sociologists and psychologists, by the endless researchers of the dreams and frustrations of the masses, all aimed at selling *movie-life*, reality as it is conceived by the ruling classes.

The first alternative to this type of cinema, which we could call the *first cinema*, arose with the so-called "author's cinema," "expression cinema," "*nouvelle vague*," "*cinema novo*," or, conventionally, the *second cinema*. This alternative signified a step forward inasmuch as it demanded that the filmmaker be free to express himself in non-standard language and inasmuch as it was an attempt at cultural decolonization. But such attempts have already reached, or are about to reach, the outer limits of what the system permits. The *second cinema filmmaker* has remained "trapped inside the fortress" as Godard put it, or is on his way to becoming trapped. The search for a market of 200,000 moviegoers in Argentina, a figure that is supposed to cover the costs of an independent local production, the proposal of developing a mechanism of industrial production parallel to that of the System but which would be distributed by the System according to its own norms, the struggle to better the laws protecting the cinema and replacing "bad officials" by "less bad," etc., is a search lacking in viable prospects, unless you consider viable the prospect of becoming institutionalized as "the youthful, angry wing of society" – that is, of neocolonialized or capitalist society.

Real alternatives differing from those offered by the System are only possible if one of two requirements is fulfilled: *making films that the System cannot assimilate and which are foreign to its needs, or making films that directly and explicitly set out to fight the System.* Neither of these requirements fits within the alternatives that are still offered by the *second cinema*, but they can be found in the revolutionary opening towards a cinema outside and against the System, in a cinema of liberation: the *third cinema*.

One of the most effective jobs done by neocolonialism is its cutting off of intellectual sectors, especially artists, from national reality by lining them up behind "universal art and models." It has been very common for intellectuals and artists to be found at the tail end of popular struggle, when they have not actually taken up positions against it. The social layers which have made the greatest contribution to the building of a national culture (understood as an impulse towards decolonization) have not been precisely the enlightened elites but rather the most exploited and uncivilized sectors. Popular organizations have very rightly distrusted the "intellectual" and the "artist." When they have not been openly used by the bourgeoise or imperialism, they have certainly been their indirect tools; most of them did not go beyond spouting a policy in favor of "peace and democracy," fearful of anything that had a national ring to it, afraid of contaminating art with politics and the artists with the revolutionary militant. They thus tended to obscure the inner causes determining neocolonialized society and placed in the foreground the outer causes, which, while "they are the condition for change, they can never be the basis for change";[10] in Argentina they replace the struggle against imperialism and the native oligarchy with the struggle of democracy against fascism, suppressing the fundamental contradiction of a neocolonialized country and replacing it with "a contradiction that was a copy of the worldwide contradiction."[11]

This cutting off of the intellectual and artistic sectors from the processes of national liberation – which, among other things, helps us to understand the limitations in which these processes have been unfolding – today tends to disappear in the extent that artists and intellectuals are beginning to discover the impossibility of destroying the enemy without first joining in a battle for their common interests. The artist is beginning to feel the insufficiency of his non-conformism and individual rebellion. And the revolutionary organizations, in turn, are discovering the vacuums that the struggle for power creates in the cultural sphere. The problems of filmmaking, the ideological limitations of a filmmaker in a neocolonialized country, etc., have thus far constituted objective factors in the lack of attention paid to the cinema by the people's organizations. Newspapers and other printed matter, posters and wall propaganda, speeches and other verbal forms of information, enlightenment, and politicization are still the main means of communication between the organizations and the vanguard layers of the masses. But the new political positions of some filmmakers and the subsequent appearance of films useful for liberation have permitted certain political vanguards to discover the importance of movies. This importance is to be found in the specific meaning of films as a form of communication and because of *their particular characteristics*, characteristics that allow them to draw audiences of different origins, many of them people who might not respond favorably to the announcement of a political speech. Films offer an effective pretext for gathering an audience, in addition to the ideological message they contain.

The capacity for synthesis and the penetration of the film image, the possibilities offered by the living document and naked reality, and the power of enlightenment of audio-visual means make the film far more effective than any other tool of communication. It is hardly necessary to point out that those films which achieve an intelligent use of the possibilities of the image, adequate dosage of concepts, language and structure that flow naturally from each theme, and counterpoints of audio-visual narration achieve effective results in the politicization and mobilization of cadres and even in work with the masses, where this is possible.

The students who raised barricades on the *Avenida 18 de Julio* in Montevideo after the showing of *Me Gustan Los Estudiantes* (*I Like Students*) (Mario Handler), those who demonstrated and sang the "Internationale" in Merida and Caracas after the showing of *La Hora De Los Hornos* (*The Hour Of The Furnaces*), the growing demand for films such as those made by Santiago Alvarez and the Cuban documentary film movement, and the debates and meetings that take place after the underground or semi-public showings of *third cinema* films are the beginning of a twisting and difficult road being traveled in the consumer societies by the mass organizations (*Cinegiornali liberi* in Italy, *Zengakuren* documentaries in Japan, etc.). For the first time in Latin America, organizations are ready and willing to employ films for political–cultural ends: the Chilean *Partido Socialista* provides its cadres with revolutionary film material, while Argentine revolutionary Peronist and non-Peronist groups are taking an interest in doing likewise. Moreover, OSPAAAL (Organization of Solidarity of the Peoples of Africa, Asia and Latin America) is participating in the production and distribution of films that contribute to the anti-imperialist struggle. The revolutionary organizations are discovering the need for cadres who, among other things, know how to handle a film camera, tape recorders, and projectors in the most effective way possible. The struggle to seize power from the enemy is the meeting ground of the political and artistic vanguards engaged in a common task which is *enriching to both*.

Some of the circumstances that delayed the use of films as a revolutionary tool until a short time ago were lack of equipment, technical difficulties, the compulsory specialization of each phase of work, and high costs. The advances that have taken place within each specialization; the simplification of movie cameras and tape recorders; improvements in the medium itself, such as rapid film that can be printed in a normal light; automatic light meters; improved audio-visual synchronization; and the spread of know-how by means of specialized magazines with large circulations and even through non-specialized media, have helped to demystify filmmaking and divest it of that almost magic aura that made it seem that films were only within the reach of "artists," "geniuses," and "the privileged." Filmmaking is increasingly within the reach of larger social layers. Chris Marker experimented in France with groups of workers whom he provided with 8mm equipment and some basic instruction in its handling. The goal was to have the worker film *his way of looking at the world, just as if he were writing it*. This has opened up unheard-of-prospects for the cinema; above all, *a new conception of filmmaking and the significance of art in our times*.

Imperialism and capitalism, whether in the consumer society or in the neocolonialized country, veil everything behind a screen of images and appearances. *The image of reality* is more important than reality itself. It is a world peopled with fantasies and phantoms in which what is hideous is clothed in beauty, while beauty is disguised as the hideous. On the one hand, fantasy, the imaginary bourgeois universe replete with comfort, equilibrium, sweet reason, order, efficiency, and the possibility to "be someone." And, on the other, the phantoms, we the lazy, we the indolent and underdeveloped, we who cause disorder. When a neocolonialized person accepts his situation, he becomes a Gungha Din, a traitor at the service of the colonialist, an Uncle Tom, a class and racial renegade, or a fool, the easy-going servant and bumpkin; but, when he refuses to accept his situation of oppression, then he turns into a resentful savage, a cannibal. Those who *lose sleep from fear of the hungry*, those who comprise the System, see the revolutionary as a bandit, robber, and rapist; the first battle waged against them is thus not on a political plane, but rather in the police context of law, arrests, etc. The more exploited a man is, the more he is placed on a plane of insignificance. The more he resists, the more he is viewed as a beast. This can be seen in AFRICA ADDIO, made by the fascist Jacopetti: the African savages, killer animals, wallow in abject anarchy once they escape from white protection. Tarzan died, and in his place were born Lumumbas and Lobegulas, Nkomos, and the Madzimbamutos, and this is something that neocolonialism cannot forgive. Fantasy has been replaced by phantoms and man is turned into an extra who dies so Jacopetti can comfortably film his execution.

I make the revolution; therefore, I exist. This is the starting point for the disappearance of fantasy and phantom to make way for living human beings. The cinema of the revolution is at the same time one of *destruction and construction*: destruction of the image that neocolonialism has created of itself and of us, and construction of a throbbing, living reality which recaptures truth in any of its expressions.

The restitution of things to their real place and meaning is an eminently subversive fact both in the neocolonial situation and in the consumer societies. In the former, the seeming ambiguity or pseudo-objectivity in newspapers, literature, etc., and the relative freedom of the people's organizations to provide their own information cease to exist, giving way to overt restriction, when it is a question of television and radio, the two most important System-controlled or monopolized communications media. Last year's May events in France are quite explicit on this point.

In a world where the unreal rules, artistic expression is shoved along the channels of fantasy, fiction, language in code, sign language, and messages whispered between the lines. Art is cut off from the concrete facts – which, from the neocolonialist standpoint, are accusatory testimonies – to turn back on itself, strutting about in a world of abstractions and phantoms, where it becomes "time-less" and history-less. Vietnam can be mentioned, but only far from Vietnam; Latin America can be mentioned, but only far enough away from the continent to be ineffective, *in places where it is depoliticized* and where it does not lead to action.

The cinema known as documentary, with all the vastness that the concept has today, from educational films to the reconstruction of a fact or a historical event, is perhaps the main basis of revolutionary filmmaking. Every image that documents, bears witness to, refutes or deepens the truth of a situation is something more than a film image or purely artistic fact; it becomes something which the System finds indigestible.

Testimony about a national reality is also an inestimable means of dialogue and knowledge on the world plane. No internationalist form of struggle can be carried out successfully if there is not a mutual exchange of experiences among the people, if the people do not succeed in breaking out of the Balkanization on the international, continental, and national planes which imperialism is striving to maintain.

There is no knowledge of a reality as long as that reality is not acted upon, *as long as its transformation is not begun on all fronts of struggle.* The well-known quote from Marx deserves constant repetition: *it is not sufficient to interpret the world; it is now a question of transforming it.*

With such an attitude as his starting point, it remains to the filmmaker to discover his own language, a language which will arise from a militant and transforming world-view and from the theme being dealt with. Here it may well be pointed out that certain political cadres still maintain old dogmatic positions, which ask the artist or filmmaker to provide an apologetic view of reality, *one which is more in line with wishful thinking than with what actually is.* Such positions, which at bottom mask a lack of confidence in the possibilities of reality itself, have in certain cases led to the use of film language as a mere idealized illustration of a fact, to the desire to remove reality's deep contradictions, its dialectic richness, which is precisely the kind of depth which can give a film beauty and effectiveness. The reality of the revolutionary processes all over the world, in spite of their confused and negative aspects, possesses a dominant line, a synthesis which is so rich and stimulating that it does not need to be schematized with partial or sectarian views.

Pamphlet films, didactic films, report films, essay films, witness-bearing films – any militant form of expression is valid, and it would be absurd to lay down a set of aesthetic work norms. *Be receptive to all that the people have to offer, and offer them the best*; or, as Che put it, *respect the people by giving them quality*. This is a good thing to keep in mind in view of those tendencies which are always latent in the revolutionary artist to lower the level of investigation and the language of a theme, in a kind of *neopopulism*, down to levels which, while they may be those upon which the masses move, do not help them to get rid of the stumbling blocks left by imperialism. The effectiveness of the best films of militant cinema show that social layers considered backward are able to capture the exact meaning of an association of images, an effect of staging, and any linguistic experimentation placed within the context of a given idea. Furthermore, revolutionary cinema is not fundamentally one which illustrates, documents, or passively establishes a situation: *rather, it attempts to intervene in the situation as an element providing thrust or rectification*. To put it another way, it provides *discovery through transformation*.

The differences that exist between one and another liberation process make it impossible to lay down supposedly universal norms. A cinema which in the consumer society does not attain the level of the reality in which it moves can play a stimulating role in an underdeveloped country, just as a revolutionary cinema in the neocolonial situation will not necessarily be revolutionary if it is mechanically taken to the metropolic country.

Teaching the handling of guns can be revolutionary where there are potentially or explicitly viable layers ready to throw themselves into the struggle to take power, but ceases to be revolutionary where the masses still lack sufficient awareness of their situation or where they already have learned to handle guns. Thus, a cinema which insists upon the denunciation of the *effects* of neocolonial policy is caught up in a reformist game if the consciousness of the masses has already assimilated such knowledge; then the revolutionary thing is to examine the *causes*, to investigate the ways of organizing and arming for the change. That is, imperialism can sponsor films that fight illiteracy, and such pictures will only be inscribed within the contemporary need of imperialist policy, but, in contrast, the making of such films in Cuba after the triumph of the Revolution was clearly revolutionary. Although their starting point was just the fact of teaching reading and writing, they had a goal which was radically different from that of imperialism: the training of people for liberation, not for subjection.

The model of the perfect work of art, the fully rounded film structured according to the metrics imposed by bourgeois culture, its theoreticians and critics, has served to inhibit the filmmaker in the dependent countries, especially when he has attempted to erect similar models in a reality which *offered him neither the culture, the techniques, nor the most primary elements for success*. The culture of the metropolis kept the age-old secrets that had given life to its models; the transposition of the latter to the neocolonial reality was always a mechanism of alienation, *since it was not possible for the artist of the dependent country to absorb, in a few years, the secrets of a culture and society elaborated through the centuries in completely different historical circumstances*. The attempt in the sphere of filmmaking to match the pictures of the ruling countries generally ends in failure, given the existence of two disparate historical realities. And such unsuccessful attempts lead to feelings of frustration and inferiority. Both these feelings arise in the first place from the fear of taking risks along completely new roads *which are almost a total denial of "their cinema."* A fear of recognizing the particularities and limitations of a dependency situation in order to discover the *possibilities inherent in that situation* by finding ways of overcoming it *which would of necessity be original.*

The existence of a revolutionary cinema is inconceivable without the constant and methodical exercise of practice, search, and experimentation. It even means committing the new filmmaker to take chances on the unknown, to leap into space at times, exposing himself to failure as does the guerrilla who travels along paths that he himself opens up with machete blows. The possibility of discovering and inventing film forms and structures that serve a more profound vision of our reality resides in the ability to place oneself on the outside limits of the familiar, to make one's way amid constant dangers.

Our time is one of hypothesis rather than of thesis, a time of works in process – unfinished, unordered, violent works made with the camera in one hand and a rock in the other. Such works cannot be assessed according to the traditional theoretical and critical canons. The ideas for *our* film theory and criticism will come to life through inhibition-removing practice and experimentation. "Knowledge begins with practice. After acquiring theoretical knowledge through practice, it is necessary to return to practice."[12] Once he has embarked upon this practice, the revolutionary filmmaker will have to overcome countless obstacles; he will experience the loneliness of those who aspire to the praise of the System's promotion media only to find that those media are closed to him. As Godard would say, he will cease to be a bicycle champion to become an anonymous bicycle rider, Vietnamese style, submerged in a cruel and prolonged war. But he will also discover that there is a receptive audience that looks upon his work as something of its own existence, and that is ready to defend him in a way that it would never do with any world bicycle champion.

Implementation

In this long war, with the camera as our rifle, we do in fact move into a guerrilla activity. This is why the work of a *film-guerrilla* group is governed by strict disciplinary norms as to both work methods and security. A revolutionary film group is in the same situation as a guerrilla unit: it cannot grow strong without military structures and command concepts. The group exists as a network of complementary responsibilities, as the sum and synthesis of abilities, inasmuch as it operates harmonically with a leadership that centralizes planning work and maintains its continuity. Experience shows that it is not easy to maintain the cohesion of a group when it is bombarded by the System and its chain of accomplices frequently disguised as "progressives," when there are no immediate and spectacular outer incentives and the members must undergo the discomforts and tensions of work that is done underground and distributed clandestinely. Many abandon their responsibilities because they underestimate them or because they measure them with values appropriate to System cinema and not underground cinema. The birth of internal conflicts is a reality present in any group, whether or not it possesses ideological maturity. The lack of awareness of such an inner conflict on the psychological or personality plane, etc., the lack of maturity in dealing with problems of relationships, at times leads to ill feeling and rivalries that in turn cause real clashes going beyond ideological or objective differences. All of this means that a basic condition is an awareness of the problems of interpersonal relationships, leadership, and areas of competence. What is needed is to speak clearly, mark off work areas, assign responsibilities, and take on the job as a rigorous militancy.

Guerrilla filmmaking proletarianizes the film worker and breaks down the intellectual aristocracy that the bourgeoisie grants to its followers. In a word, it *democratizes*. The filmmaker's tie with reality makes him more a part of his people. Vanguard layers and even masses participate collectively in the work when they realize that it is the continuity of their daily struggle. *La Hora De Los Hornos* shows how a film can be made in hostile circumstances when it has the support and collaboration of militants and cadres from the people.

The revolutionary filmmaker acts with a radically new vision of the role of the producer, teamwork, tools, details, etc. Above all, he supplies himself at all levels in order to produce his films, he equips himself at all levels, he learns how to handle the manifold techniques of his craft. His most valuable possessions are the tools of his trade, which form part and parcel of his need to communicate. The camera is the inexhaustible *expropriator of image-weapons*; the projector, *a gun that can shoot 24 frames per second.*

Each member of the group should be familiar, at least in a general way, with the equipment being used: he must be prepared to replace another in any of the phases of production. The myth of irreplaceable technicians must be exploded.

The whole group must grant great importance to the minor details of the production and the security measures needed to protect it. A lack of foresight which in conventional filmmaking would go unnoticed can render virtually useless weeks or months of work. And a failure in guerrilla cinema, just as in the guerrilla struggle itself, can mean the loss of a work or a complete change of plans. "In a guerrilla struggle the concept of failure is present a thousand times over, and victory a myth that only a revolutionary can dream."[13] Every member of the group must have an ability to take care of details; discipline; speed; and, above all, the willingness to overcome the weaknesses of comfort, old habits, and the whole climate of pseudo-normality behind which the warfare of everyday life is hidden. Each film is a different operation, a different job requiring variations in methods in order to confuse or refrain from alerting the enemy, especially as the processing laboratories are still in his hands.

The success of the work depends to a great extent on the group's ability to remain silent, on its permanent wariness, a condition that is difficult to achieve in a situation in which apparently nothing is happening and the filmmaker has been accustomed to telling all and sundry about everything that he's doing because the bourgeoisie has trained him precisely on such a basis of prestige and promotion. The watchword "constant vigilance, constant wariness, constant mobility" has profound validity for guerrilla cinema. You have to give the appearance of working on various projects, split up the materials, put it together, take it apart, confuse, neutralize, and throw off the track. All of this is necessary as long as the group doesn't have its own processing equipment, no matter how rudimentary, and there remain certain possibilities in the traditional laboratories.

Group-level cooperation between different countries can serve to assure the completion of a film or the execution of certain phases of work that may not be possible in the country of origin. To this should be added the need for a reception center for file materials to be used by the different groups and the perspective of coordination, on a continent-wide or even worldwide scale, of the continuity of work in each country: periodic regional or international gatherings to exchange experiences, contributions, joint planning of work, etc.

At least in the earliest stages, the revolutionary filmmaker and the work groups will be the sole producers of their films. They must bear the responsibility of finding ways to facilitate the continuity of work. Guerrilla cinema still doesn't have enough experience to set down standards in this area; what experience there is has shown, above all, the *ability to make use of the concrete situation of each country*. But, regardless of what these situations may be, the preparation of a film cannot be undertaken without a parallel study of its future audience and, consequently, a plan to recover the financial investment. Here, once again, the need arises of closer ties between political and artistic vanguards, since this also serves for the joint study of forms of production, exhibition, and continuity.

A guerrilla film can be aimed only at the distribution mechanisms provided by the revolutionary organizations, including those invented or discovered by the filmmaker himself. Production, distribution, and economic possibilities for survival must form part of a single strategy. The solution of the problems faced in each of these areas will encourage other people to join in the work of guerrilla filmmaking, which will enlarge its ranks and thus make it less vulnerable.

The distribution of guerrilla films in Latin America is still in swaddling clothes, while System reprisals are already a legalized fact. Suffice it to note in Argentina the raids that have occurred during some showings and the recent film suppression law of a clearly fascist character, in Brazil the ever-increasing restrictions placed upon the most militant comrades of *Cinema Novo*, and in Venezuela the banning and license cancellation of *La Hora De Los Hornos*; almost all over the continent censorship prevents any possibility of public distribution.

Without revolutionary films and a public that asks for them, any attempt to open up new ways of distribution would be doomed to failure. But both of these already exist in Latin America. The appearance of the films opened up a road which in some countries, such as Argentina, occurs through showings in apartments and houses to audiences of never more than 25 people; in other countries, such as Chile, films are shown in parishes, universities, or cultural centers (of which there are fewer every day); and, in the case of Uruguay, showings were given in Montevideo's biggest movie theater to an audience of 2,500 people, who filled the theater and made every showing an impassioned anti-imperialist event.[14] But the prospects on the continental plane indicate that the possibility for the continuity of a revolutionary cinema rests upon the *strengthening of rigorously underground base structures.*

Practice implies mistakes and failures.[15] Some comrades will let themselves be carried away by the success and impunity with which they present the first showings and will tend to relax security measures, while others will go in the opposite direction of excessive precautions or fearfulness, to such an extent that distribution remains circumscribed, limited to a few groups of friends. Only concrete experience in each country will demonstrate which are the best methods there, which do not always lend themselves to application in other situations.

In some places it will be possible to build infrastructures connected to political, student, worker, and other organizations, while in others it will be more suitable to sell prints to organizations which will take charge of obtaining the funds necessary to pay for each print (the cost of the print plus a small margin). This method, wherever possible, would appear to be the most viable, because it permits the decentralization of distribution; makes possible a more profound political use of the film; and permits the recovery, through the sale of more prints, of the funds invested in the production. It is true that in many countries the organizations still are not fully aware of the importance of this work or, if they are, may lack the means to undertake it. In such cases other methods can be used: the delivery of prints to encourage distribution and a box-office cut to the organizers of each showing, etc. The ideal goal to be achieved would be producing and distributing guerrilla films with funds obtained from expropriations of the bourgeoisie – that is, *the bourgeoisie would be financing guerrilla cinema with a bit of the surplus value that it gets from the people.* But, as long as the goal is no more than a middle- or long-range aspiration, the alternatives open to revolutionary cinema to recover production and distribution costs are to some extent similar to those obtained for conventional cinema: every spectator should pay the same amount as he pays to see System cinema. Financing, subsidizing, equipping, and supporting revolutionary cinema are political responsibilities for revolutionary organizations and militants. A film can be made, but if its distribution does not allow for the recovery of the costs, it will be difficult or impossible to make a second film.

The 16mm film circuits in Europe (20,000 exhibition centers in Sweden, 30,000 in France, etc.) are not the best example for the neocolonialized countries, but they are nevertheless a complement to be kept in mind for fundraising, especially in a situation in which such circuits can play an important role in publicizing the struggles in the Third World, increasingly related as they are to those unfolding in the metropolis countries. A film on the Venezuelan guerrillas will say more to a European public than 20 explanatory pamphlets, and the same is true for us with a film on the May events in France or the Berkeley, USA, student struggle.

A *Guerrilla Films International?* And why not? Isn't it true that a kind of new International is arising through the Third World struggles; through OSPAAAL and the revolutionary vanguards of the consumer societies?

A guerrilla cinema, at this stage still within the reach of limited layers of the population, is, nevertheless, *the only cinema of the masses possible today*, since it is the only one involved with the interests, aspirations, and prospects of the vast majority of the people. Every important film produced by a revolutionary cinema will be, explicit or not, *a national event of the masses*.

This *cinema of the masses*, which is prevented from reaching beyond the sectors representing the masses, provokes with each showing, as in a revolutionary military incursion, a liberated space, *a decolonized territory*. The showing can be turned into a kind of political event, which, according to Fanon, could be "a liturgical act, a privileged occasion for human beings to hear and be heard."

Militant cinema must be able to extract the infinity of new possibilities that open up for it from the conditions of proscription imposed by the System. The attempt to overcome neocolonial oppression calls for the invention of forms of communication; *it opens up the possibility.*

Before and during the making of *La Hora De Los Hornos* we tried out various methods for the distribution of revolutionary cinema – the little that we had made up to then. Each showing for militants, middle-level cadres, activists, workers, and university students became – without our having set ourselves this aim beforehand – a kind of enlarged cell meeting of which the films were a part but not the most important factor. We thus discovered a new facet of cinema: the *participation* of people who, until then, were considered *spectators*. At times, security reasons obliged us to try to dissolve the group of participants as soon as the showing was over, and we realized that the distribution of that kind of film had little meaning if it was not complemented by the participation of the comrades, if a debate was not opened on the themes suggested by the films.

We also discovered that every comrade who attended such showings did so with full awareness that he was infringing the System's laws and exposing his personal security to eventual repression. This person was no longer a spectator; on the contrary, from the moment he decided to attend the showing, *from the moment he lined himself up on this side* by taking risks and contributing his living experience to the meeting, he became an actor, a more important protagonist than those who appeared in the films. Such a person was seeking other committed people like himself, while he, in turn, became committed to them. *The spectator made way for the actor, who sought himself in others.*

Outside this space which the films momentarily helped to liberate, there was nothing but solitude, non-communication, distrust, and fear; within the freed space the situation turned everyone into accomplices of the act that was unfolding.

The debates arose spontaneously. As we gained in experience, we incorporated into the showing various elements (a stage production) to reinforce the themes of the films, the climate of the showing, the "disinhibiting" of the participants, and the dialogue: recorded music or poems, sculpture and paintings, posters, a program director who chaired the debate and presented the film and the comrades who were speaking, a glass of wine, a few *mates*, etc. We realized that we had at hand three very valuable factors:

1 *the participant comrade*, the man–actor–accomplice who responded to the summons;
2 *the free space* where that man expressed his concerns and ideas, became politicized, and started to free himself; and
3 *the film*, important only as a detonator or pretext.

We concluded from these data that a film could be much more effective if it were fully aware of these factors and took on the task of subordinating its own form, structure, language, and propositions to that act and to those actors – to put it another way, *if it sought its own liberation in the subordination and insertion in the others, the principal protagonists of life*. With the correct utilization of the *time* that that group of actor–personages offered us with their diverse histories, the use of the *space* offered by certain comrades, and of the *films* themselves, *it was necessary to try to transform time, energy, and work into freedom-giving energy*. In this way the idea began to grow of structuring what we decided to call the *film act*, the *film action*, one of the forms which we believe assumes great importance in affirming the line of a *third cinema*. A cinema whose first experiment is to be found, perhaps on a rather shaky level, in the second and third parts of *La Hora De Los Hornos* (*"Acto para la liberacion"*; above all, starting with *"La resistencia"* and *"Violencia y liberacion"*).

Comrades [we said at the start of *"Acto para la liberacion"*], this is not just a film showing, nor is it a show; rather, it is, above all, A MEETING – an act of anti-imperialist unity; this is a place only for those who feel identified with this struggle, because here there is no room for spectators or for accomplices of the enemy; here there is room only for the authors and protagonists of the process to which the film attempts to bear witness and to deepen. The film is the pretext for dialogue, for the seeking and finding of wills. It is a report that we place before you for your consideration, to be debated after the showing.

The conclusions [we said at another point in the second part] to which you may arrive as the real authors and protagonists of this history are important. The experiences and conclusions that we have assembled have a relative worth; they are of use to the extent that they are useful to you, who are the present and future of liberation. But most important of all is the action that may arise from these conclusions, the unity on the basis of the facts. This is why the film stops here; it opens out to you so that you can continue it.

The film act means an open-ended film; it is essentially a way of learning.

> The first step in the process of knowledge is the first contact with the things of the outside world, the stage of sensations [*in a film, the living fresco of image and sound*]. The second step is the synthesizing of the data provided by the sensations; their ordering and elaboration; the stage of concepts, judgments, opinions, and deductions [*in the film, the announcer, the reportings, the didactics, or the narrator who leads the projection act*]. And then comes the third stage, that of knowledge. The active role of knowledge is expressed not only in the active leap from sensory to rational knowledge, but, and what is even more important, in the leap from rational knowledge to revolutionary practice.... The practice of the transformation of the world.... This, in general terms, is the dialectical materialist theory of the unity of knowledge and action.[16] [*In the projection of the film act, the participation of the comrades, the action proposals that arise, and the actions themselves that will take place later.*]

Moreover, each projection of a film act presupposes *a different setting*, since the space where it takes place, the materials that go to make it up (actor–participants), and the historic time in which it takes place are never the same. This means that the result of each projection act will depend on those who organize it, on those who participate in it, and on the time and place; the possibility of introducing variations, additions, and changes is unlimited. The screening of a film act will always express in one way or another the historical situation in which it takes place; its perspectives are not exhausted in the struggle for power but will instead continue after the taking of power to strengthen the revolution.

The man of the *third cinema*, be it *guerrilla cinema* or *a film act*, with the infinite categories that they contain (film letter, film poem, film essay, film pamphlet, film report, etc.), above all counters the film industry of a cinema of characters with one of themes, that of individuals with that of masses, that of the author with that of the operative group, one of neocolonial misinformation with one of information, one of escape with one that recaptures the truth, that of passivity with that of aggressions. To an institutionalized cinema, he counterposes a guerrilla cinema; to movies as shows, he opposes a film act or action; to a cinema of destruction, one that is both destructive and constructive; to a cinema made for the old kind of human being, for them, he opposes a *cinema fit for a new kind of human being, for what each one of us has the possibility of becoming*.

The decolonization of the filmmaker and of films will be simultaneous acts to the extent that each contributes to collective decolonization. The battle begins without, against the enemy who attacks us, but also within, *against the ideas and models of the enemy to be found inside each one of us*. Destruction and construction. Decolonizing action rescues with its practice the purest and most vital impulses. It opposes to the colonialization of minds the revolution of consciousness. The world is scrutinized, unraveled, rediscovered. People are witness to a constant astonishment, a kind of second birth. They recover their early ingenuity, their capacity for adventure; their lethargic capacity for indignation comes to life.

Freeing a forbidden truth means setting free the possibility of indignation and subversion. Our truth, that of the new man who builds himself by getting rid of all the defects that still weigh him down, is a bomb of inexhaustible power and, at the same time, *the only real possibility of life*. Within this attempt, the revolutionary filmmaker ventures with *his subversive observation, sensibility, imagination, and realization*. The great themes – the history of the country, love and unlove between combatants, the efforts of a people that awakens – all this is reborn before the lens of the decolonized camera. The filmmaker feels free for the first time. He discovers that, within the System, nothing fits, while outside of and against the System, everything fits, *because everything remains to be done*. What appeared yesterday as a preposterous adventure, as we said at the beginning, is posed today as *an inescapable need and possibility*.

Thus far, we have offered ideas and working propositions, which are the sketch of a hypothesis arising from our personal experience and which will have achieved something positive even if they do no more than serve to open a heated dialogue on the new revolutionary film prospects. The vacuums existing in the artistic and scientific fronts of the revolution are sufficiently well known so that the adversary will not try to appropriate them, while we are still unable to do so.

Why films and not some other form of artistic communication? If we choose films as the center of our propositions and debate, it is because that is our work front and because the birth of a *third cinema* means, at least for us, *the most important revolutionary artistic event for our times*.

Notes

1 *The Hour of the Furnaces – Neocolonialism and Violence.*
2 Juan José Hernadez Arregui, *Imperialism and Culture.*
3 Rene Zavaleta Mercado, *Bolivia: Growth of the National Concept.*
4 *The Hour of the Furnaces.*
5 Ibid.
6 Observe the new custom of some groups of the upper bourgeoisie from Rome and Paris who spend their weekends traveling to Saigon to get a close-up view of the Vietcong offensive.
7 Irwin Silber, "USA: The Alienation of Counter Culture," *Tricontinental* 10.
8 The organization Vanguard Artists of Argentina.
9 *The Hour of the Furnaces.*
10 Mao Tse-tung, *On Practice.*
11 Rodolfo Pruigross, *The Proletariat and National Revolution.*
12 Mao Tse-tung, *On Practice.*
13 Che Guevara, *Guerrilla Warfare.*

14 The Uruguayan weekly *Marcha* organized late-night and Sunday morning exhibitions that are widely and well received.

15 The raiding of a Buenos Aires union and the arrest of dozens of persons resulting from a bad choice of projection site and the large number of people invited.

16 Mao Tse-tung, *On Practice*.

17
For an Imperfect Cinema

Julio García Espinosa

Nowadays perfect cinema – technically and artistically masterful – is almost always reactionary cinema. The major temptation facing Cuban cinema at this time – when it is achieving its objective of becoming a cinema of quality, one which is culturally meaningful within the revolutionary process – is precisely that of transforming itself into a perfect cinema.

The "boom" of Latin American cinema – with Brazil and Cuba in the forefront, according to the applause and approval of the European intelligentsia – is similar, in the present moment, to the one of which the Latin American novel had previously been the exclusive benefactor. Why do they applaud us? There is no doubt that a certain standard of quality has been reached. Doubtless, there is a certain political opportunism, a certain mutual instrumentality. But without doubt there is also something more. Why should we worry about their accolades? Isn't the goal of public recognition a part of the rules of the artistic game? When it comes to artistic culture, isn't European recognition equivalent to worldwide recognition? Doesn't it serve art and our peoples as well when works produced by underdeveloped nations obtain such recognition?

Although it may seem curious, it is necessary to clarify the fact that this disquiet is not solely motivated by ethical concerns. As a matter of fact, the motivation is for the most part aesthetic, if indeed it is possible to draw such an arbitrary dividing line between the two terms. When we ask ourselves why it is we who are the film directors and not the others, that is to say, the spectators, the question does not stem from an exclusively ethical concern. We know that we are filmmakers because we have been part of a minority which has had the time and the circumstances needed to develop, within itself, an artistic culture; and because the material resources of film technology are limited and therefore available to some, not to all. But what happens if the future holds the universalization of college level instruction, if economic and social development reduce the hours in the work day, if the evolution of film technology (there are already signs in evidence) makes it possible that this technology ceases being the privilege of a small few? What happens if the development of videotape solves the problem of inevitably limited laboratory capacity, if television systems with their potential for "projecting" independently of the central studio render the ad infinitum construction of movie theaters suddenly superfluous?

What happens then is not only an act of social justice – the possibility for everyone to make films – but also a fact of extreme importance for artistic culture: the possibility of recovering, without any kind of complexes or guilt feelings, the true meaning of artistic activity. Then we will be able to understand that art is one of mankind's "impartial" or "uncommitted"[1] activities. That art is not work, and that the artist is not in the strict sense a worker. The feeling that this is so, and the impossibility of translating it into practice, constitutes the agony and at the same time the "pharisee-ism" of all contemporary art. In fact, the two tendencies exist: those who pretend to produce cinema as an "uncommitted" activity and those who pretend to justify it as a "committed" activity. Both find themselves in a blind alley.

Anyone engaged in an artistic activity asks himself at a given moment what is the meaning of whatever he is doing. The simple fact that this anxiety arises demonstrates that factors exist to motivate it – factors which, in turn, indicate that art does not develop freely. Those who persist in denying art a specific meaning feel the moral weight of their egoism. Those who, on the other hand, pretend to attribute one to it buy off their bad conscience with social generosity. It makes no difference that the mediators (critics, theoreticians, etc.) try to justify certain cases. For the contemporary artist, the mediator is like an aspirin, a tranquilizer. Like a pill, he only temporarily gets rid of the headache. The sure thing, however, is that art, like a capricious little devil, continues to show its face sporadically in no matter which tendency.

No doubt it is easier to define art by what it is not than by what it is, assuming that one can talk about closed definitions not just for art but for any of life's activities. The spirit of contradiction permeates everything now. Nothing, and nobody lets himself be imprisoned in a picture frame, no matter how gilded. It is possible that art gives us a vision of society or of human nature and that, at the same time, it cannot be defined as a vision of society or of human nature. It is possible that a certain narcissism of consciousness – in recognizing in oneself a little historical, sociological, psychological, philosophical consciousness – is implicit in aesthetic pleasure, and at the same time that this sensation is not sufficient in itself to explain aesthetic pleasure.

Is it not much closer to the nature of art to conceive of it as having its own cognitive power? In other words, by saying that art is not the "illustration" of ideas which can also be expressed through philosophy, sociology, psychology. Every artist's desire to express the inexpressible is nothing more than the desire to express the vision of a theme in terms that are inexpressible through other than artistic means. Perhaps the cognitive power of art is like the power of a game for a child. Perhaps aesthetic pleasure lies in sensing the functionality (without a specific goal) of our intelligence and our own sensitivity. Art can stimulate, in general, the creative function of man. It can function as constant stimulus toward adopting an attitude of change with regard to life. But, as opposed to science, it enriches us in such a way that its results are not specific and cannot be applied to anything in particular. It is for this reason that we can call it an "impartial" or "uncommitted" activity, and can say that art is not strictly speaking a "job," and that the artist is perhaps the least intellectual of all intellectuals.

Why then does the artist feel the need to justify himself as a "worker," as an "intellectual," as a "professional," as a disciplined and organized man, like any other individual who performs a productive task? Why does he feel the need to exaggerate the importance of his activity? Why does he feel the need to have critics (mediators) to justify him, to defend him, to interpret him? Why does he speak proudly of "my critics"? Why does he find it necessary to make transcendental declarations, as if he were the true interpreter of society and of mankind? Why does he pretend to consider himself critic and conscience of society when (although these objectives can be implicit or even explicit in certain circumstances) in a truly revolutionary society all of us – that is to say, the people as a whole – should exercise those functions? And why, on the other hand, does the artist see himself forced to limit these objectives, these attitudes, these characteristics? Why does he at the same time set up these limitations as necessary to prevent his work from being transformed into a "tract" or a sociological essay? What is behind such pharisee-ism? Why protect oneself and seek recognition as a (revolutionary, it must be understood) political and scientific worker, yet not be prepared to run the same risks?

The problem is a complex one. Basically, it is neither a matter of opportunism nor cowardice. A true artist is prepared to run any risk as long as he is certain that his work will not cease to be an artistic expression. The only risk which he will not accept is that of endangering the artistic quality of his work.

There are also those who accept and defend the "impartial" function of art. These people claim to be more consistent. They opt for the bitterness of a closed world in the hope that tomorrow history will justify them. But the fact is that even today not everyone can enjoy the *Mona Lisa*. These people should have fewer contradictions; they should be less alienated, but in fact it is not so, even though such an attitude gives them the possibility of an alibi which is more productive on a personal level. In general they sense the sterility of their "purity" or they dedicate themselves to waging corrosive battles, but always on the defensive. They can even, in a reverse operation, reject their interest in finding tranquillity, harmony, a certain compensation in the work of art, expressing instead disequilibrium, chaos, and uncertainty which also becomes the objective of "impartial" art.

What is it, then, which makes it impossible to practice art as an "impartial" activity? Why is this particular situation today more sensitive than ever? From the beginning of the world as we know it, that is to say, since the world was divided into classes, this situation has been latent. If it has grown sharper today it is precisely because today the possibility of transcending it is coming into view. Not through a *prise de conscience*, not through the expressed determination of any particular artist, but because reality itself has begun to reveal symptoms (not at all utopian) which indicate that "in the future there will no longer be painters, but rather men who, among other things, dedicate themselves to painting" (Marx).

There can be no "impartial" or "uncommitted" art, there can be no new and genuine qualitative jump in art, unless the concept and the reality of the "elite" is done away with once and for all. Three factors incline us toward optimism: the development of science, the social presence of the masses, and the revolutionary potential in the contemporary world. All three are without hierarchical order, all three are interrelated.

Why is science feared? Why are people afraid that art might be crushed under the obvious productivity and utility of science? Why this inferiority complex? It is true that today we read a good essay with much greater pleasure than a novel. Why do we keep repeating then, horrified, that the world is becoming more mercenary, more utilitarian, more materialistic? Is it not really marvelous that the development of science, sociology, anthropology, psychology, is contributing to the "purification" of art? The appearance, thanks to science, of expressive media like photography and film made a greater "purification" of painting and the theater possible (without invalidating them artistically in the least). Doesn't modern-day science render anachronistic so much "artistic" analysis of the human soul? Doesn't contemporary science allow us to free ourselves from so many fraudulent films, concealed behind what has been called the world of poetry? With the advance of science, art has nothing to lose; on the contrary, it has a whole world to gain. What, then, are we so afraid of? Science strips art bare and it seems that it is not easy to go naked through the streets.

The real tragedy of the contemporary artist lies in the impossibility of practicing art as a minority activity. It is said – and correctly – that art cannot exercise its attraction without the cooperation of the subject. But what can be done so that the audience stops being an object and transforms itself into the subject?

The development of science, of technology, of the most advanced social theory and practice, has made possible as never before the active presence of the masses in social life. In the realm of artistic life, there are more spectators now than at any other moment in history. This is the first stage in the abolition of "elites." The task currently at hand is to find out if the conditions which will enable spectators to transform themselves into agents – not merely more active spectators, but genuine co-authors – are beginning to exist. The task at hand is to ask ourselves whether art is really an activity restricted to specialists, whether it is, through extra-human design, the option of a chosen few or a possibility for everyone.

How can we trust the perspectives and possibilities of art simply to the education of the people as a mass of spectators? Taste as defined by "high culture," once it is "overdone," is normally passed on to the rest of society as leftovers to be devoured and ruminated over by those who were not invited to the feast. This eternal spiral has today become a vicious circle as well. "Camp" and its attitude toward everything outdated is an attempt to rescue these leftovers and to lessen the distance between high culture and the people. But the difference lies in the fact that camp rescues it as an aesthetic value, while for the people the values involved continue to be ethical ones.

Must the revolutionary present and the revolutionary future inevitably have "its" artists and "its" intellectuals, just as the bourgeoisie had "theirs"? Surely the truly revolutionary position, from now on, is to contribute to overcoming these elitist concepts and practices, rather than pursuing *ad eternum* the "artistic quality" of the work. The new outlook for artistic culture is no longer that everyone must share the taste of a few, but that all can be creators of that culture. Art has always been a universal necessity; what it has not been is an option for all under equal conditions. Parallel to refined art, popular art has had a simultaneous but independent existence.

Popular art has absolutely nothing to do with what is called mass art. Popular art needs and consequently tends to develop the personal, individual taste of a people. On the other hand, mass art (or art for the masses) requires the people to have no taste. It will only be genuine when it is actually the masses who create it, since at present it is art produced by a few for the masses. Grotowski says that today's theater should be a minority art form because mass art can be achieved through cinema. This is not true. Perhaps film is the most elitist of all the contemporary arts. Film today, no matter where, is made by a small minority for the masses. Perhaps film will be the art form which takes the longest time to reach the hands of the masses, when we understand mass art as *popular* art, art created by the masses. Currently, as Hauser points out, mass art is art produced by a minority in order to satisfy the demand of a public reduced to the sole role of spectator and consumer.

Popular art has always been created by the least learned sector of society, yet this "uncultured" sector has managed to conserve profoundly cultured characteristics of art. One of the most important of these is the fact that the creators are at the same time the spectators and vice versa. Between those who produce and those who consume, no sharp line of demarcation exists. Cultivated art, in our era, has also attained this situation. Modern art's great dose of freedom is nothing more than the conquest of a new interlocutor: the artist himself. For this reason it is useless to strain oneself struggling for the substitution of the masses as a new and potential spectator for the bourgeoisie. This situation, maintained by popular art, adopted by cultivated art, must be dissolved and become the heritage of all. This and no other must be the great objective of an authentically revolutionary artistic culture.

Popular art preserved another even more important cultural characteristic: it is carried out as but another life activity. With cultivated art, the reverse is true; it is pursued as a unique, specific activity, as a personal achievement. This is the cruel price of having had to maintain artistic activity at the expense of its inexistence among the people. Hasn't the attempt to realize himself on the edge of society proved to be too painful a restriction for the artist and for art itself? To posit art as a sect, as a society within society, as the promised land where we can fleetingly fulfill ourselves for a brief instant – doesn't this create the illusion that self-realization on the level of consciousness also implies self-realization on the level of existence? Isn't this patently obvious in contemporary circumstances? The essential lesson of popular art is that it is carried out as a life activity: man must not fulfill himself as an artist but fully; the artist must not seek fulfillment as an artist but as a human being.

In the modern world, principally in developed capitalist nations and in those countries engaged in a revolutionary process, there are alarming symptoms, obvious signs of an imminent change. The possibilities for overcoming this traditional dissociation are beginning to arise. These symptoms are not a product of consciousness but of reality itself. A large part of the struggle waged in modern art has been, in fact, to "democratize" art. What other goal is entailed in combating the limitations of taste, museum art, and the demarcation lines between the creator and the public? What is considered beauty today, and where is it found? On Campbell soup labels, in a garbage can lid, in gadgets? Even the eternal value of a work of art is today being questioned. What else could be the meaning of those sculptures, seen in recent exhibitions, made of blocks of ice which melt away while the public looks at them? Isn't this – more than the disappearance of art – the attempt to make the spectator disappear? Don't those painters who entrust a portion of the execution of their work to just anyone, rather than to their disciples, exhibit an eagerness to jump over the barricade of "elitist" art? Doesn't the same attitude exist among composers whose works allow their performers ample liberty?

There's a widespread tendency in modern art to make the spectator participate ever more fully. If he participates to a greater and greater degree, where will the process end up? Isn't the logical outcome – or shouldn't it in fact be – that he will cease being a spectator altogether? This simultaneously represents a tendency toward collectivism and toward individualism. Once we admit the possibility of universal participation, aren't we also admitting the individual creative potential which we all have? Isn't Grotowski mistaken when he asserts that today's theater should be dedicated to an elite? Isn't it rather the reverse: that the theater of poverty in fact requires the highest refinement? It is the theater which has no need for secondary values: costumes, scenery, make-up, even a stage. Isn't this an indication that material conditions are reduced to a minimum and that, from this point of view, the possibility of making theater is within everyone's reach? And doesn't the fact that the theater has an increasingly smaller public mean that conditions are beginning to ripen for it to transform itself into a true mass theater? Perhaps the tragedy of the theater lies in the fact that it has reached this point in its evolution too soon.

When we look toward Europe, we wring our hands. We see that the old culture is totally incapable of providing answers to the problems of art. The fact is that

Europe can no longer respond in a traditional manner but at the same time finds it equally difficult to respond in a manner that is radically new. Europe is no longer capable of giving the world a new "ism"; neither is it in a position to put an end to "isms" once and for all. So we think that our moment has come, that at last the underdeveloped can deck themselves out as "men of culture." Here lies our greatest danger and our greatest temptation. This accounts for the opportunism of some on our continent. For, given our technical and scientific backwardness and given the scanty presence of the masses in social life, our continent is still capable of responding in a traditional manner, by reaffirming the concept and the practice of elite art. Perhaps in this case the real motive for the European applause which some of our literary and cinematic works have won is none other than a certain nostalgia which we inspire. After all, the European has no other Europe to turn to.

The third factor, the revolution – which is the most important of all – is perhaps present in our country as nowhere else. This is our only true chance. The revolution is what furnishes all other alternatives, what can supply an entirely new response, what enables us to do away once and for all with elitist concepts and practices in art. The revolution and the ongoing revolutionary process are the only factors which make the total and free presence of the masses possible – and this will mean the definitive disappearance of the rigid division of labor and of a society divided into sectors and classes. For us, then, the revolution is the highest expression of culture because it will abolish artistic culture as a fragmentary human activity.

Current responses to this inevitable future, this incontestable prospect, can be as numerous as the countries on our continent. Because characteristics and achieved levels are not the same, each art form, every artistic manifestation, must find its own expression. What should be the response of the Cuban cinema in particular? Paradoxically, we think it will be a new poetics, not a new cultural policy. A poetics whose true goal will be to commit suicide, to disappear as such. We know, however, that in fact other artistic conceptions will continue to exist among us, just as small rural landholdings and religion continue to exist.

On the level of cultural policy we are faced with a serious problem: the film school. Is it right to continue developing a handful of film specialists? It seems inevitable for the present, but what will be the eternal quarry that we continue to mine: the students in Arts and Letters at the University? But shouldn't we begin to consider right now whether that school should have a limited lifespan? What end do we pursue there – a reserve corps of future artists? Or a specialized future public? We should be asking ourselves whether we can do something now to abolish this division between artistic and scientific culture.

What constitutes in fact the true prestige of artistic culture, and how did it come about that this prestige was allowed to appropriate the whole concept of culture? Perhaps it is based on the enormous prestige which the spirit has always enjoyed at the expense of the body. Hasn't artistic culture always been seen as the spiritual part of society while scientific culture is seen as its body? The traditional rejection of the body, of material life, is due in part to the concept that things of the spirit are more elevated, more elegant, serious, and profound. Can't we, here and now, begin doing something to put an end to this artificial distinction? We should understand from here on in that the body and the things of the body are also elegant, and that material life is beautiful as well. We should understand that, in fact, the soul is contained in the body just as the spirit is contained in material life, just as – to speak in strictly artistic terms – the essence is contained in the surface and the content in the form.

We should endeavor to see that our future students, and therefore our future filmmakers, will themselves be scientists, sociologists, physicians, economists, agricultural engineers, etc., without of course ceasing to be filmmakers. And, at the same time, we should have the same aim for our most outstanding workers, the workers who achieve the best results in terms of political and intellectual formation. We cannot develop the taste of the masses as long as the division between the two cultures continues to exist, nor as long as the masses are not the real masters of the means of artistic production. The revolution has liberated us as an artistic sector. It is only logical that we contribute to the liberation of the private means of artistic production.

A new poetics for the cinema will, above all, be a "partisan" and "committed" poetics, a "committed" art, a consciously and resolutely "committed" cinema – that is to say, an "imperfect" cinema. An "impartial" or "uncommitted" one, as a complete aesthetic activity, will only be possible when it is the people who make art. But today art must assimilate its quota of work so that work can assimilate its quota of art.

The motto of this imperfect cinema (which there's no need to invent, since it already exists) is, as Glauber Rocha would say, "We are not interested in the problems of neurosis; we are interested in the problems of lucidity." Art no longer has use for the neurotic and his problems, although the neurotic continues to need art – as a concerned object, a relief, an alibi or, as Freud would say, as a sublimation of his problems. A neurotic can produce art, but art has no reason to produce neurotics. It has been traditionally believed that the concerns of art were not to be found in the sane but in the sick, not in the normal but in the abnormal, not in those who struggle but in those who weep, not in lucid minds but in neurotic ones. Imperfect cinema is changing this way of seeing the question. We have more faith in the sick man than in the healthy one because his truth is purged by suffering. However, there is no need for suffering to be synonymous with artistic elegance. There is still a trend in modern art – undoubtedly related to Christian tradition – which identifies seriousness with suffering. The specter of Marguerite Gautier still haunts artistic endeavor in our day. Only in the person who suffers do we perceive elegance, gravity, even beauty; only in him do we recognize the possibility of authenticity, seriousness, sincerity. Imperfect cinema must put an end to this tradition.

Imperfect cinema finds a new audience in those who struggle, and it finds its themes in their problems. For imperfect cinema, "lucid" people are the ones who think and feel and exist in a world which they can change; in spite of all the problems and difficulties, they are convinced that they can transform it in a revolutionary way. Imperfect cinema therefore has no need to struggle to create an "audience." On the contrary, it can be said that at present a greater audience exists for this kind of cinema than there are filmmakers able to supply that audience.

What does this new interlocutor require of us – an art full of moral examples worthy of imitation? No. Man is more of a creator than an innovator. Besides, he should be the one to give *us* moral examples. He might ask us for a fuller, more complete work, aimed – in a separate or coordinated fashion – at the intelligence, the emotions, the powers of intuition.

Should he ask us for a cinema of denunciation? Yes and no. No, if the denunciation is directed toward the others, if it is conceived that those who are not struggling might sympathize with us and increase their awareness. Yes, if the denunciation acts as information, as testimony, as another combat weapon for those engaged in the struggle. Why denounce imperialism to show one more time that it is evil? What's the use if those now fighting are fighting primarily against imperialism? We can denounce imperialism, but should strive to do it as a way of proposing concrete battles. A film which denounces, to those who struggle, the evil deeds of an official who must be brought to justice would be an excellent example of this kind of film-denunciation.

We maintain that imperfect cinema must above all show the process which generates the problems. It is thus the opposite of a cinema principally dedicated to celebrating results, the opposite of a self-sufficient and contemplative cinema, the opposite of a cinema which "beautifully illustrates" ideas or concepts which we already possess. (The narcissistic posture has nothing to do with those who struggle.) To show a process is not exactly equivalent to analyzing it. To analyze, in the traditional sense of the word, always implies a closed prior judgment. To analyze a problem is to show the problem (not the process) permeated with judgments which the analysis itself generates *a priori*. To analyze is to block off from the outset any possibility for analysis on the part of the interlocutor.

To show the process of a problem, on the other hand, is to submit it to judgment without pronouncing the verdict. There is a style of news reporting which puts more emphasis on the commentary than on the news item. There is another kind of reporting which presents the news and evaluates it through the arrangement of the item on the page or by its position in the paper. To show the process of a problem is like showing the very development of the news item, without commentary; it is like showing the multifaced evolution of a piece of information without evaluating it. The subjective element is the selection of the problem, conditioned as it is by the interest of the audience –

which is the subject. The objective element is showing the process – which is the object.

Imperfect cinema is an answer, but it is also a question which will discover its own answers in the course of its development. Imperfect cinema can make use of the documentary or the fictional mode, or both. It can use whatever genre, or all genres. It can use cinema as a pluralistic art form or as a specialized form of expression. These questions are indifferent to it, since they do not represent its real alternatives or problems, and much less its real goals. These are not the battles or the polemics it is interested in sparking.

Imperfect cinema can also be enjoyable, both for the maker and for its new audience. Those who struggle do not struggle on the edge of life, but in the midst of it. Struggle is life and vice versa. One does not struggle in order to live "later on." The struggle requires organization – the organization of life. Even in the most extreme phase, that of total and direct war, the organization of life is equivalent to the organization of the struggle. And in life, as in the struggle, there is everything, including enjoyment. Imperfect cinema can enjoy itself despite everything which conspires to negate enjoyment.

Imperfect cinema rejects exhibitionism in both (literal) senses of the word, the narcissistic and the commercial (getting shown in established theaters and circuits). It should be remembered that the death of the star-system turned out to be a positive thing for art. There is no reason to doubt that the disappearance of the director as star will offer similar prospects. Imperfect cinema must start work now, in cooperation with sociologists, revolutionary leaders, psychologists, economists, etc. Furthermore, imperfect cinema rejects whatever services criticism has to offer and considers the function of mediators and intermediaries anachronistic.

Imperfect cinema is no longer interested in quality or technique. It can be created equally well with a Mitchell or with an 8mm camera, in a studio or in a guerrilla camp in the middle of the jungle. Imperfect cinema is no longer interested in predetermined taste, and much less in "good taste." It is not quality which it seeks in an artist's work. The only thing it is interested in is how an artist responds to the following question: What are you doing in order to overcome the barrier of the "cultured" elite audience which up to now has conditioned the form of your work?

The filmmaker who subscribes to this new poetics should not have personal self-realization as his object. From now on he should also have another activity. He should place his role as revolutionary or aspiring revolutionary above all else. In a word, he should try to fulfill himself as a man and not just as an artist. Imperfect cinema cannot lose sight of the fact that its essential goal as a new poetics is to disappear. It is no longer a matter of replacing one school with another, one "ism" with another, poetry with anti-poetry, but of truly letting a thousand different flowers bloom. The future lies with folk art. But let us no longer display folk art with demagogic pride, with a celebrative air. Let us exhibit it instead as a cruel denunciation, as a painful testimony to the level at which the peoples of the world have been forced to limit their artistic creativity. The future, without doubt, will be with folk art, but then there will be no need to call it that, because nobody and nothing will any longer be able to paralyze again the creative spirit of the people.

Art will not disappear into nothingness; it will disappear into everything.

Note

1   *Una actividad desinteresada* in the original.

18

Towards a Critical Theory of Third World Films

Teshome H. Gabriel

Wherever there is a filmmaker prepared to stand up against commercialism, exploitation, pornography and the tyranny of technique, there is to be found the living spirit of New Cinema. *Wherever there is a filmmaker, of any age or background, ready to place his cinema and his profession at the service of the great causes of his time, there will be the living spirit of* New Cinema. *This is the correct definition which sets* New Cinema *apart from the commercial industry because the commitment of industrial cinema is to untruth and exploitation.*

The Aesthetics of Hunger, *Glauber Rocha [Brazil]*

Insert the work as an original fact in the process of liberation, place it first at the service of life itself, ahead of art; dissolve aesthetics in the life of society: only in this way, as [Frantz] Fanon said, can decolonisation become possible and culture, cinema, and beauty – at least, what is of greatest importance to us – become our culture, our films, and our sense of beauty.

Towards a Third Cinema, *Fernando Solanas and Octavio Gettino [Argentina]*

Frantz Fanon, in his attempts to identify the revolutionary impulse in the peasant of the Third World, accepted that culture is an act of insemination upon history, whose product is liberation from oppression.[1] In my search for a methodological device for a critical inquiry into Third World films, I have drawn upon the historical works of this ardent proponent of liberation, whose analysis of the steps of the genealogy of Third World culture can also be used as a critical framwork for the study of Third World films. This essay is, therefore, divided into two parts and focuses on those essential qualities Third World films possess rather than those they may seem to lack. The first part lays the formulation for Third World film culture and filmic institutions based on a critical and theoretical matrix applicable to Third World needs. The second part is an attempt to give material substance to the analytic constructs discussed previously.

From pre-colonial times to the present, the struggle for freedom from oppression has been waged by the Third World masses, who in their maintenance of a deep cultural identity have made history come alive. Just as they have moved aggressively towards independence, so has the evolution of Third World film culture followed a path from 'domination' to 'liberation'. This genealogy of Third World film culture moves from the First Phase in which foreign images are impressed in an alienating fashion on the audience, to the Second and Third Phases in which recognition of 'consciousness of oneself' serves as the essential antecedent for national and, more significantly, international consciousness. There are, therefore, three phases in this methodological device.

Phases of Third World Films

Phase I: The unqualified assimilation

The industry   Identification with the Western Hollywood film industry. The link is made as obvious as possible and even the names of the companies proclaim their origin. For instance, the Nigerian film company, Calpenny, whose name stands for California, Pennsylvania and New York, tries to hide behind an acronym, while the companies in India, Egypt and Hongkong are not worried being typed the 'Third World's Hollywood', 'Hollywood-on-the-Nile', and 'Hollywood of the Orient' respectively.

The theme   Hollywood thematic concerns of 'entertainment' predominate. Most of the feature films of the Third World in this phase sensationalize adventure for its own sake and concern themselves with escapist themes of romance, musicals, comedies, etc. The sole purpose of such industries is to turn out entertainment products which will generate profits. The scope and persistence of this kind of industry in the Third World lies in its ability to provide reinvestable funds and this quadruples their staying power. Therefore, in cases where a counter-cinematic movement has occurred the existing national industry has been able to ingest it. A good example is in the incorporation of the 'cinema nôvo' movement in the Brazilian Embrafilme.

The style   The emphasis on formal properties of cinema, technical brilliance and visual wizardry, overrides subject matter. The aim here is simply to create a 'spectacle'. Aping Hollywood stylistically, more often than not, runs counter to Third World needs for a serious social art.

Phase II: The remembrance phase

The industry   Indigenization and control of talents, production, exhibition and distribution. Many Third World film production companies are in this stage. The movement for a social institution of cinema in the Third World such as 'cinema moudjahid' in Algeria, 'new wave' in India and '*engagé* or committed cinema' in Senegal and Mozambique exemplifies this phase.

The theme   Return of the exile to the Third World's source of strength, i.e. culture and history. The predominance of filmic themes such as the clash between rural and urban life, traditional versus modern value systems, folklore and mythology, identifies this level. Sembene Ousmane's early film *Mandabi* about a humble traditional man outstripped by modern ways characterizes this stage. *Barravento* ('The Turning Wind'), a poetic Brazilian film about a member of a fishermen's village who returns from exile in the city, is a folkloric study of mysticism. The film from Burkina Faso (Upper Volta), *Wend Kûuni* ('God's Gift'), attempts to preserve the spirit of folklore in a brilliant recreation of an old tale of a woman who is declared a witch because of her conflicts with custom when she refused to marry after the disappearance of her husband. While the most positive aspect of this phase is its break with the concepts and propositions of Phase I, the primary danger here is the uncritical acceptance or undue romanticization of ways of the past.

It needs to be stressed that there is a danger of falling into the trap of exalting traditional virtues and racializing culture without at the same time condemning faults. To accept totally the values of Third World traditional cultures without simultaneously stamping out the regressive elements can only lead to 'a blind alley', as Fanon puts it, and falsification of the true nature of culture as an act or agent of liberation. Therefore, unless this phase, which predominates in Third World film practices today, is seen as a process, a moving towards the next stage, it could develop into opportunistic endeavours and create cultural confusion. This has been brilliantly pointed out by Luis Ospina of Colombia in his self-reflexive film *Picking on the People*, in which he criticizes the exploitative nature of some Third World filmmakers who peddle Third World poverty and misery at festival sites in Europe and North America and do not approach their craft as a tool of social transformation. An excellent case in point is the internationally acclaimed film *Pixote* by Hector Babenco. According to a *Los Angeles Times* correspondent in Rio de Janeiro, Da Silva, the young boy who played the title role of the film, was paid a mere $320. The correspondent writes: 'In a real-life drama a juvenile judge in Diadema, a suburb of São Paulo, last week released Da Silva, now 16, to the custody of his mother after his arrest on charges of housebreaking and theft.' According to Da Silva's mother, who sells lottery tickets for her living, 'after a trip to Rio when he got no work, he told me, "Mother, they have forgotten me, I am finished."' In the meantime Mr Babenco, the now famous film director, was about to shoot his next feature, *Kiss of the Spider Woman*, in collaboration with producers in Hollywood.[2]

The style   Some attempts to indigenize film style are manifest. Although the dominant stylistic conventions of the first phase still predominate here, there appears to be a growing tendency to create a film style appropriate to the changed thematic concerns. In this respect, the growing insistence on spatial representation rather than temporal manipulation typifies the films in this phase. The sense of a spatial orientation in cinema in the Third World arises out of the experience of an 'endless' world of the large Third World mass. This nostalgia for the vastness of nature projects itself into the film form, resulting in long takes and long or wide shots. This is often done to constitute part of an overall symbolization of a Third World thematic orientation, i.e. the landscape depicted ceases to be mere land or soil and acquires a phenomenal quality which integrates humans with the general drama of existence itself.

Phase III: The combative phase

The industry   Filmmaking as a public service institution. The industry in this phase is not only owned by the nation and/or the government, it is also managed, operated and run for and by the people. It can also be called a cinema of mass participation, one enacted by members of communities speaking indigenous language, one that espouses Julio García Espinosa's polemic of 'An Imperfect Cinema',[3] that in a developing world, technical and artistic perfection in the production of a film cannot be the aims in themselves. Quite a number of social institutions of cinema in the Third World, some underground like Argentina's 'Cine Liberacion' and some supported by their governments – for instance, 'Chile Films' of Allende's Popular Unity Socialist government – exemplify this phase. Two industrial institutions that also exemplify this level are the Algerian L'Office National pour le Commerce et l'Industrie Cinématographique (ONCIC) and Cuba's Institute of Film Art and Industry (ICAIC).

The theme   Lives and struggles of Third World peoples. This phase signals the maturity of the filmmaker and is distinguishable from either Phase I or Phase II by its insistence on viewing film in its ideological ramifications. A very good example is Miguel Littin's *The Promised Land*, a quasi-historical mythic account of power and rebellion, which can be seen as referring to events in modern-day Chile. Likewise, his latest film *Alsimo and the Condor* combines realism and fantasy within the context of war-torn Nicaragua. The imagery in *One Way or Another* by the late Sara Gómez Yara, of an iron ball smashing down the old slums of Havana, not only depicts the issue of women/race in present-day Cuba but also symbolizes the need for a new awareness to replace the old oppressive spirit of *machismo* which still persists in socialist Cuba. The film *Soleil O*, by the Mauritanian filmmaker Med Hondo, aided by the process of Fanonian theses, comes to the recognition of forgotten heritage in the display of the amalgam of ideological determinants of European 'humanism', racism and colonialism. The failure of colonialism to convert Africans into 'white-thinking blacks' depicted in the film reappears in a much wider symbolic form in his later film, *West Indies*, where the entire pantheon of domination and liberation unfolds in a ship symbolic of the slave-ship of yesteryear.

The style   Film as an ideological tool. Here, film is equated or recognized as an ideological instrument. This particular phase also constitutes a framework of agreement between the public (or the indigenous institution of cinema) and the filmmaker. A Phase III filmmaker is one who is perceptive of and knowledgeable about the pulse of the Third World masses. Such a filmmaker is truly in search of a Third World cinema – a cinema that has respect for the Third World peoples. One element of the style in this phase is an ideological point-of-view instead of

that of a character as in dominant Western conventions. *Di Cavalcanti* by
Glauber Rocha, for instance, is a take-off from 'Quarup', a joyous death ritual
celebrated by Amazon tribes.[4] The celebration frees the dead from the hypocritical tragic view modern man has of death. By turning the documentary of the
death of the internationally renowned Brazilian painter Di Cavalcanti into a
chaotic/celebratory montage of sound and images, Rocha deftly and directly
criticized the dominant documentary convention, creating in the process not
only an alternative film language but also a challenging discourse on the question
of existence itself. Another element of style is the use of flashback – although the
reference is to past events, it is not stagnant but dynamic and developmental. In
The Promised Land, for instance, the flashback device dips into the past to
comment on the future, so that within it a flash-forward is inscribed. Similarly,
when a flash-forward is used in Sembene's *Ceddo* (1977), it is also to convey a
past and future tense simultaneously to comment on two historical periods.

Since the past is necessary for the understanding of the present, and serves as a
strategy for the future, this stylistic orientation seems to be ideologically suited to
this particular phase.

It should, however, be noted that the three phases discussed above are not
organic developments. They are enclosed in a dynamic which is dialectical in
nature; for example, some Third World filmmakers have taken a contradictory
path. *Lucia*, a Cuban film by Humberto Solás, about the relations between the
sexes, belongs to Phase III, yet Solás's latest film, *Cecilia*, which concerns an
ambitious mulatto woman who tries to assimilate into a repressive Spanish
aristocracy, is a regression in style (glowing in spectacle) and theme (the tragic
mulatto) towards Phase I. Moving in the opposite direction, Glauber Rocha's
early Brazilian films like *Deus e O Diabo na Terra do Sol* (literally 'God and the
Devil in the Land of the Sun', but advertised in the United States as 'Black God,
White Devil'!) and *Terra em Transe* ('The Earth Trembles') reflect a Phase II
characteristic, while his last two films, *A Idade da Terra* ('The Age of Earth') and
Di Cavalcanti, both in their formal properties and subject matter manifest a
Phase III characteristic in their disavowal of the conventions of dominant cinema.
According to Glauber Rocha, *A Idade da Terra* (which develops the theme of
Terra em Transe) and *Di Cavalcanti* disintegrate traditional 'narrative sequences'
and rupture not only the fictional and documentary cinema style of his early
works, but also 'the world cinematic language' under 'the dictatorship of Coppola
and Godard'.[5]

The dynamic enclosure of the three phases posits the existence of grey areas
between Phases I and II, and II and III. This area helps to identify a large
number of important Third World films. For instance, the Indian film *Manthan*
('The Churning'), the Senegalese film *Xala* ('Spell of Impotence'), the Bolivian
film *Chuquiago* (Indian name for La Paz), the Ecuadorean film *My Aunt
Nora*, the Brazilian film *They Don't Wear Black Tie* and the Tunisian film
Shadow of the Earth occupy the grey area between Phase II and III. The
importance of the grey areas cannot be over-emphasized, for not only do they

concretely demonstrate the *process of becoming* but they also attest to the multi-faceted nature of Third World cinema and the need for the development of new critical canons.

Components of Critical Theory

From the above it can be seen that the development of Third World film culture provides a critical theory particular to Third World needs. I would like to propose at this stage an analytic construct consisting of three components that would provide an integrative matrix within which to approach and interpret the Three Phases drawn out from the Third World's cultural history. The components of critical theory can be schematized as follows:

Component 1: text

The intersection of codes and sub-codes; the chief thematic and formal characteristics of existing films and the rules of that filmic grammar. And the transformational procedures whereby new 'texts' emerge from old.

Component 2: reception

The audience: the active interrogation of images versus the passive consumption of films. The issue of alienated and non-alienated identity and the ideal/inscribed or actual/empirical spectatorship illustrates this component of critical theory.

Component 3: production

The social determination where the wider context of determinants informs social history, market considerations, economy of production, state governance and regulation composes this stage of the critical constructs. Here, the larger historical perspective, the position of the institution of indigenous cinema in progressive social taste, is contexted. The overriding critical issue at this juncture is, for instance, the unavoidable ultimate choice between the classical studio system and the development of a system of production based on the lightweight 16mm or video technology. The pivotal concern and the single most significant question at this stage, therefore, is: 'Precisely what kind of institution is cinema in the Third World?'

Confluence of Phases and Critical Theory

Each phase of the Third World film culture can be described in terms of all the three components of critical theory, because each phase is necessarily engaged in all the critical operations. For instance, Phase I is characterized by a type of film that simply mirrors, in its concepts and propositions, the status quo, i.e. the text and the rules of the grammar are identical to conventional practices. The consequence of this type of 'mimicking' in the area of 'reception' is that an alienated identity ensues from it precisely because the spectator is unable to find or recognize himself/herself in the images. The mechanisms of the systems of 'production' also acknowledge the status quo – the reliance is on the studio systems of controlled production and experimentation.

If we apply the components of critical theory to Phase II only, a slight shift in the text and the rules of the grammar is noticeable. Although the themes are predominantly indigenized, the film language remains trapped, woven and blotted with classical formal elements, and remains stained with conventional film style. In terms of 'reception' the viewer, aided by the process of memory and an amalgam of folklore and mythology, is able to locate a somewhat diluted traditional identity. The third level of critical theory also composes and marks the process of indigenization of the institution of cinema where a position of self-determination is sought.

Finally, the three components of critical theory find their dynamic wholeness in Phase III – the Combative Phase. Here, the text and sub-texts go through a radical shift and transformation – the chief formal and thematic concerns begin to alter the rules of the grammar. Another film language and a system of new codes begin to manifest themselves. With regard to 'reception' we discover that the viewer or subject is no longer alienated because recognition is vested not only in genuine cultural grounds but also in an ideological cognition founded on the acknowledgment of the decolonization of culture and total liberation.

The intricate relationships of the three *phases* of the evolution of Third World film culture and the three analytic constructs for filmic institutions help to establish the stage for a confluence of a unique aesthetic exchange founded on other than traditional categories of film conventions (see figure 18.1).

This new Third World cinematic experience, inchoate as it is, is in the process of creating a concurrent development of a new and throbbing social institution capable of generating a dynamic and far-reaching influence on the future socio-economic and educational course of the Third World.

I contend that the confluence obtained from the interlocking of the *phases* and the critical *constructs* reveals underlying assumptions concerning perceptual patterns and film viewing situations. For instance, with respect to fiction film showing in Third World theatres, rejection on cultural grounds forces incomplete transmission of meaning. That is, the intended or inscribed meaning of the film is deflected and acquires a unique meaning of its own – the mode of address of the film and the spectator behaviour undergo a radical alteration. Therefore, what has been presented as a 'fiction' film is received as if it were a 'documentary'. The same fiction film screened in its own country of origin, however, claims an ideal spectatorship because it is firmly anchored in its own cultural references, codes and symbols. A classic example of how films from one culture can be easily

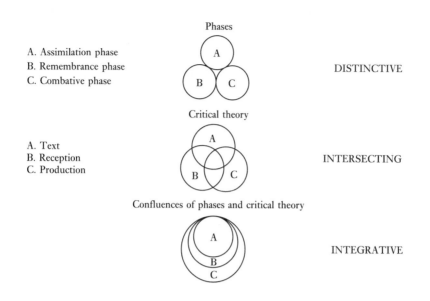

A. Assimilation phase
B. Remembrance phase
C. Combative phase

A. Text
B. Reception
C. Production

DISTINCTIVE

INTERSECTING

INTEGRATIVE

Figure 18.1   Summary of the development of film culture and filmic institutions

Here, A and B find themselves in a larger historical perspective, C. It is a wider context of indigenization and self-determination which conditions levels A and B to give up their position of dominance to C, a stage which composes and marks the union of Third World film culture and the social institutions of cinema.

misunderstood and misinterpreted by a viewer from another culture is Glauber Rocha's *The Lion Has Seven Heads* (*Der Leone Have Sept Cabezas*). The film was extensively exhibited in the West, one catalogue compiled in 1974 crediting Rocha with bringing 'the Cinema Novo to Africa for this Third World assault on the various imperialisms represented in its multilingual title. Characters include a black revolutionary, a Portuguese mercenary, an American CIA agent, a French missionary, and a voluptuous nude woman called the Golden Temple of Violence.'[6] Again, a recent compendium of reviews, *Africa on Film and Videotape, 1960–81*, dismisses the film completely with a one-liner, 'An allegorical farce noting the bond between Africa and Brazil.'[7]

Yet Glauber Rocha, in an interview given to a prominent film historian, Rachel Gerber (author of *Glauber Rocha, Cinema, Politica e a Estetica do Inconsciente*), in Rome, February 1973, and in a discussion with this author at UCLA in 1976, said that the film is a story of Che Guevara who is magically resurrected by Blacks through the spirit of Zumbi, the spiritual name of the late Amilcar Cabral. To Rocha, the film is in fact a homage to Amilcar Cabral. Thus, while the West looks at this film as an offering of clichéd images and an object of curiosity, the filmmaker is only trying to affirm the continuity of the Third World's anti-imperialist struggle from Che to Cabral (and beyond), to initiate an awareness of their lives, and the relevance to us today of what they struggled and died for. To the extent that we recognize a history of unequal exchanges between the South and the North, we must also recognize the unequal 'symbolic' exchanges involved. The difficulty of Third World films of radical social comment for Western interpretation is the result (a) of the film's resistance to the dominant conventions of cinema, and (b) of the consequence of the Western viewers' loss of being the privileged decoders and ultimate interpreters of meaning.

The Western experience of film viewing – dominance of the big screen and the sitting situation – has naturalized a spectator conditioning so that any communication of a film plays on such values of exhibition and reception. The Third World experience of film viewing and exhibition suggests an altogether different route and different value system. For instance, Americans and Europeans hate seeing a film on African screens, because everybody talks during the showings; similarly, African viewers of film in America complain about the very strict code of silence and the solemn atmosphere of the American movie-theatres.

How the system of perceptual patterns and viewing situation varies with conditions of reception from one culture to another, or how changes in the rules of the grammar affect spectator viewing habits, is part of a larger question which solidifies and confirms the issue of cultural relativism and identity.

The confluence of the phases and the constructs also converges on the technologically mediated factors of needed production apparatuses, productive relations and the mechanisms of industrial operations. It needs to be stated outright that 'technology' as such does not in itself produce or communicate meaning; but it is equally true to say that 'technology' has a dynamic which helps to create ideological carry-overs that impress discourse language, i.e. ideological discourse manifests itself in the mechanisms of film discourse. By way of an example, it is possible that a filmmaker might have the idea of 'filmic form' before having 'a content' to go along with it. Third World films are heterogeneous, employing narrative and oral discourse, folk music and songs, extended silences and gaps, moving from fictional representation to reality, to fiction – these constitute the creative part that can challenge the ideological carry-overs that technology imposes.

From the needs of Third World film criticism, contemporary film scholarship is criticized on two major fronts: first, contemporary film theory and criticism is grounded in a conception of the 'viewer' (subject or citizen) derived from psychoanalytic theory where the relation between the 'viewer' and the 'film' is determined by a particular dynamic of the 'familial' matrix. To the extent that Third World culture and familial relationships are not described through psychoanalytic theory, Third World filmic representation is open for an elaboration of the relation 'viewer'/'film' on terms other than those founded on psychoanalysis. The Third World relies more on an appeal to social and political conflicts as the prime rhetorical strategy and less on the paradigm of oedipal conflict and resolution.

Second, on the semiotic front, the Western model of filmic representation is essentially based on a literary or written conception of the scenario which implies a linear, cause/effect conception of narrative action.[8] However, Third World oral narratives, founded on traditional culture, are held in memory by a set of formal strategies specific to repeated, oral, face-to-face tellings.

It is no longer satisfactory to use existing critical criteria, which may be adequate for a film practice (Western in this case) now at a plateau of relevance,[9] to elucidate a new and dynamic film convention whose upward mobility will result in a totally new cinematic language. The Third World experience is thus raising some fundamental concerns about the methods and/or commitment of traditional film scholarship. The Third World filmic practice is, therefore, reorganizing and refining the pictorial syntax and the position of the 'viewer' (or spectator) with respect to film. The Third World cinematic experience is moved by the requirements of its social action and contexted and marked by the strategy of that action. We need, therefore, to begin attending to a new theoretical and analytic matrix governed by other than existing critical theories that claim specific applications for universal principles.

Cultural contamination is a deeply rooted human fear: it smells of annihilation. Spiritual and traditional practices have a terrific hold on the Third World rural populace. This reminds us of the maxim which was enunciated by Confucius in the sixth century BC and still prevails: 'I'm a transmitter, not an inventor.' To the Third World, spirits, magic, masquerades and rituals, however flawed they may be, still constitute knowledge and provide collective security and protection from forces of evil. Unknown forces for the rural community can only be checked or controlled if they can be identified.

One way of readily understanding what Third World culture is, is to distinguish it from what it claims not to be.[10] We call at this juncture for a thorough and comparative analysis of 'oral' or 'folk' art form and 'literate' or 'print' art form to situate the foregoing discussion on critical theory into focused attention. I propose here to examine the centrifugal as well as the centripetal cultural forces that might determine not only film, but also the media, in the Third World. This dialectical, not differential or oppositional, conception of cultural forms takes into account the dynamics of their exchange.

Several factors ensue from the examination of the two modes of cultural expression. While, for instance, the community issue is at the heart of Third World traditional culture, the issue of the individual is at the base of Western or print culture. With regard to performatory stage presentation, a Western actor interacting with the audience breaks the compact or marginal boundary. Because a special kind of magic enters a playing space, Western stage performance does not allow cross-over. While, therefore, a Western person feels his privacy violated with interactive drama, in the Third World context the understanding between the viewer and the performers is that their positions are interchangeable without notice.

Awe for the old in the Third World culture is very much in evidence. Several films reflect it. The old or the aged as repositories of Third World history is well documented in such films as *Emitai* from Senegal, *They Don't Wear Black Tie* from Brazil, *Shadow of the Earth* from Tunisia and *The In-Laws* from the People's Republic of China. The issue of the aged in Third World culture is beautifully illustrated in Safi Faye's film *Fad Jal*, where the opening sequence of the film states: 'In Africa, an old man dying is like a library burning down.'

A major area of misunderstanding (if we take into account the 'Cognitive characteristics' of the 'Folk/Print art' dichotomy in table 18.1) is the definition and replacement of 'man', the individual, within Third World societies. For any meaningful dialogue centring on Third World developmental schemes the issue of 'man/woman' in a society must be carefully debated. As Julius K. Nyerere of Tanzania puts it, 'The Purpose is Man,'[11] and as the Wolof saying goes, 'Man is the medicine of man.'

A cultural orientation of 'man', the individual, as changeable and capable of effecting change is a condition that reverberates in all advanced societies of the world, be they of capitalist or socialist persuasion. The idea that man, both in the singular and in the plural, has the capability of controlling his/her own destiny and effecting change by his/her own will is a dynamic force which can alter both the thought patterns and work habits of a people. This concept, it must be stated, is not the opposite of the Third World ideal of the primacy of the community over the individual. An excellent example is the film *Beyond the Plains* (where man is born) by Michael Raeburn, in which a young man from the Masai tribe in Tanzania was able to change his people's negative attitude towards education by not only doggedly pursuing it to the university level, but also never losing contact with his people. As he grew up he made sure he performed all the customary rites and fulfilled all the obligations demanded by his people, thus demonstrating that Western and tribal cultural education were not incompatible. From this, it can be seen that the major difference between the Third World and the West with regard to changing the community from a passive to a dynamic entity is one of approach. Whereas the former aims at changing the individual through the community, the latter wants the community changed by the individual. Only time will tell which of the two approaches makes for sustained, beneficial social progress.

Manipulation of Space and Time in Cinema

A child born in a Western society is encased, from the initial moments of birth, in purposive, man-made fabricated objects. The visual landscape he experiences is dominated by man-made forms. Even the child's dolls reflect the high technology of the environment. Nowadays, a child who is beginning to learn to spell can have a computer that can talk to him and interact with him in a human way. All of these developments are based on the insistence of a society that puts a high price on individualism, individual responsibility and achievement as most necessary.

Table 18.1 Comparison of folk and print art forms

Folk (or oral) art form	Print (or literate) art form
Conception of the value and evaluation of art	
Deeper meaning of art held by cultural groups or community. Interpretive device: one needs to belong and/or understand cultural or folk nuances.	Deeper meaning of art held as the sole property of the artist. Interpretive device: the artist proclaims 'it is for me to know and for you to find, or art is what you mean it to be.'
Recognizes general level of excellence, hence emphasis on group competence in the aesthetic judgment of art.	Recognizes exceptions, hence emphasis on individual achievement and individual responsibility.
Master artist concept – gifted but normal, and so conforms to the group.	Master artist concept – gifted but eccentric and essentially noncomformist.
Art as occasion for collective engagement.	Art as occasion for 'escape' from normal routine.
Emphasis on contextual relevance.	Emphasis on conceptual interpretation.
Art defined in terms of context.	Art defined in terms of aesthetic.
Performatory presentation	
Held in fluid boundaries, churchyards, fields, marketplaces – operating in a 360° dimension.	Boxed-in theatres and elevated to a stage – operating in a 180° dimension.
A scene flows into another. Cyclical progression linked thematically.	Each scene must follow another scene in linear progression.
Performatory effect	
Expects viewer participation, therefore arouses activity and prepares for and allows participation.	Discourages viewer participation. Puts an end to activity. Inhibits participation.
Multiple episodes that have their own centres.	Singular episode extended through detail.
Cognitive characteristics	
Man defined as 'unchangeable' alone. Change emanates from the community.	Man defined as 'man', changeable and, by virtue of his person, capable of effecting change and progress.
Individual interlinked with total social fabric. Concept of human rather than concept of 'man' as such.	Individual perceived primarily as separated from general social fabric.
Strong tradition of suggestion in the cultural symbol and in the use of linguistic formulae.	Strong tradition of detail and minute (graphic) description.

Time assumed to be a subjective phenomenon, i.e. it is the outcome of conceptualizing and experiencing movement.	Time assumed to be an 'objective' phenomenon, dominant and ubiquitous.
Wisdom is a state of intellectual maturity gained by experience. Cumulative process of knowledge, derived from the past. Characterized by slowness to judgement.	Wisdom is characterized by high degree of specialization in a particular field or discipline. Characterized by quickness of judgement based on a vast accumulation of data and information.
Earth is not a hostile world; e.g. the cult of the ancestors is an attempt at unification with the past, present and future.	Earth is a hostile world and has to be subdued. Paradise is in the future or elsewhere.

A child in a rural Third World setting is born in an unrestricted natural landscape. From the day he/she is born the child is dominated by untampered natural forms. Even the interior of the dwelling where the child is born is made to look like the natural environment: it is not unusual to see fresh grass and flowers lending nature's colour to the child's initial world setting. The child grows in this vast universe where his place within the family and in nature is emphasized. A child born and raised in this situation is taught to submerge his individuality and show responsibility to his extended family and his community. His accomplishments are measured not only by his individual achievements but by the degree to which they accomplish and contribute to the social good.

Culture, the terms on which films are based, also naturally grows from these environmental factors. An examination of oral and literate culture in terms of film brings to light two very crucial elements of cinema, namely the concepts of 'space' and 'time'. All cinema manipulates 'time' and 'space'. Where Western films manipulate 'time' more than 'space', Third World films seem to emphasize 'space' over 'time'. Third World films grow from folk tradition where communication is a slow-paced phenomenon and time is not rushed but has its own pace. Western culture, on the other hand, is based on the value of 'time' – time is art, time is money, time is most everything else. If time drags in a film, spectators grow bored and impatient, so that a method has to be found to cheat natural time. In film, this is achieved in the editing. It is all based on the idea that the more purely 'non-dramatic' elements in film are considered 'cinematic excess', i.e. they serve no unifying purpose. What is identified as 'excess' in Western cinematic experience is, therefore, precisely where we locate Third World cinema. Let me now identify those essential elements of cinematic practice that are considered cinematic excess in Western cinema but which in the Third World context seem only too natural.

The long take It is not uncommon in Third World films to see a concentration of long takes and repetition of images and scenes. In the Third World films, the slow, leisurely pacing approximates the viewer's sense of time and rhythm of life. In addition, the preponderance of wide-angle shots of longer duration deal with a viewer's sense of community and how people fit in nature. Whereas when Michelangelo Antonioni and Jean-Luc Godard use these types of shot it is to convey an existential separation and isolation from nature and self.

Cross-cutting Cross-cutting between antagonists shows simultaneity rather than the building of suspense. The power of images lies not in the expectation we develop about the mere juxtapositions or the collision itself, but rather in conveying the reasons for the imminent collision. Where, therefore, conventional cinema has too often reduced this to the collision of antagonists, on a scale of positive and negative characters, Third World films doing the same thing make it more explicitly an ideological collision.

The close-up shot A device so much in use in the study of individual psychology in Western filmmaking practice is less used in Third World films. Third World films serve more of an informational purpose than as a study in 'psychological realism'. The isolation of an individual, in tight close-up shots, seems unnatural to the Third World filmmaker because (1) it calls attention to itself; (2) it eliminates social considerations; and (3) it diminishes spatial integrity.

The panning shot Since a pan shot maintains integrity of space and time, the narrative value of such a shot renders the 'cut' or editing frequently unnecessary. The emphasis on space also conveys a different concept of 'time', a time which is not strictly linear or chronological but coexists with it. My own observation indicates that while Western films tend to pan right on a left–right axis. Middle Eastern films, for instance, tend to pan generally toward the left, as in *Alyam Alyam* (Morocco) and *Shadow of the Earth* (Tunisia). It is quite possible that the direction of panning toward left or right might be strongly influenced by the direction in which a person writes.

The concept of silence The rich potential for the creative interpretation of sound as well as the effective use of its absence is enormous in Third World films. For instance, in *Emitai* there are English subtitles for drum messages, and a rooster crows as Sembene's camera registers a low-angle shot of a poster of General de Gaulle. A neat visual pun! Silence serves as an important element of the audio track of the same film. It is 'a cinema of silence that speaks'. Silences have meaning only in context, as in the Ethiopian film *Gouma* and the Cuban film *The Last Supper*, where they contribute to the suspension of judgement which one experiences in watching a long take. Viewers wonder what will happen, accustomed as they are to the incessant sound and overload of music of dominant cinema.

Concept of 'hero' Even if a Western viewer cannot help but identify and sympathize with the black labour leader in *They Don't Wear Black Tie*, the lunatic in *Harvest: 3000 Years*, the crazy poet in *The Chronicle of the Years of Ember* and the militant party member in *Sambizanga*, the films nevertheless kill those characters. This is because wish-fulfilment through identification is not the films' primary objective; rather, it is the importance of collective engagement and action that matters. The individual 'hero' in the Third World context does not make history, he/she only serves historical necessities.

In summary, table 18.2 brings into sharper focus the differences between the film conventions of the Third World and the West and shows the dynamics of their cultural and ideological exchange.

Table 18.2 Comparison of filmic conventions (these are tendencies, not absolutes)

Western dominant conventions	Non-Western use of conventions
Lighting	
High contrast and low key, mostly Rembrandt lighting in drama while comedy uses low contrast and high-key lighting.	Lighting as a convention in Third World films is less developed, with the exception of Cuban films, whose use of lighting as a language is manifest in *Lucía* and *The Last Supper*.
Camera angle	
Mostly governed by eye-level perspective which approximates to our natural position in the world. Use of angle shots primarily for aesthetic look.	Deliberate choice of low/high-angle shots for purposes of political or social comment. Low/high-angle shots show dominance and power relations between the oppressed and oppressing classes.
Camera placement	
Distance varies according to the emotional content of the scene. Emotion, e.g. anger, is portrayed in close-up.	There is minimal use of the convention of close-up shots. This is perhaps due to lack of emphasis on psychological realism.
Camera movement	
Mostly a fixed perspective (tripod operation), promoting exposition and understanding. Often the camera moves to stay with the individual to study character development and psychological state.	Fixed perspective in African films. A moving perspective (hand-held camera) in Latin American films promotes experiential involvement and dramatic identification. If the camera moves it is to contain a scene or a sequence as a unit and not in response to individual psychology.
Set design	
A studio set. Tightens manipulatory controls, enhances fictional reality.	A location set. Location shooting relaxes manipulatory controls, and enhances documentary reality.
Acting	
A Hollywood convention, actor as icon.	Mostly non-actors acting out their real-life roles.
Parallel montage	
Shows the relations of conflicting characters/forces for dramatic and expository narrative purposes, i.e. suspense.	Cross-cutting serves an ideological purpose and denotes ironical contrast and class distinction. Consider the film *Mexico: The Frozen Revolution*.

Point of view

| Actors avoid looking directly at the camera. Actors are usually positioned or blocked so that their emotional state is easily observed by the camera. | It is not uncommon to see a look directed at the camera, hence a direct address to the audience. A shift to the conventions of oral narrative is evident. Consider the Algerian film *Omar Gatlato*. |

Note: The sum total of what is listed above as technique or elements of the filmmaking process is what expresses ideology. Films that hide the marks of production are associated with the ideology of presenting 'film as reality', the film that announces its message as an objective reflection of the way things are; whereas films which do exhibit the marks of production are associated with the ideology of presenting 'film as message'. Predominant aspect or point of view in Third World film is film announcing itself as a polemic comment on the way things are in their 'natural' reflection.

Films, therefore, in their point of view and stylistic choices, are structured to evoke a certain ideology in their production. A consequence of this, quite logically, is their different use of the conventions of time and space in cinema.

Conclusion

The spatial concentration and minimal use of the conventions of temporal manipulation in Third World film practice suggest that Third World cinema is initiating a coexistence of film art with oral traditions. Non-linearity, repetition of images and graphic representation have very much in common with folk customs. Time duration, though essential, is not the major issue because in the Third World context the need is for films, in context, to touch a sensitive cultural chord in a society. To achieve this, a general overhaul of the parameters of film form is required. Should the reorganization be successful and radical enough, a rethinking of the critical and theoretical canons of cinema would be called for, leading to a reconsideration of the conventions of cinematographic language and technique. The final result would tend towards a statement James Potts made in his article, 'Is there an international film language?':

> So, far from there being an international language of cinema, an internationally agreed UN charter of conventions and grammatical rules, we are liable to be presented, quite suddenly, with a new national school of filmmaking, which may be almost wholly untouched by European conventions and will require us to go back to square one in thinking about the principles and language of cinematography.[12]

Filmmakers in the Third World are beginning to produce films that try to restructure accepted filmic practices. There is now a distinct possibility of James Potts's perceptive remarks coming true, and it is in anticipation of the emergence of the 'new national school of filmmaking...untouched by European conventions' that this paper has been written.

Already, certain reactions from film critics may be regarded as a sign of this 'emergence'. For example, a general criticism levelled at Third World films is that they are too graphic. This spatial factor is part of a general rhythm of pictorial representation in most Third World societies. It is, therefore, precisely because graphic art creates symbols in space that it enables Third World viewers to relate more easily to their films. In the Chinese case, for example:

> The spiritual quality achieved in the supreme Chinese landscape and nature paintings is a feeling of harmony with the universe in which the inner psychic geography of the artist and the outer visual reality transcribed are fused through brush strokes into a new totality that . . . resonates with the viewer.[13]

Both the Chinese contemporary photographers and cinematographers have attempted to create similar syntax and effects to enhance the people's appreciation of their art.

Again, the most inaccessible Phase III film, the one African film that drops a curtain in front of a Western audience, and at the same time a most popular and influential film in Africa, is *Emitai* ('The Angry God'). Shot in social space by the Senegalese filmmaker Sembene, the film explores the spiritual and physical tension in a rural community. To begin with the film carries its viewers into the story without any credits, only for the entire credit to be provided some 25 minutes later. Spectators have been known to leave the screening room at this point, conditioned to read the credits as signalling the end of the film. What Sembene has provided before the credits is essentially the preface of the story like an African folktale. In addition, the ending of the film an hour and a half later is anticlimactic and this occurs at the moment the film is truly engaging – the film simply stops – what we hear is the staccato of bullet sounds against a screen gone dark. In this film the filmmaker is forcing us to forget our viewing habits and attend to the film in context instead of the experienced, framed as artistic package. A lesson is thus learned; concern should be with the language of the 'film text' in its own terms and not with the skeletal structure and chronology of the film.

Cinema, since its creation, has beguiled spectators by its manipulation of time – it expands, contracts, is lost and found, fragmented and reassembled. The resultant multiple time-perspectives have conditioned film appreciation as pure entertainment. There is perhaps some justification for this objective in a society whose stabilizing conditions can afford the use of the film medium solely for entertainment. The Third World, on the other hand, is still engaged in a desperate struggle for socio-political and economic independence and development and cannot afford to dissipate its meagre resources and/or laugh at its present political and historical situation.

The Combative Phase, in which the historical determinants of Third World culture occur, provides us with the final horizon of a cinema oriented toward a peaceful coexistence with folk-culture. That oral tradition reasserts itself in a new medium is a contribution not only to Third World societies but to the cinematic world at large.

Film is a new language to the Third World and its grammar is only recently being charted. Its direction, however, seems to be a discursive use of the medium and an appeal for intellectual appreciation. Tomás Gutiérrez Alea perhaps best exemplifies the new awareness when he says:

> If we want film to serve something higher, if we want it to fulfil its function more perfectly (aesthetic, social, ethical, and revolutionary), we ought to guarantee that it constitutes a *factor in spectators' development*. Film will be more fruitful to the degree that it pushes spectators toward a more profound understanding of reality and, consequently, to the degree that it helps viewers live more actively and incites them to stop being mere spectators in the face of reality. To do this, film ought to appeal not only to emotion and feeling but also to reason and intellect. In this case, both instances ought to exist indissolvably (*sic*) united, in such a way that they come to provoke, as Pascal said, authentic 'shudderings and tremblings of the mind'.[14]

Notes

1   F. Fanon, *The Wretched of the Earth*, New York, Grove Press, 1963, pp. 207–48. See also A. Cabral, *Return to the Source*, New York, African Information Service, 1973, pp. 42–69.

2   J. DeOnis, ' "Pixote" role proves all too real', *Los Angeles Times*, 5 June 1984.

3   J. Espinosa, 'For an imperfect cinema', in M. Chanan (ed.), *Twenty-five Years of the New Latin American Cinema*, London, BFI/Channel 4 Television, 1983, pp. 28–33.

4   R. Gerber, *Glauber Rocha, Cinema, Politica e a Esthetica do Inconsciente*, Brasil, Editore Vozes, 1982, p. 34 and *passim*.

5   G. Rocha, *Revolucão do Cinema Nôvo*, Rio de Janeiro, Alhambra/Embrafilme, 1981, p. 467.

6   From a film catalogue entitled *Films about Africa available in the Midwest*, Madison, African Studies Program, University of Wisconsin, 1974, p. 37.

7   *Africa on Film and Videotape, 1960–81: A Compendium of Reviews*, East Lansing, Michigan, African Studies Center, Michigan State University, 1982, p. 219.

8   It must be freely acknowledged that the future of art criticism and appreciation no doubt lies in the domain of semiotic inquiry. Presently, while its greater virtue lies in the attention it gives to the role of the reader, its greatest weakness is its cultural fixation with Western thought. Third World aesthetics and cultures have been ignored, making it impossible for it to occupy its premier place in a unified human science. Since the works of Lévi-Strauss and various essays and a book by Roland Barthes nothing of substance regarding semiotic inquiry into cultural studies has been offered. For a general reading on the topic, see Edith Kurzweil, *The Age of Structuralism: Lévi-Strauss to Foucault*, New York, Columbia University Press, 1980, and R. Barthes, *Mythologies*, translated by Annette Lavers, New York, Hill and Wang, 1970. For the various contending factions in the semiotic camp – structuralists, deconstructionists, reader-response critics, theories of intertextuality and narratology – the following books will serve as introductions: R. Scholes, *Semiotics and Interpretation*, New Haven, CN, Yale University Press, 1982, and J. Culler, *The Pursuit of Signs*, Ithaca, NY, Cornell University Press, 1983.

9   Recently Western filmmakers, in a bid to revitalize their film world, have made 'realistic' forays into Third World themes: *Gandhi* on India's struggle for

independence, *The Year of Living Dangerously* on Sukarno's fall from power, *Under Fire* on the Sandinista revolution in Nicaragua, and *Circle of Deceit* on the Lebanese civil war. The statement by one of the characters in *Circle of Deceit* – 'We are defending Western civilization' – is an ironic but true epigram for all the films. Far from being radical or new, therefore, these productions give us no more than Hollywood's version of the Third World. For an illuminating discussion on this recent fascination with 'the other', see John Powers, 'Saints and Savages', *American Film*, January–February 1984, pp. 38–43.

10 Various sources were consulted, including but not limited to H. Arvon's *Marxist Esthetics*, Ithaca, Cornell University Press, 1973, p. 71 and *passim*, and K. Gotrick, *Apidan Theatre and Modern Drama*, Gothenburg, Graphic Systems AB, 1984, pp. 140–63. For an elaboration of culture in the context of Third World films, see my book *Third Cinema in the Third World: The Aesthetics of Liberation*, Ann Arbor, Michigan, UMI Research Press, 1982.

11 J.K. Nyerere, *Ujamaa: Essays on Socialism*, London, Oxford University Press, 1968, pp. 91–105.

12 J. Potts, 'Is there an international film language?', *Sight and Sound*, vol. 48, no. 2, Spring 1979, pp. 74–81.

13 A. Goldsmith, 'Picture from China: the style and scope of photography are changing as outside influences mix with traditional values', *Popular Photography*, February 1984, pp. 45–50, 146 and 156.

14 T.G. Alea, *Dialéctica del Espectador*, Ciudad de la Habana, Sobre la presente edición, 1982, p. 21. The first part of the book has been translated by Julia Lesage and appears under the title 'The viewer's dialectic' in *Jump Cut* 29, February 1984, pp. 18–21, from which this quotation is taken.

19
Rethinking Women's Cinema: Aesthetics and Feminist Theory

Teresa de Lauretis

When Silvia Bovenschen in 1976 posed the question "Is there a feminine aesthetic?" the only answer she could give was, yes and no: "Certainly there is, if one is talking about aesthetic awareness and modes of sensory perception. Certainly not, if one is talking about an unusual variant of artistic production or about a painstakingly constructed theory of art."[1] If this contradiction seems familiar to anyone even vaguely acquainted with the development of feminist thought over the past fifteen years, it is because it echoes a contradiction specific to, and perhaps even constitutive of, the women's movement itself: a twofold pressure, a simultaneous pull in opposite directions, a tension toward the positivity of politics, or affirmative action in behalf of women as social subjects, on one front, and the negativity inherent in the radical critique of patriarchal, bourgeois culture, on the other. It is also the contradiction of women in language, as we attempt to speak as subjects of discourses which negate or objectify us through their representations. As Bovenschen put it, "We are in a terrible bind. How do we speak? In what categories do we think? Is even logic a bit of virile trickery?...Are our desires and notions of happiness so far removed from cultural traditions and models?" (p. 119).

Not surprisingly, therefore, a similar contradiction was also central to the debate on women's cinema, its politics and its language, as it was articulated within Anglo-American film theory in the early 1970s in relation to feminist politics and the women's movement, on the one hand, and to artistic avant-garde practices and women's filmmaking, on the other. There, too, the accounts of feminist film culture produced in the mid- to late 1970s tended to emphasize a dichotomy between two concerns of the women's movement and two types of film work that seemed to be at odds with each other: one called for immediate documentation for purposes of political activism, consciousness-raising, self-expression, or the search for "positive images" of woman; the other insisted on rigorous, formal work on the medium – or, better, the cinematic apparatus, understood as a social technology – in order to analyze and disengage the ideological codes embedded in representation.

Thus, as Bovenschen deplores the "opposition between feminist demands and artistic production" (p. 131), the tug of war in which women artists were caught between the movement's demands that women's art portray women's activities, document demonstrations, etc., and the formal demands of "artistic activity and its concrete work with material and media"; so does Laura Mulvey set out two successive moments of feminist film culture. First, she states, there was a period marked by the effort to change the *content* of cinematic representation (to present realistic images of women, to record women talking about their real-life experiences), a period "characterized by a mixture of consciousness-raising and propaganda."[2] It was followed by a second moment, in which the concern with the language of representation as such became predominant, and the "fascination with the cinematic process" led filmmakers and critics to the "use of and interest in the aesthetic principles and terms of reference provided by the avant-garde tradition" (p. 7).

In this latter period, the common interest of both avant-garde cinema and feminism in the politics of images, or the political dimension of aesthetic expression, made them turn to the theoretical debates on language and imaging that were going on outside of cinema, in semiotics, psychoanalysis, critical theory, and the theory of ideology. Thus, it was argued that, in order to counter the aesthetic of realism, which was hopelessly compromised with bourgeois ideology, as well as Hollywood cinema, avant-garde and feminist filmmakers must take an oppositional stance against narrative "illusionism" and in favor of formalism. The assumption was that "foregrounding the process itself, privileging the signifier, necessarily disrupts aesthetic unity and forces the spectator's attention on the means of production of meaning" (p. 7).

While Bovenschen and Mulvey would not relinquish the political commitment of the movement and the need to construct other representations of woman, the way in which they posed the question of expression (a "feminine aesthetic," a "new language of desire") was couched in the terms of a traditional notion of art, specifically the one propounded by modernist aesthetics. Bovenschen's insight that what is being expressed in the decoration of the household and the body, or in letters and other private forms of writing, is in fact women's aesthetic needs and impulses, is a crucial one. But the importance of that insight is undercut by the very terms that define it: the "*pre*-aesthetic realms." After quoting a passage from Sylvia Plath's *The Bell Jar*, Bovenschen comments:

> Here the ambivalence one again: on the one hand we see aesthetic activity deformed, atrophied, but on the other we find, even within this restricted scope, socially creative impulses which, however, have no outlet for aesthetic development, no opportunities for growth.... [These activities] remained bound to everyday life, feeble attempts to make this sphere more aesthetically pleasing. But the price for this was narrowmindedness. The object could never leave the realm in which it came into being, it remained tied to the household, it could never break loose and initiate communication. (pp. 132–3)

Just as Plath laments that Mrs Willard's beautiful home-braided rug is not hung on the wall but put to the use for which it was made, and thus quickly spoiled of its beauty, so would Bovenschen have "the object" of artistic creation leave its context of production and use value in order to enter the "artistic realm" and so to "initiate communication"; that is to say, to enter the museum, the art gallery, the market. In other words, art is what is enjoyed publicly rather than privately, has an exchange value rather than a use value, and that value is conferred by socially established aesthetic canons.

Mulvey, too, in proposing the destruction of narrative and visual pleasure as the foremost objective of women's cinema, hails an established tradition, albeit a radical one: the historic left avant-garde tradition that goes back to Eisenstein and Vertov (if not Méliès) and through Brecht reaches its peak of influence in Godard, and on the other side of the Atlantic, the tradition of American avant-garde cinema.

> The first blow against the monolithic accumulation of traditional film conventions (already undertaken by radical filmmakers) is to free the look of the camera into its materiality in time and space and the look of the audience into dialectics, passionate detachment.[3]

But much as Mulvey and other avant-garde filmmakers insisted that women's cinema ought to avoid a politics of emotions and seek to problematize the female spectator's identification with the on-screen image of woman, the response to her theoretical writings, like the reception of her films (co-directed with Peter Wollen), showed no consensus. Feminist critics, spectators, and filmmakers remained doubtful. For example, B. Ruby Rich:

> According to Mulvey, the woman is not visible in the audience which is perceived as male; according to Johnston, the woman is not visible on the screen.... How does one formulate an understanding of a structure that insists on our absence even in the face of our presence? What is there in a film with which a woman viewer identifies? How can the contradictions be used as a critique? And how do all these factors influence what one makes as a woman filmmaker, or specifically as a feminist filmmaker?[4]

The questions of identification, self-definition, the modes or the very possibility of envisaging oneself as subject – which the male avant-garde artists and theorists have also been asking, on their part, for almost one hundred years, even as they work to subvert the dominant representations or to challenge their hegemony – are fundamental questions for feminism. If identification is "not simply one psychical mechanism among others, but the operation itself whereby the human subject is constituted," as Laplanche and Pontalis describe it, then it must be all the more important, theoretically and politically, for women who have never before represented ourselves as subjects, and whose images and subjectivities –

until very recently, if at all – have not been ours to shape, to portray, or to create.[5]

There is indeed reason to question the theoretical paradigm of a subject–object dialectic, whether Hegelian or Lacanian, that subtends both the aesthetic and the scientific discourses of Western culture; for what that paradigm contains, what those discourses rest on, is the unacknowledged assumption of sexual difference: that the human subject, Man, is the male. As in the originary distinction of classical myth reaching us through the Platonic tradition, human creation and all that is human – mind, spirit, history, language, art, or symbolic capacity – is defined in contradistinction to formless chaos, *phusis* or nature, to something that is female, matrix and matter; and on this primary binary opposition, all the others are modeled. As Lea Melandri states,

> Idealism, the oppositions of mind to body, of rationality to matter, originate in a twofold concealment: of the woman's body and of labor power. Chronologically, however, even prior to the commodity and the labor power that has produced it, the matter which was negated in its concreteness and particularity, in its "relative plural form," is the woman's body. Woman enters history having already lost concreteness and singularity: she is the economic machine that reproduces the human species, and she is the Mother, an equivalent more universal than money, the most abstract measure ever invented by patriarchal ideology.[6]

That this proposition remains true when tested on the aesthetic of modernism or the major trends in avant-garde cinema from visionary to structural-materialist film, on the films of Stan Brakhage, Michael Snow, or Jean-Luc Godard, but is not true of the films of Yvonne Rainer, Valie Export, Chantal Akerman, or Marguerite Duras, for example; that it remains valid for the films of Fassbinder but not those of Ottinger, the films of Pasolini and Bertolucci but not Cavani's, and so on, suggests to me that it is perhaps time to shift the terms of the question altogether.

To ask of these women's films: What formal, stylistic, or thematic markers point to a female presence behind the camera? and hence to generalize and universalize, to say: This is the look and sound of women's cinema, this is its language – finally only means complying, accepting a certain definition of art, cinema, and culture, and obligingly showing how women can and do "contribute," pay their tribute, to "society." Put another way, to ask whether there is a feminine or female aesthetic, or a specific language of women's cinema, is to remain caught in the master's house and there, as Audre Lorde's suggestive metaphor warns us, to legitimate the hidden agendas of a culture we badly need to change. Cosmetic changes, she is telling us, won't be enough for the majority of women – women of color, black women, and white women as well; or, in her own words, "assimilation within a solely western-european herstory is not acceptable."[7]

It is time we listened. Which is not to say that we should dispense with rigorous analysis and experimentation on the formal processes of meaning production, including the production of narrative, visual pleasure, and subject positions, but rather that feminist theory should now engage precisely in the redefinition of aesthetic and formal knowledges, much as women's cinema has been engaged in the transformation of vision.

Take Akerman's *Jeanne Dielman* (1975), a film about the routine daily activities of a Belgian middle-class and middle-aged housewife, and a film where the pre-aesthetic is already fully aesthetic. That is not so, however, because of the beauty of its images, the balanced composition of its frames, the absence of the reverse shot, or the perfectly calculated editing of its still-camera shots into a continuous, logical, and obsessive narrative space; it is so because it is a woman's actions, gestures, body, and look that define the space of our vision, the temporality and rhythms of perception, the horizon of meaning available to the spectator. So that narrative suspense is not built on the expectation of a "significant event," a socially momentous act (which actually occurs, though unexpectedly and almost incidentally, one feels, toward the end of the film), but is produced by the tiny slips in Jeanne's routine, the small forgettings, the hesitations between real-time gestures as common and "insignificant" as peeling potatoes, washing dishes, or making coffee – and then not drinking it. What the film constructs – formally and artfully, to be sure – is a picture of female experience, of duration, perception, events, relationships, and silences, which feels immediately and unquestionably true. And in this sense the "pre-aesthetic" is *aesthetic* rather than *aestheticized*, as it is in films such as Godard's *Two or Three Things I Know about Her*, Polanski's *Repulsion*, or Antonioni's *Eclipse*. To say the same thing in another way, Akerman's film addresses the spectator as female.

The effort, on the part of the filmmaker, to render a presence in the feeling of a gesture, to convey the sense of an experience that is subjective yet socially coded (and therefore recognizable), and to do so formally, working through her conceptual (one could say, theoretical) knowledge of film form, is averred by Chantal Akerman in an interview on the making of *Jeanne Dielman*:

> I do think it's a feminist film because I give space to things which were never, almost never, shown in that way, like the daily gestures of a woman. They are the lowest in the hierarchy of film images. . . . But more than the content, it's because of the style. If you choose to show a woman's gestures so precisely, it's because you love them. In some way you recognize those gestures that have always been denied and ignored. I think that the real problem with women's films usually has nothing to do with the content. It's that hardly any women really have confidence enough to carry through on their feelings. Instead the content is the most simple and obvious thing. They deal with that and forget to look for formal ways to express what they are and what they want, their own rhythms, their own way of looking at things. A lot of women have unconscious contempt for their feelings. But I don't think I do. I have enough confidence in myself. So that's the other reason why I think it's a feminist film – not just what it says but *what* is shown and *how* it's shown.[8]

This lucid statement of poetics resonates with my own response as a viewer and gives me something of an explanation as to why I recognize in those unusual film images, in those movements, those silences, and those looks, the ways of an experience all but unrepresented, previously unseen in film, though lucidly and unmistakably apprehended here. And so the statement cannot be dismissed with commonplaces such as authorial intention or intentional fallacy. As another critic and spectator points out, there are "two logics" at work in this film, "two modes of the feminine": character and director, image and camera, remain distinct yet interacting and mutually interdependent positions. Call them feminity and feminism; the one is made representable by the critical work of the other; the one is kept at a distance, constructed, "framed," to be sure, and yet "respected," "loved," "given space" by the other.[9] The two "logics" remain separate:

> The camera look can't be construed as the view of any character. Its interest extends beyond the fiction. The camera presents itself, in its evenness and predictability, as equal to Jeanne's precision. Yet the camera continues its logic throughout; Jeanne's order is disrupted, and with the murder the text comes to its logical end since Jeanne then stops altogether. If Jeanne has, symbolically, destroyed the phallus, its order still remains visible all around her.[10]

Finally, then, the space constructed by the film is not only a textual or filmic space of vision, in frame and off – for an off-screen space is still inscribed in the images, although not sutured narratively by the reverse shot but effectively reaching toward the historical and social determinants which define Jeanne's life and place her in her frame. But beyond that, the film's space is also a critical space of analysis, a horizon of possible meanings which includes or extends to the spectator ("extends beyond the fiction") insofar as the spectator is led to occupy at once the two positions, to follow the two "logics," and to perceive them as equally and concurrently true.

In saying that a film whose visual and symbolic space is organized in this manner *addresses its spectator as a woman*, regardless of the gender of the viewers, I mean that the film defines all points of identification (with character, image, camera) as female, feminine, or feminist. However, this is not as simple or self-evident a notion as the established film-theoretical view of cinematic identification, namely, that identification with the look is masculine, and identification with the images is feminine. It is not self-evident precisely because such a view – which indeed correctly explains the working of dominant cinema – is now accepted: that the camera (technology), the look (voyeurism), and the scopic drive itself partake of the phallic and thus somehow are entities or figures of a masculine nature.

How difficult it is to "prove" that a film addresses its spectator as female is brought home time and again in conversations or discussions between audiences and filmmakers. After a screening of *Redupers* in Milwaukee (in January 1985), Helke Sander answered a question about the function of the Berlin wall in her film and concluded by saying, if I may paraphrase: "but of course the wall also represents another division that is specific to women." She did not elaborate, but again, I felt that what she meant was clear and unmistakable. And so does at least one other critic and spectator, Kaja Silverman, who sees the wall as a division other in kind from what the wall would divide – and can't, for things do "flow through the Berlin wall (TV and radio waves, germs, the writings of Christa Wolf)," and Edda's photographs show the two Berlins in "their quotidian similarities rather than their ideological divergences."

> All three projects are motivated by the desire to tear down the wall, or at least to prevent it from functioning as the dividing line between two irreducible opposites. . . . *Redupers* makes the wall a signifier for psychic as well as ideological, political, and geographical boundaries. It functions there as a metaphor for sexual difference, for the subjective limits articulated by the existing symbolic order both in East and West. The wall thus designates the discursive boundaries which separate residents not only of the same country and language, but of the same partitioned space.[11]

Those of us who share Silverman's perception must wonder whether in fact the sense of that other, specific division represented by the wall in *Redupers* (sexual difference, a discursive boundary, a subjective limit) is in the film or in our viewers' eyes. Is it actually there on screen, in the film, inscribed in its slow montage of long takes and in the stillness of the images in their silent frames; or is it, rather, in our perception, our insight, as – precisely – a subjective limit and discursive boundary (gender), a horizon of meaning (feminism) which is projected into the images, onto the screen, around the text?

I think it is this other kind of division that is acknowledged in Christa Wolf's figure of "the divided heaven," for example, or in Virginia Woolf's "room of one's own": the feeling of an internal distance, a contradiction, a space of silence, which is there alongside the imaginary pull of cultural and ideological representations without denying or obliterating them. Women artists, filmmakers, and writers acknowledge this division or difference by attempting to express it in their works. Spectators and readers think we find it in those texts. Nevertheless, even today, most of us would still agree with Silvia Bovenschen.

"For the time being," writes Gertrud Koch, "the issue remains whether films by women actually succeed in subverting this basic model of the camera's construction of the gaze, whether the female look through the camera at the world, at men, women, and objects will be an essentially different one."[12] Posed in these terms, however, the issue will remain fundamentally a rhetorical question. I have suggested that the emphasis must be shifted away from the artist behind the camera, the gaze, or the text as origin and determination of meaning, toward the wider public sphere of cinema as a social technology: we must develop our understanding of cinema's implication in other modes of cultural representation, and its possibilities of both production and counterproduction of social vision. I further suggest that, even as filmmakers are confronting the problems of transforming vision by engaging all of the codes of cinema, specific and non-specific, against the dominance of that "basic model," our task as theorists is to articulate the conditions and forms of vision for another social subject, and so to venture into the highly risky business of redefining aesthetic and formal knowledge.

Such a project evidently entails reconsidering and reassessing the early feminist formulations or, as Sheila Rowbotham summed it up, "look[ing] back at ourselves through our own cultural creations, our actions, our ideas, our pamphlets, our organization, our history, our theory."[13] And if we now can add "our films," perhaps the time has come to rethink women's cinema as the production of a feminist social vision. As a form of political critique or critical politics, and through the specific consciousness that women have developed to analyze the subject's relation to sociohistorical reality, feminism not only has invented new strategies or created new texts, but, more important, it has conceived a new social subject, women: as speakers, writers, readers, spectators, users, and makers of cultural forms, shapers of cultural processes. The project of women's cinema, therefore, is no longer that of destroying or disrupting man-centered vision by representing its blind spots, its gaps, or its repressed. The effort and challenge now are how to effect another vision: to construct other objects and subjects of vision, and to formulate the conditions of representability of another social subject. For the time being, then, feminist work in film seems necessarily focused on those subjective limits and discursive boundaries that mark women's division as gender-specific, a division more elusive, complex, and contradictory than can be conveyed in the notion of sexual difference as it is currently used.

The idea that *a film may address the spectator as female*, rather than portray women positively or negatively, seems very important to me in the critical endeavor to characterize women's cinema as a cinema for, not only by, women. It is an idea not found in the critical writings I mentioned earlier, which are focused on the film, the object, the text. But rereading those essays today, one can see, and it is important to stress it, that the question of a filmic language or a feminine aesthetic has been articulated from the beginning in relation to the women's movement: "the new grows only out of the work of confrontation" (Mulvey, p. 4); women's "imagination constitutes the movement itself" (Bovenschen, p. 136); and in Claire Johnston's non-formalist view of women's cinema as counter-cinema, a feminist political strategy should reclaim, rather than shun, the use of film as a form of mass culture: "In order to counter our objectification in the cinema, our collective fantasies must be released: women's cinema must embody the working through of desire: such an objective demands the use of the entertainment film."[14]

Since the first women's film festivals in 1972 (New York, Edinburgh) and the first journal of feminist film criticism (*Women and Film*, published in Berkeley from 1972 to 1975), the question of women's expression has been one of both self-expression and communication with other women, a question at once of the creation/invention of new images and of the creation/imaging of new forms of community. If we rethink the problem of a specificity of women's cinema and aesthetic forms in this manner, in terms of address – who is making films for whom, who is looking and speaking, how, where, and to whom – then what has been seen as a rift, a division, an ideological split within feminist film culture between theory and practice, or between formalism and activism, may appear to be the very strength, the drive, and productive heterogeneity of feminism. In their introduction to the recent collection *Re-vision: Essays in Feminist Film Criticism*, Mary Ann Doane, Patricia Mellencamp, and Linda Williams point out:

> If feminist work on film has grown increasingly theoretical, less oriented towards political action, this does not necessarily mean that theory itself is counter-produc-tive to the cause of feminism, nor that the institutional form of the debates within feminism have simply reproduced a male model of academic competition.... Fem-inists sharing similar concerns collaborate in joint authorship and editorships, cooperative filmmaking and distribution arrangements. Thus, many of the political aspirations of the women's movement form an integral part of the very structure of feminist work in and on film.[15]

The "re-vision" of their title, borrowed from Adrienne Rich ("Re-vision – the act of looking back, of seeing with fresh eyes," writes Rich, is for women "an act of survival"), refers to the project of reclaiming vision, of "seeing difference differ-ently," of displacing the critical emphasis from "images of" women "to the axis of vision itself – to the modes of organizing vision and hearing which result in the production of that 'image'."[16]

I agree with the *Re-vision* editors when they say that over the past decade, feminist theory has moved "from an analysis of difference as oppressive to a delineation and specification of difference as liberating, as offering the only possibility of radical change" (p. 12). But I believe that radical change requires that such specification not be limited to "sexual difference," that is to say, a difference of women from men, female from male, or Woman from Man. Radical change requires a delineation and a better understanding of the difference of women from Woman, and that is to say as well, *the differences among women*. For there are, after all, different histories of women. There are women who masquer-ade and women who wear the veil; women invisible to men, in their society, but also women who are invisible to other women, in our society.[17]

The invisibility of black women in white women's films, for instance, or of lesbianism in mainstream feminist criticism, is what Lizzie Borden's *Born in Flames* (1983) most forcefully represents, while at the same time constructing the terms of their visibility as subjects and objects of vision. Set in a hypothetical near-future time and in a place very much like lower Manhattan, with the look of a documentary (after Chris Marker) and the feel of contemporary science-fiction writing (the post-new-wave s-f of Samuel Delany, Joanna Russ, Alice Sheldon, or Thomas Disch), *Born in Flames* shows how a "successful" social democratic cultural revolution, now into its tenth year, slowly but surely reverts to the old patterns of male dominance, politics as usual, and the traditional Left disregard for "women's issues." It is around this specific gender oppression, in its various forms, that several groups of women (black women, Latinas, lesbians, single mothers, intellectuals, political activists, spiritual and punk performers, and a Women's Army) succeed in mobilizing and joining together not by ignoring but, paradoxically, by acknowledging their differences.

Like *Redupers* and *Jeanne Dielman*, Borden's film addresses the spectator as female, but it does not do so by portraying an experience which feels immediately one's own. On the contrary, its barely coherent narrative, its quick-paced shots and sound montage, the counterpoint of image and word, the diversity of voices and languages, and the self-conscious science-fictional frame of the story hold the spectator across a distance, projecting toward her its fiction like a bridge of difference. In short, what *Born in Flames* does for me, woman spectator, is exactly to allow me "to see difference differently," to look at women with eyes I've never had before and yet my own; for, as it remarks the emphasis (the words are Audre Lorde's) on the "interdependency of different strengths" in feminism, the film also inscribes the differences among women as *differences within women*.

Born in Flames addresses me as a woman and a feminist living in a particular moment of women's history, the United States today. The film's events and images take place in what science fiction calls a parallel universe, a time and a place elsewhere that look and feel like here and now, yet are not, just as I (and all women) live in a culture that is and is not our own. In that unlikely, but not impossible, universe of the film's fiction, the women come together in the very struggle that divides and differentiates them. Thus, what it portrays for me, what elicits my identification with the film and gives me, spectator, a place in it, is the contradiction of my own history and the personal/political difference that is also within myself.

"The relationship between history and so-called subjective processes," says Helen Fehervary in a recent discussion of women's film in Germany, "is not a matter of grasping the truth in history as some objective entity, but in finding the truth of the experience. Evidently, this kind of experiential immediacy has to do with women's own history and self-consciousness."[18] That, how, and why our histories and our consciousness are different, divided, even conflicting, is what women's cinema can analyze, articulate, reformulate. And, in so doing, it can help us create something else to be, as Toni Morrison says of her two heroines:

> Because each had discovered years before that they were neither white nor male, and that all freedom and triumph was forbidden to them, they had set about creating something else to be.[19]

In the following pages I will refer often to *Born in Flames*, discussing some of the issues it has raised, but it will not be with the aim of a textual analysis.

Rather, I will take it as the starting point, as indeed it was for me, of a series of reflections on the topic of this essay.

Again it is a film, and a filmmaker's project, that bring home to me with greater clarity the question of difference, this time in relation to factors other than gender, notably race and class – a question endlessly debated within Marxist feminism and recently rearticulated by women of color in feminist presses and publications. That this question should reemerge urgently and irrevocably now is not surprising, at a time when severe social regression and economic pressures (the so-called "feminization of poverty") belie the self-complacency of a liberal feminism enjoying its modest allotment of institutional legitimation. A sign of the times, the recent crop of commercial, man-made "woman's films" (*Lianna*, *Personal Best*, *Silkwood*, *Frances*, *Places in the Heart*, etc.) is undoubtedly "authorized," and made financially viable, by that legitimation. But the success, however modest, of this liberal feminism has been bought at the price of reducing the contradictory complexity – and the theoretical productivity – of concepts such as sexual difference, "the personal is political," and feminism itself to simpler and more acceptable ideas already existing in the dominant culture. Thus, to many today, "sexual difference" is hardly more than sex (biology) or gender (in the simplest sense of female socialization) or the basis for certain private "life styles" (homosexual and other non-orthodox relationships); "the personal is political" all too often translates into "the personal instead of the political"; and "feminism" is unhesitantly appropriated, by the academy as well as the media, as a discourse – a variety of social criticism, a method of aesthetic or literary analysis among others, and more or less worth attention according to the degree of its market appeal to students, readers, or viewers. And, yes, a discourse perfectly accessible to all men of good will. In this context, issues of race or class must continue to be thought of as mainly sociological or economic, and hence parallel to but not dependent on gender, implicated with but not determining of subjectivity, and of little relevance to this "feminist discourse" which, as such, would have no competence in the matter but only, and at best, a humane or "progressive" concern with the disadvantaged.

The relevance of feminism (without quotation marks) to race and class, however, is very explicitly stated by those women of color, black, and white who are not the recipients but rather the "targets" of equal opportunity, who are outside or not fooled by liberal "feminism," or who understand that feminism is nothing if it is not at once political and personal, with all the contradictions and difficulties that entails. To such feminists it is clear that the social construction of gender, subjectivity, and the relations of representation to experience do occur within race and class as much as they occur in language and culture, often indeed across languages, cultures, and sociocultural apparati. Thus, not only is it the case that the notion of gender, or "sexual difference," cannot be simply accommodated into the preexisting, ungendered (or male-gendered) categories by which the official discourses on race and class have been elaborated; but it is equally the case that the issues of race and class cannot be simply subsumed under some larger category labeled femaleness, femininity, womanhood, or, in the final instance, Woman. What is becoming more and more clear, instead, is that all the categories of our social science stand to be reformulated *starting from* the notion of gendered social subjects. And something of this process of reformulation – re-vision, rewriting, rereading, rethinking, "looking back at *ourselves*" – is what I see inscribed in the texts of women's cinema but not yet sufficiently focused on in feminist film theory or feminist critical practice in general. This point, like the relation of feminist writing to the women's movement, demands a much lengthier discussion than can be undertaken here. I can do no more than sketch the problem as it strikes me with unusual intensity in the reception of Lizzie Borden's film and my own response to it.

What *Born in Flames* succeeds in representing is this feminist understanding: that the female subject is en-gendered, constructed and defined in gender across multiple representations of class, race, language, and social relations; and that, therefore, differences among women are differences *within* women, which is why feminism can exist despite those differences and, as we are just beginning to understand, cannot continue to exist without them. The originality of this film's project is its representation of woman as a social subject and a site of differences; differences which are not purely sexual or merely racial, economic, or (sub)cultural, but all of these together and often enough in conflict with one another. What one takes away after seeing this film is the image of a heterogeneity in the female social subject, the sense of a distance from dominant cultural models and of an internal division within women that remain, not in spite of but concurrently with the provisional unity of any concerted political action. Just as the film's narrative remains unresolved, fragmented, and difficult to follow, heterogeneity and difference within women remain in our memory as the film's narrative image, its work of representing, which cannot be collapsed into a fixed identity, a sameness of all women as Woman, or a representation of Feminism as a coherent and available image.

Other films, in addition to the ones already mentioned, have effectively represented that internal division or distance from language, culture, and self that I see recur, figuratively and thematically, in recent women's cinema (it is also represented, for example, in Gabriella Rosaleva's *Processo a Caterina Ross* and in Lynne Tillman and Sheila McLaughlin's *Committed*). But *Born in Flames* projects that division on a larger social and cultural scale, taking up nearly all of the issues and putting them all at stake. As we read on the side of the (stolen) U-Haul trucks which carry the free women's new mobile radio transmitter, reborn as Phoenix-Regazza (girl phoenix) from the flames that destroyed the two separate stations, the film is "an adventure in moving." As one reviewer saw it,

An action pic, a sci-fi fantasy, a political thriller, a collage film, a snatch of the underground: *Born in Flames* is all and none of these. . . . Edited in 15-second bursts and spiked with yards of flickering video transfers . . . *Born in Flames* stands head and shoulders above such Hollywood reflections on the media as *Absence of Malice*, *Network*, or *Under Fire*. This is less a matter of its substance (the plot centers on the suspicious prison "suicide," à la Ulrike Meinhoff, of Women's Army leader Adelaide Norris) than of its form, seizing on a dozen facets of our daily media surroundings.[20]

The words of the last sentence, echoing Akerman's emphasis on form rather than content, are in turn echoed by Borden in several printed statements. She, too, is keenly concerned with her own relation as filmmaker to filmic representation ("Two things I was committed to with the film were questioning the nature of narrative . . . and creating a process whereby I could release myself from my own bondage in terms of class and race").[21] And she, too, like Akerman, is confident that vision can be transformed because hers has been: "Whatever discomfort I might have felt as a white filmmaker working with black women has been over for so long. It was exorcized by the process of making the film." Thus, in response to the interviewer's (Anne Friedberg) suggestion that the film is "progressive" precisely because it "demands a certain discomfort for the audience, and forces the viewer to confront his or her own political position(s) (or lack of political position)," Borden flatly rejects the interviewer's implicit assumption.

> I don't think the audience is solely a white middle-class audience. What was important for me was creating a film in which that was *not* the only audience. The problem with much of the critical material on the film is that it assumes a white middle-class reading public for articles written about a film that they assume has only a white middle-class audience. I'm very confused about the discomfort that reviewers feel. What I was trying to do (and using humor as a way to try to do it) was to have various positions in which everyone had a place on some level. Every woman – with men it is a whole different question – would have some level of identification with a position within the film. Some reviewers over-identified with something as a privileged position. Basically, none of the positioning of black characters was *against* any of the white viewers but more of an invitation: come and work with us. Instead of telling the viewer that he or she could *not* belong, the viewer was supposed to be a repository for all these different points of view and all these different styles of rhetoric. Hopefully, one would be able to identify with one position but be able to evaluate all of the various positions presented in the film. Basically, I feel this discomfort only from people who are deeply resistant to it.[22]

This response is one that, to my mind, sharply outlines a shift in women's cinema from a modernist or avant-garde aesthetic of subversion to an emerging set of questions about filmic representation to which the term *aesthetic* may or may not apply, depending on one's definition of art, one's definition of cinema, and the relationship between the two. Similarly, whether or not the terms *postmodern* or *postmodernist aesthetic* would be preferable or more applicable in this context, as Craig Owens has suggested of the work of other women artists, is too large a topic to be discussed here.[23]

At any rate, as I see it, there has been a shift in women's cinema from an aesthetic centered on the text and *its* effects on the viewing or reading subject – whose certain, if imaginary, self-coherence is to be fractured by the text's own disruption of linguistic, visual, and/or narrative coherence – to what may be called an aesthetic of reception, where the spectator is the film's primary concern – primary in the sense that it is there from the beginning, inscribed in the filmmaker's project and even in the very "making of the film."[24] An explicit concern with the audience is of course not new either in art or in cinema, since Pirandello and Brecht in the former, and it is always conspicuously present in Hollywood and TV. What is new here, however, is the particular conception of the audience, which now is envisaged in its heterogeneity and otherness from the text.

That the audience is conceived as a heterogeneous community is made apparent, in Borden's film, by its unusual handling of the function of address. The use of music and beat in conjunction with spoken language, from rap singing to a variety of subcultural lingos and non-standard speech, serves less the purposes of documentation or *cinéma vérité* than those of what in another context might be called characterization: they are there to provide a means of identification of and with the characters, though not the kind of psychological identification usually accorded to main characters or privileged "protagonists." "I wanted to make a film that different audiences could relate to on different levels – if they wanted to ignore the language they could," Borden told another interviewer, "but not to make a film that was anti-language."[25] The importance of "language" and its constitutive presence in both the public and the private spheres is underscored by the multiplicity of discourses and communication technologies – visual, verbal, and aural – foregrounded in the form as well as the content of the film. If the wall of official speech, the omnipresent systems of public address, and the very strategy of the women's takeover of a television station assert the fundamental link of communication and power, the film also insists on representing the other, unofficial social discourses, their heterogeneity, and *their* constitutive effects *vis-à-vis* the social subject.

In this respect, I would argue, both the characters and the spectators of Borden's film are positioned in relation to social discourses and representations (of class, race, and gender) within particular "subjective limits and discursive boundaries" that are analogous, in their own historical specificity, to those which Silverman saw symbolized by the Berlin wall in *Redupers*. For the spectators, too, are limited in their vision and understanding, bound by their own social and sexual positioning, as their "discomfort" or diverse responses suggest. Borden's avowed intent to make the spectator a locus ("a repository") of different points of view and discursive configurations ("these different styles of rhetoric") suggests to me that the concept of a heterogeneity of the audience also entails a heterogeneity of, or in, the individual spectator.

If, as claimed by recent theories of textuality, the Reader or the Spectator is implied in the text as an effect of its strategy – either as the figure of a unity or coherence of meaning which is constructed by the text (the "text of pleasure"), or as the figure of the division, dissemination, incoherence inscribed in the "text of *jouissance*" – then the spectator of *Born in Flames* is somewhere else, resistant to the text and other from it. This film's spectator is not only *not* sutured into the "classic" text by narrative and psychological identification; nor is it bound in the time of repetition, "at the limit of any fixed subjectivity, materially inconstant, dispersed in process," as Stephen Heath aptly describes the spectator intended by avant-garde (structural-materialist) film.[26] What happens is, this film's spectator is finally not liable to capture by the text.

And yet one is engaged by the powerful erotic charge of the film; one responds to the erotic investment that its female characters have in each other, and the filmmaker in them, with something that is neither pleasure nor *jouissance*, oedipal nor pre-oedipal, as they have been defined for us; but with something that is again (as in *Jeanne Dielman*) a recognition, unmistakable and unprecedented. Again the textual space extends to the spectator, in its erotic and critical dimensions, addressing, speaking-to, making room, but not (how very unusual and remarkable) cajoling, soliciting, seducing. These films do not put me in the place of the female spectator, do not assign me a role, a self-image, a positionality in language or desire. Instead, they make a place for what I will call me, knowing that I don't know it, and give "me" space to try to know, to see, to understand. Put another way, by addressing me as *a* woman, they do not bind me or appoint me as Woman.

The "discomfort" of Borden's reviewers might be located exactly in this disappointment of spectator and text: the disappointment of not finding oneself, not finding oneself "interpellated" or solicited by the film, whose images and discourses project back to the viewer a space of heterogeneity, differences and fragmented coherences that just do not add up to one individual viewer or one spectator–subject, bourgeois or otherwise. There is no one-to-one match between the film's discursive heterogeneity and the discursive boundaries of any one spectator. We are both invited in and held at a distance, addressed intermittently and only insofar as we are able to occupy the position of addressee; for example, when Honey, the Phoenix Radio disc jockey, addresses to the audience the words: "Black women, be ready. White women, get ready. Red women, stay ready, for this is our time and all must realize it."[27] Which individual member of the audience, male or female, can feel singly interpellated as spectator–subject or, in other words, unequivocally addressed?

There is a famous moment in film history, something of a parallel to this one, which not coincidentally has been "discovered" by feminist film critics in a woman-made film about women, Dorothy Arzner's *Dance, Girl, Dance*: it is the moment when Judy interrupts her stage performance and, facing the vaudeville audience, steps out of her role and speaks to them as a woman to a group of people. The novelty of this direct address, feminist critics have noted, is not only that it breaks the codes of theatrical illusion and voyeuristic pleasure, but also that it demonstrates that no complicity, no shared discourse, can be established between the woman performer (positioned as image, representation, object) and the male audience (positioned as the controlling gaze); no complicity, that is, outside the codes and rules of the performance. By breaking the codes, Arzner revealed the rules and the relations of power that constitute them and are in turn sustained by them. And sure enough, the vaudeville audience in her film showed great discomfort with Judy's speech.

I am suggesting that the discomfort with Honey's speech has also to do with codes of representation (of race and class as well as gender) and the rules and power relations that sustain them – rules which also prevent the establishing of a shared discourse, and hence the "dream" of a common language. How else could viewers see in this playful, exuberant, science-fictional film a blueprint for political action which, they claim, wouldn't work anyway? ("We've all been through this before. As a man I'm not threatened by this because we know that this doesn't work. This is infantile politics, these women are being macho like men used to be macho. . . . ")[28] Why else would they see the film, in Friedberg's phrase, "as a *prescription* through fantasy"? Borden's opinion is that "people have not really been upset about class and race. . . . People are really upset that the women are gay. They feel it is separatist."[29] My own opinion is that people are upset with all three, class, race, and gender – lesbianism being precisely the demonstration that the concept of gender is founded across race and class on the structure which Adrienne Rich and Monique Wittig have called, respectively, "compulsory heterosexuality" and "the heterosexual contract."[30]

The film-theoretical notion of spectatorship has been developed largely in the attempt to answer the question posed insistently by feminist theorists and well summed up in the words of B. Ruby Rich already cited above: "How does one formulate an understanding of a structure that insists on our absence even in the face of our presence?" In keeping with the early divergence of feminists over the politics of images, the notion of spectatorship was developed along two axes: one starting from the psychoanalytic theory of the subject and employing concepts such as primary and secondary, conscious and unconscious, imaginary and symbolic processes; the other starting from sexual difference and asking questions such as, How does the female spectator see? With what does she identify? Where/How/In what film genres is female desire represented? and so on. Arzner's infraction of the code in *Dance, Girl, Dance* was one of the first answers in this second line of questioning, which now appears to have been the most fruitful by far for women's cinema. *Born in Flames* seems to me to work out the most interesting answer to date.

For one thing, the film assumes that the female spectator may be black, white, "red," middle class or not middle class, and wants her to have a place within the film, some measure of identification – "identification with a position," Borden specifies. "With men [spectators] it is a whole different question," she adds, obviously without much interest in exploring it (though later suggesting that black male spectators responded to the film "because they don't see it as just about women. They see it as empowerment").[31] In sum, the spectator is addressed as female in gender and multiple or heterogeneous in race and class; which is to say, here too all points of identification are female or feminist, but rather than the "two logics" of character and filmmaker, like *Jeanne Dielman*, *Born in Flames* foregrounds their different discourses.

Second, as Friedberg puts it in one of her questions, the images of women in *Born in Flames* are "unaestheticized": "you never fetishize the body through masquerade. In fact the film seems consciously de-aestheticized, which is what gives it its documentary quality."[32] Nevertheless, to some, those images of women appear to be extraordinarily beautiful. If such were to be the case for most of the film's female spectators, however socially positioned, we would be facing what amounts to a film-theoretical paradox, for in film theory the female body is construed precisely as fetish or masquerade.[33] Perhaps not unexpectedly, the filmmaker's response is amazingly consonant with Chantal Akerman's, though their films are visually quite different, and the latter's is in fact received as an "aesthetic" work.

> Borden: "The important thing is to shoot female bodies in a way that they have never been shot before.... I chose women for the stance I liked. The stance is almost like the gestalt of a person."[34]
> And Akerman (cited above): "I give space to things which were never, almost never, shown in that way.... If you choose to show a woman's gestures so precisely, it's because you love them."

The point of this cross-referencing of two films that have little else in common beside the feminism of their makers is to remark the persistence of certain themes and formal questions about representation and difference which I *would* call aesthetic, and which are the historical product of feminism and the expression of feminist critical-theoretical thought.

Like the works of the feminist filmmakers I have referred to, and many others too numerous to mention here, *Jeanne Dielman* and *Born in Flames* are engaged in the project of transforming vision by inventing the forms and processes of representation of a social subject, women, that until now has been all but unrepresentable; a project already set out (looking back, one is tempted to say, programmatically) in the title of Yvonne Rainer's *Film about a Woman Who...* (1974), which in a sense all of these films continue to reelaborate. The gender-specific division of women in language, the distance from official culture, the urge to imagine new forms of community as well as to create new images ("creating something else to be"), and the consciousness of a "subjective factor" at the core of all kinds of work – domestic, industrial, artistic, critical, or political work – are some of the themes articulating the particular relation of subjectivity, meaning, and experience which en-genders the social subject as female. These themes, encapsulated in the phrase "the personal is political," have been formally explored in women's cinema in several ways: through the disjunction of image and voice, the reworking of narrative space, the elaboration of strategies of address that alter the forms and balances of traditional representation. From the inscription of subjective space and duration inside the frame (a space of repetitions, silences, and discontinuities in *Jeanne Dielman*) to the construction of other discursive social spaces (the discontinuous but intersecting spaces of the women's "networks" in *Born in Flames*), women's cinema has undertaken a redefinition of both private and public space that may well answer the call for "a new language of desire" and actually have met the demand for the "destruction of visual pleasure," if by that one alludes to the traditional, classical and modernist, canons of aesthetic representation.

So, once again, the contradiction of women in language and culture is manifested in a paradox: most of the terms by which we speak of the construction of the female social subject in cinematic representation bear in their visual form the prefix *de-* to signal the deconstruction or the destructuring, if not destruction, of the very thing to be represented. We speak of the de-aestheticization of the female body, the desexualization of violence, the deoedipalization of narrative, and so forth. Rethinking women's cinema in this way, we may provisionally answer Bovenschen's question thus: There is a certain configuration of issues and formal problems that have been consistently articulated in what we call women's cinema. The way in which they have been expressed and developed, both artistically and critically, seems to point less to a "feminine aesthetic" than to a feminist *deaesthetic*. And if the word sounds awkward or inelegant . . .

Notes

I am very grateful to Cheryl Kader for generously sharing with me her knowledge and insight from the conception through the writing of this essay, and to Mary Russo for her thoughtful critical suggestions.

1   Silvia Bovenschen, "Is There a Feminine Aesthetic?" trans. Beth Weckmueller, *New German Critique*, no. 10 (Winter 1977): 136. [Originally published in *Aesthetik und Kommunikation* 25 (September 1976).]

2   Laura Mulvey, "Feminism, Film, and the Avant-Garde," *Framework*, no. 10 (Spring 1979): 6. See also Christine Gledhill's account "Recent Developments in Feminist Film Criticism," *Quarterly Review of Film Studies* 3, no. 4 (1978).

3   Laura Mulvey, "Visual Pleasure and Narrative Cinema," *Screen* 16, no. 3 (Autumn 1975): 18.

4   B. Ruby Rich, in "Women and Film: A Discussion of Feminist Aesthetics," *New German Critique*, no. 13 (Winter 1978): 87.

5   J. Laplanche and J.-B. Pontalis, *The Language of Psycho-analysis*, trans. D. Nicholson-Smith, New York: Norton (1973), p. 206.

6   Lea Melandri, *L'infamia originaria*, Milan: Edizioni L'Erba Voglio (1977), p. 27; my translation. For a more fully developed discussion of semiotic theories of film and narrative, see Teresa de Lauretis, *Alice Doesn't: Feminism, Semiotics, Cinema*, Bloomington: Indiana University Press (1984).

7   See Audre Lorde, "The Master's Tools Will Never Dismantle the Master's House," and "An Open Letter to Mary Daly," in *This Bridge Called My Back: Writings by Radical Women of Color*, ed. Chérrie Moraga and Gloria Anzaldúa, New York: Kitchen Table Press (1983), p. 96. Both essays are reprinted in Audre Lorde, *Sister Outsider: Essays and Speeches*, Trumansburg, NY: Crossing Press (1984).

8   "Chantal Akerman on *Jeanne Dielman*," *Camera Obscura*, no. 2 (1977): 118–19.

9   In the same interview, Akerman said: "I didn't have any doubts about any of the shots. I was very sure of where to put the camera and when and why.... I *let* her [the character] live her life in the middle of the frame. I didn't go in too close, but I was not *very* far away. I let her be in her space. It's not uncontrolled. But the camera was not voyeuristic in the commercial way because you always knew where I was.... It was the only way to shoot that film – to avoid cutting the woman into a hundred pieces, to avoid cutting the action in a hundred places, to look carefully and to be respectful. The framing was meant to respect the space, her, and her gestures within it" (ibid., p. 119).

10 Janet Bergstrom, "*Jeanne Dielman, 23 Quai du Commerce, 1080 Bruxelles* by Chantal Akerman," *Camera Obscura*, no. 2 (1977): 117. On the rigorous formal consistency of the film, see also Mary Jo Lakeland, "The Color of Jeanne Dielman," *Camera Obscura*, nos. 3–4 (1979): 216–18.

11 Kaja Silverman, "Helke Sander and the Will to Change," *Discourse*, no. 6 (Fall 1983): 10.

12 Gertrud Koch, "Ex-changing the Gaze: Re-visioning Feminist Film Theory," *New German Critique*, no. 34 (Winter 1985): 144.

13 Sheila Rowbotham, *Woman's Consciousness, Man's World*, Harmondsworth: Penguin Books (1973), p. 28.

14 Claire Johnston, "Women's Cinema as Counter-Cinema," in *Notes on Women's Cinema*, ed. Claire Johnston, London: SEFT (1974), p. 31. See also Gertrud Koch, "Was ist und wozu brauchen wir eine feministische Filmkritik," *frauen und film*, no. 11 (1977).

15 Mary Ann Doane, Patricia Mellencamp, and Linda Williams, eds., *Re-vision: Essays in Feminist Film Criticism*, Frederick, Md.: University Publications of America and the American Film Institute (1984), p. 4.

16 Ibid., p. 6. The quotation from Adrienne Rich is in her *On Lies, Secrets, and Silence*, New York: Norton (1979), p. 35.

17 See Barbara Smith, "Toward a Black Feminist Criticism," in *All the Women Are White, All the Blacks Are Men, but Some of Us Are Brave: Black Women's Studies*, ed. Gloria T. Hull, Patricia Bell Scott, and Barbara Smith, Old Westbury, NY: Feminist Press (1982).

18 Helen Fehervary, Claudia Lenssen, and Judith Mayne, "From Hitler to Hepburn: A Discussion of Women's Film Production and Reception," *New German Critique*, nos. 24–5 (Fall/Winter 1981–2): 176.

19 Toni Morrison, *Sula*, New York: Bantam Books (1975), p. 44.

20 Kathleen Hulser, "Les Guérillères," *Afterimage* 11, no. 6 (January 1984): 14.

21 Anne Friedberg, "An Interview with Filmmaker Lizzie Borden," *Women and Performance* 1, no. 2 (Winter 1984): 43. On the effort to understand one's relation as a feminist to racial and cultural differences, see Elly Bulkin, Minnie Bruce Pratt, and

Barbara Smith, Yours in Struggle: *Three Feminist Perspectives on Anti-Semitism and Racism*, Brooklyn, NY: Long Haul Press (1984).

22 Interview in *Women and Performance*, p. 38.

23 Craig Owens, "The Discourse of Others: Feminists and Postmodernism," in *The Anti-Aesthetic: Essays in Postmodern Culture*, ed. Hal Foster, Port Townsend, Wash.: Bay Press (1983), pp. 57–82. See also Andreas Huyssen, "Mapping the Postmodern," *New German Critique*, no. 33 (Fall 1984): 5–52, now reprinted in Huyssen, *After the Great Divide: Modernism, Mass Culture, Postmodernism*, Bloomington: Indiana University Press (1986).

24 Borden's non-professional actors, as well as her characters, are very much part of the film's intended audience: "I didn't want the film caught in the white film ghetto. I did mailings. We got women's lists, black women's lists, gay lists, lists that would bring different people to the Film Forum." (Interview in *Women and Performance*, p. 43).

25 Betsy Sussler, "Interview," *Bomb*, no. 7 (1983): 29.

26 Stephen Heath, *Questions of Cinema*, Bloomington: Indiana University Press (1981), p. 167.

27 The script of *Born in Flames* is published in *Heresies*, no. 16 (1983): 12–16. Borden discusses how the script was developed in conjunction with the actors and according to their particular abilities and backgrounds in the interview in *Bomb*.

28 Interview in *Bomb*, p. 29.

29 Interview in *Women and Performance*, p. 39.

30 Adrienne Rich, "Compulsory Heterosexuality and Lesbian Existence," *Signs* 5, no. 4 (Summer 1980): 631–60; Monique Wittig, "The Straight Mind," *Feminist Issues* (Summer 1980): 110.

31 Interview in *Women and Performance*, p. 38.

32 Ibid., p. 44.

33 See Mary Ann Doane, "Film and the Masquerade: Theorising the Female Spectator," *Screen* 23, nos. 3–4 (September/October 1982): 74–87.

34 Interview in *Women and Performance*, pp. 44–5.

Part VII
The Historical Spectator/ Audience

Introduction

Toby Miller

The relationship between films and their viewers is perhaps the key to film theory, and it is referenced under many of our rubrics. There are two main forms of analysis: audience research and spectatorship theory. The former is primarily concerned with the number and conduct of people seated before screen texts: where they came from, how many there were, and what they did as a consequence of being present. The audience is understood as an empirical concept that can be known via research instruments derived from sociology, demography, social psychology, and marketing. Spectatorship theory is also concerned with speculation about the effects on people of films, but instead of questioning, testing, and measuring them, it uses psychoanalysis to explore how supposedly universal internal struggles over the formation of subjectivity are enacted on-screen and in the psyches of watchers. The spectator is understood as a narratively inscribed concept that can be known via a combination of textual analysis and Freudianism (see Part IX, on the nature of the gaze). Here, we focus more on questions of the audience.

There are three primary sites for defining the audience: the film industry, the state, and criticism. In this sense, the audience is artificial, the creature of various agencies that then act upon their creation. As John Hartley says: "The energy with which audiences are pursued in academic and industry research bespeaks something much larger and more powerful than the quest for mere data . . . the quest for knowledge about it is the search for something *special*; literally, knowledge of the *species*" (Hartley, 1992a: 84; see also Stam's essay, chapter 22, this volume).

Many discussions of the audience are signs of anxiety: laments for civic culture in the US correlate an increase in violence and a decline in membership of Parent–Teacher Associations with heavy film viewing – as true today as it was when the Payne Fund Studies of the 1930s inaugurated mass social-science panic about young people, driven by academic and familial iconophobia and the sense that large groups of people were engaged with popular culture beyond the control of the state and ruling classes, such that they might be led astray. Before even that, films were connected to gambling and horse racing in various forms of social criticism – the arts of popular commerce forever threatening an orderly conduct of urban life – or were lunged for as raw material by the emergent discipline of psychology, where obsessions with eyesight and the cinema gave professors something to do. At the same time, social reformers looked at the cinema as a potential forum for moral uplift; if film could drive the young to madness, it might also provoke a sense of social responsibility (Austin, 1989: 33–5; Webster, 1998: 192–3).

But unlike such institutions, the cultural audience is not so much a specifiable group *within* the social order as the principal site *of* that order. Audiences participate in the most global (but local), communal (yet individual), and time-consuming practice of making meaning in the history of the world. The concept and the occasion of being an audience are textual links between society and person, at the same time as viewing involves solitary interpretation as well as collective behavior (Roberts, 1995; Hartley, 1992b: 85). Production executives invoke the audience to measure success and claim knowledge of "what people want." But this focus on the audience is not theirs alone. Regulators do it to organize administration, psychologists to produce proofs, and lobby-groups to change content. "The audience" is never available in a pristine form, in that our knowledge of it always comes from these particular perspectives (Hartley, 1992b: 105). Hence the link to panics about education, violence, and apathy supposedly engendered by the screen and routinely investigated by the state, psychology, Marxism, neoconservatism, the church, liberal feminism, and others. The audience as consumer, student, felon, voter, and idiot engages such groups. This is Harold Garfinkel's notion of the "cultural dope," a mythic figure "who produces the stable features of the society by acting in compliance with preestablished and legitimate alternatives of action that the common culture provides." The "common sense rationalities . . . of here and now situations" used by people are obscured by this condescending categorization (Garfinkel, 1992: 68). When the audience is invoked as a category by the industry or its critics and regulators, it immediately becomes such a "dope." Much non-Hollywood film wants to turn such supposed "dopes" into a public of thinkers beyond the home. They are conceived of as civic-minded participants in a political and social system as well as an economy of purchasing. National cinemas in Europe, Asia, the Pacific, Latin America, and Africa are expected to win viewers and train them in a way that complements the profit-driven sector. The entertainment function is secondary to providing programs the commercial market would not deliver. Audiences are encouraged not just to watch and consume, but to act, to be better people. They are supposed to become cultural critics beyond the mall and inside the polis: citizens of a nation (Miller, 1993: 95–128; see Vasudevan's essay, chapter 23, this volume).

The crucial link between theories of the audience and spectatorship – one that abjures the idea of the "dope" – may come in a radical historicization and specification of engagement with texts, that occasion when a spectator moves from being "the hypothetical point of address of filmic discourse" to membership in "a plural, social audience"; for that moment can produce surprises (Hansen, 1994: 2; also see Pribram, 1988). The earliest US films, for example, focused on "presenting a series of views to an audience" rather than "telling stories." The fabulous possibilities of illusion provided their appeal, via a direct address of the audience. Rather than denying the process of watching, the era celebrated collusion between filmmakers and viewers. But with the first studios and the emergence of narrative technique around 1906, this "cinema of attractions" was displaced in mainstream film by storylines (Gunning, 1986: 63–4). Such stories are the most familiar form of cinema to most of us today, and it is interesting to note that the first moral panics about film audiences from conservatives, and the first promises of the political mobilization of film audiences from radicals, date from that time, when narrative met the arts of censorship and propaganda, and theaters were thought of as sites of ill-discipline. Studies were soon underway that endeavored to correlate juvenile delinquency with filmgoing (Gripsrud, 1998: 202–4).

Away from regulation, the commercially competitive nature of most cinema has led to an equally powerful concentration by producers, distributors, and exhibitors on audiences and their presumed tastes. This requires absolute numbers of viewers, information about who they are (which sectors of society they represent in terms of age, ethnicity, gender, class, and personal values), and learning what they make of what they see. Hollywood has always wanted to know who watched movies, and why they did so. In addition to the size of that viewing group, the industry wants to find out how it relates to the wider population's sexes, ages, races, tastes, patterns of consumption, and politics.

The film audience became the object of intense commercial scrutiny in the 1940s. US figures indicate that while men and women shared similar overall attendance figures, men were the most regular moviegoers. Young people were more likely than the elderly to go, and high school and college graduates went more often than people with a grade-school education. Numbers decreased from a high-point of 95 million a week in 1946 to 60 million in 1950 and 46 million in 1956. In a decade, the twin revolutions of televisualization and suburbanization had cut filmgoing in half. As more and more leisure activities became home-based across the 1960s and 1970s, movie attendance continued to decline. But late in the 1980s, when it seemed as though VCRs were going to domesticate film viewers forever, the innovation of the multiplex drew a new audience, as large cinemas met large shopping malls to form suburban heaven. At the same time, market research broadened its slicing of audiences by age, class, sex, race, and gender to "go psychographic," looking at preferences and values. In keeping with this development, the profile of the audience became older, and Hollywood moved away from films designed to appeal to young people (Wyatt, 1994: 157). Large companies make their profits from interviewing potential moviegoers as a gauge of likely attendance at specific films. Contemporary attempts to track the audience extend to an obsession by producers with Moviefone, a telephone and website movie listings service for major US cities. The number of inquiry calls received on this service precisely mirrors later ticket sales, and so it has become a surveillance device for predicting audience moves (Sreenivasan, 1997).

And on the regulation front, we are still bombarded with scientistic effects studies and moralistic diatribes about popular film and the rate of social violence, as if editing desks and script meetings were responsible for poverty, firearm availability, and masculinity. Let's consider this dynamic via a 1992 "Jump Cut" film-festival debate about texts and audiences that combined a screening and a panel discussion to deal with conflict over *Henry: Portrait of a Serial Killer* (John McNaughton, 1986), a film that gained new life as an arthouse success and a source of censors' anxiety in the early 1990s. The screening was seen to require accompanying commentary by "experts." A criminologist, a crime reporter, and a social-policy bureaucrat represented the institutions of academic law and psychology, popular journalism, and social work. The speakers announced they were not film critics and then proceeded to practice evaluative textual critique ("horrible, awful," "remarkably bad," "very, very few redeeming qualities"). The next move was to distance themselves from the paying audience in front of them ("I just can't imagine why people go to watch" and "I have no wish to voluntarily see films like this"). The three speakers discussed the inconclusiveness of media effects studies, assured us of their own detachment from the world of violence (in spite of their professional investment in it), expanded on the local history of serial killers, warned against arousal-by-video, affirmed the value of free speech, and lamented a callous world.

In question time, the audience revealed a contrasting commitment to the filmic text and the issues it raised around violence and pleasure. Some people commented on the eloquence of the film and the appropriateness of an ending that refused narrative closure. Individual members jeopardized the distinction between the normal self and the abnormal, violent other established by the panel. One person addressed the pleasure of violence, while another situated Henry's actions on a continuum of everyday violence against women. The distance from the text established by experts in law, journalism, and administration was thus broken down by the paying public. Discussion of *Henry* has at times likened it to a horror film; not surprisingly, given its title and content. Yet the text deliberately avoids many standard horror thrills. It has only minimal suspense, so the audience is not drawn into the excited-but-fearful anticipation characteristic of the horror genre. In fact, the actual time devoted to on-screen violence is probably no more than in much mainstream contemporary cinema. While Henry murders men and women with almost equal enthusiasm, the film focuses upon the killing of men, by television, shooting, and beheading. We do not witness the murder of most of Henry's female victims; rather, we see their bodies stretched out on the grass or floating in the water. Henry thematizes audience complicity in on-screen violence. One sequence shows a video recording of Henry and his colleague Ottis breaking into a suburban home and committing what seems to be rape and murder. The recording is distorted and viewers have to concentrate quite carefully to make out what is going on. McNaughton cuts to two people in front of their television, scrutinizing the videotape just as acutely and intently as we are. It is Henry and Ottis in their living-room: having recorded their own acts of violence, they are now gleefully playing them back for entertainment. The spectators' engagement is thereby brought into question. Why are we watching? What is the nature of our investment in such representations? The outcome is bewilderment on the part of those viewers who read through conventional psychological ways of seeing popular culture. The "dopes" at "Jump Cut" were alive to this.

Despite its sorrily complicitous history, there is value in analyzing spectators, providing that we see them as historical constructions of the industry and regulators, rather than as purely the creatures of the filmic apparatus or discourses of social control. Consider the history of *Crocodile Dundee* (Peter Faiman, 1986), the most popular imported film is US history. Paramount, the US distributor, worked with a particular view of North American spectators when it cut five minutes from the original version to increase the film's pace, removing scenic segments, altering the sound mix to foreground dialogue, and concentrating on the heterosexual couple (Crofts, 1989: 129, 137, 141). Here, we see different conceptions of the audience producing radically divergent versions of a film. The complexity of audiences is referenced in quite a different way by JoEllen Shively's (1992) experience of her return as a researcher to the reservation where she had grown up. She found that her fellow Native Americans had continued their practice of reading the Western genre in an actantial rather than political way, cheering for "cowboys" over the "Indians" because of narrative position, not race. Should we regard this as false consciousness, or the capacity to interpret films through their story worlds rather as well as the horizon of personal life? Actual engagement with the verbalized sense-making practices of audiences can be infinitely less mechanistic and more aware of difference than psychoanalysis, provided that it is also alive to problems with the motivated desires of measuring devices. An exemplary instance comes in Ravi Vasudevan's (1995) account of postwar Bombay cinema. He analyzes textual cues that encourage spectators to read the Hindi social film in gender, class, and national terms and how social concerns of the day about Hindu–Muslim life post-Independence influenced producers and directors.

Jacqueline Bobo's analysis of black women viewers of *The Color Purple* (Steven Spielberg, 1985) shows how watching the film, discussing it, and reading the novel drew them back to Alice Walker's writing, with all three processes invoking their historical experience in ways quite unparalleled in dominant culture – a far cry from the dismissal of Spielberg's work by critics. These women "sifted through the incongruent parts of the film and reacted favorably to elements with which they could identify" (Bobo, 1995: 3). And while Charles Chauvel's epic black–white relations melodrama *Jedda* (1955) has been criticized by some for liberal racism, to others it represents an epic if tragic moment of black masculinity on-screen, so rarely seen at all (Johnson, 1987). Similarly, gay Asian–Caribbean–Canadian video maker Richard Fung (1991) talks about searching for Asian genitals in the much-demonized genre of pornography; an account not available in conventional denunciations of porn and its impact on minorities. Shively (chapter 21, this volume) puts these paradoxes into play.

We might consider here the uptake of *Schindler's List* (Steven Spielberg, 1993). Ten years before its release, Les White unsuccessfully asked his father, a "Schindler Jew," to reminisce about the experience, opening up what had been unsayable in the family. So when Spielberg praised his scriptwriter for "inordinate restraint," White was taken back to his childhood rage at not knowing his family's past. He asked his father to "cut the bullshit." Armed with a new parental account, White takes the film to task for mitigating the horror of the real: his grandmother and aunt were shot, his grandfather and one uncle gassed, and another uncle hanged; all "indiscriminately." This is the key adverb for White, and he claims it is absent from the Spielberg version. The film text's suggestion that the Nazis targeted inefficient or resistant workers ascribes reason to what was much more a matter of chance and wilfullness. And the Hollywood account places an unrepresentative "emphasis on hope" and the prospect of survival. At the same time, White has to recognize that Spielberg's film opened up dialogue: far-distant now from familial reticence, his father is transformed into a public lecturer in schools and movie theaters (White, 1994: 3–5). Again, this type of historicized specificity is a valuable antidote to any purely textual reading.

The active audience as a group is not strong at the level of cultural production but is powerful as an interpretative community. This is the flipside to social-psychological and governmental panics that an audience may take up texts in ways that exceed their controls. This capacity to thwart the need of psychoanalytic and social-science critics to fix the meaning of text and response relates to the special skills of audiences as fans. Fans construct parasocial or imagined connexions to celebrities or actants, and are subject to intense criminological and erotomaniacal evaluation. Their chosen ones fulfill friendship functions or serve as spaces for projecting and evaluating schemas to make sense of human interaction. Umberto Eco teases out the issues in his exploration of what makes a "cult" film. In addition to adoring the text, cult-movie audiences domesticate the characters, removing them from the overall story and quoting their escapades and proclivities "as if they were aspects of the fan's private sectarian world," a world opened up to other followers through quizzes and rankings. References to segments of a movie, the behavior of actants, or the qualities of stars, become "catalyzers of collective memories," regardless of their significance for the story of the film. Sequences and tendencies are disarticulated from screen time, reshaped and redisposed as part of the cult (Leets, de Becker, and Giles, 1995: 102–4; Harrington and Bielby, 1995: 102–4, 110; Eco, 1987: 198).

There are occasions when this active-audience model celebrates readers as much as other methods patronize them, in a logocentrically interdependent mirroring effect. In reaction, Alec McHoul and Tom O'Regan have introduced the notion of "textual technologies" to bracket texts and audiences. They criticize the idea that "local instances" of people "embracing" or "refusing" the dominant interpretations preferred by global producers "guarantee any general statement about textual meaning." Aberrant decoding becomes a means of making the output of the culture industries isomorphic with a demotic, anti-capitalist, anti-patriarchal, anti-racist politics. Instead, McHoul and O'Regan propose a shift towards a "discursive analysis of particular actor networks, technologies of textual exchange, circuits of communicational and textual effectivity, traditions of exegesis, commentary and critical practice." In other words, the specific "uptake" of a text by a community should be a research referent; but not because this is guaranteed to reveal something essential to the properties of that object or its likely uptake anywhere else or at any other time. We can only ever discern a "general outline" of "interests" that can be applied to specific cases "upon a piecemeal and local inspection" that may in turn influence the wider model. Politics and texts are both about the means of communication as they function along a continuum of time and space (McHoul and O'Regan 1992: 5–6, 8–9).

Two similar approaches are available from the history of reading. One "reconstructs the diversity of older readings from their sparse and multiple traces." The other nominates "strategies by which authors and publishers tried to impose an orthodoxy or a prescribed reading on the text." The historian of the book, Roger Chartier (1989), favors a blend of these methods, focusing on "the text itself, the object that conveys it, and the act that grasps it." This tripartite system looks at how meaning is created in the interstices and interactions between and the independent function of each part: how layout, packaging, illustrations, and technology shift and determine the frames available for interpretation, especially as stories are remodeled in keeping with generic and industrial constraints and openings. Such a model of the historical spectator, derived from a blend of political economy, textual cues, and interpretative skills, seems a useful way forward for film theory.

Works Cited

Austin, Bruce A. 1989. *Immediate Seating: A Look at Movie Audiences*. Belmont: Wadsworth.

Bobo, Jacqueline 1995. *Black Women as Cultural Readers*. New York: Columbia University Press.

Chartier, Roger 1989. "Texts, Printings, Readings," *The New Cultural History*, ed. Lynn Hunt. Berkeley: University of California Press, 154–75.

Crofts, Stephen 1989. "Re-Imaging Australia: Crocodile Dundee Overseas," *Continuum 2*, no. 2: 129–42.

Eco, Umberto 1987. *Travels in Hyperreality: Essays*. Trans. William Weaver. London: Picador.

Fung, Richard 1991. "Looking for My Penis: The Eroticized Asian in Gay Video Porn," *How Do I Look? Queer Film and Video*, ed. Bad Object-Choices. Seattle: Bay Press, 145–68.

Garfinkel, Harold 1992. *Studies in Ethnomethodology*. Cambridge: Polity Press.

Gripsrud, Jostein 1998. "Film Audiences," *The Oxford Guide to Film Studies*, ed. John Hill and Pamela Church Gibson. Oxford: Oxford University Press, 202–11.

Gunning, Tom 1986. "The Cinema of Attraction: Early Film, its Spectator and the Avant-Garde," *Wide Angle* 8, nos. 3–4: 63–70.

Hansen, Miriam 1994. *Babel and Babylon: Spectatorship in American Silent Film*. Cambridge, Mass.: Harvard University Press.

Harrington, C. Lee and Denise D. Bielby 1995. *Soap Fans: Pursuing Pleasure and Making Meaning in Everyday Life*. Philadelphia: Temple University Press.

Hartley, John 1992a. *The Politics of Pictures: The Creation of the Public in the Age of Popular Media*. London: Routledge.

—— 1992b. *Tele-ology: Studies in Television*. London: Routledge.

Johnson, Colin 1987. "Chauvel and the Aboriginal Male in Australian Film," *Continuum* 1, no. 1: 47–56.

Leets, Laura, Gavin de Becker, and Howard Giles 1995. "Fans: Exploring Expressed Motivations for Contacting Celebrities," *Journal of Language and Social Psychology* 14, nos. 1–2: 102–23.

McHoul, Alec and Tom O'Regan 1992. "Towards a Paralogics of Textual Technologies: Batman, Glasnost and Relativism in Cultural Studies," *Southern Review* 25, no. 1: 5–26.

Miller, Toby 1993. *The Well-Tempered Self: Citizenship, Culture, and the Postmodern Subject*. Baltimore: Johns Hopkins University Press.

Pribram, E. Deidre (ed.) 1988. "Introduction," *Female Spectators: Looking at Film and Television*. London: Verso, 1–11.

Roberts, Sam 1995. "Alone in the Vast Wasteland," *New York Times* December 24.

Shively, JoEllen 1992. "Cowboys and Indians: Perceptions of Western Films Among American Indians and Anglos," *American Sociological Review* 57, no. 6: 725–34.

Sreenivasan, Sreenath 1997. "What is a Hit Film? Moviefone May Know," *New York Times* June 2: D9.

Vasudevan, Ravi 1995. "Addressing the Spectator of a 'Third World' National Cinema: The Bombay 'Social' Film of the 1940s and 1950s," *Screen* 36, no. 4: 305–24.

Webster, James G. 1998. "The Audience." *Journal of Broadcasting & Electronic Media* 42, no. 2: 190–207.

White, Les 1994. "My Father is a Schindler Jew," *Jump Cut* no. 39: 3–6.

Wyatt, Justin 1994. *High Concept: Movies and Marketing in Hollywood*. Austin: University of Texas Press.

20

Cowboys and Indians: Perceptions of Western Films Among American Indians and Anglos

JoEllen Shively

The dominant approach to understanding cultural products typically selects a particular popular genre for analysis in the hope of generating conclusions about the societal values expressed in the cultural product (some exceptions are Radway, 1984; Griswold, 1987; and Liebes and Katz, 1990).[1] For example, Cawelti (1970; 1976), on the basis of his reading of Western novels, concluded that these novels are a vehicle for exploring value conflicts, such as communal ideas versus individualistic impulses, and traditional ways of life versus progress. Cawelti argued that Westerns are formulaic works that provide readers with a vehicle for escape and moral fantasy.

In the major sociological study of Western films, Wright (1977) used his own viewing of the most popular Western movies from 1931 to 1972 to argue that Westerns resemble primitive myths. Drawing on Lévi-Strauss, Wright developed a cognitive theory of mythic structures in which "the receivers of the Western myth learn how to act by recognizing their own situation in it" (p. 186). Wright's main thesis is that the narrative themes of the Western resolve crucial contradictions in modern capitalism and provide viewers with strategies to deal with their economic worlds. The popularity of Westerns, Wright argued, lies in the genre's reflection of the changing economic system, which allows the viewers to use the Western as a guide for living.

These explanations of the Western's popularity attend to cultural texts but ignore the viewers, whose motives and experiences are crucial. The lack of solid data about audience interpretations of various formulas renders existing models of the cultural significance of Westerns and other genres speculative.

While growing up on an Indian reservation in the midwestern United States, I observed that fellow Indians loved Western movies and paperbacks. Subsequently, I observed this phenomenon on Indian reservations in Oregon and North Dakota, as well as among Indians who lived off the reservations. As scholars have noted (McNickle, 1973; Cornell, 1987; Snipp, 1991), American

Indians have always lived in a culturally, economically, and politically marginal subculture and are ambivalent about American values of achievement and acquisition of material wealth. Thus, it seemed unlikely that Indians who like Westerns would need them as conceptual guides for economic action as Wright alleged. The popularity of Westerns among Indians must be explained in other ways.

In an argument similar to Wright's, Swidler (1986) suggested that cultural works are tools used by people to contend with immediate problems. Swidler discussed "culture" in a broad sense as comprising "symbolic vehicles of meaning including beliefs, ritual practices, art forms, ceremonies as well as language, gossip, stories and rituals of daily life" (p. 272). Swidler was concerned with how culture shapes action and with how people "use" culture. Assuming that Western movies are a story or an art form, how do American Indians use this cultural product?

I address several issues that previous studies have made assumptions about, but have not addressed clearly. One issue is the general question of how different groups appropriate and find meaning in cultural products. In particular, does Wright's theory about the cultural use of Westerns hold true for American Indians watching a "cowboys vs. Indians" film? Is the mythic structure of a drama – the "good guy/bad guy" opposition in the Western – more salient than the ethnic aspect of the cultural product, or do Indians in the audience identify with Indians on the screen, regardless of who the good guys and bad guys are? Do Indians prefer Westerns that portray sympathetic and positive images of Indians, e.g. *Broken Arrow* and other movies described by Aleiss (1987) and Parish and Pitts (1976)? Do Indians like only Westerns that show a tribal group other than their own as the villains? Fundamentally, how do Indians link their own ethnic identity to the Western, or limit this identity so they can enter the narrative frame of the Western?

Research Design

Matched samples of 20 Indian males and 20 Anglo[2] males living in a town on an Indian reservation on the Western Plains of the United States watched a Western film, *The Searchers*. Ethnically pure groups were assembled by one Anglo informant and one Indian informant who invited five ethnically similar friends to their homes to watch the film. Written questionnaires were administered immediately after the film, followed by focus-group interviews. An Anglo female conducted the focus-group interviews with Anglos; I conducted the focus-group interviews with Indians. (I am Chippewa.) (Transcripts of the focus interviews are available from the author on request.)

Respondents were asked why they liked or did not like *The Searchers* in particular and Western movies in general. Basic demographic questions included racial identification, including "blood quantum" for Indians.

The research site is the second largest town on the reservation and has a population of about 1,200. Equal numbers of Indians and Anglos live in the town.[3] According to the Tribal Headquarters Enrollment Officer (Bighorn, May 12, 1988), of the 600 Indians, approximately 40 percent are Sioux, 10 percent are Assiniboine, 10 percent are Indians of mixed Indian origins, and approximately 40 percent of the self-identified Indians are "mixed-blood," i.e. Indian and white ancestry. Because I wanted to avoid the possible ambiguity of asking how mixed-bloods understand Westerns, all Indians in my sample claim to be "full-blood" Sioux, and all Anglos claim to be white.[4] Because the Western genre is primarily about males, only males were included in the sample.[5]

The respondents did not constitute a representative sample, but were assembled in an effort to create roughly matched groups. I attempted to match Indians and Anglos on age, income, years of education, occupation, and employment status, but succeeded in matching mainly on age, education, and occupation, and was less successful on income and employment status.[6] In the analysis, neither employment status nor income appear to affect the dependent variables. Matching Indians and Anglos on education required me to exclude college-educated respondents.[7] All subjects were between the ages of 36 and 64 – the average age of Indian respondents was 51, and the average age of Anglo respondents was 52. Most of the respondents were married.[8]

I chose *The Searchers* (1956) as the Western film to show because its major conflict is between cowboys and Indians. According to Wright (1977), *The Searchers* was one of the period's top-grossing films, a sign of mythical resonance. The film stars John Wayne – a critical advantage for a Western according to Indian and Anglo informants. Briefly, *The Searchers* is about Indian-hating Ethan Edwards's (John Wayne) and Martin Pawley's (Jeff Hunter) five-year search to find Debbie Edwards, Ethan's niece (Natalie Wood), who has been kidnapped by Comanche Chief Scar (Henry Brandon). In the end, Scar is killed, and Debbie, who was married to Scar, is taken back to the white civilized world.

Findings

I began my research with the assumption that people understand movies based on their own cultural backgrounds. Therefore, the experience of watching Western movies should be different for Indians and Anglos, especially when watching scenes in which Indians are portrayed in distorted, negative ways. My most striking finding, however, is an overall similarity in the ways Indians and Anglos experienced *The Searchers*.

All respondents – Indians and Anglos – indicated that they liked Western movies in general. Furthermore, in the focus interviews, they said they wished more Westerns were being produced in Hollywood. I asked the respondents to rank the three types of films they most liked to watch from a list of 10 (musical, gangster, horror, and so on). All 40 subjects – both Anglo and Indian – ranked

Westerns first or second; the Western was far and away the most popular genre: 75 percent ranked Westerns first. Combat movies were a distant second, and science fiction movies were third.

On both the written questionnaires and in the focus interviews, all respondents indicated that they liked *The Searchers* and considered it a typical Western. One Indian and two Anglos reported that they had seen the film before.

In response to the question, "With whom did you identify most in the film?" 60 percent of the Indians and 50 percent of the Anglos identified with John Wayne, while 40 percent of the Indians and 45 percent of the Anglos identified with Jeff Hunter.[9] None of the Indians (or Anglos) identified with the Indian chief, Scar. Indians did not link their own ethnic identity to Scar and his band of Indians, but instead distanced themselves from the Indians in the film. The Indians, like the Anglos, identified with the characters that the narrative structure tells them to identify with – the good guys. In the focus-group interviews, both Indians and Anglos reiterated their fondness for John Wayne. For both audiences, the Indians in the film were either neutral or negative. What stood out was not that there were Indians on the screen, but that the Indians were the "bad guys." For example, in the focus groups respondents were asked, "Do you ever root for the Indians?" Both Indians and Anglos consistently responded, "Sometimes, when they're the good guys." Their responses suggest that there is no strong ethnic bias governing whom the respondents root for and identify with. Instead, antagonism is directed against the bad guys. The structure of oppositions that defines the heroes in a film seems to guide viewers' identification with the characters in the film and overrides any ethnic empathy.

The Indians' identification with the good guys in the film is similar to Jahoda's (1961: 104) observations of African audiences reacting to films set in Africa that portray Africans as "rude, barbaric savages." Jahoda found that the majority of Africans did not identify with the Africans on the screen – only a minority of highly educated Africans identified with the Africans.

Although Indians and Anglos relied on cues in *The Searchers* about whom to identify with, in other ways the fictional frame of the film did not completely capture these viewers. When discussing *The Searchers*, Indians and Anglos rarely used the main characters' story names. Instead they used the actors' names – John Wayne and Jeff Hunter – which suggests a strong "star effect." Although John Wayne plays different characters in different films, these audiences associated his "cowboy" personality with the off-screen John Wayne, not with specific movie characters. On one level, they saw the actor as embodying all his movie roles. For example, when asked, "Why do you think Ethan Edwards hated the Indians in this movie?" the Indians and Anglos responded in similar ways:

Indians

Well, John Wayne might have hated Indians in this movie, but in other movies he doesn't hate them. (Mechanic, age 51)

Well, they've killed his brother and his brother's wife. He doesn't hate Indians in all his movies. (Cook, age 56)

Anglos

John Wayne doesn't like the Indians here because they've killed his brother's family. But in other movies, he's on their side. He sticks up for them. (Foreman, age 56)

Sometimes he fights for the Indians like in *Fort Apache*. (Bartender, age 48)

Both Indians and Anglos reported that they liked all of John Wayne's movies, whether he played a boxing champion, a pilot, or a cowboy. In all of his films, they see the strong personality characteristics of "the Duke," or "Dude," as some of the respondents referred to him. For both Indians and Anglos on this reservation, being called "cowboy" or one of John Wayne's nicknames, often "Dude" or "Duke," is a token of respect. Indians often see themselves as "cowboys," greeting each other with, "How ya doing, cowboy?" or "Long time no see, cowboy," and refer to their girlfriends or wives as "cowgirls." Fixico (1986) described a similar emulation of the cowboy among reservation Indians in Arizona and South Dakota.

The respondents talked about John Wayne as if he were one of them and they knew him personally – like a good friend. Believing in John Wayne the man is part of the charisma attached to the cowboy role. It is a self-reinforcing cycle: because John Wayne always plays good guys – characters with whom viewers empathize – it is easy to identify with John Wayne and all he represents. Levy (1990: 281) noted that, "because acting involves actual role playing and because of the 'realistic' nature of motion pictures, audiences sometimes fail to separate between players' roles onscreen and their real lives offscreen. The difference between life on and offscreen seems to blur." For respondents, John Wayne *is* the Cowboy, both in his movies and in real life. This focus on "John Wayne in real life" is similar to Liebes and Katz's (1990) finding that when retelling episodes of the TV series "Dallas," Americans and Kibbutzniks talk about the "real life" (behind-the-scene) personalities of the actors.

The real and the fictional: patterns of differences

Although Anglos and Indians responded in similar ways to the structure of oppositions in the narrative, the two groups interpreted and valued characteristics of the cultural product differently once they "entered" the narrative. The narrative was (re)interpreted to fit their own interests. Although both Indians and Anglos saw some aspects of *The Searchers* as real and others as fictional, the two groups differed on what they saw as authentic and what they saw as fictional.

Table 20.1 Ranks of reasons for liking *The Searchers*, by ethnicity

| | American Indians | | | | Anglos | | | |
Reason	Ranked 1st	Ranked 2nd	Ranked 3rd	Weighted sum of ranks[a]	Ranked 1st	Ranked 2nd	Ranked 3rd	Weighted sum of ranks[a]
Action/fights	2	4	5	19	2	6	4	22
John Wayne	5	3	2	23	2	3	0	12
It had cowboys and Indians	6	5	3	31	3	2	5	18
Scenery/landscape	6	3	2	26	3	5	6	25
Humor	1	5	6	19	0	1	1	3
Romance	0	0	1	1	0	0	1	1
Authentic portrayal of Old West	0	0	0	0	10	3	3	39
Other	0	0	1	1	0	0	0	0

[a] Ranks are weighted: 1st × 3; 2nd × 2; 3rd × 1.

Table 21.1 shows how the two groups responded when asked to rank their three most important reasons for liking the film. The Kendall rank-order correlation coefficient of $\tau = .29$ indicates that Indians' and Anglos' reasons often differed. The two groups agreed on the importance of "action and fights," "it had cowboys and Indians," and "the scenery and landscape" as reasons for liking the film. They also agreed that "romance" was not an important reason for liking the film. But the differences between Indians and Anglos in table 20.1 are striking: none of the Indians ranked "authentic portrayal of the Old West" as an important reason for liking the movie, while 50 percent of the Anglos ranked it as the most important reason.

The results in table 20.1 suggest that the distinctive appeal of the Western for Indians has two elements: (1) the cowboy's way of life – the idealized Western lifestyle seems to make this cultural product resonate for Indians; and (2) the setting of the film, the beauty of the landscape (Monument Valley) moves Indian viewers. When asked in the focus groups, "Why did you like this film, and what makes Westerns better (or worse) than other kinds of movies?" Indians reported: "Westerns relate to the way I wish I could live"; "The cowboy is free"; "He's not tied down to an eight-to-five job, day after day"; "He's his own man"; and "He has friends who are like him." What makes Westerns meaningful to Indians is that fantasy of being free and independent like the cowboy and the familiarity of the landscape or setting.

The setting also resonated for Anglos, but Anglos perceived these films as authentic portrayals of their past. In the focus groups, Anglos, but not Indians, talked about Westerns as accurate chronicles of their history. When asked, "Why did you like this film, and what makes Westerns better (or worse) than other kinds of movies?" Anglos said, "My grandparents were immigrants and Westerns show us the hard life they had"; "Westerns are about my heritage and how we settled the frontier and is about all the problems they had"; "Westerns give us an idea about how things were in the old days"; and "Westerns are true to life." What is meaningful to Anglos is not the fantasy of an idealized lifestyle, but that Western films link Anglos to their own history. For them, Western films are like primitive myths: they affirm and justify that their ancestors' actions when "setting this country" were right and good and necessary.[10]

Indians seemed ambivalent about how the Old West was portrayed in *The Searchers*. In the focus groups I asked Indians if the film was an authentic portrayal of the Old West and they responded:

As far as the cowboy's life goes, it's real, but you don't get to know the Indians, so it's hard to say it's totally authentic. (Bartender, age 42)

I think it's real in some ways, like when you see the cowboy and how he was. (Mechanic, age 51)

The cowboys are real to me. That's the way they were. But I don't know about the Indians 'cause you never see much of them. (Farm worker, age 50)

> Yeah, the movie is more about the good guys than the bad guys. I mean, the bad guys are there, but you don't get to know them very well. Mostly the movie is about the cowboys, the good guys, anyway. (Carpenter, age 48)

For Indians, the film was more about cowboys than about Indians. This does not hinder their enjoyment of the film or make it less meaningful, because they did not view the Indians on the screen as real Indians.

Both Indians and Anglos were asked, "Are Indians and cowboys in this film like Indians and cowboys in the past?" and, "Are they like Indians and cowboys today?" Anglos replied:

> I think the cowboys and the settlers are pretty much like those in the old days. It's hard to say if the Indians are like Indians in the past. (Mechanic, age 39)

> They're not like Indians today. (Foreman, age 56)

> Indians don't go around kidnapping white women and children these days. (Bartender, age 48)

> Probably they're similar to how some of the Indians were in the past, I mean Indians really did scalp white men. (Postal worker, age 49)

> Yeah, and they kidnapped white children and white women. My grandparents used to tell stories about how their parents told them to be careful when they played outside. They had to stay close to their homes, 'cause the Indians used to kidnap children. (Bus driver, age 49)

Anglos thought the cowboys in the Western were similar to cowboys of the past, and they suggested that Indians in the film were similar to Indians in the past. However, they did not think Indians today are like Indians in the film.

When asked the same questions about whether Indians and cowboys in the film are like Indians and cowboys today and in the past, Indians replied somewhat differently:

> The cowboys are like cowboys in the past. Maybe some Indians in the past were like the Indians in the films. (Bartender, age 58)

> They're not like Indians today. I mean, the only time Indians dress up is for powwows. (Cook, age 60)

> In this movie and other movies with Indians, you don't get to know them. I mean, they're not really people, like the cowboys are. It's hard to say they're like Indians in the past. For sure they're not like Indians today. (Bartender, age 42)

The Indians aren't at all like any of the Indians I know. (Unemployed factory worker, age 44)

Indians today are the cowboys. (Bartender, age 42)

The phrase "Indians today are the cowboys" means that contemporary Indians are more like cowboys than Anglos are, in the sense that it is Indians who preserve some commitment to an autonomous way of life that is not fully tied to modern industrial society. Indians want to be, and value being, independent and free – separate from society – more than Anglos do.

Because *The Searchers* portrays Indians not as human beings, but as "wild, blood-thirsty animals," Indians might be expected to report that the Indians on the screen are not like Indians they know today or like Indians in the past. How could they identify with the Indians on the screen when Indians are portrayed in such a caricatured fashion? The only connections that Indians made between the Indians on the screen and Indians of the past and present were with the costumes worn by the Indians on the screen.

On some deeper level, however, Indian respondents may have identified with the Indians on the screen. For example, when asked in the focus groups, "What's a bad Western like?" Indians reported that they like all Westerns except for films like *Soldier Blue*. All of the Indian respondents were familiar with this film. *Soldier Blue* is a 1970 film based on the Sand Creek massacre of 1864, when Colonel Chivington of the US Cavalry ambushed and slaughtered a village of peaceful Arapaho and Cheyenne children, women, and men in Colorado. In all of the Indian focus groups, this title was mentioned as one Western they did not like. This suggests that when films are too realistic and evoke unpleasant emotions, they are no longer enjoyable. This finding resembles Radway's (1984: 184) findings about "failed" romance novels. A "failed" romance is one that evokes overly intense feelings of anger, fear, and violence. Such novels are discarded by readers because they are not enjoyable. *Soldier Blue*, however, is sympathetic to the Indians, and the narrative leads the viewer to empathize with the Indians. Unlike the Indians, Anglos reported that they like all Westerns and could not think of an example of a bad Western.

Another striking difference revealed in table 20.1 is that Indians cited "humor" as an important reason for liking the film, while Anglos did not. In the focus groups, Indians talked about several comic scenes in the film. When asked if humor was important in Western films, they all said, "Yeah." They reported that they liked humor and wit in Western movies and valued this trait in their friends. Humor is a source of joy for them – a gift.

Anglos, in contrast, never mentioned John Wayne's humor. Why did Indians and not Anglos respond to the humor? If Anglos perceived the film as an authentic story of their past, they may have concentrated on the serious problems in the film, i.e. getting the white girl back. Perhaps Anglos were so preoccupied with the film as an affirmation of their past that they were unable to focus on the intended humor, or at least other characteristics of the film were more important. On the other hand, Indians, who did not see the film as an authentic story of their own past, may have focused more on the intended humor in the film.

Ideal heroes

Indians and Anglos also valued individual traits of the cowboy differently. Table 21.2 shows how the two groups responded when asked to rank the three most important qualities that make a good hero in a good Western. A Kendall rank-order correlation coefficient of $\tau = .167$ shows little agreement between Indian and Anglo rankings. Indians ranked "toughness" and "bravery" as the two most important qualities of a good hero in a good Western, whereas Anglos ranked "integrity/honesty" and "intelligence" as most important. Perhaps audiences look for exceptional characteristics in a good hero – qualities they would like to see in themselves. To live free and close to the land like Indians wish to live, exceptional bravery and toughness are necessary. Because Anglos do not want to live like cowboys, bravery and toughness are not as important. Responses of Indians in table 20.2 are similar to responses in table 20.1 and to the oral responses. For example, when the Indians described John Wayne as a reason why they liked *The Searchers*, they concentrated on John Wayne's toughness.

While the two groups differed on the qualities that make a good hero, Indians and Anglos tended to agree on the characteristics of a good Western. When asked what characteristics they liked in a good Western, a Kendall's rank-order correlation coefficient between Indian and Anglo responses was high, $\tau = .78$, i.e. there were no pronounced differences between Indians and Anglos. For both groups, the three most important characteristics of a good Western were: "a happy ending"; "action/fights"; and "authentic portrayal of Old West." Like the ranking of "a happy ending" as the most important ingredient in a good romance novel (Radway, 1984: 59), Indian and Anglo viewers ranked "a happy ending" as the most desirable characteristic of a good Western. The essential happy ending for my respondents may be related to Cawelti's (1976: 193) "epic moment" when the villain is conquered, the wilderness is subdued, and civilization is established. The importance of the "happy ending" may also support Wright's (1977) contention that the outcome of the Western narrative is important.

For Indians, the importance of a "happy ending" in a good Western film also reflects on their evaluation of *Soldier Blue* as a bad Western – *Soldier Blue* does not fulfill the "happy ending" criterion of a good Western. Although Indians like action or fights, they are discerning about what kinds of action or fights they enjoy.

For both Anglos and Indians, the three least liked characteristics of a good Western were: "hero rides off into the sunset alone"; "Indians as bad guys"; and "romance between hero and woman." Both groups preferred that "the hero settles down." In some ways, the characteristics the respondents like to see in a

Table 20.2 Ranks of qualities that make a good hero in a good Western, by ethnicity

Quality	American Indians				Anglos			
	Ranked 1st	Ranked 2nd	Ranked 3rd	Weighted sum of ranks[a]	Ranked 1st	Ranked 2nd	Ranked 3rd	Weighted sum of ranks[a]
Bravery	8	6	4	40	3	4	1	18
Integrity/honesty	2	2	0	10	8	9	5	47
Independence	0	0	2	2	0	0	1	1
Toughness	8	8	4	44	0	0	0	0
Sense of humor	0	2	8	12	0	1	1	3
Strength	2	0	0	6	0	0	0	0
Loyalty	0	0	0	0	1	0	0	10
Intelligence	0	2	2	6	8	6	5	41
Other	0	0	0	0	0	0	0	0

[a] Ranks are weighted: 1st × 3; 2nd × 2; 3rd × 1.

good Western support Cawelti's assumptions about the cultural significance of the Western.[11]

The Politics of Perception

Some Indians *do* identify with the Indians in the Western and are not affected by the film's signals about whom to identify with. Before taking my research procedures into the field, I pretested them with 15 American Indian college students at a West Coast university (10 males, 5 females). Because Indians in the reservation sample differed in important characteristics from the Indians in the pretests (9 of the Indian students were "mixed-bloods"), systematic comparisons were not possible.

However, Indian students responded differently from Indians in the reservation sample. Ethnicity was a salient issue for the majority of the students. The narrative of *The Searchers* did not "work" for the students and they were unable to fully enter the drama. For example, unlike the reservation Indians, a majority of the Indian students identified with and rooted for Scar and his Indians or Debbie, the kidnapped girl. They thought Debbie should have been allowed to stay with Scar and that the search should not have taken place at all.

Like the reservation Indians, the college-educated Indians did not view *The Searchers* as an authentic portrayal of the "Old West" and were quick to point out stereotypical portrayals of Indians in the film. They reacted against the negative message in the film that "the only good Indian is a dead one." They also pointed out many inaccuracies in the film, such as the use of Navajos and the Navajo language for Comanche, "Comanche" Indians wearing Sioux war bonnets, and Indians sometimes wearing war bonnets while fishing. Neither the Indians nor the Anglos in the reservation sample mentioned any of these inaccuracies.

All students but one reported that they liked Westerns in general, but preferred Westerns whose plots are about "cowboys vs. cowboys" or "Indians vs. Indians," or a "cowboys vs. Indians" plot in which the Indian point of view is shown. Several male students indicated that they and their friends often rent Western videos and named the video stores nearest the university that had the best selection of Westerns.

None of the students particularly liked John Wayne. Like the reservation sample, the students talked about John Wayne in "real life" and referred to what they considered racist statements he made off-screen in various interviews.

I asked each student, "Do Indians back home on the reservation like Westerns?" and "Do they root for the cowboys?" All of them said, "Oh yeah, sure." One Sioux student said his father had most of John Wayne's films on video, and a Chippewa said that his uncle was named after John Wayne. One Navajo said of his reservation town, "Ever since they closed down the movie theater several years ago, every Friday night they show a movie in the cafeteria room at the high school, and most of the time it's a Western. Everybody goes."

The heightened ethnic awareness of the college students interferes with, or overrides, their responses to the Western so that they do not get caught up in the structure of oppositions in the narrative. Because they identify with their ethnic group, they see *The Searchers* through a different lens. Education increases their awareness of anti-Indian bias in the film, producing a "revised eye" that frames these films in ethnic terms. In this context, ethnicity is a construct of a particular culture or subculture.

Conclusion

Although it would seem problematic for Indians to know which characters to identify with in *The Searchers*, it was not a problem for them at all – they identified with the cowboy and his lifestyle. Indians did not focus on the Indians, who are often portrayed on-screen as a faceless, screaming horde. Instead, they saw the cowboys as they want to see themselves – as the good guys.

What appears to make Westerns meaningful to Indians is the fantasy of being free and independent like the cowboy. In addition, the familiarity of the setting is important. Anglos, on the other hand, respond to the Western as a story about their past and their ancestors. The Western narrative becomes an affirmation of their own social experience – the way they are and what their ancestors strove for and imposed on the West are "good." Thus, for Anglos, the Western resembles a primitive myth. But it is not a myth in this sense for Indians – Indians do not view the Western as authentic.

Both Indians and Anglos find a fantasy in the cowboy story in which the important parts of their ways of life triumph and are morally good, validating their own cultural group in the context of a dramatically satisfying story. Perhaps this motive for ethnic group validation is more general and not peculiar to cowboy movies.

Oppositions in the Western narrative are important to viewers. Indians and Anglos both root for and identify with the good guys. The strength of the narrative lies in its Lévi-Straussian oppositions, and Wright (1977) correctly focused on them. However, Wright's thesis, that viewers see their own economic situation in Westerns and use its messages to deal with their economic world, is not supported here. Both Indians and Anglos respond to "their own situation," but not in Wright's sense. Wright's sociological explanation of the cultural significance of Westerns does not entirely contradict Cawelti (1976). Although Cawelti's discussion is too non-specific, and therefore more difficult to refute, my evidence is more compatible with Cawelti's argument that viewers use Westerns as a fantasy for exploring value conflicts (e.g. traditional ways of life versus progress) and to affirm the value of their ideals and way of life. Cawelti's non-specificity and Wright's incorrect explanation may have resulted from their failure to ask viewers or readers *why* they like Westerns.

The Indian college students, who by attending college have opted for some of the values of white society, find other meanings in *The Searchers*. Because they are immersed in the intellectual world of the university, the symbolic importance of the film for them lies in its false representation of their ancestry and history.

Notes

An earlier version of this paper was presented at the annual meeting of the American Sociological Association, August 1991, in Cincinnati. Ann Swidler and Morris Zelditch, Jr., contributed substantially to the development of the underlying research and I benefited from their valuable comments as well. I am grateful to Sarah M. Corse, James G. March, Howard Schuman, Russell Thornton, and the editor and reviewers of the *ASR* for their careful readings and insightful comments. This research was supported by a grant from the National Institute of Mental Health and by a Dean's Research Award from Stanford University.

1   Much work has involved literary and film studies. However, literary theories such as reader-response theory (Iser, 1974; Fish, 1980), pertain mostly to an "implied reader" within the text, and psychoanalyze what ethnicity, gender, religion, etc., in films mean (Friedman, 1991). This work is interesting, but irrelevant for a study of how real audiences actually respond.

2   "Anglo" refers to non-Indian white Americans and does not include those of Spanish or Mexican descent.

3   Of the approximately 50,000 residents living on the 7 federally recognized reservations in this state in 1980, 48.5 percent are Indian and 51.5 percent are Anglo (Confederation of American Indians, 1986: 125–34). Under the 1887 General Allotment Act, more than 100 Indian Reservations on the Plains, along the Pacific Coast, and in the Great Lakes states, were divided up and allotted to individual Indians. The remaining land was declared "surplus" and opened up to white homesteaders. Under the terms of this Act, Indians were eventually dispossessed of almost 90 million acres (Talbot, 1981: 111–12). Today, whites continue to own land and live on these reservations where their land is "checker-boarded" between Indian-owned land. On some of these reservations, non-Indians own as much or more land than the tribe or Indians do, and the proportion white is equal to or higher than the proportion Indian. The research site is on one of these reservations.

4   I have observed that "mixed-blood" Indians acknowledge and respect both their Indian and white ancestries. To avoid speculation about whether the findings might be associated with the self-identified Indians' "Indianness" or "whiteness," I included only full-bloods.

5   My data show that the Western genre is popular among women, but because the major focus of this study is on racial differences and because I had a limited budget, I controlled for gender by looking at males only.

6   The median annual household income for the Indians was $9,000; the median annual household income for the Anglos was $13,000. Seven of the 20 Indian men were unemployed at the time of the research compared to three of the Anglo men. Of currently employed Indians, four were working part-time; three of currently employed Anglos were working part-time. There are no significant differences between the

Indians in my study and the 1980 Census data on income and unemployment (US Bureau of the Census, 1986: tables 9, 10, 25; US Bureau of the Census, 1988: table 234). Occupations of the Indians included bartender, farm worker, mechanic, factory worker, carpenter, and food-service worker. Occupations of the Anglos included janitor, school bus driver, bartender, store clerk, factory worker, carpenter, mechanic, foreman, and postal worker.

7   Indians and Anglos differed in the proportion who completed high school, but this difference had no effect on the analysis. Among Indian respondents, 25 percent had completed high school and 60 percent had some high school. For Anglo respondents, 80 percent had completed high school and 20 percent had some high school.

8   To obtain matched 20-person samples, 11 groups comprising 30 Indians and 25 Anglos watched the film. Of these, 2 Indians and 3 Anglos had "some college education" and 8 Indians and 2 Anglos were mixed-blood. These respondents' questionnaires were not used and the respondents were not involved in the focus interviews.

9   One Anglo identified with Laurie, Martin Pawley's (Jeff Hunter's) girlfriend. It was difficult to tell why.

10 Describing the role of the myth among Trobriand Islanders, Malinowski (1948: 84–5) wrote: "The *myth* comes into play when rite, ceremony, or a social or moral rule demands justification, warrant of antiquity, reality, and sanctity."

11 I collected some data in the field on female reservation Indians and female Anglos. These data reveal gender differences as well as differences by ethnicity. For example, women identified with the women in the film, while the men did not. Women ranked "romance" as one of the most important reasons for liking the film, whereas the men ranked it as the least important reason. Women ranked "action/fights" as one of the least important reasons for liking the film, while the men ranked it as one of the most important reasons. Like Anglo men, Anglo women saw the film as an authentic portrayal of the past, while the Indian women, like the Indian men, did not. Indian women, like Indian men, also distanced themselves from the Indians on the screen.

References

Aleiss, Angela. 1987. "Hollywood Addresses Postwar Assimilation: Indian/White Attitudes in *Broken Arrow*," *American Indian Culture and Research Journal* 11: 67–79.

Bighorn, Spike N. 1988. Personal communication with author, May 12.

Cawelti, John. 1970. *The Six-Gun Mystique*. Bowling Green, OH: Bowling Green State University Popular Press.

——1976. *Adventure, Mystery and Romance*. Chicago: University of Chicago Press.

Confederation of American Indians. 1986. *Indian Reservations: A State and Federal Handbook*. Jefferson, NC: McFarland.

Cornell, Stephen. 1987. "American Indians, American Dreams, and the Meaning of Success," *American Indian Culture and Research Journal* 11: 59–70.

Fish, Stanley. 1980. *Is There a Text in This Class?* Cambridge, MA: Harvard University Press.

Fixico, Donald L. 1986. "From Indians to Cowboys: The Country Western Trend." In *American Indian Identity: Today's Changing Perspectives*, edited by C. E. Trafzer. Sacramento, CA: Sierra Oaks Publishing.

Friedman, Lester D. (ed.) 1991. *Unspeakable Images: Ethnicity and the American Cinema*. Chicago: University of Illinois Press.

Griswold, Wendy. 1987. "The Fabrication of Meaning: Literary Interpretation in the United States, Great Britain, and the West Indies," *American Journal of Sociology* 92: 1,077–117.

Iser, Wolfgang. 1974. *The Implied Reader: Patterns of Communication in Prose Fiction from Bunyan to Beckett*. Baltimore, MD: Johns Hopkins University Press.

Jahoda, Gustav. 1961. *White Man: A Study of the Attitudes of Africans to Europeans in Ghana before Independence*. London: Oxford University Press.

Levy, Emanuel. 1990. *And the Winner Is . . . : The History and Politics of the Oscar Awards*. New York: Continuum.

Liebes, Tamar and Elihu Katz. 1990. *The Export of Meaning: Cross Cultural Readings of DALLAS*. New York: Oxford University Press.

Malinowski, Bronislaw. 1948. *Magic, Science, and Religion and Other Essays*. Glencoe, IL: The Free Press.

McNickle, D'Arcy. 1973. *Native American Tribalism: Indian Survivals and Renewals*. New York: Oxford University Press.

Parish, James R. and Michael R. Pitts. 1976. *The Great Western Pictures*. Metuchen, NJ: The Scarecrow Press.

Radway, Janice A. 1984. *Reading the Romance: Women, Patriarchy, and Popular Literature*. Chapel Hill, NC: University of North Carolina Press.

Snipp, C. Mathew. 1991. *American Indians: The First of This Land*. New York: Russell Sage Foundation.

Swidler, Ann. 1986. "Culture in Action: Symbols and Strategies," *American Sociological Review* 51: 273–86.

Talbot, Steve. 1981. *Roots Of Oppression: The American Indian Question*. New York: International Publishers.

US Bureau of the Census. 1986. *1980 Census of Population. American Indians, Eskimos, and Aleuts on Identified Reservations and In the Historical Areas of Oklahoma*, vols. 1–2. Subject Report prepared by the US Department of Commerce. Washington, DC: US Government Printing Office.

—— 1988. *1980 County and City Data Book*. Prepared by the US Department of Commerce. Washington, DC: US Government Printing Office.

Wright, Will, 1977. *Sixguns and Society: A Structural Analysis of the Western*. Berkeley, CA: University of California Press.

21
Television News and Its Spectator

Robert Stam

Let us take as our point of departure something so obvious that it is often taken for granted, but something which in reality should astonish us: the fact that television news is *pleasurable*. No matter what its specific content, no matter how "bad" the news might be or how "badly" the newscasters or their presentations might offend our individual sensitivies or ideological predilections, watching the news is pleasurable. Even on a hypothetical day of worst-case scenarios – huge jumps in inflation and unemployment, imminent food shortages, nuclear leaks slouching invisibly toward our metropolitan centers – the viewing experience itself would still afford pleasure. Our first question, then, is: *Why* is the news pleasurable?; and our second, intimately linked to the first, is: To what extent can contemporary theoretical models and analytical methods elaborated largely in relation to the fiction film also illuminate television news? How can contemporary methodologies – psychoanalytic, semiotic, dialectical – disengage the operations of television news as part of what Stephen Heath, in another context, has called a "pleasure-meaning-commodity-complex"? What are the specific pleasures of the news and how can we account for them?

Epistemophilia, the love of knowing, provides but a partial explanation. We would have to ask why people *prefer* to know the news through television, and why even those who already "know" the news through alternative media *still* watch the news. Taking our cue from recent work by film theorists such as Christian Metz, Jean-Louis Baudry, and Jean-Louis Comolli, we may begin with the pleasuring capacities of the television apparatus itself.[1] By "apparatus," these theorists mean the cinema machine in an inclusive sense – not only its instrumental base of camera, projector and screen but also the spectator as the desiring subject on which the cinematic institution depends as its object and accomplice.

Metz argues in "The Imaginary Signifier" that the cinema spectator identifies first of all with his or her own act of looking, with

> himself as a pure act of perception (as wakefulness, alertness); as condition of possibility of the perceived and hence as a kind of transcendental subject, anterior to every *there is*.[2]

The "primary identification" then, is not with the events or characters depicted on the screen but rather with the act of perception that makes these secondary identifications possible, an act of perception both channeled and constructed by the anterior look of the camera and the projector that stands in for it, granting the spectator the illusory ubiquity of the all-perceiving subject.

The televisual apparatus, quite apart from its "programming," affords pleasures even more multiform and varied than those afforded by the cinema, for the viewer identifies with an even wider array of cameras and looks. The viewer of the evening news, for example, identifies with (1) film cameras and their footage shot around the world (films commissioned by the network, film from other sources, and library and archival material); (2) video cameras and their magnetic residue of images and sounds on tape; and (3) tapeless video cameras directly transmitting images and sounds (the anchors speaking the news in the studio or correspondents on location transmitting via remote). This last category is important, for television, unlike the cinema, allows us to share the literal time of persons who are elsewhere. It grants us not only ubiquity, but *instantaneous* ubiquity. The telespectator of a lunar landing becomes a vicarious astronaut, exploring the moonscape at the same time (technically a fraction of a second later) as the astronauts themselves. The viewer of a live transmission, in fact, can in some respects see better than those immediately on the scene. Multiple cameras facilitate a gratifying multiplicity of perspectives, and video tape and switcher provide the privilege of instant replay, whether of football touchdowns or political assassinations. The televisual apparatus, in short, prosthetically extends human perception, granting an exhilarating sense of visual power to its virtually "all-perceiving" spectator, stretched to the limit in the pure act of watching.

Television's "liveness" guarantees other gratifications. Live transmission makes possible real, as opposed to fabricated, suspense. Will the space mission get off the ground? Will the assassination victim survive? Unlike the cinema, television has to *tell* us, by superimposed captions, whether it is live or recorded. Talk shows *seem* to be transmitted live even when they are prerecorded, whence our occasional double take when an anachronistic allusion makes us realize that we are watching a rerun. Although live transmission forms but a tiny proportion of programming, that tiny portion sets the tone for all of television. In the news, the *part* of direct transmission – the anchor's report, conversations, occasional live special events – metonymically "contaminates" the *whole* of the news. The titles themselves – *Eyewitness News, Action News, Live at Five* – advertise this aliveness as the telos toward which the news presumably tends. In fact, this vivacity is largely fraudulent. The "fast-breaking news" is filmed hours or days before the newscast, and prerecorded correspondents' reports are fastened by rhetorical glue ("Well Walter, the feeling in Washington is...") to the directly transmitted studio reports that dominate the newscast. But this illusory feeling of presentness, this constructed impression of total immediacy, constitutes one of the news' undeniable satisfactions.[3]

The first pleasure of the news, then, is narcissistic. Television's heterogeneous resources – film, video tape, direct transmission – confer perceptual powers superior to those of the relatively sluggish and time-bound cinema, a medium that television both "includes" and surpasses with its ability to "cover the world." John Cameron Swayze anticipated this globe-trotting motif, at an earlier stage of technology, by the exotically picaresque title of his *Camel News Caravan*, and contemporary news programs call attention to it by their spherical-line globes and illuminated maps. We become, by virtue of our subject position, the audio-visual masters of the world – television transforms us into armchair imperialists, flattering and reaffirming our sense of power.

The technological supports of this intoxicating sense of power seem, at first glance, remarkably precarious. What do we see on television? We do not see John Chancellor, for he is in a studio in New York; we do not see a picture, for there is no photography involved. We see only a visual configuration, a suggestive aggregation of ionized data, what Yeshayahu Nir calls "immediate iconic presence, conjured up by an electronic scanner's promenade across a screen."[4]

Yet this low-definition image of television, often cited as a token of its "inferiority," in no way inhibits narcissistic identification. It might even be argued that in some respects identification in a medium varies in *inverse* proportion to its representational adequacy. The doubly imaginary nature of the cinema (imaginary in what it represents and imaginary by the nature of its signifier), Metz argues, heightens rather than diminishes the possibilities of identification. The impression of reality is stronger in film than in theater precisely because the phantomlike figures on the screen easily absorb our fantasies and projections.[5] Television, by this same logic, allows a more powerful identification because its signifier entails an even higher degree of imaginariness. It constitutes quintessential illusion, and it is hardly surprising that Marshall McLuhan, from a very different theoretical perspective, insists that its impoverished images, which are ultimately "not even there," make it a "cool" medium in which viewer involvement is all the more "hot" and intense.

Both cinema and television are simulation apparati which not only represent the real but also stimulate intense "subject-effects." For Baudry, the shadowy images on the screen, the darkness of the movie theater, the passive immobility of the spectator, and the womblike sealing off of ambient noises and quotidian pressures all foster an artificial state of regression not unlike that engendered by dream. The cinema, for Baudry, constitutes the approximate material realization of an unconscious goal perhaps inherent in the human mind: the regressive desire to return to an earlier state of psychic development, a state of relative narcissism in which desire could be "satisfied" through an enveloping simulated reality in which the separation between one's body and the exterior world, between ego and non-ego, is not clearly defined.

Baudry's cinescopic theory must be "scanned," admittedly, for the purposes of television. Many of the factors that nourish narcissism and regression, which foster the "realer-than-real" effect of which Baudry speaks, simply do not operate in television, at least not in its present conditions of reception. Even apart from the theoretical ambiguities in Baudry's position – the quasi-idealist positing of a trans-historical eternal wish inherent in the psyche, the monolithic model of cinema which fails to allow for either a modified apparatus or for filmic texts which "wake up" and dephantasmize the spectator, the hegemonic slighting of the aural track – his schema requires substantial modification for television. For a complex series of social and historical reasons, the cinema continues to be associated with the privileged space of theater – latter-day heir to the sacred space of ritual, games, and tragedy – while television is tied to the mundane surroundings of the average home. Its relatively aura-less presence accompanies our domestic routines. While the ciné-spectator is likely to sit "spellbound in darkness," watching in semi-reverential silence, the telespectator is more likely to be active, mobile, and verbal. The lights are more likely to be on, and the viewer exercises a certain control over channel, sound, volume, contrast, and whether or not to turn the apparatus off.

On the other hand, one should not underestimate television's own persuasiveness or its powerful encouragement of regressive and narcissistic attitudes. The smaller screen, while preventing immersion in any deep enveloping space, encourages in other ways a kind of narcissistic voyeurism. Larger than the figures on the screen, we quite literally oversee the world from a sheltered position – all the human shapes parading before us in television's insubstantial pageant are scaled down to lilliputian insignificance, two-dimensional dolls whose height rarely exceeds a foot. The very availability of television, meanwhile, entails a special kind of identification: while the fiction film works its magic over the course of an hour or two, television casts its spell over a protracted period. The ephemeral intensity of the cinematic hare ultimately yields to the slow-working efficacy of the television tortoise; it is not Plato's cave for an hour and a half, but a privatized electronic grotto, a miniature sound and light show to distract our attention from the pressure without or within.

The privileged position of the television spectator has both psychoanalytic and political implications. Television, like the cinema, is founded upon the pleasure of looking (scopophilia) and the pleasure of hearing (Lacan's "*pulsion invocante*") and both media allow us to see without being seen and hear without being heard. Quite apart from any specific voyeuristic content in the news itself (*Eyewitness News* reports on topless bars, scandals concerning celebrities, etc.) our situation as protected witnesses itself has voyeuristic overtones. Our privileged position triggers a fictitious sense of superiority, and in an atomized and hierarchical society where individuals are prodded to dreams of differential status and success, the recital of the misfortunes of others inevitably elicits an ambivalent reaction – mingling sincere empathy with mildly sadistic condescension.[6] In an economic situation where the fear of downward social mobility becomes an overriding concern, reports of industry layoffs can lead to a bizarre sense of There-but-for-the-Grace-of-God relief: "At least *I* still have a job!"

News programs are designed, on some levels, to enhance the self-image of His or Her Majesty the Spectator. The "bias" in the news often derives less from corporate manipulation or governmental pressure, although both undeniably exist, than from this inbuilt need to flatter the audience. Images of Iranian mobs implicitly contrast an objectified *Them* with a glorified *Us*, presumably as rational and humane as they are supposedly mindless and fanatical. (Europe constructed its self-image, Sartre explains in his Preface to Fanon's *Wretched of the Earth*, on the backs of its equally constructed Other: the "savage," the cannibal, the African.) Newscasters often neglect to specify the obvious for the same reason; Network News does speak of junta-style repression in Latin America, for example, but it does not usually point out that the repression is partially financed by the viewers' tax dollars. The omission does not necessarily derive only from complicity with established power or from ignorance of the facts, but also from the fact that an explicit statement that "you the viewer are in some way responsible for the atrocities you have witnessed" would not flatter and thus might hurt ratings.[7]

Apart from "primary identification" with the apparatus itself and with our own act of perception, television offers a gold mine of "secondary identifications" with the perceived human beings on the screen. Television news parades before us innumerable candidates for identification: the anchors, the correspondents, politicians and celebrities, the characters in the commercials, and the "little people" featured in the news.

At the apex of the identificatory hierarchy: the anchors. The term connotes weight and seriousness, symbolic figures who will keep us from going adrift on a stormy sea of significations. The anchors are authentic heroes, whose words have godlike efficacy: their mere designation of an event calls forth instant illustration in the form of animated miniatures or live-action footage. It has become commonplace to call them the Superstars of the News (the correspondents and reporters being minor stars and starlets), comparable in charismatic power and box office appeal to the great stars of the cinema. Almost invariably male (women being relegated to the late-night or weekend ghettoes), the anchor is Commander-in-Chief, symbolic Father, Head of the Space-Team and the Time-Team.

The anchor personae are, clearly, artful constructs. Newscasters are actors and it is quite logical that some of them should be awarded roles in fiction films – Mike Wallace in *A Face in the Crowd*, Howard K. Smith in *The Candidate*. Although newscasters play themselves, in their own name, rather than fictional characters patently not themselves, their work does involve a kind of acting. Changes of tone of voice reflect sequential changes in subject matter, and often a final summing-up recapitulates the different stances adopted throughout the newscast. The Network News style of acting, an idiosyncratic synthesis of Stanislavsky and Brecht, is above all minimalist, consisting of the orchestration of barely perceptible smiles and the delicate lowering or raising of eyebrows in conjunction with slight variations in tone or stress. The performance is built on a series of negations, a willful non-acting which simultaneously implies the presence and the denial of normal human emotions and responses (whence the scandal and admiration at Cronkite's tears over the assassination of John F. Kennedy, tears that quickly took on the status of myth precisely because of the exceptional glimpse they provided of human vulnerability behind the newscaster's mask).

"Audiences forget that movies are written," Joe Gillis tells Betty Schaefer in *Sunset Boulevard*, "they think actors make up their lines as they go along." Television audiences, similarly, forget that the news, like the fiction film, is writing (scenario, text) received as speech. Even the most "off-the-cuff" lines are often fabricated by a team of writers and researchers. The newscaster's art consists of evoking the cool authority and faultless articulation of the written or memorized text while simultaneously "naturalizing" the written word to restore the appearance of spontaneous communication. Most of the newscast, in fact, consists of this scripted spontaneity: newscasters reading from teleprompters, correspondents reciting hastily memorized notes, politicians delivering prepared speeches, commercial actors representing their roles. In each case, the appearance of fluency elicits respect while the trappings of spontaneity generate a feeling of unmediated communication.

The minimalist acting of network newscasters – the special patterns of stress and inflection, the stilted body language (assumed by North American cultural codes to connote professional competence) and the facial expressions at once intense and bland, a studied expressionlessness open to the most diverse projections – combine to trigger an effect of neutrality. The faces become empty icons, as blank and meaningless as Mozhykhin's visage in the celebrated Kuleshov experiment. We suspect the blankness to be an act, since the behind-the-scenes books tell us of the commercial break tantrums of prestigious anchors who quickly resume a tone of calm and dignity once back on the air. In reality, the calculated ambiguity of expression forms part of a commercially motivated political strategy. Since a given piece of news might be cheered by one sector of the audience but deplored by another – presidential union-busting pleases management but not labor – and since the audience is heterogeneous, traversed by tension along class, ethnic, and sexual lines, any undisguised expression of approval or disapproval would inevitably alienate part of the audience. The rhetoric of network diplomacy, consequently, favors a kind of oracular understatement, cultivating ambiguity, triggering patent but deniable meanings, encouraging the most diverse groups, with contradictory ideologies and aspirations, to believe that the newscasters are not far from their own beliefs.

In "A Short Organum for the Theater," Brecht denounces the bourgeois theater's deplorable habit of allowing the dominant actor to "star" by getting the other actors to work for him: "He makes his character terrible or wise by forcing his partners to make theirs terrified or attentive."[8] The news, similarly, fabricates its own star hierarchy. The superiority of the anchor, as we have seen, is structured into the news itself. But lesser newscasters also star. Their lines too are written, and their suave objectivity is underwritten by rehearsals and editing. Their forged articulateness, furthermore, contrasts with the inarticulateness of the "people in the street." A ritualistic montage during political campaigns, for example, features a series of voters expressing their preference for one or another of the candidates under consideration – "I like Carter, I think he's done a good job...." "I sort of like Reagan; he looks like someone you can trust...." – utterances striking largely for their apolitical and affective nature.[9] Like language, the news is built on differences. An ideologically informed and perhaps largely unconscious binarism in the news pits discursive adults (the newscasters, the politicians, the managers) against a stammering child-populace, authoritative rationality against mindless affectivity, the voiced against the voiceless. The atrophied political sense apparent in these electoral montage segments corresponds, admittedly, to a real tendency (often fostered by television itself), yet it hardly accounts for the almost total absence of articulate and politicized everyday Americans (as opposed to the diverse incarnations of the Professional Manager) on Network News. Like Brecht's star actor, the professionals get the others to work for them. While they star, the people play the supporting roles, when they are not mere backdrop or passive audience.[10]

The anchors and reporters of *Eyewitness News* are also cast for stardom. Since the news comes to us with a human face, they must be photogenic, or at least charismatic. Techniques formerly exploited for testing commercials and spotting potential rock hits are enlisted in the search for what is called the right "news flesh." "Tellback" techniques register positive and negative reactions. Guinea pig audiences are wired with electrodes that measure pulse and perspiration as indices of galvanic response to potential newscasters. "News presenters" without journalistic qualifications are hired if they pass the "skin test," and what they lack in talent or background is fabricated through image-building hype. A Baltimore station even presented a series dealing with the secret fantasies of its news team. The news, especially at the local level, is as much about the newscasters as it is about information.[11]

The individual acting styles of these local newscasters cohere into a larger representation called the "happy news team." Indeed, local *Eyewitness News* programs feature a kind of ensemble playing as cohesive as that of a Renoir film. A contrived atmosphere of self-conscious informality fosters this impression: the address is integrative; good-natured kidding implies that we all belong to a larger community sufficiently at ease to kid and joke. The happiness of the news team, we know, is a construct favored by media consultants ("news doctors") who recommend it as a tactic to boost ratings, and many icy calculations form a part of the fabrication of "warmth."

Eyewitness News exemplifies the insight (developed by Hans Magnus Enzensberger, Richard Dyer, and Fredric Jameson, among others) that to explain the public's attraction to a medium, one must look not only for the "ideological effect" that manipulates people into complicity with existing social relations, but also for the kernel of utopian fantasy reaching beyond these relations, whereby the medium constitutes itself as a projected fulfillment of what is desired and absent within the status quo. As Jameson puts it:

> The works of mass culture, even if their function lies in the legitimation of the existing order – or some worse one – cannot do their job without deflecting in the latter's service the deepest and most fundamental hopes and fantasies of the collectivity, to which they can therefore, no matter in how distorted a fashion, be found to have given voice.[12]

Indeed, *Eyewitness News* is susceptible to the same kind of analysis applied by Richard Dyer to the musical in his essay "Entertainment and Utopia." For what could be more utopian than this world of ludic productivity, where professionals seem to be having the time of their lives, where work is incessantly transformed into play? In the round of storytelling and easygoing chatter, laughter becomes the rhetorical glue between people and segments. Technical foul-ups elicit gales of laughter both from the on-screen newscasters and from the off-screen crew on the periphery of the set. In this electronically extended family romance, paternal figures preside benignly over a multi-ethnic symbolic family which stands as a metaphor for the larger community. Desirable as the amiable camaraderie of this racial utopia may be, its fictional element must be acknowledged.

Just as all films, including documentaries, can be said to be fiction films, so all of television, including the news, is inflected by fiction. But it hardly requires a semiotician to point out the fictive nature of the news, for the newscasters themselves, like journalists before them, consistently designate their work as fiction. They promise "tonight's top *stories*" not "tonight's top *facts*." Indeed, the industrial managers of the news virtually require a discourse with the attributes of fiction. Reuven Frank, president of the NBC News Division, explains:

> Every news story should, without any sacrifice of probity or responsibility, display the attributes of fiction, of drama. It should have structure and conflict, problem and dénouement, rising action and falling action, a beginning, a middle and an end. These are not only the essentials of drama; they are the essentials of narrative.[13]

The fictive nature of the news, or, more precisely, the nature of the news as a construct whose procedures resemble those of fiction, helps shed light on our initial question as to why the news is pleasurable. For stories, as a constitutive element in human life, are pleasurable because they impose the consolations of form on the flux of human experience. In this sense, all news is good news, in the same sense that all stories are good stories because they entail the pleasurability of fiction itself.

A typical news program can be seen as a weave of fictions: the individual stories, the mini-fictions called commercials, the ongoing drama of the slow revelation of the newscasters' personalities and the saga of their relation to each other and to us as spectators. The news involves macro-fictions, larger syntagmatic units such as the protracted story of American humiliation in Iran on "this, the 100th day of captivity for the American hostages" (with their homecoming orchestrated as the happy ending) and micro-fictions like the one-liners that close off the news day.[14] It is almost as if the art of storytelling, which Walter Benjamin thought to be in deep crisis, were being resurrected by an unlikely medium. And much of the pleasure of the news derives from systematic adherence to the teleological norms of storytelling.

At times, the news has more than the attributes of fiction: it literally is fiction. Following the same logic that led J. Stuart Blackton to film the sinking of the *Maine* in the bathtubs of New Jersey, networks have presented footage of military operations in Vietnam "as if" they were taking place in Cambodia.[15] At other times, the footage is authentic but its combination is fictional, as when library material and freshly shot location footage are molded into an illusory continuity. Or a single track can be fictious, as when library sound aurally buttresses the image track. Instant matting via chromakey, meanwhile, performs a kind of "creative geography," making it appear that the weatherwoman actually in the warm studio is strolling near the icy lake in Central Park.

But even apart from such clearly fictional instances, the news generally cultivates the pleasing aspect of fiction. News programs, especially local news programs, deploy what Barthes would call "hermeneutic" teasers, pieces of partial information designed to stimulate interest: "Coming Up: A Man Murders Wife and Lover . . . Actress Attempts Suicide: Details in a Minute." The stage-by-stage unfolding of the story, the orchestration of enigmas and building to a climax suggest a narrative striptease. Just as a detective story teases us with the enigma of a murder, or Hitchcock teases us with the problematic etiology of a character's unconventional sexual behavior, news titillates our curiosity and keeps us tuned in and turned on.

Television news also deploys what Barthes in *S/Z* calls "reality-effects": strategic details designed to elicit a feeling of verisimilitude. Like the nineteenth-century mimetic novel, the news orchestrates authenticating details which create the optical illusion of truth. The representational accuracy of the details is ultimately less important than the mere fact of their presence. Walter Cronkite's last-minute scribbling and paper shuffling was, presumably, pure reality-effect, since he in fact read fixed texts from a teleprompter. The noisetracks of newscasts, to take another example, often include the sounds of teletype, even though a well-equipped contemporary newsroom does not use teletype. The sounds, perhaps an elegiac homage to print media, also aurally signify work, urgency, and round-the-clock newsgathering. Those formulaic shots of correspondents posed in the White House driveway, finally, imply that the correspondent has just emerged with the news, yet in fact there are many roads to a presidential story and no guarantee at all that the correspondent physically entered the White House or even that he is actually standing in front of it.

Television news is a signifying practice with recognizable ordering procedures, an organized discourse rather than unmediated life. The news reduces the infinitude of available news items to a highly limited and predictable set of stories which it then produces and manufactures. The quite fantastic congruence of the three network news programs derives not only from shared "referential frames" and their common symbiotic relationship to established power, but also from the paradigmatic and syntagmatic operations that manufacture the news as narrative discourse.

The news, like the cinema, places images in sequence, and thus goes from shot to narrative. While newspaper readers have the freedom to fashion their own syntagmas, to determine their own itinerary through the printed text, the tele-spectator is obliged to follow a predetermined sequence. The news, in this sense, exhibits a certain syntagmatic orthodoxy. National Network News proceeds from "important" national or international stories through lesser stories and human interest features to a final anecdote providing an agreeable feeling of closure. *Eyewitness News* routinely begins with top local or national stories and proceeds to human interest, sports, and weather. It would no more begin with sports and proceed to top local news (unless a major sports event *became* the top local news) than diners in a restaurant would begin with dessert and conclude with an appetizer.

Thus the news, on some levels, has the predictable yet renewable charm of the genre film. Informational material, neatly fashioned with beginnings, middles, and ends, is poured into predictable narrative molds provided by the surrounding televisual and cinematic intertext. The murders reported on *Eyewitness News* (forever playing the B-film to the high-art seriousness of Network News), murders that amount to narrativized visualizations of statistics, differ from the murders in police or mystery shows mainly in the fact that they happened to occur in the three-dimensional world. Subjective shots suture us into the perspective of rapists and assassins. The viewer becomes voyeur and accomplice, domestic private eye, subconsciously applauding a spectacle of death and abuse.[16]

Since the news partially adopts the procedures of fiction, it is hardly surprising that it draws, to some extent, on the continuity codes of the fiction film. Cinema's way of telling stories – the specifically cinematic organization of time and space aimed at the reconstitution of a fictional world characterized by internal coherence and the appearance of flawless continuity – was partially inherited (with limitations that we shall examine subsequently) by television news. The filmed segments, especially, tend to respect this conventional decorum. New scenes are presented by a choreographed progression from more distant to closer shots (long shot of the Capitol building, then to the reporter framed next to the dome, then to the hearings room, then a zoom-in to the face of the witness). Continuity editing sutures potential gaps and continuous sounds aurally mask discontinuous images. Interviews are handled in a ritual alternation of over-the-shoulder two-shots and semi-profile medium close-ups of the interlocuters. Interview questions, often filmed or taped *after* the answers have been given, are reinserted in their logical rather than factual position in the sequence. And off-screen glances, implied to be between interviewer and interviewee or between the newscasters themselves, stitch together the newscast as a whole.

The music track also affords pleasure and guarantees continuity. Network News eschews commentative music, exploiting instead an electronic theme, a percussive *musique concrète* which opens and closes the program, and which is faded in and out to smooth the transitions between news reports and commercial breaks. The "music" programmatically evokes the electronic modernity of the newsroom, providing a tonal analogue to the urgency of fast-breaking news transmitted direct. The noises simultaneously evoke the clatter of old-fashioned teletypes and the electronic bleeps of computerized newsgathering. The music of local *Eyewitness News*, meanwhile, is more likely to pay tribute to its dual inheritance of journalism and show-biz, molding modernistic fanfares with aural evocations of the newsroom activity. Local news is more straightforwardly musical, with themes drawing on eminently urban musical forms such as jazz or disco, and is more likely to play with music for ironic effect, superimposing "It's Beginning to Look a Lot Like Christmas" on images of uncollected garbage, or accompanying space shuttle footage with the opeaning chords of *Thus Spake Zarathustra*.

While insisting on certain shared continuity procedures between television news and the conventional fiction film, we would be wrong to posit an absolute identity between the two media. In fact, as the Glasgow University Media Group points out in *Bad News*, television news inherits two distinct and in some ways contradictory discursive logics: the filmic and the journalistic. Filmic procedures are indeed present, especially in the filmed correspondents' reports, but they are constantly jostled by journalistic codes and procedures. This journalistic heritage of the news gives the lie to the myth of television's "visual imperative." In fact, television news is relatively impervious to the hegemony of the visual, for its images, more often than not, simply illustrate the spoken or written commentary. The soundtrack is in many respects more essential than the image track; the news' Echo speaks louder than its Narcissus. Since the news consists largely in newscasters speaking the news in the studio, we can grasp its essentials even when we merely hear it from another room. The news, furthermore, rather like the cinema immediately after the advent of sound, tends towards slavish devotion to the talking head, to a veritable worship of the human voice speaking in synchronous sound. In this sense it is phono- as well as logocentric, cultivating a televisual "metaphysics of presence."

In an otherwise excellent and incontrovertible article, William Gibson reaches the hasty conclusion that the fundamental aesthetic of television is naturalist:

> Why do these symbolic visions look so real? The answer begins with the aesthetic of television news, Naturalism. All network news camera placing, filming, and editing are conducted with the goal of completely erasing or minimalizing all signs of

camera placing, filming, and editing. The Naturalist film code seeks to hide the fact that it is film and instead presents itself as unmediated reality.[17]

Gibson goes on to generalize about the medium:

Network News is not the only network program to conceal its symbolic fabrications in naturalistic film. Most movies and most television series and even most commercials also present themselves as *unmediated* reality.[18]

No section of the television world, Gibson goes on to argue, shows any awareness of the existence of any other part:

For a television program to present itself as "life," it must for that very reason deny that there is any other "life." For a television show to refer to other shows or commercials would be to call attention to its own existence as a program, rather than "live." ... Such are the dynamics of Naturalism.[19]

But while the charge of naturalism applies, as we have seen, to certain features of the news, specifically to the illusionistic continuity codes of filmed reports, that charge must be revised and even reversed when extended to the news as a whole or to television in general. And here we approach the limits of the analogy between television news and the classical fiction film.

The naturalism of the filmed reports, first of all, is not total. We can dismiss one fissure in this illusion – the visible presence of the microphone – as (1) a solution to the problem of what the correspondent is to do with his or her hands, and (2) a prop or reality-effect, an iconic signifier denoting "television correspondent." But the fact that the correspondent addresses us directly cannot be so easily dismissed. Whereas the classical fiction film inherited the "fourth wall" convention from naturalistic theater, whereby the actors were not to regard or address the spectators lest they be disturbed in their position as Peeping Toms, television news more typically involves direct address by both anchor and correspondent. Although individual filmed reports may be edited as stories, they are framed as conversation, a fact whose implications, as we shall see later, are complex and far-ranging.

The view of the news aesthetic as *fundamentally* (rather than incidentally) naturalist and illusionist is misguided on a number of grounds. It is misguided, first of all, for a practical reason. Illusionistic continuity is often simply impracticable in the news; obviously not all stories permit the luxury of fiction film procedures. In such instances, it becomes virtually impossible to efface the marks of enunciation. But by a curious kind of associational boomerang, it is precisely the presence of these marks of enunciation – the blur created by the hurried movement of the camera, the inadequate focus, the awkward framing – that convinces us of the scene's authenticity, for we associate them with reportorial work on live, actual, unpredictable events. (Which is why fiction films, from

Open City through *Battle of Algiers* and *Medium Cool*, pointedly incorporate the traces of improvised, on-the-spot filmmaking into the films themselves as guarantees of verisimilitude.)

The view of television news as naturalist in style is misguided, secondly, because of the nature of the pro-textual event. Illusionism in the cinema is designed to convince the spectators that what are seeing and hearing corresponds to "something that happened." But spectators of the news *know* that something really happened, first of all because it almost invariably *did*, and secondly because alternative media such as radio and the print media have already alerted them that it did. The telespectator's credence, consequently, is less dependent on illusionistic trickery. The news is thus freed to play with what normally would be considered anti-illusionist effects. Assassination footage can be replayed in slow motion, stopped, frozen, and decorated with illustrative circles because the viewer does not doubt for one instant the reality of the event.[20]

It is only by a highly artifical feature, furthermore, that we separate the news from the commercials. The "flow" of the news program includes the commercials. Indeed, on one level, the commercials *are* the news. That sponsors have the right to interrupt essential information, for example about a narrowly averted nuclear disaster, itself conveys a powerful ideological effect. Coca-Cola is the real thing, eternal; the news is factitious and ephemeral – such is the ontology of the commercial. At the same time, the news and the commercials reciprocally influence each other, so that the commercials imitate the news and vice versa. Mobil Oil, to take one example, seats an imitation anchorman at an imitation news desk, backed by an imitation newsroom map of the world, and has him express the Mobil *Weltanschauung*. Trading on the widespread trust of the news as institution, Mobil hopes to transfer that confidence to itself and its policies. (The fact that Mobil advertises on the same program that features oil news is infinitely more important than any verifiable "bias" in the news presentation itself.) The news, meanwhile, imitates the commercials by advertising itself, its news teams and upcoming news specials, and by exploiting some of the same manipulative procedures – image enhancement, secondary identification, mini-narrative structures.[21]

Both commercials and the news fit into generic molds thrown up by the cinematic and televisual intertext, and this intertext is not intrinsically or invariably naturalist but often, surprisingly, self-referential and reflexive. Far from being hermetically sealed off from one another, there is constant circulation between the programs. The news itself does features on the popularity of shows like *Dallas* or *General Hospital*, and Walter Cronkite has a cameo appearance on *The Mary Tyler Moore Show*. At least two shows – *Mary Tyler Moore* and *Jessica Novak* – have been set in newsrooms, while the short-lived *Fly and Bones* featured the Smothers Brothers as television reporters. In the world of sitcoms, Archie Bunker, like Ralph Kramden and many others before him, performs in a television commercial, while the real-life Carroll O'Connor made commercials for Jimmy Carter. Variety shows like *Carol Burnett* or *Saturday Night Live* constantly "carnivalize" commercials and other shows. Talk shows not only display cameras and video switchers as part of their credits but also incessantly turn to talk about television itself. Johnny Carson mocks his own monologue as self-consuming artifact, while the video cameras show his producer just off-stage. Television enjoys its own "bloopers" and regularly rebroadcasts them. It even recounts its own history in *The Golden Age of Television*, and looks at itself in the mirror of *Entertainment Tonight*. In countless ways, in sum, television is self-referential and self-cannibalizing.

Television, in fact, often seems positively Brechtian rather than naturalist. Many of the distancing features characterized as Brechtian in Godard films typify television as well: the designation of the apparatus; the spatial co-presence of multiple images within the frame; the inclusion of two-dimensional materials; the direct address to the spectator; the commercial "interruptions" of the narrative flow; the juxtaposition of heterogeneous slices of discourse; the mixing of documentary and fiction modes; the subverting of visual hegemony through a dominant soundtrack; the constant recourse to written materials; the creative incorporation of errors.

Yet we know that if television is Brechtian, it is Brechtian in a peculiarly ambiguous and often debased way. While authentic Brechtianism elicits an active thinking spectator rather than a passive consumer of entertainment, most television is as narcotic and culinary as the bourgeois theater that Brecht denounced. Brecht's goal was not to satisfy audience expectations but to transform them, whereas the central impulse of commercial television (notwithstanding the creative and critical contribution of its artists) is to transform only two things: the audience's viewing habits and its buying habits. Brecht's goal was not to *be* popular in box-office terms but to *become* popular – that is, to create a new public for a new kind of theater linked to new modes of social life – whereas commercial television's goal, at least from the point of view of its managers, is to be popular in the crudely quantitative terms of "ratings." Rather than trigger "alienation effects," commercial television often simply alienates. It domesticates the horrible rather than estranging it; it often obscures the causal network of events rather than revealing it.

While television does occasionally suggest the *possibility* of authentic Brechtianism – one thinks of certain features of *The Mary Tyler Moore Show* – many of its many distancing devices, when looked at more closely, turn out to be, if not naturalist, at least anti-Brechtian.[22] The commercial interruptions that place the news "on hold," for example, are not pauses for reflection but breaks for manipulation, intended not to make us think but to make us feel and buy; rather than providing demystifying jolts, they continue the narcotic flow. The self-referentiality of commercials also serves an anti-Brechtian purpose. Commercials which parody themselves or other commercials do not demystify the product or expose hidden codes; rather, they serve both to differentiate their sponsor from other, presumably less candid sponsors who do not "confess" their commercial's status as artifact, and to weaken the spectator's defenses. From Arthur Godfrey through Johnny Carson, good-natured kidding of commercials has helped rather than hurt sales, for the humor signals the spectator that the commercial is not to be taken seriously, and this relaxed state renders the spectator more open to its message. In fact, the commercial is in deadly earnest – it is after the spectator's money.

Both the news and the commercials share one Brechtian feature which deserves a longer and deeper look: a penchant for direct address. Most of the news consists of talking heads speaking directly to the camera. Nothing, on the surface, could be farther removed from the illusionist aesthetic. A cardinal rule of the classical fiction film is that the actor must never acknowledge the camera/audience. The fictive events must unwind magically, indifferent to the presence of the audience. Illusionism hides the source of enunciation, masking its discourse as "history." The news, on the other hand, offers the image of a person, who would seem to be the source of enunciation, at a close social distance speaking directly to us.

What can we say about this apparent contradiction between illusionistic aspects of the filmed reports and the news' penchant for the same direct address favored by Brecht and Godard? First, the contradiction is real – the direct address segments *are* less illusionistic than the filmed reports. Second, this direct address is correlated with power. Newscasters share with advertisers, entertainers, and politicians this privilege which implies immense political, narrational, and discursive power. This power is correlated, furthermore, with lack of mediation. (Presidents, anchors, and advertisers address us directly in relatively close shots, correspondents address us from a slightly greater distance and regard us somewhat less insistently, and the "others" are filmed as they might be in a fiction film.)[23] Third, this direct address is itself a fiction. It is fictional in its apparent spontaneity – the implication that the newscaster has authored his or her own remarks without preformulated sources or editorial elaboration. The newscasters, furthermore, speak to an audience not present in the flesh, all the while cultivating the tacit assumption that what is said was formulated just for that audience, as if each spectator or group of spectators were the only one.

Although the apparent structure of the news is one of discourse, then, this discourse is itself fictional; it is itself *histoire*. The news is fiction, but the fiction is displaced. The "stories," although they exploit fictional procedures, are not ultimately fictional; the fiction lies, rather, in the fictive nature of the relationship between newscaster and audience. The news does not begin with "Once Upon a Time" and conclude with "They Lived Happily Ever After"; it begins with "Good Evening" and ends with "Good Night." It is framed, in other words, as a simulation of face-to-face two-person communication; the newscaster singlehandedly imitates the characteristic rhythms of dialogue. The "communication" is unilateral, not a reciprocal exchange between two transmitter–receivers but rather a powerful transmitter enjoying direct access to millions of subjects. On one level, then, we can even *reverse* the illusionistic formula. If illusionistic fictions disguise their discourse as history, television news, in certain respects, wraps up its history as discourse.

That this displaced fiction effect actually works is attested to by the immense credence given the news. Polls have shown Walter Cronkite to be the most trusted man in America and the news to be one of the country's most trusted institutions. The pseudo-intimacy of the global village fosters a confusion between the actual newscasters and their fictive personae, or, more accurately, it installs a phantasmatic relationship between the viewer and the news celebrity. People who scarcely know their own neighbors are convinced that they know the newscasters. Ted Koppel reports receiving letters which address him as if he were father, son, or lover. In a social situation of interpersonal loneliness, television becomes a meal and bedtime companion, part of the existential fabric of our lives, and newscasters become friends and confidantes.

Television news promotes what might be called – in both psychoanalytic and political terms – the regime of the "fictive We." In psychoanalytic terms, television promotes a narcissistic relationship with an imaginary other. It infant-alizes in the sense that the young child perceives everything in relation to itself; everything is ordered to the measure of its ego. Television, if it is not received critically, fosters a kind of confusion of pronouns: between "I" the spectator and "He" or "She" the newscaster, as engaged in a mutually flattering dialogue. This fictive "We" can then speak warmly about "Ourselves" and coldly about who-ever is posited as "Them." This misrecognition of mirror-like images has profound political consequences. Oil corporation commercials tell us: "We Americans have a lot of oil." The "We" is clearly fictive; most of us own no oil; we buy it at exorbitant prices in the wake of a stage-managed energy crisis. Shortly after the ill-fated "rescue attempt" in Iran, to take another example, Chuck Scarborough of New York's *Channel 4 News* began his newscast, "Well, we did our best, but we didn't make it." The "We" in this case presumably included the newscaster, the president, and a few aides. It certainly did not include the majority of Americans, even if their "support" could be artfully simulated after the fact. Television news, then, claims to speak for us, and often does, but just as often it deprives us of the right to speak by deluding us into thinking that its discourse is our own. Often it gives us the illusion of social harmony, the ersatz communication of a global village which is overwhelmingly white, male, and corporate.

The televisual institution, to slightly paraphrase Metz, is not just the televisual industry (which works to boost ratings, not to diminish them), it is also the mental machinery – another industry – which viewers "accustomed to television" have internalized historically and which has adapted them to the consumption of television as it is. The social regulation of the telespectator's metapsychology has as its function the setting up of "good object" relations with television (including television news) if at all possible, for television is watched out of desire, not reluctance, in the hope that it will please. The psychology of the spectator is linked to the financial mechanisms of television news and its possibilities of self-reproduction as Heath's "pleasure-meaning-commodity-complex." Psychoanaly-tic methods help disengage its relation to desire; semiotics helps disengage its procedures of meaning; and a critical and dialectical Marxism can disengage its status as purveyor and exemplification of commodity fetishism and its place within competing class discourse.

Only such a multi-dimensional approach can fully answer our original question: Why is the news pleasurable? Television is a libidinal as well as technological apparatus, a machine for erotic as well as financial investment. For its own self-reproduction within a capitalist system, the news must establish a good object relation with its spectator. Viewers have to "like" the news or they will not watch it, and they have to watch so that they can be sold again to sponsors. Television thus manufactures its own audience as well as the news. Through the pleasuring capacities of the apparatus, through the procedures of fiction, through attractive newscasters as the erotic subtext of the news, it manufactures itself as a good object. At the same time, to remain a good object, it must also somehow connect with the mass of people who are its audience and represent their larger social wishes and desires, for the kernel of utopianism also forms part of its constant solicitude and seduction.

It is for this reason that we would be wrong to regard television, or its news, as monolithically regressive. Manipulation and exploitation are present, but so are resistance and critique. As a matrix in which dominant and oppositional discourses do constant battle, television can never completely reduce the antagonistic dialogue of class voices to the reassuring hum of bourgeois hegemony. Television can numb consciousness, but it also drags colonial wars into the hearts of imperial beasts. While it at times amplifies the discourse of power, it also can make us aware of how social policies impinge on human beings. Television is not only its industrial managers, it is also its creative participants, the people who appear in the news, and we the audience who can resist, apply pressure to, and decode its messages. But one of our first theoretical tasks is to understand not only the alienation, but also the utopian promise of its mechanisms of pleasure.

Notes

1   For discussions of the apparatus, see Jean-Louis Baudry's "Cinéma: effets idéologiques produits par l'appareil de base," *Cinétique* No. 7–8 (1970) (published in English translation by Alan Williams as "Ideological Effects of the Basic Cinematographic Apparatus," *Film Quarterly* Vol. 28, No. 2 [Winter 1974–5], pp. 39–47), and his "Le Dispositif: approches métapsychologiques de l'impression de réalité," *Communications* No. 23 (May 1975), pp. 56–72 (published in English translation by Bertrand Augst and Jean Andrews as "The Apparatus," *Camera Obscura* No. 1 [Fall 1976], as well as his *L'Effet cinéma* (Paris: Albatross, 1978). See also Christian Metz, "Le Signifiant imaginaire," *Communications* No. 23 (May 1975), pp. 3–55 (published in English translation by Ben Brewster as "The Imaginary Signifier," *Screen* Vol. 16, No. 2 [Summer 1975], pp. 14–76), and his "Le Film de fiction et son spectateur: étude métapsychologique," also in *Communications* No. 23 (pp. 108–35), and translated by Alfred Guzzetti as "The Fiction Film and Its Spectator: A Metapsychological Study,"

New Literary History Vol. 8, No. 1 (Autumn 1976), pp. 75–105. Jean-Louis Comolli's "Machines of the Visible" is included in *The Cinematic Apparatus*, ed. Stephen Heath and Teresa de Lauretis (London: St Martin's Press, 1980).

2 Metz, "The Imaginary Signifier," p. 51.

3 The fact of live transmission also slightly alters Metz's conception of the cinematic experience as a missed rendezvous between an exhibitionist and a voyeur, in which the actor–exhibitionist is present at the filming but absent at the screening, while the spectator is present at the screening but absent at the filming. On its own terms, Metz's conception entails the problem that the film, if not the actor, is present at the screening, a fact equally true of television. But through live transmission, television at least allows the putative voyeur and exhibitionist to share the *time* of the performance.

4 I would like to express my deep appreciation to Yeshayahu Nir of Hebrew University for his stimulating comments and helpful suggestions. He will doubtless recognize certain of his examples and insights in the "shared discourse" of this essay. I would also like to thank Ann Kaplan and Brian Winston for their suggestions.

5 Jean-Louis Comolli, in "Machines of the Visible," speculates that the extreme eagerness of the first cinema spectators to recognize in the filmic images – devoid of color, depth, nuance – the literal double of life itself, derived precisely from this sense of a lack to be filled. Is there not, Comolli wonders, "in the very principle of representation, a force of disavowal which gives free reign to an analogical illusion that is as yet only weakly manifested in the iconic signifiers themselves?"

6 The cinema's most vivid object-lesson in both the illusory superiority and the voyeuristic nature of the cinematic/televisual situation is, perhaps, Alfred Hitchcock's *Rear Window*, in which the Jimmy Stewart character (significantly a mass media photojournalist) spies on his neighbors across a Greenwich Village courtyard. Stewart's eye wanders from window to window, as if he were changing channels from sit-com to police serial to soap opera. Hitchcock brilliantly undercuts his scopophilic protagonist by having the world he is watching, supposedly from a safe distance, invade his space and quite literally grab him by the throat.

7 Robert MacNeil of *The MacNeil-Lehrer Report* recalled that during the war in Vietnam, footage of American soldiers cutting off Vietnamese ears had been rejected for the program because newscasters pointed out that the evening time-slot coincided, for many families, with dinner time. Apart from this "culinary" censorship, however, he might have also pointed out that such imagery would not have flattered the American self-image as morally superior to the Vietnamese.

8 Bertolt Brecht, *Brecht on Theatre*, ed. John Willett (New York: Hill and Wang, 1964), p. 197.

9 This inarticulateness contrasts sharply with the peasants and workers interviewed on the street in Guzman's *The Battle of Chils*; their off-the-cuff remarks show a sophisticated grasp of domestic and international politics.

10 The non-professionals in the news – the interviewees on the street, the bystanders waving in the background, the individuals featured in human interest stories – at times nourish their own dreams of stardom. Indeed, the general familiarity with such media performances would enable most of us to adopt the correct persona if called upon. Jean-Luc Godard and Anne-Marie Miéville, in some of their television work, make a gesture toward taking this seriously by presenting "ordinary people" more or less directly to the viewer. The scandal of *Six Fois Deux* consists precisely in this

conjunction of ordinary people with a deliberate lack of directorial mediation or editorializing. Two schizophrenics speak, but they are neither named nor labeled as schizophrenics. No editing betrays an authorial attitude, and no newscasterly wrap-up tells us what to think. Thus Godard–Miéville hypostatize an existing feature of television – its fondness for popular vignettes – while at the same time radicalizing and subverting it.

11 For more information about the exploitation of sexual appeal in local news, see "Sex and the Anchor Person," (*Newsweek* [December 15, 1980], pp. 65–6) by Harry F. Waters with George Hackett; and Richard Corliss on "Sex Stars of the Seventies" (*Film Comment* Vol. 15, No. 4 [July–August 1979], pp. 27–9).

12 Fredric Jameson, "Reification and Utopia in Mass Culture," *Social Text* No. 1 (Winter 1979), p. 144.

13 Quoted in Edward J. Epstein, *News From Nowhere* (New York: Random House, 1974), pp. 4–5.

14 That the story of America's humiliation was partially a media construct becomes obvious when we recall that the imprisonment of the crew of the *Pueblo* in North Korea received no such buildup, nor did their homecoming elicit a heroes' welcome. The media treatment of Iran, in any case, certainly helped create an atmosphere in which the American public was quite ready for Ronald Reagan and increased defense expenditures.

15 Epstein, p. 22.

16 Christian Metz holds the fiction film itself partially responsible for the mental and motor passivity of the spectator. Norman Holland, similarly, argues in *The Dynamics of Literary Response* (New York: W. W. Norton, 1975) that the "willing suspension of disbelief depends partially on the knowledge that he or she will not be expected to act as a result of the fiction, a convention that allows a relaxation of the reality principle – the critical faculty through which we continually check what is presented as 'non-fiction' for its truth – and thus results in a pleasant blurring of what is fiction and what is self."

17 William Gibson, "Network News: Elements of a Theory," *Social Text* No. 3 (Fall 1980), p. 103.

18 Ibid., p. 106.

19 Ibid.

20 Much of the news, on the other hand, is highly pre-packaged, consisting of staged presentations or "pseudo-events": press conferences, hearings, speeches, poll results. The singularity of the Sadat assassination was, in a sense, the fact that a pseudo-event (a president reviewing his troops) was brutally interrupted by a "real" event.

21 The commercials, like the news, draw on the cinematic–televisual intertext. McDonalds' commercials draw on the codes of the musical comedy, creating an atmosphere of whimsical group-singing magically transcending spatial distance. Toy commercials incline to single frame animation and computer ads draw on science fiction. Headache remedies (see especially Excedrin commercials from the mid-seventies) pay homage to deep-focus realism à la Orson Welles, foregrounding the potion while the characters play out oedipal dramas in the "deep space." Perfume, deodorant, and jewelry commercials tend toward Lelouche romanticism (soft focus, sensuous dollies, liquid dissolves), their 30-second plots racing from meeting to *coup-de-foudre* and implied *jomissance*. Jeans commercials, meanwhile, are more straightforwardly pornographic.

22 Two shows reveal both the critical potentialities and frequent degradation of Brecht-ianism on television. *The Mary Tyler Moore Show*, with its quasi-theatrical sets, archly distanced acting, and its constant appeal to the spectator's intelligence, exhibits aspects of an authetic Brechtianism. The short-lived *Jessica Novak*, on the other hand, exploits both the image of the "new woman" (often equated with "sexually aggres-sive") and public curiosity about the behind-the-scenes truth about the newsroom and the newscasters in a show whose apparent reflexivity masks a regressive illusion-ism. In *Jessica Novak*, the self-referential becomes the self-reverential as the prot-agonist embodies Television, which is the real hero – the *deux ex machina* that solves the problems, saves lives, and heals families. The attention paid to television processes becomes merely another reality-effect, an index of profession and milieu.

23 Whence the outrage when one of the "others" – an Iranian woman militant (triply "other") – proposed to address the American public directly during the hostage crisis. The proposal elicited an instant outcry that the militants were trying to "use" the media – as indeed they were – but the accusation implied that television and its audience were not being "used" every day of the year.

22

Addressing the Spectator of a 'Third World' National Cinema: The Bombay 'Social' Film of the 1940s and 1950s

Ravi S. Vasudevan

Recent discussions of cinema and national identity in the 'third world' context have tended, by and large, to cluster around the concept of a 'third cinema'. Here the focus has been on recovering or reinventing 'national' aesthetic and narrative traditions against the homogenizing impulses of Hollywood in its domination over markets and normative standards. One of the hallmarks of third cinema theory has been its firmly unchauvinist approach to the 'national'. In its references to wider international aesthetic practices, and especially to modernist drives, third cinema asserts but problematizes the boundaries between nation and other. In the process, it also explores the ways in which the suppressed internal others of the nation, whether of class, sub- or counter-nationality, ethnic group or gender, can find a voice.[1]

A substantial lacuna in this project has been any sustained understanding of the domestic commercial cinema in the 'third world'. This is important because in countries such as India the commercial film has, since the dawn of the 'talkies', successfully marginalized Hollywood's position in the domestic market. This is not to claim that it has functioned within an entirely self-referential autarchy. The Bombay cinema stylistically integrated aspects of the world 'standard', and has also been influential in certain foreign markets. But it constitutes something like a 'nation space' against the dominant norms of Hollywood, and so ironically fulfils aspects of the role which the avant-garde third cinema proclaims as its own. Clearly, the difference in language cannot be the major explanation for this autonomy, for other national cinemas have succumbed to the rule of the Hollywood film. Instead, it is in the peculiarities of the Indian commercial film as an entertainment form that we may find the explanation for its ascendency over the home market.

The formation of a national market for the Bombay cinema was a multi-layered phenomenon. Bombay became ascendent in the home market only in the 1950s. Earlier, Pune in Maharashtra and Calcutta in Bengal were important centres of film production, catering to the Marathi and Bengali speaking 'regional' audience as well as to the Hindi audience which is the largest linguistic market in the country. While these regional markets continued to exist, Bombay became the main focus of national film production. This ascendency was curtailed by the emergence of important industries in Tamilnadu, Andhra Pradesh and Kerala, producing films in Tamil, Telugu and Malayalam. From the 1980s, these centres produced as many, and often more, films than Bombay.[2] There has been a certain equivalence in the narrative form of these cinemas, but each region contributed its distinctive features to the commercial film. In the Tamil and Telugu cases the cinema also has a strong link with the politics of regional and ethnic identity.

The achievement of the commercial cinema has had ambivalent implications for the social and political constitution of its spectator. All of these cinemas are involved in constructing a certain abstraction of national identity; by national identity I mean here not only the pan-Indian one, but also regional constructions of national identity. This process of abstraction suppresses other identities, either through stereotyping or through absence. The Bombay cinema has a special role here, because it positions other national/ethnic/religious and social identities (it has largely avoided representing the crucial question of caste) in stereotypical ways under an overarching north Indian, majoritarian Hindu identity. The stereotypes of the 'southerner' (or 'Madrasi', a term which dismissively collapses the entire southern region), the Bengali, the Parsi, the Muslim, the Sikh and the Christian occupy the subordinate positions in this universe. Bombay crystallized as the key centre for the production of national fictions just at the moment that the new state came into existence, so its construction of the national narrative carries a particular force.[3]

Indian commercial cinema has exerted an international presence in countries of Indian immigration as in East Africa, Mauritius, the Middle East and South East Asia, but also in a significant swathe of Northern Africa.[4] It has also been popular in the countries of the former Soviet Union and China. Such a sphere of influence makes one think of a certain arc of narrative form separate from, if overlapping at points with, the larger hegemony exercised by Hollywood. From the description of the cultural 'peculiarities' of the Bombay cinema which follows, one could speculate whether its narrative form has a special resonance in 'transitional' societies. The diegetic world of this cinema is primarily governed by the logic of kinship relations, and its plot driven by family conflict. The system of dramaturgy is a melodramatic one, displaying the characteristic ensemble of manichaeism, bipolarity, the privileging of the moral over the psychological, and the deployment of coincidence. And the relationship between narrative, performance sequence and action spectacle is loosely structured in the fashion of a cinema of attractions.[5] In addition to these features, the system of narration incorporates Hollywood codes of continuity editing in a fitful, unsystematic fashion, relies heavily on visual forms such as the tableau and inducts stable cultural codes of looking of a more archaic sort. Aspects of this picture echo the form of early Euro-American cinema, indicating that what appeared as a fairly abbreviated moment in the history of Western cinema has defined the long-term character of this influential cinema of 'another world'. What is required here is a comparative account of narrative forms in 'transitional' societies which might set out a different story of the cinema than the dominant Euro–American one.

In this paper I want to isolate certain aspects of this way of framing the Bombay cinema, focusing in particular on how the spectator of the 'national film' is addressed. I conceive of this as 'an analysis, even if rudimentary, of the position of the spectator within his/her cultural context, within certain large representational and belief systems'.[6] I am using examples from the 1940s and 1950s Hindi social film – the genre used to address the problems of modern life – to explain how the cinema invited the spectator to assume an identity defined along the axis of gender, class and nationhood. I want to do this primarily by identifying the way in which filmic visual culture and narrative form impinge on and shape the subjectivity of the spectator. For a large part of this paper, I will be concerned with the textual constitution of the spectator, but in the final section I will outline the dimensions of a historically significant spectatorial position that developed in the 1940s. I will focus on the way in which prevailing anxieties about the definition of a national identity at the time of the country's independence were reflected in offscreen discourses about actors and directors and how they influenced filmic reception. The popular cinema was involved in mapping a symbolic space which envisaged the national formation as being grounded in certain hierarchies. Here, I lay particular emphasis on the relations between the majority Hindu group and the minority Muslim as it was relayed through film narratives and offscreen discourses.

A Dominant Paradigm

Before turning to visual and narrative analysis, I want briefly to summarize some of the conventional viewpoints about the commercial film in India and the nature of its spectator. The dominant view is that of a tradition of film criticism associated with Satyajit Ray and the Calcutta Film Society in the 1950s. This school of criticism, which has proved influential in subsequent mainstream film criticism, assailed the popular cinema for its derivativeness from the sensational aspects of the US cinema, the melodramatic externality and stereotyping of its characters, and especially for its failure to focus on the psychology of human interaction. In these accounts, the spectator of the popular film emerges as an immature, indeed infantile, figure, one bereft of the rationalist imperatives required for the Nehru era's project of national construction.[7]

Recent analyses of the popular cinemas in the 'non-Western' world suggest to me that the melodramatic mode has, with various indigenous modifications, been a characteristic form of narrative and dramaturgy in societies undergoing the transition to modernity.[8] 'National' criticisms of this prevalent mode have taken the particular form that I have just specified, and have had both developmentalist and democratic components. The implication was that, in so far as the melodramatic mode was grounded in an anti-individualist ethos, it would undercut the rational, critical outlook required for the development of a just, dynamic and independent nation.[9]

In the Indian case, this premise of modern film criticism has been taken in rather different directions. The critic Chidananda Das Gupta emerges from the dominant tradition, being one of the founder members of the Calcutta Film Society. His recent book, *The Painted Face*,[10] argues that the commercial film catered to a spectator who had not severed his ties from the countryside and so had a traditional or premodern relationship to the image, one which incapacitated him or her from distinguishing between image and reality.[11] Das Gupta also argues that the pre-rationalist spectator was responsive to Bombay cinema's focus on family travails and identity, a focus which displaces attention from the larger social domain. He describes the spectator caught up in the psychic trauma brought about by threatened loss of the mother and the struggle for adult identity as adolescent and self-absorbed or 'totalist'.[12] We have echoes here of the realist criticism of the 1950s in its reference to the spectator of the commercial film as infantile. There is a class component to the psychological paradigm, in which the uprooted, lumpen and working class are regarded as the main audience for the Bombay film. Such a conception of the spectator ultimately has political implications. Das Gupta sees this social and psychic configuration reflecting the gullible mentality that enabled the rise to power of the actor–politicians of the south, M. G. Ramachandran and N. T. Rama Rao.[13] The naive spectator actually believed his screen idols to be capable of the prowess they displayed onscreen. In Das Gupta's view, the rational outlook required for the development of a modern nation-state is still lacking, and the popular cinema provides us with an index of the cognitive impairment of the majority of the Indian people.

This psychological and social characterization of the premodern spectator is pervasive, even if it is not used to the same ends as Das Gupta's. The social psychologist Ashish Nandy, while working outside (and, indeed, against) the realist tradition, shares some of its assumptions about the psychological address of the commercial film.[14] Nandy argues that the personality as expressed in Indian culture differed from that conceived by modern Western culture. There are two features in his conception of the psychical difference between premodern and modern forms in film narratives. For him, the dominant spectator of the popular cinema, caught in 'traditional' arenas of life and work, is quite remote from the outlook of the modern middle class; as such, this spectator is attracted to a narrative which ritually neutralizes the discomfiting features of social change, those modern thought patterns and practices which have to be adopted for reasons of survival. Regressing into a submissive familial frame of reference provides one narrative route for the traumatized spectator. But there is a second, contestatory psychic trajectory. Nandy suggests that Indian culture was defined by androgynous elements which provided the most fertile form of resisting colonial, and more broadly modern, paradigms of progress. He embraces the cultural indices of a subjectivity which is not governed by the rationalist psychology and reality orientation of that contested other. In this sense he valorizes that which Das Gupta sees as a drawback.

So a psychical matrix for understanding the address of the commercial Bombay film to its spectator, echoing in some respects the realist criticism of the 1950s, has been extended into the more explicitly psychoanalytical interpretations of spectatorial dispositions and cognitive capacities. Ironically, these premises are shared both by those critical of the commercial film and its spectator for their lack of reality orientation, and those who valorize Indian culture's resistance to modern forms of consciousness. These arguments in turn support different visions of how the relationship between psychology, class and society/nation can give rise to different dynamics of social transformation.

The popular cinema is much more complicated than these criticisms allow. Greater attention has to be paid to the relationship between family and society, between the private and the public, and especially the relations of power within which this subjectivity is produced. For instance, a marked feature of these formulations is the absence of any understanding of patriarchy, of the gendered authority which I will argue is central to understanding the sociopolitical vision of the popular film. Film studies in India will have to engage with the terms of identity offered by the cinema, its fantasy scenarios and its norms of authority and responsibility, instead of insisting that an 'adult' identity is non-negotiable or, in certain countercultural readings, undesirable. Above all, it will have to look at these questions as ones of cinematic narration.

An Indian Melodrama

On the issue of personality construction and its implications for social transformation, a useful point of departure is the elaborate Euro-American theoretical mapping of melodramatic modes of theatre and fiction. It is worth recalling that British theatre exercised considerable influence on the development of the nineteenth-century Indian urban theatre.[15] In Peter Brooks's work,[16] melodrama emerged in the nineteenth century as a form which spoke of a post-sacred universe in which the certainties of traditional meaning and hierarchical authority had been displaced. The melodramatic narrative constantly makes an effort to recover this lost security, but meaning comes to be increasingly founded in the personality. Characters take on essential, psychic resonances corresponding to family identities and work out forbidden conflicts and desires. The family is then positioned as the new locus of meaning. The spectator is addressed through the most basic registers of experience, with the narratives focusing on primal triggers of desire and anxiety. In the process, the social dimension is not displaced, but collapses into the familial and, indeed, the family itself becomes a microcosm of the social level. Melodramatic narratives therefore tend to represent the most significant characters of social life as key familial figures, father, mother and child. It would be a mistake then to categorize these narratives as bounded by the psychic universe of the inward, family-fixated adolescent. That would be to reduce the universe constructed by film narratives to their foundational address.

However, a melodramatic narrative and dramaturgy is also employed in Indian film genres such as the mythological and devotional, not only in post-sacred genres such as the social. To further confound the secular dimensions of melo-drama, even in the Bombay 'social', the genre of the modern day, women often employ a traditional Hindu idiom deifying the husband. What implications does this have for melodrama as a so-called post-sacred form?

Narrative structures and strategies are rather more complicated than these religious idioms would suggest. The sociologist Veena Das, in her article on the popular mythological film *Jai Santoshi Ma/Hail Santoshi Ma* (Vijay Sharma, 1975),[17] and the art critic Geeta Kapur, in her analysis of the 'devotional', *Sant Tukaram* (Fatehlal and Damle, 1936),[18] show that the invocation of the sacred is continuous with the reference to non-sacred space, that of the family drama and everyday activity. And Anuradha Kapur's account of the urban Indian Parsi theatre suggests that the discourse of the sacred was subordinated to an emerging discourse of the real through the adoption of realist representational strategies. In her analysis, the representation of the godly through the frontal mode of repre-sentation and direct address characteristic of ritual forms is complicated by the integration of these modes into the lateral movement of characters and by features of continuity narrative. The face of the god is in turn stripped of the ornamental features highlighted in ritual drama, and his human incarnation underlined.[19]

As far as the female devotional idiom in socials is concerned, it can paper over the powerful chasms which films open up within the ideology of masculine authority and female submission.[20] The case of the female devotee especially suggests the ambiguities which may lie beneath the invocation of male sacred authority. Feminist critics have noted that it is possible to interpret the female devotional tradition as primarily emphasizing female desire, a strategy which both circumvents patriarchy and reformulates it.[21]

In all these cases, therefore, a complication of the sacred or an outward movement into the secular form is observable. We could say that a melodramatic tendency of failed or uncertain resacralization is also at work here. An Indian melodrama, both as a phenomenon having a direct genealogy with its Western counterparts, as well as a larger cultural enterprise concerning the formation of new subjectivities, therefore has a definite existence and historical function. The concept of melodrama, straddling various types of representation and subjectivity, in which sacred and secular, the mythical and the real coexist, will help us get away from a definition of these terms as mutually exclusive. It is the *relay* between the familial, the social and the sacred in the Indian cinema's constitution of its diegetic world which complicates any straightforward rendering of the psyche of the Indian spectator.

Further specifications and distinctions about the spectator need to be made in terms of generic address. While D. G. Phalke inaugurated the popular cinema with the mythological genre, new genres very quickly emerged. These included the costume film, or the 'historical', the spectacular stunt or action-dominated film, the devotional film about the relationship between deity and devotee and, finally, the social film. Our knowledge about the terms in which the industry addressed spectators through genre, and the way spectators received genres, are as yet rudimentary. But a 1950s essay by an industry observer noted that stunt, mythological and costume films would attract a working-class audience.[22] The film industry used two hypotheses to evaluate their audience. First, that the plebeian spectators would delight in spectacle and visceral impact, uncluttered by ideas and social content. Second, that such an audience was also susceptible to a religious and moral rhetoric, indicated by their enjoyment of the mythological film. In the industry's view, therefore, the lower-class audience was motivated by visceral or motor-oriented pleasures and moral imperatives. Their susceptibility to the veracity of the image was not an issue in this discussion on attracting an audience.

On the other hand, the film industry understood the devotional and social films, with their emphasis on social criticism, to be the favoured genres of the middle class. However, by the 1950s, the industry reformulated its understanding of genre and audience appeal. After the collapse of the major studios – Bombay Talkies, Prabhat, New Theatres – the new, speculative climate of the industry encouraged an eye for the quick profit and therefore the drive for a larger audience. This encouraged the induction of the sensational attractions of action, spectacle and dance into the social film, a process explained as a lure for the mass audience.

Industry observers clearly believed the changes in the social film to be quite superficial, the genre label being used to legitimize a cobbling together of sensational attractions. And, indeed, there is something inflationary about a large number of films released in the period 1949–51 being called 'socials'. The label of the social film perhaps gave a certain legitimacy to the cinematic entertainment put together in a slapdash way. However, I will argue that these films did offer a redefinition of social identity for the spectator; the mass audiences earlier conceived of as being attracted only by sensation and themes of moral affirmation were now being solicited by an omnibus form which also included a rationalist discourse as part of its 'attractions'.[23]

Many of the formulations of the dominant paradigm refer to the cinema after the 1950s. Writers such as Das Gupta and Nandy believe that the 1950s was a transitional period between the popular culture and mixed social audience of the 1930s and 1940s and the mass audience emerging from the 1960s. However, I would suggest that the cinema of the 1950s already prefigures some of the dominant methods of the subsequent period, especially in its deployment of a rhetoric of traditional morality and identity to bind its imagining of social transformation. Perhaps it is the focus of these writers on the overt rhetoric of popular narratives that has obscured a certain dynamic in the constitution of the subject which displays dispositions other than the straightforwardly 'traditional'.

Visual Codes of Narration (1): Iconicity, Frontality and the Tableau Frame

Let me now turn to the issue of visual address. For the purposes of identifying the processes of cinematic narration, we have to turn to the Indian cinema's initial formation: a phase, from 1913, in which it not only absorbed religious and mythological narratives, but also certain modes of address. An aesthetics of frontality and iconicity has been noted for Indian films in certain phases and genres by Ashish Rajadhyaksha[24] and Geeta Kapur.[25] This aesthetic arises from mass visual culture, in instances ranging from the relationship between deity and devotee, to the enactment of religious tableaux and their representation in popular artworks such as calendars and posters. When I refer to the iconic mode, I use the term not in its precise semiotic sense, to identify a relation of resemblance, but as a category derived from Indian art-historical writing that has been employed to identify a meaningful condensation of image. The term has been used to situate the articulation of the mythic within painting, theatre and cinema, and could be conceived of as cultural work which seeks to bind a multi-layered dynamic into a unitary image. In Geeta Kapur's definition, the iconic is 'an image into which symbolic meanings converge and in which moreover they achieve stasis'.[26]

Frontal planes in cinematic composition are used to relay this work of condensation and also to group characters and objects in the space of the tableau, a visual figure which, in the Indian context, can be traced to Indian urban theatre's interactions with British melodrama in the nineteenth century. In Peter Brooks's formulation, the tableau in melodrama gives the 'spectator the opportunity to see meanings represented, emotions and moral states rendered in clear visible signs'.[27] And Barthes has noted that it is

> a pure cut-out segment with clearly defined edges, irreversible and incorruptible; everything that surrounds it is banished into nothingness, remains unnamed, while everything that it admits within its field is promoted into essence, into light, into view...[it] is intellectual, it has something to say (something moral, social) but it also says it knows how this must be done.[28]

In Barthes's argument, the tableau has a temporal dimension to it, a 'pregnant moment' caught between past and future.[29] To my mind, these observations suggest both the highly controlled work involved in the construction of the tableau and also its inbuilt possibilities of dynamization. Its constitution of a frozen dynamic implicitly suggests the possibilities of change. This means that deployment of the tableau frame does not invariably mean indifference to the problem of offscreen space. Dissections of the tableau, cut-ins to closer views on the scene, the use of looks offscreen and character movements in and out of frame serve to complicate the tableau, fulfilling the promise of its reorganization.

I will illustrate the dynamic employment of the frontal, iconic mode, and of tableau framing in a sequence from Mehboob Khan's saga of peasant life, *Mother India* (1957). This segment presents, and then upsets, a pair of relatively stable iconic instances. The mother-in-law, Sundar Chachi, is centred through a number of tableau shots taken from different angles to highlight her authority in the village just after she has staged a spectacular wedding for her son. This representation of Sundar Chachi takes place in the courtyard of her house. The other instance is of the newly wedded daughter-in-law Radha, shown inside the house, as she submissively massages her husband's feet, a classic image of the devout Hindu wife.[30] The two instances are destablized because of the information that the wedding has forced Sundar Chachi to mortgage the family land. The information diminishes her standing, causing her to leave the gathering and enter her house. Simultaneously, it also undermines Radha's iconic placement as submissive, devout wife. As she overhears the information, the camera tracks in to closeup, eliminating the husband from our view; she looks up and away, offscreen left, presumably towards the source of the information. As the larger space of the scene, the actual relationship between the inside and the outside, remains unspecified, the relationship is suggested by her look offscreen left. The likelihood of this positioning is further strengthened when Sundar Chachi enters the house and, looking in the direction of offscreen right, confesses that she has indeed mortgaged her land. The final shot, a repetition of Radha's look offscreen left, binds the two characters through an eyeline match. The women are narrativized out of their static, iconic position through narrative processes of knowledge circulation and character movement, and by the deployment of Hollywood codes of offscreen sound and eyeline match.

This deployment of tableau and icon is regularly observable in the popular cinema, even if their dispersal and reorganization is not always rendered by such a systematic deployment of the codes of continuity editing. In another, fairly systematic instance, from *Andaz/Style* (Mehboob Khan, 1949) I have suggested that the particular combination of character-centred continuity narration with the tableau plays off individual and socially coded orientations to the narrative event. The continuity codes highlight individual movement and awareness, and the tableau condenses the space of the social code. Instead of invoking themes of individual/society and modernity/tradition, I argue that such combinations present the spectator with shifting frames of visual knowledge, different sensoria of the subject.[31] Indeed, rather than attach specific forms of subjectivity to specific modes of representation in a schematic way, I believe that there are instances when certain socially and ritually coded relationships are relayed through what is, after all, the mythicized individuation of the continuity mode. Central here is a particular discourse of the image and the look in indigenous conventions.

Visual Codes of Narration (2): Looking

While visual codes deriving from mass visual culture are open to the dynamization of the sort I have described, they continue to retain a certain integrity of function, especially in the reproduction of authority structures. For example, hierarchies of power may develop around the image of a character. This character image becomes the authoritative focal point of a scene, occupying a certain privileged position which structures space as a force field of power. In contrast to formulations about looking which have become commonplace in the analysis of Hollywood cinema, the figure looked at is not necessarily subject to control but may in fact be the repository of authority. As Lawrence Babb[32] and Diana Eck[33] in their studies of looking in Hinduism have suggested, the operative terms here are *darsan dena* and *darsan lena*, the power to give the look, the privilege of receiving it. However, there may be other functions of looking in play, as when tension arises around the question of who bears authority. The look of the patriarch is privileged in such narrative moves. In a host of 1950s work, from *Awara/ The Vagabond* (Raj Kapoor, 1951), *Baazi/ The Wager* (Guru Dutt, 1951), *Aar Paar/ Heads or Tails* (Guru Dutt, 1954) through the later work of Guru Dutt in *Pyaasa/ The Thirsty One* (1957) and *Sahib, bibi aur ghulam/ King, Queen, Jack* (Abrar Alvi/Guru Dutt, 1963), the patriarchal gaze is highlighted as a dark, controlling one, seeking to arrest the shift in the coordinates of desire and authority.

In terms of visual address, the residual traces of sacralization are still observable in the reposing of authority in the male image. The family narrative that underpins the Hindi cinema resorts to a transaction of authority around this image. The patriarch gives way to the son, his successor, at the story's conclusion. This male figure's authority is placed in position by the direction of a devotional female regard.

I will cite an example from *Devdas* (Bimal Roy, 1955), a film based on a well-known Bengali novel by Sarat Chandra Chatterjee. Devdas, the son of a powerful landed family, is prohibited from marrying the girl he desires, Parvati, because of status differences. He is a classic renouncer figure of the type favoured in Indian storytelling, a figure who is unable, or refuses, to conform to the demands of society, and wastes away in the contemplation of that which he could never gain. I want to refer to a scene which employs continuity conventions to the highly 'traditional' end of deifying the male as object of desire. The sequence deals with Devdas's visit to Parvati's house, and indicates a strategy of narration whereby Parvati's point of view is used to underline the desirability and the authority exercised by Devdas's image. In this sequence, Parvati finds her grandmother and mother in the courtyard discussing Devdas's arrival from the city and the fact that he has not yet called upon them. Devdas, offscreen, calls from outside the door. From this moment, Parvati's auditory and visual attention dominates the narration. Before we can see Devdas entering the house, we withdraw with Parvati to her room upstairs, and listen to the conversation taking place below along with her. Devdas announces that he will go to see Parvati himself. In anticipation of Devdas's arrival, Parvati hurriedly starts lighting a *diya*, a devotional lamp, and the melody of a *kirtan*, a traditional devotional song expressing Radha's longing for Krishna, is played. We hear the sound of Devdas's footfall on the stairs, and Parvati's anxiety to light the lamp before Devdas enters her room is caught by a suspenseful intercutting between her lighting of the lamp and shots of the empty doorway. The doorframe in this sequence suggests the shrine in which the divine idol is housed. Devdas's entry is shown in a highly deifying way; first his feet are shown in the doorway, followed by a cut to the lighted lamp. Finally his face is revealed. There follows a cut to Parvati, suggesting that this is the order through which she has seen Devdas's arrival. As she looks at him, in a classical point of view arrangement, conch shells, traditional accompaniment to the act of worship, are sounded. The future husband as deity, object of the worshipful gaze, is established by the narration's deployment of Parvati's point of view. Her lighting of the devotional lamp and the extra-diegetic sound of the *kirtan*, and conch-shells underline the devotional nature of the woman's relationship to the male image. Guru Dutt would use the doorframe to similar effect at the climax of *Pyaasa* and the *kirtan* from *Devdas* is used again on that occasion.

I have already suggested that filmic narration is subject to ambivalence in relaying the image of masculine authority through a desiring female look. Within the *bhakti* or devotional tradition, the female devotee's energy is channelled directly into the worship of the deity, without the mediation of the priest. However, the Lord still remains a remote figure, making of the devotional act a somewhat excessive one, concentrating greater attention on the devote than the devotional object.[34] Another implication of this arrangement is that we are being invited to identify with the romantically unfulfilled woman character, a problematic position, perhaps, in terms of the gendering of spectatorship.

We need to retain a constant sense of the way the dominant tropes of narration are complicated by such features of excess. However, I still think it is necessary to acknowledge the framework of masculine authority within which female desire is finally held. And I suggest that we need to go back to the tableau and the framework of seeing provided by an iconic frontality to understand the ways in which the elaboration of filmic narration is determined by these imperatives.

In *Pyaasa* there is a scene in which the poet-hero, Vijay, refers to the prostitute, Gulab, as his wife in order to protect her from a policeman who is pursuing her. The prostitute is unaccustomed to such a respectful address, especially one suggestive of intimate ties to a man she loves, and is thrown into a sensual haze. Vijay ascends a stairway to the terrace of a building where he will pass the night. Gulab sees a troupe of devotional folk singers, *Bauls*, performing a song, *Aaj sajan mohe ang laga lo* (Take me in your arms today, O beloved), and follows Vijay up the stairs. The *baul* song is used to express Gulab's desire, and cutting and camera movement closely follow its rhythms. The scene is structured by these relations of desire, which are simultaneously relations of distance, as the woman follows, looks at and almost touches the man she loves (who is entirely unaware of all this) but finally withdraws and flees as she believes herself unworthy of him.

The relation between devotee and object of devotion determines the space of this scene, it remains the structuring element in the extension and constraining of space. The relationship here is not that of the iconic frontality of traditional worship. The desired one is not framed in this way, for continuity codes dominate the scenic construction. Even in the scene I have cited from *Devdas*, continuity codes construct space and it is a shot/reverse shot relationship which defines the ultimate moment of looking. Nevertheless, if we think of the male icon as the crucial figure towards and from which the narration moves, we can see how a 'traditional' marker of authority and desire is the anchor to the spatializing of narrative. We have here something akin to a tableau constructed over a series of shots, its constituent elements – Gulab, Vijay and the performers – being ranged in a relatively consistent spatial relationship to each other. From the point of view of the male spectator, what is being underwritten is not, or not only, the subordinate position in the act of looking, it is a moment which uses looking to relay his own desirability to him.

The Sociopolitical Referent

The relaying of patriarchal authority through reorganized tableaux, the transfer of the authoritative image from one character to another, and the presence of an empowering female look, present the essential visual–narrational transaction. In this sense there is a certain rearticulation of traditional authority and hierarchies of the visual culture into the narrational procedures of the cinema. Hollywood codes of narration, oriented to generate linear narrative trajectories motivated by character point of view and action are employed. But what is of interest is that they are used to 'enshrine' the male character in the female look as I have described, or to route the male character back to an original family identity. This latter narrative trajectory is widely observable in the series of popular crime films of the 1950s, such as *Awara*, *Baazi*, *Aar Paar* and *CID* (Raj Khosla, 1956). This circularity has something to do with the particular structures of the family narrative in the 1940s and 1950s. Something akin to a Freudian family romance was at work, in which the fantasy that the child has parents other than those who bring him up is played out. In the Hindi social film, instead of a fantasy of upward mobility, a democratizing downward spiral is set in motion, the hero being precipitated into a life of destitution and crime. The circling back, the recovery of identity, is then tied to a normalization of social experience, a recovery of the reassuring coordinates of social privilege.[35]

As a result, in line with dominant ideological currents in the wake of independence, the social film of the 1950s expanded the terms of social reference, urged an empathy towards social deprivation and invited a vicarious identification with such states. But the recovery of the hero at the conclusion finally underlines the middle-class identity that structures the narrative. However, certain shifts are observable in the nature of family narrative and the recovery of identity. In socials of the 1940s such as *Kangan/ The Bracelet* (Franz Osten, 1940) and *Kismet*, there is a proper reconciliation between son and father, and a type of joint family structure seems to be back in place. By the 1950s, however, the hero's recovery of identity and social position does not result in reconciliation with the father, but the positing of a new family space. This nuclear family is formed in alignment with the state, as if politics and personality were allied in a common project of transformation.

Indeed, while I have tried to suggest the ways the popular film seeks to integrate new forms of subjectivity into more conventional tropes, it is important that we retain the signs, however fragmentary, of other subjectivities in play, whether these express the drives of individualized perception, of an assertive masculinity, or the recovery of the popular conventions of female devotion. I have suggested elsewhere, in a study of *Andaz*, that the popular cinema of this period drew upon Hollywood narrative conventions in order to highlight the enigmatic dimensions of its female characters' desires. The film was notable for its use of hallucinations and dreams to define the heroine in terms of an ambivalent psychology and as agent of a transgressive but involuntary sexuality. Such conventions were drawn upon to be contained and disavowed. A nationalist modernizing imperative had to symbolically contain those ideologically fraught aspects of modernity that derived from transformations in the social position and sexual outlook of women. The result was a fascinatingly perverse and incoherent text, one whose ideological achievements are complicated by the subjectivities it draws upon.[36]

A 'National' Spectator

The terms of cinematic narration I have sketched here are rather different from the notions of spectatorship which have emerged from that model of the successful commodity cinema, Hollywood. Historians and theoreticians of the US cinema have underlined the importance of continuity editing in binding or suturing the spectator into the space of the fiction. The undercutting of direct address and the binding of the spectator into a hermetic universe onscreen heightens the individual psychic address and sidelines the space of the auditorium as a social and collective viewing space. This very rich historiography and textual analysis[37] speaks of the fraught process through which US cinema's bourgeois address came into being. This work describes how social and ethnic peculiarities were addressed in the relation between early cinema and its viewers. The process by which the cinema took over and came to develop its own entertainment space was a process of the formation of a national market in which the spectator had to be addressed in the broadest, non-ethnic, socially universal terms. Of course, what was actually happening was that a dominant white Anglo-Saxon norm came to be projected as universal. Along with this process, there developed the guidelines for the construction of a universal spectator placed not in the auditorium but as an imaginary figure enmeshed in the very process of narration.

The mixed address of the Hindi cinema, along with the song and dance sequences and comic skits which open up within the commercial film, suggests a rather different relationship of reception. Indeed, it recalls the notion of a 'cinema of attractions', a term developed by Tom Gunning to theorize the appeal of early Euro-American cinema.[38] In contrast to the Hollywood mode of continuity cinema or narrative integration, Gunning argues that early cinema was exhibitionist. The character's look into the camera indicated an indifference to the realist illusion that the story tells itself without mediation. The films displayed a greater interest in relaying a series of views and sensations to their audience rather than following a linear narrative logic. These elements were to be increasingly transcended in the Hollywood cinema's abstraction of the spectator as individuated consumer of its self-enclosed fictional world. In the process, the audience, earlier understood to be composed of workers and immigrants, was 'civilized' into appreciating the bourgeois virtues of a concentrated, logical, character-based narrative development.[39]

Elements of this formulation of a cinema of attractions are clearly applicable to the Bombay film. But the Bombay cinema too was engaged in creating standard, universalizing reference points. To understand the processes by which the Hindi cinema acquired certain acceptable 'national' standards, we have to be able to identify how it took over certain widespread narrational norms from the past. But alongside this, we also need to examine how it was involved in constructing certain overarching cultural norms that suppressed the representation of marginal currents in Indian narrative and aesthetic traditions.

Research into the urban theatre of the nineteenth century will provide one point of entry into the understanding of the process by which narrational norms were transmitted to the cinema. This theatre presaged the cinema in its negotiation of Western form, of technology, of narrative, even of a notion of entertainment time.[40] But it was also reputedly a great indigenizer, appropriating other traditions into Indian narrative trajectories. One narrational function that was carried from the theatre was that of a narratorial position external to the story, reminiscent of the *sutradhar* or narrator of traditional theatre. The comic, or *vidushak*, also left his mark as one of the staple figures of the commercial cinema.[41] Here he sometimes plays the role of a narrator external to the main narrative and is often engaged in a relationship of direct address to the audience. There is a certain didacticism involved in his functions. In a more commonplace function, it is the very absurdity of the comic figure, quite obviously opposed to the larger-than-life attraction of the hero, which invites a less flattering point of identification for the audience, and thereby a certain narratorial distance towards the story. Further, in the very superfluity of his functions, we could say that the comic was the spokesman within the story for a different order of storytelling, one which celebrates the disaggregative relationship to narrative.

But the main repository of such a narratorial externality to the main story and its process of narration is what I would term the 'narrational song'. This is enacted by a source other than any of the fictional characters. Through such a song, we are offered an insight into the emotional attitude of individual characters and the wider cultural and even mythic significance of certain actions and events. For example, when Devdas leaves Parvati in Bimal Roy's *Devdas*, Parvati listens to *Baul* singers as they sing of Radha's sorrow at Krishan's departure. This is a direct representation of her mood, but in addition to emotional attitudes, the song also represents a highly conventionalized cultural idiom.

The embedding of such cultural idioms offers us a stance, quite ritualistic in its intelligibility, towards the development of the narrative. We are both inside and outside the story, tied at one moment to the seamless flow of a character-based narration from within, in the next attuned to a culturally familiar stance from without. This may not be a simple, normative move on the part of the narration; indeed, we may be offered a critical view on narrative development. Significantly, such culturally familiar narratorial stances are sometimes separate from the space of the fiction. Not only are they performed by characters otherwise superfluous to the main storyline, there is often also an actual disjunction between the space of the story and that of the narrator. In this sense, the narrational song can be identified with the properties of the extra-fictional music used on the soundtrack. They both inhabit a space outside the fiction and alert us to a certain point of view or emotional disposition which we find culturally intelligible.

The disaggregation of address in Hindi cinema, such as is found in the external narrator and the comic and musical sequence, therefore integrates with a recognizable set of conventions. Further, the Bombay cinema also generates an enlarged and standardized identity across these divergent points of address. This can be located in this cinema's construction of masculine authority and its privileging of a symbolic Hindu identity. The outlines of such a masculine subjectivity were accompanied by a sharper delineation of sexual difference than that within the original cultural idiom. The androgynous aspects of Krishna's sexual identity are marginalized by fixing the male position as the object of sensual female regard and devotion.[42] For all the richness of its ambiguous use of female desire and its unconventional articulation of the hero's masculinity. Guru Dutt's *Pyaasa* is quite clear about the imperative of fixing a masculine locus of authority in its conclusion. Perhaps we have here a symbolic nationalist reformulation of culture in the cinema, undercutting the space for marginal discourses, and seeking to control ambiguity in the relationship between gender and power. Historians such as Uma Chakravarty have shown how this takes place in revisions of the Ramayana,[43] and Patricia Uberoi has suggested that a similar process, aligned to high-caste images of women as subordinate, self-effacing and motherly, took place in the culture of the calender print.[44] These patterns may help us identify the universalizing ambition of the Hindi cinema, despite its disaggregative features. The scope of universalization lies not merely in the subordination of all elements to narrative, but in ensuring that multiple and tangential tracks never exceed the limits of the dominant address. This implies that the concept of the cinema of attractions needs to be rethought when it becomes the characteristic, long-term feature of a national commodity cinema.

Identifying a Contextual Address to the Spectator

In the last part of this paper, I want to refer to a more historically specific address through which a symbolic identity was negotiated by the cinema. I will argue that, although the language of the Bombay cinema is Hindustani and therefore the product of cultural interaction between Muslim and Hindu culture, the spectator of the commercial cinema is primarily positioned in relation to the overarching Hindu symbolic identity relayed through the cinema. This is effected through the types of cultural address which I have described, through narrational song, gender idiom and modes of visual address. The strongly Hindu cultural connotation of these features is so pervasive that it is invariably thought of as the norm, rather than as a historically specific project for spectatorial identification. In the early 1940s, however, the industry became much more self-conscious about its market, and how it was to be addressed. In making this observation, I am merely sketching out certain guidelines for research rather than laying out the definite time scale and the range of resources used to put together the symbolic narrative of the Hindu nation. Preliminary findings suggest the importance of this line of enquiry.

In 1937, the All India League for Censorship, a private body, was set up to lobby for stringent measures in regard to what was perceived to be an anti-Hindu dimension in the film industry.[45] It claimed that the industry was dominated by Muslims and Parsis who wanted to show the Hindus 'in a bad light'. Muslim actors and Muslim characters were used, it declared, to offer a contrast with Hindu characters, portrayed as venal, effete and oppressive. The League evidently assumed that the government of Bombay, led by the Indian National Congress, would be responsive to their demand that certain films be banned for their so-called anti-Hindu features. Such expectations were belied by K. M. Munshi, Home Minister in the Bombay government, who dismissed the League as bigoted. Indeed, this was how the League must have appeared at the time. But their charges do bring to light the fact that certain offscreen information, that is, the religious identity of producers, directors and actors, was being related to the onscreen narrative, and in fact was seen to constitute a critical social and political level of the narrative.

It is against this background that we should situate the as yet rudimentary information which suggests that in the next decade the industry itself was coming to project an address to its market which clearly apprehended and sought to circumvent Hindu alienation. Syed Hasan Manto, who had written scripts for Hindi films, recalled that he was pressurized to leave his job in the early 1940s because he was a Muslim. Indeed, Bombay Talkies, the studio for which Manto worked from 1946 to 1948, came under threat from Hindu extremists who demanded that the studio's Muslim employees be sacked.[46] At a more symbolic level, a process seems to have been inaugurated by which the roles of hero and heroine, which normally remain outside the purview of stereotypes associated with other characters, had to be played by actors with Hindu names. In 1943, when Yusuf Khan was inducted as a male lead by Devika Rani at Bombay Talkies, his name was changed, as is well known, to Dilip Kumar. In the actor's account, the change was quite incidental.[47] But we have information about other Muslim actors and actresses who underwent name changes, such as Mahzabin, who became Meena Kumar,[48] and Nawab, who became Nimmi;[49] and, in 1950 a struggling actor, Hamid Ali Khan changed his name to Ajit on the advice of the director, K. Amarnath.[50] I am sure that this short list is but the beginning of a much longer one, and an oral history might uncover something akin to a parallel universe of concealed identities. The transaction involved seems to have been purely symbolic. Evidence from film periodicals suggests that the true identity of such actors was mostly well known, and yet an abnegation of identity was undertaken in the development of the star personality. It is as if the screen, constituting an imaginary nation space, required the fulfilment of certain criteria before the actor/actress could acquire a symbolic eligibility.

Following in the tracks of the Hindu communal censorship League of 1937, *Filmindia*, the sensationalist film periodical edited by Baburao Patel, showed that a bodily sense of communal difference had come to inflect a certain reception of film images. *Filmindia*, incensed in 1949 when demonstrations prevented the screening of *Barsaat/Monsoon* (Raj Kapoor, 1949) in Pakistan,[51] was delighted to see two Muslim actresses, Nimmi and Nargis, kiss the feet of Premnath and Raj Kapoor in the latter's *Barsaat*. In an ironic aside, the gossip columns of the periodical suggested that, to balance this act of submission, a Muslim director such as Kardar should now arrange to have a Hindu actress kiss Dilip Kumar's feet. Clearly, it was understood that such an inversion was not a likely scenario, and a vicarious pleasure was being taken in this symbolic triumph.[52] How much of these offscreen discourses actually went into the structuring of onscreen narratives? It seems to me no coincidence that in the same year in which *Filmindia* carried this dark communal reception of *Barsaat*, in *Andaz*, a film by a Muslim director Mehboob, Nargis should again be seeking to touch Raj Kapoor's feet, desperate to demonstrate her virtue as a true Indian wife, and to clear herself of charges of being involved with Dilip Kumar. The image of the star is not just reiterated in this interweaving of on- and offscreen narratives; there is an active working out and resolution of the transgressive features which have come to be attached to him/her. For example, speculations about Nargis's family background and suspicions of her chastity following her affair with Raj Kapoor seemed to repetitively feed into, and be resolved within, a host of films from *Andaz* to *Bewafa/Faithless* (M. L. Anand, 1952), *Laajwanti/Woman of Honour* (Rajinder Suri, 1957) and *Mother India*.[53]

The way in which this symbolic space was charted out by the Hindi commercial cinema is comparable to the way in which the white hero became the norm for the US commercial cinema and, preeminently, his WASP version. In both cases, the ideological construction of this space appears to be nearly effaced, but the discourses surrounding the films clearly indicate that this was not so.

In this symbolic space, the minorities too can have a presence, usually as subordinate ally of the Hindu hero. But we must not forget the specific address the industry made to the Muslim community in the form of the Muslim social film. Unfortunately, I have not seen enough of these to be able to situate them adequately within or against the grain of Hindu nationhood. *Elaan/Announcement* (Mehboob Khan, 1948) falls into this category, and it clearly urges the Muslim community to emulate its educated sections and pursue the path of modernization. Perhaps the pejorative and ideologically loaded implication of this specific address was that the wider society, comprising the Hindus, had already made this advance.

Conclusion

I have suggested that we must situate the whole project of the Hindi commercial cinema in its cultural context, that of a mass visual culture which displays certain rules of address, composition and placement. Through the deciphering of this system, we shall be able to understand the position given to the spectator, the types of identity he or she is offered. This starting point will enable us to hold on to the historical spectator as he/she is moved through regimes of subjectivity set up by generic and social address, and by the integration of a new dynamic of narration from the Hollywood cinema. In citing these imperatives of analysis, I seek to problematize a dominant paradigm in Indian criticism. This has focused on the particular familial rhetoric of the popular cinema to suggest that its address disavows the 'real' and reflects significant cognitive and political dispositions in its spectator. In a word, this is a disposition which seeks to counter a rational outlook, seen by the popular cinema's critics as the basis of a modern society and nation-state; in certain anti-modern interpretations, such failings may actually constitute a virtue.

In contrast, in my reading of cinematic narratives, we can observe the refashioning of the spectator in accordance with certain new compulsions, a streamlining of narrative form around the drives of individualized characters. Instead of an unqualified assimilation of such drives, the transformation is held within a culturally familiar visual economy centred on a transaction around the image of male authority. But there are always excessive aspects to this process of cultural 'domestication', and we need to retain a sense, however fragmentary, of the range of subjectivities which are called into play by the negotiatory features of narrative construction.

The Hindi cinema displays a disaggregative address in its structures, quite in contrast to the narrative integrity and spectatorial enmeshing of another successful commodity cinema, that of Hollywood's classical narrative cinema. However, I have argued that despite this a coherence can be discerned in the limits set by dominant discourses to otherwise diverse narrative and performative strands. Even disaggregation, I have suggested, has certain binding features in the way it articulates the spectator to earlier practices of narration and to many points of cultural institution and investment. In other words, it performs a symbolic remapping of identity and suppresses other more complicated traditions of gender, of Hinduism and other forms of culture. It is through this process of standardization that the cinema constitutes an enlarged, transcendent identity for its spectator.

Finally, I have suggested that, from the 1940s, contextual information gleaned from discourses about the cinema indicated that such a 'national' project was yoked to constructions of the Indian nation as one dominated by the Hindu, and was arrived at through symbolic transactions of offscreen identity and onscreen narrative.

Notes

Versions of this paper were presented at the Nehru Memorial Museum and Library, New Delhi, Department of Film and Television Studies, University of Amsterdam, and the *Screen* Studies Conference, June 1994. I thank Radhika Singha and Thomas Elsaesser for their comments, and the Indian Council for Historical Research, the British Council, Delhi, and the *Screen* Studies Conference organizers for enabling me to attend the *Screen* conference.

1 For a representative selection of articles, see Jim Pines and Paul Willemen (eds), *Questions of Third Cinema* (London: British Film Institute, 1989).

2 For the standard account, see E. Barnouw and S. Krishnaswamy, *Indian Film* (London and New York: Oxford University Press, 1980); also Manjunath Pendakur, 'India', in John A. Lent (ed.), *The Asian Film Industry* (London: Christopher Helm, 1990), p. 231.

3 For reflections on the subordinating implications of Bombay's national cinema, see my 'Dislocations: the cinematic imagining of a new society in 1950s India', *Oxford Literary Review*, vol. 16 (1994).

4 M. B. Billimoria, 'Foreign markets for Indian films', *Indian Talkie, 1931–56* (Bombay: Film Federation of India, 1956), pp. 53–4. A substantial deposit of Indian films distributed by Wapar France, an agency which catered to North African markets, are in the French film archives at Bois d'Arcy. For the importance of Indian film imports to Indonesia and Burma, see Lent, *The Asian Film Industry*, pp. 202, 223; and for patterns of Indian film exports at the end of the 1980s, see Pendakur, 'India', p. 240.

The Hindi film's contribution to the general sense of subordination of local products in North Africa and the Middle East is indicated in the observation that none of these cinemas [from Morocco to Kuwait] is doing well... markets are flooded with Rambos, Karate films, Hindu [sic.] musicals and Egyptian films'. Lisbeth Malkmus, 'The "new Egyptian cinema"', *Cineaste*, vol. 16, no. 3 (1988), p. 30.

5 The term comes from Tom Gunning, 'The cinema of attraction: early film, its spectator and the avant-garde', *Wide Angle*, vol. 8. nos. 3–4 (1986). There is a more elaborate discussion of this term in relation to the Bombay cinema later in this paper. For reflections on other 'attraction-based' cinemas see Laleen Jayamanne, 'Sri Lankan family melodrama; a cinema of primitive attractions', *Screen*, vol. 33, no. 2 (1992), pp. 145–53; and Gerard Fouquet, 'Of genres and savours in Thai film', *Cinemaya*, no. 6 (1989–90), pp. 4–9.

6 Nick Browne, 'The spectator of American symbolic forms: re-reading John Ford's *Young Mr. Lincoln*', *Film Reader*, part 5 (1979), pp. 180–8.

7 For an exploration of this influential critical tradition, see my 'Shifting codes, dissolving identities: the Hindi social film of the 1950s as popular culture', *Journal of Art and Ideas*, nos. 23–4 (1993), pp. 51–85.

8 See the collection of essays in Wimal Dissanayake (ed.), *Melodrama and Asian Cinema* (Cambridge: Cambridge University Press, 1993).

9 For example, Mitsushiro Yoshimoto's account of the postwar domestic criticism of Japanese cinema, 'Melodrama, post-modernism and Japanese cinema' in Dissanayake (ed.), *Melodrama and Asian Cinema*, pp. 101–26, especially pp. 110–11. Thus where late nineteenth-century Europe's discourses about melodrama helped institute a hegemonic class culture, in the context of developing societies, the 'failures' of melodrama are regarded within the imperatives of establishing a modern national configuration. For the class implications of the European context, see Christine Gledhill, *Home is Where the Heart Is: Melodrama and the Woman's Film* (London: British Film Institute, 1987), Introduction.

10 Chidananda Das Gupta, *The Painted Face* (New Delhi: Rolly Books, 1991).

11 Das Gupta, 'Seeing is believing', in *The Painted Face*, pp. 35–44.

12 Das Gupta, 'City and village' and 'The Oedipal hero', in *The Painted Face*, pp. 45–58, 70–106.

13 Das Gupta, 'The painted face of Indian politics', in *The Painted Face*, pp. 199–247.

14 All references are to Ashish Nandy, 'The intelligent film critic's guide to the Indian cinema', *Deep Focus*, vol. 1, nos 1–3 (1987–8); reprinted in Nandy, *The Savage Freud and Other Essays on Possible and Retrievable Selves* (Delhi; Oxford University Press, 1995).

15 See R. K. Yagnik, *The Indian Theatre: Its Origins and Later Development under European Influence, with Special Reference to Western India* (London: Allen and Unwin, 1933), pp. 92–117, for accounts of the influence of British melodrama on Indian urban theatre.

16 Peter Brooks, *The Melodramatic Imagination: Balzac, Henry James, Melodrama and the Mode of Excess* (New York: Columbia University Press, 1985).

17 Veena Das, 'The mythological film and its framework of meaning: an analysis of *Jai Santoshi Ma*', *India International Centre Quarterly*, vol. 8, no. 1 (1981), pp. 43–56.

18 Geeta Kapur, 'Mythic material in Indian cinema', *Journal of Arts and Ideas*, nos. 14–15 (1987), pp. 79–107.

19 Anuradha Kapur, 'The representation of gods and heroes: parsi mythological drama of the early twentieth century', *Journal of Arts and Ideas*, nos. 23–4 (1933), pp. 85–107.

20 See my '"You cannot live in society and ignore it": nationhood and female modernity in *Andaz* (Mehboob Khan, 1949)', *Contributions to Indian Sociology* (forthcoming).

21 Kumkum Sangari has noted the following effects of the female devotional voice: 'The orthodox triadic relation between wife, husband and god is broken. The wife no longer gets her salvation through her "godlike" husband . . . *Bhakti* offers direct salvation. The intermediary position now belongs not to the human husband or the Brahmin priest but to the female devotional voice. This voice, obsessed with the relationships between men and women, continues to negotiate the triadic relationship – it simultaneously transgresses and reformulates patriarchal ideologies.' Sangari, 'Mirabai and the spiritual economy of Bhakti', *Economic and Political Weekly*, vol. 25, no. 28 (1990).

22 All references are to Barnouw and Krishnaswamy, 'The Hindi film', in *Indian Talkie*, p. 81.

23 The reasons for the restructuring of the 'social' film are complex. Artists associated with the Indian People's Theatre Association (IPTA), which had ties with the Communist Party of India, had started working in the film industry from the 1940s. Among these were the actor Balraj Sahni, the director Bimal Roy and the scriptwriter K. A. Abbas. The latter was involved in *Awara/ The Vagabond* (Raj Kapoor, 1951), a film representative of the new drive to combine a social reform perspective with ornate spectacle. However, the years after independence were characterized by a broader ideological investment in discourses of social justice associated with the image of the new state and the ideology of its first prime minister, Jawaharlal Nehru.

24 Ashish Rajadhyaksha, 'The Phalke era: conflict of traditional form and modern technology', *Journal of Art and Ideas*, nos. 14–15 (1987), pp. 47–78.

25 Kapur, 'Mythic material in Indian cinema'.

26 Ibid., p. 82.

27 Brooks, *The Melodramatic Imagination*, p. 62.

28 Roland Barthes, 'Diderot, Brecht, Eisenstein', in Stephen Heath (ed. and trans.), *Image, Music, Text* (London: Fontana, 1982), p. 70.

29 Ibid.

30 See a panel from the eighteenth-century Hindu text analyzed by Julia Leslie, *The Perfect Wife: The Orthodox Hindu Woman According to the Stridharmapaddhati of Tryambakayajvan* (Delhi: Oxford University Press, 1989), for an example of this tradition.

31 Vasudevan, 'Shifting codes, dissolving identities', pp. 61–5.

32 Lawrence A. Babb, 'Glancing visual interaction in Hinduism', *Journal of Anthropological Research*, vol. 37, no. 4 (1981), pp. 387–401.

33 Diana Eck, *Seeing the Divine Image in India* (Chambersburg: Anima Books, 1981).

34 Sangari, 'Mirabai and the spiritual economy of Bhakti'.

35 For an elaboration of this narrative structure, see my 'Dislocations'.

36 Vasudevan, 'You cannot live in society – and ignore it'.

37 See Miriam Hansen, *Babel and Babylon: Spectatorship in American Silent Cinema* (Cambridge, MA: Harvard University Press, 1991); and Thomas Elsaesser (ed.), *Early Cinema: Space-Frame-Narrative* (London: British Film Institute, 1990).

38   Gunning, 'The cinema of attraction'.

39   Hansen, *Babel and Babylon*, chapters 1 and 2.

40   A. Yusuf Ali, 'The modern Hindustani drama', *Transactions of the Royal Society of Literature*, vol. 35 (1917), pp. 89–90.

41   For an account of the *sutradhar* and the *vidushak*, see M. L. Varadpande, *Traditions of Indian Theatre* (New Delhi: Abhinav Publications, 1978), pp. 84–5; also David Shulman, *The King and the Clown in South Indian Myth and Poetry* (Princeton: Princeton University Press, 1985).

42   This can be seen as part of an epochal refashioning of Krishna, suggestively presented in Nandy, 'The intelligent film critic's guide'.

43   Uma Chakravarty. 'The development of the Sita myth: a case study of women in myth and literature'. *Samya Shakti*, vol. 1, no. 1 (1983), pp. 68–75; also Paula Richman (ed.), *Many Ramayanas: The Diversity of a Narrative Tradition in South Asia* (Delhi: Oxford University Press, 1992).

44   Patricia Uberoi, 'Feminine identity and national ethos in Indian calendar art', *Economic and Political Weekly*, women's studies section, vol. 25, no. 28 (1990), pp. 41–8.

45   All references are taken from Bombay, Home Department, Political file no. 313/1940, Maharashtra State Archives.

46   See the introduction to Saadat Hasan Manto, *Kingdom's End and Other Stories*, trans. Khalid Hasan (London: Verso Books, 1987).

47   *Filmfare*, 26 April 1957, p. 77.

48   *Filmfare*, 17 October 1952, p. 19.

49   *Filmfare*, 28 November 1952, p. 18.

50   Ajit, interviewed by Anjali Joshi, *Sunday Observer*, Delhi, 16 December 1991. For some ideas about the onscreen ramifications of Hamid Ali Khan's change of name, see my 'Dislocations'.

51   *Filmindia*, April 1950, p. 13.

52   *Filmindia*, May 1950, p. 18.

53   For further reflections about Nargis's career, see Rosie Thomas, 'Sanctity and scandal in *Mother India*', *Quarterly Review of Film and Video*, vol. 11, no. 3 (1989), pp. 11–30; and Vasudevan, ' "You cannot live in society – and ignore it" '.

Part VIII

Apparatus Theory

Introduction

Toby Miller

"The apparatus" in film theory refers to the interaction between spectators, texts, and technology. Apparatus theory is concerned with the material circumstances of viewing: the nature of filmic projection (from behind the audience) or video playing (from behind or in front), the darkness of the theater or the lightness of daytime TV, the textual componentry of what is screened, and the psychic mechanisms engaged. In other words, apparatus theory inquires into the impact of the technical and physical specificity of watching films on the processing methods used by their watchers. This goes beyond issues raised in debates over technological innovation (discussed elsewhere) to focus on cinema as a "social machine." This machine is more than the obvious machines of the cinema: film, lighting, sound recording systems, camera, make-up, costume, editing devices, and projector. It goes into the realm of "demands, desires, fantasies, speculations (in the two senses of commerce and the imaginary)" (Comolli, 1985: 122). A blending of "narrativity, continuity, point of view, and identification" sees spectators become part of the very apparatus designed for them (Flitterman-Lewis, 1990: 3, 12). The apparatus takes the spectatorial illusion of seeming to experience film as "real life" and makes it a combination of power and yet relaxation, of engagement coupled with leisure: a "technique of the imaginary" that combines the realism of capitalist fiction with the "primary imaginary" of recorded sound and image (Metz, 1975: 15).

Most of the work addressing these questions was produced from the mid-1970s. It derived from semiotics, psychoanalysis, and ideology critique. The parent theorists were Christian Metz, Jacques Lacan, and Louis Althusser (the MLA), although only the first of these authors focused on film. Metz combined influences from the other two in his pioneering paper "The Imaginary Signifier" (included here). He outlined a project "to disengage the cinema-object from the imaginary and to win it for the symbolic" (1975: 14) – in other words, to make cinema's actual conditions of existence and forms of meaning available for critique, rather than remaining caught in their power–pleasure dynamic.

Apparatus theory is one of film studies' distinguishing marks from literary criticism. The concern with the occasion of consumption – the material circumstances of spectatorship – is far-distant from the fetishization of the text as a stable object that is always the same wherever and whenever it is read. At the same time, the focus on material conditions has not led to extensive empirical research. Apparatus theory has basically operated at the level of speculation, apart from a brief flurry of writing on technological history and meaning that looked at those moments when the very technology of cinema was highlighted to audiences, or that retrieved cinema's prehistory via studies of panoramas, magic lanterns, dioramas, and cineramas (de Lauretis and Heath, 1985). This is because the principal interest of apparatus theorists never diverged from those of the MLA: how subjectivity is constituted via the imaginary and the symbolic and their dance around the real. The interest in the specific technical apparatus of cinema is inextricably intertwined with an interest in Marxist theorization of prevailing ideological norms plus psychoanalytic theorization of fantasies and complexes.

The foundational social assumptions of apparatus theory come from Althusser. He sees the economic base as comprised of the productive forces and the relations of production. Its superstructure is the law, the state, and ideology. The state has two main characteristics. The first involves the use of force and its threat as a means of eliciting obedience. This characteristic is composed of the army, the police, the courts, the bureaucracy, and the prisons. Its work is done by sanction and interdiction – "the (repressive) State apparatus" ((R)SA). The second characteristic is the "Ideological State Apparatuses" (ISAs), which include religious and educational institutions, the family, the polity, the trade union, and the communications and cultural ISAs (Althusser, 1977: 136–7). So where there is one, united (R)SA, there is a "plurality" of ISAs. Althusser explains ideology as "a 'Representation' of the Imaginary Relationship of Individuals to their Real Conditions of Existence" (ibid.: 152). He argues that to criticize an ideology, for example religious faith, is to presume that this ideology is illusionary, but that it at least alludes to reality and hence has grounds which are both true and germane to itself on which it can be criticized: "(ideology = illusion/allusion)." The next presumption is that the act of interpretation can unfold this and give the lie to falsehood or underscore truth (ibid.: 153). (Here is the cue for cinematic ideology critique.)

Althusser maintains that such practices give rise to a query as to the sources and reasons for this "imaginary transposition of the real conditions of existence." Critical interpretation assumes that:

> What is reflected in the imaginary representation of the world found in an ideology
> is the conditions of existence of men, i.e. their real world . . . [when] it is not their

real conditions of existence, their real world that "men" "represent to themselves" in ideology, but above all it is their relation to those conditions of existence represented to them there. (Ibid.: 153–4)

Let us now consider a little more closely what this signifies about the category of the knowing and doing individual subject. It suggests that ideas are material practices, rituals such as the act of spectatorship (material faith in centrally projected sound and vision) or payment of a social debt (material faith in justice) that are carried out by the subject at the same time as they define that subject. For the subject is hailing and being hailed through this set of practices (ibid.: 158, 160, 162–4). So the experience of watching film would best be understood as a set of objects (the technology of the cinema and the techniques of narrative), plus relations to those objects (credulity, identification, and fantasy).

This was the animating logic behind Jean-Louis Baudry's first efforts to theorize film's capacity to be both an "impression of the real" and "more-than-the-real" (Baudry, 1986: 299). The seeming ontological hold on the real offered by cinema – a classic empiricist conceit – fitted Althusser's understanding of ideology. The subject was presented with what looked like unveiled, transparent truth, whereby the camera substituted for the eyes. Spectatorship was like "being there," but with intriguingly radical transformations of time and perspective: the distant grew near, the past became present, and points of view shifted. The spectator's loss of mobility was compensated by this promiscuous look, which traveled everywhere, to the most dangerous or painful as well as exhilarating places, and with impunity, as classical narrative ensured the ultimate restoration of equilibrium through perfect knowledge. The eye transcended the limitations of the body to roam across the multiple viewpoints and scenes of fiction feature film. Metz (1975: 5) called the cinema "a veritable psychic substitute, a prosthesis for our primally dislocated limbs." Just as ideology was the means whereby social subjects had their conditions of existence represented back to them in everyday life, masquerading as an unvarnished, transcendent truth, so film was a key mechanism for encapsulating such cultural messages. As well as generating ideology, this compressed form of making meaning offered the critic who was alive to ideology the opportunity to specify one important way that the subject and the world maintained their illusory dance (Allen, 1997: 19).

The lens positioned the viewer as the central figure of cinema; beyond the screen, yet uniquely privileged as the one who ultimately sees and knows, whose perfect knowledge is assured (at least in the case of classically closed narrative, where there may be an omniscient narrator, but omniscience is the promise of finality offered to audiences). This metaphorized the relationship of the rational, calculating consumer to objects of purchase, with the camera offering the "perfect knowledge" claimed by neo-classical economics as the foundation of its system of knowledge. But beyond that perfect knowledge comes the special capacity of the cinema to encourage identification by the spectator – an identification both with this perfect knowledge and with characters in texts.

Here we encounter the meeting-point of Althusser and Lacan via the notion of the mirror phase (mentioned in "The Nature of the Gaze"). The process of viewing is likened to the illusion of a solid-state ego given by the mirror phase. Taken together, these qualities of ideology, lens, and subjectivity blind spectators to the fact that they, like the films they watch, are thick with discourse, unknowable by themselves or others without this encrustation of meaning and interpretation, as are all social phenomena in a world of ideology. To repeat, objects, persons, and their interrelations are not knowable as empirical reality, but only through signification. But the apparatus of cinema encourages spectators to disavow this process. Moments of danger for this project of illusion come from the avant-garde and from non-continuity editing. The avant-garde rejects linear narratives and perfect knowledge from the spectator, while editing, though a necessity for mainstream narrative cinema, is risky in that it may highlight the intervention of the filmmaker, the constructedness of the image. But the conventions of Hollywood fiction film (the urge for continuity, ultimate omniscience, and closure) hide this artifice and encourage identification and mastery on the part of viewers.

Initial contributions/ripostes to apparatus theory came from feminist scholars for its failure to distinguish the different experiences and psychic mechanisms of men and women – that male viewers were principally involved in fetishizing women on screen and identifying with men on screen, which apparatus theorists had ignored. That engagement, by such writers as Constance Penley (1989), Sandy Flitterman-Lewis (1990), Joan Copjec (chapter 25, this volume), and Teresa de Lauretis (de Lauretis and Heath, 1985) enlivened apparatus theory by showing the centrality of difference to spectacle and the need for feminist filmmaking and feminist critical practice to account for and disrupt the association of the apparatus with the male gaze.

A further critique of apparatus theory is that it has no mechanism for predicting or investigating how spectators in fact process information. It cannot establish whether this disavowal occurs or does not, no way of explaining how the deception of the experience is avoided. In short, apparatus theory has no means of being falsified, because it knows the answers from the theoretical baggage that poses the questions. Any interest in the concrete meaning-making of audiences, their ability to engage actively with texts and the apparatus via personal and collective cultural history and systems of interpretation, would displace the assumption of apparatus theory that the unconscious is automatically and universally engaged by technologies of viewing. Such conflictual and manifold processes may see a proliferation of cross-identifications that go far beyond not just the limits of the body, which apparatus theory decreed, but also beyond the norms of one's psychic training and bodily awareness into entirely new territory (men identifying with women in melodramas, women identifying with male action heroes, Native Americans identifying with Western "pioneers" – in short, the theater as a site of carnival as much as machine, where viewers transcend the dross of their ordinary social and psychological lives [Stam, 1989:

224; Denzin, 1995: 102–3; Kepley, 1996]). At the same time, this interest in the ability of audiences to make meaning has seen another, seemingly conflictual paradigm emerging under the sign of Michel Foucault that considers the contemporary moment as an electronic transformation of a long history of surveillance under modernity, from the panoptic prison designs of Jeremy Bentham to the all-seeing gaze and internalization of today's mall security and virtual home cinema (Denzin, 1995). Between them, these two moves pull apart, replicate, and make empirical many of the concerns that apparatus theory sought to synthesize.

In short, apparatus theory valuably problematized the exclusive concentration on representation, demonstrating that materiality and perception, too, had their place. This emphasis on questions of ideology and the interplay of machine, text, culture, and person guaranteed that film theory would not be caught in the formalism of much literary criticism. At the same time, its very mechanistic mode of inquiry, strangely redolent of the very metaphors it so disparaged, limited its utility as a paradigm for research. When was the last time an apparatus theorist was surprised by the data he or she encountered?

Works Cited

Allen, Richard 1997. *Projecting Illusion: Film Spectatorship and the Impression of Reality*. Cambridge: Cambridge University Press.

Althusser, Louis 1977. *Lenin and Philosophy and Other Essays*, 2nd edn. Trans. Ben Brewster. London: New Left Books.

Baudry, Jean-Louis 1986. "The Apparatus: Metapsychological Approaches to the Impression of Reality in the Cinema." Trans. Jean Andres and Bertrand Augst. In *Narrative, Apparatus, Ideology: A Film Theory Reader*, ed. Phil Rosen. New York: Columbia University Press.

Comolli, Jean-Louis 1985. "Machines of the Visible." In *The Cinematic Apparatus*, ed. Teresa de Lauretis and Stephen Heath. London: Macmillan.

de Lauretis, Teresa and Stephen Heath (eds) 1985. *The Cinematic Apparatus*. London: Macmillan.

Denzin, Norman 1995. "The Birth of the Cinematic Surveillance Society," *Current Perspectives in Social Theory* no. 15: 99–127.

Flitterman-Lewis, Sandy 1990. *To Desire Differently: Feminism and the French Cinema*. Urbana: University of Illinois Press.

Kepley, Vance, Jr. 1996. "Whose Apparatus? Problems of Film Exhibition and History." In *Post-Theory: Reconstructing Film Studies*, ed. David Bordwell and Noël Carroll. Madison: University of Wisconsin Press.

Metz, Christian 1975. "The Imaginary Signifier." Trans. Ben Brewster. *Screen* 16, no. 2: 14–76.

Penley, Constance 1989. *The Future of an Illusion: Film, Feminism, and Psychoanalysis*. Minneapolis: University of Minnesota Press.

Stam, Robert 1989. *Subversive Pleasures: Bakhtin, Cultural Criticism and Film*. Baltimore: Johns Hopkins University Press.

23
The Imaginary Signifier

Christian Metz

Identification, Mirror

'What contribution can Freudian psychoanalysis make to the knowledge of the cinematic signifier?': that was the question–dream I posed (the scientific imaginary wishing to be symbolized), and it seems to me that I have now more or less *unwound* it; unwound but no more; I have not given it an answer. I have simply paid attention to what it was I wished to say (one never knows this until one has written it down), I have only questioned my question: this unanswered character is one that has to be deliberately accepted, it is constitutive of any epistemological approach.

Since I have wished to mark the places (as empty boxes some of which are beginning to fill without waiting for me, and so much the better), the places of different directions of work, and particularly of the last, the psychoanalytic exploration of the signifier, which concerns me especially, I must now begin to inscribe something in this last box; must take further, and more plainly in the direction of the unconscious, the analysis of the investigator's desire that makes me write. And to start with this certainly means asking a new question: among the specific features of the cinematic signifier that distinguish the cinema from literature, painting, etc., which ones by nature call most directly on the type of knowledge that psychoanalysis alone can provide?

Perception, imaginary

The cinema's signifier is *perceptual* (visual and auditory). So is that of literature, since the written chain has to be *read*, but it involves a more restricted perceptual register: only graphemes, writing. So too are those of painting, sculpture, architecture, photography, but still within limits, and different ones; absence of auditory perception, absence in the visual itself of certain important dimensions such as time and movement (obviously there is the time of the look, but the object looked at is not inscribed in a precise and ordered time sequence forced on the spectator from outside). Music's signifier is perceptual as well, but, like the others, less 'extensive' than that of the cinema: here it is vision which is absent, and even in the auditory, extended speech (except in song). What first strikes one then is that the cinema is *more perceptual*, if the phrase is allowable, than many other means of expression; it mobilizes a larger number of the axes of perception. (That is why the cinema has sometimes been presented as a 'synthesis of all the arts'; which does not mean very much, but considering the quantitative tally of the registers of perception, it is true that the cinema 'englobes' in itself the signifiers of other arts: it can present pictures to us, make us hear music, it is made of photographs, etc.)

Nevertheless, this as it were numerical 'superiority' disappears if the cinema is compared with the theatre, the opera and other spectacles of the same type. The latter too involve sight and hearing simultaneously, linguistic audition and non-linguistic audition, movement, real temporal progression. Their difference from the cinema lies elsewhere: they do not consist of *images*, the perceptions they offer to the eye and the ear are inscribed in a true space (not a photographed one), the same one as that occupied by the public during the performance; everything the audience hear and see is actively produced in their presence, by human beings or props which are themselves present. This is not the problem of fiction but that of the definitional characteristics of the signifier: whether or no the theatrical play mimes a fable, its *action*, if need be mimetic, is still managed by real persons evolving in real time and space, *on the same stage or 'scene' as the public*. The 'other scene', which is precisely not so called, is the cinematic screen (closer to fantasy from the outset): what unfolds there may, as before, be more or less fictional, but the unfolding itself is fictive: the actor, the 'décor', the words one hears are all absent, everything is *recorded* (as a memory trace which is immediately so, without having been something else before), and this is still true if what is recorded is not a 'story' and does not aim for the fictional illusion proper. For it is the signifier itself, and as a whole, that is recorded, that is absence: a little rolled up perforated strip which 'contains' vast landscapes, fixed battles, the melting of the ice on the River Neva, and whole life-times, and yet can be enclosed in the familiar round metal tin, of modest dimensions, clear proof that it does not 'really' contain all that.

At the theatre, Sarah Bernhardt may tell me she is Phèdre or, if the play were from another period and rejected the figurative regime, she might say, as in a type of modern theatre, that she is Sarah Bernhardt. But at any rate, I should see Sarah Bernhardt. At the cinema, she could make the same two kinds of speeches too, but it would be her shadow that would be offering them to me (or she would be offering them in her own absence). Every film is a fiction film.

What is at issue is not just the actor. Today there are a theatre and a cinema without actors, or in which they have at least ceased to take on the full and exclusive function which characterizes them in classical spectacles. But what is true of Sarah Bernhardt is just as true of an object, a prop, a chair for example. On the theatre stage, this chair may, as in Chekhov, pretend to be the chair in which the melancholy Russian nobleman sits every evening; on the contrary (in Ionesco), it can explain to me that it is a theatre chair. But in the end it is a chair. In the cinema, it will have to choose between a similar two attitudes (and many other intermediate or more tricky ones), but it will not be there when the spectators see it, when they have to recognize the choice; it will have delegated its reflection to them.

Characteristic of the cinema is not the imaginary that it may happen to represent, it is the imaginary that it *is* from the start, the imaginary that constitutes it as a signifier (the two are not unrelated; it is so apt to represent it because it is it; however, it is still it when it no longer represents it). The (possible) reduplication inaugurating the intention of fiction is preceded in the cinema by a first reduplication, always-already achieved, which inaugurates the signifier. The imaginary, by definition, combines within it a certain presence and a certain absence. In the cinema it is not just the fictional signified, if there is one, that is thus made present in the mode of absence, it is from the outset the signifier.

Thus the cinema, 'more perceptual' than certain arts according to the list of its sensory registers, is also 'less perceptual' than others once the status of these perceptions is envisaged rather than their number or diversity: for its perceptions are all in a sense 'false'. Or rather, the activity of perception in it is real (the cinema is not a fantasy), but the perceived is not really the object, it is its shade, its phantom, its double, its *replica* in a new kind of mirror. – It will be said that literature, after all, is itself only made of replicas (written words, presenting absent objects). But at least it does not present them to us with all the really perceived detail that the screen does (giving more and taking the same, i.e. taking more). – The unique position of the cinema lies in this dual character of its signifier: unaccustomed perceptual wealth, but unusually profoundly stamped with unreality, from its very beginning. More that the other arts, or in a more unique way, the cinema involves us in the imaginary: it drums up all perception, but to switch it immediately over into its own absence, which is none the less the only signifier present.

The all-perceiving subject

Thus film is like the mirror. But it differs from the primordial mirror in one essential point: although, as in the latter, everything may come to be projected, there is one thing, and one thing only that is never reflected in it: the spectator's own body. In a certain emplacement, the mirror suddenly becomes clear glass.

In the mirror the child perceives the familiar household objects, and also its object par excellence, its mother, who holds it up in her arms to the glass. But above all it perceives its own image. This is where primary identification (the formation of the ego) gets certain of its main characteristics: the child sees itself as an other, and beside an other. This other other is its guarantee that the first is really it: by her authority, her sanction, in the register of the symbolic, subsequently by the resemblance between her mirror image and the child's (both have a human form). Thus the child's ego is formed by identification with its like, and this in two senses simultaneously, metonymically and metaphorically: the other human being who is in the glass, the own reflection which is and is not the body, which is like it. The child identifies with itself as an object.

In the cinema, the object remains: fiction or no, there is always something on the screen. But the reflection of the own body has disappeared. The cinema spectator is not a child and the child really at the mirror stage (from around six to around eighteen months) would certainly be incapable of 'following' the simplest of films. Thus, what *makes possible* the spectator's absence from the screen – or rather the intelligible unfolding of the film despite that absence – is the fact that the spectator has already known the experience of the mirror (of the true mirror), and is thus able to constitute a world of objects without having first to recognize himself within it. In this respect, the cinema is already on the side of the symbolic (which is only to be expected): the spectator knows that objects exist, that he himself exists as a subject, that he becomes an object for others: he knows himself and he knows his like: it is no longer necessary that this similarity be literally *depicted* for him on the screen, as it was in the mirror of his childhood. Like every other broadly 'secondary' activity, the practice of the cinema pre-supposes that the primitive undifferentiation of the ego and the non-ego has been overcome.

But *with what*, then, does the spectator identify during the projection of the film? For he certainly has to identify: identification in its primal form has ceased to be a current necessity for him, but – on pain of the film becoming incompre-hensible, considerably more incomprehensible than the most incomprehensible films – he continues to depend in the cinema on that permanent play of identification without which there would be no social life (thus, the simplest conversation presupposes the alternation of the *I* and the *you*, hence the aptitude of the two interlocutors for a mutal and reversible identification). What form does this *continued* identification, whose essential role Lacan has demonstrated even in the most abstract reasoning ('Le temps logique et l'assertion de certitude anti-cipée,' *Ecrits*), and which constituted the 'social sentiment' for Freud (= the sublimation of a homosexual libido, itself a reaction to the aggressive rivalry of the members of a single generation after the murder of the father),[1] take in the special case of one social practice among others, cinematic projection?

Obviously the spectator has the opportunity to identify with the *character* of the fiction. But there still has to be one. This is thus only valid for the narrative-representational film, and not for the psychoanalytic constitution of the signifier of the cinema as such. The spectator can also identify with the *actor*, in more or less 'afictional' films in which the latter is represented as an actor, not a character, but is still offered thereby as a human being (as a perceived human being) and thus allows identification. However, this factor (even added to the previous one and thus covering a very large number of films) cannot suffice. It only designates secondary identification in certain of its forms (secondary in the cinematic process itself, since in any other sense all identification except that of the mirror can be regarded as secondary).

An insufficient explanation, and for two reasons, the first of which is only the intermittent, anecdotal and superficial consequence of the second (but for that reason more visible, and that is why I call it the first). The cinema deviates from the theatre in an important point that has often been emphasized: it often presents us with long sequences that can (literally) be called 'inhuman' – the familiar theme of cinematic 'cosmomorphism' developed by many film theorists – sequences in which only inanimate objects, landscapes, etc., appear and which for minutes at a time offer no human form for spectator identification: yet the latter must be supposed to remain intact in its deep structure, since at such moments the film *works* just as well as it does at others, and whole films (geographical documentaries, for example) unfold intelligibly in such conditions. – The second, more radical reason is that identification with the human form appearing on the screen, even when it occurs, still tells us nothing about the *place of the spectator's ego* in the inauguration of the signifier. As I have just pointed out, this ego is already formed. But since it exists, the question arises precisely of *where it is* during the projection of the film (the true primary identification, that of the mirror, forms the ego, but all other identifications presuppose, on the contrary, that it has been formed and can be 'exchanged' for the object or the fellow subject). Thus when I 'recognize' my like on the screen, and even more when I do not recognize it, where am I? Where is that someone who is capable of self-recognition when need be?

It is not enough to answer that the cinema, like every social practice, demands that the psychical apparatus of its participants be fully constituted, and that the question is thus the concern of general psychoanalytic theory and not of that of the cinema proper. For my *where is it?* does not claim to go so far, or more precisely tries to go slightly further: it is a question of the *point* occupied by this already constituted ego, occupied during the cinema showing and not in social life in general.

The spectator is absent from the screen: contrary to the child in the mirror, he cannot identify with himself as an object, but only with some objects which are there without him. In this sense the screen is not a mirror. This time the perceived is entirely on the side of the object, and there is no longer any equivalent of the own image, of that unique mix of perceived and subject (of other and I) which was precisely the figure necessary to disengage the one from the other. At the cinema, it is always the other who is on the screen; as for me, I am there to look at him. I take no part in the perceived, on the contrary, I am *all-perceiving*. All-perceiving as one says all-powerful (this is the famous gift of 'ubiquity' the film makes its spectator); all-perceiving, too, because I am entirely on the side of the perceiving instance: absent from the screen, but certainly present in the auditorium, a great eye and ear without which the perceived would have no one to perceive it, the *constitutive* instance, in other words, of the cinema signifier (it is I who make the film). If the most extravagant spectacles and sounds or their most improbable assembly, the one most remote from all real experience, do not prevent the constitution of meaning (and to begin with do not *astonish* the spectator, do not really astonish him, not in spirit: he simply judges the film as strange) – that is because he knows he is at the cinema.

In the cinema the *subject's knowledge* takes a very precise form without which no film would be possible. This knowledge is dual (but unique). I know I am perceiving something imaginary (and that is why its absurdities, even if they are extreme, do not seriously disturb me), and I know that it is I who am perceiving it. This second knowledge divides in turn: I know that I am really perceiving, that my sense organs are physically affected, that I am not fantasizing, that the fourth wall of the auditorium (the screen) is really different from the other three, that there is a projector facing it (and thus it is not I who am projecting, or at least not all alone) – and I also know that it is I who am perceiving all this, that this perceived-imaginary material is deposited in me as if on a second screen, that it is in me, that it forms up into an organized sequence, that therefore I am myself the place where this really perceived imaginary accedes to the symbolic by its inauguration as the signifier of a certain type of institutionalized social activity called the 'cinema'.

In other words, the spectator *identifies with himself*, with himself as a pure act of perception (as wakefulness, alertness): as condition of possibility of the perceived and hence as a kind of transcendental subject, anterior to every *there is*.

A strange mirror, very like that of childhood, and very different. Very like, as Jean-Louis Baudry has emphasized, because during the showing we are, like the child, in a sub-motor and super-perceptive state; because, like the child again, we are prey to the imaginary, the double, and are so paradoxically through a real perception. Very different, because this mirror returns us everything but ourselves, because we are wholly outside it, whereas the child is both in it and in front of it. As an *arrangement* (and in a very topographical sense of the word), the cinema is more involved on the flank of the symbolic, and hence of secondariness, than is the mirror of childhood. This is not surprising, since it comes long after it, but what is more important to me is the fact that it is inscribed in its wake with as direct and as staggered an incidence without precise equivalent in other apparatuses of signification.

Identification with the camera

The preceding analysis coincides in places with others which have already been proposed and which I shall not repeat: analyses of quattrocento painting or of the cinema itself which insist on the role of monocular perspective (hence of the *camera*) and the 'vanishing point' that inscribes an empty emplacement for the spectator–subject, an all-powerful position which is that of God himself, or more broadly of some ultimate signified. And it is true that as he identifies with himself as look, the spectator can do no other than identify with the camera, too, which has looked before him at what he is now looking at and whose *post* (= framing) determines the vanishing point. During the projection this camera is absent, but it has a representative consisting of another apparatus, called precisely a 'projector'. An apparatus the spectator has behind him, *at the back of his head*,[2] that is, precisely where fantasy locates the 'focus' of all vision. All of us have experienced our own look, even outside the supposedly obscure chamber, as a kind of searchlight turning on the axis of our own necks (like a pan) and shifting when we shift (a tracking shot now): as a cone of light (without the microscopic dust scattered through it and streaking it in the cinema) whose vicariousness draws successive and variable slices of obscurity from nothing wherever and whenever it comes to rest. (And in a double sense that is what perception and consciousness are, a *light*, as Freud put it,[3] in the double sense of an illumination and an opening, as in the arrangement of the cinema, which contains both, a limited and fabulous light that only attains a small part of the real, but in return possesses the gift of casting light on it.) Without this identification with the camera certain facts could not be understood, though they are constant ones: the fact, for example, that the spectator is not amazed when the image 'rotates' (= pan) and yet he knows he has not turned his head. The explanation is that he has no need to turn it really, he has turned it as the all-seeing, as identified with the movement of the camera, as a transcendental, not an empirical subject.

All vision consists of a double movement: projective (the 'sweeping' search-light) and introjective: consciousness as a sensitive recording surface (as a screen). I have the impression at once that, to use a common expression, I am 'casting' my eyes on to things, and that the latter, thus illuminated, arrive to be deposited within me (we then declare that it is these things that have been 'projected', on to my retina, say). A sort of stream called the look, and explaining all the myths of magnetism, has to be pumped into the world, so that objects can come back up this stream in the opposite direction (but using it to find their way), arriving at last at our perception, which is now soft wax and no longer an emitting source.

The technology of photography carefully conforms to this fantasy accompanying perception, despite its banality. The camera is 'trained' on the object like a fire-arm (= projection) and the object arrives to make an imprint, a trace on the receptive surface of the film-strip (= introjection). The spectator himself does not escape these pinchers, for he is part of the apparatus, and also because pinchers, on the imaginary plane (Melanie Klein), mark our relation to the world as a whole and are rooted in the primary figures of orality. During the performance the spectator is the searchlight I have described, duplicating the projector, which itself duplicates the camera, and he is also the sensitive surface duplicating the screen, which itself duplicates the film-strip. There are two cones in the auditorium: one ending on the screen and starting both in the projection box and in the spectator's vision in so far as it is projective, and one starting from the screen and 'deposited' in the spectator's perception in so far as it is intro-jective (on the retina, a second screen). When I say that 'I see' the film, I mean thereby a unique mixture of two contrary currents: the film is what I receive, and it is also what I release, since it does not pre-exist my entering the auditorium and I only need close my eyes to suppress it. Releasing it, I am the projector, receiving it, I am the screen; in both these figures together, I am the camera, pointed yet recording.

Thus the constitution of the signifier in the cinema depends on a series of mirror-effects organized in a chain, and not on a single reduplication. In this the cinema as a topography resembles that other 'space' the technical equipment (camera, projector, film-strip, screen, etc.), the objective precondition of the whole institution: as we know, the apparatuses too contain a series of mirrors, lenses, apertures and shutters, ground glasses, through which passes the cone of light: a further reduplication in which the equipment becomes a metaphor (as well as the real source) for the mental process instituted. Further on we shall see that it is also its fetish.

This is like the apparatus of the camera itself!

In the cinema, as elsewhere, the constitution of the symbolic is only achieved through and above the play of the imaginary: projection–introjection, presence–absence, fantasies accompanying perception, etc. Even when acquired, the ego still depends in its underside on the fabulous figures thanks to which it has been acquired and which have marked it lastingly with the stamp of the lure. The secondary process does no more than 'cover' (and not always hermetically) the primary process which is still constantly present and conditions the very possibility of what covers it.

Chain of many mirrors, the cinema is at once a weak and a robust mechanism: like the human body, like a precision tool, like a social institution. Which is to say that it is really all of these at the same time.

And I, at this moment, what am I doing if not to add to all these reduplications one more whereby theory is attempting to set itself up? Am I not looking at myself looking at the film? This *passion for seeing* (and also hearing), the foundation of the whole edifice, am I not turning it, too, on (against) that edifice? Am I not still the voyeur I was in front of the screen, now that it is this voyeur who is being seen, thus postulating a second voyeur, the one writing at present, myself again?

On the idealist theory of the cinema

The place of the ego in the institution of the signifier, as transcendental yet radically deluded subject, since it is the institution (and even the equipment) that give it this place, surely provides us with an appreciable opportunity the better to understand and judge the precise epistemological import of the idealist theory of the cinema which culminates in the remarkable works of André Bazin. Before reflecting frontally on their validity, but simply reading texts of this kind, one cannot but be struck by the great precision, the acute and directly sensitive intelligence that they often demonstrate; at the same time they give the diffuse impression of a permanent ill-foundedness (which affects nothing and yet affects everything), they suggest that somewhere they contain something like a weak point at which the whole might be overturned.

It is certainly no accident that the main form of idealism in cinematic theory has been phenomenology. Bazin and other writers of the same period explicitly appealed to it, and more implicitly (but in a more generalized fashion) all conceptions of the cinema as a mystical revelation, as 'truth' or 'reality' unfolded by full right, as the apparition of what is (*l'étant*), as an epiphany, derive from it. We all know that the cinema has the gift of sending some of its lovers into prophetic trances. However, these cosmophanic conceptions (which are not always expressed in an extreme form) register rather well the 'feeling' of the *deluded ego* of the spectator, they often give us excellent descriptions of this feeling and to this extent they are partly scientific and have advanced our knowledge of the cinema. But the *lure of the ego* is their blind spot. These theories are still of great interest, but they have, so to speak, to be put the other way round, as an optical image of the film.

For it is true that the topographical apparatus of the cinema resembles the conceptual apparatus of phenomenology, with the result that the latter can cast light on the former. (Besides, in any domain, a phenomenology of the object to be understood, a 'receptive' description of its appearances, must be the starting point; only afterwards can *criticism* begin; psychoanalysts, it should be remembered, have their own phenomenology.) – The '*there is*' of phenomenology proper (philosophical phenomenology) as an ontic revelation referring to a perceiving-subject (= 'perceptual *cogito*'), to a subject for which alone there can be anything, has close and precise affinities with the inauguration of the cinema signifier in the ego as I have tried to define it, with the spectator falling back on himself as a pure instance of perception, the whole of the perceived being 'over the way'. To this extent the cinema really is the 'phenomenological art' it has often been called, by Merleau-Ponty himself, for example ('The film and the new psychology', Lecture to the Institut des Hautes Etudes Cinématographiques, March 13, 1945, translated in *Sense and Non-sense*, North-Western University Press, Evanston, Illinois 1964, pp. 48–59). But it can only be so because its objective determinations make it so. The ego's position in the cinema does not derive from a miraculous resemblance between the cinema and the natural characteristics of all perception; on the contrary, it is foreseen and marked in advance by the institution (the equipment, the disposition of the auditorium, the mental arrangement that internalizes the two), and also by more general characteristics of the psychical apparatus (such as projection, the mirror structure, etc.), which although they are less strictly dependent on a period of social history and a technology, by no means express the sovereignty of a 'human vocation', but are rather, inversely, shaped by certain specific features of man as an animal (as the only animal that is not an animal): his primitive *Hilflosigkejt*, his dependence on another's care (the lasting source of the imaginary, of object relations, of the great oral figures of feeding), the motor prematurity of the child which condemns it to an initial self-recognition by sight (hence outside itself) anticipating a muscular unity it does not yet possess.

In other words, phenomenology can contribute to knowledge of the cinema (and it has done so) in so far as it happens to be like it, and yet it is on the cinema *and* phenomenology in their common illusion of *perceptual mastery* that light must be cast by the real conditions of society and man.

On some sub-codes of identification

The play of identification defines the cinematic situation in its generality, i.e. *the* code. But it also allows more specific and less permanent configurations, 'variations' on it, as it were; they intervene in certain coded figures which occupy precise segments of precise films.

What I have said about identification so far amounts to the statement that the spectator is absent from the screen *as perceived*, but he is also (the two things inevitably go together) present there and even 'all-present' *as perceiver*. At every moment I am in the film by my look's caress. This presence often remains diffuse, geographically undifferentiated, evenly distributed over the whole surface of the screen; or more precisely *hovering*, like the psychoanalyst's listening, ready to catch on preferentially to some motif in the film, according to the force of that motif and according to my own fantasies as a spectator, without the cinematic code itself intervening to govern this anchorage and impose it on the whole audience. But in other cases, certain articles of the cinematic codes or sub-codes (which I shall not try to survey completely here) are made responsible for suggesting to the spectator the vector along which his permanent identification with his own look should be extended temporarily inside the film (the perceived) itself. Here we meet various classic problems of cinematic theory, or at least certain aspects of them: subjective images, out-of-frame space, looks (looks and no longer the look, but the former are articulated to the latter). Nicholas Browne's article 'Rhétorique du texte spéculaire (à propos de *Stagecoach*)' in *Communications* no. 23 makes what seems to me an interesting contribution here.

There are various sorts of subjective image and I have tried elsewhere (following Jean Mitry) to distinguish between them (see section 2 of 'Current Problems of Film Theory', *Screen* vol. 14, nos. 1/2, Spring/Summer 1973, pp. 45–9). Only one of them will detain me for the moment, the one which 'expresses the viewpoint of the filmmaker' in the standard formula (and not the viewpoint of a character, another traditional sub-case of the subjective image): unusual framings, uncommon shot-angles, etc., as for example in one of the sketches which make up Julien Duvivier's film *Le Carnet de bal* (the sketch with Pierre Blanchard, shot continuously in tilted framings). In the standard definitions one thing strikes me: I do not see why these uncommon angles should express the viewpoint of the filmmaker any more than perfectly ordinary angles, closer to the horizontal. However, the definition is comprehensible even in its inaccuracy: precisely because it is uncommon, the uncommon angle makes us more aware of what we had merely forgotten to some extent in its absence: an identification with the camera (with 'the author's viewpoint'). The ordinary framings are finally felt to be non-framings: I espouse the filmmaker's look (without which no cinema would be possible), but my consciousness is not too aware of it. The uncommon angle reawakens me and (like the cure) teaches me what I already knew. And then, it obliges my look to stop wandering freely over the screen for the moment and to scan it along more precise lines of force which are imposed on me. Thus for a moment I become directly aware of the *emplacement* of my own presence–absence in the film simply because it has changed.

Now for looks. In a fiction film, the characters look at one another. As it happens (and this is already another 'notch' in the chain of identifications) a character looks at another who is momentarily out-of-frame, or else is looked at by him. If we have gone one notch further, this is because everything out-of-frame *brings us closer to the spectator*, since it is the peculiarity of the latter to be out-of-frame (the out-of-frame character thus has a point in common with him: he is looking at the screen). In certain cases the out-of-frame character's look is 'reinforced' by recourse to another variant of the subjective image, generally christened the 'character's point of view': the framing of the scene corresponds precisely to the angle from which the out-of-frame character looks at the screen. (The two figures are dissociable moreover; we often know that the scene is being looked at by someone other than ourselves, by a character, but it is the logic of the plot, or an element of the dialogue, or a previous image that tells us so, not the position of the camera, which may be very far from the presumed emplacement of the out-of-frame onlooker.)

In all sequences of this kind, the identification that founds the signifier is *twice relayed*, doubly duplicated in a circuit that leads it to the heart of the film along a line which is no longer hovering, which follows the inclination of the looks and is therefore governed by the film itself: the spectator's look (= the basic identification), before dispersing all over the surface of the screen in a variety of intersecting lines (= looks of the characters in the frame = second duplication), must first 'go through' – in the same way as an itinerary or a strait are gone through – the look of the character out-of-frame (= first duplication), himself a spectator and hence the first delegate of the true spectator, but not to be confused with the latter since he is inside, if not the frame, then at least the fiction. This invisible character, supposed (like the spectator) to be seeing, will collide obliquely with the latter's look and play the part of an obligatory intermediary. By offering himself as a crossing for the spectator, he inflects the circuit followed by the sequence of identifications and it is only in this sense that he is himself seen: as we see through him, we see ourselves not seeing him.

Examples of this kind are much more numerous and each of them is much more complex than I have described them here. At this point textual analysis of precise film sequences is an indispensable instrument of knowledge. I just wished to show that in the end there is no break in continuity between the child's game with the mirror and, at the other extreme, certain localized figures of the cinematic codes. The mirror is the site of primary identification. Identification with one's own look is secondary with respect to the mirror, i.e. for a general theory of adult activities, but it is the foundation of the cinema and hence primary when the latter is under discussion: it is *primary cinematic identification* proper ('primary identification' would be inaccurate from the psychoanalytic point of view; 'secondary identification', more accurate in this respect, would be ambiguous for a cinematic psychoanalysis). As for identifications with characters, with their own different levels (out-of-frame character, etc.), they are secondary, tertiary cinematic identifications, etc.; taken as a whole in opposition to the simple identification of the spectator with his own look, they constitute together secondary cinematic identification, in the singular (on these problems, see Michel Colin: *Le Film: transformation du texte du roman*, Mémoire de troisième cycle, 1974, to be published).

Freud noted, *vis-à-vis* the sexual act ('Inhibitions, Symptoms and Anxiety,' *Standard Edition*, Vol. XX, pp. 87–8), that the most ordinary practices depend on a large number of psychical functions which are distinct but work consecutively, so that all of them must be intact if what is regarded as a normal performance is to be possible (it is because neurosis and psychosis dissociate them and put some of them out of court that a kind of commutation is made possible whereby they can be sorted out retrospectively by the analyst). The apparently very simple act of *seeing a film* is no exception to this rule. As soon as it is subjected to analysis it reveals to us a complex, multiply interconnected imbrication of the functions of the imaginary, the real and the symbolic, which is also required in one form or another for every procedure of social life, but whose cinematic manifestation is especially impressive since it is played out on a small surface. (To this extent the theory of the cinema may some day contribute something to psychoanalysis, even if, through force of circumstances, this 'reciprocation' remains very limited at the moment, the two disciplines being very unevenly developed.)

In order to understand the fiction film, I must both 'take myself' for the character (= imaginary procedure) so that he benefits, by analogical projection, from all the schemata of intelligibility that I have within me, and not take myself for him (= return to the real) so that the fiction can be established as such (= as symbolic): this is *seeming-real*. – Similarly, in order to understand the film (at all), I must perceive the photographed object as absent, its photograph as present, and the presence of this absence as signifying. The imaginary of the cinema presupposes the symbolic, for the spectator must first of all have known the primordial mirror. But as the latter instituted the ego very largely in the imaginary, the second mirror of the screen, a symbolic apparatus, itself in turn depends on reflection and lack. However, it is not fantasy, a 'purely' symbolic–imaginary site, for the absence of the object and the codes of that absence are really produced in it by the *physis* of an equipment: the cinema is a body (a *corpus* for the semiologist), a fetish that can be loved.

The Passion for Perceiving

Cinema practice is only possible through the perceptual passions: the desire to see (= scopic drive, scopophilia, voyeurism), acting alone in the art of the silent film, the desire to hear which has been added to it in the sound cinema (this is the '*pulsion invocante*', the invocating drive, one of the four main sexual drives for Lacan – see *Le Séminaire* tome XI: *Les Quatre concepts fondamentaux de la psychanalyse*, Editions du Seuil, Paris 1973, especially pp. 164 and 178; it is well known that Freud isolated it less clearly and hardly deals with it as such).

These two sexual drives are distinguished from the others in that they are more dependent on a lack, or at least dependent on it in a more precise, more unique manner, which marks them from the outset, even more than the others, as on the side of the imaginary.

However, this characteristic is to a greater or lesser degree proper to all the sexual drives in so far as they differ from purely organic instincts or needs (Lacan), or in Freud from the self-preservation drives (the 'ego drives' which he tended subsequently to annex to narcissism, a tendency he could never quite bring himself to pursue to its conclusion). The sexual drive does not have so stable and strong a relationship with its 'object' as do for example hunger and thirst. Hunger can only be satisfied by food, but food is quite certain to satisfy it; thus instincts are simultaneously more and less difficult to satisfy than drives; they depend on a perfectly real object that cannot be deputized, but they depend on nothing else. Drives, on the contrary, can be satisfied up to a point outside their objects (this is sublimation, or else, in another way, masturbation) and are initially capable of doing without them without putting the organism into immediate danger (hence repression). The needs of self-preservation can neither be repressed nor sublimated; the sexual drives are more labile and more accommodating, as Freud insisted[4] (more radically perverse, says Lacan).[5] Inversely, they always remain more or less unsatisfied, even when their object has been attained; desire is very quickly reborn after the brief vertigo of its apparent extinction, it is largely sustained by itself as desire, it has its own rhythms, often quite independent of those of the pleasure obtained (which seemed none the less its specific aim); the lack is what it wishes to fill, and at the same time what it is always careful to leave gaping, in order to survive as desire. In the end it has no object, at any rate no real object; through real objects which are all substitutes (and all the more multiple and interchangeable for that), it pursues an imaginary object (a 'lost object') which is its truest object, an object that has always been lost and is always desired as such.

How, then, can one say that the visual and auditory drives have a stronger or more special relationship with the absence of their object, with the infinite pursuit of the imaginary? Because, as opposed to other sexual drives, the 'perceiving drive' – combining into one the scopic drive and the invocating drive – *concretely represents the absence of its object* in the distance at which it maintains it and which is part of its very definition: distance of the look, distance of listening. Psychophysiology makes a classic distinction between the 'senses at a distance' (sight and hearing) and the others all of which are exchanges between immediate neighbours and which it calls 'senses of contact' (Pradines): touch, taste, smell, coenaesthetic sense, etc. Freud notes that voyeurism, like sadism in this respect, always keeps apart the *object* (here the object looked at) and the *source* of the drive, i.e. the generative organ (the eye); the voyeur does not look at his eye ('Instincts and their Vicissitudes', *Standard Edition*, Vol. XIV, pp. 129–30). With orality and anality, on the contrary, the exercise of the drive inaugurates a certain degree of partial fusion, coincidence (= contact, tendential abolition of distance) of source and aim, for the aim is to obtain pleasure at the level of the source organ (= 'organ pleasure' – ibid., p. 138): e.g. what is called 'mouth pleasure' (see Lacan: *Le Séminaire* tome XI, p. 153).

It is no accident that the main socially acceptable arts are based on the senses at a distance, and that those which depend on the senses of contact are often regarded as 'minor' arts (= culinary arts, art of perfumes, etc.) Nor is it an accident that the visual or auditory imaginaries have played a more important part in the histories of societies than the tactile or olfactory imaginaries.

The voyeur is very careful to maintain a gulf, an empty space, between the object and the eye, the object and his own body: his look fastens the object at the right distance, as with those cinema spectators who take care to avoid being too close to or too far from the screen. The voyeur represents in space the fracture which for ever separates him from the object; he represents his very dis-satisfaction (which is precisely what he needs as a voyeur), and thus also his 'satisfaction' in so far as it is of a specifically voyeuristic type. To fill in this distance would threaten to overwhelm the subject, to bring him to orgasm and the pleasure of his own body, hence to the exercise of other drives, mobilizing the senses of contact and putting an end to the scopic arrangement. *Retention* is fully part of perceptual pleasure, which is thereby often coloured with anality. Orgasm is the object rediscovered in a state of momentary illusion; it is the fantasy suppression of the gap between object and subject (hence the amorous myths of 'fusion'). The looking drive, except when it is exceptionally well developed, is less directly related to orgasm than are the other component drives; it favours it by its excitatory action, but it is not generally sufficient to produce it by its figures alone, which thus belong to the realm of 'preparatives'. In it we do not find that illusion, however brief, of a lack filled, of a non-imaginary, of a full relation to the object, better established in other drives. If it is true of all desire that it depends on the infinite pursuit of its absent object, voyeuristic desire, along with certain forms of sadism, is the only desire whose principle of distance symbolically and spatially evokes this fundamental rent.

The same could be said, making the necessary modifications of course, about the invocating (auditory) drive, less closely studied by psychoanalysis hitherto, with the exception of writers like Lacan and Guy Rosolato. I shall merely recall that of all hallucinations – and what reveals the dissociation of desire and real object better than the hallucination? – the main ones by far are visual and auditory hallucinations, those of the senses at a distance (this is also true of the dream, another form of hallucination).

However, although this set of features seems to me to be important, it does not yet characterize the signifier of the cinema proper, but rather that of all means of expression based on sight or hearing, and hence, among other 'languages', of practically all the arts (painting, sculpture, architecture, music, opera, theatre, etc.). What distinguishes the cinema is an extra reduplication, a supplementary and specific turn to the screw bolting desire to the lack. First because the spectacles and sounds the cinema 'offers' us (offers us at a distance, hence as much *steals* from us) are especially rich and varied here: a mere difference of degree, but already one that counts: the screen presents to our apprehension, but absents from our grasp, more 'things'. (The mechanism of the perceiving drive is identical for the moment but its object is more endowed with matter; this is one of the reasons why the cinema is very suitable for handling 'erotic scenes' which depend on direct, non-sublimated voyeurism.) In the second place (and more decisive), the specific affinity between the cinematic signifier and the imaginary persists when film is compared with arts such as the theatre in which the audio-visual given is as rich as it is on the screen in the number of perceptual axes involved. Indeed, the theatre really does 'give' this given, or at least slightly more really: it is physically present, in the same space as the spectator. The cinema only gives it in effigy, inaccessible from the outset, in a primordial *elsewhere*, infinitely desirable (= never possessible), on another scene which is that of absence and which none the less represents the absent in detail, thus making it very present, but by a different itinerary. Not only am I at a distance from the object, as in the theatre, but what remains in that distance is now no longer the object itself, it is a delegate it has sent me while itself withdrawing. A double withdrawal.

What defines the specifically cinematic *scopic regime* is not so much the distance kept, the 'keeping' itself (first figure of the lack, common to all voyeur-ism), as the absence of the object seen. Here the cinema is profoundly different from the theatre as also from more intimate voyeuristic activities with a specifi-cally erotic aim (there are intermediate genres, moreover: certain cabaret acts, strip-tease, etc.): cases where voyeurism remains linked to exhibitionism, where the two faces, active and passive, of the component drive are by no means so dissociated; where the object seen is present and hence presumably complicit; where the perverse activity – aided if need be by a certain dose of bad faith and happy illusion, varying from case to case, moreover, and sometimes reducible to very little, as in true perverse couples – is rehabilitated and reconciled with itself by being as it were undividedly taken in charge by two actors assuming its constitutive poles (the corresponding fantasies, in the absence of the actions, thus becoming interchangeable and shared by the play of reciprocal identifica-tion). In the theatre, as in domestic voyeurism, the passive actor (the one seen), simply because he is bodily present, because he does not go away, is presumed to consent, to cooperate deliberately. It may be that he really does, as exhibitionists in the clinical sense do, or as, in a sublimated fashion, does that oft noted triumphant exhibitionism characteristic of theatrical acting, counterposed even by Bazin to cinematic representation. It may also be that the object seen has only accepted this condition (thus becoming an 'object' in the ordinary sense of the word, and no longer in the Freudian sense) under the pressure of more or less powerful external constraints, economic ones for example with certain poor strippers. (However, they must have consented at some point; rarely is the degree of acceptance zero, except in the case of *victimization*, e.g. when a fascist militia strips its prisoners: the specific characteristics of the scopic arrangements are then distorted by the over powerful intervention of another element, sadism.) Voyeurism which is not too sadistic (there is none which is not so at all) rests on a kind of *fiction*, more or less justified in the order of the real, sometimes institutionalized as in the theatre or strip-tease, a fiction that stipulates that the object 'agrees', that it is therefore exhibitionist. Or more precisely, what is necessary in this fiction for the establishment of potency and desire is presumed to be sufficiently guaranteed by the physical presence of the object: 'Since it is there, it must like it', such, hypocritical or no, deluded or no, is the retrenchment needed by the voyeur so long as sadistic infiltrations are insufficient to make the object's refusal and constraint necessary to him. – Thus, despite the distance inaugurated by the look – which transforms the object into a *picture* (a '*tableau vivant*')[6] and thus tips it over into the imaginary, even in its real presence – that presence which persists and the active consent which is its real or mythical correlate (but always real as myth) re-establish in the scopic space, momentarily at least, the illusion of a fullness of the object relation, of a state of desire which is not just imaginary.

It is this last recess that is attacked by the cinema signifier, it is in its precise emplacement (*in its place*, in both senses of the word) that it installs a new figure of the lack, the physical absence of the object seen. In the theatre, actors and spectators are present at the same time and in the same location, hence present one to another, as the two protagonists of an authentic perverse couple. But in the cinema, the actor was present when the spectator was not (= shooting), and the spectator is present when the actor is no longer (= projection): a failure to meet of the voyeur and the exhibitionist whose approaches no longer coincide (they have 'missed' one another). The cinema's voyeurism must (of necessity) do without any very clear mark of consent on the part of the object. There is no equivalent here of the theatre actors' final 'bow'. And then the latter could see their voyeurs, the game was less unilateral, slightly better distributed. In the darkened hall, the voyeur is really left alone (with other voyeurs, which is worse), deprived of his other half in the mythical hermaphrodite (a hermaphrodite not necessarily constituted by the distribution of the sexes but rather by that of the active and passive poles in the exercise of the drive). Yet still a voyeur, since there is something to see, called the film, but something in whose definition there is a great deal of 'flight': not precisely something that hides, rather something that *lets* itself be seen without *presenting* itself to be seen, which has gone out of the room before leaving only its trace visible there. This is the origin in particular of that 'recipe' of the classical cinema that the actor should never look directly at the audience (= the camera).

Thus deprived of rehabilitatory agreement, of a real or supposed consensus with the other (which was also the Other, for it had the status of a sanction on the plane of the symbolic), cinematic voyeurism, *unauthorized* scopophilia, is from the outset more strongly established than that of the theatre in direct line from the primal scene. Certain precise features of the institution contribute to this affinity: the obscurity surrounding the onlooker, the aperture of the screen with its inevitable keyhole effect. But the affinity is more profound. It lies first in the spectator's solitude in the cinema: those attending a cinematic projection do not, as in the theatre, constitute a true 'audience', a temporary collectivity; they are an accumulation of individuals who, despite appearances, more closely resemble the fragmented group of readers of a novel. It lies on the other hand in the fact that the filmic spectacle, the object seen, is more radically ignorant of its spectator, since he is not there, than the theatrical spectacle can ever be. A third factor, closely linked to the other two, also plays a part: the *segregation of spaces* that characterizes a cinema performance and not a theatrical one. The 'stage' and the auditorium are no longer two polar selections made in a single space; the space of the film, represented by the screen, is utterly heterogeneous, it no longer communicates with that of the auditorium: one is real, the other perspective: a stronger break than any line of footlights. For its spectator the film unfolds in that simultaneously quite close and definitively inaccessible 'elsewhere' in which the child *sees* the gambols of the parental couple, who are similarly ignorant of it and leave it alone, a pure onlooker whose participation is inconceivable. In this respect the cinematic signifier is oedipal in type.

In the set of differences between the cinema and the theatre, it is difficult to be precise about the relative importance of two sorts of conditioning facts, and yet they are definitely distinct: on the one hand the characteristics of the signifier (alone envisaged here), i.e. the supplementary degree of absence that I have analyzed, and on the other the socio-ideological circumstances that have marked the historical birth of the two arts in a divergent manner. I have broached the latter topic elsewhere in my contribution to the *Hommage à Emile Benveniste*, and I shall only recall that the cinema was born in the midst of the capitalist epoch in a largely antagonistic and fragmented society, based on individualism and the restricted family (= father–mother–children), in an especially super-egotistic bourgeois society, especially concerned with 'elevation' (or façade), especially opaque to itself. The theatre is a very ancient art, one which saw the light in more authentically ceremonial societies, in more integrated human groups (even if sometimes, as in Ancient Greece, the cost of this integration was the rejection into a non-human exterior of a whole social category, that of the slaves), in cultures which were in some sense closer to their desire (= paganism): the theatre retains something of this deliberate civic tendency towards ludico-liturgical 'communion', even in the degraded state of a worldly rendezvous around those plays known as '*pièces de boulevard*' (variety plays).

It is for reasons of this kind too that theatrical voyeurism, less cut off from its exhibitionist correlate, tends more towards a reconciled and community-orientated practice of the scopic perversion (of the component drive). Cinematic voyeurism is less accepted, more 'shame-faced'.

But there are not just the global determinations (by the signifier or by history). There are also the personal efforts of the writers, producers and actors. Like all general tendencies, the ones I have signalled are unevenly manifest from work to work. There is no need to be surprised that certain films accept their own voyeurism more plainly than do certain plays. It is at this point that the problems of political cinema and political theatre should be posed, and also those of a politics of the cinema and the theatre. The militant use of the two signifiers is by no means identical. In this respect the theatre is clearly at a great advantage, thanks to its 'lesser degree of imaginariness', thanks to the direct contact it allows with the audience. The film which aims to be a film of intervention must take this into account in its self-definition. As we know, this is by no means easy.

The difficulty also lies in the fact that cinematic scopophilia, which is 'non-authorized' in the sense I have just pointed out, is authorized however by the mere fact of its institutionalization. The cinema retains something of the peculiar prohibited character of the vision of the primal scene (the latter is always surprised, never contemplated at leisure, and the permanent cinemas of big cities, with their highly anonymous clientele entering or leaving furtively, in the dark, in the middle of the action, represent this transgression factor rather well) – but also, in a kind of inverse movement which is simply the 'reprise' of the imaginary by the symbolic, the cinema is based on the legalization and generalization of the prohibited practice. Thus it shares in miniature in the special regime of certain activities (such as the frequentation of '*maisons de tolérance*', very well named in this respect) that are both official and clandestine, and in which neither of these two characteristics ever quite succeeds in obliterating the other. For the vast majority of the audience, the cinema (rather like the dream in this) represents a kind of enclosure or 'reserve' which escapes a fully social life although it is accepted and prescribed by it: going to the cinema is one licit activity among others with its place in the admissible pastimes of the day or the week, and yet that place is a 'hole' in the social cloth, a *loophole* opening on to something slightly more crazy, slightly less approved than what one does the rest of the time.

Cinema and theatre do not have the same relation to fiction. There is a fictional cinema, just as there is a fictional theatre, a 'non-fiction' cinema just as there is a non-fictional theatre, because fiction is a great historical and social figure (particularly active in our Western tradition and perhaps in others), endowed with a force of its own which leads it to invest various signifiers (and inversely, to be more or less expelled from them on occasion). It does not follow that these signifiers have an even and uniform affinity with it (that of music, after all, is especially repugnant to it, yet there is such a thing as programme music). The cinematic signifier lends itself the better to fiction in that it is itself fictive and 'absent'. Attempts to 'defictionalize' the spectacle, notably since Brecht, have gone further in the theatre than in the cinema, and not by chance.

But what interests me here is rather the fact that this unevenness is still apparent if only the fictional theatre is compared with the fictional cinema. They are not 'fictional' in quite the same way, and it was this that I had been struck by in 1965 when I compared the 'impression of reality' produced by these two forms of spectacle ('On the Impression of Reality in the Cinema,' *Essais sur la signification au cinéma* tome I, Klincksieck, Paris 1968; translated as *Film Language*, OUP, New York 1974). At that time my approach was a purely phenomenological one, and it owed very little to psychoanalysis. However, the latter confirms me in my earlier opinion. Underlying all fiction there is the dialectical relationship between a real instance and an imaginary instance, the former's job being to *mimic* the latter: there is the representation, involving real materials and actions, and the represented, the fictional properly speaking. But the balance established between these two poles and hence the precise nuance of the *regime of credence* that the spectator will adopt varies tolerably from one fictional technique to the other. In the cinema as in the theatre, the represented is by definition imaginary; that is what characterizes fiction as such, independently of the signifiers in charge of it. But the representation is fully real in the theatre, whereas in the cinema it too is imaginary, the material being already a reflection. Thus the theatrical fiction is experienced more – it is only a matter of a different 'dosage', of a difference of economy, rather, but that is precisely why it is important – as a set of real pieces of behaviour actively directed at the evocation of something unreal, whereas cinematic fiction is rather experienced as the quasi-real presence of that unreal itself; the signifier, already imaginary in its own way, is less palpably so, it plays more into the hands of the diegesis, it tends more to be swallowed up by it, to be credited to its side of the balance-sheet by the spectator. The balance is established slightly closer to the represented, slightly further from the representation.

For the same reason, fictional theatre tends to depend more on the actor (representer), fictional cinema more on the character (represented). This difference has often been emphasized by the theory of the cinema, where it constitutes an already classical theme. In the psychoanalytic field it has also been noted, by Octave Mannoni in particular (see 'L'Illusion comique en le théâtre du point de vue de l'imaginaire' in *Clefs pour l'imaginaire ou l'autre scène*, Editions du Seuil, Paris 1969, p. 180). Even when the cinema spectator does identify with the actor rather than with the part (somewhat as he does in the theatre), it is with *the actor as 'star'*, i.e. still as a character, and a fabulous one, itself fictional: with the best of his parts.

It may be said that there are much simpler reasons for this difference, that in the theatre the same part can be interpreted by various actors from one production to another, that the actor thus becomes 'detached' from the character, whereas in the cinema there are never several productions (several 'casts') for one film, so the part and its unique interpreter are definitively associated with one another. This is quite true, and it does affect the very different balance of forces between actor and character in theatre and cinema. But it is not a 'simple' fact, nor is it independent of the distance between their respective signifiers, on the contrary, it is but one aspect of that distance (merely a very striking one). If the theatrical part can have a variety of interpreters, that is because its representation is real and mobilizes really present (and hence possibly variant) persons each evening. If the cinematic part is fastened once and for all to its interpreter, it is because its representation involves the reflection of the actor, not the actor himself, and because the reflection (the signifier) is *recorded* and hence can no longer vary.

Disavowal, Fetishism

As can be seen, the cinema has a number of roots in the unconscious and in the great movements illuminated by psychoanalysis, but they can all be traced back to the specific characteristics of the institutionalized signifier. I have gone a little way in tracing some of these roots, that of mirror identification, that of voyeurism and exhibitionism. There is also a third, that of fetishism.

Since the famous article by Freud that inaugurated the problem ('Fetishism', 1927, *Standard Edition*, Vol. XXI, pp. 152–7),[7] psychoanalysis has linked fetish and fetishism closely with castration and the fear it inspires. Castration, for Freud, and even more clearly for Lacan, is first of all the mother's castration, and that is why the main figures it inspires are to a certain degree common to children of both sexes. The child who sees its mother's body is constrained by way of perception, by the 'evidence of the senses', to accept that there are human beings deprived of a penis. But for a long time – and somewhere in it for ever – it will not interpret this inevitable observation in terms of an anatomical difference between the sexes (= penis/vagina). It believes that all human beings originally have a penis and it therefore understands what it has seen as the effect of a mutilation which redoubles its fear that it will be subjected to a similar fate (or else, in the case of the little girl after a certain age, the fear that she has already been subjected to it). Inversely, it is this very terror that is projected on to the spectacle of the mother's body, and invites the reading of an absence where anatomy sees a different conformation. The scenario of castration, in its broad lines, does not differ whether one understands it, like Lacan, as an essentially symbolic drama in which castration takes over in a decisive metaphor all the losses, both real and imaginary, that the child has already suffered (birth trauma, maternal breast, excrement, etc.), or on the contrary one tends, like Freud, to take that scenario slightly more literally. Before this *unveiling of a lack* (we are already close to the cinema signifier), the child, in order to avoid too strong an anxiety, will have to double up its belief (another cinematic characteristic) and from then on for ever hold two contradictory opinions (proof that the real perception has not been without effect for all that): 'All human beings are endowed with a penis' (primal belief) and 'Some human beings are deprived of a penis' (evidence of the senses). In other words, it will, perhaps definitively, retain its former belief *beneath* the new ones, but it will also hold to its new perceptual observation while *disavowing* it on another level (= denial of perception, disavowal, Freud's '*Verleugnung*'). Thus is established the lasting matrix, the affective prototype of all the splittings of belief which man will henceforth be capable of in the most varied domains, of all the infinitely complex unconscious and occasionally conscious interactions which he will allow himself between 'believing' and 'not believing' and which will on more than one occasion be of great assistance to him in resolving (or denying) delicate problems. (If we are all a little honest with ourselves, we will realize that a truly integral belief, without any 'underside' in which the opposite is believed, would make even the most ordinary everyday life almost impossible.)

At the same time, the child, terrified by what it has seen or glimpsed, will be tempted, more or less successfully in different cases, to *arrest* its look, for all its life, at what will subsequently become its fetish: at a piece of clothing, for example, which masks the frightening discovery, or else precedes it (underwear, stockings, boots, etc.). The fixation on this 'just before' is thus another form of disavowal, of retreat from the perceived, although its very existence is dialectical evidence of the fact that the perceived has been perceived. The fetishistic prop will become a precondition for the establishment of potency and access to orgasm (*jouissance*), sometimes an indispensable precondition (true fetishism); in other developments it will only be a favourable condition, and one whose weight will vary with respect to the other features of the erotogenic situation as a whole. (It can be observed once again that the defence against desire itself becomes erotic, as the defence against anxiety itself becomes anxiogenic; for an analogous reason: what arises 'against' an affect also arises 'in' it and is not easily separated from it, even if that is its aim.) Fetishism is generally regarded as the 'perversion' par excellence, for it intervenes itself in the 'tabulation' of the others, and above all because they, like it (and this is what makes it their model), are based on the avoidance of castration. The fetish always represents the penis, it is always a substitute for it, whether metaphorically (= it masks its absence) or metonymically (= it is contiguous with its empty place). To sum up, the fetish signifies the penis as absent, it is its negative signifier; supplementing it, it puts a 'fullness' in place of a lack, but in doing so it also affirms that lack. It resumes within it the structure of disavowal and multiple belief.

These few reminders are intended above all to emphasize the fact that the dossier of fetishism, before any examination of its cinematic extensions, contains two broad aspects which coincide in their depths (in childhood and in structure) but are relatively distinct in their concrete manifestations: these are the problems of belief (= disavowal) and that of the fetish itself, the latter more immediately linked to direct or sublimated erotogenicity.

I shall say very little about the problems of belief in the cinema. First because they are at the centre of my article in *Communications* no. 23. Second because I have already discussed them in this one *vis-à-vis* identification and the mirror: I have tried to describe, outside the special case of fiction, a few of the many and successive *twists*, the 'reversals' (reduplications) that occur in the cinema to articulate together the imaginary, the symbolic and the real; each of these twists presupposes a division of belief; in order to work, the film does not only require *a* splitting, but a whole series of stages of belief, imbricated together into a chain by a remarkable machinery. – In the third place, because the subject has already been largely dealt with by Octave Mannoni in his remarkable studies of the theatrical illusion ('L'Illusion comique en le théâtre du point de vue de l'imaginaire', *vis-à-vis* the fictional theatre. Of course, I have said above that theatrical fiction and cinematic fiction are not fictional in the same way; but this deviation concerned the representation, the signifying material, not the represented, i.e. the fiction–fact as such, in which the deviation is much smaller (at any rate so long as one is dealing with *spectacles* such as theatre and cinema – written fiction obviously presents somewhat different problems). Mannoni's analyses are just as valid for the fiction film, with the single reservation that the divergences in representation that I have already discussed are borne in mind.

I shall rest content to adapt these analyses to a cinematic perspective, and not feel obliged to repeat them (not so well) in detail. – It is understood that the audience is not duped by the diegetic illusion, it 'knows' that the screen presents no more than a fiction. And yet, it is of vital importance for the correct unfolding of the spectacle that this make-believe be scrupulously respected (or else the fiction film is declared 'poorly made'), that everything is set to work to make the deception effective and to give it an air of truth (this is the problem of *verisimilitude*). Any spectator will tell you that he 'doesn't believe in it', but everything happens as if there were none the less someone to be deceived, someone who really will 'believe in it'. (I shall say that behind any fiction there is a second fiction: the diegetic events are fictional, that is the first; but everyone pretends to believe they are true, and that is the second.) In other words, asks Mannoni, since it is 'accepted' that the audience is incredulous, *who is it who is credulous* and must be maintained in his credulousness by the perfect organization of the machinery (of the machination)? This credulous person is, of course, another part of ourselves, he is still seated *beneath* the incredulous one, or in his heart, it is he who continues to believe, who disavows what he knows (he for whom all human beings are still endowed with a penis). But by a symmetrical and simultaneous movement, the incredulous disavows the credulous: no one will admit that he is duped by the 'plot'. That is why the instance of credulousness is often projected into the outer world and constituted as a separate person, a person completely abused by the diegesis: thus in Corneille's *L'Illusion comique*, a play with a significant title, the character Pridament, the *naïf*, who does not know what theatre is, and *for whom*, by a reversal foreseen in Corneille's plot itself, the representation of the play is given. By a partial identification with this character, the spectators can sustain their credulousness in all incredulousness. This instance which believes and also its personified projection have fairly precise equivalents in the cinema: for example, the credulous spectators at the 'Grand Café' in 1895, frequently and complacently evoked by the incredulous spectators who have come *later* (and are no longer children), those spectators of 1895 who fled their seats in terror when the train entered La Ciotat station (in Lumière's famous film), because they were afraid it would run them down. Or else, in so many films, the character of the 'dreamer' – the sleeping dreamer – who during the film believed (as we did!) that it was true, whereas it was he who saw it all in a dream and who wakes up at the end of the film (as we do again). Octave Mannoni compares these switches of belief with those the ethnologist observes in certain populations in which his informers regularly declare that 'once the masks were believed in' (these masks are used to deceive children, like our Father Christmas, and adolescents learn at their initiation ceremonies that the 'masks' were in fact adults in disguise); in other words, these societies have always 'believed' in the masks, but have always rejected this belief into a 'once-upon-a-time': they still believe in them, but always in the aorist tense (like everyone). This once-upon-a-time is childhood, when one really was duped by the masks; among adults, the beliefs of once-upon-a-time irrigate the unbelief of today, but irrigate it by denegation (one could say: *by delegation*, by rejecting credence on to the child and on to former times).

Certain cinematic sub-codes inscribe disavowal into the film according to less permanent and more localized figures. They should be studied separately in this perspective. I am not thinking only of films which have been 'dreamt' in their entirety by one of their characters, but also of all the sequences accompanied by a 'voice-off' commentary, spoken sometimes by a character, sometimes by a kind of anonymous 'speaker'. This voice, precisely a voice 'off', beyond jurisdiction, represents the rampart of unbelief (hence it is the opposite of the Pridament character, yet has the same effect in the last analysis). The distance it establishes between the action and ourselves comforts our feeling that we are not duped by that action: thus reassured (behind the rampart), we can allow ourselves to be duped by it a bit longer (it is the speciality of naive distanciations to resolve themselves into alibis). – There are also all those 'films within a film' which downgear the mechanism of our belief–unbelief and anchor it in several stages, hence more strongly: the included film was an illusion, so the including film (the film as such) was not, or was so somewhat less.[8]

As for the fetish itself, in its cinematic manifestations, who could fail to see that it consists fundamentally of the equipment of the cinema (= its 'technique'), or of the cinema as a whole as equipment and as technique, for fiction films and others? It is no accident that in the cinema some cameramen, some directors, some critics, some spectators demonstrate a real 'fetishism of technique', often noted or denounced as such ('fetishism' is taken here in its ordinary sense, which is rather loose but does contain within it the analytical sense that I shall attempt to disengage). The fetish proper, like the apparatus of the cinema, is a *prop*, the prop that disavows a lack and in doing so affirms it without wishing to. A prop, too, which is as it were *deposited* on the body of the object; a prop which is the penis, since it negates its absence, and hence a partial object that makes the whole object loveable and desirable. The fetish is also the point of departure for specialized practices, and as is well known, desire in its modalities is the more 'technical' the more it is perverse.

Thus with respect to the desired body – to the body of desire rather – the fetish is in the same position as the technical equipment of the cinema with respect to the cinema as a whole. A fetish, the cinema as a technical performance, as prowess, as an *exploit*, an exploit that underlines and denounces the lack on which the whole arrangement is based (the absence of the object, replaced by its reflection), an exploit which consists at the same time of making this absence forgotten. The cinema fetishist is the person who is enchanted at what the machine is capable of, at the *theatre of shadows* as such. For the establishment of his full potency for cinematic enjoyment (*jouissance*) he must think at every moment (and above all *simultaneously*) of the force of presence the film has and of the absence on which this force is constructed.[9] He must constantly compare the result with the means set to work (and hence pay attention to the technique), for his pleasure lodges in the gap between the two. Of course, this attitude appears most clearly in the 'connoisseur', the cinephile, but it also occurs, as a partial component of cinematic pleasure, in those who just go to the cinema: if they do go it is partly in order to be carried away by the film (or the fiction, if there is one), but also in order to *appreciate* as such the machinery that is carrying them away: they will say, precisely when they have been carried away, that the film was a 'good' one, that it was 'well made' (the same thing is said of a harmonious body).

It is clear that fetishism, in the cinema as elsewhere, is closely linked to the good object. The function of the fetish is to restore the latter, threatened in its 'goodness' (in Melanie Klein's sense) by the terrifying discovery of the lack. Thanks to the fetish, which covers the wound and itself becomes erotogenic, the object as a whole can become desirable again without excessive fear. In a similar way, the whole cinematic institution is as it were *recovered* by a thin and omnipresent garment, a stimulating prop through which it is consumed: the ensemble of its equipment and its tricks – and not just the celluloid strip, the '*pellicule*' or 'little skin' which has been rightly mentioned in this connection (Roger Dadoun: ' "King Kong": du monstre comme dé-monstration,' *Littérature* no. 8, December 1972, p. 109; Octave Mannoni: *Clefs pour l'imaginaire*, p. 180) – of the equipment which *needs* the lack in order to stand out in it by contrast, but which only affirms it in so far as it ensures that it is forgotten, and which lastly (its third twist) needs it not to be forgotten none the less, for fear that at the same stroke the fact that it caused it to be forgotten will itself be forgotten.

The fetish is the cinema in its *physical* state. A fetish is always material: in so far as one can make up for it by the power of the symbolic alone one is precisely no longer a fetishist. It is important to recall here that of all the arts the cinema is the one that involves the most extensive and complex equipment; the 'technical' dimension is more obtrusive in it than elsewhere. Along with television, it is the only art that is also an industry, or at least is so from the outset (the others become industries subsequently: music through the gramophone record or the cassette, books by mass printings and publishing trusts, etc.). In this respect only architecture is a little like it: there are 'languages' that are *heavier* than others, more dependent on 'hardware'.

At the same time as it localizes the penis, the fetish represents by synecdoche the whole body of the object as desirable. Similarly, interest in the equipment and technique is the privileged representative of *love for the cinema*.

The Law is what permits desire: the cinematic equipment is the instance thanks to which the imaginary turns into the symbolic, thanks to which the lost object (the absence of what is filmed) becomes the law and the principle of a specific and instituted signifier.

For in the structure of the fetish there is another point on which Mannoni quite rightly insists and which directly concerns my present undertaking. Because it attempts to disavow the evidence of the senses, the fetish is evidence that this evidence has indeed been *recorded* (like a tape stored in the memory). The fetish is not inaugurated because the child still believes its mother has a penis (= order of the imaginary), for if it still believed it completely, as 'before', it would no longer need the fetish. It is inaugurated because the child now 'knows very well' that its mother has no penis. In other words, the fetish not only has disavowal value, but also *knowledge value*.

That is why, as I said a moment ago, the fetishism of cinematic technique is especially well developed among the 'connoisseurs' of the cinema. That is also why the theoretician of the cinema necessarily retains within him – at the cost of a new backward turn that leads him to interrogate technique, to symbolize the fetish, and hence to maintain it as he dissolves it – an interest in the equipment without which he would not have any motive for studying it.

Indeed, the equipment is not just physical (= the fetish proper); it also has its discursive imprints, its extensions in the very text of the film. Here is revealed the specific movement of theory: when it shifts from a fascination with technique to the critical study of the different *codes* that this equipment authorizes. *Concern for the signifier* in the cinema derives from a fetishism that has taken up a position as far as possible along its cognitive flank. To adapt the formula by which Octave Mannoni defines disavowal (= 'I know very well...', but all the same'), the study of the signifier is a libidinal position constituted by weakening the 'but all the same' and profiting by this saving of energy to dig deeper into the

'I know very well', which thus becomes 'I know nothing at all, but I desire to know'.

Just like the other structures that constitute the foundation of the cinema, fetishism does not intervene only in the constitution of the signifier, but also in certain of its more particular configurations. Here we have *framings* and also certain *camera movements* (the latter can anyway be defined as progressive changes in framing).

Cinema with directly erotic subject matter deliberately plays on the edges of the frame and the progressive and if need be incomplete revelations allowed by the camera as it moves, and this is no accident. Censorship is involved here: censorship of films and censorship in Freud's sense. Whether the form is static (framing) or dynamic (camera movements), the principle is the same: the point is to gamble simultaneously on the excitation of desire and its retention (which is its opposite and yet favours it), by the infinite variations made possible precisely by the studios' technique on the exact emplacement of the *boundary* that bars the look, that puts an end to the 'seen', that inaugurates that more sinister craneshot (or low-angle shot) towards the unseen, the guessed-at. The framing and its displacements (that determine the *emplacement*) are in themselves forms of 'suspense' and are extensively used in suspense films too, though they remain such forms in other cases. They have an inner affinity with the mechanisms of desire, of its postponements, its new impetus, and they retain this affinity in other places than erotic sequences (the only difference lies in the *quantum* which is sublimated and the *quantum* which is not). The way the cinema, with its wandering framings (wandering like the look, like the caress), finds the means to reveal space has something to do with a kind of permanent undressing, a generalized strip-tease, a less direct but more perfected strip-tease, since it also makes it possible to dress space again, to remove from view what it has previously shown, to *take back* as well as to retain (like the child at the moment of the birth of the fetish, the child who has already seen, but whose look beats a rapid retreat): a strip-tease pierced with 'flash-backs', inverted sequences that then give new impetus to the forward movement. These veiling–unveiling procedures can also be compared with certain cinematic 'punctuations', especially slow ones strongly marked by a concern for control and expectation (slow fade-ins and fade-outs, irises, 'drawn out' dissolves like those of Sternberg).[10]

'Theorize,' he says...(Provisional Conclusion)

The psychoanalytic constitution of the cinema signifier is a very wide problem, one containing, so to speak, a number of 'panels'. I cannot examine them all here, and there will surely be some that I have not even mentioned.

However, something tells me that (for the present) I can stop here. I wanted to give a first idea of the field I perceive, and, to begin with, to assure myself that I was indeed perceiving it (I was not certain of it all at once).

Now I shall turn back on this study itself as an unfolding of my initial dream. Psychoanalysis does not illuminate only the film, but also the conditions of desire of whoever makes himself its theoretician. Interwoven into every analytical undertaking is the thread of a self-analysis.

I have loved the cinema, I no longer love it. I still love it. What I have wished to do in these pages is to keep at a distance, as in the scopic practice I have discussed, that which in me (= in everyone) *can* love it: to retain it as *questioned*. As questioning, too, for the wish to construct the film into an object of knowledge is to extend, by a supplementary degree of sublimation, the passion for seeing that made the cinephile and the institution themselves. Initially an undivided passion, entirely occupied in preserving the cinema as a good object (imaginary passion, passion for the imaginary), it subsequently splits into two diverging and reconverging desires, one of which 'looks' at the other: this is the theoretical break, and like all breaks it is also a link: that of theory with its object.

I have used words like 'love of the cinema'. I hope I will have been understood. The point is not to restrict them to their usual meaning, the meaning suggested by 'archive rats' or fanatical 'Macmahonites' (who provide no more than exaggerated examples). Nor is the point to relapse into the absurd opposition between the affective and the intellectual. The point is to ask why many people go to the cinema when they are not obliged to, how they manage to 'assimilate' the rules of this game which is a fairly new one historically, how they themselves become cogs of the institution. For anyone who asks this question, 'loving the cinema' and 'understanding the film' are no more than two closely mingled aspects of one vast socio-psychical machinery.

As for someone who looks at this machine itself (the theoretician who desires to know it), I have said that he was of necessity sadistic. There is no sublimation, as Freud himself insisted, without 'defusion of the drives'. The good object has moved to the side of the knowledge and the cinema becomes a bad object (a dual displacement which favours the distances that enable 'science' to see its object). The cinema is 'persecuted', but this persistence is also a reparation (the knowing posture is both aggressive and depressive), a reparation of a specific kind, peculiar to the semiologist: the *restoration* to the theoretical body of what has been taken from the *institution*, from the code which is being 'studied'.

To study the cinema: what an odd formula! How can it be done without 'breaking' its beneficial image, all that idealism of film as an 'art' full and simple, the seventh of the name? By breaking the toy one loses it, and that is the position of the semiotic discourse: it feeds on this loss, it puts in its place the hoped for advance of knowledge: it is an inconsolable discourse that consoles itself, that takes itself by the hand and goes to work. Lost objects are the only ones one is afraid to lose, and the semiologist is he who rediscovers them *from the other side*: 'Il n'y a de cause que de ce qui cloche' – a cause is required only when something is not working properly.[11]

Notes

1   'The Ego and the Id,' *Standard Edition*, Vol. XIX, pp. 26 and 30 (= 'desexualized social sentiment'); see also (on paranoia) 'On Narcissism: an Introduction,' ibid., Vol. XIV, pp. 95–6, 101–2.

2   [*Derrière la tête* means 'at the back of one's mind' as well as 'behind one's head'.] See André Green: 'L'Ecran bi-face, un oeil derrière la tête,' *Psychanalyse et cinéma* no. 1, January 1970 (no further issues appeared), pp. 15–22. It will be clear that in the passage that follows my analysis coincides in places with that of André Green.

3   'The Ego and the Id,' *Standard Edition*, Vol. XIX, p. 18; 'The Interpretation of Dreams,' ibid., Vol. V, p. 615 (= consciousness as a sense organ) and p. 574 (= consciousness as a dual recording surface, internal and external); 'The Unconscious,' ibid., Vol. XIV, p. 171 (psychical processes are unconscious in themselves, consciousness is a function that *perceives* a small proportion of them), etc.

4   'Repression,' *Standard Edition*, Vol. XIV, pp. 146–7; 'Instincts and their Vicissitudes,' ibid., pp. 122 and 134n.; 'The Ego and the Id,' ibid., Vol. XIX, p. 30; 'On Narcissism: an Introduction,' ibid., Vol. XIV, p. 94, etc.

5   More precisely: lending themselves through their peculiar characteristics to a perversion which is not the drive itself, but the subject's position with respect to it (*Le Séminaire*, tome XI, pp. 165–6). Remember that for Freud as well as for Lacan, the drive is always 'componential' (the child is polymorphously perverse, etc.).

6   See the paragraph with this title in Jean-François Lyotard's article 'L'Acinéma,' *Cinéma: Théories, Lectures, Revue d'ésthétique* nos. 2/3/4, 1973, pp. 357–69.

7   See also Octave Mannoni's important study, 'Je sais bien, mais quand même...,' in *Clefs pour l'imaginaire*.

8   A startling (though only partial) resemblance with the case of 'dreams within a dream'; cf. 'The Interpretation of Dreams,' *Standard Edition*, Vol. IV, p. 338.

9   I have studied this phenomenon at slightly greater length in 'Trucage et cinéma' in *Essais sur la signification au cinéma*, tome II, Klincksieck, Paris 1972, pp. 173–92.

10 Reading this article in manuscript, Thierry Kuntzel has pointed out to me that in this paragraph I perhaps lean slightly too far towards fetishism and fetishism alone in discussing filmic figures that depend just as much on *cinematic perversion* in general: the hypertrophy of the perceptual component drive with its mises-en-scène, its progressions–retentions, its calculated postponements, etc. This objection seems to me (after the event) to be correct. I shall have to come back to it. Fetishism, as is well known, is closely linked to perversion, although it does not exhaust it. Hence the difficulty. For the cinematic effects I am evoking here (= playing on the framing and its displacements), the properly fetishistic element seems to me to be the '*bar*', the edge of the screen, the separation between the seen and the unseen, the 'arrestation' of the look. Once the seen or the unseen are envisaged rather than their intersection (their edge), we are dealing with scopic perversion itself, going beyond the strict province of the fetish.

11 [Cf. Jacques Lacan: *Le Séminaire*, tome XI, p. 25. Lacan contrasts a *cause*, as an occult property, with a *law*, in which 'causes' are smoothly absorbed as variables in a

function; the unconscious, however, will remain a cause in the occult sense, because its order exceeds any particular function: it is The Law rather than a law, *énonciation* rather than *énoncé*, '*lalangue*' rather than a *langue* – hence its privileged manifestation in the lapse, the mistake, the point at which discourse 'limps'.]

24

The Orthopsychic Subject: Film Theory and the Reception of Lacan

Joan Copjec

Through his appearance in *Television*, Lacan parodies the image of himself – of his teaching – that we have, to a large extent, received and accepted. Standing alone behind his desk, hands now supporting him as he leans assertively forward, now thrown upward in some emphatic gesture, Lacan stares directly out at us, as he speaks in a voice that none would call smooth of "quelque chose, n'est-ce pas?" This "quelque chose" is, of course, never made specific, never revealed, and so it comes to stand for a fact or a system of facts that is known, but not by us. This image recalls the one presented to Tabard by the principal in Vigo's *Zero for Conduct*. It is the product of the childish, paranoid notion that all our private thoughts and actions are spied on by and visible within a public world represented by parental figures. In appearing to us, then, by means of the "mass media,"[1] Lacan seems to confirm what we may call our "televisual" fear – that we are perfectly, completely visible to a gaze that observes us from afar (*tele* meaning both "distant" and [from *telos*] "complete").[2] That this proffered image is parodic, however, is almost surely to be missed, so strong are our misperceptions of Lacan. And, so, the significance of the words with which he opens his address and by which he immediately calls attention to his self-parody – "I always speak the truth. Not the whole truth, because there's no way to say it all. Saying the whole truth is materially impossible: words fail. Yet it's through this very impossibility that the truth holds onto the real"[3] – the significance of these words may also be missed, as they have been generally in our theories of representation, the most sophisticated example of which is film theory.

Let me first, in a kind of establishing shot, summarize what I take to be the central misconception of film theory: believing itself to be following Lacan, it conceives the screen as mirror;[4] in doing so, however, it operates in ignorance of, and at the expense of, Lacan's more radical insight, whereby the mirror is conceived as screen.

The Screen as Mirror

This misconception is at the base of film theory's formulation of two concepts – the apparatus and the gaze – and of their interrelation. One of the clearest and most succinct descriptions of this interrelation – and I must state here that it is *because* of its clarity, because of the way it responsibly and explicitly articulates assumptions endemic to film theory, that I cite this description, not to impugn it or its authors particularly – is provided by the editors of *Re-vision*, a collection of essays by feminists on film. Although its focus is the special situation of the female spectator, the description outlines the general relations among the terms *gaze*, *apparatus*, and *subject* as they are stated by film theory. After quoting a passage from Foucault's *Discipline and Punish* in which Bentham's architectural plan for the panopticon is laid out, the *Re-vision* editors make the following claim:

> the dissociation of the see/being seen dyad [which the panoptic arrangement of the central tower and annular arrangement ensures] and the sense of permanent visibility seem perfectly to describe the condition not only of the inmate in Bentham's prison but of the woman as well. For defined in terms of her visibility, she carries her own Panopticon with her wherever she goes, her self-image a function of her being for another.... The subjectivity assigned to femininity within patriarchal systems is inevitably bound up with the structure of the look and the localization of the eye as authority.[5]

The panoptic gaze defines *perfectly* the situation of the woman under patriarchy: that is, it is the very image of the structure which obliges the woman to monitor herself with a patriarchal eye. This structure thereby guarantees that even her innermost desire will always be not a transgression, but rather an implantation of the law, that even the "process of theorizing her own untenable situation" can only reflect back to her "as in a mirror," her subjugation to the gaze.

The panoptic gaze defines, then, the *perfect*, i.e. the total, visibility of the woman under patriarchy, of any subject under any social order, which is to say, of any subject at all. For the very condition and substance of the subject's subjectivity is his or her subjectivization by the law of the society which produces that subject. One only becomes visible – not only to others, but also to oneself – through (by seeing through) the categories constructed by a specific, historically defined society. These categories of visibility are categories of knowledge.

The perfection of vision and knowledge can only be procured at the expense of invisibility and non-knowledge. According to the logic of the panoptic apparatus, these last do not and (in an important sense) cannot exist. One might summarize this logic – thereby revealing it to be more questionable than it is normally taken to be – by stating it thus: since all knowledge (or visibility) is produced by society (that is, all that it is possible to know comes not from reality, but from socially constructed categories of implementable thought), since *all* knowledge is produced, *only* knowledge (or visibility) is produced, or *all* that is produced is knowledge (visible). This is too glaring a *non sequitur* – the *then* clauses are too obviously not necessary consequences of the *if* clause – for it ever to be statable as such. And yet this lack of logical consequence is precisely what must be at work and what must go unobserved in the founding of the seeing/being seen dyad which figures the comprehension of the subject by the laws that rule over its construction.

Here – one can already imagine the defensive protestations: I have overstated my argument – there *is* a measure of indetermination available even to the panoptic argument. This indetermination is provided for by the fact that the subject is constructed not by one monolithic discourse but by a multitude of different discourses. What cannot be determined in advance are the articulations that may result from the chance encounter – sometimes on the site of the subject – of these various discourses. A subject of a legal discourse may find itself in conflict with itself as a subject of a religious discourse. The negotiation of this conflict may produce a solution that was anticipated by neither of the contributing discourses. Some film theorists have underlined this part of Foucault's work in an attempt to locate possible sources of resistance to institutional forms of power, to clear a space for a feminist cinema, for example.[6] I would argue, however, that this simple atomization and multiplication of subject positions and this *partes extra partes* description of conflict does not lead to a radical undermining of knowledge or power. Not only is it the case that at each stage what is *produced* is conceived in Foucauldian theory to be a *determinate* thing or position, but, in addition, knowledge and power are conceived of as the overall effect of the *relations among* the various conflicting positions and discourses. Differences do not threaten panoptic power; they feed it.

The Lacanian argument is quite different. It states that that which is produced by a signifying system can never be determinate. Conflict in this case does not result from the clash between two different positions, but from the fact that no position defines a resolute identity. Non-knowledge or invisibility is not registered as the wavering and negotiations between two certainties, two meanings or positions, but as the undermining of every certainty, the incompleteness of every meaning and position.[7] Incapable of articulating this more radical understanding of non-knowledge, the panoptic argument is ultimately *resistant to resistance*, unable to conceive of a discourse that would refuse rather than refuel power.

My purpose here is not simply to point out the crucial differences between Foucault's theory and Lacan's, but also to attempt to explain how the two theories have failed to be perceived *as* different. How a psychoanalytically informed film theory came to see itself as expressible in Foucauldian terms, despite the fact that these very terms aimed at dispensing with psychoanalysis as a method of explanation. In Foucault's work the techniques of disciplinary power (of the construction of the subject) are conceived as capable of "materially penetrat[ing] the body in depth without depending even on the mediation of the subject's own representations. If power takes hold on the body, this isn't through its having first to be interiorized in people's consciousness."[8] For Foucault, the conscious and the unconscious are categories constructed by psychoanalysis and other discourses (philosophy, literature, law, etc.): like other socially constructed categories, they provide a means of rendering the subject visible, governable, trackable. They are categories through which the modern subject is apprehended and apprehends itself, *rather than* (as psychoanalysis maintains) processes of apprehension; they are not processes which engage or are engaged by social discourses (film texts, for example). What the *Re-vision* editors force us to confront is the fact that in film theory these radical differences have largely gone unnoticed or have been nearly annulled. Thus, though the gaze is conceived as a meta-psychological concept central to the description of the subject's psychic engagement with the cinematic apparatus, the concept, as we shall see, is formulated in a way that makes any psychic engagement redundant.

My argument is that film theory performed a kind of "Foucauldization" of Lacanian theory; an early misreading of Lacan turned him into a "spendthrift" Foucault – one who wasted a bit too much theoretical energy on such notions as the antithetical meaning of words or the repression instituted by parental inter-diction. It is the perceived frugality of Foucault (whereby every disavowal is seen to be essentially an avowal of what is being denied), every bit as much as the recent and widely proclaimed interest in history, that has guaranteed Foucault's ascendancy over Lacan in the academy.

It was through the concept of the apparatus – the economic, technical, ideological institution – of cinema that the break between contemporary film theory and its past was effected.[9] This break meant that cinematic representation was consid-ered to be not a clear or distorted reflection of a prior and external reality, but one among many social discourses that helped to construct reality and the spectatorial subject. As is well known, the concept of the apparatus was not original to film theory, but was imported from epistemological studies of science. The actual term *dispositif* ("apparatus") used in film theory is borrowed from Gaston Bachelard, who employed it to counter the reigning philosophy of phenomenology. Bachelard proposed instead the study of "phenomeno-*techno-logy*," believing that phenomena are not given to us directly by an independent reality, but are, rather, constructed (cf. the Greek *technē*, "produced by a regular method of making, rather than found in nature") by a range of practices and techniques that define the field of historical truth. The objects of science are materializable concepts, not natural phenomena.

Even though it borrows his term and the concept it names, film theory does not locate its beginnings in the work of Bachelard, but rather in that of one of his students, Louis Althusser.[10] (This history is by now relatively familiar, but since a number of significant points have been overlooked or misinterpreted, it is necessary to retrace some of the details.) Althusser was judged to have advanced and corrected the theory of Bachelard in a way that foregrounded the *subject* of science. Now, although he had argued that the scientific subject was formed in and by the field of science, Bachelard had also maintained that the subject was never *fully* formed in this way. One of the reasons for this merely partial success, he theorized, was an obstacle that impeded the subject's development; this obstacle he called the imaginary. But the problem with this imaginary, as Althusser later pointed out, was that it was itself largely untheorized and was thus (that is, almost by default) accepted by Bachelard as a *given*, as external and prior to rather than as an *effect* of historical determinations. The scientific subject was split, then, between two modes of thought: one governed by historically determined scientific forms, the other by forms that were eternal, spontaneous, and almost purely mythical.[11]

Althusser rethought the category of the imaginary, making it a part of the process of the historical construction of the subject. The imaginary came to name a process necessary for – rather than an impediment to – the ideological founding of the subject: the imaginary provided the form of the subject's lived relation to society. Through this relation, the subject was brought to accept as its own, to recognize itself in, the representations of the social order.

This last statement of Althusser's position is important for our concerns here because it is also a statement of the basic position of film theory as it was developed in the 1970s, in France and in England, by Jean-Louis Baudry, Christian Metz, Jean-Louis Comolli, and by the journal *Screen*. In sum: the screen is a mirror. The representations produced by the institution cinema, the images presented on the screen, are accepted by the subject as its own.[12] There is, admittedly, an ambiguity in the notion of the subject's "own image"; it can refer either to an image *of* the subject or an image *belonging to* the subject. Both references are intended by film theory. Whether that which is represented is specularized as an image of the subject's own body or as the subject's image of someone or something else, what remains crucial is the attribution to the image of what Lacan (not film theory, which has never, it seems to me, adequately accounted for the ambiguity) calls "that belong to me aspect so reminiscent of property."[13] It is this aspect that allows the subject to see in any representation not only a reflection of itself, but a reflection of itself as master of all it surveys. The imaginary relation produces the subject as master of the image. This insight led to film theory's reconception of film's characteristic "impression of reality."[14] No longer conceived as dependent upon a relation of verisimilitude between the image and the real referent, this impression was henceforth attributed to a relation of adequation between the image and the spectator. In other words, the impression of reality results from the fact that the subject takes the image as a full and sufficient representation of itself and its world; the subject is satisfied that it has been adequately reflected on the screen. The "reality effect" and the "subject effect" both name the same constructed impression: that the image makes the subject fully visible to itself.

The imaginary relation is defined as literally a relation of *recognition*. The subject reconceptualized as its own concepts already constructed by the Other. Sometimes the reconstruction of representation is thought to take place secondarily rather than directly, after there has been a primary recognition of the subject as a "pure act of perception." This is Metz's scenario.[15] The subject first recognizes itself by identifying with the gaze and then recognizes the images on the screen. Now, *what* exactly is the gaze, in this context? Why does it emerge in this way from the theory of the apparatus? What does it add – or subtract – from Bachelard's theory, where it does not figure as a term?[16] All these questions will have to be confronted more fully in due course; for now we must begin with the observation that this ideal point can be nothing but *the signified of the image*, the point from which the image *makes sense* to the subject. In taking up its position at this point, the subject sees itself as *supplying* the image with sense. Regardless of whether one or two stages are posited, the gaze is always the point from which identification is conceived by film theory to take place. And because the gaze is always conceptualized as an analogue of that geometral point of Renaissance perspective at which the picture becomes fully, undistortedly visible, the gaze always retains within film theory the sense of being that point at which sense and being coincide. The subject comes into being by identifying with the image's signified. Sense *founds* the subject – *that* is the ultimate point of the film theoretical concept of the gaze.

The imaginary relation is not, however, merely a relation of knowledge, of sense and recognition; it is also a relation of love guaranteed by knowledge. The image seems not only perfectly to represent the subject, it seems also to be an image of the subject's perfection. An unexceptional definition of narcissism appears to support this relation: the subject falls in love with its own image as the image of its ideal self. *Except* for the fact that narcissism becomes in this account the structure that facilitates the *harmonious* relation between self and social order (since the subject is made to snuggle happily into the space carved out for it), whereas, in the psychoanalytic account, the subject's narcissistic relation to the self is seen to *conflict with and disrupt* other social relations. I am attempting to pinpoint here no minor point of disagreement between psychoanalysis and the panoptic argument: the opposition between the unbinding force of narcissism and the binding force of social relations is one of the defining tenets of psychoanalysis.[17] It is nevertheless true that Freud himself often ran into difficulty trying to maintain the distinction and that many, from Jung on, have found it easier to merge the two forces into a libidinal monism. But easier is not better; to disregard the distinction is not only to destroy psychoanalysis but also to court determinism.

Why is the representation of the relation of the subject to the social necessarily an imaginary one? This question, posed by Paul Hirst,[18] should have launched a serious critique of film theory. That it did not is attributable, in part, to the fact that the question was perceived to be fundamentally a question about the content of the concept of the imaginary. With only a slightly different emphasis, the question can be seen to ask how the imaginary came to bear, almost exclusively, the burden of the construction of the subject – despite the fact that we always speak of the "symbolic" construction of the subject. One way of answering this is to note that in much contemporary theory the symbolic is itself structured like the imaginary, like Althusser's version of the imaginary. And thus Hirst's criticisms are aimed at our conception of the symbolic construction of the subject, in general. That this is so is made explicit once again by the frugality of Foucault, who exposes to us not only the content, but also the emptiness of some of our concepts. For he successfully demonstrates that the conception of the symbolic on which he (and, implicitly, others) relies makes the imaginary unnecessary. In a move similar to the one that refigured ideology as a positive force of the production rather than falsification of reality, Foucault rethinks symbolic law as a *purely positive* force of the production rather than repression of the subject and its desires. Offering his argument – that the law constructs desire – as a *critique* of psychoanalysis, Foucault refuses to acknowledge that psychoanalysis has itself never argued any differently.

What is the difference, then, between Foucault's and psychoanalysis's version of the law/desire relation? Simply this: Foucault conceives desire not only as an *effect*, but also as a *realization* of the law, while *psychoanalysis teaches us that this conflation of effect and realization is an error.* To say that the law is only positive, that it does not forbid desire, but rather incites it, causes it to flourish by requiring us to contemplate it, confess it, watch for its various manifestations, is to end up saying simply that the law causes us to *have* a desire – for incest, let us say. While rejecting his moralism, this position recreates the error of the psychiatrist in one of Mel Brooks's routines. In a fit of revulsion, this psychiatrist throws a patient out of his office because she reported having a dream in which she "was kissing her father!" The feeling of disgust is the humorous result of the psychiatrist's failure to differentiate the enunciative position of the dreaming patient from the stated position of the dreamed one. The elision of the difference between these positions – enunciation and statement – causes desire to be thought as realization in two ways. First, desire is conceived as an actual state resulting from a possibility allowed by law. Second, if desire is something one simply and positively has, nothing can prevent its realization except a purely external force. The destiny of desire is realization, unless it is prohibited by some external force.

Psychoanalysis denies the preposterous proposition that society is founded on desire – the desire for incest, let us say once again. Surely, it argues, it is the *repression* of this desire which is crucial. The law does not construct a subject who simply and unequivocally has a desire, but one who *rejects* its desire, one who wants not to desire it. The subject is thus split from its desire, and desire itself is conceived as something – precisely – unrealized; it does not actualize what the law makes possible. Nor is desire committed to realization, barring any external hindrance. For the internal dialectic which makes the being of the subject dependent on the negation of its desire turns the construction of desire into a self-hindering process.

Foucault's definition of the law as positive and non-repressive implies that the law is both (1) unconditional – that it *must* be obeyed, since only that which it allows can come into existence; *being is*, by definition, *obedience* – and (2) unconditioned – since nothing, i.e. no desire, precedes the law; there is no cause of the law and we must not therefore seek behind the law for its reasons. Law does not exist in order to repress desire.

Now, not only have these claims for the law been made before, they have also been previously contested.[19] For these are precisely the claims of moral conscience which Freud examines in *Totem and Taboo*. There Freud reduces these claims to what he takes to be their absurd consequences: "If we were to admit the claims thus asserted by our conscience [that desire conforms to or always falls within the law], it would follow, on the one hand, that prohibition would be superfluous and, on the other, the fact of conscience would remain unexplained."[20] On the one hand, prohibition would be superfluous. Foucault agrees: once the law is conceived as primarily positive, as producing the phenomena it scrutinizes, the concept of a negative, repressive law can be viewed as an excess – of psychoanalysis. On the other hand, the fact of conscience would remain unexplained. That is, there is no longer any reason for conscience to exist; it *should*, like prohibition, be superfluous. What becomes suddenly *in*explicable is the very *experience* of conscience – which is not only the subjective experience of the compulsion to obey, but also the experience of guilt, of the remorse that follows transgression – once we have accepted the *claims* of conscience that the law cannot fail to impose itself and cannot be caused. Foucault agrees once again: the experience of conscience and the interiorization of the law through representations is made superfluous by his theory of law.

Again: the claims of conscience are used to refute the experience of conscience. This paradox located by Freud will, of course, not appear as such to those who do not ascribe the claims *to* conscience. And yet something of the paradox *is* manifest in Foucault's description of panoptic power and film theory's description of the relation between the apparatus and the gaze. In both cases the model of self-surveillance implicitly recalls the psychoanalytic model of moral conscience even as the resemblance is being disavowed. The image of self-surveillance, self-correction, is both required to construct the subject and made redundant by the fact that the subject thus constructed is, by definition, absolutely upright, completely correct. The inevitability and completeness of its success renders the orthopedic gesture of surveillance unnecessary. The subject is and can only be inculpable. The relation between apparatus and gaze creates only the mirage of psychoanalysis. There is, in fact, no psychoanalytic subject in sight.

Orthopsychism[21]

How, then, to derive a properly psychoanalytic – that is, a split – subject from the premise that the subject is the effect rather than the cause of the social order? Before turning, finally, to Lacan's solution, it will be necessary to pause to review one extraordinary chapter from Bachelard – chapter IV of *Le Rationalisme appliqué*, titled "La Surveillance intellectuelle de soi" – where we will find some arguments that have been overlooked in more recent theorizations of the apparatus.[22]

Although Bachelard pioneered the theory of the institutional construction of the field of science, he also (as we have already said) persistently argued that the protocols of science never fully saturated nor provided the content of this field. The obstacle of the imaginary is only *one* of the reasons given for this. Besides this purely negative resistance *to* the scientific, there is also a positive condition *of* the scientific itself that prevented such a reduction from taking place. Both these reasons together guarantee that the concepts of science are never mere realizations of possibilities historically allowed, and scientific thought is never simply habit, the regulated retracing of possible paths already laid out in advance.

To say that the scientific subject is constructed by the institution of science, Bachelard would reason, is to say that it is always thereby obliged to survey itself, its own thinking, not subjectively, not through a process of introspection to which the subject has privileged access, but *objectively*, from the position of the scientific institution. So far this *orthopsychic* relation may seem no different from the panoptic relation we have been so intent on dislodging. But there *is* a difference: the orthopsychic relation (unlike the panoptic one) assumes that it is just this objective survey that allows thought to become (not wholly visible, but) *secret*; it allows thought to remain *hidden*, even under the most intense scrutiny. Let us make clear that Bachelard is not attempting to argue that there is an original, private self that happens to find in objectivity a means (among others) of concealing itself. He is arguing, rather, that the very possibility of concealment is only raised by the subject's objective relation to itself. For it is the very act of surveillance – which makes clear the fact that the subject is external to itself, exists in a relation of "extimacy" (Lacan's word) with itself – that causes the subject to appear to itself as culpable, as guilty of hiding something. The objective relation to the self, Bachelard informs us, necessarily raises the insidious question that Nietzsche formulated thus: "To everything which a man allows to become visible, one is able to demand: what does he wish to hide?" It does not matter that this "man" is oneself. The ineradicable suspicion of dissimulation raised by the objective relation guarantees that thought will never become totally coincident with the forms of the institution. Thought will be split, rather, between belief in what the institution makes manifest, and suspicion about what it is keeping secret. All objective representations, its very own thought, will be taken by the subject not as true representations of itself or the world, but as fictions: no "impression of reality" will adhere to them. The subject will appear, even to itself, to be no more than an *hypothesis of being*. Belief in the reality of representations will be suspended, projected beyond the representations themselves. And the "impression of reality" will henceforth consist in the "mass of objections to constituted reason," Bachelard says here; and elsewhere: in the conviction that "what is real but hidden has more content than what is given and obvious."[23]

The suspicion of dissimulation offers the subject a kind of reprieve from the dictates of law, the social superego. These dictates are perceived as hypotheses that must be tested rather than imperatives that must be automatically and unconditionally obeyed. The subject is not only judged by and subjected to social laws; it also judges them by subjecting them to intellectual scrutiny. Self-surveillance, then, conduces to self-correction; one thought or representation always advances another as the former's judge.

The chapter ends up celebrating a kind of euphoria of free thought. As a result of its orthopsychic relation to itself, i.e. before an image which it *doubts*, the scientific subject is jubilant. Not because its image, its world, its thought reflects its own perfection, but because the subject is thus allowed to imagine that they are all *perfectable*. It is this sense of the perfectibility of things that liberates thought from the totally determining constraints of the social order. Thought is conceived to police, and not merely to be policed by the social/scientific order, and the paranoia of the "Cassandra complex" (Bachelard's designation for the childish belief that everything is already known in advance, by one's parents, say) is thereby dispelled.

Curiously, the charge of guilt that is lodged, we were told, by the structure of surveillance, has been dropped somewhere along the way. It is now claimed, on the contrary, that surveillance enables thought to be "morally sincere." As it turns out, then, it is the very *experience* of moral conscience, the very feeling of guilt, that absolves thought of the *charge* of guilt. How has this absolution been secured? By the separation of the act of thinking from the thoughts that it thinks. So that though the thoughts may be guilty, the act of thinking remains innocent. And the subject remains whole, its intentions clear. This is the only way we can understand the apparent contradictions of this chapter. Throughout his work Bachelard maintains that "duplicity is maladroit in its address" – i.e. that they err who assume they cannot be duped, that no one is spared from deception. As a result, no thought can ever be perfectly penetrable. Yet, in this chapter he simultaneously maintains that the subject can and must penetrate its own act of thinking.

This scenario of surveillance – of the "joy of surveillance" – is consciously delineated in relation to Freud's notion of moral conscience. But Bachelard opposes his notion to the "pessimism" of that of Freud, who, of course, sees moral conscience as cruel and punishing. In Bachelard, surveillance, in seeming to offer the subject a pardon, is construed as primarily a positive or benign force. Bachelard, then, too, like Foucault and film theory, recalls and yet disavows the psychoanalytic model of moral conscience – however differently. Bachelard's orthopsychism, which is informed in the end by a psychologistic argument, cannot really be accepted by film theory as an alternative to panopticonism. Although Bachelard argues that a certain invisibility shelters the subject from what we might call "the gaze" of the institutional apparatus, the subject is nevertheless characterized by an exact legibility on another level. The Bachelardian subject may not locate *in its image* a full and upright being that it jubilantly (but wrongly) takes itself to be, but this subject does locate, *in the process of scrutinizing* this image, the joyous prospect of righting itself. Film theory's correct subject is here replaced by a self-correcting one.

Yet this detour through orthopsychism has not led only to a dead end. What we have forcibly been led to consider is the question of deception, of the suspicion of deception that must *necessarily* be raised if we are to understand the cinematic apparatus as a *signifying* apparatus, which places the subject in an external relationship to itself. Once the permanent possibility of deception is admitted (rather than disregarded, as it is by the theory of the panoptic apparatus), the concept of the gaze undergoes a radical change. For, where in the panoptic apparatus the gaze marks the subject's *visibility*, in Lacan's theory it marks the subject's *culpability*. The gaze stands watch over the *inculpation* – the faulting and splitting – of the subject by the apparatus.

The Mirror as Screen

Film theory introduced the subject into its study, and thereby incorporated Lacanian psychoanalysis, primarily by means of "The Mirror Stage as Formative of the Function of the 'I.' " It is to this essay that theorists made reference as they formulated their arguments about the subject's narcissistic relation to the film and about that relationship's dependence on "the gaze." While it is true that the mirror phase essay does describe the child's narcissistic relation to its mirror image, it is *not* in this essay but in Seminar XI that Lacan himself formulates *his* concept of the gaze. Here, particularly in those sessions collected under the heading "Of the Gaze as *Object Petit a*," Lacan *reformulates* his earlier mirror phase essay and paints a picture very different from the one painted by film theory.

Lacan tells his tale of the relation of the subject to its world in the form of a humorously recondite story about a sardine can. The story is told as a kind of mock Hegelian epic, a send-up of the broadly expansive Hegelian epic form by a deliberately "little story" that takes place in a "small boat" in a "small port" and includes a single named character, Petit-Jean. The entire overt plot consists in the sighting of a "small can." A truly short story of the object small a; the proof and sole guarantee of that alterity of the Other which Hegel's sweeping tale, in overlooking, denies.

The story sets Hegelian themes adrift and awash in a sea of bathos. A young (Hegelian) intellectual, identifying himself with the slaving class, embarks on a journey that he expects will pit him in struggle against the raw forces of a pitiless nature. But, alas, the day turns out to be undramatically sunny and fine, and the anticipated event, the meeting and match with the Master, never comes about. It is narratively replaced by what we can accurately describe as a "non-event," the spotting of the shiny, mirror-like sardine can – and an attack of anxiety. In the end, however, bathos gives way to tragedy, as we realize that in this little slice-of-life drama there is no sublation of consumption, no transcendence, only the slow dying away, through consumption, of the individual members of the slaving class. The mocking is not merely gentle, but carries in its wake this abrupt statement of consequence; something quite serious is at stake here. If we are to rewrite the tragic ending of this political tale, something will have to be retheorized.

What is it? Plainly, ultimately, it is "I" – the I that takes shape in this revised version of the mirror stage. As if to underline the fact that it is the I, and the narcissistic relation through which it is constructed, that is the point of the discussion, Lacan tells a personal story. It is he, in fact, who is the first-person of the narrative; this portrait of the analyst as a young man is his own. The cameo role in Seminar XI prepares us, then, for the starring role Lacan plays as the narcissistic "televanalyst" in *Television*. "What is at stake in both cases," Lacan says in *Television* about his performance both there and in his seminars, in general, "is a gaze: a gaze to which, in neither case, do I address myself, but in the name of which I speak."[24] What is he saying here about the relation between the I and the gaze?

The gaze is that which "determines" the I in the visible; it is "the instrument through which...[the] I [is] *photo-graphed*."[25] This might be taken to confirm the coincidence of the Foucauldian and Lacanian positions, to indicate that, in both, the gaze determines the complete *visibility* of the I, the mapping of the I on a perceptual grid. Hence the disciplinary monitoring of the subject. But this coincidence can only be produced by a precipitous, "snapshot" reading of Lacan, one that fails to notice the hyphen that splits the term *photo-graph* into *photo* – "light" – and *graph* – among other things, a fragment of the Lacanian phrase "graph of desire" – as it splits the subject that it describes.

Photo. One thing is certain: light does not enter these seminars in a straight line, through the laws of optics. Because, as he says, the geometric laws of the propagation of light map space only, and *not* vision, Lacan does not theorize the visual field in terms of these laws. Thus, the legitimate construction can*not* figure for him – as it *does* for film theory – the relation of the spectator to the screen. And these seminars cannot be used, as they are used by film theory, to support the argument that the cinematic apparatus, in direct line with the camera obscura, by recreating the space and ideology of Renaissance perspective, produces a centered and transcendent subject.[26]

This argument is critiqued in the seminars on the gaze as Lacan makes clear why the speaking subject *cannot* ever be totally trapped in the imaginary. Lacan claims, rather, that "I am not simply that punctiform being located at the geometral point from which the perspective is grasped."[27] Now, film theory, of course, has always claimed that the cinematic apparatus functions *ideologically* to produce a subject that *misrecognizes* itself as source and center of the represented world. But although this claim might seem to imply agreement with Lacan, to suggest, too, that the subject is *not* the punctiform being that Renaissance perspective would have us believe it is, film theory's notion of misrecognition turns out to be different from Lacan's in important ways. Despite the fact that the term *misrecognition* implies an error on the subject's part, a failure properly to recognize its true relation to the visible world, the process by which the subject is installed in its position of misrecognition operates without the hint of failure. The subject unerringly assumes the position perspective bids it to take. Erased from the process of construction, the negative force of error emerges later as a charge directed at the subject. But from where does it come? Film theory has only described the construction of this position of misrecognition. Though it implies that there is another *actual*, non-punctiform position, film theory has never been able to describe the *construction* of this position.

In Lacan's description, misrecognition retains its negative force in the process of construction. As a result the process is no longer conceived as a purely positive one, but rather one with an internal dialectic. Lacan does not take the single triangle that geometrical perspective draws as an accurate description of its own operation. Instead he *re*diagrams this operation by means of *two interpenetrating triangles*. Thus he represents both the way the science of optics figures the emission of light *and* the way its straight lines become refracted, diffused (the way they acquire the "ambiguity of a jewel") once we take into account the way the signifier itself interferes in this figuring. The second triangle cuts through the first, marking the elision or negation that is part of the process of construction. The second triangle diagrams the subject's mistaken belief that there is something behind the space set out by the first. It is this mistaken belief (this misrecognition) that causes the subject to *disbelieve* even those representations shaped according to the scientific laws of optics. The Lacanian subject, who doubts the accuracy of even its most "scientific" representations, is submitted to a *superegoic* law that is radically different from the optical laws to which the film theoretical subject is submitted.

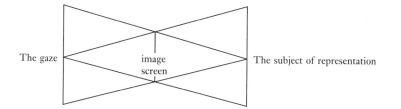

The gaze / image screen / The subject of representation

Graph. Semiotics, not optics, is the science that clarifies for us the structure of the visual domain. Because it alone is capable of lending things sense, the signifier alone makes vision possible. There is and can be no brute vision, no vision totally devoid of sense. Painting, drawing, all forms of picture-making, then, are fundamentally graphic arts. And because signifiers are material, that is, because they are opaque rather than translucent, because they refer to other signifiers rather than directly to a signified, the field of vision is neither clear nor easily traversable. It is instead ambiguous and treacherous, full of traps. Lacan's Seminar XI refers constantly, but ambiguously, to these traps. When Lacan says that the subject is trapped in the imaginary, he means that the subject can imagine nothing outside it; the imaginary cannot itself provide the means that would allow the subject to transcend it. When he says, on the other hand, that a painting, or any other representation, is a "trap for the gaze," he means that the representation *attracts* the gaze, induces us to imagine a gaze outside – and observing – the field of representation. It is this second sense of trapping, whereby representation appears to generate its own beyond (to generate, we might say, recalling Lacan's diagram, the *second* triangle, which the science of optics neglects to consider) that prevents the subject from ever being trapped in the imaginary. Where the film theoretical position has tended to trap the subject in representation (an idealist failing), to conceive of language as constructing the prison walls of the subject's being, Lacan argues that the subject sees these walls as trompe l'oeil and is thus constructed by something beyond them.

For, beyond everything that is displayed to the subject, the question is asked: what is being concealed from me? What in this graphic space does not show, does not stop *not* writing itself? This point at which something appears to be *in*visible, this point at which something appears to be missing from representation, some meaning left unrevealed, is the point of the Lacanian gaze. It marks the *absence* of a signified; it is an *unoccupiable* point, the point at which the subject disappears. The image, the visual field, then takes on a terrifying alterity that prohibits the subject from seeing itself in the representation. That "belong to me aspect" is suddenly drained from representation, as the mirror assumes the function of a screen.

Lacan is certainly *not* offering an agnostic description of the way the real object is cut off from the subject's view by language, of the way the real object escapes capture in the network of signifiers. His is not the idealist position of either Plato or Kant, who split the object between its real being and its semblance. Lacan argues, rather, that beyond the signifying network, beyond the visual field, there is, in fact, nothing at all.[28] The veil of representation actually conceals nothing. Yet the fact that representation *seems* to hide, to put a screen of aborescent signifiers in front of something hidden beneath, is not treated by Lacan as a simple error which the subject can undo; nor is this deceptiveness of language treated as something which undoes the subject, deconstructs its identity by menacing its boundaries. Rather, language's opacity is taken as the very *cause* of the subject's being, its desire. The fact that it is materially impossible to say the whole truth – that truth always backs away from language, that words always fall short of their goal – *founds* the subject. Contrary to the idealist position that makes *form* the cause of being, Lacan locates the cause of being in the *informe*: the unformed (that which has no signified, no significant shape in the visual field); the inquiry (the question posed to representation's presumed reticence). The subject is the effect of the impossibility of seeing what is lacking in the representation, what the subject, therefore, wants to see. Desire, in other words, the desire of representation, institutes the subject in the visible field.

It should be clear by now how different this description is from that offered by film theory. In film theory the subject identifies with the gaze as the signified of the image and comes into existence as the realization of a possibility. In Lacan, the subject identifies with the gaze as the signifier of the lack that causes the image to languish. The subject comes into existence, then, through a desire which is still considered to be the *effect* of the law, but not its *realization*. Desire cannot be a realization because it fulfills no possibility and has no content; it is, rather, occasioned by impossibility, the impossibility of the subject's ever coincideing with the real being from which representation cuts it off.

Narcissism, too, takes on a different meaning in Lacan, one more in accord with Freud's own. Since something always appears to be missing from any representation, narcissism *cannot* consist in finding satisfaction in one's own visual image. It must, rather, consist in the belief that one's own being exceeds the imperfections of its image. Narcissism, then, seeks the self beyond the self-image, with which the subject constantly finds fault and in which it constantly fails to recognize itself. What one loves in one's image is something *more* than the image ("in you more than you").[29] Thus is narcissism the source of the malevolence with which the subject regards its image, the aggressivity it unleashes on all its own representations.[30] And thus does the subject come into being as a transgression of, rather than in conformity to, the law. It is not the law, but the fault in the law – the desire that the law cannot ultimately conceal – that is assumed by the subject as its own. The subject, in taking up the burden of the law's guilt, goes beyond the law.

Much of this definition of narcissism I take to be compacted in Lacan's otherwise totally enigmatic sentences: "The effect of mimicry is camouflage in the strictly technical sense. It is not a question of harmonizing with the back ground, but against a mottled background, of becoming mottled – exactly like the technique of camouflage practiced in human warfare."[31] The effect of representation ("mimicry," in an older, idealist vocabulary) is not a subject who will harmonize with, or adapt to, its environment (the subject's narcissistic relation to the representation that constructs it does not place it in happy accord with the reality that the apparatus constructs for it). The effect of representation is, instead, the suspicion that some reality is being camouflaged, that we are being deceived as to the exact nature of some thing-in-itself that lies behind representation. In response to such a representation, against such a background of deception, the subject's own being breaks up between its unconscious being and its conscious semblance. At war both with its world and with itself, the subject becomes guilty of the very deceit it suspects. This can hardly, however, be called mimicry, in the old sense, since nothing is being mimed.

In sum, the conflictual nature of Lacan's culpable subject sets it worlds apart from the stable subject of film theory. But neither does the Lacanian subject resemble that of Bachelard. For while, in Bachelard, orthopsychism – in providing an opportunity for the correction of thought's imperfections – allows the subject to wander from its moorings, constantly to drift from one position to another, in Lacan "orthopsychism" – one wishes to retain the term in order to indicate the subject's fundamental dependence on the faults it finds in representation and in itself – grounds the subject. The desire that it precipitates *transfixes* the subject, albeit in a conflictual place, so that all the subject's visions and revisions, all its fantasies, merely circumnavigate the absence that anchors the subject and impedes its progress.[32] It is this desire that must be reconstructed if the subject is to be changed.

Notes

This paper was presented in Paris at a conference on "The Theory of Cinema and the Crisis in Theory" organized by Michèle Lagny, Marie-Claire Ropars, and Pierre Sorlin and held in June 1988. A translation of the paper, along with other papers from the conference and responses to them, were published in *Hors Cadre*, no. 7 (Winter 1988–9).

1   In *The Four Fundamental Concepts of Psycho-Analysis* (London, Hogarth Press, 1977, p. 274), Lacan speaks of the "phantasies" of the "mass media," as he very quickly suggests a critique of the familiar notion of "the society of the spectacle." This notion is replaced in Lacan by what might be called "the society of (formed from) the nonspecularizable."

2   *Liddell and Scott's Greek–English Lexicon*, 1906; all translations of ancient Greek terms are from this source.

3   Jacques Lacan, *Television*, trans. Denis Hollier, Rosalind Krauss, and Annette Michelson, *October*, no. 40 (Spring 1987), p. 7.

4   Mary Ann Doane points out that it is our very fascination with the model of the screen as mirror that has made it resistant to the kinds of theoretical objections which she herself makes. See Mary Ann Doane, "Misrecognition and Identity," *Ciné-Tracts*, no. 11 (Fall 1980), p. 28.

5   Mary Ann Doane, Patricia Mellencamp, and Linda Williams, eds., *Re-vision*, Los Angeles, American Film Institute, 1984, p. 14. The introduction to this very useful collection of essays also attempts to detail some of the historical shifts in feminist theories of representation; I am only attempting to argue the need for one more shift, this time away from the panoptic model of cinema.

6   See, especially, Teresa de Lauretis, *Technologies of Gender*, Bloomington, Indiana University Press, 1987.

7   In "What Is a Question," F. S. Cohen makes this important distinction clearly: "Indetermination or doubt is not, as is often maintained, a wavering between different certainties, but the grasping of an incomplete form" (*The Monist*, no. 38 [1929], p. 354, fn. 4).

8   Michel Foucault, in Colin Gordon, ed., *Power/Knowledge*, New York, Pantheon, p. 186. The interview with Lucette Finas in which this statement occurs was also published in Meaghan Morris and Paul Patton, eds., *Michel Foucault: Power, Truth, Strategy*, Sydney, Feral Publications, 1979. The statement is quoted and emphasized in Mark Cousins and Athar Hussain's excellent book, *Michel Foucault*, New York, St. Martin's Press, 1984, p. 244.

9   Although some might claim that it was the introduction of the linguistic model into film studies that initiated the break, it can be more accurately argued that the break was precipitated by a shift in the linguistic model itself – from an exclusive emphasis on the relation between signifiers to an emphasis on the relation between signifiers and the subject, their signifying effect. That is, it was not until the *rhetorical* aspect of language was made visible – *by means of the concept of the apparatus* – that the field of film studies was definitively reformed. I am arguing, however, that, once this shift was made, some of the lessons introduced by semiology were, unfortunately, forgotten.

To define a *break* (rather than a continuity) between what is often referred to as "two stages," or the first and second semiology, is analogous to defining a break between Freud's first and second concepts of transference. It was only with the second, the privileging of the analyst/analysand relationship, that psychoanalysis (properly speaking) was begun. Biography rather than theory is the source of the demand for the continuity of these concepts.

10 The best discussion of the relationship between Bachelard and Althusser can be found in Etienne Balibar, "From Bachelard to Althusser: The Concept of 'Epistemological Break,'" *Economy and Society*, vol. 5, no. 4 (November 1976), pp. 385–411.

11 This notion of the scientist discontinuous with him- or herself can be given a precise image, the alchemical image of the Melusines: creatures composed partially of inferior, fossil-like forms that reach back into the distant past (the imaginary) and partially of superior, energetic (scientific) activity. In *The Poetics of Space* (Boston, Beacon, 1969, p. 109), Bachelard, whose notion of the unconscious is more Jungian than Freudian, refers to this image from Jung's *Psychology and Alchemy*.

12 The one reservation Metz has to the otherwise operative analogy between mirror and screen is that at the cinema, "the spectator is absent from the screen: contrary to the child in the mirror" (Christian Metz, *The Imaginary Signifier*, Bloomington, Indiana University Press, 1982, p. 48). Jacqueline Rose clarified the error implied in this reservation by pointing out that "the phenomenon of transitivism demonstrates that the subject's mirror identification can be with another child," that one always locates *one's own image in another* and thus the imaginary identification does not depend on a literal mirror ("The Imaginary," in *Sexuality in the Field of Vision*, London, Verso, 1986, p. 196). What is most often forgotten, however, is the corollary of this fact: one always locates *the other in one's own image*. The effect of *this* fact on the constitution of the subject is Lacan's fundamental concern.

13 Lacan, *The Four Fundamental Concepts*, p. 81.

14 It was Jean-Louis Baudry who first formulated this definition of the impression of reality. See his second apparatus essay, "The Apparatus," in *Camera Obscura*, no. 1 (Fall 1976), especially pp. 118–19.

15 Metz's two-stage scenario is critiqued by Geoffrey Nowell-Smith in "A Note on History/Discourse," in *Edinburgh '76*, pp. 26–32; and by Mary Ann Doane in "Misrecognition and Identity."

16 I have elsewhere referred to the gaze as "metempsychotic": although it is a concept abhorrent to feminist reason, the target of constant theoretical sallies, the gaze continues to reemerge, to be reincorporated, as an assumption of one film analysis after another. The argument I am making is that it is because we have not properly determined what the gaze is, whence it has emerged, that we have been unable to

eliminate it. It is generally argued that the gaze is dependent on psychoanalytic structures of voyeurism and fetishism, presumed to be male. I am claiming instead that the gaze arises out of *linguistic* assumptions and that these assumptions, in turn, shape (and appear to be naturalized by) the psychoanalytic concepts.

17 Mikkel Borsch-Jacobsen's extremely interesting book, *The Freudian Subject* (Stanford, Stanford University Press, 1988), grapples with this *necessary* distinction in its final section – with results very different from Lacan's.

18 Paul Hirst, "Althusser's Theory of Ideology," *Economy and Society*, vol. 5, no. 4 (November 1976), pp. 385–411.

19 Mikkel Borsch-Jacobsen, in "The Law of Psychoanalysis" (*Diacritics* [Summer 1985], pp. 26–36), discusses Freud's argument with Kant in *Totem and Taboo*. This article relies, it appears, on Lacan's work in *L'Éthique de la psychanalyse* (Paris, Seuil, 1986) and the unpublished seminar on anxiety; see especially the session of December 12, 1962, where Lacan defines obsession as that which *covers over the desire in the Other with the Other's demand*. This remark relates obsessional neurosis to a certain (Kantian) concept of moral consciousness.

20 Sigmund Freud, *The Standard Edition of the Complete Psychological Works of Sigmund Freud*, trans. James and Alix Strachey, London, Hogarth Press and the Institute of Psycho-Analysis, 1953–74, vol. 13, pp. 69–70.

21 In order to dissociate his concept of science from that of idealism, conventionalism, and formalism, Bachelard formulated the concept of "applied rationalism": a scientific concept must integrate within itself the conditions of its realization. (It is on the basis of this injunction that Heisenberg could dismiss as illegitimate any talk of an electron's location that could not also propose an experimental method of locating it.) And in order to dissociate his concept of science from that of the positivists, empiricists, and realists, Bachelard formulated the concept of "technical materialism": the instruments and the protocols of scientific experiments must be theoretically formulated. The system of checks and balances according to which these two imperatives operate is what Bachelard normally means by *orthopsychism*. He extends the notion in *Le Rationalisme appliqué*, however, to include the formation of the scientific subject.

22 Gaston Bachelard, *Le Rationalism appliqué*, Paris, Presses Universitaires de France, 1949, pp. 65–81.

23 Gaston Bachelard, *The New Scientific Spirit*, Boston, Beacon Press, 1984, p. 32.

24 Lacan, *Television*, p. 7.

25 Lacan, *The Four Fundamental Concepts*, p. 106.

26 See, especially, Jean-Louis Baudry, "Ideological Effects of the Basic Cinematographic Apparatus" (first published in *Cinéthique*, nos. 7–8 [1970] and, in English, in *Film Quarterly*, no. 28 [Winter 1974–5]), and Jean-Louis Comolli, "Technique and Ideology: Camera, Perspective, Depth of Field" (first published in *Cahiers du cinéma*, nos. 229, 230, 231, and 233 [1970–1] and, in English, by the British Film Institute). This historical continuity has been taken for granted by film theory generally. For a history of the *non*continuity between Renaissance techniques of observation and our own, see Jonathan Crary, "Techniques of the Observer," *October*, no. 45 (Summer 1987). In this essay, Crary differentiates the camera obscura from the physiological models of vision that succeeded it. Lacan, in his seminars on the gaze, refers to both these models as they are represented by the science of optics and the philosophy of

phenomenology. He exhibits them as two "ways of being wrong about this function of the subject in the domain of the spectacle."

27 Lacan, *The Four Fundamental Concepts*, p. 96.

28 The questions Moustapha Safouan poses to Lacan during Seminar XI (*The Four Fundamental Concepts*, p. 103) force him to be quite clear on this point: "Beyond appearance there is nothing in itself, there is the gaze."

29 This is the title given to the last session of the seminar published as *The Four Fundamental Concepts*. Although the "you" of the title refers to the analyst, it can refer just as easily to the ideal image in the mirror.

30 Jacqueline Rose's "Paranoia and the Film System" (*Screen*, vol. 17, no. 4 [Winter 1976–7]) is a forceful critique (directed specifically at Raymond Bellour's analyses of Hitchcock, but also at a range of film theoretical assumptions) of that notion of the cinema that sees it as a successful resolution of conflict and a refusal of difference. Rose reminds us that cinema, as "technique of the imaginary" (Metz), necessarily unleashes a conflict, an aggressivity, that is irresolvable. While I am, for the most part, in agreement with her important argument, I am claiming here that Rose is wrong to make this aggressivity dependent on the shot/counter-shot structure of the film (the reversibility of the look), or to define aggressivity as the result of the imaginary relation. The gaze is threatening not because it presents the reverse (the mirror) image of the subject, but because it does not. The gaze deprives the subject of the possibility of ever becoming a fully observable being. Lacan himself says that aggressivity is not a matter of transitive retaliation: "The phenomenon of aggressivity isn't to be explained on the level of imaginary identification" (in *The Ego in Freud's Theory and in the Technique of Psychoanalysis*, New York and London, Norton, 1978, p. 22).

31 Lacan, *The Four Fundamental Concepts*, p. 99.

32 In "Another Lacan" (*Lacan Study Notes*, vol. 1, no. 3), Jacques-Alain Miller is concerned to underline the clinical dimension of Lacan's work, particularly his concept of "the pass." The difference between the "deconstructionist" and the Lacanian notion of fantasy is, thus, also made clear.

25
Feminism, Film Theory, and the Bachelor Machines

Constance Penley

"Bachelor machine" is the term Marcel Duchamp used to designate the lower part of his *Large Glass: The Bride Stripped Bare by Her Bachelors, Even*, a term aptly borrowed by Michel Carrouges to name a phenomenon that he describes in *Machines célibataires*.[1] From about 1850 to 1925 numerous artists, writers, and scientists imaginatively or in reality constructed anthropomorphized machines to represent the relation of the body to the social, the relation of the sexes to each other, the structure of the psyche, or the workings of history. His spectacular inventory of literary and artistic bachelor machines lists Mary Shelley's *Franken-stein*, Edgar Allan Poe's *The Pit and the Pendulum*, Villiers de l'Isle Adam's *L'Eve future*, almost everything of Jules Verne or Alfred Jarry, Raymond Roussel's *Impressions of Africa*, Franz Kafka's *The Penal Colony*, Fritz Lang and Thea von Harbou's *Metropolis*, and the machine–sculptures of Jean Tinguely. And as for more scientific bachelor machines, we find Freud exclaiming to Fliess of his work on the *Project for a Scientific Psychology*, "Everything fell into place, the cogs meshed, the thing really seemed to be a machine which would run of itself."[2] This "inexhaustible inventiveness and dream-like renewal of mechanical models"[3] is, however, circumscribed in a particular way. As Michel de Certeau says of the bachelor machine, "It does not tend to write the woman. . . . The machine's chief distinction is its being male."[4]

The bachelor machine is typically a closed, self-sufficient system. Its common themes include frictionless, sometimes perpetual motion, an ideal time and the magical possibility of its reversal (the time machine is an exemplary bachelor machine), electrification, voyeurism and masturbatory eroticism, the dream of the mechanical reproduction of art, and artificial birth or reanimation. But no matter how complicated the machine becomes, the control over the sum of its parts rests with a knowing producer who therefore submits to a fantasy of closure, perfect-ibility, and mastery.

It is only fitting that these characteristics should remind us of another apparatus, one that can offer impeccable credentials with respect to the bachelor machine's strict requirements for perpetual motion, the reversibility of time, mechanicalness, electrification, animation, and voyeurism: the cinema. Indeed, it is around the metaphor of the cinema as an *apparatus* that much of the most energetic contemporary thinking about film has taken place. We have only to recall the conspicuous influence of Jean-Louis Baudry's two articles about the cinematographic apparatus and Christian Metz's "The Imaginary Signifier"[5] to recognize how forcefully the idea of cinema as a technological, institutional, and psychical "machine" has shaped our current ways of understanding film. Just as influential, however, has been the theory of classical film narrative as itself a machine, and an avowedly bachelor one. On the latter point, Raymond Bellour, for example, describes the narrative mechanism of Hollywood film ("a machine of great homogeneity, due to its mode of production which is both mechanical and industrial")[6] in terms of a "massive, imaginary reduction of sexual difference to a narcissistic doubling of the masculine subject."[7] And as for the infinitely sustaining and self-sufficient qualities of the machine model, Stephen Heath argues that the classical narrative system is programmed to carry out "a perpetual retotalization of the imaginary."[8]

What are we to make, then, of Michel de Certeau's assertion that the bachelor machine "does not ... write the woman"? Or, similarly, Freud's claim that "it is highly probable that all complicated machinery and apparatus occurring in dreams stand for the genitals – and as a rule the male ones"?[9] For feminists writing about film the question of the fitness of the apparatus metaphor has been a secondary one, that is, whether or not it provides an adequate descriptive model of the way classical film functions on the basis of and for masculine fantasy (most agree that this is largely the case). They have found it more productive to ask whether this description, with its own extreme bacheloresque emphasis on homogeneity and closure, does not itself subscribe to a theoretical systematicity, one that would close off those same questions of sexual difference that it claims are denied or disavowed in the narrative system of classical film. Thus in recent feminist writing about film it is clear that this critique of the theories of the apparatus parallels the feminist challenge to two other theoretical practices which also stand accused of keeping bachelor quarters: Marxism (its awkward dealings with the "woman question") and psychoanalysis (its negative construction of "feminine sexuality").[10]

In examining the model or metaphor of the cinematic apparatus, the most useful and successful feminist approaches have been those that take film theory on its own terms – semiology, psychoanalysis, textual analysis – while questioning the capacity of each to elide the difficulties specific to feminine sexuality, if not gendered subjectivity *tout court*. Another approach to the same apparatus question in its relation to ideas like the Imaginary, identification, and repetition, would be to reject, out of hand, all the work produced by film theory on the grounds of its manifest exclusion of the woman; and then strike out along the well-worn dissident paths of a reductive biologism, sociologism, or mysticism of the feminine, resurrecting once again the expressiveness of the woman's body or "women's experience," and summoning up such pale specters as the "Electra complex," archaic pulsionality, womb envy, and the feminine principle. All of these "alternatives" represent merely another version of the easily accepted (because narcissistically desired) or the already known (the comfort of repeating the same).

The metaphor of cinema as an apparatus arose from the need to account for several aspects of film, ranging from the uniquely powerful impression of reality provided by cinema and the way the subject is positioned as a spectator, to the desire intrinsic to cinema-going itself. In this metaphor the cinematic apparatus is not merely the technological base (although the popular perception of cinema's "scientific" and technological origins are fantasmatically crucial to its reality-effect), but the entire institution of cinema, its means of promoting and distributing itself and its administration of the social spaces in which films are viewed. Broadly speaking, the cinematic apparatus achieves its specific effects (the impression of reality, the creation of a fantasmatically unified spectator–subject, the production of the desire to return to the cinema) because of its success in re-enacting or mimicking the scene of the unconscious – the psychical apparatus – and duplicating its mechanisms by way of illusion. For both Metz and Baudry, the apparatus model is effective because, like Freud's *psychischer Apparat* (which, in *The Interpretation of Dreams*, he defines in comparison to an optical apparatus), it allows us to describe the coexistence of the different systems or agencies that make up the cinematic apparatus, allot them their various functions, and even assign them a temporal order. In the earliest Freudian model, the function of the psychical apparatus was to keep the internal energy of the organism at the lowest possible level in accord with the "constancy principle." The cinematic apparatus, like the psychical system, is therefore a homeostatic model, in which all circulating energy is regulated, balanced, controlled. (Stephen Heath similarly characterizes classical film narrative as functioning according to "the capture and regulation of energy.")[11]

It is Baudry's work which most completely identifies the psychical apparatus and its topography with that of the cinematic apparatus. For Baudry, the cinema is not an extension or prosthesis of the psyche (as it is for Metz) but a faultless technological simulacrum of the systems Ucs and Pcs-Cs and their interrelations. In a grand teleological gesture, Baudry claims that all the other art forms (drawing, painting, photography, and so on) are simply rehearsals of a primordially unconscious effort to recreate the scene of the unconscious, while cinema is its most successful achievement. Baudry agrees with Metz that the success of the apparatus in its production of cinematic pleasure is due to the fact that it was, after all, "built" in conformity to strictly wish-fulfilling requirements. Thus, in Baudry's Freudian terms, the apparatus induces (as a result of the immobility of the spectator, the darkness of the theater, and the projection of the images from a place behind the spectator's head) a total regression to an earlier developmental stage in which the subject hallucinates satisfaction; or, in Metz's more Lacanian scheme, the apparatus mimes the mirror stage and therefore structures for the spectator a completely imaginary relation to the screen in which the subject is given the seamless illusion of unity and totality, as well as an identificatory feeling of mastery over the visual field.

The initial problems posed by the theories of the cinematic apparatus for a feminist consideration of film are both theoretical and practical. Jean-Louis Baudry's psyche–machine–cinema model is not only ahistorical but also strongly teleological. The shackled prisoners fascinated by the shadows on the wall of Plato's cave are the first "cinema" spectators; the only historical changes in the apparatus since then have been little more than technological modifications. If the apparatus stages an eternal, universal, and primordial wish to create a simulacrum of the psyche, then Baudry's argument is blind to the economic, social, or political determinations of cinema as well as its basic difference from other art forms (painting and photography are merely less successful versions of the cinema–machine; they are all "metonymies ... [of] the same metaphor").[12] A further problem is that Baudry's teleological argument asserts that cinema aims at pleasure alone, and that it unfailingly achieves it, an assertion, moreover, that is merely stated and not supported. *Why* does the subject necessarily seek only pleasure and its fulfillment? Surely psychoanalytic theory has offered us a more complex account of the vicissitudes of desire (the repetition compulsion and the death drive), let alone posited the desire for an unsatisfied desire (hysteria as the desire not to have one's desire satisfied). The question of pleasure has been a crucially troubling one for feminist film theory and filmmaking, and the theory of the apparatus appears to answer the question before it is even raised.

A final difficulty is that neither Metz nor Baudry (in his second article) mentions specific films. Are we then to conclude that every kind of film elicits the *same* labor in the apparatus and the same ruthlessly deterministic effects? Although it would seem important to describe the workings of the apparatus itself prior to specific inflections of it, doesn't this lead to an overwhelmingly negative and deterministic idea of the possibilities of radical experimentation in film? For if the effects of the apparatus are total, and always totally successful (for example, its creation of a unified, transcendental subject and of a completely imaginary relation of the spectator to the screen), then it begins to look like mere wish-fulfillment to imagine the kind of film that would subvert its power. There must be a way of recognizing the pervasive power of the apparatus without sacrificing this sense of acceptance on the altar of fatalism.

Beyond these general complaints about the apparatus as a model for cinema, feminists have also questioned its association with several interconnected ideas or psychic functions: the Imaginary and the mirror stage, identification, repetition, and homeostatic regulation. I want now to examine some of those specific criticisms of the apparatus theories and then point to possible ways of evicting the cinematic apparatus from its well-appointed bachelor residence.

> The imaginary, of which the cinema may well be the most privileged and efficient machine, is precisely a *machine*, an apparatus in which what is at stake is a repression or refusal of the problem or difficulty of sexuality.[13] (Jacqueline Rose)

From the evidence of the above quotation, it is clear that at least one feminist has found the machine or apparatus metaphor polemically useful or illuminating. But what is also obvious in these few lines is an attention to what is *at stake* in this configuration of sexual difference as a problem for both film and feminist theory. The psychoanalytic concept of the imaginary was formally introduced into film theory by way of Christian Metz's "The Imaginary Signifier," a lengthy essay exhaustively devoted to a discussion of the "imaginariness" of the cinematic signifier and, by extension, of the cinematic apparatus. For Metz, cinema is the art form of the imaginary par excellence, and for two reasons. First, because of its manipulation of five material components or channels of communication (analogical image, graphic image, sound, speech, dialogue) film is more sensorially *present* than any other medium. At the same time, however, that which it depicts is extremely *absent*. In contrast to theater, for example, where the actors physically share the time and space of the audience (although not necessarily in the fiction of the play, of course) film actors typically do their work far in advance of the moment of viewing and are not physically present in the same space as the cinema audience (they are on the screen but that space is, for example, a sound stage at Warner Bros.). This combination of presence and absence is characteristic of the Imaginary, as exemplified in the mirror stage of Jacques Lacan. The infant, seeing itself in the mirror, has the sense of being "there" for the first time, existing as a separate and autonomous entity at exactly the moment when it is "not there" because what it in fact sees is an *image* of a separateness and independence that it has not yet achieved. For Metz, however, the mirror identification is not a primary but a secondary form of cinematic identification. Even more fundamental in its effects is the spectator's identification with his own act of vision as it is taken up and relayed by the camera. Primary identification, then, is with the camera, or rather with the spectator himself in his own act of perceiving. This primary identification is the basis for the formation of a transcendental subject, a spectator centered for absolute mastery over the visual domain. As for the spectator's belief in the reality of the cinematic images, Metz links this to the inherent lack or absence at the heart of the cinematic signifier. By a process of fetishistic disavowal, the spectator admits that what he is perceiving is not really there, but makes himself believe it to be there nonetheless (the fetishistic formula of "I know, but": "I know that she [the mother] does not really have a penis, but I believe it to be there all the same").

In two essays on the use of the concept of the imaginary in psychoanalysis and film theory,[14] Jacqueline Rose argues that Metz makes his claims about the excessive imaginariness of the cinematic signifier on the basis of an overly schematized and reductive notion of the imaginary. What Metz disregards is that the imaginary is never purely imaginary just as the visual is never merely perceptual. In Lacan's later work on vision, particularly in the four seminars included under the heading "The Look as *object petit a*,"[15] he stresses that the imaginary is always permeated by the desire of the Other, and that it is a triangular rather than a dual relation. This triangulation can be seen most vividly when the child in front of the mirror turns to the one who is holding it and appeals with its look for an affirmation of what it sees. This appeal places the imaginary relation in the register of demand and desire, thus preempting any theoretical use of the mirror stage as an absolute or exemplary instance of unity or completion. Similarly, Metz's conclusions about the spectator's primary identi-fication and the formation of his transcendental subjectivity need to be qualified by a more subtle and intricate reading of the psychoanalytic insights into vision and subjectivity. In Lacanian thought, for example, the subject of vision is also an object of representation. Since vision always takes place in the field of the Other's vision and desire, the important look is the one that comes from outside ("What fundamentally determines me in the visible is the look which is outside").[16] The subject can be "seized by the object of its look";[17] moreover, the subject cannot see what it wants to see because the look is never a pure look (purely perceptual) but conditioned by the look (the desire) of the Other. As a third and final consideration, the subject can never see from the place from which it is seen. All of this colludes against any idea of a subject identifying with itself as a pure act of perception or that act leading to a mastery or transcendence at the level of vision. On the contrary, it suggests that the seeing subject (the subject of the unconscious) is in an extremely vulnerable position, that, if anything, the subject is more seen than seeing. Metz, in claiming that the cinema spectator is imme-diately and successfully positioned as a transcendental subject within a fantasy of omniscient perception and knowledge, confuses the actual effects of the apparatus with its aim. The apparatus may "aim" to construct a transcendental subject but it must necessarily always fail, subverted by the presence of desire in vision. This is not to discount the power of the illusionistic effects of the apparatus; it is merely to call into question the idea of an always successfully achieved subject construction that would be a purely imaginary one.

The bacheloresque cast of Metz's formulation lies in its overemphasis on the Imaginary at the expense of the Symbolic. Here, the subject, that is, the subject of the unconscious, is sexless or non-gendered. As we have seen, however, the imaginary is not to be construed as a developmental "stage" that exists "before" symbolization or desire (the triangulation of the mirror situation through the demand made to the Other) or as a moment preceding the splitting of the subject, a moment which is inseparable from sexual division. But perhaps this theoretical elision of sexual difference can be seen even more strikingly in Metz's discussion of filmic fetishism where the spectator doubles up on his belief in the image to counter the perception that the image is not real or that the depicted object is not really present. As Rose points out, however, fetishism does not bear, finally, on the image or the object but rather on the structure of subjectivity. In the psychoanalytic scenario of fetishism the traumatic moment is the boy child's perception that the mother has no penis. However, the spectator's perception of the absence of the object and thus of the unreality of the image cannot be compared directly to this traumatic perception. First, the absent object of fetish-ism is not just any object but the maternal penis. Metz fails to account for the "context" of that look, a context in which the act of perception is irremediably bound up in a structure of sexual difference. His argument, moreover, conceives the moment of perception as a moment of realization or knowledge and its disavowal. It is questionable, however, whether that moment can have any meaning in itself; more probably the meaning comes only after the fact. For Freud, the meaning of that moment is delayed and only acquired after the subject has come to recognize the value of having a penis or not. Meaning, as Rose puts it, lies "elsewhere,"[18] and not in the immediacy of perception.

Another problem with Metz's account lies in its undue emphasis on the conscious nature of the spectator's belief in the moment of perceiving. For Metz, the spectator "doubles up"[19] his belief as a defense against the anxiety caused by recognizing the absence inherent to the cinematic signifier. The result amounts to an elision of any unconscious effect because it transforms that moment into a conscious "I know, but . . . " – "I know that it's not real, but I'll pretend while I'm here that it is."[20] Rose is quick to point to the feminist consequences of such a theoretical repression of the concept of the unconscious: disavowal (of the maternal penis) must be understood as an unconscious fantasy or else we are left with the theoretically unfeasible and politically unacceptable notion that the child has a real perception of a real feminine inferiority.[21]

Finally, then, the only notable consideration of "difference" in Metz's theory of the cinematic signifier is the difference of a given image from the real object. Disavowal turns upon the spectator's recognition that the image is really lacking (in relation to the real object which it is not) and his subsequent attempt to repress that knowledge; thus the only thing that could disturb the illusion of imaginary identity would be an image that is too unreal. "Any challenge to the imaginary remains within the terms of the imaginary itself."[22] The effects of the Symbolic (or the Real, for that matter), inasmuch as they inscribe *sexual* difference, are disregarded, and Metz's "imaginary signifier" begins to assume the familiar dimensions of a bachelor apparatus.

Rose's attempt to counter the bachelor tendencies of the apparatus looks to psychoanalysis as a source of more sophisticated readings than the theory of the apparatus has provided. By contrast, Joan Copjec ("The Anxiety of the Influencing Machine"),[23] in her comparison of Metz and Baudry's theories of the apparatus with the Tauskian machine constructed by schizophrenics to deny sexual difference, chooses to engage the Derridean critique as a way of raising questions of sexual difference. Copjec argues that the theory of the apparatus constructs an anthropomorphized machine that is a projection of a libidinalized body, a phallic machine producing only male spectators. She even suggests that the theory of the apparatus is paranoid, and claims that it arose as "*the delusional defense against the alienation that the elaboration of cinema as a language opened in theory.*"[24] In other words, the theory of the apparatus sprang up in the wake of Metz's *Langage et cinéma* as a way of denying that book's most important insights for cinema, particularly its insistence on the idea that subjectivity is a linguistic construction or effect.

In "Freud and the Scene of Writing," Derrida has, in fact, written a critique of those machine metaphors of the psychical system, a critique that closely parallels our concern here with the bacheloresque tendencies of the cinematic apparatus. His essay attempts to locate and follow in Freud's text (from the *Project for a Scientific Psychology* [1985] to the "Note Upon the Mystic Writing Pad" [1925]) the path of a metaphoric investment in writing or the scriptural "which will eventually invade the entirety of the psyche" (p. 75). Derrida's interest lies in the progress of Freud's effort to find a model that could represent both the psychical system and its contents, beginning with the "neurological fable" of the *Project*, proceeding through the optical machines of the *Traumdeutung*, and concluding with the writing machine modeled on the Mystic Writing Pad. Derrida, however, is not so much concerned with the adequacy of the model (its mimetic accuracy) but rather with the question of representation itself:

> Psychical content will be *represented* by a text whose essence is irreducibly graphic. The structure of the psychical apparatus will be *represented* by a writing machine. What questions will those representations impose on us? We shall have to ask not if a writing apparatus – for example the one described in the "Note Upon the Mystic Writing Pad" – is a *good* metaphor for representing the work of the psyche; but rather what apparatus we must create in order to represent psychical writing, and what the imitation, projected and liberated in a machine, of something like psychical writing might mean. (Ibid.: 76)

What questions, indeed, will those representations impose on us?

In *The Interpretation of Dreams* Freud proposed that we picture the instrument that carries out our mental functions as resembling a compound microscope, a telescope, or a photographic apparatus. With his optical machine metaphor he hoped to overcome several limitations that had become increasingly apparent in his earlier neuron model, one based on a mode of explanation borrowed from the natural sciences, in which psychical events are characterized as states quantitatively determined by distinct material particles. Freud wanted to move away from the biologistic idea that these events take place in specific anatomical areas of the brain. To distinguish psychical locality from anatomical place, he suggested that we understand that locality as corresponding to a place inside an optical instrument where a *virtual* image forms: "In the microscope and telescope, as we know, these occur in part at ideal points, regions in which no tangible component of the apparatus is situated."[25] Freud, to give a better account of the functioning of memory, needed a model that would emphasize the temporal order rather than the spatial distribution of psychical movements, and he felt that the optical model was better able to describe the regulated timing of movements as they were "caught and localized in the parts of the mechanism" (p. 98). The shortcomings of the optical instrument metaphor were eventually to become obvious to Freud, not least because his better understanding of the workings of the psyche involved certain contradictions that the optical model could not properly represent. The psychical system, in fact, consists of two systems, one which will receive impressions and another system to permanently record those impressions. The optical machine, however, is too one-dimensional to incorporate this "double" register. Derrida notes that it was through the metaphor of the Mystic Writing Pad that Freud discovered a solution to all the cumulative problems encountered in this project. To begin with, the Mystic Pad can accommodate both systems: the top sheet (covered by a transparent protective layer) receives the impressions made by the stylus, but can be fully erased, leaving room for more marks, by simply lifting it away from the wax surface underneath; the wax layer permanently records all of the impressions made upon it. The act of writing itself solves other problems. Temporality, for example, is now inscribed in the process because of the seriality of steps involved: making the impression, lifting the second sheet to erase it, lowering the sheet, making new marks, etc. Also, the two-handed nature of the machine suggests a level of ambivalence about the agencies and origins of its *modus operandi*.

> This machine does not run by itself. It is less a machine than a tool. And it is not held with only one hand.... At least two hands are needed to make the apparatus function, as well as a system of movements, a coordination of independent initiatives, an organized multiplicity of origins. (p. 112)

As Derrida reminds us, one always writes for someone and we must be several to write and to "perceive" (p. 113). The subject of writing, then, is very different from the singular subject of the optical apparatus: "The subject of writing is a *system* of relations between strata: of the Mystic Pad, of the psyche, of society, of the world. Within that scene the punctual simplicity of the classical subject is not to be found" (p. 113).

Joan Copjec calls into question the equally punctual simplicity of the subject of the cinematic apparatus by pointing out that a more complex idea of subjectivity, of subjectivity in language, is already at work in the notion of the *dispositif* as opposed to the *appareil*. The English translation of the titles of Baudry's two articles on the apparatus hides the fact that he uses two different words: *appareil* in the first and *dispositif* in the second. Copjec reminds us that *appareil* can be translated as "apparatus" but *dispositif* would be better translated as "arrangement." The apparatus, she argues, anthropomorphizes a social construction which privileges the male, but by emphasizing the apparatus as something else, called an "arrangement," we can begin

> to question the anthropomorphic power it assumes, the functionalism it exhibits. Patriarchy can only be an effect of a particular arrangement of competing discourses, not an expressive totality which guarantees its own self-interests.... What must be analyzed is the way particular discourses inscribe sexual differences, different subject positions.... Woman produced as a category in various signifying practices...the multiformity of the construction of sexual differences. (p. 58)

In another essay, on repetition or the compulsion to repeat in film and film theory,[26] Copjec presents a second critique of the cinematic apparatus, this time from the perspective of the ideas about repetition and pleasure at work in the theories of the apparatus as well as current narrative theory of film, particularly that of Raymond Bellour. She cites Baudry's description of the apparatus as activated by a compulsion to repeat, a return to a former stage of satisfaction, and Metz's insistence that cinema is motivated by the pleasure principle, which entails the production of "good objects" only, that is, pleasurable films. "Behind" this pleasure principle, moreover, is an *a priori* intention that Baudry and Metz ascribe to the apparatus. For Baudry, the cinema *aims* to produce a hallucinated satisfaction because it is the embodiment of a primordial wish to reproduce that infantile pleasure. And for Metz, it is the *intention* of the institution which defines the success of the cinematic performance, "since the institution as a whole has filmic pleasure alone as its aim."[27] Similarly, Raymond Bellour, who, more than any other film theorist, has addressed himself to the question of repetition in the cinema, says:

> Beyond any given film, what each film aims at through the apparatus that permits it is the regulated order of the spectacle, the return of an immemorial and everyday state which the subject experiences in his dreams and for which the cinematic apparatus renews the desire.[28]

"The cinematic apparatus renews the desire": a final feature of the apparatus is its ability to reproduce itself. As Metz says, "It is the specific characteristic of every true institution that it takes charge of the mechanisms of its own reproduction."[29] Repetition, then, occurs at every level of functioning of the apparatus: it repeats for the spectator a former pleasure, and it repeats itself as it reproduces its own mechanism. In addition, at the level of classical narrative, the contradictions of that narrative system are worked through and resolved in what Bellour calls the "repetition–resolution effect" ("the fact that the film resolves itself, moves from its beginning to its end by means of differential repetition or the final integration of a certain number of elements given at the beginning and in the course of the narrative").[30] Faced with the marked emphasis of these theorists on the crucial role of repetition in film, Copjec nevertheless maintains that, for all the psychoanalytic references found in the theories of the apparatus, this is not, in fact, a very psychoanalytic idea of repetition. For psychoanalysis moved itself beyond an early understanding of repetition as either reproduction or restitution. Repetition does not reproduce past scenes, as the analysis of the Wolf Man reveals in its elaboration of the structure of fantasy; it is not necessary for an event to have taken place for it to have an existence in concrete, retrospective effects. Neither does repetition restore a lost object or a lost relationship to an object; as Freud observed of his nephew's fort/da game, mastery over the mother's absence is secondary to the primary feat of replaying the loss itself, of "returning to the ever-open gap introduced by the absence,"[31] an activity that situates itself distinctly beyond the constant, homeostatic circuit of the pleasure principle. Above all, as Lacan has shown, repetition involves alienation because of its association with the splitting of subjectivity. The mother's departure incites the infant to "multilate itself,"[32] to use a part of itself to signify her absence. This part will eventually become the *objet petit a*, the cause of desire which, to remain desire, must remain unattainable. Alienation, splitting, and the impossibility of satisfaction are a far cry from the version of repetition as pleasure that we find in the theories of the apparatus.

Again, what is at stake for feminism in the superiority of one definition over the other? For Copjec, Baudry undermines his own effort to account for the ideological determinations of cinema by attributing an unconscious aim to the apparatus and ascribing to it a kind of trans-historical agency. Desire, in this light, would be an originating force and its unquestionable aim would be satisfaction: "The cinematic apparatus becomes, once again, a tool that restores the integrity of the subject, supplies the subject's demand" (p. 50). Derrida, she says, follows Freud, and avoids this "incipient anthropomorphism" by substituting a writing machine for the optical apparatus. The Mystic Pad, as we have seen, is a vastly more complex metaphor because (and this is the problem of representation again) it can also represent the *insufficiency* of the psychical apparatus, its supplementary (rather than complementary) status: "The apparatus may be an ancient dream of man but in Derrida's analysis this dream is itself a psychic supplement, the indication within the subject of its unfulfillment" (p. 51). And to show that he, too, knows exactly what is at stake in the apparatus model, Derrida appropriately concludes "Freud and the Scene of Writing" with one of Freud's own conclusions (already cited above) concerning the dream-work: "It is highly probable that all complicated machinery and apparatus occurring in dreams stand for the genitals – and as a rule the male ones."

If, as Copjec claims, the theories of the apparatus constantly reproduce the same (that is, the male, as well as a male) point of view through their repeated emphasis on structures of masculine voyeurism, fetishism, and identification; and if, as Rose asserts, film theory's use of the concept of the imaginary tends to elide questions of sexual difference, is there any way in which the "excluded" woman can be reintroduced without falling back upon appeals to feminine identity and essence? Is it possible to dismantle, or rather debachelorize, the bachelor machine? Striking and, I would argue, symptomatically, two writers have each come to similar conclusions about ways of subverting the male narcissism of the apparatus theory. Both Mary Ann Doane[33] and Joan Copjec[34] have suggested substituting the "anaclitic" model of the drives for the account which bases itself on the fundamental importance of narcissism to the structuring of human subjectivity. The logical appeal of this is interesting not only because of the similarity of their conclusions, but also because it would seem to contradict other of their arguments, particularly those in which subjectivity is presented in terms of a linguistic or symbolic construction. I will suggest moreover that it is symptomatic because they introduce a model which ultimately risks (again) closing off questions of sexual difference.

Freud introduced the notion of anaclisis in *Three Essays on Sexuality* (1905) to describe the emergence of the sexual drives from the self-preservative instincts. In his 1915 essay, "On Narcissism," he contrasts anaclitic object-choice to narcissistic object-choice. Anaclitic choices are made along the lines of an initial attachment to the image of the parental figures, either to the woman who fed the infant or the man who protected it. In other words, the choice of love-object (the prototype of the sexually satisfying object) is determined with respect to the specific parental responsibilities for the child's feeding, care, and protection. The contrasting form of object-choice, the narcissistic one, was postulated by Freud to account for homosexual object-choice; it includes four possibilities, all of which are modeled on the subject's relation to himself rather than on a pre-existing relation to a parental figure. A narcissistic type can thus love (1) what he himself is (i.e. himself), (2) what he himself was, (3) what he himself would like to be, (4) someone who was once part of himself. (Conventionally gendered language creates a confusion here: Freud in category (4) is actually describing a woman who narcissistically loves her child because it was once part of her body.) This points up some of the difficulties inherent in the distinction between anaclitic and narcissistic. Although Freud states that male object-choice is typically anaclitic while the female's is as a rule narcissistic, he points out that this distinction is only a schematic one and that "both kinds of object-choice are open to each individual."[35] The two types of object-choice are thus purely ideal and can be alternated or combined in any actual individual case. Furthermore, in Freud's own examples, the antithesis between anaclitic and narcissistic object-choice does not always hold up. He describes as narcissistic, for example, the woman's choice of a man primarily for his love toward her, and not for her own love toward him. Here, however, the woman seems to be attempting to reproduce her relationship to the mother who fed and took care of her, which would thus be characteristic of anaclitic object-choice.

"Anaclisis" has by and large become an obsolete term, now used only descriptively or historically, because of our increased understanding of the fundamentally narcissistic nature of all object relations, even the very earliest ones. It is Lacan's mirror stage, of course, that has given us the metaphor of the narcissism underpinning all object relations: a child can only take another for an object once it has taken itself as an object. One's first love-object is oneself.

What would be the advantage then of substituting the anaclitic model of the drives for the narcissism of the apparatus, as Doane and Copjec have advocated? They each object to the central role cast for narcissism in the structuring of human subjectivity because this formula (the Lacanian account) requires both the man and the woman to define themselves in relation to a third term, a term which stands for the insufficiency or incompleteness of the subject – the phallus. They object above all to the fact that this formula supports the claim for a single libido, which Freud called masculine. Thus, in Doane's words, the narcissism/phallus

model fails to provide a theory of woman's "autonomous symbolic representation" (p. 33). While Copjec criticizes the apparatus theories for their exclusion of
the feminine body, Doane goes even further, detecting what she interprets as tell-
tale tendencies of bachelor thinking in those feminist anti-essentialist critiques
which militate against any consideration of a "natural" female body. Like the
apparatus theories, the anti-essentialist arguments (and here she is referring
specifically to the work of *m/f*) have paranoically discarded any discussion of
the body. In rejecting the idea of a natural female body, they have eliminated
questions of the body altogether. Doane fears that the very force of their
arguments will lure feminists into a one-dimensional extremist logic (one shared,
for example, by the experimental filmmaker Peter Gidal, who refuses to include
in his films any representation of a woman on the grounds that the perception of
that image is too culturally rooted in an idea of her essential (biological) difference). But we need some conception of the female body, Doane argues, in "order
to formulate the woman's different relation to speech, to language" (p. 33).
Copjec, in agreement with Doane, acknowledges that the task of putting the
body back onto film theory will "often look like a return to biologism" (p. 43);
Doane, however, reasons that, in Stephen Heath's words, "the risk of essence
may have to be taken,"[36] in order to formulate theories which provide the woman
with "an autonomous symbolic representation" (p. 33). In the attempt to find an
approach that does not irremediably separate psyche from body, or which does
not exclude the *woman's* body, Doane and Copjec, then, take up the theoretical
cause of anaclisis as a way of challenging the apparatus theorists and the anti-
essentialists. They find support for their challenge in the recently renovated
version of anaclisis found in Jean Laplanche's *Life and Death in Psychoanalysis.*[37]
Here is Mary Ann Doane's summary of Laplanche on anaclisis:

> Jean Laplanche explains the emergence of sexuality by means of the concept of
> propping or *anaclisis*. The drive, which is always sexual, leans or props itself upon
> the nonsexual or presexual instinct of self-preservation. His major example is the
> relation of the oral drive to the instinct of hunger whose object is the milk obtained
> from the mother's breast. The object of the oral drive (prompted by the sucking
> which activates the lips as an erotogenic zone) is necessarily displaced in relation to
> the first object of the instinct. The fantasmatic breast (henceforth the object of the
> oral drive) is a metonymic derivation, a symbol of the milk: "The object to be
> rediscovered is not the lost object, but its substitute by displacement; the lost object
> is the object of self-preservation, of hunger, and the object one seeks to refind is an
> object displaced in relation to that first object." Sexuality can only take form in a
> dissociation of subjectivity from the bodily function, but the concept of a bodily
> function is necessary in the explanation as, precisely, a support. (pp. 26–7)

If sexuality can be explained only in relation to the body which serves as its
"prop," then any discussion of sexuality (in filmic representation or otherwise)
will be obliged to account for the role of the body. This raises at least two
questions. First, what is *lost* by dropping narcissism from the account of the

emergence of the drives and object-relations? And second, is the "anaclitic" body necessarily a feminine body, and is this the body we need to ensure the reconceptualization of the feminine body in film theory?

Doane and Copjec's use of anaclisis to describe the emergence of the drives and the formation of subjectivity should be viewed in the context of recent feminist attempts to align the drives with the body and the body with woman: Julia Kristeva's celebration of the woman's special relation to the pre-Oedipal mother's body, Michèle Montrelay's emphasis on the "real" of the woman's own body which imposes itself prior to any act of construction, Luce Irigaray's mapping of the feminine psyche onto that body's supposedly multiple sexualities.[38] In each case the aim is to give an account of *feminine* sexuality, one which these writers believe that Freud neglected and Lacan either willfully doctored or outrageously construed in the form of a new mysticism of the feminine. "The risk of essence" unabashedly taken by these alternative theories of the feminine typically involves, however, ignoring the important psychoanalytic emphasis on the way that sexual identity is imposed from the "outside." By deriving gendered sexuality from the body, no matter how indirectly, what is in danger of disappearing is the sense of sexuality as an arbitrary identity that is imposed on the subject, as a law. And the phallus, as a sign that belongs to culture rather than to nature, is itself the sign of the law of sexual division. According to this law, each subject, male and female, must take up a position in relation to the phallus – which is *not* of a natural bodily order. In this respect, the most significant insight of psychoanalysis is the theoretical evidence it brings to bear against any notion of a "natural" sexual identity. Because sexual identity is "legislated"[39] rather than autonomously assumed, there is an ill-fit between subject and sexual identity, precisely because it is the result of an *imposition*. This insight agrees with the anti-essentialist claim that femininity is only an awkwardly donned and sometimes inappropriate garb for the woman. The anaclitic account of the emergence of the drives, put forward as an explanation of feminine subjectivity, thus risks (along with the alternative theories of femininity mentioned above) understanding femininity as naturally assumed or a simple product of the body's development. Such an understanding effaces the *difficulty* of femininity as a sexual position or category in relation to the symbolic as well as social order.

It is clear moreover that Laplanche's version of anaclisis does not seek to *substitute* anaclisis for narcissism. As we have seen he is concerned to give an account of the early emergence of the drives and the subsequent paths of object-choice. (In particular, he emphasizes that this description should not be misread as a propping on a "body," but as a propping of the drives on the instincts – p. 16.) In effect, Laplanche provides a description of the metaphorical and metonymical processes or paths leading to the choice of the object. The drives emerge metonymically from the self-preservative instincts (for example, hunger for milk/desire for the breast/desire for the mother) *and* metaphorically in the way sexuality cathects the "outside" (love of one's own double and the doubles of that original double). Laplanche stresses the *meshing* of the metaphorical–

metonymical processes; anaclisis is thus a term for him only inasmuch as it is bound up with narcissism.

A further argument against Doane and Copjec's plan for substituting anaclisis for narcissism is that the "body" in question here, if there is one at all (and for Laplanche, as we have seen, there is not), would not be a *woman's* body but a *mother's* body: the moment of the early emergence of the drives and related object choices is *before* the moment when the child can say "My mother is a woman." Once again, in the theoretical search for the "woman," we end up with the "mother," which is not at all the same thing – and feminists[40] have long recognized the crucial need to maintain that distinction, especially since the two terms have a habit of slipping into each other.

We have seen that the argument for anaclisis rests upon the notion that the drives emerge solely by differentiating themselves from the bodily functions. A final problem with this formulation is that it makes it difficult to pose the question of the status of the image or representation itself. Doane and Copjec, for example, follow up Laplanche's claim that the perception of the breast is a fantasmatic one. But what is missing from this account is precisely the whole problematic of splitting and distance that makes representation possible (the object can be represented only if it is absent), and which is provided theoretically by the structural function of narcissism. Repeatedly, then, I have demonstated the problems involved in turning to anaclisis for a more accurate account of the emergence of the drives of the feminine body, an account "uncontaminated" by the "male" preserves of narcissism and the phallic relation: if anaclisis has any claim to a theoretical existence, then it is in no way autonomous from the question of narcissism.

No matter how carefully these writers attempt to present this concept of anaclisis (or the propping of the drives on the bodily functions) as an alternative logic to that of narcissism and the phallic relation, their effort seems inevitably to reproduce the difficulties endemic to the essentialist position that they are so concerned to avoid, a position which assumes an identity rather than examining it and seeks to answer questions about sexual difference before they are asked. Clearly what we need as a counter to the "maleness" of the cinematic apparatus and its theories is not to reintroduce the *feminine body* into those theories but to insist on a way of theorizing cinema that does not eliminate the question of *sexual difference*. I would argue that the theoretical components for such a project have been presented in the recent feminist work on fantasy in relation to film.[41] An investigation of the construction of fantasy seems to provide a way of accounting for sexual difference that acknowledges difference but which in no way seeks to dictate or predetermine the subsequent distribution of that difference (in terms of sexual identity) in any given film or for any given spectator, male or female. In the psychoanalytic account of fantasy, the drives are sexualized only by way of their articulation in fantasy. The emphasis here is not on the relation to the object but on the subject's desire in relation to a scenario in which he takes part. Although the structure of these scenarios is predetermined, their contents are not. Laplanche and Pontalis, in an essay indispensable to the discussion of fantasy, "Fantasy and the Origins of Sexuality,"[42] have shown very clearly that the structure of "primal fantasies" serves to answer the subject's questions about *origins*: "The primal scene replays the origin of the individual, the fantasy of seduction pictures the emergence of sexuality; and fantasies of castration represent the origin of sexual difference."[43] The most striking feature of these fantasies though, and the one most relevant here, is that all the possible roles in the narrative are available to the subject, who can be either subject or object and can even occupy a position "outside" the scene, looking on from the spectator's point of view. Again, it is only the formal positions themselves that are fixed (there are "masculine" and "feminine" positions of desire); the subject can and does adopt these positions in relation to a variety of complex scenarios, and in accordance with the mobile patterns of his or her own desire.

The formulation of fantasy, which provides a complex and exhaustive account of *the staging and imaging of the subject and its desire*, is a model that very closely approximates the primary aims of the apparatus theory: to describe not only the subject's desire for the filmic image and its reproduction, but also the structure of the fantasmatic relation to that image, including the subject's belief in its reality. Film analysis, moreover, from the perspective of the structure of fantasy, presents a more accurate description of the spectator's shifting and multiple identifications and a more comprehensive account of these same movements within the film: the perpetually changing configurations of the characters, for example, are a formal response to the unfolding of a fantasy that is the filmic fiction itself. Finally, the model of fantasy would allow us to retain the apparatus theory's important stress on the cinema as an *institution*: in this light, all films, and not just the products of Hollywood, would be seen and studied in their fully historical and social variety as *dream-factories*. The feminist use of the psychoanalytic notion of fantasy for the study of film and its institutions can now be seen as a way of constructively dismantling the bachelor machines of film theory (no need for Luddism) or at least modifying them in accordance with the practical and theoretical demands of sexual modernity.

Notes

1   Michel Carrouges, *Les Machines célibataires* (Paris: Le Chêne, 1954); see also the catalog with essays on the "Bachelor Machines" exhibition of 1973 which appeared in 1975, *Les Machines célibataires*, eds. Jean Clair and Harald Szeemann (Venice: Alfieri, 1975).

2   Sigmund Freud, *The Origins of Psycho-Analysis: Letters to Wilhelm Fliess, Drafts and Notes 1877–1902*, eds. Marie Bonaparte, Anna Freud, and Ernst Kris, trans. Eric Mosbacher and James Strachey (New York: Basic Books, 1954), Letter 32 (10–20–95).

3   Jacques Derrida, "Freud and the Scene of Writing," trans. Jeffrey Mehlman, *Yale French Studies* no. 48 (1972): 117.

4 Clair and Szeemann: 94; the Michel de Certeau essay is titled "Arts de Mourir: Écritures anti-mystiques."

5 Jean-Louis Baudry, "Ideological Effects of the Basic Cinematographic Apparatus," trans. Alan Williams, *Film Quarterly* vol. 27, no. 2 (Winter 1974–5): 39–47; "The Apparatus: Metapsychological Approaches to the Impression of Reality in the Cinema," trans. Jean Andrews and Bertrand Augst, *Camera Obscura* no. 1 (Fall 1976): 104–26; Christian Metz, "The Imaginary Signifier," trans. Ben Brewster, *The Imaginary Signifier* (Bloomington: Indiana University Press, 1982): 3–87.

6 Janet Bergstrom, "Alternation, Segmentation, Hypnosis: Interview with Raymond Bellour," *Camera Obscura* nos. 3–4 (Summer 1979): 89.

7 Janet Bergstrom, "Enunciation and Sexual Difference," *Camera Obscura* nos. 3–4 (Summer 1979): 55.

8 Stephen Heath, "Narrative Space," *Screen* vol. 17, no. 3 (Autumn 1976): 99.

9 Sigmund Freud, *The Interpretation of Dreams*, in *The Standard Edition of the Complete Psychological Works of Sigmund Freud*, ed. and trans. James Strachey (London: Hogarth Press and the Institute of Psychoanalysis, 1958), vol. 5: 356.

10 For a recent discussion of the vicissitudes of the "woman question" in Marxism and "feminine sexuality" in psychoanalysis, see Rosalind Coward, *Patriarchal Precedents* (London: Routledge and Kegan Paul, 1983).

11 Heath, 107.

12 Derrida, 117.

13 Jacqueline Rose, conference presentation in *The Cinema in the Eighties: Proceedings of the Meeting* (Venice: Edizioni "La Biennale di Venezia," 1980): 24.

14 Jacqueline Rose, "The Imaginary," *The Talking Cure: Essays in Psychoanalysis and Language*, ed. Colin MacCabe (London and Basingstoke: Macmillan, 1981): 132–61; "The Cinematic Apparatus: Problems in Current Theory," *The Cinematic Apparatus*, eds. Teresa de Lauretis and Stephen Heath (New York: St. Martin's Press, 1980): 172–86.

15 Jacques Lacan, translated by Alan Sheridan as "Of the Gaze as *Objet Petit a*," *The Four Fundamental Concepts of Psychoanalysis* (New York W. W. Norton, 1981): 67–119.

16 Lacan, 153; translation slightly modified.

17 Rose, "The Imaginary": 154.

18 Rose, "The Cinematic Apparatus": 174.

19 Metz, 79.

20 See Metz's discussion of disavowal and fetishism, 69–78.

21 Rose, "The Cinematic Apparatus": 175.

22 Rose, "The Cinematic Apparatus": 175.

23 Joan Copjec, "The Anxiety of the Influencing Machine," *October* no. 23 (Winter 1982): 43–59.

24 Copjec, 57.

25 Freud, *The Interpretation of Dreams*: 541.

26 Joan Copjec, "*India Song/Son nom de Venise dans Calcutta désert*: The Compulsion to Repeat," *October* no. 17 (Summer 1981): 37–52.

27 Metz, 19.

28 Raymond Bellour, "Cine-Repetitions," *Screen* vol. 20, no. 2 (Summer 1979).

29 Metz, 19.

30 Bergstrom, "Alternation, Segmentation, Hypnosis": 81–2.

31 Lacan, "Tuché and Automaton," *The Four Fundamental Concepts*: 62.

32 Lacan, "Tuché and Automaton": 62.

33 Mary Ann Doane, "Woman's Stake: Filming the Female Body," *October* no. 17 (Summer 1981): 23–36.

34 Joan Copjec, "*India Song*" (see note 26 for complete reference).

35 Sigmund Freud, "On Narcissism: An Introduction," *Standard Edition*, vol. 14: 88.

36 Stephen Heath, "Difference," *Screen* vol. 19, no. 3 (Autumn 1978): 99.

37 Jean Laplanche, *Life and Death in Psychoanalysis*, trans. Jeffrey Mehlman (Baltimore and London: Johns Hopkins University Press, 1976).

38 Julia Kristeva, "Motherhood According to Giovanni Bellini," *Desire in Language* (New York: Columbia University Press, 1980); Michèle Montrelay, "Inquiry into Femininity," *m/f* no. 1 (1978); Luce Irigaray, "That Sex Which Is Not One," trans. R. Albury and Meaghan Morris (Darlington: Feral Publications, 1978). For discussions of this work see, for example, Beverley Brown and Parveen Adams, "The Feminine Body and Feminist Politics," *m/f* no. 3 (1979); Claire Pajaczkowska, "Introduction to Kristeva," *m/f* nos. 5 & 6 (1981); Mary Ann Doane, "Woman's Stake: Filming the Female Body," *October* no. 17 (Summer 1981).

39 My discussion of the narcissism/phallus model is indebted to Jacqueline Rose's introduction to *Feminine Sexuality: Jacques Lacan and the Ecole Freudienne*, eds. Juliet Mitchell and Jacqueline Rose, trans. Jacqueline Rose (London and Basingstoke: Macmillan, 1982).

40 For a recent discussion of the psychoanalytic account of the "mother" see "*L'Ane* dossier – the mother in the unconscious," trans. Ben Brewster, *m/f* no. 8 (1982). Essays by Marie-Hélène Brousse-Delancoe, Marie-Christine Hamon, Dominique Calfon, Bernard Fonty, Eric Laurent. See also in the same issue Parveen Adams, "Mothering."

41 For example see Elisabeth Lyon, "The Cinema of Lol V. Stein," *Camera Obscura* no. 6 (Fall 1980): 7–41; Janet Bergstrom, "Enunciation and Sexual Difference," *Camera Obscura* nos. 3–4 (Summer 1979), especially 56–8; Elizabeth Cowie, "Fantasia," *m/f* no. 9 (1984): 71–104.

42 Jean Laplanche and J.-B. Pontalis, "Fantasy and the Origins of Sexuality," *The International Journal of Psycho-Analysis* 49 (1968).

43 Elisabeth Lyon's formulation of Laplanche and Pontalis's description of "primal fantasies" in "The Cinema of Lol V. Stein" 12.

Part IX
The Nature of the Gaze

Introduction

Toby Miller

As is clear from Parts VII and VIII, the audience is conceived of as a group of people that is empirically knowable in its living and breathing attendance at and reactions to film. The spectator, by contrast, is generally understood in film theory as the product of two forces: first, the psychic struggles for personality that psychoanalytic theory claims are characteristic of maturation and the getting of sexuality; and second, the ways in which both the texts and the physical apparatus of cinema draw out these conflicts. Psychological battles are in the unconscious, which means that they cannot be known through the thoughts or neurones of people. Instead, they gain expression indirectly, via the repetition of various dramas about power and the self, with sexual identity at their core. Not surprisingly, these narratives find some expression in dreams, and may be sources for fiction as well; hence the similarity between filmgoing and dreams (the darkness and the abandon in story) is matched by a likeness in the texture of film narrative and the unconscious. We shall look here at the insertion of Sigmund Freud's writings into film theory, notably via the spectator's gaze at the image.

Freud's *Introductory Lectures on Psychoanalysis* stress that "psychoanalysis is a procedure for the medical treatment of neurotic patients" (Freud, 1982: 39). That might make it appear appropriate as a therapeutic method for dealing with people whose violent behavior is attributed to exposure to screen texts, or identifying anti-social conduct by on-screen characters. But it has been more central than that to screen studies. Much textual criticism is like psychoanalysis in its concern to uncover secrets and explain them: surfacing the sedimented to satisfy the analyst's professional duty and decorum and the patient's desire for accredited confession (cf. the critique by Foucault, 1984).

Psychoanalysis as a treatment is comprised, in Freud's terms, of "talk." This "talk" is very unusual. It is "intimate," with a subject matter that "socially independent" persons "must conceal from other people." More than that, the desire to have "a homogeneous personality" means that we fail to "admit" this truth even to ourselves. No surprise then that few people can hear a lecture on film theory for the first time without sensing that the reading being offered is foreign, even when it claims to explain that what is being presented can be confirmed via a close analysis of a screen text. For the very nature of spectatorship theory is to take an experience we have in common (viewing a particular movie) and show how there is more to it than meets the eye; more than meets the eye because the eye fails to query itself in the terms demanded by film theory. Once listeners admit their previous lack of preparedness to go with the flow of theory and utilize it to read texts, the mutuality of experience is restored.

The secrets of the self are emphasized in Freud's insistence that "mental processes are in themselves unconscious." He argues that "psychoanalysis cannot avoid raising this contradiction; it cannot accept the identity of the conscious and the mental." Feelings, thoughts, and desires are mental, to the extent that they can be known consciously. But they have unconscious components as well; hence the duty of psychoanalysis "to make mysteries and fish in troubled waters," where it finds a constant struggle between "the pressure of the exigencies of life" and "the satisfaction of the instincts" (Freud, 1982: 46–7).

For Freud, these "instinctual impulses . . . can only be described as sexual." They are responsible for "nervous and mental diseases," but may also contribute "to the highest cultural, artistic and social creations of the human spirit" (ibid.: 47). Clearly, this is one optic through which to view the intersection of Freud and cinema: as a means of accounting for, say, the thematic concerns of an auteur director. But it has also been a way-in to the concealed, opaque methods of Hollywood filmmaking, used as a means of clarifying how its conspicuous, clear narratives work. The feature film becomes an exemplar of cultural capitalism's efforts to render the paradigmatic into the syntagmatic, where combinations appear natural and automatic rather than cultural and selective. Craig Saper (1991: 33) argues that when our view as spectators goes beyond processing narrative cues, as we move into the text by identifying with its characters, psychoanalysis can rescue us from phantasy.

There is a further connection between textual analysis and Freud's method. He insists on intensely close readings of the underside to the stories told by his patients. This involves examining "the dregs, one might say, of the world of phenomena." The justification for doing so derives from the lack of fit between the magnitude of a problem and its representation, such that "vastness" is actually only discernible through "feeble indications" (Freud, 1982: 52). Freud mentions the skills of seduction and detection as akin to those of psychoanalysis. Both rely on "small pointers . . . comparatively slight and obscure traces of the person you were in search of" that are "small indications . . . [of] something bigger." As such, "chance and symptomatic actions" need to be understood as "valid psychical acts." This relates to his account of "forgetting," which redeems absent-mindedness as a device for secreting data. It reads remarkably like the idea of cinema as an escape from the everyday, if one that draws on that everyday to make meaning. The definition of forgetting is itself very everyday; Freud calls it "failure to carry out," which ties-in to escapism via the "intention to avoid unpleasure" (ibid.: 52, 88, 87, 100–3). This notion of avoidance becomes the animating logic behind symptomatic criticism, a form of reading that looks for structuring absences, keys to desire in both creative production and consumption that are founded on denial, displacement, and consequent overdetermination.

Freud quotes Goethe approvingly for saying of a noted eighteenth-century satirist that "where he makes a jest a problem lies concealed." This leads Freud to a "whole theory of misreading." Misreading is not an innocent mistake: like all everyday actions, it is meaningful. "Parapraxes" are small mistakes that betray profound verities. This central operating presumption, that our psyches deny stress and displace it onto other activities, arises from psychoanalysis's status as a theory of conflict. It is always on the lookout either for the suppression of personal slights and their sublimation into a civilized aggressivity, or for confusions that express internal contradictions. Freud explains denial as evidence of a truth that it seeks to contradict: "the ideas which people try to suppress in this way turn out invariably to be the most important ones." Life could be improved if "small parapraxes" were acknowledged as "auguries" that provide information about "still concealed" intentions. The point of all this is to uncover what Freud calls the "signs of an interplay of forces in the mind, as a manifestation of purposeful intentions working concurrently or in mutual oppositions." Misreading is exemplified in Freud's account of "slips of the tongue."

He attributes these to a speaker's decision not to voice certain opinions, which then achieve a distorted expression against that person's will. The "suppression of the speaker's intention to say something is the indispensable condition for the occurrence of a slip of the tongue." The crucial questions to be answered about misreading are twofold: the associations made, and the place of the error. Both of these, then, are not in the misread text so much as in the ideas it encouraged and the space in which it transpired. We could translate these, respectively, into spectators' personal histories and the climate of cinema exhibition in which they find themselves. It is also possible that "the text of what is read itself arouses the disturbing purpose" that occasions this error, when we wish to deny what is in the text and this is in conflict with our desire to understand it (ibid.: 65–6, 83, 79, 89, 146, 86, 94, 92–3, 98–9). (Incidentally, Freud actually uses the phrase "the text of the dream" as the basis for later accounts of it (ibid.: 148), and the analogy of dreaming with the filmgoing experience is obvious – no surprise that Hollywood's newest studio is "Dreamworks".)

The screen is also called to mind by Freud's concept of "scopophilia," or "the pleasure in looking." Sexual life is characterized by the "desire . . . to look at the other person or to feel him or to watch him in the performance of his intimate actions," Freud argues. Scopophilia involves the visual capture of something, a process that seeks to "make an object from the first and hold fast to it." This association with pleasure could be perverse, if taken too far, or quite ordinary if it was not the only means of obtaining sexual satisfaction (ibid.: 258, 347, 371, 364).

Scopophilia was also a major concern of Jacques Lacan, who develops these ideas into what he terms "the formation of the I," that moment when the child manages to "recognize as such his own image in a mirror." This leads to a comparison between "this virtual complex and the reality it reduplicates – the child's own body, and the persons and things, around him." This is "the mirror stage." It involves both a sexual element and the beginnings of a view of the world via "identification." The "subject . . . assumes an image," and develops the sense of being an individual, albeit one still dependent on others. Language has not yet intervened to grasp this subject and nor does it have a fully achieved sense of connection to the rest of the world, its relationship "with the other" (Lacan, 1973: 1–2). But when the child encounters its reflected image, it wrongly discerns a unified, singular person. This is the birth of the ego, a psychic condition of order and responsibility that obscures the conflictual processes that drive the person. This ego's defensive armor is permeable enough to permit identification with others. Such identification is always ambivalent and ambiguous. The image is loved for its narcissistic qualities, its resemblance to the person, but also hated for being other, for existing outside the person's physical form.

This mobile response makes us extremely adaptable to different types of characterization encountered: exhibitionists, voyeurs, slaves, masters, victims, and victimizers (Gabbard and Gabbard, 1989: 180–1). Clearly, mirrors and the processes of identification are crucial aspects to the world of cinema: we look at images, identify with parts of them, complete with all our psychic conflicts. Film is about the spectator's "perceptual identification with seeing and being seen" (Hansen, 1994: 2).

The next connection between Freudianism and film is the priority that psychoanalysis places on dreams. As noted earlier, watching is often compared to dreaming. They share darkness, imagery, and credibility. Dreams are critical objects for Freud to expound on "interpreting . . . finding a hidden sense in something." The notion of dreams-as-texts is present in his remarks on their ability to "present whole novels." And, as before, the chances are that a man confused as to the meaning of a dream "does know what his dream means: only he does not know that he knows it and for that reason thinks he does not know it." Interpretation imbued with psychoanalysis is essential, especially in its capacity to deal with the "strongly emotional thoughts and interests" informing the "unconscious," which Freud called "complexes." Interpretation differentiates the "manifest" from the "latent" to produce an integrated account of dreams (Freud, 1982: 115, 119, 130, 138, 150–1).

Apart from the simple imaging double of mirror, screen, and self, numerous stories recur in human experience, dreams, and fiction, means of working through the tensions that civilizing pressures repress. They make for excellent (and unconsciously fascinating) cinematic narratives. The Oedipus complex explains the rivalry between people of the same sex. It presumes that a son has a "special affection" for his mother, to the point of believing he owns her. This then casts his father into the role of a rival. For her part, a daughter regards her mother as an obstacle interfering with her "affectionate relation" to her father. Freud did not presume that the Oedipal complex provided a total understanding of parent–child relations, but he did see it as a necessary issue in each child's "mental life." Again, this theme has been massively treated in drama, as Freud himself points out. The complex is critical for humanity's acquisition of guilt, which Freud regards as central to a sense of mutual obligation. The prohibitions on incest and parricide become, in effect, the building blocks for civil society. We are offered Hamlet as an exemplar (ibid.: 243–4, 373, 375, 378–9).

The Oedipus complex is closely associated with the castration complex, a child's "reaction to the threats against the child aimed at putting a stop to his early sexual activities." This in turn relates to little boys' disturbance when they discover that little girls lack what Freud calls "such a precious portion." This discovery soon turns into a threat; the little boy might lose the organ, in keeping with instructions he has already received not to touch it unduly. "He comes under the sway of the castration complex" at this time, Freud argues. By contrast, little girls "feel greatly at a disadvantage" and "envy boys." They "develop a wish to be a man" (ibid.: 245, 416, 359–60). Although many film theorists work with these complexes, few if any would endorse the regressive reading offered by the notion of "penis envy."

Enough of psychoanalysis on its own terms. What about film? As Dudley Andrew (1984: 135) points out, psychoanalysis has been deployed to account for the unconscious of filmmakers and spectators, the nature of film as fantasy, the inevitability of identification for fantasy to come into play, and how the unconscious in film may intersect with wider questions of psychoanalysis and culture. Graeme Turner (1988: 113) argues that film is friendly towards psychoanalysis because of "its collapsing of the boundaries of the real." The cinema occupies the gap between what we see and what we imagine. We turn now to that uptake, focusing initially on Christian Metz's pathbreaking 1975 essay in *Screen*, "The Imaginary Signifier" (chapter 24, this volume). That paper represents his passage from the search for a technical language of cinema, towards a merger of semiotics, political economy, and psychoanalysis.

Metz seeks to "disengage the cinema-object from the imaginary and to win it for the symbolic." His project seeks to situate films within the psychic and economic context of thier signification. The aim is to explain their acceptance or rejection by audiences. Metz defines cinema as a "technique of the imaginary," in dual senses of the term. First, mainstream films depend on narrative fictions and signifiers produced through realist "photography and phonography." Second, they engage with the imaginary part of the spectating human subject, an ego that sees itself reflected in the mirror and looks for similarities and differences from what it wishes to be. The cinema screen becomes a "psychical substitute," a reflection on our failings and the reenactment of the mirror phase from childhood. The problem for theory is the way in which our love of cinema overtakes our desire to comprehend it. This is a paradox. A fascination with the screen drives us to know it and ourselves. The theorist seeks to divide the symbolic order of meaning in film from the imaginary order of meaning in the spectator, but this is constantly thwarted by the imaginary of cinema, what makes it "likeable." The conditions for theorizing about the screen – its fascination and allure – are the very qualities that incapacitate analysis. As Metz puts it, "the discourse of the object (the native discourse of the cinematic institution) insidiously comes to occupy the place of discourse about the object" (Metz, 1975: 14–16).

Metz explains the fascination of film for the spectator in terms of "voyeurism," connecting it to Lacan's explanation of the mirror phase. The ego is formed via an imaginary encounter with an image; what could better inform our understanding of cinemagoing? The film becomes an object of pleasure if it is enjoyed, unpleasure if otherwise. This is not merely a psychic internality, but an operating principle of "the cinematic institution." This term includes both the "cinema industry" and the "mental machinery," which accustom us to the products of that industry. The institution is both inside and outside us, just like the mirror-image of ourselves. Our senses of pleasure feed back to the industry as well as being shaped by it. This produces a "libidinal economy (filmic pleasure in its historically constituted form)" that intersects with a "political economy (the current cinema as a commercial enterprise)" (ibid.: 17–20).

Laura Mulvey's equally important essay "Visual Pleasure and Narrative Cinema" (1975) appeared in the next issue of *Screen*. It talked about the textual inscription of positions for spectators to adopt, and looked at the particular impact on forming gendered subjects of the gazing pleasure offered to men by classical Hollywood films. Mulvey used psychoanalytic theory enmeshed with film history as a "political weapon" that could allow readers to see how "the unconscious of patriarchal society has structured film form." So we have some significant assumptions here. The first is that society determines the formal components of film. The second is that society can be specified as dominated by men and as having an unconscious. Mulvey argues that society is paradoxically dependent on women to define itself, which it does by pointing to what it has and women do not. In other words, it pits women as castrated subjects against itself as properly phallically formed. In "the last resort," lack is all that women represent in the cinema. Men project onto these silenced creatures of their gaze their own other side, which might wish to give birth to children, but instead runs society. For their part, women look on child-bearing as compensation, cause, and replacement for their castration. Film audiences use the gaze to project onto diegetic characters their own suppressed exhibitionism. In an unequal social domain of sexual relations, this codification of the look encrypts the male gaze as active, the female as passive.

The process becomes political once women realize that while they are oppressed, they can use the tools of patriarchy – such as psychoanalysis – to discover how it works. The analysis of existing grammars of pleasure will ultimately help to subvert that pleasure. This is because – returning to the crux of Freud's thought – sexuality is always a contested norm, a continuing negotiation of heterosexuality, homosexuality, bisexuality, femininity, and masculinity inside each person. For while women on-screen lack the penis, and therefore represent the threat of castration, they help to signify, in fact they absolutely embody, sexual difference, which is comforting for men. So women are sights for sore male eyes, icons of pleasure that confirm for men their sex and their sexuality.

This understanding denied women's pleasure as spectators, assuming that the gaze in film belongs to the heterosexual male and his screen brothers. Feminist theorists and filmmakers responded by supporting and making some determinedly unpleasurable films that confronted spectators with their complicity in patriarchy. In some cases, this avant-gardism denied both women's active address and engagement with classical narrative, and crucial social differences within genders that are not about the acquisition of linguistic or familial norms or the getting of sexuality, but are to do with race and class (Pribram, 1988: 1–3; see also Doane and hooks, chapters 28 and 29, this volume).

The notion of overturning dominant forms of stitching spectators in to the text relates to criticisms of realism. For example, the conventional documentary sets the spectator's gaze up as competent, once it is guided by the knowing hand–eye–technology coordination of the director and editor. Frederick Wiseman's *Titicut Follies* (1967), by contrast, provokes an uncomfortable gaze at the self by the spectator: Where are we at any given moment? Why are we there? What is going on? Am I part of a society that endorses the brutal treatment of prisoners in this way? There is no closure. The look remains unsatisfied. We are asked to bring into question even our surveillance of the text, as viewers. Raymond Williams sees the avant-garde, in which we could include direct cinema, as acknowledging the existence of a "fragmented ego in a fragmented world," defying capitalist neatness and a unilogical realism (Williams, 1989: 93). There is, of course, intense argument about how different forms of texts can be read. In particular, the ruling Brechtian aesthetic of distantiation in 1970s film theory was archly derisive towards what became known as the "realist text" (see Part V). The notion of textually inscribed rules of reading – solid interpellations of viewers – as a function of naturalism/realism problematized the value of, for example, social realism. It was an orthodoxy that linear and resolved narratives which compelled closure were reactionary in their inevitable construction of the possibility of perfect knowledge. Instead, audiences should be confronted with the constructedness of their positioning and the seams of weaving of each text made explicit via self-referentiality. Like psychoanalytic theory, this critique made symptomatic readings of texts, assuming that spectatorship was less a practice than a by-product of being positioned and attracted by narrative and image that implied perfect knowledge and political orthodoxy in their very essence. Since that time, psychoanalytic protocols have proved to be remarkably providential for interrogating questions of masculinity, femininity, and postcoloniality. While Freud may be considered outmoded in the social sciences, his doctrine of counter-indicative reading and the centrality of sex remain magnetic to film theory.

Works Cited

Andrew, J. Dudley 1984. *Concepts in Film Theory*. Oxford: Oxford University Press.

Foucault, Michel 1984. *The History of Sexuality: An Introduction*. Trans. Robert Hurley, Harmondsworth: Penguin.

Freud, Sigmund 1982. *Introductory Lectures on Psychoanalysis*. Trans. James Strachey. Harmondsworth: Penguin.

Gabbard, Krin and Glen O. Gabbard 1989. *Psychiatry and the Cinema*. Chicago: University of Chicago Press.

Hansen, Miriam 1994. *Babel and Babylon: Spectatorship in American Silent Film*. Cambridge, Mass.: Harvard University Press.

Lacan, Jacques 1973. *Écrits: A Selection*. Trans. Alan Sheridan. New York: Norton.

Metz, Christian 1975. "The Imaginary Signifier." Trans. Ben Brewster. *Screen* 16, no. 2: 14–76.

—— 1982. *The Imaginary Signifier: Psychoanalysis and the Cinema*. Trans. Celia Britton, Annwyl Williams, Ben Brewster, and Alfred Guzzetti. Bloomington: Indiana University Press.

Mulvey, Laura 1975. "Visual Pleasure and Narrative Cinema," *Screen* 16, no. 3: 6–18.

Pribram, E. Deidre (ed.) 1988. "Introduction." *Female Spectators: Looking at Film and Television*. London: Verso.

Saper, Craig 1991. "A Nervous Theory: The Troubling Gaze of Psychoanalysis in Media Studies," *Diacritics* 21, no. 4: 33–52.

Turner, Graeme 1988. *Film as Social Practice*. New York: Routledge.

Williams, Raymond 1989. *The Politics of Modernism: Against the New Conformists*. London: Verso.

26
Visual Pleasure and Narrative Cinema

Laura Mulvey

1 Introduction

1.1 A political use of psychoanalysis

This paper intends to use psychoanalysis to discover where and how the fascination of film is reinforced by preexisting patterns of fascination already at work within the individual subject and the social formations that have molded him. It takes as starting point the way film reflects, reveals, and even plays on the straight, socially established interpretation of sexual difference that controls images, erotic ways of looking, and spectacle. It is helpful to understand what the cinema has been, how its magic has worked in the past, while attempting a theory and a practice that will challenge this cinema of the past. Psychoanalytic theory is thus appropriated here as a political weapon, demonstrating the way the unconscious of patriarchal society has structured film form.

The paradox of phallocentrism in all its manifestations is that it depends on the image of the castrated woman to give order and meaning to its world. An idea of woman stands as linchpin to the system: it is her lack that produces the phallus as a symbolic presence, it is her desire to make good the lack that the phallus signifies. Recent writing in *Screen* about psychoanalysis and the cinema has not sufficiently brought out the importance of the representation of the female form in a symbolic order in which, in the last resort, it speaks castration and nothing else. To summarize briefly: the function of woman in forming the patriarchal unconscious is twofold: she first symbolizes the castration threat by her real absence of a penis and second thereby raises her child into the symbolic. Once this has been achieved, her meaning in the process is at an end, it does not last into the world of law and language except as a memory that oscillates between memory of maternal plenitude and memory of lack. Both are posited on nature (or on "anatomy" in Freud's famous phrase). Woman's desire is subjected to her image as bearer of the bleeding wound; she can exist only in relation to castration and cannot transcend it. She turns her child into the signifier of her own desire to possess a penis (the condition, she imagines, of entry into the symbolic). Either she must gracefully give way to the word, the Name of the Father and the Law, or else struggle to keep her child down with her in the half-light of the imaginary. Woman, then, stands in patriarchal culture as signifier for the male other, bound by a symbolic order in which man can live out his fantasies and obsessions through linguistic command, by imposing them on the silent image of woman still tied to her place as bearer of meaning, not maker of meaning.

There is an obvious interest in this analysis for feminists, a beauty in its exact rendering of the frustration experienced under the phallocentric order. It gets us nearer to the roots of our oppression, it brings an articulation of the problem closer, it faces us with the ultimate challenge: how to fight the unconscious/ structured like a language (formed critically at the moment of arrival of language) while still caught within the language of the patriarchy. There is no way in which we can produce an alternative out of the blue, but we can begin to make a break by examining patriarchy with the tools it provides, of which psychoanalysis is not the only but an important one. We are still separated by a great gap from important issues for the female unconscious that are scarcely relevant to phallo-centric theory: the sexing of the female infant and her relationship to the symbolic, the sexually mature woman as non-mother, maternity outside the signification of the phallus, the vagina. . . . But, at this point, psychoanalytic theory as it now stands can at least advance our understanding of the status quo, of the patriarchal order in which we are caught.

1.2   Destruction of pleasure as a radical weapon

As an advanced representation system, the cinema poses questions of the ways the unconscious (formed by the dominant order) structures ways of seeing and pleasure in looking. Cinema has changed over the last few decades. It is no longer the monolithic system based on large capital investment exemplified at its best by Hollywood in the 1930s, 1940s, and 1950s. Technological advances (16mm, etc.) have changed the economic conditions of cinematic production, which can now be artisanal as well as capitalist. Thus it has been possible for an alternative cinema to develop. However self-conscious and ironic Hollywood managed to be, it always restricted itself to a formal mise-en-scène reflecting the dominant ideological concept of the cinema. The alternative cinema provides a space for a cinema to be born that is radical in both a political and an aesthetic sense and challenges the basic assumptions of the mainstream film. This is not to reject the latter moralistically, but to highlight the ways in which its formal preoccupations reflect the psychical obsessions of the society that produced it, and, further, to stress that the alternative cinema must start specifically by reacting against these obsessions and assumptions. A politically and aesthetically avant-garde cinema is now possible, but it can still only exist as a counterpoint.

The magic of the Hollywood style at its best (and of all the cinema that fell within its sphere of influence) arose, not exclusively but in one important aspect, from its skilled and satisfying manipulation of visual pleasure. Unchallenged, mainstream film coded the erotic into the language of the dominant patriarchal order. In the highly developed Hollywood cinema it was only through these codes that the alienated subject, torn in his imaginary memory by a sense of loss, by the terror of potential lack in fantasy, came near to finding a glimpse of satisfaction: through its formal beauty and its play on his own formative obsessions. This essay will discuss the interweaving of that erotic pleasure in film, its meaning, and in particular the central place of the image of woman. It is said that analyzing pleasure, or beauty, destroys it. That is the intention of this article. The satisfaction and reinforcement of the ego that represent the high point of film history hitherto must be attacked. Not in favor of a reconstructed new pleasure, which cannot exist in the abstract, or of intellectualized unpleasure, but to make way for a total negation of the ease and plenitude of the narrative fiction film. The alternative is the thrill that comes from leaving the past behind without rejecting it, transcending outworn or oppressive forms, or daring to break with normal pleasurable expectations in order to conceive a new language of desire.

2   Pleasure in Looking: Fascination with the Human Form

(A) The cinema offers a number of possible pleasures. One is scopophilia. There are circumstances in which looking itself is a source of pleasure, just as, in the reverse formation, there is pleasure in being looked at. Originally, in his *Three Essays on Sexuality* (1905), Freud isolated scopophilia as one of the component instincts of sexuality that exist as drives quite independently of the erotogenic zones. At this point he associated scopophilia with taking other people as objects, subjecting them to a controlling and curious gaze. His particular examples center around the voyeuristic activities of children, their desire to see and make sure of the private and the forbidden (curiosity about other people's genital and bodily functions, about the presence or absence of the penis and, retrospectively, about the primal scene). In this analysis scopophilia is essentially active. (Later, in *Instincts and Their Vicissitudes*, 1915, Freud developed his theory of scopophilia further, attaching it initially to pregenital autoeroticism, after which the pleasure of the look is transferred to others by analogy. There is a close working here of the relationship between the active instinct and its further development in a narcissistic form.) Although the instinct is modified by other factors, in particular the constitution of the ego, it continues to exist as the erotic basis for pleasure in looking at another person as object. At the extreme, it can become fixated into a perversion, producing obsessive voyeurs and peeping toms, whose only sexual satisfaction can come from watching, in an active controlling sense, an objectified other.

At first glance, the cinema would seem to be remote from the undercover world of the surreptitious observation of an unknowing and unwilling victim. What is seen of the screen is so manifestly shown. But the mass of mainstream film, and the conventions within which it has consciously evolved, portray a hermetically sealed world that unwinds magically, indifferent to the presence of the audience, producing for them a sense of separation and playing on their voyeuristic fantasy. Moreover, the extreme contrast between the darkness in the auditorium (which also isolates the spectators from one another) and the brilliance of the shifting patterns of light and shade on the screen helps to promote the illusion of voyeuristic separation. Although the film is really being shown, is there to be seen, conditions of screening and narrative conventions give the spectator an illusion of looking in on a private world. Among other things, the position of the spectators in the cinema is blatantly one of repression of their exhibitionism and projection of the repressed desire onto the performer.

(B) The cinema satisfies a primordial wish for pleasurable looking, but it also goes further, developing scopophilia in its narcissistic aspect. The conventions of mainstream film focus attention on the human form. Scale, space, stories are all anthropomorphic. Here, curiosity and the wish to look intermingle with a fascination with likeness and recognition: the human face, the human body, the relationship between the human form and its surroundings, the visible presence of the person in the world. Jacques Lacan has described how the moment when a child recognizes its own image in the mirror is crucial for the constitution of the ego. Several aspects of this analysis are relevant here. The mirror phase occurs at a time when the child's physical ambitions outstrip his motor capacity, with the result that his recognition of himself is joyous in that he imagines his mirror image to be more complete, more perfect than he experiences his own body. Recognition is thus overlaid with misrecognition: the image recognized is conceived as the reflected body of the self, but its misrecognition as superior projects this body outside itself as an ideal ego, the alienated subject, which, reintrojected as an ego ideal, gives rise to the future generation of identification with others. This mirror moment predates language for the child.

Important for this essay is the fact that it is an image that constitutes the matrix of the imaginary, of recognition/misrecognition and identification, and hence of the first articulation of the *I*, of subjectivity. This is a moment when an older fascination with looking (at the mother's face, for an obvious example) collides with the initial inklings of self-awareness. Hence it is the birth of the long love affair/despair between image and self-image that has found such intensity of expression in film and such joyous recognition in the cinema audience. Quite apart from the extraneous similarities between screen and mirror (the framing of the human form in its surroundings, for instance), the cinema has structures of fascination strong enough to allow temporary loss of ego while simultaneously reinforcing the ego. The sense of forgetting the world as the ego has subsequently come to perceive it (I forgot who I am and where I was) is nostalgically reminiscent of that presubjective moment of image recognition. At the same time the cinema has distinguished itself in the production of ego ideals as expressed in particular in the star system, the stars centering both screen presence and screen story as they act out a complex process of likeness and difference (the glamorous impersonates the ordinary).

(C) Sections (A) and (B) have set out two contradictory aspects of the pleasurable structures of looking in the conventional cinematic situation. The first, scopophilic, arises from pleasure in using another person as an object of sexual stimulation through sight. The second, developed through narcissism and the constitution of the ego, comes from identification with the image seen. Thus, in film terms, one implies a separation of the erotic identity of the subject from the object on the screen (active scopophilia), the other demands identification of the ego with the object on the screen through the spectator's fascination with and recognition of his like. The first is a function of the sexual instincts, the second of ego libido. This dichotomy was crucial for Freud. Although he saw the two as interacting and overlaying each other, the tension between instinctual drives and self-preservation continues to be a dramatic polarization in terms of pleasure. Both are formative structures, mechanisms not meanings. In themselves they have no signification, they have to be attached to an idealization. Both pursue aims in indifference to perceptual reality, creating the imagized, eroticized concept of the world that forms the perception of the subject and makes a mockery of empirical objectivity.

During its history, the cinema seems to have evolved a particular illusion of reality in which this contradiction between libido and ego has found a beautifully complementary fantasy world. In *reality* the fantasy world of the screen is subject to the law that produces it. Sexual instincts and identification processes have a meaning within the symbolic order that articulates desire. Desire, born with language, allows the possibility of transcending the instinctual and the imaginary, but its point of reference continually returns to the traumatic moment of its birth: the castration complex. Hence the look, pleasurable in form, can be threatening in content, and it is woman as representation/image that crystallizes this paradox.

3 Woman as Image, Man as Bearer of the Look

(A) In a world ordered by sexual imbalance, pleasure in looking has been split between active/male and passive/female. The determining male gaze projects its fantasy onto the female figure, which is styled accordingly. In their traditional exhibitionist role women are simultaneously looked at and displayed, with their appearance coded for strong visual and erotic impact so that they can be said to connote *to-be-looked-at-ness*. Woman displayed as sexual object is the leitmotiv of erotic spectacle: from pin-ups to strip-tease, from Ziegfeld to Busby Berkeley, she holds the look, plays to, and signifies male desire. Mainstream film neatly combined spectacle and narrative. (Note, however, how in the musical song-and-dance numbers break the flow of the diegesis.) The presence of woman is an indispensable element of spectacle in normal narrative film, yet her visual presence tends to work against the development of a story line, to freeze the flow of action in moments of erotic contemplation. This alien presence then has to be integrated into cohesion with the narrative. As Budd Boetticher [cult director of Hollywood B Westerns] has put it:

> What counts is what the heroine provokes, or rather what she represents. She is the one, or rather the love or fear she inspires in the hero, or else the concern he feels for her, who makes him act the way he does. In herself the woman has not the slightest importance.

(A recent tendency in narrative film has been to dispense with this problem altogether; hence the development of what Molly Haskell has called the "buddy movie," in which the active homosexual eroticism of the central male figures can carry the story without distraction.) Traditionally, the woman displayed has functioned on two levels: as erotic object for the characters within the screen story, and as erotic object for the spectator within the auditorium, with a shifting tension between the looks on either side of the screen. For instance, the device of the showgirl allows the two looks to be unified technically without any apparent break in the diegesis. A woman performs within the narrative, the gaze of the spectator and that of the male characters in the film are neatly combined without breaking narrative verisimilitude. For a moment the sexual impact of the performing woman takes the film into a no-man's-land outside its own time and space. Thus Marilyn Monroe's first appearance in *River of No Return* (1954) and Lauren Bacall's songs in *To Have and Have Not* (1944). Similarly, conventional close-ups of legs (Dietrich, for instance) or a face (Garbo) integrate into the narrative a different mode of eroticism. One part of a fragmented body destroys the Renaissance space, the illusion of depth demanded by the narrative, it gives flatness, the quality of a cut-out or icon rather than verisimilitude to the screen.

(B) An active/passive heterosexual division of labor has similarly controlled narrative structure. According to the principles of the ruling ideology and the psychical structures that back it up, the male figure cannot bear the burden of sexual objectification. Man is reluctant to gaze at his exhibitionist like. Hence the split between spectacle and narrative supports the man's role as the active one of forwarding the story, making things happen. The man controls the film fantasy and also emerges as the representative of power in a further sense: as the bearer of the look of the spectator, transferring it behind the screen to neutralize the extradiegetic tendencies represented by woman as spectacle. This is made possible through the processes set in motion by structuring the film around a main controlling figure with whom the spectator can identify. As the spectator identifies with the main male[1] protagonist, he projects his look onto that of his like, his screen surrogate, so that the power of the male protagonist as he controls events coincides with the active power of the erotic look, both giving a satisfying sense of omnipotence. A male movie star's glamorous characteristics are thus not those of the erotic object of the gaze, but those of the more perfect, more complete, more powerful ideal ego conceived in the original moment of recognition in front of the mirror. The character in the story can make things happen and control events better than the subject/spectator, just as the image in the mirror was more in control of motor coordination. In contrast to woman as icon, the active male figure (the ego ideal of the identification process) demands a three-dimensional space corresponding to that of the mirror recognition in which the alienated subject internalized his own representation of this imaginary existence. He is a figure in a landscape. Here the function of film is to reproduce as accurately as possible the so-called natural conditions of human perception. Camera technology (as exemplified by deep focus in particular) and camera movements (determined by the action of the protagonist), combined with invisible editing (demanded by realism), all tend to blur the limits of screen space. The male protagonist is free to command the stage, a stage of spatial illusion in which he articulates the look and creates the action.

(C1) Sections (A) and (B) have set out a tension between a mode of representation of woman in film and conventions surrounding the diegesis. Each is associated with a look: that of the spectator in direct scopophilic contact with the female form displayed for his enjoyment (connoting male fantasy) and that of the spectator fascinated with the image of his like set in an illusion of natural space, and through him gaining control and possession of the woman within the diegesis. (This tension and the shift from one pole to the other can structure a single text. Thus both in *Only Angels Have Wings* (1939) and in *To Have and Have Not* the film opens with the woman as object of the combined gaze of spectator and all the male protagonists in the film. She is isolated, glamorous, on display, sexualized. But as the narrative progresses, she falls in love with the main male protagonist and becomes his property, losing her outward glamorous characteristics, her generalized sexuality, her showgirl connotations; her eroticism is subjected to the male star alone. By means of identification with him, through participation in his power, the spectator can indirectly possess her too.)

But in psychoanalytic terms, the female figure poses a deeper problem. She also connotes something that the look continually circles around but disavows: her lack of a penis, implying a threat of castration and hence unpleasure. Ultimately, the meaning of woman is sexual difference, the absence of the penis as visually ascertainable, the material evidence on which is based the castration complex essential for the organization of entrance to the symbolic order and the Law of the Father. Thus the woman as icon, displayed for the gaze and enjoyment of men, the active controllers of the look, always threatens to evoke the anxiety it originally signified. The male unconscious has two avenues of escape from this castration anxiety: preoccupation with the reenactment of the original trauma (investigating the woman, demystifying her mystery), counterbalanced by the devaluation, punishment, or saving of the guilty object (an avenue typified by the concerns of the *film noir*); or else complete disavowal of castration by the substitution of a fetish object or turning the represented figure itself into a fetish so that it becomes reassuring rather than dangerous (hence overvaluation, the cult of the female star). This second avenue, fetishistic scopophilia, builds up the physical beauty of the object, transforming it into something satisfying in itself. The first avenue, voyeurism, on the contrary, has associations with sadism: pleasure lies in ascertaining guilt (immediately associated with castration), asserting control, and subjecting the guilty person through punishment or forgiveness. This sadistic side fits in well with narrative. Sadism demands a story, depends on making something happen, forcing a change in another person, a battle of will and strength, victory/defeat, all occurring in a linear time with a beginning and an end. Fetishistic scopophilia, on the other hand, can exist outside linear time as the erotic instinct is focused on the look alone. These contradictions and ambiguities can be illustrated more simply by using works by Hitchcock and Sternberg, both of whom take the look almost as the content or subject matter of many of their films. Hitchcock is the more complex, as he uses both mechanisms. Sternberg's work, on the other hand, provides many pure examples of fetishistic scopophilia.

(C2) It is well known that Sternberg once said he would welcome his films being projected upside down so that story and character involvement would not interfere with the spectator's undiluted appreciation of the screen image. This statement is revealing but ingenuous. Ingenuous in that his films do demand that the figure of the woman (Dietrich, in the cycle of films with her, as the ultimate example) should be identifiable. But revealing in that it emphasizes the fact that for him the pictorial space enclosed by the frame is paramount rather than narrative or identification processes. Whereas Hitchcock goes into the investigative side of voyeurism, Sternberg produces the ultimate fetish, taking it to the point where the powerful look of the male protagonist (characteristic of traditional narrative film) is broken in favor of the image in direct erotic rapport with the spectator. The beauty of the woman as object and the screen space coalesce; she is no longer the bearer of guilt but a perfect product, whose body, stylized and fragmented by close-ups, is the content of the film and the direct recipient of the spectator's look. Sternberg plays down the illusion of screen depth; his screen tends to be one-dimensional, as light and shade, lace, steam, foliage, net, streamers, etc., reduce the visual field. There is little or no mediation of the look through the eyes of the main male protagonist. On the contrary, shadowy presences like La Bessière in *Morocco* (1930) act as surrogates for the director, detached as they are from audience identification. Despite Sternberg's insistence that his stories are irrelevant, it is significant that they are concerned with situation, not suspense, and cyclical rather than linear time, while plot complications revolve around misunderstanding rather than conflict. The most important absence is that of the controlling male gaze within the screen scene. The high point of emotional drama in the most typical Dietrich films, her supreme moments of erotic meaning, take place in the absence of the man she loves in the fiction. There are other witnesses, other spectators, watching her on the screen, their gaze is one with, not standing in for, that of the audience. At the end of *Morocco*, Tom Brown has already disappeared into the desert when Amy Jolly kicks off her gold sandals and walks after him. At the end of *Dishonored* (1931), Kranau is indifferent to the fate of Magda. In both cases, the erotic impact, sanctified by death, is displayed as a spectacle for the audience. The male hero misunderstands and, above all, does not see.

In Hitchcock, by contrast, the male hero does see precisely what the audience sees. However, in the films I shall discuss here, he takes fascination with an image through scopophilic eroticism as the subject of the film. Moreover, in these cases the hero portrays the contradictions and tensions experienced by the spectator. In *Vertigo* (1958) in particular, but also in *Marnie* (1964) and *Rear Window* (1954), the look is central to the plot, oscillating between voyeurism and fetishistic fascination. As a twist, a further manipulation of the normal viewing process, which in some sense reveals it, Hitchcock uses the process of identification normally associated with ideological correctness and the recognition of established morality and shows up its perverted side. Hitchcock has never concealed his interest in voyeurism, cinematic and non-cinematic. His heroes are exemplary of the symbolic order and the law – a policeman (*Vertigo*), a dominant male possessing money and power (*Marnie*) – but their erotic drives lead them into compromised situations. The power to subject another person to the will sadistically or to the gaze voyeuristically is turned onto the woman as the object of both. Power is backed by a certainty of legal right and the established guilt of the woman (evoking castration, psychoanalytically speaking). True perversion is barely concealed under a shallow mask of ideological correctness – the man is on the right side of the law, the woman on the wrong. Hitchcock's skillful use of identification processes and liberal use of subjective camera from the point of view of the male protagonist draw the spectators deeply into his position, making them share his uneasy gaze. The audience is absorbed into a voyeuristic situation within the screen scene and diegesis that parodies his own in the cinema.

In his analysis of *Rear Window*[2] Douchet takes the film as a metaphor for the cinema. Jeffries is the audience, the events in the apartment block opposite correspond to the screen. As he watches, an erotic dimension is added to his look, a central image to the drama. His girlfriend Lisa had been of little sexual interest to him, more or less a drag, so long as she remained on the spectator side. When she crosses the barrier between his room and the block opposite, their relationship is reborn erotically. He does not merely watch her through his lens, as a distant meaningful image, he also sees her as a guilty intruder exposed by a dangerous man threatening her with punishment, and thus finally saves her. Lisa's exhibitionism has already been established by her obsessive interest in dress and style, in being a passive image of visual perfection; Jeffries's voyeurism and activity have also been established through his work as a photojournalist, a maker of stories and captor of images. However, his enforced inactivity, binding him to his seat as a spectator, puts him squarely in the fantasy position of the cinema audience.

In *Vertigo*, subjective camera predominates. Apart from one flashback from Judy's point of view, the narrative is woven around what Scottie sees or fails to see. The audience follows the growth of his erotic obsession and subsequent despair precisely from his point of view. Scottie's voyeurism is blatant: he falls in love with a woman he follows and spies on without speaking to. Its sadistic side is equally blatant: he has chosen (and freely chosen, for he had been a successful lawyer) to be a policeman, with all the attendant possibilities of pursuit and investigation. As a result, he follows, watches, and falls in love with a perfect image of female beauty and mystery. Once he actually confronts her, his erotic drive is to break her down and force her to tell by persistent cross-questioning. Then, in the second part of the film, he reenacts his obsessive involvement with the image he loved to watch secretly. He reconstructs Judy as Madeleine, forces her to conform in every detail to the actual physical appearance of his fetish. Her exhibitionism, her masochism, make her an ideal passive counterpart to Scottie's active sadistic voyeurism. She knows her part is to perform, and only by playing it through and then replaying it can she keep Scottie's erotic interest. But in the repetition he does break her down and succeeds in exposing her guilt. His curiosity wins through and she is punished. In *Vertigo*, erotic involvement with the look is disorienting; the spectator's fascination is turned against him as the narrative carries him through and entwines him with the processes that he is himself exercising.

The Hitchcock hero here is firmly placed within the symbolic order, in narrative terms. He has all the attributes of the patriarchal superego. Hence the spectator, lulled into a false sense of security by the apparent legality of his surrogate, sees through his look and finds himself exposed as complicit, caught in the moral ambiguity of looking. Far from being simply an aside on the perversion of the police, *Vertigo* focuses on the implications of the active/looking, passive/looked-at split in terms of sexual difference and the power of the male symbolic encapsulated in the hero. Marnie, too, performs for Mark Rutland's gaze and masquerades as the perfect to-be-looked-at image. He, too, is on the side of the law until, drawn in by obsession with her guilt, her secret, he longs to see her in the act of committing a crime, make her confess and thus save her. So he, too, becomes complicit as he acts out the implications of his power. He controls money and words, he can have his cake and eat it.

4   Summary

The psychoanalytic background that has been discussed in this essay is relevant to the pleasure and unpleasure offered by traditional narrative film. The scopophilic instinct (pleasure in looking at another person as an erotic object) and, in contradistinction, ego libido (forming identification processes) act as formations, mechanisms, which this cinema has played on. The image of woman as (passive) raw material for the (active) gaze of man takes the argument a step further into the structure of representation, adding a further layer demanded by the ideology of the patriarchal order as it is worked out in its favorite cinematic form – illusionistic narrative film. The argument returns again to the psychoanalytic background in that woman as representation signifies castration, inducing voyeuristic or fetishistic mechanisms to circumvent her threat. None of these interacting layers is intrinsic to film, but it is only in the film form that they can reach a perfect and beautiful contradiction, thanks to the possibility in the cinema of shifting the emphasis of the look. It is the place of the look that defines cinema, the possibility of varying it and exposing it. This is what makes cinema quite different in its voyeuristic potential from, say, strip-tease, theater, shows, etc. Going far beyond highlighting a woman's to-be-looked-at-ness, cinema builds the way she is to be looked at into the spectacle itself. Playing on the tension between film as controlling the dimension of time (editing, narrative) and film as controlling the dimension of space (changes in distance, editing), cinematic codes create a gaze, a world, and an object, thereby producing an illusion cut to the measure of desire. It is these cinematic codes and their relationship to formative external structures that must be broken down before mainstream film and the pleasure it provides can be challenged.

To begin with (as an ending), the voyeuristic–scopophilic look that is a crucial part of traditional filmic pleasure can itself be broken down. There are three different looks associated with cinema: that of the camera as it records the pro-filmic event, that of the audience as it watches the final product, and that of the characters looking at each other within the screen illusion. The conventions of narrative film deny the first two and subordinate them to the third, the conscious aim being always to eliminate intrusive camera presence and prevent a distancing awareness in the audience. Without these two absences (the material existence of the recording process, the critical reading of the spectator), fictional drama cannot achieve reality, obviousness, and truth. Nevertheless, as this essay has argued, the structure of looking in narrative fiction film contains a contradiction in its own premises: the female image as a castration threat constantly endangers the unity of the diegesis and bursts through the world of illusion as an intrusive, static, one-dimensional fetish. Thus the two looks materially present in time and space are obsessively subordinated to the neurotic needs of the male ego. The camera becomes the mechanism for producing an illusion of Renaissance space, flowing movements compatible with the human eye, an ideology of representation that revolves around the perception of the subject; the camera's look is disavowed in order to create a convincing world in which the spectator's surrogate can perform with verisimilitude. Simultaneously, the look of the audience is denied an intrinsic force: as soon as fetishistic representation of the female image threatens to break the spell of illusion, and the erotic image on the screen appears directly (without mediation) to the spectator, the fact of fetishization, concealing as it does castration fear, freezes the look, fixates the spectator, and prevents him from achieving any distance from the image in front of him.

This complex interaction of looks is specific to film. The first blow against the monolithic accumulation of traditional film conventions (already undertaken by radical filmmakers) is to free the look of the camera into its materiality in time and space and the look of the audience into dialectics, passionate detachment. There is no doubt that this destroys the satisfaction, pleasure, and privilege of the "invisible guest," and highlights how film has depended on voyeuristic active/passive mechanisms. Women, whose image has continually been stolen and used for this end, cannot view the decline of the traditional film form with anything much more than sentimental regret.

Notes

This essay is a reworked version of a paper given in the French Department of the University of Wisconsin, Madison, spring 1973.

1   There are films with a woman as main protaganist, of course. To analyze this phenomenon seriously here would take me too far afield. Pam Cook and Claire Johnston's study of *The Revolt of Mamie Stover* in Phil Hardy, ed., *Raoul Walsh* (London: Vineyard Press, 1974), shows in a striking case how the strength of this female protagonist is more apparent then real.

2   Jean Douchet, "Hitch et son public," *Cahiers du Cinéma*, 113 (November 1960), pp. 7–15.

27
Film and the Masquerade: Theorizing the Female Spectator

Mary Ann Doane

Heads in Hieroglyphic Bonnets

In his lecture on "Femininity," Freud forcefully inscribes the absence of the female spectator of theory in his notorious statement, "to those of you who are women this will not apply – you are yourselves the problem."[1] Simultaneous with this exclusion operated upon the female members of his audience, he invokes, as a rather strange prop, a poem by Heine. Introduced by Freud's claim concerning the importance and elusiveness of his topic – "Throughout history people have knocked their heads against the riddle of the nature of femininity" – are four lines of Heine's poem:

> Heads in hieroglyphic bonnets,
> Heads in turbans and black birettas,
> Heads in wigs and thousand other
> Wretched, sweating heads of humans[2]

The effects of the appeal to this poem are subject to the work of overdetermination Freud isolated in the text of the dream. The sheer proliferation of heads and hats (and hence, through a metonymic slippage, minds), which are presumed to have confronted this intimidating riddle before Freud, confers on his discourse the weight of an intellectual history, of a tradition of interrogation. Furthermore, the image of hieroglyphics strengthens the association made between femininity and the enigmatic, the undecipherable, that which is "other." And yet Freud practices a slight deception here, concealing what is elided by removing the lines from their context, castrating, as it were, the stanza. For the question over which Heine's heads brood is not the same as Freud's – it is not "What is Woman?", but instead, "what signifies Man?" The quote is taken from the seventh section (entitled "Questions") of the second cycle of *The North Sea*. The full stanza, presented as the words of "a young man,/His breast full of sorrow, his head full of doubt," reads as follows:

O solve me the riddle of life,
The teasingly time-old riddle,
Over which many heads already have brooded,
Heads in hats of hieroglyphics,
Turbaned heads and heads in black skull-caps,
Heads in perrukes and a thousand other
Poor, perspiring human heads –
Tell me, what signifies Man?
Whence does he come? Whither does he go?
Who lives up there upon golden stars?[3]

The question in Freud's text is thus a disguise and a displacement of that other question, which in the pre-text is both humanistic and theological. The claim to investigate an otherness is a pretense, haunted by the mirror-effect by means of which the question of the woman reflects only the man's own ontological doubts. Yet what interests me most in this intertextual misrepresentation is that the riddle of femininity is initiated from the beginning in Freud's text as a question in masquerade. But I will return to the issue of masquerade later.

More pertinently, as far as the cinema is concerned, it is not accidental that Freud's eviction of the female spectator/auditor is copresent with the invocation of a hieroglyphic language. The woman, the enigma, the hieroglyphic, the picture, the image – the metonymic chain connects with another: the cinema, the theater of pictures, a writing in images of the woman but not *for* her. For she is the problem. The semantic valence attributed to a hieroglyphic language is two-edged. In fact, there is a sense in which the term is inhabited by a contradiction. On the one hand, the hieroglyphic is summoned, particularly when it merges with a discourse on the woman, to connote an indecipherable language, a signifying system which denies its own function by failing to signify anything to the uninitiated, to those who do not hold the key. In this sense, the hieroglyphic, like the woman, harbors a mystery, an inaccessible though desirable otherness. On the other hand, the hieroglyphic is the most readable of languages. Its immediacy, its accessibility are functions of its status as a *pictorial* language, a writing in images. For the image is theorized in terms of a certain *closeness*, the lack of a distance or gap between sign and referent. Given its iconic characteristics, the relationship between signifier and signified is understood as less arbitrary in imagistic systems of representation than in language "proper." The intimacy of signifier and signified in the iconic sign negates the distance which defines phonetic language. And it is the absence of this crucial distance or gap which also, simultaneously, specifies both the hieroglyphic and the female. This is precisely why Freud evicted the woman from his lecture on femininity. Too close to herself, entangled in her own enigma, she could not step back, could not achieve the necessary distance of a second look.[4]

Thus, while the hieroglyphic is an indecipherable or at least enigmatic language, it is also and at the same time potentially the most universally understandable, comprehensible, appropriable of signs.[5] And the woman shares this contradictory status. But it is here that the analogy slips. For hieroglyphic languages are *not* perfectly iconic. They would not achieve the status of languages if they were – due to what Todorov and Ducrot refer to as a certain non-generalizability of the iconic sign:

> Now it is the impossibility of generalizing this principle of representation that has introduced even into fundamentally morphemographic writing systems such as Chinese, Egyptian, and Sumerian, the phonographic principle. We might almost conclude that every logography [the graphic system of language notation] grows out of the *impossibility of a generalized iconic representation*; proper nouns and abstract notions (including inflections) are then the ones that will be noted phonetically.[6]

The iconic system of representation is inherently deficient – it cannot disengage itself from the "real," from the concrete; it lacks the gap necessary for generalizability (for Saussure, this is the idea that "Signs which are arbitrary realize better than others the ideal of the semiotic process"). The woman, too, is defined by such an insufficiency. My insistence upon the congruence between certain theories of the image and theories of femininity is an attempt to dissect the *episteme* which assigns to the woman a special place in cinematic representation while denying her access to that system.

The cinematic apparatus inherits a theory of the image which is not conceived outside of sexual specifications. And historically, there has always been a certain imbrication of the cinematic image and the representation of the woman. The woman's relation to the camera and the scopic regime is quite different from that of the male. As Noël Burch points out, the early silent cinema, through its insistent inscription of scenarios of voyeurism, conceives of its spectator's viewing pleasure in terms of that of the Peeping Tom, behind the screen, reduplicating the spectator's position in relation to the woman as screen.[7] Spectatorial desire, in contemporary film theory, is generally delineated as either voyeurism or fetishism, as precisely a pleasure in seeing what is prohibited in relation to the female body. The image orchestrates a gaze, a limit, and its pleasurable transgression. The woman's beauty, her very desirability, becomes a function of certain practices of imaging – framing, lighting, camera movement, angle. She is thus, as Laura Mulvey has pointed out, more closely associated with the surface of the image than its illusory depths, its constructed three-dimensional space which the man is destined to inhabit and hence control.[8] In *Now Voyager*, for instance, a single image signals the momentous transformation of the Bette Davis character from ugly spinster aunt to glamorous single woman. Charles Affron describes the specifically cinematic aspect of this operation as a "stroke of genius":

> The radical shadow bisecting the face in white/dark/white strata creates a visual phenomenon quite distinct from the makeup transformation of lipstick and plucked eyebrows.... This shot does not reveal what we commonly call acting, especially after the most recent exhibition of that activity, but the sense of face belongs to a

plastique pertinent to the camera. The viewer is allowed a different perceptual referent, a chance to come down from the nerve-jarring, first sequence and to use his eyes anew.[9]

A "plastique pertinent to the camera" constitutes the woman not only as the image of desire but as the desirous image – one which the devoted cinéphile can cherish and embrace. To "have" the cinema is, in some sense, to "have" the woman. But *Now Voyager* is, in Affron's terms, a "tear-jerker," in others, a "woman's picture," i.e. a film purportedly produced for a female audience. What, then, of the female spectator? What can one say about her desire in relation to this process of imaging? It would seem that what the cinematic institution has in common with Freud's gesture is the eviction of the female spectator from a discourse purportedly about her (the cinema, psychoanalysis) – one which, in fact, narrativizes her again and again.

A Lass but Not a Lack

Theories of female spectatorship are thus rare, and when they are produced, seem inevitably to confront certain blockages in conceptualization. The difficulties in thinking female spectatorship demand consideration. After all, even if it is admitted that the woman is frequently the object of the voyeuristic or fetishistic gaze in the cinema, what is there to prevent her from reversing the relation and appropriating the gaze for her own pleasure? Precisely the fact that the reversal itself remains locked within the same logic. The male strip-tease, the gigolo – both inevitably signify the mechanism of reversal itself, constituting themselves as aberrations whose acknowledgment simply reinforces the dominant system of aligning sexual difference with a subject/object dichotomy. And an essential attribute of that dominant system is the matching of male subjectivity with the agency of the look.

The supportive binary opposition at work here is not only that utilized by Laura Mulvey – an opposition between passivity and activity, but perhaps more importantly, an opposition between proximity and distance in relation to the image.[10] It is in this sense that the very logic behind the structure of the gaze demands a sexual division. While the distance between image and signified (or even referent) is theorized as minimal, if not non-existent, that between the film and the spectator must be maintained, even measured. One need only think of Noël Burch's mapping of spectatorship as a perfect distance from the screen (two times the width of the image) – a point in space from which the filmic discourse is most accessible.[11]

But the most explicit representation of this opposition between proximity and distance is contained in Christian Metz's analysis of voyeuristic desire in terms of a kind of social hierarchy of the senses: "It is no accident that the main socially acceptable arts are based on the senses at a distance, and that those which depend on the senses of contact are often regarded as 'minor' arts (= culinary arts, art of perfumes, etc.)."[12] The voyeur, according to Metz, must maintain a distance between himself and the image – the cinéphile *needs* the gap which represents for him the very distance between desire and its object. In this sense, voyeurism is theorized as a type of meta-desire:

> If it is true of all desire that it depends on the infinite pursuit of its absent object, voyeuristic desire, along with certain forms of sadism, is the only desire whose principle of distance symbolically and spatially evokes this fundamental rent.[13]

Yet even this status as meta-desire does not fully characterize the cinema, for it is a feature shared by other arts as well (painting, theater, opera, etc.). Metz thus adds another reinscription of this necessary distance. What specifies the cinema is a further re-duplication of the lack which prompts desire. The cinema is characterized by an illusory sensory plenitude (there is "so much to see") and yet haunted by the absence of those very objects which are there to be seen. Absence is an absolute and irrecoverable distance. In other words, Noël Burch is quite right in aligning spectatorial desire with a certain spatial configuration. The viewer must not sit either too close or too far from the screen. The result of both would be the same – he would lose the image of his desire.

It is precisely this opposition between proximity and distance, control of the image and its loss, which locates the possibilities of spectatorship within the problematic of sexual difference. For the female spectator there is a certain over-presence of the image – she *is* the image. Given the closeness of this relationship, the female spectator's desire can be described only in terms of a kind of narcissism – the female look demands a becoming. It thus appears to negate the very distance or gap specified by Metz and Burch as the essential precondition for voyeurism. From this perspective, it is important to note the constant recurrence of the motif of proximity in feminist theories (especially those labeled "new French feminisms") which purport to describe a feminine specificity. For Luce Irigaray, female anatomy is readable as a constant relation of the self to itself, as an autoeroticism based on the embrace of the two lips which allow the woman to touch herself without mediation. Furthermore, the very notion of property, and hence possession of something which can be constituted as other, is antithetical to the woman: "*Nearness* however, is not foreign to woman, a nearness so close that any identification of one or the other, and therefore any form of property, is impossible. Woman enjoys a closeness with the other that is *so near she cannot possess it any more than she can possess herself.*"[14] Or, in the case of female madness or delirium, "women do not manage to articulate their madness: they suffer it directly in their body."[15] The distance necessary to detach the signifiers of madness from the body in the construction of even a discourse which exceeds the boundaries of sense is lacking. In the words of Hélène Cixous, "More so than men who are coaxed toward social success, toward sublimation, women are body."[16]

This theme of the overwhelming presence-to-itself of the female body is elaborated by Sarah Kofman and Michèle Montrelay as well. Kofman describes how Freudian psychoanalysis outlines a scenario whereby the subject's passage from the mother to the father is simultaneous with a passage from the senses to reason, nostalgia for the mother henceforth signifying a longing for a different positioning in relation to the sensory or the somatic, and the degree of civilization measured by the very distance from the body.[17] Similarly, Montrelay argues that while the male has the possibility of displacing the first object of desire (the mother), the female must become that object of desire:

> Recovering herself as maternal body (and also as phallus), the woman can no longer repress, "lose," the first stake of representation.... From now on, anxiety, tied to the presence of this body, can only be insistent, continuous. This body, so close, which she has to occupy, is an object in excess which must be "lost," that is to say, repressed, in order to be symbolized.[18]

This body so close, so excessive, prevents the woman from assuming a position similar to the man's in relation to signifying systems. For she is haunted by the loss of a loss, the lack of that lack so essential for the realization of the ideals of semiotic systems.

Female specificity is thus theorized in terms of spatial proximity. In opposition to this "closeness" to the body, a spatial distance in the male's relation to his body rapidly becomes a temporal distance in the service of knowledge. This is presented quite explicitly in Freud's analysis of the construction of the "subject supposed to know." The knowledge involved here is a knowledge of sexual difference as it is organized in relation to the structure of the look, turning on the visibility of the penis. For the little girl in Freud's description seeing and knowing are simultaneous – there is no temporal gap between them. In "Some Psychological Consequences of the Anatomical Distinction Between the Sexes," Freud claims that the girl, upon seeing the penis for the first time, "makes her judgement and her decision in a flash. She has seen it and knows that she is without it and wants to have it."[19] In the lecture on "Femininity" Freud repeats this gesture, merging perception and intellection: "They [girls] at once notice the difference and, it must be admitted, its significance too."[20]

The little boy, on the other hand, does not share this immediacy of understanding. When he first sees the woman's genitals he "begins by showing irresolution and lack of interest; he sees nothing or disowns what he has seen, he softens it down or looks about for expedients for bringing it into line with his expectations."[21] A second event, the threat of castration, is necessary to prompt a rereading of the image, endowing it with a meaning in relation to the boy's own subjectivity. It is in the distance between the look and the threat that the boy's relation to knowledge of sexual difference is formulated. The boy, unlike the girl in Freud's description, is capable of a re-vision of earlier events, a retrospective understanding which invests the events with a significance which is in no way linked to an immediacy of sight. This gap between the visible and the knowable, the very possibility of disowning what is seen, prepares the ground for fetishism. In a sense, the male spectator is destined to be a fetishist, balancing knowledge and belief.

The female, on the other hand, must find it extremely difficult, if not impossible, to assume the position of fetishist. That body which is so close continually reminds her of the castration which cannot be "fetishized away." The lack of a distance between seeing and understanding, the mode of judging "in a flash," is conducive to what might be termed as "over-identification" with the image. The association of tears and "wet wasted afternoons" (in Molly Haskell's words)[22] with genres specified as feminine (the soap opera, the "woman's picture") points very precisely to this type of over-identification, this abolition of a distance, in short, this inability to fetishize. The woman is constructed differently in relation to processes of looking. For Irigaray, this dichotomy between distance and proximity is described as the fact that:

> The masculine can partly look at itself, speculate about itself, represent itself and describe itself for what it is, whilst the feminine can try to speak to itself through a new language, but cannot describe itself from outside or in formal terms, except by identifying itself with the masculine, thus by losing itself.[23]

Irigaray goes even further: the woman always has a problematic relation to the visible, to form, to structures of seeing. She is much more comfortable with, closer to, the sense of touch.

The pervasiveness, in theories of the feminine, of descriptions of such a claustrophobic closeness, a deficiency in relation to structures of seeing and the visible, must clearly have consequences for attempts to theorize female spectatorship. And, in fact, the result is a tendency to view the female spectator as the site of an oscillation between a feminine position and a masculine position, invoking the metaphor of the transvestite. Given the structures of cinematic narrative, the woman who identifies with a female character must adopt a passive or masochistic position, while identification with the active hero necessarily entails an acceptance of what Laura Mulvey refers to as a certain "masculinization" of spectatorship.

> As desire is given cultural materiality in a text, for women (from childhood onwards) trans-sex identification is a *habit* that very easily becomes *second Nature*. However, this Nature does not sit easily and shifts restlessly in its borrowed transvestite clothes.[24]

The transvestite wears clothes which signify a different sexuality, a sexuality which, for the woman, allows a mastery over the image and the very possibility of attaching the gaze to desire. Clothes make the man, as they say. Perhaps this explains the ease with which women can slip into male clothing. As both Freud and Cixous point out, the woman seems to be *more* bisexual than the man. A scene from Cukor's *Adam's Rib* graphically demonstrates this ease of female transvestism. As Katherine Hepburn asks the jury to imagine the sex role reversal of the three major characters involved in the case, there are three dissolves linking each of the characters successively to shots in which they are dressed in the clothes of the opposite sex. What characterizes the sequence is the marked facility of the transformation of the two women into men in contradistinction to a certain resistance in the case of the man. The acceptability of the female reversal is quite distinctly opposed to the male reversal which seems capable of representation only in terms of farce. Male transvestism is an occasion for laughter; female transvestism only another occasion for desire.

Thus, while the male is locked into sexual identity; the female can at least pretend that she is other – in fact, sexual mobility would seem to be a distinguishing feature of femininity in its cultural construction. Hence, transvestism would be fully recuperable. The idea seems to be this: it is understandable that women would want to be men, for everyone wants to be elsewhere than in the feminine position. What is not understandable within the given terms is why a woman might flaunt her femininity, produce herself as an excess of femininity, in other words, foreground the masquerade. Masquerade is not as recuperable as transvestism precisely because it constitutes an acknowledgment that it is femininity itself which is constructed as mask – as the decorative layer which conceals a non-identity. For Joan Riviere, the first to theorize the concept, the masquerade of femininity is a kind of reaction-formation against the woman's trans-sex identification, her transvestism. After assuming the position of the subject of discourse rather than its object, the intellectual woman whom Riviere analyzes felt compelled to compensate for this theft of masculinity by over-doing the gestures of feminine flirtation.

> Womanliness therefore could be assumed and worn as a mask, both to hide the possession of masculinity and to avert the reprisals expected if she was found to possess it – much as a thief will turn out his pockets and ask to be searched to prove that he has not the stolen goods. The reader may now ask how I define womanliness or where I draw the line between genuine womanliness and the masquerade. My suggestion is not, however, that there is any such difference; whether radical or superficial, they are the same thing.[25]

The masquerade, in flaunting femininity, holds it at a distance. Womanliness is a mask which can be worn or removed. The masquerade's resistance to patriarchal positioning would therefore lie in its denial of the production of femininity as closeness, as presence-to-itself, as, precisely, imagistic. The transvestite adopts the sexuality of the other – the woman becomes a man in order to attain the necessary distance from the image. Masquerade, on the other hand, involves a realignment of femininity, the recovery, or more accurately, simulation, of the missing gap or distance. To masquerade is to manufacture a lack in the form of a certain distance between oneself and one's image. If, as Moustafa Safouan points out, "to wish to include in oneself as an object the cause of the desire of the Other is a formula for the structure of hysteria,"[26] then masquerade is anti-hysterical for it works to effect a separation between the cause of desire and oneself. In Montrelay's words, "the woman uses her own body as a disguise."[27]

The very fact that we can speak of a woman "using" her sex or "using" her body for particular gains is highly significant – it is not that a man cannot use his body in this way but that he doesn't have to. The masquerade doubles representation; it is constituted by a hyperbolization of the accoutrements of femininity. Apropos of a recent performance by Marlene Dietrich, Sylvia Bovenschen claims, "we are watching a woman demonstrate the representation of a woman's body."[28] This type of masquerade, an excess of femininity, is aligned with the *femme fatale* and, as Montrelay explains, is necessarily regarded by men as evil incarnate: "It is this evil which scandalizes whenever woman plays out her sex in order to evade the word and the law. Each time she subverts a law or a word which relies on the predominantly masculine structure of the look."[29] By destabilizing the image, the masquerade confounds this masculine structure of the look. It effects a defamiliarization of female iconography. Nevertheless, the preceding account simply specifies masquerade as a type of representation which carries a threat, disarticulating male systems of viewing. Yet, it specifies nothing with respect to female spectatorship. What might it mean to masquerade as spectator? To assume the mask in order to see in a different way?

"Men Seldom Make Passes at Girls Who Wear Glasses"

The first scene in *Now Voyager* depicts the Bette Davis character as repressed, unattractive, and undesirable or, in her own words, as the spinster aunt of the family. ("Every family has one.") She has heavy eyebrows, keeps her hair bound tightly in a bun, and wears glasses, a drab dress, and heavy shoes. By the time of the shot discussed earlier, signaling her transformation into beauty, the glasses have disappeared, along with the other signifiers of unattractiveness. Between these two moments there is a scene in which the doctor who cures her actually confiscates her glasses (as a part of the cure). The woman who wears glasses constitutes one of the most intense visual clichés of the cinema. The image is a heavily marked condensation of motifs concerned with repressed sexuality, knowledge, visibility and vision, intellectuality, and desire. The woman with glasses signifies simultaneously intellectuality and undesirability; but the moment she removes her glasses (a moment which, it seems, must almost always be *shown* and which is itself linked with a certain sensual quality), she is transformed into spectacle, the very picture of desire. Now, it must be remembered that the cliché is a heavily loaded moment of signification, a social knot of meaning. It is characterized by an effect of ease and naturalness. Yet, the cliché has a binding power so strong that it indicates a precise moment of ideological danger or threat – in this case, the woman's appropriation of the gaze. Glasses worn by a woman in the cinema do not generally signify a deficiency in seeing but an active looking, or even simply the fact of seeing as opposed to being seen. The intellectual woman looks and analyzes, and in usurping the gaze she poses a threat to an entire system of representation. It is as if the woman had forcefully moved to the other side of the specular. The overdetermination of the image of the woman with glasses, its status as a cliché, is a crucial aspect of the cinematic alignment of structures of seeing and being seen with sexual difference. The cliché, in assuming an immediacy of understanding, acts as a mechanism for the naturalization of sexual difference.

But the figure of the woman with glasses is only an extreme moment of a more generalized logic. There is always a certain excessiveness, a difficulty associated with women who appropriate the gaze, who insist upon looking. Linda Williams has demonstrated how, in the genre of the horror film, the woman's active looking is ultimately punished. And what she sees, the monster, is only a mirror of herself – both woman and monster are freakish in their difference – defined by either "too much" or "too little."[30] Just as the dominant narrative cinema repetitively inscribes scenarios of voyeurism, internalizing or narrativizing the film–spectator relationship (in films like *Psycho*, *Rear Window*, *Peeping Tom*), taboos in seeing are insistently formulated in relation to the female spectator as well. The man with binoculars is countered by the woman with glasses. The gaze must be dissociated from mastery. In *Leave Her to Heaven* (John Stahl, 1945), the female protagonist's (Gene Tierney's) excessive desire and over-possessiveness are signaled from the very beginning of the film by her intense and sustained stare at the major male character, a stranger she first encounters on a train. The discomfort her look causes is graphically depicted. The Gene Tierney character is ultimately revealed to be the epitome of evil – killing her husband's crippled younger brother, her unborn child, and ultimately herself in an attempt to brand her cousin as a murderess in order to insure her husband's future fidelity. In *Humoresque* (Jean Negulesco, 1946), Joan Crawford's problematic status is a result of her continual attempts to assume the position of spectator – fixing John Garfield with her gaze. Her transformation from spectator to spectacle is signified repetitively by the gesture of removing her glasses. Rosa, the character played by Bette Davis in *Beyond the Forest* (King Vidor, 1949), walks to the station every day simply to *watch* the train departing for Chicago. Her fascination with the train is a fascination with its phallic power to transport her to "another place." This character is also specified as having a "good eye" – she can shoot, both pool and guns. In all three films the woman is constructed as the site of an excessive and dangerous desire. This desire mobilizes extreme efforts of containment and unveils the sadistic aspect of narrative. In all three films the woman dies. As Claire Johnston points out, death is the "location of all impossible signs,"[31] and the films demonstrate that the woman as subject of the gaze is clearly an impossible sign. There is a perverse rewriting of this logic of the gaze in *Dark Victory* (Edmund Goulding, 1939), where the woman's story achieves heroic and tragic proportions not only in blindness, but in a blindness which mimes sight – when the woman pretends to be able to see.

Out of the Cinema and into the Streets: The Censorship of the Female Gaze

This process of narrativizing the negation of the female gaze in the classical Hollywood cinema finds its perfect encapsulation in a still photograph taken in 1948 by Robert Doisneau, "*Un Regard oblique*." Just as the Hollywood narratives discussed above purport to center a female protagonist, the photograph appears to give a certain prominence to a woman's look. Yet, both the title of the photograph and its organization of space indicate that the real site of scopophilic power is on the margins of the frame. The man is not centered; in fact, he occupies a very narrow space on the extreme right of the picture. Nevertheless, it is his gaze which defines the problematic of the photograph; it is his gaze which effectively erases that of the woman. Indeed, as subject of the gaze, the woman looks intently. But not only is the object of her look concealed from the spectator, her gaze is encased by the two poles defining the masculine axis of vision. Fascinated by nothing visible – a blankness or void for the spectator – unanchored by a "sight" (there is nothing "proper" to her vision – save, perhaps, the mirror), the female gaze is left free-floating, vulnerable to subjection. The faint reflection in the shop window of only the frame of the picture at which she is looking serves merely to rearticulate, *en abŷme*, the emptiness of her gaze, the absence of her desire in representation.

On the other hand, the object of the male gaze is fully present, *there* for the spectator. The fetishistic representation of the nude female body, fully in view, insures a masculinization of the spectatorial position. The woman's look is literally outside the triangle which traces a complicity between the man, the nude, and the spectator. The feminine presence in the photograph, despite a diegetic centering of the female subject of the gaze, is taken over by the picture as object. And, as if to doubly "frame" her in the act of looking, the painting situates its female figure as a spectator (although it is not clear whether she is looking at herself in a mirror or peering through a door or window). While this drama of seeing is played out at the surface of the photograph, its deep space is activated by several young boys, out-of-focus, in front of a belt shop. The opposition out-of-focus/in-focus reinforces the supposed clarity accorded to the representation of the woman's "non-vision." Furthermore, since this out-of-focus area constitutes the precise literal center of the image, it also demonstrates how the photograph makes figurative the operation of centering – draining the actual center point of significance in order to deposit meaning on the margins. The male gaze is centered, in control – although it is exercised from the periphery.

The spectator's pleasure is thus produced through the framing/negation of the female gaze. The woman is there as the butt of a joke – a "dirty joke" which, as Freud has demonstrated, is always constructed at the expense of a woman. In order for a dirty joke to emerge in its specificity in Freud's description, the object of desire – the woman – must be absent and a third person (another man) must be present as witness to the joke – "so that gradually, in place of the woman, the onlooker, now the listener, becomes the person to whom the smut is addressed."[32] The terms of the photograph's address as joke once again insure a masculinization of the place of the spectator. The operation of the dirty joke is also inextricably linked by Freud to scopophilia and the exposure of the female body:

> Smut is like an exposure of the sexually different person to whom it is directed. By the utterance of the obscene words it compels the person who is assailed to imagine the part of the body or the procedure in question and shows her that the assailant is himself imagining it. It cannot be doubted that the desire to see what is sexual exposed is the original motive of smut.[33]

From this perspective, the photograph lays bare the very mechanics of the joke through its depiction of sexual exposure and a surreptitious act of seeing (and desiring). Freud's description of the joke-work appears to constitute a perfect analysis of the photograph's orchestration of the gaze. There is a "voice-off" of the photographic discourse, however – a component of the image which is beyond the frame of this little scenario of voyeurism. On the far left-hand side of the photograph, behind the wall holding the painting of the nude, is the barely detectable painting of a woman imaged differently, in darkness – *out of sight* for the male, blocked by his fetish. Yet, to point to this almost invisible alternative in imaging is also only to reveal once again the analyst's own perpetual desire to find a not-seen that might break the hold of representation. Or to laugh last.

There is a sense in which the photograph's delineation of a sexual politics of looking is almost uncanny. But, to counteract the very possibility of such a perception, the language of the art critic effects a naturalization of this joke on the woman. The art-critical reception of the picture emphasizes a natural but at the same time "imaginative" relation between photography and life, ultimately subordinating any formal relations to a referential ground: "Doisneau's lines move from right to left, directed by the man's glance; the woman's gaze creates a line of energy like a hole in space. . . . The creation of these relationships from life itself is imagination in photography."[34] "Life itself," then, presents the material for an "artistic" organization of vision along the lines of sexual difference. Furthermore, the critic would have us believe that chance events and arbitrary clicks of the shutter cannot be the agents of a generalized sexism because they are particular, unique – "Keitesz and Doisneau depend entirely upon our recognition that they were present at the instant of the unique intersection of events."[35] Realism seems always to reside in the streets and, indeed, the out-of-focus boy across the street, at the center of the photograph, appears to act as a guarantee of the "chance" nature of the event, its arbitrariness, in short – its realism. Thus, in the discourse of the art critic the photograph, in capturing a moment, does not construct it; the camera finds a naturally given series of subject and object positions. What the critic does not consider are the conditions of reception of photography as an art form, its situation within a much larger network of representation. What is it that makes the photograph not only readable but pleasurable – at the expense of the woman? The critic does not ask what makes the photograph a negotiable item in a market of signification.

The Missing Look

The photograph displays insistently, in microcosm, the structure of the cinematic inscription of a sexual differentiation in modes of looking. Its process of framing the female gaze repeats that of the cinematic narratives described above, from *Leave Her to Heaven* to *Dark Victory*. Films play out scenarios of looking in order to outline the terms of their own understanding. And given the divergence between masculine and feminine scenarios, those terms would seem to be explicitly negotiated as markers of sexual difference. Both the theory of the image and its apparatus, the cinema, produce a position for the female spectator – a position which is ultimately untenable because it lacks the attribute of distance so necessary for an adequate reading of the image. The entire elaboration of femininity as a closeness, a nearness, as present-to-itself is not the definition of an essence but the delineation of a *place* culturally assigned to the woman. Above and beyond a simple adoption of the masculine position in relation to the cinematic sign, the female spectator is given two options: the masochism of over-identification or the narcissism entailed in becoming one's own object of desire, in assuming the image in the most radical way. The effectivity of masquerade lies precisely in its potential to manufacture a distance from the image, to generate a problematic within which the image is manipulable, producible, and readable by the woman. Doisneau's photograph is not readable by the female spectator – it can give her pleasure only in masochism. In order to "get" the joke, she must once again assume the position of transvestite.

It is quite tempting to foreclose entirely the possibility of female spectatorship, to repeat at the level of theory the gesture of the photograph, given the history of a cinema which relies so heavily on voyeurism, fetishism, and identification with an ego ideal conceivable only in masculine terms. And, in fact, there has been a tendency to theorize femininity and hence the feminine gaze as repressed, and in its repression somehow irretrievable, the enigma constituted by Freud's question. Yet, as Michel Foucault has demonstrated, the repressive hypothesis on its own entails a very limited and simplistic notion of the working of power.[36] The "no" of the father, the prohibition, is its only technique. In theories of repression there is no sense of the productiveness and positivity of power. Femininity is produced very precisely as a position within a network of power relations. And the growing insistence upon the elaboration of a theory of female spectatorship is indicative of the crucial necessity of understanding that position in order to dislocate it.

Notes

1   Sigmund Freud, "Femininity," *The Standard Edition of the Complete Psychological Works of Sigmund Freud*, ed. James Strachey, London: Hogarth Press and the Institute of Psycho-analysis (1964), p. 113.

2   This is the translation given in a footnote in *The Standard Edition*, p. 113.

3   Heinrich Heine, *The North Sea*, trans. Vernon Watkins, New York: New Direction Books (1951), p. 77.

4   In other words, the woman can never ask her own ontological question. The absurdity of such a situation within traditional discursive conventions can be demonstrated by substituting a "young woman" for the "young man" of Heine's poem.

5   As Oswald Ducrot and Tzvetan Todorov point out in *Encyclopedic Dictionary of the Sciences of Language*, trans. Catherine Porter, Baltimore and London: Johns Hopkins University Press (1979), p. 195, the potentially universal understandability of the hieroglyphic is highly theoretical and can only be thought as the unattainable ideal of an imagistic system: "It is important of course not to exaggerate either the resemblance of the image with the object – the design is stylized very rapidly – or the "natural" and "universal" character of the signs: Sumerian, Chinese, Egyptian, and Hittite hieroglyphics for the same object have nothing in common."

6   Ibid., p. 194. Emphasis mine.

7   See Noël Burch's film, *Correction Please, or How We Got Into Pictures*.

8   Laura Mulvey, "Visual Pleasure and Narrative Cinema," *Screen* 16, no. 3 (Autumn 1975), pp. 12–13.

9   Charles Affron, *Star Acting: Gish, Garbo, Davis*, New York: E. P. Dutton (1977), pp. 281–2.

10 This argument focuses on the image to the exclusion of any consideration of the soundtrack, primarily because it is the process of imaging which seems to constitute the major difficulty in theorizing female spectatorship. The image is also popularly understood as a metonymic signifier for the cinema as a whole and with good reason: historically, sound has been subordinate to the image within the dominant classical system. For more on the image/sound distinction in relation to sexual difference see my article, "The Voice in the Cinema: The Articulation of Body and Space," *Yale French Studies*, no. 60 (1980), pp. 33–50.

11 Noël Burch, *Theory of Film Practice*, trans. Helen R. Lane, New York and Washington: Praeger Publishers (1973), p. 35.

12 Christian Metz, "The Imaginary Signifier," *Screen* 16, no. 2 (Summer 1975), p. 60.

13 Ibid., p. 61.

14 Luce Irigaray, "This Sex Which is Not One," *New French Feminisms*, ed. Elaine Marks and Isabelle de Courtivron, Amherst: University of Massachusetts Press (1980), pp. 104–5.

15 Irigaray, "Women's Exile," *Ideology and Consciousness*, no. 1 (May 1977), p. 74.

16 Hélène Cixous, "The Laugh of the Medusa," *New French Feminisms*, p. 257.

17 Sarah Kofman, "Ex: The Woman's Enigma," *Enclitic* 4, no. 2 (Fall 1980), p. 20.

18 Michèle Montrelay, "Inquiry into Femininity," *m/f*, no. 1 (1978), pp. 91–2.

19 Freud, "Some Psychological Consequences of the Anatomical Distinction Between the Sexes," *Sexuality and the Psychology of Love*, ed. Philip Rieff, New York: Collier Books (1963), pp. 187–8.

20 Freud, "Femininity," p. 125.

21 Freud, "Some Psychological Consequences," p. 187.

22 Molly Haskell, *From Reverence to Rape*, Baltimore: Penguin Books (1974), p. 154.

23 Irigaray, "Women's Exile," p. 65.

24 Mulvey, "Afterthoughts...inspired by *Duel in the Sun*," *Framework* (Summer 1981), p. 13.

25 Joan Riviere, "Womanliness as a Masquerade," *Psychoanalysis and Female Sexuality*, ed. Hendrik M. Ruitenbeek, New Haven, CN: College and University Press (1966), p. 213. My analysis of the concept of masquerade differs markedly from that of Luce Irigaray. See *Ce sexe qui n'en est pas un*, Paris: Les Éditions de Minuit (1977), pp. 131–2. It also diverges to a great extent from the very important analysis of masquerade presented by Claire Johnston in "Femininity and the Masquerade: Anne of the Indies," *Jacques Tourneur*, London: British Film Institute (1975), pp. 36–44. I am indebted to her for the reference to Riviere's article.

26 Moustafa Safouan, "Is the Oedipus Complex Universal?" *m/f*, nos. 5–6 (1981), pp. 84–5.

27 Montrelay, p. 93.

28 Silvia Bovenschen, "Is There a Feminine Aesthetic?" *New German Critique*, no. 10 (Winter 1977), p. 129.

29 Montrelay, p. 93.

30 Linda Williams, "When the Woman Looks," in *Re-vision: Essays in Feminist Film Criticism*, ed. Mary Ann Doane, Pat Mellencamp, and Linda Williams, Frederick, MD: University Publications of America and the American Film Institute (1984).

31 Johnston, p. 40.

32 Freud, *Jokes and Their Relation to the Unconscious*, trans. James Strachey, New York: Norton & Co. (1960), p. 99.

33 Ibid., p. 98.

34 Weston J. Naef, *Counterparts: Form and Emotion in Photographs*, New York: E. P. Dutton and the Metropolitan Museum of Art (1982), pp. 48–9.

35 Ibid.

36 Michael Foucault, *The History of Sexuality*, trans. Robert Hurley, New York: Pantheon Books (1978).

28

The Oppositional Gaze: Black Female Spectators

bell hooks

When thinking about black female spectators, I remember being punished as a child for staring, for those hard intense direct looks children would give grown-ups, looks that were seen as confrontational, as gestures of resistance, challenges to authority. The "gaze" has always been political in my life. Imagine the terror felt by the child who has come to understand through repeated punishments that one's gaze can be dangerous. The child who has learned so well to look the other way when necessary. Yet, when punished, the child is told by parents, "Look at me when I talk to you." Only, the child is afraid to look. Afraid to look, but fascinated by the gaze. There is power in looking.

Amazed the first time I read in history classes that white slave-owners (men, women, and children) punished enslaved black people for looking, I wondered how this traumatic relationship to the gaze had informed black parenting and black spectatorship. The politics of slavery, of racialized power relations, were such that the slaves were denied their right to gaze. Connecting this strategy of domination to that used by grown folks in southern black rural communities where I grew up, I was pained to think that there was no absolute difference between whites who had oppressed black people and ourselves. Years later, reading Michel Foucault, I thought again about these connections, about the ways power as domination reproduces itself in different locations employing similar apparatuses, strategies, and mechanisms of control. Since I knew as a child that the dominating power adults exercised over me and over my gaze was never so absolute that I did not dare to look, to sneak a peep, to stare danger-ously, I knew that the slaves had looked. That all attempts to repress our/black people's right to gaze had produced in us an overwhelming longing to look, a rebellious desire, an oppositional gaze. By courageously looking, we defiantly declared: "Not only will I stare. I want my look to change reality." Even in the worse circumstances of domination, the ability to manipulate one's gaze in the face of structures of domination that would contain it, opens up the possibility of agency. In much of his work, Michel Foucault insists on describing domination in terms of "relations of power" as part of an effort to challenge the assumption that "power is a system of domination which controls everything and which leaves no room for freedom." Emphatically stating that in all relations of power "there is necessarily the possibility of resistance," he invites the critical thinker to search those margins, gaps, and locations on and through the body where agency can be found.

Stuart Hall calls for recognition of our agency as black spectators in his essay "Cultural Identity and Cinematic Representation." Speaking against the construction of white representations of blackness as totalizing, Hall says of white presence: "The error is not to conceptualize this 'presence' in terms of power, but to locate that power as wholly external to us – as extrinsic force, whose influence can be thrown off like the serpent sheds its skin." What Frantz Fanon reminds us, in *Black Skin, White Masks*, is how power is inside as well as outside:

> The movements, the attitudes, the glances of the Other fixed me there, in the sense in which a chemical solution is fixed by a dye. I was indignant; I demanded an explanation. Nothing happened. I burst apart. Now the fragments have been put together again by another self. This "look," from – so to speak – the place of the Other, fixes us, not only in its violence, hostility and aggression, but in the ambivalence of its desire.

Spaces of agency exist for black people, wherein we can both interrogate the gaze of the Other but also look back, and at one another, naming what we see. The "gaze" has been and is a site of resistance for colonized black people globally. Subordinates in relations of power learn experientially that there is a critical gaze, one that "looks" to document, one that is oppositional. In resistance struggle, the power of the dominated to assert agency by claiming and cultivating "awareness" politicizes "looking" relations – one learns to look a certain way in order to resist.

When most black people in the United States first had the opportunity to look at film and television, they did so fully aware that mass media was a system of knowledge and power reproducing and maintaining white supremacy. To stare at the television, or mainstream movies, to engage its images, was to engage its negation of black representation. It was the oppositional black gaze that responded to these looking relations by developing independent black cinema. Black viewers of mainstream cinema and television could chart the progress of political movements for racial equality via the construction of images, and did so. Within my family's southern black working-class home, located in a racially segregated neighborhood, watching television was one way to develop critical spectatorship. Unless you went to work in the white world, across the tracks, you learned to look at white people by staring at them on the screen. Black looks, as they were constituted in the context of social movements for racial uplift, were interrogating gazes. We laughted at television shows like *Our Gang* and *Amos 'n' Andy*, at these white representations of blackness, but we also looked at them critically. Before racial integration, black viewers of movies and television experienced visual pleasure in a context where looking was also about contestation and confrontation.

Writing about black looking relations in "Black British Cinema: Spectatorship and Identity Formation in Territories," Manthia Diawara identifies the power of the spectator: "Every narration places the spectator in a position of agency; and race, class and sexual relations influence the way in which this subjecthood is filled by the spectator." Of particular concern for him are moments of "rupture" when the spectator resists "complete identification with the film's discourse." These ruptures define the relation between black spectators and dominant cinema prior to racial integration. Then, one's enjoyment of a film wherein representations of blackness were stereotypically degrading and dehumanizing coexisted with a critical practice that restored presence where it was negated. Critical discussion of the film while it was in progress or at its conclusion maintained the distance between spectator and the image. Black films were also subject to critical interrogation. Since they came into being in part as a response to the failure of white-dominated cinema to represent blackness in a manner that did not reinforce white supremacy, they too were critiqued to see if images were seen as complicit with dominant cinematic practices.

Critical, interrogating black looks were mainly concerned with issues of race and racism, the way racial domination of blacks by whites overdetermined representation. They were rarely concerned with gender. As spectators, black men could repudiate the reproduction of racism in cinema and television, the negation of black presence, even as they could feel as though they were rebelling against white supremacy by daring to look, by engaging phallocentric politics of spectatorship. Given the real-life public circumstances wherein black men were murdered/lynched for looking at white womanhood, where the black male gaze was always subject to control and/or punishment by the powerful white Other, the private realm of television screens or dark theaters could unleash the repressed gaze. There they could "look" at white womanhood without a structure of domination overseeing the gaze, interpreting, and punishing. That white supremacist structure that had murdered Emmet Till after interpreting his look as violation, as "rape" of white womanhood, could not control black male responses to screen images. In their role as spectators, black men could enter an imaginative space of phallocentric power that mediated racial negation. This gendered relation to looking made the experience of the black male spectator radically different from that of the black female spectator. Major early black male independent filmmakers represented black women in their films as objects of male gaze. Whether looking through the camera or as spectators watching films, whether mainstream cinema or "race" movies such as those made by Oscar Micheaux, the black male gaze had a different scope from that of the black female.

Black women have written little about black female spectatorship, about our moviegoing practices. A growing body of film theory and criticism by black women has only begun to emerge. The prolonged silence of black women as spectators and critics was a response to absence, to cinematic negation. In "The Technology of Gender," Teresa de Lauretis, drawing on the work of Monique Wittig, calls attention to "the power of discourses to 'do violence' to people, a violence which is material and physical, although produced by abstract and scientific discourses as well as the discourses of the mass media." With the possible exception of early race movies, black female spectators have had to develop looking relations within a cinematic context that constructs our presence as absence, that denies the "body" of the black female so as to perpetuate white supremacy and with it a phallocentric spectatorship where the woman to be looked at and desired is "white." (Recent movies do not conform to this paradigm but I am turning to the past with the intent to chart the development of black female spectatorship.)

Talking with black women of all ages and classes, in different areas of the United States, about their filmic looking relations, I hear again and again ambivalent responses to cinema. Only a few of the black women I talked with remembered the pleasure of race movies, and even those who did, felt that pleasure interrupted and usurped by Hollywood. Most of the black women I talked with were adamant that they never went to movies expecting to see compelling representations of black femaleness. They were all acutely aware of cinematic racism – its violent erasure of black womanhood. In Anne Friedberg's essay "A Denial of Difference: Theories of Cinematic Identification" she stresses that "identification can only be made through recognition, and all recognition is itself an implicit confirmation of the ideology of the status quo." Even when representations of black women were present in film, our bodies and being were there to serve – to enhance and maintain white womanhood as object of the phallocentric gaze.

Commenting on Hollywood's characterization of black women in *Girls on Film*, Julie Burchill describes this absent presence:

> Black women have been mothers without children (Mammies – who can ever forget the sickening spectacle of Hattie MacDaniels waiting on the simpering Vivien Leigh hand and foot and enquiring like a ninny, "What's ma lamb gonna wear?") . . . Lena Horne, the first black performer signed to a long term contract with a major (MGM), looked gutless but was actually quite spirited. She seethed when Tallulah Bankhead complimented her on the paleness of her skin and the non-Negroidness of her features.

When black women actresses like Lena Horne appeared in mainstream cinema most white viewers were not aware that they were looking at black females unless the film was specifically coded as being about blacks. Burchill is one of the few white women film critics who has dared to examine the intersection of race and gender in relation to the construction of the category "woman" in film as object of the phallocentric gaze. With characteristic wit she asserts: "What does it say about racial purity that the best blondes have all been brunettes (Harlow,

Monroe, Bardot)? I think it says that we are not as white as we think." Burchill could easily have said "we are not as white as we want to be," for clearly the obsession to have white women film stars be ultra-white was a cinematic practice that sought to maintain a distance, a separation between that image and the black female Other; it was a way to perpetuate white supremacy. Politics of race and gender were inscribed into mainstream cinematic narrative from *Birth of A Nation* on. As a seminal work, this film identified what the place and function of white womanhood would be in cinema. There was clearly no place for black women.

Remembering my past in relation to screen images of black womanhood, I wrote a short essay, "Do You Remember Sapphire?" which explored both the negation of black female representation in cinema and television and our rejection of these images. Identifying the character of "Sapphire" from *Amos 'n' Andy* as that screen representation of black femaleness I first saw in childhood, I wrote:

> She was even then backdrop, foil. She was bitch – nag. She was there to soften images of black men, to make them seem vulnerable, easygoing, funny, and unthreatening to a white audience. She was there as man in drag, as castrating bitch, as someone to be lied to, someone to be tricked, someone the white and black audience could hate. Scapegoated on all sides. *She was not us.* We laughed with the black men, with the white people. We laughed at this black woman who was not us. And we did not even long to be there on the screen. How could we long to be there when our image, visually constructed, was so ugly. We did not long to be there. We did not long for her. We did not want our construction to be this hated black female thing – foil, backdrop. Her black female image was not the body of desire. There was nothing to see. She was not us.

Grown black women had a different response to Sapphire; they identified with her frustrations and her woes. They resented the way she was mocked. They resented the way these screen images could assault black womanhood, could name us bitches, nags. And in opposition they claimed Sapphire as their own, as the symbol of that angry part of themselves white folks and black men could not even begin to understand.

Conventional representations of black women have done violence to the image. Responding to this assault, many black women spectators shut out the image, looked the other way, accorded cinema no importance in their lives. Then there were those spectators whose gaze was that of desire and complicity. Assuming a posture of subordination, they submitted to cinema's capacity to seduce and betray. They were cinematically "gaslighted." Every black woman I spoke with who was/is an ardent moviegoer, a lover of the Hollywood film, testified that to experience fully the pleasure of that cinema they had to close down critique, analysis; they had to forget racism. And mostly they did not think about sexism. What was the nature then of this adoring black female gaze – this look that could bring pleasure in the midst of negation? In her first novel, *The Bluest Eye*, Toni

Morrison constructs a portrait of the black female spectator; her gaze is the masochistic look of victimization. Describing her looking relations, Miss Pauline Breedlove, a poor working woman, maid in the house of a prosperous white family, asserts:

> The onliest time I be happy seem like was when I was in the picture show. Every time I got, I went, I'd go early, before the show started. They's cut off the lights, and everything be black. Then the screen would light up, and I's move right on in them picture. White men taking such good care of they women, and they all dressed up in big clean houses with the bath tubs right in the same room with the toilet. Them pictures gave me a lot of pleasure.

To experience pleasure, Miss Pauline sitting in the dark must imagine herself transformed, turned into the white woman portrayed on the screen. After watching movies, feeling the pleasure, she says, "But it made coming home hard."

We come home to ourselves. Not all black women spectators submitted to that spectacle of regression through identification. Most of the women I talked with felt that they consciously resisted identification with films – that this tension made moviegoing less than pleasurable; at times it caused pain. As one black woman put it, "I could always get pleasure from movies as long as I did not look too deep." For black female spectators who have "looked too deep" the encounter with the screen hurt. That some of us chose to stop looking was a gesture of resistance, turning away was one way to protest, to reject negation. My pleasure in the screen ended abruptly when I and my sisters first watched *Imitation of Life*. Writing about this experience in the "Sapphire" piece, I addressed the movie directly, confessing:

> I had until now forgotten you, that screen image seen in adolescence, those images that made me stop looking. It was there in *Imitation of Life*, that comfortable mammy image. There was something familiar about this hardworking black woman who loved her daughter so much, loved her in a way that hurt. Indeed, as young southern black girls watching this film, Peola's mother reminded us of the hardworking, churchgoing, Big Mamas we knew and loved. Consequently, it was not this image that captured our gaze; we were fascinated by Peola.

Addressing her, I wrote:

> You were different. There was something scary in this image of young sexual sensual black beauty betrayed – that daughter who did not want to be confined by blackness, that "tragic mulatto" who did not want to be negated. "Just let me escape this image forever," she could have said. I will always remember that image. I remembered how we cried for her, for our unrealized desiring selves. She was tragic because there was no place in the cinema for her, no loving pictures. She too was absent image. It was better then, that we were absent, for when we were there it was

humiliating, strange, sad. We cried all night for you, for the cinema that had no place for you. And like you, we stopped thinking it would one day be different.

When I returned to films as a young woman, after a long period of silence, I had developed an oppositional gaze. Not only would I not be hurt by the absence of black female presence, or the insertion of violating representation, I interrogated the work, cultivated a way to look past race and gender for aspects of content, form, language. Foreign films and US independent cinema were the primary locations of my filmic looking relations, even though I also watched Hollywood films.

From "jump," black female spectators have gone to films with awareness of the way in which race and racism determined the visual construction of gender. Whether it was *Birth of A Nation* or Shirley Temple shows, we knew that white womanhood was the racialized sexual difference occupying the place of stardom in mainstream narrative film. We assumed white women knew it to. Reading Laura Mulvey's provocative essay, "Visual Pleasure and Narrative Cinema," from a standpoint that acknowledges race, one sees clearly why black women spectators not duped by mainstream cinema would develop an oppositional gaze. Placing ourselves outside that pleasure in looking, Mulvey argues, was determined by a "split between active/male and passive/female." Black female spectators actively chose not to identify with the film's imaginary subject because such identification was disenabling.

Looking at films with an oppositional gaze, black women were able to critically assess the cinema's construction of white womanhood as object of phallocentric gaze and choose not to identify with either the victim or the perpetrator. Black female spectators, who refused to identify with white womanhood, who would not take on the phallocentric gaze of desire and possession, created a critical space where the binary opposition Mulvey posits of "woman as image, man as bearer of the look" was continually deconstructed. As critical spectators, black women looked from a location that disrupted, one akin to that described by Annette Kuhn in *The Power of the Image*:

> The acts of analysis, of deconstruction and of reading "against the grain" offer an additional pleasure – the pleasure of resistance, of saying "no": not to "unsophisticated" enjoyment, by ourselves and others, of culturally dominant images, but to the structures of power which ask us to consume them uncritically and in highly circumscribed ways.

Mainstream feminist film criticism in no way acknowledges black female spectatorship. It does not even consider the possibility that women can construct an oppositional gaze via an understanding and awareness of the politics of race and racism. Feminist film theory rooted in an ahistorical psychoanalytic framework that privileges sexual difference actively suppresses recognition of race, reenacting and mirroring the erasure of black womanhood that occurs in films, silencing any discussion of racial difference – of racialized sexual difference. Despite feminist critical interventions aimed at deconstructing the category "woman" which highlight the significance of race, many feminist film critics continue to structure their discourse as though it speaks about "women" when in actuality it speaks only about white women. It seems ironic that the cover of the recent anthology *Feminism and Film Theory* edited by Constance Penley has a graphic that is a reproduction of the photo of white Rosalind Russell and Dorothy Arzner on the 1936 set of the film *Craig's Wife* yet there is no acknowledgment in any essay in this collection that the woman "subject" under discussion is always white. Even though there are photos of black women from films reproduced in the text, there is no acknowledgment of racial difference.

It would be too simplistic to interpret this failure of insight solely as a gesture of racism. Importantly, it also speaks to the problem of structuring feminist film theory around a totalizing narrative of woman as object whose image functions solely to reaffirm and reinscribe patriarchy. Mary Ann Doane addresses this issue in the essay "Remembering Women: Psychical and Historical Construction in Film Theory":

> This attachment to the figure of a degeneralizible Woman as the product of the apparatus indicates why, for many, feminist film theory seems to have reached an impasse, a certain blockage in its theorization.... In focusing upon the task of delineating in great detail the attributes of woman as effect of the apparatus, feminist film theory participates in the abstraction of women.

The concept "Woman" effaces the difference between women in specific socio-historical contexts, between women defined precisely as historical subjects rather than as *a* psychic subject (or non-subject). Though Doane does not focus on race, her comments speak directly to the problem of its erasure. For it is only as one imagines "woman" in the abstract, when woman becomes fiction or fantasy, can race not be seen as significant. Are we really to imagine that feminist theorists writing only about images of white women, who subsume this specific historical subject under the totalizing category "woman," do not "see" the whiteness of the image? It may very well be that they engage in a process of denial that eliminates the necessity of revisioning conventional ways of thinking about psychoanalysis as a paradigm of analysis and the need to rethink a body of feminist film theory that is firmly rooted in a denial of the reality that sex/sexuality may not be the primary and/or exclusive signifier of difference. Doane's essay appears in a very recent anthology, *Psychoanalysis and Cinema* edited by E. Ann Kaplan, where, once again, none of the theory presented acknowledges or discusses racial difference, with the exception of one essay, "Not Speaking with Language, Speaking with No Language," which problematizes notions of orientalism in its examination of Leslie Thornton's film *Adynata*. Yet in most of the essays, the theories espoused are rendered problematic if one includes race as a category of analysis.

Constructing feminist film theory along these lines enables the production of a discursive practice that need never theorize any aspect of black female representation or spectatorship. Yet the existence of black women within white supremacist culture problematizes, and makes complex, the overall issue of female identity, representation, and spectatorship. If, as Friedberg suggests, "identification is a process which commands the subject to be displaced by an other; it is a procedure which breaches the separation between self and other, and, in this way, replicates the very structure of patriarchy." If identification "demands sameness, necessitates similarity, disallows difference" – must we then surmise that many feminist film critics who are "over-identified" with the mainstream cinematic apparatus produce theories that replicate its totalizing agenda? Why is it that feminist film criticism, which has most claimed the terrain of woman's identity, representation, and subjectivity as its field of analysis, remains aggressively silent on the subject of blackness and specifically representations of black womanhood? Just as mainstream cinema has historically forced aware black female spectators not to look, much feminist film criticism disallows the possibility of a theoretical dialogue that might include black women's voices. It is difficult to talk when you feel no one is listening, when you feel as though a special jargon or narrative has been created that only the chosen can understand. No wonder then that black women have for the most part confined our critical commentary on film to conversations. And it must be reiterated that this gesture is a strategy that protects us from the violence perpetuated and advocated by discourses of mass media. A new focus on issues of race and representation in the field of film theory could critically intervene on the historical repression reproduced in some arenas of contemporary critical practice, making a discursive space for discussion of black female spectatorship possible.

When I asked a black woman in her twenties, an obsessive moviegoer, why she thought we had not written about black female spectatorship, she commented: "We are afraid to talk about ourselves as spectators because we have been so abused by 'the gaze'." An aspect of that abuse was the imposition of the assumption that black female looking relations were not important enough to theorize. Film theory as a critical "turf" in the United States has been and continues to be influenced by and reflective of white racial domination. Since feminist film criticism was initially rooted in a women's liberation movement informed by racist practices, it did not open up the discursive terrain and make it more inclusive. Recently, even those white film theorists who include an analysis of race show no interest in black female spectatorship. In her introduction to the collection of essays *Visual and Other Pleasures*, Laura Mulvey describes her initial romantic absorption in Hollywood cinema, stating:

> Although this great, previously unquestioned and unanalyzed love was put in crisis by the impact of feminism on my thought in the early 1970s, it also had an enormous influence on the development of my critical work and ideas and the debate within film culture with which I became preoccupied over the next fifteen

years or so. Watched through eyes that were affected by the changing climate of consciousness, the movies lost their magic.

Watching movies from a feminist perspective, Mulvey arrived at that location of disaffection that is the starting point for many black women approaching cinema within the lived harsh reality of racism. Yet her account of being a part of a film culture whose roots rest on a founding relationship of adoration and love indicates how difficult it would have been to enter that world from "jump" as a critical spectator whose gaze had been formed in opposition.

Given the context of class exploitation, and racist and sexist domination, it has only been through resistance, struggle, reading, and looking "against the grain," that black women have been able to value our process of looking enough to publicly name it. Centrally, those black female spectators who attest to the oppositionality of their gaze deconstruct theories of female spectatorship that have relied heavily on the assumption that, as Doane suggests in her essay, "Woman's Stake: Filming the Female Body," "woman can only mimic man's relation to language, that is assume a position defined by the penis–phallus as the supreme arbiter of lack." Identifying with neither the phallocentric gaze nor the construction of white womanhood as lack, critical black female spectators construct a theory of looking relations where cinematic visual delight is the pleasure of interrogation. Every black woman spectator I talked to, with rare exception, spoke of being "on guard" at the movies. Talking about the way being a critical spectator of Hollywood films influenced her, black woman filmmaker Julie Dash exclaims, "I make films because I was such a spectator!" Looking at Hollywood cinema from a distance, from that critical politicized standpoint that did not want to be seduced by narratives reproducing her negation, Dash watched mainstream movies over and over again for the pleasure of deconstructing them. And of course there is that added delight if one happens, in the process of interrogation, to come across a narrative that invites the black female spectator to engage the text with no threat of violation.

Significantly, I began to write film criticism in response to the first Spike Lee movie, *She's Gotta Have It*, contesting Lee's replication of mainstream patriarchal cinematic practices that explicitly represents woman (in this instance black woman) as the object of a phallocentric gaze. Lee's investment in patriarchal filmic practices that mirror dominant patterns makes him the perfect black candidate for entrance to the Hollywood canon. His work mimics the cinematic construction of white womanhood as object, replacing her body as text on which to write male desire with the black female body. It is transference without transformation. Entering the discourse of film criticism from the politicized location of resistance, of not wanting, as a working-class black woman I interviewed stated, "to see black women in the position white women have occupied in film forever," I began to think critically about black female spectatorship.

For years I went to independent and/or foreign films where I was the only black female present in the theater. I often imagined that in every theater in the

United States there was another black woman watching the same film wondering why she was the only visible black female spectator. I remember trying to share with one of my five sisters the cinema I liked so much. She was "enraged" that I brought her to a theater where she would have to read subtitles. To her it was a violation of Hollywood notions of spectatorship, of coming to the movies to be entertained. When I interviewed her to ask what had changed her mind over the years, led her to embrace this cinema, she connected it to coming to critical consciousness, saying, "I learned that there was more to looking than I had been exposed to in ordinary (Hollywood) movies." I shared that though most of the films I loved were all white, I could engage them because they did not have in their deep structure a subtext reproducing the narrative of white supremacy. Her response was to say that these films demystified "whiteness," since the lives they depicted seemed less rooted in fantasies of escape. They were, she suggested, more like "what we knew life to be, the deeper side of life as well." Always more seduced and enchanted with Hollywood cinema than me, she stressed that unaware black female spectators must "break out," no longer be imprisoned by images that enact a drama of our negation. Though she still sees Hollywood films, because "they are a major influence in the culture" – she no longer feels duped or victimized.

Talking with black female spectators, looking at written discussions either in fiction or academic essays about black women, I noted the connection made between the realm of representation in mass media and the capacity of black women to construct ourselves as subjects in daily life. The extent to which black women feel devalued, objectified, dehumanized in this society determines the scope and texture of their looking relations. Those black women whose identities were constructed in resistance, by practices that oppose the dominant order, were most inclined to develop an oppositional gaze. Now that there is a growing interest in films produced by black women and those films have become more accessible to viewers, it is possible to talk about black female spectatorship in relation to that work. So far, most discussions of black spectatorship that I have come across focus on men. In "Black Spectatorship: Problems of Identification and Resistance" Manthia Diawara suggests that "the components of 'difference'" among elements of sex, gender, and sexuality give rise to different readings of the same material, adding that these conditions produce a "resisting" spectator. He focuses his critical discussion on black masculinity.

The recent publication of the anthology *The Female Gaze: Women as Viewers of Popular Culture* excited me, especially as it included an essay, "Black Looks," by Jacqui Roach and Petal Felix that attempts to address black female spectatorship. The essay posed provocative questions that were not answered: Is there a black female gaze? How do black women relate to the gender politics of representation? Concluding, the authors assert that black females have "our own reality, our own history, our own gaze – one which sees the world rather differently from 'anyone else.'" Yet, they do not name/describe this experience of seeing "rather differently." The absence of definition and explanation suggests they are assuming an essentialist stance wherein it is presumed that black women, as victims of race and gender oppression, have an inherently different field of vision. Many black women do not "see differently" precisely because their perceptions of reality are so profoundly colonized, shaped by dominant ways of knowing. As Trinh T. Minh-ha points out in "Outside In, Inside Out": "Subjectivity does not merely consist of talking about oneself...be this talking indulgent or critical."

Critical black female spectatorship emerges as a site of resistance only when individual black women actively resist the imposition of dominant ways of knowing and looking. While every black woman I talked to was aware of racism, that awareness did not automatically correspond with politicization, the development of an oppositional gaze. When it did, individual black women consciously named the process. Manthia Diawara's "resisting spectatorship" is a term that does not adequately describe the terrain of black female spectatorship. We do more than resist. We create alternative texts that are not solely reactions. As critical spectators, black women participate in a broad range of looking relations, contest, resist, revision, interrogate, and invent on multiple levels. Certainly when I watch the work of black women filmmakers Camille Billops, Kathleen Collins, Julie Dash, Ayoka Chenzira, Zeinabu Davis, I do not need to "resist" the images even as I still choose to watch their work with a critical eye.

Black female critical thinkers concerned with creating space for the construction of radical black female subjectivity, and the way cultural production informs this possibility, fully acknowledge the importance of mass media, film in particular, as a powerful site for critical intervention. Certainly Julie Dash's film *Illusions* identifies the terrain of Hollywood cinema as a space of knowledge production that has enormous power. Yet, she also creates a filmic narrative wherein the black female protagonist subversively claims that space. Inverting the "real-life" power structure, she offers the black female spectator representations that challenge stereotypical notions that place us outside the realm of filmic discursive practices. Within the film she uses the strategy of Hollywood suspense films to undermine those cinematic practices that deny black women a place in this structure. Problematizing the question of "racial" identity by depicting passing, suddenly it is the white male's capacity to gaze, define, and know that is called into question.

When Mary Ann Doane describes in "Woman's Stake: Filming the Female Body" the way in which feminist filmmaking practice can elaborate "a special syntax for a different articulation of the female body," she names a critical process that "undoes the structure of the classical narrative through an insistence upon its repressions." An eloquent description, this precisely names Dash's strategy in *Illusions*, even though the film is not unproblematic and works within certain conventions that are not successfully challenged. For example, the film does not indicate whether the character Mignon will make Hollywood films that subvert and transform the genre or whether she will simply assimilate and perpetuate the norm. Still, subversively, *Illusions* problematizes the issue of race and spectatorship. White people in the film are unable to "see" that race informs their looking relations. Though she is passing to gain access to the machinery of cultural production represented by film, Mignon continually asserts her ties to black community. The bond between her and the young black woman singer Esther Jeeter is affirmed by caring gestures of affirmation, often expressed by eye-to-eye contact, the direct unmediated gaze of recognition. Ironically, it is the desiring objectifying sexualized white male gaze that threatens to penetrate her "secrets" and disrupt her process. Metaphorically, Dash suggests the power of black women to make films will be threatened and undermined by that white male gaze that seeks to reinscribe the black female body in a narrative of voyeuristic pleasure where the only relevant opposition is male/female, and the only location for the female is as a victim. These tensions are not resolved by the narrative. It is not at all evident that Mignon will triumph over the white supremacist capitalist imperialist dominating "gaze."

Throughout *Illusions*, Mignon's power is affirmed by her contact with the younger black woman whom she nurtures and protects. It is this process of mirrored recognition that enables both black women to define their reality, apart from the reality imposed upon them by structures of domination. The shared gaze of the two women reinforces their solidarity. As the younger subject, Esther represents a potential audience for films that Mignon might produce, films wherein black females will be the narrative focus. Julie Dash's recent feature-length film *Daughters of the Dust* dares to place black females at the center of its narrative. This focus caused critics (especially white males) to critique the film negatively or to express many reservations. Clearly, the impact of racism and sexism so overdetermine spectatorship – not only what we look at but who we identify with – that viewers who are not black females find it hard to empathize with the central characters in the movie. They are adrift without a white presence in the film.

Another representation of black females nurturing one another via recognition of their common struggle for subjectivity is depicted in Sankofa's collective work *Passion of Remembrance*. In the film, two black women friends, Louise and Maggie, are from the onset of the narrative struggling with the issue of subjectivity, of their place in progressive black liberation movements that have been sexist. They challenge old norms and want to replace them with new understandings of the complexity of black identity, and the need for liberation struggles that address that complexity. Dressing to go to a party, Louise and Maggie claim the "gaze." Looking at one another, staring in mirrors, they appear completely focused on their encounter with black femaleness. How they see themselves is most important, not how they will be stared at by others. Dancing to the tune "Let's get Loose," they display their bodies not for a voyeuristic colonizing gaze but for that look of recognition that affirms their subjectivity – that constitutes them as spectators. Mutually empowered they eagerly leave the privatized domain to confront the public. Disrupting conventional racist and sexist stereotypical representations of black female bodies, these scenes invite the audience to look differently. They act to critically intervene and transform conventional filmic practices, changing notions of spectatorship. *Illusions, Daughters of the Dust*, and *A Passion of Remembrance* employ a deconstructive filmic practice to undermine existing grand cinematic narratives even as they retheorize subjectivity in the realm of the visual. Without providing "realistic" positive representations that emerge only as a response to the totalizing nature of existing narratives, they offer points of radical departure. Opening up a space for the assertion of a critical black female spectatorship, they do not simply offer diverse representations, they imagine new transgressive possibilities for the formulation of identity.

In this sense they make explicit a critical practice that provides us with different ways to think about black female subjectivity and black female spectatorship. Cinematically, they provide new points of recognition, embodying Stuart Hall's vision of a critical practice that acknowledges that identity is constituted "not outside but within representation," and invites us to see film "not as a second-order mirror held up to reflect what already exists, but as that form of representation which is able to constitute us as new kinds of subjects, and thereby enable us to discover who we are." It is this critical practice that enables production of feminist film theory that theorizes black female spectatorship. Looking and looking back, black women involve ourselves in a process whereby we see our history as counter-memory, using it as a way to know the present and invent the future.

29

Looking Awry

Slavoj Žižek

Pornography

Cinema, shot with an "objective" camera, by definition views things straight on. The first association that comes to mind here is, of course, *pornography*, the genre supposed to "show everything," to hide nothing, to register "all" with an objective camera and offer it to our view. It is nevertheless precisely in pornographic cinema that the "substance of enjoyment" perceived by the view from aside is *radically lost*. Why? Let us take as our starting point the antinomic relation between the eye and the gaze as it was articulated by Lacan in his *Seminar XI*: the eye viewing the object is on the side of the subject, while the gaze is on the side of the object. When I am looking at an object, the object is always already gazing at me, and from a point at which I cannot see it:

> In the scopic field, everything is articulated between two terms that act in an antinomic way – on the side of things, there is the gaze, that is to say, things look at me, and yet I see them. This is how one should understand those words, so strongly stressed in the Gospel, *They have eyes that they might not see.* That they might not see what? Precisely, that things are looking at them.[1]

This antinomy of eye and gaze is lost in pornography. Why? Because pornography is inherently *perverse*; its perverse character lies not in the obvious fact that it "goes all the way and shows us all the dirty details"; its perversity is, rather, to be conceived in a strictly formal way. In pornography, the spectator is forced *a priori* to occupy a perverse position. According to Lacan, perversion is defined by the fact that, as a stratagem to evade his constitutive splitting, the subject itself assumes the position of an object instrumental to the enjoyment of the Other. To exemplify this perverse position, let us take *Manhunter* (1986), a film about a police detective famous for his ability to enter intuitively, by a "sixth sense," the mind of perverse, sadistic murderers. His task is to detect a particularly cruel mass-murderer who slaughtered a number of quiet provincial families. The detective reruns again and again super-8 home movies shot by each of the slaughtered families in order to arrive at the *trait unaire*, the "unique" trait, at the feature common to all of them that attracted the murderer and thus directed his choice. But all his efforts are in vain so long as he looks for this common feature on the level of content, i.e. in the families themselves. He finds a key to the identity of the murderer only when a certain inconsistency strikes his eyes. The investigation at the scene of the last crime determined that to enter the house, i.e. to break open the back door, the murderer used a kind of tool that was inappropriate and even unnecessary. The old back door had been replaced a few weeks before the crime with a new type of door. To break open the new door, another kind of tool would have been far more appropriate. So how did the murderer get this wrong – or, more precisely, out-of-date – information? The old back door could be seen clearly in the scenes from the super-8 home movie. The only common feature of all the slaughtered families, it turns out, are *the home movies themselves*. The murderer had to have had access to these private movies; there is no other link connecting them. Because these movies are private, the only possible link between them is the laboratory where they were developed. A quick check confirms that all the movies were developed in the same laboratory, and the murderer is soon identified as one of the workers in the lab.

Wherein lies the theoretical interest of this denouement? The detective looks for a common feature that will enable him to get at the murderer in the content of the home movies, thus overlooking the form itself, i.e. the crucial fact that he is all the while viewing a series of home movies. The decisive turn takes place when he becomes aware that through this very screening of the home movies, *he is already identified with the murderer*, that his obsessive gaze, surveying every detail of the scenery, coincides with the murderer's gaze. The identification is on the level of the gaze, not on the level of content. There is something extremely unpleasant and obscene in this experience of our gaze as already the gaze of the other. Why? The Lacanian answer is that such a coincidence of gazes defines the position of the pervert. (Herein consists, according to Lacan, the difference between the "feminine" and "masculine" mystique, between, let us say, Saint Theresa and Jacob Boehme. The "feminine" mystique implies a non-phallic, "not-all" enjoyment, whereas the "masculine" mystique consists precisely in such an overlap of gazes, by which we experience the way our intuition of God is at the same time the view by means of which God looks at Himself.) The final irony of *Manhunter* would then be the following: confronted with a perverse–sadistic content, the detective is able to arrive at a solution only by taking into account the fact that his very procedure is, on a formal level, already "perverse." It implies a coincidence between his gaze and the gaze of the other (the murderer).

This overlap, this coincidence of our view with the gaze of the other, brings us back to pornography. In pornography we have a kind of short circuit between the two; instead of being on the side of the viewed object, the gaze falls into ourselves, the spectators, which is why the image we see on the screen contains no spot, no sublime mysterious point from which it gazes at us. It is we who are gazing stupidly at the image that "shows all." Contrary to the commonplace according to which, in pornography, the other (the person shown on the screen) is degraded to an object of our voyeuristic pleasure, we must stress that it is the spectator him- or herself who effectively occupies the position of the object. The real subjects are the actors on the screen trying to rouse us sexually, while we, the spectators, are reduced to a paralyzed object-gaze.[2]

Pornography thus misses, reduces the point of the object-gaze in the other. This miss has precisely the form of a missed, failed encounter. That is to say, in a "normal," non-pornographic film, a love scene is always built around a certain insurmountable limit; "all cannot be shown"; at a certain point, the image blurs, the camera moves off, the scene is interrupted, we never see directly "that" (the penetration of sexual organs, etc.). In contrast to this limit of representability which defines the "normal" love story or melodrama, pornography goes beyond, "shows all." The paradox is, however, that by trespassing the limit, it always already *goes too far*, i.e. it *misses* what remained concealed in the "normal," non-pornographic love scene. This paradox is the same as that noted in the well-known phrase from Brecht's *Threepenny Opera*: if you run too fast after happiness, you might overtake it and leave happiness behind. If we proceed too hastily "to the point," if we show "the thing itself," we necessarily lose what we were after. The effect is extremely vulgar and depressing (as can be confirmed by anyone who has seen hard-core movies). Pornography is thus just another variation on the paradox of Achilles and the tortoise, which, according to Lacan, defines the relation of the subject to the object of its desire. Naturally, Achilles can easily outdistance the tortoise and leave it behind, but the point is that he cannot come up alongside it, rejoin it. The subject is always too slow or too quick, can never keep pace with the object of its desire. The unattainable/ forbidden object approached but never reached by the "normal" love story – the sexual act – exists only as concealed, indicated, "faked." As soon as we "show it," its charm is dispelled, we have "gone too far." Instead of the sublime Thing, we are stuck with a vulgar groaning and fornication. The consequence of this is that harmony, the congruence between the filmic narrative (the unfolding of the story) and the immediate display of the sexual act, is structurally impossible. If we choose one, we necessarily lose the other. In other words, if we want to have a love story that "takes," that moves us, we must not "go to the end" and "show it all" (the details of the sexual act), because as soon as we "show it all," the story is no longer "taken seriously." It starts to function only as a pretext for introducing acts of copulation.

We can further pinpoint this gap via a kind of "knowledge in the real," which determines the way actors act in different film genres. The persons included in the diegetic reality always react as if they knew in what genre of film they were. If, for example, a door creaks in a horror film, the actor will react by turning his head anxiously toward it; if a door creaks in a family comedy, the same actor will shout at his small child not to sneak around the apartment. The same is true to an even greater degree for the porno film: before we pass to the sexual activity, we need a short introduction, a normally stupid plot serving as a pretext for the actors to start to copulate (the housewife calls in a plumber, a new secretary reports to the manager, etc.). The point is that already by the manner in which they enact this introductory plot, the actors divulge that this is for them only a stupid, although necessary formality that has to be gotten over with as quickly as possible to be able to tackle the "real thing."[3]

The fantasy ideal of a perfect work of pornography would be precisely to preserve this impossible harmony, the balance between narration and explicit depicting of the sexual act, i.e. to avoid the necessary *vel* condemning us to lose one of the two poles. Let us take an old-fashioned, nostalgic melodrama like *Out of Africa*, and let us assume that the film is precisely the same as was shown in cinemas, the only change being an additional ten minutes. When Robert Redford and Meryl Streep have their first love encounter, the scene is not interrupted, the camera "shows it all," details of their aroused sexual organs, penetration, orgasm, etc. Then, after the act, the story goes on as usual. We are back in the movie we all know. The problem is that such a movie is structurally impossible. Even if it were to be shot, it simply "would not function"; the additional ten minutes would derail us; for the rest of the film we would be unable to regain our balance and follow the narration with the usual disavowed belief in the diegetic reality. The sexual act would function as an intrusion of the real undermining the consistency of this reality.

Nostalgia

In pornography, the gaze qua object falls thus onto the subject–spectator, causing an effect of depressing desublimation. Which is why, to extract the gaze-object in its pure, formal status, we have to turn to the opposite pole of pornography: nostalgia. Let us take what is today probably the most notorious case of nostalgic fascination in the domain of cinema: the American film noir of the 1940s. What, precisely, is so fascinating about this genre? It is clear that we can no longer identify with it. The most dramatic scenes from *Casablanca*, *Murder, My Sweet*, or *Out of the Past*, provoke laughter today among spectators, but nevertheless, far from posing a threat to its power of fascination, this kind of distance is its very condition. That is to say, what fascinates us is precisely a certain gaze, the gaze of the "other," of the hypothetical, mythic spectator from the 1940s who was supposedly still able to identify immediately with the universe of film noir. What we really see when we watch a film noir is this gaze of the other. We are fascinated by the gaze of the mythic "naive" spectator, the one who was "still able to take it seriously," in other words, the one who "believes in it" for us, in place of us. For this reason, our relation to a film noir is always divided, split between fascination and ironic distance – ironic distance toward its diegetic reality, fascination with the gaze.

This gaze-object appears in its purest form in a series of films in which the logic of nostalgia is brought to self-reference: *Body Heat, The Driver, Shane*. As Fredric Jameson has already observed in his well-known article "Postmodernism, or The Cultural Logic of Late Capitalism,"[4] *Body Heat* reverses the usual nostalgic procedure by which the fragment of the past that serves as the object of nostalgia is extracted from its historic context, from its continuity, and inserted in a kind of mythic, eternal, timeless present. Here, in this film noir – a vague remake of *Double Indemnity* – which takes place in contemporary Florida, the present itself is viewed through the eyes of the film noir of the 1940s. Instead of transposing a fragment of the past into a timeless, mythic present, we view the present itself as if it were part of the mythic past. If we do not take into consideration this "gaze of the 1940s," *Body Heat* remains simply a contemporary film about contemporary times and, as such, totally incomprehensible. Its whole power of fascination is bestowed upon it by the fact that it looks at the present with the eyes of the mythical past.

The same dialectic of the gaze is at work in Walter Hill's *The Driver*; its starting point is again the film noir of the 1940s, which, as such, *does not exist*. It started to exist only when, in the 1950s, it was discovered by French critics (it is no accident that even in English the term used to designate this genre is the French film noir). What was in America itself a series of often low-budget B-productions of little critical prestige, was miraculously transformed, through the intervention of the French gaze, into a sublime object of art, a kind of film pendant to philosophical existentialism. Directors who had in America the status, at best, of skilled craftsmen became auteurs, each of them staging in his films a unique tragic vision of the universe. But the crucial fact is that this French view of film noir exerted a considerable influence on French film production, so that in France itself, a genre homologous to the American film noir was established; its most distinguished example is probably Jean-Pierre Melville's *Le Samourai*. Hill's *The Driver* is a kind of remake of *Le Samourai*, an attempt to transpose the French gaze back to America itself – a paradox of America looking at itself through French eyes. Again, if we conceive of *The Driver* simply as an American film about America, it becomes incomprehensible; we must include in it the "French gaze."

Our last example is *Shane*, the classic Western by George Stevens. As is well known, the end of the 1940s witnessed the first great crisis of the Western as a genre. Pure, simple Westerns began to produce an effect of artificiality and mechanical routine; their formula, it seemed, was exhausted. Directors reacted to this crisis by overlaying Westerns with elements of other genres. Thus, we have film noir westerns (Raoul Walsh's *Pursued*, which achieves the almost impossible task of transposing into a Western the dark universe of *film noir*), musical comedy Westerns (*Seven Brides for Seven Brothers*), psychological drama Westerns (*The Gunfighter*, with Gregory Peck), historical epic Westerns (the remake of *Cimmaron*), etc. In the 1950s, André Bazin baptized this new, "reflected" genre the *meta-Western*. The way *Shane* functions can be grasped only against the background of the meta-Western. *Shane* is the paradox of a Western the "meta-" dimension of which is the *Western itself*. In other words, it is a Western that implies a kind of nostalgic distance toward the universe of Westerns, a Western that functions, so to speak, as its own myth. To explain the effect produced by *Shane*, we must again refer to the function of the gaze. That is to say, if we remain on a commonsense level, if we do not include the dimension of the gaze, a simple and understandable question arises. If the meta-dimension of this Western is the Western itself, what accounts for the distance between the two levels? Why does the meta-Western not simply overlap with the Western itself? Why do we not have a Western pure and simple? The answer is that, by means of a structural necessity, *Shane* belongs to the order of the meta-Western: on the level of its immediate diegetic contents, it is of course a Western pure and simple, one of the purest ever made. But the very form of its historical context determines that we perceive it as meta-Western; i.e. precisely because, in its diegetic contents, it is a pure Western; the dimension "beyond Western" opened up by the historical context can be filled out only by the Western itself. In other words, *Shane* is a pure Western *at a time when pure Westerns were no longer possible*, when the Western was already perceived from a certain nostalgic distance, as a lost object. Which is why it is highly indicative that the story is told from a child's perspective (the perspective of a little boy, a member of a farming family defended against violent cattle breeders by Shane, a mythic hero appearing suddenly out of nowhere). The innocent, naive gaze of the other that fascinates us in nostalgia is in the last analysis always the gaze of a child.

In nostalgic retro films, then, the logic of the gaze qua object appears as such. The real object of fascination is not the displayed scene, but the gaze of the naive "other" absorbed, enchanted by it. In *Shane*, for example, we can be fascinated by the mysterious apparition of Shane only by proxy, through the medium of the "innocent" child's gaze, never immediately. Such a logic of fascination by which the subject sees in the object (in the image it views) its own gaze, i.e. by which, in the viewed image, it "sees itself seeing," is defined by Lacan (in chapter VI of his *Seminar XI*) as the very illusion of perfect self-mirroring that characterizes the Cartesian philosophical tradition of the subject's self-reflection. But what happens here with the *antinomy* between eye and gaze? The whole point of Lacan's argument is to oppose to the self-mirroring of philosophical subjectivity the irreducible discord between the gaze qua object and the subject's eye. Far from being the point of self-sufficient self-mirroring, the gaze qua object functions like a blot that blurs the transparency of the viewed image. I can never see properly, i.e. include in the totality of my field of vision the point in the other from which it gazes back at me. Like the extended blot in Holbein's *Ambassadors*, this point throws the harmony of my vision off balance.

The answer to our problem is clear: the function of the nostalgic object is precisely to *conceal* the antinomy between eye and gaze, i.e. the traumatic impact of the gaze qua object, by means of its power of fascination. In nostalgia, the gaze of the other is in a way domesticated, "gentrified"; instead of the gaze's erupting like a traumatic, disharmonious blot, we have the illusion of "seeing ourselves seeing," of seeing the gaze itself. In a way, we could say that the function of fascination is precisely to blind us to the fact that the other is already gazing at us. . . .

Montage

Montage is usually conceptualized as a way of producing from fragments of the real – pieces of film, discontinuous individual shots – an effect of "cinematic space," i.e. a specific cinematic reality. That is to say, it is universally acknowledged that "cinematic space" is never a simple repetition or imitation of external, "effective" reality, but an effect of montage. What is usually overlooked, however, is the way this transformation of fragments of the real into cinematic reality produces, through a kind of structural necessity, a certain leftover, a surplus that is radically heterogeneous to the cinematic reality but nonetheless implied by it, part of it.[5] That the surplus of the real is, in the last resort, precisely the gaze qua object is best exemplified by the work of Alfred Hitchcock.

Pascal Bonitzer has already pointed out that the fundamental constituent of the Hitchcockian universe is the so-called "spot": the stain upon which reality revolves, passes over into the real, the mysterious detail which "sticks out," which does not "fit" into the symbolic network of reality, and which, as such, indicates that "something is amiss" (the most notorious example is the windmill turning in the wrong direction in *Foreign Correspondent*, "denaturing" the idyllic image of the Dutch countryside). The fact that this spot ultimately coincides with the threatening gaze of the other is confirmed in an almost too obvious way by the famous tennis-court scene from *Strangers on a Train*, in which Guy watches the crowd watching the match. The camera first gives us a long shot of the crowd; all the heads turn alternatively left and right, following the path of the ball, all except one, which stares with a fixed gaze into the camera, i.e. at Guy. The camera then approaches this motionless head quickly. It is Bruno, linked with Guy by a murderous pact. Here we have in a pure, as it were, distilled form the stiff, motionless gaze, sticking out like a strange body and thus disturbing the harmony of the image by introducing a threatening dimension.

The function of the famous Hitchcockian tracking or traveling shot is precisely to produce a spot. In the tracking shot, the camera moves from an establishing shot to a close-up of a detail which must remain a blurred spot, the true form of which is accessible only to the anamorphic "view from aside." The shot slowly isolates from its surroundings the element which cannot be integrated into symbolic reality, which must remain a strange body if the depicted reality is to retain its consistency.[6] But what interests us here is the fact that under certain conditions montage intervenes in the tracking shot; i.e. the continuous approach of the camera is interrupted by cuts. What are these conditions? Briefly, the tracking shot must be interrupted when it is "subjective," when the camera shows us the subjective view of a person approaching the object-spot. That is to say, whenever, in a Hitchcock film, a hero, a person around whom the scene is structured, approaches an object, a thing, another person, anything that can become uncanny in the Freudian sense, Hitchcock usually alternates the "object-ive" shot of this person in motion, his or her walking toward the uncanny Thing, with the subjective shot of what this person sees, i.e. with the subjective view of the Thing. This is, so to speak, the elementary procedure, the zero-degree of Hitchcockian montage.

Let us take a few examples. When, toward the end of *Psycho*, Lilah climbs the hill to the mysterious old house, the presumed home of "Norman's mother," Hitchcock alternates the objective shot of Lilah climbing with her subjective view of the old house. He does the same in *The Birds*, in the famous scene analyzed in detail by Raymond Bellour, when Melanie, after crossing the bay in a small rented boat, approaches the house where Mitch's mother and sister live. Again, Hitchcock alternates the objective shot of the uneasy Melanie, aware of intruding on the privacy of a home, with her subjective view of the mysteriously silent house.[7] Of the innumerable other examples we might cite, let us mention just a short, trivial scene from *Psycho* between Marion and a car dealer. Here, Hitch-cock uses his montage procedure several times (when Marion approaches the car dealer; when, toward the end of the scene, a policeman approaches who has already stopped her on the highway the same morning, etc.). By means of this purely formal procedure, an entirely trivial, everyday incident is given an uneasy, threatening dimension that cannot be sufficiently accounted for by its diegetic content (i.e. by the fact that Marion is buying a new car with stolen money and thus fears being exposed). The Hitchcockian montage elevates an everyday, trivial object into a sublime Thing. By purely formal manipulation, it succeeds in bestowing on an ordinary object the aura of anxiety and uneasiness.[8]

In Hitchcockian montage, two kinds of shots are thus permitted and two forbidden. Permitted are the objective shot of the person approaching a Thing and the subjective shot presenting the Thing the way the person sees it. Forbidden are, inversely, the objective shot of the Thing, of the "uncanny" object, and – above all – the subjective shot of the approaching person from the perspective of the "uncanny" object itself. Let us refer again to the above-mentioned scene from *Psycho* depicting Lilah approaching the house on the top of the hill. It is crucial that Hitchcock shows the threatening Thing (the house) exclusively from the point of view of Lilah. If he were to have added a "neutral," objective shot of the house, the whole mysterious effect would have been lost. We (the spectators) would have to endure a radical desublimation. Suddenly we would become aware that there is nothing uncanny in the house as such, that the house is – like the "black house" from Patricia Highsmith's short story – just an ordinary old house. That is, the effect of uneasiness would be radically "psychologized," we would say to ourselves, "This is just an ordinary house, all the mystery and anxiety attached to it is just an effect of the heroine's psychic turmoil!"

The effect of uncanniness would also be lost if Hitchcock had immediately added a shot "subjectifying" the Thing, i.e. a subjective shot from inside the house. Let us imagine that, as Lilah approached the house, there had been a trembling shot showing Lilah through the window curtains, accompanied by the sound of hollow breathing, indicating thus that somebody from the house was watching her. Such a procedure (used regularly in standard thrillers) would, of course, intensify the strain. We would say to ourselves, "This is terrible! There is somebody in the house (Norman's mother?) watching Lilah, she is in mortal danger without knowing it!" But such a subjectivization would again suspend the status of the gaze *qua object*, reducing it to a subjective point-of-view of another diegetic personality. Sergei Eisenstein himself once risked such a direct subject-ivization in a scene from *The Old and the New* (1929), a film celebrating the successes of the collectivization of Soviet agriculture in the late 1920s. It is a somewhat Lysenkist scene demonstrating how nature itself finds pleasure in subordinating itself to the new rules of collective farming, how, for example, even cows and bulls mate more ardently once they are included into *kolkhozes*. In a quick tracking shot, the camera approaches a cow from behind, and in the next shot it becomes clear that this view of the camera is that of a bull mounting a cow. Needless to say, the effect of this scene is so obscene that it is almost nauseating. What we have here is really a kind of Stalinist pornography.

So it would therefore be wise to return to the Hollywood decency of Hitch-cock; let us again take the scene from *Psycho* in which Lilah approaches the house where "Norman's mother" presumably lives. In what does its uncanny dimension consist? Could we not best describe the effect brought about by this scene precisely by rephrasing the words of Lacan and say that, in a way, *it is already the house which gazes at Lilah*? Lilah sees the house, but nonetheless she cannot see it at the point from which it gazes back at her. Here the situation is the same as that in Lacan's recollection from his youth reported in chapter VIII of *Seminar XI*. As a student on holiday Lacan joined a fishing expedition. Among the fishermen on the boat, there was a certain Petit-Jean, who pointed out an empty sardine can glittering in the sun, tossed around by the waves, and said to him, "You see that can? Do you see it? Well, it doesn't see you!" Lacan's comment: "If what Petit-Jean said to me, namely that the can did not see me, had any meaning, it was because, in a sense, it was looking at me, just the same."[9] It was gazing at him because, as Lacan explains, using a key notion of the Hitchcockian universe, "I was rather out of place in the picture." Among these uneducated fishermen, he was, effectively, "the man who knew too much."

The Death Drive

The examples we have analyzed thus far were purposefully elementary, so let us conclude with an analysis of a scene in which Hitchcockian montage is part of a complex totality, the scene from *Sabotage* (1936) in which Sylvia Sidney kills

Oscar Homolka. The two characters are dining together at home; Sylvia is still in a state of shock, having learned recently that Oscar, her husband, is the "saboteur" responsible for the death of her younger brother, blown up by a bomb on a bus. When Sylvia brings the vegetable platter to the table, the knife on the platter acts as a magnet. It is almost as if her hand, against her will, is compelled to grab the knife, yet she cannot make up her mind. Oscar, who up to this point has pursued banal, everyday table conversation, perceives that she is spellbound by the knife and becomes aware of what it may mean to him. He stands up and walks round the table toward her. When they are face to face, he reaches for the knife but, unable to complete the gesture, lets *her* grab it. The camera then moves in tighter showing only their faces and shoulders, so that it is not clear what is happening with their hands. Suddenly Oscar utters a short cry and falls down, without our knowing whether she stabbed him or he, in a suicidal gesture, impaled himself upon the blade.

The first thing that deserves notice is the way the act of murder results from the encounter of two thwarted threatening gestures.[10] Both Sylvia's move forward with the knife and Oscar's move toward it correspond to the Lacanian definition of the threatening gesture: it is not a gesture that is interrupted, i.e. a gesture intended to be carried out but prevented from reaching its goal by an external obstacle. It is, on the contrary, something that was already begun in order *not* to be accomplished, not to be brought to its conclusion.[11] The very structure of the threatening gesture is thus that of a theatrical, hysterical act, of a split, self-hindered gesture, of a gesture that cannot be accomplished not because of an external obstacle but because it is in itself the expression of a contradictory, self-conflicting desire – in this case, of Sylvia's desire to stab Oscar and, at the same time, of the prohibition that blocks the realization of this desire. Oscar's move (when, after becoming aware of her intention, he stands up and comes forward to meet her) is again contradictory, split into his "self-preserving" desire to snatch the knife from her and master her, and his "masochistic" desire to offer himself to the stab of the knife, a desire conditioned by his morbid feeling of guilt. The successful act (the stabbing of Oscar) results thus from the encounter of the two failed, hindered, split acts. Her desire to stab him is met by his own desire to be killed and punished. Apparently, Oscar moves forward to defend himself, but this move is at the same time supported by the desire to be stabbed. So, ultimately, it is of no importance which of the two "really" carried out the crucial gesture (did she push the knife in or did he throw himself on the blade?). The murder results from the overlap, from the coincidence of his and her desire.

In relation to the structural place of Oscar's "masochistic" desire, we should refer to the logic of fantasy elaborated by Freud in "A Child Is Being Beaten." Freud explains here how the final form of the fantasy scene ("A child is being beaten") presupposes two previous phases. The first phase is "My father is beating the child (my brother, somebody who is my rival double)." The second is the "masochistic" inversion of the first, "sadistic" one ("I am being beaten by my father"). The third phase, the final form of the fantasy, renders indistinct, neutralizes the subject ("who is doing the beating?") as well as the object ("which child is being beaten?") in the impersonal "A child is being beaten." According to Freud, the crucial role belongs to the *second*, "masochistic" phase. This is where the real trauma lies, the phase that is radically "repressed." We find no trace of it in the child's fantasizing. We can only *construct* it retroactively on the basis of "clues" pointing to the fact that *there is something missing* between "My father is beating the child" and "A child is being beaten," i.e. that we cannot immediately transform the first form into the third, definite one; an intermediate form must intervene:

> This second phase is the most important and the most momentous of all. But we may say of it in a certain sense that it has never had a real existence. It is never remembered, it has never succeeded in becoming conscious. It is a construction of analysis, but it is no less a necessity on that account.[12]

The second form of the fantasy is thus the Lacanian real: a point which never took place "in (symbolic) reality," which was never inscribed into the symbolic texture, but which must nonetheless be presupposed as a kind of "missing link" guaranteeing the consistency of our symbolic reality. And our thesis is that Hitchcockian murders (in addition to Oscar's murder in *Sabotage*, let us mention at least the final fall of the saboteur from the Statue of Liberty in *Saboteur* and Gromek's murder in *Torn Curtain*) are governed by a homologous fantasy logic. The first phase is always "sadistic"; it consists in our identification with the hero, who finally has the opportunity to have done with the villain. We cannot wait to see Sylvia finish off the evil Oscar, to see the decent American push the Nazi saboteur over the railing, to see Paul Newman get rid of Gromek. The final phase is, of course, the compassionate inversion. When we see that the "villain" is really a helpless, broken being, we are overwhelmed with compassion and guilt; we are punished for our previous "sadistic" desire. In *Saboteur*, the hero tries desperately to *save* the villain suspended by his sleeve, the seams of which tear one by one; in *Sabotage*, Sylvia compassionately embraces the dying Oscar, preventing him from hitting the floor; in *Torn Curtain*, the very long duration of the act of murder, the clumsiness of Paul Newman, and the desperate resistance of the victim render the whole affair extremely painful.

At first it may seem that it is possible to pass directly from the first to the last phase, i.e. from sadistic pleasure at the imminent destruction of the villain to a sense of guilt and compassion. But if this were all, Hitchcock would be simply a kind of moralist, presenting us with the price to be paid for our "sadistic" desire: "You wanted the villain to be killed, now you've got it and can suffer the consequences!" But there is in Hitchcock always an intermediate phase. The "sadistic" desire for the villain to be killed is followed by a sudden awareness that it is actually already the "villain" himself who is, in a stifled but nonetheless unequivocal way, disgusted with his own corruption and wants to be "delivered" from this unbearable pressure through his own punishment, his own death. This is the delicate moment in which we become aware that the hero's (and thus our, the spectators') desire to annihilate the "villain" *is already the desire of the "villain" himself.* In *Sabotage*, for example, it is the moment at which it becomes clear that Sylvia's desire to stab Oscar overlaps with Oscar's desire to exculpate himself through his death. This constant implicit presence of a tendency to self-annihilation, of an enjoyment found in provoking one's own ruin, in short, of the "death drive," is what bestows upon the Hitchcockian "villain" his ambiguous charm, and it is at the same time what prevents us from passing immediately from an initial "sadism" to a final feeling of compassion for the villain. The compassion is based upon the awareness that the villain himself knows about his guilt and wants to die. In other words, the compassion arises only when we become aware of the *ethical* attitude contained in the villain's subjective position. . . .

We might also approach from this perspective the figure of the *femme fatale* in film noir – ruining the lives of men and at the same time victim of her own lust for enjoyment; obsessed by lust for power, endlessly manipulating her partners, and at the same time slave to some third, ambiguous person, sometimes even to an impotent or sexually ambivalent man. What bestows on her an aura of mystery is precisely the fact that she cannot be clearly located in the opposition between master and slave. When she seems permeated with intense pleasure, it suddenly becomes apparent that she suffers immensely. When she seems to be the victim of some horrible and unspeakable violence, it suddenly becomes clear that she enjoys it. So we can never be quite sure if she enjoys or suffers, if she manipulates or is herself manipulated. Thus the deeply ambiguous character of those moments in film noir (or in the hard-boiled detective novel) when the *femme fatale* breaks down and becomes the victim of her own game. Let us mention only the first model of such a breakdown, the final confrontation between Sam Spade and Brigid O'Shaughnessy in *The Maltese Falcon*. When she begins to lose her firm grasp of the situation, Brigid suffers a hysterical breakdown. Passing immediately from one strategy to another, she threatens, then cries and maintains that she did not know what was really happening to her. Suddenly she again assumes an attitude of cold distance and disdain, etc. In short, she dons the whole inconsistent array of hysterical masks. This final breakdown of the *femme fatale*, the moment when she appears as an entity without substance, as a series of inconsistent masks without a coherent ethical attitude, this moment when our fascination with her changes suddenly into a feeling of aversion at such a filthy, amorphous, slimy being, i.e. – to refer again to Shakespeare's *Richard II* – when we see "nought but shadows of what is not" where, previously, we had seen a clear and distinct form exerting tremendous seductive power – this moment of reversal is at the same time the moment of triumph for the hard-boiled detective. Now, when the fascinating figure of the *femme fatale* disintegrates into an inconsistent bric-a-brac of hysterical masks, he is finally capable of gaining a kind of distance toward her and of rejecting her.

The destiny of the *femme fatale* in film noir, her final hysterical breakdown, exemplifies perfectly the Lacanian proposition that "Woman does not exist." She is nothing but "the symptom of man." Her power of fascination masks the void of her non-existence, so when she is finally rejected, her whole ontological consistency is dissolved. But precisely as non-existing, i.e. at the moment at which, through the hysterical breakdown, she *assumes* her non-existence, she constitutes herself as a "subject." What is waiting for her *beyond* hysterization is the death drive at its purest.

In feminist writings on film noir we often encounter the thesis that the *femme fatale* presents a mortal threat to the man (the hard-boiled detective), i.e. that her boundless enjoyment menaces his very identity as subject. By rejecting her at the end, he regains his sense of personal integrity and identity. This thesis is true, but in a sense that is the exact opposite of the way it is usually understood. What is so menacing in the *femme fatale* is not the boundless enjoyment overwhelming the man and making of him woman's plaything or slave. It is not Woman as the object of fascination causing us to lose our sense of judgment and moral attitude but, on the contrary, that which remains hidden beneath this fascinating mask, what appears when the mask falls off – the dimension of the pure subject fully assuming the fact of the death drive. To use Kantian terminology, woman is not a threat to man insofar as she embodies pathological enjoyment, insofar as she enters the frame of a particular fantasy. The real dimension of the threat is revealed when we "traverse" the fantasy, when the coordinates of the fantasy space are lost through hysterical breakdown. In other words, what is really menacing about the *femme fatale* is not that she is fatal for *men* but that she presents a case of a "pure," non-pathological subject fully assuming *her own* fate. When the woman reaches this point, there are only two attitudes left to the man. Either he "cedes his desire," rejects her, and regains his imaginary, narcissistic identity (Sam Spade at the end of *Maltese Falcon*), or he *identifies* with the woman qua his symptom and meets his fate in a suicidal gesture (the act of Robert Mitchum in what is perhaps the crucial film noir, Jacques Tourneur's *Out of the Past*).[13]

But what has all this to do with Hitchcockian montage? Let us return to the scene from his *Sabotage* analyzed above. The decisive feature of this scene is that, although its emotional center is Sylvia, her terrible tension, she is the object and Oscar the subject. It is *his* subjective perspective, the rupture in this perspective, that articulates the rhythm of the scene, spells its deployment, so to speak. In the beginning, Oscar pursues the usual dinner conversation and entirely fails to notice Sylvia's extreme inner tension. When Sylvia becomes transfixed by the knife, the astonished Oscar glances at her and becomes aware of her desire. This introduces the first scansion. It is the end of the empty chatter; it becomes clear to Oscar that Sylvia is at the point of stabbing him. Thereupon, he stands up and steps forward to meet her. This part of the action is shot in the manner of Hitchcockian montage, i.e. the camera first shows us Oscar approaching Sylvia, then Oscar's view of the paralyzed, inflexible Sylvia, staring at him with a desperate look, as if asking him to help her make up her mind. When they find themselves face to face, he himself is paralyzed and lets *her* grab the knife. Then we pass to a shot of their heads exchanging intense glances, i.e. we do not see what is going on below their waists. Suddenly, he utters an incomprehensible cry. Next shot: a close-up of her hand holding the knife plunged deep into his chest. Thereupon she embraces him, as in an act of compassion, before he collapses to the floor. So he helped her indeed: by moving close to her, he lets her know that he has accepted her desire as his own, i.e. that he also wants to die. No wonder, then, that afterward, Sylvia embraces him compassionately. He has, so to speak, met her halfway, delivered her from an unbearable tension.[14]

The moment of Hitchcockian montage – the moment at which Oscar advances toward Sylvia – is thus the moment at which Oscar accepts her desire as his own, or – to refer to the Lacanian definition of the hysteric's desire as the desire of the other – the moment at which Oscar is hysterized. When we see Sylvia through Oscar's eyes, in the subjective shot of the camera approaching her, we witness the moment at which Oscar becomes aware that her desire overlaps with his own, i.e. that he himself yearns to die – the moment at which he takes upon himself the lethal gaze of the other.

Notes

1   Jacques Lacan, *The Four Fundamental Concepts of Psycho-Analysis*, London, Hogarth Press, 1977, p. 109.
2   It is precisely because in pornography the picture does *not* gaze back at us – i.e. because it is "flat," without any mysterious "spot" that must be looked at "awry" in order to assume distinct form – that the fundamental prohibition determining the direction of the look of the actors on the screen is suspended. In a pornographic film, the actor – usually a woman – in the moment of intense sexual pleasure, looks directly into the camera, addressing us, the spectators.
3   This paradox of the "impossible knowledge" inscribed into the way persons react on screen is far more interesting than it may appear at first sight. For example, it offers us a clue to the logic of Hitchcock's cameo appearances in his own films. In *Topaz*, without doubt his worst film, Hitchcock appears in a wheelchair in an airport lounge, as if wishing to inform us that his creative power is crippled. In his last film, *Family Plot*, he appears as a shadow on the windowpane of the death registry office, as if wishing to inform us that he is already close to death. Every one of his cameo appearances reveals such an "impossible knowledge," as if Hitchcock were capable of assuming for an instant a position of pure meta-language, of taking an "objective look" at himself and locating himself in the picture.
4   Fredric Jameson, "Postmodernism, or The Cultural Logic of Late Capitalism," *New Left Review*, no. 146 (July–August 1984), pp. 53–92.
5   This problematic was first articulated by Noël Burch in his theory of *hors-champ*, i.e. of a specific exterior implied, constituted by the very interplay of the *champ* and *contre-champ*; see Noël Burch, *Theory of Film Practice*, London, Praeger, 1973.
6   See Slavoj Žižek, "Hitchcock," *October*, no. 38 (Fall 1986), pp. 99–111.
7   It is by no means a pure coincidence that, in both cases, the object approached by the hero is a *house*. For *Notorious*, Pascal Bonitzer developed a detailed theory of the house

as a place of an incestuous secret in Hitchcock's work; see Pascal Bonitzer, *Le Champ aveugle*, Paris, Gallimard, 1982.

8 In his ironic, amiably sadistic teasing of the spectator, Hitchcock takes into account precisely this gap between the formal procedure and the content it is applied to, i.e. the fact that anxiety results from a purely formal procedure. First, by means of formal manipulation, Hitchcock bestows upon an everyday, trivial object the aura of mystery and anxiety. Afterwards, it becomes clear that this object effectively *is* just an everyday object. The best-known case is to be found in the second version of *The Man Who Knew Too Much*: on a suburban London Street, James Stewart approaches a stranger. As they silently exchange glances, an atmosphere of tension and anxiety is created. It seems that the stranger is threatening Stewart, but soon afterwards we discover that Stewart's suspicion was entirely unfounded. The stranger was just an accidental passer-by.

9 Lacan, p. 95.

10 See Mladen Dolar, "L'Agent secret: le spectateur qui en savait trop," in Slavoj Žižek, ed., *Tout ce que Vous avez toujours voulu savoir sur Lacan, sans jamais oser le demander à Hitchcock*, Paris, Navarin, 1988.

11 Lacan, p. 114.

12 Sigmund Freud, *The Standard Edition of the Complete Psychological Works*, trans. James Strachey, London, Hogarth Press and the Institute of Psycho-Analysis, 1955, vol. XVII, p. 185.

13 The fact that this had to do with a post-fantasy "purification" of desire is attested by an ingenious detail. In the final scene, the wardrobe of Jane Greer unmistakably resembles that of a nun.

14 It was François Truffaut who not only pointed out that this scene "almost suggests suicide rather than murder," but also drew the parallel between Oscar's and Carmen's deaths: "It's as if [Oscar] Homolka were allowing himself to be killed by Sylvia Sidney. Prosper Merimée staged Carmen's death on the same dramatic principle, with the victim thrusting her body forward to meet the slayer's fatal stab" (François Truffaut, *Hitchcock*, New York, Simon & Schuster, 1984, p. 77).

Part X
Class and the Culture
Industries

Introduction

Toby Miller

Class

Class is an uncomfortable topic in film theory. Class conflicts and solidarities make their mark as clearly in most people's lives as do those of religion, gender, nation, sexuality, race, and age. But the concept of class is dogged by its associations with state socialism and totalitarian government. The weakness of US academic Marxism also helps explain this *lacuna* along with sociology's empiricist and functionalist heritage and the humanities' concentration on personal identity (on this point, see James, 1996: 2). Most cultural theory simply denies the relevance of class, in a way that would seem bizarre even to readers of the *New York Times*, where class distinctions are a matter of daily speculation. In Third World countries, the issue of colonialism is more pressing than internal inequality, and has been a focus for film. This is not to suggest an absence of class consciousness: consider *Kaddu Beykat* (Safi Faye, 1975), Ousmane Sembène's *Mandabi* (1968), or Clarence Delgado's *Niiwam* (1992), which address the experiences of peasants in dealing with the bureaucratic class of the postcolonial order (Diawara, 1992: 46; Cham, 1996: 6, 8). Britain has produced a goodly body of film theory that relates to class, but even there, the Althusserian turn took Marxism away from the labor process of film, audience segmentation, and control of the film industry, and towards more textual approaches that concentrated on ideology (see Part VIII on the apparatus).

Yet capitalist narrative films frequently evoke class politics, from the transcendent notion of continental or hemispheric migration in search of self-improvement to the make-over sequences that transform shop girls into princesses. Sometimes this makes a pretty point. In *The Lady from Shanghai* (Orson Welles, 1948), Welles's escape from a murder trial is aided by his fellow-workers, as another seaman and a cook add to the diversion he has created. Theirs is an instinctive response to the plight of their own class; the "legitimacy" of bourgeois law drops away in the face of interpersonal familiarity linked to a shared experience of financial domination. In *Gone With the Wind* (Victor Fleming, 1939), the connections and disarticulations that tie Confederate whites to one another are about owning land as well as sharing race. The tragic lack of connectedness between the warders and inmates of *Titicut Follies* (Frederick Wiseman, 1967) sees potential class links obscured by the power of the state to decree good and evil and divide the working class accordingly. *My Fair Lady* (George Cukor, 1964) is about the linguistic make-over that a (male) intellectual fraction of the ruling class can provide for a (female) worker: accent is an immediate signifier of social location, all-powerful yet also mutable in the hands of official knowledge and training. Alec Guinness's character in *The Man in the White Suit* (Alexander MacKendrick, 1951) is fatally compromised by his lack of clear adherence to a class: his accent and training mark him out as privileged, but his industrial position is that of a blue-collar employee. He is thus accepted by neither segment of society, quite apart from his invention of an indestructible fabric that will leave the textile industry without the gift of built-in product obsolescence.

Apart from these obvious examples, class differs from those categories with signifiers that are easily read against signifieds in the material world (think of gender, as shown by Patrice Petro, chapter 33). As a theoretical object, class is somewhat inimical to immediate referentiality in social identity. It is not an already-constituted group of people, but frequently exists as a "class on paper." Its members may have similar jobs, opinions, and dispositions, but their existence as a unified class is a theoretical one that manufactures a "space of social relations" as a heuristic tool of social theory. It is not always self-consciously occupied by people, and in particular, is a "difficult" thing to say in much cultural politics. And it is also increasingly awkward to use class as a category of identifiable agency. When and how does a class "act?" One moment when it makes itself evident is via what Pierre Bourdieu calls "the labor of representation," work done to produce and promote a view of the world, as per culture (Rosenthal, 1988: 30–1; Bourdieu, 1994: 113–15).

The word "class" derives from a classical Latin term referring to the division of Roman citizens by wealth (Martin, 1986: 70). There are two principal ways of conceptualizing class: the categorical and the generative. Categorical systems rely on people's opinions of their social location and a number of non-economic factors such as status and power, as well as their position in the labor market. Generative definitions, by contrast, focus on people's relationships to the means of production. So whereas the first looks at wealth, public standing, authority over others, politics, and culture, the second is concerned with who owns labor power and the fruits of its investment in goods and services. Leaving to one side the accounts of class derived from self-apportionment of attributes through questionnaire sociology, or the Weberian stress on position within the labor market and the additional grids of status and authority, the Marxist tradition offers discontinuities in this area. There is a division (1) between those with or without property; (2) between those with or without power or authority; (3) between those with or without control of the forces of production (technology); and (4) between persons in differing relationships to a shifting set of processes in the production, appropriation, and distribution of surplus value (for non-Marxist accounts, see Inkeles, 1964: 84–6; Weber, 1952; for Marxism, see Resnick and Wolff, 1988: 2–4).

The arts have long been crucial to class societies. For instance, the very model of the patron of the arts derives from the cultural subvention provided to ruling-class iconography by the absolutist monarchs of mid- to late-millennial Europe, up to the advent of bourgeois democracy. The principal concern of the old absolutism was "a high standard of culture within a very narrow context," in part via the reproduction of ruling classes by training their progeny (Vitanyi, 1983: 98). The appearance of laissez-faire capitalism marked the desire to supplant automatic transfer of privilege with its earned equivalent. Capital was to take priority over the former system of inherited control of land and state. Although there have been cities for 6,000 years, capitalism accelerated their growth dramatically. With the modern city of the Industrial Revolution came notions of public opinion and a public culture (Bauer, 1932: 670). Production and its infrastructure formed the stimulus to networks such as libraries and theaters and the need to train a proletariat to manufacture and to consume; and hence, to appreciate. Equally, there was the need to form a sense of belonging in the wider populace. This wider populace included new types of person and "new spheres of life.... The diffusion of culture to the middle class and the formation of a broader educated public interested in the arts" (Habermas, 1989: 8). Sometimes in imitation of aristocracy, and sometimes as an act of its own invention, the bourgeoisie became an innovator, striving for a "consciously constructed culture" as a means of building a new social order (Marshall, 1976: 290).

In the absence of the "controlling paternosters of kin, clan or indenture" (Wilson, 1991: 6), the modern city provided the first comparatively open cultural site for people to meet promiscuously, if sometimes with additional policing of bourgeois women (de Swaan, 1990: 142). (You get a sense of this in a postcolonial context when Jimmy Cliff goes to Kingston in search of transcendence from rural Jamaican life in *They Harder They Come* (Perry Henzell, 1972), and in sequences in *Jom* (Samb Makharam, 1982) that show young women leaving the African desert to become maids for the urban elite (Cham, 1996: 13).) The nineteenth-century sociologist Georg Simmel's account of the "touch-and-go elements of metropolitan life" underscores the polysemous "reserve with its overtone of hidden aversion" that offered an anonymous history and new "individual independence and differentiation" along with the "right to distrust" (Simmel, 1976: 88–9). As the great migrations towards European cities took place in the nineteenth- and early twentieth centuries, time and space were reordered by contrast with the comparatively sealed-off worlds of rural management (Lash, 1990: 17).

For the city required a "cognitive map" as well as a strictly spatial one, encompassing all the "vaster and properly unrepresentable totality" of the social (Jameson, 1991: 51). As a set of texts and a set of buildings, cinema provides just such class maps and streetscapes, just that mixture of seamless anonymity with careful social gradation that the capitalist city produced. On the one hand, this led to social criticisms of movie theaters as houses of mayhem. On the other, it led to the push for government participation in filmmaking, either as censor or producer.

Class critiques have been dubious about government participation in culture, as per national cinemas, even as antidotes to market capitalism. In 1848 Marx and his collaborators regarded "the executive of the modern state as but a committee for managing the common affairs of the whole bourgeoisie" (Marx and Engels, 1976: 239). To Engels, the "state was the official representative of the whole of society, its concentration in a visible body, but it was so only in so far as it was the state of that class which in its time represented the whole of society" (ibid.: 362–3). As the possibilities of action by the left within parliamentary democracy emerged with time, this position periodically seemed to soften.

Film has been a focus for competing ideas about class society, as evidenced by the debates over audiences described elsewhere. The editor of several movie magazines in the 1920s, for example, hailed the cinema as dedicated "to serve all peoples and all classes" by moving among "the great illiterate and semiliterate strata where words falter, fail, and miss" (Ramsaye, 1947: 11, 1). Film requires massive finance, always at the production stage but especially now at the level of distribution and promotion – so it is the province of the wealthy. But it also needs a mass audience to succeed, and must appeal across class tastes. The fact that so many stockbrokers attacked Oliver Stone's *Wall Street* (1987) for being meaningless to "ordinary" Americans and mistreating the ruling elite is some evidence that it touched a class nerve (Denzin, 1991: 87). The class aspects of film do not begin and end with textual content and spectator response: conditions of production, distribution, promotion, and exhibition are part of a labor process. Consider the classic indictment of Depression social policy, *Housing Problems* (Edgar Anstey and Arthur Elton, 1935). It could be interpreted as "radical ethnography," in that the underclass is given voice and vision. But looking at the conditions of existence of the text encourages us to note its status as a promotional device for the gas industry and the project of governmental intervention in homes and the creation of asocial "project" accommodation (Corner, 1996: 64).

Foregrounding the working class in Hollywood narrative is also no guarantee of a progressive politics. As Michael Ryan and Douglas Kellner (1988: 109) point out, *Rocky* (John G. Avildsen, 1976), *Flashdance* (Adrian Lyne, 1983), and *Saturday Night Fever* (John Badham, 1977) assuredly address and focus on working people and their desire to transcend the misery of class society, but always in an individualistic way that relies on personal traits and determination ("making dreams come true") rather than favoring solidarity and collective political action: think also of *Coal Miner's Daughter* (Michael Apted, 1980). Love, sex, commodities, and occupational mobility are the elixir, not union organizing, voting, lobbying, or media activism. An engagement with structural inequality is subordinated to a conservative notion of self-improvement and the denigration of lived working experience. Working-class white folks are easy targets for redneck, conservative labels, as per the Vietnam War issues raised in *Easy Rider* (Dennis Hopper, 1969) or *Joe* (John G. Avildsen, 1970). When unionism, for example, is foregrounded, it is as often in the context of corruption or racial divisions within labor – *On the Waterfront* (Elia Kazan, 1954), *F.I.S.T.* (Norman Jewison, 1978), or *Blue Collar* (Paul Schrader, 1978) – as it is to do with communal successes – *Norma Rae* (Martin Ritt, 1979). There are significant exceptions, notably the work of John Sayles, but the general trend is clear.

Attempts to do class analysis in film involve a number of moves: literally observing how a class acts (its clothing, gestures, movements, work, leisure, home-life); seeing who controls the means of communication (technicians, producers, directors, censors, shareholders); analyzing the ideological message of stories (personal transcendence versus collective solidarity, the legitimacy of capitalist "freedoms," or the compensations in family and community for social inequality); and noting which interests are served by government-sponsored national film industries (local bourgeoisies, men, whites, distributors, "the people"). In textual terms, those films that foreground class through theme or identification (many 1960s British documentaries and the British New Wave of that period, Michael Apted's *7 Up* series, classic Soviet silent-era cinema, and Gillo Pontecorvo's *The Battle of Algiers* (1966), for example) do not exhaust the list of films ready for class readings. Here, patterns of speech or costume may not only signify the immediate referent of social position, but go beyond that to the trappings, logic, and operation of capitalism: how the clothes were made, or the housing conditions that go along with the accent; we might think here of the James Bond series' obsession with small differentiations of social position through food, alcohol, cars, and the way that hotel staff and other employees are easily ordered about. Some of us deem it important that Sean Connery orders the Dom Perignon '52, while George Lazenby orders the '57.

Drawing attention to class is not always a radical initiative. Consider the "polite" side to national art cinemas and their oft-expressed opposition to the export of US screen products and infrastructure. British tourism targets and TV export opportunities to the US encourage a screen focus on the ruling-class frippery of a lost age (Hoggart, 1995: 52), what Rupert Murdoch (1989: 5) calls "drama run by the costume department". Anxieties about American entertainment are frequently expressed under the guise of concern for repressive or phantasmatic "national cultures." Governments that see themselves as responsible for the provision of culture have a long tradition of state support for – and not just censorship of – the cinema. But the extraordinary puritanism of some cultural protection denies the liberatory aspects of much US entertainment for stifling class structures. In 1945 J. M. Keynes addressed the BBC radio audience on the need for decentralized, publicly financed culture to avoid "the excessive prestige of metropolitan standards and fashions" engendered by the cinema's powers of mimetic desire: "Let every part of Merry England be merry in its own way. Death to Hollywood" (quoted in Mayer, 1946). What could this mean, other than keeping the provinces in their place and ensuring that only certain aspects of the culture industries were given state funds to assist their work?

The Culture Industries

Approaches to film and class often draw on the notion of cultural industries, generally understood as "institutions in our society which employ the characteristic modes of production and organization of industrial corporations to produce and disseminate symbols in the form of cultural goods and services, generally, although not exclusively, as commodities" (Garnham, 1987: 25). The goods produced are often regarded as "non-material," in that they satisfy aesthetically rather than in a utilitarian way (Hirsch, 1972: 639). But traces of the capitalist urge that animated them are present, nevertheless.

There are three basic critiques of this process:

> that mass culture is an industry organized for profit; that in order for this industry to be profitable, it must create a homogeneous and standardized product that appeals to a mass audience; and that this requires a process in which the industry transforms the creator into a worker on a mass production assembly line, requiring him or her to give up the individual expression of his own skill and values. (Gans, 1974: 20)

The idea that culture industries "impress . . . the same stamp on everything" derives from the Frankfurt School, a group of scholars interested in what they called "critical theory." In the 1930s, leading Frankfurters Theodor Adorno and Max Horkheimer migrated from Germany to the United States, where they found a political acquiescence that reminded them of what they thought they had left behind (Adorno and Horkheimer, 1977). Their explanation for this concentrates on the production-line development of culture. The excitement of millions in the face of entertainment encourages business to use systems of reproduction that ensure the identical nature of what is offered. Because demand is dispersed and supply is centered, management organizes itself through a clear administrative logic. This central administration of cultural output is socially acceptable because it is said to reflect the tastes and desires of audiences. For Adorno and Horkheimer, this denies a cycle of power in which consumers are manipulated through the mobilization of cultural technology by those at the economic apex of production. Coercion is mistaken for free will and culture becomes one more industrial process, subordinated to dominant economic forces within society that call for standardization.

In the 1970s the filmmaker Alexander Kluge (then a Frankfurt School fellow-traveler, prior to a career in TV that saw him change his mind on such matters) offered the following:

> In order to cheat spectators on an entrepreneurial scale, the entrepreneurs have to designate the spectators themselves as entrepreneurs. The spectator must sit in the movie house or in front of the TV set like a commodity owner: like a miser grasping every detail and collecting surplus on everything.... Understanding a film completely is conceptual imperialism which colonizes its objects. If I have understood everything then something has been emptied out. (Kluge, 1981–2: 210–11)

The one element that might stand against crass uniformity is "individual consciousness." But that consciousness, according to Adorno and Horkheimer (1977), has itself been customized to the dictates of the economy. In its pre-capitalist and modernist forms, this authentic spirit of creativity produced and appreciated forms of art that both expressed and surpassed the conditions of their existence. But as the culture industries are structured like any other capitalist industrial sector, their special role is to provide ideological legitimacy for the dominant mode of production by hailing social subjects as members of a society (Kellner, 1995: 29). As Ross Gibson says, this discourse elevates "true art" by allowing it the virtues of courage, innovation, and energy. The popular, by contrast, is construed as "lazy and craven in its 'contentment' to deal with prefabricated signs and materials" (Gibson, 1992: 201).

The nomenclature of the culture industries brings to mind a non-organic, distanced, remotely conceived but locally delivered sense of culture. For all the loss of organic unity when religion was replaced by the economy as a dominant organizing principle in modern capitalist society, this culture is far from chaotic. The imperative of generating consumption through spectacle means that for Guy Debord, writing in the 1960s, quality is always forgone in favor of quantity and regularity, in ways that deny the actual conditions of factory production that make objects for sale through labor power. Commodities become the totality of life, hiding not only the role of work in their own creation, but the rest of real life. Commodities are designated with human characteristics (beauty, tastefulness, serenity, and so on) as compensations for the absence of these qualities in everyday life under capitalism: a "permanent opium war" (Debord, 1995: 26–7, 29–30).

The price paid for attending a film (exchange-value) takes over from the desires exhibited in the actual practical utility of what is being purchased (use-value). This price expresses the momentary monetary value of that need, rather than its lasting practical utility for people. That notion of built-in obsolescence and value bestowed via a market is in fact a key to all commodities, popular or otherwise. They elicit desire by wooing consumers, glancing at them sexually, and smelling and looking nice in ways that are borrowed from romantic love but then reverse that relationship: people learn about correct forms of romantic love from commodities, such as love scenes in movies. Wolfgang Haug's term, "commodity aesthetics," is about the division between what commodities promise by way of seduction and what they are actually about (Haug, 1986: 17, 19, 35).

While much of the Enlightenment disappointment characteristic of the Frankfurt School is shared by conservatives in their negativity towards the notion of "the masses," for some 1960s theorists, mass culture represents the absolute apex of modernity. Far from being supremely alienating, it stands for the expansion of civil society, the first moment in history when central political organs and agendas are receptive to and part of the broad mass of the community. The population is now part of the social, rather than excluded from the means and politics of political calculation. Such formulations claim that the number of people classed as outsiders is diminished in mass society, along with the lessening of authority, the promulgation of individual rights and respect, and the intensely interpersonal, large-scale human interaction necessitated by industrialization and aided by systems of mass communication. The spread of advertising breaks down social barriers between high and low culture (Shils, 1966: 505–6, 511).

On the left, latter-day Frankfurter Hans Magnus Enzensberger (1970; see chapter 31, this volume) views the mass media as a new opportunity and site for mass participation in making meaning, a breakaway from high-cultural dominance and feudal patterns of owning and controlling culture. Walter Benjamin, a contemporary of Adorno and Horkheimer, is best known for this more positive position, welcoming film as an end to individualistic notions of genius and the arcane in favor of materialist criticism. The infinitely reproducible nature of mechanical (and now, electronic) art meant that authenticity and authority were also brought into question. The intimidating aura of high-cultural quality was endangered, making for a potentially liberatory culture that addressed the needs of ordinary people. Tradition was blasted away like the foundations to an outmoded building. Benjamin opposes the efforts of fascism to render politics artistic to a radical riposte that will politicize art (Benjamin, 1985: 216–21, 242).

Writing today, Jean Baudrillard maintains that all products purchased within capitalist societies involve the consumption of advertising, rather than objects themselves, such is the contest for newness and currency. The culture industries are central to this model of the compulsion to buy, through the double-sided nature of advertising and "the good life" of Hollywood luxury: they encourage competition between people at the same time as they standardize processes to manufacture unity in the face of diversity. For all the seeming affluence and proliferation of material goods, the idea of people achieving transcendence has been displaced by the overwhelming force of objects rather than people in determining life. Commodities dominate a formerly human and natural landscape. The corollary of this is the simultaneous triumph and emptiness of the sign as a source and measure of value. Baudrillard discerns four "successive phases of the image." It begins as a reflection of reality. This is transformed into a perversion of reality, as representation of the truth is displaced by false information. Then these two delineable phases of truth and lies become indistinct, as underlying reality is lost. Finally, the sign refers to itself, with no residual need of correspondence with the real. The sign is its own simulation (Baudrillard, 1988c: 10–11; 1988a: 29; 1988b: 170).

What has the culture industries paradigm done for film theory? It has alerted us to the fact that organizations train, finance, describe, circulate, and reject actors and activities that go under the signs "filmmaker" and "film." Governments, trade unions, colleges, social movements, community groups, and businesses aid, fund, control, promote, teach, and evaluate creative persons. They define and implement criteria that make possible the use of the word "creative," through law courts that permit erotica on the grounds that they are works of art, schools that require pupils to study film on the grounds that it is improving, film commissions that sponsor scripts on the grounds that they reflect society back to itself, or studios that invite Academy Award voters to parties as promotions for their movies. In turn, these criteria may themselves derive, respectively, from legal doctrine, citizenship or tourism aims, and profit plans. This industrial infrastructure has implications for what it actually means to produce culture:

> The popular notion of a struggling artist working isolated in a lonely garret is extremely misleading as a representation of the norm. Creators often struggle economically, but in modern societies most of them work in organizational settings – either directly in an organization or indirectly dependent upon one or more organizations to distribute or exhibit their work...even culture production by individuals occurs in collective contexts...networks of functionally interdependent individuals, groups, and organizations. (Zollars and Cantor, 1993: 3)

Of course, film combines aspects of artisanal labor with a dense process of division of labor, legal regulation, multiple ownership of different but related industrial structures, and so on. Douglas Gomery (1989: 44) proposes that "At the final accounting, it is the industrial organization of media entertainments – at all points on the circuit of planning, production, distribution, exhibition and circulation – that determines the text."

Consider this "culture industries" account of Hollywood. In the decade from 1946, suburbanization, televisualization, and anti-trust decisions compelled changes to the vertically integrated studio system. There was a decrease of a third in the number of Hollywood-made films and more than a doubling of imports. Production went overseas as location shooting became a means of differentiating stories, and studios purchased facilities around the world to utilize cheap labor. Between 1950 and 1973, just 60 percent of Hollywood films in production began their lives in the US, with global presales garnering funds from distributors around the world in advance of production in Los Angeles. This opened the door to the US for European producers. And American financial institutions are now long-practiced at purchasing foreign theaters and distribution companies and sharing risk and profit with local businesses. By the end of the 1980s overseas firms were crucial suppliers of funds invested in Hollywood or loans against distribution rights in their countries of origin. Joint production arrangements are well-established between US firms and French, British, Swedish, and Italian companies, with connections to theme parks, cabling, and home video. Hollywood production is undertaken by small editing, lighting, and rental studio companies that work with independent producers and sell their services across a variety of audio-visual industries. Films may be shot across the world, but decision-making and post-production are concentrated in the LA entertainment sector (although animation work is frequently undertaken in Southeast Asia and Europe by employees at lower rates of pay than US workers) (Wasko, 1994: 33; Miège, 1989: 46). Filmmaking needs to be understood in terms of investment patterns and industrial infrastructure as well as texts, and this is true of distribution and exhibition as well as production. The screen industries employ over a million working people in the US alone, most of whom have low weekly earnings. These groups have important internal divisions between so-called "talent" and "craft" and between heavily unionized film and broadcast workers and non-union cable employees; but their numerical growth and willingness to strike during the dominance of Republican union-busting was a beacon through the 1980s and should gain greater attention from conventional film theory (Gray and Seeber, 1996a: 34; 1996b: 4, 7; Christopherson, 1996: 87, 105–6).

There has been recent interest in the concept of the culture industries as a way to economic renewal rather than a category of critique, even for many on the left. With manufacturing industry departing much of Europe, efforts have been made by local governments and the European Union to develop the services sector (Frith, 1991). In keeping with this, some influential film and media critics (Sylvia Harvey, Richard Collins, Stuart Cunningham, Angela McRobbie, and Jacques Attali, for example), have shifted from textual analysis to policy analysis. Their discussions of industry structure avoid the purity of Frankfurt and represent a shift from conventional film theory's lack of interest in the who, what, when, where, and how of filmmaking. On the other hand, the powerful moral suasion of Frankfurter critique is always looking over their shoulder.

Works Cited

Adorno, Theodor W. 1991. "Culture Industry Reconsidered." In *Culture and Society: Contemporary Debates*, ed. Jeffrey C. Alexander and Steven Seidman. Cambridge: Cambridge University Press.

——and Max Horkheimer 1977. "The Culture Industry: Enlightenment as Mass Deception." In *Mass Communication and Society*, ed. James Curran, Michael Gurevitch, and Janet Woollacott. London: Edward Arnold.

Baudrillard, Jean 1988a. "Consumer Society." Trans. Jacques Mourrain. In *Selected Writings*, ed. Mark Poster. Stanford: Stanford University Press.

——1988b. "Simulacra and Simulations." Trans. Paul Foss, Paul Patton, and Philip Beitchman. In *Selected Writings*, ed. Mark Poster. Stanford: Stanford University Press.

——1988c. "The System of Objects." Trans. Jacques Mourrain. In *Selected Writings*, ed. Mark Poster. Stanford: Stanford University Press.

Bauer, W. 1932. "Public Opinion." In *Encyclopaedia of the Social Sciences*, ed. E. Seligman. New York: Macmillan.

Benjamin, Walter 1985. *Illuminations: Essays and Reflections*. Trans. Harry Zohn, ed. Hannah Arendt. New York: Schocken.

Bourdieu, Pierre 1994. "Social Space and Symbolic Power." In *The Polity Reader in Social Theory*. Cambridge: Polity Press.

Cham, Mbye B. 1996. "Introduction." In *African Experiences of Cinema*, ed. Imruh Bakari and Mbye Cham. London: BFI.

Christopherson, Susan 1996. "Flexibility and Adaptation in Industrial Relations: The Exceptional Case of the US Media Entertainment Industries." In *Under the Stars: Essays on Labor Relations in Arts and Entertainment*, ed. L. S. Gray and R. L. Seeber. Ithaca, NY: Cornell University Press.

Corner, John 1996. *The Art of Record: A Critical Introduction to Documentary*. Manchester: Manchester University Press.

de Swaan, Abram 1990. *The Management of Normality*. London: Routledge.

Debord, Guy 1995. *The Society of the Spectacle*. Trans. Donald Nicolson-Smith. New York: Zone.

Denzin, Norman K. 1991. *Images of Postmodern Society: Social Theory and Contemporary Cinema*. London: Sage.

Diawara, Manthia 1992. *African Cinema: Politics and Culture*. Bloomington: Indiana University Press.

Engels, Frederick 1976. *Anti-Dühring: (Herr Eugen Dühring's Revolution in Science)*. Peking: Foreign Languages Press.

Enzensberger, Hans Magnus 1970. "Constituents of a Theory of the Media," *New Left Review* no. 64: 13–36.

Frith, Simon 1991. "The Culture of Culture Industries," *Cultural Studies Birmingham* no. 1: 134–55.

Gans, Herbert J. 1974. *Popular Culture and High Culture: An Analysis and Evaluation of Taste*. New York: Basic.

Garnham, Nicholas 1987. "Concepts of Culture: Public Policy and the Cultural Industries," *Cultural Studies* 1, no. 1: 23–37.

Gibson, Ross 1992. *South of the West: Postcolonialism and the Narrative Construction of Australia*. Bloomington: Indiana University Press.

Gomery, Douglas 1989. "Media Economics: Terms of Analysis," *Critical Studies in Mass Communication* 6, no. 1: 43–60.

Gray, L. S. and R. Seeber 1996a. "The Industry and the Unions: An Overview." In *Under the Stars: Essays on Labor Relations in Arts and Entertainment*, ed. L. S. Gray and R. L. Seeber. Ithaca, NY: Cornell University Press. 15–49.

——1996b. "Introduction." *Under the Stars: Essays on Labor Relations in Arts and Entertainment*, ed. L. S. Gray and R. L. Seeber. Ithaca, NY: Cornell University Press.

Habermas, Jürgen 1989. *The New Conservatism: Cultural Criticism and the Historians' Debate*. Trans. and ed. Shierry Weber Nicholsen. Cambridge, Mass.: MIT Press.

Haug, W. F. 1986. *Critique of Commodity Aesthetics: Appearance, Sexuality and Advertising in Capitalist Society*. Trans. Robert Bock. Cambridge: Polity Press.

Hirsch, Paul 1972. "Processing Fads and Fashions: An Organization-Set Analysis of Cultural Industry Systems," *American Journal of Sociology* 77, no. 4: 639–59.

Hoggart, Richard 1995. "Power, Throne, and Rank," *Society* 33, no. 1: 51–2.

Inkeles, Alex 1964. *What is Sociology? An Introduction to the Discipline and Profession*. Englewood Cliffs, NJ: Prentice-Hall.

James, David 1996. "Introduction: Is There Class in this Text?" In *The Hidden Foundation: Cinema and the Question of Class*, ed. David James and Rick Berg. Minneapolis: University of Minnesota Press.

Jameson, Fredric 1991. *Postmodernism, or the Cultural Logic of Late Capitalism*. London: Verso.

Kellner, Douglas 1995. *Media Culture: Cultural Studies, Identity and Politics Between the Modern and the Postmodern*. New York: Routledge.

Kluge, Alexander 1981–2. "On Film and the Public Sphere." Trans. Thomas Y. Levin and Miriam B. Hansen. *New German Critique* nos. 24–5: 206–20.

Lash, Scott 1990. *Sociology of Postmodernism*. London: Routledge.

Marshall, T. H. 1976. "The Nature and Determinants of Social Order." In *Sociological Perspectives: Selected Readings*, ed. Kenneth Thompson and Jeremy Tunstall. Harmondsworth: Penguin.

Martin, Pete 1986. "The Concept of Class." In *Classic Disputes in Sociology*, ed. R. J. Anderson, J. A. Hughes, and W. W. Sharrock. London: Allen & Unwin.

Marx, Karl and Friedrich Engels 1976. "Bourgeois and Proletarians." In *Sociological Perspectives: Selected Readings*, ed. Kenneth Thompson and Jeremy Tunstall. Harmondsworth: Penguin.

Mayer, J. P. 1946. *Sociology of Film: Studies and Documents*. London: Faber and Faber.

Miège, Bernard 1989. *The Capitalization of Cultural Production*. Trans. Josiane Hay, Nicholas Garnham, and UNESCO. New York: International General.

Murdoch, Rupert 1989. "Freedom in Broadcasting." MacTaggart Lecture at the Edinburgh Film Festival. N. p.: News Limited Corporation.

Ramsaye, Terry 1947. "The Rise and Place of the Motion Picture," *Annals of the American Academy of Political and Social Science* no. 254 (November): 1–11.

Resnick, Stephen and Richard Wolff 1988. "Radical Differences Among Radical Theories," *Review of Radical Political Economics* 20, nos. 2–3: 1–6.

Rosenthal, John 1988. "Who Practices Hegemony?: Class Division and the Subject of Politics," *Cultural Critique* 9: 25–52.

Ryan, Michael and Douglas Kellner 1988. *Camera Politica: The Politics and Ideology of Contemporary Hollywood Film*. Bloomington: Indiana University Press.

Shils, Edward 1966. "Mass Society and its Culture." In *Reader in Public Opinion and Communication*, 2nd edn, ed. Bernard Berelson and Morris Janowitz. New York: Free Press; London: Collier-Macmillan.

Simmel, Georg 1976. "The Metropolis and Mental Life." Trans. Kurt H. Wolff. In *Sociological Perspectives: Selected Readings*, ed. Kenneth Thompson and Jeremy Tunstall. Harmondsworth: Penguin.

Vitanyi, Ivan 1983. "Typology and Effects of Cultural Policies," *Cultures* 33: 97–106.

Wasko, Janet 1994. *Hollywood in the Information Age: Beyond the Silver Screen*. Cambridge: Polity Press.

Weber, Max 1952. *From Max Weber: Essays in Sociology*. Trans. and ed. H. H. Gerth and C. Wright Mills. London: Routledge and Kegan Paul.

Wilson, Elizabeth 1991. *The Sphinx in the City: Urban Life, the Control of Disorder, and Women*. London: Virago Press.

Zollars, Cheryl L. and Muriel Goldsman Cantor 1993. "The Sociology of Culture Producing Occupations: Discussion and Synthesis," *Current Research on Occupations and Professions* vol. 8: 1–29.

30
Constituents of a Theory of the Media

Hans Magnus Enzensberger

If you should think this is Utopian, then I would ask you to consider why it is Utopian.
Brecht, Theory of Radio

With the development of the electronic media, the industry that shapes consciousness has become the pacemaker for the social and economic development of societies in the late industrial age. It infiltrates into all other sectors of production, takes over more and more directional and control functions, and determines the standard of the prevailing technology.

In lieu of normative definitions, here is an incomplete list of new developments which have emerged in the last twenty years: news satellites, color television, cable relay television, cassettes, videotape, videotape recorders, video-phones, stereophony, laser techniques, electrostatic reproduction processes, electronic high-speed printing, composing and learning machines, microfiches with electronic access, printing by radio, time-sharing computers, data banks. All these new forms of media are constantly forming new connections both with each other and with older media like printing, radio, film, television, telephone, teletype, radar, and so on. They are clearly coming together to form a universal system.

The general contradiction between productive forces and productive relationships emerges most sharply, however, when they are most advanced. By contrast, protracted structural crises, as in coal mining, can be solved merely by getting rid of a backlog, that is to say, essentially they can be solved within the terms of their own system, and a revolutionary strategy that relied on them would be short-sighted.

Monopoly capitalism develops the consciousness-shaping industry more quickly and more extensively than other sectors of production; it must at the same time fetter it. A socialist media theory has to work at this contradiction, demonstrate that it cannot be solved within the given productive relationships – rapidly increasing discrepancies, potential destructive forces. "Certain demands of a prognostic nature must be made" of any such theory (Benjamin).

A "critical" inventory of the status quo is not enough. There is danger of underestimating the growing conflicts in the media field, of neutralizing them, of interpreting them merely in terms of trade unionism or liberalism, on the lines of traditional labor struggles or as the clash of special interests (program heads/executive producers, publishers/authors, monopolies/medium sized business, public corporations/private companies, etc.). An appreciation of this kind does not go far enough and remains bogged down in tactical arguments.

So far there is no Marxist theory of the media. There is therefore no strategy one can apply in this area. Uncertainty, alternations between fear and surrender, mark the attitude of the socialist Left to the new productive forces of the media industry. The ambivalence of this attitude merely mirrors the ambivalence of the media themselves without mastering it. It could only be overcome by releasing the emancipatory potential which is inherent in the new productive forces – a potential which capitalism must sabotage just as surely as Soviet revisionism, because it would endanger the rule of both systems.

The Mobilizing Power of the Media

The open secret of the electronic media, the decisive political factor, which has been waiting, suppressed or crippled, for its moment to come, is their mobilizing power.

When I say *mobilize* I mean *mobilize*. In a country which has had direct experience of fascism (and Stalinism) it is perhaps still necessary to explain, or to explain again, what that means – namely, to make men more mobile than they are. As free as dancers, as aware as football players, as surprising as guerrillas. Anyone who thinks of the masses only as the object of politics cannot mobilize them. He wants to push them around. A parcel is not mobile; it can only be pushed to and fro. Marches, columns, parades, immobilize people. Propaganda, which does not release self-reliance but limits it, fits into the same pattern. It leads to depoliticization.

For the first time in history, the media are making possible mass participation in a social and socialized productive process, the practical means of which are in the hands of the masses themselves. Such a use of them would bring the communications media, which up to now have not deserved the name, into their own. In its present form, equipment like television or film does not serve communication but prevents it. It allows no reciprocal action between transmitter and receiver; technically speaking, it reduces feedback to the lowest point compatible with the system.

This state of affairs, however, cannot be justified technically. On the contrary. Electronic techniques recognize no contradiction in principle between transmitter and receiver. Every transistor radio is, by the nature of its construction, at the same time a potential transmitter; it can interact with other receivers by circuit reversal. The development from a mere distribution medium to a communications medium is technically not a problem. It is consciously prevented for understandable political reasons. The technical distinction between receivers and transmitters reflects the social division of labor into producers and consumers, which in the consciousness industry becomes of particular political importance. It is based, in the last analysis, on the basic contradiction between the ruling class and the ruled class – that is to say, between monopoly capital or monopolistic bureaucracy on the one hand and the dependent masses on the other.

This structural analogy can be worked out in detail. To the programs offered by the broadcasting cartels there correspond the politics offered by a power cartel consisting of parties constituted along authoritarian lines. In both cases marginal differences in their platforms reflect a competitive relationship which on essential questions is non-existent. Minimal independent activity on the part of the voter/viewer is desired. As is the case with parliamentary elections under the two-party system, the feedback is reduced to indices. "Training in decision making" is reduced to the response to a single, three-point switching process: Program 1; Program 2; Switch off (abstention).

"Radio must be changed from a means of distribution to a means of communication. Radio would be the most wonderful means of communication imaginable in public life, a huge linked system – that is to say, it would be such if it were capable not only of transmitting but of receiving, of allowing the listener not only to hear but to speak, and did not isolate him but brought him into contact. Unrealizable in this social system, realizable in another, these proposals, which are, after all, only the natural consequences of technical development, help towards the propagation and shaping of that *other* system." . . .

Cultural Archaism in the Left Critique

The New Left of the 1960s has reduced the development of the media to a single concept – that of manipulation. This concept was originally extremely useful for heuristic purposes and has made possible a great many individual analytical investigations, but it now threatens to degenerate into a mere slogan which conceals more than it is able to illuminate, and therefore itself requires analysis.

The current theory of manipulation on the Left is essentially defensive; its effects can lead the movement into defeatism. Subjectively speaking, behind the tendency to go on the defensive lies a sense of impotence. Objectively, it corresponds to the absolutely correct view that the decisive means of production are in enemy hands. But to react to this state of affairs with moral indignation is naive. There is in general an undertone of lamentation when people speak of manipulation which points to idealistic expectations – as if the class enemy had ever stuck to the promises of fair play it occasionally utters. The liberal superstition that in political and social questions there is such a thing as pure, unmanipulated truth seems to enjoy remarkable currency among the socialist Left. It is the unspoken basic premise of the manipulation thesis.

This thesis provides no incentive to push ahead. A socialist perspective which does not go beyond attacking existing property relationships is limited. The expropriation of Springer is a desirable goal but it would be good to know to whom the media should be handed over. The Party? To judge by all experience of that solution, it is not a possible alternative. It is perhaps no accident that the Left has not yet produced an analysis of the pattern of manipulation in countries with socialist regimes.

The manipulation thesis also serves to exculpate oneself. To cast the enemy in the role of the devil is to conceal the weakness and lack of perspective in one's own agitation. If the latter leads to self-isolation instead of mobilizing the masses, then its failure is attributed holus-bolus to the overwhelming power of the media.

The theory of repressive tolerance has also permeated discussion of the media by the Left. This concept, which was formulated by its author with the utmost care, has also, when whittled away in an undialectical manner, become a vehicle for resignation. Admittedly, when an office-equipment firm can attempt to recruit sales staff with the picture of Che Guevara and the text *We would have hired him*, the temptation to withdraw is great. But fear of handling shit is a luxury a sewerman cannot necessarily afford.

The electronic media do away with cleanliness; they are by their nature "dirty." That is part of their productive power. In terms of structure, they are antisectarian – a further reason why the Left, insofar as it is not prepared to re-examine its traditions, has little idea what to do with them. The desire for a cleanly defined "line" and for the suppression of "deviations" is anachronistic and now serves only one's own need for security. It weakens one's own position by irrational purges, exclusions, and fragmentation, instead of strengthening it by rational discussion.

These resistances and fears are strengthened by a series of cultural factors which, for the most part, operate unconsciously, and which are to be explained by the social history of the participants in today's Left movement – namely their bourgeois class background. It often seems as if it were precisely because of their progressive potential that the media are felt to be an immense threatening power; because for the first time they present a basic challenge to bourgeois culture and thereby to the privileges of the bourgeois intelligentsia – a challenge far more radical than any self-doubt this social group can display. In the New Left's opposition to the media, old bourgeois fears such as the fear of "the masses" seem to be reappearing along with equally old bourgeois longings for pre-industrial times dressed up in progressive clothing.

At the very beginning of the student revolt, during the Free Speech Movement at Berkeley, the computer was a favorite target for aggression. Interest in the Third World is not always free from motives based on antagonism towards civilization which has its source in conservative culture critique. During the May events in Paris the reversion to archaic forms of production was particularly characteristic. Instead of carrying out agitation among the workers with a modern offset press, the students printed their posters on the hand presses of the École des Beaux Arts. The political slogans were hand-painted; stencils would certainly have made it possible to produce them *en masse*, but it would have offended the creative imagination of the authors. The ability to make proper strategic use of the most advanced media was lacking. It was not the radio headquarters that were seized by the rebels, but the Odéon Theatre, steeped in tradition.

The obverse of this fear of contact with the media is the fascination they exert on left-wing movements in the great cities. On the one hand, the comrades take refuge in outdated forms of communication and esoteric arts and crafts instead of occupying themselves with the contradiction between the present constitution of the media and their revolutionary potential; on the other hand, they cannot escape from the consciousness industry's program or from its aesthetic. This leads, subjectively, to a split between a puritanical view of political action and the area of private "leisure"; objectively, it leads to a split between politically active groups and subcultural groups.

In Western Europe the socialist movement mainly addresses itself to a public of converts through newspapers and journals which are exclusive in terms of language, content, and form. These newssheets presuppose a structure of party members and sympathizers and a situation, where the media are concerned, that roughly corresponds to the historical situation in 1900; they are obviously fixated on the *Iskra* model. Presumably the people who produce them listen to the Rolling Stones, watch occupations and strikes on television, and go to the cinema to see a Western or a Godard; only in their capacity as producers do they make an exception, and, in their analyses, the whole media sector is reduced to the slogan of "manipulation." Every foray into this territory is regarded from the start with suspicion as a step towards integration. This suspicion is not unjustified; it can however also mask one's own ambivalence and insecurity. Fear of being swallowed up by the system is a sign of weakness; it presupposes that capitalism could overcome any contradiction – a conviction which can easily be refuted historically and is theoretically untenable.

If the socialist movement writes off the new productive forces of the consciousness industry and relegates work on the media to a subculture, then we have a vicious circle. For the Underground may be increasingly aware of the technical and aesthetic possibilities of the disc, of videotape, of the electronic camera, and so on, and is systematically exploring the terrain, but it has no political viewpoint of its own and therefore mostly falls a helpless victim to commercialism. The politically active groups then point to such cases with smug *Schadenfreude*. A process of unlearning is the result and both sides are the losers. Capitalism alone benefits from the Left's antagonism to the media, as it does from the depoliticization of the counterculture.

Democratic Manipulation

Manipulation – etymologically, "handling" – means technical treatment of a given material with a particular goal in mind. When the technical intervention is of immediate social relevance, then manipulation is a political act. In the case of the media industry, that is by definition the case.

Thus every use of the media presupposes manipulation. The most elementary processes in media production, from the choice of the medium itself to shooting, cutting, synchronization, dubbing, right up to distribution, are all operations carried out on the raw material. There is no such thing as unmanipulated writing, filming, or broadcasting. The question is therefore not whether the media are manipulated, but who manipulates them. A revolutionary plan should not require the manipulators to disappear: on the contrary, it must make everyone a manipulator.

All technical manipulations are potentially dangerous; the manipulation of the media cannot be countered, however, by old or new forms of censorship, but only by direct social control, that is to say, by the mass of the people, who will have become productive. To this end, the elimination of capitalistic property relationships is a necessary but by no means sufficient condition. There have been no historical examples up until now of the mass self-regulating learning process which is made possible by the electronic media. The Communists' fear of releasing this potential, of the mobilizing capabilities of the media, of the interaction of free producers, is one of the main reasons why even in the socialist countries, the old bourgeois culture, greatly disguised and distorted but structurally intact, continues to hold sway.

As a historical explanation, it may be pointed out that the consciousness industry in Russia at the time of the October Revolution was extraordinarily backward; their productive capacity has grown enormously since then, but the productive relationships have been artificially preserved, often by force. Then, as now, a primitively edited press, books, and theater were the key media in the Soviet Union. The development of radio, film, and television is politically arrested. Foreign stations like the BBC, the Voice of America, and the *Deutschland Welle*, therefore, not only find listeners, but are received with almost boundless faith. Archaic media like the hand-written pamphlet and poems orally transmitted play an important role.

The new media are egalitarian in structure. Anyone can take part in them by a simple switching process. The programs themselves are not material things and can be reproduced at will. In this sense the electronic media are entirely different from the older media like the book or the easel painting, the exclusive class character of which is obvious. Television programs for privileged groups are certainly technically conceivable – closed-circuit televison – but run counter to the structure. Potentially, the new media do away with all educational privileges and thereby with the cultural monopoly of the bourgeois intelligentsia. This is one of the reasons for the intelligentsia's resentment against the new industry. As for the "spirit" which they are endeavoring to defend against "depersonalization" and "mass culture," the sooner they abandon it the better.

Properties of the New Media

The new media are orientated towards action, not contemplation; towards the present, not tradition. Their attitude to time is completely opposed to that of bourgeois culture, which aspires to possession, that is to extension in time, best of all, to eternity. The media produce no objects that can be hoarded and auctioned. They do away completely with "intellectual property" and liquidate the "heritage," that is to say, the class-specific handing-on of non-material capital.

That does not mean to say that they have no history or that they contribute to the loss of historical consciousness. On the contrary, they make it possible for the first time to record historical material so that it can be reproduced at will. By making this material available for present-day purposes, they make it obvious to anyone using it that the writing of history is always manipulation. But the memory they hold in readiness is not the preserve of a scholarly caste. It is social. The banked information is accessible to anyone, and this accessibility is as instantaneous as its recording. It suffices to compare the model of a private library with that of a socialized data bank to recognize the structural difference between the two systems.

It is wrong to regard media equipment as mere means of consumption. It is always, in principle, also means of production and, indeed, since it is in the hands of the masses, socialized means of production. The contradiction between producers and consumers is not inherent in the electronic media; on the contrary, it has to be artificially reinforced by economic and administrative measures.

An early example of this is provided by the difference between telegraph and telephone. Whereas the former, to this day, has remained in the hands of a bureaucratic institution which can scan and file every text transmitted, the telephone is directly accessible to all users. With the aid of conference circuits, it can even make possible collective intervention in a discussion by physically remote groups.

On the other hand, those auditory and visual means of communication which rely on "wireless" are still subject to state control (legislation on wireless installations). In the face of technical developments, which long ago made local and international radio-telephony possible, and which constantly opened up new wavebands for television – in the UHF band alone, the dissemination of numerous programs in one locality is possible without interference, not to mention the possibilities offered by wired and satellite television – the prevailing laws for control of the air are anachronistic. They recall the time when the operation of a printing press was dependent on an imperial license. The socialist movements will take up the struggle for their own wavelengths and must, within the foreseeable future, build their own transmitters and relay stations.

One immediate consequence of the structural nature of the new media is that none of the regimes at present in power can release their potential. Only a free socialist society will be able to make them fully productive. A further characteristic of the most advanced media – probably the decisive one – confirms this thesis: their collective structure.

For the prospect that in future, with the aid of the media, anyone can become a producer, would remain apolitical and limited were this productive effort to find an outlet in individual tinkering. Work on the media is possible for an individual only insofar as it remains socially and therefore aesthetically irrelevant. The collection of transparencies from the last holiday trip provides a model of this.

That is naturally what the prevailing market mechanisms have aimed at. It has long been clear from apparatus like miniature and 8-mm movie cameras, as well as the tape recorder, which are in actual fact already in the hands of the masses, that the individual, so long as he remains isolated, can become with their help at best an amateur but not a producer. Even so potent a means of production as the shortwave transmitter has been tamed in this way and reduced to a harmless and inconsequential hobby in the hands of scattered radio hams. The programs which the isolated amateur mounts are always only bad, outdated copies of what he in any case receives.

Private production for the media is no more than licensed cottage industry. Even when it is made public it remains pure compromise. To this end, the men who own the media have developed special programs which are usually called "Democratic Forum" or something of the kind. There, tucked away in the corner, "the reader (listener, viewer) has his say," which can naturally be cut short at any time. As in the case of public-opinion polling, he is only asked questions so that he may have a chance to confirm his own dependence. It is a control circuit where what is fed in has already made complete allowance for the feedback.

The concept of a license can also be used in another sense – in an economic one: the system attempts to make each participant into a concessionaire of the monopoly that develops his films or plays back his cassettes. The aim is to nip in the bud in this way that independence which video equipment, for instance, makes possible. Naturally, such tendencies go against the grain of the structure, and the new productive forces not only permit but indeed demand their reversal.

The poor, feeble, and frequently humiliating results of this licensed activity are often referred to with contempt by the professional media producers. On top of the damage suffered by the masses comes triumphant mockery because they clearly do not know how to use the media properly. The sort of thing that goes on in certain popular television shows is taken as proof that they are completely incapable of articulating on their own.

Not only does this run counter to the results of the latest psychological and pedagogical research, but it can easily be seen to be a reactionary protective formulation; the "gifted" people are quite simply defending their territories. Here we have a cultural analogue to the familiar political judgments concerning a working class which is presumed to be "stultified" and incapable of any kind of self-determination. Curiously, one may hear the view that the masses could never govern themselves out of the mouths of people who consider themselves socialists. In the best of cases, these are economists who cannot conceive of socialism as anything other than nationalization.

A Socialist Strategy

Any socialist strategy for the media must, on the contrary, strive to end the isolation of the individual participants from the social learning and production process. This is impossible unless those concerned organize themselves. This is the political core of the question of the media. It is over this point that socialist concepts part company with the neo-liberal and technocratic ones. Anyone who expects to be emancipated by technological hardware, or by a system of hardware however structured, is the victim of an obscure belief in progress. Anyone who imagines that freedom for the media will be established if only everyone is busy transmitting and receiving is the dupe of a liberalism which, decked out in contemporary colors, merely peddles the faded concepts of a preordained harmony of social interests.

In the face of such illusions, what must be firmly held on to is that the proper use of the media demands organization and makes it possible. Every production that deals with the interests of the producers postulates a collective method of production. It is itself already a form of self-organization of social needs. Tape recorders, ordinary cameras, and movie cameras are already extensively owned by wage-earners. The question is why these means of production do not turn up at factories, in schools, in the offices of the bureaucracy, in short, everywhere where there is social conflict. By producing aggressive forms of publicity which were their own, the masses could secure evidence of their daily experiences and draw effective lessons from them.

Naturally, bourgeois society defends itself against such prospects with a battery of legal measures. It bases itself on the law of trespass, on commercial and official secrecy. While its secret services penetrate everywhere and plug in to the most intimate conversations, it pleads a touching concern for confidentiality, and makes a sensitive display of worrying about the question of privacy when all that is private is the interest of the exploiters. Only a collective, organized effort can tear down these paper walls.

Communication networks which are constructed for such purposes can, over and above their primary function, provide politically interesting organizational models. In the socialist movements the dialectic of discipline and spontaneity, centralism and decentralization, authoritarian leadership and anti-authoritarian disintegration has long ago reached deadlock. Network-like communications models built on the principle of reversibility of circuits might give indications of how to overcome this situation: a mass newspaper, written and distributed by its readers, a video network of politically active groups.

More radically than any good intention, more lastingly than existential flight from one's own class, the media, once they have come into their own, destroy the private production methods of bourgeois intellectuals. Only in productive work and learning processes can their individualism be broken down in such a way that it is transformed from morally based (that is to say, as individual as ever) self-sacrifice to a new kind of political self-understanding and behavior.

An all too widely disseminated thesis maintains that present-day capitalism lives by the exploitation of unreal needs. That is at best a half-truth. The results obtained by popular American sociologists like Vance Packard are not un-useful but limited. What they have to say about the stimulation of needs through advertising and artificial obsolescence can in any case not be adequately explained by the hypnotic pull exerted on the wage-earners by mass consumption. The hypothesis of "consumer terror" corresponds to the prejudices of a middle class, which considers itself politically enlightened, against the allegedly integrated proletariat, which has become petty bourgeois and corrupt. The attractive power of mass consumption is based not on the dictates of false needs, but on the falsification and exploitation of quite real and legitimate ones without which the parasitic process of advertising would be redundant. A socialist movement ought not to denounce these needs, but take them seriously, investigate them, and make them politically productive.

That is also valid for the consciousness industry. The electronic media do not owe their irresistible power to any sleight-of-hand but to the elemental power of deep social needs which come through even in the present depraved form of these media.

Precisely because no one bothers about them, the interests of the masses have remained a relatively unknown field, at least insofar as they are historically new. They certainly extend far beyond those goals which the traditional working-class movement represented. Just as in the field of production, the industry which produces goods and the consciousness industry merge more and more, so too, subjectively, where needs are concerned, material and non-material factors are closely interwoven. In the process old psycho-social themes are firmly embedded – social prestige, identification patterns – but powerful new themes emerge which are utopian in nature. From a materialistic point of view, neither the one nor the other must be suppressed.

Henri Lefèbvre has proposed the concept of the *spectacle*, the exhibition, the show, to fit the present form of mass consumption. Goods and shop windows, traffic and advertisements, stores and the world of communications, news and packaging, architecture and media production come together to form a totality, a permanent theater, which dominates not only the public city centers but also private interiors. The expression "beautiful living" makes the most commonplace objects of general use into props for this universal festival, in which the fetishistic nature of the commodities triumphs completely over their use value. The swindle these festivals perpetrate is, and remains, a swindle within the present social structure. But it is the harbinger of something else. Consumption as spectacle contains the promise that want will disappear. The deceptive, brutal, and obscene features of this festival derive from the fact that there can be no question of a real fulfillment of its promise. But so long as scarcity holds sway, use-value remains a decisive category which can only be abolished by trickery. Yet trickery on such a scale is only conceivable if it is based on mass need. This need – it is a utopian one – is there. It is the desire for a new ecology, for a breaking down of environmental barriers, for an aesthetic which is not limited to the sphere of "the artistic." These desires are not – or are not primarily – internalized rules of the game as played by the capitalist system. They have physiological roots and can no longer be suppressed. Consumption as spectacle is – in parody form – the anticipation of a utopian situation.

The promises of the media demonstrate the same ambivalence. They are an answer to the mass need for non-material variety and mobility – which at present finds its material realization in private car ownership and tourism – and they exploit it. Other collective wishes, which capital often recognizes more quickly and evaluates more correctly than its opponents, but naturally only so as to trap them and rob them of their explosive force, are just as powerful, just as unequivocally emancipatory: the need to take part in the social process on a local, national, and international scale: the need for new forms of interaction, for release from ignorance and tutelage; the need for self-determination. "Be everywhere!" is one of the most successful slogans of the media industry. The readers' parliament of *Bild-Zeitung* [the Springer press mass publication] was direct democracy used against the interests of the *demos*. "Open spaces" and "free time" are concepts which corral and neutralize the urgent wishes of the masses.

There is corresponding acceptance by the media of utopian stories: e.g. the story of the young Italo-American who hijacked a passenger plane to get home from California to Rome was taken up without protest even by the reactionary mass press and undoubtedly correctly understood by its readers. The identification is based on what has become a general need. Nobody can understand why such journeys should be reserved for politicians, functionaries, and businessmen. The role of the pop star could be analyzed from a similar angle; in it the authoritarian and emancipatory factors are mingled in an extraordinary way. It is perhaps not unimportant that beat music offers groups, not individuals, as identification models. In the productions of the Rolling Stones (and in the manner of their production) the utopian content is apparent. Events like the Woodstock Festival, the concerts in Hyde Park, on the Isle of Wight, and at Altamont, California, develop a mobilizing power which the political Left can only envy.

It is absolutely clear that, within the present social forms, the consciousness industry can satisfy none of the needs on which it lives and which it must fan, except in the illusory form of games. The point, however, is not to demolish its promises but to take them literally and to show that they can be met only through a cultural revolution. Socialists and socialist regimes which multiply the frustration of the masses by declaring their needs to be false, become the accomplices of the system they have undertaken to fight.

Summary

Repressive use of media	Emancipatory use of media
Centrally controlled program	Decentralized program
One transmitter, many receivers	Each receiver a potential transmitter
Immobilization of isolated individuals	Mobilization of the masses
Passive consumer behavior	Interaction of those involved, feedback
Depoliticization	A political learning process
Production by specialists	Collective production
Control by property owners or bureaucracy	Social control by self-organization

The Subversive Power of the New Media

As far as the objectively subversive potentialities of the electronic media are concerned, both sides in the international class struggle – except for the fatalistic adherents of the thesis of manipulation in the metropoles – are of one mind. Frantz Fanon was the first to draw attention to the fact that the transistor receiver was one of the most important weapons in the Third World's fight for freedom. Albert Hertzog, ex-Minister of the South African Republic and the mouthpiece of the right wing of the ruling party, is of the opinion that "television will lead to the ruin of the white man in South Africa." American imperialism has recognized the situation. It attempts to meet the "revolution of rising expectations" in Latin America – that is what its ideologues call it – by scattering its own transmitters all over the continent and into the remotest regions of the Amazon basin, and by distributing single-frequency transistors to the native population. The attacks of the Nixon Administration on the capitalist media in the USA reveal its understanding that their reporting, however one-sided and distorted, has become a decisive factor in mobilizing people against the war in Vietnam. Whereas only 25 years ago the French massacres in Madagascar, with almost 100,000 dead, became known only to the readers of *Le Monde* under the heading of "Other News" and therefore remained unnoticed and without sequel in the capital city, today the media drag colonial wars into the centers of imperialism.

The direct mobilizing potentialities of the media become still more clear when they are consciously used for subversive ends. Their presence is a factor that immensely increases the demonstrative nature of any political act. The student movements in the USA, in Japan, and in Western Europe soon recognized this and, to begin with, achieved considerable momentary success with the aid of the media. These effects have worn off. Naive trust in the magical power of reproduction cannot replace organizational work; only active and coherent groups can force the media to comply with the logic of their actions. That can be demonstrated from the example of the Tupamaros in Uruguay, whose revolutionary practice was implicit in it publicity for their actions. Thus the actors become authors. The abduction of the American ambassador in Rio de Janeiro was planned with a view to its impact on the media. It was a television production. The Arab guerrillas proceed in the same way. The first to experiment with these techniques internationally were the Cubans. Fidel appreciated the revolutionary potential of the media correctly from the first. Today illegal political action demands at one and the same time maximum security and maximum publicity.

Revolutionary situations always bring with them discontinuous, spontaneous changes brought about by the masses in the existing aggregate of the media. How far the changes thus brought about take root and how permanent they are demonstrates the extent to which a cultural revolution is successful. The situation in the media is the most accurate and sensitive barometer for the rise of bureaucratic or Bonapartist anticyclones. So long as the cultural revolution has the initiative, the social imagination of the masses overcomes even technical backwardness and transforms the function of the old media so that their structures are exploded. . . .

In the 1920s the Russian film reached a standard that was far in advance of the available productive forces. Pudovkin's *Kinoglas* and Dziga Vertov's *Kinopravda* were no "newsreels" but political television magazine programs *avant l'écran*. The campaign against illiteracy in Cuba broke through the linear, exclusive, and isolating structure of the medium of the book. In the China of the Cultural Revolution, wall newspapers functioned like an electronic mass medium – at least in the big towns. The resistance of the Czechoslovak population to the Soviet invasion gave rise to spontaneous productivity on the part of the masses, which ignored the institutional barriers of the media. Such situations are exceptional. It is precisely their utopian nature, which reaches out beyond the existing productive forces (it follows that the productive relationships are not to be permanently overthrown), that makes them precarious, leads to reversals and defeats. They demonstrate all the more clearly what enormous political and cultural energies are hidden in the enchained masses and with what imagination they are able, at the moment of liberation, to realize all the opportunities offered by the new media.

31
Ideology, Economy and the British Cinema

John Hill

Analysis of the cinema's place within capitalism can broadly be seen to have entailed a double focus for Marxists, both generated and legitimated by a sense of what constitutes a proper and recognizable Marxist concern. In general terms this might be characterized as a concern both with determination and with effectivity. On the one hand, a 'materialist' concern to place cinema via its social and economic determinants whether grasped in terms of technology, economy (cinema's subservience to the logic of capital accumulation), class base or conjunctural complex. On the other, a 'critical' concern to place the cinema via its role within the social formation, to account for cinema in its ideological clothes, its complicity with a continuing structure of domination. Yet the articulation of these twin foci has remained problematic. The emphasis here is on articulation, with its demand for a structured combination which is more than mere addition or a setting of the two beside each other as equal but alternative choices (precisely the language of 'on the one hand' and 'on the other'). Such difficulty is not merely the product of bad analysis or conceptual confusion (though this may of course be the case) but is symptomatic of a more generalized problem of emphasis within Marxist analysis with its polar temptations of economism and idealism. In both cases the problem of articulation is effectively displaced through a dissolution of one of the terms into the other: the effect of ideology becomes directly 'readable' in the sum of its determinations (the ownership of the cinematic means of production, the logic of the market, and so on) or alternatively the determinative complex becomes evacuated from the ideological scene, 'unreadable' either directly or indirectly. And in occupation of the hinterland is the compromise whereby ideology and economy are seen to coalesce, but in some unexplained liaison whose specific parameters and modalities remain occluded (take, for example, the Comolli/Narboni (1971) formulation: 'every film...is determined by the ideology which produces it...but is all the more thoroughly and completely determined because...its very manufacture mobilizes powerful economic forces' (p. 30)). Indeed, the necessity to resort to such ultimately evasive formulations such as 'all the more' seems almost to be the condition upon which such work can begin: how 'relative', for example, is the 'relative' in 'relative autonomy' and what precisely is 'relative' to what; and just what is 'mediating' what in the notion of 'mediation'? And it may be precisely because of this that, when attempts are inaugurated to combine the twin modes of analysis, the 'balance' so often tends to be lost and one is emphasized at the expense of the other. This would seem to be the case in the two examples discussed here: both set out with the broad ambition of examining textual ideology through an analysis of its conditions of production, but both end up by giving one privilege over the other. Thus in the case of Murdock and Golding (1977a; but see also 1974a and 1974b and their contribution to this volume) media (and ideological) specificity is largely collapsed into economy while for *Cahiers du Cinéma* (1972) the reverse is true – film (and ideological) specificity is largely evacuated of its determinations.

In 'Capitalism, Communication and Class Relations', Graham Murdock and Peter Golding explicitly attack those brands of Marxist theory which have placed cultural criticism above economic analysis, beginning with cultural artefacts and then working backwards to the economic base rather than vice versa. Although for them this proclivity can be accounted for in terms of a reaction against economic determinism and the popularity of 'critical philosophy', Murdock and Golding none the less argue that by abandoning any sustained analysis of the economic base we are 'thereby jettisoning the very elements that give Marxist sociology its distinctiveness and explanatory power' (1977a, p. 17) and that while not wishing to return to economic determinism would nevertheless claim 'that control over material resources and their changing distribution are ultimately the most powerful of the many levers in cultural production' (p. 20). The thesis is fleshed out with material on media integration and diversification and concludes with two general consequences for cultural production of the economic processes outlined: '(1) the range of material available will tend to decline as market forces exclude all but the commercially successful and (2) this evolutionary process is not random, but systematically excludes those voices lacking economic power and resources' (p. 37).

It is of course possible to quibble with Murdock and Golding at the level of empirical observation – their under-emphasis on the need for originality in the drive for media expansion and similar under-emphasis on the possibility of oppositional viewpoints within the commercial media, consequent upon their problematic conflation of the long-term interest of capital in general and short-term interest of the individual entrepreneur[1] – but the concern here is rather with the way the general problem of ideology and economy is established and resolved by them. The concern here circulates around the 'gap' which remains for Murdock and Golding between economic production on the one hand and media forms on the other, which is only overcome for them through the dissolution of media specificity (the particular organizations of matters of expression) and consequent reduction of the media to transcriptions of socio-political ideologies originated elsewhere. Thus, for example, Murdock and Golding criticize a large proportion of media studies for concentrating almost entirely on news and failing to address themselves to 'the main dramatic, fictional and entertainment forms which make up the bulk of most people's media fare' (p. 36) – yet it is precisely these forms which Murdock and Golding themselves would seem unable to account for in the absence of any provision of the means for their conceptualization. At most their concluding theses would allow them to account for the repetition and exclusion of particular forms once constituted but not for their dominance within the media nor for their particular operations. Or they can only do so through an attribution of unproblematic transparency to these forms whereby the difference between the various media in terms of matters of expression and conventions can be elided and the way formal conventions actually work in meaning-production be ignored. Thus when Murdock and Golding discuss the 'readings' of media imagery presented by others such as Poulantzas, Berger and Barthes, judging it a 'bald beginning', it is in turn difficult to see how Murdock and Golding can even reach such a bare starting point purely from their perspective. For 'imagery' is not only the end product of an economic process, but the product of a work of signification as well with its own internal dynamics and operations (and internal history), which is precisely the domain then that Murdock and Golding ignore.

It is this field which Stephen Heath has tried to capture in his use of the term 'machine': 'cinema itself seized exactly between industry and product as the stock of constraints and definitions from which film can be distinguished as a specific signifying practice' (1976, p. 256), where 'specificity' implies not only a sense of media peculiarity but also a semiotic particularity (signification through both codes unique to the cinema and broader socio-cultural ones) and 'practice' stresses process: 'film as a work of production of meanings'. That is to say, film does not merely 'express' or 'represent' but is itself an active process of signification through which meaning is produced. Two consequences for a consideration of ideology seem to follow. First, that the media are not merely 'empty' forms which neutrally transcribe socio-political ideologies, but enjoy their own level of effectivity which is the property of the cinematic 'machine' and not the cinematic institution. One attempt to theorize this, for example, at a general level can be seen in the work of Jean-Paul Fargier (1971) where cinema is considered not merely as a vector of ideologies already in circulation, but as producing its own specific ideology: 'the impression of reality'. Now whether or not we accept fully this formulation (for example, it is not at all clear that the 'impression' is fundamental to 'bourgeois cinema' or that its appearance is irreducibly ideological), it does none the less help clarify the point that the 'ideological effect' of the cinema cannot be understood outside of the operation of its particular conventions and constraints which then, because they carry their own specific effectivities, cannot be seen necessarily to correspond to a maker's personality or 'intentions' nor likewise his or her social and political beliefs. As Francis Mulhern has argued for literature, so with reservations (considered below) it would here be accepted for film: 'the formal characteristics of a literary text cannot be considered as the aesthetic expression of its author's pre-existing ideological positions . . . Moreover, the ideological positions affirmed by a literary text need not even coincide with the positions formally adopted by its author. They are the determinate effects of the form of the text, and may in fact be deeply inconsistent with the latter' (1975, p. 85). Second, it follows that if the media do not merely express ideologies, they must then be considered as actively constitutive of ideologies. That is to say, ideologies are not merely ingredients to be detected in the media, but also its products. And again, as active productions, ideologies are not merely to be seen as sets of positivities but also as processes of exclusion – with these 'exclusions' potentially being able to feed back to disturb or deform their progenitive system (and thereby furnishing our analysis with a notion of 'contradiction' retrieved from both a reductionism which would merely place it as a reflection of contradictions determined at the level of the economic and the homeostasis of a reproduction-orientated Marxist functional-ism – though as we shall see later not then without difficulties). For Murdock and Golding, however, it is the former relationship (ideologies as ingredients): 'The first task is to spell out the nature of the ruling ideology, and to specify the propositions and assumptions of which it is composed. Secondly, the appearance and entrenchment of such propositions and assumptions in media output needs to be clearly demonstrated' (1977a, p. 35). But the ruling ideology is not just 'entrenched' in the media: it is actually produced. For there is no general or abstract system which is the ruling ideology: rather the ruling ideology is only constituted in and through the concrete: '[Ideology] is there and yet it is not there. It appears indeed as if the general structure of a dominant ideology is almost impossible to grasp, reflexively and analytically as a whole. The dominant ideology always appears, precisely, in and through the particular' (Hall 1972b, p. 82). Indeed, as Hall and his colleagues at the Centre for Contemporary Cultural Studies at Birmingham University have gone on to show, the task of the media as part of the State may indeed be to create an ideological unity where none before existed (Hall et al., 1976; Chambers et al., 1977): 'Far from expres-sing or reflecting an already given class interest, television is one of the sites where ideological elements and positions are articulated into a specific type of political class discourse' (Chambers et al., 1977, p. 114). And this may be part of the problem. For Murdock and Golding classes are by and large seen as already constituted, with their own social and economic identities which can then be reflected or not reflected within the media, rather than as complex and contra-dictory unities without any necessary homogeneity at the cultural level but rather 'represented' through a variety of forms.

However, given the impossibility of grasping ideology purely in terms of class origins we must then avoid evacuating class from our analysis altogether. Thus, from beginning with similar premises, one tendency has been to define ideology neither by its class base nor its reproduction of the social formation but merely as that part of the social formation that exists when we subtract the political and economic levels. Raymond Williams (1973) has argued that if the concept of 'social totality' is to be retrieved from a mere sociology of interconnections, then it must include a notion of 'domination'. Likewise I would wish to argue that if ideology is to be rescued from a significatory egalitarianism (and conjunctural analysis from a new form of empiricism) it must also include a notion of ideologies not just as discursive systems but as ultimately maintaining a structure of dominance. Not of course directly or crudely, but in complex and contradictory ways whose specific potencies and inflections have to be analyzed in particular and concrete ways. This is not then to imply a subscription to the thesis of cultural transparency. It is quite possible to concede that human beings may always be subjects in so far as they are constituted in and through discursive practices of whose grounds they are not conscious, but this does not then imply that they will always be subjected (in the sense of subjection) to the particular discursive practices of capitalism. For here cultural opacity is not necessarily allied to relations of domination, just as ideology is not then coterminous with discourse.

Likewise I would not wish these conclusions to lead to an abandonment of the problem of determination (and here I would part company with Hindess (1977) and Hirst (1976b) whose either/or choice of total autonomy or total determination can find no theoretical coherence for this in-between). Just as we cannot read off cinema's signifying practices from its material conditions of existence, so we cannot provide a coherent account of cinema which evacuates such material agencies and apparatuses. Because they don't tell it all, it does not follow that they then tell us nothing (likewise 'creators'' intentions and socio-political ideologies). But just as class is not a monolith, so determination must not be conceived as single-layered and uni-directional, but rather multi-layered and complex and operant within 'ideology' (the constraints of the 'machine') as well as between 'ideology' and 'economy'.

Returning to Golding and Murdock via their more recent paper it can be seen that they address themselves to a number of the problems posed here largely to reassert their initial position of the privileging of the economic but with the novel input of a specific polemic against 'textural [sic] analysis'. As this can be read as both a 'defence' of their own position and an 'attack' on some of the positions posed here, their three main arguments may well merit further investigation. Golding and Murdock firstly maintain that textual analysis cannot provide an adequate account of the relations of production governing a text's construction. This is undoubtedly correct, but none the less turns the pertinent issue on its head: for while indeed production relations may not be able to be read back from textual analysis this does not then imply the converse – that textual processes can then be read forward from those same relations of production.[2] Golding and Murdock's second argument refers to inference. Textual analysis is a form of 'content analysis' (a label hardly doing justice to the significant advances of much textual analysis over content analysis as classically understood) and is thus necessarily 'circumstantial' and 'qualitative'. Again the argument is carried on by means of a reversal. A thesis on methodological capabilities is made to do service instead of the required conceptual analysis. Rather than the problems of theory generating demands of methodological procedure, technical possibilities adjudicate the value of theory instead. Furthermore it is an argument that can really only make sense if we are to assume that inference is something peculiar to content analysis rather than a condition general to sociology. It would indeed be a barren and denuded sociology (at best an operationism whereby concepts become fully defined by their procedures of measurement) that could lay claim to have resolved the problems of inference. The third argument of Golding and Murdock is that exclusive concentration on textual analysis would necessarily be truncated and partial in its explanation of ideological production. This is, of course, true – but in establishing the opposite case Golding and Murdock are in danger of an equal partialness and truncation. They themselves recognize that economic analysis cannot be sufficient in itself, but then fail to theorize that very 'insufficiency' thereby themselves 'bracketing off' the very issues which are at stake.

If then it can be argued that Golding and Murdock devalue the significatory level of the media and that this has effects for how they can formulate a theory of ideology, let us now look at the reverse tendency in the work of the *Cahiers du cinéma* editorial group (1972) and its implications. An increasingly common response to this analysis of 'Young Mr. Lincoln' is to note the inadequacy of *Cahiers'* attempt to define the historical determinations of the film but none the less to applaud the actual textual analysis as if the two were quite happily separable (Campbell, 1977, p. 30; Caughie, 1977–8, p. 93) despite the defined object of the piece:

> to distinguish the historicity of [a number of 'classic' films including 'Young Mr. Lincoln's'] inscription: the relation of these films to the codes (social, cultural . . .) for which they are a site of intersection, and to other films themselves held in an intertextual space: therefore, the relation of these films to the ideology which they convey, a particular 'phase' which they represent, and to the events (present, past, historical, mythical, fictional) which they aimed to represent. (*Cahiers du cinéma*, 1972, p. 6)

While agreeing with such writers in their diagnosis of a certain failure, I would none the less not want to gloss this over in terms of 'the intrinsic difficulty of the task' or an 'unhappy contingency' but rather I would see the imbalance as consequent on the premises founding the analysis and thus necessarily undermining the original 'object'.

Unlike Golding and Murdock, whose object was to account for fairly general features of the media in terms of the structural principles of the economy, *Cahiers* selected a specific media artefact – one film – which they sought to account for in fairly specific ways. This they then did through a rather 'unmaterialist' mode of operation – accounting for the movie's appearance in terms of the intention of one man: the Republican Zanuck wanted to make a film about the Republican Lincoln in order to promote a Republican victory in the presidential election of

1940. Brewster (1973) suggests that, faced with the difficulty of substantiating such a thesis, this specific ideological purpose is ignored in favour of the more general one of 'the reformulation of the historical figure of Lincoln on the level of the myth and the eternal' (*Cahiers du cinéma*, 1972, p. 13). However, it seems that this division is more than a symptom of intellectual difficulty, but rather of theoretical choice. Thus a division can be seen being made between the ideological determinations of the film (Zanuck's purpose) and the ideological undertaking actualized in the film, the latter not in fact being a property of the former, and hence clarifying *Cahiers*' distinction between their own analysis and that which they call 'demystification' whereby 'an artistic product' is 'linked to its socio-historical context according to a linear, expressive, direct causality' (p. 7).

The consequence of this then is that political and economic analysis can only have a limited function and can only loosely, if at all, place the film's ideological role (which is not to question the essential 'correctness' of *Cahiers*' refusal to 'read off' ideology from its social determinants, but rather to examine its theoretical effects). And this conjoins with the other object that *Cahiers* set themselves. For in differentiating themselves from other types of reading (commentary, interpretation, mechanistic structuralism and demystification) *Cahiers* specify their project as that of an 'active reading'. At one level this can be seen as according recognition to the 'work' of the text, its process of signification. *Cahiers* are not content merely to abstract broad 'ideological statements' in one simultaneous operation, but rather wish to follow 'the film's process of becoming-a-text', its 'dynamic inscription'. This might be seen as an operation which traces the audience's diachronic experience of watching a film, but for *Cahiers* it involves more: 'A process of active reading is to make them say what they have to say within what they leave unsaid, to reveal their constituent lacks' (p. 8). In such terms, then, the initial concern with a socio-historical situating can be seen to be misplaced, for there is no textual meaning to be discovered independent of consumption anyway, which becomes in fact of more decisive importance than the moment of production: 'We do not hesitate to force the text, even to rewrite it in so far as the film only constitutes itself as a text by integration of the reader's knowledge' (p. 37). But the dilemmas are in the very formulation. For if the text only exists through 'integration of the reader's knowledge' in what sense can they be said to be 'forcing' or 'rewriting'? Does the object-text have an existence independent of the knowing subject after all, or is there at least some recognition of 'correctness' in the process of 'meaning-extraction'? The problem can be posed in terms of validity – does the by and large correct observation that the text only exists through the 'integration of the reader's knowledge' allow *carte blanche* in analysis, or do there remain 'controls' or 'limit-positions' which continue to govern the analyzing discourse?

Clearly *Cahiers* are concerned that their reading should not be viewed as a purely personal or idiosyncratic one (they make recurring references to readings being 'authorized', of occurrences in the film bringing out its 'true meaning', and so on); but they are equally clearly, through their use of the language of psychoanalysis, not attempting to reproduce a 'lay' reading or any actual historical reading. Indeed, they pose their critical activity as exactly opposite to the norms of conventional consumption: 'a kind of non-reading' (p. 6) governed by the 'transparence' and 'presence' of 'classic' representation and narrative. The problem is then not only of what guarantees their reading (can the methodological licence apparently legitimated by their founding premises be overcome without theoretical circularity?)[3] but perhaps more importantly for our purposes, what this might mean in relation to our understanding of ideology. What are we told about the ideological project of the film, whether successful or failed, if the reading which *Cahiers* locates was never in fact accessible to a general audience? (A claim referring us back to the privileged warrant of psychoanalysis to explicate the unconscious workings of ideology would, apart from problems of validity, still have to cope with the problems of the dehistoricized and decontextualized versions of the unconscious and ideology it sought to work with). A division could perhaps be made between the film's general ideological undertaking – the reformulation of the historical figure of Lincoln – which could then be viewed as fairly accessible to an audience ('transparent' and 'present') – and *Cahiers*' analysis of the costs of producing that ideological formulation, the repressions involved. But what then is the significance of *Cahiers*' formulation to the effect that 'a distortion of the ideological project by the writing of the film' is manifested within the film (1972, p. 37)? For whom is the ideological project distorted if it takes a skilled reading based on psychoanalysis to reveal it, and in just what way is our understanding of the film's ideological effectivity altered?

Subsequent work (Willemen, 1971 and 1972–3; Johnston, 1975) which has built upon *Cahiers*' protocols has then evaded such issues by necessarily abandoning historical analysis altogether and deriving its legitimacy either from its use-value for contemporary criticism (the institution of a more 'progressive' mode of reading texts) or for contemporary filmmaking (the strategies it might suggest). Readings are then quite self-consciously constructed in opposition to actual historical readings (whether skilled or lay), the evidence of which then becomes irrelevant (though Willemen (1972–3) at once conjoins an acceptance of the audience's non-awareness of textual contradictions with the demand for a historical sensitivity if contemporary critics are not to 'misread' Sirk's films just as the claims of relevance for aesthetic strategies, unnoticed in their own day, rest on an unexplicated assumption as to their pertinence for a contemporary audience). As such then it is clear that the attempt to combine economic and ideological analysis has been effectively removed from the agenda (Kuhn, 1975). Accompanying such 'revisions' has been a 'stronger' repudiation of the possibility at all of the enterprise here called for, made in terms of current work on the theory of history, whereby film analysis can only be carried on in and for the present with validity being guaranteed by political knowledge of the current conjuncture (Hindess and Hirst, 1975; Tribe, 1977–8; McCabe, 1977; Ellis, 1977). As yet however it is difficult to see whether such work has been adequately able to resolve its own problems of relativism and political opportunism (the ritual invocation of the 'current conjuncture' remaining as yet peculiarly empty of foundational concepts).

It is in this way then that the *Cahiers* analysis reveals a complementary set of problems to those considered in relation to Murdock and Golding. Whereas Murdock and Golding fail to pay adequate attention to significatory processes, *Cahiers* conversely emphasize these to the point of accrediting them an almost total autonomy. This is in turn allied to the problem of consumption. For Murdock and Golding the problem did not arise – for them the audience can by and large be 'read out' from the media texts themselves. *Cahiers*, on the other hand, correctly refuse to see the audience as locked into some preordained textual meaning, but in doing so tend to dissolve the text altogether and ignore the socio-historical context in which it is received. The importance here is to suggest that just as the text cannot be read off directly from production, so audience response cannot be read back from properties of the text only. The emphasis on significa-tion breaks with notions of the passive consumer – audiences are rather seen as actively productive of meaning through a knowledge and activation of codes (but not then as self-conscious 'decoders') – but this must then be understood in actual conditions of social and historical readership. Neale (1977) has argued in the case of propaganda that 'it can't simply be a matter of reading off a set of textual characteristics. What has to be identified is the use to which a particular text is put, to its function within a particular situation, to its place within cinema conceived as a social practice' (p. 39). This is the case for Neale because he wants to see propaganda as a form of address which 'produces a position of social struggle' (p. 32) and, for him, such a position cannot be purely the product of textual address. However, while Neale himself would not want to do this, it does seem possible to generalize this to notions of textual 'effectivity' (including ideological effectivity) beyond those which imply forms of social action. And thus an analysis of media ideology could not rest with an analysis of production and text alone but must in turn include a theory of readership and analysis of consumption (indeed outside of which there is no text at all). So just as produc-tion and text are articulated through the 'machine' of social and historical cinematic conventions and constraints, so the 'machine' of socially and historic-ally placed readership cuts across the text and its audience.

The 'meaning' then of a film is not something to be discovered purely in the text itself (into which the spectator may or may not be bound) but is constituted in the interaction between the text and its users. The early claim of semiotics to be in some way able to account for a text's functioning through an immanent analysis was essentially misfounded in its failure to perceive that any textual system could only have meaning in relation to codes not purely textual, and that the recognition, distribution and activation of these would vary socially and historically. On the other hand the fact that we are concerned with codes, that is systems of regularity, should indicate that this does not then imply textual meaning to be dispersed altogether whereby all readings become equal and novelty becomes a virtue in itself. Likewise it does not abandon us to uses and gratifications theory with its collapse of the text into an individualistic and psychologistic problematic. Rather we would want to argue that readership must be understood in terms of broader patterns of socio-cultural consumption whereby texts are read both 'aesthetically', in terms of codes specifically 'artistic', and 'socially', in relation to the broader contours of life-experience engendered via class, race, sex and nation, where again these are not conceived as homogeneous but variegated (and thereby resisting the associated assumptions often governing analysis of the passive consumer of the development of society itself towards a 'mass' homogeneity; as Swingewood argues, 'capitalist economy and technology and capitalist culture – have achieved new principles of economic and cultural richness and diversity . . . the development of the capitalist mode of production has served to augment, not destroy, civil society' (1977, p.x.). If a notion such as 'preferred reading' then is to have a value, it is not as a means of fixing one interpretation over and above others, but rather a means of accounting for how, under certain conditions, a text will tend to be read in particular ways because of the way meaning is placed through the articulation of particular aesthetic, social and historical codes.

In this we can see that the task of ideological analysis is not the production of new meanings but rather of accounting for how old meanings are generated for and through particular audiences (which is not then to posit the unified sign-community of much early semiotics), the novelty lying in this analysis and the new problematic in which it is placed. Following from this it is clear that the readings which such analysis predicates should not be so fashioned as to contradict the evidence of actual socio-historical readings. Indeed, there is a real danger that as film analysis develops an ever more complex and sophisticated battery of methodological tools it loses sight of social analyses in favour of the institution of its own skilled community of readers with its own particular credentials (the codes of academia and advanced interdisciplinary discourses such as semiotics and psychoanalysis). This is not to deny the importance of such disciplines, but to argue that their value lies not in the discovery of some new signified (a new way of capturing the text's 'true meaning'), or the liberation of the signifier in the interests of subversion, but in accounting for the processes of signification through which particular meanings are produced in specific contexts. As Barthes puts it in his influential *S/Z*: 're-reading is an operation contrary to the commercial and ideological habits of our society' (1975, p. 15). But then whether his own multiple re-reading is an analysis of how the form of realism is textually produced with all its concomitant difficulties, or merely the introduction of a new (more 'writerly') mode of consumption, would be open to dispute. Likewise this is not then to argue that each and every meaning is to be found raised to the level of consciousness. Obviously within our culture certain very central types of meaning surround us without being explicitly recognized – but the identification of such "non-consciousness" is not then arbitrary and unless some 'control' at the level of experience (which does not thereby become privileged in analysis) is exercised a licence is spawned which in all likelihood may only have the remotest of links with an understanding of the production and reproduction of ideologies. Put another way, because our methodology is anti-phenomenological, it does not then make phenomenology irrelevant: a confusion which seems to vitiate the critiques of phenomenology in Metz and Culler respectively by Henderson (1975) and Tribe (1976).

Notes

1   Cf. Murdock and Golding's position that oppositional views 'are easily swamped by the volume of mainstream output' (p. 38) with Alvin Gouldner's claim for the 'contradictions' internal to a system of producing accounts of social reality that is grounded in private ownership: 'The hegemonic class's profit imperative therefore ends by undermining the very culture on which its own legitimacy rests' (1976, p. 157). The obverse of this can also be formulated – commercial imperatives will not necessarily lead to an investment in that which would appear conducive to capital's long-term interests. Take, for example, the case of *The Angry Silence*. In *Film World* Ivor Montagu (1964) argues 'Seeing the income level of those who control the controlling circuits in this country, such a film, had it been ten times cruder than it was, must inevitably have been certain of distribution and exhibition before ever it was begun' (p. 271). Yet this was precisely what it was not. Only one company could be found with any interest at all in the film and only then after £40,000 had been lopped off the bill through a sacrifice of fees by many of the leading participants in favour of a share of the profits, such as they might be.

2   Indeed, the whole issue is something of a red herring relying on a peculiar selection of a representative for semiotics (Terry Eagleton) and an assumed unproblematic reading of a rather confused claim. Far from being a 'very reasonable' assertion it is unclear what a text's 'internalization' of its production relations might mean (if to be more than a mere axiom of the sort that every text is produced within a particular set of production relations). Eagleton himself reveals a hesitancy, and through his unsure employment of the notion of 'literary mode of production' tends to effect an unhappy elision of two distinct types of relations under the category of 'literary relations of production' – relations largely understood as those of the mode of production proper and those operant between text and audience. And thus while probably attempting a 'stronger' and thus more tenuous claim he is likely to be more correctly seen as constructing an argument about relations of consumption and not relations of production at all and hence to be reading forward from text to audience (interestingly one of the relations submerged in Murdock and Golding's analysis) rather than back from text to production relations, as full quotation of the relevant passage reveals: 'One might add, too, that every literary text in some sense internalizes its social relations of production – that every text intimates by its very conventions the way it is to be consumed, encodes within itself its own ideology of how, by whom and for whom it was produced. Every text obliquely posits a putative reader, defining its productability in terms of a certain capacity for consumption' (Eagleton, 1976, p. 48).

3   Brewster (1973) attempts this by establishing rules of pertinence in accordance with motivations generated within the textual system itself (though in so far as the 'implicit reader' which this is supposed to predicate is never empirically found not altogether

without contradiction). Henderson (1973/74) rightly criticizes Brewster for his attempt to impose Metzian terms within a foreign problematic, but in re-stating *Cahiers*' own rules of pertinence he hardly resolves the issue which Brewster was at least attempting to face: 'The *Cahiers* reading goes beyond the text relating what is present to what is absent, thereby defining its own principles of pertinence' (Henderson, 1973/74, p. 43). The rules of pertinence then may be the properties of the studying discourse (*Cahiers*' reading) rather than of the text itself ('Young Mr. Lincoln'), but then that hardly exempts that discourse from the demands of validity and coherence.

32
Mass Culture and the Feminine:
The "Place" of Television in Film
Studies

Patrice Petro

The fear of the vulgar is the obverse of the fear of excellence, and both are aspects of the fear of difference.[1]

The final session of the 1984 Society for Cinema Studies Conference held in Madison, Wisconsin was devoted to the question of "The Place of Television in Film Studies." The question of television's "place" in film studies was nevertheless soon displaced by an intense debate over the "proper" object for scholarly attention, a debate which encouraged some conference participants to voice their fears about the precarious status of film within the academy and to express their anxieties over television's potential threat to that status.

To begin with, some conference participants feared that once television was incorporated into film studies, a return to various positivist methodologies would soon follow, thereby undermining the more sophisticated approaches to spectatorship and textuality carried over from continental philosophy and literary theory to film studies proper. Furthermore, the emphasis upon content analysis, audience survey, and controlled experiment in mainstream television study, in short, the "number crunching" empiricism of communication research, was seen by some to threaten the already beleaguered position of film study within the university by moving it further away from the humanities and in the direction of the social sciences.

In addition to this was a second, less articulated, fear that the study of the "vulgar," popularized medium of television would undercut the artistic and educational goals of film study within the university. In support of this fear, and serving as further evidence to indict television as medium, were quoted the apparently different modes of reception assumed to follow from "viewing a film" and "watching television." As many theorists have pointed out, when viewing a film, the spectator centers attention on the screen, becoming absorbed in the narrative and with the characters. When watching television, however, viewing seems to be marked by discontinuous attention, by the spectator's participation in several activities at once in which televiewing may not even rank as third in importance.[2] Drawing upon these assumed differences between perception and spectatorship in film and television viewing, the debate over television's place in film studies came to rest upon the (unexamined) assumption that while film encourages attention to the work itself, television merely contributes to the tendency toward distracted and indiscriminate reception.

It would be hasty to dismiss the fears outlined here as entirely illusory or to generalize about all film scholars' tunnel vision with respect to their discipline (thus overlooking the extremely productive work on television carried out by film scholars in both Britain and the United States).[3] It nevertheless seems to me that the anxiety expressed over the prospect and consequences of positivist methodologies inundating film studies is rather misplaced. For a start, not only have such methodologies long existed in film studies (as represented by the work of I. C. Jarvie, for instance), but they have in no significant way obstructed the development or refinement of film theoretical concerns. It is for this reason that the second fear, expressed in terms of television "debasing" the cultural and educational goals of film studies, seems to me highly suggestive in its assumption of what, precisely, constitutes knowledge, education, and value. As Hélène Cixous has remarked, every theory of culture, "every theory of society, the whole conglomeration of symbolic systems – everything, that is, that's spoken, everything that's organized as discourse, art, religion, family, language, everything that seizes us, everything that acts on us – it is all ordered around hierarchical oppositions that can only be sustained by means of a difference posed by cultural discourses as 'natural,' the difference between activity and passivity."[4]

The difference between art and mass culture – understood by means of a "natural" opposition between activity and passivity – has long been assumed in our theories of culture. And it is remarkable how theoretical discussions of art and mass culture are almost always accompanied by gendered metaphors which link "masculine" values of production, activity, and attention with art, and "feminine" values of consumption, passivity, and distraction with mass culture. To be sure, this dichotomy is not exclusive to those seeking to valorize high art. As Tania Modleski has persuasively argued, even theorists of mass culture continually make "mass culture into the 'other' of whatever, at any given moment, they happen to be championing – and, moreover, to denigrate that other primarily because it allegedly provides pleasure to the consumer."[5] Given the tenacity of hierarchical gender oppositions both in our culture and our theoretical discourses, it is not surprising that debates over the "place" of television in film studies should echo the oppositions between activity and passivity when assigning value to different representational practices. What is surprising is that some film scholars assign a place to television outside the domain of legitimate culture, outside the arena of academic respectability, particularly since this was (and in some cases, continues to be) precisely the "place" assigned to cinema by educators, intellectuals, and artists.

In the following discussion, I would like to suggest possible reasons for the attribution of "feminized" values (with their implicitly pejorative connotations) to television by analyzing developments within film criticism as well as within critical theories of television. I must emphasize, however, that I am not concerned to argue that either television or film is in fact "feminized." While at least one film scholar has valorized television as psychically and essentially feminine,[6] thereby providing television with an ontology to match the masculine ontology of film provided by Baudry and Metz, I believe that this kind of approach not only collapses the historical and theoretical issues raised by television as a social technology, but also replicates the very terms which ally femininity with passivity, consumption, and distraction. In my view, it is precisely these terms which must be called into question if television theorists are to avoid reproducing the problems already encountered by theorists of film. Indeed, what I would like to argue is that before we can begin to theorize the historical and perceptual difference between film and television viewing, we need first to scrutinize our critical vocabularies which assign hierarchical and gender-specific value to difference. My aim in this essay will thus be less to advance a new theory of television than to demonstrate how critics of mass culture, from civic reformers to postmodern theorists, employ gender-specific oppositions in order to evaluate the differences between art and mass culture. In this way, I hope to suggest why debate over the "place" of television in film studies may have been necessary to begin with.

Cinema and Mass Culture

Since its beginnings, the cinema has been interrogated in almost every Western society for its function and meaning in culture. Rather than presume to give an extensive account of the various discourses on cinema as a manifestation of mass culture, I will merely suggest a pervasive preoccupation with gender-oppositions in mass culture criticism. In fact, before turning to television directly, it is useful to look at how debates over television have not only borrowed from, but have also virtually replicated, earlier debates over film.

Quite consciously, I have chosen to draw my examples from Anglo-American and German mass cultural criticism and to divide various approaches into three major areas: (1) moral and educational discourses – concerned to discuss cinema's effects upon children (those presumably unable to distinguish "reality" from "fantasy") and marked by an analogous inability to distinguish representation from presentation, given their assumption that film maintains an immediate and direct relation to the real; (2) artistic and intellectual discourses – generally concerned to distinguish "artistic" from "popular" practices and to defend the status of art by setting it in opposition to mass culture's triviality and vulgarity;

and (3) political and cultural discourses – usually involving critics on the political left and distinguished by an attempt to discern the social and ideological effects of mass-produced forms on audiences themselves produced by an increasingly industrialized culture. At this point I must emphasize that these categories are not mutually exclusive, since moral evaluations of the cinema are never confined to the discourses of reformers, just as analyses of the effects of industrial culture are not limited to critics on the left.

I must also make explicit my reasons for privileging examples from Anglo-American and German mass cultural criticism. Most obviously, institutional and historical factors have made possible the interchange between Anglo-American and German intellectuals (e.g. the impact of the German university on American intellectual life in the late nineteenth century and the influence of the Institute for Social Research on American sociology and communications research in the 1940s and 1950s). Furthermore, it seems to me that early German film theory may have much to offer contemporary film and television scholars.[7] Without a doubt, problems of translation (both literal and cultural) have often stood in the way of sophisticated assessments of early Germany theory; the narrow and predominantly formal understanding of that theory as either "realist" (Kracauer), "modernist" (Adorno), or "postmodernist" (Benjamin) may indeed be attributed to this. And although early German film theory does not escape the patriarchal bias found in its Anglo-American counterpart, I do believe that it holds out perhaps the most promise for any historical analysis of perception and identification in film and television media. For instance, Benjamin's discussion of aura and its demise provides an important historical and ideological explanation (rather than a formal or epistemological one) for the current denigration of television by scholars who have only recently succeeded in restoring aura to the study of film art.

The writings of American educators and reformers in the early twentieth century are especially revealing in their construction of the differences between "education" and "mass culture" through their reference to the "demands" of national traditions and the "seductions" of popular entertainment forms. As early as 1926, Donald Young, a sociologist at the University of Pennsylvania, argued that the cinema was helping to promote a "reckless appreciation of true values," and this precisely because it was designed to be cheap, available, and easy to understand.[8] Following from the observations advanced by Young, and popularizing the research of prominent sociologists and psychologists, Henry James Foreman, author of *Our Movie-Made Children* (1933), explicitly distinguished between the "rigors" of national education and the "promiscuity" of the cinema. Foreman acknowledged that the cinema may one day provide instruction more valuable "than the present text-book variety." For the time being, however, he believed the cinema to be "vast, haphazard, promiscuous...[and] ill-chosen" in its output, and thus "extremely likely to create a haphazard, promiscuous, and undesirable national consciousness."[9]

The concern of American academics and reformers with regulating the cinema for the good of "national consciousness" found similar expression in the writings of German educators and reformers. As Miriam Hansen forcefully demonstrates in her recent essay, "Early Silent Cinema: Whose Public Sphere?," educators and literary commentators in Germany in the early twentieth century aimed to establish the educational mission of the cinema by curbing what they saw as the explicitly sexual excesses inherent in its appeal.[10] Cautioning against the irrational tendencies of mass tastes, German cinema reformers specifically warned against what they perceived as the increasing – and much deplored – sexualization of cinema audiences. The high percentage of women in film audiences, combined with an apparently sensual and intoxicating atmosphere of the cinema auditorium, was perceived, in fact, as such an alarming phenomenon that, as Hansen explains, the fear of mass culture was translated into a fear of femininity more generally, "of female presence on both a pragmatic and metaphoric level."[11] Quoting from Alfred Döblin, Hansen makes this point especially clear:

> Inside the pitch-black, low ceilinged space a rectangular screen glares over a monster of an audience, a white eye fixating the mass with a monotonous gaze. Couples making out in the background are carried away and withdraw their undisciplined fingers. Children wheezing with consumption quietly shake with the chills of evening fever; badly smelling workers with bulging eyes; women in musty clothes, heavily made-up prostitutes leaning forward, forgetting to adjust their scarves. Here you can see "panem et circenses" fulfilled; spectacle as essential as bread; the bullfight as popular need.[12]

As this quote from Döblin suggests, the polemic against the cinema's "monstrous," "devouring" pleasures was not limited to civic-minded reformers alone: a number of established artists and intellectuals also decried the cinema's function as "vulgar" alternative to the cultural heritage of genuine art. Franz Pfemfert, editor of the expressionist journal *Aktion*, for example, called the cinema "barbaric," arguing that while "the torchbearers of culture hasten to new heights, the people ... listen to the babbling of the cinema and place a new record on the phonograph."[13] Significantly, many German artists and intellectuals directed their attack against the cinema by way of an attack on the American film, that form of cinematic representation not only emblematic of mass, industrialized culture, but also most threatening to the maintenance of a uniquely German cultural heritage. As one German publisher wrote in 1926: "The number of people who see films and don't read books has reached into the millions ... They all surrender to American tastes, they conform, they become uniform. The American film is the new world militarism. It is more dangerous than the Prussian world militarism. It doesn't devour single individuals, it devours whole peoples."[14] Not only is a dividing line drawn here between book culture and film culture, between a traditional mode of written expression and an emerging mode of visual expression, but it is also remarkable how the metaphorized threat slides from the masculine, the militaristic, and the national to the feminine, the insidious, and the all-enveloping. (The comparison between residual and emerging modes of representation, and the values attached to each, will, of course, find similar articulation when television is discussed as a threat to the dominance of film.)

Metaphors that refer to the cinema's insatiable appetite, to its appeal to the most promiscuous and undiscerning of tastes, can also be discerned in the writings of leftist cultural critics. As Heide Schlüpmann points out in her brilliant essay, "Kinosucht" (literally, "Cinema Addiction"), the writings of Kracauer, Benjamin, and Adorno are instructive both in their attack on bourgeois notions of artistic value and in their simultaneous contempt for "feminized" reception.[15] For example, in contrast to Kracauer's later work, *From Caligari to Hitler* (1947), where mass culture is associated with a specifically male mob psychology, Kracauer's early writings often focus upon female spectators and the potentially liberating effects of mass culture. (This is not to say, however, that femininity and liberation are ever equated, a point to which I will return shortly.) As Kracauer writes in his 1927 essay, "The Mass Ornament":

> What is entertainment for the masses is judged by intellectuals as distraction of the masses. Contrary to such a position, I would argue that the aesthetic pleasure gained from the ornamental mass movements is legitimate.... When great amounts of reality-content are no longer visible in our world, art must make do with what is left.... No matter how low one rates the value of the mass ornament, its level of reality is still above that of artistic productions which cultivate obsolete noble sentiments in withered forms – even when they have no further significance.[16]

As Kracauer makes clear, the perceptual "distraction" structured by the mass media carries with it a double meaning. On the one hand, distraction in the cinema is "progressive," since it translates forms of industrial organization into a sensory, perceptual, and highly self-conscious discourse: "in the pure externality of the cinema, the public meets itself, and the discontinuous sequence of splendid sense impressions reveals to them their own daily reality. Would it be concealed to them, it couldn't be attacked or changed."[17] On the other hand, distraction in the cinema contains "reactionary" tendencies, since it encourages passivity and mindless consumption on the part of the spectator which work to block the imagination and "distract" from the necessity to change the present order: "reason is impeded...when the masses into which it should penetrate yield to emotions provided by the godless, mythological cult."[18] The emotionality and irrationality of the cinematic spectacle, those apparently "reactionary" effects of distraction, are in turn linked by Kracauer to an overidentified and specifically female mode of spectatorship. As he argues in his essay, "The Little Shopgirls Go to the Movies" (1927): "Many people sacrifice themselves nobly because they are too lazy to rebel; many tears are shed and they only flow because to cry is sometimes easier than to think. . . . Clandestinely the little shopgirls wipe their eyes and powder their noses before the lights come up."[19]

In this passage, Kracauer implies that a truly progressive cinema must encourage an intellectual distance if the spectator is to guard against the lure of a passive, emotional, or "feminized" reception. Kracauer's emphasis upon an active or intellectual stance toward cinematic distraction, moreover, clearly informs the discussion of mass culture one finds in the writings of Benjamin and Brecht.[20] While all three theorists sought to redeem mass culture, and this in spite of the apparent irrationalism of its appeal, their all too easy linkage of irrationalism with the feminine poses a serious problem for any re-evaluation of their writings.

It should nevertheless be remembered that early German film theorists directed their attention to the social function of representation and thus their analyses of mass culture remain far more dialectical, far more historical, than what one finds in much contemporary film theory. For example, in their well-known essay, "Cinema/Ideology/Criticism," Jean-Louis Comolli and Paul Narboni restate the distinction between art and mass culture one finds in the writings of early German film theorists, only now this distinction is displaced onto a formal opposition between "radical practice" and "classical Hollywood cinema," where Hollywood cinema becomes virtually synonymous with "ideology," with mass culture as the expression of a thoroughly degraded consciousness.[21] In marked contrast to early German film theorists, Comolli and Narboni also maintain that the perceptions afforded by mainstream cinema simply reproduce a closed-system, a "mystified," "illusory," and one-dimensional perceptual experience: "The notion of a public and its tastes was created by the ideology to justify and perpetuate itself. And this public can only express itself via the thought-patterns of ideology. The whole thing is a closed-circuit, endlessly repeating the same illusion. . . . Nothing in these films jars against the ideology, or the audience's mystification by it. They are very reassuring for audiences for there is no difference between the ideology they meet every day and the ideology on the screen."[22]

To be sure, Comolli and Narboni recognize that some "classical" films do escape the dominant ideology in which they are inscribed. Nevertheless, because they conceive of classical cinema as a monolith and a closed system, without any attention to the dynamics of reception, they must resort to text-bound notions in order to theorize that which is transgressed; i.e. that which ruptures, displaces, or disperses the "false and easy pleasures" of the Hollywood system is seen as a strictly formal gesture. However formalistic Comolli's and Narboni's theory of perception in the cinema may now seem, their understanding of transgressive practice continues to hold sway in even the most sophisticated of film theories. Stephen Heath, for example, defines the classical system as that which regulates, binds, and unifies the viewing subject. And fundamental to this binding, this all-consuming – again, "devouring" – process, is the system of suture, defined by Heath, somewhat unguardedly, as a "stitching or typing as in the surgical joining of the lips of a wound."[23] Heath theorizes an aesthetics able to transgress or

"rupture" this dominant visual economy through recourse to a modernist practice which radically exposes the contradictions or "gaps" in the classical system.
To quote Heath, once denied the pleasures of unity, coherence, and binding in,
"the individual as spectator loses his epicentral role and disappears...'he is no
longer a simple consumer, he must also produce'...the spectator, that is, is to be
divided, displaced, pulled into the radical exteriority of his/her process as subject
which poses the construction of subjectivity in the objective contradictions of the
class struggle."[24] Heath's emphasis upon work and production, and his invocation of the mutilated self in the service of the class struggle, serve as explicit
contrast to the unified, consuming product of bourgeois ideology. The gendered
metaphors here are clear: masculinity, production, and the divided self are again
valorized in opposition to femininity, consumption, and the unified body.

The modernist and explicitly formalist impulse of Heath's argument has
recently been questioned by theorists of postmodernism who are skeptical of
claims for the transgressive or negative potential of mass cultural forms.[25] And
yet even postmodern theorists tend to reproduce rigidly text-bound distinctions
between spectatorial perceptions of "unity" (or realism), "transgression" (or
modernism), and "dispersion" (or postmodernism). In an essay which concludes
a volume dedicated to Frankfurt School debates, for example, Fredric Jameson
argues that since modernism has "become the dominant style of commodity
production," it has now lost its political, contestatory, and perceptual value.[26]
"In these circumstances," Jameson writes, "there is some question whether the
ultimate renewal of modernism, the final dialectical subversion of the now
automatized conventions of an aesthetic of perceptual revolution, might not
simply be...realism itself! For when modernism and its accompanying techniques of 'estrangement' have become the dominant style whereby the consumer is
reconciled with capitalism, the fragmentation itself needs to be 'estranged' and
corrected by a more totalizing way of viewing phenomena."[27] In a more recent
essay, "Postmodernism and Consumer Society," Jameson checks the utopia of
this realist solution and argues against all forms of mass culture which he sees as
debasing the critical or emancipatory potential of art. "The erosion of the older
distinction between high-culture and so-called mass or popular culture," Jameson
now writes, "is perhaps the most distressing development of all from an academic
standpoint, which has traditionally had a vested interest in preserving a realm of
high or elite culture against the surrounding environment of philistinism, of
schlock and kitsch, of TV series and *Reader's Digest* culture, and in transmitting
difficult and complex skills of reading, listening, and seeing to its initiates."[28]

Given the history of mass culture criticism, Jameson's remarks hardly seem
original, reproducing as they do the familiar distinctions between art's "complex"
and "difficult" skills and mass culture's "cheap" and "easy" pleasures which
consume, incorporate, and trivialize everything. At this point we might want to
question the rigid distinctions between art and mass culture which organize our
critical discourses. More precisely, we may even want to ask whether mass
culture is really as monolithic and all-consuming as it has been frequently

constructed to be, or whether, in fact, it is mass cultural *criticism* that has a vested interest in consuming and trivializing the different experiences of mass cultural reception. Before answering this question directly, I would now like to turn to television and to the discourses generated by this mass cultural form, perhaps considered to be the most vulgar and most implicated in the "environment of philistinism" that Jameson describes.

Television and Mass Culture

"Television," writes Jerry Mander, "has so enveloped and entered us, it is hard for most of us to remember that it was scarcely a generation ago that there was no such thing as television."[29] Mander's use of the metaphor of penetration to describe and condemn television as medium evokes an audience for television that is passive, vulnerable, and inherently "feminized." And not only is Mander's discourse representative of a great deal of television criticism, but it also reaffirms the real and metaphoric fear of femininity previously articulated by critics of cinema – a fear that simultaneously directs itself against women as viewers and against the perceptual distraction assumed to follow from mass cultural reception.

The earliest studies of television, for example, were conducted by sociologists and psychologists concerned with uncovering the effects of television violence on children, on those viewers most easily "seduced" by aggressive behavior presented on the screen.[30] Similar to early studies of the cinema, early studies of television aimed to intervene in the shaping of consumer tastes so as to regulate television programs and to educate television viewers by presenting "themes and characterizations which are morally and socially more worthwhile."[31] What "morally" and "socially" worthwhile might have meant to early television reformers may be gleaned from the response of one television producer to the pressures for television regulation. Worthington Miner, executive producer of National Telefilm Associates, wrote in 1961 that any censorship of televisual reality will merely effect the return of a repressed, and presumably more detrimental, violence than that which currently organizes social relations:

> When all searching into politics, religion, and sex is removed – when every "damn" and "hell" is gone – when every Italian is no longer a "wop" and every Negro is no longer a "nigger" – when every gangster is renamed Adams or Bartlett, and every dentist an incipient Schweitzer, when indeed, every advertiser and account execut- ive smiles – what is left? For this the censor must answer. What is left? Synthetic hogwash and violence! Shot through the guts, the head, or the back – the bloodier the better – Nielsen and Trendex demand it! Let woman blast her man in the face with a shotgun – but please, no cleavage. Tears? Oh, yes – lots of tears – for the poor misunderstood woman, or man, who just happened on the side to be selling heroin – or themselves. And in the daytime – Woman! The backbone of the home, the family, the business, the works. Oh, yes, within the censor's acceptance, the woman is forever a giant of integrity, loyalty, force – while generally misunderstood

and abused. Man – a poor, fumbling, well-meaning idiot – or a martyr. This is what the censor declares every American adolescent should know about his father.[32]

The racism and sexism of Miner's remarks are outrageous in their very explicitness. And yet the conservatism implicit in Miner's belief that television programs and social relations are best left the way they are can also be detected in the writings of less hysterical television commentators. Paul Robinson, professor of history and author of an essay entitled "TV Can't Educate," reverts to the familiar distinctions between "education" and "entertainment" in order to argue that attempts to regulate or promote educational values through TV are fundamentally misguided since television is "structurally unsuited to learning." In learning, Robinson maintains, "one must be able to freeze the absorption of fact or proposition at any moment to make mental comparisons." And since television is always "a matter of seconds, minutes, and hours... it can never teach." Significantly, Robinson does not confine his critical remarks to the educational pretensions of TV, nor to television alone. "There is a new form of slumming among intellectuals," Robinson writes, "watching 'bad' (i.e. commercial) TV and even writing books about it." This trend, Robinson argues, should not be taken seriously, for if television and film are equipped to "entertain, divert, above all to amuse," they cannot provide the time or absorption required for true knowledge. The opposition between the absorption of learning and the distraction of television thus leads Robinson to conclude that there is, in fact, "only one way to learn: by reading."[33] (Following this line of argument, one wonders why universities require professors to lecture at all.)

Robinson's argument clearly aims to preserve the traditional boundaries that define educational value in the academy and, in this, his position is hardly much less conservative than Miner's. Furthermore, it is important to stress that the terms and oppositions which organize Robinson's discourse also pervade writings on television by critics on the political left. For example, in his essay, "Of Happiness and Of Despair We Have No Measure," Ernest van den Haag, a critic indebted to the pessimistic strain of Frankfurt School theory, also denies any educational function to television since education is itself implicated in the logic of commodity production. Van den Haag goes one step further than Robinson, however, by claiming that television (and mass culture more generally) cannot offer genuine pleasure either, for pleasure, too, has been commodified and drained of its true significance: "Condemned to pleasure, people often find themselves out on parole, craving to be distracted from distraction by distraction." In van den Haag's view, the commodification of labor under capitalism "depletes people psychologically and makes them weary and restless." And, in their desperate search for genuine experience and involvement, the mass media offer them only vulgar, duplicitous, and vacuous pleasures. The bonds that once existed between producers and consumers, van den Haag continues, have been severed with the advent of the impersonal market system which increases the sense of "violation [that] springs from the same thwarting of individuality that makes prostitution (or promiscuity) psychologically offensive." Not surprisingly, van den Haag's characterization of the "promiscuous" marketplace lends itself to a description of the relationship between producers and consumers of mass culture more generally: "The cost of cheap and easy availability, of mass production, is wide appeal; and the cost of wide appeal is de-individualization of the relationship between those who cater and those who are catered to; and of the relationship between both to the object of transaction. By using each other indiscriminately... the prostitute and her client sacrifice to seemingly more urgent demands the self which, in order to grow, needs continuity, discrimination and completeness in relationships." The "cheap and easy" pleasures which lead van den Haag to personify mass culture as a prostitute also serve him to identify the values of genuine art. Like love, he argues, "art can only be experienced as a cumulative relationship." That is to say, in contrast to the promiscuity and non-involvement of mass cultural reception, the reception of art encourages a continuous and individualized devotion to the work itself. "New, doubtful, and difficult" in its appreciation, art therefore negates mass culture's "loud, broad, and easy charms."[34] While van den Haag does acknowledge that mass culture may provide pleasure to some, he maintains that this pleasure is only a "substitute" for the true pleasures of art which restore man's need for unity and "penetrate deeper experience and lead to a fuller confrontation of man's predicament."[35]

"Man's" predicament and "man's" need for unity are recurring themes in much mass culture criticism. And given the pervasive expression of these themes, it is hardly surprising that the televisual form most condemned in mass culture criticism is the soap opera, that form which makes its appeal explicitly to women. In his essay, "Soap Time: Thoughts on a Commodity Art Form," Dennis Porter argues that soap time is "for and of pleasure, the time of consumption, of a collectivized and commercially induced American Dream." In Porter's view, the consumption of soap operas is thoroughly mystified and illusory, for soap operas completely efface the traces of their production and thus deny the distance that would "subvert [their] commercial function." Porter continues: "Not only is [the soap opera] itself made to be sold for a profit on the open market, it is also designed as a purveyor of commodities, an indiscriminate huckster for freeze-dried coffee, pet food, and Carefree panty shields. As a consequence, it mystifies everything it touches...." Although Porter does not state it directly, it is clear from his argument that the soap opera primarily mystifies its audience – an audience implicitly coded as female. (Indeed, the presumed consumers for panty shields and, perhaps, for coffee and pet food are women; hence, women are those consumers who are, according to Porter, most easily duped by the phony spell of the commodity.) Porter does express his moral disgust with the function of soap operas in perpetuating the domestication of American women. And yet, he nevertheless condemns women's pleasure in watching soap operas, and goes so far as to suggest that "the speech of the soap opera... is voiceless."[36] In so doing, Porter assumes his experience of watching soap operas to be the same

for women, thus silencing the voice that may speak to women in even the most
highly privatized and commodified of forms.

A similar inability to acknowledge the function of television for different kinds
of audiences marks Noël Burch's discussion of television in his essay, "Narrat-
ive/Diegesis – Thresholds, Limits." Like Porter, Burch is also concerned to
emphasize how television's commodification of pleasure makes it the newest and
most "potent weapon in the media arsenal of capitalism." And yet, unlike Porter,
Burch adopts a postmodern stance which does not allow for the hope of distanciation to guard against television's hypnotic, consuming, and narcotizing
effects. In striking contrast to his earlier, modernist stance, Burch argues that
television's return to the dispersed structures of identification that marked the
primitive cinema is "anything but innocent." "For years," Burch continues, "we
have assumed that the alienation effect was necessarily enlightening, liberating,
that anything which undercut the empathetic power of the diegetic process was
progressive." Now, "having observed the way in which Americans relate to a
television," however, Burch is forced to conclude, like Jameson, that "distanciation . . . has been coopted." The incorporation of a variety of genres in American
network television, while apparently innovative or modernist in its mixture of
styles, is thus for Burch "designed to place everything on the same plane of
triviality . . . in which the repression in El Salvador is no more nor less involving
than 'The Price is Right.'" The television spectator is not encouraged to think,
to know, to take action, but instead to become entranced by a "fascinated non-
involvement which is several removes in passivity away from the 'spell of motion
pictures.'" Explicitly set in opposition to the cinema, television for Burch
becomes the "bad object" from which to promote radical practice. And given
television's alleged modernism, now Burch, too, argues for a return to realism, to
a strong diegetic effect characteristic of classical narrative forms which will
restore spectatorial unity and "elicit some kind of emotional, intellectual, and
perhaps even ideological commitment."[37] With Burch, as with Jameson, mass
culture criticism comes full circle: from an attack on unity or realism, to a
privileging of negativity or modernism, to a call for involvement through realist
forms.

In this circular movement, however, the "place" accorded to the feminine
remains constant, forever made to bear the composite marks of passivity, mystification, and vulgarity. To quote from Cixous, it seems as though everything
"must return to the masculine," to the realm of the "proper" which sustains
itself only by locating a place for the feminine outside the realm of respectability,
outside the sphere of activity and knowledge.[38]

And yet, if the eternal return of the masculine may pervade our theories of
mass culture, it would be both a mistake and a serious omission on my part to
suggest that all contemporary writings on mass culture are caught within the
terms of a repetitive, masculinized discourse. A brief look at recent film and
television scholarship will serve to emphasize that a certain shift is underway in
contemporary writings on mass culture, a shift which contests the traditional

view of mass culture as essentially passive, or, when used as a term of oppro-brium, "feminized" in its modes of consumption and address.

For a start, what contemporary theorists have diagnosed as our "postmodern condition" – a condition marked by an apparent erosion of older distinctions between high and low culture – has been implicitly questioned by theorists who demonstrate that mass culture, from the nineteenth-century novel to the TV serial, has always quoted from high art or "legitimate" forms. Rather than situate either film or television as the privileged metaphor for the (often deplored) proliferation, overproduction, or diffusion of signs, some recent theorists of mass culture have attempted to analyze the function of intertextuality historically and in relation to competing representational forms. Jane Feuer's work on the Hollywood musical, for example, traces the quotation and erasure of high art intertexts as central to the development of the musical as a genre.[39] The elision of boundaries between popular and elite forms, Feuer emphasizes, is by no means an invention of the last several decades nor the mark of our postmodern, despairing condition. Instead, Feuer argues that the Hollywood musical's process of inter-textual appropriation (or "quotation") from both legitimate and popular forms (i.e. theater, popular recordings, television) marks that genre as a hybrid from its very inception. Furthermore, as Feuer emphasizes, the self-consciously hybrid character of the Hollywood musical is itself a form of self-promotion, an attempt at product differentiation in an intensely competitive entertainment market. And, as Feuer concludes, a narrowly formal evaluation of the Hollywood musical's textual effects will not suffice to explain its complex social function. As she puts it, "unless we put the Hollywood musical in its proper place in the history of entertainment, we may mistake it for a modernist film, or, worse, we may never see what its revelations are trying to conceal."[40] Feuer's work on the Hollywood musical, along with other theorists' work on popular forms, also casts doubt upon the pervasive view of mass culture as either formally or ideologically homoge-neous. Recent scholarship on the woman's film and the maternal melodrama, for example, has insisted upon a differentiated view of the so-called classical Holly-wood cinema so as to understand its historically variable structures of address and modes of reception.[41]

What is true of recent film scholarship is also true of recent writing on television. Tania Modleski's work on daytime soaps, for example, examines the assumption that they are "feminized" forms by analyzing the construction of women as social readers and the construction of soap operas as social texts.[42] Proceeding from the assumption that soap operas are organized differently from popular forms aimed at a masculine visual pleasure, Modleski maintains that the discontinuous, often fragmented rhythm of soaps is organized around the rhythm of women's work. Although she quotes approvingly from Benjamin, who claims that reception in a state of distraction marks the experience of mass cultural consumption, Modleski does not then glibly endorse a reading of daytime soaps as simply "progressive," but stresses instead their function in habituating women to "interruption, distraction, and spasmodic toil."[43] At the same time, however,

Modleski's negative appraisal of the effects of daytime soaps does not lead her to argue that they are irredeemably "reactionary." On the contrary, she maintains that soap operas serve as the site for the expression of repressed desires which, if openly articulated, "would challenge the psychological and social order of things."[44] The contradictory social function of daytime soaps brings Modleski, finally, to question the patriarchal bias in theories of spectatorship and identification. Indeed, Modleski argues that while the female viewer of soaps may lack the "distance" supposedly required for mastery over the image, she does not pathologically over-identify with soap opera characters, "but rather relates to them as intimates, as extensions of her world."[45] And, as Modleski concludes, we must not condemn this empathetic mode of identification if we are ever to understand how mass culture "speaks to women's pleasure at the same time it puts it in the service of patriarchy, keeps it working for the good of the family."[46]

Following from Modleski's remarks, we may now want to pursue a different reading of mass culture, one which begins from the assumption that mass culture is neither intrinsically "progressive" nor "reactionary," but highly contradictory and historically variable in its form, its meanings, and its effects. It is here that early German film theory, when combined with a feminist perspective, may provide a more precisely social and historical explanation for the construction of subjectivity and identification in film and television viewing as at once dispersed and distracted while at the same time intensely preoccupied and absorbed. In other words, rather than revert to uncomplicated or merely formal oppositions in our analyses of textual and subject effects, we must attend to the complex interplay between psychic, social, and cultural processes in the construction of visual pleasure and identification. From this perspective, if female spectators find it difficult to assume a fetishistic distance from the image (as feminist theorists and theorists like Kracauer have claimed), then it would no longer follow that they therefore lack the ability to attain pleasure or a critical understanding of the image. Indeed, rather than subscribe to an epistemology that privileges the masculine, to the notion that an emotional identification is always regressive, we would do better to understand that different spectators may recognize themselves differently, and that this recognition, itself an effect of cultural and institutional processes, may entail a complex response of concentration, distraction, and emotional identification. While in some instances an empathetic mode of identification may very well put women's pleasures in the service of patriarchy, in others it may in fact encourage an understanding that leads to strong emotional response which, in turn, may lead to recognition and to action.

Theorists of film and television must begin to acknowledge the complex and competing modes of perception and identification in mass cultural practices and avoid theorizing in an immanently textual or formal manner. As we have seen, not only is such an approach fundamentally ahistorical, but it also lends itself to a pernicious patriarchal bias that elides the social function of representation by continually returning to an epistemology that privileges the masculine and, by extension, "legitimate" cultural forms. This is not to suggest, however, that we embrace mass culture uncritically or assume it to be inherently liberating, progressive, or somehow problem-free. Neither do I mean to deny the real perceptual and historical differences between film and television viewing or to dismiss the important institutional changes resulting from differences between, for example, collective and privatized reception. I would only insist that these differences be theorized historically and not through recourse to essences which reduce the question of difference to a mere application of gendered metaphors and man-made oppositions.[47]

Notes

1 Leslie A. Fiedler, "The Middle Against Both Ends," in *Mass Culture: The Popular Arts in America*, ed. Bernard Rosenberg and David Manning White (New York: Free Press, 1957), 547.

2 For an elaboration of this argument, see Rick Altman, "The Sound Track in Television," paper read at the 1984 SCS Conference, March 28–31, 1984, Madison, Wisconsin; forthcoming in a collection of essays on mass culture edited by Tania Modleski.

3 See, for example, the collection of essays edited by E. Ann Kaplan entitled, *Regarding Television*, American Film Institute Monograph Series, vol. 3 (Frederick, Md.: University Publications of America, 1984), and especially Kaplan's introductory essay.

4 Hélène Cixous, "Castration or Decapitation," trans. Annette Kuhn, *Signs: Journal of Women in Culture and Society* 7, no. 1 (Autumn 1981): 44.

5 Tania Modleski, "The Terror of Pleasure: The Contemporary Horror Film and Postmodern Theory," forthcoming in *Theories of Contemporary Culture*, Indiana University Press, vol. 7. Modleski's feminist critique of mass culture criticism has inspired my own thinking about film and television criticism. For a more elaborate discussion of the "feminization of culture" in mass culture criticism, see Modleski's essay, "Femininity as Mas(s)querade: A Feminist Approach to Mass Culture," forthcoming in *High Theory/Low Culture*, ed. Colin MacCabe, University of Manchester Press.

6 I am referring here to Beverle Houston's analysis of television spectatorship in her essay, "Viewing Television: The Metapsychology of Endless Consumption," *Quarterly Review of Film Studies* 9, no. 3 (Summer 1984): 183–95.

7 Miriam Hansen and Thomas Elsaesser have both provided extremely subtle and sophisticated reassessments of early German film theory. They are also in the process of editing a volume of *New German Critique* devoted to a re-examination of early German film theory in light of contemporary theoretical concerns in film and television study.

8 Donald Young, "Social Standards and the Motion Picture," *The Annals of the American Academy of Political and Social Sciences* 128 (November 1926): 147; quoted in Robert Sklar, *Movie-Made America* (New York: Random House, 1975), 123.

9 Henry James Foreman, *Our Movie-Made Children* (1933), 64–5; quoted in Sklar, 137.

10 I am merely summarizing part of Hansen's argument here. For a more complete, and extremely illuminating discussion of German mass culture debates, see Hansen's

essay, "Early Silent Cinema: Whose Public Sphere?," *New German Critique*, no. 29 (Spring–Summer 1983): 147–83.

11 Hansen, 175.

12 Alfred Döblin, "Das Theater der kleinen Leute," in *Kino-Debatte: Literatur und Film, 1909–1929*, ed. Anton Kaes (Tübingen: Niemeyer, 1978), 38; quoted in and translated by Hansen, 174.

13 Franz Pfemfert, quoted in Anton Kaes's introduction to the anthology *Kino-Debatte*, 10; translation mine. All translations are mine unless otherwise noted.

14 Herbert Jhering, "UFA und Buster Keaton," (1926); quoted in Anton Kaes's introduction to the anthology, *Kino-Debatte*, 15.

15 Heide Schlüpmann's essay, which links intellectual attitudes towards the cinema (especially those of Kracauer, Benjamin, and Adorno) with a pervasive patriarchal bias, has been central to my own thinking about theories of cinematic and televisual spectatorship. See her "Kinosucht," *Frauen und Film*, no. 33 (October 1982): 45–52.

16 Siegfried Kracauer, "Das Ornament der Masse," in *Das Ornament der Masse* (Frankfurt am Main: Suhrkamp, 1963), 50–1. This essay is available in translation in *New German Critique*, no. 5 (Spring 1975): 67–76.

17 Kracauer, "Kult der Zerstreuung," ibid., 315.

18 Kracauer, "Das Ornament der Masse," ibid., 62.

19 Kracauer, "Die kleinen Ladenmädchen gehen ins Kino," ibid., 292–3.

20 In saying this, I do not mean to imply that either Kracauer, Benjamin, or Brecht settled upon a simple, or one-sided interpretation of perception and distraction in the cinema. While the emphasis in their writings seems to me to fall upon an active or intellectual meaning of distraction which, in turn, is combined with a suspicion towards emotional response and identification, all three theorists were alert to the need for identification, recognition, and pleasure in the cinema. (Indeed, as Heide Schlüpmann has recently argued, Kracauer's own fascination for the cinema was in fact often projected on to the little shopgirls he discusses.)

21 Jean-Louis Comolli and Paul Narboni, "Cinema/Ideology/Criticism," reprinted in translation in *Screen* 12, no. 1 (Spring 1971): 27–36; also reprinted in *Movies and Methods*, ed. Bill Nichols (Berkeley: University of California Press, 1976), 23–30.

22 Comolli and Narboni, *Movies and Methods*, 26.

23 Stephen Heath, "Narrative Space," *Screen* 17, no. 3 (Autumn 1976); reprinted in *Questions of Cinema* (Bloomington: Indiana University Press, 1981), 52.

24 Stephen Heath, "From Brecht to Film – Theses, Problems," *Screen* 16, no. 4 (Winter 1975–6): 39.

25 See the anthology of essays, *The Anti-Aesthetic: Essays on Postmodern Culture*, ed. Hal Foster (Port Townsend, Washington: Bay Press, 1983).

26 Fredric Jameson, "Reflections in Conclusion," in *Aesthetics and Politics*, ed. Ronald Taylor (London: New Left Books, 1977), 209.

27 Jameson, "Reflections in Conclusion," 211. It should be noted that Jameson's conclusion here is much in line with the conclusion reached by Kracauer and Benjamin.

28 Fredric Jameson, "Postmodernism and Consumer Society," in *The Anti-Aesthetic*, 112.

29 Jerry Mander, *Four Arguments For the Elimination of Television* (New York: William Morrow, 1978), 350–1. As a number of feminist theorists have pointed out, the metaphorics of penetration and rape pervade a number of critical and representational

discourses. See, for example, Tania Modleski's remarks regarding Baudrillard's theory of mass communication and Cronenberg's horror films in her essay, "The Terror of Pleasure: The Contemporary Horror Film and Postmodern Theory." See also Teresa de Lauretis's critique of the patriarchal bias in Derrida and Foucault in her essay, "Between the Rhetoric of Violence and the Violence of Rhetoric," forthcoming in a special issue of *Semiotica* (1984), edited by Nancy Armstrong.

30　The number of sociological and psychological studies of television's effects on children are too numerous to list. For a useful overview of these approaches, as well as an extensive bibliography, see Paul M. Hirsch, "The Role of Television and Popular Culture in Contemporary Society," in *Television: The Critical View*, Third Edition, ed. Horace Newcomb (New York: Oxford University Press, 1982), 280–310.

31　Hilde T. Himmelweit, *Television and the Child*, 220; quoted in Robert S. Alley, "Television Drama," in *Television: The Critical View*, 91.

32　Worthington Miner, "The Terrible Toll of Taboos" (March 1961); reprinted in *Television and Radio*, ed. Poyntz Tyler, *The Reference Shelf*, vol. 33, no. 6 (New York: H. W. Wilson, 1961), 171.

33　Paul Robinson, "TV Can't Educate," *The New Republic* (August 12, 1978); reprinted in *The Little, Brown Reader*, Third Edition, ed. Marcia Stubbs and Sylvan Barnett (Boston: Little, Brown, 1983), 216–19.

34　Ernest van den Haag, "Of Happiness and Of Despair We Have No Measure," in *Mass Culture: The Popular Arts in America*, ed. Bernard Rosenberg and David Manning White, 505, 512, 513, 516.

35　Ibid., 533. Van den Haag also writes, and no less revealingly, that while "no pin-up girl can surfeit appetite for a real one . . . the pin-up can spoil the appetites for other images of girls . . ." (525).

36　Dennis Porter, "Soap Times: Thoughts on a Commodity Art Form," in *Television: The Critical View*, 129–31.

37　Noël Burch, "Narrative/Diegesis – Thresholds, Limits," *Screen* 23, no. 2 (July–August 1982): 16–33.

38　Cixous, "Castration or Decapitation," 41–55.

39　Jane Feuer, *The Hollywood Musical* (Bloomington: Indiana University Press, 1982).

40　Ibid., 47.

41　See Linda Williams, "Something Else Besides a Mother: *Stella Dallas* and the Maternal Melodrama," *Cinema Journal* 24, no. 1 (Fall 1984), 2–27; and Tania Modleski, "Time and Desire in the Woman's Film," *Cinema Journal* 23, no. 3 (Spring 1984), 19–30.

42　Tania Modleski, "The Search for Tomorrow in Today's Soap Operas," in *Loving with a Vengeance: Mass Produced Fantasies for Women* (New York: Methuen, 1984), 85–109. Part of this chapter has been reprinted as "The Rhythms of Reception: Daytime Television and Women's Work," in *Regarding Television*, ed. Kaplan, 67–75.

43　Modleski, "The Rhythms of Reception," 71.

44　Modleski, "The Search for Tomorrow in Today's Soap Operas," 30.

45　Modleski, "The Rhythms of Reception," 69.

46　Ibid.

47　I would like to thank Carol Flinn for her critical and close reading of this essay.

Part XI

Stars and Performance

Introduction

Toby Miller

Stars are crucial to writing on film. Douglas Gomery (1991) divides traditional film history between survey books and biographies. Surveys allow the facts to speak for themselves – or claim they do – by recounting sequences of events, mostly in cause-and-effect relation. The questions posed by such histories include: How did a technology develop? Who ran the powerful companies? What was the role of the state? What part did the public play? And what was the relationship between the screen and national, local, and other forms of culture? The biography is much more populist. Its readership is the screen audience itself. More a fan's genre, it is both positive and negative about stars and managers. The biographical genre tends to privilege the thesis that "great men" make history, with destiny determined by the struggle of individuals and their imagined interiorities.

We divide our discussion here between four facets of stardom: how to theorize stars, their history, their economic value, and their gendered status. As the industry magazine *Variety* puts it, a star is "a curious amalgam consisting of a person wrapped in a certain body of work at a particular moment in time" (Bart, 1997: 4). Stars are actors whose "names becomes assets in the production of films, and drawing powers in attracting audiences." They tend to operate via the following division: character is "a notational entity," personality a "private biographical reality," and persona "the public image of the actor as a concrete person that is inferred from his or her screen presence and associated publicity." Four attributes are generally correlated with stardom: looks, age, ability, and screen image. These are often said to engage spectators in a mixture of sadistic voyeurism and masochistic self-denial. Each quality can be studied through a blend of semiotic and sociological analysis. At the same time, we need to acknowledge the differential uptake of star symbols among audiences –

distinctions between high and low affective investments. Stars do not have a universal meaning, and the attributes attached to them may vary by role rather than persona (Levy, 1990: 247–50; King, 1987: 160; McDonald, 1995: 86–7; Dyer, 1986; Stacey, 1994: 136; Thompson, 1978).

The star is a marketing method, a social sign, a national emblem, a product of capital and individualism, and an object of personal as much as collective consumption. All of these involve an imbrication of private and public, non-performativity and performativity, intimacy and publicity; and the opportunity for appropriation by marginal groups. Stars "personalize social meanings and ideologies." Actors become stars when their off-screen life-styles and personalities equal or surpass their acting ability in importance. Stardom represents power and material success. Stars are implicated in consumerism and social stereotyping. They are sites of "cultural politics" (Gledhill, 1991: xii–xiii). For instance, an editorial covering the death of Laurence Olivier claimed he was "a mirror in which the public sees the world as it really is or should be." This references the public fascination with the private and public aspects of artists' lives, endowing them with "totemic significance.... As a star, he was the property of the world" ("Death of an Artist," 1989). But this notion of property is a complicated one. As Rosemary J. Coombe says, "the law...produces the possibility of the celebrity signifier's polysemy," such that people are permitted to own exclusive rights to the public utilization of their "nickname, signature, physical pose, body parts, frequently used phrases, car, performance style, mannerism, and gestures" (Coombe, 1992: 59–61, 66).

For Barry King (1987; 1992) arguments to the effect that stars who die young symbolize the inevitable rebelliousness of the youth of a generation (Montgomery Clift or James Dean, for example) and thereby become mythic, install the populist biography of the star as both academic artefact and guarantor of academic access to populist status: they function as a demotic warrant. No general account of stardom can be derived from an absolute concentration on audiences, on the responses and appropriations that help to subtend the interpretation and take-up of star-texts. Stars tend, on these interpretations, to embody so many contradictions of capital and gender, and be capable of so many decodings by various minorities and subcultures, that they are endlessly plural and have no form of their own.

King seeks to overcome this problem by returning to "the site of production," concentrating on "the formation of the performance commodity." The intertextuality of the private and the public in the case of the star is especially interesting given Marx's understanding of commodity fetishism, whereby reification drives persons to divide themselves between the private agency of personal characteristics and the public domain of socially meaningful activity. The human personality is discounted in the latter. Processes of exchange conventionally devalue the particular features of the individual in preference for substitutable, generic, general qualities; such is the process of the abstraction of labor. The star is "ambiguously located between capital and labor," a free agent that repeatedly binds itself to contractual arrangements but obtains wealth, status, and power. Stars may establish companies, "profiting from the sale of their own personae." This necessitates maintaining "a personal monopoly over his or her persona." The technology of visual reproduction enables a multiplicity of personalized perspectives inside a world of commodity reproduction. Stars stand in for the power of labor in a spectacularized fashion; hence their hold on "popular consciousness" (King, 1987: 146–60).

As we have noted elsewhere, the adoption of psychoanalysis by film theory involved an investigation of mechanisms of desire in spectators and texts, the means of identification between audience and actor. This identification was criticized for its conventional sexism and commodity fetishism and welcomed for its potential to deliver positive points of identification for marginalized groups (Gledhill, 1991: xiv–xv). Accounts of the valorization of film stars in India focus on their capacity to "offer audiences whose lives are limited in various ways – materially and emotionally – the vicarious pleasure of identification with and exploration of the realm of the extraordinary." There is a merger of the transgressive and the ideal in their off-screen mores (Gandhy and Thomas, 1991: 107–8). John G. Cawelti (1980) contends that performance is more integral to popular culture than "fine or elite work." Hence the need to "articulate an aesthetic of performance" to comprehend popular culture. There is no referent beyond performance, in the sense of a preconditioned, preexistent work that is well- or ill-performed; the work and the performance are a unity. The reproducibility of virtuosic performance provided by electronic technology has produced an era of performativity, via instantaneous reception and long archival life. Popular art is marked out by its "simplicity, familiarity and strong impact." The star's capacity to be both the bearer of an institutional–diegetic legend and a personal-life legend, goes guarantor of comprehendability and emotion. Stars can provide both superhuman and quintessentially human weight (consider John Wayne and Will Rogers within the genre of the Western). Genres produce characteristics for the star personae which they carry and are then mutually informed and invigorated by (James Bond/Sean Connery). Performance also helps to differentiate products which are, in many ways, classically conventional, derivative, and mechanical. A performer is thus a presence, a mediation, and a set of skills. Performance attracts artistic categorization as transformative or interpretative, rather than recitational or incantatory. It is best understood as an amalgam of the real, an abstraction from that real which is the work performed, and the self. Improvisations on the self equate with improvising the textual work that originated the performance (Cawelti, 1980: 4–10).

James Naremore (chapter 37, this volume) argues that acting happens when "persons held up for show have become agents in a narrative" (1988: 23). Thomas Kavanagh (1979) asks whether stars are a means of generic classification and a way into understanding the relationship of spectator to text. The social text of Marlon Brando that informs a reading of *The Wild One*

(Laslo Benedeck, 1954) is chronologically, thematically, and politically different from the text mobilized to read *Superman* (Richard Donner, 1978), yet intimately related to it. Kavanagh borrows from Émile Benveniste's concept of the "middle voice." In earlier Indo-European form, the antinomy to active was middle, not passive, with a referentiality of the verb to the subject rather than the object. The middle voice bespeaks interiority as the "within" of the subject, describing actions that take place and remain inside that space. This is not an opposition between doing and being, but the relationship of the subject to action. Homologously, stars-on-screen confront diegetic difficulties but do so with another interaction occurring, between their film subjectivity and their extra-textual – albeit still textually derived and publicly known – personae. The star-subject is both the agent who makes things happen and the core who centers all this activity and is its diegetic referent. Clint Eastwood eponymizes narratives even as his characters inform and are informed by them both physically and actantially. When the subject transforms a process from its interior and onto the stage of action, this is a move into the transitive. Star-films are, *inter alia*, "the 'acting out' of a synchronic structure within the actor as actor." This removes the process from inside the subject; it is transitive because the film's narrative is exteriorized onto what the star does to objects. So the narrative of star-films is the outcome of certain processes. Stars are act*ants* as diegetic characters and act*ors* as "organizing presence" of screen material for spectators (Kavanagh, 1979: 54–61).

What is the history to stardom? Stars emerged in American theater of the 1820s, as actors and independent producers, visible because theaters advertised actors above and beyond titles (Gledhill, 1991: xii; Staiger, 1991: 8). Movie actors' names were unknown until about 1912, since "names" cost more money, but then a battle between independent producers and Edison/Biograph created a struggle for product differentiation through publicity, films, and magazines (Gamson, 1994: 24–5). There were three successive transformations into the star: (1) a "discourse on acting"; (2) a notion of the "picture personality"; and (3) the mature form – "the star." The first occurred alongside a transition from concentrating on technology – the wonder of the apparatus – to the issue of visible labor and hence personality. The star was present when there was "a fairly thoroughgoing articulation of the paradigm professional life/private life." The domain of screen knowledge deemed suitable for the audience extended outside the picture theater, with private lives "a new site of knowledge and truth" from about 1914. The moral standing of film came to be carried by stars and their families. The development of the narrative fiction film in the first decade of the century assisted the individuation of actors: close-ups psychologized the diegetic characters and performers. At the same time, a cross-culture-industry development intertextually evidenced the nexus between the star system of Hollywood payments and the appearance of columns of prose and pictures dedicated to biographical details of actors in the American daily press towards the close of the century's first decade (Musser, 1986: 59–60).

Production houses were effectively "building a public personality" via their stars, each of whom by the 1930s had authorized biographical legends circulating that intertwined with their roles in narrative features. A personality was required to permeate screen roles and publicity materials. The economic background is that by the turn of the century, over-production in American business had created a crisis. Manufactured goods were on inventory, not in homes. By the 1920s moves to right this situation had extended beyond management and into consumption: to market, to market. Large banks were now funding Hollywood, and they sought coordination. Two adjacent changes occurred through the mid-1930s: Hollywood stars showcasing make-up, clothing, and other items of dress-up sensibility; and direct tie-ins between screen texts and particular products. The latter might see a soft-drink or automobile advertised in a magazine by a movie star or utilized in a film, with stars' personal preferences in diet, clothing, and cosmetics closely published/monitored (and freely available). By the Depression, Hollywood stars were the third biggest source of news in the United States. Early tales of stars as American aristocrats were carefully supplanted by myths about merit and luck. With the break up of the Hollywood studios' vertical integration in the 1950s, stars could own their labor more fully and were no longer subject to quite the same degree of compulsory fit between the private and the public (Harris, 1991: 40; Eckert, 1991: 30, 32, 36; Gamson, 1994: 27, 29, 31, 41).

What is a star worth? During the 1940s George Gallup's Audience Research Inc. surveyed marquee attraction of stars, arguing that 16 percent of revenue came from recognition value. Later research suggested the figure was more like 2 percent. By the 1950s the idea was to use actors who appealed across American society rather than in one target group; hence the 1959 casting of Ricky Nelson (age 19) alongside Dean Martin (42) and John Wayne (52) in Howard Hawks's *Rio Bravo* (Izod, 1988: 158). Studies of films from the late 1960s suggest stars may benefit from the marquee signage of a successful film, rather than the other way around. Wallace et al. (1993) evaluated over 100 stars and 1,600 recent movies. Their question was: what accounts for the popularity of films within the US? In terms of parental sanctions, family anxieties about films can remove up to $2 million from the box office, depending on the severity of the panic. Other negative factors are patrimony: foreign films deduct about $5.6 million from rentals. Eight genres have positive effects: adventure ($8M), comedy ($6M), disaster ($31M), horror ($14M), musical ($8.8M), religion ($17.5M), science fiction ($25.6M), and spy ($7.8M). On the star front, of course, the cost of hiring certain actors is critical. The research used regression analysis to correlate certain stars with success (Burt Reynolds, Danny DeVito, Dustin Hoffman, Barbra Streisand, and Bill Murray), others with steady increase in impact over many years (Brando, James Coburn, Tom Cruise, Eastwood, Bette Midler, and Sylvester Stallone), some with success–decline–success stories (Julie Andrews, Kevin Bacon, Robert De Niro, and Charlton Heston), and a final group of initial achievement followed by decline (Richard Dreyfuss, Harrison Ford, Tom

Laughlin, Eddie Murphy, Paul Newman, and Robert Redford). Once other variables are removed, stars appear to account for approximately 22 percent of rental value (Wallace et al., 1993: 2–4, 11, 16, 21).

Emanuel Levy (1990) matched the looks, age, ability, and screen image of 81 men and 48 women against the major box-office attractions between 1932 and 1984. His findings were as follows: all the women were defined as conventionally attractive, and half the men. Most women were blonde, most men dark. Male leads could be old, but not female. Professional training was insignificant, but more common among women, who were mostly excluded from the action-adventure genre. Women lasted two years as major stars on average; men lasted four (ibid.: 247–51, 253–6).

Clearly, mainstream Hollywood constructs "sexuality as stable, with well-defined characteristics, and the alignment of masculinity with men and femininity with women" (Holmlund, 1986: 31; for a similar focus see Straayer and Rowe chapters 35 and 36, this volume). But Stéphane Brisset (1989) argues that American cinema has produced extraordinary variation in the representation of women: eroticism, Machiavellianism, voluntarism, and seduction. Although rarely the active motors of narrative, women tend to pose the problem, the crux of a difficulty around which turns the fate of a male protagonist in becoming either villain or hero. This changed slightly in the 1980s, with determining female protagonists in *Bagdad Café* (Percy Adlon, 1988), *Babette's Feast* (Gabriel Axel, 1987), *Norma Rae* (Martin Ritt, 1979), *Gorillas in the Mist* (Michael Apted, 1988), *A Fish Called Wanda* (Charles Crichton, 1988), and others. The accompanying change in male roles sees a selection of options from supportive, lost, dismissive, angry, and constant colleague (Brisset, 1989: 6–7). On the other hand, Elayne Rapping (1989: 4) sees a progression through the 1980s away from autonomous women making their own lives and towards a reconciliation of self with conventional family.

Yvonne Tasker (1993) has provided us with a detailed overview of male stars in contemporary action-adventure feature films, such as the *Rambo* cycle (Ted Kotcheff, George Pan Cosmatos, and Peter MacDonald, 1982–8), Arnold Schwarzenegger's vehicles, and *Basic Instinct* (Paul Verhoeven, 1992). She suggests that the public circulation of the Adonis star is split between two incommensurate discourses. One locates this brand of heroism as a triumphalist masculinity that places physical force at its center, a vulgar assertion of traditional male authority against the travails of life and femininity. The second reads this as a hysterical hypothesization of maleness. This is the man "in crisis," a bodily form and social identity that protests too much to be at home with himself and in control of "his" world. Both discourses underscore that the form is concerned with a "reinscription of difference"; hence Tasker's proposal that the "either/or" notion of assertion versus mourning be linked. The high-budget 1980s macho Hollywood action cinema is not so much about natural male bodies making their way through the world as it is concerned with built bodies that move between the labor that creates and maintains them and the chaos that leaves them in need of repair. Male strength is always in need of renewal, forever required to verify its capacities (Tasker, 1993: 109, 2, 9, 3). There is both the promise of instability and the valuing of violence in the animating hypothesis of today's big-budget stars.

Throughout the 1990s Hollywood put its faith in a renewed star system, including stars afflicted with hyper-musculature and the new, "softer" leads such as Ethan Hawke and Brad Pitt alongside Julia Roberts and Sandra Bullock, with the latter less physically passive than their predecessors. Controversy over the public and private intermingling of their lives was as important a publicity tool as it had been at any point in the previous century.

Works Cited

Bart, Peter 1997. "Showbiz Star Wars," *Variety* September 29–October 5: 4, 75.

Brisset, Stéphane 1989. "Les Femmes de l'Oncle Sam," *Cinéma* 49: 6–7.

Cawelti, John G. 1980. "Performance and Popular Culture," *Cinema Journal* 20, no. 1: 4–13.

Coombe, Rosemary J. 1992. "The Celebrity Image and Cultural Identity: Publicity Rights and the Subaltern Politics of Gender," *Discourse* 14, no. 3: 59–88.

"Death of an Artist" 1989. *The Australian* July 13: 12.

Dyer, Richard 1986. *Heavenly Bodies: Film Stars and Society*. New York: St Martin's Press.

Eckert, Charles 1991. "The Carole Lombard in Macy's Window." In *Stardom: Industry of Desire*, ed. Christine Gledhill. London: Routledge.

Gamson, Joshua 1994. *Claims to Fame: Celebrity in Contemporary America*. Berkeley: University of California Press.

Gandhy, Behroze and Rosie Thomas 1991. "Three Indian Film Stars." In *Stardom: Industry of Desire*, ed. Christine Gledhill. London: Routledge.

Gledhill, Christine 1991. "Introduction." *Stardom: Industry of Desire*, ed. Christine Gledhill. London: Routledge.

Gomery, Douglas 1991. "Methods for the Study of the History of Broadcasting and Mass Communication," *Film & History* 21, nos. 2–3: 55–63.

Harris, Thomas 1991. "The Building of Popular Images: Grace Kelly and Marilyn Monroe." In *Stardom: Industry of Desire*, ed. Christine Gledhill. London: Routledge.

Holmlund, Christine 1986. "Sexuality and Power in Male Doppelganger Cinema: The Case of Clint Eastwood's *Tightrope*," *Cinema Journal* 20, no. 1: 31–42.

Izod, John 1988. *Hollywood and the Box Office 1895–1986*. New York: Columbia University Press.

Kavanagh, Thomas M. 1979. "The Middle Voice of Film Narration," *Diacritics* (September): 54–61.

King, Barry 1987. "The Star and the Commodity: Notes Towards a Performance Theory of Stardom," *Cultural Studies* 1, no. 2: 145–61.

—— 1992. "Stardom and Symbolic Degeneracy: Television and the Transformation of the Stars as Public Symbols," *Semiotica* 92, nos. 1–2: 1–47.

Levy, Emanuel 1990. "Social Attributes of American Movie Stars," *Media, Culture & Society* 12, no. 2: 247–67.

McDonald, Paul 1995. "Star Studies." In *Approaches to Popular Film*, ed. Joanne Hollows and Mark Jancovich. Manchester: Manchester University Press.

Musser, Charles 1986. "The Changing Status of the Film Actor." In *Before Hollywood: Turn-of-the-Century Film from American Archives*, ed. Jay Leyda and Charles Musser. New York: American Federation of Arts.

Naremore, James 1988. *Acting in the Cinema*. Berkeley: University of California Press.

Rapping, Elayne 1989. "Liberation in Chains: 'The Woman Question' in Hollywood," *Cineaste* 17, no. 1: 4–8.

Stacey, Jackie 1994. *Star Gazing: Hollywood Cinema and Female Spectatorship*. London: Routledge.

Staiger, Janet 1991. "Seeing Stars." In *Stardom: Industry of Desire*, ed. Christine Gledhill. London: Routledge.

Tasker, Yvonne 1993. *Spectacular Bodies: Gender, Genre and the Action Cinema*. London: Routledge.

Thompson, John O. 1978. "Screen Acting and the Commutation Test," *Screen* 19, no. 2: 55–69.

Wallace, W. Timothy, Alan Seigerman, and Morris B. Holbrook 1993. "The Role of Actors and Actresses in the Success of Films: How Much is a Movie Star Worth?" *Journal of Cultural Economics* 17, no. 1: 1–27.

33
Heavenly Bodies: Film Stars and Society

Richard Dyer

Introduction

Eve Arnold's portrait of Joan Crawford gathers into one image three dimensions of stardom. Crawford is before two mirrors, a large one on the wall, the other a small one in her hand. In the former we see the Crawford image at its most finished; she is reduced to a set of defining features: the strong jaw, the gash of a mouth, the heavy arched eyebrows, the large eyes. From just such a few features, an impressionist, caricaturist or female impersonator can summon up 'Joan Crawford' for us. Meanwhile, in the small mirror we can see the texture of the powder over foundation, the gloss of the lipstick, the pencilling of the eyebrows – we can see something of the means by which the smaller image has been manufactured.

Neatly, we have two Crawford reflections. The placing of the smaller one, central and in sharpest focus, might suggest that this is the one to be taken as the 'real' Crawford. Eve Arnold is known as a photographer committed to showing women 'as they really are', not in men's fantasies of them. This photo appears in her collection *The Unretouched Woman* (1976), the title proclaiming Arnold's aim; it is accompanied by the information that Crawford wanted Arnold to do the series of photos of her to show what hard work being a star was. The style and context of the photo encourage us to treat the smaller image as the real one, as do our habits of thought. The processes of manufacturing an appearance are often thought to be more real than the appearance itself – appearance is mere illusion, is surface.

There is a third Crawford in the photograph, a back view slightly less sharply in focus than the mirror images. Both the large and the small facial images are framed, made into pictures. The fact that the different mirrors throw back different pictures suggests the complex relationship between a picture and that of which it is a picture, something reinforced by the fact that both mirrors reflect presentation: making-up and decorating the face. Both mirrors return a version of the front of the vague, shadowy figure before them. Is this third Crawford the real one, the real person who was the occasion of the images? This back view of Crawford establishes her as very much there, yet she is beyond our grasp except through the partial mirror images of her. Is perhaps the smaller mirror image the true reflection of what the actual person of Crawford was really like, or can we know only that there was a real person inside the images but never really know her? Which is Joan Crawford, really?

We can carry on looking at the Arnold photo like this, and our mind can constantly shift between the three aspects of Crawford; but it is the three of them taken together that make up the phenomenon Joan Crawford, and it is the insistent question of 'really' that draws us in, keeping us on the go from one aspect to another.

Logically, no one aspect is more real than another. How we appear is no less real than how we have manufactured that appearance, or than the 'we' that is doing the manufacturing. Appearances are a kind of reality, just as manufacture and individual persons are. However, manufacture and the person (a certain notion of the person, as I'll discuss) are generally thought to be more real than appearance in this culture. Stars are obviously a case of appearance – all we know of them is what we see and hear before us. Yet the whole media construction of stars encourages us to think in terms of 'really' – what is Crawford really like? which biography, which word-of-mouth story, which moment in which film discloses her as she really was? The star phenomenon gathers these aspects of contemporary human existence together, laced up with the question of 'really'.

The rest of this chapter looks at this complex phenomenon from two angles – first, the constitutive elements of stars, what they consist of, their production; secondly, the notions of personhood and social reality that they relate to. These are not separate aspects of stardom, but different ways of looking at the same overall phenomenon. How anything in society is made, how making is organized and understood, is inseparable from how we think people are, how they function, what their relation to making is. The complex way in which we produce and reproduce the world in technologically developed societies involves the ways in which we separate ourselves into public and private persons, producing and consuming persons and so on, and the ways in which we as people negotiate and cope with those divisions. Stars are about all of that, and are one of the most significant ways we have for making sense of it all. That is why they matter to us, and why they are worth thinking about.

Making Stars

The star phenomenon consists of everything that is publicly available about stars. A film star's image is not just his or her films, but the promotion of those films and of the star through pin-ups, public appearances, studio hand-outs and so on, as well as interviews, biographies and coverage in the press of the star's doings and 'private' life. Further, a star's image is also what people say or write about him or her, as critics or commentators, the way the image is used in other contexts such as advertisements, novels, pop songs, and finally the way the star can become part of the coinage of everyday speech. Jean-Paul Belmondo imitating Humphrey Bogart in À bout de souffle is part of Bogart's image, just as anyone saying, in a mid-European accent, 'I want to be alone' reproduces, extends and inflects Greta Garbo's image.

Star images are always extensive, multimedia, intertextual. Not all these manifestations are necessarily equal. A film star's films are likely to have a privileged place in her or his image, and I have certainly paid detailed attention to the films in the analyses that follow. However, even this is complicated. In the case of Robeson, his theatre, recording and concert work were undoubtedly more highly acclaimed than his film work – he was probably better known as a singer, yet more people would have seen him in films than in the theatre or concert hall. Later, in the period not covered here, he became equally important as a political activist. Garland became more important in her later years as a music hall, cabaret and recording star, although, as I argue in the Garland chapter, that later reputation then sent people back to her old films with a different kind of interest. Again, Monroe may now have become before everything else an emblematic figure, her symbolic meaning far outrunning what actually happens in her films.

As these examples suggest, not only do different elements predominate in different star images, but they do so at different periods in the star's career. Star images have histories, and histories that outlive the star's own lifetime. In the chapters that follow I have tried to reconstruct something of the meanings of Robeson and Monroe in the period in which they were themselves still making films – I've tried to situate them in relation to the immediate contexts of those periods. Robeson and Monroe have continued to be ethnic and sexual emblems as they were in their lifetime, but I have wanted to situate them in relation to the specific ways of understanding and feeling ethnic and sexual questions which were available in the 1930s and 1950s respectively, rather than in relation to what they mean in those terms now, although this would be an equally proper enquiry. (I did not, by the way, put ethnic and sexual in relation to Robeson and Monroe 'respectively', because Robeson is importantly situated in relation to ideas of sexuality just as Monroe is a profoundly ethnic image.) With Garland I have done the opposite – I have tried to look at her through a particular world-view, that of the white urban male gay subculture that developed in relation to her after her major period of film stardom and as she was becoming better known as a cabaret, recording and television star (and subject of scandal). The studies of Monroe, Robeson and Garland that follow are partial and limited, not only in the usual sense that all analyses are, but in being deliberately confined to particular aspects of their images, at particular periods and with a particular interest in seeing how this is produced and registered in the films.

Images have to be made. Stars are produced by the media industries, film stars by Hollywood (or its equivalent in other countries) in the first instance, but then also by other agencies with which Hollywood is connected in varying ways and with varying degrees of influence. Hollywood controlled not only the stars' films but their promotion, the pin-ups and glamour portraits, press releases and to a large extent the fan clubs. In turn, Hollywood's connections with other media industries meant that what got into the press, who got to interview a star, what clips were released to television was to a large extent decided by Hollywood. But this is to present the process of star making as uniform and oneway. Hollywood, even within its own boundaries, was much more complex and contradictory than this. If there have always been certain key individuals in controlling positions (usually studio bosses and major producers, but also some directors, stars and other figures) and if they all share a general professional ideology, clustering especially around notions of entertainment, still Hollywood is also characterized by internecine warfare between departments, by those departments getting on with their own thing in their own ways and by a recognition that it is important to leave spaces for individuals and groups to develop their own ideas (if only because innovation is part of the way that capitalist industries renew themselves). If broadly everyone in Hollywood had a sense of what the Monroe, Robeson and Garland images were, still different departments and different people would understand and inflect the image differently. This already complex image-making system looks even more complex when one brings in the other media agencies involved, since there are elements of rivalry and competition between them and Hollywood, as well as co-operation and mutual influence. If the drift of the image emanates from Hollywood, and with some consistency within Hollywood, still the whole image-making process within and without Hollywood allows for variation, inflection and contradiction.

What the audience makes of all this is something else again – and, as I've already suggested, the audience is also part of the making of the image. Audiences cannot make media images mean anything they want to, but they can select from the complexity of the image the meanings and feelings, the variations, inflections and contradictions, that work for them. Moreover, the agencies of fan magazines and clubs, as well as box office receipts and audience research, mean that the audience's ideas about a star can act back on the media producers of the star's image. This is not an equal to-and-fro – the audience is more disparate and fragmented, and does not itself produce centralized, massively available media images; but the audience is not wholly controlled by Hollywood and the media, either. In the case, for example, of feminist readings of Monroe (or of John Wayne) or gay male readings of Garland (or Montgomery Clift), what those particular audiences are making of those stars is tantamount to sabotage of what the media industries thought they were doing.

Stars are made for profit. In terms of the market, stars are part of the way films are sold. The star's presence in a film is a promise of a certain kind of thing that you would see if you went to see the film. Equally, stars sell newspapers and magazines, and are used to sell toiletries, fashions, cars and almost anything else.

This market function of stars is only one aspect of their economic importance. They are also a property on the strength of whose name money can be raised for a film; they are an asset to the person (the star him/herself), studio and agent who controls them; they are a major part of the cost of a film. Above all, they are part of the labour that produces film as a commodity that can be sold for profit in the market place.

Stars are involved in making themselves into commodities; they are both labour and the thing that labour produces. They do not produce themselves alone. We can distinguish two logically separate stages. First, the person is a body, a psychology, a set of skills that have to be mined and worked up into a star image. This work, of fashioning the star out of the raw material of the person, varies in the degree to which it respects what artists sometimes refer to as the inherent qualities of the material; make-up, coiffure, clothing, dieting and body-building can all make more or less of the body features they start with, and personality is no less malleable, skills no less learnable. The people who do this labour include the star him/herself as well as make-up artists, hairdressers, dress designers, dieticians, body-building coaches, acting, dancing and other teachers, publicists, pin-up photographers, gossip columnists, and so on. Part of this manufacture of the star image takes place in the films the star makes, with all the personnel involved in that, but one can think of the films as a second stage. The star image is then a given, like machinery, an example of what Karl Marx calls 'congealed labour', something that is used with further labour (scripting, acting, directing, managing, filming, editing) to produce another commodity, a film.

How much of a determining role the person has in the manufacture of her or his image and films varies enormously from case to case and this is part of the interest. Stars are examples of the way people live their relation to production in capitalist society. The three stars examined in subsequent chapters all in some measure revolted against the lack of control they felt they had – Robeson by giving up feature filmmaking altogether, Monroe by trying to fight for better parts and treatment, Garland by speaking of her experiences at MGM and by the way in which her later problems were credited to the Hollywood system. These battles are each central parts of the star's image and they enact some of the ways the individual is felt to be placed in relation to business and industry in con-temporary society. At one level, they articulate a dominant experience of work itself under capitalism – not only the sense of being a cog in an industrial machine, but also the fact that one's labour and what it produces seem so divorced from each other – one labours to produce goods (and profits) in which one either does not share at all or only in the most meagre, back-handed fashion. Robeson's, Monroe's, Garland's sense that they had been used, turned into something they didn't control is particularly acute because the commodity they produced is fashioned in and out of their own bodies and psychologies.

Other stars deliver different stories, of course. June Allyson, in interviews and in her biography 'with Frances Spatz-Leighton', sings the praises of the job security provided by the studio system, of big capital, just as in her movies she perfected the role of the happy stay-at-home housewife who saw it as her role to support her man in his productive life, whether he produced music (as in *The Glenn Miller Story*) or profits (as in *Executive Suite*). There is a consistency between her 'contented housewife' screen image, her satisfaction with her working conditions, the easygoing niceness in the tone of the biography and interviews. She thus represents the possibility of integrated, mutually supporting spheres of life, not the tension between screen image, manufacture and real person that Monroe, Garland and Robeson suggest.

Many male stars – Clark Gable, Humphrey Bogart, Paul Newman, Steve McQueen – suggest something else again. In each, sporting activity is a major – perhaps the major – element in their image; they are defined above all as people for whom having uncomplicated fun is paramount, and this is implicitly carried over into their reported attitude to their work. But equally work isn't important, it's just something you do so as to have the wherewithal to play polo, sail yachts, race cars. This is, then, an instrumental attitude towards manufacture, not the antagonistic one of Garland, Robeson and Monroe, nor the integrated one of Allyson, nor yet again the committed one of, for example, Fred Astaire, Joan Crawford or Barbra Streisand. These last three suggest different relations of commitment to work – Astaire to technical mastery, in the endless stories of his perfectionist attitude towards rehearsal and the evidence of it on the screen; Crawford in her total slogging away at all aspects of her image and her embodiment of the ethic of hard work in so many of her films; Streisand in her control over the films and records she makes, a reported shopfloor control that also shows in the extremely controlled and detailed nature of her performance style. Whatever the particular inflection, stars play out some of the ways that work is lived in capitalist society. My selection of Monroe, Robeson and Garland is different only in that there is in them an element of protest about labour under capitalism which you do not find in Allyson, Gable, Astaire, Streisand and the rest.

The protests of Robeson, Monroe and Garland are individual protests. Robeson and Monroe could be taken as protests emblematic of the situation of black people and women respectively, and have been properly used as such. But they remain individualized, partly because the star system is about the promotion of the individual. Protest about the lack of control over the outcome of one's labour can remain within the logic of individualism. The protests of Robeson, Monroe and Garland are of the individual versus the anomic corporation; they are protests against capitalism that do not recognize themselves as such, protests with deep resonances within the ideologies of entrepreneurial capitalism. They speak in the name of the individual and of the notion of success, not in the name of the individual as part of a collective organization of labour and production. (Robeson alone began to move in that direction in his ensemble theatre work, and in his deliberately emblematic role in political activity in later years.)

A star image consists both of what we normally refer to as his or her 'image', made up of screen roles and obviously stage-managed public appearances, and also of images of the manufacture of that 'image' and of the real person who is the site or occasion of it. Each element is complex and contradictory, and the star is all of it taken together. Much of what makes them interesting is how they articulate aspects of living in contemporary society, one of which, the nature of work in capitalist society, I've already touched on. In the chapters that follow I want to look at the ways in which three particular stars relate to three aspects of social life – sexuality, ethnicity and sexual identity. Even being that specific, it is still complicated, I'm still wanting to keep some sense of the multiplicity of readings even of those stars in those terms. In the rest of this chapter, however, I want to risk even wider generalizations. Work, sexuality, ethnicity and sexual identity themselves depend on more general ideas in society about what a person is, and stars are major definers of these ideas.

Living Stars

Stars articulate what it is to be a human being in contemporary society; that is, they express the particular notion we hold of the person, of the 'individual'. They do so complexly, variously – they are not straightforward affirmations of individualism. On the contrary, they articulate both the promise and the difficulty that the notion of individuality presents for all of us who live by it.

'The individual' is a way of thinking and feeling about the discrete human person, including oneself, as a separate and coherent entity. The individual is thought of as separate in the sense that she or he has an existence apart from anything else – the individual is not just the sum of his or her social roles or actions. He or she may only be perceived through these things, may even be thought to be formed by them, yet there is, in this concept of the person, an irreducible core of being, the entity that is perceived within the roles and actions, the entity upon which social forces act. This irreducible core is coherent in that it is supposed to consist of certain peculiar, unique qualities that remain constant and give sense to the person's actions and reactions. However much the person's circumstances and behaviour may change, 'inside' they are still the same individual; even if 'inside' she or he has changed, it is through an evolution that has not altered the fundamental reality of that irreducible core that makes her or him a unique individual.

At its most optimistic, the social world is seen in this conception to emanate from the individual, and each person is seen to 'make' his or her own life. However, this is not necessary to the concept. What is central is the idea of the separable, coherent quality, located 'inside' in consciousness and variously termed 'the self', 'the soul', 'the subject' and so on. This is counterposed to 'society', something seen as logically distinct from the individuals who compose it, and very often as inimical to them. If in ideas of 'triumphant individualism' individuals are seen to determine society, in ideas of 'alienation' individuals are seen as cut adrift from and dominated, battered by the anonymity of society. Both views retain the notion of the individual as separate, irreducible, unique.

It is probably true to say that there has never been a period in which this concept of the individual was held unproblematically throughout society. The notion of the individual has always been accompanied by the gravest doubts as to its tenability. It is common, for instance, to characterize Enlightenment philosophy as one of the most shiningly optimistic assertions of individuality; yet two of its most sparkling works, Hume's *An Essay on Human Understanding* and Diderot's *Rameau's Nephew*, fundamentally undercut any straightforward belief in the existence of the coherent, stable, inner individual; Hume by arguing that all we can know as our self is a series of sensations and experiences with no necessary unity or connection, Diderot by focusing on the vital, theatrical, disjointed character of Rameau's nephew, so much more 'real' than Diderot, the narrator's stodgily maintained coherent self.

If the major trend of thought since the Renaissance, from philosophical rumination to common sense, has affirmed the concept of the individual, there has been an almost equally strong counter-tradition of ideas that have severely dented our confidence in ourselves: Marxism, with its insistence that social being determines consciousness and not vice versa, and, in its economist variant, with its vision of economic forces propelling human events forward; psychoanalysis, with its radical splitting of consciousness into fragmentary, contradictory parts; behaviourism, with its view of human beings controlled by instinctual appetites beyond consciousness; linguistics and models of communication in which it is not we who speak language, but language which speaks us. Major social and political developments have been understood in terms of the threat they pose to the individual: industrialization can be seen to have set the pace for a whole society in which people are reduced to being cogs in a machine; totalitarianism would seem to be the triumph, easily achieved, of society over the individual; the development of mass communications, and especially the concomitant notion of mass society, sees the individual swallowed up in the sameness produced by centralized, manipulative media which reduce everything to the lowest common denominator. A major trajectory of twentieth-century high literature has examined the disintegration of the person as stable ego, from the fluid, shifting self of Woolf and Proust to the minimal self of Beckett and Sarraute. 'Common sense' is no less full of tags acknowledging this bruised sense of self: the sense of forces shaping our lives beyond our control, of our doing things for reasons that we don't understand, of our not recognizing ourself in actions we took yesterday (to say nothing of years ago), of not seeing ourselves in photographs of ourselves, of feeling strange when we recognize the routinized nature of our lives – none of this is uncommon.

Yet the idea of the individual continues to be a major moving force in our culture. Capitalism justifies itself on the basis of the freedom (separateness) of anyone to make money, sell their labour how they will, to be able to express opinions and get them heard (regardless of wealth or social position). The openness of society is assumed by the way that we are addressed as individuals – as consumers (each freely choosing to buy, or watch, what we want), as legal subjects (free and responsible before the law), as political subjects (able to make up our mind who is to run society). Thus even while the notion of the individual is assailed on all sides, it is a necessary fiction for the reproduction of the kind of society we live in.

Stars articulate these ideas of personhood, in large measure shoring up the notion of the individual but also at times registering the doubts and anxieties attendant on it. In part, the fact that the star is not just a screen image but a flesh and blood person is liable to work to express the notion of the individual. A series of shots of a star whose image has changed – say, Elizabeth Taylor – at various points in her career could work to fragment her, to present her as nothing but a series of disconnected looks; but in practice it works to confirm that beneath all these different looks there is an irreducible core that gives all those looks a unity, namely Elizabeth Taylor. Despite the elaboration of roles, social types, attitudes and values suggested by any one of these looks, one flesh and blood person is embodying them all. We know that Elizabeth Taylor exists apart from all these looks, and this knowledge alone is sufficient to suggest that there is a coherence behind them all.

It can be enough just to know that there was one such person, but generally our sense of that one person is more vivid and important than all the roles and looks s/he assumes. People often say that they do not rate such and such a star because he or she is always the same. In this view, the trouble with, say, Gary Cooper or Doris Day, is that they are always Gary Cooper and Doris Day. But if you like Cooper or Day, then precisely what you value about them is that they are always 'themselves' – no matter how different their roles, they bear witness to the continuousness of their own selves.

This coherent continuousness within becomes what the star 'really is'. Much of the construction of the star encourages us to think this. Key moments in films are close-ups, separated out from the action and interaction of a scene, and not seen by other characters but only by us, thus disclosing for us the star's face, the intimate, transparent window to the soul. Star biographies are devoted to the notion of showing us the star as he or she really is. Blurbs, introductions, every page assures us that we are being taken 'behind the scenes', 'beneath the surface', 'beyond the image', there where the truth resides. Or again, there is a rhetoric of sincerity or authenticity, two qualities greatly prized in stars because they guarantee, respectively, that the star really means what he or she says, and that the star really is what she or he appears to be. Whether caught in the unmediated moment of the close-up, uncovered by the biographer's display of ruthless uncovering, or present in the star's indubitable sincerity and authenticity, we have a privileged reality to hang on to, the reality of the star's private self.

The private self is further represented through a set of oppositions that stem from the division of the world into private and public spaces, a way of organizing space that in turn relates to the idea of the separability of the individual and society:

private	public
individual	society
sincere	insincere
country	city
small town	large town
folk	urban
community	mass
physical	mental
body	brain
naturalness	artifice
sexual intercourse	social intercourse
racial	ethnic

When stars function in terms of their assertion of the irreducible core of inner individual reality, it is generally through their associations with the values of the left-hand column. Stars like Clark Gable, Gary Cooper, John Wayne, Paul Newman, Robert Redford, Steve McQueen, James Caan establish their male action-hero image either through appearing in Westerns, a genre importantly concerned with nature and the small town as centres of authentic human behaviour, and/or through vivid action sequences, in war films, jungle adventures, chase films, that pit the man directly, physically against material forces. It is interesting that with more recent examples of this type – Clint Eastwood, Harrison Ford – there has been a tendency either to give their films a send-up or tongue-in-cheek flavour (Eastwood's chimp films, Ford as Indiana Jones) or else a hard, desolate, alienated quality (Eastwood in *Joe Kidd*, Ford in *Blade Runner*), as if the values of masculine physicality are harder to maintain straight-facedly and unproblematically in an age of microchips and a large scale growth (in the USA) of women in traditionally male occupations.

The private self is not always represented as good, safe or positive. There is an alternative tradition of representing the inner reality of men, especially, which stretches back at least as far as the romantic movement. Here the dark, turbulent forces of nature are used as metaphors for the man's inner self: Valentino in *The Son of the Sheik*, the young Laurence Olivier as Heathcliff in *Wuthering Heights* and as Maxim de Winter in *Rebecca*. In the 1940s and 1950s the popularization of psychoanalysis added new terms to the private–public opposition. Thus:

private	public
subconscious	conscious
Id	Ego

and in the still more recent Lacan inflection:

Imaginary   Symbolic

These have been particularly important in the subsequent development of male
stars, where the romantic styles of brooding, introspective, mean-but-vulnerable
masculinity have been given Oedipal, psychosexual, paranoid or other crypto-
psychoanalytical inflections with stars like Montgomery Clift, James Dean,
Marlon Brando, Anthony Perkins, Jack Nicholson, Richard Gere. Recent black
male stars such as Jim Brown, Richard Roundtree and Billy Dee Williams are
interesting in that their fiercely attractive intensity seems closer to the 'dangerous' romantic tradition proper; at the same time they also draw on the old
stereotype of the black man as brute, only now portraying this as attractive rather
than terrifying; and they are almost entirely untouched by the psychoanalytical
project of rationalizing and systematizing and naming the life of the emotions and
sensations. All these male stars work variations on the male inner self as negative,
dangerous, neurotic, violent, but always upholding that as the reality of the man,
what he is really like.

The stars analysed in the rest of this book also have strong links with the left-
hand, 'private' column. Monroe was understood above all through her sexuality –
it was her embodiment of current ideas of sexuality that made her seem real,
alive, vital. Robeson was understood primarily through his racial identity,
through attempts to see and, especially, hear him as the very essence of the
Negro folk. Both were represented insistently through their bodies – Monroe's
body was sexuality, Robeson's was the nobility of the black race. Garland too
belongs with the left-hand column, initially through her roles as country or small-
town girl, later through the way her body registered both her problems and her
defiance of them. All the descriptions of her from her later period begin by
describing the state of her body and speculating from that on what drugs, drink,
work and temperament have done to it, and yet how it continues to be animated
and vital. Not only are Monroe, Robeson, Garland stars who are thought to be
genuine, who reveal their inner selves, but the final touchstone of that genuine-
ness is the human body itself. Stars not only bespeak our society's investment in
the private as the real, but also often tell us how the private is understood to be
the recovery of the natural 'given' of human life, our bodies. Yet as the chapters
that follow argue, what we actually come up against at this point is far from
straightforwardly natural; it is particular, and even rather peculiar, ways of
making sense of the body. The very notions of sexuality and race, so apparently
rooted in the body, are historically and culturally specific ideas about the body,
and it is these that Monroe and Robeson, especially, enact, thereby further
endowing them with authenticity.

What is at stake in most of the examples discussed so far is the degree to
which, and manner in which, what the star really is can be located in some inner,
private, essential core. This is how the star phenomenon reproduces the

overriding ideology of the person in contemporary society. But the star phenomenon cannot help being also about the person in public. Stars, after all, are always
inescapably people in public. If the magic, with many stars, is that they seem to
be their private selves in public, still they can also be about the business of being
in public, the way in which the public self is endlessly produced and remade in
presentation. Those stars that seem to emphasize this are often considered
'mannered', and the term is right, for they bring to the fore manners, the stuff
of public life. When such stars are affirmative of manners and public life they are
often, significantly enough, European or with strong European connections –
stars to whom terms like suave, gracious, debonair, sophisticated, charming
accrue, such as Fred Astaire, Margaret Sullavan, Cary Grant, David Niven,
Deborah Kerr, Grace Kelly, Audrey Hepburn, Rex Harrison, Roger Moore.
These are people who have mastered the public world, in the sense not so
much of being authentically themselves in it nor even of being sincere, as of
performing in the world precisely, with poise and correctness. They get the
manners right. An additional example might be Sidney Poitier, only with him the
consummate ease of his public manners comes up against the backlog of images
of black men as raging authenticities, with the result that in his films of the 1950s
and 1960s he is not really able to be active in public, he is a good performer who
doesn't perform anything. It is only with *In the Heat of the Night* that something
else emerges, a sense of the tension attendant on being good in public, a quality
that brings Poitier here into line with a number of other stars who suggest
something of the difficulty and anxiety attendant upon public performance.

Many of the women stars of screwball comedy – Katharine Hepburn, Carole
Lombard, Rosalind Russell, and more recently Barbra Streisand – have the
uncomfortable, sharp quality of people who do survive and succeed in the public
world, do keep up appearances, but edgily, always seen to be in the difficult
process of doing so. Bette Davis's career has played variations on this representation of public performance. Many of her films of the 1930s and 1940s exploit her
mannered style to suggest how much her success or survival depends upon an
ability to manipulate manners, her own and those of people around her, to get her
own way (*Jezebel, The Little Foxes*), to cover her tracks out of courage (*Dark
Victory*) or guilt (*The Letter*), to maintain a public presence at all costs for a
greater good than her own (*The Private Life of Elizabeth and Essex*), to achieve
femininity (*Now Voyager*) and so on. If being in public for Davis in these films is
hypertense, registered in her rapid pupil movements, clenching and unclenching
fists, still in the 1930s and 1940s she is enacting the excitement, the buzz of
public life, of being a person in public. Later films become something like the
tragedy of it. *All About Eve* details the cost of keeping up appearances, maintaining an image. *Whatever Happened to Baby Jane?* evokes the impossibility of
achieving again the public role that made her character feel good. Yet the end
of *Baby Jane* affirms the public self as a greater reality than the private self
cooped up in the dark Gothic mansion – we learn that it is Crawford not Davis
who is the baddie; away from the house, on the beach, surrounded by people, the

ageing Jane can become the public self she really is, Baby Jane. Davis's career thus runs the gamut of the possibilities of the private individual up against public society; from, in the earlier films, triumphant individualism, the person who makes their social world, albeit agitatedly, albeit at times malignantly, to, in the later films, something like alienation, the person who is all but defeated by the demands of public life, who only hangs on by the skin of their teeth – until the up-tempo happy ending.

The private/public, individual/society dichotomy can be embodied by stars in various ways; the emphasis can fall at either end of the spectrum, although it more usually falls at the private, authentic, sincere end. Mostly too there is a sense of 'really' in play – people/stars are really themselves in private or perhaps in public but at any rate somewhere. However, it is one of the ironies of the whole star phenomenon that all these assertions of the reality of the inner self or of public life take place in one of the aspects of modern life that is most associated with the invasion and destruction of the inner self and corruptibility of public life, namely the mass media. Stars might even seem to be the ultimate example of media hype, foisted on us by the media's constant need to manipulate our attention. We all know how the studios build up star images, how stars happen to turn up on chat shows just when their latest picture is released, how many of the stories printed about stars are but titillating fictions; we all know we are being sold stars. And yet those privileged moments, those biographies, those qualities of sincerity and authenticity, those images of the private and the natural can work for us. We may go either way. As an example, consider the reactions at the time to John Travolta in *Saturday Night Fever*. I haven't done an audience survey, but people seemed to be fairly evenly divided. For those not taken with him, the incredible build-up to the film, the way you knew what his image was before you saw the film, the coy but blatant emphasis on his sex appeal in the film, the gaudy artifice of the disco scene, all merely confirmed him as one great phoney put-on on the mass public. But for those for whom he and the film did work, there were the close-ups revealing the troubled pain behind the macho image, the intriguing off-screen stories about his relationship with an older woman, the spontaneity (= sincerity) of his smile, the setting of the film in a naturalistically portrayed ethnic subculture. A star's image can work either way, and in part we make it work according to how much it speaks to us in terms we can understand about things that are important to us.

None the less, the fact that we know that hype and the hard sell do characterize the media, that they are supreme instances of manipulation, insincerity, inauthenticity, mass public life, means that the whole star phenomenon is profoundly unstable. Stars cannot be *made* to work as affirmations of private or public life. In some cases, the sheer multiplicity of the images, the amount of hype, the different stories told become overwhelmingly contradictory. Is it possible still to have any sense of Valentino or Monroe, their persons, apart from all the things they have been made to mean? Perhaps, but at best isn't it a sense of the extraordinary fragility of their inner selves, endlessly fragmented into what everyone else, including us, wanted them to be? Or it may be that what interests us is the public face, accepting the artifice and fantasy for what it is – do we ask for sincerity and authenticity from Jayne Mansfield or Diana Ross, Groucho, Harpo or Chico Marx?

Or we may read stars in a camp way, enjoying them not for any supposed inner essence revealed but for the way they jump through the hoops of social convention. The undulating contours of Mae West, the lumbering gait and drawling voice of John Wayne, the thin, spiky smile of Joan Fontaine – each can be taken as an emblem of social mores: the ploys of female seduction, the certainty of male American power, the brittle niceness of upper-class manners. Seeing them that way is seeing them as appearance, as image, in no way asking for them to be what they are, really.

On rare occasions a star image may promote a sense of the social constructed-ness of the apparently natural. The image of Lena Horne in her MGM films does this in relation to ideas of black and female sexuality. Her whole act in these films – and often it is no more than a turn inserted into the narrative flow of the film – promotes the idea of natural, vital sexuality, with her flashing eyes, sinuous arm movements and suggestive vocal delivery. That people saw this as the ultimate in unfettered feminine libido is widely attested, yet as an act it has an extraordinary quality, a kind of metallic sheen and intricate precision that suggests the opposite of animal vitality. In an interview with Michiko Kakutani in the *New York Times* (Sunday, 3 May 1981, section D, pp. 1, 24), Lena Horne discussed her image in this period in relation to her strategy of survival in the period as a black woman:

> Afraid of being hurt, afraid of letting her anger show, she says she cultivated an image that distanced her from her employers, her colleagues, and from her audi-ences as well. If audience members were going to regard her as no more than an exotic performer – 'Baby, you sure can sing, but don't move next door' – well, then, that's all they'd get. By focusing intently on the notes and lyrics of a song, she was able to shut out the people who were staring at her, and over the years, she refined a pose of sophisticated aloofness, a pose that said, 'You're getting the singer, but not the woman.' 'I used to think, "I'm black and I'm going to isolate myself because you don't understand me," ' she says. 'All the things people said – sure, they hurt, and it made me retreat even further. The only thing between me and them was jive protection.'

It is rare for a performer to understand and state so clearly both how they worked and the effect of it, but this catches exactly Horne's image in the 1940s and 1950s, its peerless surface, its presentation of itself *as* surface, its refusal to corroborate, by any hint of the person giving her self, the image of black sexuality that was being wished on her. This could not, did not stop audiences reading her as transparently authentic sexuality; but it was some sort of strategy of survival that could also be seen for what it was, a denaturalizing of the ideas of black sexuality.

I have been trying to describe in this chapter some of the ways in which being interested in stars is being interested in how we are human now. We're fascinated by stars because they enact ways of making sense of the experience of being a person in a particular kind of social production (capitalism), with its particular organization of life into public and private spheres. We love them because they represent how we think that experience is or how it would be lovely to feel that it is. Stars represent typical ways of behaving, feeling and thinking in contemporary society, ways that have been socially, culturally, historically constructed. Much of the ideological investment of the star phenomenon is in the stars seen as individuals, their qualities seen as natural. I do not wish to deny that there are individuals, nor that they are grounded in the given facts of the human body. But I do wish to say that what makes them interesting is the way in which they articulate the business of being an individual, something that is, paradoxically, typical, common, since we all in Western society have to cope with that particular idea of what we are. Stars are also embodiments of the social categories in which people are placed and through which they have to make sense of their lives, and indeed through which we make our lives – categories of class, gender, ethnicity, religion, sexual orientation, and so on. And all of these typical, common ideas, that have the feeling of being the air that you breathe, just the way things are, have their own histories, their own peculiarities of social construction.

Because they go against the grain of the individualizing, naturalizing emphasis of the phenomenon itself, these insistences on the typical and social may seem to be entirely imported from theoretical reflection. Yet ideas never come entirely from outside the things they are ideas about, and this seems particularly so of the star phenomenon. It constantly jogs these questions of the individual and society, the natural and artificial, precisely because it is promoting ideas of the individual and the natural in media that are mass, technologically elaborated, aesthetically sophisticated. That central paradox means that the whole phenomenon is unstable, never at a point of rest or equilibrium, constantly lurching from one formulation of what being human is to another. This book is an attempt to tease out some of those formulations in particular cases, to see how they work, to get at something of the contradictions of what stars are, really.

34

The She-Man: Postmodern Bi-Sexed Performance in Film and Video

Chris Straayer

The historic absence of the penis from cinema's view has allowed the male body an independence from anatomical verification according to sex and has situated the male costume simply to reflect a heroic (phallic) narrative purpose.[1] It is his charging about that has identified a male film character as male, yet it is his penis that has invested man with the cultural right to charge about – the signifier in absentia. Richard Dyer and Peter Lehman have written about the difficulty of maintaining the penis–phallus alliance in the event that the penis is seen on-screen.[2] In actuality, the penis (man's hidden "nature") cannot compare to the phallus (man's cultural power). Male sexuality, as a representational system, depends on displacing the penis with the phallus.

In mainstream cinema, the female costume delivers sexual anatomy whereas the male costume abandons it. Sex is "present" in both the masquerade of femininity and the female body, doubly absent for the male. Male sex is (mis)represented by the phallus. Instead of a body with a penis, the male character's entire body, through its phallic position and action, becomes a giant (substitute) penis – a confusion of standing erect with erection. Although sliding signification is integral to the representation of both female and male sexuality, the first effectively relies more on iconographic and indexical relations and the second on symbolic relations. This "visible difference" in the representation systems of female sex and male sex allows the *potential* for an intense double signification of sexuality in the male cross-dresser – composed of both macho male sexuality via phallic action and the unseen penis, and female sexuality signaled by the masquerade's visible display.

In contrast to the traditional conditions and compromises of transvestism in classical film and television, a phenomenon in contemporary popular culture, which I term the "She-man," exploits cross-dressing's potential for intense double sexual signification.[3] I refer to the appropriation of female coding by a male performer as a straightforward empowering device, rather than as an emasculating comic ploy. The transgressive figure of the She-man is glaringly bi-sexed rather than obscurely androgynous or merely bisexual. Rather than under-going a downward gender mobility, he has enlarged himself with feminine gender and female sexuality.

In her book *Mother Camp*, Esther Newton relates the drag queen's reliance on visible contradictions, as opposed to the transvestite's attempt to pass as the other sex.[4] Laying bare his feminine masquerade by baring a hairy chest, the drag queen makes obvious the superficiality and arbitrariness of gender costuming. In John Waters's film *Pink Flamingos*, a "transbreastite" squeezes this contradiction onto the body, disrupting sexual as well as gender signification. The sight of "his" hormonally produced breasts is followed by "his" exposed penis, an icongruity that overflows its own binary opposition. Likewise, the bisexual, transsexual Dr. Frank N. Furter (Tim Curry) of *The Rocky Horror Picture Show* makes lipstick seem macho as he undulates a black garter belt in aggressive, seductive exhibitionism. A nude male dancer in *Pink Flamingos* executes anal acrobatics with phallic nerve and Medusan humor, and Divine puts a steak between her legs to simultaneously parody the rhetoric of women as meat and embody the taboo of menstruation, thus pushing the transgression of sex bound-aries beyond anatomy to physiology.[5] *La ley de deseo (Law of Desire)* gives us the "slutty" male-to-female transsexual Tina (played by a woman – Carmen Maura) under a jet of water and clinging dress, who harks back to a classical harlot, then later outslugs a policeman like a "real" man. *Shadey*'s Oliver (Anthony Sher), a "woman trapped in a man's body," is stabbed in the testicles with a kitchen knife and responds with a look of *jouissance*. In the era of music television, both Boy George and Michael Jackson make louder *scenes* as Boy-Girls.

As these examples suggest, rather than diminishing his phallic power, or amplifying it via a contrast with weakness, female coding lends additional strength to the She-man. The male body's "staying power" remains unchallenged by feminine dress, makeup, and gestures which, in popular media, have become one and the same with female sexuality. More indexical than symbolic, the feminine costume utilizes conventions of spatial and temporal contiguity to deliver its referent. The determined geometry of Tim Curry's bra and garters bestows a female anatomy on him, even as the bulge in the crotch of his body corset indexes his male sex.[6] The power of the She-man, then, is emphatically sexual.

What is the origin of this "feminine" power? Is not the penis the dominant signifier which defines woman by her lack thereof? Is not the penis the dominant sexual signifier, reigning by virtue of a proclaimed anatomical visibility (which nevertheless remains covered)? Perhaps this powerful invisible visibility is born from an exaggerated persona – the Freudian phallic symbol. The empowered feminine, however, must have a different source.

Writing about the early twentieth-century mannish lesbian (for example, Radclyffe Hall and her character Stephen in the 1928 novel *The Well of*

Loneliness) in the context of other second-generation Victorian women who were presumed to be empty of sexuality, Esther Newton has argued that male clothing served as a means for women to proclaim their de facto sexuality.

> By "mannish lesbian"...I mean a figure who is defined as lesbian *because* her behavior or dress (and usually both) manifest elements designated as exclusively masculine. From about 1900 on, this cross-gender figure became the public symbol of the new social/sexual category "lesbian."...Hall and many other feminists like her embraced, sometimes with ambivalence, the image of the mannish lesbian and the discourse of the sexologists about inversion primarily because they desperately wanted to break out of the asexual model of romantic friendship....
>
> The bourgeois woman's sexuality proper was confined to its reproductive function: the uterus was its organ. But as for lust, "the major current in Victorian sexual ideology declared that women were passionless and asexual, the passive objects of male sexual desire."...Sex was seen as phallic, by which I mean that, conceptually, sex could only occur in the presence of an imperial and imperious penis....
>
> How could the New Woman lay claim to her full sexuality? For bourgeois women, there was no developed female sexual discourse; there were only male discourses – pornographic, literary, and medical – *about* female sexuality. To become avowedly sexual, the New Woman had to enter the male world, either as a heterosexual on male terms (a flapper) or as – or with – a lesbian in male body drag (a butch).[7]

The signification of sexuality was under male control: women declared their own active libidos by means of male clothing codes.

How is it that the contemporary She-man is then sexually empowered by female coding? How did female imagery come to signify sexuality and power? Along with the contributions of sexology, sexual liberation, and the feminist and gay activist movements, feminist artists (rather than She-men performers) must be credited for this empowerment of the "feminine." Whether "on our backs" or "off our backs," female sexual responses and desires are now seen as powerful by men. No longer only feared, female sexuality is envied.

Ironically, cinema's sexualization of woman's image is also partly responsible for making possible a representation of femaleness as sexual power. Following a long history of visual representations that established woman's body as the conventional marker of sexual difference, cinema made this body the carrier of sexuality in both visuals and narrative. Woman's image became the visible site of sexuality that was obtained by the male hero – that is, male sexuality was projected onto, represented by, and obtainable through her body. Although quite different from the Victorian woman who announced her sexuality via the male image, contemporary woman's "sexual" image in classical cinema also has the potential to be seen as an involuted image of sexual power.

But the most forceful paradigms for active female sexuality – which deconstruct involution and assert realignment – are found in contemporary women's performance art where artists expose their bodies for purposes of direct address.

Such bodily discourse constructs both a new "speaking subject" position and an aesthetics of female sexual presence. Utilizing classic examples from 1970s body art, two concepts relating to the She-man's origin can be narrativized. In practice, however, the two seem inseparable. The first is the story of the phallic femme which evolves from the feminine masquerade; the second story is that of the Medusan femme which evolves from the female body. These are the two powers that are appropriated by the She-man and merge in his/her signifying formation.

Early in the present feminist era, Lynda Benglis attacked the art world's discrimination against women with a self-portrait published in *Artforum* (December 1974) in which she manually "props" a dildo onto her nude body. In this act of appropriation she effectively identified the phallus as the basic qualification for artistic success and she explicitly collapsed the phallus with the penis – via body/object/photo collage art.

This inspires a first narrative: in the late 1960s and early 1970s, second-wave feminists (in dress-for-success suits) abandoned "femininity," disrupting feminine signification to steal the phallus, which, soon afterwards, they laterally passed on to self-conscious feminist femmes (in leather miniskirts). Through a process quite the reverse of fetishism, these feminists created the phallic-femme whose phallus was locked into a new feminine mode of signification. Today, sex role stereotypes are up for grabs. The attitude of Tina Turner's *What's Love Got to Do with It?* has reversed the cries of sexual oppression once embodied in Janis Joplin's screeching romantic masochism. And, in her *One Man Show*, Grace Jones, "feeling like a woman, looking like a man," gives a new bodily relevance to Marlene Dietrich's transvestite persona. Women spike their hair to match their heels, apply 1950s pink lipstick to "talk back" to the silence imposed on their mothers, hang crosses from their ears instead of from their necks. Indeed skirts are worn (and torn) self-reflexively; the accoutrements of femininity are used to parody patriarchal culture. In an attempt to reconquer phallic signification, the male performer now assumes postfeminist drag. When he is successful, he becomes the She-man, his phallus marked in the feminine.

In "Film and the Masquerade," Mary Ann Doane describes the feminine masquerade as a distancing device.

> The masquerade, in flaunting femininity, holds it at a distance. Womanliness is a mask which can be worn or removed. The masquerade's resistance to patriarchal positioning would therefore lie in its denial of the production of femininity as closeness, as presence-to-itself, as, precisely, imagistic. The transvestite adopts the sexuality of the other – the woman becomes a man in order to attain the necessary distance from the image. Masquerade, on the other hand, involves a realignment of femininity, the recovery, or more accurately, simulation, of the missing gap or distance. To masquerade is to manufacture a lack in the form of a certain distance between oneself and one's image. . . .
>
>   The very fact that we can speak of a woman "using" her sex or "using" her body for particular gains is highly significant – it is not that a man cannot use his body in

this way but that he doesn't have to. The masquerade doubles representation; it is constituted by a hyperbolization of the accoutrements of femininity.[8]

An excess of femininity, then, enables woman to stand back from her image and read it better. The pertinent question to this discussion is where does woman's "sexuality" reside in this improbable separation – in the cultural construction of femininity which she now consciously manipulates as a "persona," or in some nature within her but beyond her reading? This question is parallel to the situation of women in relation to language. Can women better speak by parodying patriarchal language (Benglis's phallic femme), or by narrating their own sexual bodies (the Medusan femme)?

A second process, which can be postulated to explain the feminine power that the She-man usurps, spans this distance between culture and nature. Vagina envy, as evidenced in some She-men performers, suggests that female sexuality challenges the position of the phallus as the dominant signifier. In her early feminist performance "Interior Scroll" (1975), Carolee Schneeman defended the suitability of personal experience as material for art by reading a "diary" scroll withdrawn from her vagina. Thus she asserted the female body to be a producer of meaning.[9]

Female sexuality is now neither simply the sign of lack, as Laura Mulvey has identified it, inciting castration anxiety and thus necessitating fetishization and narrative punishment, nor a generator of signs within Lévi-Strauss's parameters.[10] Female sexuality is erupting into contemporary culture like a volcano in the suburbs. Hélène Cixous's laughing Medusa, who haughtily displays her sex to men's horrified reactions, provides a paradigm for an empowering bodily address.[11] Furthermore, this "imagined" figure, the Medusan femme, exerts a specifically feminine body-signifying process – a multiplying, questioning, disgressing, fragmenting language that corresponds to the indefinable plurality of female sexuality spread over a woman's body, as described by Luce Irigaray.

> So woman does not have a sex organ? She has at least two of them, but they are not identifiable as ones. Indeed she has many more. Her sexuality, always at least double, goes even further: it is *plural*. Is this the way culture is seeking to characterize itself now? . . .
>
> *Woman has sex organs more or less everywhere*. She finds pleasure almost anywhere. Even if we refrain from invoking the hystericization of her entire body, the geography of her pleasure is far more diversified, more multiple in its differences, more complex, more subtle, than is commonly imagined – in an imaginary rather too narrowly focused on sameness. . . .
>
> Thus what [women] desire is precisely nothing, and at the same time everything. Always something more and something else besides that *one* – sexual organ, for example – that you give them, attribute to them. Their desire is often interpreted, and feared, as a sort of insatiable hunger, a voracity that will swallow you whole. Whereas it really involves a different economy more than anything else, one

that upsets the linearity of a project, undermines the goal-object of a desire, diffuses the polarization toward a single pleasure, disconcerts fidelity to a single discourse.[12]

Rebelling against the symbolic order, contemporary sexual culture demands a "plural" sight/site that can be seen *and* felt. The phallus, a mere abstraction that hides the organ which might go limp, is a holdover from the Victorian age. Today's Medusan femme expresses her sexuality with her entire body, spreading her legs and stomping her feet to join the postmodern laughter.

In "Form and Female Authorship in Music Video" Lisa Lewis has written about the opportunity afforded to female musicians by the music video form. Not only does their role as singers suggest authorship and assign narrative importance to them, but they are enabled by performance strategies to express gender-specific attitudes or viewpoints. She states:

> Female musicians are actively participating in making the music video form work in their interest, to assert their authority as producers of culture and to air their views on female genderhood. The generic emphasis in music video on using the song as a soundtrack, together with the centrality of the musician's image in the video, formally support the construction of female authorship....
>
> Many female musicians have proved to be quite adept at manipulating elements of visual performance in their video act, thereby utilizing music video as an additional authorship tool. In "What's Love Got To Do With It?," the gestures, eye contact with the camera and with other characters, and the walking style of Tina Turner add up to a powerful and aggressive on-screen presence.[13]

This new visual music format requires specific performance talents from male musicians as well. As Richard Goldstein states in "Tube Rock: How Music Video Is Changing Music" these musicians have to learn to communicate with their bodies.

> Tube rock forces musicians to act. Not that they haven't been acting since Jerry Lee Lewis learned to stomp on a piano and Chuck Berry essayed his first duckwalk; but on MTV, musicians have to emote the way matinee idols once did if they're to establish the kind of contact tube rockers covet – the heightened typology of a classic movie star. What once made a rock performer powerful – the ability to move an arena with broad gesture and precision timing – has been supplanted by a new strategy: the performer must project in close-up.[14]

Because of their different relations to bodily expression, females and males have adjusted differently to the music video form. While MTV's emphasis on body and presence seems to have provided women performers an avenue for gaining authorship, males have attempted to "master" the facial expression of sensuality as well as the language of exhibitionism, efforts which have themselves recast gender and asked new questions about sexuality. As Simon Frith writes in *Music for Pleasure*:

> The most important effect of gender-bending was to focus the problem of sexuality onto males. In pop, the question became, unusually, what do men want? And as masculinity became a packaging problem, then so did masculine desire.... On video, music can be mediated through the body directly.[15]

These three authors are identifying and analyzing the same phenomenon. The music video form has instigated repositionings by/of both female and male performers; it has made direct address and personal display necessary for a star persona. These repositionings often result in ambiguous reversals, such as that evident in two Bananarama videos, *I Can't Help It* and *Love in the First Degree*. In each video, the three female vocalists sing in the first-person, to the camera as well as to a male "you" within the fictional performance space. In each, the male body is exploited as visual object at the same time that the song lyrics admit female dependency. "I can't help it," Bananarama sings as a shirtless male dances. "I'm captivated by your honey. Move your body. I need you. I won't give up." Similarly, as a group of males dance (at times down on their hands and knees) in prison-striped briefs and crop-tops, the "fully dressed" female Bananarama trio sings, "Only you can set me free." As one of these singers shakes a dancer's head and then pushes him away, they continue, "'cause I'm guilty of love in the first degree." The bare legs of the men contrast strikingly with the women's covered legs.

This new reversal of subjectivity and exhibitionism between female and male performers incorporates ambiguity that satisfies multiple audience identifications and desires. When the She-man collects all this ambiguity on "his" body, subjectivity and exhibitionism reverberate in a "contradictory" assemblage of gender and sexual codes. In this case, the male performer adopts sexualized female body language to achieve a powerful exhibitionistic subjectivity.

What happens when the male performer (metaphoric possessor of the dominant, if out-of-style, signifier) exercises his prerogative to appropriate the phallic femme's masquerade or the Medusan body? He finds himself a split personality, a schizophrenic sign, a media image combining disbelief and an aesthetic of "hysteric," ricocheting signifiers. This is the She-man, whose sexual power depends not on the ostensibly stable male body but on embraced incongruity. And with this incongruity, he is the site of a "nervous" breakdown, the utter collapse of the most basic binary opposition (male and female) into postmodern irrelevance.

The She-man's performance engulfs and rewrites the conventional heterosexual narrative, suturing the viewer into unending alterations of absence and presence, desire and pleasure. First we see a woman. Where's the man? Then we see a man. Where's the woman? Simultaneously we are given the pleasure of conventional reading and the pleasure of subverting convention. The woman *is* the man. The She-man is the shot-reverse shot. Performance is the *nouveau narrative*.

A discussion of the She-man in music videos and video art calls for a return to modernist concerns. For two reasons, the video medium is especially suitable for the She-man's scheme. Historically, video art has shown an affinity with performance art, perhaps because of what Rosalind Krauss called the medium's property of narcissism.[16] In addition, as Douglas Davis has pointed out, the experience of viewing the small video monitor contains its own particular physicality that seems appropriate for performance.[17] Instead of identifying with some larger-than-life idealized Lacanian "mirror" image, video viewers experience the medium's McLuhanesque tactility or, in Davis's terms, its subtle existentialism. When they do use it as a mirror, as Krauss suggests, it is not to mistake themselves for ideal images, but to check their makeup. Video's mobile viewers, whether in their living rooms or in dance bars, are likely to feel that they are cruising, not dreaming. Video music actually benefits from the viewing logistics of the medium, engaging viewers in a physical/rhythmic identification. Rather than an empty vessel for empathic identification, the performer is a surrogate dance partner, and often this is reinforced by the genre's mobile aesthetics – the artist's continual movement interacts with and against the editing and camera movement.[18]

In contrast to commercial music video, video art is produced with relatively small budgets by independent artists. Expressing the individual artists' concerns, video artworks may break radically in form and content from mainstream conventions. Often they present ideas and images not included in mass media. In the two examples which follow, traditional sexual iconography is upset by explicitly gay dynamics. Conventional boundaries between the sexes become blurred.

John Greyson's *The Kipling Trilogy: Perils of Pedagogy* (1984, Canada) is a humorous commentary on the relation between desire, fantasy, and status differentials between men. The female's position as object of the erotic gaze is assumed by a young male character who flaunts himself exhibitionistically before his male mentor. Thus the conventional representation of desire – directed at women by men – is adopted for a man–boy interaction. The tape cuts between images of the boy dressing up in a number of costumes and the older man watching: however, in many shots, the boy directs a flirtatious look at the camera/video viewer. By lip-synching the song "To Sir With Love," the boy "appropriates" its woman vocalist's voice. The appropriation is assisted technologically as the song is slowed down to lower the pitch of "her" voice. Although the boy is actually standing upright (in the pro-filmic arena), unusual camera positioning has determined that his monitored image be horizontal; that is, he is technologically "laid." In three ways, then, video technology has been used to confuse "male" and "female": the boy is situated as object of the camera gaze, he is turned on his side to imply a "reclining" position, and a recorded voice is "converted" from female to male by altering its pitch. In addition to being acted upon, however, the boy actively corroborates in his feminization. Conscious of and adept with the specific powers of his female position, he both accommodates and controls the viewer's desire. With his own self-assured seductive look, he fixes the viewer's gaze. As he "sings," he directs the viewer's sexual longings by pointing his finger at his open mouth. Later, lying nude on a floor, he smiles at the camera/viewer and then "gratuitously" turns onto his stomach.

In *Chinese Characters* (1986, Canada), video artist Richard Fung also uses technology to intervene in conventional gender positioning. First he video-keys himself into a pornographic film where he then poses as the lure for a desiring "stud." His presence as both performer and character constructs two different identificatory positions for viewers. In voice-over, he tells us, as the artist, how he learned to make appropriate sounds during sex by listening to women in pornographic films. As a character, he purposefully fondles his nipples. The tape alternates between images of this activity and shots of the conventionally well-endowed porn stud. Camera angles and framing, inherited from the source film, foreground the upper part of Fung's body and the lower part of the stud's body. Hardcore pornography is the only genre that consistently shows the penis, and its convention of featuring large penises can be seen as an attempt to uphold the phallus in the realm of the physical. Twisting this convention, Fung uses performance and technology in this tape to create a She-man whose breasts offer a visual equivalent – as much an alternate as a complement – to the porn star's "cock." Objects of each other's (and our) gazes, both male characters are seductive, desiring subjects.

Because they circulate more in the mainstream (in video clubs and/or on television) and assume a mass (although young) audience, music videos that subvert gender conventions often do so within representations of heterosexuality. Although their gender alterations (especially when accompanied by a camp aesthetics) may connote a gay dynamics or desire, their heterosexual illusion, maintained by heterosexual characters and plots, finally attributes the She-man construction to a wider, popular desire. The She-man can be seen as representing a desire for sexual fluidity (to be both sexes, as well as both genders) rather than simply representing gay desire through an unsuitable but dominant (heterosexual) iconography.

In his music video *When You're a Boy*, David Bowie appears as lead singer as well as (in drag) three backup female singers. As a man he sings, "Nothing stands in your way when you're a boy.... Other boys check you out.... You get a girl.... Boys keep swinging. Boys always work it out." As the female chorus, he echoes himself with, "Boys!" The video ends, not on the handsome Bowie in suit and tie, but with each of the three female singers walking forward on a stage. The first two dramatically remove their wigs and smear their lipstick with the backs of their hands as if attempting to wipe it off. They establish a single Bowie identity beneath the girl group facade; from their duplicated "unmasking" actions we induce that the third female is also Bowie. However, the third backup singer, an older female character who walks forward slowly with a cane, does not "unmask." Instead, she blows a kiss to the camera/audience, thus insuring an open ending to this already ironic declaration about gender and sex.

In *Walk Like a Man*, Divine (who is best known as the transvestite star of several John Waters films) achieves a most convincing gender/sexual transformation – via costume, makeup, gestures, and a look suggestive of Mae West.[19] As Divine stands on a wagon/car singing, swinging, and whipping her imaginary horses, the camera places viewers in the position of the missing horses. Combined with music video's reinforcement of the viewers' physicality, this situates them well for her whipping. The diegetic audience/chorus encourages viewers to "join in the song," yet when we do, we enter into camp S&M theater.

Divine's very corporality – her assertively displayed female (soft and excessive)[20] flesh – along with the accenting of her stomach by the "outline" design of her costume, tend to posit the woman in his/her body. The fact that the costume also covers his male genital anatomy further facilitates the conversion of Divine's image from that of the transvestite to that of the transsexual. Finally, the rapid editing between different subject-camera distances mimics a *fort-da* game, which, combined with her whipping action, suggests Divine as a phallic mother in relation to the audience.[21]

The examples of appropriation in these video works demonstrate a tentative collapse of the phallic femme and the Medusan femme on the She-man's body. Female sexuality originally carried either by the masquerade or by the body abandons these boundaries to slip back and forth between the male performer's body and his masquerade, constantly threatening to engulf and dissolve him. Divine's costume is a masquerade that generates a womb on/in his/her body.

Interestingly, a trace of masculinity is deliberately maintained in these videos, as if this threatened engulfment necessitates the shy penis to peek out. In *Perils of Pedagogy*, the penis of the flirting, feminized boy is once shown and once indicated by a bulge in his undershorts. The eroticization of nipples supplements rather than displaces the "masculinized" anatomy of the "well-endowed" porn star in *Chinese Characters*. Though triply female, Bowie's drag personas ostensibly serve as back-up support for the (currently) real Bowie – the *GQ* male whose pretty looks and fashion stretch gender rather than sex. And, as Divine swings her hips, a cut-in shot briefly focuses on a male masturbatory gesture she enacts with the horses' reins. This copresence of feminine and masculine elements creates the internal distance which establishes the She-man's image as bi-sexed rather than transsexual.

In Dead or Alive's *Save You All My Kisses*, the lead (male) singer appears extremely androgynous but emanates a distinctly feminine sexual energy. This sexuality is both emphasized and checked by an ornate silver codpiece prominently shown during a vertical track up his/her body. Also signaling maleness is the singer's Adam's apple. Coexisting female signals include his/her "dominatrix" whip and long, obviously styled hair. Dressed in black leather jacket and tights, he/she walks, dances, and sings in front of a wire fence while a gang of boys climbs the other side of the fence attempting to get at him/her. The boys' enthusiastic approach displays much ambivalence – they seem both attracted to and angered by him/her. At times their postures and glances seem to signify lust, but at other times they seem to be mocking him/her. While one swings his baseball bat in a way that threatens a fag-bashing, another rips open his T-shirt as if stripping for him/her. A male alter-ego character is also present, also dressed in black leather and resembling his "female" counterpart except that he wears more masculine pants, presents a more masculine posture, and carries a baseball bat. Again it is unclear whether he is attracted to "her" or threatening to attack "her." The contradictory reactions of this diegetic audience confuse straight and gay subjectivities and emphasize the She-man as simultaneously female and male.

It must be emphasized that, although gay audiences may have more to gain from the She-man's radical display of gender *and* sex constructions, the She-man is not a specifically gay figure, nor an effeminate male, nor a hermaphrodite. The She-man, as enacted by both gay and straight performers, is a fully functional figuration signifying both woman and man.

In *The Desire to Desire*, an analysis of 1940s women's films, Mary Ann Doane identifies proper makeup and dress as indicators of a woman's stable narcissism.[22] If that makeup is smeared or that dress torn, the woman is marked with the pathetic condition of impaired narcissism. This is a narcissism marked by too much self-love or brazen love for a man.

Narcissism becomes quite different, however, when two sexes are present in the same body. This condition can signal both heterosexual coupling and bisexuality. When performer Mike Monroe of Hanoi Rocks sweats through his makeup, for instance, a return of the male and a *successful* narcissism is signaled. Doane has argued for seeing a predilection in women for tactility and overidentification, in contrast with the male tendency for voyeurism and fetishism, both of which require distance.[23] Mike Monroe's narcissistically bi-sexed figure makes over-identification a moot point. As sweat seeps through cosmetics, distance abandons difference.

Is there a complementary bi-sexed figure, a reverse of the She-man, built from woman's body and man's masquerade? I think not. Because female sexuality is conventionally imaged and indexed by the female masquerade, and because the male "costume" conventionally serves to mask rather than indicate male (genital) sexuality, there is no mechanism by which a "He-woman" could be produced predominantly via appropriation of masquerade. Even more than the She-man performer's use of gesture to make transvestism corporeal, the "incorporation" of action is essential for a woman performer's successful sex crossing. In order to construct an empowering position and achieve a transgression similar to those of the She-man, women would need to entirely disrupt the "*men act* and *women appear*" sex roles described by John Berger.[24] In short, without also appropriating "male" action (a more difficult accomplishment), women's transvestism fails to achieve the double sexuality of the She-man. Nevertheless, several examples of transgressive transvestism by women suggest possibilities.

Annie Lennox of Eurythmics deliberately recalls/retains the female masquerade when cross-dressing via her bright red lipstick – which, even on young girls, signals *adult* female sexuality. This lipstick sexualizes her image while her *act* of wearing a suit (rather than the mere presence of a suit) pushes it toward a bi-sexed image. Her assertive masculine behavior – speech, gestures, and posture – "invests" the suit with transgressive power. Similarly, when Lily Tomlin impersonates her character Tommy Velour, a working-class, Italian nightclub singer, her sexual come-ons to "girls" in the audience validate and sexualize the hair on "his" chest.

The portrait of Madonna that appeared on the cover of the 1990 issue of *Interview* magazine successfully employs reversal, contradiction, and action to disrupt gender and sex. Wearing dark lipstick, exaggerated eyelashes, fish-net stockings, hot pants, and a polka-dotted blouse with bell-shaped collar and cuffs, Madonna thrusts forward her pelvis, grabs her crotch, and squeezes her thigh muscle in a gesture that young men often use playfully to suggest a gigantic-sized penis. Madonna's "girlish" clowning-around both mocks machismo and usurps the penis. Psycho-sexologists have long referred to penis envy in women and described the clitoris as an underdeveloped penis. Women have been positioned alongside boys, their "lack" diminishing them and disqualifying them for adulthood. Traditionally, when cross-dressing, they achieved boyishness rather than manliness. By plagiarizing a male fantasy, Madonna ironically reassigns and complicates penis envy.

Woman's "counterpart" to the She-man would likely require appropriation of male sexual prerogatives in two areas. First, she needs to trespass the boundaries of sexual segregation relating to pornography and sexual information, erotica, expression of libido, and sexual joking. (Here we might think of Mae West.) Second, she must aggressively expose the untamed sexual imagery of her body. For instance, a woman's unruly mature pubic hair contrasts sharply with the image of female genitals in conventional pornography, where shaving or partially shaving the public hair converts a physical characteristic into masquerade and enforces an image of feminine youth.

Instead of a He-woman, this transgressive figure might better be imagined as a "She-butch." In contrast to the She-man's image-actions (actions on images), the She-butch would perform action-images (images containing action). One contemporary figure that might qualify for the status of action-image (a qualification supported by her disturbing, disruptive impression on mainstream culture) is the female bodybuilder. As Laurie Schulze states,

> The female bodybuilder threatens not only current socially constructed definitions of femininity and masculinity, but the system of sexual difference itself.... A female body displaying "extreme" muscle mass, separation and definition, yet oiled up, clad in a bikini, marked with conventionally "feminine"-styled hair and carefully applied cosmetics juxtaposes heterogeneous elements in a way that frustrates ideological unity and confounds common sense.... Muscle mass, its articulation, and the

strength and power the body displays, is clearly an achievement, the product of years of intense, concentrated, deliberate work in the gym, a sign of activity, not passivity.[25]

As might be expected, the arena of avant-garde performance also holds possibilities for the emerging She-butch. Following the taboo-breaking work of performance artists such as Lynda Benglis and Carolee Schneeman, Karen Finley appropriates male prerogatives in her "id-speak" performances. Finley's dirty talk/dirty acts such as "I Like to Smell the Gas Passed from your Ass," "I'm an Ass Man," and "Don't Hang the Angel" use the language of pornography for radical "feminine" misbehavior.[26]

Another ripe-for-action figure, which I have termed the "nouveau lesbian butch," is the contemporary lesbian who updates the Victorian era's mannish lesbian/female transvestite with a transgressive handling of dildos. Self-consciously appropriating the dominant image of sexual agency, the nouveau lesbian butch attains a shocking difference that is nonetheless compatible with the concept of femininity as construction. Combining visual dominance with bodily audacity, her mocking, dildoed body identifies the penis's cosmetic potential. Simultaneously constructing and deconstructing the male "body," she claims the speaking position in bodily discourse to confess the male facade – a bulge that might just as well be silicone as flesh. Whether such avant-garde/ underground transgressions will ever be reflected in mainstream culture will no doubt depend on economic determinants as well as the industry's ability to negotiate as well as package the She-butch's sexual subjectivity in a way that doesn't directly challenge society's prevailing concept of passive/image/ woman.

Evident in popular music culture as well as underground film and experimental video, the She-man is currently the most powerful signifying formation transgressing the male–female sex dichotomy. This figure suggests the collapse of the phallus as the dominant signifier and recognizes a new empowered female sexuality which cannot be reduced to boyishness. Although the She-man is obviously a result of male prerogative, his/her dependency on female sexual imagery for a powerful impact is also evidence of the phallic femme's effectivity and the Medusan femme's signifying power. More importantly, the She-man disrupts the very concept of male–female discontinuity. Through his/her appropriations of femininity and female physicality, the She-man not only achieves a postmodern dismantling of gender and sex differences, but also adopts a *greater* sexuality.

Notes

The core of this article was originally presented at a television and postmodernism seminar at the University of Wisconsin-Milwaukee Center for Twentieth-Century Studies in 1988.

Earlier versions occur in my dissertation, *Sexual Subjects: Signification, Viewership, and Pleasure in Film and Video* (Northwestern University, 1989), and in *Screen* 31.3 (1990).

1 Working definitions for sex, gender, and sexuality are in order. Most feminist theorists use the term "sex" to refer to male and female biology and the term "gender" to refer to masculine and feminine attributes which are culturally and historically constructed. The term "sexuality" refers to sexual desire and behavior which also is understood to be socially constituted. See Gayle Rubin, "The Traffic in Women," in *Toward an Anthropology of Women*, ed. Rayna R. Reiter (New York, 1975); and "Thinking Sex: Notes for a Radical Theory of the Politics of Sexuality," in *Pleasure and Danger: Exploring Female Sexuality*, ed. Carole S. Vance (Boston, 1984). Following Michel Foucault, *History of Sexuality, Volume 1: An Introduction* (New York, 1980), I assume the sexes to be mediated rather than natural. Although science relies on biology to define sex, biology itself does not provide any single all-inclusive and fixed demarcation between male and female persons. The exceptions and ambiguities in anatomical assignment become even more pervasive and disruptive when chromosome patterns, hormones, secondary sex characteristics, and behaviors are considered. The persistent concept of sex – that is, of two opposite and distinct sexes – is pressed upon ever-changing information about biology. Sex is thus a product of discourse rather than a natural condition. In this article, I use the word sex to refer to conventionally defined and discursively employed genital anatomy. Obviously, the construction of male and female sexes relies on gender operations as much as biology. Therefore, I am purposely playing with the slippery status of all the above terminology to expose its artificiality, unreliability, and manipulability. (Indeed, as much as sorting out these terms, my current project calls for moving with them.)

2 Richard Dyer, "Male Sexuality in the Media," in *The Sexuality of Men*, ed. Andy Metcalf and Martin Humphries (London, 1985), 28–43; and Peter Lehman, "*In the Realm of the Senses*: Desire, Power, and the Representation of the Male Body," *Genders* 2 (Summer 1988): 91–110.

3 See "Redressing the Natural: The Temporary Transvestite Film" (ch. 6 of my dissertation cited above). In this chapter, I identify and analyze a subgenre of temporary transvestite films in which male and female characters cross-dress for sexual disguise. (Examples of such films include *Some Like It Hot*, *Victor/Victoria*, *Tootsie*, and *Sylvia Scarlett*.) I note that male transvestism is portrayed in mainstream film as undesired, impractical, and laughable. At the same time that these films question gender construction, attempts to cross boundaries of sex "prove" futile.

4 Esther Newton, *Mother Camp: Female Impersonators in America* (Chicago, 1972), 97–111. For additional discussion of drag in relation to cross-dressing and transvestism, see ch. 6 of my dissertation.

5 My use of the term "Medusan" throughout this paper is inspired by Hélène Cixous's radical description of the mythological Medusa who aggressively exposes her genitals and laughs at the terror this causes to men. See "The Laugh of the Medusa," in *New French Feminisms*, ed. Elaine Marks and Isabelle de Courtivron (New York, 1981).

6 This indexical male bulge is becoming a more common sight in contemporary fashion where the male image is increasingly sexualized. However, it still is associated predominantly with motivated costume – as in exercise culture – and is *not* associated with a subsequent exposure of the penis itself. We shall find in the discussion that follows that, just as the drag queen's gender deconstruction depends on

a contradictory display of sexual codes, female iconography in the bi-sexed She-man often instigates a display of the male sex as well.

7　Esther Newton, "The Mythic Mannish Lesbian: Radclyffe Hall and the New Woman," *Signs* 9 (Summer 1984): 560–1, 573.

8　Mary Ann Doane, "Film and the Masquerade: Theorising the Female Spectator," *Screen* 23, 3–4 (September–October 1982): 81–2.

9　A photograph of this performance can be found in *The Amazing Decade: Women and Performance Art in America 1970–1980*, ed. Moira Roth (Los Angeles, 1983), 15.

10　See Laura Mulvey, "Visual Pleasure and Narrative Cinema," *Screen* 16.3 (1975): 6–18; and Claude Lévi-Strauss, *Structural Anthropology*, trans. Claire Jacobson and Brooke G. Schoepf (Garden City, 1967).

11　Woman writing her sexual body is a thematic concern throughout Hélène Cixous's work. See Marks and Courtivron, eds., *New French Feminisms*: and "Castration or Decapitation," trans. Annette Kuhn, *Signs* 7 (Autumn 1981): 41–55.

12　Luce Irigaray, *This Sex Which Is Not One*, trans. Catherine Porter and Carolyn Burke (Ithaca, NY: 1985), 23–33.

13　Lisa Lewis, "Form and Female Authorship in Music Video," in *Media in Society: Readings in Mass Communication*, ed. Caren Deming and Samuel Becker (Glenview, Il., 1988), 140, 143.

14　Richard Goldstein, "Tube Rock: How Music Video Is Changing Music," in Deming and Becker, eds., *Media in Society*, 50–1.

15　Simon Frith, *Music for Pleasure* (Cambridge, 1988), 166–7.

16　Rosalind Krauss, "Video: The Aesthetics of Narcissism," in *New Artists Video*, ed. Gregory Battcock (New York, 1978), 43–64.

17　Douglas Davis, "Filmgoing/Videogoing: Making Distinctions," in *Artculture: Essays on the Post-Modern*, ed. Douglas Davis (New York, 1977), 79–84.

18　A good example of this is the Communards' "Never Can Say Good-bye" in which constant sweeping camera movements "bring" viewers to the singers/stars, and swirling camera movements incorporate both stars and viewers into a large group of dancers. The stars are both center and part of the dynamic social group. This accomplishes a "live and let live" solidarity in which it no longer matters if one is gay or straight as long as he/she can dance. (The Communards are openly gay; the diegetic audience is composed primarily of heterosexual couplings, though the rapid pace achieved by cinematography and editing fragments this coupling.)

19　Parker Tyler raises the interesting question of who is imitating whom between Mae West and the drag queen. "Miss West's reaction to comments that connected her with female impersonators . . . was reported as the boast that, of course, she 'knew that female impersonators imitated her.' It is often hard, as everyone knows, to establish primacy of claims to originality, whether actually asserted or only indicated statistically. Perhaps one ought simply to say that Miss West's style as a woman fully qualifies her – as it always did – to be a Mother Superior of the Faggots." See Tyler's *Screening the Sexes: Homosexuality in the Movies* (New York, 1972), I. This question is relevant to my evaluation of the She-man as a new and separate entity that transcends/abandons any original male agency.

20　For further discussion of this, see Gaylyn Studlar, "Midnight Excess: Cult Configurations of 'Femininity' and the Perverse," *Journal of Popular Film and Television* 17 (Spring 1989): 2–13, esp. 6. Discussing Divine's film appearances, Studlar argues that "we believe Divine is a woman primarily because she is fat. As Noelle Caskey observes, fat is 'a direct consequence of her [woman's] sexuality.... Fat and femininity cannot be separated physiologically.'" Her Noelle Caskey quote is taken from "Interpreting Anorexia Nervosa," in *The Female Body in Western Culture*, ed. Susan Rubin Suleiman (Cambridge, Mass., 1986), 176, 178, 66–7.

21 See Jane Gallop, *The Daughter's Seduction: Feminism and Psychoanalysis* (Ithaca, NY, 1982), for an elaboration of the concept of phallic mother.

22 Mary Ann Doane, *The Desire to Desire: The Woman's Film of the 1940s* (Bloomington, 1987).

23 See Doane, "Film and the Masquerade" and *Desire to Desire*.

24 John Berger, *Ways of Seeing* (London, 1972), 47.

25 Laurie Schulze, "On the Muscle" in *Fabrications: Costume and the Female Body*, ed. Jane Gaines and Charlotte Herzog (New York, 1990), 59, 68, 70.

26 C. Carr, "Unspeakable Practices, Unnatural Acts: The Taboo Art of Karen Finley," *Village Voice*, 1986, 24 June, 17–20, 86.

35

Roseanne: Unruly Woman as Domestic Goddess

Kathleen K. Rowe

Sometime after I was born in Salt Lake City, Utah, all the little babies were sleeping soundly in the nursery except for me, who would scream at the top of my lungs, trying to shove my whole fist into my mouth, wearing all the skin off on the end of my nose. I was put in a tiny restraining jacket. . . . My mother is fond of this story because to her it illustrates what she regards as my gargantuan appetites and excess anger. I think I was probably just bored.

Roseanne: *My Life As A Woman*[1]

Questions about television celebrities often centre on a comparison with cinematic stars – on whether television turns celebrities into what various critics have called 'degenerate symbols' who are 'slouching toward stardom' and engaging in 'dialogues of the living dead'.[2] This chapter examines Roseanne Barr, a television celebrity who has not only slouched but whined, wisecracked, munched, mooned, and sprawled her way to a curious and contradictory status in our culture explained only partially by the concept of stardom, either televisual or cinematic. Indeed, the metaphor of decay such critics invoke, while consistent with a strain of the grotesque associated with Barr, seems inappropriate to her equally compelling vitality and *jouissance*. In this study I shall be using the name 'Roseanne' to refer to Roseanne Barr-as-sign, a person we know only through her various roles and performances in the popular discourse. My use follows Barr's lead in effacing the lines among her roles: Her show, after all, bears her name and in interviews she describes her 'act' as 'who she is'.

Nearing the end of its second season, her sitcom securely replaced *The Cosby Show* at the top of the ratings. The readers of *People Weekly* identified her as their favourite female television star and she took similar prizes in the People's Choice award show this spring. Yet 'Roseanne', both person and show, has been snubbed by the Emmies, condescended to by media critics and trashed by the tabloids (never mind the establishment press). Consider *Esquire*'s solution of how to contain Roseanne. In an issue on its favourite (and least favourite) women, it ran two stories by two men, side by side – one called 'Roseanne – Yay', the other 'Roseanne – Nay'. And consider this from *Star*. 'Roseanne's Shotgun "Wedding from Hell"' – 'Dad refuses to give pregnant bride away – 'Don't wed that druggie bum!"'; 'Maids of honor are lesbians – best man is groom's detox pal'; 'Ex-hubby makes last-ditch bid to block ceremony'; 'Rosie and Tom wolf two out of three tiers of wedding cake' (6 Feb. 1990). Granted that tabloids are *about* excess, there's often an edge of cruelty to that excess in Roseanne's case, and an effort to wrest her definition of herself from the comic to the melodramatic.

Such ambivalence is the product of several phenomena. Richard Dyer might explain it in terms of the ideological contradictions Roseanne plays upon – how, for example, the body of Roseanne-as-star magically reconciles the conflict women experience in a society that says 'consume' but look as if you don't. Janet Woollacott might discuss the clash of discourses inherent in situation comedy – how our pleasure in Roseanne's show arises not so much from narrative suspense about her actions as hero, nor from her one-liners, but from the economy or wit by which the show brings together two discourses on family life: one based on traditional liberalism and the other on feminism and social class. Patricia Mellencamp might apply Freud's analysis of wit to Roseanne as she did to Lucille Ball and Gracie Allen, suggesting that Roseanne ventures farther than her comic foremothers into the masculine terrain of the tendentious joke.[3]

All of these explanations would be apt, but none would fully explain the ambivalence surrounding Roseanne. Such an explanation demands a closer look at gender and at the historical representations of female figures similar to Roseanne. These figures, I believe, can be found in the tradition of the 'unruly woman', a topos of female outrageousness and transgression from literary and social history. Roseanne uses a 'semiotics of the unruly' to expose the gap she sees between the ideals of the New Left and the Women's Movement of the late 1960s and early 1970s on the one hand, and the realities of working-class family life two decades later on the other.

Because female unruliness carries a strongly ambivalent charge, Roseanne's use of it both intensifies and undermines her popularity. Perhaps her greatest unruliness lies in the presentation of herself as *author* rather than actor and, indeed, as author of a self over which she claims control. Her insistence on her 'authority' to create and control the meaning of *Roseanne* is an unruly act *par excellence*, triggering derision or dismissal much like Jane Fonda's earlier attempts to 'write' her self (but in the genre of melodrama rather than comedy). I will explain this in three parts: the first takes a brief look at the tradition of the unruly woman; the second, at the unruly qualities of *excess* and *looseness* Roseanne embodies; and the third, at an episode of her sitcom which dramatizes the conflict between female unruliness and the ideology of 'true womanhood'.

The Unruly Woman

The unruly woman is often associated with sexual inversion – 'the woman on top', according to social historian Natalie Zemon Davis, who fifteen years ago first identified her in her book *Society and Culture in Early Modern France*. The sexual inversion she represents, Davis writes, is less about gender confusion than about larger issues of social and political order that come into play when what belongs 'below' (either women themselves, or their images appropriated by men in drag) usurps the position of what belongs 'above'. This topos isn't limited to Early Modern Europe, but reverberates whenever women, especially women's bodies, are considered excessive – too fat, too mouthy, too old, too dirty, too pregnant, too sexual (or not sexual enough) for the norms of conventional gender representation. For women, excessive fatness carries associations with excessive wilfulness and excessive speech ('fat texts', as Patricia Parker explains in *Literary Fat Ladies*, a study of rhetoric, gender, and property that traces literary examples of this connection from the Old Testament to the twentieth century).[4] Through body and speech, the unruly woman violates the unspoken feminine sanction against 'making a spectacle' of herself. I see the unruly woman as prototype of woman as subject – transgressive above all when she lays claim to her own desire.

The unruly woman is multivalent, her social power unclear. She has reinforced traditional structures, as Natalie Davis acknowledges.[5] But she has also helped sanction political disobedience for men and women alike by making such disobedience thinkable. She can signify the radical utopianism of undoing all hierarchy. She can also signify pollution (dirt or 'matter out of place', as Mary Douglas might explain). As such she becomes a source of danger for threatening the conceptual categories which organize our lives. For these reasons – for the power she derives from her liminality, her associations with boundaries and taboo – she evokes not only delight but disgust and fear. Her ambivalence, which is the source of her oppositional power, is usually contained within the licence accorded to the comic and the carnivalesque. But not always.

The unruly woman has gossiped and cackled in the margins of history for millennia, from Sarah of the Old Testament who laughed at God (and figures in Roseanne's tribute to her grandmother in her autobiography), to the obstinate and garrulous Mrs Noah of the medieval Miracle Plays (who would not board the Ark until she was good and ready), to the folk figure 'Mère Folle' and the subject of Erasmus's *The Praise of Folly*. Her more recent incarnations include such figures as the screwball heroine of the 1930s film, Miss Piggy, and a pantheon of current female grotesques and sacred monsters: Tammy Faye Bakker, Leona Helmsley, Imelda Marcos, and Zsa Zsa Gabor. The media discourse around these women reveals the same mixed bag of emotions I see attached to Roseanne, the same cruelty and tendency to carnivalize by pushing them into parodies of melodrama, a genre which, unlike much comedy, punishes the unruly woman for asserting her desire. Such parodies of melodrama make the unruly woman the target of *our* laughter, while denying her the power and pleasure of her own.

The disruptive power of these women – carnivalesque and carnivalized – contains much potential for feminist appropriation. Such an appropriation could enable us to problematize two areas critical to feminist theories of spectatorship and the subject: the social and cultural norms of femininity, and our understanding of how we are constructed as gendered subjects in the language of spectacle and the visual. In her essay 'Female Grotesques', Mary Russo asks: 'In what sense can women really produce or make spectacles out of themselves? . . . The figure of female transgressor as public spectacle is still powerfully resonant, and the possibilities of redeploying this representation as a demystifying or utopian model have not been exhausted.'[6] She suggests that the parodic excesses of the unruly woman and the comic conventions surrounding her provide a space to act out the dilemmas of femininity, to *make visible* and *laughable* what Mary Ann Doane describes as the 'tropes of feminity'.

Such a sense of spectacle differs from Laura Mulvey's. It accepts the relation between power and visual pleasure but argues for an understanding of that relation as more historically determined, its terms more mutable. More Foucaldian than Freudian, it suggests that visual power flows in multiple directions and that the position of spectacle isn't entirely one of weakness. Because public power is predicated largely on visibility, men have traditionally understood the need to secure their power not only by looking but by being seen – or rather, by fashioning, as author, a spectacle of themselves. Already bound in a web of visual power, women might begin to renegotiate its terms. Such a move would be similar to what Teresa de Lauretis advocates when she calls for the strategic use of narrative to 'construct other forms of coherence, to shift the terms of representation, to produce the conditions of representability of another – and gendered – social subject'.[7] By returning the male gaze, we might expose (make a spectacle of) the gazer. And by utilizing the power already invested in us as image, we might begin to negate our own 'invisibility' in the public sphere.

Roseanne as Spectacle

The spectacle Roseanne creates is *for* herself, produced *by* herself from a consciously developed perspective on ethnicity, gender, and social class. This spectacle derives much of its power from her construction of it as her 'self' – an entity which, in turn, she has knowingly fashioned through interviews, public performances, and perhaps most unambiguously her autobiography. This book, by its very existence, enhances the potency of Roseanne-as-sign because it grants a historicity to her 'self' and a materiality to her claims for authorship. The autobiography describes key moments in the development of 'Roseanne' – how she learned about female strength when for the first time in her life she saw a woman (her grandmother) stand up to a man, her father; how she learned about marginality and fear from her childhood as a Jew in Utah under the shadow of the Holocaust, and from her own experience of madness and institutionalization. Madness is a leitmotif both in her autobiography and in the tabloid talk about her.[8] Roseanne's eventual discovery of feminism and counter-culture politics led to disillusionment when the women's movement was taken over by women unlike her, 'handpicked', she writes, to be acceptable to the establishment.

Coexisting with the pain of her childhood and early adulthood was a love of laughter, the bizarre, a good joke. She always wanted to be a writer, not an actor. Performance, however, was the only 'place' where she felt safe. And because, since her childhood, she could always say what she wanted to as long as it was funny, *comic* performance allowed her to be a writer, to 'write' herself. While her decision to be a comedian was hampered by a difficulty in finding a female tradition in which to locate her own voice, she discovered her stance (or 'attitude') when she realized that she could take up the issue of female oppression by adopting its language. Helen Andelin's *Fascinating Womanhood* (1974) was one of the most popular manuals of femininity for the women of her mother's generation. It taught women to manipulate men by becoming 'domestic goddesses'. Yet, Roseanne discovered, such terms might also be used for 'self-definition, rebellion, truth-telling', for telling a truth that in her case is both ironic and affirmative. And so she built her act and her success on an exposure of the 'tropes of femininity' (the ideology of 'true womanhood', the perfect wife and mother) by cultivating the opposite (an image of the unruly woman).

Roseanne's disruptiveness is more clearly paradigmatic than syntagmatic, less visible in the stories her series dramatizes than in the image cultivated around her body: Roseanne-the-person who tattooed her buttocks and mooned her fans, Roseanne-the-character for whom farting and nose-picking are as much a reality as dirty dishes and obnoxious boy bosses. Both in body and speech, Roseanne is defined by *excess* and by *looseness* – qualities that mark her in opposition to bourgeois and feminine standards of decorum.

Of all of Roseanne's excesses, none seems more potent than her weight. Indeed, the very appearance of a 200-plus-pound woman in a weekly prime-time sitcom is significant in itself. Her body epitomizes the grotesque body of Bakhtin, the body which exaggerates its processes, its bulges and orifices, rather than concealing them as the monumental, static 'classical' or 'bourgeois' body does. Implicit in Bakhtin's analysis is the privileging of the female body – above all the *maternal* body which, through pregnancy and childbirth, participates uniquely in the carnivalesque drama of inside-out and outside-in, death-in-life and life-in-death. Roseanne's affinity with the grotesque body is evident in the first paragraph of *Roseanne: My Life as a Woman*, where her description of her 'gargantuan appetites' even as a newborn brings to mind Bakhtin's study of Rabelais.[9] Roseanne compounds her fatness with a 'looseness' of body language and speech – she sprawls, slouches, flops on furniture. Her speech – even apart from its content – is loose (in its 'sloppy' enunciation and grammar) and excessive (in tone and volume). She laughs loudly, screams shrilly, and speaks in a nasal whine.

In our culture, both fatness and looseness are violations of codes of feminine posture and behaviour. Women of 'ill-repute' are described as loose, their bodies, especially their sexuality, seen as out of control. Fatness, of course, is an especially significant issue for women, and perhaps patriarchy nowhere inscribes itself more insidiously and viciously on female bodies than in the cult of thinness. Fat females are stigmatized as unfeminine, rebellious, and sexually deviant (under or over-sexed). Women who are too fat or move too loosely appropriate too much space, and femininity is gauged by how little space women take up.[10] It is also gauged by the intrusiveness of women's utterances. As Henley notes, voices in any culture that are not meant to be heard are perceived as loud when they do speak, regardless of their decibel level ('shrill' feminists, for example). Farting, belching, and nose-picking likewise betray a failure to restrain the body. Such 'extreme looseness of body- focused functions' is generally not available to women as an avenue of revolt but, as Nancy Henley suggests, 'if it should ever come into women's repertoire, it will carry great power'.[11]

Expanding that repertoire is entirely consistent with Roseanne's professed mission.[12] She writes of wanting 'to break every social norm... and see that it is laughed at. I chuckle with glee if I know I have offended someone, because the people I intend to insult offend me horribly.'[13] In an interview in *People Weekly*, Roseanne describes how Matt Williams, a former producer on her show, tried to get her fired: 'He compiled a list of every offensive thing I did. And I do offensive things.... *That's who I am. That's my act.* So Matt was in his office making a list of how gross I was, how many times I farted and belched – taking it to the network to show I was out of control' (my emphasis). Of course she was out of control – *his* control. He wanted to base the show on castration jokes, she says, recasting it from the point of view of the little boy. She wanted something else – something different from what she sees as the norm of television: a 'male point of view coming out of women's mouths... particularly around families'.[14]

Roseanne's ease with her body, signified by her looseness, triggers much of the *unease* surrounding her. Such ease reveals what Pierre Bourdieu describes as 'a sort of indifference to the objectifying gaze of others which neutralizes its powers' and 'appropriates its appropriation'.[15] It marks Roseanne's rebellion against not only the codes of gender but of class, for ease with one's body is the prerogative of the upper classes. For the working classes, the body is more likely to be a source of embarrassment, timidity, and alienation, because the norms of the 'legitimate' body – beauty, fitness, and so on – are accepted across class boundaries while the ability to achieve them is not. In a culture which defines nature negatively as 'sloppiness', physical beauty bears value that is not only aesthetic but moral, reinforcing a sense of superiority in those who put some effort into enhancing their 'natural' beauty (p. 206).

Roseanne's indifference to conventional readings of her body exposes the ideology underlying those readings. Concerning her fatness, she resists the culture's efforts to define and judge her by her weight. Publicly celebrating the libidinal pleasure of food, she argues that women need to take up more space in the world, not less. And her comments about menstruation similarly attack the 'legitimate' female body, which does not menstruate in public. On an award show she announced that she had 'cramps that could kill a horse'. She startled Oprah Winfrey on her talk show by describing the special pleasure she took from the fact that she and her sister were 'on their period' – unclean, according to Orthodox law – when they were allowed to bear their grandmother's coffin. And in her autobiography she writes about putting a woman (her) in the White House: 'My campaign motto will be "Let's vote for Rosie and put some new blood in the White House – every 28 days"' (p. 117). Rather than accepting the barrage of ads that tell women they can never be young, thin, or beautiful enough and that their houses – an extension of their bodies – can never be immaculate enough, she rejects the 'pollution taboos' that foster silence, shame, and self-hatred in women by urging them to keep their genitals, like their kitchen appliances, deodorized, antisepticized, and 'April fresh'. Instead she reveals the social causes of female fatness, irritability, and messiness in the strains of working-class family life, where junk food late at night may be a sensible choice for comfort after a day punching out plastic forks on an assembly line.

Demonic Desires

The episode I'm going to talk about (7 November 1989) is in some ways atypical because of its stylistic excess and reflexivity. Yet I've chosen it because it so clearly defines female unruliness and its opposite, the ideology of the self-sacrificing wife and mother. It does so by drawing on and juxtaposing three styles: a realist sitcom style for the arena of ideology in the world of the working-class wife and mother; a surreal dream sequence for female unruliness; and a musical sequence within the dream to reconcile the 'real' with the unruly. Dream sequences invariably signal the eruption of unconscious desire. In this episode, the dream is linked clearly with the eruption of *female* desire, the defining mark of the unruly woman.

The episode begins as the show does every week, in the normal world of broken plumbing, incessant demands, job troubles. Roseanne wants ten minutes alone in a hot bath after what she describes as 'the worst week in her life' (she just quit her job at the Wellman factory). But between her husband Dan and her kids, she can't get into the bathroom. She falls asleep while she'll waiting. At this point all the marks of the sitcom disappear. The music and lighting signal 'dream'. Roseanne walks into her bathroom, but it's been transformed into an opulent, Romanesque pleasure spa where she is pampered by two bare-chested male attendants ('the pec twins', as Dan later calls them). She's become a glamorous redhead.

Even within this dream, however, she's haunted by her family and the institution that stands most firmly behind it – the law. One by one, her family appears and continues to nag her for attention and interfere with her bath. And one by one, without hesitation, she kills them off with tidy and appropriate means. (In one instance, she twitches her nose before working her magic, alluding to the unruly women of the late 1960s/early 1970s sitcom *Bewitched*.) Revenge and revenge fantasies are of course a staple in the feminist imagination (Marleen Gorris's *A Question of Silence* (1982), Nelly Kaplan's *A Very Curious Girl* (1969), Cecilia Condit's *Possibly in Michigan* (1985), Karen Arthur's *Lady Beware* (1987)). In this case, however, Roseanne doesn't murder for revenge but for a bath.

Roseanne's unruliness is further challenged, ideology reasserts itself, and the dream threatens to become a nightmare when she is arrested for murder and brought to court. Her family really *isn't* dead, and with her friends they testify against her, implying that because of her shortcomings as a wife and mother she's been murdering them all along. Her friend Crystal says: 'She's loud, she's bossy, she talks with her mouth full. She feeds her kids frozen fish sticks and high calorie sodas. She doesn't have proper grooming habits.' And she doesn't treat her husband right even though, as Roseanne explains, 'The only way to keep a man happy is to treat him like dirt once in a while.' The trial, like the dream itself, dramatizes a struggle over interpretation of the frame story that preceded it: the court judges her desire for the bath as narcissistic and hedonistic, and her barely suppressed frustration as murderous. Such desires are taboo for good self-sacrificing mothers. For Roseanne, the bath (and the 'murders' it *requires*) are quite pleasurable for reasons both sensuous and righteous. Everyone gets what they deserve. Coincidentally, ABC was running ads during this episode for the docudrama *Small Sacrifices* (12–14 November 1989), about a real mother, Diane Downs, who murdered one of her children.

Barely into the trial, it becomes apparent that Roseanne severely strains the court's power to impose its order on her. The rigid oppositions it tries to enforce begin to blur, and alliances shift. Roseanne defends her kids when the judge – Judge Wapner from *People's Court* – yells at them. Roseanne, defended by her sister, turns the tables on the kids and they repent for the pain they've caused her. With Dan's abrupt change from prosecutor to crooner and character witness, the courtroom becomes the stage for a musical. He breaks into song, and soon the judge, jury, and entire cast are dancing and singing Roseanne's praises in a bizarre production number. Female desire *isn't* monstrous; acting on it 'ain't misbehavin'', her friend Vanda sings. This celebration of Roseanne in effect vindicates her, although the judge remains unconvinced, finding her not only guilty but in contempt of court. Dreamwork done, she awakens, the sound of the judge's gavel becoming Dan's hammer on the plumbing. Dan's job is over too, but the kids still want her attention. Dan jokes that there's no place like home but Roseanne answers 'Bull'. On her way, at last, to her bath, she closes the door to the bathroom to the strains of the chorus singing 'We Love Roseanne'.

The requirements for bringing this fantasy to an end are important. First, what ultimately satisfies Roseanne isn't an escape from her family but an acknowledgement from them of *her* needs and an expression of their feeling for her – 'We love you, Roseanne'. I am not suggesting that Roseanne's series miraculously transcends the limitations of prime-time television. To a certain degree this ending does represent a sentimental co-opting of her power, a shift from the potentially radical to the liberal. But it also indicates a refusal to flatten contradictions. Much of Roseanne's appeal lies in the delicate balance she maintains between individual and institution and in the impersonal nature of her anger and humour, which are targeted not so much at the people she lives with as at what makes them the way they are. What Roseanne *really* murders here is the ideology of 'perfect wife and mother', which she reveals to be murderous in itself.

The structuring – and limits – of Roseanne's vindication are also important. Although the law is made ludicrous, it retains its power and remains ultimately indifferent and immovable. Roseanne's 'contempt' seems her greatest crime. More important, whatever vindication Roseanne does enjoy can happen only within a dream. It cannot be sustained in real life. The realism of the frame story inevitably reasserts itself. And even within the dream, the reconciliation between unruly fantasy and ideology can be brought about only by deploying the heavy artillery of the musical and its conventions. As Rick Altman has shown, few forms embody the utopian impulse of popular culture more insistently than the musical, and within musicals, contradictions difficult to resolve otherwise are acted out in production numbers. That is what happens here. The production number gives a fleeting resolution to the problem Roseanne typically plays with: representing the unrepresentable. A fat woman who is also sexual; a sloppy housewife who's a good mother; a 'loose' woman who is also tidy, who hates matrimony but loves her husband, who hates the ideology of 'true womanhood' yet considers herself a domestic goddess.

There is much more to be said about Roseanne and the unruly woman: about her fights to maintain authorial control over (and credit for) her show; her use of the grotesque in the film *She Devil* (1989); her performance as a stand-up comic; the nature of her humour, which she calls 'funny womanness'; her identity as a Jew and the suppression of ethnicity in her series; the series' move toward melodrama and its treatment of social class. A more sweeping look at the unruly woman would find much of interest in the Hollywood screwball comedy as well as feminist avant-garde film and video. It would take up questions about the relation between gender, anger, and Medusan laughter – about the links Hélène Cixous establishes between laughing, writing, and the body and their implications for theories of female spectatorship. And while this article has emphasized the oppositional potential of female unruliness, it is equally important to expose its misogynistic uses, as in, for example, the Fox sitcom *Married . . . With Children* (1988). Unlike Roseanne, who uses female unruliness to push at the limits of acceptable female behaviour, Peg inhabits the unruly woman stereotype with little distance, embodying the 'male point of view' Roseanne sees in so much television about family.

Roseanne points to alternatives. Just as 'domestic goddess' can become a term of self-definition and rebellion, so can spectacle-making – when used to seize the visibility that is, after all, a precondition for existence in the public sphere. The ambivalence I've tried to explain regarding Roseanne is evoked above all, perhaps, because she demonstrates how the enormous apparatus of televisual star-making can be put to such a use.

Notes

With thanks to Ellen Seiter for her helpful comments on an earlier draft of this article.

1 Roseanne Barr, *Roseanne: My Life as a Woman* (New York: Harper and Row, 1989), 3.
2 The phrase 'slouching towards stardom' is Jeremy Butler's.
3 Janet Woollacott, 'Fictions and Ideologies: The Case of the Situation Comedy', in Tony Bennett, Colin Mercer, and Janet Woollacott, *Popular Culture and Social Relations* (Philadelphia: Open University Press, 1986), 196–218; Patricia Mellencamp, 'Situation Comedy, Feminism, and Freud', in Tania Modleski (ed.), *Studies in Entertainment* (Bloomington: Indiana University Press, 1986), 80–95.
4 Patricia Parker, *Literary Fat Ladies: Rhetoric, Gender, Property* (New York: Methuen, 1987).
5 Natalie Zemon Davis, *Society and Culture in Early Modern France* (Stanford: Stanford University Press, 1975), 124–51.
6 Mary Russo, 'Female Grotesques', in Teresa de Lauretis (ed.), *Feminist Studies, Critical Studies* (Bloomington: Indian University Press, 1986), 217.
7 Teresa de Lauretis, *Technologies of Gender* (Bloomington: Indiana University Press, 1987), 109.
8 For example 'Roseanne goes nuts!', in the *Enquirer*, 9 Apr. 1989, and 'My insane year', in *People Weekly*, 9 Oct. 1989: 85–6. Like other labels of deviancy, madness is often attached to the unruly woman.
9 Mikhail Bakhtin, *Rabelais and His World*, trans. Helene Iswolsky (Bloomington: Indiana University Press, 1984).
10 Nancy M. Henley, *Body Politics: Power, Sex and Non-verbal Communication* (Englewood Cliffs, NJ: Prentice-Hall, 1977), 38.
11 Ibid. 91.
12 In 'What am I anyway, a Zoo?', *New York Times*, 31 July 1989, she enumerates the ways people have interpreted what she stands for – the regular housewife, the mother, the postfeminist, the 'Little Guy', fat people, the 'Queen of Tabloid America', 'the body politic', sex, 'angry womankind herself', 'the notorious and sensationalistic La Luna madness of an ovulating Abzugienne woman run wild', etc.
13 *Roseanne*, 51.
14 *People Weekly*, 85–6.
15 Pierre Bourdieu, *Distinction: A Social Critique of the Judgement of Taste*, trans. Richard Nice (Cambridge, Mass.: Harvard University Press, 1984), 208.

36

Marlon Brando in *On the Waterfront*

James Naremore

Unlike the other stars I have been discussing, Marlon Brando is commonly associated with an innovative "school," a theoretical approach to acting that gives us an opportunity to compartmentalize him. The technical distinction between Brando and his predecessors, however, is sometimes more apparent than real. The more one studies Brando's work, the more one doubts that it can be explained as the result of a pedagogy or that the pedagogy itself can be neatly separated from the main tradition of American film acting.

Consider one of the most celebrated moments in Brando's career. Early in *On the Waterfront*, he and Eva Marie Saint are walking through a children's school yard. She accidentally drops one of her white gloves, and Brando picks it up. They pause, and he sits on a playground swing in the center of the composition; as they talk, he casually slips the glove over his hand. Critics frequently cite this piece of business as a *locus classicus* of Method technique (see, for example, Higson, 12). Director Elia Kazan once discussed it at length in response to an interviewer who asked how the work of the Actors' Studio had influenced his films; the incident, he suggested, was at least partly improvised, revealing an important psychological subtext:

> The glove was his way of holding her. Furthermore, whereas he couldn't, because of this tension about her brother being killed, demonstrate any sexual or loving feeling towards her, he could towards the glove. And he put his hand inside the glove, you remember, so that the glove was both his way of holding on to her against her will, and at the same time he was able to express through the glove something he couldn't express to her directly. So the object, in that sense, did it all. (Ciment, 45–46)

Brando's handling of the glove is clearly an impressive moment, a little more flirtatious than Kazan's description indicates. Why it should exemplify the Method, however, is not clear: the idea of a subtext was not new in Hollywood performances, and every form of realist acting (especially the older, silent, movie form) encourages the use of expressive objects.

I shall return to the problem of recognizing the Method in practice, but for now I would like to suggest that the truly striking aspect of the scene has more to do with Brando's persona than with the Actors' Studio. The fact is, few virile male leads before him (with the possible exception of Cagney) would so effortlessly have slipped on a woman's glove. Quite apart from its narrative implications or its presumptive sources in the Method, the gesture helps point up what Kazan has elsewhere described as the "bisexual" effect of Brando's image (Downing, 21). Even when he is playing a slightly punchy ex-boxer, there is something deeply sensual about him, an Olivier-like delicacy in the movement of his hands that makes an effective contrast with his weight-lifter's torso and his Roman head. (The same quality can be seen in his eyes and mouth, and it is interesting that the eye makeup he uses for the Terry Malloy character makes him look both punched-out and somewhat "feminine.") Consider also the pose on the swing, which establishes Malloy's childlike nature and at the same time typifies the star – a relaxed, "cool" posture, suggesting macho power mixed with sexy, graceful indolence. Brando creates the same feeling in later movies, well after he has grown heavy and middle aged. Watch him in *The Chase* (1966), when he saunters out on the front steps of his sheriff's office and pauses briefly to survey the town; his Stetson is slanted forward and he rests his weight on one leg, cocking his knee forward in a Michelangelo pose. Or notice the famous poster for *Last Tango in Paris* (1973), which shows his body in silhouette, seated in a reclining chair, his knees bent and his legs crossed like those of a gloomy decadent.

All of which may help to explain why Brando was so effective as the stud of Tennessee Williams's dramas (*A Streetcar Named Desire* [1951] and *The Fugitive Kind* [1959]), and why he has appeared so memorably in the roles of homosexual fantasy figures – a biker in *The Wild One* (1954) and an unusually dandified cowboy in *One-Eyed Jacks* (1961). Later he seemed to exaggerate this tendency, playing a foppish Mr Christian in *Mutiny on the Bounty* (1962), a closet gay in *Reflections in a Golden Eye* (1967), and a polymorphously perverse villain who cross-dresses and talks seductively to his horse in *The Missouri Breaks* (1976). He also lends a frighteningly eroticized quality to violence; he is frequently depicted as a sadistic character (*Streetcar*, *Last Tango*, *The Nightcomers* [1972], and *The Missouri Breaks*), or he is shown being horribly maimed or beaten by people who take pleasure in giving out punishment (*Waterfront*, *The Chase*, and *One-Eyed Jacks* – the last a film in which he plays a young man named "Kid" who gets his fingers crushed in public by "Dad" Longworth.)

A high contrast to the utterly straight Waynes, Gables, and Pecks of the 1940s, Brando is symptomatic of the period that produced Montgomery Clift, James Dean, Elvis Presley, and Marilyn Monroe – all of them brooding, ostensibly inarticulate types who suggested a scandalous sexuality and who signaled American entertainment's drift toward adolescent audiences in the decades after the war. Indeed Brando's relation to this particular group of stars can be demonstrated more easily than his indebtedness to the Method. For example, the accent he uses in *One-Eyed Jacks* seems to have been modeled on Presley's, and he and Presley together virtually taught Dean how to play the quintessential sexy teenager of the 1950s. Dean's performance in *Rebel without a Cause* (1955) – a far cry from Andy Hardy – contains several obvious "borrowings" from *Waterfront*, including a scene where he uses a girl's compact for much the same purpose as Brando had used a woman's glove. The equally important influence of Presley on *Rebel without a Cause* is only slightly less apparent, perhaps because Warner Brothers was nervous about the implications of rock and roll: whenever the rebellious kids turn on a radio, we hear a big band.

Among the "rebel" stars of his day Brando always seemed the most gifted and intelligent, the least inclined to romantic excess or self-destruction. He was, however, contemptuous of celebrity and increasingly guilty about acting. He has probably appeared in more bad pictures than any important thespian since Orson Welles, and his disdain for show business has given a somewhat veiled effect to his work. Even in *Last Tango*, the most "biographical" of his performances, there is a deliberate coyness about the way his body is presented to the camera. As Norman Mailer once pointed out, Brando had been a virtual walking phallus in his early pictures; yet here, where the role is to some extent parodic and where we expect to see him stripped down and demystified, he is photographed in a gauzy light with his back turned.[1]

Unlike the typical Stanislavskian, Brando has also tended to hide behind changes of accent and makeup. He has been a Mexican in *Viva Zapata* (1952), an Oriental in *Teahouse of the August Moon* (1956), a southerner in at least six pictures, and a white-haired Nazi officer in *The Young Lions* (1958). In the 1950s he was Stanley Kowalski, Napoleon, Marc Antony, and Sky Masterson all within a few years of each other – as if he were trying to escape both a "realist" tag and the fixed image of a movie star. Ultimately he adopted the shaggy-dog manner of a theatrical ham, choosing pictures that allowed him to play stylized imperialist villains (*The Ugly American* [1963], *Burn!* [1969], *Apocalypse Now* [1979]) or that earned him large sums of money for campy performances (*Candy* [1968], *The Night of the Following Day* [1969], *Superman* [1978]). Somehow he was able to retain enough respect for his artistic ability to create interest simply by being a famous man who does a cotton-in-cheek act, donning funny clothes and speaking in strange voices. His reliance on mimicry is particularly ironic in the context of *The Godfather* (1972), Hollywood's most self-conscious tribute to the Method. The cast in both parts of that film consists largely of players from the Actors' Studio; Brando and Strasberg, separated by parts one and two, are given the roles of patriarchs, but Brando gives a stronger sense than anyone of "putting on" his characterization.

At the time of *On the Waterfront* Brando's ambivalence about his work and his rather playful theatrically were less apparent: he was a sensational, slightly scary sex object, and he quickly became known as what Andrew Sarris has called an "axiom of the Method." Although the first of these attributes is obvious, the second is problematic. Critics often invoke Brando's name as they do Picasso's, to denote both an individual style and an artistic movement; yet Brando himself has disclaimed any significant influence from the Actors' Studio, and no one has come forward with an explanation of Method acting that would allow us to recognize every instance of it on the screen. Undoubtedly Hollywood saw commercial value in associating stars with a new style (even one that fostered an image of "artistic" outsiders who disdained the usual publicity), but where criticism is concerned, the word Method has always been vague, capable of indicating a variety of phenomena. Thus in books on the subject, Brando is sometimes lumped together with such different people as Joanne Woodward, David Wayne, and Shelly Winters, all of whom worked extensively with Lee Strasberg.[2] The result, as Richard Dyer has remarked, is that "the formal differences between the Method and, say, the repertory/Broadway style are less clear than the known differences between how the performances were arrived at" (154). Given these problems, a study of Brando's work in *Waterfront* needs to be prefaced by a brief history of the Method, both as a practice and as a critical term.

Perhaps one reason why the Method has dubious value as a term denoting a style is that it was never intended to refer to a performing technique in the strict sense. It consisted of a series of quasi-theatrical exercises, often resembling psychological therapy, designed to "unblock" the actor and put him or her in touch with sensations and emotions. Most of all, it tried to develop an "affective" or "emotional memory" that functioned rather like an onion concealed in a handkerchief, producing real rather than artificial tears. Players who used the Method continued to work in their own emotional idiolect, but they learned to manipulate buried sensory recollections and the Stanislavskian "as if," thus appearing more natural and spontaneous. Technically, they were not "living the part," and they were warned against using emotional memories during actual performances (advice they did not always follow – hence the slightly abstracted look associated with some actors). The point of the training was simply to put performers in a receptive state, thereby facilitating what was *already* recognized as "good" realistic drama. Lee Strasberg's claims could sometimes sound quite modest: "The entire purpose of the 'Method' or our technique or whatever you want to call it," he wrote, "is to find a way to start in each of us [a] creative process so that a good deal of the things we know but are not aware of will be used on the stage to create what the author sets for us to do" (Cole and Chinoy, 629).

Where film is concerned, we can speak of an intuitive Method that was at work from the beginning, helping to shape the classic narrative cinema. Consider the affinities between Stanislavsky and Griffith: both were part of a turn-of-the-century attempt to make proscenium framing and blocking seem less artificial: both were interested in a subtext of intimate, emotionally charged acting: and both were attracted to a mixture of local color and melodrama (one of Stanislavsky's favorite plays was *The Two Orphans*). Alla Nazimova, a Hollywood star in the years 1916–20, had been one of Stanislavsky's pupils, and, as noted previously,

Pudovkin's classic treatise on film acting had advocated an explicitly Stanislavskian technique. Hence there was a good deal of truth in Strasberg's well-known remark that Gary Cooper resembled a Method actor. Strasberg later qualified the statement, but aren't the movies the place above all others where actors have perfected the art of playing "themselves"? And couldn't *High Noon* (1952) be described as a Stanislavskian Western?

The term "Method" became fashionable in American dramatic criticism during the 1930s, with Lee Strasberg's adaptation of what was then called the "Stanislavsky System" to the productions of the Group Theater. The word appears in the subsequent writing of various members of the Group, including Robert Lewis, Stella Adler, and Elia Kazan: but above all it was nourished by Strasberg himself, who used it more than anyone else. When the Actors' Studio was established in 1947 by Kazan, Lewis, and Cheryl Crawford, Strasberg was given the job of full-time teacher or "moderator," and in that capacity he began to elaborate what was initially a *politique* into a kind of theory. By the mid 1950s, he had turned the Studio into an institution that was related to Stanislavsky in roughly the same way that psychoanalysis is related to Freud. But even though the Studio was often associated with a new American style, its work was easily assimilated into the mainstream of expressive-realist acting, and its specific achievements are difficult to assess. For example, Brando and Marilyn Monroe are often singled out as two of the Studio's "pupils," but they barely qualify. Brando was trained chiefly at Erwin Piscator's Dramatic Workshop, where he encountered both Lewis and Strasberg but where he also learned about Brecht. His most influential teacher was the eclectic, politically committed Stella Adler (who must have been amused when he yelled "Stella!" every night on the stage in *A Streetcar Named Desire*). As for Monroe, she did little more than attend a few sessions at the Studio when she was already a star, sitting in the back row and helping Strasberg to become a celebrity.[3]

Strasberg's romanticism, his emphasis on ego psychology rather than on training for the voice and body, his courting of celebrities in his guise of philosopher and therapist – all these things were retrograde developments in a richer, more productive Stanislavskian tradition that precedes him. The Master's own "theory" had been little more than a distillation of commonplaces that governed Western theater since the seventeenth century, combined with structures against pantomime and a series of training aids adapted from behaviorist psychology. Unlike Strasberg, however, Stanislavsky was a brilliant director who codified techniques for producing naturalist ensembles and who influenced generations after him. In the rather parochial teaching of the Actors' Studio, Stanislavsky's approach had been narrowed down to a quasi-Freudian "inner work" fueled by an obsession with the "self." Strasberg claimed to be teaching outside the theatrical event, and yet his moderating sessions were themselves performances, theatricalized encounters played out before a coterie audience, with Strasberg taking on the role of analyst. They helped make him a cult figure, but a case could be made that they impoverished the theater – feeding the star system, promoting conventional realism at the expense of the avant-garde, and giving American drama a less forceful social purpose.[4]

In this regard, we need to distinguish between the Studio and the earlier Group Theater, which mixed realistic social plays such as *The House of Connelly* with agitational, semi-Brechtian productions of *1931*, *Waiting for Lefty*, and *Johnny Johnson* (the last directed by Strasberg). In later years Strasberg de-emphasized the political basis of the Method, and, like most Stanislavkians, he always undervalued performances in the alternative comic, modernist, or decon-structive modes. Furthermore, his rather analytic approach to the actor's "self" was different from the Group Theater's stress on the ensemble and on the relationship between individual players and society as a whole. Here is Stella Adler describing the first principle of acting for the Group:

> We asked the actor to become aware of himself. Did he have any problems? Did he understand them in relation to his whole life? To society? Did he have a point of view in relation to these questions?
>
> A point of view was necessary, he was told. The actor should begin to question and learn to understand a great many things. A better understanding of himself would inevitably result. It would be of great artistic use for the actors to have a common point of view which they could share with the other co-workers of the theater. The actor was told that it was necessary and important to convey this point of view through plays to audiences: that theatrical means and methods had to be found to do this in a truthful and artistic way. (Cole and Chinoy, 602–3)

By contrast, the Actors' Studio was much less interested in a "point of view," and its jargon had a familiar ring: "private moment," "freedom," "naturalness," "organic" – the keywords of romantic individualism.

Whatever the Studio's limitations, Strasberg was unquestionably a gifted teacher who inspired actors and provided ways of producing "lifelike" perfor-mances in contemporary settings. Furthermore, under his direction, the Studio never completely lost sight of its origins in the socially critical atmosphere of the 1930s. From the beginning Strasberg's teaching manifested a tendency toward the kind of theater for which Stanislavskian aesthetics had been originally designed, thus contributing to a proliferation of naturalistic social drama in the 1950s. Because there was a recognizable look to the male stars of these dramas, the term Method soon acquired a critical life of its own, associated with a dramatic genre and an actorly "personality."

As a description of film acting, the Method therefore seems most useful when it points to something at once broader and more specific than either Brando or the teaching of the Actors' Studio – that is, when it indicates a stylistic or ideological leaning within 1950s culture, which has left its traces on contemporary Holly-wood. In the context of a discussion of film noir, David Bordwell has pointed out that most words denoting style function in this way. They usually begin as negative assertions, signaling the "repudiation of a norm," but when critics later use them as positive definitions, they become unwieldy, making sense only when they refer to "particular patterns of non-conformity" within a dominant mode (75). Hence when Brando is described as a "Method actor" in *Waterfront*, the term can be taken to mean – correctly – that he was exposed to ideas of the Group Theater and the Actors' Studio during the late 1940s and 1950s; but it also implies some combination of the following non-conformist "patterns," each of which helps to describe his image:

(1) He appears in a naturalistic setting. *Waterfront* belongs in company with a series of "social problem" films, most of them shot on location and directed by Kazan, that began to appear in Hollywood after World War II. During the 1950s, such films were usually produced independently, with black-and-white formats that resembled those of prestigious television shows rather than big-screen movies. They frequently involved Actors' Studio personnel (*A Face in the Crowd* [1957], *A Hatful of Rain* [1957], *The Strange One* [1958]), or they were based on scripts by writers like Odets and Chayefsky (*The Big Knife* [1955], *Marty* [1955], *The Sweet Smell of Success* [1957]). They had a good deal in common with a slightly later outpouring of British neorealism (*Room at the Top* [1959], *Saturday Night and Sunday Morning* [1960]), and despite their sometimes naive or compromised politics, they represented a turn toward what Raymond Williams has defined as "authentic naturalism" as opposed to mere "bourgeois physical representation." "Naturalism," Williams writes, "was always a critical movement, in which the relation between men and their environments was not merely *represented* but *actively explored* . . . it is quite evidently a bourgeois form, [but] it is also, on its record, part of the critical and self-critical wing of the bourgeoise" (*Culture*, 170, my emphasis).

(2) He acts out the "existential paradigm." In certain ways, Brando's Terry Malloy is a typical 1950s protagonist, resembling not only the three characters played by Dean but also such ostensibly different fellows as John Osborne's Jimmy Porter in *Look Back in Anger*. Thus he is an "outsider," resentful of bourgeois society and "existentially" rebellious. As Fredric Jameson remarks, this is a "middle-brow media usage" of existentialism, entailing the favorite liberal theme of "the inability to communicate." Whether the character is a laborer, an upwardly mobile son of a wage-earning family, or an affluent teenager, he has the same problem: an uneasiness with official language and no words for his love or rage. At the same time, he brims over with sensitivity and feeling, the intensity of his emotion giving him a slightly neurotic aspect. The Method's stress on "affective memory" probably fuels his emotionalism. "The agonies and exhalations of method acting," Jameson notes, "were perfectly calculated to render [an] asphyxiation of the spirit that cannot complete its sentence." Ironically, however (especially in second-generation graduates of the Actors' Studio like Al Pacino), inarticulateness becomes what Jameson calls "the highest form of expressiveness . . . and the agony over uncommunicability suddenly turns out to be everywhere fluently comprehensible" (80–1).

(3) He deviates from the norms of classical rhetoric. Looked at today, Brando hardly seems unusual, but at the time of *Waterfront*, he was known for his

"slouch" and "mumble." Like Dean, he spoke softly, sometimes departed slightly from scripted dialogue, and used regional or "ethnic" accents (many of them never heard in movies except in comedy).[5] At the same time, his body was almost self-consciously loose, and many of the working-class or outlaw characters he played allowed him to mock the "good manners" of traditional theater. In *One-Eyed Jacks*, for example, he eats Sunday dinner with Karl Malden and makes a great show of talking with his mouth full: later in the same film, he keeps a matchstick in his mouth during a barroom conversation, even drinking tequila around it; still later, in the midst of a romantic encounter with a young woman, he abstractedly cleans his ear with his finger. It should be stressed, however, that Brando's work is always fluently representational and "centered," in keeping with the basic demands of narrative cinema. He never breaks the illusion, he never departs radically from the script, and his movements are never as casual as they seem. For instance, in *Waterfront*, he makes an amusing and nicely calculated turn when one of the federal investigators (Martin Balsam) calls out to Terry Malloy amid a crowd of men on the docks: we see him reluctantly glance over his shoulder that is nearest the voice; he starts to move but then changes direction, slowly revolving the long way around to make his response look contemptuous. Here and in other places he is conscious of the way people "revise" actions in everyday life; even so, he takes care to observe the spatial dynamics of ordinary movie acting. If he seemed unusual in his day, it was chiefly because he often gazed downward or off into space during conversations and because his posture and speaking style made other actors look politely stiff.

Only the last of these three "patterns of non-conformity" is concerned exclusively with what Richard Dyer has called "performance signs," and only at this level can we speculate on the relation between Brando's work and the specifics of Method teaching. For example, the "truth" of emotions in Stanislavskian drama was frequently elicited by improvisational techniques, which brought a feeling of halting spontaneity and verisimilitude to performances. The exercises in "affective memory," which Robert Lewis and Lee Strasberg first discovered in the teachings of Stanislavsky's disciple Richard Boleslavsky, may have indirectly contributed to Brando's hipsterish posture: Lewis had emphasized that one of the essential means of inducing emotional recall was "complete physical relaxation" (Cole and Chinoy, 631). Boleslavsky (who was influenced by a nineteenth-century behavioral psychologist named Theodule Ribot) encouraged relaxation not only in the training exercises but also on the stage; he had even devised a formula for achieving the best results: "Think [of your muscles] constantly, to relax them as soon as you feel any tension...you must watch yourself all day long, at whatever you do, and be able to relax each superfluous tension" (Cole and Chinoy, 513).

In more general terms, Brando's emotionality and slight abstractedness has something in common with the Method's valuation of expression over rhetoric – an essentially romantic attitude that reaches its ultimate form in what Strasberg called the "private moment." In the Actors' Studio, Strasberg frequently requested professional actors to imagine or relive an experience for themselves alone, ignoring their audience. Paradoxically, this stress on inwardness some-times resulted in a shrill, almost hysteric quality – for example, in the work of the entire cast of *Splendor in the Grass* (1961) or in any performance by Rod Steiger. It gave Hollywood acting an emotionalism not seen since the days of Griffith, but it reversed Griffith's priorities, viewing characters in somewhat clinical rather than purely moral terms and (in its first stages at least) centering on male rather than female stars. As Andrew Higson has observed. "In some ways you can read the Method as a reinvestment of emotionality into the narrative film, where emotionality is conventionally associated with the feminine" (19).

In fact, Method-trained players seemed to relish the opportunity to weep (partly, one suspects, because emotionality is associated with "fine acting"), and in the process they helped establish what Virginia Wexman describes as the selective "softness" of 1950s male protagonists.[6] Except in *Last Tango*, Brando himself seldom sheds tears on screen – in *Waterfront*, for example, his deepest pain is registered off camera, during the scene where he mourns the death of his beloved pigeons. But as Peter Biskind has remarked, other Method stars of the decade seemed to adopt Johnny Ray's "Cry" as their theme song: James Dean's incessant tearfulness in *East of Eden* (1955) even forces a rebuke from Julie Harris: "Do you want to cry all your life?" The persistence of Method training into the 1970s ultimately resulted in Jack Nicholson's traumatic weeping in *Five Easy Pieces* (1970) – a moment that Nicholson says he conceived himself, using personal associations with a speech the character makes to his father. "I think it was a breakthrough," he told a writer for the *New York Times*. "I don't think they'd had this level of emotion, really, in almost any male character until that point" (Rosenbaum, 19). By the 1970s, a reemergent feminism and a relaxation of censorship had enabled women (who were always allowed tears) to use the same hesitant, potentially rebellious, neurotically intense expressiveness as the Method males. Ann-Margret's slightly Monroe-like Bobbie in *Carnal Knowledge* (1971) is one qualified example, but consider also three female stars who were more systematically exposed to Actors' Studio teaching: Faye Dun-away, Jane Fonda, and Diane Keaton. They are as good as James Dean at using "affective memory," and like him they are fond of indicating a brooding, restless emotionalism that their characters struggle to repress.

All of which brings us back to Brando's indolent pose on the child's swing in *Waterfront* and to his manipulation of a woman's glove. We can never know if he is truly feeling the emotions he acts, and we have only Kazan's suggestion that some of his behavior was improvised. There is, in fact, good reason to doubt that the action was purely spontaneous: the whiteness of the garment and Brando's position at the exact center of the composition seem calculated to make his gestures especially visible. Nevertheless, the sequence contains readable attri-butes of Method cinema, including a mise-en-scène that is nearly indistinguish-able from documentary, and – in the case of Brando – a relaxed, sexy, sensitive performance filled with sidelong glances and unverbalized emotion. The function of the glove as an expressive object is also somewhat different from what it would be in the typical movie. If George Raft flips a coin in *Scarface* (1932), it becomes a motif associated with his character. If Dana Andrews plays with a child's toy in *Laura* (1944), it is referred to in the dialogue and shown in an insert, becoming an obvious sign of the character's need to maintain control. If Cary Grant pulls a matchbook from his pocket or handles Eva Marie Saint's travel razor in *North by Northwest*, these objects are not only singled out by the camera but used later in the narrative. The glove in *Waterfront* also has a purpose, but one that seems relatively unmotivated, more like an actor's than a writer's choice; Brando's handling of the garment is not prompted by anything but accident, and for that reason it looks spontaneous, contributing to the naturalistic cinema's love of verisimilitude.[7]

This verisimilar quality is in many ways evident throughout *Waterfront*. An independent production featuring actors from the New York stage rather than movie stars, the film was shot in a New Jersey locale that cameraman Boris Kaufman never glamorizes. On the surface it resembles Italian neo-realism and some of the Group Theater projects of the 1930s, although in other ways it is quite typical, recalling melodramas like *Angels with Dirty Faces*. (Budd Schulberg's script is based on a real-life character, but many people have noted that a film about a dockworker who cooperates with a federal investigation was an expedient project for Kazan; not long before the making of the film, he had served as a "friendly" witness before the House UnAmerican Activities Committee.) Like most other Hollywood films about social problems, *Waterfront* declares an evil – in this case, gangsterism in the New York labor unions – but avoids systemic analysis. Partly because of difficulties Kazan encountered with censors, the political attitudes beneath the gritty surface of his film seem especially familiar: a sentimental Christian populism mixed with a longing for a strong male hero to guide the masses. What gives the story its real novelty and interest is Brando, who brings a feeling of troubled adolescence to the central character, an attitude that would influence movies for years afterward.

Surprisingly, Brando was not the chief contender to play Malloy. Frank Sinatra, having established himself in *From Here to Eternity* (1953) as an actor of scrappy urban types, was under strong consideration and was reportedly furious when Kazan chose Brando instead. Brando himself seems to have approached the movie with a certain truculence, even though he turned in a performance so technically adept and intense that it energized the film and affected whole generations of actors. It is difficult to watch Newman in *The Left-Handed Gun* (1958), Beatty in *All Fall Down* (1962), Pacino in *Serpico* (1973), Stallone in *Rocky* (1976), Travolta in *Saturday Night Fever* (1977), Gere in *Bloodbrothers* (1978), or indeed any of Hollywood's proletarian sex symbols down to the present day (a more recent example is Sean Penn in *At Close Range* [1985]), without being reminded in some way of Brando in this role. He is a decisive moment in American cinema, one of those actors who represents a type so forcefully that it becomes a persistent feature of the culture.

In effect, Brando gives his working-class character a sex appeal based on the same fantasy that would later make James Dean the hero of a young cult: in Brando's hands *Waterfront* becomes the study of a tough but confused and sensitive male who wins his way to adulthood by overcoming brutal or misguided parent figures in an indifferent society. True, Brando plays an overweight former boxer who is pushing thirty: nevertheless, he is also a character who has been patronized and manipulated by older men and who acts as a kind of big brother to a group of street kids called the Golden Warriors. Brando lends to this plot situation his introspective manner and a sensual delicacy and sweetness that are all the more attractive for the way they coexist with the stocky, almost burly power of his head and physique; he is thus able to generate a remarkable sense of adolescent beauty and pathos. His shy but streetwise remarks, the sway of his walk, the absent-minded look in his eye as he chews gum, the way he sprawls on a pile of gunnysacks and flips through the pages of a girlie magazine – all these things function to establish him as a sort of child, in appealing contrast to the stereotypical and sententious "adults" who surround him.

Brando's every look, movement, and gesture is keyed to the essentially adolescent confusion of the character. Throughout, he oscillates between violence and childlike bewilderment, making visible Terry's conflict between the Social Darwinism of his criminal father-substitutes and the ideals of community inculcated by Edie Doyle and Father Barry. The film's strategy is to make Terry a synthesis of these two groups: a hero virile and independent enough to beat up the mobsters yet sensitive and caring enough to win the heart of Edie. As a structural ploy, the characterization works to maintain traditional patriarchal values while softening the male image; but Brando's performance and the particular thematic of *Waterfront* also yield more socially progressive effects than the usual movie. In *Rebel without a Cause*, for instance, the delinquent boy comes to embody the norms of a bourgeois family. The Brando film puts the rebel character in a different context, showing him choosing between cut-throat capitalism and the ethic of cooperation; it poses the selfishness of the paternalistic gangster–businessmen against the communal values of industrial labor and the church; and it falters only slightly by suggesting that Terry's "manhood" is achieved through a toe-to-toe slugging match. (The original ending was to have been different. Rod Steiger has said in an interview that Kazan and Schulberg wanted to close with "a shot of the dead boy floating down the river" [Leyda, 441], but the Hays Office insisted that crime could not triumph.)

Brando helps the central dynamic of the film succeed by letting us see a play of conflicts in his behavior. He gives an ambiguous significance to nearly all the objects he touches – for example, in one scene he angrily brandishes a pistol and then cradles it sadly against his cheek, converting it suddenly from a phallus into a breast. Notice also the way he uses the short jacket he wears, which is as obviously symbolic as James Dean's red windbreaker in *Rebel*. Sometimes Brando turns up the collar, drapes a loading hook around the neck, and stuffs his hands in the pockets; this rough-trade style contrasts with other moments when the jacket becomes a sign of his vulnerability, a thin line of defense against cold air and psychological pain. As Leo Braudy has noted, one of the most effective images in the film is Brando's wounded, solitary walk at the conclusion, the jacket "zippered tightly to keep the blood invisible inside" (242).

Brando's love scenes with Eva Marie Saint have a similar but more threatening dynamic, ranging in psychological effect from the moment when he tries on her glove like a child to the moment when he breaks down her door like a rapist. As a result, she alternately mothers him and shrinks away in fear. When they meet he wrestles playfully with her until she slaps his face; then when he discovers she is the sister of the man he inadvertently fingered for the mob, he stops in his tracks and does a beautifully understated double take, his eyes confused and anxious. Later he takes her to a dockside bar, teaches her how to drink a boilermaker, and proudly announces the philosophy of life he has learned from Johnny Friendly: "Do it to him before he does it to you." Only a moment afterward the camera closes in on his face to catch a glimpse of uncertainty as he mutters "I'd like ta help." Frustrated, he raises a hand to his chin, holding the thumb stiffly, almost as if he were going to suck it; then he pinches the chin between thumb and forefinger, pulling at it like a goatee. The gesture is more important than anything he says, expressing in one fluid movement the anguish of a child trying to be "manly."

"Some people just got faces that stick in your mind," Brando tells Saint in one of the film's most touching scenes. His own face is a fascinating blend of the pug and the poet – slightly ducktailed hair combed back to reveal a high forehead, battered but eloquent eyes, and full sensual lips. His nose is too straight for a boxer, but the width of his jaw and his slightly flattened profile make him look imposing, larger than in fact he is. Especially when standing still, he has a dancer's instinct for line and space, and he is good at calling attention to himself by being slightly quieter than the other actors. Contrary to what was first written about him, he does not mumble or scratch his way through the role. His "Method" consists of a softly articulated, sometimes repetitive speech, an abstracted stroking of his body as he talks, a troubled reluctance to look anyone in the eye, and a series of relaxed poses that imply athletic grace and sexuality.

Brando is less disassociated from his body than the typical leading man of his day, and his eyes are able to express a wide range of understated emotions in an instant of time. Like most male stars in Hollywood drama, however, he is required to be less animated than the secondary players, who are presented as vivid stereotypes. His occasional reserve helps to signify a power and stoicism similar to those of every action hero from John Wayne to Clint Eastwood, but when his reluctance to speak is combined with his emotional glances and his particular body language, he seems to be working subtly against the grain – not only of Hollywood in general but of everyone else in the film. Indeed, as Virginia Wexman has remarked, early Method acting became so heavily associated with star images that a picture like *Waterfront* often deliberately accentuates Brando's low-key behavior, marking him off from the other players.

Consider, for example, the way Brando contrasts with Lee J. Cobb and the rest of the cast in an early scene in the Union Hall. Cobb is wildly overstated – stalking around a pool table at the center of the room, staring with Neanderthal fascination at a boxing match on TV, chewing great hunks of a sandwich, and complaining that "there's nobody tough anymore." Brando enters slowly, head slightly bowed, wearing a dark pullover that makes him look slim and subdued. He responds to Cobb's "Hiya, Slugger!" with slight embarrassment, shyly holding out a hand to shake. Cobb ducks the hand, feints, and begins a mock boxing match that foreshadows the real combat at the end of the film, circling behind Brando to lift him in a fatherly bear hug. Throughout all this, Brando's movements are half-hearted, his smile wan and forced. While Cobb tells how he fought his way to the top of the union, yanking his collar open to reveal his battle scars, Brando reacts as though he knows the story all too well. Then he turns his back to the camera and leans against the pool table, playing most of the scene from a "weak" position typical of naturalistic drama. His head droops like that of a child trying to avoid attention, but meanwhile he stands at the center of the composition, gazed at by the other players; light from above models his hunched shoulders, giving him the power-in-repose look of classical statuary.

Brando's one partly assertive moment comes later in the scene, when he complains about the Joey Doyle incident. "I just figure I shoulda been told," he says, eyebrows raised in mock innocence, eyes meeting Cobb's and then sliding off to a distant horizon, palms rubbing together slowly but nervously. "Here, kid, here's half a bill," Cobb says, stuffing money into the collar of the pullover. In a flash, several expressions cross Brando's face: defensive shock, a flinch as if the money were burning his skin, and nearly imperceptible nausea – communicated by a curl of his upper lip, which he quickly hides by turning his head from our view and Cobb's. He exits as quietly as he arrived, tossing a jacket over his shoulder and sauntering off into the smoky light of an anteroom.

The same naturalistic rhetoric and the same feeling of power and nobility hidden beneath a vulnerable, inarticulate surface, help to account for Brando's impact in the celebrated taxicab scene, which encapsulates the film's major themes in a single, virtually self-contained, episode and forever establishes one definition of the Method. On the level of classical plot structure, the encounter between Charlie and Terry Malloy has been perfectly written, with a strong "through line" and a series of emotional changes that mark a beginning, middle, and end. For his part, Steiger's character has a compelling dramatic purpose: he has been ordered to stop Brando from cooperating with a federal crime commission or else to kill him – an action that ultimately involves a choice between saving himself and saving his brother. Steiger therefore undergoes a variety of quick, apparently spontaneous changes as the scene progresses: at first he smiles nervously, trying to be paternalistic and manipulative; when this fails, he becomes by turns abusive, threatening, and distraught, at last falling back in guilt, exhaustion, and fear as he lets Brando go free. By contrast, Brando operates from a fairly secure position, largely *reacting* to events. Wise to Steiger's patronizing attitude, he tolerates everything until the scene provides him with what one contemporary manual of Stanislavskian acting calls a "beat change" – a sudden reversal of the action, motivated by the character's discovery of new information.[8] When Brando realizes that Steiger is "taking him for a ride," a close-up marks his shocked response. Painfully and almost gently, he begins lecturing Steiger, charging him with having betrayed their relationship years before. His quiet speech leads to a climatic moment of recognition, and the scene ends in silence as each man contemplates what has happened.

The physical and rhetorical requirements of this scene are minimal, with the two actors placed in relatively "gestureless" positions, so that inflections and tones of voice carry the meaning. In fact, Brando and Steiger are hunched together to the point where they can barely move, their every glance and twitch microscopically studied. Venetian blinds have been drawn over the car's rear window to heighten the feeling of claustrophobia, and Leonard Bernstein's overinsistent score keeps pounding away on the soundtrack; the result is a feeling of almost hallucinatory, over-heated naturalism, a sense of hysteria held in check by the tiny enclosure and the muttered New-Yorkese. Of the two performances, however, Brando's is noticeably more recessive, calculated to gain strength in relation to Steiger's inherent shrillness.

At the beginning of the scene, Steiger sits bundled up in his topcoat, his snap-brim hat and beady eyes pointed intently at Brando, who slouches back, glancing away out the side window, his hands relaxed on his knees. The conversation starts in a fairly innocuous way, with Steiger's nervousness and Brando's slightly knowing smile revealing its subtext. Finally, in near panic over Brando's impending betrayal of the union gang, Steiger's voice begins to rise while Brando responds in a still, almost sleepy tone that gives his dialogue a poetic flavor. When Steiger calls him a "rubber-lipped ex-tanker" and warns him to change his mind before they reach 437 River Street, Brando reacts. We can see the new information registering, leading to a kind of shock. In medium shot, he frowns at Steiger, and then he begins slowly, quietly, and intently shaming him, characteristically repeating a line to make it seem a spontaneous sign of Terry's bewilderment and growing anger: "Before we get to *where*, Charlie? Before we get to *where?*" In desperation, Steiger pulls out a gun, holding it so ineptly that we immediately feel his lack of conviction. Brando's face modulates from disbelief to disgust, and then breaks into a weary, disappointed smile. "Oh, Charlie, *wow!*" he says – the last banal word, softly sighed, becoming an eloquent reproach.

The scene's climatic speeches derive much of their power from Brando's rhythms and gestures, which reveal tides of emotion running beneath Terry Malloy's supposedly clumsy talk. When he recalls how he was forced to take a dive, he reaches out and touches Steiger gently on the shoulder with the tips of his fingers, a shadow of bitterness and sarcasm crossing his eyes. "It was you," he says in a near whisper. "You was my brother, Charlie. You shoulda looked out for me a little bit." Then he glances away and raises his right hand in the air, palm toward his face, fingers spread and curled like those of an actor playing Hamlet. All of Brando's energy seems collected in that hand, the rest of his body held in languid abeyance. Turning to Steiger, he gives the gesture an angry inflection. "You don't understand!" he says in an urgent undertone. His puffy eyes look up toward some imagined ideal, and his mouth twists in pain at the memory of a wasted life. Again he whispers, turning the sentences into a litany: "I coulda had *class!* I coulda been a contender! I coulda been somebody!" He savors the poetic, musicalized flavor of the three lines – not only the chanting repetition of "coulda," but the alliteration, internal rhyme, and subtle augmentation in "coul*da* bee*na* conten*da*." Then he expels breath and lets the rest of the speech out in a rapid, prosaic fall: "... instead of just a bum, which is what I am, let's face it."

At this point, the relationship between the two men has been partly reversed, and their postures indicate the change. Steiger, the well-heeled, guiltily protective older brother, is reduced to a child who squirms in his seat as Brando speaks a saddened adult truth. Finally Steiger clutches his gloved fingers together and slumps back almost tearfully, his hat pushed up from his forehead. On the opposite side of the screen, Brando rests his chin in his palm and turns his gaze out the window. Silence descends, marking the exchange as a touchstone of American film acting, and as one of the best-remembered moments in either player's career.

The taxicab scene eventually became a part of folklore, the "contender" speech being alluded to in other films. The sequence also contributed heavily to what Richard De Cordova, borrowing from Foucault, has called the "discourse on acting," partly because it was so neatly self-contained, so observant of classical unities, and so completely centered on the two players. In such a context, naturalistic inflections of performance – always consistent with an underlying logic of well-made theater – tended to stand out in sharp relief. The irony, of course, was that an apparent search for "truth" and "authenticity" had turned into a showcase for technique.

We should not be surprised at this phenomenon: any slight departure from well-established convention quickly becomes evident as a stylistic choice. Moreover, naturalistic social drama has always been faced with contrary demands. On the one hand, it wants to persuade us that "the world is like this," but on the other, it wants to make moral or ethical judgments about the world. As a result, such drama tends to undermine stage rhetoric selectively while adhering to melodramatic structures of character and action. *Waterfront*, for example, was conceived as a documentary-like exposé but maintains the traditions of the gangster movie; in the case of Method acting, a system of training that aims to transcend mere playacting depends, at bottom, on a star system.

Looked at today, what seems distinctive about the taxicab scene between Brando and Steiger is not its underlying approach to cinema but its mannerisms, especially the timing and emotional "beat" of the conversation, which differs from the more regular give-and-take of 1940s Hollywood rhetoric. This – combined with the slouched postures, the quiet but intense emotionalism, and the "ethnic" accents – has always been the popular idea of the Method. Brando's own cleverness fostered such a definition. The Method was articulated in terms of "essences," but audiences looked at surfaces; for them, the much-talked-about new technique was associated with behavioral tics and a star image. Thus, while the Actors' Studio valued emotional freedom and individuality, it soon elevated Brando's work to an ideal. In subsequent years, a good many aspiring male actors approached the Studio like a shrine, hoping to make their performances more "real"; in practice, however, they often imitated the early Brando, who became godfather to several generations of players.

Notes

1   Bertolucci allows Brando to improvise in a casual way, and he merges the character of Paul with the roles and biography of the star: "You know he was a boxer? That didn't work . . . so he became an actor, then a racketeer on the waterfront in New York . . . It didn't last long . . . played the bongo drums . . . revolutionary in South America . . . One day lands in Tahiti." This sometimes playful self-referentiality, however, does not result in a Brechtian distanciation. Like the Method teachers, Bertolucci is an idealist, hoping to fuse the actor and character, thereby arriving at a psychological truth. He has claimed that he was looking for the "roots of human behavior," and for "absolute authenticity"; Brando, meanwhile, has called his work in the film a "violation of my innermost self." Despite such mystic pronouncements, *Last Tango* tends to romanticize both Brando and Hollywood cinema. Bertolucci said that he could not reveal Brando's genitals because he felt so much identification with the character: "To show him naked would have been like showing myself naked." Apparently he had no such qualms about Maria Schneider, who is not only shown in full frontal nudity, but is also assigned the role of a typical *femme fatale*. (For a complete, more sympathetic account of the film in light of contemporary theory, see Yosefa Loshitsky. "The Radical Aspect of Self-Reflexive Cinema," Ph.D. diss., Indiana University, 1987. The quotations above are taken from this source.)

2   For a history of Method acting in the United States (though it makes somewhat broad claims for the Actors' Studio), see Foster Hirsch, *A Method to Their Madness: The History of the Actors' Studio* (New York: Norton, 1984).

3   The list of movie stars who actually worked with Strasberg is impressive: James Dean, Paul Newman, Jack Nicholson, Bruce Dern, Al Pacino, Jane Fonda, etc. Nevertheless, the very fact that the Studio became an entry point for Hollywood is an indication of how far Strasberg had moved from the repertory ideals of the Moscow Art Theater and from his own original aims.

4   In fact, Strasberg found himself in one of the most contradictory positions in American theater. The Studio had been established as a place where professional actors could work on their craft apart from the dictates of the marketplace: but the actors' lives were determined by a capitalist economy, and any school they attended could not help but become what D. H. Lawrence would have called an adjunct of the "factory."

5 Some viewers took Brando's slur in *Streetcar* as the sign of an untutored primitive; later, in a move virtually designed to prove he was an actor, he played Shakespeare alongside Gielgud, and it became apparent that he was an accomplished mimic with a soft but quite musical voice. His films are filled with artful uses of dialect and playful turns of phrase. Like many of the best poets, he seems to have listened well to demotic speech. Sometimes his accent mocks the film – in *The Chase*, for example, he slyly calls the Robert Redford character "Bubber," even though everyone else pronounces it "Bubba." My favorite of his impersonations is *One-Eyed Jacks*, in which he speaks such insults as "Git up, you skum-suckin pig!" Calder Wallingham's script is keyed to the voices of players like Slim Pickens and Ben Johnson, and Brando's drawl is similar to theirs, as in the moment when he explains why he had to shoot a man in a bar: "He didn't gimme no selection."

6 "Softness" in male performance often functions to persuade the audience of a virile player's belief in his role. On July 20, 1987, the *New Yorker* magazine quoted an anonymous foreign observer of Lt. Col. Oliver North's televised appearance before the congressional Iran–Contra hearings: " 'He has the oblique, diagonal eyebrows of Lillian Gish. . . . and that same American quality of always seeming about to burst into tears' " (19).

7 Brando's decision to wear the glove may or may not have been prompted by Method teaching; it is nonetheless a good instance of his sheer cleverness. His career is filled with small, inventive, if less richly functional pieces of business – for instance, in a conversation during *The Chase*, he slowly rubs the bowl of a pipe along the side of his nose to oil the wood.

8 See Bruder et al., *A Practical Handbook for the Actor*, 87. This text is derived from what is sometimes called the "Mamet method," or the teachings of playwright David Mamet. The "beat change" describes any emotional fluctuation in a dramatic scene. In movies, such changes are often marked by a close-up; for example, in Wyler's *Jezebel* (1938), when Bette Davis discovers that the man she loves has married someone else. The change can also occur within a long take; compare Wyler's *The Letter* (1940), when Bette Davis's lawyer visits her in prison and calmly tells her that a piece of evidence has been found that might convict her of murder. In long shot, we see a shadow of unease cross her face, and then her attempt to mask the emotion.

Part XII

Permutations of Difference

Introduction

Robert Stam

Although autonomous individuals participate in the cinema, these individuals are traversed by social force fields, and specifically by relations of social domination and subordination. Film producers and receivers are not just individuals in the abstract; they are of a specific nationality, class, gender, and sexuality. Much of recent film theory/analysis has focused on these axes of social identity and oppression, the diverse forms of stratification which mold both art and social life. Which brings up the issue of the relation between all these distinct axes of social representation. The very language which we use to address oppression, Elisabeth Young-Bruehl explains, comes to us from distinct discursive traditions: (1) the tradition of anti-colonialist and anti-racist writing; (2) postwar discussions of antisemitism and Nazism; and (3) the Women's Liberation movement (Young-Bruehl, 1996: 23–5). We have to ask whether one of the axes of oppression is primordial, the root of all the others. Is class the foundation of all oppressions, as canonical Marxism had suggested? Or is patriarchy ultimately more fundamental to social oppression than classism and racism, as some versions of feminism might suggest? Or is race the overarching determinant? Can one "allegorize" one kind of oppression, say racism, through another form of oppression, such as sexism? Are there "analogical structures of feeling" which would lead one oppressed group to identify with another? What are the analogies between antisemitism, anti-black racism, sexism, and homophobia? Both homophobia and antisemitism have in common a penchant for projecting enormous power on to their targeted victims: "they" control everything, or "they" are trying to take over. But what is unique and specific to each of these forms of oppression? A person can be the victim of homophobia within his/her own family, for example, something far less likely in the case of antisemitism or anti-black racism. To what extent can one "ism" hang out, as it were, with other isms? Sexism, racism, and classism can all tinge themselves with homophobia, for example. What is essential is not to ghettoize these axes of representation, to see that race is classed, that gender is raced, and so forth. In Part XII we will treat some of these issues, with special emphasis on issues of race.

What is most striking about film theory's relation to "race" is that for so long it sustained a remarkable silence on the subject. For most of this century film theory seems to have had the illusion of being "raceless." There are few references to race in the film theorists of the silent period, for example, even though that period coincided with the heights of European imperialism and of scientific racism, and with myriad colonialist films like *King of the Cannibals* and *Le Musulman Rigolo*. (Ella Shohat focuses on such representations in chapter 38.)

Most of the protesting about such representations was left to the community newspapers of racialized communities, and to organizations such as the NAACP. Much of the community-related work on ethnic/racial stereotypes, for example in African American newspapers like *The Californian Eagle*, was devoted to demonstrating that films had misrepresented the community in question. Native Americans, very early on, vocally protested misrepresentations of their culture and history. A 1911 *Moving Picture World* (August 3) reports a Native American delegation to President Taft protesting erroneous representations and even asking for a Congressional Investigation. In the same vein, the NAACP protested *Birth of a Nation*, Chicanos protested the "*bandido*" films, Mexicans protested *Viva Villa!* (1934), Cubans protested *Cuban Love Song* (1931), and Latin Americans generally protested the caricaturing of their culture even in the films of the "Good Neighbor" period.

Contemporary racism, although hardly unique to the West, has historically been both an ally of and a partial product of colonialism. The most obvious victims of racism are those whose identity was forged within the colonial cauldron: Africans, Asians, and the indigenous peoples of the Americas as well as those displaced by colonialism or neo-colonialism such as Arabs in France. For our purposes, cinematic racism refers to all the contextual and textual practices whereby racialized difference is transformed into "otherness" and exploited or penalized by and for those with institutionalized media power. The hair-trigger sensitivity about racial stereotypes partially derives from what James Baldwin called the "burden of representation." On the symbolic battlegrounds of the mass media, the struggle over representation in the simulacral realm homologizes that of the political sphere, where questions of imitation and representation easily slide into issues of delegation and voice. Any negative behavior by any member of the oppressed community is instantly generalized as typical, as pointing to a perpetual backsliding toward some presumed negative essence. Representations thus become allegorical; within hegemonic discourse every sub-altern performer/role is seen as synecdochically summing up a vast but puta-tively homogenous community. Socially empowered groups need not be unduly concerned about "distortions and stereotypes," since even occasionally negative images form part of a wide spectrum of representations. Each negative image of an under-represented group, in contrast, becomes sorely overcharged with allegorical meaning.

The sensitivity around stereotypes and distortions largely arises, then, from the powerlessness of historically marginalized groups to control their own representation. A full understanding of filmic representation therefore requires a comprehensive analysis of the institutions that generate and distribute mass-mediated texts as well as of the audience that receives them. Whose stories are being told? By whom? How are they manufactured, disseminated, received? Who controls production, distribution, exhibition in the film industry? (See, for example, Jesse Rhine's *Black Films/White Money*). Despite the success of celebrities like Oprah Winfrey and Bill Cosby, for example, only a handful of blacks hold executive positions with film studios and television networks.[1] And blacks are not the only disadvantaged group in this respect. While producers assume that Italian American directors should direct films about Italian Americans, for example, they choose Anglos to direct films about Latinos.[2]

Film casting, as an immediate form of representation, constitutes a kind of delegation of voice with political overtones. Here too Europeans and Euro-Americans have played the preponderant role, relegating non-Europeans to supporting roles and the status of extras. Within Hollywood cinema, Euro-Americans have historically enjoyed the unilateral prerogative of acting in "blackface," "redface," "brownface," and "yellowface." From the nineteenth-century vaudeville stage through such figures as Al Jolson in *Hi Lo Broadway* (1933), Fred Astaire in *Swing Time* (1936), and Bing Crosby in *Dixie* (1943), the tradition of blackface recital furnished one of the most popular of American pop-cultural forms. African Americans were not the only "people of color" to be played by Euro-Americans; the same law of unilateral privilege functioned in relation to other groups. Rock Hudson, Boris Karloff, Elvis Presley, Cyd Charisse, Dame Judith Anderson, and Douglas Fairbanks Jr. are among the many Euro-American actors who have represented Native American roles, while Paul Muni, Charlton Heston, Marlon Brando, and Natalie Wood are among those who have played Latino characters. This asymmetry in representational power has generated intense resentment among minoritarian communities, for whom the casting of a non-member of the minority group is a triple insult, implying (a) you are unworthy of self-representation; (b) no one from your group is capable of representing you, and (c) we, the producers of the film, care little about your offended sensibilities, for we have the power and there is nothing to be done about it.

Important work has already been done on ethnic/racial representation and stereotypes, especially within Hollywood cinema (see Neale, 1979; Hilger, 1986; Miller, 1980; Pettit, 1980; Richard, 1992; Woll and Miller, 1987; Churchill, 1992; Guerrero, 1993; Shohat and Stam, 1994). Critics such as Vine Deloria (1969), Ralph and Natasha Friar (1972), Ward Churchill (1992) and many others have discussed the binaristic splitting that has turned Native Americans into bloodthirsty beasts or noble savages. Native American critics have pointed to the innumerable representational blunders of Hollywood films, which have had Indians perform grotesque dog-eating rituals (*The Battle at Elderbush Gulch*, 1913), wrist-cutting ceremonies (*Broken Arrow*, 1950), and misascribed specific ceremonies to the wrong tribes (Sioux sun-dance presented as the *okipa* ceremony of the Mandans). (See Ward Churchill's essay, p. 717.)

A number of other scholars, notably Donald Bogle (1988; 1989), Daniel Leab (1976), James Snead (1992), Ed Guerrero (1993), Clyde Taylor (1999), and Thomas Cripps (1977; 1979; 1993) have explored how preexisting stereotypes – for example the jiving sharpster and shuffling stage sambo – were transferred from antecedent media to film. In *Toms, Coons, Mulattoes, Mammies and Bucks*, Bogle surveys representations of blacks in Hollywood cinema. Bogle's title already announces five major stereotypes, but Bogle's book goes beyond stereotypes to focus on the ways African American performers have "signified" and subverted the roles forced on them. For Bogle, the history of black performance is one of battling against confining types and categories, a battle homologous to the quotidian struggle of three-dimensional blacks against the imprisoning conventions of an apartheid-style system. Throughout, Bogle emphasizes the resilient imagination of black performers obliged to play against script and studio intentions, their capacity to turn demeaning roles into resistant performance.

Important work has also been done on the stereotypes of other ethnic groups such as Latinos (see Noriega, 1992; Fregoso, 1993; Ramirez-Berg, 1995). In *The Latin Image in American Film*, Allen Woll (1980) points to the substratum of male violence common to Latino male stereotypes – the bandido, the greaser, the revolutionary, the bullfighter. Latina women, meanwhile, call up the heat and passionate salsa evoked by the titles of the films of Lupe Velez: *Hot Pepper* (1933), *Strictly Dynamite* (1934), and *Mexican Spitfire* (1940). Arthur G. Pettit (1980), in *Images of the Mexican American in Fiction and Film*, traces the intertext of such imagery to the Anglo "Conquest fiction" of writers like Ned Buntline and Zane Grey. Already in conquest fiction, Pettit argues, the Mexican is defined negatively, in terms of "qualities diametrically opposed to an Anglo prototype." Anglo conquest authors transferred to the mestizo Mexicans the prejudices previously directed toward the native American and the black. Morality, in such works, is color-coordinated; the darker the color, the worse the character.[3]

There is no point in summarizing the work on stereotypes here; rather, I would like both to defend the importance of such work and raise some methodological questions about the underlying premises of character or stereotype-centered approaches. To begin, stereotype analysis, the analysis of repeated, ultimately pernicious constellations of character traits, has made an indispensable contribution by (1) revealing oppressive *patterns* of prejudice in what might at first glance have seemed random and inchoate phenomena; (2) by highlighting the psychic devastation inflicted by systematically negative portrayals on those groups assaulted by them, whether through internalization of the stereotypes themselves or through the negative effects of their dissemination; (3) signaling the social *functionality* of stereotypes, demonstrating that stereotypes are not an error of perception but rather a form of social control, intended as what Alice Walker calls "prisons of image."[4] The call for "positive images," in the same way, corresponds to a profound logic which only the representationally privileged can fail to understand. Given a dominant cinema that trades in heroes and heroines, minority communities rightly ask for their fair share of the representational pie as a simple matter of representational parity.

At the same time, the stereotype approach entails a number of pitfalls from a theoretical–methodological standpoint. First, the exclusive preoccupation with images, whether positive or negative, can lead to a kind of *essentialism*, as less subtle critics reduce a complex variety of portrayals to a limited set of reified formulae. This essentialism generates in its wake a certain *ahistoricism*; the analysis tends to be static, not allowing for mutations, metamorphoses, changes of valence, altered function; it ignores the historical instability of the stereotype and even of language. Stereotypic analysis is likewise covertly premised on *individualism*, in that the individual character, rather than larger social categories (race, class, gender, nation, sexual orientation), remains the point of reference. The focus on individual character also misses the ways in which whole cultures, as opposed to individuals, can be caricatured or misrepresented without a single character being stereotyped. The flawed mimesis of many Hollywood films dealing with the Third World, with their innumerable ethnographic, linguistic, and even topographical blunders, which have Brazilians wear Mexican sombreros, for a "tango," for example, has less to do with stereotypes per se than with the tendentious ignorance of colonialist discourse.

A moralistic approach also sidesteps the issue of the relative nature of "morality," eliding the question: positive for whom? It ignores the fact that oppressed people might not only have a *different* vision of morality, but even an *opposite* vision. What is seen as "positive" by the dominant group (for example, the acts of those "Indians" in Westerns who spy for the whites), might be seen as treason by the dominated group. The taboo in classical Hollywood was not on "positive images" but rather on images of racial equality, images of anger and revolt.

The privileging of positive images also elides the patent differences, the social and moral heteroglossia, characteristic of any social group. A cinema of contrivedly positive image betrays a lack of confidence in the group portrayed, which usually itself has no illusions concerning its own perfection. It is often assumed, furthermore, that control over representation leads automatically to the production of "positive images." But African films like *Laafi* (1991) and *Finzan* (1990) do not offer positive images of African society; rather, they offer *African* perspectives on African society. "Positive images," in this sense, can be a sign of insecurity. Hollywood, after all, has never worried about depicting the US as a land of gangsters, rapists, and murderers.

A privileging of social portrayal, plot, and character often leads to a slighting of the specifically cinematic dimensions of the films; often the analyses might as easily have been of novels or plays. A thoroughgoing analysis has to pay attention to "mediations": narrative structure, genre conventions, cinematic style. Euro-centric discourse in film may be relayed not by characters or plot but by lighting, framing, mise-en-scène, music. Some basic issues of mediation have to do with the *rapports de force*, the balance of power as it were, between foreground and background. The cinema translates correlations of social power into registers of foreground and background, on-screen and off-screen, speaking and silent. To speak of the "image" of a social group, we have to ask precise questions about images: How much space do they occupy in the shot? Are they seen in close-ups or only in distant long shots? How often do they appear compared with the Euro-American characters and for how long? Are they active, desiring characters or decorative props? Do the eyeline matches identify us with one gaze rather than another? How do body language and character positionings communicate social distance or differences in status? Is there an aesthetic segregation whereby one group is haloed and the other villainized? What homologies inform artistic and ethnic/political representation? Questions of address are as crucial as questions of representation. Who is speaking through a film? Who is imagined as listening? Who is actually listening? Who is looking? And what social desires are mobilized by the film?

The critique-of-stereotypes approach is implicitly premised on the desirability of "rounded" three-dimensional characters within a realist–dramatic aesthetic. Given the cinema's history of one-dimensional portrayals, the hope for more complex and "realistic" representations is completely understandable, but should not preclude more experimental, anti-illusionistic alternatives. Realistic "positive" portrayals are not the only way to fight racism or to advance a liberatory perspective. Within a Brechtian aesthetic, for example, (non-racial) stereotypes can serve to generalize meaning and demystify established power, while characters are presented as the sites of contradiction. Parody of the kind theorized by Bakhtin, similarly, favors decidedly negative, even grotesque images to convey a deep critique of societal structures. Satirical or parodic films may be less concerned with constructing positive images than with challenging the stereotypical expectations an audience may bring them. On the other hand, what one might call the generic defense against accusations of racism – "It's only a comedy!," "All the characters are caricatures!," "But it's a parody!" – is highly ambiguous, since it all depends on the modalities and the objects of the lampoon, parody, and so forth.

The 1990s have witnessed an attempt to move beyond ghettoized studies of isolated groups – Native Americans, African Americans, Latinos – in favor of a relational and contrapuntal approach (both Shohat and Gaines provide examples in their essays). The period has also witnessed the emergence of "whiteness studies." This movement responds to the call by scholars of color for an analysis of the impact of racism not only on its victims but also on its perpetrators. The "whiteness" scholars questioned the quiet yet overpowering normativity of whiteness, the process by which "race" was attributed to others while whites were tacitly positioned as unmarked norm. Although whiteness (like blackness) was on one level merely a cultural fiction without any scientific basis, it was also a social fact with all-too-real consequences for the distribution of wealth, prestige, and opportunity (Lipsitz, 1998: vii). Thus whiteness studies "outed" whiteness as just another ethnicity, but one historically accorded inordinate privilege. This movement – it is hoped – signals the end of "the innocent white subject," and an end to the venerable practice of unilaterally racializing the Third World or minority "others," while casting whites as somehow "raceless." Toni Morrison, bell hooks, Coco Fusco, George Lipsitz, and Richard Dyer are among the many who have problematized normative notions of "whiteness." Dyer's book *White* (1997) focuses on the representation of white people in Western culture. The term "people of color" as a designation for "non-whites," Dyer points out, implies that whites are "colorless" and thus normative: "Other people are raced, we are just people" (ibid.: 1). Even lighting technologies, and the specific mode of movie lighting, Dyer points out, have racial implications, and the assumption that the "normal" face is the white face runs through most of the manuals on cinematography.

"Whiteness studies" at its best denaturalizes whiteness as unmarked norm, calling attention to the taken-for-granted privileges (e.g. not to be the object of media stereotypes) that go with whiteness. At the same time, "whiteness studies" runs the risk of once again recentering white Narcissism, of changing the subject back to the assumed center – a racial version of the Show Business dictum: "speak ill of me but speak."

While "stereotypes and distortions" analysis poses legitimate questions about social plausibility and mimetic accuracy, about negative stereotypes and positive images, it is often premised on an exclusive allegiance to an aesthetic of ver-isimilitude.[5] An obsession with "realism" casts the question as simply one of "errors" and "distortions," as if the "truth" of a community were unproblematic, transparent, and easily accessible, and "lies" about that community easily unmasked. Yet the issue is less one of fidelity to a preexisting truth or reality, than one of a specific orchestration of ideological discourses and communitarian perspectives. While on one level film is mimesis, representation, it is also utterance, an act of contextualized interlocution between socially situated produ-cers and receivers. It is not enough to say that art is constructed. We have to ask "constructed for whom" and in conjunction with which ideologies and dis-courses? In this sense, art is a representation in not so much a mimetic as a political sense, as a delegation of voice.[6]

Indeed, the very term "image studies" symptomatically elides the oral and the "voiced." A more nuanced discussion of race in the cinema would emphasize less a one-to-one mimetic adequacy to historical truth than the interplay of voices, discourses, perspectives. The task of the critic would be to call attention to the cultural voices at play, not only those heard in aural "close-up" but also those distorted or drowned out by the text. The question is not of pluralism but of multi-vocality, an approach that would strive to cultivate and even heighten cultural difference while abolishing socially generated inequalities.

Notes

1 See *New York Times* (September 24, 1991).

2 See Gary M. Stern, "Why the Dearth of Latino Directors?" *Cineaste* XIX, Nos. 2–3 (1992).

3 Analysts have also performed extended analyses of specific films from within this perspective. Charles Ramirez Berg analyzes *Bordertown* (1935), the first Hollywood sound film to deal with Mexican–American assimilation and the film which laid down the pattern for the Chicano Social Problem Film. Among the narrative and ideological features Berg isolates are: (1) stereotypical inversion (i.e. the upgrading of Chicanos coupled with the denigration of the Anglos, portrayed as oversexed blondes (Marie), materialistic socialites (Dale), and inflexible authority figures (the judge); (2) undiminished stereotyping of other marginalized groups (for example, Chinese Americans); (3) the assimilationist idealization of the Chicana mama as the "font of genuine ethnic values;" (4) the absent father (Anglo families are complete and ideal; Chicano families are fragmented and dysfunctional); and (5) the absent non-maternal chicana (implying the inferiority of Chicanas to Anglo women). See Charles Ramirez Berg, "*Bordertown*, the Assimilation Narrative and the Chicano Social Problem Film," in Chon Noriega, ed., *Chicanos and Film* (New York: Garland, 1992).

4 Quoted in *Prisoners of Image: Ethnic and Gender Stereotypes*, publication of the Alternative Museum, New York City (1989).

5 Steve Neale points out that stereotypes are judged simultaneously in relation to an empirical "real" (accuracy) and an ideological "ideal" (positive image). See "The Same Old Story: Stereotypes and Difference," *Screen Education*, Nos. 32–3 (Autumn/Winter 1979–80).

6 Kobena Mercer and Isaac Julien, in a similar spirit, distinguish between "representation as a practice of depicting" and "representation as a practice of delegation." See Mercer and Julien (1988).

37

Gender and Culture of Empire: Toward a Feminist Ethnography of the Cinema

Ella Shohat

Although recent feminist film theory has acknowledged the issue of differences among women, there has been little attempt to explore and problematize the implications of these differences for the representation of gender relations within racially and culturally non-homogeneous textual environments.[1] While implicitly universalizing "womanhood," and without questioning the undergirding racial and national boundaries of its discourse, feminist film theory, for the most part, has not articulated its generally insightful analyses *vis-à-vis* the contradictions and assymetries provoked by (post)colonial arrangements of power. This elision is especially striking since the beginnings of cinema coincided with the height of imperialism between the late nineteenth century and World War I. Western cinema not only inherited and disseminated colonial discourse, but also created a system of domination through monopolistic control of film distribution and exhibition in much of Asia, Africa, and Latin America. The critique of colonialism within cinema studies, meanwhile, has tended to downplay the significance of gender issues, thus eliding the fact that (post)colonial discourse has impinged differently on the representation of men and women. It is between these two major theoretical frameworks that my essay is situated, attempting to synthesize feminist and postcolonial cultural critiques.

In this essay I explore Western cinema's geographical and historical constructs as symptomatic of the colonialist imaginary generally but also more specifically as a product of a gendered Western gaze, an imbrication reflective of the symbiotic relations between patriarchal and colonial articulations of difference. I emphasize the role of sexual difference in the construction of a number of superimposed oppositions – West/East, North/South – not only on a narratological level but also on the level of the implicit structuring metaphors undergirding colonial discourse. While referring to some resistant counter-narratives, I also examine the structural analogies in the colonialist positioning of different regions, particularly in sexual terms, showing the extent to which Western representation of otherized territories serves diacritically to define the "West" itself.

Gendered Metaphors

Virgins, Adams, and the Prospero complex

An examination of colonial discourse reveals the crucial role of gendered metaphors in constructing the colonial "subaltern." Europe's "civilizing mission" in the Third World is projected as interweaving opposing yet linked narratives of Western penetration into inviting virginal landscape[2] *and* resisting libidinal nature. The early exaltation of the New World paradise, suggested for example by Sir Walter Raleigh's report – "a country that hath yet her mayden head, never sakt, turned, nor wrought"[3] – and by Crèvecoeur's letters – "Here nature opens her broad lap to receive the perpetual accession of new comers, and to supply them with food"[4] – gradually centered around the idealized figure of the pioneer. Linked to nineteenth-century westward expansionism, the garden symbol embraced metaphors related to growth, increase, cultivation, and blissful agricultural labor.[5] At the same time, the discourse of Empire suggests that "primitive" landscapes (deserts, jungles) are tamed; "shrew" peoples (Native Americans, Africans, Arabs) are domesticated; and the desert is made to bloom, all thanks to the infusion of Western dynamism and enlightenment. Within this Promethean master-narrative, subliminally gendered tropes such as "conquering the desolation," and "fecundating the wilderness," acquire heroic resonances of Western fertilization of barren lands. The metaphoric portrayal of the (non-European) land as a "virgin" coyly awaiting the touch of the colonizer implied that whole continents – Africa, America, Asia, and Australia – could only benefit from the emanation of colonial praxis. The revivification of a wasted soil evokes a quasi-divine process of endowing life and meaning ex nihilo, of bringing order from chaos, plenitude from lack. Indeed, the West's *Prospero complex* is premised on an East/South portrayed as a Prospero's isle, seen as the site of superimposed lacks calling for Western transformation of primeval matter. The engendering of "civilization," then, is clearly phallo-centric, not unlike the mythical woman's birth from Adam's Ribs.[6]

The American hero, as R. W. B. Lewis points out, has been celebrated as prelapsarian Adam, as a New Man emancipated from history (i.e. European history) before whom all the world and time lay available.[7] The American Adam archetype implied not only his status as a kind of creator, blessed with the divine prerogative of naming the elements of the scene about him, but also his fundamental innocence. Here colonial and patriarchal discourses are clearly interwoven. The biblical narration of Genesis recounts the creation of the World; the creation of Adam from earth (*adama* in Hebrew) in order for man to rule over nature. The power of creation is inextricably linked to the power of naming – God lends his naming authority to Adam as mark of his rule, and the woman is "called Woman because she was taken out of man." The question of naming played an important role not only in gender mythology but also in colonial narratives in which the "discoverer" gave names as a mark of possession ("America" as celebrating Amerigo Vespucci) or as bearers of a European global perspective ("Middle East," "Far East"). "Peripheral" places and their inhabitants were often stripped of their "unpronounceable" indigenous names and outfitted with names marking them as the property of the colonizer. The colonial explorer as depicted in *Robinson Crusoe* creates, demiurge-like, a whole civilization and has the power of naming "his" Islander "Friday," for he "saves" his life on that day; and Friday, we recall, is the day God created Adam, thus further strengthening the analogy between the "self-sufficient" Crusoe and God.

The notion of an American Adam elided a number of crucial facts, notably that there were other civilizations in the New World; that the settlers were not creating "being from nothingness"; and that the settlers had scarcely jettisoned all their Old World cultural baggage, their deeply ingrained attitudes and discourses. Here the notion of "virginity," present for example in the etymology of Virginia, must be seen in diacritical relation to the metaphor of the (European) "motherland." A "virgin" land is implicitly available for defloration and fecundation. Implied to lack owners, it therefore becomes the property of its "discoverers" and cultivators. The "purity" of the terminology masks the dispossession of the land and its resources. A land already fecund, already producing for the indigenous peoples, and thus a "mother," is metaphorically projected as virgin, "untouched nature," and therefore as available and awaiting a master. Colonial gendered metaphors are visibly rendered in Jan Van der Straet's pictorial representation of the discovery of America, focusing on the mythical figure of Amerigo Vespucci, shown as bearing Europe's emblems of meaning (cross, armor, compass).[8] Behind him we see the vessels which will bring back to the Occident the treasures of the New World Paradise. In front of him we see a welcoming naked woman, the Indian American. If she is an harmonious extension of nature, he represents its scientific mastery.[9] Here the conqueror, as Michel de Certeau puts it, "will write the body of the other and inscribe upon it his own history."[10]

In Nelson Pereira dos Santos's *How Tasty Was My Frenchman* (*Como Era Gostoso Meu Françes*, 1970), the patriarchal discourse on the encounter between Europeans and Native Americans is subverted.[11] Partly based on a diary written by the German adventurer, Hans Staden, the film concerns a Frenchman who is captured by the Tupinamba tribe and sentenced to death in response to previous massacres inflicted by Europeans upon them. Before his ritualized execution and cannibalization, however, he is given a wife, Sebiopepe (a widow of one of the Tupinamba massacred by the Europeans) and he is allowed to participate in the tribe's daily activities.[12] In the last shot, the camera zooms into Sebiopepe's face as she is emotionlessly devouring her Frenchman, despite the fact that she has developed a close relationship with him. This final image is followed by a citation from a report on Native American genocide by Europeans, which undermines the possibly disturbing nature of the last shot.[13] If pictorial representations of the "discovery" tend to center on a nude Native American woman as metaphorizing the welcoming "new-found-land," in *How Tasty Was My Frenchman* the Native American woman is far from being an object of European discourse. Presented as linked to her communal culture and history, she herself becomes part of history. Her nudity is not contrasted with the discoverer's heavy clothing; rather, she is part of an environment where nudity is not a category. The fact that the film employs largely longshots in which characters appear nude in the performance of their banal daily activities undermines voyeurism and stands in contrast to the fetishistic Hollywood mode that tends to fragment the (female) body in close shots.[14] In her interaction with the Frenchman, Sebiopepe represents, above all, the voice of the Native American counter narrative.[15] In one scene, for example, a myth of origins prefigures the symbolic revolt of the Tupinamba. Sebiopepe begins to narrate in Tupi a Tupinamba Promethean myth concerning the God, Mair, who brought them knowledge. The Frenchman, at one point, takes over the narration and, in French, further recounts the deeds of the God, while we see him performing the divine deeds. The Whitening of the Tupinamba God on the image track evokes the Promethean colonial discourse concerning the redemption of the Natives, but here that discourse is relativized, especially since the Native American woman ends the myth in Tupi, recounting the rebellion of the people against the God, while the image track shows the destruction of the Frenchman's work. Her voice, then, recounts the tale of the people who revolted, undercutting the masculinist myth of availability, submissiveness, and redemption.

Graphological tropes

The inclination to project the non-Occident as feminine is seen even in the nineteenth century Romantic depiction of the ancient Orient of Babylonia and Egypt, reproduced in films such as D. W. Griffith's *Intolerance* (1916) and Cecil B. DeMille's *Cleopatra* (1934). In *Intolerance* Babylon signifies sexual excess, building on the Book of Revelation as "Babylon, the Great, the Mother of Harlots and of the Abominations of the Earth." DeMille's *Cleopatra* explicitly expresses this view by having the sexually manipulative Cleopatra addressed as Egypt[16] and by presenting the Orient as exclusively the scene of carnal delights. The ultimate subordination of the woman Cleopatra and her country Egypt is not without contemporary colonial overtones, suggested for example in the Anglo-aristocratic "Roman" court where sarcastic jokes are made at the expense of a presumably Black Cleopatra, asserting that Rome could never be turned into the Orient, or ruled by an Egyptian. (The historically dark Cleopatra is turned by Hollywood conventions of Beauty into a European looking White woman, just as the iconography of Christ has gradually de-Semitized him.)[17] The visual infatuation with Babylon and Egypt's material abundance emphasized through a mise-en-scène of monumental architecture, domestic detail, and quasi-pornographic feasts, cannot be divorced from the intertext of colonial travel literature whose reports also obsessively recounted the details of Oriental sensual excesses.

Cinema, in this sense, enacted a historiographical and anthropological role, writing (in-light) the cultures of others. The early films' penchant for graphological signifiers such as hieroglyphs (in the different versions of *Cleopatra*), Hebrew script (*Intolerance*), or the image of an open book as in "The Book of Intolerance" and the marginal "notes" accompanying the intertitles (which pedagogically supply the spectator with additional information) imply Hollywood as a kind of a Western popular griot. By associating itself with writing, and particularly with "original" writing, early cinema lent a pedagogical, historical, and artistic aura to a medium still associated with circus-like entertainments. (It is not a coincidence, perhaps, that Siegfried Kracauer, for example, referred to films as "visible hieroglyphs.") And by linking a new apprentice art to ancient times and "exotic" places cinema celebrated its ethnographic and quasi-archaeological powers to resuscitate forgotten and distant civilizations, a celebration implicit in the construction of pseudo-Egyptian movie palaces. The "birth" of cinema itself coincided with the imperialist moment, when diverse colonized civilizations were already shaping their conflicting identities *vis-à-vis* their colonizers. These films about the ancient world suggest, perhaps, a Romantic nostalgia for a "pure" civilization prior to Western "contamination." They also represent a Romantic search for the lost Eastern origins of Western civilizations, analogous to Schlieman's excavations in Troy. It is within this context that we can understand the "structuring absence" – in the representation of Egypt, Babylonia, and the (biblical) Holy Land – of the contemporary colonized Arab Orient and its nationalist struggles.[18] Through a historiographical gesture, the films define the Orient as ancient and mysterious, participating in what Jacques Derrida in another context calls the "hieroglyphist prejudice." The cinematic Orient, then, is best epitomized by an iconography of Papyruses, Sphinxes, and Mummies, whose existence and revival depend on the "look" and "reading" of the Westerner. This rescue of the past, in other words, suppresses the voice of the present and thus legitimizes by default the availability of the space of the Orient for the geopolitical maneuvers of the Western powers.

The filmic mummified zone of ancient civilizations, then, is dialectically linked to the representation of the historical role of the West in the imperial age. Reproducing Western historiography, First World cinema narrates European penetration into the Third World through the figure of the "discoverer."[19] In most Western films about the colonies (such as *Bird of Paradise* (1932), *Wee Willie Winkie* (1937), *Black Narcissus* (1947), *The King and I* (1956), *Lawrence of Arabia* (1962), and even Buñuel's *Adventures of Robinson Crusoe* (1954)) we accompany, quite literally, the explorer's perspective. A simple shift in focalization to that of the "natives," as occurs in the Australian–Aboriginal *Nice Coloured Girls* (1987)[20] or in the Brazilian *How Tasty Was My Frenchman* where the camera is placed on land with the "natives" rather than on ship with the Europeans, reveals the illusory and intrusive nature of the "discovery." More usually, however, heroic status is attributed to the voyager (often a male scientist) come to master a new land and its treasures, the value of which the "primitive" residents had been unaware.[21] It is this construction of consciousness of "value" as a pretext for (capitalist) ownership which legitimizes the colonizer's act of appropriation. The "discovery," furthermore, has gender overtones.[22] In this exploratory adventure, seen in such films as *Lawrence of Arabia* and the *Indiana Jones* series, the camera relays the hero's dynamic movement across a passive, static space, gradually stripping the land of its "enigma," as the spectator wins visual access to Oriental treasures through the eyes of the explorer–protagonist. *Lawrence of Arabia* provides an example of Western historical representation whereby the individual Romantic "genius" leads the Arab national revolt, presumed to be a passive entity awaiting T. E. Lawrence's inspiration. (Arab sources obviously have challenged this historical account.)[23] The unveiling of the mysteries of an unknown space becomes a *rite de passage* allegorizing the Western achievement of virile heroic stature.

Mapping terra incognita

The masculinist desire of mastering a new land is deeply linked to colonial history and even to its contemporary companion, philosophy, in which epistemology partially modeled itself on geography. The traditional discourse on nature as feminine – for example Francis Bacon's idea that insofar as we learn the laws of nature through science, we become her master, as we are now, in ignorance, "her thralls"[24] – gains, within the colonial context, clear geopolitical implications. Bacon's search for expanding scientific knowledge is inseparable from the contemporaneous European geographical expansion, clearly suggested by his language of analogies and metaphors: "As the immense regions of the West Indies had never been discovered, if the use of the compass had not first been known, it is no wonder that the discovery and advancement of arts hath made no greater progress, when the art of inventing and discovering of the sciences remains hitherto unknown."[25] And Bacon finds it "disgraceful," that "while the regions of the material globe...have been in our times laid widely open and revealed, the intellectual globe should remain shut up within the narrow limits of old discoveries."[26] Traveling into the indefiniteness of the ocean, the Faustian overreacher's voyage beyond the Pillars of Hercules aims at the possibility of a *terra incognita* on the other side of the ocean. Studying topography, systematizing the paths, as Hans Blumenberg points out, guarantees that the accidents of things coming to light ultimately lead to a universal acquaintance with the world. "So much had remained concealed from the human spirit throughout many centuries and was discovered neither by philosophy nor by the faculty of reason but rather by accident and favorable opportunity, because it was all too different and distant from what was familiar, so that no preconception (*praenotio aliqua*) could lead one to it."[27] The logic of explorers from Robinson Crusoe to Indiana Jones is, in this sense, based on the hope that "nature" conceals in its "womb" still more, outside the familiar paths of the power of imagination (*extra vias phantasiae*). It is within this broader historical and intellectual context that we may understand the symptomatic image of penetration into a cave placed in a non-European land to discover that "Unknown," seen for example in the Rudyard Kipling-based *The Jungle Book* (1942), *Raiders of the Lost Ark* (1981), *Indiana Jones and the Temple of Doom* (1984), and the E. M. Forster-based *A Passage to India* (1984).

Colonial narratives legitimized the embarking upon treasure hunts by lending a scientific aura, encapsulated especially by images of maps and globes. Detailed descriptions of maps were probably inspired by the growing science of geography which determined the significance of places through its power of inscription on the map, with the compass on top as the signature of scientific authority. Geography, then, was microcosmically reflected in the map-based adventures which involved the drawing or deciphering of a map, and its authentication through the physical contact with the "new" land. Western cinema, from the earliest anthropological films through *Morocco* (1930) to the *Indiana Jones* series, has relied on map imagery for plotting the Empire, while simultaneously celebrating its own technological power – implicitly *vis-à-vis* the novel's reliance upon words or static drawings, and later still photographs – to illustrate vividly the topography. For example, venture-narrative films mark maps with moving arrows to signify the progress of the Westerner in his world-navigation, a practice characterizing even the recent *Raiders of the Lost Ark* and *Indiana Jones and the Temple of Doom*. By associating itself with the visual medium of maps, cinema represents itself scientifically, as being a twentieth-century continuation of Geography.

Films often superimposed illustrative maps on shots of landscapes, subliminally imposing the map's "claim" over the land, functioning as a legal document. *King Solomon's Mines* (1937, 1950, 1985), as Anne McClintock suggests in her discussion of Rider Haggard work, explicitly genderizes the relation between the explorer and the topography.[28] Menahem Golan's version, for example, reveals in the second shot of the film a small nude female sculpture engraved with Canaanite signs, explained by the archeologist to be a map leading to the twin mountains, the Breasts of Sheba, below which, in a cave, are hidden King Solomon's diamond mines. The camera voyeuristically tilts down on the female body/map, scrutinizing it from the excited perspective of the archeologist and the antique dealer. The road to utopia involves the deciphering of the map, of comprehending the female body; the legendary twin mountains and the cave metaphorize the desired telos of the hero's mission of plunder. The geology and topography of the land, then, is explicitly sexualized to resemble the physiology of a woman.

The recurrent image of the spinning globe, similarly, entitles the scientist to possess the world, since the globe, as the world's representation, allegorizes the relationship between creator and creation. Cinema's penchant for spinning globe logos serves to celebrate the medium's kinetic possibilities as well as its global ubiquity, allowing spectators a cheap voyage while remaining in the metropolitan "centers" – Lumières' location shootings of diverse Third World sites, such as India, Mexico, and Palestine being symptomatic of this visual national-geographics mania. The spinning globe virtually became the trade-mark of the British Korda brothers' productions, many of whose films, such as *Sanders of the River* (1935), *The Drum* (1938), *The Four Feathers* (1939), and *The Jungle Book*, concerned colonial themes.[29] The overarching global point-of-view sutures the spectator into a Godlike cosmic perspective. Incorporating images of maps and globes, the Jules Verne-based film *Around the World in 80 Days* (1956), for example, begins by its omniscient narrator hailing the "shrinking of the world" as Verne was writing the book.[30] The "shrinking" relates the perspective of upper-class British men whose scientific confidence about circling the world in eighty days is materialized, thus linking the development of science to imperialist control: "Nothing is impossible. When science finally conquers the air it may be feasible to circle the globe in eighty hours," says the David Niven character.

Science, knowledge, and technology can also be read allegorically as linked to imperial expansionism in the film's citation of Georges Méliès's film *A Trip to the Moon* (*Le Voyage dans la lune*, 1902) (based on Verne's *From the Earth to the Moon*, 1865) in which the "last frontier" explored is seen first in the imagistic phallic penetration of the rounded moon.[31] This imagination of the "last frontier," in a period when most of the world was dominated by Europe, reproduces the historical discourse of the "first frontier." The narrative is structured similarly to the colonial captivity narrative where the skeleton creatures carrying spears burst from the moon's simulacrum of a jungle but are defeated by the male explorers' umbrella-like guns which magically eliminate the savage creatures. Such a film, not in any obvious sense "about" colonialism, but one produced in a period when most of the world was dominated by Europe, can thus be read as an analogue of imperial expansion.[32] Similarly in recent films such as *Return of the Jedi* (1983) the conquest of outer space exists on a continuum with an imperial narrative in which the visualization of the planet provides the paradigm for the representation of Third World "underdevelopment" (deserts, jungles, and mountains). The Manichean relationship between the American hero and the new land and its natives involves exotic creatures, teddy-bear-like Ewoks whose language remains a mystery throughout the film, who worship the technologically well-equipped hero and who defend him against evil ugly creatures who have unclear motives. The American hero's physical and moral triumph legitimizes the destruction of the enemy, as does the paternal transformation of the friendly "elements" into servile objects, along with his assumed right to establish new outposts (and implicitly to hold on to old outposts, whether in Africa, Asia, or America).

The dark continent

The colonial films claim to initiate the Western spectator into an unknown culture. This is valid even for films set in "exotic" lands and ancient times which do *not* employ Western characters (for example, *Intolerance*,[33] *The Ten Commandments* (1923, 1956), *The Thief of Baghdad* (1924), and *Kismet* (1944), yet whose Oriental heroes/heroines are played by Western stars. The spectator is subliminally invited on an ethnographic tour of a celluloid-"preserved" culture, which implicitly celebrates the chronotopic magical aptitude of cinema for panoramic spectacle and temporal voyeurism, evoking André Bazin's formulation of cinema as possessing a "mummy complex."[34] Often the spectator, identified with the gaze of the West (whether embodied by a Western male/female character or by a Western actor/actress masquerading as an Oriental), comes to master, in a remarkably telescoped period of time, the codes of a foreign culture shown, as Edward Said suggests, as simple, unselfconscious, and susceptible to facile apprehension. Any possibility of dialogic interaction and of a dialectical representation of the East/West relation is excluded from the outset. The films thus reproduce the colonialist mechanism by which the Orient, rendered as devoid of any active historical or narrative role, becomes the object of study and spectacle.[35]

The portrayal of a Third World region as undeveloped, in this same vein, is reinforced by a topographical reductionism, for example the topographical reductionism of the Orient to desert, and metaphorically, to dreariness. The desert, a frequent reference in the dialogues and a visual motif throughout the Orientalist films, is presented as the essential unchanging decor of the history of the Orient. While the Arabs in such films as *Lawrence of Arabia*, *Exodus* (1960), and the *Raiders of the Lost Ark* are associated with images of underdevelopment, the Westerner, as the antithesis of the Oriental desert, is associated with productive, creative pioneering, a masculine redeemer of the wilderness. The films reflect a culturally overdetermined geographical–symbolic polarity; an East/West axis informs many films on the Oriental theme. As if in a reversion to deterministic climate theories such as those of Madame de Staël or Hippolyte Taine, the films present the East as the locus of irrational primitivism and uncontrollable instincts. The exposed, barren land and the blazing sands, furthermore, metaphorize the exposed, unrepressed "hot" passion and uncensored emotions of the Orient, in short, as the world of the out-of-control Id.

The Orient as a metaphor for sexuality is encapsulated by the recurrent figure of the veiled woman. The inaccessibility of the veiled woman, mirroring the mystery of the Orient itself, requires a process of Western unveiling for comprehension. Veiled women in Orientalist paintings, photographs, and films expose flesh, ironically, more than they conceal it.[36] It is this process of exposing the female Other, of literally denuding her, which comes to allegorize the Western masculinist power of possession, that she, as a metaphor for her land, becomes available for Western penetration and knowledge. This intersection of the epistemological and the sexual in colonial discourse echoes Freud's metaphor of the "dark continent." Freud speaks of female sexuality in metaphors of darkness and obscurity often drawn from the realms of archeology and exploration – the metaphor of the "dark continent," for example, deriving from a book

by the Victorian explorer Stanley.[37] Seeing himself as explorer and discoverer of
new worlds, Freud in *Studies on Hysteria* compared the role of the psychoanalyst
to that of the archeologist "clearing away the pathogenic psychical material layer
by layer" which is analogous "with the technique of excavating a buried city."[38]
The analogy, made in the context of examining a woman patient, Fräulein
Elisabeth Von R., calls attention to the role of the therapist in locating obscure
trains of thought followed by penetration, as Freud puts it in the first person: "I
would penetrate into deeper layers of her memories at these points carrying out
an investigation under hypnosis or by the use of some similar technique."[39]

Speaking generally of "penetrating deeply" into the "neurosis of women"
thanks to a science which can give a "deeper and more coherent" insight into
femininity,[40] Freud is perhaps unaware of the political overtones of his optical
metaphor. Penetration, as Toril Moi suggests, is very much on Freud's mind as
he approaches femininity,[41] including, one might add, the "dark continent of
female sexuality." The notion of the necessary unveiling of the unconscious
requires an obscure object in order to sustain the very desire to explore, penetrate, and master. David Macey's suggestion that psychoanalysis posits femininity
as being in excess of its rationalist discourse, and then complains that it cannot
explain it,[42] is equally applicable to the positing of the Other in colonial discourse. Furthermore, Freud uses the language of force; for example, "we force
our way into the internal strata, overcoming resistances at all times."[43] Looking
at the Eastern roots of civilizations, Freud employs ancient myths and figures
such as the Sphinx and Oedipus to draw parallels between the development of
the civilization and that of the psyche. (Although Freud did not speculate at any
great length on Egyptian mythology, over half of his private collection of anti-
quities reportedly consisted of ancient Egyptian sculptures and artifacts.)[44] The
psychoanalyst who heals from the suppressed past (most of Freud's studies of
hysteria were conducted in relation to women) resembles the archeologist who
recovers the hidden past of civilization (most of which was "found" in Third
World lands). As in archeology, Freud's epistemology assumes the (white) male
as the bearer of knowledge, who can penetrate woman and text, while she, as a
remote region, will let herself be explored till truth is uncovered.

The interweaving of archeology and psychoanalysis touches on a nineteenth-
century motif in which the voyage into the origins of the Orient becomes a
voyage into the interior colonies of the "self." ("Un voyage en Orient [était]
comme un grand acte de ma vie intérieure," Lamartine wrote.)[45] The origins of
archeology, the search for the "roots of civilization" as a discipline are, we know,
inextricably linked to imperial expansionism. In the cinema, the *Indiana Jones*
series reproduces exactly this colonial vision in which Western "knowledge" of
ancient civilizations "rescues" the past from oblivion. It is this masculinist rescue
in *Raiders of the Lost Ark* that legitimizes denuding the Egyptians of their
heritage, confining it within Western metropolitan museums – an ideology
implicit as well in the Orientalist *Intolerance*, *Cleopatra*, and the *Mummy* series.
(These films, not surprisingly, tend to be programmed in museums featuring

Egyptological exhibitions.) *Raiders of the Lost Ark*, symptomatically, assumes a disjuncture between contemporary and ancient Egypt, since the space between the present and the past can "only" be bridged by the scientist. The full significance of the ancient archeological objects within the Eurocentric vision of the Spielberg film is presumed to be understood only by the Western scientists, relegating the Egyptian people to the role of ignorant Arabs who happen to be sitting on a land full of historical treasures – much as they happen to "sit" on oil. Set in the mid-1930s when most of the world was still under colonial rule, the film regards the colonial presence in Egypt, furthermore, as completely natural, eliding a history of Arab nationalist revolts against foreign domination.

The American hero – often cinematically portrayed as a Cowboy – is an archeologist implicitly searching for the Eastern roots of Western civilization. He liberates the ancient Hebrew ark from illegal Egyptian possession, while also rescuing it from immoral Nazi control, subliminally reinforcing American and Jewish solidarity *vis-à-vis* the Nazis and their Arab assistants.[46] The geopolitical alignments here are as clear as in the inadvertent allegory of *The Ten Commandments*, where a WASPish Charlton Heston is made to incarnate Hebrew Moses struggling against the Egyptians, thus allegorizing in the context of the 1950s the contemporary struggle of the West (Israel and the US) against Egyptians/Arabs.[47] That at the end of *Raiders of the Lost Ark* it is the American Army which guards the "top secret" ark – with the active complicity of the ark itself – strengthens this evocation of geopolitical alliances.[48] *Raiders of the Lost Ark* significantly develops parallel linked plots in which the female protagonist, Marion, and the ark become the twin objects of the hero's search for harmony. The necklace which leads to the ark is first associated with Marion who becomes herself the object of competing nationalist male desires. She is abducted by the Nazis and their Arab assistants much as the ark is hijacked by them, followed by Dr Jones's rescue of Marion and the ark from the Nazis. The telos of the voyage into unknown regions – whether mental or geographical – then, is that the Westerner both knows the Orient (in the epistemological and biblical senses) and at the same time brings it knowledge, rescuing it from its own obscurantism. . . .

Textual/Sexual Strategies

The colonial gaze

Still playing a significant role in postcolonial geopolitics, the predominant trope of "rescue" in colonial discourse forms the crucial site of the battle over representation. Not only has the Western imaginary metaphorically rendered the colonized land as a female to be saved from her environ/mental disorder, it has also projected rather more literal narratives of rescue, specifically of Western and non-Western women – from African, Asian, Arab, or Native American men. The figure of the Arab assassin/rapist, like that of the African cannibal, helps produce the narrative and ideological role of the Western liberator as integral to the colonial rescue phantasy. This projection, whose imagistic avatars include the polygamous Arab, the libidinous Black buck, and the macho Latino, provides an indirect apologia for domination. In the case of the Orient, it carries with it religious/theological overtones of the inferiority of the polygamous Islamic world to the Christian world as encapsulated by the monogamous couple. The justification of Western expansion, then, becomes linked to issues of sexuality.

The intersection of colonial and gender discourses involves a shifting, contradictory subject positioning, whereby Western woman can simultaneously constitute "center" and "periphery," identity and alterity. A Western woman, in these narratives, exists in a relation of subordination to Western man and in a relation of domination toward "non-Western" men and women. This textual relationality homologizes the historical positioning of colonial women who have played, albeit with a difference, an oppressive role toward colonized people (both men and women), at times actively perpetuating the legacy of Empire.[49] This problematic role is anatomized in Ousmane Sembène's *Black Girl* (*La Noire de . . .*, 1966) in the relationship between the Senegalese maid and her French employer, and to some extent by Mira Hamermesh's documentary on South Africa *Maids and Madams* (1985), in contrast to the White-woman's-burden ideology in films such as *The King and I* (1956), *Out of Africa* (1985), and *Gorillas in the Mist* (1989). In many films, colonial women become the instrument of the White male vision, and are thus granted a gaze more powerful than that not only of non-Western women but also of non-Western men.

In the colonial context, given the shifting relational nature of power situations and representations, women can be granted an ephemeral "positional superiority" (Edward Said), a possibility exemplified in *The Sheik* (1921). Based on Edith Hull's novel, George Melford's *The Sheik* first introduces the spectator to the Arab world in the form of the "barbarous ritual" of the marriage market, depicted as a casino lottery ritual from which Arab men select women to "serve as chattel slaves." At the same time, the Western woman character, usually the object of the male gaze in Hollywood films, tends to be granted in the East an active (colonial) gaze, insofar as she now, temporarily within the narrative, becomes the sole delegate, as it were, of Western civilization. The "norms of the text" (Boris Uspensky) are represented by the Western male but in the moments of His absence, the white woman becomes the civilizing center of the film.[50] These racial and sexual hierarchies in the text are also clearly exemplified in Michael Powell and Emeric Pressburger (*Black Narcissus*), where most of the narrative is focalized through the British nuns and their "civilizing mission" in India. But ultimately the "norms of the text" are embodied by the British man, whose initial "prophecy" that the wild mountains of India are not suitable for and are beyond the control of the Christian missionaries is confirmed by the end of the narrative, with the virtual punishment of the nuns as catastrophes and mental chaos penetrate their order. Yet in relation to the "Natives" (both Indian men and women) the British women are privileged and form the "filter" and "center of consciousness" (Gérard Genette) of the film.

The discourse on gender within a colonial context, in sum, suggests that Western women can occupy a relatively powerful position on the surface of the text, as the vehicles less for a sexual gaze than a colonial gaze. In these friction-producing moments between sexual and national hierarchies, particularly as encapsulated through the relationship between Third World men and First World women, national identity (associated with the white female character) is relatively privileged over sexual identity (associated with the dark male character). At the same time, the same ambivalence operates in relation to Third World men, whose punishment for inter-racial desire is simultaneously accompanied by spectatorial gratification for a male sexual gaze as ephemerally relayed by a darker man. These contradictions of national and sexual hierarchies, present in embryo in early cinema, are accentuated in the recent nostalgia-for-empire (liberal) films which foreground a female protagonist, presumably appealing to feminist codes, while reproducing colonialist narrative and cinematic power arrangements. The desexualization of the "good" African or Indian (servant) man in *Gorillas in the Mist*, *A Passage to India*, and *Out of Africa*, not unlike the desexualization of the female domestic servant as in *The Birth of a Nation* (1915) and *Gone with the Wind* (1939), is dialectically linked to the placement of the Western woman in the (White) "Pater" paradigm *vis-à-vis* the "natives."

Rape and the rescue phantasy

The chromatic sexual hierarchy in colonialist narratives, typical of Western racial conventions, has White women/men occupy the center of the narrative, with the White woman as the desired object of the male protagonists and antagonists. Marginalized within the narrative, Third World women – when not inscribed as metaphors for their virgin land as in *Bird of Paradise* – appear largely as sexually hungry subalterns.[51] In one scene in *The Sheik*, Arab women – some of them Black – fight quite literally over their Arab man. While the White woman has to be lured, made captive, and virtually raped to awaken her repressed desire, the Arab/Black/Latin women are driven by a raging libido. Here one encounters some of the complementary contradictions in colonial discourse whereby a Third World land and its inhabitants are the object of the desire for chastity articulated in the virgin metaphors, while also manifesting Victorian repression of sexuality, particularly female sexuality, through unleashing its pornographic impulse.[52]

The positing of female sexual enslavement by polygamous Third World men becomes especially ironic when we recall the subjection of African American women slaves on Southern plantations with the daily lived polygamy of White men slaveowners.[53] Images of Black/Arab woman in "heat" versus "frigid" White woman also indirectly highlight the menacing figure of the Black/Arab rapist and therefore mythically elide the history of subordination of Third World women by First World men. The hot/frigid dichotomy, then, implies three interdependent axioms within the sexual politics of colonialist discourse: (1) the sexual interaction of Black/Arab men and White women can *only* involve rape (since White women, within this perspective, cannot possibly desire Black men); (2) the sexual interaction of White men and Black/Arab women cannot involve rape (since Black/Arab women are in perpetual heat and desire their White master); and (3) the interaction of Black/Arab men and Black/Arab women also cannot involve rape, since both are in perpetual heat. It was this racist combinatoire that generated the (largely unspoken) rationale for the castration and lynching of African American men and the non-punishment of White men for the rape of African American women.

It is within this logic that *The Birth of a Nation* obsessively links sexual and racial phobias. The animalistic "Black," Gus, attempts to rape the virginal Flora, much as the "mulatto" Lynch tries to force Elsie into marriage, and the "mulatta" Lydia blames an innocent White man of sexual abuse, while simultaneously manipulating the unaware politician Stoneman through sexuality. The threat of African American political assertion is subliminally linked to Black sexual potency. It is not surprising, therefore, that the only non-threatening Black figure, the "loyal" mammy, is portrayed as completely desexualized. The thematization of Blacks' hyper-sexuality diacritically foils (White) masculinist acts of patriotism. It is the attempted rape of Flora that catalyzes the grand act of White "liberation". The opening intertitle, which states that the very presence of the African in America "planted the first seed of disunion," and the portrayal of idealized harmony between North and South (and Masters and Slaves) before the abolition suggest that libidinal Blacks destroyed the nation. The rescue of Flora, of Elsie, and of the besieged Northerners and Southerners (who are now once again united "in common defence of their Aryan Birthright"), operates as a didactic allegory whose telos is the Klansmen's vision of the "order of things." The closure of "mixed"-marriage between North and South confirms national unity and establishes a certain sexual order in which the virginal desired White woman is available only to White man. The superimposition of the Christ figure over the celebrating family/nation provides a religious benediction on the "birth." This abstract, metaphysical Birth of the Nation masks a more concrete notion of birth – no less relevant to the conception of the American nation – that of children from raped Black women, just as the naming of the mulatto as "Lynch" crudely blames the victims. Furthermore, the White man, who historically raped Third World women, manifests latent rapist desires toward innocent White women via a projected Black man, here literally masked in black-face.

Even when not involving rape, the possibilities of erotic interaction in films prior to the 1960s were severely limited by apartheid-style ethnic/racial codes. The same Hollywood that at times could project mixed love stories between Anglo-Americans and Latins and Arabs (especially if incarnated by White American actors and actresses such as Valentino in *The Sheik*, Dorothy Lamour in *The Road to Morocco* (1942), or Maureen O'Hara in *They Met in Argentina* (1941) was completely inhibited in relation to African, Asian, or Native American sexuality.

This latent fear of blood-tainting in such melodramas as *Call Her Savage* (1932) and *Pinky* (1949) necessitates narratives where the "half breed" ("Native American" in *Call Her Savage* and "Black" in *Pinky*) female protagonists are prevented at the closure of the films from participating in mixed-marriage, ironically despite the roles being played by "pure White" actresses. It is therefore the generic space of melodrama that preoccupies itself with "inter-racial" romantic interaction. The trajectory of constituting the couple in the musical comedy, for example, could not allow for a racially "subaltern" protagonist.

The Production Code of the Motion Picture Producers and Directors of America, Inc.: 1930–1934, an even stricter version of the Hays Office codes of the 1920s, explicitly states: "Miscegenation (sex relation between the white and black races) is forbidden."[54] The delegitimizing of the romantic union between "white" and "black" "races" is linked to a broader exclusion of Africans, Asians, and Native Americans from participation in social institutions. Translating the obsession with "pure blood" into legal language, Southern miscegenation laws, as pointed out by African American feminists as early as the end of the last century,[55] were designed to maintain White (male) supremacy and to prevent a possible transfer of property to Blacks in the post-abolition era. "Race" as a biological category, as Hazel Carby formulates it, was subordinated to race as a political category.[56] It is within this context of an exclusionary ideology that we can understand the Production Code's universal censorship of sexual violence and brutality where the assumption is one of purely individual victimization, thus undermining a possible portrayal of the racially–sexually based violence toward African Americans, and implicitly wiping out the memory of the rape, castration, and lynching from the American record.[57] The Production Code, in other words, eliminates a possible counter-narrative by Third World people for whom sexual violence has often been at the kernel of their historical experience and identity. . . .[58]

The imaginary of the harem

As with voyeuristic anthropological studies and moralistic travel literature concerning non-normative conceptions of sexuality, Western cinema diffused the anachronistic but still Victorian obsession with sexuality through the cinematic apparatus. The outlet for Western male heroic desire is clearly seen in *Harum Scarum* (1965), a reflexive film featuring a carnival-like Orient reminiscent of Las Vegas, itself placed in the burning sands of the American desert of Nevada, and offering harem-like nightclubs. The film opens with Elvis Presley – attired in an "Oriental" head wrap and vest – arriving on horseback in the desert. Upon arrival Presley leaps off his horse to free a woman from two evil Arabs who have tied her to a stake. The triumphant rescuer later sings:

> I'm gonna go where desert sun is; where the fun is; go where the harem girls dance;
> go where there's love and romance – out on the burning sands, in some caravan. I'll

find adventure where I can. To say the least, go East, young man. You'll feel like the Sheik, so rich and grand, with dancing girls at your command. When paradise starts calling, into some tent I'm crawling. I'll make love the way I plan. Go East – and drink and feast – go East, young man.

Material abundance in Orientalist discourse, tied to a history of imperial enterprises, here functions as part of the generic utopia of the musical, constituting itself, in Jamesonian terms, as a projected fulfillment of what is desired and absent within the socio-political status quo. Yet the "absence" is explicitly within the masculinist imaginative terrain. The images of harems offer an "open sesame" to an unknown, alluring, and tantalizingly forbidden world, posited as desirable to the instinctual primitive presumably inhabiting all men. In *Kismet* (1955), for example, the harem master entertains himself with a panopticon-like device which allows him to watch his many women without their knowledge. Authorizing a voyeuristic entrance into an inaccessible private space, the Harem dream reflects a masculinist utopia of sexual omnipotence.[59]

The topos of the harem in contemporary popular culture draws, of course, on a long history of Orientalist phantasies. Wester voyagers had no conceivable means of access to harems – indeed, the Arabic etymology of the word "harem," Kharim, refers to something "forbidden." Yet Western texts delineate life in the harems with great assurance and apparent exactitude, rather like European Orientalist studio paintings, for example the famous *Turkish Bath* (1862) which was painted without Ingres ever visiting the Orient. The excursions to the Orient, and on-location paintings by painters such as Ferdinand-Victor-Eugene Delacroix, similarly, served largely to authenticate an *a priori* vision. Inspired by the Arab popular tradition of fantastic tales, the travelers recounted the Orient to fellow-Westerners according to the paradigms furnished by European translations of *A Thousand and One Nights* (*Alf Laila wa Laila*), tales which were often translated quite loosely in order to satisfy the European taste for a passionately, violent Orient.[60] This Orient was perhaps best encapsulated in the figure of Salomé, whose Semitic origins were highlighted by the nineteenth-century Orientalist ethnographic vogue (e.g. Hugo von Habermann, Otto Friedrich).

The historical harem – which was largely an upper-class phenomenon – was in fact most striking in its domesticity. Memoirs written by Egyptian and Turkish women[61] depict the complex familial life and a strong network of female communality horizontally and vertically across class lines. The isolated but relatively powerful harem women depended on working-class women who were freer to move, and therefore became an important connection to the outside world.[62] Despite their subordination, harem women, as Leila Ahmed points out, often owned and ran their property, and could at times display crucial political power, thus revealing the harem as a site of contradictions.[63] Whereas Western discourse on the harem defined it simply as a male-dominated space, the accounts of the harem by Middle Eastern women testify to a system whereby a man's female relatives also shared the living space, allowing women access to other women, providing a protected space for the exchange of information and ideas safe from the eyes and the ears of men. (Contemporary Middle Eastern vestiges of this tradition are found in regular all-female gatherings, whereby women, as in the harems, carnivalize male power through jokes, stories, singing, and dancing.) In other words, the "harem," though patriarchal in nature, has been subjected to an ahistorical discourse whose Eurocentric assumptions left unquestioned the sexual oppression of the West. The Middle Eastern system of communal seclusion, then, must also be compared to the Western system of domestic "solitary confinement" for upper-middle class women.[64]

European women constituted an enthusiastic audience for much of the nineteenth-century Orientalist poetry written by Beckford, Byron, and Moore, anticipating the spectatorial enthusiasm for exoticist films. As travelers, however, their discourse on the harems oscillates between Orientalist narratives and more dialogical testimonies. Western women participated in the Western colonial gaze; their writings often voyeuristically dwell on Oriental clothes, postures, and gestures, exoticizing the female "other."[65] If male narrators were intrigued by the harem as the locus of lesbian sexuality, female travelers, who as women had more access to female spaces, undermined the pornographic imagination of the harem. Interestingly, the detailed description of Turkish female bodies in Lady Mary Wortley Montagu's letters, particularly those drawn from her visit to the *hammam* (baths), points to a subliminal erotic fascination with the female "other," a fascination masquerading, at times, as a male gaze:

> I perceiv'd that the Ladys with the finest skins and most delicate shapes had the greatest share of my admiration, th'o their faces were sometimes less beautiful than those of their companions. To tell you the truth, I had the wickedness enough to wish secretly that Mr. Gervase had been there invisible. I fancy it would have very much improv'd his art to see so many fine Women naked in different postures.[66]

Female travelers, furthermore, were compelled to situate their own oppression *vis-à-vis* that of Oriental women. Lady Mary Wortley Montagu often measures the freedom endowed to English *vis-à-vis* Turkish women, suggesting the paradoxes of harems and veils:

> 'Tis very easy to see that they have more liberty than we have, no woman of what rank soever being permitted to go in the streets without two muslins, one that covers her face all but her eyes and another that hides the whole dress ... You may guess how effectually this disguises them, that there is no distinguishing the great lady from her slave, and 'tis impossible for the most jealous husband to know his wife when he meets her, and no man dare either touch or follow a woman in the streets ... The perpetual masquerade gives them entire liberty of following their inclinations without danger of discovery.[67]

In fact, Lady Mary Wortley Montagu implicitly suggests an awareness, on the part of Turkish women, not simply of their oppression but also of that of

European women. Recounting the day she was undressed in the *hamman* by the lady of the house, who was struck at the sight of the stays, she quoted the lady's remark that "the Husbands in England were much worse than in the East; for they ty'd up their wives in boxes, of the shape of their bodies."[68]

The popular image-making of the Orient internalized, in other words, the codes of male-oriented travel-narratives. The continuities between the representation of the native body and the female body are obvious when we compare Hollywood's ethnography with Hollywood's pornography. Ironically, we find a latent inscription of harems and despots even in texts not set in the Orient. *Harem structures*, in fact, permeate Western mass-mediated culture. Busby Berkeley's musical numbers, for example, project a harem-like structure reminiscent of Hollywood's mythical Orient. Like the harem, his musical numbers involve a multitude of women who, as Lucy Fischer suggests, serve as signifiers of male power over infinitely substitutable females.[69] The mise-en-scène of both harem scenes and musical numbers is structured around the scopic privilege of the master and his limitless pleasure in an exclusive place inaccessible to other men. Berkeley's panopticon-like camera links visual pleasure with a kind of surveillance of manipulated female movement. The camera's omnipresent and mobile gaze, its magic-carpet-like air-borne prowling along confined females embodies the over-arching look of the absent/present master – i.e. of both the director/producer, and vicariously of the spectator. The production numbers tend to exclude the male presence, but allow for the fantasies of the spectator, positioning his/her gaze as that of a despot entertained by a plurality of females. Rendered virtually identical, the women in Berkeley's numbers evoke the analogy between the musical show and the harem not only as a textual construct but also as a studio practice whose patriarchal structure of casting is conceived as a kind of beauty contest (a "judgment of Paris"). Speaking of his casting methods, Berkeley himself recounted a day in which he interviewed 723 women in order to select only three: "My sixteen regular girls were sitting on the side waiting; so after I picked the three girls I put them next to my special sixteen and they matched just like pearls."[70]

The desert odyssey

The exoticist films allow for subliminally transsexual tropes. The phantasm of the Orient gives an outlet for a carnivalesque play with national and at times gender identities. Isabelle Adaani in *Ishtar* is disguised as an Arab male-rebel and Brooke Shields as an American male racer in the Sahara desert, while Rudolph Valentino (*The Sheik* and *Son of the Sheik*), Douglas Fairbanks (*The Thief of Baghdad*), Elvis Presley (*Harum Scarum*), Peter O'Toole (*Lawrence of Arabia*), Warren Beatty and Dustin Hoffman (*Ishtar*) wear Arab disguise. Masquerading manifests a latent desire to transgress fixed national and gender identities. In *The Sheik*, the Agnes Ayres character, assisted by Arab women, wears an Arab female dress in order to penetrate the Oriental "marriage market," assuming the "inferior" position of the Arab woman in order, paradoxically, to empower herself with a gaze on Oriental despotism. The change of gender identities of female characters in more recent films such as *Sahara* and *Ishtar* allows as well for harmless transgressions of the coded "feminine" body-language. In counter-narratives such as *The Battle of Algiers* (*La Battaglia di Algeri*, 1966), however, gender and national disguises take on different signification.[71] FLN Algerian women wear Western "modern" dress, dye their hair blonde, and even act coquettishly with French soldiers.[72] Here it is the Third World which masquerades as the West, not as an act of self-effacing mimicry but as a way of sabotaging the colonial regime of assimilation.

Since clothing over the last few centuries, as a result of what J. C. Flugel calls "the Great Masculine Renunciation,"[73] has been limited to austere, uncolorful, and unplayful costumes, the projection to the phantastic locus of the Orient allows the imagination to go exuberantly "native." Historically, the widely disseminated popular image in newspapers and newsreels of T. E. Lawrence in flowing Arab costume have partially inspired films such as *The Sheik* and *Son of the Sheik*, whose bi-sexual appeal can be located in the closet construction of Western man as "feminine."[74] The coded "feminine" look, therefore, is played out within the safe space of the Orient, through the "realistic" embodiment of the "Other." David Lean's Lawrence, despite his classical association with norms of heroic manliness, is also portrayed in a homoerotic light. When he is accepted by the Arab tribe he is dressed all in white, and at one point set on a horse, moving delicately, virtually captured like a bride. Drawing a sword from his sheath, the Peter O'Toole character shifts the gendered signification of the phallic symbol by using it as a mirror to look at his own newly acquired "feminine" Oriental image. More generally, the relationship between Lawrence and the Omar Sharif character gradually changes from initial male rivalry to an implied erotic attraction in which Sharif is associated with female imagery, best encapsulated in the scene where Sharif is seen in close-up with wet eyes, identifying with the tormented Lawrence. The inter-racial homoerotic subtext in *Lawrence of Arabia* forms part of a long tradition of colonial narratives from novels such as *Robinson Crusoe* (Crusoe and Friday), and *Huckleberry Finn* (Huck and Jim) to filmic adaptations such as *Around the World in 80 Days* (Phileas Fogg and his dark servant Passepartout).[75] Most texts about the "Empire," from the Western genre to recent nostalgia-for-Empire films such as *Mountains of the Moon* (1989), however, are pervaded by White homoeroticism in which male explorers, deprived of women, are "forced" into physical closeness, weaving bonds of affection and desire, in the course of their plights in an unknown, hostile land.

Homoeroticism, then, can simultaneously permeate homophobic colonialist texts. Within this symptomatic dialectic we may also understand the textual (dis)placement of the heterosexual African/Arab/Latino man, as playing the Id to the Western masculinist Superego. In *The Sheik*, for example, Valentino, as long as he is known to the spectator only as Arab, acts as the Id, but when he is revealed to be the son of Europeans, he is transformed into a superego figure who nobly risks his life to rescue the English woman from "real" Arab rapists.[76] And the English woman overcomes her sexual repression only in the desert, after being sexually provoked repeatedly by the Sheik. Valentino, the "Latin lover," is here projected into another "exotic" space where he can act out sexual phantasies that would have been unthinkable in a contemporaneous American or European setting. The desert, in this sense, functions narratively as an isolating element, as sexually and morally separate imaginary territory. The Orientalist films tend to begin in the city – where European civilization has already tamed the East – but the real dramatic conflicts take place in the desert where women are defenseless, and White woman could easily become the captive of a romantic sheik or evil Arab. The positioning of rapeable White woman by a lustful male in an isolated desert locale gives voice to a masculinist fantasy of complete control over the Western woman, the woman "close to home," without any intervening protective code of morality. Puritanical Hollywood thus claims to censure female adventurousness, and the male tyranny of harems and rapes – but only, paradoxically, as a way of gratitiying Western inter-racial sexual desires.

In the more recent reworking of *The Sheik* and *Son of the Sheik*, in Menahem Golan's *Sahara*, the male rescue phantasy and the punishment of female rebellion undergird the film. In *Sahara* the central figure, Dale (Brooke Shields), feisty race-car driving and only-daughter of a 1920s car manufacturer, is presented as reckless, daring, and assertive for entering the male domain of the Oriental desert and for entering the "men only" race. She also literally disguises herself as a man, and adopts His profession and His mastery of the desert land through technology. Captured by desert tribesmen, she becomes a commodity fought over within the tribe and between tribes; the camera's fetishization of her body, however, is the ironic reminder of the Western projection of stars' bodies as commodity. Scenes of Brooke Shields wrestling with her captors not only suture the Western spectator to a national rescue operation but also invite the implied spectator into an orgiastic voyeurism. The desire for the Western woman and the fear of losing control over her is manifested in her punishment through several attempted rapes by Arabs. But at the end the courageous winner of the race decides "on her own" to return to the noble light-skinned sheik who had rescued her from cruel Arabs at the risk of his own life. The woman, who could have won independence, still "voluntarily" prefers the ancient ways of gender hierarchies.

At times, it is implied that women, while offended by Arab and Muslim rapists, actually *prefer* masterful men like Valentino.[77] Following the screening of *The Sheik*, newspaper columnists were asking "Do women like masterful men?" To which Valentino replied: "Yes." "All women like a little cave-man stuff. No matter whether they are feminists, suffragettes or so-called new women, they like to have a masterful man who makes them do things he asserts."[78] Edith Hull expressed similar opinions. "There can be only one head in a house. Despite modern desire for equality of sexes I still believe that physically and morally it is better that the head should be the man."[79] Edith Hull's novel and Monic Katterjohn's adaptation, gratify, to some extent, a projected Western female desire for an "exotic" lover, for a Romantic, sensual, passionate, but non-lethal, play with the *Liebestod*, a release of the Id for the (segregated) upper-middle class occidental woman.[80] (The author of the source novel claimed to have written the book for relaxation when her husband was in the war and she was alone in India. She decided to visit in Algeria, where she was impressed with the fine work the French government was doing.) In this sense the phantasm of the Orient can be incorporated by Western women, forming part of the broader colonial discourse on the "exotic," while simultaneously constituting an imaginary locus for suppressed sexual desires.

The rescue phantasy, when literalized through the rescue of a woman from a lascivious Arab, has to be seen not only as an allegory of saving the Orient from its libidinal, instinctual destructiveness but also as a didactic *Bildungsroman* addressed to women at home, perpetuating by contrast the myth of the sexual egalitarianism of the West. The exoticist films delegitimize Third World national identities and give voice to anti-feminist backlash, responding to the threat to institutionalized patriarchal power presented by the woman's suffrage movements and the nascent feminist struggle. In this sense the narrative of Western women in the Third World can be read as a projected didactic allegory insinuating the dangerous nature of the "uncivilized man" and by implication lauding the freedom presumably enjoyed by Western women. In *The Sheik* and *Sahara* the Western woman directly rebels against the "civilized tradition" of marriage at the beginning of the film, calling it "captivity," only to later become literally captive of lusting Dark men. Transgressing male space (penetrating the marriage market by masquerading as an Arab woman in *The Sheik*, and participating in a male race by masquerading as a young man in *Sahara*), the female protagonist begins with a hubris *vis-à-vis* her Western male protectors (against the Arabians from the desert), and then goes through the "pedagogical" experience of attempted rapes. The telos, or quite literally, "homecoming" of this desert Odyssey is the disciplinary punishment of female desire for liberation and renewed spectatorial appreciation for the existing sexual, racial, and national order.

My discussion of colonial constructions of gender has aimed at analyzing the crucial role of sexual difference for the culture of Empire. Western popular culture, in this sense, has operated on the same Eurocentric discursive continuum as such disciplines as Philosophy, Egyptology, Anthropology, Historiography, and Geography. From the erotic projections of *The Sheik* to the spectacular historiography of *Lawrence of Arabia*, or from the fantastic tale of *The Mummy* (1932) to the Egyptological mission of *Raiders of the Lost Ark*, my reading has tried to suggest that despite some differences, having to do with the periods in which the films were produced, hegemonic Western representation has been locked into a series of Eurocentric articulations of power. Although a feminist reading of (post)colonial discourse must take into account the national and historical specificities of that discourse, it is equally important also to chart the broader structural analogies in the representation of diverse Third World cultures. (Post)colonial narratives, as we have seen, serve to define the "West" through metaphors of rape, phantasies of rescue, and eroticized geographies. The popular culture of Empire has tended to rely on a structurally similar genderized discourse within different national and historical moments, a discourse challenged by resistant counter-narratives such as *How Tasty Was My Frenchman*, *Nice Coloured Girls*, and *The Mummy/The Night of Counting the Years*.

Notes

1   Different sections of this essay were presented at several conferences: Third World Film Institute, New York University (1984); The Middle East Studies Association, University of California, Los Angeles (1988); Humanities Council Faculty Seminar on Race and Gender, New York University (1988); The Society for Cinema Studies, Iowa University (1989); The Conference on "Gender and Colonialism," University of California, Berkeley (1989); The Conference on "Rewriting the (Post)Modern: (Post)-Colonialism/Feminism/Late Capitalism," University of Utah, Humanities Center (1990).

2   Here some of my discussion is indebted to Edward Said's notion of the "feminization" of the Orient, *Orientalism* (New York: Vintage, 1978). See also Francis Barker, Peter Hulme, Margaret Iversen, Diana Loxley, eds. *Europe and Its Others* Vols. 1 and 2. Colchester: University of Essex, 1985, especially Peter Hulme, "Polytropic Man: Tropes of Sexuality and Mobility in Early Colonial Discourse" (Vol. 2); Jose Rabasa, "Allegories of the Atlas" (Vol. 2). Some of my discussion here on gendered metaphors appears in Ella Shohat, "Imagining Terra Incognita: The Disciplinary Gaze of Empire," *Public Culture*, Vol. 3, No. 2.

3   Sir Walter Raleigh, "Discovery of Guiana." Cited in Susan Griffin, *Woman and Nature: The Roaring Inside Her* (New York: Harper & Row, 1978), p. 47.

4   St. John de Crèvecoeur, *Letters from an American Farmer*, 1782. Cited in Henry Nash Smith, *Virgin Land: The American West as Symbol and Myth* (Cambridge, Massachusetts: Harvard University Press, 1950), p. 121.

5   See Henry Nash Smith, *Virgin Land: The American West as Symbol and Myth*. For nineteenth-century North American expansionist ideology, see Richard Slotkin, *The Fatal Environment: The Myth of the Frontier in the Age of Industrialization, 1800–1890* (Middletown, Connecticut: Wesleyan University Press, 1985).

6   For an examination of the representation of the American frontiers and gender issues see Annette Kolodny, *The Lay of the Land: Metaphors as Experience and History in American Life and Letters* (Chapel Hill: University of North Carolina Press, 1975); and *The Land Before Her: Fantasy and Experience of the American Frontiers, 1630–1860* (Chapel Hill: University of North Carolina Press, 1984).

7   R. W. B. Lewis, *The American Adam: Innovecre, Tragedy, and Thirteen in the Nineteenth Century* (Chicago: University of Chicago Press, 1959.) Hans Blumenberg, interestingly, points out in relation to Francis Bacon that the resituation of Paradise, as the goal of history, was supposed to promise magical facility. The knowledge of

nature for him is connected to his definition of the Paradisiac condition as mastery by means of the word. (*The Legitimacy of the Modern Age*. Translated by Robert Wallace. Cambridge, Massachusetts. MIL Press, 1980.)

8   Jan Van der Straet's representation of America has been cited by several scholars: Michel de Certeau "Avant propos" in *L'Écriture de l'histoire*. Paris: Gallimard, 1975; Olivier Richon, "Representation, the Despot and the Harem: Some Questions Around an Academic Orientalist Painting by Lecomte-du-Nouy" (1885) in *Europe and Its Others* (Vol. 1).

9   The gendering of colonial encounters between a "feminine" nature and "masculine" scientist draws on a pre-existing discourse which has genderized the encounter between "Man and Nature" in the West itself. For a full discussion see, for example, Susan Griffin, *Woman and Nature: The Roaring Inside Her*.

10   Michael de Certeau, "Avant propos" in *L'Écriture de l'histoire*.

11   The film was distributed in the US as *How Tasty Was My Little Frenchman*.

12   For a close analysis of *How Tasty was My Frenchman* see Richard Peña, "How Tasty Was My Little Frenchman," in Randal Johnson and Robert Stam, *Brazilian Cinema*. East Brunswick, New Jersey: Associated University Presses, 1982 (reprinted by University of Texas Press, 1985).

13   The report concerns another tribe, the Tupiniquim who were massacred by their "allies," the Portuguese, confirming the Native American stance, mediated in the film through the Tupinamba tribe, that despite tactical alliances, the Europeans, whether French or Portuguese, have similar desires in relation to the Native American Land.

14   The film which was shot in Parati (Brazil) has the actors and actresses mimic Native American attitudes towards nudity by living nude throughout the duration of the shooting. This production method is, of course, different from the industrial approach to shooting scenes of nudity. *How Tasty Was My Frenchman* can also be seen as part of a counterculture of the late 1960s, and its general interest in non-Western societies as alternative possibilities.

15   *How Tasty Was My Frenchman* does not criticize patriarchal structures within Native American societies.

16   Although Cleopatra was addressed as Egypt in the *Antony and Cleopatra* play: Shakespeare here and in *The Tempest* offers a complex dialectics between the West and "its Others."

17   Colonialist representations have their roots in what Martin Bernal calls the "Aryan model," a model which projects a presumably clear and monolithic historical trajectory leading from classical Greece (constructed as "pure," "Western," and "democratic") to Imperial Rome and then to the metropolitan capitals of Europe and the United States. (See *Black Athena: The Ajnasnath Roots of Classical Civilization. Volume 1, The Fabrication of Ancient Greece 1785–1985*. New Brunswick: Rutgers University Press, 1987.) "History" is made to seem synonymous with a linear notion of European "progress." This Eurocentric view is premised on crucial exclusions of internal and external "others": the African and Semitic cultures that strongly inflected the culture of classical Greece; the Islamic and Arabic-Sephardi culture which played an invaluable cultural role during the so-called "dark" and "middle" ages; and the diverse indigenous peoples, whose land and natural resources were violently appropriated and whose cultures were constructed as "savage" and "irrational."

18 Egyptology's mania for a mere ancient Egypt, for example, is ironic in an Arab context where Egypt is often perceived as *the* model of an Arab country.

19 This is true even for those films produced after the great wave of national liberation movements in the Third World.

20 Tracey Moffatt's *Nice Coloured Girls* explores the relocations established between White settlers and Aboriginal women over the last two hundred years, juxtaposing the "first encounter" with present-day urban encounters. Conveying the perspective of Aboriginal women, the film situates their oppression within a historical context in which voices and images from the past play a crucial role.

21 Female voyagers occupy very rarely the center of the narrative (*The King and I, Black Narcissus*). In contrast to scientist heroes, they tend to occupy the "feminine" actantial slot: educators and nurses.

22 The passive/active division is, of course, based on stereotypically sexist imagery.

23 See for example Suleiman Mousa, *T. E. Lawrence: An Arab View*. Translated by Albert Butros. New York: Oxford University Press, 1966.

24 See Francis Bacon, *Advancement of Learning* and *Novum Organum*, New York: Colonial Press, 1899.

25 Francis Bacon, *Advancement of Learning* and *Novum Organum. In Advancement of Learning*, p. 135.

26 Francis Bacon, *Novum Organum* in *The Works of Francis Bacon*. James Spedding, Robert Ellis and Douglas Heath, eds. London: Longmans, 1870, p. 82.

27 Hans Blumenberg, *The Legitimacy of the Modern Age*, p. 389.

28 For an illuminating reading of Haggard's *King Solomon's Mines* see Anne McClintock, "Maidens, Maps, and Mines: The Reinvention of Patriarchy in Colonial South Africa." *The South Atlantic Quarterly*, Vol. 87, No. 1 (Winter 1988).

29 Television has incorporated this penchant for spinning globe logos especially in news programs, displaying its authority over the world.

30 *Around the World in 80 Days* feminizes national maps by placing images of "native" women on the backs of maps of specific countries. The balloon used by the protagonist is referred to as "she" and called "La Coquette."

31 The feminine designation of "the moon" in French, "La Lune," is reproduced by the "feminine" iconography of the moon.

32 Georges Méliès's filmography includes a relatively great number of films related to colonial explorations and Orientalist phantasies such as *Le Fakir-Mystère Indien* (1896), *Vente d'Esclaves au Harem* (1897), *Cleopatre* (1899), *La Vengeance de Bouddah* (1901), *Les Aventures de Robinson Crusoe* (1902), *Le Palais des Milles et Une Nuits* (1905). Interestingly, Méliès's early fascination with spectacles dates back to his visits to the Egyptian Hall shows, directed by Maskelyne and Cooke and devoted to fantastic spectacles.

33 I am here referring especially to the Babylon section.

34 Bazin's Malraux-inspired statement in the opening of "The Ontology of the Photographic Image" suggests that "at the origin of painting and sculpture there lies a mummy complex" (*What Is Cinema*, translated by Hugh Gray, Berkeley: University of California Press, 1967, p. 9). The ritual of cinema, in this sense, is not unlike the Egyptian religious rituals which provided "a defence [*sic*] against the passage of time," thus satisfying "a basic psychological need in man, for death is but the victory of time." In this interesting analogy Bazin, it seems to me, offers an existentialist

interpretation of the mummy, which, at the same time, undermines Egyptian religion itself; since the ancient Egyptians above all axiomatically assumed the reality of life after death – toward which the mummy was no more than a means.

35   In this essay, I refer to some of the various subgenres of the Hollywood Orientalist film of which I have identified seven: (1) stories concerning contemporary Westerners in the Orient (*The Sheik* (1921), *The Road to Morocco* (1942), *Casablanca* (1942), *The Man Who Knew Too Much* (1956), *Raiders of the Lost Ark* (1981), *Sahara* (1983), *Ishtar* (1987)); (2) films concerning "Orientals" in the first world (*Black Sunday* (1977), *Back to the Future* (1985)); (3) films based on ancient history such as the diverse versions of *Cleopatra*; (4) films based on contemporary history (*Exodus* (1960), *Lawrence of Arabia* (1962)); (5) films based on the Bible (*Judith of Bethulia* (1913), *Samson and Delilah* (1949), *The Ten Commandments* (1956)); (6) films based on *The Arabian Nights* (*The Thief of Baghdad* (1924), *Oriental Dream* (1944), *Kismet* (1955)); (7) films in which ancient Egypt and its mythologized enigmas serve as pretext for contemporary horror–mystery and romance (the *Mummy* series). I view these films partially in the light of Edward Said's indispensable contribution to anti-colonial discourse, i.e. his genealogical critique of Orientalism as the discursive formation by which European culture was able to manage – and even produce – the Orient during the post-Enlightenment period.

36   Mallek Alloula examines this issue in French postcards of Algeria. See *The Colonial Harem*. Translated by Myrna Godzick and Wlad Godzich. Minneapolis: University of Minnesota Press, 1986.

37   Freud associates Africa and feminity in *The Interpretation of Dreams* when he speaks of Haggard's *She* as "a strange book, but full of hidden meaning...the eternal feminine...*She* describes an adventurous road that had scarcely even been trodden before, leading into an undiscovered region...." *The Standard Edition of the Complete Psychological Works of Sigmunal Freud*, ed. James Strachey. London: Hogarth Press, 1953–74, SE IV–V, pp. 453–4.

38   Joseph Breuer and Sigmund Freud, *Studies on Hysteria*. Translated by James Strachey in collaboration with Anna Freud. New York: Basic Books, 1957, p. 139.

39   Breuer and Freud, *Studies on Hysteria*, p. 193.

40   Sigmund Freud, "On Transformations of Instinct as Exemplified in Anal Erotism," in *The Standard Edition of the Complete Psychological Works of Sigmund Freud*, SE XVII, pp. 129, 135.

41   Toril Moi, "Representation of Patriarchy: Sexuality and Epistemology in Freud's Dora," in Charles Brenheimer and Claire Kahane, eds. *In Dora's Case: Freud, Hysteria, Feminism*. London: Virago, 1985, p. 198.

42   David Macey, *Lacan in Contexts*. London, New York: Verso, 1988, pp. 178–80.

43   Breuer and Freud, *Studies on Hysteria*, p. 292.

44   Stephan Salisbury, "In Dr. Freud's Collection, Objects of Desire," *The New York Times*, September 3, 1989.

45   "My voyage to the Orient was like a grand act of my interior life."

46   Linking Jews to the history, politics, and culture of the West must be seen as continuous with Zionist discourse which has elided the largely Third World Arab history and culture of Middle Eastern Sephardic Jews. For a full discussion of the problematics generated by Zionist discourse, see Ella Shohat, "Sephardim in Israel: Zionism from the Standpoint of Its Jewish Victims," *Sejal Text* 1920 (Fall 1988). This

debate was partially continued in *Critical Inquiry* Vol. 15, No. 3 (Spring 1989) in the section "An Exchange on Edward Said and Difference." See especially, Edward Said, "Response," pp. 634–46.

47 *The Ten Commandments*, partially shot on location in Egypt, was banned by the Egyptian government.

48 On another level we might discern a hidden Jewish substratum undergoing the film. In the ancient past Egypt dispossessed the Hebrews of their ark and in the present (the 1930s) it is the Nazis; but in a time tunnel Harrison Ford is sent to fight the Nazis in the name of a Jewish shrine (the word "Jewish" is of course never mentioned in the film) and in the course of events the rescuer is rescued by the rescuee. A phantasy of liberation from a history of victimization is played out by Steven Spielberg, using biblical myths of wonders worked against ancient Egyptians this time redeployed against the Nazis – miracles absent during the Holocaust. The Hebrew ark itself performs miracles and dissolves the Nazis, saving Dr Jones and his girlfriend Marion from the Germans who, unlike the Americans, do not respect the divine law of never looking at the Holy of Holies. The Jewish religious prohibition of looking at God's image and the prohibition of graven images (with the consequent cultural de-emphasis on visual arts) is triumphant over the Christian predilection for religious visualization. The film, in the typical paradox of cinematic voyeurism, punishes the hubris of the "Christian" who looks at divine beauty while at the same time nourishing the spectator's visual pleasure.

49 See for example Cynthia Enloe, *Bananas, Beaches and Bases: Making Feminist Sense of International Politics* (Berkeley: University of California Press, 1989), pp. 19–41.

50 See Boris Uspensky, *A Poetics of Composition* (Berkeley: University of California Press, 1973).

51 For a critical discussion of the representation of Black female sexuality in the cinema see Jane Gaines, "White Privilege and Looking Relations – Race and Gender in Feminist Film Theory," *Screen* Vol. 29, No. 4 (Autumn 1988). On Black spectatorship and reception of dominant films see for example Jacqueline Bobo, "*The Color Purple*: Black Women as Cultural Readers" in Diedre Pridram, ed. *Female Spectators: Looking at Films and Television* (New York: Verso, 1988); Manthia Diawara, "Black Spectatorship: Problems of Identification and Resistance" in *Screen* Vol. 29, No. 4 (Autumn 1988).

52 The mystery in the *Mummy* films which often involves a kind of Liebestod or haunting heterosexual attraction – for example *The Mummy* (1932), *The Mummy's Curse* (1944), *The Mummy's Hand* (1940) – can be seen in this sense as allegorizing the mysteries of sexuality itself.

53 In her striking autobiography, Harriet Jacobs, for example, recounts the history of her family, focusing especially on the degradation of slavery and the sexual oppression she suffered as a slave woman. Her daily struggle against racial/sexual abuse is well illustrated in the cases of her master, who was determined to turn her into his concubine, his jealous wife, who added her own versions of harassments, and the future congressman, who, after fathering her children, did not keep his promise to set them free. *Incidents in the Life of a Slave Girl Written by Herself*, Fagan Yellin, ed. (Cambridge, Massachusetts: Harvard University Press, 1987).

54 Citations from The Production Code of the Motion Picture Producers and Directors of America, Inc.: 1930–1934 are taken from Garth Jowett, *Film: The Democratic Art* (Boston: Little, Brown and Company, 1976).

55　Here I am especially thinking of Anna Julia Cooper and Ida B. Wells.

56　Hazel V. Carby, "Lynching, Empire, and Sexuality." *Critical Inquiry* Vol. 12, number 1 (Autumn 1985).

57　For discussion of rape and racial violence see for example Jacquelyn Dowd Hall, " 'The Mind that Burns in Each Body': Women, Rape, and Racial Violence" in Ann Snitow, Christine Stansell and Sharon Thompson, eds., *Powers of Desire* (New York: Monthly Review Press, 1983).

58　Haile Gerima's *Bush Mama* anatomizes contemporary American power structure in which rape performed by a white policeman is subjectivized through the helpless young Black woman.

59　Fellini's $8\frac{1}{2}$, meanwhile, self-mockingly exposes this pornographic imagination of the King Solomon style harem as merely amplifying the protagonist's actual lived polygamy.

60　For the Orientalist ideology undergirding the translations of *A Thousand and One Nights* to European languages see Rana Kabbani, *Europe's Myths of Orient* (Bloomington: Indiana University Press, 1986).

61　See for example Huda Shaarawi, *Harem Years: The Memoirs of an Egyptian Feminist (1879–1924)*. Translated by Margot Badran. (New York: Feminist Press at the City University of New York, 1987.)

62　See Lois Beck and Nikki Keddie, eds. *Women in the Muslim World* (Cambridge, Massachusetts: Harvard University Press, 1978); Mervat Hatem, "The Politics of Sexuality and Gender in Segregated Patriarchal Systems: The Case of Eighteenth- and Nineteenth-Century Egypt." *Feminist Studies* 12, No. 2 (Summer 1986).

63　For a critique of Eurocentric representation of the Harem see Leila Ahmed, "Western Ethnocentrism and Perceptions of the Harem," *Feminist Studies* 8, No. 3 (Fall 1982).

64　The artistic representation of the solitary confinement of upper-middle class Western women within the household is fascinatingly researched and analyzed by Bram Dijkstra, *Idols of Perversity* (New York: Oxford University Press, 1986).

65　Protofeminist Western women such as Hubertine Auclert, Françoise Correze, Mathea Gaudry, and Germaine Tillion, as Marnia Lazreg suggests, reproduced Orientalist discourse in their writings. For a critique of Western feminism and colonial discourse see for example Marnia Lazreg "Feminism and Difference: The Perils of Writing as a Woman on Women in Algeria," *Feminist Studies* 14:3 (Fall 1988): Chandra Talpade Mohanty, "Under Western Eyes: Feminist Scholarship and Colonial Discourses." *Boundary* 2:12 (Spring/Fall 1984); Gayatri Chakravorty Spivak, "French Feminism in an International Frame," *Yale French Studies* 62 (1981); *In Other Worlds: Essays in Cultural Politics*, chapter 3 "Entering the Third World" (New York and London: Methuen, 1987).

66　Robert Halsband, ed., *The Complete Letters of Lady Mary Wortley Montagu*, Vol. 1 (London: Oxford University Press, 1965), p. 314.

67　Robert Halsband, ed., *The Selected Letters of Lady Mary Wortley Montagu* (New York: St. Martin's Press, 1970), pp. 96–7.

68　Robert Halsband, ed., *The Complete Letters of Lady Mary Wortley Montagu*, Vol. 1, pp. 314–15.

69　For an analysis of the "mechanical reproduction" of women in Busby Berkeley's films, see Lucy Fischer, "The Image of Woman As Image: The Optical Politics of

Dames," in Patricia Erens, ed. *Sexual Stratagems: The World of Women in Film* (New York: Horizon Press, 1979).

70 Quoted in Lucy Fischer, "The Image of Woman As Image: The Optical Politics of *Dames*," p. 44.

71 For a detailed analysis of *The Battle of Algiers*, see Robert Stam, "Three Women, Three Bombs: *The Battle of Algiers*, Notes and Analysis" *Film Study Extract* (MacMillan Press, 1975). See also Barbara Harlow's introduction to Malek Alloula, *The Colonial Harem*, pp. ix–xxii.

72 In *Battle of Algiers* FLN Algerian men at one point wear Arab female dress – a disguise whose ultimate goal is to assert Algerian national identity. This ephemeral change of gender identities within anti-colonial texts requires a more elaborate analysis of the Third World masculine rescue operation of Third World women from the violation of First World men. Such feminist criticism directed at the works of Frantz Fanon and Malek Alloula within the Algerian/French context has been addressed, in the Black/White North American context, at Malcolm X and the Black Panthers.

73 See J. C. Flugel, *The Psychology of Clothes* (London: Hogarth Press, 1930). For an extended discussion of Flugel writing on fashion see Kaja Silverman, "The Fragments of a Fashionable Discourse," in *Studies in Entertainment: Critical Approaches to Mass Culture*, ed. Tania Modleski (Bloomington: Indiana University Press, 1986); also Silverman, *The Acoustic Mirror: The Female Voice in Psychoanalysis and Cinema* (Bloomington: Indiana University Press, 1988), pp. 24–7.

74 The American journalist Lowell Thomas was instrumental in the popularization of T. E. Lawrence in the West; his show, which consisted of lecture and footage he shot from the Middle East front, was, after a short time, moved to Madison Square Garden. See John E. Mack, *A Prince of Our Disorder: The Life of T. E. Lawrence* (Boston: Little Brown and Company, 1976).

75 Leslie Fielder argues that homoerotic friendship between White men and Black or indigenous men is at the core of the classical American novel. See *Love and Death in the American Novel* (New York: Criterion Books, 1960).

76 Interestingly Leslie Fiedler's *The Inadvertent Epic* comments on another white woman novelist, Margaret Mitchell, whose *Gone With the Wind* is structured according to scenarios of inter-ethnic rapes.

77 For an analysis of Valentino and female spectatorship, see Miriam Hansen, "Pleasure, Ambivalence, Identification: Valentino and Female Spectatorship," *Cinema Journal* 25, No. 4 (Summer, 1986).

78 *Movie Weekly*, November 19, 1921.

79 *Movie Weekly*, November 19, 1921.

80 Denis de Rougemont partially traces the *liebestod* motif to Arabic poetry. See *Love in the Western World*, translated by Montgomery Belgion (New York: Harper & Row, 1974).

38

Fantasies of the Master Race:
Categories of Stereotyping of
American Indians in Film

Ward Churchill

*Now those movie Indians wearing all those feathers can't come out as human beings.
They're not expected to come out as human beings because I think the American people do
not regard them as wholly human. We must remember that many, many American
children believe that feathers grow out of Indian heads.*

Stephan Feraca, Motion Picture Director, 1964

The handling of American Indians and American Indian subject matter within
the context of commercial US cinema is objectively racist on all levels, an
observation which extends to television as well as film. In this vein, it is linked
closely to literature, both fictional and non-fictional, upon which many if not
most movie scripts are at least loosely based. In a very real sense, it is fair to
observe that all modes of projecting concepts and images of the Indian before the
contemporary US public fit the same mold, and do so for the same fundamental
"real world" reasons. This essay will attempt to come to grips with both the
method and the motivation for this, albeit within a given medium and examining
a somewhat restricted range of the tactics employed. The medium selected for
this purpose is commercial film, the technique examined that of stereotypic
projection. The matter divides itself somewhat automatically into three major
categories of emphasis. These may be elucidated as follows.

The American Indian as a Creature of Another Time

We are all aware of the standard motion picture technique of portraying the
Native American with galloping pony and flowing headdress. We have seen the
tipi and the buffalo hunt, the attack on the wagon train and the ambush of
the stagecoach until they are scenes so totally ingrained in the American

consciousness as to be synonymous with the very concept of the American Indian (to non-Indian minds at any rate and, unfortunately, to many Indian minds as well). It is not the technical defects of the scenes depicted here – although often they are many – which present the basic problem. Rather, it is that the historical era involved spans a period scarcely exceeding 50 years' duration. Hence, the Indian has been restricted in the public mind, not only in terms of the people portrayed (the Plains Nations), but in terms of the time of their collective existence (roughly 1825–80).

The essential idea of Native America instilled cinematically is that of a quite uniform aggregation of peoples (in dress, custom, and actions) which flourished with the arrival of whites upon their land and then vanished somewhat mysteriously, along with the bison and the open prairie. There is no "before" to this story, and there is no "after." Such is the content of *They Died With Their Boots On, Boots and Saddles, Cheyenne Autumn, Tonka Wakan* and *Little Big Man*, to list but five examples from among hundreds. Of course, commercial film has – albeit in many fewer cases – slightly expanded the scope of the stereotype. The existence of the peoples of the Northeast receive recognition in such epics as *Drums Along the Mohawk* and *The Deerslayer*. The peoples of the Southwest have been included, to some extent, in scattered fare such as *Broken Arrow, Fort Apache*, and *Tell Them Willie Boy Is Here*. The Southeastern nations even claim passing attention in efforts such as the Walt Disney *Davy Crockett* series and biographical features about the lives of such Euroamerican heroes as Andrew Jackson and Sam Houston.

The latter deviations from the Plains stereotype – which has assumed proportions of a valid archetype in the public consciousness – drives the timeline back some 75 years at most. A century-and-a-quarter selected for depiction is hardly better than a fifty-year span. Further, it should be noted that, costuming aside, literally all the geographical/cultural groups presented are portrayed in exactly the same manner, a matter we will consider in the following two sections. The point of the historical confines involved in this category, however, is that indigenous people are defined exclusively in terms of certain (conflict and demise) interactions with Euroamericans. There is no cinematic recognition whatsoever of a white-free and autonomous native past. Similarly, no attention is paid at all to the myriad indigenous nations not heavily and dramatically involved in the final period of Anglo-Indian warfare. US audiences know no Aztec, Inca, or Anasazi parallel to *Cleopatra, The Robe*, or *Ben Hur*. Small wonder the public views the native as some briefly extant, mythic, and usually hostile apparition. As a consequence, the public perception of the historical existence of Native Americans is of beings who spent their time serving as little other than figurative pop-up targets for non-Indian guns.

Nor is there an abundance of films attempting to deal with contemporary Indian realities. In effect, the native ceased to exist after the onset of the reservation period of the Plains peoples. This is evidenced by the fact that the author could find only two films listed – biographies of Jim Thorpe and Ira

Hayes, both starring Burt Lancaster – released prior to 1980 which featured the indigenous experience after 1880 in any meaningful way at all. As to current events, well... There's always the *Billy Jack* series: *Born Losers, Billy Jack, The Trial of Billie Jack* and *Billie Jack Goes to Washington* (the latter, thankfully, was shelved before release), utilizing the vehicle of an ex-Special Forces mixed-blood karate expert to exploit the grisly mystique of Shaft and Superfly-type super-heroes (or anti-heroes, if you prefer). The result is a predictably shallow and idiotic parallel to the *Batman* TV series.

The single (lackluster) attempt by Hollywood to equal for American Indians what *Sounder* and *Lady Sings the Blues* have achieved for African Americans was rapidly withdrawn from circulation as an "embarrassment." So steeped in celluloid myopia are filmdom's critics – so full, that is, of their own self-perpetuating stereotyping – that they panned the characters in *Journey Through Rosebud* as "wooden Indians." This, despite the fact that most Native Americans viewing them ranked them as the most accurate and convincing ever to come from the studios. Possibly, other films of the stature of *Journey Through Rosebud* have been made but not released, in effect doing nothing to alter the time-warp involving American Indians in film. A result is that the US mainstream population finds itself under no particular moral or psychic obligation to confront the fact of Native America, as either an historical or topical reality.

Native Cultures Defined by Eurocentric Values

An Anishinabe (Chippewa) friend of mine once visited the Field Museum in Chicago. While examining the exhibits of American Indian artifacts located there, she came across an object which she immediately recognized as being her grand-mother's root digger, an item the museum's anthropological "experts" had identified and labeled as a "Winnebago hide scraper." She called the mistake to the attention of the departmental director and was told that she, not the museum, was wrong. "If you knew anything at all about your heritage," he informed her, "you'd know that tool is a hide scraper." My friend, helpless to correct this obvious (to her) misinformation, went away. "They never listen to the people who really know these things," she said later. "And so they never understand what they think they know."

The above sad-but-true story is not unusual. It serves to illustrate a pattern in Euroamerican dealings with indigenous people which extends vastly beyond the mere identification of objects. In terms of commercial cinema and acting, the problem may be considered on the basis of "context" and "motivation." Put most simply, the question of context is one in which specific acts of certain American Indians are portrayed in scenes devoid of all cultural grounding and explanation. From whence is comprehension of the real nature of these acts to come? The viewing audience is composed overwhelmingly of non-Indians who obviously hold no automatic insight into native cultures and values, yet somehow they must affix meaning to the actions presented on the screen. Scenes such as those presented in the John Ford "classic," *Stagecoach*, are fine examples of this stereotyping approach. Thus, the real acts of indigenous people – even when depicted more-or-less accurately – often appear irrational, cruel, unintelligent, or silly when displayed in film.

Motivation is a more sophisticated, and consequently more dangerous, consideration. Here, a cultural context of sorts is provided, at least to some degree, but it is a context comprised exclusively of ideas, values, emotions, and other meanings assigned by Euroamerica to the native cultures portrayed. Insofar as indigenous American and Euro-derived worldviews are radically and demonstrably different in almost every way, such a projection can only serve to misrepresent dramatically the native cultures involved and render them nonsensical at best. Such misrepresentation serves two major stereotyping functions. Since the complex of dominant and comparatively monolithic cultural values and beliefs of Eurocentrism presently held by the bulk of the US population are utilized to provide motivation for virtually all American Indians portrayed in commercial film, all native values and beliefs appear to be lumped together into a single homogeneous and consistent whole, regardless of actual variances and distinctions (the following section discusses the result of this phenomenon).

Given that the cultural values and beliefs extended as the contextual basis for motivation are misrepresentative of the actual cultural context of Native America – and are thus totally out of alignment with the actions portrayed – the behavior of American Indians is often made to appear more uniformly vicious, crude, primitive, and unintelligent than in cases where context and motivation are dispensed with altogether.

A primary device used by Hollywood to attach Eurocentric values to native acts has been to script a white character to narrate the story-line. Films such as *Cheyenne Autumn*, *A Man Called Horse* (and its sequels), *Soldier Blue*, and *Little Big Man* exemplify the point. Each purports to provide an "accurate and sympathetic treatment of the American Indian" (of yesteryear) while utterly crushing native identity under the heel of Euroamerican interpretation. To date, all claims to the contrary notwithstanding, there has not been one attempt to put out a commercial film which deals with native reality through native eyes.

"Seen One Indian, Seen 'em All"

This third category is, in some ways, a synthesis of the preceding two. It has, however, assumed an identity of its own which extends far beyond the scope of the others. Within this area lies the implied assumption that distinctions between cultural groupings of indigenous people are either non-existent (ignorance) or irrelevant (arrogance). Given this attitude regarding the portrayal of Indians in film, it is inevitable that the native be reduced from reality to a strange amalgamation of dress, speech, custom, and belief. All vestiges of truth – and thereby of intercultural understanding – give way here before the onslaught of movieland's mythic creation.

The film *A Man Called Horse* may serve as an example. This droll adventure, promoted as "the most authentic description of North American Indian life ever filmed," depicts a people whose language is Lakota, whose hairstyles range from Assiniboin through Nez Percé to Comanche, whose tipi design is Crow, and whose Sun Dance ceremony and the lodge in which it is held are both typically Mandan. They are referred to throughout the film as "Sioux," but to which group do they supposedly belong? Secungu (Brûlé)? Oglala? Santee? Sisseton? Yanktonai? Minneconjou? Hunkpapa? Those generically – and rather pejoratively – called "Sioux" were/are of three major geographic/cultural divisions: the Dakotas of the Minnesota woodlands, the Nakotas of the prairie region east of the Missouri River, and the Lakotas of the high plains proper. These groups were/are quite distinct from one another, and the distinctions *do* make a difference in terms of accuracy and "authenticity."

The source material utilized to create the cinematic imagery involved in *A Man Called Horse* was the large number of portraits of American Indians executed by George Catlin during the first half of the nineteenth century and now housed in the Smithsonian Institution. However, while Catlin was meticulous in attributing tribal and even band affiliations to the subjects of his paintings, the filmmakers were not. The result is a massive misrepresentation of a whole variety of real peoples, aspects of whose cultures are incorporated, gratuitously, into that of the hybrid "Indians" who inhabit the movie.

Nor does the dismemberment of reality in this "most realistic of Westerns" end with visual catastrophe. The door to cultural reduction is merely opened by such devices. Both the rationale and spiritual ramifications of the Sun Dance are voided by the film's Eurocentric explanation of its form and function. Thus is the Lakota's central and most profoundly sacred of all ceremonies converted into a macho exercise in "self-mutilation," a "primitive initiation rite" showing that the Indian male could "take it." It follows that the film's Anglo lead (Richard Harris) must prove that he is "as tough as the Sioux" by eagerly seeking out his fair share of pain during a Sun Dance. He does this in order to be accepted as "one of them." Just bloody up your chest and no further questions will be asked. How quaint.

This, of course, paves the way for the Harris character to become leader of the group. The Sioux, once they have been reduced to little more than a gaggle of prideful masochists, are readily shown to be possessed of little collective intellect (surprise, surprise). Hence, it becomes necessary for the Anglo captive to save his savage captors from an even more ferocious group of primitives coming over the hill. He manages this somewhat spectacular feat by instructing his aboriginal colleagues in the finer points of using the bow, a weapon in uninterrupted use by the people in question for several hundred generations, and out of use by the English for about 200 years at the time the events in the film supposedly occur.

But no matter the trivial details. The presumed inherent superiority of Eurocentric minds has once again been demonstrated for all the world to witness. All that was necessary to accomplish this was to replace a *bona fide* native culture with something else.

The technique employed in *A Man Called Horse* is by no means novel or unique. Even the highly touted (in terms of making Indians "the good guys") *Billy Jack* series could never lock in any specific people it sought to portray. The Indians depicted remain a weird confluence of Navajos and various Pueblos, occasionally practicing what appear to be bastardizations of Cheyenne and Kiowa ceremonies. All the better to trot them around as props for every non-Indian fad from the benefits of macrobiotic cookery to those of Haikido karate.

It is elementary logic to realize that when the cultural identity of a people is symbolically demolished, the achievements and very humanity of that people must also be disregarded. The people, as such, disappear, usually to the benefit – both material and psychic – of those performing the symbolic demolition. There are accurate and appropriate terms which describe this: dehumanization, obliteration or appropriation of identity, political subordination and material colonization are all elements of a common process of imperialism. This is the real meaning of Hollywood's stereotyping of American Indians.

Conclusion

It should be relatively easy at this point to identify film stereotyping of American Indians as an accurate reflection of the actual conduct of the Euroamerican population *vis-à-vis* Native America in both historical and topical senses. North American indigenous peoples have been reduced in terms of cultural identity within the popular consciousness – through a combination of movie treatments, television programming, and distortive literature – to a point where the general public perceives them as extinct for all practical intents and purposes. Given that they no longer exist, that which *was* theirs – whether land and the resources on and beneath it, or their heritage – can *now* be said, without pangs of guilt, to belong to those who displaced and ultimately supplanted them. Such is one function of cinematic stereotyping within North America's advanced colonial system.

Another is to quell potential remorse among the population at large. Genocide is, after all, an extremely ugly word. Far better that the contemporary mainstream believe their antecedents destroyed mindless and intrinsically warlike savages, devoid of true culture and humanity, rather than that they systematically exterminated whole societies of highly intelligent and accomplished human beings who desired nothing so much as to be left in peace. Far better for their descendants if the Euroamerican invader engaged in slaughter only in self-defense, when confronted with hordes of irrationally bloodthirsty heathen beasts, rather than coldly and calculatedly committing mass murder, planning step by step the eradication of the newest-born infants. "Nits make lice," to quote US Colonel John M. Chivington.

Filmdom's handling of "history" in this regard is, with only a few marginal exceptions, nothing more or less than an elaborate denial of European/Euroamerican criminality on this continent over the past 350 years. Implicitly then, it is an unbridled justification and glorification of the conquest and subordination of Native America. As such, it is a vitally necessary ingredient in the maintenance and perfection of the Euroempire which began when the Pilgrims landed in 1620. Hollywood's performance on this score has been, overall, what one might have legitimately expected to see from the heirs to Leni Riefenstahl, had the Third Reich won its War in the East during the 1940s.

As the Oneida comedian Charlie Hill has observed, the portrayal of Indians in the cinema has been such that it has made the playing of "Cowboys and Indians" a favorite American childhood game. The object of the "sport" is for the "cowboys" to "kill" all the "Indians," just like in the movies. A bitter irony associated with this is that Indian as well as non-Indian children heatedly demand to be identified as cowboys, a not unnatural outcome under the circumstances, but one which speaks volumes to the damage done to the American Indian self-concept by movie propaganda. The meaning of this, as Hill notes, can best be appreciated if one were to imagine that the children were instead engaging in a game called "Nazis and Jews."

That movieland's image of the Indian is completely false – and often shoddily so – is entirely to the point. Only a completely false creation could be used to explain in "positive terms" what has actually happened here in centuries past. Only a literal blocking of modern realities can be used to rationalize present circumstances. Only a concerted effort to debunk Hollywood's mythology can alter the situation for the better. While it's true that the immortal words of General Phil Sheridan – "The only good Indian is a dead Indian" – have continued to enjoy a certain appeal with the American body politic, and equally true that dead Indians are hardly in a position to call the liars to account for their deeds, there are a few of us left out here who just might be up to the task.

39
Cultural Identity and Cinematic Representation

Stuart Hall

Both the new 'Caribbean cinema', which has now joined the company of the other 'Third Cinemas', and the emerging cinemas of Afro-Caribbean blacks in the 'diasporas' of the West, put the issue of cultural identity in question. Who is this emergent, new subject of the cinema? From where does it speak? The practices of representation always implicate the positions from which we speak or write – the positions of *enunciation*. What recent theories of enunciation suggest is that, though we speak, so to say 'in our own name', of ourselves and from our own experience, nevertheless who speaks, and the subject who is spoken of, are never exactly in the same place. Identity is not as transparent or unproblematic as we think. Perhaps, instead of thinking of identity as an already accomplished historical fact, which the new cinematic discourses then represent, we should think, instead, of identity as a 'production', which is never complete, always in process, and always constituted within, not outside, representation. But this view problematizes the very authority and authenticity to which the term 'cultural identity' lays claim.

In this paper, then, I seek to open a dialogue, an investigation, on the subject of cultural identity and cinematic representation. The 'I' who writes here must also be thought of as, itself, 'enunciated'. We all write and speak from a particular place and time, from a history and a culture which is specific. What we say is always 'in context', *positioned*. I was born into and spent my childhood and adolescence in a lower-middle class family in Jamaica. I have lived all my adult life in England, in the shadow of the black diaspora – 'in the belly of the beast'. I write against the background of a lifetime's work in cultural studies. If the paper seems preoccupied with the diaspora experience and its narratives of dis-placement, it is worth remembering that all discourse is 'placed', and the heart has its reasons.

There are at least two different ways of thinking about 'cultural identity'. The first position defines 'cultural identity' in terms of the idea of one, shared culture, a sort of collective 'one true self', hiding inside the many other, more superficial or artificially imposed 'selves', which people with a shared history and ancestry hold in common. Within the terms of this definition, our cultural identities reflect the common historical experiences and shared cultural codes which provide us, as 'one people', with stable, unchanging and continuous frames of reference and meaning, beneath the shifting divisions and vicissitudes of our actual history. This 'oneness', underlying all the other, more superficial differences, is the truth, the essence, of 'Caribbeaness'. It is this identity which a Caribbean cinema must discover, excavate, bring to light and express through cinematic representation.

Such a conception of cultural or national identity played a critical role in all the post-colonial struggles which have so profoundly reshaped our world. It lay at the centre of the vision of the poets of 'Negritude', like Aimee Ceasire and Leopold Senghor, and of the Pan-African political project, earlier in the century. It continues to be a very powerful and creative force in emergent forms of representation amongst hitherto marginalized peoples. In post-colonial societies, the rediscovery of this identity is often the object of what Frantz Fanon once called a 'passionate research...directed by the secret hope of discovering beyond the misery of today, beyond self-contempt, resignation and abjuration, some very beautiful and splendid era whose existence rehabilitates us both in regard to ourselves and in regard to others.' New forms of cultural practice in these societies address themselves to this project for the very good reason that, as Fanon puts it, in the recent past, 'Colonization is not satisfied merely with holding a people in its grip and emptying the native's brain of all form and content. By a kind of perverted logic, it turns to the past of the oppressed people, and distorts, disfigures and destroys it' (Fanon, *Wretched of the Earth*, 'On National Culture').

The question which Fanon's observation poses is, what is the nature of this 'profound research' which drives the new forms of visual and cinematic representation? Is it only a matter of unearthing that which the colonial experience buried and overlaid, bringing to light the hidden continuities it suppressed? Or is a quite different practice entailed – not the rediscovery but the *production* of identity? Not an identity grounded in the archaeology, but in the *re-telling* of the past?

We cannot and should not, for a moment, underestimate or neglect the importance of the act of imaginative rediscovery. 'Hidden histories' have played a critical role in the emergence of some of the most important social movements of our time. The photographic work of a visual artist like Armet Francis, a Jamaican-born photographer who has lived in Britain since the age of eight, is a testimony to the continuing creative power of this conception of identity within the practices of representation. His photographs of the peoples of The Black Triangle, taken in Africa, the Caribbean, the US and the UK, attempt to reconstruct in visual terms 'the underlying unity of the black people whom, colonization and slavery distributed across the African diaspora.' His text is an act of imaginary re-unification.

Crucially, his images find a way of imposing an imaginary coherence on the experience of dispersal and fragmentation, which is the history of all enforced diasporas. He does this by representing or 'figuring' Africa as the mother of these different civilizations. His Triangle is, after all, 'centred' in Africa. Africa is the name of the missing term, the great aporia, which lies at the centre of our cultural identity and gives it a meaning which, until recently, it lacked. No one who looks at these textual images now, in the light of the history of transportation, slavery and migration, can fail to understand how the rift of separation, the 'loss of identity', which has been integral to the Caribbean experience only begins to be healed when these forgotten connections are once more set in place. Such texts restore an imaginary fullness or plenitude, to set against the broken rubric of our past. They are resources of resistance and identity, with which to confront the fragmented and pathological ways in which that experience has been reconstructed within the dominant regimes of cinematic and visual representation of the West.

There is, however, a related but different view of cultural identity, which qualifies, even if it does not replace, the first. This second position recognizes that, as well as the many points of similarity, there are also critical points of deep and significant *difference* which constitute 'what we really are': or rather – since history has intervened – 'what we have become'. We cannot speak for very long, with any exactness, about 'one experience, one identity', without acknowledging its other side – the differences and discontinuities which constitute, precisely, the Caribbean's 'uniqueness'. Cultural identity, in this second sense, is a matter of 'becoming' as well as of 'being'. It belongs to the future as much as to the past. It is not something which already exists, transcending place, time, history and culture. Cultural identities come from somewhere, have histories. But, like everything which is historical, they undergo constant transformation. Far from being eternally fixed in some essentialized past, they are subject to the continuous 'play' of history, culture and power. Far from being grounded in a mere 'recovery' of the past, which is waiting to be found, and which, when found, will secure our sense of ourselves into eternity, identities are the names we give to the different ways we are positioned by, and position ourselves within, the narratives of the past.

It is only from this second position that we can properly understand the truly traumatic character of 'the colonial experience'. The ways we have been positioned and subjected in the dominant regimes of representation were a critical exercise of cultural power and normalization, precisely because they were not superficial. They had the power to make us see and experience ourselves as 'Other'. Every regime of representation is a regime of power formed, as Foucault reminds us, by the fatal couplet, 'power/knowledge'. And this kind of knowledge is internal, not external. It is one thing to place some person or set of peoples as the Other of a dominant discourse. It is quite another thing to subject them to that 'knowledge', not only as a matter of imposed will and domination, by the power of inner compulsion and subjective conformation to the norm. That is the lesson – the sombre majesty – of Fanon's insight into the colonizing experience in *Black Skin, White Masks*.

This expropriation of cultural identity cripples and deforms. If its silences are not resisted, they produce, in Fanon's vivid phrase, 'individuals without an anchor, without horizon, colourless, stateless, rootless – a race of angles' (Fanon, *Wretched of the Earth*). Nevertheless, it also changes our conception of what 'cultural identity' is. In this perspective, cultural identity is not a fixed essence at all, lying unchanged outside history and culture. It is not some universal and transcendental spirit inside us on which history has made no fundamental mark. It is not once-and-for-all. It is not a fixed origin to which we can make some final and absolute Return. Of course, it is not a mere phantasm, either. It is *something* – not a mere trick of the imagination. It has its histories – and histories have their real, material and symbolic effects. The past continues to speak to us. But this is no longer a simple, factual 'past', since our relation to it is, like the child's relation to the mother, always-already 'after the break'. It is always constructed through memory, fantasy, narrative and myth. Cultural identities are the points of identification, the unstable points of identification or suture, which are made, within the discourses of history and culture. Not an essence but a *positioning*. Hence, there is always a politics of position, which has no absolute guarantee in an unproblematic, transcendental 'law of history'.

This second view of cultural history is much less familir, and unsettling. But it is worth spending a few moments tracing its formations. We might think of Caribbean identities as 'framed' by two axes or vectors, simultaneously operative: the vector of similarity and continuity; and the vector of difference and rupture. Caribbean identities always have to be thought of in terms of the dialogic relationship between these two axes. The one gives us some grounding in, some continuity with, the past. The second reminds us that what we share is precisely the experience of a profound discontinuity. The peoples dragged into slavery by the triangulate Atlantic trade came predominantly from Africa – though when that supply ended, it was temporarily refreshed by indentured labour from the Asian sub-continent. This neglected fact explains why, when you visit Guyana or Trinidad, you suddenly see, symbolically inscribed in the faces of their peoples, the paradoxical 'truth' of Christopher Columbus's mistake: you *can* find 'Asia' by sailing west, if you know where to look! The great majority of slaves were from Africa – already figured, in the European imaginary, as 'the Dark Continent'. But they were also from different countries, tribal communities, villages, languages and gods. African religion, which has been so profoundly formative in Caribbean spiritual life, is precisely *different* from Christian monotheism in having, not one, but a proliferation of gods. These gods live on, in an underground existence, in the pantheon of black Saints which people the hybridized religious universe of Latin American Catholicism. The paradox is that it was the uprooting of slavery and transportation and the insertion into the plantation economy (as well as the symbolic economy) of the Western world that 'unified' these peoples across their differences, in the same moment as it cut them off from direct access to that past.

Difference, therefore, persists – in and alongside continuity. And this is so, not only for the past but in the present. To return to the Caribbean after any long absence is to experience again the shock of the 'doubleness' of similarity and difference. As a Jamaican returning for the First Caribbean Film Festival, I 'recognized' Martinique instantly, though I was seeing it for the first time. I also saw at once how different Martinique is from, say, Jamaica: and this is no mere difference of topography or climate. It is also a profound difference of culture and history. And the difference *matters*. It positions Martiniquains and Jamaicans as *both* the same *and* different. Moreover, the boundaries of difference are continually repositioned in relation to different points of reference. *Vis-à-vis* the developed West, we are very much 'the same'. We belong to the marginal, the underdeveloped, the periphery, the 'Other'. We are at the outer edge, the 'rim', of the metropolitan world – always 'South' to someone else's *El Norte*.

At the same time, we do not stand in the same relation of 'otherness' to the metropolitan centres. Each has negotiated its economic, political and cultural dependency differently. And this 'difference', whether we like it or not, is already inscribed in our cultural identities. In turn, it is this negotiation of identity which makes us, *vis-à-vis* other Latin American people, with a very similar history, different. Caribbeans – *les Antilliennes*: 'islanders' to their mainland. And yet, *vis-à-vis* one another, Jamaican, Haitian, Cuban, Guadeloupean, Barbadian, etc. . . .

How, then, to describe this play of 'difference' within identity? The common history – transportation, slavery, colonization – has been profoundly formative. It was also, metaphorically as well as literally, a translation. The inscription of difference is also specific and critical. I use the word 'play' because the double meaning of the metaphor is important. It suggests, on the one hand, the instability, the permanent unsettlement, the lack of any final resolution. On the other hand, it reminds us that the place where this 'doubleness' is most powerfully to be heard is 'playing' within the varieties of Caribbean musics. This cultural 'play' could not be represented, cinematically, as a simple, binary opposition – 'past/present', 'them/us'. Its complexity exceeds this binary structure of representation. At different places, times, in relation to different questions, the boundaries are re-sited. They become, not only what they have, at times, certainly been – mutually excluding categories: but also, what they sometimes are – differential points along a sliding scale.

One trivial example is the way Martinique both *is* and *is not* 'French'. Superficially, Fort de France is a much richer, more 'fashionable' place than Kingston – which is not only visibly poorer, but itself at a point of transition between being 'in fashion' in an Anglo-African and Afro-American way – for those who can afford to be in any sort of fashion at all. Yet, what is distinctively 'Martiniquais' can only be described in terms of that special and peculiar supplement which the black and mulatto skin adds to the 'refinement' and sophistication of a Parisian-derived *haute couture*: that is, a sophistication which, because it is black, is always transgressive.

To capture this sense of difference which is not pure 'otherness', we need to deploy the play on words of a theorist like Jacques Derrida. Derrida uses the anomalous a in his way of writing 'difference' – *differance* – as a marker which sets up a disturbance in our settled understanding or translation of the concept. It sets the word in motion to new meanings without obscuring the trace of its other meanings. His sense of *difference*, as Christopher Norris puts it, thus 'remains suspended between the two French verbs "to differ" and "to defer" (postpone), both of which contribute to its textual force but neither of which can fully capture its meaning. Language depends on difference, as Saussure showed . . . . the structure of distinctive propositions which make up its basic economy. Where Derrida breaks new ground . . . is in the extent to which "differ" shades into "defer" . . . the idea that meaning is always deferred, perhaps to the point of an endless supplementarity, by the play of signification' (Norris, 1982: 32). This second sense of difference challenges the fixed binaries which stabilize meaning and representation and show how meaning is never finished or completed in this way, but keeps on moving to encompass other, additional or supplementary meanings, which, as Norris puts it elsewhere (Norris, 1987: 15) 'disturb the classical economy of language and representation.' Without relations of difference, no representation could occur. But what is then constituted within representation is always open to being deferred, staggered, serialized.

Where, then, does identity come in to this infinite postponement of meaning? Derrida does not help us as much as he might here – and this is precisely where, in my view, he has permitted his profound theoretical insights to be reappropriated into a celebration of formal 'playfulness', which evacuates it of its political meaning. For if signification depends upon the endless repositioning of its differential terms, meaning, in any specific instance, depends on the contingent and arbitrary stop – the necessary and temporary 'break' in the infinite semiosis of language. This does not detract from the original insight. It only threatens to do so if we mistake this 'cut' of identity – this *positioning*, which makes meaning possible – as a natural and permanent, rather than an arbitrary and contingent 'ending'. Whereas, I understand every such position as 'strategic'. And arbitrary, in the sense that there is no permanent equivalence between the particular sentence we close, and its true meaning, as such. Meaning continues to unfold, so to speak, beyond the arbitrary closure which makes it, at any moment, possible. It is always either over- or undetermined – either an excess or a supplement. There is always something 'left over'.

It is possible, with this conception of 'difference', to rethink the positionings and repositionings of Caribbean cultural identities in relation to at least three 'presences', to borrow Aimee Cesaire's and Leopold Senghor's metaphor: Presence Africaine, Presence Europeanne, and the third, most ambiguous, presence of all – the sliding term, 'Presence American'. I mean America, here, not in its 'first-world' sense – the big cousin to the North whose 'rim' we occupy, but in the second, broader sense: America, the New Found Land, the 'New World', *terra incognita*.

'Presence Africaine' is the site of the repressed. Apparently silenced beyond memory by the power of the new cultures of slavery, it was in fact present everywhere: in the everyday life and customs of the slave quarters, in the languages and patois of the plantations, in names and words, often disconnected from their taxonomies, in the secret syntactical structures through which other languages were spoken, in the stories and tales told to children, in religious practices and beliefs, in the spiritual life, the arts, crafts, musics and rhythms of slave and post-emancipation society. Africa, the signified which could not be represented, remained the unspoken, unspeakable 'presence' in Caribbean culture. It is 'hiding' behind every verbal inflection, every narrative twist of Caribbean cultural life. It is the secret code with which every Western text was 're-read'. *This* was – is – the 'Africa' that 'is alive and well in the diaspora' (Hall, 1976).

When I was growing up as a child in Kingston, I was surrounded by the signs, music and rhythms of this Africa of the diaspora, which only existed as a result of a long and discontinuous series of transformations. But, although almost everyone around me was some shade of brown or black (Africa 'speaks'!), I never once heard a single person refer to themselves or to others as, in some way, or as having been at some time in the past, 'African'. It was only in the 1970s that this Afro-Caribbean identity became historically available to the great majority of Jamaican people, at home and abroad. In this historic moment, the great majority of Jamaicans discovered themselves to be 'black' – just as they discovered themselves to be the sons and daughters of 'slavery'.

This profound cultural discovery, however, was not, and could not be, made directly, without 'mediation'. It could only be made through the impact on popular life of the post-colonial revolution, the civil rights struggles, the culture of Rastafarianism and the music of reggae – the metaphors, the figures or signifiers, of a new construction of 'Jamaican-ness'. This is a 'new' Africa, grounded in an 'old'. Africa, now, as part of a spiritual journey of discovery that led, in the Caribbean, to an indigenous cultural revolution. 'Africa', as we might say, necessarily 'deferred' – as a spiritual, cultural and political metaphor.

It is the presence/absence of the 'otherness' of Africa, in this form, which made it also the privileged signifier of new conceptions of Caribbean identity. Everyone in the Caribbean, of whatever ethnic background, must sooner or later come to terms with this African Presence. Black, brown, mulatto, white – all must look 'Presence Africaine' in the face, speak its name. But whether it is, in this sense, an *origin* of our identities, unchanged by 400 years of displacement, dismemberment, transportation, to which we could in any final or literal sense, return, is more open to doubt. The original 'Africa' is no longer there. It too has been transformed. History is, in that sense, irreversible. We must not collude with the West which, precisely, 'normalizes' and appropriates Africa by freezing it into some timeless zone of the 'primitive, unchanging past'. Africa must at last be reckoned with, by Caribbean people. But it cannot in any simple sense be merely recovered. It belongs irrevocably, for us, to what Edward Said once called an 'imaginative geography and history', which helps 'the mind to intensify its own sense of itself by dramatizing the difference between what is close to it and what is far away' (Said, *Orientalism*). It 'has acquired an imaginative or figurative value we can name and feel' (ibid.). Our belongingness to it constitutes what Benedict Anderson calls 'an imagined community'. To *this* 'Africa', which is a necessary part of the Caribbean imaginary, we can't literally go home again.

The character of this displaced 'homeward' journey – its length and complexity – comes across vividly, not yet in the Caribbean cinemas, but in other texts. Tony Sewell's text and documentary archival photographs, *Garvey's Children: The Legacy of Marcus Garvey*, tells the story of a 'return' to an African identity for Caribbean people which went, necessarily, by the long route – through London and the United States. It 'ends', not in Ethiopia, but with Garvey's statue in front of the St Ann Parish Library in Jamaica, with the music of Burning Spear and Bob Marley's Redemption Song. This is our 'long journey' home. Derek Bishton's remarkably courageous visual and written text, *Black Heart Man*, the story of the journey of a *white* photographer 'on the trail of the promised land', starts in England, and goes, through Sashamene, the place in Ethiopia to which many Jamaican people have found their way on their search for the Promised Land, and the story of slavery; but it ends in Pinnacle, Jamaica, where the first Rastafarian settlement was established, and 'beyond' – among the dispossessed of twentieth-century Kingston and the streets of Handsworth, where Bishton's voyage of discovery first began. This symbolic journey is necessary for us all – and necessarily circular.

This is the Africa we must return to but 'by another route': what Africa has *become* in the New World, what we have made of 'Africa'. 'Africa' – as we re-tell it through politics, memory and desire.

What of the second, troubling term in the identity equation – the European Presence? For many of us, this is a matter, not too little but of too much. Where Africa was a case of the unspoken, Europe was a case of that which is endlessly speaking – and endlessly speaking *us*. The European Presence thus interrupts the innocence of the whole discourse of 'difference' in the Caribbean by introducing the question of power. 'Europe' belongs irrevocably to the question of power, to the lines of force and consent, to the pole of the *dominant* in Caribbean culture. In terms of colonialism, underdevelopment, poverty and the racism of colour, the European Presence is that which, in visual representation, has positioned us within its dominant regimes of representation: the colonial discourse, the literatures of adventure and exploration, the romance of the exotic, the ethnographic and travelling eye, the tropical languages of tourism, travel brochure and Hollywood and the violent, pornographic languages of *ganja* and urban violence.

The error is not to conceptualize this 'presence' in terms of power, but to locate that power as wholly external to us – an extrinsic force, whose influence can be thrown off like the serpent sheds its skin. What Frantz Fanon reminds us, in *Black Skin, White Masks*, is how its power is inside as well as outside: 'the movements, the attitudes, the glances of the other fixed me there, in the sense in which a chemical solution is fixed by a dye. I was indignant; I demanded an explanation. Nothing happened. I burst apart. Now the fragments have been put together again by another self.' This 'look', from – so to speak – the place of the Other, fixes us, not only in its violence, hostility and aggression, but in the ambivalence of its desire. This brings us face to face, not simply with the dominating European Presence as the site or 'scene' of integration where those other presences which it had actively disaggregated were recomposed – reframed, put together in a new way; but as the site of a profound splitting and doubling: what Homi Bhabba has called 'the ambivalent identifications of the racist world'...the ' "otherness" of the self inscribed in the perverse palimpsest of colonial identity'.

The dialogue of power and resistance, of refusal and recognition, with and against 'Presence Europeanne' is almost as complex as the so-called 'dialogue' with Africa. In terms of popular cultural life, it is nowhere to be found in its pure, pristine state. It is always already fused, syncretized, with other cultural elements. It is always-already creolized. Not 'lost beyond the Middle Passage, but ever-present, the harmonics in our musics to the ground-bass of Africa, traversing and intersecting our lives at every point. How can we stage this dialogue so that, finally, we can place it, without terror, rather than being forever placed by it? Can we ever recognize its irreversible influence, whilst resisting its imperializing eye? The enigma is impossible, so far, to resolve. It requires the most complex of cultural strategies. Think, for example, of the dialogue of every Caribbean filmmaker, one way or another, with the dominant cinemas of the 'West' – of European and American filmmaking. Who could describe this tense and tortured dialogue as a 'one way trip'?

I think of the third, 'New World' Presence, not so much in terms of power, as of ground, place, territory. It is the juncture-point where the other cultural tributaries met, the 'empty' land (the European colonizers emptied it) where strangers from every other part of the globe met. None of the people who now occupy the islands – black, brown, white, African, European, American, Spanish, French, East Indian, Chinese, Portuguese, Jew, Dutch – originally 'belonged' there. It is the space where the creolizations and assimilations and syncretisms were negotiated. The New World is the third term – the primal scene where the fateful/fatal encounter was staged between Africa and the West. It has to be understood as the place of displacements: of the original pre-Columbian inhabitants, the Arawaks, permanently displaced from their homelands; of peoples displaced in different ways from Africa, Asia and Europe; the displacements of slavery, colonization and conquest. It stands for the endless ways in which Caribbean people have been destined to 'migrate'; it is the signifier of migration itself – of travelling, voyaging, and return as fate, as destiny; of the Antillean as the prototype of the modern or postmodern New World nomad, continually moving between centre and periphery. This preoccupation with movement and migration Caribbean cinema shares with many other 'Third Cinemas', but it is one of our defining themes, and is destined to cross the narrative of every film script or cinematic image.

Presence Americaine also has its silences, its suppressions. Peter Hulme, in his essay on 'Islands of Enchantment' (*New Formations*, no. 3, Winter, 1987) reminds us that the word 'Jamaica' is the Hispanic form of the indigenous Arawak name of the island – 'land of wood and water' – which Columbus's renaming ('Santiago') never replaced. The Arawak 'presence' remains a ghostly one, visible in the islands mainly in their museums and archeological sites, part of the barely knowable or usable 'past'. It is not represented in the emblem of the Jamaican National Heritage Trust, for example, which chose, instead, the figure of Diego Pimienta, 'an African who fought for his Spanish masters against the English invasion of the island in 1655' – a deferred, metonymic, sly and sliding representation of Jamaican identity if ever there was one! Peter Hulme recounts the story of how Prime Minister Edward Seaga tried to alter the Jamaican coat-of-arms, which consists of two Arawak figures holding a shield with five pineapples, surmounted by an alligator. 'Can the crushed and extinct Arawaks represent the dauntless character of Jamaicans? Does the low-slung, near extinct crocodile, a cold-blooded reptile, symbolize the warm, soaring spirit of Jamaicans?' Prime Minister Seaga asked, rhetorically (*Jamaica Hansard*, vol. 9, p. 363: 1983–4. Quoted in Hulme). There can be few political statements which so eloquently testify to the complexities entailed in the process of trying to represent a diverse peoples with a diverse history through a single, hegemonic 'identity'. Fortunately, Mr Seaga's invitation to the Jamaican people, who are overwhelmingly of African descent, to start their 'remembering' by first 'forgetting' something else, got the comeuppance it so richly deserved.

Thus I think of the New World Presence – America, *terra incognita* – as itself the beginning of diaspora, of diversity, of difference: as what makes Afro-Caribbean people already the people of a diaspora. I use this term here metaphorically, not literally. I do not mean those scattered tribes whose identity can only be secured in relation to some sacred homeland to which they must at all costs return, even if it means pushing other people into the sea. This is the old, the imperializing, the hegemonizing form of 'ethnicity'. We have seen the fate of the people of Palestine at the hands of this backward-looking conception of diaspora – and the complicity of the West with it. The diaspora experience as I intend it here is defined, not by essence or purity, but by the recognition of a necessary heterogeneity, diversity; by a conception of 'identity' which lives with and through, not despite, difference; by *hybridity*. Diaspora identities are those which are constantly producing and reproducing themselves anew, through transformation and difference. One can only think here of what is uniquely – 'essentially' – Caribbean: precisely the mixes of colour, pigmentation, physiognomic type; the 'blends' of tastes that is Caribbean cuisine; the aesthetics of the 'cross-overs', of 'cut-and-mix', to borrow Dick Hebdige's telling phrase, which is the heart and soul of black music.

Young black cultural practitioners and critics in Britain are increasingly coming to acknowledge and explore in their work this 'diaspora aesthetic': 'Across a whole range of cultural forms there is a "syncretic" dynamic which critically appropriates elements from the master-codes of the dominant culture and "creolizes" them, disarticulating given signs and rearticulating their symbolic meaning. The subversive force of this hybridizing tendency is most apparent at the level of language itself where creoles, patois and black English decentre, destabilize and carnivalize the linguistic domination of "English" – the nation-language of master-discourse – through strategic inflections, reaccentuations and other performative moves in semantic, syntactic and lexical codes' (Kobena Mercer, *Blackframes*).

It is because this 'New World' is constituted for us as place, a narrative of displacement, that it gives rise so profoundly to a certain imaginary plenitude, recreating the endless desire to return to 'lost origins', to be one again with the mother, to go back to the beginning. Who can ever forget, when once seen rising up out of that blue-green Caribbean, those islands of enchantment. And yet, this 'return to the beginning' is like the Imaginary in Lacan – it can neither be fulfilled nor requited, and hence is the beginning of the symbolic, of representation, the infinitely renewable source of desire, memory, myth, search, discovery – in short, the reservoir of our cinematic narratives.

I have been trying, in a series of metaphors, to put in play a different sense of our relationship to the past, and thus a different way of thinking about cultural identity, which might begin to constitute new points of recognition in the discourses of the emerging Caribbean cinema. I have been trying to speak of identity as constituted, not outside but within representation; and hence of cinema, not as a second-order mirror held up to reflect what already exists, but as that form of representation which is able to constitute us as new kinds of subjects, and thereby enable us to discover who we are. Communities, Benedict Anderson argues in *Imagined Communities*, are to be distinguished, not by their falsity/genuineness, but by the style in which they are imagined. This is the vocation of a modern Caribbean cinema: by allowing us to see and recognize the different parts and histories of ourselves, to construct those points of identification, those positionalities we call 'a cultural identity'.

'We must not therefore be content', Fanon warns us, 'with delving into the past of a people in order to find coherent elements which will counteract colonialism's attempts to falsify and harm. . . . A national culture is not a folklore, nor an abstract populism that believes it can discover a people's true nature. A national culture is the whole body of efforts made by a people in the sphere of thought to describe, justify and praise the action through which that people has created itself and keeps itself in existence' (*The Wretched of the Earth*).

40

White Privilege and Looking Relations: Race and Gender in Feminist Film Theory

Jane Gaines

Born in Flames, a feminist science fiction film set ten years after a Social-Democratic "revolution" in the US, provides an abrupt reminder of the place of theory in the context of social change. Toward the end of the film, with the women's takeover of New York communications channels in progress, the voice of theory is heard over the image, insisting that women also need to take over the production of language. Although the film gives credence to the voice of theory (a white female British-accented voice), it is clear that the militant Women's Emergency Brigade and the martyred Black lesbian leader are carrying the revolutionary moment. What strikes me about the juxtaposition – images of women hot-wiring U-Haul trucks and the voice of theory urging women to take control of their own images – is that the voice sounds so crisply detached and arid.[1]

What I want to discuss is not so much the scene as the tenor of the female intellectual voice, which immediately recalls for me the tone of feminist film theory – firm in its insistence on attention to cinematic language and strict in its prohibition against making comparisons between "actuality" and the text. Let me be clear that this is something of a caricature of a stance which many of us who work on feminist film theory find less and less tenable.[2] Certainly, the intense concentration on cinema as language has helped to remedy a naiveté about form which characterized early feminist film criticism. However, as interest in the operations of the cinematic text increased, we witnessed the banishment of sociological reference points and historical detail from criticism. From this viewpoint it seems that one can only analyze the ideological through its encoding in the conventions of editing or the mechanics of the motion picture machine.[3]

For Marxists, this textual detachment, as I will call it, has special implications: concentration on the functioning of discourse creates the impression that developments in an ideological realm are unrelated to developments elsewhere in social life. As feminist film theory has emphasized the irresistible allure and captivating power of classical narrative cinema, it has located determination exclusively in the ideological realm. At the center of this difficulty has been the effort to understand the ideological work of mainstream cinema in terms of the psychoanalytic concept of sexual difference, which has largely meant casting formal structures such as narrative and point of view as masculine, and locating the feminine, the opposite term, in the repressed or excluded. Since this theory has focused on sexual difference, class and racial differences have remained outside its problematic, divorced from textual concerns by the very split in the social totality that the incompatibility of these discourses misrepresents. Adorno has remarked on this split, although in the context of an argument for the merger of sociology and psychology:

> The separation of sociology and psychology is both correct and false. False because it encourages the specialists to relinquish the attempt to know the totality which even the separation of the two demands; and correct insofar as it registers more intransigently the split that has actually taken place in reality than does the premature unification at the level of theory.[4]

In the interest of understanding the social totality, I am suggesting that our criticism should work to demystify this apparent separation by raising questions of race and class exactly where they have been theoretically disallowed.

Here I want to show how a theory of the text and its spectator, based on the psychoanalytic concept of sexual difference, is unequipped to deal with a film which is about racial difference and sexuality. Immediately, the Diana Ross star-vehicle, *Mahogany* (Berry Gordy, 1975), suggests a psychoanalytic approach because the narrative is organized around the connections between sadism, voyeurism, and photographic acts. Furthermore, it is a perfect specimen of classical narrative cinema which has been so fully theorized in Freudian terms. The psychoanalytic mode, however, works to block out considerations which take a different configuration. For instance, the Freudian scenario, based on the male/female distinction, is incongruous with the scenario of racial and sexual relations in Afro-American history. Where we use a psychoanalytic model to explain Black family relations, we force an erroneous universalization, and inadvertently reaffirm white middle-class norms.

Since it has taken gender as its starting point in the analysis of oppression, feminist theory has helped to reinforce white middle-class values, and to the extent that it works to keep women from seeing other structures of oppression, it functions ideologically. In this regard, bell hooks specifically criticizes a feminism which seems unable to imagine women's oppression in terms other than gender:

> Feminist analyses of woman's lot tend to focus exclusively on gender and do not provide a solid foundation on which to construct feminist theory. They reflect the dominant tendency in Western patriarchal minds to mystify women's reality by insisting that gender is the sole determinant of woman's fate.[5]

This gender analysis illuminates the condition of white middle-class women rather exclusively, hooks explains, and its centrality in feminist theory suggests that the women who have contributed to the construction of this theory have been ignorant of the way women in different racial groups and social classes experience oppression. How should the white middle-class feminist who does not want to be racist in her work respond to this criticism? In her essay "On Being White," one of the few considerations of this delicate dilemma, Marilyn Frye urges us not to do what middle-class feminists have historically done: to assume responsibility for everyone. To take it upon oneself to rewrite feminist theory so that it encompasses our differences is another exercise of racial privilege.[6] What one can, with conscience, do is to undertake the difficult study of our own "determined ignorance"; one can begin to learn about the people whose history cannot be imagined from a position of privilege.[7] In this context, my argument takes two directions. One juxtaposes Black feminist theory with those aspects of feminist theory which have a tendency to function as normative; the other transposes these issues, as Marxist theory would understand them, into the question of how we are to grasp the interaction of the various levels.

The feminist commitment to revealing the patriarchal assumptions behind familiar cinematic language dates from the mid-1970s with the appearance of Claire Johnston's "Women's Cinema as Counter-Cinema"[8] and Laura Mulvey's often reprinted "Visual Pleasure and Narrative Cinema."[9] The latter essay, coinciding as it did with the publication of Christian Metz's "The Imaginary Signifier," paired with a supporting theoretical statement from the editors of the British *Screen*, helped introduce psychoanalytic concepts into contemporary film theory where they quickly streamlined a Marxist problematic which dealt awkwardly with the social individual.[10] The terms of psychoanalysis, introduced through the permission of Althusserian Marxism, made it possible to investigate the sites outside the workplace where oppression is experienced. For Marxist feminists, this connection between Marxism and psychoanalysis immediately enriched the study of the construction of subjectivity in its prime location – the family.

Althusser's antidote to empiricism and economic reductionism has been welcomed by Marxists working in cultural studies, and the appeal is understandable. If materiality is no longer elsewhere, scholars are suddenly free to concentrate on textual matters without having to concern themselves simultaneously with economic specificity. Marxists in cultural studies outside *Screen*, however, believe that Althusser's understanding of ideology as having a materiality of its own contradicts basic Marxist tenets.[11] Within British cultural studies, then, psychoanalysis is held in check by the larger debates around Althusserian Marxism. This is not, however, the case in the US, where these traditions are often a distant point of reference. Thus the *Screen* film theory imported to the US comes furnished with idealist assumptions that are mistaken for Marxist underpinnings. Because traditional Marxist terms do not support the critical context in film and television studies in the US as they do in Britain, the challenge to psychoanalytic film theory here may have to come from other critical vantage points.

Lesbian feminists in the US have already raised objections to the way in which contemporary film theory explains the operation of the classic realist text in terms of tensions between masculinity and femininity. Drawing on Freud and Lacan, this position (which is basically Mulvey's) defines the classic cinema as an expression of the patriarchal unconscious in the way it constructs points of view or "looking positions." At issue here is the way these viewing vantage points control the female body on the screen and privilege the visual position (the gaze) of the male character(s) within the film. The governing "look" of the male character in the film merges with the spectator's viewing position in such a way that the spectator sees as that character sees. This theory goes beyond the understanding of the text as producing its own ideal reader; the text is also able to specify the gender of the imputed subject, which in the classic cinema is male.

This understanding of the viewing pleasure in classical cinema as inherently male has drawn an especially sharp response from critics who have argued that this response cancels the lesbian spectator whose viewing pleasure would never be male pleasure. Positing a lesbian spectator would significantly change the trajectory of the gaze since the eroticized star body might be the visual objective of another female character in the film with whose "look" the viewer might identify. (Marilyn Monroe and Jane Russell in *Gentlemen Prefer Blondes*, according to this argument, are "only for each other's eyes.")[12] Following the direction of an early lesbian reading of *Gentlemen Prefer Blondes*, studies of *Personal Best* show lesbian readership as subverting dominant meanings and confounding textual structures.[13] Consistently, lesbians have charged that cultural theory posed in psychoanalytic terms is unable to conceive of desire or explain pleasure without reference to the binary oppositions male/female. This is, as Monique Wittig sees it, the function of the heterosexual assumption, or the "straight mind," that unacknowledged structure built not only into Lacanian psychoanalysis, but underlying the basic divisions of Western culture, organizing all knowledge, yet escaping any close examination:

> With its ineluctability as knowledge, as an obvious principle, as a given prior to any science, the straight mind develops a totalizing interpretation of history, social reality, culture, language....I can only underline the oppressive character that the straight mind is clothed in its tendency to immediately generalize its production of concepts into general laws which claim to hold true for all societies, all epochs, all individuals.[14]

I want to suggest further that the male/female opposition, so seemingly fundamental to feminism, may actually lock us into modes of analysis which will continually misunderstand the position of many women.

Women of color, like lesbians, have been added to feminist analysis as an afterthought. Standard feminist anthologies consistently include articles on Black female and lesbian perspectives as illustration of the liberality and the inclusiveness of feminist work. However, the very concept of "different perspectives," while validating distinctness and maintaining a common denominator (woman), still places the categories of race and sexual preference in theoretical limbo. Our political etiquette is correct, but our theory is not so perfect. A familiar litany in our work is the broad-minded conclusion to a feminist argument: "Of course, the implications are somewhat different if race, class, and sexual preference are considered." In Marxist feminist analysis, the factors of race and sexual preference often remain loose ends because these categories of oppression do not fit easily into a model based on class relations in capitalist society. Some gay historians have been able to determine a relationship between the rise of capitalism and the creation of the social homosexual.[15] However, only with a very generous notion of sexual hierarchies, such as the one Gayle Rubin uses in her recent work on the politics of sexuality, can sexual oppression (as different from gender oppression) be *located in relation* to a framework based on class.[16] Race has folded more neatly than sexual preference into Marxist models, but the orthodox formulation which understands racial conflict as class struggle is unsatisfactory to Marxist feminists who want to know exactly how gender intersects with race. The oppression of *women* of color remains incompletely grasped by this paradigm.

Just as the classic Marxist model of social analysis based on class has obscured the function of gender, the feminist model based on the male/female division under patriarchy has obscured the function of race. The dominant feminist paradigm actually encourages us *not to think* in terms of any oppression other than male dominance and female subordination. Feminism seems, as Barbara Smith states, "blinded to the implications of any womanhood that is not white womanhood."[17] Black feminists agree that for purposes of analysis, class is as significant as race; however, if these feminists hesitate to emphasize gender as a factor, it is in deference to the way Black women describe their experience.[18] Historically, Afro-American women have formulated political allegiance and identity in terms of race rather than gender or class.[19] Feminism, however, has not registered the statements of women of color who realize oppression first in relation to race rather than to gender: for them exploitation is personified by a white female.[20] Even more difficult for feminist theory to digest is Black female identification with the Black male. On this point, Black feminists diverge from white feminists as they repeatedly remind us that Black women do not necessarily see the Black male as patriarchal antagonist but feel instead that their racial oppression is "shared" with men.[21] In the most comprehensive analysis, Black lesbian feminists have described race, class, and gender oppression as "interlocking" in reference to the way these oppressions are synthesized in the lives of Black women.[22]

The point here is not to rank the structures of oppression in a way that implies the need for Black women to choose between solidarity with men or with women and between race or gender as the basis for a political strategy. At issue is the question of the fundamental antagonism relevant to any Marxist feminist theory.[23] Where we have foregrounded one antagonism in our analysis, we have misunderstood another, and this is most dramatically illustrated in the applications of the notion of patriarchy. Feminists have not been absolutely certain what they mean by patriarchy: alternately it has referred to either father right or to the domination of women;[24] but what is consistent about the use of the concept is the rigidity of the structure it describes. Patriarchy is incompatible with Marxism where it is used trans-historically without qualification and where it becomes the source to which all other oppressions are tributary, as in the radical feminist theory of patriarchal order which sees oppression in all forms and through all ages as derived from the male/female division.[25] Unfortunately, this deterministic model, which in Sheila Rowbotham's analysis almost functions like a "feminist base-superstructure," has the disadvantage of leaving us with no sense of movement, or no idea of how women have acted to change their condition, especially in comparison with the fluidity of the Marxist conception of class.[26] The radical feminist notion of absolute patriarchy has also one-sidedly portrayed the oppression of women through an analogy with slavery, and since this theory has identified woman as man's savage or repressed Other it competes with theories of racial difference which understand the Black as the "unassimilable Other."[27] Finally, the notion of patriarchy is most obtuse when it disregards the position white women occupy over Black men as well as Black women.[28] In order to rectify this tendency in feminism, Black feminists refer to "racial patriarchy," based on an analysis of the white patriarch/master in American history and his dominance over the Black male as well as the Black female.[29]

For Black feminists, history also seems to be the key to understanding Black female sexuality. "The construction of the sexual self of the Afro-American women," says Rennie Simson, "has its roots in the days of slavery."[30] Looking at this construction over time reveals a pattern of patriarchal phases and women's sexual adjustments that has no equivalent in the history of white women in the US. In the first phase, characterized by the dominance of the white master during the period of slavery, Black men and women were equal by default. To have allowed the Black male any power over the Black woman would have threatened the power balance of the slave system. Thus, as Angela Davis explains social control in the slave community, "The man slave could not be the unquestioned superior within the 'family' or community, for there was no such thing as the 'family provided' among the Slaves."[31] The legacy of this phase has involved both the rejection of the pedestal the white female has enjoyed and the heritage of retaliation against white male abuse. If the strategy for racial survival was resistance during the first phase, it was accommodation during the following phase. During Reconstruction, the Black family, modeled after the white bourgeois household, was constituted defensively in an effort to preserve the race.[32] Black women yielded to their men in deference to a tradition that promised respectability and safety. Reevaluating this history, Black feminists point out that during Reconstruction the Black male, following the example of the white patriarch, "learned" to dominate. The position consistently taken by Black feminists, that patriarchy was originally foreign to the Afro-American community and was introduced into it historically, then, represents a significant break with feminist theories which see patriarchal power invested in all men throughout history.[33]

Black history also adds another dimension to the concept of rape which has emerged as the favored metaphor for defining women's jeopardy in the second wave of feminism.[34] The charge of rape, conjuring up a historical connection with lynching, is always connected with the myth of the Black man as archetypal rapist. During slavery, this abuse provided an opportunity to strike a blow at Black manhood, but the increase in the sexual violation of Black women during Reconstruction reveals its political implications. After emancipation, the rape of Black women was a "message" to Black men which, as one historian describes the phenomenon, could be seen as "a reaction to the effort of the freedman to assume the role of patriarch, able to provide for and protect his family."[35] If, as feminists have argued, women's sexuality evokes an unconscious terror in men, then Black women's sexuality represents a special threat to white patriarchy; the possibility of its "eruption" stands for the aspirations of the Black race as a whole. The following analysis poses the questions raised when race complicates sexual prohibition. In the context of race relations in US history, sexual looking carries with it the threat of actual rather than symbolic castration.

In *Mahogany*, the sequel to *Lady Sings the Blues*, Diana Ross plays an aspiring fashion designer who dreams of pulling herself up and out of her Chicago South Side neighborhood through a high-powered career. During the day, Tracy Chambers is assistant to the modeling supervisor for a large department store resembling Marshall Field & Company. At night she attends design school where the instructor reprimands her for sketching a cocktail dress instead of the assignment, the first suggestion of the exotic irrelevance of her fantasy career. Although she loses her job with the department store, the renowned fashion photographer Sean McEvoy (Tony Perkins) discovers her as a model and whisks her off to Rome. There Tracy finally realizes her ambition to become a designer when a wealthy Italian admirer gives her a business of her own. After the grand show, unveiling her first line of clothes, she decides to return to Chicago where she is reunited with community organizer Brian Walker (Billy Dee Williams) whose political career is organized as a kind of counterpoint to Tracy's.

With its long fashion photography montage sequences temporarily interrupting the narrative, *Mahogany* invites a reading based on the alternation between narrative and woman-as-spectacle as theorized in "Visual Pleasure and Narrative Cinema." To the allure of pure spectacle these sequences add the fascination of masquerade and transformation. Effected with wigs and make-up colors, the transformations are a play on and against "darkness"; Diana Ross is a high-tech Egyptian queen, a pale medieval princess, a turbaned Asiatic, and a body-painted blue nymph. As her body color is washed out in bright light or powdered over, and as her long-haired wigs blow around her face, she becomes suddenly "white."

Motion pictures seem never to exhaust the narrative possibilities associated with the metaphor of the camera-as-deadly-weapon; *Mahogany* adds to this the sadomasochistic connotations of high fashion photography with reference to the mid-1970s work of Guy Bourdin and Helmut Newton that is linked to the tradition of "attraction by shock."[36] The montage sequences chronicling Tracy's career, from perfume ads to high fashion magazine covers, equate the photographic act with humiliation and violation. Camera zoom and freeze frame effects translate directly into aggression, as in the sequence in which Sean pushes Tracy into a fountain: her dripping image solidifies into an Italian Revlon advertisement. Finally, the motif of stopping-the-action-as-aggression is equated with the supreme violation – the attempt to murder. Pressing his favorite model to her expressive limits, Sean drives her off an expressway ramp. Since this brutality escalates after the scene in which he fails with Tracy in bed, the film represents her punishment as a direct consequence of his impotence.[37]

With its classic castration threat scenario, its connection between voyeurism and sadism, and its reference to fetishization as seen in Sean's photographic shrine to the models he has abused, *Mahogany* is the perfect complement to a psychoanalytic analysis of classical Hollywood's "visual pleasure." The film feeds further into the latter by producing its own "proof" that there is only an incremental difference between voyeurism (fashion photography) and the supreme violation – murder. The black and white photographic blow-ups of Tracy salvaged from the death car seem undeniable evidence of the fine line between looking and killing, or, held at another angle, between advertising imagery and pornography. These, then, are the points that the analysis of cinema as patriarchal makes when it characterizes classical film form as ideologically insidious in its control of the female image, its assuagement of women's threat, and its denial of its own complicity in this signifying activity.

To explain the ideological function of this film in terms of the construction of male pleasure, however, is to "aid and abet" the film's other ideological project. Following this line of analysis, one is apt to step into an ideological signifying trap set up by the chain of meanings that lead away from seeing the film in terms of black and white conflict. Because there are so many connotative paths – photographer exploits model, madman assaults woman, voyeur attempts murder – we may not immediately see white man as the aggressor against Black woman. Other strategies encourage the viewer to forget or not notice racial issues. For instance, the narrative removes Tracy from racially polarized Chicago to Rome where the brown Afro-American woman with Caucasian features is collected by the photographer who names his subjects after inanimate objects. Losing her Black community identity, Tracy becomes *Mahogany*, a dark, rich, valuable substance; that is, her Blackness becomes commodified.

Mahogany functions ideologically for Black viewers in the traditional Marxist sense, that is, in the way the film obscures the class nature of social antagonisms. This has certain implications for working-class Black viewers who would benefit the most from seeing the relationship between race, gender, and class oppression.

This film experiences the same problem in its placement of Black femaleness that the wider culture has had historically; a Black female is either all woman and tinted Black, or mostly Black and scarcely woman. These two expectations correspond roughly to the two worlds and two struggles the film contrasts: the struggle over the sexual objectification of Tracy's body, targeting commercial exploiters, and the class struggle of the Black community, targeting slum landlords. The film identifies this antagonism as the hostility between fashion and politics, corresponding roughly with Tracy and Brain and organizing their conflict and reconciliation. Intensifying the conflict between the two characters, the film brings "politics" and "fashion" together in one daring homage to the aesthetic of "attraction by shock." Sean arranges his models symmetrically on the back stairwell of a run-down Chicago apartment building and plants the confused tenants and street people as props. Flamboyant excess, the residue of capital, is juxtaposed with a kind of dumbfounded poverty. For a moment, the scene figures the synthesis of gender, class, and race, but the political glimpse is fleeting. Forced together as a consequence of the avant-garde's socially irresponsible quest for new outrage, the political antagonisms are suspended – temporarily immobilized as the subjects pose.

The connection between gender, class, and race oppression is also denied as the ghetto photography session illustrates the analogy between commercial and race/class exploitation which registers on the screen as visual incongruity. Visual discrepancy, which is finally used for aesthetic effect, also makes it difficult to grasp the confluence of race, class, and gender oppression in the image of Tracy Chambers. Her class background magically becomes decor in the film; it neither radicalizes her nor drags her down – rather it sets her off. Diana Ross is alternately weighed down by the glamour iconography of commercial modeling and stripped to a Black body essence. But the *haute couture* iconography ultimately dominates the film. Since race is decorative and class does not reveal itself to the eye, she can only be seen as "exploited" in terms of her role as a model.

If the film plays down race, it does so not only to accommodate white audiences. While it worships the success of the Black cult star and treats aspiring young Blacks to Diana Ross's dream come true – a chance to design all the costumes in her own film, *Mahogany* also hawks the philosophy of Black enterprise. Here it does not matter where you come from, but you should ask yourself, in the words of the theme song, "Where are you going to, do you know?"[38] Race is like any other obstacle – to be transcended through diligent work and dedication to a goal. Supporting the film's self-help philosophy is the related story of Diana Ross's discovery as a skinny teenager singing in a Baptist Church in Detroit. With *Mahogany*, Motown president and founder Berry Gordy (who fired Tony Richardson to take over the film's direction himself) helps Diana Ross make something of herself again (on a larger scale) just as he helped so many aspiring recording artists by coaching them in money management and social decorum in his talent school.[39]

The phenomenon of Motown Industries comments less on the popularity of the self-help philosophy and more on the discrepancy between the opportunity formula and the social existence of Black Americans. Ironically, Black capitalism's one big success thrives on the impossibility of Black enterprise: soul entertainment as compensation and release sells because capitalism cannot deliver well-being to all.[40] Black music and performance, despite the homogenization of the original forms, represent a utopian aspiration for Black Americans as well as white suburbanites. Simon Frith describes the "need" supplied by rock fantasy:

> Black music had a radical, rebellious edge: it carried a sense of possibility denied in the labor market; it suggested a comradeship, a sensuality, a grace and joy and energy lacking in work . . . the power of rock fantasy rests, precisely, on utopianism.[41]

Here I am drawing on a theory of culture which sees capitalism as erratically supplying subversive "needs" as well as "false" desires, often through the same commodities which produce the ideological effect. Given that popular culture can accommodate the possibility of both containment and resistance in what Stuart Hall calls its "double movement," I want to turn, then, to the ways *Mahogany* can be seen to move in the other direction.[42]

Racial conflict surfaces or recedes in this film rather like the perceptual trick in which, depending on the angle of view, one swirling pattern or the other pops out at the viewer. Some ambiguity, for instance, is built into the confrontation between Black and white, as in the scene where Sean lures Brian into a struggle over an unloaded weapon. The outcome, in which Sean, characterized as a harmless eccentric, manipulates Brian into pulling the trigger, could be read as confirming the racist conception that Blacks who possess street reflexes are murderous aggressors. *Ebony* magazine, however, features a promotional still of the scene (representing Brian holding a gun over Sean), with a caption describing how Brian is tricked but still wins the fight.[43] Viewers, who choose the winners of ambiguous conflicts, may also choose to inhabit "looking" structures. The studies of lesbian readership already cited show that subcultural groups can interpret popular forms to their advantage, even without "invitation" from the text. Certainly more work needs to be done with the positioning of the audience around the category of race, considering, for instance, the social prohibitions against the Black man's sexual glance, the interracial intermingling of male "looks," and other visual taboos related to sanctions against interracial sexuality, but these issues are beyond the scope of this essay.

What I do find is that one of the basic tenets of contemporary feminist film theory – that the (male) spectator possesses the female indirectly through the eyes of the male protagonist (his screen surrogate) – is problematized in a film in which racial difference structures a hierarchy of access to the female image. These racial positions relate to other scenarios which are unknown by psychoanalytic categories. Considering the racial categories which psychoanalysis does not recognize, we see that the white male photographer monopolizes the classic patriarchal look controlling the view of the female body, and that the Black male protagonist's look is either repudiated or frustrated. The sumptuous image of Diana Ross is made available to the spectator via the white male character (Sean) but *not* through the look of the Black male character (Brain). In the sequence in which Tracy and Brian first meet outside her apartment building, his "look" is renounced. In each of the three shots of Tracy from Brian's point of view, she turns from him, walking out of his sight and away from the sound of his voice as he shouts at her through a megaphone. The relationship between the male and female protagonists is negotiated around Brian's bullhorn, emblem of his charismatic Black leadership, through which he tries to reach both the Black woman and his constituents. Thus both visual and audio control is denied the Black male, and the failure of his voice is consistently associated with Tracy's publicity image. The discovery by Brian's aides of the Mahogany ad for Revlon in *Newsweek* coincides with the report that the Gallup polls show the Black candidate trailing in the election. Later, the film cuts from Mahogany on the *Harper's Bazaar* cover to Brian's limping campaign where the sound of his voice magnified through a microphone is intermittently drowned out by a passing train as he makes his futile pitch to white factory workers. The manifest goal of the film, the reconciliation of the Black heterosexual couple, is thwarted by the commercial appropriation of her image, but, in addition, her highly mediated form threatens the Black political struggle.

Quite simply, then, there are structures relevant to any interpretation of this film which override the patriarchal scenario feminists have theorized as formally determining. From Afro-American literature, for instance, we should consider the scenario of the talented and beautiful mulatta who "passes" in white culture, but decides to return to Black society.[44] From Afro-American history, we should recall the white male's appropriation of the Black woman's body which weakened the Black male and undermined the community. We need to develop a theory of Black female representation which takes account of "passing" as an eroticizing alternation and a peculiar play on difference, and the corresponding double consciousness it requires of those who can seem either Black or White. Further, we need to reconsider the woman's picture narrative convention – the career renounced in favor of the man – in the context of Black history. Tracy Chambers's choice recapitulates Black aspiration and the white middle-class model which equates stable family life with respectability, but Tracy's decision is complicated since it favors Black community cooperation over acceptance by white society. Finally, one of the most difficult questions raised by Afro-American history and literature has to do with interracial heterosexuality and sexual "looking." *Mahogany* suggests that, since a Black male character is not allowed the position of control occupied by a white male character, race could be a factor in the construction of cinema language. More work on looking and racial taboos might determine whether or not mainstream cinema can offer the spectator the pleasure of looking at a white female character via the gaze of a Black male character. Framing the question of male privilege and viewing pleasure as the "right to look" may help us to rethink film theory along more materialist lines, considering, for instance, how some groups have historically had the license to "look" openly while other groups have "looked" illicitly.[45] Or, does the psychoanalytic model allow us to consider also the prohibitions against homosexuality and miscegenation?

Feminists who use psychoanalytic theory are careful to point out that "looking" positions do not correlate with social groups, and that ideological positioning is placement in a representational system which has no one-to-one correspondence with social reality. This, of course, keeps the levels of the social totality hopelessly separate. While I would not want to argue that form is ideologically neutral, I would suggest that we have overemphasized the ideological function of "signifying practice" at the expense of considering other ideological implications of the conflicting meanings in the text. Or, as Terry Lovell puts it, "While interpretation depends on analysis of the work's signifying practice, assessment of its meanings from the point of view of its validity, or of its ideology, depends on comparison between those structures of meaning and their object of reference, through the mediation of another type of discourse."[46] The impetus behind Marxist criticism, whether we want to admit it or not, is to make comparisons between social reality as we live it and ideology as it does not correspond to that reality. This we attempt to do knowing full well the futility of looking for real relations that are completely outside ideology.

Thus, while I am still willing to argue, as I did in earlier versions of this essay, that we can see the *Mahogany* narrative as a metaphor for the search for Black female sexuality, I see something else in hindsight. I would describe this as the temptation in an emerging Black feminist criticism, much like an earlier tendency in lesbian criticism, to place sexuality safely out of patriarchal bounds by declaring it outside culture, by furtively hiding it in subcultural enclaves where it can remain its "essential self," protected from the meaning-making mainstream culture. *Mahogany*, then, is finally about the mythical existence of something elusive. We know it through what white men do to secure it, and what black men are without it. It is the ultimate substance to the photographer – Tony Perkins's character – who dies trying to record its "trace" on film. It is known by degree – whatever is most wild and enigmatic, whatever cannot be conquered or subdued – the last frontier of female sexuality. Although it is undetectable to the advertising men who can analyze only physical attributes, it is immediately perceptible to a lesbian (Gavina herself, the owner of the Italian advertising agency), who uses it to promote the most inexplicable and subjective of commodities – perfume. Contrary to the suggestion that black female sexuality might still remain in excess of culture, and hence unfathomed and uncodified, it is worked over again and again in mainstream culture because of its apparent elusiveness, and in this context it is rather like bottled scent, which is often thought to convey its essence to everyone but the person wearing it.

To return to my main point, as feminists have theorized women's sexuality, they have universalized from the particular experience of white women, thus effecting what Hortense Spillers has called a "deadly metonomy."[47] While white feminists theorize the female image in terms of objectification, fetishization, and symbolic absence, their black counterparts describe the body as the site of symbolic resistance and the "paradox of non-being," a reference to the period in African–American history when black female did not signify "woman."[48] What strikes me still in this comparison is the stubbornness of the terms of feminist discourse analysis, which has not been able to deal, for instance, with what it has meant historically to be designated as not-human, and how Black women, whose bodies were legally not their own, fought against treatment based on this determination. Further, feminist analysis of culture as patriarchal cannot conceive of any connection between the female image and class or racial exploitation that includes the male. Historically, Black men and women, although not equally endangered, have been simultaneously implicated in incidents of interracial brutality. During two different periods of African American history, sexual assault, "symbolic of the effort to conquer the resistance the black woman could unloose," was a warning to the entire Black community.[49] If, as feminists have argued, women's sexuality evokes an unconscious terror in men, then Black women's sexuality represents a special threat to white patriarchy; the possibility of its eruption stands for the aspirations of the Black race as a whole.

My frustration with the feminist voice that insists on change *at the level of language* is that this position can deal with the historical situation described above only by turning it into discourse, and even as I write this, acutely aware as I am of the theoretical prohibitions against mixing representational issues with real historical ones, I feel the pressure to transpose people's struggles into more discursively manageable terms. However, a theory of ideology that separates the levels of the social formation in such a way that it is not only inappropriate but theoretically impossible to introduce the category of history into the analysis cannot be justified with Marxism. This has been argued elsewhere by others, among them Stuart Hall, who finds the "universalist tendency" found in both Freud and Lacan responsible for this impossibility. The incompatibility between Marxism and psychoanalytic theory is insurmountable at this time, he argues, because "the concepts elaborated by Freud (and reworked by Lacan) cannot, *in their in-general and universalist form*, enter the theoretical space of historical materialism."[50] In discussions within feminist film theory, it has often seemed the other way around – that historical materialism could not enter the space theorized by discourse analysis drawing on psychoanalytic concepts. Sealed off as it is (in theory), this analysis may not comprehend the category of the real historical subject, but its use will always have implications *for* that subject.

Notes

1 Feminist discussions around Lizzie Borden's 1983 feature, such as the one in June, 1985, at the Society for Cinema Studies Conference at New York University, actually exemplify my argument. Holding ourselves to consideration of the film's representational system was a frustrating exercise since crucial issues of subcultural reception and feminist political strategy were also at stake.

2 For an overview, see my "Women and Representation: Can We Enjoy Alternative Pleasure?" in Entertainment as Social Control, ed. Donald Lazere, Berkeley: University of California Press, forthcoming.

3 In "Aesthetics and Politics," New Left Review 107 (1978): 23, Terry Eagleton describes his exasperation with Screen, the journal which introduced this analytical style into British criticism:

> And yet, persuing still another article in that journal on the complex mechanisms by which a shot/reverse shot reinstates the imaginary, or the devices by which a particular cinematic syntagm permits the interruption of symbolic heterogeneity into the positioned perceptual space of the subject, one is forced to query with certain vehemence why ideological codes have been so remorselessly collapsed back into the intestines of the cinematic machine.

4 T. W. Adorno, "Sociology and Psychology," New Left Review 46 (November–December 1967): 78.

5 Feminist Theory: From Margin to Center, Boston: South End Press (1984), 12.

6 The Politics of Reality, Trumansburg, New York: The Crossing Press (1984), 113.

7 Frye, 118.

8 Notes on Women's Cinema, ed. Claire Johnston, London: Society for Education in Film and Television (1973); rpt. Sexual Stratagems, ed. Patricia Erens, New York: Horizon (1979), 133–43; Movies and Methods, ed. Bill Nichols, Berkeley and Los Angeles: University of California Press (1976), 208–17.

9 Screen 16, no. 3 (Autumn 1975): 6–18; rpt. Women and Cinema, eds. Karyn Kay and Gerald Peary, New York: E. P. Dutton (1977), 412–28; Film Theory and Criticism, eds. Gerald Mast and Marshall Cohen, 3rd edn., New York: Oxford (1985).

10 Trans. Ben Brewster, Screen 16, no. 2 (Summer 1975): 14–76.

11 Examples include Simon Clarke, Victor Jeleniewski Seidler, Kevin McDonnell, Kevin Robins, and Terry Lovell, One-Dimensional Marxism, London: Alison & Busby (1980); Kevin Robins, "Althusserian Marxism and Media Studies: The Case of Screen," Media, Culture and Society 1, no. 4 (October 1979): 355–70; Ed Buscombe, Christine Gledhill, Alan Lovell, Christopher Williams, "Statement: Psychoanalysis and Film," Screen 20, no. 1 (Spring 1979): 121–33; Christine Gledhill, "Recent Developments in Feminist Criticism," Quarterly Review of Film Studies 3, no. 4 (Fall 1978); 457–93; rpt. Re-Vision, eds. Mary Ann Doane, Patricia Mellencamp, and Linda Williams, Frederick, Maryland: University Publications of America (1984), 18–48.

12 Lucie Arbuthnot and Gail Seneca, "Pre-Text and Text in Gentlemen Prefer Blondes," Film Reader 5 (Winter 1981): 13–23.

13 Chris Straayer, "*Personal Best*: Lesbian/Feminist Audience," *Jump Cut* 29 (February 1984): 40–4; Elizabeth Ellsworth, "The Power of Interpretive Communities: Feminist Appropriations of *Personal Best*," paper delivered at Society for Cinema Studies Conference, University of Wisconsin-Madison, March, 1984.

14 "The Straight Mind," *Feminist Issues* (Summer 1980): 107–11.

15 See, for instance, John D'Emilio's *Sexual Politics, Sexual Communities*. Chicago: University of Chicago Press (1984).

16 In "Thinking Sex: Notes for a Radical Theory of the Politics of Sexuality," in *Pleasure and Danger*, ed. Carol Vance, Boston and London: Routledge & Kegan Paul (1984), 307, Rubin stresses the need to make this distinction because feminism does not immediately apply to both oppressions. As she clarifies this: "Feminism is the theory of gender oppression. To automatically assume that this makes it the theory of sexual oppression is to fail to distinguish between gender, on the one hand, and erotic desire, on the other."

17 *Towards a Black Feminist Criticism*, Trumansburg, New York: Out and Out Books (1977), 1.

18 Bonnie Thornton Dill, "Race, Class, and Gender: Prospects for an All-Inclusive Sisterhood," *Feminist Studies* 9, no. 1 (Spring 1983): 134; for a slightly different version of this essay, see " 'On the Hem of Life': Race, Class, and the Prospects for Sisterhood," in *Class, Race, and Sex: The Dynamics of Control*, eds. Amy Swerdlow and Hanna Lessinger, Boston: G. K. Hall (1983).

19 Margaret Simons, "Racism and Feminism: A Schism in the Sisterhood," *Feminist Studies* 5, no. 2 (Summer 1979): 392.

20 Adrienne Rich, in *On Lies, Secrets, and Silence*, New York: W. W. Norton (1979), 302–3, notes that while Blacks link their experience of racism with the white woman, this is still patriarchal racism working through her. It is possible, she says, that "a black first grader, or that child's mother, or a black patient in a hospital, or a family on welfare, may experience racism most directly in the person of a white woman, who stands for those service professions through which white male supremacist society controls the mother, the child, the family, and all of us. It is *her* racism, yes, but a racism learned in the same patriarchal school which taught her that women are unimportant or unequal, not to be trusted with power; where she learned to mistrust and hear her own impulses for rebellion; to become an instrument."

21 Gloria Joseph, "The Incompatible Menage à Trois: Marxism, Feminism, and Racism," in *Women and Revolution*, ed. Lydia Sargent, Boston: South End Press (1981), 96; Combahee River Collective in "Combahee River Collective Statement," in *Home Girls*, ed. Barbara Smith, New York: Kitchen Table Press (1983), 275, compares their alliance with Black men with the negative identification white women have with white men:

> Our situation as Black people necessitates that we have solidarity around the fact of race, which white women of course do not need to have with white men, unless it is their negative solidarity as racial oppressors. We struggle together with Black men against racism, while we also struggle with Black men about sexism.

22 "Combahee River Collective Statement," 272.

23 E. Ann Kaplan, in *Women and Film*, New York and London: Methuen (1983), 140, says the danger for Marxists in employing the connection between Althusser and Lacan is that "the theories do not accommodate the categories of either class or race: economic language as the primary shaping force replaces socioeconomic relations and institutions as the dominant influence. Sexual difference becomes the driving force of history in place of the Marxist one of class contradictions."

24 Michèle Barrett, *Women's Oppression Today*, London: Verso (1980), 15.

25 For a comparison between radical feminism, liberal feminism, Marxism, and socialist feminism, see Alison Jaggar, *Feminist Politics and Human Nature*, Sussex: Harvester Press (1983).

26 "The Trouble with Patriarchy," in *People's History and Socialist Theory*, ed. Raphael Samuel, London and Boston: Routledge & Kegan Paul (1981), 365.

27 Frantz Fanon, *Black Skin, White Masks*, trans. Charles Lam Markmann, Paris, 1952; rpt. New York: Grove Press (1967), 161.

28 Simons, 387.

29 Barbara Omolade, "Hearts of Darkness," in *Powers of Desire*, eds. Ann Snitow, Christine Stansell, and Sharon Thompson, New York: Monthly Review Press (1983), 352.

30 "The Afro-American Female: The Historical Context of the Construction of Sexual Identity," in *Powers of Desire*, 230. The "days of slavery" is a recurring reference point in the writings of Black feminists. Although I am arguing that studying the Black condition *in history* is the antithesis of theorizing subjectivity ahistorically, I can also see how the "days of slavery" might function as an ideological construct. We do the evolving work of Black feminists a disservice if we do not subject it to the same critique we would apply to white middle-class feminism. How, for instance, can equal subjugation during slavery have anything to do with ideals of male/female equality? I am indebted to Brackette Williams for calling this to my attention.

31 "The Black Woman's Role in the Community of Slaves," *The Black Scholar* (December 1971): 5–6.

32 Omolade, 352.

33 Joseph, 99; Audre Lorde, in *Sister Outsider*, Trumansburg, New York: The Crossing Press (1984), 119, sees sexism in Black communities as not original to them, but as a plague that has struck. She argues:

> Because of the continuous battle against racial erasure that Black women and Black men share, some Black women still refuse to recognize that we are also oppressed as women, and that sexual hostility against Black women is practiced not only by the white racist society, but implemented within our Black communities as well. It is a disease striking the heart of Black nationhood, and silence will not make it disappear.

34 Linda Gordon and Ellen DuBois, in "Seeking Ecstasy on the Battlefield: Danger and Pleasure in Nineteenth Century Feminist Sexual Thought," *Feminist Review* 13 (Spring 1983): 43, note that in its two stages the feminist movement has developed two major themes which have expressed women's sexual danger. Whereas prostitution articulated women's fears in the nineteenth century, rape summarizes the contemporary terror.

35   Jacquelyn Dowd Hall, " 'The Mind That Burns in Each Body': Women, Rape, and Racial Violence," in *Powers of Desire*, 332.

36   Nancy Hall-Duncan, *The History of Fashion Photography*, New York: Alpine Books (1979), 196.

37   White reviewer Jay Cocks, in "Black and Tan Fantasy," *Time*, 27 October, 1975, 71, interprets the scene in which Tony Perkins is represented as severely devastated after his failure in bed with Diana Ross as a "romantic interlude," and the "one pearl" in the entire film.

38   Simon Frith, in "Mood Music," *Screen* 25, no. 3 (May–June 1984): 78, says that theme songs are more significant than critics have realized. It is the last of the motion picture experience to touch us as we leave the theater, and it works to "rearrange our feelings."

39   Stephen Birmingham, *Certain People*, Boston and Toronto: Little, Brown (1977), 262–63.

40   Manning Marable, in *How Capitalism Underdeveloped Black America*, Boston: South End Press (1983), 157, lists Motown Industries as the largest grossing Black-owned corporation in the US, which did $64.8 million in business in 1979.

41   *Sound Effects*, New York: Pantheon (1981), 264.

42   "Notes on Deconstructing 'The Popular'," in *People's History and Socialist Theory*, 228.

43   "Spectacular New Film for Diana Ross: *Mahogany*," *Ebony*, October 1975, 146.

44   See, for instance, Jessie Fauset's *There is Confusion*, New York: Boni and Liveright (1924), and *Plum Bun*, New York: 1928: rpt. New York and London: Routledge and Kegan Paul (1985); Nella Larsen's *Quicksand*, New York: 1928; and *Passing*, New York: 1929; rpt. New Bunswick, NJ: Rutgers University Press, 1986.

45   Fredric Jameson, in "Pleasure: A Political Issue," *Formations of Pleasure*, Boston and London: Routledge & Kegan Paul (1983), 7, interprets Mulvey's connection between viewing pleasure and male power as the conferral of a "right to look." He does not take this further, but I find the term suggestive and at the same time potentially volatile. I refer to the current division in the women's movement over the need for anti-pornography legislation. Feminist supporters of the legislation argue that male pornographic reading and "looking" should be illegal because it is an infringement of women's civil rights. For an overview of the debates around pornography as they relate to film theory see Chuck Kleinhans and Julia Lesage, "The Politics of Sexual Representation," in *Jump Cut* 30 (March, 1985): 24–6. In the same issue, two articles argue the political significance of sexual looking for the gay male subculture (Richard Dyer's "Coming to Terms," 28–9, and Tom Waugh's "Men's Pornography: Gay vs. Straight," 30–3.) For one of the most provocative analyses of the feminist position on pornography, see Joanna Russ, *Magic Mommas, Trembling Sisters, Puritans, and Perverts*, Trumansburg, New York: The Crossing Press (1985).

46   *Pictures of Reality*, London: British Film Institute (1980), 90.

47   Spillers, 78. It is very tempting to contrast the colonized (the body or other cultural terrain) with a notion of the "authentic," as though something has escaped or eluded colonization. We often argue for the integrity of people's indigenous culture or alternative experience by characterizing it as "pure"; we hope that the colonizer will find the alien culture incomprehensible or "unfathomable." Feminists have recently slipped into this position as they have created a new mystique based on women's

"unrealized" sexuality – a wild place as yet uncharted by the dominant culture. The problem is that even this space is filled out with well-worn notions of pleasure and fulfilment. Given the opportunity to symbolize, to codify sexuality, the sexual subordinate can never represent or experience in complete cultural isolation. In borrowing Spillers's argument, I have made a case for Black women's sexuality that I would never have made for female sexuality as a whole. Brackette Williams has corrected me here again.

48 Spillers, 77.
49 Davis, 11.
50 "Debate: Psychology, Ideology and the Human Subject," *Ideology and Consciousness* 2 (October 1977): 118–19.

41
White

Richard Dyer

This is an article about a subject that, much of the time as I've been writing it, seems not to be there as a subject at all. Trying to think about the representation of whiteness as an ethnic category in mainstream film is difficult, partly because white power secures its dominance by seeming not to be anything in particular but also because, when whiteness qua whiteness does come into focus, it is often revealed as emptiness, absence, denial or even a kind of death.

It is, all the same, important to try to make some headway with grasping whiteness as a culturally constructed category. 'Images of' studies have looked at groups defined as oppressed, marginal or subordinate – women, the working class, ethnic and other minorities (e.g. lesbians and gay men, disabled people, the elderly). The impulse for such work lies in the sense that how such groups are represented is part of the process of their oppression, marginalization or subordination. The range and fertility of such work has put those groups themselves centre-stage in both analytical and campaigning activity, and highlighted the issue of representation as politics. It has, however, had one serious drawback, long recognized in debates about women's studies. Looking, with such passion and single-mindedness, at non-dominant groups has had the effect of reproducing the sense of the oddness, differentness, exceptionality of these groups, the feeling that they are departures from the norm. Meanwhile the norm has carried on as if it is the natural, inevitable, ordinary way of being human.

Some efforts are now being made to rectify this, to see that the norm too is constructed, although only with masculinity has anything approaching a proliferation of texts begun. Perhaps it is worth signalling here, before proceeding, two of the pitfalls in the path of such work, two convolutions that especially characterize male writing about masculinity – guilt and me-too-ism. Let me state that, while writing here as a white person about whiteness, I do not mean either to display the expiation of my guilt about being white nor to hint that it is also awful to be white (because it is an inadequate, limiting definition of being human, because feeling guilty is such a burden). Studies of dominance by the dominant should not deny the place of the writer in relation to what s/he is writing about it, but nor should they be the green light for self-recrimination or trying to get in on the act.

Power in contemporary society habitually passes itself off as embodied in the normal as opposed to the superior (cf. Marcuse, 1964). This is common to all forms of power, but it works in a peculiarly seductive way with whiteness, because of the way it seems rooted, in commonsense thought, in things other than ethnic difference. The very terms we use to describe the major ethnic divide presented by Western society, 'black' and 'white', are imported from and natur- alized by other discourses. Thus it is said (even in liberal textbooks) that there are inevitable associations of white with light and therefore safety, and black with dark and therefore danger, and that this explains racism (whereas one might well argue about the safety of the cover of darkness and the danger of exposure to the light); again, and with more justice, people point to the Judaeo-Christian use of white and black to symbolize good and evil, as carried still in such expressions as 'a black mark', 'white magic', 'to blacken the character' and so on (cf. Jordan, 1969 and Fryer, 1984). I'd like to look at another aspect of commonsensical conflations of black and white as natural and ethnic categories by considering ideas of what colour is.

I was taught the scientific difference between black and white at primary school. It seemed a fascinating paradox. Black, which, because you had to add it to paper to make a picture, I had always thought of as a colour, was, it turned out, nothingness, the absence of all colour; whereas white, which looked just like empty space (or blank paper), was, apparently, all the colours there were put together. No doubt such explanations of colour have long been outmoded; what interests me is how they manage to touch on the construction of the ethnic categories of black and white in dominant representation. In the realm of categories, black is always marked as a colour (as the term 'coloured' egregiously acknowledges), and is always particularizing; whereas white is not anything really, not an identity, not a particularizing quality, because it is everything – white is no colour because it is all colours.

This property of whiteness, to be everything and nothing, is the source of its representational power. On the one hand, as one of the people in the video *Being White*[1] observes, white domination is reproduced by the way that white people 'colonize the definition of normal'. Paul Gilroy similarly spells out the political consequences, in the British context, of the way that whiteness both disappears behind and is subsumed into other identities. He discusses the way that the language of 'the nation' aims to be unifying, permitting even socialists an appeal in terms of 'we' and 'our' 'beyond the margins of sectional interest', but goes on to observe that:

> there is a problem in these plural forms: who do they include, or, more precisely for our purposes, do they help to reproduce blackness and Englishness as mutually exclusive categories? . . . why are contemporary appeals to 'the people' in danger of transmitting themselves as appeals to the white people? (Gilroy, 1987: 55–6)[2]

On the other hand, if the invisibility of whiteness colonizes the definition of other norms – class, gender, heterosexuality, nationality and so on – it also masks whiteness as itself a category. White domination is then hard to grasp in terms of the characteristics and practices of white people. No one would deny that, at the very least, there are advantages to being white in Western societies, but it is only avowed racists who have a theory which attributes this to inherent qualities of white people. Otherwise, whiteness is presented more as a case of historical accident, rather than a characteristic cultural/historical construction, achieved through white domination.

The colourless multi-colouredness of whiteness secures white power by making it hard, especially for white people and their media, to 'see' whiteness. This, of course, also makes it hard to analyse. It is the way that black people are marked as black (are not just 'people') in representation that has made it relatively easy to analyse their representation, whereas white people – not there as a category and everywhere everything as a fact – are difficult, if not impossible, to analyse qua white. The subject seems to fall apart in your hands as soon as you begin. Any instance of white representation is always immediately something more specific – *Brief Encounter* is not about white people, it is about English middle-class people; *The Godfather* is not about white people, it is about Italian American people; but *The Color Purple* is about black people, before it is about poor, southern US people.

This problem clearly faced the makers of *Being White*, a pioneering attempt to confront the notion of white identity. The opening vox pop sequence vividly illustrates the problem. Asked how they would define themselves, the white interviewees refer easily to gender, age, nationality or looks but never to ethnicity. Asked if they think of themselves as white, most say that they don't, though one or two speak of being 'proud' or 'comfortable' to be white. In an attempt to get some white people to explore what being white means, the video assembles a group to talk about it and it is here that the problem of white people's inability to see whiteness appears intractable. Sub-categories of whiteness (Irishness, Jewishness, Britishness) take over, so that the particularity of whiteness itself begins to disappear; then gradually, it seems almost inexorably, the participants settle in to talking with confidence about what they know: stereotypes of black people.

Yet perhaps this slide towards talking about blackness gives us a clue as to where we might begin to see whiteness – where its difference from blackness is inescapable and at issue. I shall look here at examples of mainstream cinema whose narratives are marked by the fact of ethnic difference. Other approaches likely to yield interesting results include: the study of the characterization of whites in Third World or diaspora cinema; images of the white race in avowedly racist and fascist cinema; the use of the 'commutation test' (Thompson, 1978), the imaginary substitution of black for white performers in films such as *Brief Encounter*, say, or *Ordinary People* (if these are unimaginable played by black actors, what does this tell us about the characteristics of whiteness?) or, related to this, consideration of what ideas of whiteness are implied by such widespread observations as that Sidney Poitier or Diana Ross, say, are to all intents and purposes 'white'. What all these approaches share, however, is reference to that which is not white, as if only non-whiteness can give whiteness any substance. The reverse is not the case – studies of images of blacks, Native Americans, Jews and other ethnic minorities do not need the comparative element that seems at this stage indispensable for the study of whites.

The representation of white qua white begins to come into focus – in mainstream cinema, for a white spectator – in films in which non-white characters play a significant role. I want to look at three very different examples here – *Jezebel* (USA, Warner Brothers, 1938), *Simba* (GB, Rank Studios, 1955) and *Night of the Living Dead* (USA, 1969). Each is characteristic of the particular genre and period to which it belongs. *Jezebel* is a large-budget Hollywood feature film (said to have been intended to rival *Gone with the Wind*) built around a female star, Bette Davis; its spectacular pleasures are those of costume and decor, of gracious living, and its emotional pleasures those of tears. *Simba* is a film made as part of Rank's bid to produce films that might successfully challenge Hollywood at the box office, built around a male star, Dirk Bogarde; its spectacular pleasures are those of the travelogue, its emotional ones excitement and also the gratification of seeing 'issues' (here, the Mau-Mau in Kenya) being dealt with. *Night of the Living Dead* is a cheap, independently produced horror film with no stars; its spectacular and emotional pleasures are those of shock, disgust and suspense, along with the evident political or social symbolism that has aided its cult reputation.

The differences between the three films are important and will inform the ways in which they represent whiteness. Yet there is some point in trying to see continuity across three, none the less significantly different, films. There is no doubt that part of the strength and resilience of stereotypes of non-dominant groups resides in their variation and flexibility – stereotypes are seldom found in a pure form and this is part of the process by which they are naturalized, kept alive (Perkins, 1979; Neale, 1979/80). Yet the strength of white representation, as I've suggested, is the apparent absence altogether of the typical, the sense that being white is coterminous with the endless plenitude of human diversity. If we are to see the historical, cultural and political limitations (to put it mildly) of white world domination, it is important to see similarities, typicalities, within the seemingly infinite variety of white representation.

All three films share a perspective that associates whiteness with order, rationality, rigidity, qualities brought out by the contrast with black disorder, irrationality and looseness. It is their take on this which differs. *Simba* operates with a clear black–white binarism, holding out the possibility that black people can learn white values but fearing that white people will be engulfed by blackness. *Jezebel* is far more ambivalent, associating blackness with the defiance of its female protagonist, whom it does not know whether to condemn or adore. *Night* takes the hint of critique of whiteness in *Jezebel* and takes it to its logical conclusion, where whiteness represents not only rigidity but death.

What these films also share, which helps to sharpen further the sense of whiteness in them, is a situation in which white domination is contested, openly in the text of *Simba*, and explicitly acknowledged in *Jezebel*. The narrative of *Simba* is set in motion by the Mau-Mau challenge to British occupation, which also occasions set pieces of debate on the issues of white rule and black responses to it; the imminent decline of slavery is only once or twice referred to directly in *Jezebel*, but the film can assume the audience knows that slavery was soon ostensibly to disappear from the southern states. Both films are suffused with the sense of white rule being at an end, a source of definite sorrow in *Simba* but in *Jezebel* producing that mixture of disapproval and nostalgia characteristic of the white representation of the ante-bellum South. *Night* makes no direct reference to the state of ethnic play but, as I shall argue below, it does make implicit reference to the black uprisings that were part of the historical context of its making, and which many believed would alter irrevocably the nature of power relations between black and white people in the USA.

The presence of black people in all three films allows one to see whiteness as whiteness, and in this way relates to the existential psychology that is at the origins of the interest in 'otherness' as an explanatory concept in the representation of ethnicity (Fanon, 1986; Said, 1978; Bhabha, 1983). Existential psychology, principally in the work of Jean-Paul Sartre, had proposed a model of human growth whereby the individual self becomes aware of itself as a self by perceiving its difference from others. It was other writers who suggested that this process, supposedly at once individual and universal, was in fact socially specific – Simone de Beauvoir arguing that it has to do with the construction of the male ego, Frantz Fanon relating it to the colonial encounter of white and black. What I want to stress here is less this somewhat metaphysical dimension (cf. Parry, 1987), more the material basis for the shifts and anxieties in the representation of whiteness suggested by *Simba*, *Jezebel* and *Night*.

The three films relate to situations in which whites hold power in society, but are materially dependent upon black people. All three films suggest an awareness of this dependency – weakly in *Simba*, strongly but still implicitly in *Jezebel*, inescapably in *Night*. It is this actual dependency of white on black in a context of continued white power and privilege that throws the legitimacy of white domination into question. What is called for is a demonstration of the virtues of whiteness that would justify continued domination, but this is a problem if whiteness is also invisible, everything and nothing. It is from this that the films' fascinations derive. I shall discuss them here in the order in which they most clearly attempt to hang on to some justification of whiteness, starting, then, with *Simba* and ending with *Night*.

Simba

Simba is a characteristic product of the British cinema between about 1945 and 1965 – an entertainment film 'dealing with' a serious issue (Hill, 1986). It is a colonial adventure film, offering the standard narrative pleasures of adventure with a tale of personal growth. The hero, Alan (Bogarde), arrives in Kenya from England to visit his brother on his farm, finds he has been killed by the Mau-Mau and stays to sort things out (keep the farm going, find out who killed his brother, quell the Mau-Mau). Because the Mau-Mau were a real administrative and ideological problem for British imperialism at the time of the film's making, *Simba* also has to construct a serious discursive context for these pleasures (essentially a moral one, to do with the proper way to treat native peoples, toughness versus niceness). It does this partly through debates and discussions, partly through characters clearly representing what the film takes to be the range of possible angles on the subject (the bigoted whites, the liberal whites, the British-educated black man, the despotic black chief) but above all through the figure of the hero, whose adventures and personal growth are occasioned, even made possible, through the process of engaging with the late colonial situation. The way this situation is structured by the film and the way Alan/Bogarde rises to the occasion display the qualities of whiteness.

Simba is founded on the 'Manicheism delirium' identified by Fanon as characteristic of the colonialist sensibility (1986: 1); it takes what Paul Gilroy refers to as an 'absolutist view of black and white cultures, as fixed, mutually impermeable expressions of racial and national identity, [which] is a ubiquitous theme in racial "common sense"' (1987: 6). The film is organized around a rigid binarism, with white standing for modernity, reason, order, stability, and black standing for backwardness, irrationality, chaos and violence. This binarism is reproduced in every detail of the film's mise-en-scène. A sequence of two succeeding scenes illustrates this clearly – a meeting of the white settlers to discuss the emergency, followed by a meeting of the Mau-Mau. The whites' meeting takes place in early evening, in a fully lit room; characters who speak are shot with standard high-key lighting so that they are fully visible; everyone sits in rows and although there is disagreement, some of it hot-tempered and emotional, it is expressed in grammatical discourse in a language the British viewer can understand; moreover, the meeting consists of nothing but speech. The black meeting, on the other hand, takes place at dead of night, out of doors, with all characters in shadow; even the Mau-Mau leader is lit with extreme sub-expressionist lighting that dramatizes and distorts his face; grouping is in the form of a broken, uneven circle; what speech there is is ritualized, not reasoned, and remains untranslated (and probably in no authentic language anyway), and most vocal sounds are whooping, gabbling and shrieking; the heart of the meeting is in any case not speech, but daubing with blood and entrails and scarring the body. The return to whiteness after this sequence is once again a return to daylight, a dissolve to the straight lines of European fencing and vegetable plots.

The emphasis on the visible and bounded in this mise-en-scène (maintained throughout the film) has to do with the importance of fixity in the stereotyping of others – clear boundaries are characteristic of things white (lines, grids, not speaking till someone else has finished and so on), and also what keeps whites clearly distinct from blacks. The importance of the process of boundary establishment and maintenance has long been recognized in discussions of stereotyping and representation (Bhabha, 1983; Dyer, 1992; Gilman, 1985). This process is functional for dominant groups, but through it the capacity to set boundaries becomes a characteristic attribute of such groups, endlessly reproduced in ritual, costume, language and, in cinema, mise-en-scène. Thus, whites and men (especially) become characterized by 'boundariness' (cf. Chodorow, 1978).

Simba's binarism is in the broadest sense racist, but not in the narrower sense of operating with a notion of intrinsic and unalterable biological bases for differences between peoples (Banton, 1977).[3] It is informed rather by a kind of evolutionism, the idea of a path of progress already followed by whites but in principle open to all human beings – hence the elements in the binarism of modernity versus backwardness. Such evolutionism raises the possibility of blacks becoming like whites, and it is the belief in this possibility that underpins the views of the liberal characters in the film, Mary (Virginia McKenna) and Dr Hughes (Joseph Tomelty), the latter pleading with his fellow settlers at the meeting to 'reason', not with the Mau-Mau but with the other Africans, who are not beyond the reach of rational discussion. The possibility is further embodied in the character of Peter Karanja (Earl Cameron), the son of the local chief (Orlando Martins), who has trained to be a doctor and is now running a surgery in the village. The film is at great pains to establish that Peter is indeed reasonable, rational, humane, liberal. It is always made quite clear to the viewer that this is so and the representatives of liberalism always believe in him; it is the other whites who do not trust him, and one of Alan's moral lessons is to learn to respect Peter's worth. It seems then that part of the film is ready to take the liberal evolutionist position. Yet it is also significant that the spokespeople for liberalism (niceness and reason) are socially subordinate: a woman and a Welsh doctor (played for comic eccentricity most of the time); and that liberalism fails, with its representatives (Mary, Peter and now won-over Alan) left at the end of the film crouched in the flames of Alan's farm, rescued from the Mau-Mau in the nick of time by the arrival of the white militia, and Peter dying from wounds inflicted on him by the Mau-Mau (represented as a black mob). Although with its head, as it were, the film endorses the possibility of a black person becoming 'white', this is in fact deeply disturbing, setting in motion the anxiety attendant on any loosening of the fixed visibility of the colonized other. This anxiety is established from the start of the film and is the foundation of its narrative.

As is customary in colonial adventure films, *Simba* opens with a panoramic shot of the land, accompanied here by birdsong and the sound of an African man singing. While not especially lush or breathtaking, it is peaceful and attractive. A cry of pain interrupts this mood and we see the man who has been singing stop, get off his bicycle and walk towards its source to find a white man lying covered in blood on the ground. The black man kneels by his side, apparently about to help him, but then, to the sound of a drum-roll on the soundtrack, draws his machete and plunges it (off screen) into the wounded man. He then walks back to his bike and rides off. Here is encapsulated the fear that ensues if you can't see black men behaving as black men should, the deceptiveness of a black man in Western clothes riding a bike. This theme is then reiterated throughout the film. Which of the servants can be trusted? How can you tell who is Mau-Mau and who not? Why should Alan trust Peter?

This opening sequence is presented in one long take, using panning. As the man rides off, the sound of a plane is heard, the camera pans up and there is the first cut of the film, to a plane flying through the clouds. There follows (with credits over) a series of aerial shots of the African landscape, in one of which a plane's shadow is seen, and ending with shots of white settlement and then the plane coming to land. Here is another aspect of the film's binarism. The credit sequence uses the dynamics of editing following the more settled feel of the pre-credit long take; it uses aerial shots moving through space, rather than pans with their fixed vantage point; it emphasizes the view from above, not that from the ground, and the modernity of air travel after the primitivism of the machete. It also brings the hero to Africa (as we realize when we see Bogarde step off in the first post-credit shot), brings the solution to the problems of deceptive, unfixed appearances set up by the pre-credit sequence.

Simba's binarism both establishes the differences between black and white and creates the conditions for the film's narrative pleasures – the disturbance of the equilibrium of clear-cut binarism, the resultant conflict that the hero has to resolve. His ability to resolve it is part of his whiteness, just as whiteness is identified in the dynamism of the credit sequence (which in turn relates to the generic expectations of adventure) and in the narrative of personal growth that any colonial text with pretensions also has. The empire provided a narrative space for the realization of manhood, as both action and maturation (Hall, 1981). The colonial landscape is expansive, enabling the hero to roam and giving us the entertainment of action; it is unexplored, giving him the task of discovery and us the pleasures of mystery; it is uncivilized, needing taming, providing the spectacle of power; it is difficult and dangerous, testing his machismo, providing us with suspense. In other words, the colonial landscape provides the occasion for the realization of white male virtues, which are not qualities of being but of doing – acting, discovering, taming, conquering. At the same time, colonialism, as a social, political and economic system, even in fictions, also carries with it challenges of responsibility, of the establishment and maintenance of order, of the application of reason and authority to situations. These, too, are qualities of white manhood that are realized in the process of the colonial text, and very explicitly in Simba. When Alan arrives at Nairobi, he is met by Mary, a woman to whom he had proposed when she was visiting England; she had turned him down, telling him, as he recalls on the drive to his brother's farm, that he had 'no sense of responsibility'. Now he realizes that she was right; in the course of the film he will learn to be responsible in the process of dealing with the Mau-Mau, and this display of growth will win him Mary.

But this is a late colonial text, characterized by a recognition that the empire is at an end, and not unaware of some kinds of liberal critique of colonialism. So

Simba takes a turn that is far more fully explored by, say, *Black Narcissus* (1947) or the Granada television adaptation of *The Jewel in the Crown* (1982). Here, maturity involves the melancholy recognition of failure. This is explicitly stated, by Sister Clodagh in *Black Narcissus*, to be built into the geographical conditions in which the nuns seek to establish their civilizing mission ('I couldn't stop the wind from blowing'); it is endlessly repeated by the nice whites in *The Jewel in the Crown* ('There's nothing I can do!') and symbolized in the lace shawl with butterflies 'caught in the net' that keeps being brought out by the characters. I have already suggested the ways in which liberalism is marginalized and shown to fail in *Simba*. More than this, the hero also fails to realize the generically promised adventure experiences: he is unable to keep his late brother's farm going, nor does he succeed in fighting off a man stealing guns from his house; he fails to catch the fleeing leader of the Mau-Mau, and is unable to prevent them from destroying his house and shooting Peter. The film ends with his property in flames and – a touch common to British social conscience films – with a shot of a young black boy who symbolizes the only possible hope for the future.

The repeated failure of narrative achievement goes along with a sense of white helplessness in the face of the Mau-Mau (the true black threat), most notably in the transition between the two meeting scenes discussed above. Alan has left the meeting in anger because one of the settlers has criticized the way his brother had dealt with the Africans (too soft); Mary joins him, to comfort him. At the end of their conversation, there is a two-shot of them, with Mary saying of the situation, 'it's like a flood, we're caught in it'. This is accompanied by the sound of drums and is immediately followed by a slow dissolve to black people walking through the night towards the Mau-Mau meeting. The drums and the dissolve enact Mary's words, the whites 'caught' in the encroachment of blackness.

Simba is, then, an endorsement of the moral superiority of white values of reason, order and boundedness, yet suggests a loss of belief in their efficacy. This is a familiar trope of conservatism. At moments, though, there are glimpses of something else, achieved inadvertently perhaps through the casting of Dirk Bogarde. It becomes explicit in the scene between Mary and Alan just mentioned, when Alan says to Mary, 'I was suddenly afraid of what I was feeling', referring to the anger and hatred that the whole situation is bringing out in him and, as Mary says, everyone else. The implication is that the situation evokes in whites the kind of irrational violence supposedly specific to blacks. Of course, being white means being able to repress it and this is what we seem to see in Alan throughout the film. Such repression constitutes the stoic glory of the imperial hero, but there is something about Bogarde in the part that makes it seem less than admirable or desirable. Whether this is suggested by his acting style, still and controlled, yet with fiercely grinding jaws, rigidly clenched hands and very occasional sudden outbursts of shouting, or by the way Rank was grooming him against the grain of his earlier, sexier image (including its gay overtones) (Medhurst, 1986), it suggests a notion of whiteness as repression that leads us neatly on to *Jezebel*.

Jezebel

Like *Simba*, *Jezebel* depicts a white society characterized by order and rigidity, here expressed principally through codes of behaviour and rules of conduct embodied in set piece receptions, dinner parties and balls. This does contrast with the bare glimpses we get of black life in the film, but *Jezebel* also explores the ways in which whiteness is related to blackness, materially and emotionally dependent on it yet still holding sway over it.

Compositionally, *Jezebel* frequently foregrounds black people – scenes often open with the camera moving from a black person (a woman selling flowers in New Orleans, a servant carrying juleps, a boy pulling on a rope to operate a ceiling fan) across or towards white characters; black people often intrude into the frame while white characters talk. This is particularly noticeable during a dinner-table discussion of the future of slavery; when one of the characters, Pres (Henry Fonda), says that the South will be defeated by machines triumphing over 'unskilled slave labour', the chief black character, Cato (Lou Payton), leans across our field of vision to pour Pres's wine, literally embodying the fact of slave labour. The film's insistence upon the presence of black people is important in its perception and construction of the white South. As Jim Pines puts it, 'black characters do not occupy a significant dramatic function in the film, but their social role nevertheless plays an explicit and relevant part in the conflict that arises between the principal white characters' (Pines, 1975: 59).

Jezebel is distantly related, through the sympathies of its stars, director and production studio, to progressive ideas on race, making it, as Pines says, 'within the plantation movie tradition...undoubtedly the most liberal-inclined' (ibid.: 55; cf. Cripps, 1977: 299, 304). These ideas have to do with the belief or suspicion that black people have in some sense more 'life' than whites. This idea, and its ambivalences, have a very long history which cannot detain us here. It springs from ideas of the closeness of non-European (and even non-metropolitan) peoples to nature, ideas which were endemic to those processes of European expansion variously termed exploration, nation building and colonialism (Robinson, 1983). Expansion into other lands placed the humans encountered there as part of the fauna of those lands, to be construed either as the forces of nature that had to be subjugated or, for liberals, the model of sweet natural Man uncontaminated by civilization. At the same time, ideas of nature have become central to Western thought about being human, such that concepts of human life itself have become inextricable from concepts of nature. Thus the idea that non-whites are more natural than whites also comes to suggest that they have more 'life', a logically meaningless but commonsensically powerful notion.

Jezebel relates to a specific liberal variation on this way of thinking, a tradition in which *Uncle Tom's Cabin* and the Harlem Renaissance are key reference points (Fredrickson, 1972; Lewis, 1981), as is the role of Annie in Sirk's *Imitation of Life*. Ethel Mannin's statement may be taken as emblematic:

It is of course that feeling for life which is the secret of the Negro people, as surely as it is the lack of it, and slow atrophy of the capacity to live emotionally, which will be the ultimate decadence of the white civilized people. (Mannin, 1930: 157)

'Life' here tends to mean the body, the emotions, sensuality and spirituality; it is usually explicitly counterposed to the mind and the intellect, with the implication that white people's over-investment in the cerebral is cutting them off from life and leading them to crush the life out of others and out of nature itself. The implicit counterposition is, of course, 'death', a point to which I shall return in the discussion of *Night of the Living Dead*.

Jezebel is generally, and rightly, understood to be about the taming of a woman who refuses to live by the Old South's restrictive codes of femininity. It is a clear instance of Molly Haskell's characterization of one of the available models for strong women's roles in classic Hollywood movies, the 'superfemale', who is 'too ambitious and intelligent for the docile role society has decreed she play' but remains 'exceedingly "feminine" and flirtatious' and 'within traditional society', turning her energies on those around her, 'with demonic results' (1974: 214). Davis's character, Julie, is strong, defiant of convention (for example, striding into the bank, a place that women do not enter), refusing to behave in the genteel way her fiancé, Pres, requires of her. The trajectory of the narrative is her punishment and moral growth, in two stages. She learns to conceal her defiance and energy beneath an assumption of femininity, but this is still not enough, since it is still there in the malignant form indicated by Haskell; it is only by literally sacrificing herself (accompanying Pres, who has caught yellow jack fever, to Red Island, where fever victims are isolated) that the film is able to reach a satisfactory, transcendentally punishing climax. All of this is entirely understandable within a gender frame of reference; but the film also relates Julie's energies to blackness, suggesting that her trajectory is a specifically white, as well as female, one.

The most famous scene in the film is the Olympus Ball, at which all the unmarried women wear white. Julie, to embarrass Pres and to cock a snook at out-dated convention ('This is 1852, not the Dark Ages – girls don't have to simper about in white just 'cos they're not married'), decides to wear a red dress. The immediate scandal is not just the refusal to conform and uphold the celebration of virginity that the white dress code represents but the sexual connotations of the dress itself, satin and red, connotations made explicit in a scene at the dressmaker's ('Saucy, isn't it?', says Julie; 'And vulgar', says her aunt, with which Julie enthusiastically concurs). This is the dress of Julie's that her black maid Zette (Theresa Harris) most covets, and after the ball Julie gives it to her. It is precisely its *colourfulness* that, stereotyping informs us, draws Zette – the dress is 'marked' as coloured, a definite, bold colour heightened by a flashy fabric, just as black representation is. Thus what appears to be symbolism (white for virginity, colour for sex) within a universally applicable communication circuit becomes ethnically specific. The primary association of white with chastity is inextricably tied to not being dark and colourful, not being non-white, and the defiance and vitality narratively associated with Julie's wearing of the dress is associated with the qualities embodied by black women, qualities that Julie as a white woman must not display, or even have. Of course, the red dress looks merely dark in this black and white film.

Wearing the dress causes a rift between Julie and Pres; shortly after, he leaves for the North on business. By the time he returns, Julie has learned to behave as a white woman should. Once again, the specific whiteness of this is revealed through the figure of Zette. There is, for instance, a scene in which Julie is getting ready for the arrival of Pres at a house party at her aunt's plantation. In her room she moves restlessly about, with Zette hanging on to her as she tries to undo Julie's dress at the back; Zette's movements are entirely determined by Julie's but Zette is attending to the basic clothing while Julie is just fussing about. When Julie thinks she hears a carriage coming, she sends Zette to check; Zette runs from the room, and the film cuts to the huge hallway, showing us all of Zette's rapid descent of the stairs and run to the door, before cutting again to show her calling out to the man and boy in livery waiting for carriages at the gate. This apparently unnecessarily elongated sequence not only helps whip up excitement and anticipation at Pres's arrival, but also gives Julie time to take off one dress and put on another, a potentially titillating sight that would not be shown in this kind of film in this period. But using a sequence centred on a black woman is not only a device to heighten suspense and bypass a taboo image – it works as seamlessly well as it does because it is also appropriate to show a black woman here.

By this stage in the film, Julie has learned the behaviour appropriate to a white woman in her position. Earlier in the film she openly expressed her passion and defiance; now, awaiting Pres, she has learned to behave as she should. She no longer expresses feeling – she 'lives' through Zette. Zette has to express excited anticipation, not in speech but in physical action, running the length of a long stair and spacious hallway. It is Zette's excited body in action that we see, instead of Julie's body disrobed and enrobed. When Julie hears the servants at the gate call out, 'Carriage is coming!', she sends Zette to the window to see if it is Pres. The excitement mounts as the carriage draws near. There is a rapid montage of black people: Zette shot from below at a dynamic angle looking for the carriage, the servants at the gate no longer still but the man moving about, the boy leaping in anticipation, and crowds of hitherto unseen black children running to the gate, jumping and cavorting. Meanwhile Julie remains perfectly still, only her eyes, in characteristic Davis fashion, darting and dilating with suspense; perfectly, luminously lit, she says nothing, expresses nothing with her body – it is black people who bodily express her desire.

This use of black people to express, to 'live', the physical dimension of Julie's life is found throughout the film, most notably after her manipulations have gone awry to the point that one of her old flames, Buck (George Brent), is about to duel with Pres's brother. The black plantation workers have gathered at the house to entertain the white guests ('a quaint old custom down here', says Julie to Pres's new, and Northern, wife, Amy). As they arrive they sing a song about marrying, heard over shots of Julie, a bitterly ironic counterpoint. She shushes the chorus and tells them to start singing, 'Gonna Raise a Ruckus To-night', then goes to the edge of the verandah and sits down, beckoning the black children to gather close round her, before joining in with the singing. The song is a jolly one and the shots of the black singers show them in happy-go-lucky Sambo style, but the last shot of the sequence closes on Julie, near to tears against the sound of this cheerful singing. The power of the sequence does not come from this ironic counterpoint alone but also from the way that Julie, by merging as nearly as possible with the singers and joining in the song, is able to express her pent-up feelings of frustration, anger, jealousy and fear, feelings for which there is no white mode of expression, which can only be lived through blacks.

The point of *Jezebel* is not that whites are different from blacks but that whites live by different rules. Unlike the two women with whom she is compared, her aunt and Amy, Julie cannot be 'white'. It is her aunt and Amy who confirm that whites are calm, controlled, rational; Julie transgresses, but in the process reveals white calm as an imposition, a form of repression of life. The film's ambivalence lies in its being a vehicle for Davis. She/Julie is a 'Jezebel', a byword for female wickedness, but none the less a star with a huge female following and shot here with the kind of radiance and glow Hollywood reserved for its favoured women stars. There is no doubt that what Julie does is wicked and that her punishment is to be understood as richly deserved; but there is also no doubt that she is to be adored and precisely, as I've tried to argue, because she does not conform to notions of white womanhood.

Night of the Living Dead

If blacks have more 'life' than whites, then it must follow that whites have more 'death' than blacks. This thought has seldom been explored so devastatingly as in the living dead films directed by George Romero – *Night of the Living Dead* (1969), *Dawn of the Dead* (1978) and *Day of the Dead* (1985).

The *Dead* films are unusual among horror films for the explicitness of their political allegory and unique for having as their heroes 'positive' black men. In general, the latter have been applauded merely as an instance of affirmative action, casting colour blind a black man in a part which could equally well have gone to a white actor. As Robin Wood notes, however, 'it is not true that [their] colour is arbitrary and without meaning'; Ben's blackness in *Night* is used 'to signify his difference from the other characters, to set him apart from their norms' (1986a: 116), while Peter's in *Dawn* again indicates 'his separation from the norms of white-dominated society and his partial exemption from its constraints' (ibid.: 120). In all three films, it is significant that the hero is a black man, and not just because this makes him 'different' but because it makes it possible to see that whites are the living dead. I shall confine detailed discussion here to the first film of the trilogy.

All the dead in *Night* are whites. In a number of places, the film shows that living whites are like, or can be mistaken for, the dead. The radio states that the zombies are 'ordinary looking people', and the first one we see in the film does look in the distance like some ordinary old white guy wandering about the cemetery, somehow menacing, yet not obviously abnormal, John, the brother in the opening sequence, recalls pretending to be something scary to frighten Barb when they visited the graveyard as children; he imitates the famous zombie voice of Boris Karloff to scare her now. Halfway through the film, Barb becomes catatonic, like a dead person. The other developed white characters emerge from where they have been hiding, 'buried' in the cellar. Towards the end of the film, there is an aerial shot from the point of view of a helicopter involved in the destruction of the zombies; it looks down on a straggling line of people moving forward uncertainly but inexorably, in exactly the same formation as earlier shots of the zombies. It is only with a cut to a ground level shot that we realize this is a line of vigilantes, not zombies.

Living and dead whites are indistinguishable, and the zombies' sole raison d'être, to attack and eat the living, has resonances with the behaviour of the living whites. The vigilantes shoot and destroy the zombies with equanimity ('Beat 'em or burn 'em – they go up pretty good', says their leader, Chief McLelland), finally including the living – the hero, Ben (Duane Jones) – in their single-minded operations. Brother John torments Barb while living, and consumes her when he is dead. Helen and Harry Cooper bicker and snipe constantly, until their dead daughter Carrie first destroys, then eats them. The young couple, Tom and Judy, destined generically to settle down at the end of the film, instead go up in flames through Tom's stupidity and Judy's paralysed response to danger.

If whiteness and death are equated, both are further associated with the USA. That the film can be taken as a metaphor for the United States is established right at the start of the film. It opens on a car driving through apparently unpopulated back roads suggesting the road tradition of 1950s and 1960s US culture, the novel *On the Road* (1957) and the film *Easy Rider* (1969) with its idea of the 'search for America'. When the car reaches the graveyard (the USA?), a Stars and Stripes flag flutters in the foreground. The house in which the characters take shelter is archetypally middle, backwoods North American – a white wooden structure, with lace curtains, cut-glass ornaments, chintz arm-chairs. It, too, is immediately associated with death, in a series of shock cuts from Barb, exploring the house, to stuffed animal heads hung on the walls. Casting further heightens the all-Americanness of these zombie-like living whites. Barb is ultra-blonde and pale, and her name surely suggests the USA's best-selling doll; John is a preppy type, clean cut with straight fair hair, a white shirt with pens in the pocket, straight out of a Brooks Brothers advertisement. Judy too is dazzlingly blonde, though Tom and the Coopers are more nondescript whites.

What finally forces home the specifically white dimension of these zombic–US links are the ways in which the zombies can be destroyed. The first recalls the liberal critique of whites as ruled by their heads; as the radio announcer says, 'Kill the brain and you kill the ghoul' since, it seems, zombies/whites are nothing but their brains. The film diverges from earlier representations of the black/ white, life/death opposition by representing Ben's 'life' quality in terms of practical skill, rather than innate qualities of 'being'. Particularly striking is a scene in which Ben talks about what they need to do as he dismantles a table to make boards for the windows, while Barb takes the lace cloth from it, folds and cradles it, hanging on uselessly to this token of white gentility while Ben tries to ensure their survival.

The alternative way of destroying the zombies is burning. Some of the imagery, particularly the molotov cocktails going up around empty cars, seems to recall, in its grainy black-and-white texture, newspaper coverage of the ghetto uprisings of the late 1960s, and the 'fire', as an image of Black Power's threat to white people, had wide currency (most notably in the title of James Baldwin's 1963 novel *The Fire Next Time*). The zombies are scared of light as well as fire, and Ben is associated with both, not only because of his skill in warding off the zombies with torches, but in the way he is introduced into the film. Barb wanders out of the house into the glare of a car's headlights, out of which Ben seems to emerge; a shot of the lights glaring into the camera is followed by another with Ben moving into the frame, his white shirt first, then his black face filling the frame in front of the light, in a reversal of the good/bad, white/black, light/ darkness antinomies of Western culture.

The film ends with the white vigilantes (indistinguishable from the zombies, remember) killing Ben, the representative of life in the film. Much of the imagery of *Night* carries over into *Dawn*, despite their many differences (most notably the latter's strong vein of humour). The opening sequence has white militia gleefully destroying living blacks and Hispanics who refuse to leave their tenement homes during the zombie emergency; as in *Night*, the black hero, Peter (Ken Foree), emerges from the light (this time from behind a white sheet with strong, bright light flooded unnaturalistically behind it); it is his practical skills that enable him to survive, skills that only the white woman, Fran (Gaylen Ross), is ultimately able to emulate. Zombieness is still linked with whiteness, even though some of the dead are black or Hispanic – a black zombie who attacks a living black man in the tenement is whited up, the colour contrast between the two emphasized in a shot of the whitened black zombie biting the living black man's neck; in the shopping mall, an overt symbol of the US way of life, editing rhymes the zombies with the shop mannequins, all of whom are white.

Day extends the critique of US values to the military–industrial complex, with its underpinnings in masculine supremacy. As Robin Wood (1986b) argues, the white men and the zombies alike are characterized by 'the conditioned reflex', the application to human affairs of relentless rationality; the scientist, Logan, teaches one of the zombies to be human again, which in practice means killing the military leader, Rhodes, out of atavistic loyalty to Logan. When Logan earlier tells Rhodes that what he is teaching the zombies is 'civility', to make them like the living, there is a sudden cut to a sequence of the men gleefully, sadistically corraling the zombies to be specimens for Logan's crazed experiments. The whiteness of all this is pointed, as before, by the presence of a black character, John (Terry Alexander), who is even more dissociated from both zombies and white male values than were Ben and Peter in the earlier films. He is not only black but West Indian, and he offers the idea of finding an island as the only hope for the two white characters (a WASP woman, Sarah, and an Irish man, Billy) not irrevocably implicated in white male values. He and Billy are not only socially marginal but also live separately from the soldiers and scientists, having set up a mock home together in the outer reaches of the underground bunker they all share. All the other living characters are redneck males, and although there is a power struggle between them, they are both more like each other and like the zombies than they are like John, Sarah or Billy. At the end of one scene, where Rhodes has established his authority over Logan, there is a final shot of John, who has looked on saying nothing; he rubs the corner of his mouth with his finger ironically, then smiles sweetly at Rhodes, an expression of ineffably insolent refusal of the white boys' games.

The *Dead* films are of course horror movies and there is a danger, as Pete Boss has pointed out, that the kind of political readings that I and others have given them may not be easy 'to integrate . . . with the fantasies of physical degradation and vulnerability' characteristic of the contemporary horror film (1986: 18). However, the use of 'body horror' in the *Dead* films to represent whiteness is not simply symbolism, making use of what happens to the genre's current conventions. On the contrary, body horror is the horror of whiteness and the films' gory pleasures are like an inverted reprise of the images of whiteness that are touched on in *Simba* and *Jezebel*.

The point about Ben, Peter and John is that in their different ways they all have control over their bodies, are able to use them to survive, know how to do things with them. The white characters (with the exception of Fran, Sarah and Billy) lose that control while alive, and come back in the monstrously uncontrolled form of zombiness. The hysterical boundedness of the white body is grotesquely transgressed as whites/zombies gouge out living white arms, pull out organs, munch at orifices. The spectre of white loss of control is evoked by the way the zombies stumble and dribble in their inexorable quest for blood, often with intestines spilling out or severed limbs dangling. White over-investment in the brain is mercilessly undermined as brains spatter against the wall and zombies flop to the ground. 'The fear of one's own body, of how one controls it and relates to it' (Brophy 1986: 8) and the fear of not being able to control other bodies, those bodies whose exploitation is so fundamental to capitalist economy, are both at the heart of whiteness. Never has this horror been more deliriously evoked than in these films of the *Dead*.

Because my aim has been to open up an area of investigation, I shall not even attempt a rounded conclusion. Instead, let me start off again on another tack, suggested by the passing references to light and colour above. I suspect that there is some very interesting work to be done on the invention of photography and the development of lighting codes in relation to the white face, which results in the technicist ideology that one sometimes hears of it being 'more difficult' to photograph black people. Be that as it may, it is the case that the codes of glamour lighting in Hollywood were developed in relation to white women, to endow them with a glow and radiance that has correspondences with the transcendental rhetoric of popular Christianity.

Of no woman star was this more true than Marilyn Monroe, known by the press at the time as 'the Body'. I've argued elsewhere that her image is an inescapably and necessarily white one (Dyer, 1986: 42–5); in many of her films this combines with the conventions of glamour lighting to make her disappear as flesh and blood even more thoroughly than is the case with other women stars. Her first appearance in *The Seven Year Itch* (1955), for instance, is a classic instance of woman as spectacle caught in a shot from the male protagonist's point of view. It opens on Richard (Tom Ewell), on his hands and knees on the floor looking for something, bottom sticking up, a milk bottle between his legs – the male body shown, as is routine in sex comedies, as ludicrously grotesque; he hears the door-bell and opens the door to his flat; as the door opens light floods in on him; he looks and there is a cut to the hall doorway, where the curvy shape of a woman is visible through the frosted glass. The woman's shape is placed exactly within the frame of the door window, the doorway is at the end of the hall, exactly in the centre of the frame; a set of enclosing rectangles create a strong sense of perspective, and emphasize the direction of Richard's/our gaze. The colouring of the screen is pinky-white and light emanates from behind the doorway where the woman is. All we see of her is her silhouette, defining her proportions, but she also looks translucent. The film cuts back to Richard, his jaw open in awe, bathed in stellar light. Later in the film, when the Monroe character's tomato plant crashes on to Richard's patio, we have another shot of her from Richard's point of view. He looks up, and there is a cut to Monroe looking down from her balcony, apparently nude; the wall behind her is dark, as is the vegetation on the balcony, so her face and shoulders stand out as white. Such moments conflate unreal angel-glow with sexual aura.

The Seven Year Itch is a very smart film. Through innumerable gags and crossreferences, it lets on that it knows about male fantasy and its remote relation to reality. Yet it is also part of the Monroe industry, peddling an impossible dream, offering another specifically white ideal as if it embodies all heterosexual male yearning, offering another white image that dissolves in the light of its denial of its own specificity.

White women are constructed as the apotheosis of desirability, all that a man could want, yet nothing that can be had, nor anything that a woman can be. But, as I have argued, white representation *in general* has this everything-and-nothing quality.

Notes

1 Made by Tony Dowmunt, Maris Clark, Rooney Martin and Kobena Mercer for Albany Video, London.
2 See also the arguments about feminism and ethnicity in Carby (1982).
3 This restrictive definition of racism has been disputed by, among others, Hall (1980).

References

Banton, Michael (1977) *The Idea of Race*, London: Tavistock.

Bhabha, Homi K. (1983) 'The Other Question – the Stereotype and Colonial Discourse', *Screen* 24 (6): 18–36.

Boss, Pete (1986) 'Vile Bodies and Bad Medicine', *Screen* 27 (1): 14–25.

Brophy, Philip (1986) 'Horrality – the Textuality of Contemporary Horror Films', *Screen* 27 (1): 2–13.

Carby, Hazel (1982) 'White Woman Listen! Black Feminism and the Boundaries of Sisterhood', in Centre for Contemporary Cultural Studies (ed.) *The Empire Strikes Back*, London: Hutchinson, 212–23.

Chodorow, Nancy (1978) *The Reproduction of Mothering*, Berkeley: University of California Press.

Cripps, Thomas (1977) *Slow Fade to Black*, New York: Oxford University Press.

Dyer, Richard (1986) *Heavenly Bodies*, London: Macmillan.

Dyer, Richard (1992) 'The Role of Stereotypes', chapter 3 above.

Fanon, Frantz (1986) *Black Skin, White Mask*, London: Pluto.

Fisher, Lucy (ed.) (1992) *Imitation of Life*, New Brunswick: Rutgers University Press.

Fredrickson, George (1972) *The Black Image in the White Mind*, New York: Harper & Row.

Fryer, Peter (1984) *Staying Power*, London: Pluto.

Gilman, Sandor L. (1985) *Pathology and Difference*, Ithaca, NY: Cornell University Press.

Gilroy, Paul (1987) *There Ain't No Black in the Union Jack*, London: Hutchinson.

Hall, Stuart (1980) 'Race, Articulation and Societies Structured in Dominance', in UNESCO *Sociological Theories: Race and Colonialism*, Paris: UNESCO.

Hall, Stuart (1981) 'The Whites of their Eyes', in George Bridges and Rosalind Brunt (eds) *Silver Linings*, London: Lawrence & Wishart, 28–52.

Haskell, Molly (1974) *From Reverence to Rape*, New York: Holt, Rinehart & Winston.

Hill, John (1986) *Sex, Class and Realism in British Cinema*, London: British Film Institute.

Jordan, Winthrop (1969) *White over Black*, Harmondsworth: Penguin.

Lawrence, Errol (1982) 'In the Abundance of Water the Fool is Thirsty: Sociology and Black Pathology', in Centre for Contemporary Cultural Studies (ed.) *The Empire Strikes Back*, London: Hutchinson, 95–142.

Lewis, David Levering (1981) *When Harlem Was in Vogue*, New York: Knopf.

Mannin, Ethel (1930) *Confessions and Impressions*, New York: Doubleday Doran.

Marcuse, Herbert (1964) *One Dimensional Man*, Boston: Beacon Press.

Medhurst, Andy (1986) 'Dirk Bogarde', in Charles Barr (ed.) *All Our Yesterdays*, London: British Film Institute, 346–54.

Neale, Steve (1979/80) 'The Same Old Story', *Screen Education* 32/3: 33–8.

Parry, Benita (1987) 'Problems in Current Theories of Colonial Discourse', *Oxford Literary Review* 9 (1/2): 27–58.

Perkins, T. E. (1979) 'Rethinking Stereotypes', in Michèle Barrett, Philip Corrigan, Annette Kuhn and Janet Wolff (eds) *Representation and Cultural Practice*, London: Croom Helm, 135–59.

Pines, Jim (1975) *Blacks in Films*, London: Studio Vista.

Robinson, Cedric (1983) *Black Marxism*, London: Zed Books.

Said, Edward (1978) *Orientalism*, London: Routledge & Kegan Paul.

Thompson, John O. (1978) 'Screen Acting and the Commutation Test', *Screen* 19 (2): 55–70.

Wood, Robin (1986a) *Hollywood from Vietnam to Reagan*, New York: Columbia University Press.

Wood, Robin (1986b) 'The Woman's Nightmare: Masculinity in *The Day of the Dead*', *Cine Action!* 6: 45–9.

Further Reading

Blackburn, Julia (1979) *The White Men: The First Response of Aboriginal People to the White Man*, London: Orbis.

Bruckner, Pascal (1983) *Les Sanglots de l'homme blanc*, Paris: Editions du Seuil.

Frye, Marilyn (1983) 'On Being White', in *The Politics of Reality*, Trumansburg, NY: The Crossing Press.

hooks, bell (1991) 'Representing Whiteness: Seeing Wings of Desire', in *Yearning: Race, Gender and Cultural Politics*, London: Turnaround, 165–72.

hooks, bell (1992) 'Representations of Whiteness', in *Black Looks: Race and Representation*, Boston: South End Press, 165–78.

Malbert, Roger and Coates, Julia (1991) *Exotic Europeans*, London: South Bank Centre.

Malcolmson, Scott L. (1991) 'Heart of Whiteness', *Voice Literary Supplement*, March: 10–14.

Michaels, Walter Benn (1988) 'The Souls of White Folk', in Elaine Scarry (ed.) *Literature and the Body: Essays on Populations and Persons*, Baltimore: Johns Hopkins University Press, 185–209.

Roediger, David (1991) *The Wages of Whiteness*, London: Verso.

Saxton, Alexander (1990) *The Rise and Fall of the White Republic*, London: Verso.

Ware, Vron (1992) *Beyond the Pale: White Women, Racism and History*, London: Verso.

Part XIII

The Politics of Postmodernism

Introduction

Robert Stam

Contemporary film theory has of necessity to confront the phenomena summed up in the slippery and polysemic term "postmodernism," a term which implies the global ubiquity of market culture, a new stage of capitalism in which culture and information become key terrains for struggle. The term "postmodernism" itself has a long prehistory in studies of painting (John Watkins Chapman in 1870 spoke of "postmodern painting"); in literary study (Irving Howe in 1959 spoke of "postmodern fiction"); and in architecture (Charles Jencks). Postmodernism was anticipated (without the term) in Guy Debord's *Society of the Spectacle* (1967), where the French situationist argued that everything that had once been directly lived had in the contempory world transmuted into a representation. By shifting attention from political economy *per se* into the economy of the sign and the spectacularization of everyday life, Debord clearly anticipated similar later moves by Jean Baudrillard.

"Postmodernism" is on one level not an event but a discourse, a conceptual grid which has by now been "stretched" to the breaking point. As Dick Hebdige points out in *Hiding in the Light* (1988), postmodernism has shown a protean capacity to change meaning in different national and disciplinary contexts, coming to designate a host of heterogeneous phenomena, ranging from details of architectural decor to broad shifts in societal or historical sensibility. Hebdige discerns three "founding negations" within postmodernism: (1) the negation of totalization, i.e. an antagonism to discourses which address a transcendental subject, define an essential human nature, or proscribe collective human goals; (2) the negation of teleology (whether in the form of authorial purpose or historical destiny); and (3) the negation of utopia, i.e. a skepticism about what Lyotard calls the "grands recits" of the West, the faith in progress, science, or class struggle. (A *boutade* summed up this position as: "God is dead, so is Marx, and I'm not feeling too well myself.") The empty sequentiality of the "post" corresponds to a preference for prefixes such as *de* or *dis* – *de*centering, *dis*placement – which suggest the demystification of preexisting paradigms. Postmodernism is fond of terms which connote openness, multiplicity, plurality, heterodoxy, contingency, hybridity.

In Jameson's paradoxical formulation, postmodernism is "a unified theory of differentiation," torn between an impulse to unify its fields with totalizing assertions and a contrary impulse to proliferate differences (Jameson, 1998: 37). In general, postmodernism foregrounds the fragmented and heterogenous nature of socially constituted identity in the contemporary world, where subjectivity becomes "nomadic" (Deleuze) and "schizophrenic" (Jameson). Some other leitmotifs in postmodernist writing are (1) the dereferentialization of the real, whereby the linguistic referent is bracketed (Saussure), the psychoanalytic patient's actual history is substituted by an imaginary history (Lacan), where "there is no outside-the-text" (Derrida) and where no history exists without "prior textualization" (Jameson) or rhetorical "emplotment" (Hayden White); (2) the desubstantialization of the subject: the transmutation of the old, stable ego into a fractured, discursive construct fashioned by the media and by social discourses; (3) the dematerialization of the economy, the shift from the production of objects (metallurgy) to the production of signs and information (semiurgy); (4) the breakdown of the high/low art distinction (Huyssens) evidenced in the commercial cooptation of high modernism and "the surrealist takeover of the pop sensibility" (Sontag), for example Daliesque perfume commercials; (5) an atrophied historical sense (Jameson's "depthlessness" and the "waning of affect"); and (6) dissensus rather than consensus, as diverse communities endlessly negotiate their differences.

Postmodernism and its relation to film theory depends very much on whether we see it as (1) a *discursive/conceptual grid*; (2) a *corpus of texts* (both those which theorize postmodernism (e.g. Jameson, Lyotard, etc.) and those which are theorized by it (e.g. *Blade Runner*); (3) a *style or aesthetic* (characterized by self-conscious allusiveness, narrational instability and nostalgic recycling and pastiche); (4) an *epoch* (roughly the post-industrial, transnational information age); (5) a *prevailing sensibility* (nomadic subjectivity, historical amnesia); or (6) a *paradigm shift*: the end of Enlightenment meta-narratives of Progress and Revolution. Some theorists, such as Fredric Jameson, take a multidimensional approach which sees postmodernism as *simultaneously* a style, a discourse, and an epoch.

The term "postmodernism" has been mobilized almost in opposite political senses. One current retools "ideology critique" for a new era, thus enabling the critical demystification of media texts. Some see postmodernism as decreeing the death of utopian alternatives, while using a utopian language to describe "actually existing capitalism." For some, Postmodernism was seen as the aging of Aquarius, a symptom of the battle fatigue of tenured leftists, a signal of the obsolesence of left politics, now seen as uptight and puritanical. Since everyone now participates in the system, the system is no longer visible qua system. Hal Foster, in his preface to *The Anti-Aesthetic* (1983), discerns contradictory political tendencies within postmodern discourse, distinguishing between neo-conservative, anti-modernist, and critical postmodernisms, arguing, finally, for a postmodern "culture of resistance" as a "counter-practice not only to the official culture of modernism but also to the 'false narrativity' of a reactionary postmodernism" (Foster, 1983: xii).

A foundational, and in many ways quite problematic, text for the theory of the postmodern was Jean-François Lyotard's *The Postmodern Condition* (published in French in 1979 and in English in 1984). The point of departure for Lyotard's book was the epistemology of the natural sciences in the academy, a subject about which Lyotard confessed that he knew very little. The book became disproportionately influential because of its uncanny timing and title. For Lyotard, post-modernism represented a crisis of knowledge and legitimation, one which led to a historically conditioned skepticism toward the "grands recits," i.e. the meta-narratives of the Enlightenment concerning scientific progress and political liberation. Echoing many third worldist critiques of European "humanism" and "rationality," as well as Adorno's remarks on the impossibility of poetry after Auschwitz, Lyotard questioned whether any thought could "sublate Auschwitz in a general process toward universal emancipation" (Lyotard, 1984: 6).

While many of the postmodernists were lapsed radicals like Baudrillard and Lyotard, Fredric Jameson theorized postmodernism from within an unabashedly neo-Marxist framework. As the title of his essay "Postmodernism, or the Cultural Logic of Late Capitalism" implies, for Jameson "postmodernism" is a periodizing concept. Building on Ernest Mandel's account of the three phases of capitalism (market, monopoly, and transnational), and borrowing from the terminology of the Russian Formalists, Jameson posited postmodernism as the "cultural domin-ant" of late capitalism. Positions on postmodernism, for Jameson, carry with them a specific stance on transnational capitalism. While many postmodern critics stress the aesthetic, Jameson shows the inextricable connections between the economic and aesthetic in an era where specters of free-floating capital vie against each other "in a vast worldwide disembodied phantasmagoria" (Jameson, 1998: 142) and where electronic capital transfers abolish space and time and where capital achieves its ultimate dematerialization in a globalized cyberspace (ibid.: 154).

In the postmodern era the conflation of the economic with the cultural results in the "aestheticization of everyday life" (ibid.: 73). The most typical aesthetic expression of postmodernism is not parody but pastiche, a blank, neutral practice of mimicry, without any satiric agenda or sense of alternatives, nor for that matter any mystique of "originality" beyond the ironic orchestration of dead styles, whence the centrality of "intertextuality" and what Jameson calls the "random cannibalization of all the styles of the past" (Jameson, 1991: 65). TV programs like *The Daily Show*, where the news of the day – famine in Ethiopia, massacres in Rwanda, Bill Clinton and Monica Lewinsky – becomes the trampoline for smirky humor, offers evidence of Jameson's point. Here irony becomes not only "blank" but auto-telic, a self-satisfied "yeah, whatever" response to history.

The work of Jean Baudrillard, meanwhile, both extends and revises semiotic and Marxist theory, while incorporating the provocations of the situationists and the anthropological theories of Marcel Mauss and Georges Bataille. Baudrillard argues that the contemporary world of mass-mediated commodification entails a new economy of the sign, and a consequently altered attitude toward representation. (In *The Mirror of Production*, Baudrillard had already argued against the productivist logic of Marxism, with its tendency to valorize the economy *per se* while ignoring the more subtle economies of the sign). The new era, for Baudrillard, is characterized by semiurgy, i.e. the process by which the production of objects as the motor of social life has given way to the production and proliferation of mass-mediated signs. In "The Precession of Simulacra" (Baudrillard, 1983), Baudrillard posited four stages through which representation had passed on its way to unqualified simulation; a first stage where the sign "reflects" a basic reality; a second stage where the sign "masks" or "distorts" reality; a third stage where the sign masks the *absence* of reality; and a fourth stage where the sign becomes mere simulacrum, i.e. a pure simulation bearing no relation whatsoever to reality. With hyperreality, the sign becomes more real than reality itself. The disappearance of the referent and even of the signified leaves in its wake nothing but an endless pageant of empty signifiers. Los Angeles becomes a bad copy of Disneyworld, presented as imaginary in order to convince us that the rest is real. The photo is cuter than the baby. John Hinkley recapitulates Travis Bickle's rescue fantasy in *Taxi Driver*, while Reagan confounds his real life with his reel life. The masses, in an era of the death of the social, become an implosive force that can no longer be spoken for, articulated, or represented.

Baudrillard's critics, such as Douglas Kellner and Christopher Norris, accuse him of fake, risk-free radicalism, blasé nihilism, and "sign fetishism." For Kellner (1989) Baudrillard is a "semiological idealist" who abstracts signs from their material underpinnings, while Norris (1990) describes Baudrillard's project as resulting in an "inverted Platonism," a discourse that systematically promotes what for Plato were negative terms (rhetoric, appearance, ideology) over their positive counterparts. The descriptive fact that we currently inhabit an unreal world of mass-media manipulation and hypoerreal politics, as evidenced by the Persian Gulf War and as mocked in the film *Wag the Dog*, does not mean that no alternative is possible. One cannot so easily jump from a descriptive account of contemporary conditions to a blanket rejection of all truth claims and political agency. Baudrillard has only provided a meta-narrative in reverse, a negative teleology of the progressive emptying out of the social.

On another level, Baudrillard's work is a symptom of Parisian provincialism, the assumption that when Paris sneezes, the whole world catches a cold. Indeed, Third World critics have argued that "postmodernism" was merely another way of the West naming itself, passing off its provincial concerns as universal conditions. "For the African," writes Denis Epko, "the celebrated postmodern condition [is] nothing but the hypocritical self-flattering cry of overfed and spoiled children" (Epko, 1995: 122). Latin American intellectuals, meanwhile, pointed out that neologistic Latin American culture (for example, Brazilian modernism and Mexican *mesticaje* in the 1920s), in its precocious embrace of hybridity and syncretism, had been postmodern *avant la lettre*.

How we see Postmodernism aesthetically depends on how we see its relation to modernity (the move beyond feudal structures provoked by the interrelated operations of colonialism and capitalism in the fifteenth century and industrialism and imperialism later) and to modernism (the movement beyond conventional mimetic representation and plausible plots and characters in the arts), all of which varies depending on which art or medium is being discussed, in relation to which national context, and which discipline. Dominant cinema, for example, despite its technological razzle-dazzle, i.e. its modernity, largely adopted a premodernist aesthetic (see Stam, 1985; Friedberg, 1993). Television and video and computer technologies, in contrast, seem like postmodern media *par excellence*, and they are very avant-garde in aesthetic terms.

Postmodernism as a discursive/stylistic grid has enriched film theory and analysis by calling attention to a stylistic shift toward a media-conscious cinema of multiple styles and ironic recyclage – for example the relation between Madonna's "Material Girl" and *Gentlemen Prefer Blondes*. Much of the work on postmodernism in film has involved the positing of a postmodern aesthetic, exemplified in such influential films as *Blue Velvet* (1982), *Blade Runner* (1987) and *Pulp Fiction* (1994). Jameson discerns in such "Neo-noir" films as *Body Heat* a "nostalgia for the present." Films like *American Graffiti* for Americans, *Indochine* for the French, and the "raj nostalgia" films (*Heat and Dust*, *A Passage to India*) for the English, convey a wistful sense of loss for what is imagined as a simpler and grander time. For this stylistically hybrid postmodern cinema, both the modernist avant-garde modes of analysis – with the cinema as the instigator of epistemological breakthroughs – and the modes of analysis developed for "classical" cinema, no longer quite "work." Instead, libidinal intensities compensate for the weakening of narrative time, as the older plots are replaced by an "endless string of narrative pretexts in which only the experiences available in the sheer viewing present can be entertained" (Jameson, 1998: 129).

The important point that postmodernism makes is that virtually all political struggles take place nowadays on the symbolic battleground of the mass media. Instead of the 1960s slogan "the revolution will not be televised" it seems in the 1990s that the *only* revolution will be televisual. The struggle over representation in the realm of the simulacra homologizes that of the political sphere, where questions of representation slide into issues of delegation and voice. At its worst, postmodernism reduces politics to a passive spectator sport where the most we can do is react to pseudo-events (but with real-world effects) like the "Bill and Monica show" through polls or call-in tabloid news programs. At its best, postmodernism alerts us that new times demand new strategies.

42
Television and Postmodernism

Jim Collins

The development of some kind of working relationship between television and postmodernism within the realm of critical studies is inevitable, almost impossible, and absolutely necessary. Inevitable, because television is frequently referred to as the quintessence of postmodern culture, and postmodernism is just as frequently written off as mere 'television culture.' Close to impossible, because of the variability of both television and postmodernism as critical objects; both are currently undergoing widespread theorization in which there are few, if any, commonly agreed-upon first principles. Necessary, because that very lack, the absence of inherited critical baggage, places television studies in a unique position *vis-à-vis* postmodernism. Unlike the critical work devoted to other media, television studies does not have to 'retrofit' critical paradigms developed in modernist or premodernist periods and therefore should ideally be able to provide unprecedented insights into the complex interrelationships between textuality, subjectivity, and technology in contemporary cultures.

There is no short definition of *postmodernism* that can encompass the divergent, often contradictory ways the term has been employed. One reason for this divergence is that the term is used to describe: (1) a distinctive style; (2) a movement that emerged in the 1960s, 1970s, or 1980s, depending on the medium in question; (3) a condition or milieu that typifies an entire set of socioeconomic factors; (4) a specific mode of philosophical inquiry that throws into question the givens of philosophical discourse; (5) a very particular type of 'politics'; and (6) an emergent form of cultural analysis shaped by all of the above.

This terminological confusion is exacerbated by the contentiousness of the various definitions. As Jonathan Arac has written, 'It remains even now typically the case that to 'have a position' on postmodernism means not just to offer an analysis of its genesis and contours, but to let the world know whether you are for it or against it, and in fairly bold terms.'[1] One could argue that the chief drawback of most of this work is that the latter inevitably takes precedence over the former, producing little in the way of actual description but a great deal in the way of critical ax grinding. But although easy moralizing about postmodernism may often reveal little besides the presuppositions of the critical languages used to demonize or valorize it, the contested nature of the term – the fact that no definition of contours can ever be ideologically neutral, that description is inseparable from evaluation – reveals one of the most significant lessons of postmodern theory: all of our assumptions concerning what constitutes 'culture' and 'critical analysis' are now subject to intense debate.

If there is a common denominator in all of these contentious definitions of postmodernism, it is the determination to define it as something other than *modernism*, a term that is likewise given variable status. Modernism is generally characterized in one of two ways, depending on the individual critic's perspective on postmodernism: as a heroic period of revolutionary experimentation that sought to transform whole cultures, in which case postmodernism is seen as a neoconservative backlash; or as a period of profound elitism, in which case postmodernism signals a move away from the self-enclosed world of the avant-garde back into the realm of day-to-day life....

Although it is possible to list the tell-tale stylistic features of postmodern design – the move away from abstraction and geometrics to the overly familiar and mass-produced; the replacement of purity with eclecticism, internationalism with cultural specificity, and invention with rearticulation – the cultural significance of these changes and their ideological ramifications remains a matter of intense debate. It is also especially difficult to relate television to these debates in any kind of one-to-one correspondence. Television, unlike architecture, literature, or painting, never had a modernist phase that could serve as a point of departure for postmodern television. The emergence of postmodernism is decidedly an 'uneven' development; its appearance and eventual impact vary from one medium to another.

Because neither an etymology, nor an evolutionary schema, nor an all-encompassing theoretical paradigm can provide an adequate working definition of postmodernism that allows for diverse applications to television, I will set forth a series of recurring themes developed by theoreticians working in different media that, in aggregate, provide a sense of the conflictedness but also the potential cohesiveness of postmodern theory. These themes, considered together, allow for a reconsideration of the semiotic, technological, and ideological dimensions of television.

A Semiotics of Excess: 'The Bombardment of Signs'

One of the key preconditions of the postmodern condition is the proliferation of signs and their endless circulation, generated by the technological developments associated with the information explosion (cable television, VCRs, digital recording, computers, etc.). These technologies have produced an ever increasing surplus of texts, all of which demand our attention in varying levels of intensity. The resulting array of competing signs shapes the very process of signification, a context in which messages must constantly be defined over and against rival forms of expression as different types of texts frame our allegedly common reality according to significantly different ideological agendas.

Television is obviously a central factor in this information explosion. Many critics on both the left and the right insist that television is likewise instrumental in the devaluation of meaning – the reduction of all meaningful activity to mere 'non-sense', to a limitless televisual universe that has taken the place of the real. Such critics as Allan Bloom and Jean Baudrillard have made grandiose claims about the destructive power of mass culture (most especially television).[2] The former has claimed that television has brought about the ruination of true learning and morality. The latter has claimed that contemporary culture *is* television culture – endless simulations in which reality simply disappears. In Bloom's view, the culprit is not television alone, but the more general democratization of culture, which threatens the elite values that once formed the basis of real learning: the acquisition of Truth. But to Baudrillard (who is no more a postmodernist than Bloom), television is cause as well as symptom, allegedly constructing a seamless realm of simulations that hinder our acquisition of the *really real*.

The problem with these critiques is their contention that all signs are encoded and decoded according to exactly the same logic, or encoded so differently that, as a whole, they produce one and only one effect. They insist that the technological developments of the recent past have made 'meaning' an antiquated concept, because all signs are supposedly exhausted, mere electronic pulses disconnected from any referent. The chief limitation of these critics who are so anxious to demonize television is that they insist on making dire predictions about the devastating effects of this technological explosion (which alters everything, everywhere, in the same way), but they fail to recognize that the rate of absorption of those technological changes has increased commensurately. The medium may indeed be the message, but twenty minutes into the future the technological novelty is already in the process of being absorbed. In the same way that a figure of speech enjoys a certain novelty at its initial appearance but then begins to become absorbed into the category of the already familiar, the 'figures of technology' that produce an initial disorientation are quickly made manageable (*secondarized*) through different strategies of absorption as they are worked over by popular texts and popular audiences. This absorption/secondarization process involves the manipulation of the array by texts operating within it – television programs (as well as rock songs, films, bestsellers, and so forth) that demonstrate an increasingly sophisticated knowledge of the conditions of their production, circulation, and eventual reception.

A recent episode of *Northern Exposure* illustrates this absorption process quite clearly. When Holling, the local tavern owner, acquires a satellite dish that receives two hundred worldwide channels, his girlfriend Shelley quickly becomes a television addict, her entire life suddenly controlled by the new technology. She becomes maniacal in the process, and we see her calling the shopping channel to order thousands of dollars' worth of kitsch items. The determination of her character by television programs is stressed repeatedly, as she dances to music videos or dresses up as a Vanna White wannabe to watch *Wheel of Fortune*. But by the end of the program she has confessed her televisual sins, in a mock confessional to the local disk jockey-priest, and resolves to watch selectively. Meanwhile the central character, Dr. Joel Fleischmann, envisions his failed love affair in terms of old black-and-white Hollywood films, including a silent-movie version of the final scene from *The Graduate*, with himself as the star. Other characters recognize his need for what they call 'closure' in his relationship, and they decide to provide this by enacting a movie fantasy of how his relationship should have ended. The closure of both plot lines epitomizes the absorption of media culture, not just through parody but through its secondarization by texts and audiences that rearticulate it according to their own needs, a process thematized by the program itself.

Irony, Intertextuality, and Hyperconsciousness

The all-pervasiveness of different strategies of rearticulation and appropriation is one of the most widely discussed features of postmodern cultural production. Umberto Eco has argued that this ironic articulation of the 'already said' is the distinguishing feature of postmodern communication. In his often-quoted example, he insists that we can no longer make innocent statements. A lover cannot tell his beloved, 'I love you madly,' because it would very probably produce only a laugh. But if he wants to make such a declaration of love, he could say, 'As Barbara Cartland would put it, "I love you madly."' The latter indicates a mutual awareness of the 'already said,' a mutual delight in ironically manipulating it for one's own purposes.[3] This emphasis on irony is often written off as mere 'camp' recycling, but such a view fails to account for the diversity of possible strategies of rearticulation, which range from the simple revivalism found in the buildings of Robert Stern, the interior design collections of Ralph Lauren, or the clothing of Laura Ashley to the more explicitly critical reworking of the 'already said' in films like *Thelma and Louise*, the photographs of Barbara Kruger, or the radicalized cover versions of pop standards by the Sex Pistols or The Clash, in which the past is not just accessed but 'hijacked,' given an entirely different cultural significance than the antecedent text had when it first appeared. What is postmodern in all of this is the simultaneity of these competing forms of rearticulation – the 'already said' is being constantly recirculated, but from very different perspectives ranging from nostalgic reverence to vehement attack or a mixture of these strategies. Linda Hutcheon argues very convincingly that what distinguishes postmodern rearticulations of the past is their ambivalent relationship to the antecedent text, a recognition of the power of certain texts to capture the imagination, but at the same time a recognition of their ideological or stylistic limitations (this ambivalent parody will be discussed in more detail below).[4]

There is no other medium in which the force of the 'already said' is quite so visible as in television, primarily because the already said is the 'still being said.' Television programming since the 1950s has depended on the recycling of Hollywood films and the syndication of past prime-time programs. The proliferation of cable channels that re-present programs from the past four decades of television history marks the logical extension of this process, in which the various pasts and presents of television now air simultaneously. Television programming as accessing of the accumulated past of popular culture ranges from K-Tel offers for old *Honeymooners* and *I Love Lucy* episodes to the explicitly parodic demolitions of television programs to be found on *In Living Color, David Letterman*, and *Saturday Night Live*. This diversity in the forms and motivations of televisual rearticulation is even more apparent in the simultaneous but conflictive 're-presentations' of early sitcoms on rival cable networks. The Christian Broadcasting Network and Nickelodeon both broadcast series from the late 1950s and early 1960s, but whereas the former presents these series as a model for family entertainment the way it used to be, the latter offers them as fun for the contemporary family, 'camped up' with parodic voice-overs, super-graphics, and reediting designed to deride their quaint vision of American family life, which we all know never really existed even 'back then.'

The foregrounding of intertextual references has become a marker of 'quality television' (for example, prime-time network programs like *Hill Street Blues* and *St. Elsewhere*, which reflect a more sophisticated 'cinematic style,' feature ensemble casts, etc.) as well. Jane Feuer has traced this self-conscious intertextuality as it developed in the MTM style, but more recently, as 'quality television' has developed across production companies and networks, the explicit referencing has played a vital role in situating a given program in relation to other forms of quality and non-quality programs.[5] During the 1990 fall season, for example, Michael and Hope of ABC's *thirtysomething* referred to watching *L.A. Law*, while on NBC's *L.A. Law*, attorney Anne Kelsey spoke of wanting to get home and watch *thirtysomething* because it was 'responsible television.'

This sort of referencing-as-positioning is not restricted to quality TV. On a recent episode of *Knots Landing* (a nighttime soap that airs opposite *L.A. Law* and makes no claims whatsoever to be quality television), two minor characters argue about their favorite TV programs. One states that he has to turn down a dinner invitation because 'I forgot to set my VCR. I gotta see what Corbin Bernsen is wearing tonight.' When his friend states that he 'never watches that show' because he's a 'newshound,' the *L.A. Law* fan says derisively, 'News my foot. You're crazy about Diane Sawyer.' When his colleague protests that 'she's very intelligent,' his friend responds, 'Right, you're in love with her mind.' The referencing here, within the context of an evening soap, presupposes three important factors: (1) that viewers will possess a televisual literacy developed enough to recognize programs from the actors' names and that they will know the television schedule well enough to appreciate the reference to the programs that air opposite *Knots Landing* on the two other major networks (*L.A. Law* and *Prime Time Live*); (2) that

VCR time-shifting is now commonplace, especially for dedicated viewers of *L.A. Law* but also for those fans who exist within the fictional world of programs that air on competing channels; and (3) that the 'irresponsible,' non-quality program informs us why viewers *really* like quality television – for the wardrobes and the sexiness of the stars involved, which, as the characters of *Knots Landing* know, constitute the *real* pleasure of the televisual text.

These intertextual references are emblematic of the *hyperconsciousness* of postmodern popular culture: a hyperawareness on the part of the text itself of its cultural status, function, and history, as well as of the conditions of its circulation and reception. Hyperconsciousness involves a different sort of self-reflexivity than that commonly associated with modernist texts. Highly self-conscious forms of appropriation and rearticulation have been used by postmodern painters, photographers, and performance artists (David Salle, Cindy Sherman, Laurie Anderson, and others), and their work has enjoyed a great deal of critical attention. In the 'meta-pop' texts that we now find on television, on newsstands, on the radio, or on grocery store book racks, we encounter, not avant-gardists who give 'genuine' significance to the merely mass cultural, but a hyperconscious rearticulation of media culture by media culture.[6]

The self-reflexivity of these popular texts of the later 1980s and early 1990s does not revolve around the problems of self-expression experienced by the anguished creative artist so ubiquitous in modernism but instead focuses on antecedent and competing programs, on the ways television programs circulate and are given meaning by viewers, and on the nature of televisual popularity. A paradigmatic example of this is the opening scene of *The Simpsons' Thanksgiving Special* (1990), in which Bart and his father, Homer, are watching television in their living room on Thanksgiving morning. *The Simpsons*, as a concept, is already a mean-spirited parody of the traditional family sitcom, and this particular scene adds an attack on the imbecilic chatter of 'color commentators.' But the scene goes beyond simple parody. As they watch the Thanksgiving Day parade, Bart keeps asking Homer to identify the balloon float characters, complaining that they could use some characters that 'were made in the last fifty years.' His father tells him that the parade is a tradition, that if 'you start building a balloon for every flash-in-the-pan cartoon character, you'll turn the parade into a farce.' At this point the television-within-the-television depicts a Bart Simpson balloon floating by while the 'real' Bart Simpson looks on. Thus Bart watches himself as a popular phenomenon on television. *The Simpsons* television program thereby acknowledges its own characters' status as popular icons whose circulation and reception are worked back into the 'text' itself.

Subjectivity, *Bricolage*, and Eclecticism

The 'Bart watches Bart' example may be emblematic of a postmodern textuality, but what are the effects of this hyperconscious irony on television viewers? Is its ultimate effect emancipatory, leading to a recognition that television's representations are social constructions rather than value-neutral reflections of the 'real' world? Or does this irony produce a disempowering apathy, in which no image is taken at all seriously? John Caughie has described this problem very effectively:

> The argument, then, is that television produces the conditions of an ironic knowingness, at least as a possibility...[which] may offer a way of thinking subjectivity free of subjection....Most of all, it opens identity to diversity, and escapes the notion of cultural identity as a fixed volume....But if it does all this, it does not do it in that utopia of guaranteed resistance which assumes the progressiveness of naturally oppositional readers who will get it right in the end. It does it, rather, with terms hung in suspension...tactics of empowerment, games of subordination with neither term fixed in advance.[7]

The crux of the matter here is the notion of the subject that is presupposed. Caughie's insightful point about irony *vis-à-vis* subjectivity suggests that television viewers are individual subjects neither completely programmed by what they are watching nor completely free to choose as self-determining individuals, captains of their fates, masters of their souls.[8] One of the significant developments in postmodern theory (put forward in an increasing number of disciplines) is the recognition that a new theory of the subject must be developed, one that can avoid the deterministic conception of the individual as programmable android without resurrecting a romantic 'Self' that operates as a free agent, unfettered and uninfluenced by ideology....

The concept of the postmodern subject as multiple and contradictory, acted upon but also acting upon, has also led to reconsideration of the 'effects' that popular culture, most especially television, has on its viewers. The *hypodermic* model of media effects (in which mass media allegedly 'injects' values directly into passive viewers) has been challenged by John Fiske, Ien Ang, and others who share a cultural studies perspective.[9] Many of them use de Certeau's concept of 'poaching' to characterize audiences' skillful abduction of televisual texts, focusing on the ways in which audiences make the meanings they want or need out of television programs.[10] It is at this point that British cultural studies begins to share a number of concerns with postmodern theory *per se*, positing a subject who operates as a technologically sophisticated *bricoleur*, appropriating and recombining according to personal need. The term *bricolage*, developed by anthropologists to describe the ways primitive tribespeople piece together a meaningful cosmogony (or simply a way of operating) out of random elements they encounter in their day-to-day lives, has recently been applied to the behavior of individuals in contemporary media cultures. The culturalist and postmodernist positions differ, however, in regard to 'mass culture.' The former presupposes that mass culture may still be pernicious and homogeneous, but that it may be transformed into something resembling a genuine folk culture at the moment of reception because viewers tend to disregard the intended effects of television and take from it what best fits into their lives. This is a very attractive political position in that it allows for the continued demonization of capitalism and mass culture while it celebrates the resourcefulness of ordinary people. However, it fails to recognize the eclecticism of postmodern cultural *production*.

Many television programs, films, popular songs, and other manifestations of popular culture are already the result of sophisticated forms of *bricolage*, already conscious of the multiple ways they might be understood. As I have mentioned above, Charles Jencks insists that one of the distinguishing features of postmodern architecture is 'radical eclecticism.'[11] The work of Charles Moore, James Stirling, and Hans Hollein juxtaposes styles, materials, and conventions hitherto thought to be thoroughly incompatible. Michael M. J. Fisher and George Lipsitz contend very convincingly that this eclecticism, this creation as *bricolage*, is also a feature of the ethnic and racial subcultures that are so prominent in American popular culture. 'It is on the level of commodified mass culture that the most popular, and often the most profound, acts of cultural *bricolage* take place. The destruction of established canons and the juxtaposition of seemingly inappropriate forms that characterize the self-conscious postmodernism of "high culture" have long been staples of commodified popular culture.'[12]

The eclecticism associated with postmodernism takes on a more complicated dimension in regard to television. Individual programs like *Pee-Wee's Play House*, *Max Headroom*, and *Twin Peaks* are as radically eclectic in their use of diverse stylistic conventions as any postmodern building. Furthermore, the eclecticism of television textuality operates on a technological/institutional level as well because it has been institutionalized by cable television and the VCR, which together produce infinite programming variations. Postmodernist eclecticism might only occasionally be a preconceived design choice in individual programs, but it is built into the technologies of media-sophisticated societies. Thus television, like the postmodern subject, must be conceived as a *site* – an intersection of multiple, conflicting cultural messages. Only by recognizing this interdependency of *bricolage* and eclecticism can we come to appreciate the profound changes in the relationship of reception and production in postmodern cultures. Not only has reception become another form of meaning production, but production has increasingly become a form of reception as it rearticulates antecedent and competing forms of representation.

Commodification, Politics, Value

Another major concern of postmodern cultural analysis has been the impact of consumerism on social life. Fredric Jameson argues that postmodernism is best understood as the end result of capitalism's relentless commodification of all phases of everyday existence. He sees pop culture's radical eclecticism as mere 'cannibalization' of the past and as 'sheer heterogeneity' without 'decidable' effects.[13] For Jameson, all such cultural activity is driven by the logic of 'late' capitalism, which endlessly develops new markets that it must neutralize politically by constructing a vision of success and personal happiness, expressible solely through the acquisition of commodities.

The relevance of Jameson's work for television studies has already been explored by a number of critics, not surprising given the advertiser-driven nature of the medium in the United States, where commercials not only interrupt programs but have actually emerged as a form of programming. The blurring of the distinction between programs and commercials has become even greater with the development of 'infomercials,' shopping channels, product lines generated by Saturday morning cartoons (as well as by evening soaps like *Dynasty*), and so on. If television is defined by its semiotic complexity, its intertextuality, and its eclecticism, it is also just as surely defined by its all-pervasive appeals to consumerism.

The problem for television studies, as it tries to come to terms with postmodernism, is how to reconcile the semiotic and economic dimensions of television. Stressing the semiotic to the exclusion of the economic produces only a formalist game of 'let's count the intertexts,' but privileging the economic to the point that semiotic complexity is reduced to a limited set of moves allowed by a master system is just as simplistic. The attempt to turn television into a master system operating according to a single logic is a fundamentally nostalgic perspective; the culture of the 1990s, though judged to be the sheer noise of late capitalism, is nevertheless expected to operate according to nineteenth-century models of culture as homogeneous totality.

Making postmodernism coterminous with late capitalism offers a theoretical neatness by providing an all-purpose, master explanation: postmodern culture is a symptom of more fundamental economic and political trends. But this position is fraught with a number of problems. The limitations of this view of postmodernism become especially apparent in Jameson's notion of 'cognitive mapping'.[14] He argues that a new aesthetics that will make sense of multinational capitalism has yet to emerge and that there exists as yet no way of mapping the chaotic spaces of postmodern cultures. But the 'map' he hopes will be drawn will not be acceptable to him unless it envisions this space according to the contours of traditional Marxist theory. Jameson doesn't entertain the notion that mere mass culture may itself provide a mapping function or that television is not just a chaotic terrain in need of mapping but is itself a proliferation of maps. Lifetime, MTV, Black Entertainment Television, and the Family Channel all envision contemporary cultural life from specific generational, racial, and gendered perspectives. Taken together, they don't coalesce into one big picture but rather a composite of overlapping views that visualize the terrain of contemporary life in reference to its specific uses. The desire to formulate one master map, despite the multiple ways that the terrain can be envisioned and put to use by individual subjects as *bricoleurs*, exposes not just the limitations of traditional Marxist paradigms, but also the need to develop far more sophisticated forms of materialist analysis that recognize the multiple uses and effects of consumerism.[15]

... Within this politics of diversity and difference, 'value' is not abandoned – only absolute 'truth values,' or what Herrnstein Smith has called the automatic 'axiomatics' of traditional critical theory that relied on transcendent, universal qualities as proof or verification for all evaluation. She insists that both value and evaluation are radically contingent. 'That which we call "value" may be seen neither as an inherent property of objects, nor an arbitrary projection of subjects but, rather, as the product of the dynamics of some economy or, indeed, of any number of economies (that is, systems of apportionment and circulation of "goods") in relation to a shifting state, of which an object or entity will have a different (shifting) value.'[16]

The ramifications of this point for television study – specifically for developing a theory of postmodern television – are far reaching, because Smith argues that we need to continue to debate the value of any given text but also insists on the contingent nature of those judgments. Evaluation always depends on criteria that are culturally determined and therefore culturally specific rather than transcendent. This is a vitally important point, because it allows for an analysis of television that recognizes the variable nature of televisual signs. Their value cannot be explained in reference to one logic but will be channel-, program-, and audience-sensitive. Even more important, by focusing on the dynamics of the economies that determine these shifting values, we can begin to understand the interconnectedness of the semiotic and the economic dimensions of postmodern television.

Twin Peaks

In order to demonstrate how the various themes of postmodern theory might be considered together in reference to a single television series, I will focus on *Twin Peaks*, because it became a cultural phenomenon that epitomizes the multiple dimensions of televisual postmodernism. *Twin Peaks* was not 'postmodernist' just because it involved David Lynch, a bona fide postmodernist filmmaker, or because it depended on a number of postmodern stylistic conventions, or because it generated so many commodity intertexts (*The Secret Diary of Laura Palmer*, *Dale Cooper: My Life, My Tapes*, and a soundtrack album, among other things). Rather, the circumstances that allowed for its development and the ways in which it circulated are emblematic of postmodern culture and represent the confluence of a number of factors that give postmodern television its historical specificity.

The appearance of *Twin Peaks* on prime-time network television was due in large part to the impact of cable and VCR technology. The advent of cable systems that offer dozens of alternatives to the 'big three' networks and the ubiquity of the VCR, which offers an even broader range of entertainment, led to a significant decline in the networks' share of the total viewing audience. In 1979, 91 percent of viewers were watching network programs during prime time, but by 1989 the number had dropped to 67 percent.[17] This viewer migration to cable and videocassettes has been portrayed in near-catastrophic terms by the networks, because those households that are able to afford cable and VCRs are precisely the households network advertisers most want to reach. Particularly prized within this audience segment are 'yuppie' viewers, who not only purchase expensive consumer goods but also tend to consume other forms of entertainment – on broadcast television, videotape, cable, and pay-per-view and at movie theaters.

The development of *Twin Peaks* reflects a fundamental change in the way the entertainment industries now envision their publics. The audience is no longer regarded as a homogeneous mass but rather as an amalgamation of microcultural groups stratified by age, gender, race, and geographic location. Therefore, appealing to a 'mass' audience now involves putting together a series of interlocking appeals to a number of discrete but potentially interconnected audiences. The promotion of *Batman: The Movie* by the various components of Warner Communications serves as the paradigmatic example here. D.C. Comics were used to secure the preteen and early teen audience, while MTV and Prince helped to lure the female teen audience. The original development of *Twin Peaks* involved exactly this sort of appeal to a number of distinct audiences. As producer Mark Frost himself acknowledged, he hoped the series would appeal to 'a coalition of people who may have been fans of *Hill Street*, *St. Elsewhere*, and *Moonlighting*, along with people who enjoyed the nighttime soaps' – along with, of course, the people who watch neither anymore, now that cable and VCR have become household fixtures.[18] The emergence of 'coalition audiences' as a marketing strategy parallels the development of 'coalition politics' in contemporary political theory. Culture industries and political activists both recognize the fragmentary nature of 'the public' and realize that effective mobilization of 'public opinion' is possible only through strategies of amalgamation.

The media blitz that surrounded the premiere of *Twin Peaks* is quite literally a textbook example of the skillful manipulation of the discourses of cultural legitimation that have hitherto been used to attribute value to media other than television. The full-page ad that appeared in the *New York Times* the day the pilot premiered (April 6, 1990) is a case in point. In bold, oversized letters we are told: 'Twin Peaks – the series that will change TV,' according to *Connoisseur* magazine. Two evaluative criteria are reiterated throughout the glowing reviews quoted in the ad – a romantic–modernist glorification of originality and the shock of the new it produces, and an all-purpose notion of connoisseurship. Throughout this initial wave of reviews in the popular press, *Twin Peaks* is valorized in cinematic terms, a medium that, judging by these reviews, enjoys a far higher degree of cultural status than television, especially when it involves David Lynch, already promoted as a genius director.

Many reviews bestowed automatic status on the program because it was the product of an *auteur* – a filmmaker with a recognizable signature. Richard Zoglin's review in *Time* (April 9, 1990), entitled 'Like Nothing Else on Earth:

David Lynch's *Twin Peaks* may be the most original show on TV,' describes the 'Lynchian touches' and the director's art school training. The notion that great television might be made only by a great filmmaker also pervades Terence Rafferty's review in *The New Yorker* (April 9, 1990). After referring to Lynch as an 'all-American surrealist,' Rafferty states that 'within five minutes of the opening of *Twin Peaks* we know we're in David Lynch's world – unmistakable even on a small screen.' The reliance on this evaluative criteria appears in its most bald-faced form in *Newsweek*'s cover story (October 1, 1990) on Lynch, in which an 'avant-garde' portrait of the director is accompanied by the graphic, 'David Lynch – The Wild at Art Genius Behind *Twin Peaks*'.

The discrete filmlike nature of the pilot was emphasized explicitly in an ad quoted in the television spot that ran during the week of the premiere: 'It's must-see, must-tape television,' a statement that stresses the singularity of the program. After the first few episodes had appeared, however, the avant-garde *auteur* mode of evaluation began to dissipate as *Twin Peaks* came to be conceived no longer as a discrete cinematic pilot, but rather as a television serial. The next major article in *Time* (7 May 1990) concerns the *Twin Peaks* 'mania,' how it has become a topic of 'coffee wagon' conversation around offices. The article refers to the show's 'trendiness' and includes a chart detailing the character configuration, complete with cutesy hearts and coffee cups, all of which emphasize its soap opera dimensions. The article features, interestingly, this quote from a regular viewer: 'It's only a TV show, but you feel like a cultural idiot if you can't quote it on Fridays.' At this point, when *Twin Peaks* is no longer being described as 'hauntingly original' it returns to being just TV.

The issue of 'cultural literacy,' raised indirectly by the viewer's statement, involves this very shift in evaluative criteria. What does it mean to be 'culturally literate' about *Twin Peaks*? Should one regard it as an unprecedented *auteurist/avant-gardist* incursion into the vast wasteland of mere TV? Or should one adopt a sense of knowing detachment that asserts, 'I know it's just all TV trash, but I enjoy it ironically'?[19] The answer is not a matter of either/or but *both*, because a postmodern cultural literacy recognizes exactly this kind of variability. *Twin Peaks* is a polysemic phenomenon alternately valorized as would-be cinema and would-be soap opera. The cover stories on *Twin Peaks* that appeared in *Newsweek*, *Rolling Stone*, and *Soap Opera Weekly* (October 16, 1990) reflect the polysemic nature of signs that constitute this program. The *Newsweek* 'Wild at Art' cover features only Lynch as mad genius, whereas the *Rolling Stone* cover shows three of the program's stars vamping it up. *Soap Opera Weekly* features a large photo of Lynch with smaller inset photos of the stars, but surrounds both with other soap stories and photos – 'Behind the scenes at *The Bold and the Beautiful*,' 'It's not all Romance at *Lovings* Dual Wedding' – in addition to the 'curious Revelations' from *Peaks* cast members. In each case, the significance or cultural resonance of the series changes fundamentally in accordance with the evaluative criteria employed by each magazine as it frames the phenomenon according to its own discursive agenda.

Although the press coverage of the *Twin Peaks* phenomenon accentuates its polysemic, multi-accentual nature, the semiotic variability of the program is not restricted to the diverse ways it is given significance at the point of reception. The style of *Twin Peaks* is aggressively eclectic, utilizing a number of visual, narrative, and thematic conventions from Gothic horror, science fiction, and the police procedural as well as the soap opera. This eclecticism is further intensified by the variable treatment each genre receives in particular scenes. At one moment, the conventions of a genre are taken 'seriously'; in another scene, they might be subjected to the sort of ambivalent parody that Linda Hutcheon associates with postmodern textuality. These generic and tonal variations occur within scenes as well as across scenes, sometimes oscillating on a line-by-line basis, or across episodes when scenes set in paradigmatic relationship to one another (through the use of the same character, setting, or soundtrack music) are given virtually antithetical treatments. The movement in and out of parodic discourse is common in all of the episodes. For example, in the pilot, when Dale Cooper and Harry Truman are going through Laura Palmer's diary and personal effects, the dialogue, delivery, and soundtrack music all operate according to the conventions of the Jack Webb police procedural. But the 'just the facts, ma'am' tone of Cooper's discourse about cocaine, safety deposit boxes, and court orders is shattered by the concluding line of the scene, which is delivered in exactly the same manner: 'Diane, I'm holding in my hand a box of chocolate bunnies.'

This sort of tonal variation has led a number of critics to conclude that *Twin Peaks* is mere camp, an ironic frolic among the rustic bumpkins and the TV trash they devour along with their doughnuts. But the series is never just camp; the parodic perspective alternates with more straightforward presentation, encouraging an empathetic response rather than the ironic distance of the explicitly parodic. In the third episode, for example, when Dale Cooper explains his 'deductive technique involving mind–body coordination' – complete with a blackboard, a map of Tibet, and rock throwing the scene becomes a thorough-going burlesque of the traditional final scene of detective novels, films, or television programs when the detective explain how he/she solved the crime, usually through a hyperrational deduction process. The introduction of the Dalai Lama, dream states, and rocks transports ratiocination (crime solving by rational deduction) into the realm of irrational spirituality, thereby parodying one of the fundamental 'givens' of detective fiction. The absurd misuse of conventions defies the viewer to take the scene seriously. However, the scene at the end of episode fifteen in which Leland, possessed by Bob, brutally murders Maddie is one of the most horrifying murder scenes ever to appear on prime-time television; it defies the viewer *not* to empathize with the innocent victim, not to be deeply disturbed by the insanity and violence, which are intensified by the editing and sound distortions.

The death of Leland at the end of episode seventeen exemplifies not just this scene-to-scene variation but also the paradigmatic variation mentioned above, in which the same textual elements from earlier episodes are repeated but given completely different inflections. As Leland dies in Cooper's arms, he realizes that he has killed three young women, including his daughter Laura, and in the moments when he is dying, the framing, dialogue, acting style, reaction shots, and non-diegetic music all contribute to the pathetic nature of the scene, encouraging the viewer to empathize wholeheartedly with the horrified father. Particularly interesting here is that two key elements contributing to this pathos were used parodically in earlier episodes: Cooper's Tibetan spiritualism, previously used as a signifier of his goofiness, is here given integrity as something that comforts the dying man, describing what he apparently sees at the point of death; and 'Laura Palmer's Theme,' previously used parodically to accompany any number of 'soap opera' love scenes, here accompanies a scene of tragic paternal love.

It could be argued that this tonal oscillation and generic amalgamation, in which viewers are encouraged to activate ever-shifting sets of expectations and decoding strategies, is simply one of those 'Lynchian tricks' – that in *Twin Peaks*, as in *Blue Velvet*, Lynch labors to catch his viewers *between* sets of expectations, producing the shock of the newly juxtaposed. Although this oscillation in tonality is undeniably a characteristic of Lynch's more recent projects, it is also reflective of changes in television entertainment and of viewer involvement in that entertainment. That viewers would take a great deal of pleasure in this oscillation and juxtaposition is symptomatic of the 'suspended' nature of viewer involvement in television that developed well before the arrival of *Twin Peaks*. The ongoing oscillation in discursive register and generic conventions describes not just *Twin Peaks* but the very act of moving up and down the televisual scale of the cable box. While watching *Twin Peaks*, viewers may be overtly encouraged to move in and out of an ironic position, but watching other television soap operas (nighttime or daytime) involves for many viewers a similar process of oscillation in which emotional involvement alternates with ironic detachment. Viewing perspectives are no longer mutually exclusive, but set in perpetual alternation.[20]

What distinguishes *Twin Peaks* from, say, *Dallas* or *Knots Landing* is not that it encourages this alternation in viewing positions but that it explicitly acknowledges this oscillation and the suspended nature of television viewing. In other words, *Twin Peaks* doesn't just acknowledge the multiple subject positions that television generates; it recognizes that one of the great pleasures of the televisual text is that very suspension and exploits it for its own ends.

If the postmodern condition is one in which we as individual subjects are constantly engaged in the process of negotiating the array of signs and subject positions that surround us, *Twin Peaks* and other forms of hyperconscious popular culture address themselves directly to this condition, situating themselves exactly in the arcs and gaps that result when these positions don't coalesce. By taking the array as their 'setting' and redefining 'narrative action' in terms of the exploitation of the array, these texts redefine the nature of entertainment in contemporary cultures. The concerns of postmodern television and postmodern theory, then, are thoroughly intertwined, because both are responses to the contingent, conflicted set of circumstances that constitute cultural life at the end of the twentieth century.

Notes

1 Jonathan Arac, *Critical Genealogies* (New York, Columbia University Press, 1987), p. 284.

2 Allan Bloom, *The Closing of the American Mind* (New York, Simon & Schuster, 1987); Jean-Louis Baudrillard, 'The Implosion of Meaning in the Media and the Information of the Social in the Masses', in Kathleen Woodward, ed., *Myths of Information: Technology and Post-Industrial Culture* (Madison, WI, Coda Press, 1980), pp. 137–48.

3 Umberto Eco, postscript to *The Name of the Rose* (New York, Harcourt Brace Jovanovich, 1984).

4 Linda Hutcheon, 'The Politics of Postmodernism, Parody, and History'. *Cultural Critique*, 5 (Winter 1986–7), pp. 179–207.

5 Jane Feuer, 'The MTM Style', in Jane Feuer, Paul Kerr, and Tise Vahimagi, eds, *MTM: 'Quality Television'* (London, British Film Institute, 1984), pp. 32–60.

6 Jim Collins, 'Appropriating Like *Krazy*. From Pop Art to Meta-Pop', in James Naremore and Patrick Brantlinger, eds, *Modernity and Mass Culture* (Bloomington, IN, Indiana University Press, 1991), pp. 203–23.

7 John Caughie, 'Playing at Being American. Game and Tactics', in Patricia Mellencamp, ed., *Logics of Television: Essays in Cultural Criticism* (Bloomington, IN, Indiana University Press, 1990), pp. 54–5.

8 For a detailed analysis of the changes in theories of the subject, see Paul Smith, *Discerning the Subject* (Minneapolis, MN, University of Minnesota Press, 1988).

9 John Fiske, 'Popular Discrimination', in James Naremore and Patrick Brantlinger, eds, *Modernity and Mass Culture* (Bloomington, IN, Indiana University Press, 1991), pp. 103–16; Ien Ang, *Watching 'Dallas': Soap Opera and the Melodramatic Imagination*, trans. Della Couling (London, Methuen, 1985).

10 Michel de Certeau, *The Practice of Everyday Life* (Berkeley, CA, University of California Press, 1984).

11 Charles Jencks, *The Language of Post-Modern Architecture*, 5th edn (New York, Rizzoli, 1987).

12 George Lipsitz, 'Cruising around the Historical Bloc: Postmodernism and Popular Music in East Los Angeles', *Cultural Critique*, 5 (Winter 1986–7), p. 161.

13 See Fredric Jameson, 'Postmodernism, or, the Cultural Logic of Late Capitalism', *New Left Review*, 146 (July/August 1984), and 'Postmodernism and Consumer Society', in Hal Foster, ed., *The Anti-Aesthetic: Essays on Postmodern Culture* (Port Townsend, WA, Bay Press, 1983), pp. 111–25.

14 Fredric Jameson, 'Cognitive Mapping', in Cary Nelson and Lawrence Grossberg, eds, *Marxism and the Interpretation of Culture* (Urbana, IL, University of Illinois Press, 1988), pp. 347–57.

15 See especially Hilary Radner, *Shopping Around: Feminine Culture and the Will to Pleasure* (New York, Routledge, 1992).

16 Barbara Herrnstein Smith, 'Value without Truth Value', in John Fekete, ed., *Life after Postmodernism* (New York, St. Martin's Press, 1987), p. 1.

17 *Entertainment Weekly*, March 4, 1990.

18 *Time*, April 9, 1990, p. 97.

19 Ang, *Watching 'Dallas'*.

20 Jane Feuer, 'Reading *Dynasty*: Television and Reception Theory', *South Atlantic Quarterly*, 88: 2 (Spring 1989), pp. 443–60.

I would like to thank Ava Preacher Collins and Hilary Radner for their contributions to the completion of this manuscript.

43
Critical and Textual
Hypermasculinity

Lynne Joyrich

I'd like to begin my discussion of TV, postmodernism, and the cultural connotations of femininity by referring to an image from David Cronenberg's film *Videodrome*. In this film, video signals are used to literally open their viewers to total control: exposure to these signals transforms the human body into a living VCR which can then be penetrated by videotapes, preventing the subject from differentiating reality from video simulation. Not only does this illustrate the worst fears of mass culture critics (fears concerning the power of the media to seduce and rape the viewer), but it clearly and violently marks the receptive TV body as feminine – the tapes are thrust into a gaping wound that pierces the hero's stomach. *Videodrome* thus brings together the image of the cyborg body – a postmodern hybrid of human, animal, and machine – and the image of the 'feminine body' – a body yielding to manipulation, too close to the image to properly evaluate it.[1]

Such conceptual ties between TV, postmodernism, and femininity (or, more accurately, the meanings our culture assigns to 'femininity') are symptomatic of shifting gender relations in our technologically mediated culture. Television, today's cyborgian 'machine-subject,'[2] can be seen as playing out these relations in all their contradictions, revealing a terrain in which gender figures prominently in a network of differences we have only begun to explore. By 'reading' several television texts against texts marking TV's critical reception, I will attempt to map out the connections forged between TV and postmodern culture, focusing on the veiled references to sexual difference and the figuration of gender constituted within this field.

Noting the ways in which TV has been portrayed as feminine in both film and mass culture criticism – a situation exacerbated by the fluctuating ground of postmodernism – I argue that while such tropes of analysis are seductive, they are also potentially dangerous, encouraging critics to ignore the complexities and contradictions of gender inscription as well as the other fields of difference (race, class, age, and so on) which traverse the TV text and audience alike.[3] In fact, attending to the complex dynamics of gender within both television and TV criticism might lead us to a very different conclusion from that implied by *Videodrome*'s sexual imagery. Despite the prevalence of such figures and images in accounts of TV, we cannot simply claim that television is itself either feminine or feminizing. Rather, this ontological premise recuperates the feminine and the critical insights of feminism within a new version of masculinity which inhabits television studies as well as television texts. In other words, the focus on TV as 'feminine' masks a deeper cultural concern with masculinity – a concern which may express itself through the construction of a 'hypermasculinity' that renders the presence of women within TV representation and TV criticism unnecessary.

Several theorists have noted that consumer culture and the culpable masses blamed for its existence have often been figured as feminine. Tania Modleski examines this aspect of historical accounts and emphasizes the problems involved in either simply condemning or celebrating these feminine inscriptions.[4] Andreas Huyssen has also explored attacks on sentimental culture – slurs based on fears of the engulfing ooze of the masses which provoked the 'reaction formation' of a virile and authorial modernism. Yet he concludes his analysis by claiming that such gendered rhetoric has diminished with the decline of modernism: 'mass culture and the masses as feminine threat – such notions belong to another age, Jean Baudrillard's recent ascription of femininity to the masses notwithstanding.'[5] Nonetheless, despite Huyssen's optimistic conclusion, such gendered imagery can still be seen in many analyses of television. While, as Huyssen argues, the 'great divide' between art and mass culture may have narrowed (or even imploded) in the postmodern age, this rupture does not necessarily extend to a generalized dissolution of binary categories of analysis. Rather than an age in which bipolar thinking is no longer operative, we exist in a transitional space in which new dichotomies are erected as fast as the old ones break down. In fact, the very rupture of traditional modes of thought provokes a panicked attempt to create new divisions rather than working to dispel our society's felt need for oppositions. Thus, the kind of binary divisions used to discount mass art by the modernist critics Huyssen discusses continue to exert an influence over critics associated with the rise of postmodern theory in spite of their apparent reluctance to condemn all forms of mass and subcultural production. In other words, distinctions of value seem to hold sway within the realm of mass texts themselves even if the grand opposition between high and low art can no longer describe today's aesthetic theory or practice. Television theorists regularly define their object through such polarities; by constructing a duality in which television is placed in opposition to some other, more 'respected' medium, these theorists articulate cultural and textual difference in terms that are reminiscent of what is still posed as the dominant binarism of our culture – sexual difference.

In *Understanding Media*, for example, Marshall McLuhan compares today's media to the previously dominant print, arguing that the new holistic and participatory modes promote a 'global embrace' and the implosion of margin to center. Associating these media with the non-conformity of criminals, children, blacks, cripples, and women, McLuhan distinguishes the heterogeneity of television from the regularity of book culture.[6] The 'rational' form of print, allied with 'literate man,' is uniform, linear, and isolated – it is, like film, a 'hot' medium based on exclusion. It thus creates the centralized, autonomous subject motivated toward impersonal domination, expansionism, and departmental organization. On the other hand, the 'irrational' media of the electric age, particularly television, return us to the distance between subjects as well as the distance between sign and referent – is abolished. The mosaic of TV requires the involvement of all senses in a tactile, primitive intimacy that produces, according to McLuhan, retribalization, organic interlacing, proximity, and empathy.

These qualities are clearly drawn from sterotypes of femininity, and while McLuhan values them, he nonetheless believes that what he terms the 'threat from within the gates' (the new media) must be kept under control by the masculine logic of print.[7] This phrase comes from Hegel who, in theorizing the disruption provoked by Woman, writes that the community 'creates its enemy for itself within its own gates, creates it in what it suppresses, and what is at the same time essential to it – womankind in general. Womankind – the everlasting irony in the life of the community – changes by intrigue the universal purpose of government into a private end.'[8] McLuhan's metaphor for the disruptive media then clearly genders television as feminine – intrinsically feminine if 'the medium is the message.' Any enthusiasm he expresses for the organic qualities of television thus evades important historical questions. For example, McLuhan's claim that TV is inherently decentralized allows him to ignore the fact that it is very much economically centralized and that its femininity consists more in the gender of its primary consumers than in its moral or aesthetic nature. Ignoring the particular social construction of both TV and femininity, McLuhan produces a celebratory reading of television in which sexual difference, once again polarized and essentialized, is made to uphold a historically specific mode of consumption.

Several other critics comparing television to earlier media similarly figure opposition in gendered terms. John Fiske and John Hartley, for example, use McLuhan to support their theory of television as our culture's bard, also describing it as immediate and illogical, failing to support the individualism upheld by linear, abstract print. Arguing that TV is criticized merely because it fails to conform to the standards of 'Rational Man,' they too employ unacknowledged gender codes in their evaluation of television as a 'separate but equal' medium. While Fiske and Hartley do not recognize their oppositions as gendered ones, their description of television as an intimate, personal, familiar medium, working to bond all viewers in an inclusive world, repeats common sexual stereotypes.[9] The cultural denigration of television is thus related to the marginality of an unnamed femininity – as Fiske and Hartley claim, TV is scorned merely for being TV: non-linear, illogical, and unmasculine.[10]

Similarly, John Ellis compares television to the cinema, arguing that today, the culturally respectable is equated with the cinematic. According to Ellis, cinema's mode of narration constructs a scenario of voyeurism, granting the spectator power over the image and centering the look on the female body. TV, on the other hand, has little narration in the cinematic sense: it offers itself as an immediate presence, failing to produce a sufficiently voyeuristic position for its viewers. TV involves what Ellis calls 'the glance' – a look without power – rather than cinema's gaze. The viewer then delegates his/her look to television itself, forging a sense of intimacy as events are shared rather than witnessed.[11] In other words, the glance of the TV viewer is a domestic, distracted, and powerless look that implies continuous copresence – a 'feminine' look that is too close to the object to maintain the gap essential to desire and full subjectivity.

As this brief survey shows, the use of feminine imagery to describe our 'lowest' cultural form (in opposition to whatever is held up as more respectable and 'masculine' – print or film) has not faded away with the passing of modernism.[12] In fact, such gender implications take on new meaning in the postmodern age as the threat of fluctuating signs, unstable distinctions, and fractured identities provokes a retreat toward nostalgia for firm stakes of meaning.[13] As the ' "natural" grounding principle' once seemingly offered by sexual difference erodes, new anxieties are created which are often projected onto television (a medium which stands as the ultimate in fluctuating signs even as it tries to remain a bastion of family values). Describing television in a world in which distance and contemplation are impossible, for example, Baudrillard writes, 'the opposing poles of determination vanish according to a nuclear contraction... of the old polar schema which has always maintained a minimal distance between a cause and an effect, between the subject and an object.'[14] In the circular logic of simulation, classical reason threatens to vanish, and separate positions merge. In Baudrillard's words, 'positivity and negativity engender and overlap... there is no longer any active or passive... linear continuity and dialectical polarity no longer exist.'[15] As dialectics collapse, the oppositions which maintain sexual difference and the stability of the sexed gaze seem to shift, if not fully disappear.

This collapse of the oppositions which have always upheld the primacy of the masculine subject is further suggested in Baudrillard's description of television as he discards what film theory has taken to be the terms of sexual difference: 'TV is no longer the source of an absolute gaze... no longer... a system of scrutiny ... playing on the opposition between seeing and being seen.'[16] In rejecting the applicability of the categories subject/object, active/passive, and seeing/being seen, Baudrillard rejects the divisions that have been seen by many feminist film critics as constitutive of the male spectator.[17] In other words, for Baudrillard, postmodernism – and television in particular – seems to disallow the security and mastery of the masculine position, and as this stable site disappears, we are all left floating in a diffuse, irrational space – a space traditionally coded as feminine.

In the essay 'In the Shadow of the Silent Majorities,' Baudrillard describes the masses as soft and sticky, lacking attribute and reference. They are like a black hole that engulfs all meaning in an implosion of the social, an overpresence that collapses inward, producing a lack of distance or defining feature, and through this account, the masses are figured in clichés of femininity. But like women, the masses have access to a certain excess – they over-conform and over-consume, reduplicating the logic of the media. Referring, like McLuhan, to Hegel's analysis of 'womankind,' Baudrillard writes that this 'destructive hyper-simulation' is 'akin to the eternal irony of femininity of which Hegel speaks – the irony of false fidelity, of an excessive fidelity to the law, an ultimately impenetrable simulation of passivity and obedience...which annuls...the law governing them.'[18] This theorization of subversive hyperconformity is very familiar. It mimics both Luce Irigaray's analysis of feminine mimicry – a playful repetition in which women resubmit themselves to a masculine discourse so as to show they remain 'elsewhere' – and the notion of feminine masquerade elaborated, for example, by Mary Ann Doane in which women flaunt their femininity in order to hold it at a distance.[19]

Yet as many critics have noted, Baudrillard (unlike Irigaray and Doane) is not advocating acts of political resistance – he assumes the position of the feminine in order to stress the vacuum of the enveloping mass rather than the possible differences that may be constituted within it. He thus argues against those theorists who 'would like to make a new source of revolutionary energy (in particular in its sexual and desire version). They would like to...reinstate it in its very banality, as historical negativity. Exaltations of micro-desires, small differences, unconscious practices, anonymous marginalities...and to transfer it back to political reason.'[20] For Baudrillard, the goal of politicizing such fields is an impossible one. Substituting the fear of an all-consuming mass for the older notion of an all-controlling industry, he insists upon the anonymity of the feminized masses who are neither subject nor object.[21] In rejecting any theory of subjectivity which might valorize the deconstruction of identity (in a play of differences) as politically progressive, Baudrillard sentences the political (and political resistance) to annihilation. Nonetheless, as 'a direct defiance of the political,' the masses' feminine hyperconformity, their ironic excess, is still a show of strength, a mode of resistance escaping control.[22] In this way, Baudrillard employs the concept of the feminine, but deprives it of the progressive force suggested by some feminist critics – he simply recasts the division between mass culture and high culture in terms of a routine gender dichotomy.

Baudrillard is not the first male theorist to claim the position of the feminine as a way to signify ironic strength (whether deemed political or not). His analysis of hyperaffirmation recalls Jacques Derrida's discussion of the feminine in *Spurs* (part of which occurs, interestingly, in a section entitled 'Simulations'). Considering Nietzsche's 'affirmative woman,' Derrida writes, 'she plays at dissimulation, at ornamentation, deceit, artifice, at an artist's philosophy. Here is an affirmative power.' Woman is thus an indeterminable identity, 'a non-figure, a simulacrum.'[23] It is the very breakdown in logic that dismays readers of Baudrillard's *Simulations* that delights Derrida here, and the creation of a space between the self and the image through an exaggeration of this breakdown, the hypersimulation associated with feminine irony, is the only 'hopeful' possibility that even Baudrillard seems to offer.

Yet feminists must approach a hope figured as feminine salvation with suspicion. As Modleski points out, figuring both the masses and their subversive mode as feminine does not necessarily give feminists concerned with the historical and cultural position of women any cause for celebration. Noting the (masculine) sexual indifference that arises when the position of feminine difference is claimed by everyone, Modleski insists that the ascription of femininity to the anonymous mass glosses over crucial distinctions.[24] Attending similarly to Nancy Miller's warning, we must not lose sight of the ways in which a theoretical position that deems the question 'who speaks?' irrelevant can also maintain the institutional silencing of women. As Miller states, 'Only those who have it can play with not having it.'[25]

Not only must we be leery of male theorists playing with the demise of a social and political representation that we have never had, but we must not obscure the differences that do exist for men and women within the realm of mass culture. Returning to Huyssen's claim that images of a feminized mass culture no longer apply to the postmodern world, let me continue his point: 'If anything, a kind of reverse statement would make more sense: certain forms of mass culture, with their obsession with gendered violence, are more of a threat to women than to men. After all, it has always been men rather than women who have had real control over the productions of mass culture.'[26] In other words, while television spectatorship may be figured as generically feminine, two crucial differences are overlooked: the historical split between consumption and production (in which women are the primary consumers while men largely control television production) and TV's reaction against the feminine through the construction of a violent hypermasculinity.

Turning first to the issue of a gendered consumption, many television critics and historians have explored the material conditions of female consumption, women's viewing patterns, and advertisers' address to this audience.[27] Furthermore, several theorists suggest a relationship between constructions of femininity and the consumer subject. Elsewhere, I have argued that such theoretical accounts of femininity accord in many ways with popular images of women in relation to looking and buying.[28] In the popular imagination, the woman is too close to what she sees – she is so attached that she is driven to possess whatever meets her eye (or, as the pun suggests, her 'I'). The labels commonly applied to film and television genres addressing a female audience – 'weepies' and 'tearjerkers' – convey the same assessment: there is an almost physical closeness assumed to exist between the overinvolved female spectator and the image which forces her tearful response. Such everyday appraisals of women as subjects who lack the distance required for 'proper' reasoning and viewing are mirrored by theoretical and psychoanalytic accounts of femininity which similarly stress women's lack of subject/object separation.[29]

While feminist theorists may offer these tropes of female proximity, fluidity, and 'nearness' as a subversive or hopeful alternative to the masculine model of identity, such overpresence cannot be divorced from consumer desires. As several critics have remarked, it is the emphasis on self-image that invites the consumer to attend to the images of advertised products, and the woman who must purchase in order to enhance her own status as valued commodity becomes the prototypical consumer – the same overpresence that ties her to the image allows her to be situated as both the subject and the object of consumerism at once.[30] It is thus no coincidence that (what has been seen as) the particular 'feminine' textuality of television supports the psychology of the perfect consumer. One of TV's most devalued genres, the soap opera, clearly exposes this intersection of cultural notions of femininity and consumerism: within the form seen by many critics as emblematic of female subjectivity, there are almost twice as many commercials as occur on prime-time TV. Furthermore, television theorists have suggested a relationship between soap opera form – a continuously interrupted present which refuses closure – and the effectivity of its commercials which, rather than truly interrupting the soap opera, continue its narrative patterns while offering 'oases of narrative closure.'[31]

Yet the conditions that link consumerism and femininity (both related to an overidentification with the image and commodity object) affect all of postmodern culture – today men also attend to self-image and their value of exchange, similarly losing the distinction between subject and object that has characterized the female consumer. Not only, then, are women presumed to be the best of consumers, but all consumers are figured as feminized – a situation yielding tension in a culture desperately trying to shore up traditional distinctions even as its simulations destabilize such attempts. As the distance between subject and object diminishes in the weightless space of postmodern culture, the threat of feminization as well as an all-encompassing consumerism hangs over all subjects, and television (discussed, like femininity, through tropes of proximity, overpresence, and immediacy) is central to this process.

While TV's appeal then does not stop with women, its consumers have been belittled in such terms in the critical and popular imagination alike, provoking contemptuous assessments of genres in addition to those traditionally associated with female audiences. Music Television, for example – a form which also addresses a culturally devalued (but economically desirable) audience, youths in this case – further reveals the relations between a fractured Oedipal logic, postmodern form, and consumerism: these videos completely dissolve the distinction between program, product, and ad in texts which can only be described as commercials for themselves.[32] TV soap operas and music videos, the programs most disparaged, are thus in many ways the most telling, displaying the conventions of continuity and difference, presence and interruption, viewing and consuming invoked by the television apparatus. In other words, the forms that seem to best illustrate TV's specificity also reveal a consumerism associated with the address to an audience deemed infantile or feminine, a spectator 'not fully a man.'

Yet as the 'feminine' connotations attached to television and consumer closeness are diffused onto a general audience, contradictions of gender and spectatorship emerge, and television is placed in a precarious position as it attempts to induce consumer overpresence even as it tries to achieve cultural status by mimicking the more respectable cinema. It is interesting in this context to look at texts which exaggerate or foreground the specific representational strategies and discursive configurations of contemporary television. For example, a program such as ABC's on-again, off-again series *Max Headroom* rejects the cinematic model as it self-consciously announces television's difference, and as it calls attention to the characteristics of television (which are, as we have seen, shot through with connotations of gender), it would also seem to be among the shows most vulnerable to charges of feminization.

Max Headroom does, in many ways, raise this fear as it both extends and defends itself against the vacuum of simulation and the threat of a feminized world. In the premiere episode, for example, we are introduced to Max, a computer-generated 'video subject' who is born in an attempt to answer an enigma. The enigma at the root of this 'birth' centers on a mysterious death and cover-up – an event investigated by ace news reporter Edison Carter, the man who furnished the mind given to Max. In the scene in which this enigma is made visible, we see a large and lazy man at home in his armchair, watching television as an ad comes on the air. The ad he sees makes use of a diegetically new representational form – instead of presenting a logical and linear argument, a miniature narrative, or a coherent series of associational images, it involves a rapid flow of sound and images, chaotically thrown together so that nothing can be clearly identified or isolated. In other words, this ad is simply an intensified microcosm of TV as we, the home viewers, know it. The effect of this commercial on the diegetic viewer, however, is that of a literal inflation – the man swells up as consumer s(t)imulation builds inside of him until he actually explodes (or, for Baudrillard, implodes). What we witness, then, can almost be described as a form of hysterical pregnancy – TV provokes a generation of sensations, meaning, and animated force until this energy short-circuits and bursts to the surface, destroying the human body but providing the narrative origin of the cyborg, Max. Because Edison Carter has seen this event (although on videotape), he is captured, and his brain is scanned by a computer in order to disclose the full extent of his knowledge. In the process, Max Headroom is created. Eventually, of course, Edison recovers, solves the case, and reports the crime through another simulation – he broadcasts the contents of Max's memory which contains the videotape of the viewer explosion.

Exploring the sexual and textual issues raised in this episode, it is first of all apparent that TV is caught up in a web of simulations – any access to 'the real' is mediated through a series of video images (the original video ad, the videotape of the ad and explosion, the computer scan of Edison's memory of the tape, and finally, Edison's retaping of Max's computerized memory of the tape – a broadcast which is at that point at least four times removed). In the show's brief second run, such simulations are even further exaggerated. While Max gained Edison's mind in the opening season, in the 'second premiere' Max returns the favor, allowing Edison to be programmed with the contents of his computerized memory in order to save Edison from 'going out of his head' after being brainwashed by some junk food and its accompanying prize.[33] The question, then, of whose mind either Edison or Max can go out of (or into) raises the ultimate problem of simulation and its twisted yet seemingly all-encompassing order. *Max Headroom*, in other words, presents a completely technologically mediated world, the ultimate in postmodern hyperreality that, as the program's logo tells us, is only twenty minutes into our own future. Furthermore, in its form as well as content, this show draws on postmodern textual devices – the program is known for the ways in which it refuses to subordinate its visual effects to a clear narrative progression and multiplies the look through a dense layering of simulated images and a fractured diegesis. As this program plays with TV's multiplicity of signs, time flow and shifting space, editing techniques derived from advertising, and fluctuating levels of reality/reproduction/fabrication, it carries TV form to its limits, shifting the critique of television into a celebration of its specificity.

But like critical accounts of television, *Max Headroom*'s depiction of TV simulation is not divorced from questions of gender: this scene figures both the receptive TV body and the threat of a simulated world in terms of denigrating images of femininity. The viewer-victim, while a man, is an emasculated one – pregnancy that ultimately results in Max. As (literally) a 'talking head,' Max himself is likewise feminized – he lacks the body of a man and constantly tries to sort out a man's sexual memories that he can't really understand. While Max masquerades as male, his constantly shifting contours provide him with a fluctuation of being that refuses even the illusion of unity and stability. Unable to differentiate himself from the matrices that bear him, he does not master the order of hyperreality but can only flow within it, losing the distinction between self and other that is (however fictionally) required to attain the status of a man. This condition, however, is not confined to Max – even the experts of this simulation, the computer operators who help Edison solve his cases, lack powerful masculinity: Max is created by a pre-adolescent (and pre-sexual) whiz kid, while Edison's computer guide is female. Here, as in Baudrillard's vision, the dangers of hyperreality, as well as its perpetrators, are feminized.

Yet while it plays with textual figures and devices that have been theoretically linked not only to postmodernism but also to feminine subjectivity, various strategies with which to contain TV's 'feminine' connotations are also employed. *Max Headroom* literally splits its hero in two, displacing postmodern consumer consciousness onto Max and leaving Edison Carter free to play the role of traditional hero. While Max is there for comic effect (much of the show's humor is based on his lack of a stable identity and his literal existence in the perpetual present of the TV mosaic – in the show's jargon, Max is 'in the system,' essentially bound to the flow of TV), it does, nonetheless, take a 'real man' to free us from the adverse effects of this simulated world. Edison Carter, a typical melodramatic hero, battles crime and exposes wrongdoing in order to keep his world in line. This program thus exists in the tension between modern and postmodern forms, projecting the 'feminine' cyborgian elements onto a dominated other (Max) while still allowing its male protagonist to control the diegetic space and the flow of the narrative.

In a similar way, television as a whole exists in an odd tension, balanced between the modern and the postmodern (its reliance on melodrama, for example, in the midst of its own self-referential texts) and between culturally constituted notions of the feminine and the masculine (both sustaining and rejecting the positions offered by critical, as well as commercial, discourses). This places television in a curious bind – a situation perhaps most evident in many prime-time programs which, in order to be 'culturally respectable' and appeal to male viewers, attempt to elevate the infantile and deny the feminine conventionally associated with television (particularly with the texts I have noted). A common strategy of television is thus to construct a violent hypermasculinity – an excess of 'maleness' that acts as a shield. In this way, TV's defense against the feminine may be seen to correspond with television theory's attempts to dispense with the same – by their either resisting the feminine position (as many television texts do) or else incorporating and so speaking for it (as occurs in many recuperative critical texts, as discussed above), the real presence of women within these particular TV representations and critical texts is deemed unnecessary.

Within the realm of TV itself, there are a number of possible methods of defense. By aiming for the status of 'quality' television (producing texts that can function under the name of an author), creating 'proper' spectator distance by mimicking cinematic conventions, or obsessively remarking the masculinity of their thematics, some programs attempt to evade TV's feminization. Yet attempts at denial and male masquerade can produce problems which emerge on the surface of 'masculine' texts.[34] Faced with the contradictions created by the imperative to inscribe order in a medium that disallows resolution and the demand to be 'manly' in the 'feminized' world of TV, these texts yield a realm of masculine excess that demonstrates their fragile position within both TV's hyperreality and a 'hypermasculinity' that is its defense.

In her article on televised sports, Margaret Morse notes that despite cultural inhibition, 'the gaze at "maleness" would seem necessary to the construction and . . . replenishment of a shared . . . ideal of masculinity'[35] – an ideal that, in the light of my earlier remarks on consumer culture, particularly needs replenishing. Morse examines the discourse on sport as 'a place of "autonomous masculinity," freed even from dependence on woman-as-other to anchor identity.'[36] Sport, however, is not the only area in which the male body is displayed. In her analysis of *Magnum, p.i.*, for example, Sandy Flitterman traces the mobilization of the male spectacle, revealing the ways in which an eroticized masculinity is foregrounded.[37] Furthermore, such displays do not necessarily establish a masculinity free from relation to the feminine, despite their location within the (generally) all-male preserves of sports and the cop/detective show. They can instead be seen as an attempt to save masculinity even in the 'feminized' world of TV, even in the vacuum of a crisis-ridden postmodernism (which, not incidentally, also includes the crisis of Vietnam – a crisis in masculinity which has been dealt with explicitly in several cop/detective shows, including *Magnum, p.i.*, and which may also be partially responsible for the popularity of the genre in general).[38]

Even more than *Magnum, p.i.*, *Miami Vice* is a show of male excess and display which can be analyzed as a response to a feminine 'contagion.' In his insightful analysis, Jeremy Butler reveals the ways in which *Miami Vice* aspires to the cultural position of the cinema through its use of *film noir* conventions.[39] Yet *Vice* differs from *film noir* in some important ways. In place of the duplicitous woman – the trouble that sets the cinematic plot in motion – the motivating forces in *Miami Vice* are all men. Women may be visible as background detail or decor, but in a world in which male criminals are the primary enigmas and objects of voyeurism, the woman is divested of all potency, including, and most importantly, her power of masquerade, her ability to manipulate her femininity. Here, the power of masquerade belongs to men, most frequently Crockett and Tubbs who display themselves as criminals in order to lure their prey into captivity. (This display can also be seen in the ways in which the images of Crockett and Tubbs have been taken up by advertising and fashion – again, it is the male image which is now the focus, the men who masquerade.) While film noir investigates female identity and masquerade, *Miami Vice*'s central dilemma revolves around the identity of 'V/vice' and the possibility of differentiating between the cops and the crooks, the men and their roles.[40] Clearly at stake here is a question of masculinity in a world in which all stable distinctions have dissolved, in which shared by everyone. This is a crucial question for postmodern, post-Vietnam America as well as an issue for television – the 'feminine' cultural form of our time.

An episode entitled 'Duty and Honor' (one of the episodes confronting Vietnam) exemplifies the textual disturbances provoked by such displays of manliness. The narrative traces the paths of both an assassin – a black Vietnam veteran, called only 'the Savage,' who is responsible for a series of prostitute murders (all of the victims are marked by the words 'VC Whore' despite the fact that most of them are not Vietnamese) – and a Vietnamese police officer, a former friend of Lieutenant Castillo who comes to Miami to solve the murders that have haunted the two since their meeting in Vietnam. From our first sight of the Savage, he is marked as an object of the gaze as he appears before a mirror, eyeing himself and rehearsing a pose. He is thus constituted as spectacle – the spectacle of a perfect machine, a cyborg weapon of war, and a feminized icon demanding to be looked at.

Discussing the spectacle of the cyborg body as well as the aesthetic of slow motion, Morse analyzes the athlete in terms of the cultural fantasy of the perfect machine body, a body moved by an 'inner logic' beyond space and time, at one with nature and 'unimpeded by acts of the ego.' In the ritualized experience of this unified 'flow,' she writes, 'man can overcome his separateness from nature, God, other men and his own body, and achieve grace, signified by slow motion.'[41] In other words, as a cyborg body, an object displayed for the fascinated gaze, the male athlete can ritually experience a subjectivity usually coded as feminine. This analysis of slow motion applies to the visual style of *Miami Vice*, and specifically here to the cyborg, the Savage, who is positioned as both a (feminized) visual object and a perfect machine of death. His status as image is constantly emphasized as we see him primp in a black leather coat, repeating a gesture of smoothing his hair. In one scene, he even competes with a televised display of male body-building as he yells at his landlady for watching too much TV and failing to look at him when she speaks.

As both spectacle and object of the investigatory gaze, the Savage is assigned the role traditionally aligned with femininity. In fact, as the narrative progresses, we learn that he is literally feminized; he has been castrated in Vietnam, the reason for his hatred of Vietnamese women and their simulated stand-ins. Hypermasculinity as a response to such feminization, the underlying structure of texts of male spectacle, is then made manifest in the episode's central murder scene.[42] The scene is marked by a flattened pictorial space fully dominated by the Savage. Staring into the camera, he is posed against a stark wall, apparently naked, with an enormous knife emerging from the bottom of the frame. Sharing the prostitute's point of view, we see the Savage approach and almost leap into the camera, returning the look of the spectator with a violent retribution that obscures our vision and concretizes the excess of his status as spectacle as well as the discord of such hypermasculinity, a reaction to castration.

In the logic of the episode, this castration is infectious – after the introductory flashback to the initial crime in Vietnam, the episode begins as Sonny Crockett is interrupted at the height of a sexual encounter by the news of the latest homicide. Sonny is also a Vietnam vet, and there is an odd mirroring thus established between two 'couples': Sonny and the Savage, and Castillo and Nguyen Van-Trang, Castillo's former partner. In both couples, each 'partner' has immediate knowledge of the other which goes beyond language but is distorted by a masquerade. Furthermore, in these 'pairs,' the conventional terms of sexual difference have been displaced onto racial difference, a situation also key to *Miami Vice*'s primary partnership – that of Crockett and Tubbs. In this episode, however, the focus shifts to the couples Sonny and Savage, Castillo and Trang – two familiar heroes and their 'others.' Sonny mirrors the Savage in two scenes as shots of his search for the killer are intercut with shots of the Savage looking for prostitutes. Finally, Sonny exhibits the contagion of feminization by smoothing his hair in the characteristic gesture of his prey moments before the Savage arrives and is instantly recognized through the crowd (although Sonny has never seen him before) while making the same gesture.

While the chase scene locates Sonny and the Savage as (literally) moving down 'parallel roads,' the successful joining of Castillo and Trang is located in the hope for an impossible future world. It is only after Trang has saved

Castillo from attack, tenderly examined his wound, and quickly disappeared that Castillo reads of his friend's masquerade – Trang is an alias, assumed for undercover work in South Vietnam and Miami. While he remains unnamed, his voice-over explains his real status as colonel in the Army of the Republic of Vietnam, his new understanding of the Savage as victim (of the true savages in both of their countries who nurture war), and his appreciation of Castillo's care despite the masquerade. He ends his letter asking for friendship: 'I dream of a more perfect world in which we could also be comrades.' The dream of male bonding, occurring against a backdrop in which it is impossible to distinguish opposing sides, assert right or wrong, or secure masculinity apart from a violent defense, is here played out in all its excess and contradiction.

While the politically progressive 'message' of this episode is striking in relation to the usual fare of TV cop shows, it exposes the problematic of which I am speaking in chillingly clear terms, embodying the hypermasculine defense against a feminization associated with TV, postmodernism, and post-Vietnam America in the cyborg character of the Savage. As such, it reveals TV's masquerade of masculinity – a masquerade which may be seen as a violent response to the feminine connotations attached to television and its receptive viewers. In other words, while theoretical and popular discourses alike may figure television in terms of femininity, we should not accept such views uncritically, failing then to notice other crucial differences which run through television – differences related to class and racial positioning, for example – as well as the contradictions of gender that do exist within television's multiple address. While the gender inscriptions of US broadcast television are complex, intertwined, and unstable, it is important to note that even the temporary securities offered in shows of male spectacle require the neutralization or absence of women (while still disavowing any overt homosexual eroticism). The family offered is a family of man, and the gender positions cast are significant for both the men and women watching. In a medium in which the familial is the dominant theme as well (current theories of sexual and textual difference – the masculine threat that) current theories of sexual and textual difference – the masculine threat that lurks 'within the gates' of a medium deemed feminine.

Notes

1   The concept of the cyborg body comes from Donna Haraway, 'A Manifesto for Cyborgs: Science, Technology, and Socialist Feminism in the 1980s', *Socialist Review*, 80 (Mar.–Apr. 1985), pp. 65–107. See also Tania Modleski's discussion of *Videodrome* in 'The Terror of Pleasure: The Contemporary Horror Film and Postmodern Theory' in Tania Modleski, ed., *Studies in Entertainment: Critical Approaches to Mass Culture* (Bloomington, IN, Indiana University Press, 1986), p. 159.

2 The term 'machine-subject' comes from Margaret Morse who analyzes the ways in which TV seems to address its viewers from a position of subjectivity in 'Talk, Talk, Talk – The Space of Discourse in Television', *Screen*, 26: 2 (Mar.–Apr. 1985), p. 6.

3 For a related analysis see Patrice Petro, 'Culture and the Feminine: The "Place" of Television in Film Studies', *Cinema Journal*, 25: 3 (Spring 1986), pp. 5–21.

4 Tania Modleski, 'Femininity as Mas(s)querade: A Feminist Approach to Mass Culture', in Colin MacCabe, ed., *High Theory/Low Culture* (New York, St. Martin's Press, 1986), pp. 37–52.

5 Andreas Huyssen, 'Mass Culture as Woman: Modernism's Other', in *After the Great Divide: Modernism, Mass Culture, Postmodernism* (Bloomington, IN, Indiana University Press, 1986), pp. 62 and 53–5.

6 Marshall McLuhan, *Understanding Media: The Extensions of Man* (New York, McGraw, 1964), pp. 16–17.

7 McLuhan, *Understanding Media*, p. 17.

8 Georg W. F. Hegel, *Phenomenology of Mind*, trans. J. B. Baillie (New York, Harper, 1967), p. 496.

9 John Fiske and John Hartley, *Reading Television* (New York, Methuen, 1978). See, for example, pp. 15, 85–7, 112, and 116–26. The chart of oppositions between television and literate media that Fiske and Hartley offer in this book (pp. 124–5) mirrors the one that Fiske employs to differentiate feminine and masculine forms in *Television Culture* (New York, Methuen, 1987), p. 203.

10 According to Fiske and Hartley, it is in the space between TV's irrational mode and the masculine logic of print that the viewer can position him/herself so as to decode TV differently. Through the (unspoken) metaphors of sexual difference, then, these theorists construct a theory of television's difference – a view that echoes a common position in literary theory which has also aligned textual difference with figures of femininity.

11 John Ellis, *Visible Fictions* (London, Routledge, 1982). See, for example, pp. 57, 116, 137–9, 141–3, 146.

12 Perhaps the most obvious case of this tendency to associate television with the feminine is the Lacanian reading offered by Beverle Houston in the article 'Viewing Television: The Metapsychology of Endless Consumption', *Quarterly Review of Film Studies*, 9: 3 (Summer 1984), pp. 183–95. I don't discuss this analysis in the text precisely because the thesis that TV is feminine is so clear in her work. The more interesting cases, in my opinion, are those in which gendered metaphors creep into discussions of television by critics not expressly making this claim.

13 See, for example, Huyssen's discussion of nostalgia as a response to postmodernism's 'various forms of "otherness"' (including feminism) on pp. 199 and 219–20. Janice Doane and Devon Hodges discuss the anxiety provoked by the erosion of traditional categories of gender in *Nostalgia and Sexual Difference: The Resistance to Contemporary Feminism* (New York, Methuen, 1987).

14 Jean Baudrillard, *Simulations* (New York, Semiotext[e], 1983), p. 56.

15 Baudrillard, *Simulations*, pp. 30–1. See also pp. 52, 54.

16 Baudrillard, *Simulations*, pp. 52, 54.

17 See in particular, Laura Mulvey, 'Visual Pleasure and Narrative Cinema', *Screen*, 16 (3): (Autumn 1975), pp. 6–18. Recently, many feminist film theorists have retheorized

spectatorship so as to account for shifting and contradictory identifications and more powerful and pleasurable positions for the female viewer. See, for example, Elizabeth Cowie, 'Fantasia', *m/f*, 9 (1984), pp. 71–105; Teresa de Lauretis, *Alice Doesn't: Feminism, Semiotics, Cinema* (Bloomington, IN, Indiana University Press, 1984); Tania Modleski, *The Women Who Knew Too Much: Hitchcock and Feminist Theory* (New York, Methuen, 1988); Kaja Silverman, *The Acoustic Mirror: The Female Voice in Psychoanalysis and Cinema* (Bloomington, IN, Indiana University Press, 1988); and Linda Williams, 'Something Else Besides a Mother: *Stella Dallas* and the Maternal Melodrama', *Cinema Journal*, 24 (1): (Fall 1984), pp. 2–27.

In discussing the female spectator in the latter part of this paper in terms of narcissism and tropes of proximity, I am not claiming that these are the only or essential positions available for an actual female viewer. Rather, I am focusing on the *representation* of women in both popular and critical accounts of cinematic spectatorship. In other words, the historically and culturally sanctioned positions for female viewers are quite limited even though other constructions of viewing pleasure are certainly possible, particularly for viewers who have been positioned 'differently' by the discourses of feminism.

18 Jean Baudrillard, *In the Shadow of the Silent Majorities... or The End of the Social and Other Essays* (New York, Semiotext[e], 1983), p. 33.

19 Luce Irigaray, *This Sex Which Is Not One*, trans. Catherine Porter (Ithaca, NY, Cornell University Press, 1985), pp. 76, 150–1; and Mary Ann Doane, 'Film and the Masquerade: Theorizing the Female Spectator', *Screen*, **23**: 3–4 (Sept.–Oct. 1982), pp. 74–88. Doane employs and expands the concept of masquerade developed by Joan Riviere in 'Womanliness as Masquerade', in Henrik Ruitenbeek, ed., *Psychoanalysis and Female Sexuality* (New Haven, CT, College and University Press, 1966), pp. 209–20. Also see Mary Ann Doane, 'Masquerade Reconsidered: Further Thoughts on the Female Spectator', *Discourse*, **11** (1): (Fall–Winter 1988–9), pp. 42–54.

20 Baudrillard, *In the Shadow*, pp. 40–1. See also p. 39.

21 Rey Chow, 'Tofu: The Protein and Protean Dietetics', Cornell Graduate Student Conference on the Culture Industry, Cornell University, New York, April 1987.

22 See Baudrillard, *In the Shadow*, p. 39.

23 Jacques Derrida, *Spurs: Nietzsche's Styles*, trans. Barbara Harlow (Chicago, IL, University of Chicago Press, 1978), pp. 67, 57, 49.

24 Modleski, *The Women Who Knew Too Much*, pp. 50–1.

25 Nancy Miller, 'The Text's Heroine: A Feminist Critic and Her Fictions', *Diacritics*, 12: 2 (Summer 1982), p. 53. Also addressing this issue is Naomi Schor, 'Dreaming Dissymmetry: Barthes, Foucault, and Sexual Difference', in Alice Jardine and Paul Smith, eds, *Men in Feminism* (New York, Methuen, 1987), pp. 98–110; and Patricia Mellencamp who examines sit-com simulations that are inflected differently by the female voice in 'Situation Comedy, Feminism, and Freud: Discourses of Gracie and Lucy', in Modleski, *Studies in Entertainment*, especially p. 87.

26 Huyssen, 'Mass Culture as Woman', p. 205. The 'threat to women' revealed by mass culture's gendered violence can also be seen in my example of *Videodrome* – a film that thus demonstrates how TV has been figured as feminine as well as how this figuration masks a violent hypermasculinity.

27 See, for example, the essays in *Camera Obscura*'s special issue on 'Television and the Female Consumer', *Camera Obscura*, 16 (Jan. 1988), and in the anthology *Boxed In:*

Women and Television, ed. Helen Baehr and Gillian Dyer (New York, Pandora Press, 1987).

28 Lynne Joyrich, 'All That Television Allows: TV Melodrama, Postmodernism, and Consumer Culture', *Camera Obscura*, 16 (Jan. 1988), pp. 141–7.

29 See, for example, Nancy Chodorow, *The Reproduction of Mothering: Psychoanalysis and the Sociology of Gender* (Berkeley, CA, University of California Press, 1978); Carol Gilligan, *In a Different Voice: Psychological Theory and Women's Development* (Cambridge, MA, Harvard University Press, 1982); Irigaray, *This Sex Which Is Not One*; and Michèle Montrelay, 'Inquiry into Femininity', *m/f*, 1 (1978), pp. 83–102. For an illuminating discussion of such tropes of feminine proximity, see Mary Ann Doane, *The Desire to Desire: The Woman's Film of the 1940s* (Bloomington, IN, Indiana University Press, 1987).

30 On advertising and self-image, see T. J. Jackson Lears, 'From Salvation to Self-realization: Advertising and the Therapeutic Roots of Consumer Culture, 1880–1930', in Richard Wightman Fox and T. J. Jackson Lears, eds, *The Culture of Consumption: Critical Essays in American History, 1880–1980* (New York, Pantheon, 1983), pp. 3–38. Relating this to the specific position of women is Rosalind Coward, *Female Desires: How They Are Sold, Bought, and Packaged* (New York, Grove Press, 1985), and Doane, *The Desire to Desire*, especially pp. 13 and 22–33.

31 See Sandy Flitterman, 'The *Real* Soap Operas: TV Commercials', in E. Ann Kaplan, ed., *Regarding Television: Critical Approaches – An Anthology* (Frederick, MD, University Publications of America, 1983), pp. 84, 94. See also the essays on soap by Tania Modleski, Charlotte Brunsdon, and Robert Allen in the same volume.

32 On MTV and postmodernism, see, for example, E. Ann Kaplan, *Rocking Around the Clock: Music Television, Postmodernism, and Consumer Culture* (New York, Methuen, 1987); Peter Wollen, 'Ways of Thinking about Music Video (and Postmodernism)', *Critical Quarterly*, **28**: 1–2 (Spring–Summer 1986), pp. 167–70; and the essays on music video in *Journal of Communication Inquiry*, 10 (1) (1986).

33 After *Max Headroom*'s initial introduction in the US on March 31, 1987 (a remake of the original British text), its 'second premiere' aired on ABC on April 28, 1988. Throughout this episode, we witness an argument between the two heroes which erupts when Max (who gets better ratings) steals Edison's airtime. When Max is later projected into Edison's brain in order to provide what is referred to as 'a jumpstart' (a phrase which implies that Edison too is a technological being, another cyborg), they continue the argument. Edison exclaims, 'You're always in my way – you're too close to me,' and Max responds, 'I can't help being that close and being a threat to you.' Edison then asks, 'Have you any idea what it's like having a part of me competing against me?' to which Max replies, 'And have you any idea what it's like just being a part?' This exchange, coupled with the plot concerning the power of consumerism, is interesting for the ways in which it explicitly employs the tropes of 'nearness' and overpresence that have been raised in both popular and critical portrayals of the cyborg, the female, and the 'consuming' body. Furthermore, it reveals the threat to a (presumed) separate and unified male subject that is posed by such 'feminized' objects as well as by the operations of postmodern culture which confuse the distinction between part and whole, self and 'other.'

34 The analysis of such shows as 'hysterical' texts that yield contradictions emerging as textual fissures suggests a reading of these programs as 'male melodramas.' Noting

that melodrama's search for clearly marked oppositions historically arises in periods of crisis, one can analyze television – the medium of hyperreality which is defined as *the age of crisis* – as the melodramatic forum of postmodernism. Because of both the specific suitability of melodrama for television and the demands of postmodernism, even genres not typically associated with the melodrama – such as the cop show – have turned toward the more personal issues associated with melodramatic form, thereby inheriting some of this genre's tensions as well as the tensions provoked by such generic hybrids. See Joyrich, 'All That Television Allows', pp. 129–53.

35 Margaret Morse, 'Sport on Television: Replay and Display', in Kaplan, *Regarding Television*, p. 45.

36 Morse, 'Sport on Television', p. 44.

37 Sandy Flitterman, 'Thighs and Whiskers – the Fascination of *Magnum, p.i.*', *Screen*, **26** (2) (Mar.–Apr. 1985), pp. 42–58.

38 The crisis in masculinity provoked by Vietnam has also been discussed by Andrew Ross, 'Masculinity and *Miami Vice*: Selling In'. *Oxford Literary Review*, 8: 1–2 (1986), p. 150. Comparing *Miami Vice* to film noir, Jeremy Butler reminds us of the historical connection between noir style and postwar disillusionment – a connection which suggests that the popularity of *Miami Vice* may be related to post-Vietnam despair. See '*Miami Vice*: The Legacy of Film Noir', *Journal of Popular Film and Television*, **13** (3) (Fall 1985), p. 129.

39 For Butler's analysis of these issues of sexual difference, see pp. 129–30, 132–3.

40 On this core dilemma, see Butler, '*Miami Vice*', pp. 131–2. On the double meaning of 'Vice' as it relates to masquerade and the 'right stuff' of masculinity, see Ross, 'Masculinity and *Miami Vice*', p. 152.

41 Morse, 'Sport on Television', pp. 44, 56.

42 In other words, in 'Duty and Honor' (which NBC first aired on February 6, 1987) hypermasculinity can be seen as a response to (or defense against) the literal embodiment of the Oedipal structure and the castrating woman.

44
"In My Weekend-Only World...":
Reconsidering Fandom

Henry Jenkins

In an hour of make-believe
In these warm convention halls
My mind is free to think
And feels so deeply
An intimacy never found
Inside their silent walls
In a year or more
Of what they call reality.

In my weekend-only world,
That they call make-believe,
Are those who share
The visions that I see.
In their real-time life
That they tell me is real,
The things they care about
Aren't real to me.
        (T.J. Burnside Clapp, Weekend-Only World)

"Get a life," William Shatner told *Star Trek* fans. "I already have a life," the fans responded, a life which was understood both in terms of its normality by the standards of middle-class culture and by its difference from that culture. This book maps some major dimensions of that "life." If fans are often represented as antisocial, simple-minded, and obsessive, I wanted to show the complexity and diversity of fandom as a subcultural community.

This account offers a conception of fandom that encompasses at least five levels of activity:

(*a*) Fandom involves a particular mode of reception. Fan viewers watch television texts with close and undivided attention, with a mixture of emotional proximity and critical distance. They view them multiple times, using their videotape players to scrutinize meaningful details and to bring more and more of the series narrative under their control. They translate the reception process into social interaction with other fans. John Fiske (1991) distinguishes between semiotic productivity (the popular construction of meanings at the moment of reception) and enunciative productivity (the articulation of meaning through dress, display, and gossip). For the fan, this otherwise theoretically useful distinction breaks down since the moment of reception is often also the moment of enunciation (as is literally true within the group viewing situations described here). Making meanings involves sharing, enunciating, and debating meanings. For the fan, watching the series is the beginning, not the end, of the process of media consumption.

(b) Fandom involves a particular set of critical and interpretive practices. Part of the process of becoming a fan involves learning the community's preferred reading practices. Fan criticism is playful, speculative, subjective. Fans are concerned with the particularity of textual detail and with the need for internal consistency across the program episodes. They create strong parallels between their own lives and the events of the series. Fan critics work to resolve gaps, to explore excess details and undeveloped potentials. This mode of interpretation draws them far beyond the information explicitly present and toward the construction of a meta-text that is larger, richer, more complex and interesting than the original series. The meta-text is a collaborative enterprise; its construction effaces the distinction between reader and writer, opening the program to appropriation by its audience.

(c) Fandom constitutes a base for consumer activism. Fans are viewers who speak back to the networks and the producers, who assert their right to make judgments and to express opinions about the development of favorite programs. Fans know how to organize to lobby on behalf of endangered series, be they *Twin Peaks* fans exploiting the computer networks to rally support for a show on the verge of cancelation or *Beauty and the Beast* fans directing anger against a producer who violated their basic assumptions about the program. Fandom originates, at least in part, as a response to the relative powerlessness of the consumer in relation to powerful institutions of cultural production and circulation. Critics claim that fans are little more than an extension of the market logic of commercial broadcasting, a commodity audience created and courted by the culture industries (Tulloch and Jenkins, forthcoming). Such a position is false to the reality fans experience when they come into contact with systems of cultural production: media corporations do indeed market to fans, target them for program merchandizing, create official fan organizations that work to regularize audience responses, and send speakers to conventions to promote new works or to squash unwanted speculations. Yet network executives and producers are often indifferent, if not overtly hostile, to fan opinion and distrustful of their input into the production process. Fan response is assumed to be unrepresentative of general public sentiment and therefore unreliable as a basis for decisions. The media conglomerates do not want fans who make demands, second-guess creative decisions and assert opinions; they want regular viewers who accept what they are given and buy what they are sold. Official fan organizations generate and maintain the interests of regular viewers and translate them into a broader range of consumer purchases; i.e. spinoff products, soundtracks, novelizations, sequels, etc. Fandom (i.e. the unofficial fan community) provides a base from which fans may speak about their cultural preferences and assert their desires for alternative developments.

(*d*) Fandom possesses particular forms of cultural production, aesthetic traditions and practices. Fan artists, writers, videomakers, and musicians create works that speak to the special interests of the fan community. Their works appropriate raw materials from the commercial culture but use them as the basis for the creation of a contemporary folk culture. Fandom generates its own genres and develops alternative institutions of production, distribution, exhibition, and consumption. The aesthetic of fan art celebrates creative use of already circulating discourses and images, an art of evoking and regulating the heteroglossia of television culture.

The nature of fan creation challenges the media industry's claims to hold copyrights on popular narratives. Once television characters enter into a broader circulation, intrude into our living rooms, pervade the fabric of our society, they belong to their audience and not simply to the artists who originated them. Media texts, thus, can and must be remade by their viewers so that potentially significant materials can better speak to the audience's cultural interests and more fully address their desires.

Fan art as well stands as a stark contrast to the self-interested motivations of mainstream cultural production; fan artists create artworks to share with other fan friends. Fandom generates systems of distribution that reject profit and broaden access to its creative works. As Jeff Bishop and Paul Hoggett have written about subcultural communities organized around common enthusiasms or interests, "The values...are radically different from those embedded within the formal economy; they are values of reciprocity and interdependence as opposed to self-interest, collectivism as opposed to individualism, the importance of loyalty and a sense of 'identity' or 'belonging' as opposed to the principle of forming ties on the basis of calculation, monetary or otherwise" (Bishop and Hoggett, 1986: 53). Fanzines are most often sold at cost; the circuit stories are made available for fans to make their own copies; fan videos are exchanged on a tape-for-tape basis; filk songs traditionally circulated through word-of-mouth. There is evidence that these practices are beginning to change – and not necessarily for the better. Witness the emergence of semiprofessional publishers of zines and distributors of filktapes, yet even these companies originate within the fan community and reflect a desire to achieve a better circulation of its cultural products.

Fandom recognizes no clear-cut line between artists and consumers; all fans are potential writers whose talents need to be discovered, nurtured, and promoted and who may be able to make a contribution, however modest, to the cultural wealth of the larger community. In researching this book, I spoke to many who had discovered skills and abilities that they had not recognized before entering fandom; they received there the encouragement they had found lacking from their interactions with other institutions. They often gained subsequent opportunities on the basis of these developed skills.

(*e*) Fandom functions as an alternative social community. The song lyrics that open this chapter, like the filk songs discussed in the previous chapter, capture something essential about fandom, its status as a utopian community. *Weekend-Only World* expresses the fans' recognition that fandom offers not so much an escape from reality as an alternative reality whose values may be more humane and democratic than those held by mundane society. T.J. Burnside Clapp contrasts the intimacy and communalism of fandom to the alienation and superficiality of mundane life:

> I see them daily, months on end.
> The surface all I see.
> Do they hold the things in their hearts
> That I do in mine?
> We talk of mortgages and sports
> And what's new on TV
> But we grow no closer
> With the passing time.

She can spend far less time in the company of fans, in that "weekend-only world" of the con, yet she has "lived a lifetime in those few but precious hours" and has felt closeness to many who were strangers before fandom brought them together. She gains power and identity from the time she spends within fan culture; fandom allows her to maintain her sanity in the face of the indignity and alienation of everyday life: "It keeps me safe through weeks so long between."

Writers such as Hans Magnus Enzensberger (1974), Frederic Jameson (1979), and Richard Dyer (1985), have pointed toward the utopian dimension of popular culture; its appeal to the consumer is linked to its ability to offer symbolic solutions to real-world problems and felt needs. Jameson has shown how mass-culture texts must evoke and manage social and political anxieties and fantasies. Traces of these countercultural impulses remain present, even within texts that otherwise seem reactionary: "Genuine social and historical content must first be tapped and given some initial expression if it is subsequently to be the object of successful manipulation and containment" (Jameson, 1979: 144). Richard Dyer has similarly argued that entertainment offers us an "image of something better" than the realm of everyday experience; entertainment gratifies because it holds open the imagined possibility of satisfying spectators' actual lacks and desires. Entertainment, Dyer asserts, teaches us "what utopia would feel like" (Dyer, 1985: 222). In a discussion of the American musical, Dyer contrasts popular entertainment with real-world problems: popular entertainment promises abundance instead of scarcity, energy instead of exhaustion, intensity instead of dreariness, transparency instead of manipulation, community instead of fragmentation. Science fiction has often been discussed as providing readers with the image of a better world, an alternative future, an ideal against which to measure contemporary life but also a refuge from drudgery and constraint (Lefanu, 1988).

Fan culture finds that utopian dimension within popular culture a site for constructing an alternative culture. Its society is responsive to the needs that draw its members to commercial entertainment, most especially the desire for affiliation, friendship, community. Mass culture provides many images of such a world – the tunnel community of *Beauty and the Beast*, the expanded family of the Enterprise Crew, the political commitment of the Liberator, the ideal partnership of countless cop shows, the merry men of Sherwood Forest, the dedicated members of the Blackwood project. The characters in these programs devote their lives to goals worth pursuing and share their hours with friends who care for them more than life itself. The fans are drawn to these shows precisely because of the vividness and intensity of those relationships; those characters remain the central focus of their critical interpretations and artworks.

Life, all too often, falls far short of those ideals. Fans, like all of us, inhabit a world where traditional forms of community life are disintegrating, the majority of marriages end in divorce, most social relations are temporary and superficial, and material values often dominate over emotional and social needs. Fans are often people who are overeducated for their jobs, whose intellectual skills are not challenged by their professional lives. Fans react against those unsatisfying situations, trying to establish a "weekend-only world" more open to creativity and accepting of differences, more concerned with human welfare than with economic advance. Fandom, too, falls short of those ideals; the fan community is sometimes rife with feuds and personality conflicts. Here, too, one finds those who are self-interested and uncharitable, those who are greedy and rude, yet, unlike mundane reality, fandom remains a space where a commitment to more democratic values may be renewed and fostered. Non-communal behavior is read negatively, as a violation of the social contract that binds fans together and often becomes the focus of collective outrage.

Nobody can live permanently within this utopia, which becomes recognizable as such only against the backdrop of mundane life; fans must come and go from fandom, finding this "weekend-only world" where they can, enjoying it for as long as possible, before being forced to return to the workaday world. Within the few short hours they spend each month interacting with other fans, they find something more than the superficial relationships and shoddy values of consumer culture. They find a space that allows them to discover "what utopia feels like."

In a telling critique of the politics of postmodernism, Lawrence Grossberg notes that while we often think of political resistance in negative terms – as a rejection or repudiation of existing conditions – it may also have a more positive or celebratory dimension:

> Opposition may be constituted by living, even momentarily, within alternative practices, structures and spaces, even though they may take no notice of their relationship to existing systems of power. In fact, when one wins some space within the social formation, it has to be filled with something, presumedly something one cares for passionately.... And it is here that questions of desire and pleasure must be raised as more than secondary epiphenomena. (Grossberg, 1988: 169–70)

Fandom constitutes such a space, one defined by its refusal of mundane values and practices, its celebration of deeply held emotions and passionately embraced pleasures. Fandom's very existence represents a critique of conventional forms of consumer culture. Yet fandom also provides a space within which fans may articulate their specific concerns about sexuality, gender, racism, colonialism, militarism, and forced conformity. These themes regularly surface within fan discussions and fan artworks. Fandom contains both negative and positive forms of empowerment. Its institutions allow the expression both of what fans are struggling against and what they are struggling for; its cultural products articulate the fans' frustration with their everyday life as well as their fascination with representations that pose alternatives.

In making this claim, I am not asserting that fandom necessarily represents a progressive force or that the solutions fans propose are ideologically consistent and coherent. A poached culture, a nomadic culture, is also a patchwork culture, an impure culture, where much that is taken in remains semi-digested and ill-considered. As Grossberg asserts, a politics of consumption:

> does not say that people always struggle or that when they do, they do so in ways we condone. But it does say, both theoretically and politically, that people are never merely passively subordinated, never totally manipulated, never entirely incorporated. People are engaged in struggles with, within and sometimes against real tendential forces and determinations in their efforts to appropriate what they are given. Consequently, their relations to particular practices and texts are complex and contradictory: they may win something in the struggle against sexism and lose something in the struggle against economic exploitation; they may both gain and lose something economically; and although they lose ideological ground, they may win some emotional strength. (Ibid.: 169–70)

The irony, of course, is that fans have found the very forces that work to isolate us from each other to be the ideal foundation for creating connections across traditional boundaries; that fans have found the very forces that transform many Americans into spectators to provide the resources for creating a more participatory culture; that fans have found the very forces that reinforce patriarchal authority to contain tools by which to critique that authority. We should not be surprised that in doing so, fans absorb much that we as leftist academics may find aesthetically dubious and politically suspect. What *is* surprising, particularly in the face of some fifty years of critical theories that would indicate otherwise, is that fans find the ability to question and rework the ideologies that dominate the mass culture they claim as their own. A character in Lizzie Borden's *Born in Flames* describes political alchemy as "the process of turning shit into gold"; if this claim is true, there may be no better alchemists on the planet than fans.

I am not claiming that there is anything particularly empowering about the texts fans embrace. I am, however, claiming that there is something empowering about what fans do with those texts in the process of assimilating them to the particulars of their lives. Fandom celebrates not exceptional texts but rather exceptional readings (though its interpretive practices make it impossible to maintain a clear or precise distinction between the two).

This is a book about fans and fan culture. It is not about the media industry and it is not about popular texts. I have no particular objections to studying these topics and have done so on other occasions; both seem necessary to a full understanding of mass culture and media consumption. Only by analyzing the structures of the primary text can we fully understand what fan interpretation contributes in the process of appropriating these programs for their own uses (thus, for example, my account of *Beauty and the Beast* acknowledges generic features of the program and aspects of its production history as well as the categories by which fan critics evaluated and interpreted it). Only by locating the market conditions that block fan access to the means of mass cultural production can we understand the political dimensions of their relationship with the media. I am not privileging the fan here, because I want to decenter the text or even prioritize consumption over production. Indeed, my hope is that fan critical practice may provide a model for a more specifically drawn, more exploratory and speculative style of media criticism: one alive to the pleasures of the text but retaining some critical distance from its ideological structures. What I want to reject is a tradition that reads the audience from the structures of the text or in terms of the forms of consumption generated by the institutions of production and marketing. What I want to challenge is the tendency to create a theoretical fiction that masks rather than illuminates the actual complexities of audience–text relations.

Media theorists have always made claims about the audience. What audience research contributes to this debate, then, is not the focus on the audience but rather a reconsideration of the most productive methods for making meaningful generalizations about the nature and character of audience response. Media scholars cannot help but talk about the audience in relationship to media culture; the question is what types of audience(s) we will talk about and whether they will be allowed to talk back. Much of what passes for critical theory lacks even the most rudimentary grounding in empirical reality, drawing its assumptions about spectatorship through a combination of personal introspection and borrowed authority. The result is a curious theory that cannot be tested and must be taken on blind faith. I question what forms of popular power can be founded on theories that require our unquestioning acceptance of hierarchical knowledge and which become accessible only to an educated elite.

The problem I confronted upon entering media studies, having already spent a number of years in the company of fans, was that the dominant conceptions of television spectatorship seemed radically at odds with my own experience of the media. The sweeping claims of ideological critics were totally implausible in their dismissal of popular readers as positioned by the text and unable to resist its demands. Such approaches cannot begin to account for the writing and circulation of fanzines or the mixture of fascination and frustration that runs through fan discourse. As Ien Ang writes:

> Ethnographic work, in the sense of drawing on what we can perceive and experience in everyday settings, acquires its critical mark when it functions as a reminder that reality is always more complicated and diversified than our theories can represent, and that there is no such thing as "audience" whose characteristics can be set once and for all. The critical promise of the ethnographic attitude resides in its potential to make and keep our interpretations sensitive to the concrete specificities, to the unexpected, to history.... What matters is not the certainty of knowledge about audiences, but an ongoing critical and intellectual engagement with the multifarious ways in which we constitute ourselves through media consumption. (Ang, 1990: 110)

In other words, ethnography may not have the power to construct theories, but it can disprove them or at least challenge and refine them. While I have drawn on theory as a tool for understanding fandom as a set of cultural, social, and interpretive practices, I have not drawn upon fandom as a means of developing a new theory of media consumption. I distrust the move which takes concrete, culturally situated studies of particular fan practices, of specific moments in the ongoing relationship between audience(s) and texts, and translates them into data for the construction of some general theory of the media audience. Fan culture differs in a qualitative way from the cultural experience of media consumption for the bulk of the population. It is not simply that fan interpretations are more accessible to analysis, more available for observation than the transitory meanings produced by non-fan viewers, but rather, participating within fandom fundamentally alters the ways one relates to television and the meanings one derives from its contents. The fan audience is in no sense representative of the audience at large, nor can we go from an understanding of a specific subculture to an account of *the active spectator* (a phrase which necessarily remains a theoretical rather than an ethnographic construct). I am not even sure that the types of fans I have discussed here, fans of a particular configuration of popular narratives, are necessarily identical with other varieties of fans, fans of specific media personalities, rock performers, sports teams, or soap operas. These groups will have some common experiences as well as display differences that arise from their specific placement within the cultural hierarchy and their interests in different forms of entertainment.

It strikes me as ironic, however, that before Cultural Studies began to research fan culture, fans were dismissed as atypical of the media audience because of their obsessiveness and extreme passivity; now that ethnographic accounts of fan culture are beginning to challenge those assumptions, fans are dismissed as atypical of the media audience because of their activity and resistance. Both positions portray the fan as radically "Other" rather than attempting to understand the complex relationship between fan culture and mainstream consumer culture. We cannot afford to dodge that question; we can neither afford to move from the extreme case to the general (as has been true of some recent work within the Cultural Studies tradition), nor can we afford to ignore the connection that places fan culture on a continuum with other media consumption. We can, however, insist that any theory that is constructed to account more generally for the relationship between spectators and texts not preclude the existence of the practices documented here. We can even hope for theories that can explain their persistence in the face of strong countervailing pressures. A model that sees only media effects on passive spectators falls short of this test; a model that allows for different forms of interaction, that posits a more active relationship in which textual materials are appropriated and fit to personal experience does not. Fandom does not prove that all audiences are active; it does, however, prove that not all audiences are passive.

Select Bibliography

Compiled by
Toby Miller and Robert Stam

This Select Bibliography and the reference lists appended in individual chapters include most of the work cited.

Books

Abel, Richard 1988. *French Film: Theory and Criticism 1907–1939*, 2 vols. Princeton: Princeton University Press.

——(ed.) 1996. *Silent Film*. Brunswick: Rutgers University Press.

Adams, Parveen 1996. *The Emptiness of the Image: Psychoanalysis and Sexual Differences*. London: Routledge.

Adams, Parveen and Elizabeth Cowie (eds) 1990. *The Woman in Question*. Cambridge, MA: MIT Press.

Adorno, T. W. 1978. *Minima Moralia: Reflections From a Damaged Life*. Trans. E. F. Jeph. London: Verso.

Adorno, T. W. and Max Horkheimer 1997. *Dialectic of Enlightenment*. Trans. John Cummings. New York: Verso.

Affron, Charles 1982. *Cinema and Sentiment*. Chicago: University of Chicago Press.

Affron, Charles and Mirella Jona Affron 1995. *Sets in Motion: Art Direction and Film Narrative*. New Brunswick: Rutgers University Press.

Ahmad, Aijaz. "Jameson's Rhetoric of Otherness and the National Allegory," *Social Text* 17 (Fall 1987).

Alea, Tomas Gutierrez 1982. *Dialectica Del Espectador*. Havana: Ediciones Union.

Allen, Richard 1989. *Representation, Meaning, and Experience in the Cinema: A Critical Study of Contemporary Film Theory*. Ph.D. Dissertation, University of California Los Angeles.

——1993. "Representation, Illusion, and the Cinema," *Cinema Journal* No. 32, Vol. 2 (winter).

——1995. *Projecting Illusion: Film Spectatorship and the Impression of Reality*. New York: Cambridge University Press.

Allen, Richard and Murray Smith (eds) 1997. *Film Theory and Philosophy*: Oxford: Clarendon Press.

Allen, Robert C. (ed.) 1992. *Channels of Discourse: Television and Contemporary Criticism, Reassembled*, 2nd edn. Chapel Hill: University of North Carolina Press.

Allen, Robert C. and Douglas Gomery 1985. *Film History: Theory and Practice*. New York: Alfred A. Knopf.

Alternative Museum of New York 1989. *Prisoners of Image: Ethnic and Gender Stereotypes*. New York: The Museum.

Althusser, Louis 1969. *For Marx*. Trans. Ben Brewster. New York: Pantheon Books.

Althusser, Louis and Étienne Balibar 1979. *Reading Capital*. Trans. Ben Brewster. London: Verso.

Altman, Rick (ed.) 1981. *Genre: The Musical*. London: Routledge and Kegan Paul.

—— 1984. "A Semantic/Syntactic Approach to Film Genre," *Cinema Journal* 23, 3: 6–18.

—— 1987. *The American Film Musical*. Bloomington: Indiana University Press.

—— (ed.) 1992. *Sound Theory, Sound Practice*. New York: Routledge.

Alvarado, Manuel and John O. Thompson (eds) 1990. *The Media Reader*. London: British Film Institute Publishing.

Alvarado, Manuel, Edward Buscombe, and Richard Collins (eds) 1993. *The Screen Education Reader: Cinema, Television, Culture*. New York: Columbia University Press.

Anderson, Benedict 1991. *Imagined Communities: Reflexions on the Origins and Spread of Nationalism*, 2nd edn. London: Verso.

Anderson, Perry 1998. *The Origins of Postmodernity*. New York: Verso.

Andrew, Dudley 1976. *The Major Film Theories*. New York: Oxford University Press.

—— 1978a. "The Neglected Tradition of Phenomenology in Film," *Wide Angle* 2, No. 2.

—— 1978b. *André Bazin*. New York: Oxford University Press.

—— 1984. *Concepts in Film Theory*. New York: Oxford University Press.

Ang, Ien 1985. *Watching "Dallas": Soap Opera and the Melodramatic Imagination*. Trans. Della Couling. London: Methuen.

—— 1996. *Living Room Wars: Rethinking Media Audiences for a Postmodern World*. London: Routledge.

Appadurai, Arjun 1990. "Disjunction and Difference in the Global Cultural Economy," *Public Culture*, Vol. 2, No. 2 (Spring).

Armes, Roy 1974. *Film and Reality: An Historical Survey*. Harmondsworth: Penguin.

—— 1987. *Third World Film Making and the West*. Berkeley: University of California Press.

Armstrong, Dan 1989. "Wiseman's Realm of Transgression: *Titicut Follies*, the Symbolic Father and the Spectacle of Confinement," *Cinema Journal* 29, No. 1 (Fall).

Arnheim, Rudolf 1958. *Film*; repr. as *Film as Art*. London: Faber.

—— 1997. *Film Essays and Criticism*. Trans. Brenda Benthien. Madison: University of Wisconsin Press.

Auerbach, Erich 1953. *Mimesis: The Representation of Reality in Western Literature*. Trans. Willard R. Trask. Princeton: Princeton University Press.

Aumont, Jacques 1987. *Montage Eisenstein*. Trans. Lee Hildreth, Constance Penley, and Andrew Ross. Bloomington: Indiana.

—— 1997. *The Image*. Trans. Claire Pajackowska. London: British Film Institute.

Aumont, Jacques and J. L. Leutrat 1980. *Théorie du film*. Paris: Albatross.

Aumont, Jacques and Michel Marie 1989. *L'Analyse des films*. Paris: Nathan-Université.

—— 1989. *Histoire du cinéma: nouvelles approches*. Paris: Publications de la Sorbonne.

Aumont, Jacques, Alain Bergala, Michel Marie, and Marc Vernet 1983. *Esthetique du film*. Paris: Fernand Nathan.

Austin, Bruce A. 1989. *Immediate Seating: A Look at Movie Audiences*. Belmont: Wadsworth.

Avelar, Jose Carlos 1995. *A Ponte Clandestina: Teorias de Cinema na America Latina*. São Paulo: Edusp.

Bad Object-Choices (eds) 1991. *How do I look? Queer Film and Video*. Seattle: Bay Press.

Bailble, Claude, Michel Marie, and Marie-Claire Ropars 1974. *Muriel, histoire d'une recherche*. Paris: Galilee.

Bailey, R. W., L. Matejka, and P. Steiner (eds) 1978. *The Sign: Semiotics Around the World*. Ann Arbor: Michigan Slavic Publications.

Bakari, Imruh and Mbye Cham (eds) 1996. *BlackFrames: African Experiences of Cinema*. London: British Film Institute.

Baker Jr., Houston, Manthia Diawara, and Ruth H. Lindeborg (eds) 1996. *Black British Cultural Studies: A Reader*. Chicago: University of Chicago Press.

Bakhtin, Mikhail 1981. *The Dialogical Imagination*. Trans. Michael Holquist, ed. Caryl Emerson and Michael Holquist. Austin: University of Texas Press.

——1986. *Speech Genres and other Late Essays*. Trans. Vern W. McGee, ed. Caryl Emerson and Michael Holquist. Austin: University of Texas Press.

——and P. M. Medvedev 1985. *The Formal Method in Literary Scholarship*. Trans. Albert J. Wehrle. Cambridge: Harvard University Press.

Bal, Mieke 1985. *Narratology: Introduction to the Theory of Narrative*. Toronto: University of Toronto Press.

Bálász, Bela 1930. *Der Geist des Films*. Frankfurt: Makol.

——1970. *Theory of the Film*. Trans. Edith Bone. New York: Dover.

Barnouw, Erik 1992. *Documentary: A History of the Non- Fiction Film*. New York: Oxford University Press.

Barnouw, Erik and S. Krishnaswamy 1980. *Indian Film*. New York: Oxford University Press.

Barsam, Richard Meran (ed.) 1976. *Nonfiction Film Theory and Criticism*. New York: E. P. Dutton.

——1992. *Nonfiction Film: A Critical History*. Bloomington: Indiana University Press.

Barthes, Roland 1967. *Elements of Semiology*. Trans. Annette Lavers and Colin Smith. New York: Hill & Wang.

——1972. *Mythologies*. Trans. Annette Lavers. New York: Hill & Wang.

——1974. *S/Z*. New York: Hill & Wang.

——1975. *The Pleasure of the Text*. Trans. Richard Miller. New York: Hill & Wang.

——1977. *Image/Music/Text*. Trans. Stephen Heath. New York: Hill & Wang.

——1980. *Camera Lucida*. New York: Hill & Wang.

——1985. *The Grain of the Voice*. New York: Hill & Wang.

Bataille, Gretchen, M. and Charles L. P. Silet (eds) 1980. *The Pretend Indians: Image of Native Americans in the Movies*. Ames: Iowa State University Press.

Baticle, Yveline 1973. *Clés et codes du cinema*. Paris: Magnard Université.

Baudrillard, Jean 1975. *The Mirror of Production*. St. Louis: Telos Press.

——1983. *Simulations*. Trans. Paul Foss, Paul Patton, and Phillip Beitchman. New York: Semiotext(e).

——1987. *Forget Foucault*. New York: Semiotext(e).

——1988. *The Ecstasy of Communication*. Trans. Bernard Schutze and Caroline Schutze. New York: Semiotext(e).

—— 1991a. "The Reality Gulf," The *Guardian*, Jan. 11.

—— 1991b. "La Guerre du Golfe n'a pas eu lieu," *Libération*, March 29.

Baudry, Jean-Louis. "Écriture/Fiction/Ideologie," *Tel Ouel*, 31 (Autumn 1967). Trans. Diana Matias. *Afterimage*, 5 (Spring 1974).

Bazin, André 1967. *What is Cinema?* 2 Vols. Trans. and ed. Hugh Gray. Berkeley: University of California Press.

Beauvoir, Simone de 1952. *The Second Sex*. Trans. H. M. Parshley. New York: Knopf.

Beckmann, Peter 1974. *Formale und Funktionale Film und Fernsehanalyse*. Stuttgart: Diss. Phil.

Bell-Metereau, Rebecca 1993. *Hollywood Androgyny*, 2nd edn. New York: Columbia University Press.

Bellour, Raymond 1979. *L'Analyse du film*. Paris: Albatross.

—— (ed.) 1980. *Le Cinéma américain: analyses de films*. 2 vols. Paris: Flammarion.

Belton, John (ed.) 1995. *Movies and Mass Culture*. New Brunswick: Rutgers University Press.

Benjamin, Walter 1968. *Illuminations*. Trans. Harry Zohn. New York: Harcourt and Brace & World.

—— 1973. *Understanding Brecht*. Trans. A. Bostock. London: New Left Books.

Bennett, Tony, Susan Boyd-Bowman, Colin Mercer, and Janet Woollacott (eds) 1981. *Popular Television and Film*. London: British Film Publishing and Open University Press.

Bentele, Gunter (ed.) 1981. *Semiotik und Massenmedien*. Munich: Olschlager.

Bentele, Gunter, and Ivan Bystrina 1978. *Semiotik*. Stuttgart: Kohlhammer.

Benveniste, Emile 1971. *Problems in General Linguistics*. Trans. Mary Elizabeth Meek. Coral Gables: University of Miami Press.

Berenstein, Rhona Joella 1995. *Attack of the Leading Ladies: Gender, Sexuality, and Spectatorship in Classic Horror Cinema*. New York: Columbia University Press.

Berg, Charles Ramirez 1992. *Cinema of Solitude: A Critical Study of Mexican Film, 1967–1983*. Austin: University of Texas Press.

Bernardet, Jean-Claude 1994. *O Autor No Cinema*. São Paulo: Editora Brasilienese.

Bernardi, Daniel (ed.) 1996a. *The Birth of Whiteness: Race and the Emergence of US Cinema*. New Brunswick: Rutgers University Press.

—— (ed.) 1996b. *Looking at Film History in "Black and White"*. New Brunswick: Rutgers University Press.

Bernstein, Matthew, and Gaylyn Studlar (eds) 1996. *Visions of the East: Orientalism in Film*. New Brunswick: Rutgers University Press.

Berry, Chris (ed.) 1991. *Perspectives on Chinese Cinema*. London: British Film Institute.

Best, Steven and Douglas Kellner 1991. *Postmodern Theory: Critical Interrogations*. New York: Guilford Press.

Bettetini, Gianfranco, 1971. *L'indice del realismo*. Milan: Bompiani.

—— 1973. *The Language and Technique of the Film*. The Hague: Mouton.

—— 1975. *Produzione del senso e messa in scena*. Milan: Bompiani.

Betton, Gerard, 1971. *L'Indice del realismo*. Milan: Bompiani.

—— 1987. *Esthetique du cinéma*. Paris: Presses Universitaires du France.

Bhabha, Homi K. 1990. *Nation and Narration*. London: Routledge.

Bidaud, Anne-Marie 1994. *Hollywood et le rêve américain: cinema et idéologie aux etats-unis*. Paris: Masson.

Bobo, Jacqueline 1995. *Black Women as Cultural Readers*. New York: Columbia University Press.

Bogle, Donald 1989. *Toms, Coons, Mulattoes, Mammies, and Bucks: An Interpretive History of Blacks in American Films*. New York: Continuum.

—— 1988. *Blacks in American Films and Television: An Illustrated Encyclopedia*. New York: Simon and Schuster.

Bordwell, David 1985. *Narration in the Fiction Film*. Madison: University of Wisconsin Press.

—— 1989. *Making Meaning: Inference and Rhetoric in the Interpretation of Cinema*. Cambridge, MA: Harvard University Press.

—— 1997. *On the History of Film Style*. Cambridge, MA: Harvard University Press.

Bordwell, David and Noël Carroll (eds) 1996. *Post-Theory: Reconstructing Film Studies*. Madison: University of Wisconsin Press.

Bordwell, David and Kristin Thompson 1996. *Film Art: An Introduction*, 5th ed. New York: McGraw-Hill.

Bordwell, David, Janet Staiger, and Kristin Thompson 1985. *The Classical Hollywood Cinema: Film Style and Mode of Production to 1960*. New York: Columbia University Press.

Bourdieu, Pierre 1998. *On Television*. New York: New Press.

Boyd, Todd 1996. *Am I Black Enough for You? Popular Culture from the Hood and Beyond*. Berkeley: University of California Press.

Branigan, Edward, 1984. *Point of View in the Cinema: A Theory of Narration and Subjectivity in Classical Film*. The Hague: Mouton.

—— 1992. *Narrative Comprehension and Film*. New York: Routledge.

Bratton, Jacky, Jim Cook, and Christine Gledhill (eds) 1994. *Melodrama: Stage, Picture, Screen*. London: British Film Institute.

Braudy, Leo 1976. *The World in a Frame*. New York: Anchor Press.

Braudy, Leo, Marshall Cohen, and Gerald Mast (eds) 1999. *Film Theory and Criticism*, 5th edn. New York: Oxford University Press.

Brecht, Bertolt 1964. *Brecht on Theatre*. New York: Hill & Wang.

Brennan, Teresa and Martin Jay (eds) 1996. *Vision in Context: Historical and Contemporary Perspectives on Sight*. New York: Routledge.

Brooker, Peter and Will Brooker (eds) 1997. *Postmodern After-images: A Reader in Film, Television and Video*. London: Arnold.

Brooks, Virginia 1984. "Film, Perception, and Cognitive Psychology," *Millennium Film Journal* 14.

Brown, Royal S. 1994. *Overtones and Undertones: Reading Film Music*. Berkeley: University of California Press.

Browne, Nick 1982. *The Rhetoric of Film Narration*. Ann Arbor: UMI.

—— (ed.) 1990. *Cahiers du Cinéma 1969–1972: The Politics of Representation*. Cambridge, MA: Harvard University Press.

—— (ed.) 1997. *Refiguring American Film Genres: History and Theory*. Berkeley: University of California Press.

Brunette, Peter and David Wills 1989. *Screen/Play: Derrida and Film Theory*. Princeton: Princeton University Press.

Brunsdon, Charlotte and David Morley 1978. *Everyday Television: "Nationwide"*. London: British Film Institute.

Bryson, Norman, Michael Ann Holly, and Keith Moxey 1994. *Visual Culture: Images and Interpretations.* Hanover: Wesleyan University Press.

Buckland, Warren (ed.) 1995. *The Film Spectator: From Sign to Mind.* Amsterdam: Amsterdam University Press.

Bukatman, Scott 1993. *Terminal Identity: The Virtual Subject in Postmodern Science Fiction.* Durham, NC: Duke University Press.

Burch, Noël 1973. *Theory of Film Practice.* Trans. Helen R. Lane. New York: Praeger.

——1990. *Life to Those Shadows.* Trans. and ed. Ben Brewster. Berkeley: University of California Press.

Burger, Peter 1984. *Theory of the Avant-Garde.* Trans. Michael Shaw. Minneapolis: University of Minneapolis Press.

Burgoyne, Robert A. 1990. *Bertolucci's 1900: A Narrative and Historical Analysis.* Detroit: Wayne State University Press.

Burnett, Ron (ed.) 1991. *Explorations in Film Theory: Selected Essays from Ciné-Tracts.* Bloomington: Indiana University Press.

Burton, Julianne, 1985. "Marginal Cinemas," *Screen* Vol. 26, Nos. 3–4 (May–August).

——(ed.) 1986. *Cinema and Social Change.* Austin: University of Texas.

——(ed.) 1990. *The Social Documentary in Latin America.* Pittsburgh: University of Pittsburgh Press.

Buscombe, Edward 1970. "The Idea of Genre in the American Cinema," *Screen* 11, 2: 33–45.

——(ed.) 1988. *The BFI Companion to the Western.* New York: Da Capo.

Butler, Jeremy G. (ed.) 1995. *Star Texts: Image and Performance in Film and Television.* Detroit: Wayne State University Press.

Butler, Judith P. 1990. *Gender Trouble: Feminism and the Subversion of Identity.* New York: Routledge.

Caldwell, John Thornton 1994. *Televisuality: Style, Crisis and Authority in American Television.* New Brunswick: Rutgers University Press.

Carroll, John, M. 1980. *Toward a Structural Psychology of Cinema.* The Hague: Mouton.

——1988. "A Program for Film Theory," *Journal of Aesthetics and Art Criticism*, 35, 3.

Carroll, Noël 1982. "The Future of an Allusion: Hollywood in the Seventies and (Beyond)," *October*, Vol. XX (Spring).

——1988a. *Mystifying Movies: Fads and Fallacies in Contemporary Film Theory.* New York: Columbia University Press.

——1988b. *Philosophical Problems of Film Theory.* Princeton: Princeton University Press.

——1996. *Theorizing the Moving Image.* Cambridge: Cambridge University Press.

——1998. *A Philosophy of Mass Art.* Oxford: Clarendon Press.

Carson, Diane, Linda Dittmar, and Janice R. Welsh (eds) 1994. *Multiple Voices in Feminist Film Criticism.* Minneapolis: University of Minnesota Press.

Carter, Angela, 1978. *The Sadeian Woman and the Ideology of Pornography.* New York: Harper & Row.

Casebier, Allan 1991. *Film and Phenomenology: Toward a Realist Theory of Cinematic Representation.* Cambridge: Cambridge University Press.

Casetti, Francesco, 1977. *Semiotica.* Milan: Edizione Academia.

——1986. *Dentro lo Sguardo, il Filme e il suo Spettatore.* Rome: Bompiani.

——1990. *D'un Regard l'autre.* Lyon: Presses Universitaires de Lyon.

——1993. *Teorie del cinema (1945–1990).* Milan: Bompiani.

Caughie, John (ed.) 1981. *Theories of Authorship: A Reader*. London: Routledge and Kegan Paul.

Cavell, Stanley 1982. *Pursuits of Happiness*. Cambridge, MA: Harvard University Press.

Cesaire, Aimé 1972. *Discourse on Colonialism*. Trans. Joan Pinkham. New York: MR.

Cha, Theresa Hak Kyung (ed.) 1980. *Apparatus*. New York: Tanam Press.

Chakravarty, Sumita 1993. *National Identity in Indian Popular Cinema*. Austin: University of Texas Press.

Cham, Mbye B. and Claire Andrade-Watkins (eds) 1988. *Critical Perspectives on Black Independent Cinema*. Cambridge: MIT Press.

Chanan, Michael 1976. *Chilean Cinema*. London: British Film Institute.

—— 1980. *Santiago Alvarez*. London: British Film Institute.

—— (ed.) 1983. *Twenty-Five Years of the New Latin American Cinema*. London: British Film Institute.

—— 1985. *The Cuban Image*. London: British Film Institute.

Charney, Leo and Vanessa R. Schwartz (eds) 1995. *Cinema and the Invention of Modern Life*. Berkeley: University of California Press.

Chateau, Dominique and François Jost 1979. *Nouveau cinéma, nouvelle sémiologie*. Paris: Union Generale d'Editions.

Chateau, Dominique, André Gardies, and François Jost 1981. *Cinémas de la modernité: films, théories*. Paris: Klincksieck.

Chatman, Seymour 1978. *Story and Discourse: Narrative Structure in Fiction and Film*. Ithaca, NY: Cornell University Press.

Chatterjee, Partha 1993. *Nationalist Thought and the Colonial World*. Minneapolis: University of Minnesota Press.

Chion, Michel 1982. *La Voix au cinéma*. Paris: Cahiers du Cinéma/Editions de l'Etoile.

—— 1985. *Le Son au cinéma*. Paris: Cahiers du Cinéma/Editions de l'Etoile.

—— 1988. *La Toile trouée*. Paris: Cahiers du Cinéma/Editions de l'Etoile.

—— 1994. *Audio-Vision: Sound on Screen*. Trans. and ed. Claudia Gorbman. New York: Columbia University Press.

Chomsky, Noam 1957. *Syntactic Structures*. The Hague: Mouton.

—— 1972. *Language and Mind*. New York: Harcourt Brace.

Chow, Rey 1995. *Primitive Passions: Visuality, Sexuality, Ethnography, and Contemporary Chinese Cinema*. New York: Columbia University Press.

Christian, Barbara 1985. *Black Feminist Criticism: Perspectives on Black Women Writers*. New York: Pergamon.

Church Gibson, Pamela and Roma Gibson (eds) 1993. *Dirty Looks: Women, Pornography, Power*. London: British Film Institute.

Churchill, Ward 1992. *Fantasies of the Master Race: Literature, Cinema and the Colonization of American Indians*. Ed. M. Annette Jaimes. Monroe: Common Courage Press.

Cixous, Hélène and Catherine Clement 1975. *La jeune née*. Paris: Union Générale d'Editions.

Clark, VeVe A., Millicent Hodson, and Catrina Neiman (eds) 1946/1988. *The Legend of Maya Deren: A Documentary Biography and Collected Works, vol. 1, part 2*. New York: Anthology Film Archives and Film Culture.

Clerc, Jeanne-Marie 1993. *Littérature et cinéma*. Paris: Editions Nathan.

Clover, Carol J. 1992. *Men, Women, and Chain Saws: Gender in the Modern Horror Film*. Princeton: Princeton University Press.

Cohan, Steve 1997. *Masked Men: Masculinity and the Movies in the Fifties*. Bloomington: Indiana University Press.

—— and Ina Rae Hark (eds) 1992. *Screening the Male: Exploring Masculinities in the Hollywood Cinema*. New York: Routledge.

Colin, Michel 1985. *Language, film, discourse: prolégomènes à une sémiologie génerative du film*. Paris: Klincksieck.

Collet, Jean, Michel Marie, Daniel Percheron, Jean-Paul Simon, and Marc Vernet 1975. *Lectures du film*. Paris: Albatross.

Collins, Jim 1989. *Uncommon Cultures: Popular Culture and Post-Modernism*. London: Routledge.

Collins, Jim, Hillary Radner, and Ava Preacher Collins (eds) 1993. *Film Theory Goes to the Movies*. New York: Routledge.

Comolli, Jean-Louis and Narboni, Jean 1969. "Cinema/Ideology/Criticism," *Cahiers du cinéma*.

Cook, Pamela 1985. *The Cinema Book*. London: British Film Institute.

—— 1996. *Fashioning the Nation: Costume and Identity in British Cinema*. London: British Film Institute.

Cook, Pamela and Philip Dodd (eds) 1993. *Women and Film: A Sight and Sound Reader*. Philadelphia: Temple University Press.

Copjec, Joan 1989. "The Orthopsychic Subject: Film Theory and the Reception of Lacan," *October* 49.

—— (ed.) 1993. *Shades of Noir*. New York: Verso.

Corrigan, Timothy 1991. *Cinema without Walls: Movies and Culture after Vietnam*. New Brunswick: Rutgers University Press.

Cowie, Elizabeth 1997. *Representing the Woman: Cinema and Psychoanalysis*. Minneapolis: University of Minnesota Press.

Crary, Jonathan 1995. *Techniques of the Observer*. Cambridge: MIT Press.

Creed, Barbara 1993. *The Monstrous-Feminine: Film, Feminism, Psychoanalysis*. New York: Routledge.

Creekmur, Corey K. and Alexander Doty (eds) 1995. *Out in Culture: Gay, Lesbian and Queer Essays on Popular Culture*. Durham, NC: Duke University Press.

Cripps, Thomas 1979. *Black Film as Genre*. Bloomington: Indiana University Press.

Culler, Jonathan 1975. *Structuralist Poetics: Structuralism, Linguistics and the Study of Literature*. Ithaca, NY: Cornell University Press.

—— 1981. *The Pursuit of Signs: Semiotics, Literature, Deconstruction*. Ithaca, NY: Cornell University Press.

Custen, George 1992. *Bio/Pics*. New Brunswick: Rutgers University Press.

Dates, J. and W. Barlow (eds) 1990. *Split Image: African-Americans in the Mass Media*. Washington: Howard University Press.

David, Joel 1995. *Fields of Vision: Critical Applications in Recent Philippine Cinema*. Quezon City: Ateneo de Manila University Press.

Debord, Guy 1967. *Society of the Spectacle*. Paris: Éditions Champ Libre.

de Certeau, Michel 1984. *The Practice of Everyday Life*. Trans. Steven Rendall. Berkeley: University of California Press.

de Cordova, Richard 1990. *Picture Personalities: The Emergence of the Star System in America*. Urbana: University of Illinois Press.

de Lauretis, Teresa 1985. *Alice Doesn't: Feminism, Semiotics, Cinema*. Bloomington: Indiana University Press.

——1989. *Technologies of Gender: Essays on Theory, Film and Fiction*. Bloomington: Indiana University Press.

——1994. *The Practice of Love: Lesbian Sexuality and Perverse Desire*. Bloomington: Indiana University Press.

de Saussure, Ferdinand 1966. *Course in General Linguistics*. Trans. Wade Baskin. New York: McGraw Hill.

Deleuze, Gilles 1977. *Anti-Oedipus: Capitalism and Schizophrenia*. Trans. Robert Hurley, Mark Seem, and Helen R. Lane. New York: Viking Press.

——1986. *Cinema 1: The Movement-Image*. Trans. Hugh Tomlinson and Barbara Habberjam. London: Athlone Press.

——1989. *Cinema 2: The Time-Image*. Trans. Hugh Tomlinson and Robert Galeta. Minneapolis: University of Minnesota Press.

——1990. *Negotiations*. Trans. Martin Joughin. New York: Columbia University Press.

Deloria, Vine, Jr. 1969. *Custer Died For Your Sins*. New York: Avon Books.

Dent, Gina (ed.) 1992. *Black Popular Culture*. Seattle: Bay Press.

Denzin, Norman K. 1991. *Images of Postmodern Society: Social Theory and Contemporary Cinema*. London: Sage Publications.

——1995. *The Cinematic Society: The Voyeur's Gaze*. London: Sage Publications.

Dermody, Susan and Elizabeth Jacka 1988. *The Screening of Australia, ii: Anatomy of a National Cinema*. Sydney: Currency Press.

Derrida, Jacques 1976. *Of Grammatology*. Trans. Gayatri Chakravorty Spivak. Baltimore: Johns Hopkins University Press.

——1978. *Writing and Difference*. Trans. Alan Bass. Chicago: University of Chicago.

Desnos, Robert 1923. "Le Rêve et le cinéma," *Paris Journal*, April 27.

Diawara, Manthia 1992. *African Cinema: Politics and Culture*. Bloomington: Indiana University Press.

——(ed.) 1993. *Black American Cinema*. New York: Routledge.

Dienst, Richard 1994. *Still Life in Real Time: Theory after Television*. Durham, NC: Duke University Press.

Dissanayake, Wimal (ed.) 1988. *Cinema and Cultural Identity: Reflections on Films from Japan, India, and China*. Lanham: University Press of America.

——(ed.) 1993. *Melodrama and Asian Cinema*. Cambridge: Cambridge University Press.

——(ed.) 1994. *Colonialism and Nationalism in Asian Cinema*. Bloomington: Indiana University Press.

Doane, Mary Ann 1987. *The Desire to Desire: The Woman's Film of the 1940's*. Bloomington: Indiana University Press.

Doane, Mary Ann, Patricia Mellencamp, and Linda Williams (eds) 1984. *Revision: Essays in Feminist Film Criticism*. Frederick, MD: University Publications of America.

Donald, James (ed.) 1990. *Psychoanalysis and Cultural Theory: Thresholds*. London: Macmillan.

Dorfman, Ariel 1983. *The Empire's Old Clothes: What the Lone Ranger, Babar, and Other Innocent Heroes do to our Minds*. New York: Pantheon.

Dorfman, Ariel and Armand Mattelart 1975. *How to Read Donald Duck: Imperialist Ideology in the Disney Comic*. London: International General.

Dosse, François 1997. *History of Structuralism*, 2 vols. Trans. Deborah Glassman. Minneapolis: University of Minnesota Press.

Doty, Alexander 1993. *Making Things Perfectly Queer: Interpreting Mass Culture*. Minneapolis: University of Minnesota Press.

Downing, John D. H. (ed.) 1987. *Film and Politics in the Third World*. New York: Praeger.

Dreyfus, Hubert L. and Paul Rabinow (eds) 1982. *Michel Foucault: Beyond Structuralism and Hermeneutics*. Brighton: Harvester.

Drummond, Phillip, et al. (eds) 1979. *Film as Film: Formal Experiment in Film 1910–1975*. London: Arts Council of Great Britain.

Ducrot, Oswald and Tzvetan Todorov (eds) 1972. *Encyclopedic Dictionary of the Sciences of Language*. Trans. Catherine Porter. Baltimore: Johns Hopkins University Press.

Duhamel, Georges 1931. *America, the Menace: Scenes from the Life of the Future*. Trans. Charles M. Thompson. Boston: Houghton Mifflin.

Dyer, Richard 1986. *Heavenly Bodies: Film Stars and Society*. New York: St. Martin's Press.

—— 1990. *Now You See It: Studies on Lesbian and Gay Film*. New York: Routledge.

—— 1993. *The Matter of Images: Essays on Representations*. London: Routledge.

—— 1997a. *Stars*, 2nd revd edn. London: British Film Institute.

—— 1997b. *White*. London: Routledge.

Eagle, Herbert (ed.) 1981. *Russian Formalist Film Theory*. Ann Arbor: Michigan Slavic Publications.

Easthope, Anthony 1986. *What a Man's Gotta Do: The Masculine Myth in Popular Culture*. London: Paladin.

—— (ed.) 1993. *Contemporary Film Theory*. London: Longman.

Eco, Umberto 1975. *A Theory of Semiotics*. Bloomington: Indiana University Press.

—— 1979. *The Role of the Reader: Explorations in the Semiotics of Texts*. Bloomington: Indiana University Press.

—— 1984. *Semiotics and the Philosophy of Language*. Bloomington: Indiana University Press.

Ehrlich, Victor 1981. *Russian Formalism: History–Doctrine*. London: Yale University Press.

Eikhenbaum, Boris (ed.) 1982. *The Poetics of Cinema*. In *Russian Poetics in Translation*, Vol. 9, trans. Richard Taylor. Oxford: RPT Publications.

Eisenstein, Sergei 1957. *Film Form and Film Sense*. Cleveland: Merieian.

—— 1988. *Selected Works, Vol. 1: Writings 1922–1934*. Trans. and ed. Richard Taylor. Bloomington: Indiana University Press.

—— 1992. *Selected Works, Vol. 2: Towards a Theory of Montage*. Trans. Michael Glenny, ed. Richard Taylor and Michael Glenny. Bloomington: Indiana University Press.

Eisler, Hans and Theodor W. Adorno 1947. *Composing for the Films*. New York: Oxford University Press.

Ellis, John 1992. *Visible Fictions: Cinema, Television, Video*, 2nd edn. London: Routledge & Kegan Paul.

Elsaesser, Thomas 1973. "Tales of Sound and Fury: Observation on the Family Melodrama," *Monogram* No. 4.

—— 1989. *New German Cinema: A History*. New Brunswick: Rutgers University Press.

—— (ed.) 1990. *Early Cinema Space, Frame, Narrative*. London: British Film Insitute Publishing.

Enzensberger, Hans Magnus 1974. *The Consciousness Industry: On Literature, Politics & the Media*. New York: Seabury Press.

Epko, Denis 1995. "Towards a Post-Africanism," *Textual Practice* No. 9 (Spring).

Epstein, Jean 1974–5. *Écrits sur le cinéma, 1921–1953: édition chronologique en deux volumes*. Paris: Seghers.

—— 1977. "Magnification and Other Writings," *October* No. 3 (Spring).

Erens, Patricia 1979. *Sexual Stratagems: The World of Women in Film*. New York: Horizon.

—— 1984. *The Jew in American Cinema*. Bloomington: Indiana University Press.

—— (ed.) 1990. *Issues in Feminist Film Criticism*. Bloomington: Indiana University Press.

Fanon, Frantz 1963. *The Wretched of the Earth*. Trans. Constance Farrington. New York: New Grove Press.

—— 1965. *Studies in a Dying Colonialism*. New York: Monthly Review Press.

—— 1967a. *Black Skin, White Masks*. New York: Grove Press.

—— 1967b. *Toward the African Revolution*. New York: Monthly Review Press.

Fell, John L. 1974. *Film and the Narrative Tradition*. Norman: University of Oklahoma Press.

Ferro, Marc 1985. *Cinema and History*. Berkeley: University of California Press.

Feuer, Jane 1993. *The Hollywood Musical*, 2nd edn. Bloomington: Indiana University Press.

Fischer, Lucy 1989. *Shot/Countershot: Film Tradition and Women's Cinema*. Princeton: Princeton University Press.

Fiske, John 1987. *Television Culture*. London: Methuen.

—— 1989a. *Understanding Popular Culture*. Boston: Unwin Hyman.

—— 1989b. *Reading The Popular*. Boston: Unwin Hyman.

Fiske, John and John Hartley 1978. *Reading Television*. London: Methuen.

Flinn, Caryl 1992. *Strains of Utopia: Gender, Nostalgia, and Hollywood Film Music*. Princeton: Princeton University Press.

Flitterman-Lewis, Sandy 1990. *To Desire Differently: Feminism and the French Cinema*. Urbana: University of Illinois Press.

Forgacs, David and Robert Lumley (eds) 1996. *Italian Cultural Studies: An Introduction*. New York: Oxford University Press.

Foster, Hal 1983. *The Anti-Aesthetic: Essays on Postmodern Culture*. Port Townsend: Bay Press.

Foucault, Michel 1971. *The Order of Things: An Archeology of the Human Sciences*. New York: Pantheon.

—— 1978. *The History of Sexuality*. New York: Pantheon.

—— 1979. *Discipline and Punishment: Birth of the Prison*. New York: Vintage.

Frank, Lisa and Paul Smith (eds) 1993. *Madonnarama: Essays on Sex and Popular Culture*. Pittsburgh: Cleiss Press.

Freeland, Cynthia A. and Thomas E. Wartenberg (eds) 1995. *Philosophy and Film*. New York: Routledge.

Fregoso, Rosa Linda 1993. *The Bronze Screen: Chicana and Chicano Film Culture*. Minneapolis: University of Minnesota Press.

Freud, Sigmund 1954. *The Origins of Psychoanalysis: Letters to Wilhelm Fleiss*, Trans. Eric Mosbacher and James Strachey. New York: Basic Books.

—— 1958. *On Creativity and the Unconscious*. Trans. Joan Riviere. New York: Harper and Row.

—— 1959. *Beyond the Pleasure Principle*. Trans. James Strachey. New York: Bantam.

—— 1963a. *Sexuality and the Psychology of Love*. New York: Collier Books.

—— 1963b. *Three Case Histories*. New York: Collier Books.

—— 1965. *New Introductory Lectures*. Trans. W. J. H. Sprott. New York: W. W. Norton.

Friar, Ralph E. and Natasha A. Friar 1972. *The Only Good Indian: The Hollywood Gospel*. New York: Drama Book Specialist.

Friedan, Betty 1963. *The Feminine Mystique*. New York: Norton.

Friedberg, Anne 1993. *Window Shopping: Cinema and the Postmodern*. Berkeley: University of California Press.

Friedman, Lester 1982. *Hollywood's Image of the Jew*. New York: Ungar.

—— (ed.) 1991a. *Unspeakable Images: Ethnicity and the American Cinema*. Chicago: University of Illinois Press.

—— 1991b. *American Cinema*. Urbana: University of Illinois Press.

Fusco, Coco 1987. *Reviewing Histories: Selections from New Latin American Cinema*. Buffalo: Hallwalls.

—— 1988. *Young British and Black*. Buffalo: Hallwalls.

Fuss, Diana 1989. *Essentially Speaking: Feminism, Nature and Difference*. New York: Routledge.

—— 1991. *Inside/ Out: Lesbian Theories, Gay Theories*. New York: Routledge.

Gabbard, Krin and Glen O. Gabbard 1989. *Psychiatry and the Cinema*. Chicago: University of Chicago Press.

Gabriel, Teshome H. 1982. *Third Cinema in the Third World: The Aesthetics of Liberation*. Ann Arbor: UMI Research Press.

Gaines, Jane 1991. *Contested Culture: The Image, the Voice, and the Law*. Chapel Hill: University of North Carolina Press.

—— (ed.) 1992. *Classical Hollywood Narrative: The Paradigm Wars*. Durham, NC: Duke University Press.

Gaines, Jane and Charlotte Herzog (eds) 1990. *Fabrications: Costume and the Female Body*. London: Routledge.

Gamman, Lorraine and Margaret Marshment (eds) 1988. *The Female Gaze: Women as Viewers of Popular Culture*. London: Women's Press.

Garber, Marjorie 1992. *Vested Interests: Cross-Dressing and Cultural Anxiety*. New York: Routledge.

Garcia, Berumen and Frank Javier 1995. *The Chicano/ Hispanic Image in American Film*. New York: Vantage Press.

Garroni, Emilio 1972. *Progetto di Semiotica*. Bari: Laterza.

Gates, Jr., Henry Louis 1984. *Black Literature and Literary Theory*. London and New York: Methuen.

—— (ed.) 1986. *"Race," Writing, and Difference*. Chicago: University of Chicago Press.

—— 1987. *Figures in Black*. New York: Oxford University Press.

—— 1988. *The Signifying Monkey*. New York: Oxford University Press.

Gaudreault, André and François Jost 1990. *Le Récit cinématographique*. Paris: Nathan.

Gehring, Wes (ed.) 1988. *Handbook of American Film Genres*. Westport: Greenwood Press.

Genette, Gérard 1976. *Mimologiques: voyages en cratylie*. Paris: Seuil.

—— 1980. *Narrative Discourse: An Essay in Method*. Ithaca, NY: Cornell University Press.

—— 1982a. *Figures of Literary Discourse*. New York: Columbia University Press.

—— 1982b. *Palimpsestes: la littérature au second degré*. Paris: Seuil.

Gever, Martha, John Greyson, and Pratibha Parmar (eds) 1993. *Queer Looks: Perspectives on Lesbian and Gay Film Videos.* New York: Routledge.

Gidal, Peter (ed.) 1978. *Structural Film Anthology.* London: British Film Institute.

——1989. *Materialist Film.* London: Routledge.

Gledhill, Christine (ed.) 1987. *Home is Where the Heart Is: Studies in Melodrama and the Woman's Film.* London: British Film Institute.

——(ed.) 1991. *Stardom: Industry of Desire.* London: Routledge.

Godard, Jean-Luc 1958. "Bergmanorama," *Les Cahiers du cinéma*, No. 85 (July).

Gorbman, Claudia 1987. *Unheard Melodies: Narrative Film Music.* Bloomington: Indiana University Press; London: British Film Institute.

Gramsci, Antonio 1992. *Prison Notebooks.* New York: Columbia University Press.

Grant, Barry Keith (ed.) 1986. *The Film Genre Reader.* Austin: University of Texas Press.

——(ed.) 1995. *Film Genre Reader II.* Austin: University of Texas Press.

Grant, Barry Keith and Jeannette Sloniowski (eds) 1998. *Documenting the Documentary: Close Readings of Documentary Film and Video.* Detroit: Wayne State University Press.

Greenaway, Peter 1998. "Virtual Irreality," *Cinemais*, No. 13, Sept./Oct.

Greenberg, Harvey Roy 1993. *Screen Memories: Hollywood Cinema on the Psychoanalytic Couch.* New York: Columbia University Press.

Greimas, Algirdas Julien. *Du Sens.* Paris: Seuil.

Griffin, Gabrielle and Andermahr, Sonya (eds) 1997. *Straight Studies Modified: Lesbian Interventions in the Academy.* London: Cassell.

Grodal, Torben Krogh 1997. *Moving Pictures: A New Theory of Film Genres, Feelings, and Cognition.* Oxford: Oxford University Press.

Gross, Larry, John Stuart Katz, and Jay Ruby (eds) 1988. *Image Ethics: The Moral Rights of Subjects in Photographs, Film, and Television.* New York: Oxford University Press.

Grossberg, Lawrence W., Cary Nelson, and Paula A. Treicheler (eds) 1992. *Cultural Studies.* New York: Routledge.

Guerrero, Ed 1993. *Framing Blackness: The African American Image in Film.* Philadelphia: Temple University Press.

Gunning, Tom 1990. *D. W. Griffith and the Origins of American Narrative Film.* Champaign: University of Illinois Press.

Gurevitch, Michael, Tony Bennett, James Curran, and Janet Woollacott (eds) 1982. *Culture, Society and the Media.* London: Routledge.

Guzzetti, Alfred 1981. *Two or Three Things I Know About Her: Analysis of a Film by Godard.* Cambridge, MA: Harvard University Press.

Hall, Stuart and Paul du Gay (eds) 1996. *Questions of Cultural Identity.* London: Sage Publications.

Hall, Stuart, Dorothy Hobson, Andrew Lowe, and Paul Willis (eds) 1980. *Culture, Media, Language.* London: Hutchinson.

Hammond, Paul (ed.) 1978. *The Shadow and its Shadow: Surrealist Writings on the Cinema.* London: British Film Institute.

Handel, Leo 1950. *Hollywood Looks at its Audience.* Urbana: University of Illinois Press.

Hansen, Miriam 1991. *Babel and Babylon: Spectatorship in American Silent Film.* Cambridge, MA: Harvard University Press.

Harding, Colin and Simon Popple (eds) 1997. *In the Kingdom of Shadows: A Companion to the Early Cinema.* Madison: Fairleigh Dickenson University Press.

Harvey, Sylvia 1978. *May '68 and Film Culture.* London: British Film Institute.

Haskell, Molly 1987. *From Reverence To Rape: The Treatment of Women in the Movies*, 2nd edn. New York: Holt, Rinehart and Winston.

Hays, Michael and Anastasia Nikolopoulou (eds) 1996. *Melodrama: The Cultural Emergence of a Genre*. New York: St. Martin's Press.

Hayward, Phillip and Tana Wollen (eds) 1993. *Future Visions: New Technologies of the Screen*. London: British Film Institute.

Hayward, Susan 1996. *Key Concepts in Cinema Studies*. London: Routledge.

Heath, Stephen 1981. *Questions of Cinema*. Bloomington: Indiana University Press.

—— 1982. *The Sexual Fix*. London: MacMillan.

Heath, Stephen and Teresa de Lauretis (eds) 1980. *The Cinematic Apparatus*. London: MacMillan.

Heath, Stephen and Patricia Mellencamp (eds) 1983. *Cinema and Language*. Frederick, MD: University Publications of America.

Hebdige, Dick, 1979. *Subculture: The Meaning of Style*. London: Methuen.

—— 1988. *Hiding in the Light: On Images and Things*. London: Routledge.

Hedges, Inez 1991. *Breaking the Frame: Film Language and the Experience of Limits*. Bloomington: Indiana University Press.

Henderson, Brian 1980. *A Critique of Film Theory*. New York: E. P. Dutton.

Hervey, Sandor G. J. 1982. *Semiotic Perspectives*. London: Allen & Unwin.

Hilger, Michael 1986. *The American Indian in Film*. Metuchen, NJ: Scarecrow Press.

—— 1995. *From Savage to Nobleman: Images of Native Americans in Film*. Lanham: Scarecrow Press.

Hill, John and Pamela Church Gibson (eds) 1998. *The Oxford Guide to Film Studies*. Oxford: Oxford University Press.

Hillier, Jim (ed.) 1985. *Cahiers du cinéma: The 1950s: Neo-Realism, Hollywood, New Wave*. Cambridge, MA: Harvard University Press.

Hobsbawm, E. J. and Ranger, Terrence (eds) 1983. *The Intervention of Tradition*. Cambridge: Cambridge University Press.

Hockings, Paul (ed.) 1975. *Principles of Visual Anthropology*. The Hague: De Gruyter.

Hodge, Robert and Gunther Kress 1988. *Social Semiotics*. Ithaca, NY: Cornell University Press.

Hollows, Joanne and Mark Jancovich (eds) 1995. *Approaches to Popular Film*. Manchester: Manchester University Press.

hooks, bell 1992. *Black Looks: Race and Representation*. Boston: South End Press.

—— 1996. *Reel to Real: Race, Sex and Class at the Movies*. New York: Routledge.

Horton, Andrew and Stuart Y. McDougal, (eds) 1998. *Play It Again, Sam: Retakes on Remakes*. Berkeley: University of California Press.

Humm, Magie 1997. *Feminism and Film*. Bloomington: Indiana University Press.

Hutcheon, Linda 1988. *A Poetics of Postmodernism: History, Theory, Fiction*. New York: Routledge.

Irigaray, Luce 1985a. *Speculum of the Other Woman*. Trans. Gillian C. Gill. Ithaca, NY: Cornell University Press.

—— 1985b. *This Sex Which Is Not One*. Trans. Catherine Porter with Carolyn Burke. Ithaca, NY: Cornell University Press.

Jackson, Jr., Earl 1995. *Strategies of Deviance: Studies in Gay Male Representation*. Bloomington: Indiana University Press.

Jacobs, Lewis 1960. *An Introduction to the Art of the Movies*. New York: Noonday.

Jakobson, Roman 1971. *Selected Writings*. The Hague: Mouton Press.

Jakobson, Roman and Morris Halle 1956. *Fundamentals of Language*. The Hague: Mouton Press.

James, David E. 1989. *Allegories of Cinema: American Film in the Sixties*. Princeton: Princeton University Press.

James, David E. and Rick Berg (eds) 1996. *The Hidden Foundation: Cinema and the Question of Class*. Minneapolis: University of Minnesota Press.

Jameson, Fredric 1972. *The Prison-house of Language: A Critical Account of Structuralism and Russian Formalism*. Princeton: Princeton University Press.

—— 1981. *The Political Unconscious: Narrative as a Socially Symbolic Act*. Ithaca, NY: Cornell University Press.

—— 1986. "Third World Literature in the Era of Multinational Capitalism," *Social Text* No. 15 (Fall).

—— 1991. *Postmodernism, or, The Cultural Logic of Late Capitalism*. Durham, NC: Duke University Press.

—— 1992. *The Geopolitical Aesthetic: Cinema and Space in the World System*. Bloomington: Indiana University Press.

—— 1998. *The Cultural Turn: Selected Writings on the Postmodern 1983–1998*. London: Verso.

Jarvie, Ian 1970. *Sociology of the Movies*. New York: Basic.

—— 1978. *Movies as Social Criticism*. Metuchen: Scarecrow Press.

—— 1987. *Philosophy of the Film: Epistemology, Ontology, Aesthetics*. New York: Routledge and Kegan Paul.

Jay, Martin 1994. *Downcast Eyes: The Denigration of Vision in Twentieth Century French Thought*. Berkeley: University of California Press.

Jeancolas, Jean-Pierre 1995. *Histoire du cinéma Français*. Paris: Nathan.

Jeffords, Susan 1994. *Hard Bodies: Hollywood Masculinity in the Reagan Era*. New Brunswick: Rutgers University Press.

Jenkins, Henry 1992. *What Made Pistachio Nuts? Early Sound Comedy and the Vaudeville Aesthetic*. New York: Columbia University Press.

Jenkins, Henry and Kristine Brunovska Karnick (eds) 1994. *Classical Hollywood Comedy*. New York: Routledge.

Jenks, Chris (ed.) 1995. *Visual Culture*. London: Routledge.

Johnson, Randal and Robert Stam (eds) 1982 *Brazilian Cinema*. Rutherford, NJ: Fairleigh Dickinson University Press. (Republished Texas 1987, Columbia University Press 1994.)

Johnston, Claire 1973. *Notes on Women's Cinema*. London: Society for Education in Film and Television.

—— (ed.) 1975. *The Work of Dorothy Arzner: Toward a Feminist Cinema*. London: British Film Institute.

Jost, François 1987. *L'Oeil – camera: entre film et roman*. Lyon: Presses Universitaires de Lyon.

Jullier, Laurent 1997. *L'Ecran post-moderne: un cinéma de l'allusion et du feu d'artifice*. Paris: L'Hartmattan.

Kabir, Shameem 1997. *Daughters of Desire: Lesbian Representations in Film*. London: Casell Academic.

Kael, Pauline 1963/1966. *I Lost it at the Movies*. New York: Bantam.

Kaes, Anton 1989. *From Hitler to Heimat: The Return of History as Film*. Cambridge, MA: Harvard University Press.

Kalinak, Kathryn 1992. *Settling the Score: Music and the Classical Hollywood Film*. Madison: University of Wisconsin Press.

Kaminsky, Stuart M. 1974. *American Film Genres: Approaches to a Critical Theory of Popular Film*. Dayton: Pflaum.

Kaplan, E. Ann (ed.) 1988. *Postmodernism and its Discontents: Theories and Practices*. London: Verso.

—— 1990. *Psychoanalysis and the Cinema*. London: Routledge.

—— 1997. *Looking for the Other*. London: Routledge.

—— (ed.) 1998. *Women in Film Noir*, 4th edn. London: British Film Institute.

Kay, Karyn and Gerald Pear (eds) 1977. *Women and the Cinema*. New York: E. P. Dutton.

Kellner, Douglas 1995. *Media Culture*. London: Routledge.

King, John, Ana M. Lopez, and Manuel Alvarado (eds) 1993. *Mediating Two Worlds: Cinematic Encounters in the Americas*. London: British Film Institute.

Kipnis, Laura 1993. *Ecstasy Unlimited: On Sex, Capital, Gender and Aesthetics*. Minneapolis: Minnesota University Press.

—— 1996. *Bound and Gagged: Pornography and the Politics of Fantasy in America*. New York: Grove.

Kirkham, Pat and Janet Thumin (eds) 1993. *You Tarzan: Masculinity, Movies, and Men*. New York: St. Martin's Press.

Kitses, Jim 1969. *Horizons West*. London: Secker and Warburg/British Film Institute.

Klinger, Barbara 1994. *Melodrama and Meaning: History, Culture and the Films of Douglas Sirk*. Bloomington: Indiana University Press.

Koch, Walter A. 1971. *Varia Semiotica*. Hidesheim: Olms.

Kozloff, Sarah 1988. *Invisible Storytellers*. Berkeley: University of California Press.

Kracauer, Siegfried 1947. *From Caligari to Hitler: A Psychological History of the German Film*. Princeton: Princeton University Press.

—— 1965. *Theory of Film: The Redemption of Physical Reality*. New York: Oxford University Press.

—— 1995. *The Mass Ornament: Weimar Essays*. Trans. and ed. Thomas Y. Levin. Cambridge, MA: Harvard University Press.

Kress, Gunther and Theo van Leeuwen 1996. *Reading Images: The Grammar of Visual Design*. London: Routledge.

Kristeva, Julia 1969. *Semeiotike: récherches pour une sémanalyse*. Paris: Seuil.

—— 1980. *Desire in Language: A Semiotic Approach to Literature and Art*. Trans. Thomas Gora, Alice Jardine, and Leon S. Roudiez. New York: Columbia University Press.

—— 1984. *Revolution in Poetic Language*. Trans. Margaret Waller. New York: Columbia University Press.

Krutnik, Frank 1991. *In a Lonely Street: Film Noir, Genre, Masculinity*. London: Routledge.

Kuhn, Annette 1982. *Women's Pictures: Feminism and Cinema*. London: Routledge.

—— 1985. *The Power of the Image: Essays on Representation and Sexuality*. London: Routledge and Kegan Paul.

Kuhn, Annette and Susannah Radstone (eds) 1990. *Women in Film: An International Guide*. New York: Fawcett Columbine.

Kuleshov, Lev 1974. *Kuleshov on Film: Writings of Lev Kuleshov*. Trans. and ed. Ronald Levaco. Berkeley: University of California Press.

Lacan, Jacques 1977. *Écrits: A Selection*. Trans. Alan Sheridan. New York: W. W. Norton.

—— 1978. *The Four Fundamentals of Psycho-Analysis*. Trans. Alan Sheridan. New York: W. W. Norton.

Lagny, Michele 1976. *La Révolution figurée: film, histoire, politique*. Paris: Albatross.

—— 1992. *De l'histoire du cinéma: méthode historique et histoire du cinéma*. Paris: Armand Colin.

Lagny, Michele, Marie-Claire Ropars, and Pierre Sorlin 1976. *Octobre: écriture et idéologie*. Paris: Albatross.

Landow, George P. (ed.) 1994. *Hyper/ Text/ Theory*. Baltimore: Johns Hopkins University Press.

Landy, Marcia (ed.) 1991. *Imitations of Life: A Reader on Film and Television Melodrama*. Detroit: Wayne State University Press.

—— 1994. *Film, Politics and Gramsci*. Minneapolis: University of Minnesota Press.

—— 1996. *Cinematic Uses of the Past*. Minneapolis: University of Minnesota Press.

Lang, Robert 1989. *American Film Melodrama*. Princeton: Princeton University Press.

Langer, Suzanne 1953. *Feeling and Form*. New York: Scribner.

Lapierre, Marcel 1946. *Anthologie du cinéma*. Paris: La Nouvelle Edition.

Laplanche, J. and J. B. Pontalis 1978. *The Language of Psycho-Analysis*. Trans. Donald Nicholson-Smith. New York: Norton.

Lapsley, Robert and Michael Westlake 1988. *Film Theory: An Introduction*. Manchester: Manchester University Press.

Lawrence, Amy 1991. *Echo and Narcissus: Women's Voices in Classical Hollywood*. Berkeley: University of California Press.

Lebeau, Vicky 1994. *Lost Angels: Psychoanalysis and Cinema*. London: Routledge.

Lebel, J. P. 1971. *Cinéma et idéologie*. Paris: Editions Sociales.

Lehman, Peter. (ed.) 1990. *Close Viewings: An Anthology of New Film Criticism*. Sarasota: University of Florida Press.

—— 1993. *Running Scared: Masculinity and the Representation of the Male Body*. Philadelphia: Temple University Press.

—— 1997. (ed.) *Defining Cinema*. New Brunswick: Rutgers University Press.

—— 1998. "Reply to Stuart Minnis," *Cinema Journal* 37, No. 2 (Winter)

Lemon, Lee T. and Marion J. Reis (eds) 1965. *Russian Formalist Criticism: Four Essays*. Lincoln: Nebraska University Press.

Lev, Peter 1993. *The Euro-American Cinema*. Austin: University of Texas Press.

Lévi-Strauss, Claude 1967. *Structural Anthropology*. Trans. Claire Jacobson and Brooke Grundfest Schoepf. Garden City, NY: Doubleday.

—— 1990. *The Raw and the Cooked*. Trans. John and Doreen Weightman. Chicago: University of Chicago Press.

Lewis, Jon 1992. *The Road to Romance and Ruin: Teen Films and Youth Culture*. New York: Routledge.

L'Herbier, Marcel 1946. *Intelligence du cinématographe*. Paris: Ed. Correa.

L'Herminier, Pierre 1960. *L'Art du cinéma*. Paris: Seghers.

Liebman 1980. *Jean Epstein's Early Film Theory, 1920–1922*. Ann Arbor: University Microfilms.

Lindermann, Bernhard 1977. *Experimentalfilm als Metafilm*. Hildesheim: Olms.

Lindsay, Vachel 1922. *The Art of the Moving Image*. New York: MacMillan.

Lipsitz, George 1998. *The Possessive Investment in Whiteness: How White People Profit From Identity Politics*. Philadelphia: Temple University Press.

Lister, Martin (ed.) 1995. *The Photographic Image in Digital Culture*. London: Routledge.

Loisoz, Peter 1992. *Innovation in Ethnographic Film: From Innocence to Self-Consciousness, 1955–1985*. Chicago: University of Chicago Press.

Lotman, Juri 1976. *Semiotics of Cinema*. Trans. Mark E. Suino. Ann Arbor: Michigan Slavic Contributions.

Lovell, Terry 1980. *Pictures of Reality: Aesthetics, Politics and Pleasure*. London: British Film Institute.

Lowry, Edward 1985. *The Filmology Movement and Film Study in France*. Ann Arbor: UMI.

Lyotard, Jean-François 1984. *The Postmodern Condition*. Trans. Geoff Bennington and Brian Massumi. Minnesota: University of Minnesota Press.

MacCabe, Colin 1985. *Tracking the Signifier: Theoretical Essays: Film, Linguistics, Literature*. Minneapolis: University of Minnesota Press.

——(ed.) 1986. *High Theory/Low Culture: Analyzing Popular Television and Film*. New York: St. Martin's Press.

MacDonald, Scott 1993. *Avant-Garde Film: Motion Studies*. Cambridge: Cambridge University Press.

Machado, Arlindo 1997. *Pre-Cinema e Pos-Cinemas*. São Paulo: Papirus.

Macharey, Pierre 1978. *Theory of Literary Production*. Trans. Geoffrey Wall. London: Routledge.

Manchel, Frank 1992. *Film Study: Analytical Bibliography Vols. 1–4*. Madison: Fairleigh Dickinson University Press.

Mannoni, Octave 1969. *Clefs pour l'imaginaire*. Paris: Editions du Seuil.

Marchetti, Gina 1994. *Romance and the "Yellow Peril": Race, Sex, and Discursive Strategies in Hollywood Fiction*. Berkeley: University of California Press.

Marie, Michel and Marc Vernet 1990. *Christian Metz et la théorie du cinéma*. Paris: Meridiens Klincksieck.

Marks, Elaine and Isabelle de Courtivron (eds) 1980. *New French Feminisms*. Amherst: University of Massachusetts Press.

Martin, Michael T. 1993. *Cinemas of the Black Diaspora: Diversity, Dependence and Oppositionality*. Detroit: Wayne State University Press.

——(ed.) 1997. *New Latin American Cinema*, 2 vols. Detroit: Wayne State University Press.

Masson, Alain 1994. *Le Récit au cinéma*. Paris: Editions de l'Etoile.

Matejka, Ladislav and Irwin R. Titunik (eds) 1976. *Semiotics of Art: Prague School Contributions*. Cambridge, MA: MIT Press.

Mattelart, Armand and Michele Mattelart 1992. *Rethinking Media Theory: Signposts and New Directions*. Trans. James A. Cohen and Marina Urquidi. Minneapolis: University of Minnesota Press.

——1994. *Mapping World Communication: War, Progress, Culture*. Trans. Susan Emanuel and James A. Cohen. Minneapolis: University of Minnesota Press.

Mauduy, J. and G. Henriet 1989. *Geographies du western*. Editions Nathan.

Mayne, Judith 1987. *Private Novels, Public Films*. Atlanta: University of Georgia Press.

—— 1989. *Kino and the Woman Question: Feminism and Soviet Silent Film*. Columbus: Ohio State University Press.

—— 1990. *The Woman at the Keyhole: Feminism and Women's Cinema*. Bloomington: Indiana University Press.

—— 1993. *Cinema and Spectatorship*. London: Routledge.

—— 1995. *Directed by Dorthy Arzner*. Bloomington: Indiana University Press.

Mellen, Joan 1974. *Women and their Sexuality in the New Film*. New York: Dell.

Mellencamp, Patricia 1990. *Indiscretions: Avant-Garde Film, Video and Feminism*. Bloomington: Indiana University Press.

—— 1995. *A Fine Romance: Five Ages of Film Feminism*. Philadelphia: Temple University Press.

Mellencamp, Patricia and Philip Rosen (eds) 1984. *Cinema Histories/Cinema Practices*. Frederick, MD: University Publications of America.

Mercer, Kobena and Isaac Julien 1988. "Introduction: De Margin and De Center," *Screen* Vol. 29, No. 4.

Merck, Mandy (ed.) 1992. *The Sexual Subject: Screen Reader in Sexuality*. New York: Routledge.

Merquior, J. G. 1986. *From Prague to Paris*. London: Verso.

Messaris, Paul 1994. *Visuals Literacy: Image, Mind, and Reality*. Boulder: Westview Press.

Metz, Christian 1972. *Essais sur la signification au cinéma*. Paris: Editions Klincksieck

—— 1974a. *Film Language: A Semiotics of the Cinema*. Trans. Michael Taylor. New York: Oxford University Press.

—— 1974b. *Language and Cinema*. Trans. Donna Jean. The Hague: Mouton.

—— 1977. *Essais sémiotiques*. Paris: Klincksieck.

—— 1982. *The Imaginary Signifier: Psychoanalysis and the Cinema*. Trans. Celia Britton, Annwyl Williams, Ben Brewster, and Alfred Guzzetti. Bloomington: Indiana University Press.

—— 1991. *La Naration impersonelle, ou le site du film*. Paris: Klincksieck.

Michelson, Annette 1972. "*The Man With the Movie Camera*: From Magician to Epistemologist," *Artforum* (March).

—— 1984. Introduction to *Kino-Eye: The Writing of Dziga Vertov*. Berkeley: University of California Press.

—— 1990 "The Kinetic Icon in the Work of Mourning: Prolegomena to the Analysis of a Textual System," *October* 52 (Spring).

Miller, Randall (ed.) 1980. *The Kaleidoscopic Lens: How Hollywood Views Ethnic Groups*. Englewood, NJ: Jerome S. Ozer.

Miller, Toby 1993. *The Well-Tempered Self: Citizenship, Culture, and the Postmodern Subject*. Baltimore: Johns Hopkins University Press.

—— 1998. *Technologies of Truth: Cultural Citizenship and the Popular Media*. Minneapolis: University of Minnesota.

Miller, Toby and Robert Stam (eds) 1999. *Film Theory: A Companion*. Oxford: Blackwell Publishers.

Mirzoeff, Nicholas (ed.) 1998. *Visual Culture Reader*. London: Routledge.

Mitchell, Juliet 1974. *Psychoanalysis and Feminism*. New York: Vintage.

Mitchell, Juliet and Jacqueline Rose (eds) 1982. *Feminine Sexuality: Jacques Lacan and the Ecole Freudienne*. New York: W. W. Norton.

Mitchell, William J. 1992. *The Reconfigured Eye: Visual Truth in the Post-Photographic Era.* Cambridge, MA: MIT Press.

Mitry, Jean 1963, 1965. *Esthetique et psychologie du cinéma*, 2 vols. Paris: Ed. Universitares.

—— 1987. *La Sémiologie en question: language et cinéma.* Paris: Les Editions du Cerf.

—— 1997. *The Aesthetics and Psychology of the Cinema.* Trans. Christopher King. Bloomington: Indiana University Press.

Modleski, Tania 1988. *The Women Who Knew Too Much.* New York: Methuen.

—— 1991. *Feminism Without Women: Culture and Criticism in a "Postfeminist" Age.* New York: Routledge.

Moller-Nap, Karl-Dietmar 1986. *Fimsprache.* Munster: Maks.

Monaco, James 1981. *How to Read a Film: The Art, Technology, Language, History, and Theory of Film and Media*, revd edn. New York: Oxford University Press.

Mora, Carl J. 1988. *Mexican Cinema: Reflections of a Society 1896–1988.* Berkeley: University of California Press.

Morin, Edgar 1958. *Le Cinéma ou l'homme imaginaire: essai d'anthropologie.* Paris: Editions de Minuit.

—— 1960. *The Stars: An Account of the Star-System in Motion Pictures.* Trans. Richard Howard. New York: Grove Press.

Morley, David 1980. *The Nationwide Audience: Structure and Decoding.* London: British Film Institute.

—— 1992. *Television Audiences and Cultural Studies.* London: Routledge.

Morley, David and Kuan-Hsing Chen (eds) 1996. *Stuart Hall: Critical Dialogues in Cultural Studies.* London: Routledge.

Morse, Margaret 1998. *Virtualities: Television, Media Art and Cyber-Cultures.* Bloomington: Indiana University Press.

Mukarovsky, Jan 1936/1970. *Aesthetic Function, Norm and Value as Social Facts.* Ann Arbor: University of Michigan.

Mulvey, Laura 1989. *Visual and Other Pleasures.* Bloomington: Indiana University Press.

—— 1996. *Fetishism and Curiosity.* Bloomington: Indiana University Press.

Munsterberg, Hugo 1970. *Film: A Psychological Study.* New York: Dover.

Murray, Janet H. 1997. *Hamlet on the Holodeck: The Future of Narrative in Cyberspace.* Cambridge, MA: MIT Press.

Naficy, Hamid 1993. *The Making of Exile Cultures: Iranian Television in Los Angeles.* Minneapolis: University of Minnesota Press.

Naremore, James 1988. *Acting in the Cinema.* Berkeley: University of California Press.

—— 1998. *On the Dark Side.* Berkeley: University of California Press.

Naremore, James and Patrick Brantlinger (eds) 1991. *Modernity and Mass Culture.* Bloomington: Indiana University Press.

Nattiez, J. J. 1975. *Fondéments d'une sémiologie de la musique.* Paris: Union Generale d'Editions.

Neale, Steve 1979–80. "The Same Old Story: Sterotypes and Difference," *Screen Education* Nos. 32–3 (Autumn/Winter).

—— 1980. *Genre.* London: British Film Institute.

—— 1985. *Cinema and Technology: Image, Sound, Colour.* Bloomington: Indiana University Press.

Neupert, Richard 1995. *The End: Narration and Closure in the Cinema.* Detroit: Wayne State University Press.

Nichols, Bill 1981. *Ideology and the Image*. Bloomington: Indiana University Press.

——(ed.) 1985. *Movies and Methods*, 2 vols. Berkeley: University of California Press.

——1991. *Representing Reality*. Bloomington: Indiana University Press.

Nochlin, Linda 1971. *Realism*. Harmondsworth: Penguin.

Noguez, Dominique 1973. *Cinéma: théorie, lectures*. Paris: Klincksieck.

Noriega, Chon A. (ed.) 1992. *Chicanos and Film: Essays on Chicano Representation and Resistance*. Minneapolis: University of Minnesota Press.

Noriega, Chon A. and Ana M. Lopez (eds) 1996. *The Ethnic Eye: Latino Media Arts*. Minneapolis: University of Minnesota Press.

Norris, Christopher 1982. *Deconstruction: Theory and Practice*. London and New York: Methuen.

——1990. *What's Wrong With Postmodernism: Critical Theory and the Ends of Philosophy*. Baltimore: Johns Hopkins University Press.

——1992. *Uncritical Theory: Postmodernism, Intellectuals, and the Gulf War*. Amherst: University of Massachusetts Press.

Noth, Winfried 1995. *Handbook of Semiotics*. Bloomington: Indiana University Press.

Nowell-Smith, Geoffrey 1967. *Visconti*. London: Secker & Warburg.

O'Sullivan, Danny, John Fiske, John Hartley, and Danny Saunders 1994. *Key Concepts in Communication*, 2nd edn. London and New York: Routledge.

Odin, Roger 1983. "Pour une sémio-pragmatique du cinéma," *Iris* 1, 1.

——1990. *Cinéma et production de sens*. Paris: Armand Colin.

Ory, Pascal and Jean-François Sirinelli 1986. *Les Intellectuels en France, de l'affaire Dreyfus à nos jours*. Paris: Armand Colin.

Pagnol, Marcel 1933. "Dramaturgie de Paris," *Cahiers du film* No. 1 (December 15).

Palmer, R. Bartond (ed.) 1989. *The Cinematic Text: Methods and Approaches*. New York: AMS Press.

Panofsky, Erwin 1939. *Studies in Iconology*. Oxford: Oxford University Press.

Parry, Benita 1994. *Third Text* 28/29 (Autumn/Winter).

Pearson, Roberta 1992. *Eloquent Gestures: The Transformation of Performance Style in the Griffith Biograph Films*. Berkeley: University of California Press.

Pechey, Graham (ed.) 1986. *Literature, Politics and Theory: Papers from the Essex Conference 1976–84*. London: Methuen.

Peirce, Charles Sanders 1931. *Collected Papers*, 8 vols. ed. Charles Hartshorne and Paul Weiss. Cambridge, MA: Harvard University Press.

Penley, Constance (ed.) 1988. *Feminism and Film Theory*. London: Routledge.

——1989. *The Future of an Illusion: Film, Feminism and Psychoanalysis*. Minneapolis: University of Minnesota Press.

Penley, Constance and Sharon Wills (eds) 1993. *Male Trouble*. Minneapolis: University of Minnesota Press.

Perkins, V. F. 1972. *Film as Film: Understanding and Judging Movies*. Harmondsworth: Penguin.

Petro, Patrice 1989. *Joyless Streets, Women and Melodramatic Representation in Weimar Germany*. Princeton: Princeton University Press.

——(ed.) 1995. *Fugitive Images: From Photography to Video*. Bloomington: Indiana University Press.

Pettit, Arthur G. 1980. *Images of the Mexican American in Fiction and Film*. College Station: Texas A & M University Press.

Philippe, Claude-Jean 1983. *La Nouvelle vagues 25 ans après*. Paris: Cerf.

Piaget, Jean 1970. *Structuralism*. Trans. and ed. Chaninah Maschler. New York: Harper/ Colophon.

Pietropaolo, Laura and Ada Testaferri (eds) 1995. *Feminisms in the Cinema*. Bloomington: Indiana University Press.

Pines, Jim and Paul Willemen (eds) 1989. *Questions of Third Cinema*. London: British Film Institute.

Polan, Dana 1985. *The Political Language of Film and the Avant-Garde*. Ann Arbor: UMI Research Press.

—— 1986. *Power and Paranoia: History, Narrative and the American Cinema, 1940–1950*. New York: Columbia University Press.

Pollock, Griselda 1988. *Vision and Difference: Feminism, Femininity, and the History of Art*. London: Routledge.

Powdermaker, Hortense 1950. *Hollywood: The Dream* Factory. Boston: Little Brown.

Prendergast, R. M. 1992. *Film Music: A Neglected Art*, 2nd edn. New York: W. W. Norton.

Presnell, Michael 1983. *Sign, Image, and Desire: Semiotic Phenomenology and the Film Image*. Ann Arbor: UMI.

Pribram, Deidre (ed.) 1988. *Female Spectators: Looking at Film and Television*. London: Verso.

Prince, Gerald 1987. *A Dictionary of Narratology*. Lincoln: University of Nebraska Press.

Propp, Vladimir 1968. *Morphology of the Folktale*. Trans. Laurence Scott. Austin: University of Texas Press.

Pudovkin, V. I. 1960. *Film Technique*. New York: Grove.

Ray, Robert B. 1995. *The Avant-Garde Finds Andy Hardy*. Cambridge, MA: Harvard University Press.

—— 1998. "The Bordwell Regime and the Stake of Knowledge," *Strategies* I (Fall).

Real, Michael R. 1996. *Exploring Media Culture: A Guide*. Thousand Oaks: Sage Publications.

Reeves, Geoffrey 1993. *Communications and the "Third World"*. London: Routledge.

Reid, Mark A. 1993. *Redefining Black Film*. Berkeley: University of California Press.

Renov, Michael (ed.) 1993. *Theorizing Documentary*. New York: Routledge.

Renov, Michael and Erika Suderburg (eds) 1995. *Resolutions: Contemporary Video Practices*. Minneapolis: University of Minnesota Press.

Rich, Adrienne 1979. *On Lies, Secrets, and Silence*. New York: Norton

Rich, Ruby 1992. "New Queer Cinema," *Sight and Sound* (September).

—— 1998. *Chick Flicks: Theories and Memories of the Finest Film Movement*. Durham, NC: Duke University Press.

Riffaterre, Michel 1979. *La Production du texte*. Paris: Seuil.

—— 1982. *Sémiotique de la poésie*. Paris: Seuil.

Rimmon-Kenan, Shlomith 1983. *Narrative Fiction: Contemporary Poetics*. London: Methuen.

Ritchin, Fred 1990. *In Our Own Image: The Coming Revolution in Photography*. New York: Aperature Foundation.

Rocha, Glauber 1963. *Rivisão Critica do Cinema Brasileiro*. Rio de Janeiro: Editora Civilizacão Brasileira.

Rodowick, D. N. 1988. *The Crisis of Political Modernism: Criticism and Ideology in Contemporary Film Theory*. Urbana: University of Illinois Press.

—— 1991. *The Difficulty of Difference: Psychoanalysis, Sexual Difference and Film Theory*. New York: Routledge.

—— 1997. *Deleuze's Time Machine*. Raleigh, NC: Duke University Press.

Rogin, Michael 1996. *Blackface, White Noise: Jewish Immigrants in the Hollywood Melting Pot*. Berkeley: University of California Press.

Romney, Jonathan and Adrian Wooton (eds) 1995. *Celluloid Jukebox: Popular Music and the Movies Since the 50s*. Bloomington: Indiana University Press.

Ropars-Wuilleumier, Marie-Claire 1981. *Le Texte divisé*. Paris: Presses Universitaires de France.

Rose, Jacqueline 1980. "The Cinematic Apparatus: Problems in Current Theory." In Teresa de Lauretis and Stephen Heath (eds) *Feminist Studies/Critical Studies*. New York: St. Martin's Press.

—— 1986. *Sexuality in the Field of Vision*. London: Verso.

Rosen, Marjorie 1973. *Popcorn Venus: Women, Movies and the American Dream*. New York: Coward McCann & Geoghegan.

Rosen, Philip (ed.) 1986. *Narrative, Apparatus, Ideology: A Film Theory Reader*. New York: Columbia University Press.

Rosenbaum, Jonathan 1997. *Movies as Politics*. Berkeley: University of California Press.

Rosenstone, Robert A. 1995a. *Visions of the Past: The Challenge of Film to Our Idea of History*. Cambridge, MA: Harvard University Press.

—— (ed.) 1995b. *Revisioning History: Film and the Construction of a New Past*. Princeton: Princeton University Press.

Ross, Harris 1987. *Film as Literature, Literature as Film*. New York: Greenwood Press.

Rowe, Kathleen 1995. *The Unruly Woman: Gender and the Genres of Laughter*. Austin: University of Texas Press.

Rushdie, Salman 1992. *The Wizard of Oz*. London: British Film Institute.

Rushing, Janice Hocker and Thomas S. Frentz 1995. *Projecting the Shadow: The Cyborg Hero in American Film*. Chicago: University of Chicago Press.

Russo, Vito 1998. *The Celluloid Closet: Homosexuality in the Closet*. New York: Harper & Row.

Ryan, Michael 1982. *Marxism and Deconstruction: A Critical Articulation*. Baltimore: Johns Hopkins University Press.

Ryan, Michael and Douglas Kellner 1988. *Camera Politica: The Politics and Ideology of Contemporary Hollywood Film*. Bloomington: Indiana University Press.

Salt, Barry 1993. *Film Style and Technology: History and Analysis*, revd edn. London: Starword.

Sarris, Andrew 1968. *The American Cinema: Directors and Directions 1929–1968*. New York: Dutton.

—— 1971. "Notes on the Auteur Theory in 1962." In P. Adams Sitney (ed.) *Film Culture Reader*. London: Secker & Warburg.

—— 1973. *The Primal Screen: Essays in Film-Related Subjects*. New York: Simon and Schuster.

Schapiroo, Mark 1992. "Bollywood Babylon," *Image* (June 28).

Schatz, Thomas 1981. *Hollywood Genres: Formulas, Filmmaking, and the Studio System*. Philadelphia: Temple University Press.

——1998. *The Genius of the System: Hollywood Filmmaking in the Studio Era*, 2nd edn. New York: Pantheon Books.

Schefer, Jean-Louis 1981. *L'Homme ordinaire du cinéma*. Paris: Gallimard.

Schneider, Cynthia and Brian Wallis (eds) 1988. *Global Television*. New York: Wedge Press.

Schwarz, Roberto 1987. *Que Horas Sao?: Ensaios*. São Paulo-SP: Compania das Letras.

Schwichtenberg, Cathy (ed.) 1993. *The Madonna Connection*. Boulder: Westview Press.

Screen: Incorporating Screen Education 1985. Vol. 26, Nos. 3–4 (May–August).

Screen Reader I: Cinema/Ideology/Politics 1977. London: SEFT.

Screen Reader II: Cinema & Semiotics 1981. London: SEFT.

Sebeok, Thomas A. 1979. *The Sign and Its Masters*. Austin: University of Texas Press.

——1986. *The Semiotic Sphere*. New York: Plenum.

Sedgwick, Eve Kosofsky 1985. *Between Men: English Literature and Male Homosocial Desire*. New York: Columbia University Press.

——1991. *Epistemology of the Closet*. London: Harvester Wheatsheaf.

Seiter, Ellen, Hans Borchers, Gabriele Kreutzner, and Eva-Marie Warth (eds) 1991. *Remote Control: Television, Audiences and Cultural Power*. London: Routledge.

Seldes, Gilbert 1924. *The Seven Lively Arts*. New York and London: Harper & Brothers.

——1928 "The Movie Commits Suicide," *Harpers* (November).

Shaviro, Steven 1993. *The Cinematic Body*. Minneapolis: University of Minnesota Press.

Shohat, Ella 1992. "Notes on the Postcolonial," *Social Text* Nos. 31–2.

——1989. *Israeli Cinema: East/West and the Politics of Representation*. Austin: University of Texas Press.

——1999. *Talking Visions: Multicultural Feminism in a Transnational Age*. Cambridge, MA: MIT Press.

Shohat, Ella and Robert Stam 1994. *Unthinking Eurocentrism*. London: Routledge.

Short, K. R. M. (ed.) 1981. *Feature Films as History*. London: Croom Helm.

Silverman, Kaja 1983. *The Subject of Semiotics*. New York: Oxford University Press.

——1988. *The Acoustic Mirror: The Female Voice in Psychoanalysis and Cinema*. Bloomington: Indiana University Press.

——1992. *Male Subjectivity at the Margins*. New York: Routledge.

——1995. *The Threshold of the Visible World*. New York: Routledge.

Sinclair, John, Elizabeth Jacka, and Stuart Cunningham (eds) 1996. *New Patterns in Global Television: Peripheral Vision*. Oxford: Oxford University Press.

Sitney, Adams 1978. *The Avant-Garde Film: A Reader of Theory and Criticism*. New York: New York University Press.

Sklar, Robert 1975. *Movie Made America: A Social History of American Movies*. New York: Random House.

Sklar, Robert and Charles Musser (eds) 1990. *Resisting Images: Essays on Cinema and History*. Philadelphia: Temple University Press.

Smith, Jeff 1998. *The Sounds of Commerce: Marketing Popular Film Music*. New York: Columbia University Press.

Smith, Murray 1995. *Engaging Characters: Fiction, Emotion, and the Cinema*. Oxford: Clarendon Press.

Smith, Paul (ed.) 1976. *The Historian and Film*. Cambridge: Cambridge University Press.

Smith, Valerie 1996. *Black Issues in Film*. New Brunswick: Rutgers University Press.

——(ed.) 1997. *Representing Blackness Issues in Film and Video*. New Brunswick: Rutgers University Press.

Snead, James 1992. *White Screens/ Black Images: Hollywood from the Dark Side*. New York: Routledge.

Snyder, Ilana 1997. *Hypertext: The Electronic Labyrinth*. Washington Square: New York University Press.

Sobchack, Thomas and Vivian Sobchack 1987. *An Introduction to Film*, 2nd edn. Boston: Little, Brown.

Sobchack, Vivian 1992. *The Address of the Eye: A Phenomenology of Film Experience*. Princeton: Princeton University Press.

Soloman, Stanley J. 1976. *Beyond Formula: American Film Genres*. New York: Harcourt Brace.

Sorlin, Pierre 1977. *Sociologie du cinéma: ouverture pour l'histoire de demain*. Paris: Editions Aubier Mongaigne.

——1980. *The Film in History: Restaging the Past*. New Jersey: Barnes & Noble Books.

Spigel, Lynn 1992. *Make Room for TV: Television and the Family Ideology in Postwar America*. Chicago: University of Chicago Press.

Spivak, Gayatri Chakravorty 1987. *In Other Worlds: Essays in Cultural Politics*. New York: Routledge.

Stacey, Jackie 1994. *Star Gazing: Hollywood Cinema and Female Spectatorship*. London: Routledge.

Staiger, Janet 1992. *Interpreting Films: Studies in the Historical Reception of American Cinema*. Princeton: Princeton University Press.

——1995a. *Bad Women: Regulating Sexuality in Early American Cinema*. Minneapolis: University of Minnesota Press.

——(ed.) 1995b. *The Studio System*. New Brunswick: Rutgers University Press.

Stallabrass, Julian 1996. *Gargantua: Manufactured Mass Culture*. New York: Verso.

Stam, James H. 1976. *Inquiries into the Origin of Language*. New York: Harper & Row.

Stam, Robert 1985. *Reflexivity in Film and Literature*. Ann Arbor: University of Michigan Press. (Reprinted Columbia University Press, 1992.)

——1989. *Subversive Pleasures: Bakhtin, Cultural Criticism and Film*. Baltimore: Johns Hopkins University Press.

——1992. "Mobilizing Fictions: The Gulf War, the Media, and the Recruitment of the Spectator," *Public Culture* Vol. 4, No. 2 (Spring).

——1998. *Tropical Multiculturalism: A Comparative History of Race in Brazilian Cinema and Culture*. Durham, NC: Duke University Press.

——1999. *Film Theory: An Introduction*. Oxford: Blackwell Publishers. Storey, John (ed.) 1996. *What is Cultural Studies? A Reader*. London: Arnold.

Stam, Robert and Roberta Pearson 1983. "Hitchcock's *Rear Window*: Reflexivity and the Critique of Voyeurism," *Enclitic* Vol. 7, No. 1.

Stam, Robert, Robert Burgoyne, and Sandy Flitterman-Lewis 1992. *New Vocabularies in Film Semiotics: Structuralism, Post-Structuralism and Beyond*. London: Routledge.

Storey, John (ed.) 1996. *What is Cultural Studies? A Reader*. London: Arnold.

Straayer, Chris 1996. *Deviant Eyes, Deviant Bodies: Sexual Re-Orientations in Film and Video*. New York: Columbia University Press.

Strinati, Dominic 1995. *An Introduction to Theories of Popular Culture*. London: Routledge.

Studlar, Gaylyn 1988. *In The Realm of Pleasure*. Urbana: University of Illinois Press.

—— 1996. *This Mad Masquerade: Stardom and Masculinity in the Jazz Age*. New York: Columbia University Press.

Suarez, Juan A. 1996. *Bike Boys, Drag Queens, and Superstars: Avant-Garde*. Bloomington: Indiana University Press.

Tan, Ed S. H. 1996. *Emotion and the Structure of Narrative Film: Film as an Emotion Machine*. Mahwah: Lawrence Erlbaum.

Tasker, Yvonne 1993. *Spectacular Bodies: Gender, Genre and the Action Cinema*. New York: Routledge.

Taylor, Clyde 1998. *The Mask of Art: Breaking the Aesthetic Contract in Film and Literature*. Bloomington: Indiana University Press.

Taylor, Lucien (ed.) 1994. *Visualizing Theory: Selected Essays from V. A. R. 1990–1994*. New York: Routledge.

Taylor, Richard (ed.) 1927/1982. *The Poetics of Cinema, Russian Poetics in Translation*, IX. Oxford: RPT Publications.

Taylor, Robert Brent (ed.) 1993. *Hollywood as Mirror: Changing View of Outsiders and Enemies in American Movies*. Westport, CT: Greenwood Press.

Thompson, Kristin 1981. *Ivan the Terrible: A Neo-Formalist Analysis*. Princeton: Princeton University Press.

—— 1988. *Breaking the Glass Armor*. Princeton: Princeton University Press.

Todorov, Tzvetan 1977. *The Poetics of Prose*. Ithaca, NY: Cornell University Press.

Tomlinson, John 1991. *Cultural Imperialism: A Critical Introduction*. London: Pinter.

Toplin, Robert Brent 1993. *Hollywood as Mirror: Changing View of Outsiders and Enemies in American Movies*. Westport, CT: Greenwood Press.

—— 1996. *History by Hollywood: The Use and Abuse of the American Past*. Champaign: University of Illinois Press.

Trinh, T. Min-Ha 1991. *When the Moon Waxes Red: Representation, Gender and Cultural Politics*. New York: Routledge.

Tulloch, John (ed.) 1977. *Conflict and Control in the Cinema*. Melbourne: Macmillan.

Turim, Maureen 1989. *Flashbacks in Film: Memory and History*. New York: Routledge.

Turovskaya, Maya 1989. *Cinema as Poetry*. London: Faber.

Tyler, Parker 1972. *Screening the Sexes: Homosexuality in the Movies*. New York: Holt, Rinehart and Winston.

Ukadike, Nwachukwu Frank 1994. *Black African Cinema*. Berkeley: University of California Press.

Ulmer, Gregory 1985. *Applied Grammatology*. Baltimore: Johns Hopkins University Press.

—— 1989. *Teletheory: Grammatology in the Age of Video*. London: Routledge.

Vanoye, Francis 1989. *Récit ècrit/récit filmique*. Paris: Nathan.

Vernet, Marc 1988. *Figures de l'absence*. Paris: Cahiers du cinéma.

Veron, Eliseo 1980. *A Producão De Sentido*. São Paulo: Editora Cultrix.

Vertov, Dziga 1984. *Kino-Eye: The Writings of Dziga Vertov*. Trans. Kevin O'Brien, ed. Annette Michelson. Berkeley: University of California Press.

Viano, Maurizio 1993. *A Certain Realism: Making Use of Pasolini's Film Theory and Practice*. Berkeley: University of California Press.

Virilio, Paul 1989. *War and Cinema: The Logistics of Perception*. Trans. Patrick Camiller. London: Verso.

—— 1994. *The Vision Machine*. Bloomington: Indiana University Press.

Virmaux, Alain and Odette Virmaux 1976. *Les Surréalistes et le cinéma*. Paris: Seghers.

Volosinov, V. N. 1976. *Marxism and the Philosophy of Language*. Trans. Ladislav Matejka and I. R. Titunik. Cambridge, MA: Harvard University Press.

Vygotsky, Lev 1987. *Thought and Language*. Trans. Eugenia Hanfmann and Gertrude Vakar. Cambridge, MA: MIT Press.

Walker, Janet 1993. *Couching Resistance: Women, Film, and Psychoanalytic Psychiatry*. Minneapolis: University of Minnesota Press.

Walsh, Martin 1981. *The Brechtian Aspect of Radical Cinema*. London: British Film Institute.

Waugh, Thomas (ed.) 1984. *"Show Us Life!": Toward a History and Aesthetics of the Committed Documentary*. Metuchen: Scarecrow Press.

—— 1996. *Hard to Imagine: Gay Male Eroticism in Photography and Film from their Beginnings to Stonewall*. New York: Columbia University Press.

Wees, William C. 1991. *Light Moving in Time: Studies in the Visual Aesthetics of Avant-Garde Film*. Berkeley: University of California Press.

Weis, Elizabeth and John Belton 1985. *Theory and Practice of Film Sound*. New York: Columbia University Press.

Weiss, Andrea 1992. *Vampires and Violets: Lesbians in the Cinema*. London: Jonathan Cape.

Wexman, Virginia Wright 1993. *Creating the Couple: Love, Marriage, and Hollywood Performance*. Princeton: Princeton University Press.

Whittock, Trevor 1990. *Metaphor and Film*. Cambridge: Cambridge University Press.

Wiegman, Robyn 1995. *American Anatomies: Theorizing Race and Gender*. Durham, NC: Duke University Press.

Willemen, Paul 1994. *Looks and Frictions: Essays in Cultural Studies and Film Theory*. Bloomington: Indiana University Press.

Williams, Christopher (ed.) 1980. *Realism and the Cinema: A Reader*. London: Routledge and Kegan Paul.

—— (ed.) 1996. *Cinema: The Beginnings and the Future*. London: University of Westminster Press.

Williams, Linda 1984. *Figures of Desire*. Urbana: University of Illinois Press.

—— 1989. *Hard Core: Power, Pleasure and the Frenzy of the Visible*. Berkeley: California University Press.

—— (ed.) 1994. *Viewing Positions: Ways of Seeing Film*. New Brunswick: Rutgers University Press.

Williams, Raymond 1982. *The Sociology of Culture*. New York: Schocken Books.

—— 1985. *Keywords: A Vocabulary of Culture and Society*. New York: Oxford University Press.

Williamson, Judith 1978. *Decoding Advertisements: Ideology and Meaning in Advertising*. London: Marion Boyars.

Wilson, George M. 1986. *Narration in Light: Studies in Cinematic Point of View*. Baltimore: Johns Hopkins University Press.

Wilton, Tamsin (ed.) 1995. *Immortal Invisible: Lesbians and the Moving Image*. London: Routledge.

Winston, Brian 1995. *Claiming the Real*. London: British Film Institute.

—— 1996. *Technologies of Seeing: Photography, Cinematography and Television*. London: British Film Institute.

Wolfe, George C. 1988. *The Colored Museum*. New York: Grove Weidenfeld.

Wolfenstein, Martha and Nathan Leites 1950. *Movies: A Psychological Study*. Glencoe, IL: Free Press.

Woll, Allen L. 1980. *The Latin Image in American Film*. Los Angeles: UCLA Latin American Center Publications.

Woll, Allen L. and Randall M. Miller (eds) 1987. *Ethnic and Racial Images in American Film and Television*. New York: Garland.

Wollen, Peter 1982. *Readings and Writings: Semiotic Counter-Strategies*. London: Verso.

—— 1993. *Raiding the Icebox: Reflections on Twentieth-Century Culture*. Bloomington: Indiana University Press.

—— 1998. *Signs and Meaning in the Cinema*, 4th edn. London: BFI Publishing.

Wong, Eugene Franklin 1978. *On Visual Media Racism: Asians in American Motion Pictures*. New York: Arno Press.

Wood, Ellen Meiksins and John Bellamy Foster 1997. *In Defense of History: Marxism and the Postmodern Agenda*. New York: Monthly Review Press.

Wright, Will 1975. *Sixguns and Society*. Berkeley: University of California Press.

Wuss, Peter 1986. *Die Tiefenstruktur des Filkunstwerks*. The Hague: Mouton.

Wyatt, Justin 1994. *High Concept: Movies and Marketing in Hollywood*. Austin: University of Texas Press.

Xavier, Ismail 1977. *O Discurso Cinematografico*. Rio de Janeiro: Paz e Terra.

—— 1983. *A Experiencia do Cinema*. Rio da Janeiro: Graal.

—— 1996. *O Cinema No Seculo*. ed. Arthur Nestrovski. Rio de Janeiro: Imago.

—— 1997. *Allegories of Underdevelopment*. Minneapolis: University of Minnesota Press.

Young, Lola 1996. *Fear of the Dark: "Race," Gender and Sexuality in the Cinema*. London: Routledge.

Young-Bruehl, Elisabeth 1996. *The Anatomy of Prejudices*. Cambridge, MA: Harvard University Press.

Zizek, Slavoj 1991. *Looking Awry: An Introduction to Jacques Lacan Through Popular Culture*. Cambridge, MA: MIT Press.

—— (ed.) 1992 *Everything You Always Wanted to Know About Lacan But Were Afraid To Ask Hitchcock*. London: Verso.

—— 1993. *Enjoy Your Symptom! Jacques Lacan in Hollywood and Out*. New York: Routledge.

—— 1996. *For They Know Not What They Do: Enjoyment as a Political Factor*. New York: Verso.

Special Issues of Journals

"Audiences." *Journal of Film and Video* 43, Nos. 1–2 (1991).

"The Black Image in Film." *Film and History* 25, Nos. 1–2 (1990).

CA: Cinema. Special Issue on Christian Metz. No. 32 (May 1975).

"Christian Metz et la théorie du cinéma." *Iris* 6, No. 1 (1990).

CINÉMACTION. 20 ans de théories féministes sur le cinéma. ed. Guy Hennebelle. No. 67. Condé-sur-Noireau: CinémAction-Corlet (1993).

—— *Les Théories du cinéma aujourd'hui.* No. 47. Paris: Cerf-Corlet (1988).

—— *Cinéma et histoire autour de Marc Ferro.* No. 65. CinémaAction-Corlet (1992).

"Cinema and Cognitive Psychology." *Iris* No. 9 (Spring 1989).

"Cinema & Narration 1" and "Cinema & Narration 2." *Iris* No. 7 (1986); No. 8 (1988).

"Cinema/Sound." *Yale French Studies* No. 60 (1980).

"Dix années d'analyses textuelles de films. Bibliographie analytiques." *Linguistique et semiologie*, No. 3 (1977).

"Do You Read Me? Queer Theory and Social Praxis." *Spectator* 15, No. 1 (1994).

"Early Cinema Audiences/Les Spectateurs au début du cinéma." *Iris* 6, No. 2 (1990).

'Enonciation et cinéma'. *Communications* No. 38. Paris: Seuil (1983).

"Exploitation Film." *Film History* 6, No. 3 (1994).

"The Female Spectator." *Camera Obscura* Nos. 20–1 (1989).

"Feminist Film Criticism." *Film Criticism* 13, No. 2 (1989).

"Feminist Film Criticism" and "Film and Cultural Studies." *Film Reader* No. 5 (1982).

"Film Comedy." *Journal of Film and Video* 46, No. 3 (1994).

"Film Genre." *Film Reader* No. 3 (1978).

"Film Genres." *Journal of Film and Video* 48, Nos. 1–2 (1996).

"Film and History." *Radical History Review* No. 41 (April 1988).

"Film/Narrative/The Novel." *Cinetracts* No. 13 (1981).

"Film and Psychoanalysis." *Persistence of Vision* No. 10 (1993).

"Film as Text." *Forum for Modern Language Studies* 31, No. 1 (1995).

"Gender and Film." *Women's Studies* 25, No. 2 (1996).

"The Hollywood Indian: Stereotypes of Native Americans in Films." Trenton, NJ: New Jersey State Museum (1980).

"Interpretation, Inc.: Issues in Contemporary Film Studies." *Film Criticism* 17, Nos. 2–3 (1993).

"Literature and Film: Models of Adaption." *Canadian Review of Comparative Literature* 23, No. 3 (1996).

"Metahistory of Film." *Film Reader* No. 4 (1979).

"The Movies: A Centennial Issue." *Michigan Quarterly Review* 34, No. 4 (Fall 1995/ Winter 1996).

"Narrative/Non-Narrative." *Wide Angle* 8, Nos. 3–4 (1986).

"The New Auteurism." *Film Criticism* 19, No. 3 (1995).

"New Masculinities." *Velvet Light Trap* No. 38 (Fall 1996).

"Melodrama." *Journal of the University Film and Video Association* 35, No. 1 (1983).

"New Queer Cinema." *Sight and Sound* 2, No. 5 (1992).

"On the Soundtrack." *Screen* 25, No. 3 (1984).

"La Parole au cinéma/Speech in Film." *Iris* 3, No. 1 (1985).

"Philosophy and Film." *Journal of Value Inquiry* 29, No. 4 (1995).

"Philosophy of Film History." *Film History* 6, No. 1 (1994).

"Psychanalyse et cinéma." *Communications* No. 23 (1975).

"Psychoanalysis and Cinema." *Free Associations* 4, No. 3 (1994).

"Psychoanalysis and Cinema." *Journal of Popular Film and Television* 18, No. 1 (1990).

"Psychoanalysis and Film" and "Psychoanalysis and Film II." *American Imago* 50, No. 4 (1993); 52, No. 2 (1995).

"Psychoanalysis and Film." *Journal of Film and Video* 46, No. 2 (1994).

"The Rediscovery of a Kuleshov Experiment: A Dossier." *Film History* 8, No. 3 (1996).

"L'Effet Kulechov/The Kuleshov Effect." *Iris* 4, No. 1 (1986).
"Screening Cultural Studies." *Continuum, The Australian Journal of Media & Culture* 7, No. 2 (1994).
"Sex and Sexuality." *Journal of Popular Film and Television* 22, No. 4 (1995).
Sites: The Journal of 20th Century Contemporary French Studies 1, No. 1 (1995).
"Sound & Cinema." *Film Journal* 100, No. 9 (1997).
"Sound and Music in the Movies." *Cineaste* 21, Nos. 1–2 (1995).
"Special Issue on Children's Film." *The Lion and the Unicorn* 20, No. 1 (1996).
"Special Issue on the Western." *Film Criticism* 20, No. 3 (1996).
"Style in Cinema." *Style* 32, No. 3 (1998).
"The Trial(s) of Psychoanalysis." *Critical Inquiry* Vol. 13, No. 2 (1987).
"US Latinos and the Media, Parts 1 and 2." *Jump Cut* No. 38 (June 1993); No. 39 (June 1994).

Useful Journals for General Reference

Advertising Age, Afterimage, American Cinema Editor, American Cinematographer, Animation Journal, Art and Text, Artforum, Arts and Humanities Citation Index, Asian Cinema, Australian Journal of Communication, Australian Journal of Cultural Studies, Australian Journal of Screen Theory, Billboard, Black Film Review, Black Renaissance Noire, Body and Society, boundary 2, Box Office, Broadcasting and Cable, Camera Obscura, Canadian Journal of Film Studies/revue canadienne d'ritudes cinimatographiques, Cineaste, Cinefantastique, Cinema, Cinema Canada, Cinema Journal, Cinema Papers, Cinematograph, Cinemaya, Communication Abstracts, Continuum, Convergence, Critical Inquiry, Critical Quarterly, *Critical Studies in Mass Communication, Cultural Critique, Cultural Studies, Culture and Policy, Diasporas, Differences, Discourse, Dissertation Abstracts International, Dox, East–West Film Journal, Emmy, European Journal of Communication, European Journal of Cultural Studies, Film Comment, Film Criticism, Film Culture, Film and History, Film History, Film Journal, Film Literature Index, Film and Philosophy, Film Quarterly, Film Threat, Films and Filming, Films in Review, Framework, French Cultural Studies, Genders, Historical Journal of Film, Radio and Television, Humanities Index, Independent, IMCS: The International Journal for Media and Communication Studies Online* at: http://www.aber.ac.uk/~jmcwww, *International Index to Film Periodicals, International Index to Television Periodicals, International Journal of Cultural Studies, Iris, Journal of Broadcasting and Electronic Media, Journal of Communication, Journal of Communication Inquiry, Journal of Film and Video, Journal of Popular Culture, Journal of Popular Film and Television, Jump Cut, Lightstruck, Literature/Film Quarterly, Media Culture & Society, Media International Australia, Metro, m/f, Millennium Film Journal, Montage, Monthly Film Bulletin, Movie, Movieline, New Formations, October, Off Hollywood Report, Persistence of Vision, Pix, Post Script, Premiere, Psychotronic Video, Public Culture, Quarterly Review of Film, Television & New Media, Television and Video, Queens Quarterly, Screen, Screen Education, Sight and Sound, Sightlines, Social Sciences Citation Index, Social Sciences Index, Social Text, Southern Review, Spectator, Studies in Visual Communication, Television Quarterly, Theory, Culture and Society, Variety, Velvet Light Trap, Visions, Visual Anthropology, Visual Anthropology Review, Western Humanities Review,* and *Wide Angle.*

Internet Resources

Internet Movie Database <http://www.cs.cf.ac.uk/Movies/search.html>, <h-film@uicv-m.uic.edu, screen–ll@ualvm.ua.edu>

All-Movie Guide <http://allmovie.com/amg/movie-Root.html>

Cinemedia <http://www.afionline.org/CineMedia/cmframe.html>

Movie Review Query Engine at Telerama <http://www.cinema.pgh.pa.us/movie/reviews>

The Cinema Connection <http://www.social change.net.au/TCC/>

LSU Libraries Webliography: Film and Media <http://www.lib.lsu.edu/hum/film.html>

UCLA Arts Library Selected Internet Sources in Film <http://www.lilbrary.ucla.edu/libraries/arts/websites/www.mov.htm>

International FilmArchive CD-ROM of the International Federation of Film Archives

Film Index International CD-ROM of the British Film Institute

MLA International Bibliography of Books and Articles on the Modern Languages and Literatures CD-ROM.

Other useful on-line sources can be found listed in Bert Delvert, "Shots in Cyberspace: Film Research on the Internet." *Cinema Journal* 35, No. 1 (1995): 103–24; Bert Eievert and Dan Harries (1996) *Film & Video on the Internet: The Top 500 Sites.* Studio City: Michale Weise Productions, and Sarah Berg and Toby Miller, *The Blackwell Cultural Theory Website* <http://www.blackwellpublishers.co.uk cultural>.

Index

Note: "n." after a page reference indicates the number of a note on that page.